Margaret Kelner
Rt / Box 98
East Bernard, Tx 77435
or
215 Kirkley 1431
Huntsville, Tx.

Child
Psychology

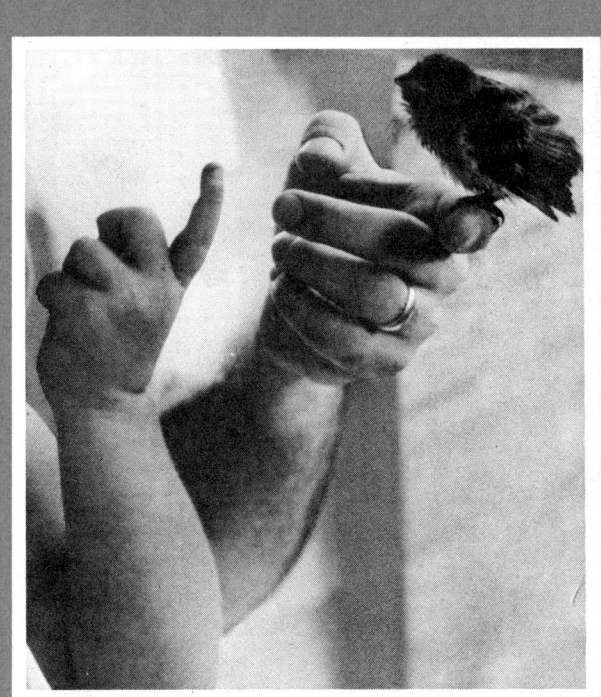

Child Psychology

Brian Sutton-Smith
*Teachers College
Columbia University*

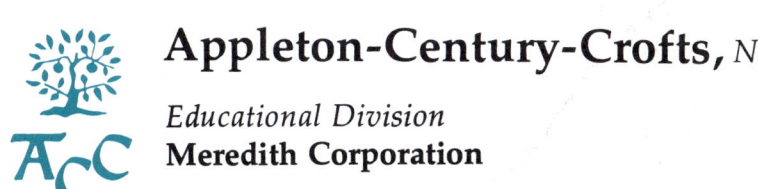
Appleton-Century-Crofts, New York
Educational Division
Meredith Corporation

Copyright © 1973 by MEREDITH CORPORATION

All rights reserved

This book, or parts thereof, must not be used or reproduced in any manner without written permission. For information address the publisher, Appleton-Century-Crofts, Educational Division, Meredith Corporation, 440 Park Avenue South, New York, N.Y. 10016.

73 74 75 76 77 / 10 9 8 7 6 5 4 3 2 1

Library of Congress Card Number: 72-90948

PRINTED IN THE UNITED STATES OF AMERICA

Illustrations: *Danmark & Michaels, Inc.*
Picture Editor: *Mira Schachne*
Frontis Photos: *Florence Dara Silverman*
Cover Art: *Judith Sugar*

390-81867-4

Contents

Preface xii

Dimensions of Child Psychology 1

1 Theory and Methods 3

What Are Children? 3
The First Task of Child Psychology 4
A Historical Overview 5
Contemporary Theories of Child Psychology 8
Methods of Research in Child Psychology 15
The Importance of Child Psychology 21

2 Learning and Development   26

Learned and Unlearned Behavior   26
Classical Conditioning   30
Operant Conditioning   32
Variable Factors that Affect Learning   36
Observational Learning   41
Conditions that Affect Learning   47

II The Prenatal Period   55

3 Genetics and Development   57

The Nature–Nurture Controversy   57
The Science of Genetics   58
The Principles of Genetics   59
The Nature of Genetic Influence   65
Methods of Studying Genetic Influence   67
Specific Effects of Heredity on Human Development   68

4 Prenatal Environmental Influences   83

Prenatal Development   84
Effects of Prenatal Environment and Birth   89
Conditions during Pregnancy   90
Conditions during Birth   99

III Infancy 111

5 Motor Development and Sensory Experience 113

The State of the Newborn   114
Growth in Infancy   118
Visual Perception   121
Other Sensory and Perceptual Development   127
Motor Development   129
The Differences in Infants   136

6 Mental, Cognitive, and Language Development 144

Language Development   145
Intelligence and the Infant   156
Piaget: Intelligence in Infancy   160
Voluntary Behavior   170

7 Social Development 182

Child–Parent Interaction   184
Attachment to the Parent   190
Anxieties Related to Attachment   194

The Institutionalized Infant **199**
Socialization in Infancy **206**
Cultural Differences in Child Rearing **210**
Prediction of Behavior **211**

IV Toddlerhood Ages 2 and 3 221

8 Motor, Cognitive, and Language Development 223

Physical and Motor Development **224**
Intelligence and Its Measurement **226**
Cognitive Development **228**
Language Development **234**
How Are Language and Cognition Related? **242**
Environmental Influences on Language and Cognition **245**

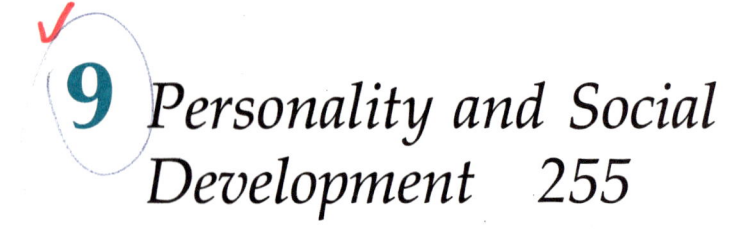

9 Personality and Social Development 255

The Home Environment **256**
Identification **260**
Dependency **262**
Conscience **267**

Aggression   **269**
Sex-Typing   **278**
Sexual Curiosity   **283**
Development of the Self   **285**

V *Early Childhood Ages 4 through 7*   **297**

10 *Intellectual and Cognitive Development*   **299**

The Preoperational Stage: The Period of Intuitive Thought   **301**
Problem–Solving Processes   **306**
Mental Imagery   **315**
Perceptual Growth   **317**
Changes in Thinking and Learning   **322**
Intelligence and I.Q.   **323**
Correlates of I.Q. and School Performance   **327**

11 *Personality and Social Development*   **337**

Patterns of Interaction with Peers   **338**
Peers as Agents of Socialization   **344**

Effects of Nursery School Attendance   349
Emotional Development   354
Behavior Problems and Disorders   362

VI The Middle Years Ages 8 through 12   377

12 Cognitive and Moral Development and Social Perception   379

Cognitive Changes in Middle Childhood   380
Cognitive Aspects of Moral Development   383
Social Cognition   392
The Development of the Peer Group   400

13 Personality and Social Development   414

Personality Themes of the Middle Years   415
Personality Variables of the Middle Years   418
Peers: Acceptance and Friendship   421
Influences on Personality   425
Social Class Influences   429

VII Adolescence 447

14 Physical and Cognitive Development and Role Changes 449

Adolescence — A Time of Change 449
Physical and Sexual Development 451
Intellectual and Cognitive Development 458
Social and Cultural Changes 462
Peer Relationships and the Peer Culture 469

15 Personality and Social Development 478

Theories of Adolescent Personality 479
Dependence versus Independence 481
Development of Values in Adolescence 483
Self-concept and Self-esteem 486
Atypical Groups 490
Maturity 497

Indexes 507

Preface

This text is designed for developmental psychology courses at the college level. It is comprehensive and systematic in its coverage of basic concepts and principles, important trends in research, and applications of this research. Emphasis is on the clear presentation of all theoretical and applied research, in part by introducing concepts and theories within their philosophical perspective and by developing readable descriptions that are easily accessible to student discussion.

Every textbook writer must realize that there is no single right way to teach a course; a good teacher will adapt the material to suit his own special abilities and interests and his students' needs. Thus, this book includes detailed information on cognitive, social, and emotional development, as well as the different approaches to these areas of study. A special effort has been made to use many current resources that will help the reader keep abreast of recent developments with significance for the future. For example, discussions of cognitive development have been expanded to reflect the recent growth of research in this area.

This book further concentrates on development in a way that involves the student, in a way that makes psychology more a part of his world. The normative approach that is emphasized in most textbooks provides generalities and averages, but people must deal with individuals and specific incidents. The case studies that appear at the end of most chapters are intended not only to illustrate the general influences, but also to provide specific examples of unique combinations of these general laws.

Features of the Text

Every good textbook, whether it is introductory or advanced, must be able to satisfy the needs of professors and students alike. The satisfaction of these needs—for clear, readable, up-to-date, and relevant material—would make a book that is more interesting and useful to students and a better teaching tool for professors. Appleton-Century-Crofts has attempted with this book to achieve that goal for child psychology courses.

Readability. A first step in producing this book was to define "readability" in the context of the teaching situation and to determine how it might be achieved. After much discussion and analysis, and with the help of professionals, it was decided that a readable text is a text that organizes material clearly, in a teachable sequence; a text that draws upon a wealth of psychological detail and yet elucidates general principles and themes; a text that selects examples and experimental data with regard for both scientific importance and probable interest value; and a text that conveys some of the excitement of developmental psychology through graphics, without skimping or overwhelming the text itself.

Summaries. Each chapter is summarized clearly and concisely. The main highlights are reiterated in such a way that the student can easily review and remember the material he has just read. Students may also use the summaries for immediate recall of material in preparation for an examination.

Case Studies. Many of the chapters are followed by two case studies. These illustrations pick up general concepts of the chapter and apply them to individual children, demonstrating the unique interaction of the various genetic and environmental influences on the child. The interested student might refer to *Carmichael's Manual of Child Psychology*, edited by Paul Mussen, for more information on these and related research topics.

Illustrations. Modern society is increasingly oriented toward visual images. This book contains photographs and line drawings where appropriate, to give visual impact and support to the text. For example, the actual sequence of motor development is made clear in a series of pertinent photographs.

Tables and Graphs. Since psychology is a science, and thus has an empirical base, it is important for the student to be able to understand how data are organized. All the tables and graphs in this text have been designed to make this data attractive, graphic, and readily comprehensible.

Acknowledgments

To my wife, Shirley, and the children, Katherine, Mark, Leslie, Mary, and Emily, many thanks for their anecdotes included herein. It is a pleasure to surreptitiously illustrate a textbook with bits of family biography. I might also say that they have not let this book interfere with their lives and so are not conscious of any sacrifice to be expunged by some brief sanctimonious acknowledgment from me. I suppose that this is because there are different games in my family, just as there are in this book.

Over the years I have been indebted to a number of people for fostering my particular dreams about psychology. On a cash basis, a Ph.D. fellowship from the New Zealand government comes first, followed by subsequent support by a Fulbright Travel Award, a Smith-Mundt postdoctoral fellowship, support from The Family Study Center at the University of Chicago, The American Philosophical Society, The Bowling Green State University Scholarship Fund, The National Science Foundation, The Office of Education, The National Association of Mental Health, Horace Mann Lincoln Institute at Teachers College, The Ford Foundation, and, above all, The National Institute of Mental Health, which has, more than any other body, made the life of research a reality for me.

As they say in popular novels, the following names have contributed to, but are not in any way responsible for the issue. In New Zealand, I remember in particular Sir Thomas Hunter, Professors Ernest Beaglehole, Colin Bailey, Arthur Fieldhouse, and H. C. D. Somerset. In the United States, Harold Jones, Fritz Redl, Paul Gump, Nelson Foote, David Riesman, Bernard Kaplan, John Roberts, and George Rand. Credit also goes to several members of the publisher's staff, especially to the editor, Julie Small, and to the production editor, Eleanor Perz. And, in particular, I would like to thank my long-time research collaborator Ben Rosenberg of Bowling Green State University, whose enthusiasm and involvement have meant that doing research has always been fun.

B.S-S.

Dimensions of Child Psychology

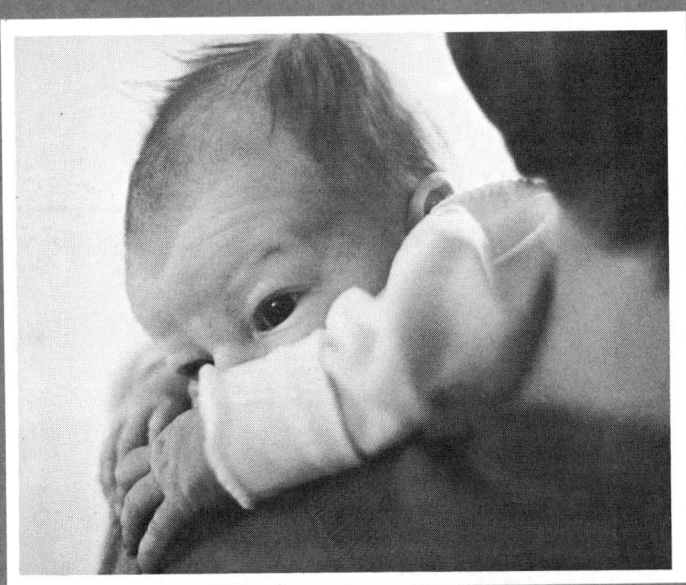

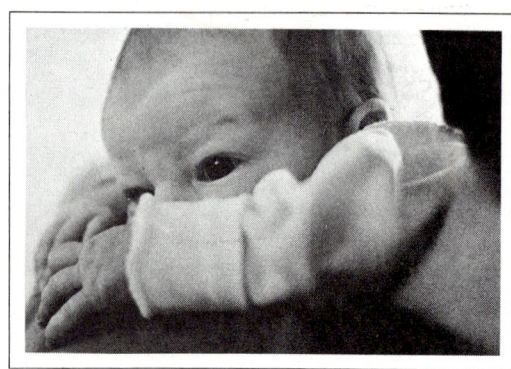

Ed Lettau—Black Star

Theory and Methods   1

What Are Children?

When we look at children we usually perceive human beings that are small, lacking in knowledge, immature, cute, weak, vulnerable, demanding, literal-minded, messy, innocent, affectionate, and so forth. Rarely do we look beyond such commonplace notions for a more meaningful understanding of what children really are. Most of our everyday contact and familiarity with children reinforces our naive beliefs about the nature of childhood. These beliefs, in turn, influence our behavior toward children and, ultimately, the behavior of children themselves.

Many standard nursery rhymes and jokes about children point up just how ingrained our ideas about children are, as does this familiar joke:

"Johnny," says the Sunday school teacher, "who defeated the Philistines?"
"I don't know," says Johnny. "If they don't play the Dodgers, I don't keep track of them."

The humor in this story lies in the contrast between adult thinking and what we suppose to be a young child's thought processes. It focuses on the limited range of the child's knowledge, on his inability to use the word *defeat* outside of one narrow context—in short, on the traits that distinguish him from an adult.

When we begin the scientific study of children, however, we become interested in precisely what stories such as this tell us about children, aside from the fact that children are not as capable in various ways as adults are. For example, we become interested in the nature of the children's cognitive and verbal processes that underlie a story of this kind. We become interested in the theories of childhood that may explain children's stories and rhymes. Consider the following jingle:

> First grade, baby,
> Second grade, tot,
> Third grade, angel,
> Fourth grade, snot.

This jingle tells us how children view each other, and it might possibly reflect the way adults view children. We can see here an implicit theory about how children mature, how they develop their identity, and how they develop group feelings. Underlying our casual beliefs and perceptions, then, is a whole network of theory which can be made explicit and examined.

Familiar Notions Need Questioning

Most of our common attitudes about children, as well as the more complex beliefs underlying them, are transmitted to us by our own families. Our ideas about childhood in general are usually based upon private memories of our own childhood experiences.

Other major influences on our perception of children are the representations of them that we see in magazines, newspapers, television, radio, movies, books, even in toys. The work of child psychologists and other theorists of human nature also contributes to the views we hold. Sometimes whole generations are strongly influenced by the work of a few men. For example, in recent decades, many children have been raised somewhat according to Dr. Spock. In addition, many tenets of Sigmund Freud's psychoanalytic theory have become so ingrained in our culture that we are hardly aware of them. We take them for granted.

However, it is these assumptions and beliefs that we must make explicit and that we must begin to question if we are ever to gain any hard, scientific knowledge about the nature of children. For, upon investigation, we may find that some of our firmest beliefs are certainly not true of children everywhere, and may not even apply to all children in our own society.

Modern anthropology has shown us that it is fruitless to study adults of so-called primitive cultures by using the same set of questions that we apply to adults of our own technological, industrialized culture. Yet, when it comes to children, we often assume that they are the same everywhere, that they live in a universal world of their own. Even within our own society, however, there is great variation in children's behavior, personality, and development between the various classes and racial and ethnic groups. Furthermore, it is now known that in the history of Western society, children were not always regarded and treated in the same manner as they are at present. Indeed, at one time, childhood was scarcely recognized as a distinct phase of life.

We must always be aware of the cultural context of the child under study if we want to make accurate generalizations about his behavior. When, for instance, we say that a child is "immature," we must remember that this may be true only within our own social and cultural framework and not necessarily true outside of it. The characteristics we attribute to the child and his world are largely products of our own unreflective everyday relationship with children in our culture; they may not always stand up under rigorous conceptual analysis.

The First Task of Child Psychology

In order to be in a position to study the child with some degree of objectivity, it is necessary to define terms and make explicit all of our hidden assumptions and beliefs about childhood. In doing this, we must realize that child psychology is not alone in this task. All the natural sciences and all the other human sciences have had to clarify the definitions and concepts of their subject matter and determine which of the things that they were talking about really existed, at the same time as they undertook the scientific work of experimentation, collection of data, and proof or disproof of hypotheses about the way things worked.

The history of Western physics is a dramatic example of this point. Beginning about 2500 years ago, the early Greek philosophers began to ask what were the basic materials of the universe. Earth, air, fire, and water were generally viewed as the basic substances. By a long series of developments, through Plato and Aristotle, medieval and Renaissance philosophers, through the work of Newton in the seventeenth century, down to the twentieth-century revolution in physics (Einstein, Bohr, and others), we have moved far beyond this primitive conception. As the physical sciences have developed, men's ideas about the components of the universe have changed drastically.

The sciences of man, however, undertook the essential task of clarification of their subject matter, of definition and redefinition of terms, much later in their history. For centuries, scientific progress was hampered by a confusion of the scientific question "What is man?" with either the ethical question "What ought man to be?" or the religious question "What is the meaning of life?" The human sciences are clearly at an earlier stage of development than the natural and physical sciences. In this age of scientific sophistication, it would not be quite correct to put child psychology at the level of Aristotelian speculative physics; yet it still has a long way to go. The different schools of psychological theory have quite disparate and often conflicting pictures of what children (and adults) are. We are far from attaining a unified framework for experimental work.

But the task of achieving greater clarity and general agreement about what basically exists is even more complicated in the human sciences than it is in the natural sciences. Many more complex variables affect the state of man. Men's theories and beliefs about themselves tend to affect their behavior and character. Men—and especially children—become what they, and others, think they are.

The effort to create a unified theory of child development, then, is bound to be a very difficult task. In a sense, it is tempting to say that there are no such things as "children" at all. There is only the distorting lens of centuries of accumulated habits, beliefs, and myths which affect all of our views of what children are. As we approach this new science from the starting point of our familiar notions—exchanging myths for facts or finding factual bases for myths—we need to examine what these commonplace beliefs are and what they have been in the past.

A Historical Overview

The Concept of the Child

Two main currents of thinking and social custom have led to our present-day concept of children. One of them is the gradual separation, during the course of Western history, of child from adult. (The notion of childhood as a separate and distinct stage of life became dominant only in the seventeenth century.) The other current of thought is the result of philosophical arguments about the nature of man, which also began to flower in the seventeenth century in Europe. This notion focused on children as pure human beings who had not yet been corrupted by life. Arguing on the basis of childhood's supposed innocence, many philosophers sought to prove various theses about man's fundamental nature, in his pure, unadulterated form, untouched by society and convention.

These two views of childhood are, in a sense, opposites. The first represents a growing belief that children form a distinct class of human beings with marked differences from adults, whereas the second, although it does not deny outright that children are different from adults, is more concerned with the similarities between child and man.

The Separation of Child and Adult

It was not until the seventeenth century that children came to be regarded and treated very differently from adults. To be sure, many thinkers before that time had been aware that what happens to a human being in the early years of his life has very important consequences for his later development. Among the Greeks, Plato stressed the importance of education and training of children to fit different roles in society. Saint Augustine, at the beginning of the Christian era, wrote about the impact of early training and example on man's later moral development. In daily life, however, children generally were not treated in special ways. After the period of infancy, they became small adults working and playing with older people.

The foremost documentarian of this historical fact is the French historian Philippe Ariès. In his book *Centuries of Childhood* (1962), he notes that, after a late weaning (around the age of 7 years), the children of medieval Europe made the transition directly into the adult community, sharing in all adult activities. The child left his natural parents early in life to be an apprentice in another household. Schools were open to people of all ages seeking to learn a trade or specialized skill, and all ages were taught together. Children were not considered as innocent and thus were exposed to sexual matters at an early age. There were no such things as distinctive children's clothing or children's toys. Children wore scaled-down versions of the adult dress of whatever socioeconomic class they were born into. (In family portraits of the sixteenth century, the children often were depicted as miniatures of their parents.) Even today there are still many parts of the world where children live this way (Whiting 1963).

The seventeenth century saw a marked change in the way society treated children, from the basic step of recognizing them as distinct from adults, to the more particular changes in their education. It is likely that the moral influence of the Protestant Reformation and the Catholic Counter-Reformation contributed significantly to the new attitude toward children. It is also probable that economic factors were involved—the huge medieval manors were declining and being supplanted to an extent by the nuclear family—the group composed of husband, wife, and their children—as an economic unit. Children at this time began to be separated from adults and adolescents. The growth of rigid sexual morality led to the concept of childhood as an innocent, uncorrupted time of life. Educators, clergymen, and humanitarian thinkers of the time influenced whole generations to raise their children differently, to shield them from the corruption seen in the adult world.

It was at this time that children began to wear special clothing that distinguished them from other age groups. Schools taught morality and religion along with reading and writing, and students were separated into grades according to their ages, as is done today. The periods of training were extended, and the child's entry into the work force was postponed to a later age.

The clergymen, moralists, and teachers of the seventeenth century tried, for the most part successfully, to influence human nature and society by means of child training. In order to do this, they had to attempt to understand the growth and behavior of the child. It is out of these early efforts to understand and influence children's behavior and character that the child psychology of today has evolved.

The First Theories of Childhood

As more attention came to be focused on the practices of child rearing, new literature developed about the nature of the child. Some writers asked which characteristics in children were inherent and which could be taught. Debates developed between educators, reformers, and moralists over whether children were "naturally evil" or whether they were basically good until corrupted by society.

At the same time as these moral debates were taking place, a somewhat related philosophical discussion about the nature of man was developing. Here, the question was not so much whether children were naturally good or evil, but whether children were naturally anything at all. How much of human nature was inherent in the child and how much was the product of environmental influences? Did the human being actively develop according to his own internal order, or did he merely react to the outside world as it impinged upon his senses?

British thinkers of the time generally adopted the environmentalist viewpoint. They looked for the causes of the child's behavior outside the child, believing that every action is caused by some prior external action or condition. This stand was in keeping with the mechanistic world view, present in England at that time, which was brought about by Isaac Newton's discoveries in physics.

Foremost among these British philosophers was John Locke, who is considered the founder of

DIMENSIONS OF CHILD PSYCHOLOGY

the philosophical doctrine known as *empiricism*. The view of empiricism is that all knowledge comes through experience. Writing at the end of the seventeenth century, Locke maintained that the infant's mind is a *tabula rasa* — a blank tablet — on which the environment makes its impressions; he held that there is nothing in the mind that does not enter through the senses.

This empirical view was developed further in the mid-eighteenth century by another British philosopher, David Hume, who also believed that the environment was all-important in determining the child's nature. Hume broke down mental events into basic units called impressions or sensations. These were the building blocks of human thought. Man's higher cognitive processes, such as reasoning and judgment, arose as a result of repeated associations of impressions. This associationistic psychology of the early British empiricists has become a trend that has dominated British and, to some extent, American psychological theorizing ever since Hume's day.

One consequence of Locke's and Hume's views of man was a strong emphasis on systematic child training. If the child was nothing but the product of his environment, his character could be determined by consistent teaching. The method of training, according to Locke, was to be reward and punishment. By rewarding some behaviors and punishing others, parents could teach the child to control his appetites rationally, to undergo self-denial, in order to attain higher, less immediate goals.

A quite different tendency among theories of human nature developed with continental thinkers of the time. The German philosopher Immanuel Kant, writing a few decades after Hume, held the position that all organisms, including man, had their own built-in principles of development by which they used their environment to survive and grow. He called these principles "natural purposes," arguing that this was the only way in which we could understand the behavior of organic systems. Whereas Hume and Locke sought the antecedent causes of action, Kant looked for the reasons for the action, what functions the action served.

Kant also believed that human beings in particular had innate perceptual and logical categories or structures, such as space and time, by which they could order the welter of impressions they received through their senses. This view is in distinct contrast to Hume's associationism, which holds that impressions are ordered by repeated connections until they become habit. Kant believed man to be a more active, purposive organism, and further held that man possessed a moral structure that commanded him always to try to choose the morally correct course of action. As applied to children, this view posits not a *tabula rasa* but, by contrast, a young being who is born with the psychological equipment necessary to organize and make sense of his world.

Another eighteenth-century philosopher who adopted this viewpoint was the Frenchman Jean Jacques Rousseau. Like Kant, Rousseau believed that children were endowed with an intuitive sense of right and wrong. He believed that children should, for the most part, be left alone and allowed to follow their own course of development.

Rousseau also saw the child as an active, self-developing being, not merely a passive recipient of the environment's influences. According to Rousseau, the child actively seeks out what he needs from the world for each of his stages of mental and physical growth. These stages, although subject to environmental pressure, are originally determined inwardly and will unfold naturally if they are allowed to do so.

The theories of Locke, Rousseau, and other philosophers have continued to be important influences on psychological thought to the present time. In their original form, however, these theories were not conceived as testable hypotheses, nor were they based on systematic observation or controlled experimentation. Much of the child psychology of today is an attempt to reformulate and further develop these basic philosophical theories so that they can then be tested by current scientific methods.

The First Scientific Work

As more attention came to be fixed on children, many philosophers and scientific thinkers began to observe their own children more systematically. Toward the end of the eighteenth century and throughout the nineteenth century, a number of baby biographies began to appear.

THEORY AND METHODS 7

One of the most interesting and famous of these accounts of a child's motor, sensory, and cognitive growth was written by Charles Darwin, who is best known for his formulation of the theory of evolution. Darwin saw the child as a rich source of scientific information about man. His theory of evolution, suggesting that different species could develop from a common ancestor, led people to apply similar notions of development to the different stages of the human species. If the origin of mankind could be seen in the lower orders of animals, perhaps the human adult could be better understood by the study of his origin as a child. Many investigators thus began to ask when and how the various adult functions, such as language, logic, and perception of objects, developed in children.

As a result of Darwin's influence, many educators, biologists, and other scientists began to study children even more systematically. Soon their work expanded from biographical accounts of individual children to studies of larger groups of children. This development, of course, was of great scientific importance, for it enabled psychologists to make more reliable generalizations based on larger populations of subjects.

One of the pioneers in the scientific study of large groups of children was the American psychologist G. Stanley Hall. Hall is generally credited with devising and refining the questionnaire as a research technique. By obtaining information about children's personality traits, abilities, problems, and backgrounds from a broad selection of subjects, Hall was able to get more reliable and representative data than had previously been obtained. Although his approach would not be considered as controlled or objective as today's methods, it represented a great advance over the sketchy philosophical speculation that preceded his work.

Since Hall's time, there has been a great growth in scientific psychology. The empirical tradition of Locke and Hume was carried into twentieth-century psychology by such men as Pavlov in Russia and Watson in the United States. Their work focused on learning and the conditioning of responses. In laboratory experiments they used rewards and punishments to establish and measure various behaviors in animals and human subjects. Their contributions paved the way for the learning theories of such psychologists as B. F. Skinner, Clark Hull, John Dollard, Neal Miller, and others.

The tradition of Rousseau and Kant, on the other hand, is reflected, in different ways, in the cognitive-developmental theory of the Swiss child psychologist Jean Piaget and the organismic theory of Heinz Werner. Also largely in this tradition is the work of Sigmund Freud, the founder of psychoanalysis, who illuminated the immense influence of childhood experiences on later development and behavior.

These three principal types of theory—learning theory, stemming from the tradition of British empiricism and associationist psychology; developmental theory, stemming from the ideas of Kant and Rousseau; and psychoanalytic theory, stemming from the work of Freud—dominate the field of child psychology at present. To gain an understanding of today's science of children, we must have a somewhat more detailed acquaintance with each of these types of theory.

Contemporary Theories of Child Psychology

The Different World Models

Our present-day theories in child psychology have grown out of several long-standing traditions concerning the nature of man. The two main trends that we have considered are the view of Locke and Hume, that man is essentially passive, and the contrasting ideas of Rousseau and Kant, who maintained that man takes an active part in his own development.

The psychological theory that derives from Locke and Hume is referred to as the *mechanistic model*, which holds that behavior operates according to mechanical principles and can best be understood in terms of environmental cause and behavioral effect. This approach tries to analyze human behavior on the basis of simple units which can be measured quantitatively for change over a period of time. Adherents of this view tend

8 DIMENSIONS OF CHILD PSYCHOLOGY

to be skeptical about the use of such abstract terms as thought, desire, or purpose which do not point to anything clearly observable or measurable. They tend to concentrate on observed behavior, and thus have often been tagged with the label *behaviorist*.

This position, which clearly derives from the thinking prevalent in the natural and physical sciences, possesses certain definite strengths. It promotes rigorous analysis, as opposed to speculation, and encourages the use of controlled experiments and the careful sifting of evidence essential to scientific progress.

The contrasting model, deriving from the philosophy of Rousseau and Kant, is the *structural model*. This viewpoint concerns itself with the total organism rather than with isolated behaviors and, for this reason, it is also referred to as *organismic*.

Structural (or organismic) theorists are less interested in questions of mechanical cause and effect than in the structures of the organism. Like Kant and Rousseau, they hold that man makes active use of his environment rather than merely reacting to it. The child is born with its own plan of development, and the environment serves to nourish or limit the child's growth. Rather than viewing man's complicated psychological structures as being built up out of simple basic elements, structural theorists tend to see the more complex processes as qualitative changes that come into being all at once. The strength of this model is the richness of hypotheses it has generated about child development through the work of such men as Jean Piaget and Heinz Werner.

The third major type of psychological theory is that of Freudian psychoanalysis. The theories of Freud generally seem to imply a structuralist world picture. The psychoanalytic thinkers are concerned with internal structures in adults and children, with qualitative changes, and especially with problems of wish and motivation. However, the Freudians do give somewhat more weight to the role that environmental factors play in the development of human functions. In this sense, they are the most "behaviorist" of the structural theorists.

Having looked at some of the major conceptual features that distinguish the different types of contemporary theory in child psychology, we now are prepared to examine each of these theories in greater detail.

Mechanistic Theory

LEARNING THEORY. Learning theory, also called *social learning theory* or *behaviorism*, is essentially a theory about how behavior is acquired. According to this view, the behavior of all organisms consists of responses to the multitude of stimuli in the environment. Stimulus-response (S–R) is the basis of all behavior. The S–R pattern is further broken down into types of S–R conditioning—classical stimulus conditioning and operant conditioning—which are treated more fully in Chapter 2. That chapter is devoted to a detailed account of the contributions of learning theory to our understanding of the child's development, and analyzes such key concepts as reward, punishment, generalization, extinction, discrimination, and observational learning.

Because behaviorists believe in an atomistic or analytic approach to development as well as in a strictly scientific approach, the methodology most widely advocated is that of the controlled laboratory experiment. A certain type of behavior is isolated and given a precise definition. An experimental process is then devised either to induce this behavior in the experimental subject or to discourage it. It is then hypothesized that something like the experimental procedure actually takes place in the normal experience of the child. It should be emphasized that the strategy of S–R theorists is always to "operationalize" psychological concepts. By this we mean that they define by observable behavioral operations; for example, thirst is defined as deprivation of water. Many S–R theorists even attempt to give operational definitions of such mental states as thinking, feeling, willing, hoping, and so on. In this way they can give an S–R account of how human beings acquire these higher mental processes.

Structural Theory

Whereas learning theory views the child as a relatively, if not completely, passive, reactive being responding to environmental stimuli, structural theories present a comparatively active picture of child development. The child is driven by an internal tendency to grow and develop more complicated structures, both psychological and biological, for dealing with the environment. Although the environment still plays an important role, it mainly provides the material that the child uses in developing himself. The environment is not the determinant of the child's nature.

The way in which the child's adaptive structures unfold is internally determined. Where behaviorism sees human development as the continuous accumulation of quantitative changes in behavior, structural theory sees changes as qualitative leaps—whole new structures make their appearances at different stages. The crawling baby becomes the walking baby; the concrete-thinking child becomes the adolescent capable of abstraction. Each higher development is quite different in quality from the stage that preceded it. Development is thus discontinuous.

The two major structural approaches are the cognitive-developmental theories of Jean Piaget and the organismic theories of Heinz Werner. Both of these thinkers are squarely in the European tradition stemming from Kant and Rousseau.

JEAN PIAGET'S THEORY. The work of the Swiss psychologist Jean Piaget has roots in the biological sciences as well as in philosophy. Partly as a result of its comprehensive theoretical foundations, his work has influenced people in all fields of psychology, not child theorists alone. From his early interest in biology Piaget moved into the study of psychoanalysis, and from there he began making connections between the various branches of science and applying his knowledge to questions of how children's thought processes come into being. His close observations of his own three children in the 1920s provided some of the first source material for the formulation of his cognitive theories.

Although the empirical results of his observations have been fascinating, much of his experimental work with cognition is not as strictly controlled as the work of some S–R theorists. Still, it is Piaget's argument that if we wish to understand how a child's mind is operating, we must keep asking searching questions to find out how he is thinking. For that reason, we cannot always use the same questions with each child (Piaget termed this the *clinical method*). What Piaget's method lacks in scientific precision, however, is often compensated for by the richness of his theory, which will be considered more fully in the next chapter as well as in later chapters of the book.

Structuralist assumptions about the nature of children have led in other directions as well. Heinz Werner, for example, takes into account not only cognitive development, but also the importance of the aesthetic dimension. Freud and his followers, on the other hand, delved into the emotional realm of human development.

HEINZ WERNER'S THEORY. Werner is a psychologist who came to America when Hitler rose to power in the 1930s. His theory, like Piaget's, is in the European tradition and draws heavily on biology and aesthetics for its insights.

For Werner, the concept of the development of the total organism is all-important. This is to say, we do not simply read development from the "book of nature," as his collaborator Bernard Kaplan once expressed it. All that is given in nature is that people change over a period of time, and the term for that is *ontogeny*. Development, however, has to do with whether people change for better or for worse. The difference is easily understood if it is realized that when we reach old age we often decline and sometimes grow senile. Therefore, if we use the term *development* for that process, we use it in a contradictory sense, for senility cannot truly be regarded as development. It is, therefore, more accurate to use the term *ontogeny* for these age changes, whatever direction they may take.

The concept of development includes the idea of positive direction, which clearly is defined by the culture of which we are a part or by the philosopher who uses it. What people regard as development is what they want to happen as children get older. When children do not behave according to the culture's expectations, they are called "immature," a term of disapproval. We cannot escape the fact that our ideas about development also include the values we place on that process. Nevertheless, Werner, reviewing individual and historical development, thinks it is

DIMENSIONS OF CHILD PSYCHOLOGY

possible to state certain abstract truths about it, wherever it may occur. He called his principle of development the *orthogenetic* principle.

In orthogenetic development, the system (a human child, for instance) develops from a primitive level of activity— one that is *global, undifferentiated,* and *unarticulated*—to a state of *differentiation, articulation,* and *hierarchic integration*.

An example of global behavior is the movement of a salamander embryo. At first the whole organism curls to one side and then to the other. Gradually, it starts to move its top half and bottom half independently and in different directions.

An example of an undifferentiated system is the amoeba. It has one cell that performs all of its functions. This contrasts quite obviously with the human body with its many different kinds of cells all performing different functions. These cells are organized or integrated to work with each other and insure the survival of the total organism.

Human behavior, says Werner, develops from the global and undifferentiated to the differentiated and integrated. The development of human speech illustrates this process. The infant at first makes random sounds. Gradually, these sounds are formed into words; the words become articulated into parts of speech which are used in characteristic ways. These parts of speech are then coordinated and integrated with each other in definite ways to form sentences. Thus, there is increasing complication and structure, and the organism is able to perform increasingly complex tasks.

Werner, who originally was interested in aesthetics, is relatively unique among developmental psychologists in considering development to be multilinear. That is, he believes development occurs along many different lines (forms of functioning) at the same time but not always at the same levels. A person can be developmentally quite "primitive" in his management of the graphic arts or in his understanding of music, while he is at the same time very complex and well organized in his control of, say, chemistry or psychology. It is in this sense that Werner is quite different from Piaget, who considers development almost entirely in terms of cognition alone. Werner was concerned with all types of development, not just man as a rational being, which is Piaget's basic approach.

In this respect Werner owes a historical debt to the philosopher Ernst Cassirer. Cassirer, like Kant, felt that there were many ways in which a man knows the world (categories of space and categories of time, for instance), but Cassirer extended the idea to suggest that man knows this world also through music, through dance, through play, through myth, and through language, as well as through the categories of reason. It is this more extensive concept of the forms of knowing which a child must gradually acquire that Werner brings into developmental psychology. Most developmental psychologists have been concerned only with the development of such traditional forms of growth as physical growth, social growth, and perceptual and cognitive growth. How a person grows expressively and aesthetically has been much neglected because these have been considered "irrational" aspects of human life, not as alternative methods of "knowing" the world in which we live.

Another important principle of Werner's is the idea that the developed person will have "mobility of operations." He will not be just an adult who is more "rational" and controlled than children are (our traditional puritanical idea); rather, he will be capable of many types of knowing and control. He will be able to approach life in different ways (aesthetic as well as cognitive), and he will be able to use the more undifferentiated as well as the differentiated functions when he needs them. According to Werner, for example, the creative person often must deal with his subject in an undifferentiated way before he can come up with novel differentiations. The poet must immerse himself in his subject matter before he can represent it with his novel verbal articulations. The psychotherapist must virtually identify with his patient and share his subjective life, at some quite primitive or intuitive level, before he can reunite the feelings thus garnered with his more abstract theoretical insights. It is when a psychiatrist does not do this that we recognize that his pronouncements are arbitrary and abstract and do not have the touch of truth for his patient. Being mobile enough to shift backward and forward in one's developmental level is quite different from the idea that an adult's responses are always "adult" in nature. Werner would contend that some responses we have characteristically called adult are actually conventional, rigid, or inflexible. The mature adult, to Werner, is flexible. He knows how to work, but also how to play.

Psychoanalytic Theory of Development

The third theory of child development to be considered here is psychoanalytic theory, which is based on the revolutionary work of Sigmund Freud at the turn of the century. Freud's ideas have had such great impact on man's view of himself and the world that they have transcended academic and clinical circles to become a familiar part of our common knowledge—although his theories often are distorted as they are popularized.

Psychoanalytic theory derives from clinical work with patients suffering from various mental disorders and neurotic symptoms. The Freudian theory of the development of the human personality extrapolates from findings about abnormal functioning. Because psychoanalysts rely on patients' reports about their feelings and thoughts, the theory tends to concentrate on thought and emotion and to a lesser degree, on everyday, routine behavior.

DRIVES. Like S–R theory, Freudian theory makes use of the concept of drive. However, the drives that it deals with are general and instinctual. Drives are conceptualized as excitations that must be reduced. The drive, arising in some part of the body, pushes the organism into behavior designed to obtain an object that will gratify the instinct or drive—that is, lessen the excitation. The main drives, according to Freud, are hunger, aggression, and sex.

Sex, for Freud, is one of man's most important drives. The sex drive is conceived in a very general sense, however; Freud associated it with many behaviors that are not considered as sexual outside of the psychoanalytic framework. For instance, most physical pleasure, according to the Freudian view, has a sexual element to it.

ID. The term that Freud gave to sexual energy is *libido*. The libidinal drives are those pleasure-seeking drives of the organism that are among the first to develop. Freud called the structure in the personality that includes these drives the *id*. The id is the earliest structure to make its appearance in the child. It is controlled by the pleasure principle. The drives of the young child require immediate satisfaction. The child cannot accept any delay of gratification. He cannot think rationally about his situation or try to achieve long-range goals. All he knows is his immediate need. For this reason the processes of the id have been called primary processes, as opposed to the more developed secondary processes of the older child and the adult.

EGO. In contrast to the primary processes of the id are the secondary processes of rational calculation of long-range pain and pleasure. These processes belong to the element of the personality that Freud called the *ego*. The ego develops as an adaptive mechanism under the pressure of events in the life of the child. It is governed by the reality principle. Instead of immediately discharging libidinal energy in the form of such primitive behaviors as sucking on almost any available object or having a temper tantrum when the object of the drive is not available, the ego of the older child or the adult controls and channels this energy. One method of control is repression. *Repression* means that the ego does not allow certain ideas to enter into consciousness. Another method of channeling energy is logical thinking. Instead of opting for immediate pleasure, the ego selects a behavioral strategy that will maximize long-term pleasure.

SUPEREGO. The third element of the personality, one that develops along with the ego, is the *superego*. The superego is essentially conscience. Whereas both the ego and the id are concerned with achieving drive satisfaction, either through rational or irrational means, the superego is concerned with the restriction of drive satisfaction. The superego represents the moral restrictions of the culture that have been transmitted to the child by his parents and have become a part of the child's own makeup.

CATHEXIS. In addition to drive, id, ego, and superego, one other concept is crucial to psychoanalytic theory—the concept of *cathexis*. Cathexis is the process whereby objects receive the power to gratify desires. All drives need objects for their gratification. In Freudian theory, the number of possible objects is not as limited as it is in behaviorist or learning theory. Not only primary objects such as food or love objects (other people), but also ideas or fantasies of drive objects, as well as other representatives of drives, have the power to reduce drive energies. In general, then, cathexis is the investing of any object with the power to arouse or gratify some drive.

PSYCHOSEXUAL STAGES. According to classical psychoanalytic theory, cathexis focuses on different parts of the body at successive psychosexual stages of the child's development. The first stage is the oral stage. Here the cathexis focuses on the mouth, the breast, and the mother as the supplier of food and warmth. The oral stage is characterized by dependence, passivity, and the desire to take in and totally incorporate the drive object.

The second stage of development is the anal stage. During this period, libidinal cathexis is focused on the anal region of the body. Some psychoanalysts believe that this takes place because of toilet training, while others view it as an inevitable development regardless of what processes of child training occur. Some personality traits associated with the anal stage are possessiveness and neatness.

The third and fourth stages of development, in Freud's view, are the phallic and Oedipal stages. Here attention shifts to the genitals as a source of satisfaction. This process takes place at the same time as increased ego development. It is in this stage that children begin to solidify their sexual identities and to regard persons of the opposite sex (initially parents and later peers) as possible drive objects. This is followed by a period of latency, or sexual quiescence, then by the adolescent stage, and the genital stage, and finally adulthood.

According to Freud, each stage of psychosexual development is attended by a certain amount of repression of ideas of drive objects and repression of actual desires, feelings, and drive-directed behaviors. This takes place because the object of the drive cannot always be attained. The organism must develop ways other than immediate gratification for dealing with its drives.

Repression has two important consequences. The first is that the ego begins to develop its powers for dealing with the environment. These powers include the various adult functions such as speech, logic, and social ability. The second consequence of repression is that a certain amount of libidinal cathexis becomes fixated at each stage of development. Thus, a typical adult personality will at times exhibit traits that could be classified as oral and anal, as well as traits from the genital stage of development.

ERIKSON'S THEORY. Erik Erikson, who is perhaps the most famous child psychoanalyst in this country today, has extended Freud's psychosexual development theory to include eight complementary psychosocial stages, which often are referred to as "the eight stages of man." Erikson places a major emphasis on the importance of social and cultural factors in the determination of each stage; yet he makes use of Freud's ideas of psychosexual development at each level. Whereas Freud's stages are linked to organs of the body, Erikson's are more closely associated with the types of psychosocial learning that occur at different ages. Erikson sees each stage as representing a "psychosocial crisis" that must be resolved successfully before the next stage can be adequately managed.

Freud's oral stage of infancy corresponds to the stage in Erikson's view when the infant develops either a basic trust or mistrust of his world and the people in it, depending on how well his basic needs are met in the first year. The anal stage in Freudian theory coincides roughly with the period in which Erikson believes the child learns either autonomy or shame, depending on how his parents have reacted to his strivings for autonomy. In the years from about 3 to 6, which span Freud's phallic and Oedipal stages, Erikson believes the child either learns initiative or is immobilized by guilt. Next, in Freud's latency period, Erikson sees the school-age child developing either a sense of mastery and industry or a sense of inferiority. In adolescence, the child experiences the psychosocial crisis of identity. It was the popular accounts of Erikson's theory of

THEORY AND METHODS 13

the identity crisis which brought his name into public prominence during the last twenty years. Adult life comprises three stages: intimacy (versus isolation), productivity or generativity (versus self-absorption), and—if all other crises have been successfully resolved—integrity (versus despair). Erikson's ideas will be examined in greater detail in later chapters.

In the psychoanalytic view, we can see, then, that a normal person is usually a combination of partly resolved, partly unresolved conflicts to which he has adapted more or less adequately. As his subsequent years present him with life crises that evoke these conflicts, so his adequacy rises or falls. In this view the human person is likely to change a great deal as his circumstances and his challenges change. A person apparently at ease with life one year, may next year be distraught with his inability to handle the new crises that have arisen in his life, crises that may have evoked some earlier failure to handle such situations. While psychoanalysis does not seem as influential in developmental psychology as it was in earlier years, partly because it has been difficult to investigate scientifically, it is still the theoretical system which comes closest to conveying the turbulence of human growth as many of us experience it personally.

In summary, we should note that psychoanalytic theory puts a great emphasis on the emotions, thoughts, and basic needs of the individual. Psychoanalysis bases its account of human development on the individual case history. It attempts to trace how a human being, in the course of encountering a sometimes rewarding and sometimes frustrating environment, develops adult means for coping with his drives.

A Comparison of the Major Theories

The vitality of the science of child psychology is due in part to the fact that marked dissimilarities prevail in the major theories that delineate the field. The theories discussed here disagree fundamentally on the determinants of human nature. The behaviorist outlook is the most economical since it breaks down human activity into patterns of stimulus and response. The other theories all posit more complicated structures and seem generally willing to grant the existence of mental entities such as ideas, feelings, wishes, and so on. However, the structures that each of the theories deals with are vastly dissimilar in nature.

Since all the theories focus on different aspects of child development, it may seem as if they are all speaking different languages. The behaviorists are concerned primarily with how behavior becomes habit and how new habits are acquired by selective reinforcement of the old. Their language is scientific and quantitative, couched in terms of cause and effect. By and large, this approach to development is inductive—that is, it is open-ended. There is a desire among behaviorists to avoid too many assumptions about development in general. The only fixed terms are intended to be the laws of learning, which should be the same at all age levels. Accordingly, development proceeds where it may go. Where it may go is not decided beforehand.

The theories of Piaget focus on the development of logic and cognitive structures. Piaget is concerned less with habitual action and more with the forms of thought. His language tends toward the abstractly logical, philosophical, and mathematical. Indeed, borrowing a term from philosophy, Piaget has called his work "genetic epistemology," which could be taken to mean, roughly, the natural and historical origins of the theory of knowledge. Studying the child according to Piaget is studying how a person gradually develops an intellect that ultimately may become capable of abstract thought, ideally, as a physicist might use his intellect.

Werner is more concerned with the concept of what development itself is than are any of the other theorists. He has a broader view of its various domains, including the aesthetic as well as the cognitive and physical functions in his concern. The mature adult for Werner would be more than Piaget's rationalist. He would be an aesthetician as well, and also someone with a flexible capacity to make use of functions, often thought of as "childish," when they were necessary to a more complete understanding.

Finally, Freudian psychoanalytic theory deals primarily with the emotions, thoughts, instinctual drives, and the conquest of conflicts, rather than with cognitive structure or routine behavior. The mature Freudian adult has lived much

14 DIMENSIONS OF CHILD PSYCHOLOGY

more dangerously and made many more conquests and liberations of his personal nature and needs than any of the others. The other accounts are relatively passionless when compared with the Freudian one.

Given these differences in emphasis, there seems to be little prospect for bridging the gaps between the various theories of human development at present. Recent attempts to mix Piagetian language with learning theory (Berlyne 1965), and older attempts to combine Freudian theory and behaviorism (Dollard and Miller 1941), are the exception rather than the rule.

The different subjects that the present-day theories of child psychology deal with, and the opposing world outlooks behind these theories (the mechanistic viewpoint and the structural viewpoint), dictate very different methods of research for each theory. In order to appreciate contemporary child psychologists more fully, it will be useful to examine some of the methodologies currently in use.

Methods of Research in Child Psychology

The Scientific Method

When people talk about children, they generally use vague, loosely defined terms. "Johnny is a slow learner," a parent might say; or "Margaret is shy," or "Nancy is very bright." Such terms, however, convey little concrete information on which to base predictions or explanations of the phenomena of child development. We need to know in much more detail what is meant by a term such as "shy." What behaviors are "shy"? What other personality traits and environmental factors is shyness related to?

The general means that we use to find answers to these questions is the scientific method. As was pointed out earlier, other sciences have had to examine what their basic, everyday concepts really meant in terms of observable and measurable phenomena. Once data had been gathered and experimental tests had been performed which showed regular relations between different types of events, laws could be formulated about the workings of nature. Although psychology faces some special problems in gathering data about the human personality and behavior and measuring different aspects of it, nevertheless it, too, must use the scientific method.

Before we consider the various methods that psychologists use, we must understand two basic scientific terms. One of these is the concept of the *variable*. A variable is any event or set of events or conditions that can change or can be changed by the researcher. Most scientific work is aimed at demonstrating regular relationships between variables—for instance, by showing that the degree of thirst in a rat will affect how fast it learns to press a bar to obtain water.

The second term is *control*. When scientists set up an experiment to study one variable, they attempt to control—or hold constant—all other variables. When all variables are held constant except for the one being studied, they have a sounder basis for saying that any changes they then observe come from the variable being studied.

The Experimental Method

The methods of research that a scientist will use follow from his basic assumptions about his subject matter. The behaviorists or learning theorists, for instance, who tend to deal with isolated, distinct pieces of behavior, will use the most rigorous scientific methods of experiment. In the experimental situation, the scientists control the experimental variables. In the field of psychology, these variables are usually external stimuli and/or various easily manipulated states of the organism under study, such as thirst and hunger.

In order to make sure that his results are significant, the scientist will use two groups of subjects—an experimental group and a control group. The experimental group is subjected to the particular stimulus being studied, whereas the control group is not. The scientist observes the differences between the two groups with respect to the behavior under study. A hypothetical example of the use of a control group is one that would try to determine if praise from adults increases a child's rate of learning. Two groups of children, as similar in every way as possible, would be asked to learn a certain new task, perhaps a new puzzle. One group—the experimental group—would be praised by the investigators as they tried to learn, and the control group would receive no praise. If the children in the praised group learned to solve the puzzle more quickly, it could be concluded that praise was instrumental in their faster learning.

Another important characteristic of the experimental method as it is applied to research in child behavior is its focus on behavior that can be quantitatively measured. Rather than using subjective terms to characterize behavior, the behavioral scientist will concern himself with precise matters such as rates of acquisition of behavior, amount of reinforcement, reaction time, and so forth. In order to measure elements such as these, the behavioral scientist relies on instruments rather than on his own observation. This further rules out the possibility of subjective distortion of the facts.

The experimental method has many obvious advantages. Since the experimenter can control all the conditions under study, he is in a position to obtain unambiguous results. With such clear results, he is then able to make certain predictions about the behavior under study. Prediction, of course, has always been one of the primary aims of scientific work in any field of science because it allows us to understand how to control and possibly improve the future. In developmental psychology, prediction is particularly important in achieving an understanding—and sometimes a control—of how the child will develop in the future. If mental retardation or even learning disabilities can be foreseen, it may then become possible to prevent or at least reduce them.

Finally, an experiment can always be repeated and thus is open to reexamination by the scientific community. Without clear and explicit methodology which enables duplication or reevaluation of results, an experiment is less valuable.

The laboratory experiment also has some disadvantages, however, when it is used in the study of human development. The most obvious problem is that laboratory conditions are somewhat artificial. Most of what we want to know concerning child development takes place in the child's natural environment, which cannot be duplicated in a laboratory. Thus, for the most part, in artificially isolating simple human behaviors and controlling all external factors, the experimenter cuts down on the relevance of his work for real-life situations.

Another problem in laboratory work is that of measurement. At present, only relatively simple, overt responses can be accurately measured. For more complex responses such as thinking, there are no precise means of measurement. Much of human behavior is thus still beyond the reach of exact quantitative study.

Finally, a third problem is that of measuring change in a given individual's behavior over a period of time. Child psychology by its very nature is concerned with changes that take place in an individual over a number of years. In a laboratory situation, however, an individual is subjected to controlled conditions for a very short period of time. If one wants to see how his behavior has changed by repeating the same experiment a year later, one is faced with the possibility that the subject may have learned something from the previous experiment. For example, a child may have learned that performing a certain action will bring him a reward. If one repeats the experiment later in the child's life, it is possible that he will learn the action to be performed much more quickly the second time. This may have nothing to do with his normal development, but it may simply reflect the fact that he recalls the previous experiment. If the experimenter tries to avoid this problem by performing the same experiment with many different age groups, he is faced with the difficulty that the differences between age groups are not differences in age alone. Each age level has a different history.

Other Methods

In order to study the child as he really exists in his natural environment, many researchers have found it necessary to sacrifice some of the precision of laboratory work for the greater scope of other methods of research. Thus, they can obtain more information about their subjects by asking them questions (through questionnaires or interviews), by giving them tests (intelligence or aptitude tests), or by observing them in their natural circumstances. It is often difficult, however, to know very clearly what this information means. The circumstances frequently are far too complex to allow a definitive explanation of the responses that are seen.

A method that has been particularly favored over the years by developmental psychologists is the observational method. One group from the Midwest has, in fact, collected complete "day studies" on many children. In this procedure the researcher follows the children around all day, recording his observations (Barker 1968). What results is a rich yield of data on the lives of these children—a great deal more than could have been learned by other techniques. Understandings seem clear and evident because some events later in the day appear to follow naturally from what happened earlier in the day. Unfortunately, however, we cannot be certain that our understandings from this kind of data are correct. What we think we understand is not proven to be so. For that proof, we would need to test this "hunch" by some experimental method.

Correlational Research

All of the methods discussed so far, other than the experimental method, are, in effect, *correlational methods*. As its name indicates, methods of correlation try to show relationships between two or more personality or behavioral variables. This type of research technique differs from the laboratory or experimental method in that the experimenter is not manipulating the variables himself, nor is he trying so hard to control all possible factors. Rather, he is gathering data by the various methods of observation and testing, and then establishing correlations among his results. Sometimes the researcher has a very good idea of what he is looking for before he starts to collect data; sometimes hypotheses occur to him only during the course of his work. Rarely does he proceed on ideas as precise or as limited as those of the laboratory researcher.

Essentially a correlational study tells the investigator when two variables are systematically associated with each other in the population he is studying—for example, that members of a lower socioeconomic group tend to score lower on verbal tests of intelligence. Such a study, unlike the experimental study, does not tell him why this is so. For this reason correlational studies often yield much data but little certainty. The fact that two conditions or events are closely correlated does not necessarily indicate that there is a cause-and-effect relationship. If we find that members of lower socioeconomic groups also prefer a certain brand of soft drink, we cannot assume that the soft drink is the reason for their lower social status. What we can hope to do is to clarify various alternative hypotheses through correlational study; we can then expose these hypotheses to more precise experimental testing.

The correlations of greatest interest to developmental psychologists are those in which some form of functioning varies with changes in age (a 10-month-old crawls, a 15-month-old walks); or those in which there are different correlations between two functions across age levels (cognitive competence precedes linguistic competence at 18 months; linguistic competence often precedes cognitive competence at 30 months); or those in which there are different correlations between stimulus and response variables across age levels (4-year-olds respond to salient stimuli in probability learning experiments, but 8-year-olds tend to distribute their responses more evenly across the possible stimuli).

RETROSPECTION. In attempting to establish such age correlations, the developmental psychologist has a number of alternative strategies. One technique that has been used to collect data on child rearing and human development is the method of *retrospection*, or the *clinical method*. When this technique is used, people are asked to recall their own childhoods or those of their children. They are asked specific questions about their development, such as whether they were happy in school, whether their parents punished them, and so on.

As a method of gathering information, it is one that is quite easy to use: the experimenter asks people to talk. As a way of gaining reliable information, however, it is fraught with difficulties. This method is used primarily in psychoanalysis but is not limited to it. Piaget's very special use of the clinical method does not probe into the subject's background, for instance, but seeks instead to determine the character of his thinking processes.

A hypothetical example will illustrate the advantages and disadvantages of retrospection.

Suppose we interviewed a number of schizophrenics and their families about their upbringing. We might be able to arrive at a number of hypotheses about the relationship of schizophrenia to certain child-rearing practices. If, instead of using this method, we used the opposite approach, known as the *prospective* method, we would study the present child-rearing practices of many families and wait to see if any produced schizophrenics. We might be spending a great deal of time and money for very limited results, however, for we would have no way of knowing which families, if any, would produce schizophrenics. Thus, it would seem that the retrospective method possesses a clear advantage.

The disadvantages of retrospection, however, are in fact overwhelming, primarily because retrospection depends on the person being interviewed knowing and telling the truth. It is known that although people do not often intentionally lie, it is virtually impossible to eliminate distortion in personal accounts of upbringing and family history. We need consider only the problem of memory failure to realize that such interviews are generally unreliable.

Various studies have been conducted to evaluate the use of retrospection. In their book *Child Rearing*, Yarrow, Campbell, and Burton (1968) compared data on child rearing collected by contemporaneous observation with data collected by interviewing the same mothers and children at a later date.

The results showed some interesting points. Although there was a certain degree of correlation between the "memory" data and the earlier "baseline" data, there were significant and systematic differences. It was found that mothers generally painted a more favorable picture of the child's upbringing than was warranted by the data collected at the time child raising was observed. In addition, it was found that the greater the number of years since the collection of the baseline data, the more the memories differed from the baseline data. Thus, distortion increased with time. Moreover, it was found that mothers modified their memories of the earlier characteristics of their children to conform to character traits based on sex-linked stereotypes. Boys, for example, were seen as more aggressive than they had appeared in earlier baseline data. Finally, recollections of the child's past characteristics were changed to conform to present perceptions about the child's personality.

It is clear that the retrospective method has serious disadvantages. For this reason it is rarely used any longer in academic psychology, though it does have a certain value as a tool for suggesting rough hypotheses which may then be tested by other means.

THE CROSS-SECTIONAL METHOD. One way to study the changes that may or may not occur in children as they pass from one age to the next is the *cross-sectional method*. In this method, a group of children are studied who are matched in all respects, such as socioeconomic class, culture, and education, but who represent all the ages the psychologist wishes to study. The range of age-linked changes or characteristics is thus observed in a cross section of ages, rather than in single individuals studied over many years as they mature.

An example of the cross-sectional method would be a study of how dependent behavior changes with age. By this method, a group of younger children and a group of older children are rated for dependent behavior; if there is a decrease in dependency on adults in the older age groups, we can conclude that dependent behavior does change with age.

The cross-sectional method is convenient in that it does not require a great investment of time or money and often suggests many interesting hypotheses. It, too, has serious disadvantages, however, when applied to a wide range of ages. The main problem with the method is that culture and history influence people's attitudes and behavior enormously. Traits that were common to one generation may not be as widespread in the next generation. Therefore, the change that is seen cannot always be attributed directly to age differences, but may be due to historical and cultural differences.

This statement from a cross-sectional study of people in old age (Cavan 1949) illustrates such a problem:

. . . the percentage of both men and women with favorable attitudes towards religion increases with age: the increase is especially marked for the women in their nineties.

Does this really mean that a person's involvement with religion increases with age? Or is there, perhaps, a historical element at work? The first 50 years of this century witnessed a steady decrease in religious membership and interest. The older a person is today, the greater the chance that he grew up in a time when religion was a much more important force than at present. People today are brought up with far less religious training or influence than the people of 50 years ago.

It is possible, then, that we cannot conclude a person grows more religious as he grows older. Perhaps all we can say is that the younger people in the sample of this study were less religious than the older people. The differences observed between the younger and the older people may reflect a change in history and culture more than a change that characteristically accompanies an individual's maturation.

Two other problems of wide-ranging cross-sectional studies are that the individuals in a sample cannot be successfully matched for survival ability, and that the younger persons may not remain "matched" to all significant characteristics of the older persons as they mature. The older age group is naturally composed of people who have survived a longer time, while the younger population may include many who will not survive as long. The two populations, therefore, are unmatched in any of a number of factors that may determine a person's survival, and these factors may be significant for the question that is being studied. In addition, the sample of younger people will also include many who will change in some possibly important way before aging—such as by improving their socioeconomic status or education. Differences in behavior would then be attributable not only to age change but to other variables as well.

Although the question of religiousness across such a broad age span may be a slightly exaggerated example, it serves to point out problems that are faced to a lesser extent by all cross-sectional studies. Generally, cross-sectional studies are most useful when a limited age span is being considered and when relatively quick results are desired.

THE LONGITUDINAL METHOD. One of the most theoretically sound and valuable methods of correlational research is the *longitudinal method*. This is the method of making repeated observations of the same individual or group of individuals as they grow older, over an extended period of time.

This method has several advantages. First, all factors except age changes can be held constant, since the same individuals are always being studied. Second, individual forms of child development such as early or late maturation are easily observable when one individual's growth is followed over a span of time. Third, it is possible to detect "sleeper effects"—changes that jump age periods—because again one individual is under more or less constant study.

The longitudinal method also presents some problems. The main one is that often we do not know exactly which variables to study. In performing a longitudinal study of schizophrenia, for example, we would test and measure a sample of apparently normal children and then follow them through life to see which ones become schizophrenics. We would then note those who become schizophrenic and review the earlier data to see how the eventual schizophrenics differed from the other children.

This procedure may seem fairly simple; however, a problem arises when we try to decide what to measure at the beginning of the study. Which factors would be relevant to the problem? I.Q.? Probably. Should we also study hair color or height? It seems clear that these factors are irrelevant, but the problem with using the longitudinal method alone is that we have no way of knowing for certain. In other words, this method does not suggest any hypotheses about which factors may lead to schizophrenia. We could spend a great deal of time and money, only to find that we were studying irrelevant variables.

There are a number of other practical problems in conducting longitudinal studies. One of them is the great amount of time and patience necessary for gathering data about individuals over a long span of their (and the researcher's) life. Few people want to devote that much time to studying one problem. Moreover, it is not easy to find subjects who will cooperate with such a study over a lengthy time period. Those who do cooperate tend to come from a higher socioeconomic level, and this fact in itself will make the sample of people studied unrepresentative of the population as a whole.

Another disadvantage of the longitudinal method is that the culture, in this country at least, is constantly changing at an ever faster rate, and these changes may accelerate developmental changes as they are being studied, again confusing historical shifts with age shifts. There is, as well, the quite practical concern that any study that is attempting to establish stages of development over a long span of time runs the danger of becoming outmoded before it is completed. Still, in general, the longitudinal method is the most theoretically sound of all the methods of correlation that we have discussed.

Given the advantages and disadvantages of each of the principal methods of research, the most effective technique would be to combine the strengths of all three. Thus, on a given question, such as childhood factors leading to schizophrenia, we would first employ the retrospective method in an effort to uncover the important variables. We would then check our results with a number of cross-sectional studies. Finally, we would make several small-scale longitudinal studies — that is, studies using limited age spans of about five years — with each study overlapping the one before it.

If we have conducted our retrospective and cross-sectional studies thoroughly and accurately, we will know which kinds of families and which years of an individual's life are most likely to show up as significant in a longitudinal study. The longitudinal study in which the subjects are thus carefully selected will then give us a fairly accurate picture of schizophrenic development.

Relationship of Theories and Methods

Each theory of child development that we have discussed, by the nature of the issues it deals with and because of its general world view, tends to favor a given method of investigation, although it may not necessarily restrict itself to that method.

Learning theory, as we have seen, is concerned with the ultimate bits of behavior that are routine or habit; it is also an offshoot of the major traditions of scientific study. Thus, learning theory tends to employ methods that will yield strict scientific results about simple behavior, results that can be controlled and manipulated. To this end, it will use the laboratory method.

Structural theorists like Piaget and Werner are concerned with the development of more complex behaviors that are not easily studied in the laboratory alone. Piaget, in particular, is concerned with the structure of human thought and how such structure develops. His fundamental interest in stages of growth leads him to use interviews, informal "experiments," and naturalistic observation at different age levels, as well as more formal experiments, in order to discover the basic stages of development.

Werner introduced the innovative technique of paralleling the experiment with the more naturalistic real-life data. He sought to show in this way that the general principles of orthogenesis that he observed naturalistically could be replicated within particular experiments — as, for example, when subjects are asked to make responses to a picture that is flashed on a screen for a split second at increasing time intervals. The picture that is first flashed in front of them is seen quite diffusely and in an undifferentiated way. As the time interval of presentation is lengthened, perception becomes more precise and the bits are articulated together more meaningfully. According to Werner, this shows that microgenesis (perception in the microworld of the experiment) parallels orthogenesis.

Freudian psychoanalytic theory is concerned with conflict and neurosis. It develops its view of child development by interpreting and extrapolating information, not from experimental subjects, but from patients who are seeking to understand and resolve conflicts in their lives. This theory, then, focuses mainly on such conflicts, the motivations (often unconscious) of behavior. Getting at these hidden springs of action requires a great deal of intensive clinical work; Freudians therefore rely heavily on the retrospective clinical method.

Thus we can see that each theory leans toward a characteristic world view, a particular set of problems, a particular methodology to deal with these problems, and particular types of data to which it gives primary attention. It follows that the uses of each theory will be slightly different. In sum they provide a wide-ranging, if still incomplete, view of human development. Before examining the main body of research on child development—the goal of this book—let us look briefly at the uses of these different theories and methods.

The Importance of Child Psychology

Why Study Children?

The science of child development is a relatively new phenomenon in human cultural history. Although children have been a topic of interest at least since the seventeenth century, the truly experimental study of children did not begin until approximately 50 years ago. This burgeoning of a whole new field of scientific endeavor is in part the result of a culture that seeks to find alternative ways of child rearing. More exact knowledge of how children grow will give us the power to adopt new ways of child training.

This aspect of our culture—the desire to find new and better ways of rearing children—is clearly related to other more general cultural developments. The general information explosion makes us realize how relative most of our customs and traditional behavior patterns are; the increased mobility of people in our society gives many people direct experience of other ways of life; and increased leisure time gives people the time to question matters, such as child rearing, that they were too busy to reflect on in the past. In addition, the study of children is to a great extent also the study of man. Our increased interest in our psychological selves in this age necessitates an understanding of our personal psychic origins. We study children, then, in order to increase our own consciousness and better understand the culture of our children.

The practical answers to questions of child rearing obviously will change as the scientific "truths" change. In recent years, many parents and teachers have used the ideas of Arnold Gesell and Benjamin Spock. As the science of child psychology evolves, however, other effective techniques and philosophies are bound to develop.

One of the most valuable applications of child psychology today is the diagnosis and treatment of learning disabilities in school children. Partly because of developmental norms and partly because of increased knowledge of cognitive and physiological functions, psychologists now can recognize such difficulties long before they become evident to most teachers or parents as clinical conditions. This early diagnosis (usually by a school psychologist) often can mean the difference between improved learning and irreversible decline.

We now know, for instance, that a child who literally cannot sit still in a classroom—and consequently will not be able to pay attention to, and learn, much of what is taught in that room—may be suffering from a treatable condition known as *hyperkinesis*. The cause of his extreme overactivity may be physiological or it may be psychological. Tests of the child and an evaluation of his home and school environment can determine the probable origins. Instead of being written off by parents and teachers as a troublemaker or a slow learner, the hyperkinetic child now may be taught, through S–R techniques, how to moderate his excessive responses to the surrounding stimuli. Or—depending on the cause of his overactivity—he can be given corrective medication or placed in a learning situation that is less distracting than the average classroom. Through simple measures such as these, derived from research in child psychology, many children who might have spent restless, unproductive years in classrooms that overstimulated them beyond control, now may be able to enjoy their school days and learn as readily as others.

Aside from the immediate practical importance of child psychology, of course, there is the more theoretical scientific interest in the origins of various processes of human behavior. The acquisition of knowledge for its own sake is a motive in all fields of science, and certainly child psychology is no exception. The study of children can have great theoretical implications for the science of psychology as a whole.

Just as the entire field of medicine benefits from the specialized medical study of how each life begins as one cell and develops into an intricately functioning human infant, so all areas of psychology are influenced by what is found to be true of the psychological development of the human being in his first two decades of life. The work of Freud has supported the view that the earliest years of a person's life are the most influential in forming his personality and subsequent behavior. The more we learn about these early years, therefore, the more thoroughly we can understand the later years.

What to Study in Children

As American culture and trends in psychological theory have changed through the years, the focus of childhood study also has shifted. Both the questions that were asked and the method used to find the answers have changed.

The early period of scientific child study in this country, for example, was devoted mainly to studying the measurable elements of a child's development at various stages. Psychologists were striving to find average and mean patterns of development for each age level. The establishment of developmental norms was among the first major contributions of the new science of child psychology.

Theoretical interest then shifted to learning theory and behaviorism, which has had its effects on child-rearing practices. The behaviorist's principles of conditioning through reward and punishment were often applied at home to implement firm discipline and training. Over the years, however, trends have swung back and forth from strictness to permissiveness, from bottle-feeding to breast-feeding, from early to late toilet training.

Psychoanalytic theory, as well as behaviorism, has been concerned with how to produce certain types of overt behavior. Both schools of thought are interested in the question of what qualities define a "normal" child and what can be done to foster these qualities, but the approach of psychoanalysis has produced quite a different answer from that of behaviorism. When Freudian theory was most popular as a guide to child rearing, people generally believed that unqualified love and acceptance alone would produce a "normal" child. In line with this has been the counseling of Gesell, who has stressed that parents should let their children learn various habits and skills at their own pace; rarely should they attempt to force any behavior on their children at an early age. Gesell's meticulous descriptions of normative development—week to week in the infant and year to year in the older child—have provided parents and teachers with a valuable guide through the sometimes puzzling territory of childhood (Gesell and Ilg 1943).

More recently there has been a move away from trying to establish age trends and differences, and greater emphasis on the processes and mechanisms of development. This change has gone hand in hand with a shift from a purely descriptive approach to a more analytical and theoretical approach. Instead of merely detailing the stages of growth in verbal behavior, for instance, the child psychologist will try to uncover the process whereby one stage develops out of the previous stage, as a result of the structural character of the organism and the conditions that change it.

While this trend is in part a direct outcome of the increasingly scientific nature of the field, it is also in part impelled by a new cultural awareness of the tremendous effects of poverty and experiential deprivation on many of our children. If we are indeed moving into a culture where most citizens will earn their living by their capacity for mastering symbolic skills—reading, writing, thinking, computerizing, advertising—and very few can earn theirs by manual or physical mastery, as automation displaces them, then failure in schooling becomes increasingly disastrous.

For this reason, much of the research today in developmental psychology concentrates on the causes and the ways of remedying such failure. The focus tends to be on learning and cognition in infancy and early childhood because this is where the difficulties are most obvious and where they must be corrected. Behaviorist theories of change and the Piagetian theory of cognition are currently of greatest moment in this field because they have a direct bearing on such problems. This is not to imply, however, that the problems to which Werner and Freud have addressed themselves may not return to greater prominence again at some later date.

Briefly, our aim in this book will be to present the findings that have come out of the recent trends in child psychology, using the most important and significant theoretical and practical conclusions from present-day research. We shall also try to indicate what questions remain to be solved, what are the areas of research that need to be more fully explored.

Our focus throughout will be on the origins and development of psychological processes. We shall trace the various stages of growth, but we shall also try to give an account of the process of growth—that is, how one stage evolves out of another, as a result both of conditions internal to the child (structures) and of conditions impinging on him (S-R).

Summary

In medieval Europe, children were treated as miniature adults. In the seventeenth century, they began to be treated as a distinct class. As more attention came to be focused on practices of child rearing, philosophers began to ask questions about the nature of the child and, more generally, about the nature of man. Two contrasting views developed: one, set forth by Locke and Hume, held that man is essentially passive or receptive; the other, set forth by Rousseau and Kant, argued that man takes an active part in his own development.

Present-day theories in child psychology tend to stem from these contrasting views. They are mechanistic, as is the first, or structural, as is the second. From mechanistic thinking, learning theory, or behaviorism, has developed. This theory maintains that the behavior of all organisms can be understood in terms of responses to stimuli in the environment. Structural theories postulate that the individual is governed by internal structures which determine his methods for dealing with the environment.

The two major structural approaches are the cognitive-developmental theory of Jean Piaget and the organismic theory of Heinz Werner. Piaget focuses on how a person gradually becomes capable of abstract thought. Werner believes that human behavior develops from the global and undifferentiated to the differentiated and integrated. He is concerned with various types of development—aesthetic as well as perceptual and cognitive.

Psychoanalytic theory, based on the work of Sigmund Freud, also may be classed with the structural theories. It places great emphasis on the emotions, thoughts, and basic needs of the individual. It attempts to trace how a human being, encountering his environment, develops adult means for coping with his drives.

Because each of these theories of child development differs in its general world view and in the specific issues with which it is concerned, each also tends to favor particular methods of investigation.

Learning theory tends to employ the laboratory method, which yields controlled information about simple behavior.

Structural theorists like Piaget and Werner are concerned with the development of more complex behaviors that are not easily studied in the laboratory alone. Piaget's investigative tools have included the interview and naturalistic observation. Werner favored the technique of paralleling experiments with more naturalistic real-life data.

Freudian theory, concerned with conflict and neurosis, interprets and extrapolates information from patients; it relies on the retrospective clinical method. Behaviorist theories of change and the Piagetian theory of cognition have a direct bearing on children's learning difficulties and ways of remedying them. To benefit children is indeed one of the most important reasons for studying them, but the acquisition of understanding is also important. The study of children seems to be a preoccupation of our cultural era and is perhaps related to our desire to increase both self-understanding and self-control in both our personal and intimate family lives.

References

Ariès, P. *Centuries of childhood.* New York: Vintage Books, 1962.

Ausubel, D. P., and Sullivan, E. V. *Theory and problems of child development.* (2nd ed.) New York: Grune & Stratton, 1970.

Baldwin, A. *Theories of child development.* New York: Wiley, 1967.

Bandura, A. Social-learning theory of identificatory processes. In D. A. Goslin (Ed.), *Handbook of socialization theory and research.* Chicago: Rand McNally, 1968.

Bandura, A., Ross, D., and Ross, S. A. Imitation of film-mediated aggressive models. *J. abnorm. soc. Psychol.*, 1963, 66, 3–11.

Bandura, A., and Walters, R. H. *Social learning and personality development.* New York: Holt, Rinehart & Winston, 1963.

Barker, R. G. *Ecological psychology.* Stanford, Calif.: Stanford Univer. Press, 1968.

Bayley, N. Research in child development: A longitudinal perspective. *Merrill-Palmer Quart.*, 1965, 11, 183–208.

Benjamin, J. Methodological considerations in the validation and elaboration of psychoanalytical personality theory. *Amer. J. Orthopsychiat.*, 1950, 20, 139–156.

Berlyne, D. E. *Structure and direction in thinking.* New York: Wiley, 1965.

Berrien, F. K. Methodological and related problems in cross-cultural research. *Intl. J. Psychol.*, 1967, 2(1), 33–34.

Bijou, S. W., and Baer, D. M. *Child development. Vol. 1. A systematic and empirical theory.* New York: Appleton-Century-Crofts, 1961.

Bijou, S. W., and Baer, D. M. The laboratory-experimental study of child behavior. In P. H. Mussen (Ed.), *Handbook of research methods in child development.* New York: Wiley, 1960.

Braithwaite, R. B. *Scientific explanation.* New York: Cambridge Univer. Press, 1955.

Breland, K., and Breland, M. The misbehavior of organisms. *Amer. Psychologist*, 1961, 16, 681–684.

Bruner, J. S. The course of cognitive growth. *Amer. Psychologist*, 1964, 19, 1–15.

Cassirer, E. *An essay on man.* New Haven, Conn.: Yale Univer. Press, 1948.

Cavan, R. S. *Personal adjustment in old age.* Chicago: Science Research Associates, 1949.

Chess, S., Thomas, A., Buick, H. G., and Hertzig, M. Implications of a longitudinal study of child development for child psychiatry. *Amer. J. Psychiat.*, 1960, 117, 434–441.

Cofer, C. N., and Appley, M. H. *Motivation: Theory and research.* New York: Wiley, 1964.

Cronbach, L. J. The two disciplines of scientific psychology. *Amer. Psychologist*, 1957, 12, 671–684.

Dennis, W. *Current trends in psychology.* Pittsburgh: Univer. of Pittsburgh Press, 1947.

Dollard, J., and Miller, N. *Social learning and imitation.* New Haven, Conn.: Yale Univer. Press, 1941.

Elkind, D. Naturalistic methods in psychological research. *Human Develpm.*, 1967, 10.

Erikson, E. H. *Childhood and society.* (2nd ed.) New York: Norton, 1963.

Erikson, E. H. Identity and the life cycle. *Psychological Issues*, 1959, 1, 18–164.

Freud, A. *The ego and the mechanisms of defense.* New York: International Universities Press, 1946.

Freud, A. The mutual influences in the development of ego and id: Introduction to the discussion. *Psychoanalytic Study of the Child*, 1952, 7, 42–50.

Freud, S. *A general introduction to psychoanalysis.* New York: Liveright, 1935.

Gesell, A. The ontogenesis of infant behavior. In L. Carmichael (Ed.), *Manual of child psychology.* New York: Wiley, 1946.

Gesell, A. L. *Infancy and human growth.* New York: Macmillan, 1928.

Gesell, A. L., and Ilg, F. L. *Infant and child in the culture of today.* New York: Harper, 1943.

Glass, D. C. *Environmental influences.* New York: Rockefeller Univer. Press, 1968.

Hartmann, H. *Ego psychology and the problem of adaptation.* New York: International Universities Press, 1958.

Heider, F. *The psychology of interpersonal relations.* New York: Wiley, 1958.

Hume, D. *On human nature and the understanding.* New York: Macmillan, 1962.

Hume, D. *Treatise of human nature.* New York: Penguin, 1970.

Inhelder, B., Bovet, M., Sinclair, H., and Smock, C. D. On cognitive development. *Amer. Psychologist*, 1966, 21, 160–164.

Inhelder, B., and Piaget, J. *Early growth of logic in the child.* New York: Norton, 1969.

Jones, H. E. The longitudinal method in the study of personality. In I. Iscoe and H. W. Stevenson (Eds.), *Personality development in children.* Austin, Tex.: Univer. of Texas Press, 1960.

Jones, H. E. Problems of method in longitudinal research. *Vita Humana*, 1958, 1(2), 93–99.

Kagan, J. American longitudinal research on psychological development. *Child Develpm.*, 1964, 35, 1–32.

Kagan, J., and Howard, A. M. *Birth to maturity.* New York: Wiley, 1962.

Kant, I. *The analytic of the beautiful.* Trans. by Walter Cerf. Incl. *The feeling of pleasure and displeasure.* Indianapolis: Bobbs-Merrill, 1965.

Kant, I. Doctrine of virtue. In *The metaphysics of morals.* Part 2. Trans. by M. J. Gregor. Philadelphia: Univer. of Pennsylvania Press, 1971.

Langer, J. *Theories of development.* New York: Holt, Rinehart & Winston, 1969.

Langer, S. K. *Philosophy in a new key.* (3rd ed.) Cambridge, Mass.: Harvard Univer. Press, 1957.

Lewin, K. *Field theory in social science.* New York: Harper & Row, 1951.

Lippitt, R., and White, R. K. The social climate of children's groups. In R. G. Barker, J. Kounin, and H. F. Wright (Eds.), *Child behavior and development.* New York: McGraw-Hill, 1943.

Loevinger, J. The meaning and measurement of ego development. *Amer. Psychologist*, 1966, *21*, 195–206.

Malzmann, I. Thinking: From a behavioristic point of view. *Psychol. Rev.*, 1955, *62*, 275–286.

Merton, R. K. *Social theory and social structure.* New York: Free Press, 1949.

Mowrer, O. H. *Learning theory and behavior.* New York: Wiley, 1960.

Murray, H. A. *Explorations in personality.* New York: Oxford, 1938.

Mussen, P. H. (Ed.) *Handbook of research methods in child development.* New York: Wiley, 1960.

Mussen, P. H., Langer, J., and Covington, M. (Eds.) *Trends and issues in developmental psychology.* New York: Holt, Rinehart & Winston, 1969.

Penk, W. E. Developmental patterns of conceptual styles. *Psychol. Reports*, October 1971, *29*(2), 635–639.

Piaget, J. *The origins of intelligence in children.* New York: International Universities Press, 1952.

Rapaport, D. Psychoanalysis as a developmental psychology. In B. Kaplan and S. Wapner (Eds.), *Perspectives in psychological theory: Essays in honor of Heinz Werner.* New York: International Universities Press, 1960.

Rapaport, D. The structure of psychoanalytic theory. *Psychol. Issues*, 1960, *2*(2).

Rogers, C. *On becoming a person: A therapist's view of psychotherapy.* Boston: Houghton Mifflin, 1961.

Schachter, S., and Singer, J. E. Cognitive, social and physiological determinants of emotional state. *Psychol. Rev.*, 1962, *69*, 379–399.

Sears, R. R. A theoretical framework for personality and social behavior. *Amer. Psychologist*, 1951, *6*, 476–483.

Skinner, B. F. Are theories of learning necessary? *Psychol. Rev.*, 1950, *57*, 193–216.

Skinner, B. F. Psychology: A behavioral reinterpretation. Man. *Proceedings of the American Philosophical Association*, 1964, *108*, 482–485.

Spock, B. M. *The common sense book of baby and child care.* New York: Duell, Sloan & Pearce, 1946.

Stevenson, H. W., et al. (Eds.) *Early behavior: Comparative and developmental approaches.* New York: Wiley, 1967.

Storm, L. H. Psychodiagnosis: The measurement of organicity. *J. Clinical Psychol.*, January 1972, *28*(1), 54–60.

Wapner, S., and Werner, H. Perceptual development. Worcester, Mass.: Clark Univer. Press, 1957.

Werner, H. *Comparative psychology of mental development.* (Rev. ed.) New York: International Universities Press, 1957.

Werner, H. The concept of development from a comparative and organismic point of view. In D. B. Harris (Ed.), *The concept of development: An issue in the study of human behavior.* Minneapolis: Univer. of Minnesota Press, 1957.

Werner, H., and Kaplan, B. The developmental approach to cognition. *Amer. Anthrop.*, 1956, *58*, 866–880.

Werner, H., and Kaplan, B. *Symbol formation.* New York: Wiley, 1964.

White, S. H. A contemporary perspective on learning theory and its relation to education. Unpublished manuscript, Harvard Univer., 1967.

Whiting, B. B. (Ed.) *Six cultures: Studies of child rearing.* New York: Wiley, 1963.

Williams, E. P., and Rausch, H. L. (Eds.) *Naturalistic viewpoints in psychological research.* New York: Holt, Rinehart & Winston, 1969.

Witkin, H. A., Dyk, R. B., Faterson, H. F., Goodenough, D. R., and Karp, S. A. *Psychological differentiation: Studies of development.* New York: Wiley, 1962.

Yarrow, M., Campbell, J. D., and Burton, R. V. *Child rearing.* San Francisco: Jossey-Bass, 1968.

Young, P. V. *Scientific social surveys and research.* Englewood Cliffs, N.J.: Prentice-Hall, 1966.

2 Learning and Development

Learning is crucial in the life of a child—crucial for his physical survival as well as his mental growth. Almost from the moment he takes his first breath, the infant is learning how to adapt to the world around him. He learns how to nurse effectively, how to gain attention, and how to distinguish between his mother and father. Later he learns how to feed and dress himself, and finally he comes to learning as it is generally thought of: the ABCs and counting to 10. But learning is not limited to skills and information. A child also learns fears, wants, and attitudes.

Nearly everything a person does is a result of learning, and his learning is limited only by his biological nature and his own set of genes. Because he is human, for instance, he will never fly like a falcon or climb like a koala bear. If he should inherit one of the forms of mental retardation, he will never master the complexities of mathematics; yet, even here, because of the dramatic advances in our knowledge of how children learn, he may still be taught what he needs to know to live in society.

Learned and Unlearned Behavior

Although it obviously is a vital part of a child's development, learning itself is hard to define. Psychologists cannot always agree on exactly how learning takes place. Generally, *learning is a process in which experience or practice results in relatively permanent changes, or the capacity for changes, in a child's responses.* A change in behavior is the most likely evidence of learning. Of course, some changes are not a result of learning, but come from growth, a child's genetic makeup, fatigue, temporary moods, or illness. We are not concerned here with this sort of change but with those that result from experience. Changes may result from random experience—the child who burns his fingers will avoid open flames—or organized experience, or training, such as toilet training.

Psychologists in the twentieth century have discovered a good deal about how children learn. However, most of their work has been based on earlier studies of learning in animals and adults. Also, most of the actual research work has been done in clinical settings, rather than in surroundings more natural to the child—a classroom, for example, or a playroom. Despite these drawbacks, much has been learned and more is published each year about how and when the child learns.

The earliest studies were based on the principles of classical conditioning—Pavlov's dog salivating at the sound of a buzzer is the famous example. From the knowledge that began accumulating, some researchers developed other theories about the learning process that are grouped under the label of *operant conditioning* (as distinct from classical, or Pavlovian, conditioning). Still others are investigating an area of learning known as *cognitive learning*. No one approach is completely independent of the knowledge gained by any other. They are all interrelated.

As the science of child psychology progressed, experimenters continued to find a great many variable factors affecting learning. These differed in effects depending on the child's age and maturation level. Effects of variables also fluctuate with a child's health, experience, emotions, and motivations. All these changeable factors make it hard to build neat theories. In fact, no single theory of child learning has ever met the test of all the accumulated data. Each theory can deal with a small stack of information; none can accept all the findings and remain a coherent theory. Trying to build a comprehensive theory would be like packing a dozen garden rakes, a hundred bricks, forty pounds of nails, and fifty pounds of corn seed in a single plastic bag. Either something falls out or the bag is torn and distorted.

Unlearned Behavior

INSTINCT. Not all child behavior is learned. *Instinctive* responses are unlearned and can be seen when a child blinks or jumps at the drop of a dish or a pan. However, such instinctive reflex actions are much more complex in animals and play a more influential role in animal than in human behavior. When a female cat has her first litter, she eats the placenta, kills any deformed kittens, and then nurses the remaining offspring. This type of behavior would be called *instinctive*, rather than learned, by ethologists, scientists who study the behavior of animals, especially in relation to their natural habitat.

Ethologists and other scientists have debated for many years whether certain behavior in animals and humans is learned or instinctive. One attempt to clarify the distinction has been to use the term *species-specific* to describe behavior that appears to be unlearned and instinctive in an entire species (the behavior is specific to that species).

While use of the term *species-specific* avoids the more controversial one of *instinctive* and helps to narrow the focus of the discussion somewhat, it still does not provide any answers about what produces this type of behavior. Some studies have shown, however, that an animal's environment can affect his behavior—perhaps in ways parallel to the ways that a man's environment affects his behavior.

Much behavior that used to be thought "instinctive" has been shown recently to depend on "normal" conditions for that animal. Harlow's now famous studies have shown, for example, that if rhesus monkeys are "reared" by machines that provide food, rather than by other monkeys, they later fail to show a range of mating and other social responses that had been considered instinctive (Harlow 1958; Harlow and Zimmerman 1959). Much that we think of as instinct in a given species now begins to look more like learned adaptive habits for those groups that practice them.

Traits of Instinctive Acts. While we still do not understand the origins of instinct, we do have more basic information than before. For example, we know that what is usually called instinctive behavior (but may be the species' "adaptive habits") shares three characteristics. First, all members of any species have the same behavior patterns. (In the case of sexual behavior, all members of the same sex in one species have the same patterns.) Second, the behavior does not appear to be learned in obvious ways—at a certain level of maturation, for instance, cats will mate, give birth, and nurse their kittens. Third, the behavior is complex and holds to a set pattern.

Human behavior does not fit these three qualifications. Even motherhood, that fondly regarded bastion of instinctive warmth, is often challenged as to its instinctive nature in humans. Women throughout the world care for their babies in many different ways. Some breast-feed their newborn, some use bottles, and some turn their infants over to a communal nursing pool. A few mothers even abandon their children at birth. While these responses may be prompted by cultural habits or emotional disturbances, the fact remains that all human mothers do not behave the same. It is hard to see, therefore, how instinct or rigid species' habits can be a controlling force in human motherhood.

The same is true of self-preservation, often cited as the basic human instinct. A glance through Fox's *Book of Martyrs* will turn up hundreds of cases of men and women who have gone against the natural desire for life and chosen, instead, to die for what they believed was a greater good.

More important than instinct, man has the capacity to change and adapt his behavior to suit his needs in new environments and new situations. If the human child is born with any instinctive patterns of behavior, his learning quickly takes precedence over them. If they remain in the mature man, they are very well hidden. However, while instincts may not be important in man, it should be kept clear that other innate factors have considerable influence in man's development.

IMPRINTING. Most unlearned behavior in animals or humans would seem to be easily identified as such. The infant begins to make sucking motions without any help from his mother (some even suck their thumbs before they are born, as X-rays have revealed). A female cat will know how to mate, give birth, and nurture her first litter of kittens even though she may not have seen another cat since her own birth.

However, there is a form of behavior in some newborn animals, known as the "following response," which has characteristics of both learned and unlearned behavior. In certain species, the newborn or newly hatched, during the first few hours after birth, will always follow its mother; if the mother is absent at this time—either because of an accident of nature or because of experimental conditions—the newborn will follow the first moving object it sees. This phenomenon was first recorded by the distinguished ethologist Konrad Lorenz. He found that if he separated a mother goose from her new goslings, the flock of goslings would accept him as their mother and dutifully follow him wherever he led. Professor Lorenz coined the word *imprinting* to describe this following response, referring to the lasting impression he had made on his subjects the goslings (Lorenz 1952).

After birth, imprinting has only a short time to take effect. A mallard duckling, for example, will follow a moving wooden decoy (or even a human) most readily when it appears about 16 hours after hatching. Older ducklings are much less inclined to follow, and ducklings 36 to 48 hours old are already hardened nonfollowers if no mother-object has appeared by this time. These latter ducklings will always be socially maladjusted, insofar as the lack of mother-following affects their lives with other ducks (Hess 1964).

Because imprinting takes place when an outside stimulus—the decoy for the duckling—is presented to the subject, imprinting resembles a learned response. Yet, others maintain that it is not learned, but rather instinctive, because the freshly hatched duckling was not trained to follow. The question is unresolved. Though experimenters have studied imprintings other than mother-following, none of them has firmly proved that these behaviors are either learned or instinctive.

Critical Period for Learning. Common as it is in animals, imprinting has not yet been found in humans. But some psychologists believe that there are times when a child, like a gosling or mallard duckling, can more easily learn certain specific actions best. In animals—most of which have shorter lives than man—these periods of readiness are brief, as we saw with the mallards. For a child, though, a critical period for learning a particular bit of behavior may be a matter of months or years; yet, if the skill is not learned at that time, he may never be able to master it—at least not

Figure 2.1 Imprinting. The goslings, exposed to Konrad Lorenz during the optimal period, follow him as they would their mother. (Thomas McAvoy—LIFE Magazine © Time Inc.)

with the ease he once could have shown. His lack of learning at the right growth stage also may erect an emotional barrier to other learning.

Teaching children to swim is usually easy. They are eager to slip into the water and their bodies are ready to learn. With some practice, they will become good swimmers. Teaching an adult is often another story. Both his attitude and his body are different. Some psychologists would say that the adult is more difficult to teach because his readiness period for learning to swim has been missed. Others, however, might argue that he is slower to learn because he may have become afraid of water, or because he may be less energetic, or at least less limber, than he was as a child. Probably the only sound generalizations we can make at this time are that (1) young children are generally more eager to learn, (2) some skills require the maturation and learning of prior capacities and skills before they can be learned, and (3) if skills are not learned at the time which is thought to be culturally appropriate, many intervening factors occur to decrease the probability that they will be learned as easily as time goes by. It is probably only in this limited sense that we can speak of critical periods for learning in human development.

MATURATION. A child is born with many body systems, but not all of them begin working at birth. Some, though visible in the newborn infant, will begin to work only as the child grows older. A child's legs—his locomotive system—are useless for walking until he is 12 to 18 months old. By then he has developed his leg muscles by crawling, while his baby bones have hardened enough to support his weight. This system-by-system development of both biological and neurophysiological components of the body is referred to as *maturation*. The child's genes ultimately determine that each system will be activated in a precise order, related to the child's age and the length of time the previously developed system has been in operation.

Infant stages of maturation are easy to see. A pediatrician can roughly predict when a child will raise its head, sit up, crawl, or walk. Maturation does not stop when a child becomes an adult. In the human, it continues from conception to death.

Learning and Maturation. The different roles that maturation and learning play in the appearance of certain basic behavior patterns have been investigated for many years in an effort to determine just how each process affects a child's or an animal's development. A study of salamanders has indicated the importance of maturation for some basic patterns of behavior.

Two groups of newborn salamanders were placed in separate tanks, Group A in the usual water-filled tank and Group B in a tank containing water and an anesthetic. The Group B salamanders lay motionless, their bodies feeding on their yolk sacs. After Group A had been swimming in its plain water for five days, Group B was transferred to plain water. In less than half an hour, Group B was swimming as well as Group A—proving that maturation is more important than learning or practice in this basic behavior (Carmichael 1927).

Learning and maturation interact and affect each other, but maturation does more to establish basic behavior sequences than learning does. Before he can learn to hold a spoon or tie his shoe, a child must reach a particular stage of maturation of hands and fingers. At that optimum stage, he will learn quickly even though he has little training. Knowing maturation's strong role in a child's performance, you would naturally conclude that older children perform most tasks better than their juniors. Experimenters have found that when young children, all equally trained, were asked to cut paper, button their shirts, and walk upstairs, the more mature children always did better than the younger ones. Of course, regardless of age, it goes without saying that a child can only perform tasks within his repertoire as a human being. Asking an unsteady, year-old infant to kick up his heels and cavort like a year-old colt would be about as successful as asking the colt to take up walking on its hind legs.

Still, in discussing maturation, we must be careful that we do not attribute to it results which are really the outcome of accumulated learning that has not been studied. It is only by trying to help children learn a skill in every way possible, and in ways tailored to their level of maturation, that we can really discover what actually are the limits imposed by maturation. A study in which a group of 4-year-olds were taught to discriminate left from right illustrated this approach.

The children were shown two cards, each with a stick figure pointing either to its left or to its right. They first were asked to learn that the figure pointing off to their left was called "Jack" and that the one pointing off to their right was called "Jill." After as many as 80 trials, with the usual rewards for correct answers, the responses were no better than chance guesses.

Rather than assuming that this skill was simply below the maturation level of 4-year-olds, the researcher modified his technique. He showed the same cards to the same children, but this time he asked them to respond to the card with the figure pointing to their left by reaching out to their left and touching a push button on the left side of the table at which they were seated. He asked them to reach to their right in the same way when they saw a card with the figure pointing to their right. The 4-year-olds who had failed to make the correct *verbal* responses to the figures now quickly learned to make the correct *reaching* responses to them. And after learning to distinguish left from right in this fashion, without words, they were returned to the original "Jack and Jill" naming problem, which most of them readily mastered (Jeffrey 1958).

This study, then, along with others, indicated that children can learn certain skills sooner than is usually expected—if the training takes into account exactly what skills the children already have and do not yet have. What has previously been considered the limits of maturation may in some cases be limitations in the methods of training or teaching.

Classical Conditioning

Of the many ways in which a child learns, conditioned learning is certainly the most familiar. Since Ivan Pavlov's famous experimental work with dogs near the turn of the century, *conditioned* has become a widely bantered catchword. It usually summons up the image of Fido dashing into the kitchen to be fed every time he hears the crunch of the can opener, no matter how recently he has eaten. Like most stereotypes, this one captures only a part, but an important part, of the truth.

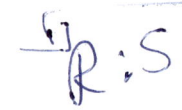

Conditioned learning appears in two different forms—classical conditioning and operant conditioning. Basic to both types of conditioned learning is the subject's response to a stimulus. A *stimulus* can be anything, physical or mental, to which the subject reacts or responds. The *response* is what the subject does when he perceives the stimulus. The *stimulus* of a red traffic light will produce the *response* of putting your foot on the brake of your car; the smell of popcorn will probably make you salivate. When an infant smiles on seeing his mother's face, he is responding to a stimulus. Conditioned learning establishes a bond or association between a stimulus and a response. The bond is the regular, measurable relationship between the stimulus and the response.

Classical conditioning was the first learning process to draw the attention of researchers. For years, psychologists have assumed it to be the basic and, therefore, the most important learning process, particularly during infancy. While this has not been proved, it does seem likely, for instance, that the thousands of times parents change a baby's diapers, feed him, and put him to bed, would clearly establish associations for the infant. If his mother always scowls in disgust when she changes his diapers, the baby may link disgust with diaper changing, or perhaps with bowel movements. Unfortunately, we do not know for certain that he does, since attempts by child-rearing studies to associate such behaviors have not produced much firm evidence. Nevertheless, the apparent common sense behind the assumption makes it seem likely that a baby does pick up this kind of "learning" by association.

Because learning by association is a basic learning process, child psychologists are strongly drawn to the work of Pavlov, who did basic work in classical conditioning. Classical conditioning can be defined as a form of learning in which the subject establishes a new association between an outside stimulus and a response that, for him, is basically a natural reflex action. A baby may gurgle a hundred times a day for no apparent reason since gurgling is a natural reflex action for an infant. But when he gurgles promptly and regularly at the sight of his bottle, he has developed a new association between the stimulus of the bottle and his reflex of gurgling.

Pavlov's Work

The work of this Russian physiologist (1849–1936) with salivation in dogs is the most famous model of classical conditioning. Pavlov's basic discovery was that a dog can be taught to salivate at the sound of a buzzer. A dog normally will salivate only when it senses food. In his experiment, Pavlov sounded a buzzer immediately before giving food to a dog. Soon the sound of the buzzer alone made the dog salivate (Pavlov 1927). In this experiment, the food is an *unconditioned, or unlearned, stimulus* because it naturally produces the *unconditioned, or unlearned, response* of salivation. The buzzer is the *conditioned stimulus* because the animal was taught, or conditioned, to respond to it. The response of salivating at the sound of a buzzer is a *conditioned response* because it is produced by a conditioned stimulus. The animal had learned a new association between the conditioned stimulus of the buzzer—previously only a noise to the dog—and its natural salivation reflex. The learning of that new association is the essence of classical conditioning.

Infant Conditioning

Following Pavlov's discovery, many experimenters have tried to discover whether the responses of infants could be conditioned. For example, Lipsitt and Kaye designed an experiment to determine if newborn infants could be conditioned to make sucking motions at the sound of a tone, which would indicate that infant conditioning is possible. They sounded a tone (a conditioned stimulus) for one second before giving the infants a pacifier (an unconditioned stimulus) to suck on. The tone was left on for the 15 seconds the infants were allowed to suck on the pacifiers. At first, the sucking on the pacifier was an unconditioned response—infants will automatically suck on pacifiers or almost any objects placed in their mouths. After twenty 15-second trials in which the tone and the pacifier were presented together, however, the infants began sucking in response to only the tone. The sucking reflex was now a conditioned one—it could be elicited by the conditioned stimulus alone (Lipsitt and Kaye 1964). On the basis of this experiment, Lipsitt and Kaye concluded that infants can indeed be conditioned.

Other infant reflexes, such as head-turning, eye-moving (Kasatkin et al. 1953; Koch 1965; Mirzoiants 1954), and mouth-opening (Kaye 1965), also have been conditioned successfully, even though the infants generally did not remain conditioned for long.

This lack of stability and persistence in the

conditioned responses of young babies has been a major argument against the view that conditioning is the most important form of infant learning. On the other hand, the fact that the infant can indeed be conditioned is necessary evidence for those who argue that early experiences are important in determining later development.

AGE AFFECTS CONDITIONING. During the first four years of childhood, the older a child is, the more quickly he can be conditioned. But after age 4, the relation between the speed of conditioning and age disappears (Mateer 1918). Some researchers have thought that the speed of conditioning might be related to a child's intelligence. However, studies show little evidence that the rapidly conditioned child has any greater learning capacity than the child who becomes conditioned slowly.

Operant Conditioning

In the second learning model—*operant conditioning*—a new association between a stimulus and a response is developed, as it also was in classical conditioning. But that is the end of the similarity between the two models. In operant conditioning, the action the learner takes is voluntary—under his own control; it is not a natural reflex, such as blinking or salivating, as in classical conditioning. The learner's response—solving a problem correctly, for instance—*operates* in the process. The response is *instrumental* in producing a reward, such as praise from a teacher or parent, which is why the process is called *operant* or *instrumental conditioning*.

There are other differences, too. In classical conditioning, the experimenter has almost complete control over the stimuli and the rewards he gives his subject. He does not rely on the voluntary responses of the subject. In operant conditioning, however, the opposite is true. The subject is rewarded or punished because of what he does or fails to do. A reward is given only if he gives the specific response the experimenter wants. The experimenter also can use what might be called a negative reward—he can remove an irritating stimulus, such as a very bright light, when the subject performs the desired response.

While the two conditioning techniques are distinct, some researchers have argued that the subjects' actual behavior and learning processes may be quite similar (Grant 1964; Kimmel 1965; Prokasy 1965). For example, in classical conditioning of eyelid movements, the subject, not the experimenter, may be controlling the relation between his eye blinks and an unconditioned stimulus like a bright light by timing his eye blinks to avoid the light. Thus, the subject may be controlling his own response as he does in operant conditioning. It is possible, therefore, that classical and operant conditioning are only different forms of labeling quite similar processes.

Operant Conditioning in Animals

Rats and pigeons are favorite subjects for operant conditioning. They invariably find them-

Figure 2.2 A Skinner box used in operant learning experiments. To the right of the chamber is a device that records the responses of the rats. (Hugh Rogers—Monkmeyer)

selves housed in a contraption called the Skinner box, named for B. F. Skinner, the American psychologist who invented it and developed many of the techniques of instrumental conditioning. Made of metal and glass and about as big as a hatbox, the Skinner box may also have a floor of metal rods that can deliver electric shocks. An inside wall holds a lever for rats or a pecking key for pigeons, and below it is either a tray or an opening. This is where the animal gets his reward—food pellets or water for the rat and grain for the pigeon. Outside the box is a measuring device that records the number of times the rat presses the lever or the pigeon pecks the key.

In his first experiment in operant conditioning, Skinner set up a small lever which the rat had to press to get his food pellet. Skinner's aim, of course, was to reward and strengthen the lever-pressing response. First, he let his animal become accustomed to the box, frequently feeding him in it. Then he removed the rat and withheld its food for 24 hours. When the rat was returned to the box, it poked about and soon found the lever and pressed it. A pellet fell into the tray. As the rat ate it, a device outside recorded the lever-pressing response. The rat pressed the lever again and ate. Soon it was pressing and eating like the starved rat it was, and the recording device was noting each course in its meal (Skinner 1932).

Skinner had successfully trained the animal to perform a specific action, pressing the lever, which was not a natural reflex and was new to the animal for this purpose in this setting. Pressing the lever, the instrument of conditioning, resulted directly in the reward of food. The positive reward of food pellets continually strengthened the lever-pressing response. Once the rat learned to press the lever, its rate of response became steady. If a rat made the box its permanent home, the rodent would probably eat at regular intervals, and more slowly, since it would know where its next meal was coming from.

Operant Conditioning in Infants

B. F. Skinner and his followers were the first to popularize operant conditioning. But earlier, in the late 1920s, other experimenters had made systematic studies of such conditioning with children (Ivanov-Smolensky 1927). A 1959 study of the conditioning of infant vocal sounds also employed techniques of operant conditioning. Here, the experimenters rewarded the vocal sounds of 3-month-old babies by smiling, saying "tssk, tssk," and touching the infants' stomachs. When they did this, the babies made sounds more often. The experiment, conducted in nine 3-minute sessions daily over six days, seemed to show clear signs of conditioning (Rheingold, Gewirtz, and Ross 1959). However, these signs have been read another way—the smiling, clucking, and touching may have aroused the infants' responses instead of reinforcing them. Still other experiments (Weisberg 1963; Brackbill 1958) have backed the conclusion that the infants had actually been conditioned to make the vocal sounds.

If further proof of the possibility of operant conditioning in infants was required, an experiment to condition head-turning provided it. The reward in this case was a three-second nip at a nursing bottle filled with milk. Group A was rewarded for head turns of 45 degrees to the right, Group B for the same kind of turn to the left. Infants in Group C, the control group, were rewarded no matter which way they turned and even if they did not turn at all. To prevent distraction, the experimenters laid the babies in a white-walled room, facing straight up. During a three-minute conditioning period, head turns were rewarded. For the next two minutes, they were not. Next came a two-minute session with the reward restored.

The results were clear. Groups A and B turned their heads to the right or left significantly more often than under normal conditions. During the no-reward period, both groups showed definite declines in the head turns. But in the two-minute refresher session, they rebounded from their lapse and did even more head-turning than before the unrewarded period. Predictably, the control group showed none of these fluctuations in behavior (Siqueland 1964).

Shaping: Little by Little

Instead of rewarding a single completed action, a person can gradually *shape* a child's behavior. In shaping, he would reward the child for actions that come close to the final act he wants from

LEARNING AND DEVELOPMENT 33

the child. It is probably this process that is at work when parents praise or reward their children for at least trying to hang up their coats, or making a serious effort at washing their faces. Every now and then the child comes a little closer. By slowly demanding a more complete version of the desired behavior before rewarding the child, and by not rewarding acts that are contrary to this behavior, the adult can shape the child's existing responses into a new behavior.

This gradual process of shaping a new behavior through successive approximations explains the development of many new patterns of behavior. While they seem spontaneous, they may result from a fairly long period of operant conditioning. Skinner has used the image of a sculptor in describing this process:

Operant conditioning shapes behavior as a sculptor shapes a lump of clay. Although at some point the sculptor seems to have produced an entirely novel object, we can always follow the process back to the original undifferentiated lump, and we can make the successive stages by which we return to this condition as small as we wish. At no point does anything emerge which is very different from what preceded it. The final product seems to have a special unity or integrity of design, but we cannot find a point at which this suddenly appears. In the same sense, an operant is not something which appears full grown in the behavior of the organism. It is the result of a continuous shaping process. (Skinner 1953)

Behavior of adults as well as children can be shaped. A psychology class decided one day to practice what they had learned by conditioning their teacher. When he stepped to the left of his lectern, they coughed, shuffled notes, yawned, and dropped books. When he moved to the right, they fixed their eyes on him in silent, rapt attention. By midterm, the professor was all but riveted to the right side of his lectern. Standing in that position, he was positively rewarded by his students' attention and negatively rewarded by the lack of class disturbances. His students had shaped his behavior.

Conditioning of Attitudes

Attitudes as well as physical reflexes or voluntary responses can be conditioned. This helps to explain the curious prejudices some people exhibit. A woman says she could never become engaged to a man named Harry. A man in his forties says he would never eat any meat identified as lamb. These odd aversions suggest the man and woman were negatively conditioned to the words *Harry* and *lamb*. The learning process that can influence attitudes actually falls somewhere between the two models of classical and operant conditioning.

An experiment of Staats and Staats illustrates conditioning of attitudes. Two groups of people learned a list of words, including *Swede* and *Dutch*. Group A heard Swede and Dutch followed by positive words, such as *pretty*, *happy*, and *nice*. Group B heard Swede and Dutch succeeded by negative words—*ugly*, *dirty*, and *mean*. When both groups rated the national names on a scale ranging from very pleasant to very unpleasant, Group A rated Swede and Dutch as pleasant. Group B rated them as unpleasant. Obviously, both groups' attitudes had been conditioned successfully (Staats and Staats 1958).

This simple process of association is often used for political purposes. The people in power attempt to link their political opponents to attitudes and goals that seem to threaten the populace. The opponents become the enemy, and everything related to the opposition becomes just as bad. Or, as the well-worn legal phrase puts it, the opposition is convicted of guilt by association. Here, too, an effective even if unpleasant kind of conditioning has been used.

Applications

As the preceding cases make clear, operant conditioning has uses beyond the laboratory. Since some mental processes can be changed through operant conditioning, it has been applied in psychotherapy for a few conditions and in the treatment of minor social problems, such as shyness and timidity. When used in these ways it is sometimes referred to as *behavior therapy*. Perhaps the most important part of this kind of conditioning is discovering the reward—praise, candy, cash—that best reinforces the subject's behavior. When the psychotherapist finds the right reward, he uses it to encourage behavior that gradually moves closer to the desired behavior—whether it is speaking audibly or learning to meet strangers.

The more difficult the case, the more often behavior shaping must begin with tangible rewards. With progress, these material rewards may be increasingly replaced by abstract rewards. In the most fortunate outcomes, the subject eventually rewards himself, using the types of verbal rewards he once received from others. There have been some impressive documentations of such a "developmental" series occurring with disturbed children (Hamblin et al. 1971).

Conditioning has been especially effective in breaking an undesirable habit such as thumb-sucking. In an experiment cited by Baer, two young children who were steady thumb-suckers were seated side by side and shown cartoon films, which they enjoyed. When the first child sucked his thumb, the projector was stopped. Only when he removed his thumb from his mouth did the film continue. Thumb-sucking soon became less attractive to him and he stopped. But the second child did not stop because the experimenters had deliberately not cued the cartoon's stops and starts to his thumb-sucking (Baer 1962). Thus, the first child's habit was broken by regularly withdrawing the reward to punish thumb-sucking.

Another case tackled a child's fear of getting a haircut. An 18-month-old child, Bud, feared the barber because it seemed he linked the barber's white smock, starched cloth, chrome-trimmed chair, and shears with the doctor who had given him some painful injections. Bud's nursery school teacher, Miss L., and her assistant, Miss W., involved Bud's friend Bill, who liked the barbershop, to help condition Bud.

Phase one of their plan was an effort to dispel Bud's fear of the barber's paraphernalia. The morning before they were to take Bud to the barbershop for his first visit, his teachers buttoned on starched white smocks in place of their flowered ones. Miss L. showed Bud and the others how a hair clipper and shears work, along with standard scissors; she demonstrated the shears by clipping off a bit of Bill's hair. Miss L. then playfully wrapped up Bud and Bill in white cotton sheets resembling a barber's cloth. None of these vignettes fazed Bud.

Phase two was expected to show Bud that the barber was friendly and harmless. Miss L. had planned a two-minute "social" visit to the barber that afternoon, but Bud refused to leave the car when he spotted the barbershop. So Bud and the barber merely waved "bye-bye" to each other.

On the way to school the second morning, the children and teachers drove by the barbershop; Bud waved to the barber along with the others. At noon, on the way home, Miss L. carried Bud into the shop, where they discussed the barber's clock, since Bud was currently fascinated by clocks. They also spoke briefly about the shop's more threatening furnishings.

When the foursome made their visit on the third day, Bud watched Miss L. spin around in one of the chairs. She invited Bill to climb up and spin with her. Miss W. got into another chair and helped Bud onto her knee; then they all spun around a few times. The barber then demonstrated that his chairs also went up and down and gave Bud and Miss W. a couple of rides. Finally he set the chair at working height, and Miss W. told Bud she was going to wrap him up in the barber's cloth. The barber gingerly began cutting Bud's hair; to his surprise and relief, he finished without so much as a nicked ear (Landreth and Read 1942).

PROGRAMMED INSTRUCTION. The idea behind teaching machines and programmed instruction grew out of Skinner's and Pressey's experiments in operant conditioning. As it is used in some schools today, programmed instruction breaks down an area of knowledge—the sex life of the fruit fly, for example—into small steps or units of information. It presents these in logical sequence, with each unit followed by questions. When a child answers, the machine (or the answer section of the book, if a machine is not used) immediately tells him if he is right or wrong. For the average student, knowing he gave the correct answer is reward enough.

Programmed instruction has not turned out to be suitable for total education as some proponents at first thought it might be. However, it can be valuable in teaching some subjects, such as arithmetic. The machine also is helpful to the student who finds it hard to learn in a classroom. With the machine, he can work alone and undistracted, at his own speed. And, of course, the teaching machine's knobs, keys, screen, and other hardware act as an incentive to some students who are quite uninterested in education's less tangible aspects. For these uses there is clearly value in programmed instruction. However, as a tool for the total education process, it has proved disappointing, at least partly, because it cannot account for all kinds of attitudes toward learning. For many learners, part of their incentive is the enjoyment of their *own* control of the conditions and outcomes of learning, rather than control by a program.

Pavlov, Skinner, and scores of other scientists and researchers have explored the two basic learning models of classical and operant conditioning. From their studies, which deal extensively with animals, we know first of all that there is much we do not understand about human learning and that even in the very young child, learning is an extremely complex activity. Because psychologists studying infants have been more successful with operant conditioning than with the classical conditioning, we may assume, perhaps, that operant conditioning is more important during infancy. This would not be a surprise to those who emphasize the great importance of the child's own voluntary activity in his learning—Piaget, for example, whom we shall discuss later in this chapter.

Variable Factors that Affect Learning

Classical and operant conditioning involve several variable factors that change from one situation to the next. We already are familiar with the basic factors in the conditioning process—stimulus, response, and reward. But there are a few subtleties we should examine.

Psychologists first used the words *stimulus* and *response* as labels for physical actions, gestures, or objects that could be measured. In time, however, they came to use the labels to describe such intangibles as mental images and feelings, which they began to speak of as internal stimuli or responses. Though real, images and feelings cannot be seen, so psychologists have to estimate changes in them from measurable changes in the body or in behavior. For example, an increase in a hungry child's heartbeat might indicate he was imagining a juicy hamburger. Although *response* and *stimulus* now have broader meanings, psychologists have generally kept these words rather than using the more abstract terms such as *image* and *emotion*. Retaining the earlier concrete labels may be merely a habit of language among psychologists. Or it may reflect a professional insistence on *empiricism*—that all information come from experience and be measurable. In this approach the psychologist says: "I'll believe it when I see it"—or touch, taste, hear, or smell it. He insists on being able to measure the outcomes of the variables he uses.

Stimulus and Response

A stimulus can be any of an infinite variety of things. In fact, every *thing* in the universe can be considered a stimulus. And then there is an equal number of *nonthings*—such as gestures, noises, memories—that also can be stimuli. Broadly, stimuli can be divided into two kinds: internal and external. The food Pavlov gave his dog was an external stimulus—it came from outside the dog, the subject of the experiment. The buzzer also was an external stimulus. For the hungry child, the stimulus to eat is internal—his stomach is growling.

Responses fall into two categories—*natural* and *learned* responses. An infant who turns his head is making a natural response, one he would make on his own. On the other hand, the child who responds to the internal stimulus of hunger by raiding the refrigerator is making a learned response. But learning is more than either a stimulus or a response. Making a link or association between the two produces the learning. For example, through association, the child learns to name the things around him. By hearing a particular one-syllable word whenever a certain furry, four-legged creature appears, the child learns who the family cat is.

Reinforcement

Reinforcement is a third variable that affects learning in conditioned learning experiments. In operant conditioning, *reinforcement* is a reward given to the subject as soon as he makes the desired response to a stimulus. It encourages a learner to repeat a response, and thereby reinforces the bond between stimulus and response. The pigeon that pecks the key in a Skinner box gets a few grains of wheat. More than likely the bird will peck the key again soon. The infant who turns his head is encouraged to do it again by a drink of warm milk. In classical conditioning, the learner's response is not thought to be under his control. Reinforcement in this case means strengthening an association the learner has made between a reflexive response (salivation in Pavlov's dog) and a conditioned stimulus (the buzzer). Pavlov argued that this association could be strengthened, or reinforced, by repeatedly pairing the conditioned stimulus with the unconditioned or natural stimulus (food)—the greater the number of pairings, the stronger the conditioning.

PRIMARY AND SECONDARY REWARDS. Reinforcement has been classed as either primary or secondary. *Primary reinforcers* or rewards in general compel the subject to respond without the help of other rewards. There are two categories of rewards that are considered to be capable of doing this—those that satisfy needs which are basic for survival and those which are innately satisfying in themselves. Water, food, sleep, and the avoidance of pain are primary rewards, for example, because they satisfy primary, survival, needs. Tactile contact in infancy and stimulation of the genital area also would be considered primary rewards by some psychologists because they provide pleasure independent of any earlier association with other rewards.

A *secondary reinforcer* or reward can influence the learner only after he links it with some primary reinforcer. The food Pavlov's dog eats is a primary reinforcer—it satisfies a basic need, hunger. The buzzer that is paired with the food is a secondary reinforcer because the dog has learned to associate it with the satisfaction of hunger. Secondary rewards are also called learned rewards. Money would have no reward value for a young child; the child must first learn that money can buy candy or toys before the money can operate as a reward. High grades in school and promotions on a job are also secondary or learned reinforcers—they have acquired value because a person has learned to associate them with specific primary rewards.

Working with a chimpanzee, Wolfe demonstrated that a secondary reinforcer could be used to condition behavior. First, he gave a poker chip to the chimp. When the chimp put the chip into a vending machine, a grape tumbled out. After the animal had bought itself several grape snacks, the researcher trained it to raise a lever and pull a small tray by a cord. He paid the chimp in poker chips. Interestingly, the chimp performed these two tasks eagerly even though it could not buy grapes for itself until later (Wolfe 1936). The chimp had linked a primary and secondary re-

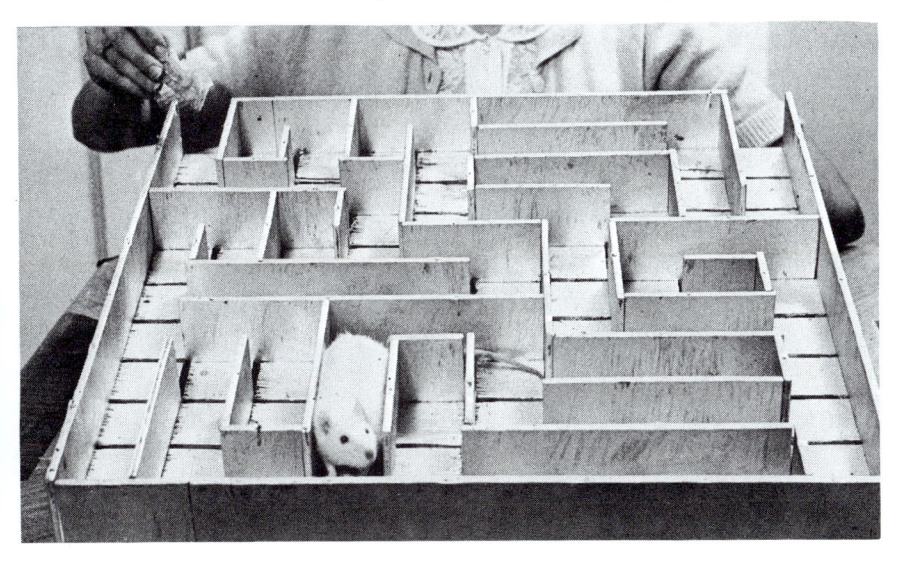

Figure 2.3 The rat is being conditioned to learn the maze. When it finds its way out of the maze, it will receive a reward of food. (Robert J. Smith—Black Star)

LEARNING AND DEVELOPMENT 37

ward; the poker chip acquired value for the chimp because it represented the primary reward—the grape.

TIMING OF REINFORCEMENT. In some studies, researchers have delayed giving the reward or reinforcement, for varying lengths of time, until after the subject completes his response. Their attempts have been to discover what, if any, effects the timing of the reinforcement has on the learning process. Studies of this nature have provided much dependable information, telling us, for example, that the time lag between response and reward affects how fast the rat will press the lever or the baby will turn its head. Generally, the sooner the reward is given, the faster the subject learns the response. Accordingly, a delay in reward delays the rate of response. One theory suggests that the response rate is slowed because during the period of delay, other, different responses, which the experimenter does not want, may rise to the surface. These will compete with the desired response and delay or eliminate it. The rat may become intrigued with a flea in his haunch, the child with a patch of sunlight on the ceiling. In both cases, the desired response will be delayed.

PARTIAL REINFORCEMENT. Reinforcement can be continuous or irregular. A rat may get a food pellet every time it presses the lever, or it may get one every third time. Given the inconsistent nature of most parents, the practice of partial reinforcement is probably widespread. Experiments show that *partially or irregularly rewarded animals and children respond faster and keep their responses longer than consistently rewarded subjects*. Some observers have suggested that partial reinforcement creates an incentive to respond, much like the "next time" conviction of the inveterate gambler. Yet studies have shown that incentive itself, when it is one variable factor in an experiment, does not influence a subject's rate of response. Why partially reinforced subjects respond faster and longer remains unanswered.

THE ROLE OF REINFORCEMENT. Not everyone agrees that a reward is important at all in the learning process. A group called the *contiguity theorists* maintains that the subject will learn, without a reward, if only the response takes place while the stimulus is present, that is, if the stimulus and response are contiguous. Opposing this view are the reinforcement theorists, who staunchly insist that whether the contiguity theorist knows it or not, a reward is always present when learning takes place. A third group takes another stand, saying that a reward is important in operant but not classical conditioning.

Latent Learning. Contiguity theorists may draw some support from an experiment that demonstrates learning can occur without a reward, though the reward is needed to make the subject *show* what it has learned. Tolman and Honzik allowed rats to run freely in a labyrinth, and left half the rodents unfed for several days. However, they rewarded the other half, the control group, each day for successfully threading the byways of the maze—a task at which they outperformed the unfed group. When the unfed rats began to get food rewards, though, their performance in the maze suddenly shot up to the level of the control group. The starved rats apparently had learned as much during their unrewarded travels in the maze as the well-rewarded rodents. Since they did not demonstrate this knowledge—until they were rewarded—their learning is called *latent learning* (Tolman and Honzik 1930).

SOCIAL VARIABLES. Frequently, in experiments of conditioned learning, praise is the reward used. Many complex factors are involved in the effects of praise. Is the experimenter male or female? Which sex is the subject, and how old is the child? These, and more, are important social variables.

The following experiment with preschool boys illustrates how the sex of both the subject and the experimenter can influence learning. Two researchers—a male and a female—conditioned several boys to answer "Mother" or "Father" to a series of simple questions about a family of four dolls. The boys were selected from among the highest and lowest scorers on a test that measured whether they identified more strongly with males or females at that stage in their lives. In the experiment, the researchers were able to condition all the boys to some extent, but boys who identified strongly with a masculine figure were conditioned more easily by a male than a female. Similarly, praise from the male experimenter more strongly reinforced the behavior of boys who identified with the masculine figure. Finally, it is interesting—and consistent—that only when boys with low masculine identification were tested by a male experimenter did "Mother" fare better as a conditioned response than "Father" (Epstein and Liverant 1963). In this experiment, the sex of the experimenter and child was important. Other variables, such as the experimenter's looks and behavior and the child's previous contact with him—if any—also help to determine how easily the child will learn (Stevenson 1970).

Stimulus Generalization

While a child who has been conditioned to a particular stimulus will respond to that stimulus, he also may respond to a stimulus that resembles the right one. This is called *stimulus generalization* because the child's "definition" of the original stimulus has broadened or become generalized enough to include other stimuli that now will trigger the same response. However, generalization will not occur to just any stimulus. As a rule, the more a new stimulus looks like the old one, the more likely the child is to perform the act the old one prompted.

An experiment with an infant named Albert and a white rat illustrates the process of stimulus generalization. When Albert was given a rat as a playmate, the boy showed no signs of fear. However, as Albert played with the rodent, the experimenters made a loud noise that frightened the boy. After the rat and the noise were paired a few times, Albert wanted nothing more to do with his pet. But his fear was not limited to the rat. It became generalized and Albert was quickly intimidated by other objects—his mother's mink neckpiece, a dog, wool, human hair—that were "furry" like the rat. While he definitely had developed a fear of fur, Albert remained quite cool when the experimenters checked the extent of his stimulus generalization by giving him objects that had no fur and did not resemble a rat (Watson and Raynor 1920).

Generalization, of course, operates in all of us, not only in children. It can be seen in the worker who argues heatedly with his foreman because his superior reminds him of his feared father, or in the man who is compulsively or excessively polite to women because they all remind him of his mother, whom he adored.

Stimulus Discrimination

In addition to generalizing, a child can learn the opposite process—discriminating among stimuli. He can be trained to respond only to a single, very particular stimulus—high C on a Stradivarius, for example. Such learning is called *discrimination*. To condition a child to discriminate, the experimenter presents several stimuli to him, but he rewards the child only when he responds to the "correct" one. Eventually, the child will learn to identify which stimulus is the appropriate one and will respond only to it. This type of learning occurs countless times during the course of a child's early years: he learns to discriminate between water and other clear liquids such as vinegar or oil, between spoons and knives, between candy and bits of crayons. Of course, the speed with which a child learns to discriminate is affected by the subtlety of the differences he is asked to detect, as well as by other variables such as how close, in both time and space, the stimulus is to the child's response and reward.

Stimulus Familiarization

A child's familiarity with a stimulus also affects his response to it. As a child grows more familiar with a conditioned stimulus, he responds to it more and more slowly. One pair of experimenters worked with two kindergarten classes. With Class A, they sounded a two-second buzzer 40 times, and with Class B, they switched on a two-second light 40 times. All the children then played a lever-pulling game in which both buzzer and light were conditioned stimuli. When Class A members played the game, they responded much more quickly to the new stimulus of the light than to the old one of the buzzer. However, Class B, for whom the light was the familiar stimulus, responded only slightly faster to the new stimulus of the buzzer than they had to the light (Cantor and Cantor 1964). In this study and in later ones, experimenters also found that as the trials wore on, children responded progressively more slowly

LEARNING AND DEVELOPMENT 39

to both familiar and new stimuli. The repetition or familiarity of the "game" itself also may have caused their interest to drop, resulting in slower responses.

Extinction

Responses may be completely eliminated from a person's repertoire. *The elimination of a response is called extinction. Extinction takes place when the association between the stimulus and the child's response breaks down.* This may happen when a particular response goes unrewarded for a period of time. As important as extinction is in behavior theory, it has not been widely studied in children. One series of studies shows it takes longer to extinguish the response of the child who was rewarded only partially during conditioning (Bijou 1957; Lewis 1952; Myers 1960). Two more studies conclude that more training (Siegel and Foshee 1953) and more incentives (Pumroy and Pumroy 1961) also make a child's response harder to extinguish.

The fact that behavior learned in a conditioning experiment can be extinguished does not mean, however, that behavior learned in early childhood cannot be lasting, as some would maintain. Parents are generally more persistent in training and rewarding their children and exert their influence over a longer period of time than experimenters do. Once experimenters have shown that their learning principles do indeed operate in children, they move on to other things. Parents do not. Parents also are apt to be less consistent in their rewards than experimenters, thereby providing partial reinforcement most of the time. These two elements—increased training and rewards and partial reinforcement—both tend to produce behavior that is the most difficult to extinguish.

Satiation and Deprivation

Short of extinction, a child's response may be affected by either of two opposites—*satiation* or *deprivation*. An experiment, with praise as the reward, shows how this operates. Three groups of preschool children were asked to drop marbles into two holes in a box. After testing to find a "baseline response"—how the children per-

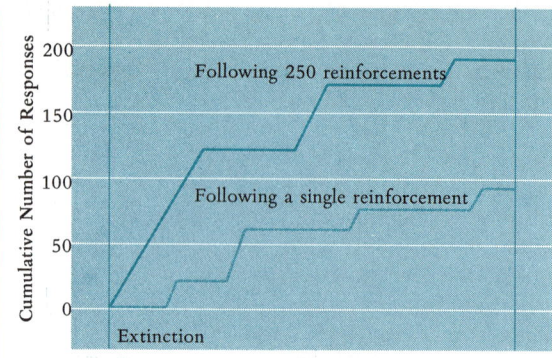

Figure 2.4 Extinction of the bar-pressing response of rats in relation to the number of reinforcements. The number of responses is several times greater after 250 reinforcements than after a single reinforcement. (After B. F. Skinner. *The behavior of organisms.* New York: Appleton-Century-Crofts, 1938.)

formed unrewarded—the experimenters began the project itself. They left Group A alone in an empty room for 20 minutes. During the same time, they satiated Group B by periodically praising the children while they did a simple task. Then came the marble-dropping game. They praised each child every fifth time he dropped a marble into the hole least preferred in the last minute of baseline play. The isolated children of Group A, when rewarded at last with the experimenters' praise, outperformed both Groups B and C (who had not yet been involved in any way). In fact, the children of Group B who were satiated performed barely more often than in the baseline play (Gewirtz and Baer 1958a, 1958b). Clearly, the reward of praise was more effective with the deprived group than with the satiated group. Primary rewards, such as food, produce roughly the same results, with the hungry child responding faster and more often than his well-fed peer.

Response Hierarchy

A conditioned child can usually respond to a stimulus in several ways, including, of course, the way he has learned. However, if this conditioned response is weakened—because of a long unrewarded spate, for example—one of his earlier responses may raise its head. The various available responses are called the *response hierarchy* since each has a different relative strength or probability of occurring. The most strongly established response will occur first.

During extinction, the rat presses the lever and gets nothing to eat. The rodent presses again. And again. Nothing. The rat slams down the lever. It throws itself against the lever. Finally, in a frenzy of frustration, it hurls itself against the wall until it lies in a panting heap. Such behavior is made up of responses the rat possessed before it learned lever-pressing. When lever-pressing failed to produce food pellets, the earlier responses welled up, overpowered, and replaced it.

Early responses also surface in humans. They often seem to emerge in subway, train, and bus stations, where tired people are in a hurry and appealing vending machines promise a little pleasure. A perspiring man, with his tie pulled down, approaches a cold-drink machine. He drops in his coins and pulls the lever. A dull clank follows, but no drink. He pulls the lever again, sighing. Nothing happens. He pulls the coin-return, but it is jammed. He smashes the coin-return with the heel of his hand and howls in pain—still no money. He slams the machine with his good hand. He kicks it and sprains his foot. He seizes the machine in both hands and tries to rock it, but it is bolted to the floor. He throws a shoulder block, smashing three plastic panels, and stalks away, having displayed several early, or primitive, responses.

Anticipatory Responses

When a child has learned that an unconditioned stimulus, such as food, will follow a conditioned stimulus, such as a bell, he may begin to anticipate the food and thus respond to the bell earlier and earlier, well before the experimenter can give him the food. When a person begins to react to a stimulus before it actually appears, his response is referred to as *anticipatory*. Marquis found that newborn infants—2 to 9 days old—were capable of anticipatory responses. She sounded a buzzer five seconds before they were fed at each meal. At first they began sucking only when they were given their bottles, but within five days, 8 of the 10 babies began opening their mouths and sucking—the natural responses to stimulation by a nipple—as soon as they heard the buzzer (Marquis 1931). This study indicated that newborns can learn more than response to a conditioned stimulus; their response will gradually appear sooner as the trials repeat—the response will anticipate the natural stimulus of the food.

Anticipatory responses are common in adults, too. The tightwad husband scowls when his wife describes her friend's new mink. He is responding before she actually introduces the dreaded unconditioned stimulus: the announcement that she wants one, too. The flutist who stands in front of the cymbal player in the orchestra is another anticipatory responder. He knows that in the eighth bar of the school song, the cymbals clash 10 inches from his head. The first time he nearly swallowed his flute. Now, as the orchestra moves into the fourth bar, he tilts forward and knots his neck muscles as he anticipates the cymbalist's enthusiastic contribution.

Observational Learning

A child learns much of his behavior by watching how adults and his peers behave and by noting the results of particular behavior. In social situations, imitation of observed behavior is very apparent, but it is difficult to analyze because of the many variable factors in such uncontrolled settings. Nonetheless, some of imitative learning's basic processes have been studied.

Experiments by Bandura et al. have shown that aggressive behavior can be learned through imitation. In one series of studies, three groups of preschool children saw three versions of adult aggression. Group A saw an adult punch, kick, hammer, and shout at an inflated doll. Group B watched this same adult, but on film, abuse the doll in the same way. Group C saw a cartoon character, also on film, take similar aggressive action toward the doll. Afterward, the experimenters frustrated the children mildly by taking away their toys. They then led them to a room. In it were the tools of aggression they had just seen used—and, of course, the inflated doll. All three groups—those who had seen cartoons and the filmed as well as the "live" adults—beat up the dolls with equal gusto and showed more aggression than children who had not seen any of these models. However, the boys were generally fiercer than the girls, as were the children whose model had been an aggressive male rather than a female (Bandura, Ross, and Ross 1963).

The Effective Model

Strong and immediate as imitative learning can be, it always depends on the many variables in both the model and the child. Generally, a model will be successfully imitated if:

1. He is a person to which the child can link himself in some way, whether he is a peer or a parent—two models a child quickly imitates. Younger children seldom interest older ones. A 5-year-old will ignore the aggression of a 2-year-old because he does not think much of feisty toddlers—"They're just little kids."
2. He has prestige in the child's eyes. Tests taken after another study using filmed aggression show that while a male peer model of the viewing children evoked strong and immediate imitations, it was the adult male—generally a revered figure—who made the most lasting impression (Hicks 1965).
3. He is rewarded for his behavior, since studies have shown that preschool children imitate more if they see the model well treated for his actions. Conversely, children imitate less if the model is punished, or if nothing at all happens to him.
4. The model is active, or better yet, clearly aggressive, for children seem to enjoy imitating aggressive behavior more than passive behavior. This may be due simply to children's natural high spirits and love of action, or, according to some theorists, it may be a needed release from tension that children share at certain stages of maturation.

The Model Learner

Characteristics of the child, the other half of the model-learner team, will also affect his imitative learning. As a rule, imitation of a model by the child is more likely if:

1. He is *motivated* to observe and imitate the model because he has been rewarded at home and at school for imitating his parents, teachers, and friends.
2. He is disposed to notice specific aspects of the model's behavior because of his own experience. For example, a child who has been spanked is *ready* to notice a model who administers a spanking.
3. Before the experiment, the child is told to pay close attention to the model, and is urged to imitate him closely. This warm-up turns the child's attention to the model and gives him an *incentive* to imitate later.
4. He is promised a *reward* for imitating the model.
5. He delivers a blow-by-blow *verbal description* of the model's behavior as he watches it unfold. Studies show that the child who gives such a narrative account imitates better than a child who simply pays close attention or a child who performs a rigid, mental-verbal activity, such as counting, while the model behaves or misbehaves. Perhaps the act of describing makes it easier for the child to recall and imitate actions.

Latent Learning in Children

In the aggression experiment, the children were "set up"—mildly frustrated and then shown the doll—to imitate the model. And they quickly complied. However, a child will not always behave this way. He may not imitate immediately, even though he has learned the behavior. He may store his learned response for weeks or months—even years, if the behavior made a deep impression on him—and then one day suddenly put his latent learning into action in a situation very different from the model's. He may turn on an irksome fellow first-grader and bloody his nose with a brisk right cross.

While a child will more readily imitate a rewarded model, he may also learn from a punished model. However, he probably will not imitate that behavior. This was demonstrated with the same children who viewed the mayhem committed on the inflated doll. Group A saw the model rewarded and imitated his behavior enthusiastically. Group B saw the model punished for pummeling the doll and did few imitations. Group C, the control group, saw the model go unrewarded and unpunished and did more imitations than Group B, but not nearly as many as Group A. However, when all three groups were later promised rewards if they could imitate the model's actions, they all beat the doll to a frazzle.

Cognitive Learning

If we could recapture the precise feelings we had about adults at age 6, we might well find our dominant feeling was that adults knew what they wanted and how to get it. They planned, they took definite, sometimes mysterious, steps. They were organized. In large part, this was a sound perception. An adult is organized. He makes a clear distinction between his ambitions and his achievements, between his dreams and his daily life, between the Rolls-Royce he wants and the Chevrolet he owns. He knows the social world of people in the same way, and he knows that all objects and people in the world outside himself somehow relate to each other and affect each other, and often him.

Grouping and Relating Objects

All objects fall into certain classes. Cars, buses, and trains are all means of transportation. Cannons, swords, and guided missiles are all weapons. More mysteriously, other objects are linked by action. A turn of a car's ignition key relates to the gasoline burning in the carburetor. The electrical impulse fed into a Teletype machine in Manhattan is related to the words appearing on paper coming out of another Teletype machine in San Francisco.

An adult knows that some objects which look different are actually the same. He understands that the snowball a boy throws in January is made of water like the rain that drenches him in an August downpour. The raw Idaho potato is also the fluffy mashed food he eats for dinner. He knows that certain symbols such as "1" and "one" mean the same thing.

These attributes of the adult mind seem obvious to us—we take them for granted most of the time. Yet, natural as it is to the mature human, the adult outlook is not an accident. The everyday categorizing of objects into real and imaginary, the knowledge of superficial differences and changes in objects, the understanding of cause-effect relationships—all result from a process stretching over perhaps 20 years of a human's life. This process of knowing is another kind of learning called *cognitive learning*.

Cognition is a subtle and continuous process. It is a person's way of getting to know his world. He simplifies his understanding of the many different things he encounters by finding similarities and relationships among them. He anticipates the future by relating it to what he already knows. The study of cognitive learning deals with the process by which people come to understand and organize their world. In particular, it deals with the role that concepts, images, symbols, principles, and rules play in this process.

Concept Learning

Concepts are the building blocks of cognitive learning. A child forms a concept when he places objects in a class and treats that class as a separate whole. A person presented with a hammer, a saw, and a drill puts all three in the class called tools because they are all used to make or change other objects. They have an abstract trait in common. To learn concepts, a child must necessarily be able to discriminate, that is, to isolate an object and notice its characteristics. Otherwise, he will not be able to put, say, an apple, a banana, and a tangerine—three unlike objects—into the same class, fruit. Similarly, to be able to put a horse, an elephant, and a yak into one class, a child must be able to ignore the superficial differences between the three and detect the common trait—in this case, four-leggedness.

Concept learning does not have to involve the spoken word. A child conditioned to get bubble gum by pressing a lighted square—and ignoring unlighted ones—may press a lighted triangle and ignore unlighted ones. When he does so, he places lighted shapes in a separate class and treats them differently from unlighted shapes. Some writers have preferred to call such concepts without words *action concepts*, *schemas*, or *sensorimotor operations*. Words, however, are often used in learning concepts. In fact, all the objects in man's world assume their places through words which label them by class. A chair is not just this wing chair or that lawn chair, it is also a class. So is *house.* It includes the 4-room bungalow and the 400-room mansion, just as *bird* encompasses the tiny hummingbird and the enormous soaring condor.

Besides concepts of objects, there are concepts of actions—fold, drop, stop, go. And concepts of location—beside, over, under, through. Complicated as these concepts may seem, most 4-year-olds have a good grasp of these concepts as a result of their intense activity with the environment. And this is essential for full human development. For only through concept learning can the child free his mind from what would be the overpowering and, finally, maddening task of absorbing and retaining a worldful of unique objects.

Discovering Patterns

A child often discovers a concept with sudden realization or insight. An experiment with children 7 to 8 years old shows how this may take place. Directly in front of the seated children, the experimenters placed three dot-dash patterns, each composed of one dot and two dashes. The patterns stayed the same throughout the experiment. On a small screen above the patterns, the experimenters flashed a series of patterns composed of three different shapes, for example, two circles and a square. This combination of two like objects and one unlike was always the same. However, the one unlike object changed places in the lineup of shapes. The child's job was to press a button under the dot-dash pattern whose dot was in the same position in its pattern as the unlike shape was in its lineup. The children learned the concept and matched the patterns fairly quickly; and once they understood the concept behind the patterns they made no errors. Because only the physical stimuli were changed, and the relationship (two similar and one dissimilar object) remained constant, the child could be said to have learned a concept and not only a response to a given stimulus (Suppes 1966).

THE DEFINING TRAIT. Interestingly, when children younger than first- or second-graders took part in such pattern studies, they usually had trouble clearly isolating the traits that identified their concepts. Consequently, their concepts often fell apart when an irrelevant trait was changed. A very young boy may base his concept of *horse* on a palomino. When he encounters a bay or a chestnut, he may not immediately absorb this "new" animal into his concept, even though coloring is a purely accidental—and therefore irrelevant—trait of the concept *horse.* The child who does not yet sift out irrelevant traits will classify objects inconsistently. His unstable concepts may topple when he meets objects that do not fit neatly into these concepts.

Investigating the way a child defines traits, Vygotsky studied conceptual behavior in young Russian children. He asked them to sort 32 blocks into four classes. The objects differed in four ways: they were five distinct colors, six shapes, two heights, and two widths. The experimenter gave the children 4 blocks as concepts and asked them to select related blocks from the 32 and add them to each of the 4. He set up the task so that height and width were the defining traits for the four concepts; the children had to disregard shape and color. It was found that the younger children often formed concepts on an inconsistent basis. A child presented with a tall, narrow orange oblong added a squat orange oval. He had chosen color as the defining trait of his concept. Next the child added a tall, narrow blue oval—shifting his concept base from color to shape (Vygotsky 1962).

Forming groups or classes of objects on a different concept base is called *conceptual chaining.* A child may build such chains longer and longer, changing the base each time he adds a new object. Obviously, such concepts, like a tower built of lead pipes, soda straws, spaghetti, pipe cleaners, and pencils, will topple before they reach the real, organized world. Toward 7 years of age, children increasingly form such concepts on a consistent basis.

Components of Cognition

We have discussed cognitive learning as an organizing force in our world. A closer look will highlight cognitive learning's important components. Besides concepts, which we have discussed rather thoroughly, cognitive learning depends on images, symbols, rules, and insight. Like concepts, these components are abstract qualities of the human mind, much as temperature is a quality of air. Unsubstantial as they may sound, these qualities are the foundation for such basic mental processes as encoding, remembering, hypothesizing, evaluating, and deducting, which we will deal with later.

IMAGES. *Images* are probably the first mental furniture a child acquires toward the end of the first year of life. The image records a specific thing—a fire, a Christmas tree, a bow tie—not as in a photograph, but more like a blueprint. The image is an arrangement of salient elements of the child's experience. If you try to remember the kitchen of your childhood home, you will find certain things stand out clearly. Perhaps a red clock over the sink or a yellow flower painted on the wall. These prominent elements give the image its vivid character and distinguish it from your grandmother's kitchen or your friend's kitchen.

SYMBOLS. *Symbols* are names for objects and qualities. The names of letters, numbers, objects, or persons are all symbols. They are not the things themselves; they stand for the things. They are more abstract than the image, which "freezes" a specific sight or sound. The child who can name the letter *E* and point to an E knows the symbol for the sound *E*. By the time he turns 6, he will know both the letter images and the symbols of the entire alphabet. Symbols, it must be clear, are the mind's workhorses. They are used to name concepts. Without the symbolic, generalized name of *horse*, the young boy could not form a verbal class called *horse*. He would simply have a lifetime collection of racehorses, cowboy nags, Indian ponies, police mounts, and circus Percherons. Taken alone, not one of these could help him form the verbal concept of *horse*. He would be left with a stableful of separate images.

PRINCIPLES OR RULES. *Principles or rules* underlie the relationships between things. The child who knows that cars go on roads does not try to put a toy car on train tracks or float it like a boat. He knows, when he grasps the principle "cars go on roads," that cars behave in certain ways. He has learned the principle by putting together the concepts—cars, roads, on, and go. As he matures, he will be able to put together sets of concepts to form larger principles. He will be able to grasp the complex rules that make up the study of chemistry or other sciences. And he will begin combining old principles with new ones to solve problems that are new to him. When a person does come up with a completely new solution, we call this creativity.

INSIGHT. A person stumped by a problem often seems to be making no headway toward a solution. Then, in a flash, he suddenly sees a way out. This sudden realization is *insight*. According to many psychologists, during the no-action period the person actually is rummaging unconsciously through his mental files and drawers of experience with similar problems, looking for an answer to the new one. The flash of insight takes place in the instant when the recalled images, symbols, and principles fuse with the new problem.

Jean Piaget: The Need to Know

One of the major forces behind the study of cognitive development has been the work of the Swiss psychologist Jean Piaget and his associates. Piaget believes that a child learns and develops because of his own drive to be active and explore, rather than as a result of outside forces acting upon him. This sets Piaget apart from others we have discussed earlier who have been primarily concerned with things that affect a child's behavior from the outside.

Piaget agrees, of course, that the environment exerts an important influence on the child, but he does not feel this answers all questions. He does not see the child as a passive subject who waits for stimuli to act upon him. Instead, he sees the child as active, seeking more and more stimulation from his environment. Piaget regards himself as an "interactionist" because his approach focuses on the interplay between internal and external forces; it is this interaction, he feels, that results in cognitive development.

ESTABLISHING EQUILIBRIUM. The child's inclination to explore and learn leads him to new stimuli and then to the process of establishing what Piaget calls *equilibrium* with his now enlarged environment. When a child encounters something that is partly familiar and partly new, he tries to respond to it by using the habits and techniques

LEARNING AND DEVELOPMENT

he has already developed. When he finds that these methods are not quite adequate, he gropes around and tries out new ones until he establishes a satisfactory relationship, or equilibrium, with that new, unsettling stimulus.

This process of seeking equilibrium can be seen in the infant who is given a new toy that is not really good for sucking—a hollow wooden cylinder with a bell inside it, for example. The infant will probably explore it first with his mouth and try to suck on it. He is using his existing responses, but they are not adequate—they are not paying off. This bottle-shaped thing is not giving milk or juice or even tactile pleasure. The baby's environment is "unbalanced" now. He has to try something new to establish an *equilibrium* with this unsettling object. After fiddling around with it for a while, he eventually may shake it or drop it or bang it on the floor. These acts will produce satisfying results that will amuse him: he will hear the pleasant jingle of the bell, or the clunk of wood on wood, and may see the toy roll across the floor. The infant has made certain discoveries about this new object and his relationship to it.

For Piaget, the child's drive to establish equilibrium when he finds himself in disequilibrating circumstances is more basic to cognitive development than either maturation or learning. It is because the child is trying to put things in order in his actions and thoughts that he is ready to learn relevant associations, to be conditioned, to have his learning reinforced, and to learn by observation. If he does not see an association as relevant to his present situation, he does not learn it. Learning is always secondary to development, according to Piaget. For Piaget, the phenomena of chaining, discovering patterns, and developing images, which we have discussed, are merely examples of the way in which the child as a *rule-seeking* organism gropes for a more adequate equilibrium with his world.

Partly because of Piaget, many investigators have become interested in investigating the way children's learning results from their own voluntary behavior. Some have felt that the child's desire for learning is so strong that it could be attributed to a motive for competence or knowledge. Others have suggested a broader idea of reinforcement that includes intrinsic reinforcement—that is, actions that are carried out by the child simply because he finds them satisfying, rather than because of the reward he will receive from someone else.

CONCEPT OF OPERATIONS. One of the basic ways in which a person comes to know something is described by Piaget as an *operation*. Piaget has defined this important concept as follows:

To understand the development of knowledge, we must start with an idea which seems central to me—the idea of an *operation*. Knowledge is not a copy of reality. To know an object, to know an event, is not simply to look at it and make a mental copy, or image, of it. To know an object is to act on it. To know is to modify, to transform the object, and to understand the process of this transformation, and as a consequence to understand the way the object is constructed. An operation is thus the essence of knowledge; it is an interiorized action which modifies the object of knowledge. For instance, an operation would consist of joining objects in a class, to construct a classification. Or an operation would consist of ordering, or putting things in a series. Or an operation would consist of counting, or of measuring. In other words, it is a set of actions modifying the object, and enabling the knower to get at the structures of the transformation. (Piaget 1964)

PIAGET'S FOUR STAGES. The concept of the operation forms the basis for the four stages of cognitive development that Piaget has defined. From birth to about 2 years the baby is in the *sensorimotor stage*. He is involved basically in physical contact with the objects around him; he is developing sensorimotor operations. At about the age of 2, with the beginnings of language, he enters a stage in which his operations advance from simple action to the use of representations—the use of images, symbols, and language. The period from about 7 to 11 years is called the *concrete operational stage*, when the child begins using concepts and becomes capable of operations on concrete objects but not yet on verbal hypotheses. The stage of *formal operations* ("operations on operations"), finally, characterizes adolescent and adult thought. Each stage, then, encompasses different developmental tasks that are solved at each level and provide the foundation for the next. (These stages will be discussed in the chapter dealing with cognitive development for that particular age level.)

Because Piaget's tradition is based more on biology and mathematics than the other theories we have discussed in this chapter, the terms he uses and the approach he takes are radically different from them. The differences, however, do not make any one theory less important in the total picture of child development. From the stimulus-response theorists we can learn a great deal about how behavior and learning can be influenced, while from Piaget's work we can learn much about the workings of a child's mind when he is solving problems or is involved in cognitive learning.

Conditions that Affect Learning

As many experiments have shown, all children do not perform the same at the same task. Clearly, the instructions the experimenter gives, the incentives, the models, and the extent of training all influence the child's responses at a particular age. But no one can assume from this that all children will respond as the experimental children did. The variable factors are too numerous and too strong. A child's health, his intelligence, his readiness to learn, his emotional state, and his motivation, all will affect his learning. Individual differences always continue to confound experimentally derived generalities.

Physical State

Temporary physical disorders such as a stomachache, as well as more serious illnesses and physical handicaps, can affect a child's learning. Similarly, fatigue and poor nutrition can interfere with a child's interest in activity and his ability to learn. While some interfering physical conditions are easily detected, others, like malnutrition, may go unnoticed as a source of a learning problem.

At any given moment a child's readiness for learning can be critical, as we have seen earlier in the chapter. Attainment of a certain maturational level as well as prior skills, both mental and physical, is necessary for particular learning to take place.

Emotional State

The child's emotional state, such as a state of anxiety and fear, is one of the major variables that affect his learning. For many children—motivated perhaps by a fear of losing affection—anxiety and fear can be either considerable blocks or equally strong incentives to learning.

Apparently children are born fearless. They learn all the fears they possess, and these fears become part of their learning equipment. The fearful child wants to escape or avoid the dreaded object, event, or person, and thereby reduce the fear that troubles him. A new stimulus need not be painful in itself to be feared. But linked to a past pain, it can produce fear. The child who choked on a pill may vehemently refuse to take another. He may recall his choking, which terrified him, when he sees the second pill. Of course, it works the other way around, too. The child who gulped his first pill without a gasp may never flinch from his daily vitamin tablets.

Some psychologists make a distinction between fear and anxiety. For them, fear is provoked by real threats from the environment—a fall from a tree, a bite from a dog, a burn from a stove. Anxiety, on the other hand, is prompted by less tangible, internal stimuli—a man feels he will lose his job, a woman thinks her meeting will be a bore, a student is convinced he will fail his final exam.

Whether or not we make this distinction between fear and anxiety, some common sources of fear for children of 3 years or more are the expectation of withdrawn food or affection, physical harm, or a clash between their beliefs or behaviors and set rules or "manners." Some psychologists would add a fourth fear source—a drastic change in a stimulus. This source of fear comes into play sufficiently early that the mechanism (if not the particular fear) seems to have an innate basis in the character of the organism. As they grow, children gain a sense of the rightness of things through their cognitive learning. Reinforcement is associated with the mother's face, not the stranger's. Clouds belong in the sky, cats meow, fires burn. The child who meets a one-armed man is startled. The amputee violates the child's concept of man as two-armed. And, as many an embarrassed parent will testify, the child has to immediately and loudly ask: "How come that man's got only one arm, Mommy?" Similarly, the father who grows a mustache while away for a week may find his return welcome marred when his 3-year-old bawls in his face in terror. Again, the stimulus has been changed.

Motivation

Motivation is a concept that refers to the needs, goals, or desires that spur a person to action. Motivation ranges from specific primary needs like the need to eat, to learned or secondary motives such as the wish for money, peer acceptance, affection, and good grades. These motives prompt the child to behave in particular ways. He learns to obey and be polite because he wants his parents' affection. He learns to pay attention in class and do his homework because he wants good grades. However, important as motives are in determining behavior, their presence alone does not insure that they will be satisfied. How many men want a more meaningful career and more respect from their colleagues or fellow workers? How many women want a more gracious home or a prettier face? They may get what they want, but just as often, they may not. Such thwarted desires create much of the anxiety and tension that people feel.

ROLE OF MOTIVATION IN LEARNING. Since motivation produces a condition, an aroused or attentive state, fixed on the satisfaction of its particular need or goal, it is easy to see how this state of arousal is important in learning. A child told to watch until the light turns green will be more disposed, at that moment, to learn to cross the street safely. The boy cautioned to "pay attention to this problem" will be ready to watch the blackboard as his teacher explains improper fractions. The level of his motivation is a key element in his learning, as you might expect. Experiments comparing children who have fairly strong motivation with others who have weaker motivation have shown that the more motivated children respond more often and more strongly, and deal with their surroundings more frequently and more effectively. These behaviors are vital learning assets.

While practically no psychologist will deny motivation's importance, not all can agree on how it really works in the learning process. Many believe that it sensitizes the child to particular stimuli. For example, he presses the red button in order to get the piece of peanut brittle. Those who disagree say that the child's reinforcement of his behavior comes from his response or achievement itself, not from the peanut brittle. This view is supported by the study described earlier of 6-month-old infants who performed certain acts—moving a rattle, knocking over a bottle—for the pure pleasure of doing them.

CURIOSITY AS MOTIVATION. Why do dogs bark? How do trees get so tall? Why do grandmothers say "Oh my!" Simple curiosity motivates a child to learn, perhaps as much as training does. The child does not learn his curiosity. But this spontaneous drive does affect his learning. And his learning, in turn, affects his level of curiosity. Some children show more curiosity than others—they explore more, physically or with questions. They enter more and more new areas—areas that the less curious child may overlook.

Butler designed a study to see if a monkey could find all the reward it needed in simply satisfying its curiosity. He gave several monkeys a mechanical puzzle consisting of a pin, a hook and eye, and a clasp. The puzzle could be disconnected only in a certain order. If a monkey touched one of the pieces out of that order, his move was counted an error. After a few tries, the monkeys were disassembling their puzzles with no mistakes. The experimenter then reassembled them. One monkey was so fascinated by the puzzle that he went on taking it apart for 10 hours and would have continued longer if the experimenter had not quit from fatigue. Obviously, the act of disassembling the puzzle was in itself rewarding to the monkey (Butler 1954).

SATISFYING GOALS. A child may wish, and work, for his goal of good grades. But if he is to succeed, the following factors must be present in the right degrees. First, the child must have learned the responses that will be good tools to help him satisfy his desire for A's. A child who cannot read well can hardly hope to grasp the subtleties of essays or novels and thereby get an A in

English. Second, the child must expect that he will achieve his goal of academic standing. A boy who has piled up a D record in arithmetic for three years is likely to despair of A's. While he still might want to succeed, he is not likely to behave as though he does. He is more likely to pretend that he does not care, that grades are not important, and that his teacher would not give him an A anyway because she does not like the way he parts his hair. The less he believes he can earn the grades, the weaker his efforts will become. Some children give up completely. They "drop out," even though they still fill a chair in class.

The third factor that helps determine success is the degree of anxiety the child feels about reaching for the goal. Can he earn better grades in arithmetic? Will his parents still love him if he fails? Will he look ludicrous to his peers if he tries and fails? The 2-year-old does not have the same source of anxiety as the older child. He gratifies himself quickly because he has not yet learned that his parents may disapprove of his eating the chocolate Easter bunny before breakfast. The older child knows his mother would be angry if he ate the bunny, so he refrains from doing so and thereby keeps his mother's affection. The more anxiety a child feels about doing something, the less likely he is to do it, even though the desire is just as strong.

Finally, the child's success in his desire hinges on the situation in which the motive arouses him. If he is sitting in church and is suddenly seized by the desire to sing his ABC's, he more than likely will not. If he is outside or playing at his nursery school, he probably will sing. All these factors—knowing the right responses, expecting to succeed, being anxious about trying, and being able to adapt his response to the immediate situation—influence whether a child will attempt to attain a goal and whether he will succeed.

As we noted earlier, there is no single, all-embracing theory of learning. There are, however, prominent elements that are common to most theories. For instance, it is clear that a child learns from his earliest days, and that at every age individual children will learn at different speeds. These differences can be attributed to any number of variable factors, such as intelligence, motivation, the child's reaction to the situation or the person he is learning from, or the child's emotional or physical state.

While this chapter has dealt primarily with learning, we have entitled it *Learning and Development*. As used in this chapter, the word *development* refers to the results or effects on the organism of many learnings over a period of time. However, this is only one use of the term *development*. It is important to emphasize that development is much more than the effects of learning alone. We have already discussed the important role that maturation plays in development. The genetic influences on development will become clear in the next chapter. And having introduced Piaget we must argue further that development is more than the sum of genetics, maturation, and learning. Piaget would contend that development involves more centrally the organism's struggle to bring all these forces into some equilibrium. Thus, development precedes learning for Piaget. From our point of view it is clear, then, that learning is a more specific term than development. The latter is a broader term and this book is devoted to its many meanings.

Summary

Learning, the changes resulting from both random and organized experiences, is determined by one's biological nature and genetic makeup as well as environmental influences. Learning is not limited only to skills and information; fears, wants, and attitudes are also learned. While studies have exposed a great variability of factors involved, no single theory of how children learn has ever met the test of all the accumulated data.

Not all behavior is learned. Instinctive responses are unlearned complex responses that hold to set patterns and are shared by all members of any species. However, learning quickly takes precedence over instinct. The "following response"—a form of imprinting in which a baby animal will follow the first moving object it sees during an early critical period of growth—straddles the line between instinctive and learned behavior.

Maturation, a system-by-system development of the body determined by a child's genes, does more to establish basic behavior sequences than learning does. Learning and maturation, however, do interact and directly affect each other. Because of this interaction, it is important not to attribute to maturation results which may instead be the outcome of accumulated learning.

Conditioned learning, whether classical or operant conditioning, establishes a new association or relationship (a measurable bond) between a stimulus, internal or external, and a response, natural or learned. In classical conditioning, the basic theories of which were formed by Pavlov, the bond is basically a natural reflex action, while in operant conditioning, popularized by B. F. Skinner, the action taken is voluntary and performed to produce a reward or to avoid punishment. Operant conditioning has been applied in many practical situations such as programmed instruction and psychotherapy.

While there is disagreement about the significance of reinforcement in the conditioned learning process, responses do vary depending on whether the reinforcement is primary or secondary, delayed or partial. Stimulus generalization, familiarization, and discrimination, as well as extinction, are also response variables that may be initiated by conditioning.

In addition to conditioning, much behavior in children is learned by watching and imitating a model. The most effective model may be a parent, a teacher, a sibling, or a playmate, at various stages in the child's life. The extent of his learning will depend on the degree of prestige the model has in the child's eyes, and whether or not the model and the child are rewarded or punished for the behavior in question.

The process of coming to know anything—relationships of objects or the categorizing of objects, for example—is still another kind of learning, called cognitive learning. It is the process by which people come to organize and understand their world.

Jean Piaget, a Swiss psychologist and a major force in the study of cognitive development, stresses the child's own drive to learn and to establish equilibrium with what he encounters, rather than the action of outside forces on the child, as the more significant powers involved in learning. We are able to know something, according to Piaget, by performing operations or sets of actions that modify objects. Piaget divides cognitive growth into four stages, based on the concept of the operation.

Learning, whether conditioned, observational, or cognitive, is greatly affected by the child's health, nutrition, and emotional state, and by intelligence. A child's readiness, physical and mental, and his level of maturation also directly affect his ability to learn.

Motivation causes an aroused state energizing a person's behavior and directly influencing his learning. Curiosity, the satisfaction of goals, and the desire to gain approval are all forms of motivational forces.

Learning is not the same thing as development. The latter is a broader term that encompasses not only the results of learning but of genetics, maturation, and internal forces of the organism.

References

Achenbach, T., and Zigler, E. Cue-learning and problem-learning strategies in normal and retarded children. *Child Develpm.*, 1968, 39, 827–848.

Baer, D. M. A technique of social reinforcement for the study of child behavior: Behavior avoiding reinforcement withdrawal. *Child Develpm.*, 1962, 33, 847–858.

Bandura, A., Grusec, J. E., and Menlove, F. L. Some social determinants of self-modeling reinforcement systems. *J. pers. soc, Psychol.*, 1967, 5, 449–455.

Bandura, A., Ross, D., and Ross, S. A. Imitation of film-mediated aggressive models. *J. abnorm. soc. Psychol.*, 1963, *66*, 3–11.

Bijou, S. W. Patterns of reinforcement and resistance to extinction in young children. *Child Develpm.*, 1957, *28*, 47–54.

Brackbill, Y. Extinction of the smiling response in infants as a function of reinforcement schedules. *Child Develpm.*, 1958, *29*, 115–124.

Brearley, M., and Hitchfield, E. *A teacher's guide to reading Piaget.* London: Routledge & Kegan Paul, 1966.

Butler, R. A. Curiosity in monkeys. *Scientific Amer.*, February 1954.

Caldwell, E. C., and Hall, V. C. The influence of concept training on letter discriminations. *Child Develpm.*, 1969, *40*, 63–71.

Cantor, G. N., and Cantor, J. H. Effects of conditioned-stimulus familiarization on instrumental learning in children. *J. exp. child Psychol.*, 1964, *1*, 71–78.

Carmichael, L. A further study of the development of behavior in vertebrates experimentally removed from the influence of environmental stimulation. *Psychol. Rev.*, 1927, *34*, 34–47.

Church, R. M., and Campbell, B. A. (Eds.) *Punishment and avoidance behavior.* New York: Appleton-Century-Crofts, 1969.

Elkind, D., and Flavell, J. H. *Studies in cognitive development.* Oxford: Oxford Univer. Press, 1969.

Ellis, H. C. *Fundamentals in human learning.* Dubuque, Ia.: Brown, 1971.

Epstein, R., and Liverant, S. Verbal conditioning and sex-role identification in children. *Child Develpm.*, 1963, *34*, 99–106.

Estes, W. K. *Learning theory and mental development.* New York: Academic Press, 1970.

Flavell, J. H. *The developmental psychology of Jean Piaget.* New York: Van Nostrand, 1963.

Furth, H. G. *Piaget and knowledge: Theoretical foundations.* Englewood Cliffs, N.J.: Prentice-Hall, 1969.

Gagné, R. M. *Conditions of learning.* New York: Holt, Rinehart & Winston, 1965.

Gagné, R. M. Contribution of learning to human development. *Psychol. Rev.*, 1968, *75*, 177–191.

Gewirtz, J. L. Mechanisms of social learning: Some roles of stimulation and behavior in early human development. In D. A. Goslin (Ed.), *Handbook of socialization theory and research.* Chicago: Rand McNally, 1969.

Gewirtz, J. L., and Baer, D. M. Deprivation and satiation of social reinforcers as drive conditions. *J. abnorm. soc. Psychol.*, 1958, *57*, 165–172. (a)

Gewirtz, J. L., and Baer, D. M. The effects of brief social deprivation on behaviors for a social reinforcer. *J. abnorm. soc. Psychol.*, 1958, *56*, 49–56. (b)

Gordon, I. J. *On early learning: The modifiability of human potential.* Washington, D.C.: Association for Supervision and Curriculum Development, 1971.

Goss, A. E., and Nodine, C. F. *Paired-associates learning: The role of meaningfulness, similarity and familiarization.* New York: Academic Press, 1965.

Goulet, L. R. Training, transfer and the development of complex behavior. *Human Develpm.*, 1970, *13*(4), 213–240.

Grant, D. A. Classical and operant conditioning. In A. W. Melton (Ed.), *Categories of human learning.* New York: Academic Press, 1964.

Hall, J. F. (Ed.) *Readings in the psychology of learning.* Philadelphia: Lippincott, 1967.

Hamblin, R. L., Buckholdt, D., Ferritor, O., Kozloff, M., and Blackwell, L. *The humanization process.* New York: Wiley, 1971.

Harlow, H. F. The nature of love. *Amer. Psychologist*, 1958, *13*, 673–685.

Harlow, H. F., and Zimmerman, R. R. Affectional responses in the infant monkey. *Science*, 1959, *130*, 421–423.

Harris, T. L., and Schwahn, W. (Eds.) *Selected readings on the learning process.* New York: Oxford Univer. Press, 1961.

Hess, E. H. Imprinting in birds. *Science*, 1964, *146*, 1129–1139.

Hicks, D. J. Imitation and retention of film-mediated aggressive peer and adult models. *J. pers. soc. Psychol.*, 1965, *2*, 97–100.

Ivanov-Smolensky, A. G. On the methods of examining the conditioned food reflexes in children and mental defectives. *Brain*, 1927, *50*, 138–141.

Jeffrey, W. E. Variables in early discrimination learning: Motor response in the training of left-right discrimination. *Child Develpm.*, 1958, *29*, 269–275.

Johnson, P. E. (Ed.) *Learning: Theory and practice.* New York: Crowell, 1971.

Kasatkin, N. I., Mirzoiants, N. S., and Khokhitva, A. Conditioned orienting responses in children in the first year of life. Trans. from the Russian, 1953. In *The central nervous system and behavior.* Princeton, N.J.: Josiah Macy, Jr., Foundation, 1960.

Kaye, H. The conditioned Babkin response in human newborns. *Psychon. Sci.*, 1965, *2*, 287–288.

Keller, F. S. *Learning: Reinforcement theory.* (2nd ed.) New York: Random House, 1969.

Kendler, H. H., and Kendler, T. S. Development of mediating responses in children. In J. C. Wright and J. Kagan (Eds.), Basic cognitive processes in children. *Monogr. Soc. Res. Child Develpm.*, 1962, *28*(2), Serial 86, 33–52.

Kimmel, H. D. Instrumental inhibitory factors in classical conditioning. In W. F. Prokasy (Ed.), *Classical conditioning.* New York: Appleton-Century-Crofts, 1965.

Kintsch, W. *Learning, memory and conceptual processes.* New York: Wiley, 1970.

Klausmeier, H. J., and Ripple, R. E. *Learning and human abilities: Educational psychology.* (3rd ed.) New York: Harper & Row, 1971.

Koch, J. The development of the conditioned orienting reaction to humans in 2–3 month infants. *Act. Nerv. Sup.*, 1965, *7*(2), 141–142.

Landreth, C., and Read, K. H. *Education of the young child: A nursing school manual.* New York: Wiley, 1942.

Lawson, P. R. *Learning and behavior.* New York: Macmillan, 1960.

Lewis, D. J. Partial reinforcement in a gambling situation. *J. exp. Psychol.*, 1952, *43*, 447–450.

Lewis, M. A developmental study of information processing within the first three years of life. *Child Develpm. Monogr.*, 1969, No. 133.

Lipsitt, L. P., and Kaye, H. Conditioned sucking in the human newborn. *Psychon. Sci.*, 1964, *1*, 29–30.

Lipsitt, L. P., and Spiker, C. C. (Eds.) *Advances in child development and behavior.* Vol. I. New York: Academic Press, 1963.

Lipsitt, L. P., and Spiker, C. C. *Advances in child development and behavior.* Vol. II. New York: Academic Press, 1965.

Lipsitt, L. P., and Spiker, C. C. *Advances in child development and behavior.* Vol. III. New York: Academic Press, 1967.

Logan, F. A. *Fundamentals of learning and motivation.* Dubuque, Ia.: Brown, 1970.

Lorenz, K. Z. *King Solomon's ring.* London: Methuen, 1952.

Marquis, D. P. Can conditioned responses be established in the newborn infant? *J. genet. Psychol.*, 1931, *39*, 479–492.

Marx, M. H. *Learning: Interactions.* New York: Macmillan, 1970.

Mateer, F. *Child behavior.* Boston: Badger, 1918.

Miller, N. E., and Dollard, J. *Social learning and imitation.* New Haven, Conn.: Yale Univer. Press, 1941.

Mirzoiants, N. S. The conditioned orienting reflex and its differentiation in the child. *Zhurnal Vysshei Nervoi Deyatel' nosti imeni. I. P. Pavlova,* 1954, *4,* 616–619.

Mowrer, O. H. *Learning theory and behavior.* New York: Wiley, 1960.

Mowrer, O. H. *Learning theory and personality dynamics.* New York: Ronald Press, 1950.

Munn, N. L. *The evolution and growth of human behavior.* (2nd ed.) Boston: Houghton Mifflin, 1965.

Myers, N. A. Extinction following partial and continuous primary and secondary reinforcement. *J. exp. Psychol.*, 1960, *60*, 172–179.

Papousek, H. Conditioning during early post-natal development. In Y. Brackbill and S. G. Thompson (Eds.), *Behavior in infancy and early childhood.* New York: Free Press, 1967.

Pavlov, I. P. *Conditioned reflexes.* New York: Macmillan, 1927.

Piaget, J. Development and learning. In R. E. Ripple and V. N. Rockcastle (Eds.), *Piaget rediscovered. A report of the conference on cognitive studies and curriculum development, March 1964.* Ithaca, N.Y.: Cornell Univer. School of Education, 1964.

Piaget, J. *Six psychological studies.* Ed. by D. Elkind. New York: Random House, 1967.

Prokasy, W. F. Classical eyelid conditioning: Experimenter operations, task demands, and response shaping. In W. F. Prokasy (Ed.), *Classical conditioning: A symposium.* New York: Appleton-Century-Crofts, 1965.

Pumroy, D. K., and Pumroy, S. S. Effect of amount and percentage of reinforcement on resistance to extinction in preschool children. *J. genet. Psychol.*, 1961, *98*, 55–62.

Rheingold, H. L., Gewirtz, J. L., and Ross, H. W. Social conditioning of vocalization in the infant. *J. comp. physiol. Psychol.*, 1959, *52*, 68–73.

Siegel, P. S., and Foshee, J. G. The law of primary reinforcement in children. *J. exp. Psychol.*, 1953, *45*, 12–14.

Sigel, I. The attainment of concept. In M. L. Hoffman and L. W. Hoffman (Eds.), *Review of child development research.* New York: Russell Sage Foundation, 1964.

Sigel, I., and Hooper, F. *Logical thinking in children.* New York: Holt, Rinehart & Winston, 1968.

Simmons, M. W. Operant discrimination learning in human infants. *Child Develpm.*, 1964, *35*, 737–748.

Siqueland, E. R. Operant conditioning of head turning in four-month infants. *Psychon. Sci.*, 1964, *1*, 223–224.

Skinner, B. F. On the rate of formation of a conditioned reflex. *J. genet. Psychol.*, 1932, *7*, 274–285.

Skinner, B. F. *The behavior of organisms.* New York: Appleton-Century-Crofts, 1938.

Skinner, B. F. *Science and human behavior.* New York: Macmillan, 1953.

Sluckin, W. *Imprinting and early learning.* Chicago: Aldine-Atherton, 1967.

Spence, K. W. *Behavior theory and learning.* Englewood Cliffs, N.J.: Prentice-Hall, 1960.

Spence, K. W., and Spence, J. T. (Eds.) *The psychology of learning and motivation.* 3 vols. New York: Academic Press, 1967–1970.

Staats, A. W. *Human learning: Studies extending conditioning principles to complex behavior.* New York: Holt, Rinehart & Winston, 1964.

Staats, C. K., and Staats, A. W. Attitudes established by classical conditioning. *J. abnorm. soc. Psychol.*, 1958, *57*, 37–40.

Stevenson, H. W. Learning in children. In P. H. Mussen (Ed.), *Carmichael's manual of child psychology.* Vol. I. (3rd ed.) New York: Wiley, 1970.

Suppes, P. Mathematical concept formation in children. *Amer. Psychologist,* 1966, *21*, 139–150.

Tempone, V. J. Mediational processes in primary stimulus generalization. *Child Develpm.*, 1966, *37*, 687–696.

Tolman, E. C., and Honzik, C. H. Introduction and removal of reward, and maze performance in rats. *Univer. of Calif. Publ. Psychol.*, 1930, *4,* 257–275.

Vygotsky, L. S. *Thought and language.* Cambridge, Mass.: M.I.T. Press, 1962.

Wallach, M. Research in children's thinking. In H. W. Stevenson (Ed.), *Child psychology.* N.S.S.E. Yearbook. Chicago: Univer. of Chicago Press, 1963.

Watson, J. B., and Raynor, R. Conditioned emotional reactions. *J. exp. Psychol.*, 1920, *3*, 1–4.

Weisberg, P. Social and nonsocial conditioning of infant vocalization. *Child Develpm.*, 1963, *34*, 377–388.

Wolfe, J. B. Effectiveness of token rewards for chimpanzees. *Comp. Psychol. Monogr.*, 1936, *12*(60).

Zeaman, D., and House, B. J. The relation of IQ and learning. In R. M. Gagné (Ed.), *Learning and individual differences.* Columbus, Ohio: Merrill, 1967.

Zigler, E. Developmental versus difference theories of mental retardation and the problem of motivation. *Amer. J. ment. Def.*, 1969, *73*, 536–556.

Zigler, E. An overview of research in learning, motivation, and perception. *Except. Children*, 1962, *28*(9), 455–458.

The Prenatal Period

II

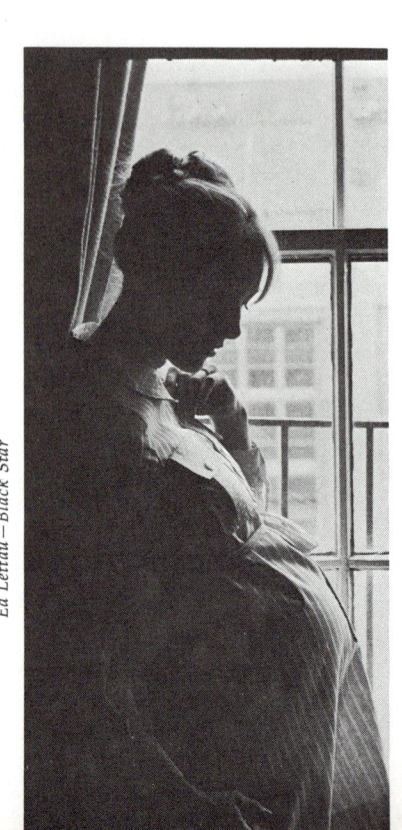

Ed Lettau—Black Star

Genetics and Development 3

THE FIRST influences upon a child's development take place before he is born. These prenatal influences fall into two basic categories: (1) genetic inheritance and (2) environmental forces. Psychologists are becoming increasingly aware of the important role of prenatal factors on the child's total development. In this chapter and the next we shall be concerned with both the genetic and environmental prenatal elements, the way they operate, and their effects on the individual. We begin in this chapter by considering the mechanisms of heredity and then the extent to which heredity and environmental forces may interact to affect specific traits and areas of behavior.

At the very moment of conception, that first, single fertilized cell contains all the genetic information that will make the child a unique individual, in his appearance and in his behavior. Yet, the fact that the genetic blueprint is preestablished at the moment of conception does not mean that the child will develop precisely according to this inherited plan. The ultimate appearance of nearly every genetic trait is subject to modification even in the earliest hours of prenatal life.

The Nature–Nurture Controversy

For centuries, parents, philosophers, and scientists have debated the question of which has the greater influence on a child's development and behavior: his genetic inheritance (considered as "nature") or his environment, both before and after birth ("nurture"). As the science of psychology has become more and more sophisticated, however, research has shown that neither group of influences completely dominates the other. A human being, in his mother's womb as well as in the prime of his mature life, is a complex, changing blend of the genetic potential he inherited from his parents, of other biological influences, and of the environmental forces that can either inhibit or nourish his potential. The questions that are now being researched concern the varying, and relative, degrees of influence that specific genetic, biological, and social forces exert on specific traits and forms of behavior.

Intelligence has long been a popular subject of argument in the nature-versus-nurture discussion, and it continues to be. As recently as 1969, a leading behavioral scientist, Arthur R. Jensen, reviewed studies which supported his theory that racial genetic factors affect human intelligence (Jensen 1969). Jensen's theory raised a furor among psychologists and other professionals concerned with human potential, who generally agree that it is the interaction between heredity and environment that determines intelligence. They also believe that the relative degree of influence of these forces cannot be precisely predicted or measured. Jensen's critics maintain that we cannot conclude, at this stage in our understanding, that measured differences in I.Q. between large cultural or racial groups are necessarily determined by genetics, certainly not until all members of the groups to be compared have had equal opportunities for maximum environmental stimulation.

It is difficult to discover exactly what causes high or low intelligence. It is held, for example, that biological variables, either genetic or nongenetic in origin, affect a child's potential intelligence, but the environment in the mother's body, and later in the child's home and school, also exerts a significant influence. Low intelligence could result from such prenatal conditions as insufficient oxygen in utero; brain damage during delivery; disease, drugs, or nutritional deficiencies in the mother during pregnancy, or in the child himself. Later in life, regardless of a child's genetic inheritance, his behavior and intellectual performances are bound to be affected—for good or ill— by the influence of parents, teachers, classmates, playmates, and society in general. For example, outstanding scientific ability in a child whose parents are scientists might be assumed to be an inherited aptitude, but frequent exposure to scientific ideas, the natural desire to imitate his parents, and time spent working on his own junior experiments and school lessons to win their approval are also important influences.

The question of intelligence is a good illustration of the complexity of assessing the varying combinations of hereditary and environmental influences. It might be useful here to think of the relationship between the two forces in terms of a person and the changing contexts in which he finds himself throughout his life. At any one moment the person is a distinct, ongoing force, but he is continually adapting to, or being modified by, his social and physical surroundings. He has predispositions, ambitions, talents, and learned responses, but these are the products of earlier moments of his life, and they are subject to change at any time. In a similar way, the original sources of a person's nature, his genes, are undergoing modification from the first instant of conception. The fact that the genes exert the primary influence on a person's development tends to make them seem more important and removed from the rest of a person's life than they actually are.

The Science of Genetics

One of the most exciting, complex, and revolutionary of modern sciences—*genetics*—is concerned with the mechanisms of heredity and the reasons for variety in inherited traits within a family. The geneticist, like the psychologist, is interested not only in determining which traits are transmitted from parent to child, but in learning why children of the same parents show some family resemblances and not others. A brother and sister might both have their mother's red hair, freckled skin, and blue eyes, yet the sister might be tall and thin like her parents and her brother short and pudgy like no one else in this family of "bean poles." We assume they both inherited their freckles, blue eyes, and red hair, but should we discount the possibility of heredity in the brother's roly-poly stature simply because he is the only family member to exhibit this trait? On the contrary, science has learned enough about genetics to tell us that the brother can look different, and be different in many respects, because each child inherits a particular combination of his parents' genes that differs in varying degrees from his brother's or sister's genetic inheritance. Another possibility is that the chubby brother's prenatal environment also could have altered the blueprints for his physique.

The study of genetics is so new that it did not receive its name until 1902 when a Danish botanist, O. S. Johannsen, coined the word *gene* (meaning origin of life), from which the word *genetics* was later derived. With the advent of the field of molecular genetics and the understanding it has given us of the structure and function of the gene, this science has progressed so far that men now have it in their power to influence not only the development of plants and insects, but of animals, including man. Not surprisingly, improvement of the human race by selective breeding has largely been confined to theoretical discussions and science fiction. With the tragic exception of experiments conducted in Nazi Germany as part of Hitler's abortive efforts to produce a master race, geneticists have been restrained from tampering with human heredity by ethical considerations as well as by their awareness of the limits of their knowledge.

The interaction of numerous environmental factors upon inherited characteristics further complicates the highly complex study of genetics in the human race. Nevertheless, researchers have come a long way in their understanding of the relative degree of the influence of heredity and environment in determining various traits. A measure of this advance can be seen in the classic study of the "Jukes" family, conducted in 1875 by Richard L. Dugdale, which supposedly showed that criminal and asocial traits are inherited. The evidence it provided, however, now appears to offer as strong a case for environment as it does for heredity. Dugdale traced seven generations descended from a shiftless loafer and a prostitute and found them generally a sorry lot of criminals, degenerates, prostitutes, and other undesirable types (Dugdale 1910). Later it was found that he relied heavily on his imagination and local gossip for his facts. Even if his data were reliable, we now realize it would be impossible to know how much of the Jukeses' behavior was due to parentage and how much to unfortunate surroundings and influences.

Many more recent—and more reliable—studies have shown that genetic inheritance can be a strong influence in certain areas of psychological development. One such study has found that even in old age, identical twins (twins with identical gene inheritance) were more alike than fraternal twins, mentally as well as physically (Kallmann and Sander 1949). The use of twin studies as a tool in genetic and psychological research will be discussed at greater length later in this chapter.

The Principles of Genetics

Conception

The inheritance of traits begins with conception, when a sperm cell, or *spermatozoon*, from the male unites with an egg cell, or *ovum*, from the female, following sexual intercourse. The sex or reproductive cells that come from parents are known as *gametes*, and together they form a *zygote*. Each gamete contains 23 distinctively different chromosomes, which carry genetic material. Thus a life begins as heir to 46 chromosomes bearing instructions for the formation of an individual with unique characteristics and potentials.

Each germ cell contains 23 single chromosomes.

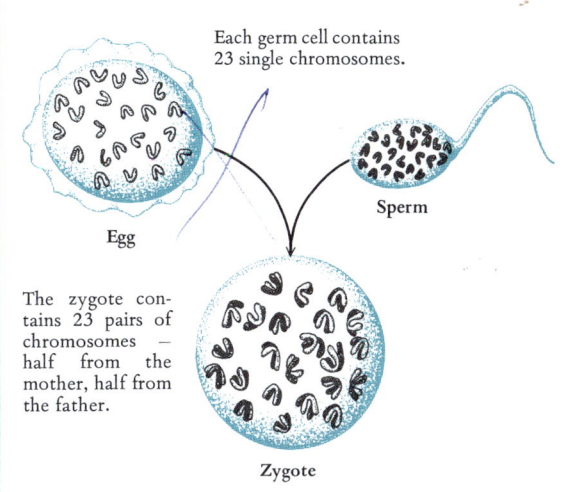

Egg

Sperm

The zygote contains 23 pairs of chromosomes — half from the mother, half from the father.

Zygote

Figure 3.1 The inheritance of genetic material.

GENETICS AND DEVELOPMENT 59

The Beginnings of Growth

Following the fertilization of an ovum by a spermatozoon, the one-celled zygote divides into two cells, the two become four, and so the embryo starts to develop. But before the first cell, or any later body cell, actually divides, its 46 threadlike chromosomes duplicate themselves. Then, in the course of a process called *mitosis*, the two complete sets of 46 collect on opposite sides of the cell. When the cell divides to form two cells, the new cells will contain identical reproductions of the chromosomes in the original. The replication of chromosomes and division of cells repeats and repeats, eventually producing the complete human being. These two processes continue throughout our entire life, as some of the body's billions of cells (as in our skin) are constantly replaced as they die.

Gametes

There is one vital exception to the statement that each of a person's cells contains replicas of the original 46 chromosomes. Gametes, which are sperm and ova, contain only 23. How does the exception occur? When a child reaches sexual maturity, some cells become completed sperm or ova. These special cells are called *reproductive cells*, as distinct from *body cells*, which go to make up bones, nerves, muscles, and organs. When it is time for the sperm or ova to develop, a process called gametogenesis occurs. During gametogenesis, a special kind of cell division, called *meiosis*, takes place. In meiosis, chromosome replication occurs once, but a mitosislike division occurs twice, leaving four cells, each with 23 chromosomes, half the number found in body cells. These cells, with 23 chromosomes each, become sperm and eggs, or *gametes*.

Chromosomes, Genes, and DNA

CHROMOSOMES. All living things receive their genetic inheritance through the chromosomes transmitted from the parents at the moment of conception. A *chromosome* is a threadlike structure contained in the nucleus or "brain" of every cell, and it carries genetic information from the parents to every cell of the child. In effect, a chromosome is a vehicle for the genes. As mentioned earlier, there are 46 chromosomes in every human body cell, and 23 in every gamete.

We are accustomed to thinking of a set of chromosomes as a master plan for a person's physical growth and potential for other traits. But the inheritance that is handed down from the parents through their chromosomes is actually a set of specifications that will direct the production of proteins from the amino acids in the child's body from the moment he is conceived and throughout his life; these proteins eventually result in a unique person. We say that a child's appearance

1. The body cells contain 46 chromosomes, or 23 pairs. (Only 4 are shown here for simplification.)

2. Before the cell divides, each chromosome duplicates itself.

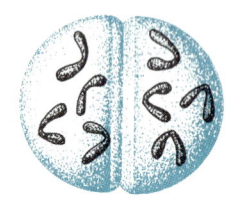

3. The halved chromosomes separate and go to opposite sides of cell; there are now 46 on each side.

4. When the cell divides, each new cell contains 46 chromosomes and is identical to the original cell.

Figure 3.2 Mitosis, or the formation of new body cells. When body cells divide, each new cell contains the same number of chromosomes as the original cell.

Figure 3.3 Meiosis, or the cell division in which sperm and ova are formed. A reduction of chromosomes occurs when reproductive cells divide.

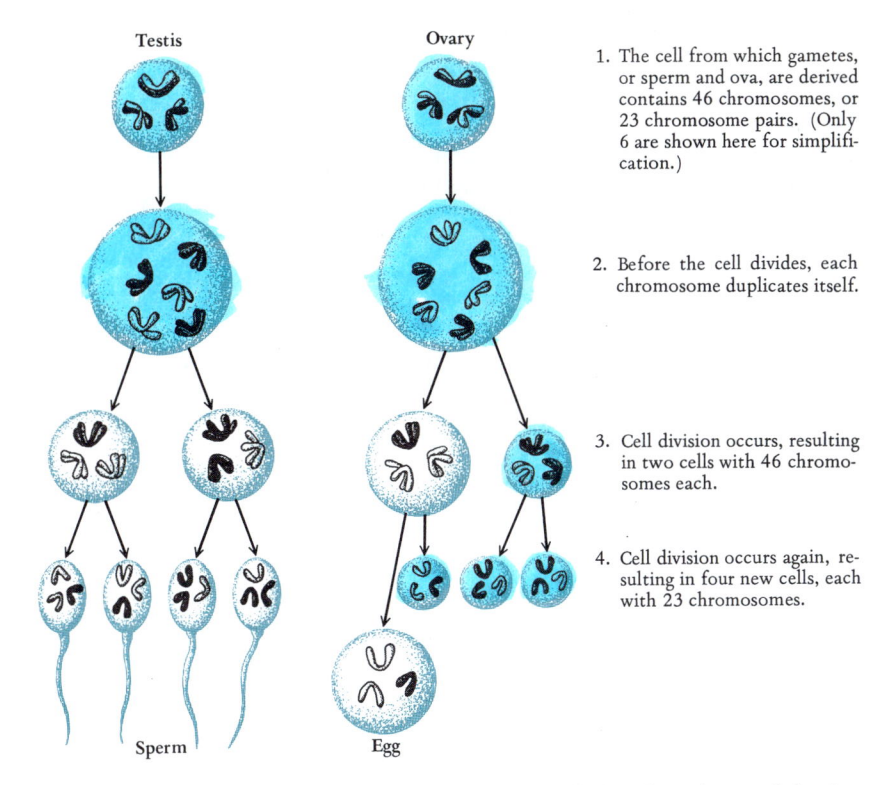

1. The cell from which gametes, or sperm and ova, are derived contains 46 chromosomes, or 23 chromosome pairs. (Only 6 are shown here for simplification.)

2. Before the cell divides, each chromosome duplicates itself.

3. Cell division occurs, resulting in two cells with 46 chromosomes each.

4. Cell division occurs again, resulting in four new cells, each with 23 chromosomes.

and abilities and behavior are inherited, but, strictly speaking, only the instructions for the formation of particular building blocks of the body are inherited.

GENES. Each chromosome is made up of units called genes. *Genes* are the segments of the chromosomes where the specific sets of instructions we call "heredity" are recorded. There are about 20,000 genes in one chromosome, and they are arranged along the length of the chromosome, each with a fixed position. Each gene carries a specification for a series of chemical processes, the results of which will ultimately be seen as some aspect of the person—the curve of the nose, the size of the brain, various traits that give the individual potential for special abilities. The development of a single organ or trait, however, may be specified by a combination of many genes, and is therefore called a *polygenic* trait.

DNA. Until about 20 years ago scientists did not know exactly what a gene was made of, or even if it actually existed. In 1953, however, J. D. Watson and F. H. Crick developed a model—the double helix—that explained the structure of a much-investigated chemical called *deoxyribonucleic acid*, or *DNA* for short. It was already known that DNA was present in all body cells and in the chromosomes, and some scientists suspected that the genes themselves might be made of this substance. But it was not until scientists began to use Watson and Crick's now famous *double helix* model of the DNA molecule that they could understand how genes could duplicate themselves at each cell division. It is primarily this understanding of DNA's structure that led to the agreement that it must be the main substance of genes.

Watson and Crick's double helix model looks like a ladder that has been twisted into a coil (*helix* means coil); see Figure 3.4. The coiled parallel strands are made up of sugar and phosphate, and the rungs connecting them are composed of a pair of chemical bases—*adenine* paired with *thymine* in some rungs, or *guanine* paired with *cytosine* in other rungs. The chemicals are always paired in

GENETICS AND DEVELOPMENT **61**

this fashion, but the sequence of pairs along the "ladder" will vary. The pattern of this sequence is, in effect, the language of the genetic code.

The transmission of the variety of traits that passes from generation to generation is made possible by the ingenious disassembling and reassembling procedure that takes place in the DNA molecule. As the zygote, or fertilized egg, divides and redivides to form an ever growing and ever more complex organism, the two spirals of the DNA molecules unwind, each strand taking with it one-half of each pair of bases. Each single strand and its attached chemicals then come in contact with chemicals present in its own cell—adenine, thymine, guanine, cytosine, a sugar, and phosphate. The appropriate partner for each chemical base attaches itself, and two new coiled strands form. Now each half of the original spiral ladder has created a new half; each new cell has its own two-stranded molecule of DNA, and thus its own set of genes.

The information coded in each DNA molecule, however, must be communicated from the cell nucleus to the rest of the cell in order for the genetic instructions to be put into effect. This "messenger" function is performed by another substance in the gene, ribonucleic acid, or *RNA*. A single-stranded ribbon molecule, RNA is composed of sugar, phosphate, and the same bases as those in DNA, with the exception of thymine, which is replaced by uracil. The patterns formed by the sequence of DNA base pairs are imprinted on the RNA, which moves out of the cell nucleus into the *cytoplasm*, the substance that constitutes the cell's internal environment. Another abbreviated form of RNA, called *transfer RNA*, collects the specific chemicals and assembles them along the messenger RNA. The specifications carried by these two forms of RNA determine which proteins are produced from the amino acids available to the cell. Each gene carries instructions for one type of protein chain, or polypeptide. Since these proteins make up much of the structure and chemical machinery of every cell of the body, the genetic instructions profoundly affect the activities of the body. A defect in a single gene may mean that the body cannot synthesize an important substance. For example, cretinism, a form of

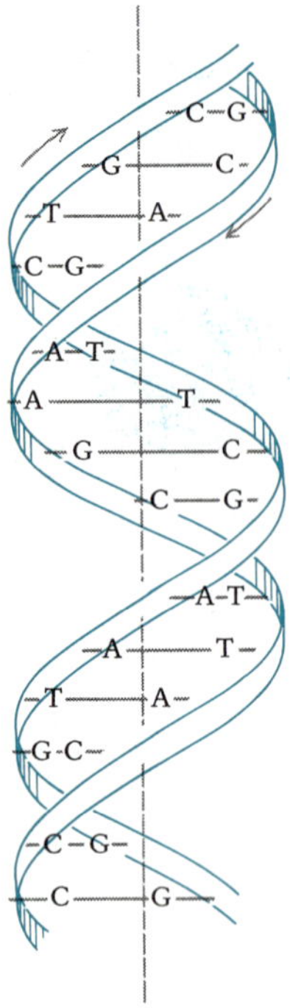

Figure 3.4 Portion of the double helix model of the DNA molecule proposed by Watson and Crick. Each "rung" on the molecule has a pair of chemicals—either adenine (A) plus thymine (T), or cytosine (C) plus guanine (G). (From J. D. Watson and F. H. C. Crick. *Nature,* 1953, Vol. 171. By permission.)

mental retardation, is caused by the lack of a protein enzyme that releases iodine essential to the formation of thyroid hormones.

The Mendelian Laws of Heredity

Our current understanding of how inherited traits can be so varied, and why one trait may seem to disappear but will show up a generation or so later, owes a great deal to the revolutionary work of an Austrian monk, Gregor Mendel, in the 1850s.

In his monastery garden Mendel experimented with two strains of peas, red-flowering and white-flowering. (During the course of his work he was to use other strains bearing other characteristics as well.) When he mated pure-bred red plants with pure-bred white ones, he found that all offspring of that mating were red. When he mated these red offspring with each other, however, they produced an average of three red plants to one white one.

After eight years of scrupulously noting the appearance of characteristics in one generation after another, Mendel arrived at certain principles that apparently governed the transmission of these traits. These principles of heredity are known as the *Mendelian laws* and apply to all living organisms.

The Mendelian laws can be summarized as follows:

1. The individual units of heredity—which are now called genes—do not usually change as they are passed from generation to generation, even across centuries. This constancy in our genes explains why we can see striking similarities between our own baby pictures and tintypes or early photographs of our great-grandparents as babies. When genes from two parents combine in their child, the genes are not blended, as paint pigments would be, but maintain their own identity, like bits of colored glass in a mosaic. Rather, it is the *combination of genes* that changes from generation to generation.
2. An individual has two genes coded for each inherited characteristic or portion of it. These two genes that make a pair are now called *alleles* (from *allelon*, of one another). One allele of each pair comes from the mother and one from the father. Alleles for a certain trait may be alike (a child might inherit alleles for blue eyes from both his mother and father, and he would be called *homozygous* for that trait), or the alleles may hold different instructions for a trait, and are then called *heterozygous*. If the alleles are not alike, one usually will dominate the other—that allele's instructions alone will be expressed in the organism—and so it is referred to as *dominant;* the weaker allele or half of the gene pair is called *recessive.*

   For instance, one gene in a pair may carry instructions for straight hair and the other for curly hair. Because straight hair is a recessive trait and curly hair a dominant one, a child carrying both alleles (the child is said to be heterozygous) will have curly hair. But the child may pass on his recessive gene to his children. Thus, if he mates with another heterozygous curly-haired person, there is a 25 percent chance of their having a straight-haired child—one who shows the recessive trait. Furthermore, because of the first law described above, there is a greater chance that their children will be heterozygous for curly hair, like themselves, and will carry the recessive gene for straight hair for at least another generation, although they do not express it themselves.
3. The two members of each pair of genes separate from each other when the organism forms gametes—sperm or eggs. In the case of humans, a heterozygous curly-haired person, one carrying both the dominant and recessive alleles for hair shape, can produce sperm (or eggs) with either the straight-hair or the curly-hair gene. This is called the *law of segregation* because Mendel used the term *segregation* to describe the separation of gene pairs into different gametes.
4. Finally, Mendel proposed a *law of random assortment*, which states that gene pairs for different traits, such as eye color and blood type, segregate independently of each other— unless they happen to be closely associated with each other on the same chromosome. This random assortment is one of the major reasons for the great variety of possible combinations of traits from one person to the next. Thus, a person with blue eyes can have any of several blood types, for instance.

Genotype and Phenotype

The visible expression of an individual's overall genetic makeup is called his *phenotype*. It includes thousands of characteristics, such as intelligence, height, pulse rate, sociability. *Genotype*, on the other hand, refers only to the genetic pattern that was inherited at conception. In theory, a person's genotype may indicate he will grow to be over six feet tall, but if his mother was malnourished during pregnancy, or if he did not eat the right foods as a baby, his growth may be severely stunted. His phenotype would show small stature, although his genotype held the potential for tallness. The distinction between genotype and phenotype becomes more and more difficult to draw, however, as scientists discover how early in the zygote's existence certain alterations of heredity may occur. Strictly speaking, all we can accu-

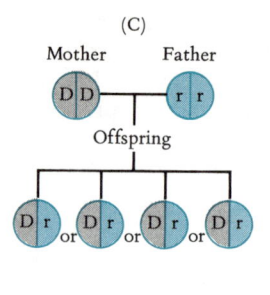

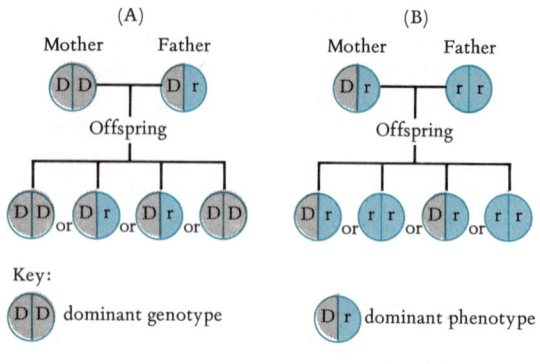

Figure 3.5 Possible makeup of offspring when dissimilar genes mate: (A) both parents have dominant phenotypes; (B) the mother's phenotype is dominant, the father's is pure recessive; (C) the mother's phenotype is pure dominant, the father's is pure recessive.

rately know is a person's phenotype, unless his original set of genes were to be analyzed at the moment of conception, which is impossible with current technology.

Genetic Uniqueness

Anthropologists have shown that each of us, through the mating of men and women from different races and geographic areas over the centuries, is the product of a fantastically rich genetic inheritance. Still, each of us (except identical twins) possesses a unique pattern of genes.

We have seen how the random separation of gene pairs during meiosis contributes to the uniqueness of every individual. Every sperm or ovum created will probably carry different combinations of genes. Yet, there is still another event that takes place in the reproductive cells during meiosis, before the sperm and ova are produced, which further insures that each new child will be different from any other. It is a process referred to as *crossing over*. As the chromosomes (with the genes they carry) line up in pairs at the beginning of meiosis, both genes of any pair may cross over to opposite chromosomes. In this way, then, the members of chromosome pairs usually exchange many genes before separating and becoming part of a sperm or ovum cell. This associates new genes with each other on a chromosome.

When we consider the several complex processes that in effect "scramble" the genes transmitted from parents to their children—crossing over, the random assortment of genes in each sperm and ovum, and the random union of any one of millions of sperm with any ovum—it is not difficult to see how each new individual is certain to be unique, like no other person.

We can better understand the occurrence of different traits within a family if we keep in mind that a heritage of possible gene combinations has come down from preceding generations, and that, as Mendel's experiments showed, a characteristic may disappear for a generation or more, only to reappear later.

Sex Determination

Chance also operates in establishing whether a baby will be a boy or a girl. Sex is determined by one of the 23 chromosomes in the spermatozoon when it penetrates the ovum at conception. Each body and germ cell carries a specialized chromosome pair—the sex chromosomes. In females, the

Figure 3.6 Diagram to illustrate the appearance of a characteristic from one generation to the next. In this hypothetical model, it is assumed that the first set of parents have pure genotypes and that each member of the succeeding generations marries someone who does not possess the original characteristic. The appearance of the characteristic is diminished by half in each succeeding generation.

Generation	Appearance of Characteristic
Parents	100% (in one parent)
Children	50%
Grandchildren	25%
Great-grandchildren	12½%

64 THE PRENATAL PERIOD

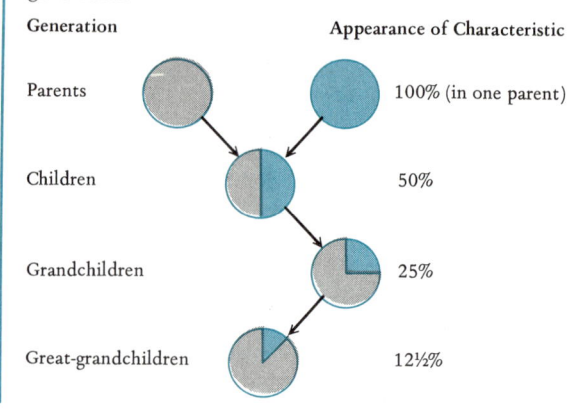

pair is an *XX*, and in males an *XY*. When the germ cells divide to produce sperm and ova and the chromosome pairs separate, half of the sperm carry the X chromosomes, half the Y's; the ovum bears only the X kind. When the gametes unite, if the sperm carries the X chromosome, the baby is destined to be a girl; if the sperm carries a Y chromosome, a boy will be born. These are the two normal combinations. Later in this chapter, we shall discuss the results of an XXY and an XYY combination, abnormalities almost certain to bring a confusion of gender identity to anyone so unlucky as to inherit them.

The Nature of Genetic Influence

The genes an individual inherits are not ordinarily affected by any events or conditions in a person's life. This means that we cannot alter our genes by the skills and traits we acquire during our lifetime. We may be aided or limited in acquiring characteristics by our genetic constitution. If our influence on our children is strong enough, they may imitate these characteristics; but this will not alter the genes they transmit to their children.

The idea that a man who develops a spectacular set of biceps can pass his big muscles on to his progeny has been relegated to the scrap heap of science. Mr. America's muscles were enlarged by his own weight-lifting efforts, although his inherited body structure, and perhaps even his partially inherited persistence, helped serve his purpose. The notion that a woman might fulfill her desire to give birth to a potential concert pianist by listening to classical piano music during her pregnancy has been similarly discredited.

While genetic material ordinarily cannot be changed, alteration in genes can occur under certain abnormal conditions. (An altered gene produces *mutations*—changes in a species.) Evidence of genetic changes caused by exposure to X-rays has been presented, and there is some indication that psychoactive drugs like LSD can change genetic material in the sperm and egg cells.

When we speak of inherited traits, it is with the understanding that what is actually transmit-

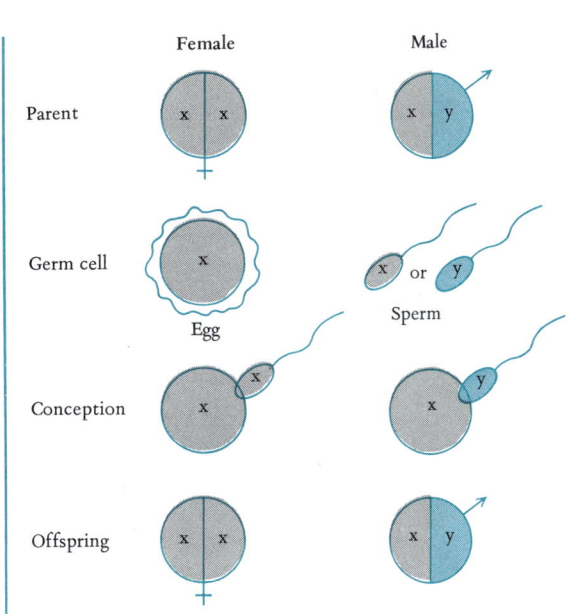

Figure 3.7 The mating of sex chromosomes and the resultant sex of the offspring.

ted from parent to child are genes that have the *potential* to produce certain traits under certain conditions. A case in point is an experiment with Himalayan rabbits that shows how the appearance of an inherited characteristic is changed in response to an environmental influence. This rabbit's fur is white except at its extremities, the ears, nose, tips of paws, and tail, where it is black. This characteristic pattern (which apparently has survival value to the rabbit living in the snow-covered Himalayan Mountains) is passed from one generation to the next. In a laboratory experiment, when a patch of white fur was shaved from the back of one of these rabbits and an ice pack kept on the patch, the fur that grew back was black instead of white. This experiment demonstrated that the pattern itself is not inherited; rather, the rabbit inherits the *capacity* to produce black pigment in parts of its body where the temperature is lowest. And, according to this theory, since the temperature at the extremities is normally lower than elsewhere in the body, the pigmentation there is black. We might make a comparison with the factor of height in human beings; while stature basically is established in the genes, height can be increased or stunted by nutrition

(Witkin 1967). The potential is inherited, but its fulfillment is subject to environmental influences.

With regard to the inheritance of traits in humans, Gerald E. McClearn has written:

The key concept . . . necessarily involves the simultaneous consideration of both genetic and environmental determinants. With this formulation, an attempt to describe a trait as being "genetic" or "environmental" in origin is seen to be meaningless. . . . Depending simultaneously upon environmental and genetic variance sources, the heritability [of any trait] will change as a given population is subjected to different environmental circumstances, or as its genetic composition changes. Thus a heritability value refers to a given trait in a given population at a given time in a given environment. (McClearn 1970)

We have learned that genetic traits may fail to appear in one generation, only to crop up in the next. In the individual as well, genetic traits do not necessarily become evident at any given time; the effect of gene action can *manifest* itself at any time. Our developmental processes are subject to the continuing influences of heredity; moreover, there are specific genes which are effective at specific times. For instance, the susceptibility to Huntington's chorea is present in the genes from birth because it is inherited, but the disease itself usually appears some time in adulthood. By contrast, another characteristic, phenylketonuria, shows up at birth but remains the same thereafter.

Whether or not a certain trait shows up in an individual, and the extent to which it does appear, frequently depends on circumstances in the person's environment and on the specific trait in question. If medical tests indicate that a baby has inherited an allergic sensitivity to a certain food, such as chocolate, or even cow's milk, that food can be withheld and the baby will be spared the rashes or intestinal trouble associated with it. Later in his life he might be able to tolerate the food. Similarly, a desirable trait could remain latent if circumstances in the child's life did not serve to activate its development. A child might inherit the potential for musical talent, but his musicality might go untapped and unrecognized if he had foster parents who failed to provide him with an opportunity to exercise it, or who discouraged any musical attempts he made on his own. On the other hand, if this child were raised in a home where musical talent was highly valued and encouraged, and where music was an integral part of family life, he might become a more accomplished musician than the child with only average musical ability raised in the same home.

Genes can influence or alter a child's behavior in much more profound and unfortunate ways, too. Some of these genetic influences—for instance, certain birth defects—can be changed in varying degrees in some cases; in others they cannot be changed at all. Amaural idiocy, a result of hereditary metabolic disorders, is among those defects that cannot be improved by environment—the affected person remains mentally defective. Hereditary deafness, although it will continue to provide difficulties, can be offset by training. Deaf persons who are not reached by education because no one has taken the trouble to break through the wall of silence that separates them from the society of those who hear, may be mistakenly assumed to be mentally deficient. Many children born deaf have in the past been doomed to bear this stigma. Now we know that as the training of deaf children improves, their intelligence quotient rises, and an increasing number are being helped to lead more normal lives (Anastasi 1958).

The isolation enforced by certain physical diseases and long bouts of illness can act as a deterrent to intellectual development or, depending on factors in the home and the individual's social environment, may have the opposite effect of enabling him to develop his intellectual powers more fully. Genetically inherited conditions can also affect personality; physical suffering makes some people more sympathetic to misfortune and others more hostile and bitter.

By their effect on physical appearance, genes may increase an individual's chances for success or, conversely, may set limits to his social acceptance and opportunities. Society tends to form preconceptions and make judgments based on stereotypes; its attitudes and expectations are reflected in the image the individual forms of himself, so that he tends generally to act as society expects him to act. Thus, racial stereotypes, long ingrained in the American consciousness, have served to obstruct opportunities for the black American, creating in him a self-concept of inferiority, now changing as he understands the forces that have prevented him from fulfilling his potential.

Methods of Studying Genetic Influence

Psychologists dealing with the perceptible problem of child growth and behavior continue to look for answers to two fundamental questions: How can we study the influence of genetics on behavior and development? How do we understand the many combinations of interaction between heredity and environment?

It might be possible to set up the ideal research situation to answer these questions in regard to insects or lower animals, but certainly not for the human child. Scientists cannot breed humans, manipulate their development, and control their environment as they do that of the fruit fly or the rat. Human research of this type occurs only in grade-B science fiction and horror movies. But even without the ethical restraints that prevent work of this sort in real life, experimentation with human heredity would be impractical since humans reproduce slowly and bear relatively few offspring. Furthermore, with a creature as complex as a human, the number of variables present in the body and the environment that must be dealt with scientifically becomes enormous. Since researchers cannot direct or influence human heredity for their purposes, or even observe the genes in action, they must infer what happens from the evidence they can observe in the growing human, in his natural environment.

Research Using Twins

In the absence of controlled breeding experiments in human genetics, twins have been a boon to research. Identical (*monozygotic*) twins are ideal subjects for some types of studies. Because they are born from a single, divided fertilized ovum, they inherit the same chromosomes. The genetic potential of identical twins is identical, and therefore any differences that are observed in their development or behavior are attributable to environmental influences. In other words, the variables of heredity are held constant by the fact that the subjects are identical twins, and this enables researchers to assess the effects of environmental variables more accurately. Besides comparing identical twins with each other, researchers have compared twin pairs reared together with twin pairs reared apart. All of these studies have revealed much about the interaction and overlapping of inherited and environmental influences, as will be discussed in greater detail later.

Fraternal (*dizygotic*) twins also have been subjects of many studies. Fraternal twins are conceived at the same time but develop from different fertilized egg cells. Their genetic inheritance is therefore no more alike than that of their siblings (brothers and sisters), but their prenatal environment and experience are similar. Studies of fraternal twins usually relate their similarities and differences in development and behavior to those of identical twins and to their own nontwin siblings.

In studying the influence of environment on inherited tendencies, whether in the case of twins or nontwin siblings, exact judgments are always difficult to make. Even identical twins reared in the same household may be affected by different experiences, exposure to different diseases, and different interpersonal relationships inside of the family as well as away from it.

When identical twins are reared apart, a difference in certain traits may become apparent. Charlotte Auerbach, an English geneticist, cited a study of separately reared identical twins which showed a variation in weight. The average weight difference of 50 pairs of identical twins reared together was 4.1 pounds, while that between the members of 20 pairs reared apart was 9.9 pounds. "Average differences in intelligence quotient, scholastic performance, and personality traits were also increased by separation, the more so the greater the difference between the social and cultural backgrounds of the two foster homes"

(Auerbach 1961). These differences in identical twins indicate that a child's environment does exert a significant influence on specific areas of his development and behavior.

Specific Effects of Heredity on Human Development

Physical Traits

Heredity is most clearly evident in the way an individual looks. His facial features, height, skin, eye and hair color, distribution of body hair, body form, and countless other details of his physical makeup are established for him at birth by the genes handed down by his parents. Environmental factors, such as a birth injury, diet, geography, occupation, and disease, can change his appearance and alter his anatomy, but under ordinary circumstances his physical traits will continue to show the strong influence of genes. This was clearly seen by Kallmann and Sander in their 1949 study of elderly twins mentioned earlier.

In this study, the identical twins, all over 60 years old, were still physically alike to a startling degree: equally enfeebled or strong for their years, showing the same extent of thinning or graying of the hair, the same pattern of skin wrinkling, and the same kind of eye, ear, and teeth changes. The identical twins tended to live to about the same age, frequently dying within a period of days or weeks of each other. In one remarkable case, twin sisters developed similar symptoms of mental senility, although their social and marital histories were very different. They became blind and deaf in the same month and died five days apart, before their eighty-sixth birthday (Kallmann and Sander 1949).

When a child's facial features closely resemble those of one of his parents, it can be assumed that the different genes involved were almost all dominant over those transmitted by the other parent. Not merely a single gene but several may carry instructions for the formation of a feature. In the nose formation, one "key" gene is believed to control the general shape of the nose, while several others influence the formation of the bridge, nostrils, root, and tip.

Polygenic (many-gene) inheritance apparently is also involved in the design of the ears: they are either large or small, with rims that are rolled or flat, lobes that hang free or are attached to the head. Chins, jaws, and teeth also show the influence of several genes.

Stature depends on growth in many separate parts of the body—the vertebrae, neck, trunk, legs, and other areas whose length is dictated by the genes. All-over shortness or tallness may be inherited, yet there are indications that the environment may exert a strong influence. A study made in 1916 of the children of Japanese and Jewish immigrants to the United States found they were taller than their parents on the average by two inches. Something in the new country—probably diet—caused the younger generation to shoot up like seeds transplanted in enriched soil.

Evidence of the influence of heredity on such physiological traits as blood pressure, pulse rate, and breathing rate, although less apparent than on anatomical features, has been offered by various investigators. The body's total physiological and neurological functioning—its metabolism, its reactions to stimuli, its power to resist disease, its ability to withstand stress—all are determined by the interaction of genes and the environment. In some instances the genes are the major determinant; in others it is the environment.

The onset of puberty, the first menstrual period, and the length of a person's life, barring fatal accident or illness, are matters that appear to be strongly affected by genetic constitution.

Disease Tendencies

At least 1500 diseases in man are now classified as genetic in origin, and 92 of them are known to be caused by deficiencies of specific enzymes (McKusick 1970, 1971). Many of these diseases are rare, but when considered as a group, genetic diseases constitute an increasingly significant medical problem. Diabetes is perhaps the most widespread disease linked to heredity: there are about four million diabetics in the United States today (Friedmann and Roblin 1972).

In diabetes, as in most genetically determined diseases, however, it is a predisposition to the disorder, not the disease itself, that is inherited. In some cases, aspects of the person's environment (his diet, for instance) can be controlled in such a way as to avert the onset of the disease.

Table 3.1 Hereditary Diseases and Defects

Dominant	Sex-Linked	Recessive
Huntington's chorea Nerve deafness (middle age)	Hemophilia Color-blindness Sweat-gland defects Pattern baldness	Diabetes mellitus Phenylketonuria Progressive muscular dystrophy, childhood and early adolescent types Glaucoma Infantile congenital deafness

Source: Data condensed and selected from A. Scheinfeld, *Your Heredity and Environment*, Lippincott, 1965. Used by permission.

The susceptibility to a defect or disease can be produced in several ways. The genes may cause production of the wrong amount or the wrong form of a particular enzyme or other chemical needed by the body, or they may fail to "order" a vital substance altogether. Table 3.1 lists a few disorders that can be caused by such abnormalities of the body chemistry; environmental variables, however, can affect the appearance of genetically determined diseases.

Certain blood diseases that have been linked to heredity are seen only in particular ethnic groups. This pattern of occurrence would indicate that some environmental elements must have played a role even in the genetic origin of such diseases in the population. For instance, the abnormal gene that is responsible for sickle-cell anemia, which largely afflicts persons of African background, provides a defense against malaria at the same time that it produces a form of red blood cells that cannot completely perform their function of distributing oxygen through the body. If a person inherits the sickle-cell trait from only one parent, the effects of anemia will be relatively mild and, if he lives in Africa, he will benefit from a resistance to malaria. Only if the trait is inherited from both parents will the anemia overtake the advantages of malaria resistance. Then the person is almost certain to die earlier than would otherwise be the case.

It is easy to see how the sickle-cell trait was, in effect, an evolutionary adaptation to the environment for persons living in Africa. For descendants living in the United States, however, there is no particular advantage in being immune to malaria, so carriers do not necessarily outlive noncarriers; in fact, their mild anemia may make them weaker than the general population and so lessen their survival and therefore their number in the population. Consequently, the incidence of the disease in the United States is proportionately lower than in countries such as Africa where malaria resistance provides a strong advantage for survival.

Although a cure has not yet been found for sickle-cell anemia, this and other genetic diseases usually can be treated by drugs, by modifying the diet, or by replacing the faulty product of the defective genes. An exciting recent development in biological research may make it possible eventually to replace the defective gene itself with healthy DNA material (Friedmann and Roblin 1972). Certain genetic diseases could then be prevented altogether.

Reactions to Drugs

We have seen that an inherited deficiency in, or an inappropriate form of, an enzyme in the body may produce a tendency for a particular disease. In a similar way, abnormalities or even normal variations in body chemistry may cause serious abnormalities in a person's reactions to drugs.

Doctors are discovering that what is considered to be the proper dose of a drug (based on a person's age, weight, sex, and stage of disease) can be toxic to some people or ineffective in others. Many now feel it is a person's genetic makeup that largely determines these unexpected reactions (La Du 1971).

In some cases of abnormal drug reactions, a meticulous family medical history might predict the patient's resistance to the drug in question.

For example, an elderly man who had suffered a heart attack was given the usual anticoagulant drug to prevent blood clots from forming. When the standard dosage did not produce the desired result, the amounts were steadily increased. Eventually he was receiving 20 times the normal amount before his body would respond "normally." When his relatives, including an identical twin, were tested and questioned, it was found that five others among them had similar resistance to that drug, and his twin had shown the same reaction after similar heart trouble of his own. The entire family history was then analyzed, and it was discovered that this particular reaction was indeed an inherited trait. A specialized area of medicine known as *pharmacogenetics* is involved in identifying such abnormal and unexpected drug reactions that are caused by genetically determined variations or deficiencies in the body's enzymes.

Mental Disease and Retardation

BRAIN DAMAGE. When a gene fails to produce a specific enzyme, the brain is one of the vital areas that may be impaired. One such form of genetically caused brain damage is *phenylketonuria* (or PKU); it results from a defect or error in the body's metabolism. Children with PKU lack an enzyme needed to metabolize or process the acid produced in the digestion of a protein factor known as phenylalanine, which is found in milk and many other foods. Consequently, toxic quantities of the acid (phenylpyruvic acid) accumulate in the body and cause brain damage. Fortunately, hospitals in most states are required by law to perform a simple test to detect abnormal concentrations of this substance in newborn infants; those affected can then be placed on a diet low in phenylalanine until the danger of brain damage is past.

Another form of brain damage and retardation caused by abnormalities in the genetic material is mongolism, or *Down's syndrome*, which afflicts about 1 in 600 babies born in the United States. In this case, it is the incorrect number and pairing of the chromosomes that somehow produces the damage. Mongoloid babies have 47 chromosomes although their parents carry the normal 46; the extra chromosome attaches itself to a member of pair number 21.

The mongoloid is mentally retarded and is recognized by certain distinct physical characteristics: a peculiar skin fold in the inner corner of the eyes giving an Oriental look, a broad nose, a protruding tongue, and a single crease across the palm. Mongoloid births occur with greater frequency among older women.

The detection of chromosomal aberrations that cause such conditions as mongolism during early pregnancy has been made possible by a new technique known as *amniocentesis*. Through a needle inserted into the uterus, fluid containing fetal cells can be withdrawn, and the cells can be examined in the laboratory for a chromosome count. If the chromosomes show that the fetus is seriously abnormal, a woman might choose to terminate the pregnancy. At the moment, amniocentesis is generally performed only in pregnancies where there is known to be a high risk of chromosomal defect; the technique still holds possible dangers for the fetus. Moreover, because the development of amniocentesis is so recent, not many physicians have yet acquired the specialized training necessary to perform the test.

GENETIC COUNSELING. Before a couple decides to have children, however, it is now possible for them to have their own chromosomes analyzed. In this way, through what is known as genetic counseling, a person can learn whether or not he or she carries genes that would transmit to future offspring certain defects that are detectable in the parents' chromosomes. A woman who had given birth to a severely damaged baby might learn from an analysis of her and her husband's chromosomes that this would almost certainly happen again with any future pregnancies. This information, disturbing as it might be, could spare her the anguish of repeatedly bearing, and perhaps soon losing, babies with extreme birth defects. She and her husband might choose to adopt children rather than take such a risk.

On the other hand, genetic counseling can provide reassurance to prospective parents who are worried about their chances for having normal children. A woman who knows that mongolism has occurred in her mother's family might be reluctant to have children for fear that she, too, would give birth to a mongoloid baby. Chromosome analysis might well show that she does not carry the peculiar genetic pattern that often produces the 47 chromosomes of the mongoloid.

MENTAL ILLNESS. Many circumstances, in addition to the known genetic factors, accounted for the 6,000,000 cases of mental illness recorded in the United States in 1971. In cases that are not the apparent result of specific injury to the brain, but instead are psychoneurological and related to a personality breakdown, authorities tend to disagree about the causative factors. The greatest disagreement has arisen over schizophrenia. So many symptoms of mental disorder have been attributed to this disease that in this country more hospital beds are occupied by persons diagnosed as schizophrenics than by patients with any other kind of disease.

In children, schizophrenia may be a disease different from the adult illness; in fact, there seem to be at least two types of childhood schizophrenia. The first, called autism, usually appears in the first two years of life and is considered chronic; the second type tends to appear intermittently beginning at about the age of 6 and is called schizophrenia. In both cases, the affected child often behaves much like one who has been brain-damaged either in a birth accident or by a genetic defect. Some authorities insist the origin of this disease is genetic, affecting the body's biochemistry; others disagree, blaming it on psychological difficulties encountered early in life. Some believe schizophrenia involves a number of disease processes, with the participation of several genetic factors.

A strong case for the genetic origin of schizophrenia was made by Kallmann (1946, 1953), who examined pairs of twins, full siblings, half-siblings, and step-siblings. In each pair, one member had been hospitalized for schizophrenia. The highest proportion of concordance, or likeness, in regard to schizophrenia, 85.8, appeared in the group of identical twins, with a marked drop to 14.7 shown for the fraternal twins. The proportion of schizophrenic concordance continued to drop in direct ratio to the decrease in family relationship or genetic inheritance. Knowing as we do that identical twins are born with the same genetic potential, we can see why the Kallmann studies offer a good case for heredity.

At the moment, another group is investigating the possibility that schizophrenia can be caused by the interaction between an especially stressful family life and an abnormally sensitive and rapid-firing autonomic nervous system (Mednick and Schulsinger 1971). This unusual type of nervous system activity (which might be inherited) tends to make a person increasingly irritable when faced with even mild stress—he is unable to become accustomed to stress and to moderate his response to it. At the same time, however, this same overactive nervous system provides a special aptitude for learning to avoid distressing situations or thoughts altogether. The affected child learns that the most self-protective way he can deal with either internal or external stress is to block it out—to turn off the signals since he cannot turn them down. If the child is subjected to repeated and prolonged stress in his home, he would then develop more and more extreme tactics for avoiding that pain, to the point where his behavior might eventually be diagnosed as schizophrenic.

The evidence that is accumulating from all sides about this little-understood disease (or complex of diseases) leads away from the notion of simply either a genetic or an environmental cause. Instead, as with more and more diseases, and even with variations of standard behavior, there appears to be an extremely complicated and delicate interaction between genetic potential and environmental forces. It is possible that a child inherits certain physiologic traits that would make him predisposed to schizophrenic behavior; yet he could be protected from the disease if his family life and schooling were especially fortunate, or were adjusted to meet his needs. Some researchers are currently hoping to use this idea of the interaction of probable causal forces to prevent the disease. They are trying to improve certain crucial living conditions for a group of children who, because of their medical and family histories, would be expected to develop some form of schizophrenia (Mednick and Schulsinger 1971).

Intelligence

As is commonly thought, intelligence involves the ability to acquire knowledge. But learned information is useful only if the individual also has the ability to use it properly. In our evaluation of intelligence, can we exclude the ability to adjust to new situations? Questions and qualifications such as these have made it difficult to formulate an exact psychological definition of intelligence. In the presence of such immeasurable aspects of intelligence as adaptability, creativity, and wit, it is virtually impossible to establish criteria for testing and comparing intelligence. The most familiar criterion is the I.Q. test; yet it has its shortcomings as a measure of intelligence. For example, Theodosius Dobzhansky, a foremost geneticist, says:

what is measured by the I.Q. is not necessarily the same as what is referred to in everyday language as intelligence, cleverness, aptitude, or wit. Still less does the I.Q. give an estimate of the value or worth of the person. The I.Q. as administered to school children is regarded as a measure of their ability to handle verbal symbols. This ability shows a fairly high correlation with scholastic success, and this is what makes the I.Q. measurements useful, but at the same time suggests the limitations of their usefulness. The I.Q. is certainly not independent of the environment, of the family background, schooling and the circumstances under which the test is administered. (Dobzhansky 1964)

The intelligence quotient is thus disputed as a valid measure of allover intelligence because it is based on acquired knowledge. Investigators nevertheless regard it as valuable, within its limitations, in studies to determine genetic influence.

A number of studies in recent years have attempted to separate factors in intelligence by testing subjects in various areas of ability. Thus, Vandenberg (1966) conducted large-scale twin studies in which he was able to show that the influence of heredity was greater in respect to some abilities involved in intelligence and lower in others. In tests pertaining to word skills, in the ability to visualize spatial relationships (as in recognizing a design in a different context), and the ability to work with numbers, heredity appeared to play a significant part. In respect to the ability to reason or remember, he found no evidence of genetic determination.

Many other studies, however, support the assumption that under normal circumstances intelligence potential is established by the genes.

Studies that have compared twins reared together in the same family with twins who had been separated and reared apart, with one or both in a foster home, have been a fruitful source of data on the relative influences of heredity and environment.

Before examining some of their findings, we should know something about an important tool used in psychology, the statistical correlation, or *correlation coefficient*, used to show the degree to which two factors or circumstances are related to one another. For example, a person might want to know, "What is the relationship between the intelligence quotient and school grades?" The purpose would be to determine whether a high I.Q. necessarily results in high academic achievement. The researcher would record the subjects' scores for I.Q. and their school grades on different scales. The degree to which the ratings for the two factors were alike or different would be indicated as the correlation coefficient. If both ratings were exactly alike for every person tested, the figure would be +1.00. This perfect positive correlation would be highly improbable, however, as would a perfect negative one (−1.00), which would indicate that all persons demonstrated the highest possible intelligence scores and at the same time the lowest possible scholastic scores, or vice versa. A correlation coefficient of .90 or above indicates a very high correlation or similarity; coefficients around .50 indicate a lesser correlation, and those under .30 indicate that the correlation may be more a result of coincidence than any reliable relationship between the two factors being measured.

The value of this tool can be seen in studies that compare the similarity of identical twins raised together with the similarity found in those who are raised apart, or in fraternal twins or in nontwin siblings.

One such study, conducted by Newman, Freeman, and Holzinger (1937), found a correlation coefficient of .77 in I.Q. for identical twins who had been separated and raised in different homes, as compared with .63 for fraternal twins raised in a single household. Thus, despite differences in environment, the identical twins scored closer to one another in the intelligence test than did the nonidentical twins who shared a home situation.

The same team, in another twin study, found an average difference in I.Q. of only 5.9 between twins in identical pairs, as compared with 9.9 for fraternal twins. They concluded that heredity is a significant factor in intellectual ability.

A later work by a British researcher, Shields (1962), confirmed these findings. Shields conducted a television search for three groups of twins (the same categories used by the Newman team)—identical twins reared together, identical twins reared apart, and fraternal twins reared together—and he examined them for intelligence, height, weight, extroversion, and neuroticism. He found that identical twins were more alike than fraternal twins regardless of whether they were brought up together or apart. The correlation in intelligence between identical twins reared together (.76) varied only slightly from that of identical twins reared apart (.77), in contrast to the figure for fraternal twins (.51).

Another British investigator, Cyril Burt (1966), in a survey of his own and other studies of genetic determinants in intelligence and achievement, has offered convincing evidence for environmental determinants in regard to achievement and for genetic influence in regard to intelligence. Altogether, he used six different groups: identical twins reared together; identical twins reared apart; fraternal twins reared together; siblings (not twins) reared together; siblings (not twins) reared apart; unrelated children reared together. The children in each pair were compared with each other on intelligence, educational achievement, and physical development, and correlation scores were then computed. In each trait, identical twins reared together had the highest correlation scores. The high correlation coefficient for intelligence and physical factors in identical twins reared apart was considered as even more significant proof of genetic influence.

In examination for scholastic achievement, however, a higher correlation coefficient was found in fraternal twins reared together than in identical twins reared apart, thereby indicating that educational attainment, as distinguished from innate ability, is influenced to a great extent by environment. However, identical twins reared together scored a higher correlation than either fraternal twins reared together or siblings reared together, a result indicating that educational attainment is not entirely free of genetic influence. It is interesting to note that environment influenced the verbal part of the test more than the arithmetic part.

In his paper, Burt compared his results with those of other investigators, including the 1937 Newman study. The correlations in I.Q. that he found (.93 for identical twins reared together, .88 for identical twins reared apart, and .45 for fraternal twins reared together) correspond closely to the data of the Newman team (.88, .77, and .63), supporting the conclusion that I.Q. is in large measure affected by heredity. Table 3.2 summarizes the findings of the twin I.Q. studies discussed here.

Burt also replied to those who cite the great differences in I.Q. test scores found between some twins reared apart as an argument against the genetic origin of intelligence. Thus, for example, he pointed to a pair of identical twins in the Newman study who were reared apart, one girl in an isolated part of the Rockies which had no schools, and the other in an area where she was fully educated, reaching college. The uneducated girl scored only 92 on the I.Q. test, her sister, 116. Burt pointed out that the tests were mainly of ver-

Table 3.2 Correlations of I.Q. Scores of Twins

Group	Newman et al. (1937)	Shields (1962)	Burt (1966)
Identical twins reared together	.88	.76	.93
Identical twins reared apart	.77	.77	.88
Fraternal twins reared together	.63	.51	.45

bal ability and not "culture free"; hence, they were biased in favor of the educated sister. He suggested that environmental influences be evaluated by an examination of the correlations between test-score differences for identical twins and the differences in their home conditions. If a great number of twins who scored differently on tests were found to be raised under different conditions, we should get a high correlation between test differences and environmental differences, signifying environmental influences. Burt did such a correlation and found high correlations between school attainment differences and home conditions, but not between individual score differences and home conditions. Thus, as noted before, intelligence seems mainly to be genetically determined, whereas school attainment is influenced largely by environment.

Personality

A variety of personality traits make us react to the environment in distinctively different ways. A number of studies show that genetic factors affect such personality traits as sociability, assertiveness, and temperament, but also that the influence of heredity may be overshadowed by a multitude of environmental factors, including social and cultural pressures and health and nutrition. Generally speaking, it is difficult to measure the degree to which personality is "inborn" or formed by outside factors.

One of the personality traits that has been measured with some degree of reliability is sociability—the extent to which a person is introverted or extroverted. Introversion is the term used to describe the characteristics of the shy, reclusive person, and extroversion the outgoing, gregarious quality one finds in the sociable person who is always the last to leave a party.

Studies that have followed children from birth to adulthood show that whether a person is generally introverted or extroverted tends to remain remarkably the same, and especially so in girls. Most investigators feel that genetic, biologic factors therefore determine this characteristic, but they also agree that certain behavior of the parents can alter a child's sociability at certain ages (Schaefer 1964).

A study of sociability in grade-school twin girls has shown that heredity accounted for about 60 to 80 percent of the individual's style of social responsiveness (Scarr 1965). This report also summarized the findings of other investigators and found that a high degree of heritability in extroversion and introversion held true regardless of sex, age, social class, and cultural differences.

Infants also have been measured for social responsiveness and dependency. Freedman (1965) observed the ways in which infants in the first 5 months of life responded to others, and then he measured the frequency and intensity of these babies' fear of strangers between 5 and 12 months, noting the age at which this fear became apparent. Identical twins were much more similar in their social behavior and fear of strangers than were the fraternal twins, which led Freedman to conclude that genetics does play some role in determining a baby's dependency.

Asocial and neurotic behavior are other aspects of human personality that some investigators have shown to be genetically determined. H. J. Eysenck (1964) found a high incidence of genetic determinants in criminal and asocial behavior, as well as in neurotic behavior. Selecting his subjects from twin pairs, he found that in adult criminal behavior, childhood behavior disorders, and alcoholism, identical twins were alike in about twice as many cases as fraternal twins (see Table 3.3). Eysenck has noted that other studies show, "Much the same is true in relation to neurotic complaints and emotional disorders."

A more recent study supports Eysenck's evidence of genetic influence in alcoholism. It found that the incidence of alcoholism was higher among persons who had alcoholic natural parents but were raised by nonalcoholic foster parents, than it was among persons who did not have an alcoholic natural parent but were raised by alcoholic persons (Schuckit 1972).

The difficulty of measuring the relative influence of genes and environment on personality is complicated by the unavoidable establishment of behavior patterns early in the lives of children. One study showed, for example, that assertiveness may be affected by early rearing. In a paper on the effect that parent-child relationships have

Table 3.3 Similarity in Various Types of Criminal, Antisocial, and Asocial Behavior Among Twins

	Number of Twin Pairs	Identical	Fraternal	Proportion of Similarity Identical	Fraternal
Adult Crime	225	107	118	71	34
Juvenile Delinquency	67	42	25	85	75
Childhood Behavior Disorder	107	47	60	87	43
Homosexuality	63	37	26	100	12
Alcoholism	82	26	56	65	30

Source: Adapted from H. J. Eysenck, *Crime and Personality*. Boston: Houghton Mifflin, 1964. Used by permission.

on the child's personality, Richard Bell noted that parents tend to use harsher means to control highly assertive, active children, but can be easier on docile children who present fewer care problems. The noisy child who is "always getting into things" is less likely to pay attention to parental curbs, so that an exasperated parent may resort to verbal and physical punishment when, for example, Junior has gleefully tossed his bowl of oatmeal off the table for the second or third time. In the case of the quiet, introverted child, reasoning alone or threats of withdrawal of love can usually inhibit further mischief. A child accustomed to abusive disciplinary measures from his parents will tend, when he has power, to deal more harshly with others. Very likely he will always be more aggressive than his more introverted brother, partly because of his genetic constitution and partly because he elicited a different kind of response from his parents.

Assuming that a genetic determinant for sociability is also present in children, Bell noted that "children high in person orientation attend to the behavior of their parents and reinforce social responses emanating from them." The behavior of children low in person orientation "is controlled less by variations in social response from parents. They are interested in physical activity and inanimate objects" (Bell 1968).

Sexuality

If children's behavior and personalities—even what is considered their "femininity" or "masculinity"—can be affected by their parents' responses and demands, it is reasonable to ask if the behavior of adult men and women also is molded to a certain degree by the concepts and stereotypes society has established regarding sex roles. Or do men and women behave differently because something in their respective gene instructions makes them respond to the environment in peculiarly masculine or feminine ways? Recently this has become, if not a new issue, then one of the most hotly debated social issues of our time. The Women's Liberation Movement maintains that society dictates the roles men and women are expected to play; its adversaries retort that the role of woman is biologically, if not divinely, ordained, and "by God, she should stick to it." Scientific authorities are taking sides in this argument, and we find ourselves engaged once more in the old nature–nurture argument.

While there is considerable evidence and agreement regarding the influence of heredity in the sexually distinctive behavior of animals, the evidence regarding human beings is less compelling. Some authorities argue that men and women are born with traits that make them behave according to their sex; others are equally insistent that we are sexually molded by the environment. The most widely held position, however, is that in all males and females an interaction takes place between biological sexuality and the environment. The question that needs to be explored now is how various combinations of these influences result in different forms of behavior and degrees of masculinity and femininity in a person.

HEREDITY POSITION. In 1968, a time when women were beginning to organize to protest sexual discrimination which assigned them to the kitchen or the typewriter, a team of investigators led by D. M. Broverman came up with a controversial, and now widely contested, study to show that cognitive ability, the capacity to learn, is related to sexual differences. According to this research team, differences in male and female behavior reflect differences in neurological processes, in one case as a reaction to the androgens, the biochemical substances that produce masculine characteristics, and in the other to estrogen, the female hormone. The investigators asserted that the differences in behavior they attributed to different hormonal reactions caused men and women to perform at different levels of competence, and concluded that women would be better at typing and men at problem solving.

Other studies, as yet insufficiently replicated, have also supported the argument for genetic influence by showing that sex differences are present at birth. One such study showed that newborn girls respond more readily to comforting than boys and hence receive more comforting than irritable baby boys. As a result, a more mutually rewarding relationship is established between mothers and their infant daughters than with their newborn sons (Moss 1967). Various other studies have shown that male infants are larger, more muscular, more active, less susceptible to pain, less sensitive to touching than girls, and have higher metabolism rates.

Because of these apparent differences in infants, mothers might well handle them differently and so shape certain facets of the behavior of each in different ways. Mothers might tend to spend more time cooing and smiling at affectionate, responsive daughters, and would perhaps be inclined to limit the time spent in these activities with more difficult infant sons. Sons would learn that forceful, aggressive behavior was needed to win Mother's attention, whereas daughters could easily gain attention by smiling and babbling.

Inherited Sexual Anomalies. While the average man or woman may debate the relative influences of heredity and environment on his own feelings and expressions of masculinity or femininity, there is a small segment of the human population for whom there is no doubt that heredity has influenced, rather than a clearly defined sex role, a confusion of sexual identity. These are the individuals born with chromosomal aberrations that cause them to develop abnormally. Serious disturbances can take place in the development of a person's testes or ovaries, or in secondary sex characteristics of the individual, if one of the inherited gametes contains more or fewer than the normal 23 chromosomes.

In the 1950s it was learned that improper distribution of the sex chromosomes can result in sexual anomalies or abnormalities. As we have seen, whether a child is to be a boy or a girl is designated before birth by one of the 23 chromosomes in the sperm of the father. If the chromosome in the ovum unites with an X chromosome, the resulting organism will be female; if a Y, male. The absence of a sex chromosome or the addition of a superfluous one in the fertilized ovum can cause a variety of deviations.

Much of our understanding of the action of the chromosomes in sex designation was made possible by the work of Murray L. Barr and his colleagues. In 1948, they found a way to distinguish body cells destined to be female from those destined to be male. The female cell contains a substance called sex chromatin—a material not present in the male cell—which can be seen in the laboratory. The Barr team developed a technique involving microscopic examination of skin tissues, mucous scrapings, or blood films, to ascertain the absence or presence of sex chromatin in nuclei—thereby making it possible to learn whether an individual is genetically male or female, as well as to determine sex before birth. Abnormalities in sex chromosome structure were found to result in chromatin-negative (absent) females and chromatin-positive (present) males (Barr and Carr 1960). Thus, the Barr test became of value in identifying certain abnormal conditions, such as *Klinefelter's syndrome*, whose origin had hitherto been a mystery.

In *Klinefelter's syndrome*, the individual has male external sex organs but female body contours. There is no production of spermatozoa, so the afflicted person is sterile. Characteristic of this abnormality is the presence of 47 chromosomes, with the extra one attached to the pair of sex chromosomes, producing an XXY group. Klinefelter's syndrome shows up in about 1 in 800 live births, and, like mongolism, it occurs more often among babies born to women who are over 40.

In *Turner's syndrome*, which affects girls, in 1 out of 8,000 births, there is irregular growth and no development of secondary sexual characteristics. The abnormality results from the inaction of one of the chromosomes, and the Barr test shows an absence of the sex chromatin.

The presence of an extra Y chromosome, another irregularity, has been held accountable in some cases of criminality in males. P. A. Jacobs and his colleagues (1965) conducted a survey of mentally retarded patients in a maximum-security prison who had committed crimes of violence. Of the 197 patients examined, seven had an XYY sex chromosome group. (They were also unusually tall.) The greater incidence of this unusual chromosome group among criminals than in the general population was regarded as significant. In a follow-up on these patients, Price and Whatmore (1967) found that the prisoners with the XYY chromosomes differed from those with a normal sex chromosome pair in several ways. They committed fewer crimes than the XY inmates, and their violent acts were generally directed at property rather than persons; their behavior problems began at a younger age, and their siblings were significantly less likely to have antisocial records than the siblings of XY inmates. The basic difference appeared to be a lack of impulse control in XYY prisoners rather than any increased proneness to criminal behavior as such.

Homosexuality. Demands of homosexuals to be treated without discrimination have been another source of revival of the nature-nurture argument. A twin study that points to hereditary influences was made by Kallmann (1952). He examined 40 pairs of identical twins and 45 pairs of fraternal twins in which one member in each pair was an overt homosexual. In 39 of the identical twin pairs he found both members homosexual, while in the fraternal twins the frequency of homosexuality in the alternate members was no higher than its rate of occurrence in the general male population. Kallmann also found that in identical twin pairs, the character and extent of sexual deviance was dramatically similar. In a comparable test, where homosexuality occurred in 113 twin pairs, Schlegel (1962) found that 95 percent of the identical twins examined were both homosexual, while among fraternal twins the figure was only 5 percent. Both studies were offered to support the notion of genetic determination of maleness and femaleness. Yet, there is still no evidence of exactly how these differences might be determined by genes, whether through effects on the central nervous system or on the hormonal system. Also needed is more research on environmental forces that undoubtedly are at work here as in most other areas of human behavior.

ENVIRONMENTAL POSITION. An articulate opponent of traditional sex roles and spokeswoman for Women's Liberation, Kate Millett, has asserted that most sexual behavior is learned and not inherited. In her popular book *Sexual Politics*, she has written:

Psychosexually there is no differentiation between the sexes at birth. Psychosexual personality is therefore postnatal and learned. . . . Because of our social circumstances, male and female are really two cultures and their life experiences are utterly different—and this is crucial. Implicit in all the gender identity development which takes place through childhood is the sum total of the parents', the peers', and the culture's notions of what is appropriate to each gender by way of temperament, character, interests, status, worth, gesture and expression. Every moment of the child's life is a clue to how he or she must think and behave to attain or satisfy the demands which gender places upon one. In adolescence, the merciless task of conformity grows to crisis proportions, generally cooling and settling in maturity. (Millett 1971)

Millett relied on the authority of John Money, a leading investigator of psychosexual differences.[1] Money argued against biology as the principal determinant of sexual behavior. He maintained that human beings are neutral at birth in regard to sex role and asserted that "the power and permanence of something learned has been underestimated" (Money 1965). He arrived at this position through studies he has made since 1955

---

1. The following discussion is based on B. G. Rosenberg and B. Sutton-Smith, *Sex and Identity* (New York: Holt, Rinehart & Winston, 1972).

with J. L. Hampson and J. G. Hampson. Their work is based on the hypothesis that human beings, like animals, go through an early critical period of *imprinting* during which important, irreversible social behavior learning takes place that will dictate the way they behave for the rest of their lives (Money, Hampson, and Hampson 1955). In Money's opinion, two critical periods for imprinting gender role occur in humans: during the first two and one-half to three years of life, and again at puberty. In sex-role development, he maintains, sex established by experience has more influence than sex established by heredity (Money 1961).

In their investigations, Money, Hampson, and Hampson have studied subjects with contradictory sex characteristics, such as hermaphrodites, who have both male and female physical sex traits, evident in the appearance of external genitals, a sex chromatin pattern, gonads, or internal reproductive organs. Intensive studies were made in 1961 of such persons, using clinical interviews, life data, observations of mannerisms, demeanor, interests, and so on. The sex role each took on, whether as boy or girl, or man or woman, was examined in relation to six factors: chromosomal sex, gonadal sex, hormonal sex, internal accessory organs (uterus, prostate, and seminal vessels), external genital appearance, and assigned sex and rearing. Without exception, the gender role the person had adopted reflected the assigned sex rather than chromosomal sex. In regard to all other variables of sex, where a contradiction existed between a biologic sex factor and the sex rearing of the subject, there was an overwhelming tendency to act in accordance with rearing rather than biological assignment. In only 7 out of 110 cases examined was rearing different from the gender role adopted by the subject. In their summation, the authors wrote:

There is no such biologic entity as sex. What exists in nature is a dimorphism within species into male and female individuals, which differ with respect to contrasting characters for each of which in any given species we recognize a male form and a female form. . . . Sex is not a force that produces these contrasts; it is merely a name for our total impression of the differences. . . . Psychologic sex or gender role appears to be learned. . . . In place of a theory of innate constitutional psychologic bisexuality we can substitute a concept of psychosexual neutrality in humans at birth. (Money 1965)

This investigative team was criticized in a paper by M. Diamond (1965), who doubted conclusions based on subjects showing clinical deviations from the normal. Furthermore, Diamond pointed out that if man is assumed to be sexually neutral at birth, man's sexual patterns must be basically different from those of other animals, whose sexual behavior is known to be fixed from birth. Diamond believed it was improbable that man is this different from other animals. He did, however, acknowledge the significance of learning in the development of the gender role:

Undoubtedly we are dealing with an interaction of genetics and experience; the relative contribution of each, however, may vary with the particular behavior pattern and individual concerned. . . . It is the genetic heritage of an individual which predisposes him to react in a particular manner so that the learning of a gender role can occur. . . . Sexual predisposition is only a potentiality setting limits to a pattern that is greatly modifiable by ontogenetic experiences. Life experiences most likely act to differentiate and direct a flexible sexual disposition and to mold the prenatal organization until an environmentally (socially or culturally) acceptable gender role is formulated and established. (Diamond 1965)

Another study, made in 1967 by J. J. Baker and R. J. Stoller, raised other questions about the "neutrality" position. As young children, the persons in their study appeared to be normal. However, five subjects born and reared as boys showed interest only in activities generally regarded as typically feminine; a sixth subject, born and raised as a girl, had always shown masculine tendencies. All the subjects were anatomically normal at birth and were brought up in the normal way for their sex. At puberty, however, they did not develop normally; the boy subjects showed physical changes of a feminine nature, and the girl manifested masculine physical traits. Baker and Stoller held that the latent biological abnormalities had affected the children's earlier behavior. The evidence in this study has since been disputed, but the authors concluded that such cases "appear to be exceptions to the general rule that postnatal psychological forces overpower the biological in the development of gender identity."

Both of the investigative teams cited here have dealt with persons born with sexual abnormalities. It is difficult to accept the conclusions of either as correct in reference to normal human development. Do we really have sufficient proof to assume that the normal individual is psychosexually neutral at the time of conception or that, to the contrary, the sexual behavior of the normal individual is predetermined by genetic constitution?

Neither extreme position is satisfactory. We have seen some evidence both that behavioral differences between boys and girls can be measured in the earliest days of life, and, on the other hand, that what is considered "feminine" or "masculine" behavior can be shaped by mothers' reactions to such differences in infants. The most reasonable conclusion at this point would be that male and female children are born showing degrees of behavioral differences, but the powers of culture seem to have much greater weight than any innate differences in the final expression of masculine or feminine behavior. A person is likely to develop a sex role that fits most comfortably with both his biologic inheritance and the responses and teaching he receives from those around him.

Summary

By the time a child is born, his development has already been influenced for approximately nine months by (1) his genetic inheritance ("nature") and (2) environmental forces ("nurture"). The old debate over whether nature or nurture exerts more influence on a child has largely been abandoned today in favor of a search for the relative degrees of each influence, and the specific ways in which each force interacts with others to produce individual traits and forms of behavior.

The relatively new science of genetics is discovering precisely how traits, and which traits, are inherited. All of a person's genetic inheritance (his *genotype*), we now know, is present in the nucleus of the one-celled zygote from which his life begins when an egg from his mother is fertilized by a sperm from his father. This genetic information is transmitted on 46 threadlike *chromosomes* (23 pairs, with half of each pair coming from each parent).

Each time a body cell divides, in forming the embryo or in replacing dead cells throughout a person's life, the chromosomes duplicate themselves; this process is called *mitosis*. Every cell of the body thus has its own copy of the original genetic code. When the reproductive cells begin to form ova or sperm, however, the chromosome pairs are duplicated once and then the pair-members separate from each other; one member of each pair goes to each of four new cells. This type of cell division, which results in sperm and ova (*gametes*) with 23 chromosomes, is called *meiosis*.

Each chromosome carries about 20,000 *genes*, which hold the information that directs the multitude of highly precise processes in the body's development. Genes are composed largely of *DNA*, and the patterns of the chemicals in making DNA are essentially the language of the genetic code. These patterns determine the chemical processes that eventually produce the human being and contribute to his functioning throughout life.

The random separation of chromosome pairs during meiosis, along with the random union of any sperm with any ovum, and the crossing over of genes from one chromosome to another, all virtually insure that every individual (except identical twins) is unique.

What is inherited through genes is a potential for certain traits, rather than ready-made traits themselves. The appearance of inherited traits (a person's *phenotype*), even physical traits such as stature, can be hindered or encouraged by numerous environmental forces, both biological (illness or nutrition, for example) and psychosocial (relationships with family, friends, and teachers).

In order to explore the mechanisms of genetic inheritance and the effects of environmental forces, psychologists often study sets of identical and fraternal twins. Sometimes sets raised together are compared with those raised apart, or degrees of similarity in identical twins are compared with those found in fraternal twins. Twin studies have revealed much about the interaction and overlapping of inherited and environmental influences on certain traits.

Intelligence, for instance, appears to be significantly determined by heredity, but the application of intelligence to scholastic achievement is primarily influenced by a child's parents, teachers, friends, or other environmental elements. Recent studies indicate also that sociability is inherited (extroverted babies usually become extroverted adults), although this and other inherited personality traits are subject to modification by a child's personal surroundings. In the matter of sexual identity and sex roles, behavioral differences between newborn girls and boys have been measured, suggesting that males and females do inherit some different modes of behavior. Evidence in other studies, however, points to the conclusion that the culture in which the child lives exerts a greater influence on the development of his sexual identity. Heredity is known also to determine, to varying degrees, a person's tendencies to certain diseases, his reactions to drugs, and, of course, his physical appearance.

References

Anandalakshany, S. G., and Grinder, R. E. Conceptual emphasis in the history of developmental psychology: Evolutionary theory, teleology and the nature-nurture issue. *Child Develpm.*, Dec. 1970, *41*(4), 1113–1123.

Anastasi, A. Heredity, environment, and the question "how?" *Psychol. Rev.*, 1958, *65*, 197–208.

Anastasi, A. On the formation of psychological traits. *Amer. Psychologist*, October 1970, *25*(10), 899–910.

Anderman, S., Barclay, A., Kahana, B., and Yates, A. Intelligence and serum phenylalanine in levels in phenylketonuric children. *Proc. Ann. Conv. Am. Psychol. Assoc.*, 1971, *6*, Pt. 2, 613–614.

Ashley, M. *Direction of human development*. (Rev. ed.) New York: Hawthorn, 1970.

Auerbach, C. *The science of genetics*. New York: Harper, 1961.

Baker, H. J., and Stoller, R. J. Biological force postulated as having role in gender identity. *Roche reports: Frontiers of hospital psychiatry*, 1967, *4*, 3.

Barr, M. L., and Carr, D. H. Sex chromatin, sex chromosomes, and sex anomalies. *Canadian Med. Ass. J.*, 1960, *83*, 979–986.

Bell, R. Q. A reinterpretation of the direction of effects in studies of socialization, *Psychol. Rev.*, 1968, *75*, 84–88.

Biass-Ducroux, F. *Glossary of genetics*. New York: American Elsevier, 1970.

Biller, H. B. *Father, child and sex role: Paternal determinants in personality development*. Lexington, Mass.: Heath, 1971.

Bloom, B. S. *Stability and change in human characteristics*. New York: Wiley, 1964.

Blumberg, B. S., and Hesser, J. L. Loci differently affected by selection in two American black populations. *Proc. Natl. Acad. Sci. U.S.A.*, 1971, *68*(10), 2554–2558.

Broverman, D. M., Klaiber, E. L., Kobayashi, T., and Vogel, W. Rules of activation and inhibition in sex difference in cognitive abilities. *Psychol. Rev.*, 1968, *75*, 23–50.

Burt, C. The genetic determination of differences in intelligence: A study of monozygotic twins reared together and apart. *Brit. J. Psychol.*, 1966, *57*, 137–153.

Carey, M. J., Tischler, B., and Sandercock, J. Structural aberrations of autosomes in a mentally retarded population. *Amer. J. ment. Def.*, January 1971, *75*(4), 487–498.

Cattell, R. B. Statistical methods and logical considerations in investigating inheritance. *Proc. International Congress Human Genet.*, 1963, *3*, 1712–1717.

Cord, E. L. Proprioceptive and motor functions in schizophrenic, normal and adoptive families: A behavior-genetic analysis. *Dissert. Abstr.*, January 1971, *75*(4), 487–498.

Dallapiciola, B. Identification of the human sex chromosome complement in polymorphonuclear leukocytes: A new technique. *J. Lab. Clin. Med.*, 1971, *78*(1), 88–93.

Darlington, C. D., and Mather, K. *Elements of genetics*. New York: Schocken, 1969.

DeFries, J. C., and Hegmann, J. P. Genetic analysis of open-field behavior. In G. Lindzey and D. D. Thiessen (Eds.), *Contributions to behavior-genetic analysis: The mouse as a prototype.* New York: Appleton-Century-Crofts, 1970.

Demerec, M. (Ed.) *Advances in genetics.* Vol 15. New York: Academic Press, 1970.

Diamond, M. A critical evaluation of ontogeny of human sexual behavior. *Quart. Rev. Biol.*, 1965, *40*, 147–175.

Dobzhansky, T. *Heredity and the nature of man.* New York: Harcourt Brace Jovanovich, 1964.

Doris, J. Science action and values in familial retardation. *J. spec. Educ.*, Spring 1970, *4*(2), 161–170.

Dugdale, R. L. *The Jukes: A study in crime, pauperism, disease and heredity.* New York: Putnam's, 1910.

Elandt-Johnson, R. C. *Probability models and statistical methods in genetics.* New York: Wiley, 1971.

Eysenck, H. J. *Crime and personality.* Boston: Houghton Mifflin, 1964.

Fraser, A. *Heredity, genes and chromosomes.* New York: McGraw-Hill, 1966.

Freedman, D. G. Heredity control of early social behavior. In B. M. Foss (Ed.), *Determinants of infant behavior.* Vol III. New York: Wiley, 1965.

Friedmann, T., and Roblin, R. Gene therapy for human genetic disease? *Science*, 1972, *175*, 949–954.

Gilmour, G., Bloom, A. D., Kusum, P. L., Robbins, E. S., and Maximilian, C. Chromosomal aberrations in users of psychoactive drugs. *Arch. Gen. Psychiat.*, March 1971, *24*(3), 268–272.

Goldstein, H. J., Pardes, H., Small, A. M., and Steinberg, M. D. Psychological differentiation and specificity of response. *J. nerv. ment. Dis.*, August 1970, *151* (2), 97–103.

Hauschka, R. S., Hasson, J. E., Goldstein, M. N., Koepf, G. F., and Sondberg, A. A. An XYY man with proprz indicating familial tendency to nondisjunction. *Amer. J. human genet.*, 1962, *14*, 22–30.

Heston, L. L. The genetics of schizophrenic and schizoid disease. *Science,* January 1970, *4*(1), 21–28.

Hirschhorn, K., and Harris, H. (Eds.) *Advances in human genetics.* Vol. 2. New York: Plenum, 1971.

Jacobs, P. A., Brunton, M., and Melville, M. M. Aggressive behavior, mental subnormality and the XYY male. *Nature*, 1965, *208*, 1351–1352.

Jensen, A. R. How much can we boost I.Q. and scholastic achievement? *Harv. educ. Rev.*, 1969, *39*, 1–123.

Kallmann, F. J. *Heredity and health in mental disorders.* New York: Norton, 1953.

Kallmann, F. J. Twin and sibship study of overt male homosexuality. *Amer. J. human genet.*, 1952, *4*, 136–146.

Kallmann, F. J., and Sander, G. Twin studies on senescence. *Amer. J. Psychiat.*, 1949, *106*, 29–36.

Kay, H. E. M., and Margoles, C. Chromosomes of human fetus by lymphocytes: Frequency of abnormalities and absence of maternal cells. *Lancet*, 1971, *2*(7727), 733–735.

Kranz, P. L. A psychological investigation of seven hermaphroditic children. *Dissert. Abstr.*, May 1970, *30* (11–13), 5223.

Kruskal, W. H., and Haberman, S. Chromosomal effect and LSD: Samples of four. *Science*, December 1968, *162*(3861), 1508–1509.

LaDu, B. N., Jr. The genetics of drug reactions. *Hospital practice*, June 1971, 97–106.

Lindzey, G., and Thiessen, D. D. (Eds.) *Contributions to behavior-genetic analysis: The mouse as a prototype.* New York: Appleton-Century-Crofts, 1970.

Lonsdale, D., and Forest, M. Normal mental development in treated phenylketonuria. *Amer. J. Dis. Child.*, 1970, *45*(239), 5–12.

McClearn, G. Behavioral genetics. *Behavioral Science*, 1970, *16*, 64–81.

McClearn, G. Genetic influences on behavior and development. In P. H. Mussen (Ed.), *Carmichael's manual of child psychology.* Vol. I. (3rd ed.) New York: Wiley, 1970.

McKusick, V. A. Human genetics. *Annu. rev. genet.*, 1970, *4*, 1–46.

McKusick, V. A. *Mendelian inheritance in man.* (3rd ed.) Baltimore: Johns Hopkins Press, 1971.

Manosevitz, M., Lindzey, G., and Thiessen, D. (Eds.) *Behavioral genetics: Method and research.* New York: Appleton-Century-Crofts, 1969.

Manosevitz, M., and Lindzey, G. Genetics of hoarding: A biometrical analysis. *J. comp. physiol. Psychol.*, 1967, *63*, 142–144.

Mednick, S., and Schulsinger, F. Studies of children at high risk for schizophrenia. Unpublished manuscript.

Millett, K. *Sexual politics.* New York: Doubleday, 1971.

Money, J. Psychosexual differentiation. In J. Money (Ed.), *Sex research: New developments..* New York: Holt, Rinehart & Winston, 1965.

Money, J. *Cognitive defects in Turner's syndrome.* Second Invitational Conference on Human Behavior Genetics. Louisville: Univer. of Kentucky Press, 1966.

Money, J. Components of eroticism in man: The hormones in relation to sexual morphology and sexual desire. *J. nerv. ment. Dis.*, 1961, *132*, 239–248.

Money, J., Hampson, J. L., and Hampson, J. G. An examination of some basic sexual concepts: The evidence of human hermaphroditism. *Bull. Johns Hopkins Hosp.*, 1955, *97*, 301–319.

Moss, H. A. Sex, age and state as determinants of mother–infant interaction. *Merrill-Palmer Quart.*, 1967, *13*, 19–36.

Newman, H. H., Freeman, R. N., and Holzinger, K. J. *Twins: A study of heredity and environment.* Chicago: Univer. of Chicago Press, 1937.

Nielson, J. Criminality among patients with Klinefelter's syndrome and the XYY syndrome. *Brit. J. Psychiat*, October 1970, *117*(539), 365–369.

Nielson, J., Bjarnason, S., Friedrich, U., Froland, A., Hanson, V. H., and Sørenson, A. Klinefelter's syndrome in children. *J. child Psycho. and Psychiat. and Allied Dis.*, November 1970, *11*(2), 109–119.

O'Grady, D. J., Berry, H. K., and Sutherland, B. J. Phenylketonuria: Intellectual development and early treatment. *Develpm. Med. and Child Neurol.*, 1970, *12*(3), 343–347.

Price, W. H., and Whatmore, P. B. Criminal behavior and the XYY male. *Nature*, 1967, *210*, 213, 815.

Rosenberg, B. G., and Sutton-Smith, B. *Sex and identity*. New York: Holt, Rinehart & Winston, 1972.

Russell, E. W. A reexamination of Halstead's biological intelligence factors. *Proc. Ann. Conv. Amer. Psychol. Assoc.*, 1971, *6*, Pt. 1, 461–462.

Scarr, S. *The inheritance of sociability*. College Park, Md.: Univer. of Maryland, 1965.

Schaefer, E. S. An analysis of consensus in longitudinal research on personality consistency and change. *Vita Humana*, 1964, *7*, 143–146.

Schlegel, W. S. Die konstitutionsbiologischen Grundlagen der Homosexualität. *Zeitschrift für menschliche Vererbung*, Konstitutionslehre, 1962, *36*, 341–364.

Schuckit, M. A., Goodwin, D. A., and Winokur, G. Genetics and alcoholics. *Science News*, 1972, *101*, 170.

Segrames, R. T. Personality, body build and adrenocortical activity. *Brit. J. Psychiat.*, October 1970, *117*(539), 405–411.

Shields, J. *Monozygotic twins*. Oxford: Oxford Univer. Press, 1962.

Stony, R. R. The etiology of Parkinson's disease. *Diseases nerv. Syst.*, June 1970, *31*, 381–390.

Thiessen, D. D. *Gene organization and behavior*. New York: Random House, 1971.

Thiessen, D. D. The genetic determination of behavior. *Science Teach.*, April 1970, *37*(4), 53–54.

Tijo, J. H., Pahnhe, W. N., and Kurlord, A. A. LSD and chromosomes: A controlled experiment. *J. Amer. Med. Ass.*, 1969, *210*(5), 849–856.

Vandenberg, S. G. Multivariate analysis of twin differences. In S. G. Vandenberg (Ed.), *Methods and goals in human behavior genetics*. New York: Academic Press, 1965.

Vandenberg, S. G. *The nature and nurture of intelligence*. Paper presented at Conference on Biology and Behavior, Rockefeller Univer., New York, 1966.

Vandenberg, S. G. (Ed.) *Progress in human behavior genetics: Recent reports of genetic syndromes*. Baltimore: Johns Hopkins Univer. Press, 1968.

Weir, M. W., and DeFries, J. C. Prenatal maternal influence on behavior in mice: Evidence of a genetic basis. *J. comp. physiol. Psychol.*, 1964, *58*, 412–417.

Weyl, N. Some possible genetic implications of Carthaginian child sacrifice. *Persp. in Bio. and Med.*, Fall 1968, *12*(1), 69–78.

Whittinghill, M. *Human genetics and its foundations*. New York: Van Nostrand-Reinhold, 1965.

Witkin, E. M. Mutations and evolution. *The Atlantic*, October 1957, 140.

Prenatal Environmental Influences 4

IT IS ACCEPTED without question that an individual's development is greatly influenced by his environment. But until fairly recent times, environmental influences were thought to come into play only at birth. For a long time, the unborn baby was considered to be all but isolated from the outside world. However, in recent years, evidence has indicated that prenatal events can influence the development of an individual's inherited potential. Today, prenatal studies comprise a very active area of research.

The fetus inherits more than its genetic make-up. In a sense, it inherits an environment, one that depends upon the health and welfare of the fetus' mother. The mother who is physically well developed, free of diseases, well nourished, and given good prenatal care provides the best possible environment for the developing fetus. Conversely, the mother who is undernourished, takes the wrong drug (or too much of the right drug), or contracts certain diseases endangers the fetus she carries. The result can range from mildly disturbing to totally disastrous.

The fetus receives its food and oxygen through the mother's bloodstream, and thus can be affected by any drugs the mother takes. Hormones and other chemicals produced in the mother's body can also reach the fetus. For example, if the mother is continually upset, the chemicals formed or released during these periods may impose a stress on the fetus.

A better understanding of prenatal influences seems likely to shed some light on problems children can have in making the necessary physical and mental adjustments as they develop. Although not all cases of maladjustment will reveal a prenatal cause, it remains true that an examination of a troubled child's prenatal and birth history can often reveal the causes of the child's maladjustment.

Prenatal Development

The fertilized egg takes nine months to grow into an infant ready to be born. During this gestation or *intrauterine period*, the fetus lives in the protective environment that has developed inside the mother's uterus. Using growth as a criterion, the intrauterine period can be divided into three parts.

The first, *the period of the ovum*, begins with conception and lasts until the first tiny, floating cell mass attaches to the uterus wall—usually after 10 to 14 days.

The second growth period, *the period of the embryo*, extends from the attachment date until the end of the eighth week. In this important period, the essential body systems—the circulatory, pulmonary, and digestive systems, for example—begin forming, and the developing fetus begins to resemble a human being.

The third and final growth stage is *the period of the fetus*. It is by far the longest of the three stages, lasting from the start of the ninth week until birth—about 30 weeks later. During the fetal period, the fetus increases substantially in size. In addition, the body systems that appeared in the embryo develop completely.

Conception

About 400 times in the normal woman's life her body prepares itself to conceive life. Once every 28 days, on a schedule maintained by secreted hormones, an *ovum* or egg cell matures in one of her two ovaries and is released. The 23 chromosomes in this ovum carry the mother's contribution to her offspring's gene structure.

The father's *sperm cells* carry another 23 chromosomes, his share of the fetus' genetic heritage. Every day, a man's body produces a huge number of sperm cells—several hundred million of them. Great numbers of sperm are necessary for conception, for the overwhelming majority of them die as they swim along the route to the female's ovum. Many times no sperm cells at all reach the egg.

While the egg cells are some of the largest cells that either males or females produce, they are all but invisible. Sperm cells are even smaller. About 90,000 of them weigh the same as one ovum, ranking the sperm among the smallest cells produced by either sex.

When the mature ovum is released by the ovary, it enters one of the two Fallopian tubes where conception can occur. As tiny hairlike bristles propel the ovum toward the uterus, the sperm cell is moving from the vagina through the uterus and up the Fallopian tube. The instant the sperm pierces the ovum, the egg is fertilized. Life begins.

Immediately after fertilization of the ovum—now called the *zygote*—the nuclei of the sperm and ovum unite. Each one's chromosomes align to form 23 pairs, an arrangement that will be repeated in every one of the new individual's billions of cells. While these chromosomes are the individual's genetic potential, they are not the sole determinants of his development. Even this early in life, the environment of the new human being has begun to impinge on its future development.

Period of the Ovum

Barely 24 hours after conception, the zygote has divided into two 46-chromosome cells. Cell division continues as the zygote moves through the Fallopian tube. By the time it reaches the uterus, the zygote may contain as many as 32 cells. Meanwhile, the uterine lining has been prepared to receive the zygote. Tissues of the uterine wall have thickened and the flow of blood to the

Figure 4.1 A human ovum at the moment of fertilization. (Dr. L. B. Shettles—Columbia Presbyterian Medical Center)

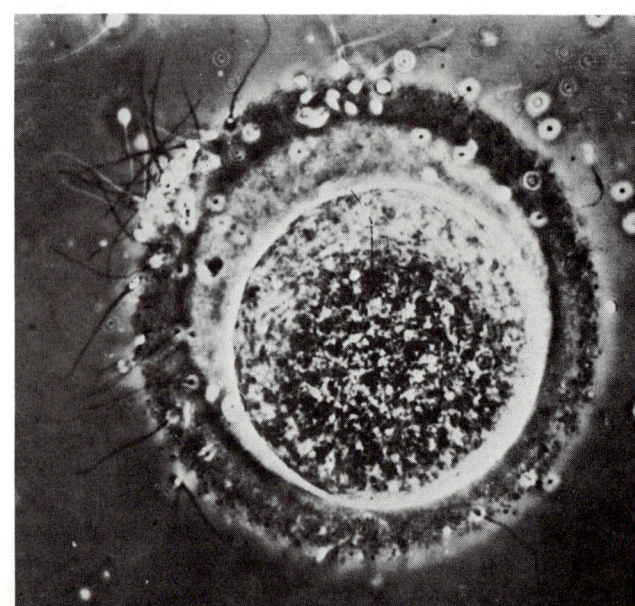

uterus has increased—as it does in the monthly menstrual cycle. If no zygote had arrived, the extra tissue would again have disintegrated and left the body in the usual menstrual flow.

While it is descending the Fallopian tube and floating in the uterus before attaching itself, the zygote is nourished by the ovum's yolk. On its arrival in the uterus, the zygote's cells already have begun to *differentiate*—that is, to separate into groups according to their future functions. Specifically, at this early point of differentiation—in which the zygote becomes the *blastocyst*—two kinds of cells are forming. Those on the blastocyst's outer layer will develop into the protective and nourishing structures—the placenta, the umbilical cord, and the amniotic sac. The inner cell cluster will become the embryo.

After floating for a time, the blastocyst implants itself in the blood-rich uterine wall, using tendrils to anchor itself. Within two weeks after conception, the ovum is completely embedded, and the offspring's dependent relationship with the mother has begun.

To survive, the blastocyst must implant itself properly. Otherwise, it will quickly die and pass out of the body with the menstrual flow. Implantation could be thwarted by a number of events. The blastocyst's trip down the Fallopian tube may last too long, causing the fertilized ovum to miss the optimum time for implantation; or, the ovum may not have enough yolk to feed the floating blastocyst until it implants. It also is possible that the uterine walls may be inadequate—because of a hormonal imbalance—to support the blastocyst.

Period of the Embryo

Implantation begins the period of the embryo. During this six-week span—from implantation to eight weeks after conception—the embryo develops very rapidly. From a cell mass smaller than a salt grain, it grows to a length of over 1 inch and a weight of one-thirtieth of an ounce. By the end of the embryonic period almost all of the newborn's structures and systems have begun to develop.

An 8-week-old embryo already resembles a human being. Its face has a mouth, a nose, and eyes. Its head, with a protruding brow, makes up

Figure 4.2 Fertilization and implantation. The mature egg leaves the ovary and is fertilized in the Fallopian tube. The fertilized egg continues through the Fallopian tube to the uterus, where it is implanted in the endometrium.

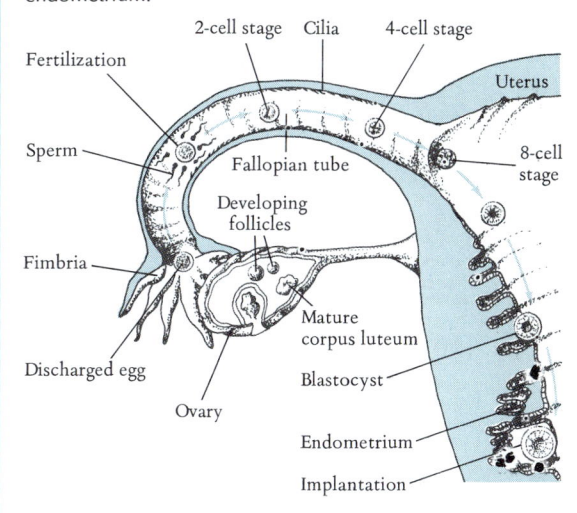

about half its body's length. Arms and legs, with blunt fingers and toes, are bent at elbow and knee. Ribs, made of cartilage at this stage, show under the skin. This tiny, 1-inch creature grew out of the blastocyst's inner cell cluster.

While this transformation was taking place, the outer cell layer was differentiating into two fetal membranes, the *chorion* and *amnion*. These membranes, along with another called the *decidua capsularis*, which extends from the uterine wall, form the structures which perform the crucial functions of protection, respiration, nutrition, and excretion. The *umbilical cord* and the *placenta* make nutrition, respiration, and waste disposal possible. The third structure, the *amniotic sac*, provides protection.

The sac, which completely surrounds the embryo by the end of the eighth week, is filled with watery amniotic fluid which insulates the embryo from jostling and other moderate physical impacts that the pregnant woman may encounter, and which prevents it from sticking to the amniotic membrane. The fluid also supports the embryo within the uterus and provides a constant ambient temperature.

PRENATAL ENVIRONMENTAL INFLUENCES   85

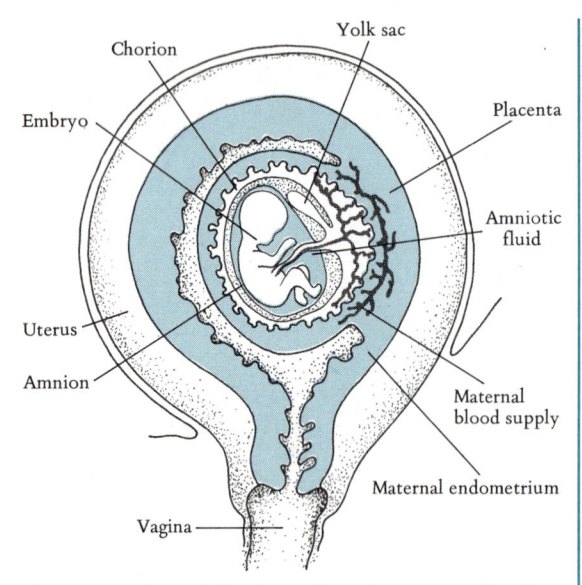

Figure 4.3 An early human embryo in uterus enclosed within its supportive membranes—the amnion, the chorion, and the placenta.

It is in this setting that the embryo takes nourishment, produces its bodily wastes, and grows. The embryo carries out these life processes through the *umbilical cord*, which is its link to the placenta. The cord enters the fetus' abdomen—eventually growing as thick as a man's thumb—bearing inside it two blood vessels, one flowing to the embryo and the other to the placenta.

The placenta, which works in conjunction with the umbilical blood vessels, is a thick mass of tissue. It develops adjacent to the uterus and acts as a two-way filter between the bloodstreams of mother and embryo. In the placenta, the blood vessels from the connecting umbilical cord fan out like the roots of a tree. The finest vessels intertwine with capillaries carrying the mother's blood from the uterine wall. Some of the mother's capillaries break open, and rootlike projections, peculiar to the embryo's blood system, dip into the mother's blood. Thus, food and oxygen are exchanged for waste products.

Contrary to earlier belief, the bloodstreams of mother and embryo do not mix. They are separated by the placenta's cell walls, which are semipermeable membranes that act like sieves with holes the size of small molecules. Although blood cells are too large to pass through this "strainer," other cells are not. Through the membrane, the embryo takes in oxygen, sugar, fats, and other foods. At the same time, the embryo rids its bloodstream of carbon dioxide and other wastes which move out through the membrane.

Investigators now are doing considerable research to determine what other substances can enter the embryo's bloodstream through the placenta's membrane. The effects that these substances may have on the embryo are of particular interest—an interest strongly prompted by tragic experiences with the drug thalidomide in the early 1960s. Thalidomide had been prescribed, mainly in Europe, to reduce the "morning sickness" normal among pregnant women. While the drug may have benefited the expectant mothers, the benefits were gained at a disastrous cost to their offspring.

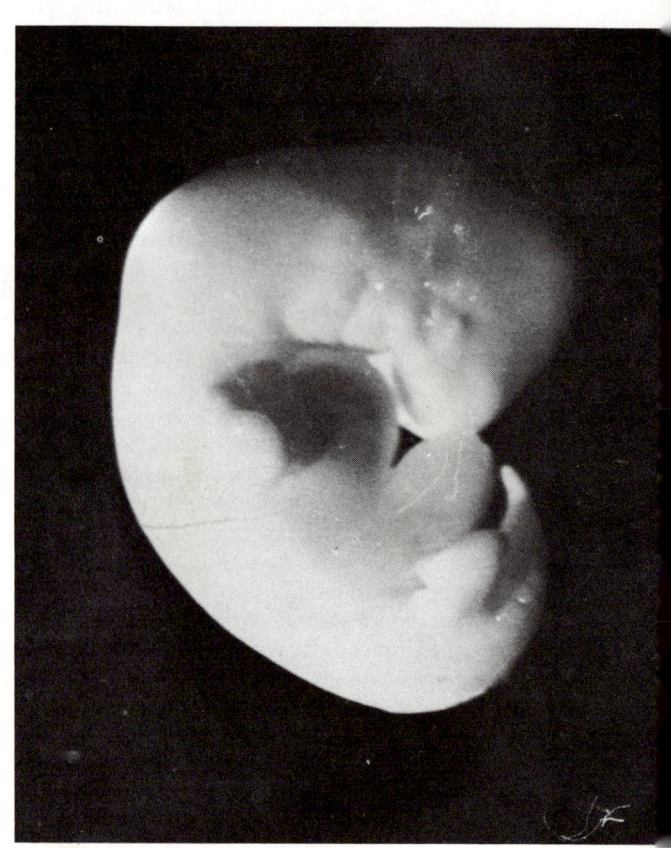

A

86 THE PRENATAL PERIOD

Natural substances—such as hormones—in the mother's bloodstream also can affect the embryo. Therefore, even though nerves themselves do not link mother to embryo, a mother's emotional state may influence the embryo because of chemicals which her emotional condition sets loose in her bloodstream. Of course, the molecules of all such blood-borne chemical substances must be small enough to pass through the placental membrane. Otherwise they cannot reach the embryo, and therefore cannot affect it.

We can see, then, that well before birth the embryo is affected by its immediate environment. So far, the most direct influences that have been discovered are chemicals, drugs, hormones, and some viruses, which also are small enough to slip through the placental membrane.

THE EMBRYO. In the six-week embryonic period, the first miniscule cluster of cells is transformed into a distinctly human organism. Obviously, changes occur in a rapid yet orderly manner. Were it possible to blueprint them, the construction plans for the embryo's growth probably would be more complicated than those for a towering skyscraper.

The growth begins very early. Shortly after implantation, three distinct cell layers begin to differentiate in the embryo. All body systems evolve from these three cell layers. These layers are called:

1. The ectoderm, or outer layer, which will become the sensory cells, the skin, and the nervous system;
2. The mesoderm, or middle layer, which will develop into muscles, blood, and the excretory system; and
3. The endoderm, or inner layer, which will emerge as the digestive system, the lungs, and the thyroid and thymus glands.

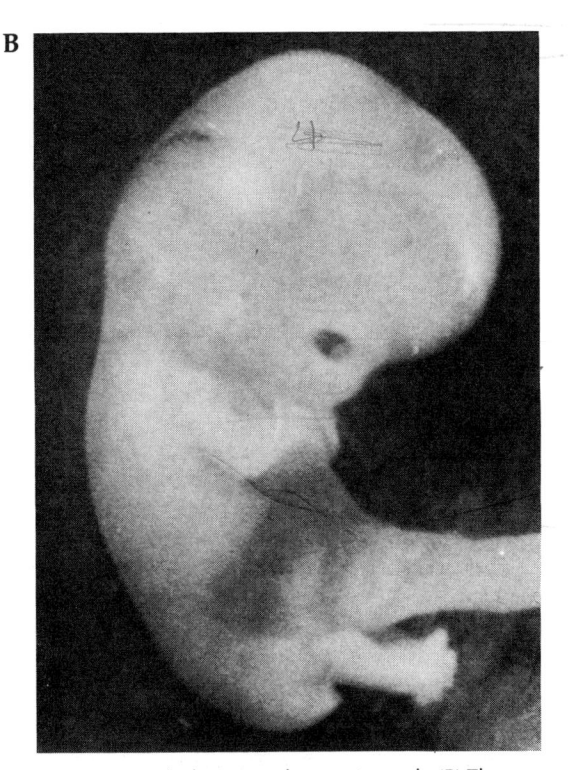

Figure 4.4 (A) The human embryo at 1 month. (B) The human embryo at 3 months. (C) The human embryo at 6 months. (Dr. L. B. Shettles—Columbia Presbyterian Medical Center)

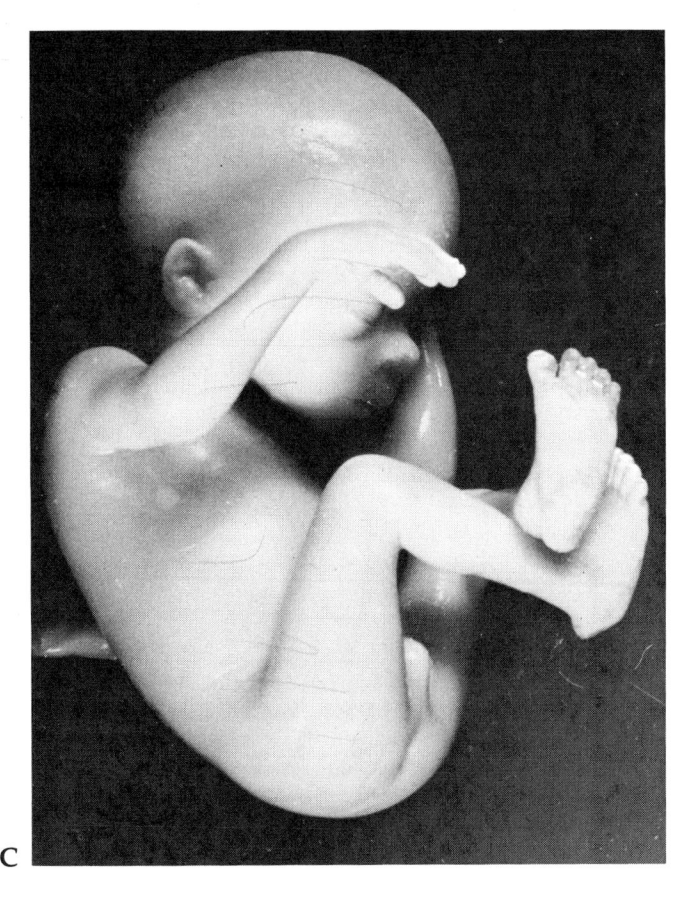

PRENATAL ENVIRONMENTAL INFLUENCES 87

By the end of the third week of embryonic development, the three layers have become basic systems that are functioning. The neural tube, which becomes the spinal cord and part of the brain, has formed. The heart is beating. The nervous system, too, has begun a period of intense development which will last through the twenty-eighth day.

At four weeks, the embryo is about as big as a pea and lies curled, head and tail almost touching. Though no face has formed yet, the eye has emerged as a dark circle. During the next two weeks, arms and legs appear and the muscles and skeleton begin to form. The embryo's primitive tail, which will become the lower tip of its backbone, is visible. The stomach and intestine are developing. The head is growing rapidly as the brain expands.

In both the embryonic and fetal stages, growth follows the law of cephalocaudal direction—that is, development proceeds from the top down. Thus, the embryo's head grows fastest and constitutes almost half the length of its body during the embryonic period.

At the close of the eight weeks of embryonic growth, all major organs are present, at least in primitive forms, and some are functioning. The liver is making blood cells and the kidneys are extracting waste. The glands have begun to secrete hormones and sex organs are distinguishable.

The 8-week-old embryo also has reflexes. A light touch to the mouth will cause an embryo's whole body to convulse. The movement is a reflex reaction, an automatic response to the touch. Spontaneous movements begin a few weeks later.

THE IMPORTANCE OF THE EMBRYONIC PERIOD. Though it is little more than 1 inch long, the 8-week-old embryo is a fully equipped human being. While an enormous amount of growth and development lies ahead—particularly in the seven remaining prenatal months—all subsequent growth will be merely expansion of the basic systems already present.

Bringing those basic systems to the eight-week point of development demands a crowded timetable during the embryonic period. Because physical development is so closely scheduled in this period, the embryo is more vulnerable now than in later weeks. A serious environmental disruption could impair the body system that is growing fastest at this point. Such a system, deformed or slowed in its growth, may never get another opportunity to correct the deformity or complete the growth. So tight is the schedule that if the same environmental disturbance were to occur only a few days later, it would pass without harm. Given the vulnerable nature of the embryo in the first eight weeks, it is understandable that German measles, as well as certain drugs and chemicals, can be most harmful during this time. The presence of destructive drugs, chemicals, or diseases can result in such major defects as blindness, deafness, mental deficiency, heart abnormality, or physical deformity.

Miscarriage is another hazard during the first three prenatal months. When a miscarriage occurs, the embryo separates from the uterine wall and is expelled by the uterus. The embryo also can be deliberately expelled through the artificially induced miscarriage known as abortion. Until the late 1960s, abortions were illegal unless a woman's life was threatened by her pregnancy. Today, the law has been changed in several states, and pregnant women in those areas can obtain legal abortions on request. Strong arguments have been advanced for and against abortion. Among the latter is the contention that abortion can induce serious psychological problems in women who terminate a pregnancy in this manner. For our purposes, it should be noted that if an abortion is to be performed, it is most easily and safely done during the first three months of pregnancy, provided that it is done by a doctor with hospital or clinic facilities at hand.

Period of the Fetus

In the period of the fetus, the embryo grows and becomes more articulated, finally resulting in the newborn baby, who usually is about 20 inches long and slightly over 7 pounds (birth weights ranging from 5 to 12 pounds are normal).

Physical changes in the fetus make several general stages in the fetal period clearly identifiable. In the third and fourth months, the muscles develop rapidly and the fetus begins to move. It can open and close its mouth, swallow, and move its head in the "oral reflex" motion which it will use when it feeds as a newborn. Sophisticated muscular action begins. The fetus opens and closes its fist, moves its thumb independently, and even sucks its thumb. By the end of the fourth month, the mother usually can feel the fetus moving about.

The fetus grows more in the fourth month than in any other. It almost doubles its length, reaching 6 inches from crown to rump, and a weight of about 4 ounces. Since the trunk and limbs have developed more — in accordance with the law of developmental direction — the head is now only one-third of the body length. Each day, the 4-month-old fetal heart circulates 25 quarts of blood. At this stage, the fetus reacts more specifically to stimulation. A particular limb, instead of the whole body, will move at a touch. Fingers or toes, too, will curl when the palm or sole is stimulated, and a facial expression will change at the touch of a cheek.

At five months the fetus' internal organs lie in positions similar to those in an adult, and its skin is fully developed. The fetus sleeps and wakes, and occasionally hiccoughs. Hair, nails, and sweat glands appear. In the sixth month, the eyelids open and the fetus moves its eyes. At the end of this month, the unborn infant measures 10 inches from crown to rump and weighs 24 ounces — six times its weight two months earlier. Though a premature infant of six months can cry weakly and grasp a rod firmly (Hooker 1952), it cannot perform more basic functions, such as regulating its body temperature or its breathing. Therefore, its chances of survival are poor.

In the seventh month, the fetal brain develops further, extending and refining its control of body systems. The eyes now can distinguish light from dark. With proper care — especially precautions to avoid infection — an infant born prematurely at seven months has a fair chance to survive.

The last three months of pregnancy are the fetus' most active period. Only in the last weeks, when its own size limits movement, does the fetus reduce its activity. During these last two months, the fetus gains about 8 ounces a week as the body accumulates fat. Seventy percent of the fetuses born at eight months survive.

Growth slows down in the last two weeks as the placenta begins to degenerate and the uterus drops lower in the mother's body in preparation for birth.

Effects of Prenatal Environment, and Birth

While the prenatal environment seems to affect the unborn child, it is often difficult to establish direct relationships between specific stimuli and observed effects. Physicians have no doubt that if a mother has German measles during the first three months of pregnancy, the fetus may well be affected. Statistics give the odds in favor of deformity and even predict that the defect most probably will be deafness, a heart malfunction, or an eye abnormality. However, a few other environmental factors have equally predictable effects — smoking, for example. More women who smoke are known to have premature babies than nonsmokers. While these early births could be a result of smoking, it also is possible that the factors in a woman's personality or body chemistry which cause her to smoke also cause her to have a premature baby. Similarly, women who are nervous and upset during pregnancy often have irritable babies. Again, it is possible that the pregnant woman's emotional state could be communicated to her unborn infant. On the other hand, it seems equally possible that soon after birth the infant could begin learning nervous behavior from its mother. There are many other unanswered questions about prenatal stimuli and their effects on the fetus, and research in these areas is continuing. Meanwhile, we can examine pregnancy and birth — the two processes during which the unborn infant can be affected by what occurs in its environment. As we consider some of the prenatal conditions that affect the developing infant, it is important to remember that in most cases the birth of an infant is normal and without complications.

Conditions of Pregnancy

A woman in good health, given good prenatal care, is likely to have a healthy baby who surmounts the trauma of birth and makes a rapid adjustment to life outside the womb. But many factors contribute to the *good* health of the mother and the *good* prenatal care given the fetus. The mother's diet is important, but so is the ingestion of anything that might pass through the placental filtering system. During pregnancy, the effects of drugs on the fetus as well as on the expectant mother must be considered. Several additional factors, including the pregnant woman's emotions, also seem to influence her infant's physical and emotional condition at its birth and later in its development.

AGE OF THE MOTHER. Many healthy babies are born every day to teen-agers and women in their forties. Yet, statistical evidence shows that the safest time for childbearing is from 21 to 29 years of age.

Why this is true is not clear. In younger women, the reproductive system may not be completely ready to function. Conversely, in older women, the system already may have begun to slow down. Whatever the biological reason, it is true that near both ends of the age span from sexual maturity to menopause, the chances for miscarriage, premature birth, and complications of delivery increase. Mothers under 20 and those over 35 also have a higher proportion of mentally retarded children (Pasamanick and Lilienfeld 1955) — possibly because of more complicated deliveries. Older mothers, particularly those whose first pregnancy occurs after age 35, also are more likely to have illnesses during pregnancy as well as more difficult labors. In addition, Down's disease, more commonly known as mongolism, is more often found in the offspring of older mothers. Mothers between 15 and 25 years of age have 1 chance in 3,000 of giving birth to a mongoloid infant. Between ages 45 and 49, the odds increase to 1 in 300 (Gruenberg 1964).

DISEASES AND DISORDERS. Viruses, as well as radiation and certain drugs, are *teratogenes* — that is, agents which can produce malformations in the developing fetus. For this reason German measles, or rubella, is the most widely feared disease among pregnant women. Rubella's direct link to birth defects was first recognized in 1941, but the range and severity of its teratogenic effects on the fetus became clear only during the rubella epidemic of 1964-1965 when about 20,000 infants died in the womb and 30,000 more were born with defects.

Rubella's threat is strongest in the first three prenatal months. In the first four weeks, the disease has a 50-50 chance of causing major defects. The likelihood of damage diminishes to 17 percent during the third month, and to near zero thereafter (Rhodes 1961). In addition to fetal deafness, congenital heart disease, and eye defects, the fetus whose mother contracts rubella in the first three months stands a 10 to 20 percent chance of miscarriage.

In 1964, Sheridan studied over 200 children whose mothers had contracted rubella in the first 16 weeks. While 30 percent of the infants suffered various deformities, the disease apparently did not affect their intelligence. The distribution of high, medium, and low I.Q.'s was the same among the experimental children as among the general population.

In recent years, a rubella vaccine has been developed, and in the early 1970s an extensive campaign was begun to immunize children, the carriers of the disease. The hope, of course, is to reduce the threat to pregnant women by reducing the number of potential rubella carriers. Because the vaccine contains a live rubella virus, it is not safe for women during pregnancy or even shortly before conception.

Influenza and *mumps* are two more viruses which, though less widely feared, also can cause malformations in the fetus. Like rubella, these viruses are more dangerous during the first three months. However, the actual likelihood of fetal defects is smaller — 23 percent for mumps and 7 percent for influenza. In addition, the defects are not as serious as those caused by rubella — Rhodes in his 1961 study has described them as "run-of-the-mill defects."

Since rubella, influenza, and mumps all infect

the pregnant woman, the fetus itself may sometimes become infected. Infants have been born with smallpox, chickenpox, mumps, and malaria—although this is relatively rare. It may be that such viruses are small enough to pass through the placental filtering system and infect the fetus in the uterus. Or, on the other hand, the infant may have contracted the disease at birth.

Syphilis in the pregnant woman is a potent threat to the fetus after the fifth month. Over half the fetuses infected with syphilis are stillborn, aborted, or die shortly after birth. Survivors face possible deformity or mental retardation. Sometimes the child may carry the disease for several years after birth without displaying any symptoms. Fetal infection from a syphilitic mother is not inevitable. If the mother receives antibiotics before the eighteenth week of her pregnancy, the fetus usually can escape the disease.

Some maternal chronic disorders—as opposed to diseases—also can harm the fetus. *Diabetes* is a common example of such a disorder. A diabetic woman's shortage of insulin and consequent inability to metabolize sugar can lead to miscarriages, stillbirths, malformations, or later problems of physical adjustment for the newborn infant. A woman who carries the potential for diabetes—without ever having been diabetic—may develop the disorder during pregnancy. However, with proper medical care, diabetes, too, can be controlled and the threat to the fetus considerably reduced.

Toxemia can be more dangerous. In pregnant women, the disease causes a malfunction of the kidneys, high blood pressure, and swollen limbs. Uncorrected, toxemia can lead to convulsions, coma, and the failure of the kidneys and liver. Such cases may be fatal to both the expectant mother and the fetus.

THE RH FACTOR. Another condition that can affect the infant prenatally is the Rh-positive factor—an inherited, genetically dominant trait in the blood. In the great majority of conceptions, the Rh factor is not a concern. Specifically, there is no danger to a fetus conceived by an Rh-positive woman and an Rh-positive man, an Rh-negative woman and an Rh-negative man, or an Rh-positive woman and an Rh-negative man. Only when the woman is Rh negative and the man is Rh positive is the fetus endangered. Because the Rh factor is genetically dominant, the child conceived by such a couple will have the father's Rh positive—which is incompatible with the expectant mother's Rh negative. When certain substances, called *antigens*, in the blood of the Rh-positive fetus, slip through the placental filter, the pregnant woman's bloodstream reacts immediately by producing antibodies to combat the foreign blood factor. When sufficient numbers of these antibodies are produced, they enter the fetal bloodstream and attack its red blood cells. This condition in the fetus is called *erythroblastosis*. As a result, the fetus may die *in utero* or shortly after birth. Surviving infants may have suffered brain damage which could paralyze them or reduce their mental powers.

Because the expectant mother's antibodies are not yet present in great numbers, the first Rh-positive offspring of an Rh-negative woman is not threatened. While the number of antibodies, and therefore the chance of fetal damage, increases with each pregnancy, physicians cannot predict whether a potent count will appear in a particular pregnancy. However, a physician who is aware of potential Rh incompatibility will monitor the woman's antibody count. If it becomes too large, he may attempt to save the baby by inducing labor and giving the newborn infant an immediate and complete blood transfusion. Of course, the success of such a procedure presumes a fetus mature enough to survive outside the womb. For those that are not, another alternative has been found in recent years: an intrauterine blood transfusion. It is worth noting that the A, B, and O factors in the blood (from which the common blood types get their names) also can be incompatible between mother and fetus. However, a drastic reaction to such incompatibility occurs far less frequently than in the case of Rh incompatibility.

NUTRITION. Unlike other factors damaging to the fetus, poor nutrition apparently is not detrimental in the first few prenatal months. The young fetus seems to satisfy its needs by drawing on the vitamins and minerals stored in the pregnant woman's body. This situation changes as the fetus matures. Particularly in the last three months when the fetus is growing rapidly, the nutritional needs of mother and child increase. If the woman's reserves are exhausted at this point, and her diet does not replace the depleted nutrients, both the expectant mother and the infant may suffer ill effects.

In their 1942 study of about 200 women attending a prenatal clinic, Ebbs and his colleagues illustrated the importance of the diet in the later months of pregnancy (Ebbs, Tisdall, and Scott 1942). The experimental group consisted of pregnant women who were inadequately nourished by their diets. After the first four or five months of pregnancy, the diets of half the women were enriched, while those of the other half were not. In comparing the two groups, the investigators found that the women with enriched diets were healthier and developed fewer complications of pregnancy, such as toxemia and anemia. They also had fewer threatened or actual miscarriages, fewer premature births, and fewer stillbirths. They enjoyed one more benefit: their labor periods averaged five hours less than those of the poorly nourished women.

For six months, the same investigators followed the progress of both groups' offspring. Good diet seemed to affect the infants as well. Babies of the well-fed mothers developed fewer serious diseases, such as pneumonia and rickets, and also had fewer colds and other minor illnesses.

Effects of Vitamins. In studies of both humans and animals, investigators have attempted, with some degree of success, to discover which dietary deficiencies cause which defects. The lack of vitamin B seems to affect mental ability. Vitamin C and D shortages are involved in physical abnormalities, and an inadequate supply of protein affects birth weight. In rats, vitamin deficiencies have caused stunted growth and diminished the ability to learn mazes, while encouraging excessive emotionalism and antisocial behavior (Chow et al. 1971). When excessive vitamin A was given to rats and mice in early pregnancy, their offspring displayed physical abnormalities; later in pregnancy, heavy doses of vitamin A seemed to diminish both the offsprings' motivation and their attention span (Hutchings and Gibbon 1971).

While these instances of vitamin excess and deficiency seem to be identifiable, other relationships between dietary lacks and infant behavior are difficult to establish. A study which sought to link the mother's diet to the child's intelligence illustrates this difficulty. In 1955, Harrell and several associates gave three vitamin supplements—plus a control supplement containing no vitamins—to one group of women in Virginia and another in Kentucky. Late in pregnancy, each woman was given one of the three kinds of tablets, which remained her sole vitamin supplement for the remainder of her term. The children's I.Q.'s were tested at ages 3 and 4. In the Virginia group, the investigators found no significant differences between the different vitamins. However, at 3 years of age, the mean, or average, I.Q.'s of all children whose mothers had taken vitamins were about 4 points higher than those of children whose mothers had taken the nonvitamin supplement. At age 4, the difference was 5 points. On the other hand, tests of the Kentucky mothers' children showed no significant I.Q. differences among any of the groups. Harrell and his colleagues explained the apparently contradictory results in terms of the mothers' nutritional histories. The Virginia women were city slum residents, assumed to have had poorer diets than the Kentucky women—isolated mountain dwellers who grew their own food. Thus, the investigators concluded, the vitamins had the greatest effect on the Virginia women because they were in more dire need of basic nourishment.

Regardless of specific nutritional cause-effect relationships, it is an established fact that a woman whose diet has been poor throughout her life is less well prepared for childbearing. It is well known, too, that children of mothers who maintain nourishing diets grow taller than those whose mothers have poor nutritional habits. Improved nutrition may be one reason why American-born children of immigrants often are taller than their parents.

Physical Size of Mother. Maternal size also appears to be a factor influencing fetal well-being. The mother's size is often related to her early nutritional history, as well as to the nutritional habits of her own mother. Several studies among Scottish women have demonstrated that short women have more complications in delivery, premature babies, and infant deaths shortly after birth. One reason for these difficulties is that short women often have a pelvic shape which can make delivery difficult. Specifically, Bernard, in his 1952 study, found that 34 percent of the short women had poor pelvic shape, as opposed to only 7 percent of the well-grown women. Complications at birth were found by Baird (1964) to exist in a constant relationship with short stature, regardless of the woman's social or economic status. In an earlier study, Baird (1949) found that out of 13,000 first deliveries in Aberdeen, Scotland, twice as many premature births occurred among mothers under 5 feet 1 inch tall as among mothers over 5 feet 4 inches tall. The shorter mothers also had twice as many fetal deaths.

A report prepared by Birch in 1971 for the United States Office of Economic Opportunity provided an apt summary of information about faulty maternal nutrition and childbearing. The report noted that:

We have no definitive answer to the question of the degree to which maternal nutrition during pregnancy contributes to pregnancy outcome. Clearly, whether or not nutritional lacks experienced by the mother during pregnancy will affect fetal growth is dependent upon the size and physical resources of the mother herself. Well-grown women are most likely to have tissue reserves which can be diverted to meet the nutritional needs of the fetus even when pregnancy is accompanied by significant degrees of contemporary undernutrition. Conversely, under the same set of circumstances, poorly grown women with minimal tissue reserves could not be expected to be able to provide adequately for the growing infant.

EMOTIONAL STATE OF MOTHER. Strong maternal emotions—fear or anger, for example—affect the chemical balance of the pregnant woman's body. When such strong emotions are aroused, the endocrine glands pump adrenalin and other hormones into the bloodstream. In addition, the autonomic nervous system, which directs involuntary reactions, releases other chemicals. The metabolic rate of cells is altered as well.

These changes in the bloodstream of an emotionally upset pregnant woman affect the fetus. Secretions of the woman's glands and nervous system cross the placental barrier, reproducing the woman's physiological state in the fetus. Early in pregnancy, severe emotional disturbance can cause physical abnormalities. For example, it appears that two fairly common deformities, the cleft palate and the harelip, result from excessive emotional stress in the seventh to tenth weeks. At this time, the palate (which is the roof of the mouth) and the bones of the upper jaw are forming. Glandular secretions released by emotional stress interrupt this development (Strean and Peer 1956).

Later in pregnancy, emotional stress is less likely to cause deformities, but it does seem to affect the offspring's behavior. *In utero*, a fetus responds to the woman's stress by moving excessively. However, severe and prolonged stress seems to affect the infant after birth as well. Sontag, in a 1941 study, found that women emotionally taxed during pregnancy have irritable, overactive infants who have considerable difficulty adjusting their sleeping and eating habits. This phenomenon is still being studied. How a fetus can acquire a disturbed nervous system is hard to explain since direct hormonal effects usually wear off a few hours after birth. In addition, experiments have not shown conclusively that the infant does not learn his irritability from his nervous and agitated mother in his first few days of life.

Other investigators have probed other aspects of maternal anxiety. In 1963, McDonald and his colleagues used standard psychological tests to examine the relationship between such anxiety and the complications of pregnancy and birth, as well as the newborn infant's health and disposition. The researchers tested women of the lower socioeconomic class in their last three months of pregnancy for their anxiety levels. All of the women were similar in age, intelligence, and previous numbers of pregnancies. After they had delivered their babies, the women were divided into a "normal" and an "abnormal" group on the basis of their delivery results. The abnormal women had difficulties—bleeding or a breast abscess, prolonged labor, premature or stillborn infants, or infants who displayed such irregularities as poor heart rate or muscle tone. These women comprised about half of the total tested. When anxiety scores and delivery results were compared, the abnormal women, comprising about half of the total tested, were found to have registered substantially higher anxiety levels on the prebirth psychological tests. They also were found to have spent more time in labor and to have had more male babies than the normal mothers.

Maternal Attitude toward Pregnancy. In another anxiety-related study, Ferreira (1960) tested women in their last four weeks of pregnancy to discover their attitudes toward pregnancy and their level of fear of harming their babies in caring for them. For the first five days after birth, the investigator observed the women's babies and rated them according to their behavior in five areas: crying frequency and duration, amount of sleep, irritability, bowel movements, and feeding. The rating classified one in five of the infants as deviant. Comparing the results of the mothers' attitudinal tests and the infants' postnatal behavior, the investigator found that the mothers of the deviant babies had shown significantly higher fear that they would harm their babies. Ferreira interpreted this maternal fear as a sign of hostility toward the unborn infants—a hostility which exerted its influence on the fetus during the prenatal period. However, this may not be the case. As Moss pointed out in his 1970 commentary, nothing in Ferreira's experiment conclusively eliminates postnatal mother–infant interaction as the cause of the infants' deviation. Thus, it remains possible that in his first five days of life, the infant learned his deviations from his experiences with a hostile mother. (As in McDonald's study, the abnormal group in Ferreira's study included more male than female infants. We shall discuss the greater natural vulnerability of the male more fully at the end of this chapter.)

While maternal anxiety about pregnancy, and particularly about birth, is not uncommon, women who have had certain childhood experiences are more likely to view pregnancy negatively. Despres discovered this in 1937 when he gave an attitudinal questionnaire to a group of pregnant women. The women's answers indicated that those who regarded pregnancy negatively shared several traits: they were poorly adjusted to marriage; ignorant of sex; emotionally deprived in childhood; deprived of close contact with their mothers; and charged with the care of younger brothers and sisters. Opposite traits—such as good marital adjustment, compatibility, and warm family relationships in childhood—typified women who had positive attitudes toward pregnancy.

Animal Studies. Research on maternal stress in humans has so far yielded little in terms of reliable, consistent prediction of offspring behavior. Experimentation on human subjects is, of course, limited for ethical and moral reasons. Rats, on the other hand, have been used extensively to study the effects of the female's emotions on her offspring. Nonetheless, this research, too, is inadequate to permit predictions—even for rats. Too many contradictory behavior results remain unexplained. Good examples of such contradictions can be found in stress experiments by Hockman (1961) and Thompson (1957). Hockman conditioned a group of rats to a stress-inducing situation. When the rats became pregnant, he repeated the stress situation at regular intervals until the rats gave birth. The litters were divided for rearing. Some pups were raised by their mothers, some by other rats who had experienced stress conditioning, and the rest by a control group with no stress training. All of the pups, except those raised by their own mothers, displayed excessive emotion and exhibited disturbed behavior when they were young. However, this behavior gradually disappeared as the rats matured.

In his study, Thompson produced fear in pregnant rats by preventing them from fleeing from a signal they associated with electric shock. In this study, all the offspring displayed increased emotionality, whether or not they were raised by their own mothers. Thus, as a comparison of these experiments makes clear, it is difficult to predict offspring behavior on the basis of prenatal emotional stress on the pregnant female.

Physical as well as emotional stress on the mother can cause changes of behavior in rat offspring. For example, Keely in his 1962 study found that pregnant mice who lived in crowded conditions had offspring who responded slowly and were generally less active. But in the case of physical stress, too, it is difficult at present to predict offspring behavior.

In rats, prenatal stress apparently has varying effects, depending on the intensity and amount of stress and the prenatal age at which the rats experience the stress. Moreover, specific stresses do not inevitably result in correspondingly specific behaviors in the offspring. Instead, these behavioral effects may result from stress in general. In their discussion of the subject, Thompson and Grusec (1970) concluded on this same note:

> . . . there is every reason to believe that any treatment that can produce a stress response in a pregnant female and in the fetus is likely to leave residua that will later become manifest in various forms of behavior.

As we have stated, the emotional stress of the mother may be transmitted to the fetus by way of an excess of various hormonal substances, such as adrenalin, in her bloodstream. Hormones created by the fetus itself may also affect its prenatal environment and development.

HORMONAL INFLUENCES. Some of the most dramatic research concerning the prenatal effects of hormones on the fetus has centered around the sex hormones, androgen and estrogen, which are produced within the fetus itself. As soon as the fetal gonads differentiate into either testes in the male or ovaries in the female, they begin to secrete the corresponding hormone. That these hormones have profound effects on the development of the fetus is now a well-established fact. Their influence can be so strong as to override even the genetic coding for gender determination.

Particular attention has been given the male hormone, androgen, for without it there would be no males. Androgen must be secreted by the testes for a male to differentiate, while neither the ovaries nor estrogen, the female hormone, need be present for a female to develop. For example, when neither hormone is present, whether because of surgical removal of the fetal gonads before differentiation, or the lack of gonads due to a genetic defect such as Turner's syndrome, the resulting offspring, regardless of its genetic sex, is always a female. Androgen apparently acts as an inhibitor of this natural tendency toward female differentiation, and therefore much research has centered around this particular hormone.

Animal Studies. When pregnant guinea pigs were injected with androgen so as to affect the fetuses, the female offspring were found to exhibit masculine characteristics, both in their physical development and their adult sexual behavior (Grady, Phoenix, and Young 1965; Young, Goy, and Phoenix 1964). Similarly, when pregnant rhesus monkeys were injected with androgen, their female fetuses were virilized to the extent of developing a malelike penis and an empty scrotum, instead of a clitoris and a vagina. The androgen injections were specifically timed in this study to coincide with the critical period for brain differentiation in the fetal monkey. Since the social and sexual behavior of the resulting "female" more closely resembled that of their normal male peers than that of their normal female peers, it was strongly suggested that the androgen not only exerted influence on the development of the sexual organs, but also affected the sexual differentiation of the brain (Goy 1968; Goy 1971; Young, Goy, and Phoenix 1964).

Experiments on rats have supported this suggestion. Grady, Phoenix, and Young (1965) used rats to discover if males would differentiate similarly to females in behavior, as well as in physical development, if deprived of androgens during the critical period for brain differentiation. This critical period in rats occurs postnatally (within one to five days after birth) so that by castrating the newly born males, their undifferentiated brains would receive no androgen. The results showed that the castrated males behaved and looked more like normal females than males, while no similar phenomena took place when intact males were injected with female hormones or were castrated at a later time.

These and other animal studies have provided compelling evidence that, at least in animals, fetal androgen exerts influence on the sexual differentiation of the brain, in addition to inhibiting the development of normal female sexual organs and genitalia—even when this development runs counter to the chromosomal gender coding.

Effects of Androgen on the Human Fetus. As it is obviously not possible to inject pregnant human females with androgen to see what happens to their fetuses and offspring, investigators have studied pertinent cases of aberrant development in humans. Certain rare genetic deviations, such as Turner's syndrome and androgen-insensitivity syndrome, involve the prenatal absence of androgen or its effects, providing a situation similar to that in the experiments on rats. In Turner's syndrome, for instance, the fetus develops no gonads and thus does not produce any sex hormones. Since the fetus develops as a phenotypic female, this seems to confirm the condition that without the masculinizing effects of androgen, the tendency is toward feminine differentiation (Young, Goy, and Phoenix 1964).

Androgen-insensitivity syndrome illustrates the extreme importance of androgen to male differentiation. In this syndrome, a genetic male, with properly differentiated and functioning fetal testes, develops completely female external genitalia because the body cells are genetically unresponsive to androgen. Thus, there is no inhibition of the tendency towards female differentiation, and the baby is born for all appearances as a female, is certified as such, and continues to develop as such, complete with female secondary characteristics at puberty. Only then, because of failure to begin menstruation, is the discrepancy discovered between her female sexual appearance and her genetically male gender and testes (Money 1970).

Two other rare clinical syndromes found in humans, adrenogenital syndrome and progestin-induced hermaphroditism, involve the fetal masculinization of females. In adrenogenital syndrome, an excessive production of adrenal androgens in the fetus causes masculinizing effects on the female both prenatally and at puberty. The clitoris is enlarged and the labia is partially fused. The masculinized genitalia have to be surgically feminized after birth. Progestin-induced hermaphroditism sometimes occurs when the pregnant mother is given synthetic progestin—a chemical resembling androgen—to prevent a possible miscarriage. The virilizing effects on the female fetus are similar to those in adrenogenital syndrome, though not so severe.

Studies on the postnatal and adult behavior of individuals with any of these deviations again suggest that fetal androgen may influence the differentiation process in brain tissue, as well as that in the sexual organs. In cases of both Turner's syndrome and androgen-insensitivity syndrome, the individuals developed a gender identity that was unquestionably female (Ehrhardt, Greenberg, and Money 1970; Money, Ehrhardt, and Masica 1968). Investigations into the behavior and self-identity concepts of girls with either adrenogenital syndrome or progestin-induced hermaphroditism, both of which involve an excess of androgen in the fetus, revealed an emphasis on tomboy behavior in childhood. Compared to control groups matched in age, sex, race, I.Q., and parents' socioeconomic level, these girls exhibited more interest in athletic and outdoor play and less interest in such activities as doll play and household chores. They were also less concerned than were the control groups in child rearing and more interested in careers (Ehrhardt, Epstein, and Money 1968; Ehrhardt and Money 1967).

Of course, whether these behavior patterns were the result of the presence or absence of prenatal androgen or were molded by the individual's postnatal environment is not by any means certain. As we discussed in the preceding chapter, the suggestion that any sexually dimorphic behavior is prenatally determined has aroused great controversy. However, there is at least some evidence to suggest that the presence or absence of androgen in the fetal environment may, by influencing the initial organization and differentiation of fetal brain tissue, perhaps create a bias toward the "acquisition and expression of behavior patterns and styles and the constellation of characteristics which later identify that individual as masculine or feminine" (Reinisch, in press).

Increased Androgen and I.Q. Perhaps the most striking findings in studies of fetally androgenized humans concerns I.Q. In 1967, Money and his associates found that out of 70 subjects with adrenogenital syndrome, 60 percent (as compared to 25 percent in a normal population) had I.Q.'s above 110, and 13 percent (as compared to 2 percent in a normal population) had I.Q.'s above 130. In another study, using a sample of 10 progestin-induced hermaphrodites, 60 percent had I.Q.'s above 130 (Ehrhardt and Money 1967).

The evidence in both studies does not conclusively prove that fetal androgenization alone was responsible for the high I.Q.'s. In the case of adrenogenital syndrome particularly, it is conceivable that a genetic factor—perhaps the trait responsible for the condition itself—might also produce the higher I.Q.'s. In the progestin-induced hermaphroditism, there is a possibility that the progestin treatment given the mothers might be related to the high I.Q. scores.

DRUGS. Until 1961, not much thought had been given to testing drugs for their effects on unborn infants. However, in that year, the attention of the medical profession, scientists, and the general public was dramatically focused on prenatal medication by a tragic event. In West Germany, hundreds of babies were born with limb deformities—stunted arms, useless hands, disproportionate legs—and with a variety of deformities of the heart, blood vessels, digestive tract, and ears. The limb deformities were a rare kind which might otherwise occur in West Germany perhaps 15 times in a decade (Taussig 1962).

The evidence was finally collected in the last few months of 1961. It all pointed to thalidomide, a drug sold without prescription. It was widely used in West Germany as a sleeping pill and as a nausea-preventative for pregnant women. It was found that mothers of deformed babies had taken thalidomide between the fourth and sixth weeks.

The story was repeated in every country where thalidomide had been sold. Many thousands of infants, in all, were affected. Two-thirds of these will survive for many years; most of the survivors will have normal intelligence (Taussig 1962).

American families were spared the misfortune of widespread infant deformity by one woman in the federal government's Food and Drug Administration. Frances Kelsey became suspicious of the drug's possible side effects and requested more information before approving the drug for sale in this country. During the subsequent delay, the news came in from West Germany.

Drug Research Expanding. The thalidomide incident carried one overriding lesson—that every drug to be taken during pregnancy must be examined for its possible teratogenic effects on the unborn infant. Pregnant women, as well as women who suspect they are pregnant, should be extremely cautious about taking any drugs, especially new ones. The rule applies particularly during the first three months.

Since the 1960s, research on prenatal drug effects has expanded, but progress has been slow. Much of the information is new and untested. At this stage a discussion of medication and drugs in pregnancy would amount to a listing of chemical compounds and a detailing of the abnormalities which the chemicals have caused or are suspected of causing. For example, sex hormones given early in pregnancy will distort the development of masculine and feminine traits; diuretics may cause kidney disease; excessive aspirin may cause blood-system abnormalities; quinine leads to deafness, reserpine to respiratory problems, novobiocin to jaundice, and chloromycetin to leukemia and chromosome damage (Kelsey 1969).

In the 1960s, addictive drugs, such as heroin, and psychoactive drugs, such as LSD, became the best known of the harmful prenatal drugs. It became evident that the baby of a morphine or heroin addict is born addicted to the drug. As soon as it is born, the infant begins to undergo symptoms of withdrawal—fever, tremors, convulsions, breathing difficulties, and intestinal disturbance (Brazelton 1970). The severity of the infant's heroin withdrawal is proportionate to the period of the mother's addiction, the size of her doses, and the proximity of her last dose to her time of delivery (Burnham 1972).

Withdrawal symptoms can be treated at birth. But the later effects on the children of addicts are still unknown. It is possible that the fate of these children will include brain damage, chromosome impairment, and increased vulnerability to addiction.

"Heroin babies" are small. About half of the infants of heroin addicts weigh 5½ pounds or less. Such diminished weights may be the result of the heroin or of poor prenatal care. Prematurity, too, may be the reason for the small babies. However, because heroin distorts the menstrual cycle, doctors cannot tell whether a heroin baby is premature or simply a small but full-term infant (Burnham 1972).

Addiction to methadone has recently been discovered in newborn babies. The drug methadone is sometimes used as a substitute for heroin in the treatment of addicts. Even though methadone is an addictive drug, it was hoped that methadone would not affect the unborn baby. This is not the case. Of 23 babies born to methadone-addicted mothers in Washington, D.C., researchers found that 17 suffered from methadone withdrawal symptoms. The newborn babies were irritable, twitched violently, and had cold sweats.

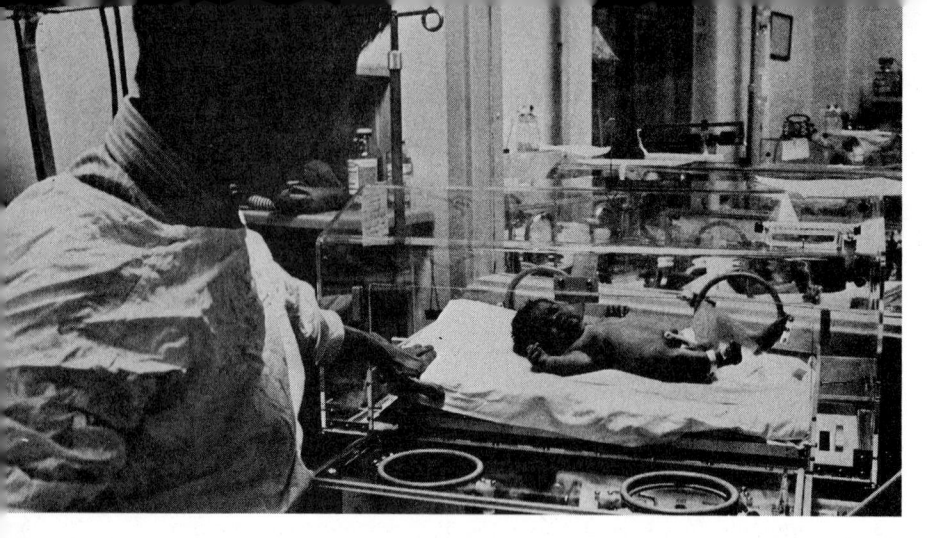

Figure 4.5 In a hospital ward for babies born as drug addicts, a doctor tests an infant's reflexes. If the newborn is an addict, his movements will be very jerky. (Arnold Hinton —Nancy Palmer Photo Agency)

Hospital treatment to free them from their inborn addiction to methadone lasted up to 90 days (*Science News* 1972).

Other addictive drugs also have negative effects, but their extent is less well known. LSD (lysergic acid diethylamide) seems to cause chromosome abnormalities in offspring. Such damage may not be permanent, but, on the other hand, LSD may pose a direct threat to the infant's postnatal survival. In one experiment, four pregnant rhesus monkeys were given LSD. All the mothers showed chromosome damage which subsequently repaired itself. In addition, all the females delivered late. One offspring had "no significant increase" in chromosome damage. However, the other three died not long after birth (Kato et al. 1970).

Apparently, even drugs taken before conception can influence the offspring's development. In 1972, Friedler and Cochin treated rats with morphine until five days before mating. Three to four weeks after birth, the rat pups began to show retarded growth. Thus, as this experiment and the others indicate, the human reproductive system appears to be quite sensitive to many ingested nonfood substances, whether the mother uses them before or during pregnancy. In reviewing animal studies related to prenatal drugs and behavior, Thompson and Grusec (1970) similarly concluded, "Almost any compound put into a pregnant animal by any route seems to have effects on a variety of behaviors provided the dosage is sufficient."

Effects of Smoking. Elements in cigarette smoke constitute drugs that also affect the unborn. For example, when an expectant mother smokes, the fetal heartbeat accelerates. In 1957, Simpson found that women who are steady smokers are twice as likely to deliver prematurely. In their 1961 study, Frazier and his colleagues compared the smoking habits of 2,736 pregnant black women and obtained similar results. For nonsmokers the rate of premature deliveries was 11.2 percent, while for women who began smoking during pregnancy the rate rose to 13.6 percent. For long-time smokers the rate was as high as 18.6 percent. Chances of premature birth also were found to increase in proportion to the amount of smoking done by the expectant mother. Moreover, smokers' offspring weighed less than the infants of nonsmokers born at the same premature stage. These findings, however, are not conclusive. It is possible that prematurity may not be a direct result of smoking, but, rather, of another factor, as yet unknown, that may cause both the need to smoke and the premature births.

IRRADIATION. External treatment, as well as ingested substances, can affect the human fetus. Exposure to ionizing radiation from X-rays, fluoroscopes, radioactive elements, or other sources may do serious harm. However, animal experiments have indicated that 10 roentgens or less of radiation will not damage a fetus. Thus, a dental X-ray or a simple pelvic X-ray of a pregnant woman, both of which are about one-tenth of a roentgen, are considered harmless. The large doses sometimes used in cancer treatments are much more powerful and can lead to both physical and mental abnormalities. In Denmark, radiation is considered a substantial threat. Exposure to over 10 roentgens is sufficient legal reason for a Danish woman to obtain an abortion.

Large-scale studies of prenatal radiation effects in humans were conducted with the cooperation of the Japanese victims of the World War II atomic bombing of that country. Many thousands of Japanese were contaminated by the radiation from those enormous explosions. Investigators found that a great number of women less than 20 weeks pregnant who were within one-half mile of the heart of the Hiroshima explosion suffered miscarriages and stillbirths. Among the infant survivors, there was a high proportion of abnormal babies. Many were afflicted with leukemia (cancer of the blood), stunted growth, and abnormally small skulls and brains (microcephaly) (Neel 1953).

Excessive radiation seems to most commonly result in defects of the central nervous system. Of the 30 types of abnormalities that Rugh listed in his 1962 study as caused by the X-irradiation of human fetuses, the microcephalic defect, which directly affects the central nervous system, was reported most often.

Radiation in Nature. Measuring the effects of radiation in varying doses is not feasible with human subjects. But in a 1959 experiment, Gentry, Parkhurst, and Bulin developed an approach that approximated a study of dosage effects, by correlating infant abnormalities with the amount of radiation emitted by natural surroundings—such as rocks—in the areas in which they lived. In this particular study, the experimenters found that there was a measurable correlation between the incidence of infant abnormalities and the amount of radiation in an area. Animal studies have confirmed that even a low level of radiation affects behavior. Radiation of pregnant rats resulted in pups that displayed more fear and less intelligence than normal, according to Furchtgott's 1963 study. His experiment also showed that the earlier in pregnancy the radiation dose was administered, the less radiation was needed to affect learning ability.

Conditions of Birth

From the start of labor contractions to the actual emergence of the newborn infant, most births take about 15 hours. Generally, the first child takes longer to be born than will its younger brothers or sisters. In normal births, 40 weeks after conception, the baby leaves the uterus head first. The mother's strong abdominal muscles push it out of her body. With a sharp cry, it breathes air for the first time.

The few minutes immediately after the baby's emergence may be the most crucial in its life. The infant must begin to breathe or the lack of oxygen may damage its brain.

MEDICATION DURING LABOR. Labor, like the entire pregnancy, is a period of vulnerability for the unborn infant. Drugs are the usual influences that affect it at this point. Sedative drugs or anesthetics sometimes are given to a woman in labor, particularly if the labor is painful. If the dosage is substantial and near delivery, the newborn infant may show signs of sedation for several days. Stechler (1964a) demonstrated this phenomenon by measuring the alertness of babies 2 to 4 days old. The mothers of some of the infants had taken drugs within 90 minutes before delivery that reached their maximum potency before delivery time. The entire group of newborn infants was shown three different pictures a total of nine times. The duration of their fixed looks at the pictures was recorded, and the cumulative totals for each were registered as the measure of individual attentiveness. Infants whose mothers had taken no drugs in the 90 minutes immediately before birth looked longer at the pictures than infants whose mothers had taken sedative drugs within the same predelivery period. In addition, the infants whose mothers had taken larger sedative dosages closer to delivery time did less looking than any of the infants.

In 1961, Brazelton had made other such discoveries—this time they were about the effects of heavy labor-period medication on infants. Heavy medication taken by the mothers clearly affected the offspring. The infants were slower to gain weight, less adept at breast-feeding, and disorganized for a longer period of time than infants whose mothers had taken light dosages of medication. Similarly, in 1948, Hughes and his colleagues found—through the use of electroencephalograms—that infants whose mothers had taken barbiturates during labor showed decreased brain activity for two full days after birth (Hughes, Ehemann, and Brown 1948).

Though excessive drugs during labor can decrease the oxygen reaching the fetal bloodstream or suppress the newborn's breathing, moderate

Table 4.1 Effect of Premedication on the Neonate

	33 Babies of Medicated Mothers	8 Babies of Nonmedicated Mothers
Behavioral state		
Impaired	29	1
Not impaired	4	7
Newborn EEG		
Altered	28	1
Not altered	5	7
Both behavior and EEG		
Altered	24	1
Not altered	1	7

Source: A. D. Borgstedt and M. G. Rosen. Medication during labor correlated with behavior and EEG of the newborn. *Amer. J. Dis. Child.*, 1968, *115*, 21.

drug dosages should not permanently affect an infant—any effects generally wear off within a short time. However, it is conceivable that the infant's groggy and inept behavior in the first few days could influence the mother's attitude toward the baby, thus possibly getting their relationship off to a bad start—which could then lead to continuing difficulties between them.

ANOXIA. All the cells of the body need oxygen, but the cells of the central nervous system need it most. A shortage of oxygen for even a brief time can bring damage or even death to brain cells. An infant is most vulnerable to oxygen shortage, or *anoxia*, during birth, when excessive pressure on the head of the fetus can cause hemorrhaging—a rupturing of the blood vessels in the brain. In addition, there is the particular danger of anoxia if any delay occurs between the time the infant's maternal oxygen supply ceases and the moment his own lung-breathing takes over.

Fetal Anoxia. It is difficult to study anoxia apart from other complications of pregnancy and birth. For example, while the relationship between prematurity and anoxia has not yet been discovered, a link between the two seems plausible. Some have suggested that anoxia may be a *cause* of prematurity (Joffe 1969). Anoxia may be a cause of other prenatal and birth difficulties as well.

In the fetal stage, anoxia can be caused by a decline of oxygen in the mother's blood or a poor blood supply to the placenta. Maternal high blood pressure would reduce the blood flow to the placenta, while maternal anemia—which is more likely during pregnancy—would reduce the amount of the blood's iron, which is needed to transport oxygen. Either event could cause fetal anoxia.

The geographical location in which prenatal development takes place may also be linked to anoxia. Babies of mothers living in the Andes Mountains at altitudes of over 10,000 feet above sea level almost always receive a poor oxygen supply during their intrauterine development (Hultgren and Spickard 1960). Among such infants, heart abnormalities are more common than usual.

To examine the effects of altitude, Vierck and his colleagues (1966) kept pregnant rats in a simulated atmosphere of 33,000 feet for six hours. The rat pups, tested for emotionality and activity at 30 and 44 days, were less emotional and more active than those in a control group. After they had combined these results with the findings of other studies, the experimenters suggested that animals born after anoxia are overactive under stress but sluggish in familiar surroundings.

In 1960, Meier and his associates, also working with rats, found that prenatal anoxia's effect on the offspring depended on the point in pregnancy at which the anoxia occurred. Anoxia induced early in gestation seemed to improve the off-

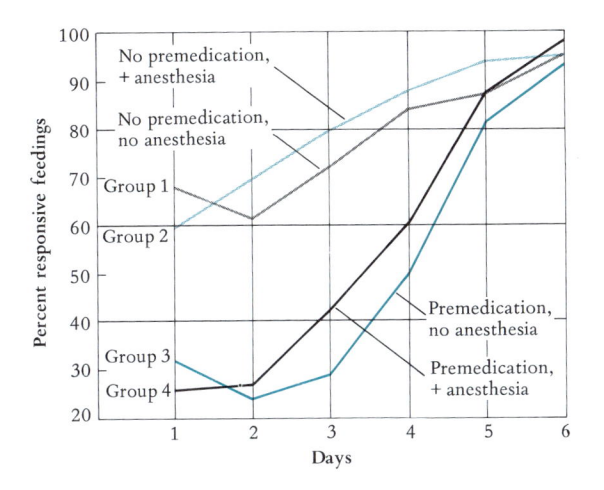

Figure 4.6 Responsive feedings in neonates. (From T. B. Brazelton. Psychophysiologic reactions in the neonate: II. Effects of maternal medication on the neonate and his behavior. *J. Pediat.*, 1961, *58*, 513–518.)

Figure 4.7 Weight gain in babies. (From T. B. Brazelton. Psychophysiologic reactions in the neonate: II. Effects of maternal medication on the neonate and his behavior. *J. Pediat.*, 1961, *58*, 513–518.)

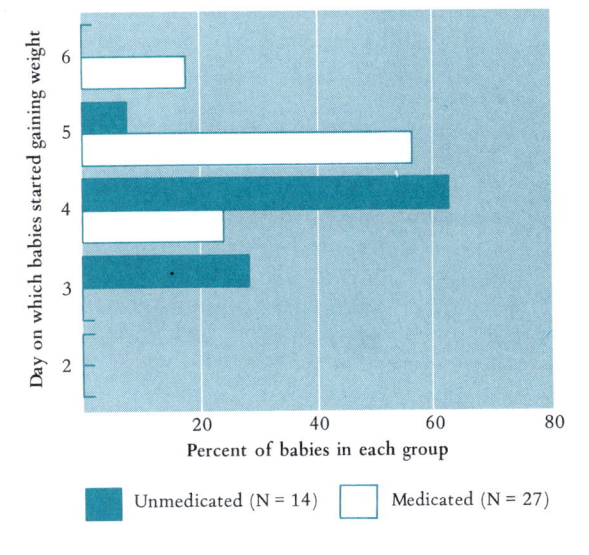

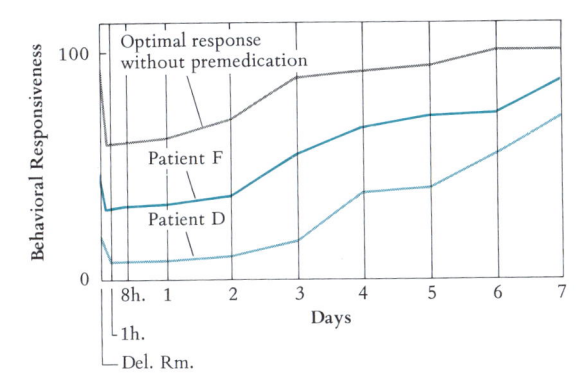

Figure 4.8 Behavior responsiveness of neonates (includes neurological responses, sensory responses, and motor activity state behavior). (From A. D. Borgstedt and M. G. Rosen. Medication during labor correlated with behavior and EEG of the newborn. *Amer. J. Dis. Child.*, 1968, *115*, 21.)

PRENATAL ENVIRONMENTAL INFLUENCES   **101**

spring's ability to learn—as their performance in a maze indicated—while later exposure led to diminished performance.

Anoxia at Birth. When a birth is long and difficult, the danger of anoxia increases. Thus, the frequent length of premature births is one reason why anoxia and prematurity are related. In addition, every minute that delays the start of breathing subjects the newborn infant to greater damage from anoxia. Premature babies are again more susceptible because they often have difficulty establishing regular breathing.

Anoxia can cause brain damage. In 1962, Teuber and Rudel showed that a severe lack of oxygen in the newborn can damage the cells of the brainstem, the region that controls motor activities. Brainstem damage may lead to muscular tremors, paralysis of the arms and legs, or difficulty in speaking. The term *cerebral palsy* is generally used to describe such lack of muscular control.

Mild anoxia has proportionate effects. Infants who have undergone brief shortages of oxygen are irritable and tense during their first week of postnatal life (Graham, Matarazzo, and Caldwell 1956). However, the effects apparently do not vanish with the symptoms. In their first year, these infants scored below normal infants on standard tests of motor development (Stechler 1964b). They also proved less attentive to moving lights (Lewis et al. 1967).

After many studies of problems of pregnancy and birth, Pasamanick and his fellow investigators correlated infants' problems with their measurable effects. Their conclusion was that in a continuum ranging from severe to minor brain damage, there is a corresponding range of effects. From death or such serious defects as cerebral palsy, epilepsy, and mental retardation, the range of effects runs down to such difficulties as behavior problems, learning blocks, disorganized conduct, and greater sensitivity to stress (Pasamanick and Knobloch 1960). Children who develop the less serious problems have suffered *minimal brain damage*. Much remains to be learned about this subject. In time, we may find that it is a more widespread defect than is now realized. Some reading difficulties may be explained in this way, for while a child can have trouble reading for many reasons, it does seem likely that minimal brain damage may be the primary cause in a number of cases.

BRAIN DAMAGE AND LEARNING. In a 1956 study, Pasamanick and his colleagues provided some support for the alleged link between minimal brain damage and learning difficulty. They obtained the records of children reported to the Baltimore Department of Education for behavior disorders. First, the investigators examined the pregnancy and birth conditions for over 1,000 of these children. Then they assembled the same information on a control group whose members had no behavior problems, but who matched the experimental children in age, sex, race, and socioeconomic status. The investigators found that the children with behavior problems had experienced significantly more pregnancy and birth complications than the control children. More important to our point, the investigators discovered that children with the type of disorder often specifically associated with minimal brain damage—that is, confused, disorganized, or hyperactive behavior—had undergone a higher rate of pregnancy and birth complications than the disorder group as a whole (Pasamanick, Rogers, and Lilienfeld 1956). Presumably, these seemingly brain-damaged children were reported to the Department of Education because of their learning problems in addition to—or more probably as a result of—their observed behavior disorders. On the basis of this evidence, minimal brain damage appears to be linked to learning difficulty.

The duration of mild anoxia's effects on an individual is not predictable. Generally, however, as mildly anoxic children grow older, they differ less from normal children. One group that had suffered mild anoxia at birth was tested for its progress at ages 3 and 7. At 3, the anoxic children did not perform as well as normal children on conceptualization tests. At 7, the average I.Q.'s of the two groups were equal, but the anoxic children were more easily distracted. They also had difficulty copying designs, a reflection of continuing deficiencies in motor coordination (Corah et al. 1965; Ernhart et al. 1960).

The Premature Infant

UNREADY FOR LIFE. A baby weighing under 5½ pounds at birth is considered premature. Because such a child is born too soon, his growth and development are incomplete. His brain is not ready to control all of his functions. He breathes irregularly and must be given extra oxygen. He cannot adjust his body temperature to ambient temperature changes. He cannot suck well and therefore must be fed intravenously. The more premature the infant, the more serious these problems are.

Because they are underdeveloped, premature babies are more susceptible to several damaging phenomena. In 1966, Braine and his colleagues studied a group of premature babies in the first days after birth. These babies, it was found, suffered from anoxia, weight loss, and infection more often than a similar group of full-term infants. At 13 months, the same premature babies performed at a level well below the full-term infants in a test of their gross motor development. Among the premature infants, the poorest performance corresponded with the lightest birth weights.

Premature infants often carry their developmental disadvantages with them into childhood. They tend to remain slightly smaller than the average, full-term child; this disadvantage frequently endures all the way through to maturity (Drillien and Ellis 1964). In addition, their motor and intellectual abilities develop more slowly.

PREMATURITY AND DISORDERS. In 1955, Lilienfeld and Pasamanick identified a relationship between prematurity and cerebral palsy. Their procedure was to examine the birth records of all children with cerebral palsy born in New York State between 1940 and 1947. They found that 22 percent of those with cerebral palsy were born prematurely. In further work, Pasamanick and his colleagues found that low birth weight and prematurity were among the most common early factors associated with later behavioral difficulties. They followed the development of 500 premature children until age 9, comparing them with full-term children matched for race, maternal age, parity (rank by age among children in a family), season of birth, and socioeconomic status. The premature children were both intellectually and physically retarded, relative to the full-term children, at ages 3 to 5; and at ages 7 and 9, the premature children still earned lower scores on standard I.Q. tests (Harper et al. 1959; Knobloch et al. 1956, 1959; Wiener et al. 1965, 1968).

Prematurity has been related to mental disorders as well as physical disabilities. In 1964, Zitrin and his associates examined the records of 450 children under 12 who were admitted to the Psychiatric Division of Bellevue Hospital in New York City. Disturbed children were matched with a control group for age, sex, race, hospital of birth, and hospital accommodations (private, semiprivate, ward). Whereas only 6 percent of the normal white children were premature, 13 percent of the disturbed white children were born early—a statistically significant difference. For nonwhites the difference was smaller—16 percent of the disturbed children and 10 percent of the normal children were premature. To explain the difference between the races, the authors suggested that the institutionalized white children were more severely disturbed and displayed the effects of prematurity more clearly because white parents generally allow their children to reach a greater degree of disturbance before committing them to an institution such as Bellevue.

In 1970, McNeil performed a similar study of premature children and their behavior disorders. He examined the birth histories of a group of disturbed children for complications of pregnancy and birth. Again it was found that the disturbed children had experienced significantly more complications than the control group. The children's disorders related particularly to prematurity and weak or delayed breathing. Other complications of pregnancy and birth were slightly more frequent among the more seriously disturbed subjects.

From these experiments, it is clear that prematurity exercises a substantial influence on infants. Among the defects it can cause are retardations in gross motor development, reduced physical size, retarded intellectual abilities, and mental disorders which often are manifested in aberrant behavior. In drawing this conclusion, we should not overlook the possibility that premature children's behavior disorders also may be due to the mother's reaction to the underdeveloped infant. His deficiencies may have prompted his mother to treat him in a certain way, thereby affecting his development. For example, the small and delicate premature baby needs extra protection and care. The mother of such a child may persist in her protective attitude even though the child has outgrown his need for it. In doing so, the mother may deny the child opportunities to perform actions and learn certain skills and concepts. It is conceivable that some of the deviations of premature children may arise from such restrictive mother–infant relationships.

Birth Complications and Other Variables

THE VULNERABLE MALE. Boys are not as resilient as girls—at least not early in life. Three boys are conceived for every two girls, and yet women outnumber men by a substantial proportion in the general population. The apparent contradiction is resolved in part by what happens to the conceived male infants between conception and their first year of postnatal life. By the time of birth, miscarriages and other intrauterine mishaps have reduced the 3-to-2 ratio to nearly 1-to-1 (Serr and Ismajovich 1963). The male half of the ratio decreases still further because more male babies die in their first postnatal year, particularly among premature babies. Finally, more males have difficulties beginning their lung-breathing in the minutes after birth (Stechler 1964b). This disability makes them more susceptible to the further handicap of brain damage.

Hyperanxious mothers more often give birth to males than to females. In an earlier discussion of maternal stress, we described two studies which examined the relationships between the mother's prenatal anxiety, her labor and delivery problems, and the physical condition of her offspring. In both studies, more male than female babies were born to mothers with high anxiety during pregnancy, and the majority of newborn infants with poor health and disposition were male. For example, in the 1963 study by McDonald and his colleagues, out of the 44 babies classified as abnormal, 31 were males. Pasamanick's Baltimore study of behavior disorders, cited in our discussion of anoxia and learning, revealed the same factor of vulnerability in the male. Males constituted a larger proportion in the group of infants who had suffered brain damage (Pasamanick, Rogers, and Lilienfeld 1956).

Why the predominance of males among the offspring of prenatally anxious women, as well as among brain-damaged infants? One theory maintains that it is *because* the mother is carrying a less than healthy fetus—which is likely to be a male—that she feels anxious (Moss 1970). If the fetus is functioning poorly, the woman may have unpleasant symptoms during pregnancy. Because she does not feel well, she may become anxious for her own well-being as well as that of her unborn infant. Therefore, the anxiety may not be the cause of problems in pregnancy and birth, but rather the result of them.

SOCIOECONOMIC STATUS. Children born to mothers of a low socioeconomic class have two strikes against them even before they are delivered. First, these poorer infants are more likely to have undergone unpleasant prenatal experiences, and second, once they are born, their new environment offers them less help in overcoming the difficulties caused by those prenatal experiences. A comparison of two basic groups in the American population—the whites and the nonwhites—illustrates the point. In 1967, 14 percent of the infants of nonwhite Americans—who predominate in the United States' lower socioeconomic class—weighed less than 5½ pounds at birth, the weight below which an infant is considered premature. In the same year, only 7 percent of the white American infants weighed less than 5½ pounds.

The entire environment of the unborn nonwhite infant works against him. His mother's nutrition and prenatal care often are substandard. Complications of pregnancy and delivery occur with a greater frequency among nonwhites than whites (Pasamanick, Knobloch, and Lilienfeld 1956). In addition, both the prenatal and postnatal problems of the nonwhite offspring are reflected in the infant death rate: twice as many nonwhite babies die in their first postnatal year.

A 1967 study by Hendricks clearly demonstrated that these statistics reflect a socioeconomic class standing rather than an ethnic or genetic difference. He compared the births in a group of upper-class whites with those in a group of upper-class nonwhites, and contrasted these with births in lower-class whites and nonwhites. The upper classes in both ethnic groups resembled each other more than either resembled the lower classes of its own ethnic group. Notably, fewer infant deaths and fewer premature births occurred in the upper-class groups of both whites and nonwhites.

These results are disturbing when they are considered with the gloomy findings on prematurity and class standing that Birch pointed out in his 1971 report for the U.S. Office of Economic Opportunity. In that report, Birch stated that children of lower socioeconomic classes who are born prematurely have poorer school performance and lower I.Q.'s than premature children born into homes with higher social and economic status. Thus, it seems possible that with a good home environment, a child can overcome the disadvantages he may have suffered prenatally and in birth. However, this is not possible for the infants born into lower-class homes. On the contrary, as Birch noted, "Prematurity is most frequent in the very groups in which its depressing effects on intelligence are greatest."

Birch has outlined the odds which a child of low socioeconomic class must struggle against. According to Birch, the odds against the infant start with its mother's generally poor nutritional history. Birch noted that because the pregnant woman has been undernourished as a child and adult, her growth has been stunted and her efficiency as a reproducer diminished. These deficits mean she is more likely to provide a poor prenatal environment for the infant, and runs a greater risk of complications in delivery as well. Consequently, her infant may be poorly prepared for life. Finally, the infant's chances are further decreased by the continued poor nutrition of the mother during her pregnancy and of her baby after he is born.

Improvements in the rather simple rudiments of prenatal care could give many children a much better chance to live their lives at the maximum level of their physical and intellectual powers. If this is to be accomplished, however, it is necessary to educate prospective mothers on their own prenatal needs. The maintenance of good health and nutritional habits, plus the avoidance of known hazards to prenatal life, would be a major contribution to the goal of providing a sound prenatal environment for the infant growing toward the day of his birth.

Summary

Even before birth, an individual's development is influenced by his environment. The fetus' environment depends on the health and welfare of his mother; a mother who is physically well developed, free of disease, well nourished, and given good prenatal care provides the best possible environment.

Many factors contribute to the good health of the mother and the good prenatal care given the fetus. One important factor is nutrition. In the first few prenatal months, the fetus satisfies its needs by drawing on the vitamins and minerals stored in its mother's body. In the last three months, the nutritional needs of mother and child increase. If the woman's diet does not replace her depleted nutrients at this point, both the expectant mother and the infant may suffer. It has been shown that pregnant women given enriched diets have fewer complications during pregnancy, fewer miscarriages, and shorter labor periods. Their babies develop fewer diseases.

The fetus receives its food and oxygen through the mother's bloodstream and thus can be affected by any substances that pass through the placental filtering system. Drugs are one such substance. Pregnant women should be extremely cautious about taking any medication or drug, as the thalidomide tragedy of the early 1960s illustrates. Addictive and psychoactive drugs are also harmful to infants. Babies of heroin addicts are born addicted to the drug and exhibit withdrawal symptoms at birth. LSD may cause chromosome abnormalities in offspring. Cigarettes may also be classed as drugs affecting the unborn. Steady smokers are twice as likely to have premature babies.

Hormones and other chemicals produced in the mother's body can also reach the fetus. This explains the effect of maternal emotions. When strong emotions are aroused, adrenalin and other hormones are pumped into the bloodstream. Early in pregnancy, these chemicals may cause physical abnormalities in the fetus. Anxious mothers also have difficulties in delivery which may affect the child.

The mother who contracts a virus may also produce a defective infant. During the first three prenatal months, rubella is particularly dangerous; the fetus may be born with congenital heart disease, eye defects, or deafness. Influenza and mumps are other diseases which may cause malformations. Untreated syphilis in the pregnant woman is another threat; over half the fetuses infected with syphilis are stillborn, aborted, or die shortly after birth, while others may be deformed or mentally retarded.

External treatment, too, can affect the fetus. Exposure to excessive radiation can do serious harm, especially to the central nervous system of the fetus.

The conditions of its birth are also important to an infant's well-being. Then the baby is most vulnerable to oxygen shortage, which may cause permanent damage to brain cells. Premature babies are particularly susceptible to anoxia, as well as to weight loss and infection.

Research has proved that a healthy prenatal environment is vital to the developing infant. While we have considered a number of conditions during pregnancy and birth that may be harmful, it should be remembered that most pregnancies result in the birth of normal, healthy infants.

References

Abrams, S. The upper weight level premature child. *Dis. Nerv. Syst.*, 1969, *30*(6), 414–417.

Ader, R., and Deitchman, R. Effects of prenatal maternal handling on the maturation of rhythmic processes. *J. comp. physiol. Psychol.*, 1970, *71*(3), 492–496.

Arena, J. M. Drug dangers to the fetus from maternal medications. *Clin. Pediat.*, 1964, *3*, 450–465, 471.

Assali, N. S. *Biology of gestation*. 2 vols. New York: Academic Press, 1968.

Babson, S., et al. *Management of high-risk pregnancy and intensive care of the neonate*. (2nd ed.) St. Louis, Mo.: Mosby, 1971.

Bacon, H. M. Psychiatric aspects of therapeutic abortion. *Canada's Ment. Health*, 1969, *17*(1), 18–21.

Baird, D. Social class and foetal mortality. *Lancet*, 1947, *253*, 531–535.

Baird, D. Social factors in obstetrics. *Lancet*, 1949, *1*, 1079–1083.

Baird, D. The epidemiology of prematurity. *J. Pediat.*, 1964, *65*, 909–924.

Baird, D., and Illsley, R. Environment and childbearing. *Proceedings of the Royal Society of Medicine*, 1953, *46*, 53–59.

Baker, A. A. *Psychiatric disorders in obstetrics practice*. Worcester, Mass.: Davis, 1970.

Barnet, A. B., et al. Click-evoked EEG responses in normal and developmentally retarded infants. *Nature*, 1967, *214*, 252–255.

Bench, J., and Parker, A. Hyper-responsivity to sounds in the short gestation baby. *Develpm. Med. and Child Neurol.*, February 1971, *13*(1), 15–19.

Benton, J. W., Moser, H. W., Dodge, P. R., and Carr, S. Modification of the schedule of myelinization in the rat by early nutritional deprivation. *Pediatrics*, 1966, *38*, 801–804.

Berkman, P. L. Painless motherhood, psychological stress, and physical morbidity. *J. Health and Soc. Behav.*, 1969, *10*(4), 323–334.

Bernard, R. M. The shape and size of the female pelvis. Transactions of the Edinburgh Obstetrical Society. *Edinburgh Med. J.*, 1952, *59*(2), 1–16.

Beyer, T. E. The effects of maternal protein restriction on offspring behavior. *Dissert. Abstr.*, April 1971, *3* (10-B), 6252.

Birch, H. G. Malnutrition, learning, and intelligence. In E. Grotberg (Ed.), *Designs and proposals for early childhood research: A new look*. Washington, D.C.: U.S. Government Printing Office, 1971.

Blinick, G. Menstrual function and pregnancy in narcotics addicts treated with methadone. *Nature*, 1968, *219*(5150), 180.

Borgstedt, A. D., and Rosen, M. G. Medication during labor correlated with behavior and EEG of the newborn. *Amer. J. Dis. Child.*, 1968, *115*, 21–24.

Bradley, R. A. *Husband-coached childbirth*. New York: Harper & Row, 1965.

Braine, M. D. S., Heimer, C. B., Wortis, H., and Freedman, A. M. Factors associated with impairment of the early development of prematures. *Monogr. Soc. Res. Child Develpm.*, 1966, *31*, 1–92.

Brazelton, T. B. Effect of prenatal drugs on the behavior of the neonate. *Amer. J. Psychiat.*, 1970, *126*, 1261–1266.

Brazelton, T. B. Psychophysiologic reactions in the

neonate. II. Effect of maternal medication on the neonate and his behavior. *J. Pediat.*, 1961, *58*, 513–518.

Broen, B. B. Evolution of a group therapeutic approach to school-age pregnant girls. *Proc. 77th Ann. Conv. Am. Psychol. Assoc.*, 1969, *4*, Pt. 2, 547–548.

Burnham, S. The heroin babies are going cold turkey. *New York Times Magazine*, January 9, 1972.

Cannings, C. A discussion of Wanberg's rule on the zygosity of twins. *Ann. Hum. Genet.*, 1969, *32*(4), 403–406.

Chow, B. F., Simonson, M., Hanson, H. M., and Roeder, L. M. Behavioral measurements in nutritional studies. *Conditional Reflex*, 1971, *6*, 36–40.

Corah, N. L., Anthony, E. J., Painter, P., Stern, J. A., and Thurston, D. Effects of perinatal anoxia after 7 years. *Psychol. Monogr.*, 1965, *79*, 1–34.

Davison, A. N., and Dobbing, J. Myelinization as a vulnerable period in brain development. *Brit. Med. Bull.*, 1966, *22*, 40–45.

Despres, M. A. Favorable and unfavorable attitudes toward pregnancy in primaparae. *J. genet. Psychol.*, 1937, *51*, 241–254.

Drillien, C. M., and Ellis, R. W. B. *The growth and development of the prematurely born infant.* Baltimore: Williams & Wilkins, 1964.

Dubignon, J., Campbell, O., Curtis, M., and Partington, M. W. The relation between laboratory measures of sucking, food intake, and perinatal factors during the newborn period. *Child Develpm.*, 1969, *40*(4), 1107–1120.

Ebbs, J. H., Tisdall, F. F., and Scott, W. A. The influence of prenatal diet on the mother and child. *Millbank Memorial Fund Quart.*, 1942, *20*, 35–36.

Ehrhardt, A. A., Epstein, R., and Money, J. Fetal androgens and female gender identity in the early-treated adrenogenital syndrome. *Johns Hopkins Med. J.*, 1968, *122*, 160–167.

Ehrhardt, A. A., Greenberg, N., and Money, J. Female gender identity and absence of fetal gonadal hormones: Turner's syndrome. *Johns Hopkins Med. J.*, 1970, *126*, 237–248.

Ehrhardt, A. A., and Money, J. Progestin-induced hermaphroditism: I.Q. and psychosexual identity in a study of ten girls. *J. Sex Research*, 1967, *3*, 83–100.

Ernhart, C. B., Graham, F. K., and Thurston, D. Relationship of neonatal apnea to development at three years. *Arch. Neurol.*, 1960, *2*, 504–510.

Everett, J. W. "Delayed pseudopregnancy" in the rat, a tool for the study of central neural mechanism in reproduction. In M. Diamond (Ed.), *Perspectives in reproduction and sexual behavior.* Bloomington: Indiana Univer. Press, 1969.

Ferreira, A. J. The pregnant woman's emotional attitude and its reflection on the newborn. *Amer. J. Orthopsychiat.*, 1960, *30*, 553–561.

Frazier, T. M., Davis, G. H., Goldstein, H., and Goldberg, I. D. Cigarette smoking and prematurity: A prospective study. *Amer. J. Obst. and Gynec.*, 1961, *81*, 988–996.

Friedler, G., and Cochin, J. Growth retardation in offspring of female rats treated with morphine prior to conception. *Science*, 1972, *175*, 654–656.

Furchtgott, E. Behavioral effects of ionizing radiations: 1955–61. *Psychol. Bull.*, 1963, *60*(2), 157–199.

Garn, S. M. Growth and development. In E. Ginzberg (Ed.), *The nation's children.* New York: Columbia Univer. Press, 1960.

Gentry, J. T., Parkhurst, E., and Bulin, G. V., Jr. An epidemiological study of congenital malformations in New York State. *Amer. J. Public Health*, 1959, *49*, 1–22.

Goedie, L., Svedsen-Rhodes, U., Easton, J., and Robertson, N. R. The development of innate sleep rhythms in short gestation infants. *Develp. Med. and Child Neurol.*, February 1971, *13*(1), 40–50.

Goodwin, B. An investigation of the relationship between psychoprophylaxis in childbirth and changes in concept of self and concept of husband. *Dissert. Abstr.*, May 1971, *31*(11–13), 6714.

Goy, R. W. Organizing effects of androgen on the behavior of rhesus monkeys. In R. P. Michael (Ed.), *Endocrinology and human behavior.* London: Oxford Univer. Press, 1968.

Goy, R. W. Early hormonal influences on the development of sexual and sex-related behavior. In T. Melnechuk and F. O. Schmitt (Eds.), *Neurosciences: A study program.* New York: Rockefeller Univer. Press, 1971.

Grady, K. L., Phoenix, C. H., and Young, W. C. Role of the developing rat testis in differentiation of the neural tissues mediating mating behavior. *J. comp. physiol. Psychol.*, 1965, *59*, 176–182.

Graham, F. K., Matarazzo, R. G., and Caldwell, B. M. Behavioral differences between normal and traumatized newborns. *Psychol. Monogr.*, 1956, *70*, No. 5.

Gruenberg, E. M. Epidemiology. In H. A. Stevens and R. Heber, *Mental retardation: A review of research.* Chicago: Univer. of Chicago Press, 1964.

Harper, P. A., Fisher, L. K., and Rider, R. V. Neurological and intellectual status of prematures at three to five years of age. *J. Pediat.*, 1959, *55*, 679–690.

Harrell, R. F., Woodyard, E., and Gates, A. E. *The effects of mothers' diets on the intelligence of offspring: A study of the influence of vitamin supplementation of the diet of pregnant and lactating women on the intelligence of their children.* New York: Teachers College, Columbia Univer., 1955.

Hendricks, C. H. Delivery patterns and reproductive efficiency among groups of differing socioeconomic status and ethnic origins. *Amer. J. Obst. and Gynec.*, 1967, *97*, 608–624.

Hockman, C. H. Prenatal maternal stress in the rat: Its effects on emotional behavior in the offspring. *J. comparat. and physiol. Psychol.*, 1961, *54*, 679–684.

Hooker, D. *The prenatal origin of behavior.* Lawrence: Univer. of Kansas Press, 1952.

Houston, K. B. Review of the evidence and qualifications regarding the effects of hallucinogenic drugs on chromosomes and embryos. *Amer. J. Psychiat.*, 1969, *126*, 251–254.

Hughes, J. G., Ehemann, B., and Brown, U. A. Electroencephalography of the newborn. *Amer. J. Dis. Child.*, 1948, *76*, 626–633.

Hultgren, H. H., and Spickard, W. Medical experiences in Peru. *Stanford Medical Bulletin*, 1960, *18*, 76–95.

Humphrey, T. The development of human fetal activity and its relation to postnatal behavior. In H. W. Reese and L. P. Lipsitt (Eds.), *Advances in child development and behavior*. Vol. 5. New York: Academic Press, 1970.

Hutchings, D. E., and Gibbon, J. Effects of vitamin A excess administered in late pregnancy on discrimination learning in offspring. *Proc. 79th Ann. Conv. Amer. Psychol. Assoc.*, 1971, *6*, 211–212.

Illsley, R. Early prediction of perinatal risk. *Proceedings of the Royal Society of Medicine*, 1966, *59*, 181–184.

James, W. H. The effect of maternal psychological stress on the foetus. *Brit. J. Psychiat.*, 1969, *115*(524), 811–825.

Joffe, J. M. *Prenatal determinants of behavior*. London: Pergamon Press, 1969.

Kaelther, C. T., and Pugh, T. F. Influence of intrauterine relations on the intelligence of twins. *New England J. Med.*, 1969, *280*, 1030–1037.

Karacon, J., et al. Some implications of the sleep patterns of pregnancy for postpartum emotional disturbances. *Brit. J. Psychiat.*, 1969, *115*(525), 929–935.

Kato, T., Jarvik, L. F., Roizin, L., and Moralishvili, E. Chromosome studies in pregnant rhesus macaque given LSD-25. *Diseases nerv. Syst.*, 1970, *31*, 245–250.

Keeley, K. Prenatal influence on behavior of offspring of crowded mice. *Science*, 1962, *135*, 44–45.

Kelsey, F. O. Drugs and pregnancy. *Ment. Retardation*, 1969, *7*, 7–10.

Knobloch, H., Rider, R., Harper, P., and Pasamanick, B. Neuropsychiatric sequelae of prematurity: A longitudinal study. *J. Amer. Med. Ass.*, 1956, *161*, 581–585.

Knobloch, H., Pasamanick, B., Harper, P., and Rider, R. The effect of prematurity on health and growth, *Amer. J. Public Health*, 1959, *49*, 1164–1173.

Lapidus, L. B. Cognitive control and reaction to stress: Conditions for mastery in the anticipatory phase. *Proc. 77th Ann. Conv. Amer. Psychol. Ass.*, 1969, *4*, Pt. 2, 569–570.

Lewis, M., Martels, B., Campbell, H., and Goldberg, S. Individual differences in attention. *Amer. J. Dis. Child.*, 1967, *113*, 461–465.

Lilienfeld, A. M., and Pasamanick, B. The association of prenatal and paranatal factors with the development of cerebral palsy and epilepsy. *Amer. J. Obst. and Gynec.*, 1955, *70*, 93–101.

McDonald, R. L., Gynther, M. D., and Christakos, A. C. Relation between maternal anxiety and obstetric complications. *Psychosom. Med.*, 1963, *25*, 357–363.

McNeil, T. F., Wiegerink, R., and Dozier, J. E. Pregnancy and birth complications in the births of seriously, moderately, and mildly behaviorally disturbed children. *J. nerv. ment. Dis.*, 1970, *15*, 24–34.

Malmquist, A., Kaij, L., and Nilsson, A. Psychiatric aspects of spontaneous abortion: I. A matched control study of women with living children. *J. Psychosom. Res.*, 1969, *13*(1), 45–51.

Meier, G. W., Bunch, M. E., Nolan, C. T., and Scheidler, C. H. Anoxia, behavioral development and learning ability: A comparative experimental approach. *Psychol. Monogr.*, 1960, *1* (Whole No. 488).

Money, J. Matched pairs of hermaphrodites: Behavioral biology of sexual differentiation from chromosomes to gender identity. *Engineering and Science*, 1970, *33*, 34–39.

Money, J., Ehrhardt, A. A., and Masica, D. N. Fetal feminization induced by androgen insensitivity in the testicular feminization syndrome: Effect of marriage and maternalism. *Johns Hopkins Med. J.*, 1968, *123*, 105–114.

Moore, J. M., and Kendall, D. G. Children's concepts of reproduction. *J. Sex. Res.*, February 1971, *7*(1), 42–61.

Moss, H. A. Early environmental effects: Mother–child relations. In T. D. Spencer and H. Kass (Eds.), *Perspectives in child psychology*. New York: McGraw-Hill, 1970.

Munroe, R. L., and Munroe, R. H. Male pregnancy symptoms and cross-sex identity in three societies. *J. soc. Psychol.*, June 1971, *84*(1), 11–25.

Neel, J. V. The effect of exposure to the atomic bombs on pregnancy termination in Hiroshima and Nagasaki: Preliminary report. *Science*, 1953, *118*, 537–541.

Noyes, R. W. Perspectives in human fertility. In M. Diamond, *Perspectives in reproduction and sexual behavior*. Bloomington: Indiana Univer. Press, 1969.

Pasamanick, B., and Knobloch, H. Brain damage and reproductive casualty. *Amer. J. Orthopsychiat.*, 1960, *30*, 298–305.

Pasamanick, B., Knobloch, H., and Lilienfeld, A. M. Socioeconomic status and some precursors of neuropsychiatric disorders. *Amer. J. Orthopsychiat.*, 1956, *26*, 594–601.

Pasamanick, B., and Lilienfeld, A. M. Association of maternal and fetal factors with development of mental deficiency. 1. Abnormalities in the prenatal and paranatal periods. *J. Amer. Med. Ass.*, 1955, *159*, 155–160.

Pasamanick, B., Rogers, M. E., and Lilienfeld, A. M. Pregnancy experience and the development of behavior disorder in children. *Amer. J. Psychiat.*, 1956, *112*, 613–618.

Reinisch, J. Fetal hormones, the brain, and human sex differences. *Arch. sexual behav.* (In press)

Rhodes, A. J. Virus infections and congenital malformations. In *Congenital malformations: Papers and discussions presented at the first international conference on congenital malformations*. Philadelphia: Lippincott, 1961, 106–116.

Richardson, S. A. The influence of social, environmental and nutritional factors on mental ability. In N. S. Scrimshaw and J. E. Gordon (Eds.), *Malnutrition, learning and behavior*. Cambridge, Mass.: M. I. T. Press, 1968.

Rugh, R. Low levels of X-irradiation and the early mammalian embryo. *Amer. J. Roentgenology*, 1962, *87*, 559–566.

Rutt, C. N., and Offord, D. R. Prenatal and perinatal

complications in childhood schizophrenics and their siblings. *J. nerv. ment. Dis.*, May 1971, *152*, 324–331.

Science News. Methadone addiction in babies. March 1972, *101*(11), 170.

Serr, D. M., and Ismajovich, B. Determination of primary sex ratio from human abortions. *Amer. J. Obst. and Gynec.*, 1963, *87*, 63–65.

Sheridan, M. D. Final report of a prospective study of children whose mothers had rubella in early pregnancy. *Brit. Med. J.*, 1964, *2*, 536–539.

Simpson, W. J. A preliminary report on cigarette smoking and the incidence of prematurity. *Amer. J. Obst. and Gynec.*, 1957, *73*, 808–815.

Sontag, L. W. The significance of fetal environmental differences. *Amer. J. Obst. and Gynec.*, 1941, *42*, 996–1003.

Stechler, G. A longitudinal follow-up of neonatal apnea. *Child Develpm.*, 1964, *35*, 333–348. (a)

Stechler, G. Newborn attention as affected by medication during labor. *Science*, 1964, *144*, 315–317. (b)

Stoller, A., and Collmann, R. D. Grand maternal age at birth of mothers of children with Down's syndrome (mongolism). *J. ment. def. Res.*, 1969, *13*(3), 201–205.

Strean, L. P., and Peer, A. Stress as an etiologic factor in the development of cleft palate. *Plastic and Reconstructive Surgery*, 1956, *18*, 1–8.

Taussig, H. B. The thalidomide syndrome. *Scientific Amer.*, 1962, *207*, 29–35.

Teuber, H. L., and Rudel, R. G. Behavior after cerebral lesions in children and adults. *Develpm. Med. and Child Neurol.*, 1962, *4*, 3–20.

Thompson, W. R. Influence of prenatal maternal anxiety on emotionality in young rats. *Science*, 1957, *125*, 698–699.

Thompson, W. R., and Grusec, J. A. Studies of early experience. In P. H. Mussen (Ed.), *Carmichael's manual of child psychology.* Vol. I. (3rd ed.) New York: Wiley, 1970.

Vierck, C. J., Jr., King, F. A., and Ferm, V. H. Effects of prenatal hypoxia upon activity and emotionality of the rat. *Psychon. Sci.*, 1966, *4*, 87–88.

Werner, E. Cumulative effect of perinatal complications and deprived environment on physical, intellectual and social development of preschool children. *Pediatrics*, 1967, *39*, 490–505.

Wiener, G., Rider, R. V., Oppel, W. C., Fischer, L. K., and Harper, P. A. Correlates of low birth weight: Psychological status at 6–7 years of age. *Pediatrics*, 1965, *35*, 434–444.

Wiener, G., Rider, R. V., Oppel, W. C., and Harper, P. A. Correlates of low birth weight: Psychological status at eight to ten years of age. *Pediatrics Research*, 1968, *2*, 110–118.

Young, W. C., Goy, R. W., and Phoenix, C. H. Hormones and sexual behavior. *Science*, 1964, *143*, 212–218.

Zitrin, A., Ferber, P., and Cohen, D. Pre- and paranatal factors in mental disorders of children. *J. nerv. ment. Dis.*, 1964, *139*, 357–361.

III

Infancy

Burk Uzzle — Magnum

Motor Development and Sensory Experience 5

TODAY's newborn baby has come a long way from the popular sixteenth-century notion of the infant as a rather insensitive and bumbling being. Nevertheless, the infant's detractors were not confined to the sixteenth century; in the twentieth, one researcher labeled the infant "neurologically insufficient" (Flechsig 1920). Another—on the threshold of this century—called him "cognitively confused" (James 1890). In the years since, the infant has advanced considerably in the regard of psychologists, and with good cause. In what other terrestrial species could we find a helpless, bleating mammal that, within less than 18 months, has become a remembering, discriminating being who walks on his hind legs, speaks so he can be understood, and carries on a complex social life with his peers and parents?

The average child of 18 months is a free and capable agent. He can walk, perhaps even run. If he is especially well-developed he can creep up and down stairs. He can climb into a chair for dinner and, just as likely, stand up on it and rock a little. He can jump off small rocks and step over toys, kick his teddy bear and drag a doll by the hair. He can pull off his socks and some of his other clothes; unzipping is fun, but zipping up defeats him. He can step into his slippers—no shoe-tying yet. With urging, he will sometimes collect his toys and dump them into a chest, though he would much prefer to empty the chest, and the wastebaskets, and the dresser drawers. He can drink from his sister's china tea set, usually without breaking a cup, and occasionally without spilling a drop of his apple juice. He knows his name is Alex, but Alex what?—he does not understand the question. He can name his dog, his bike, his ball and plastic bat. He knows his coat from his hat. He can sit or lie; he can take

113

a pencil and paper and make squiggles, a few curved lines, and perhaps one or two deflated open circles.

At around 18 months to 2 years, the child also begins to develop his own meaningful sentences and to show in other ways that he is starting to use symbols in thinking about, and reacting to, what is going on around him. He may play at being mother, or pretend to drink from his hand. He becomes a dramatically different type of being from what he was as an infant. Because this symbolic capacity usually emerges at some time around the second birthday and transforms the child in such a substantial way, the time from birth to 2 years of age is considered a logical and convenient unit for study. It is the child in roughly this time period of life that is the subject of the three chapters in this section. Although the infant's physical, cognitive, and social development are discussed in separate chapters, these three aspects of growth themselves are not separable. In life, a child's body, mind, and personality develop together, and each affects the other two.

As a psychologist observes a newborn infant, he asks himself several questions. What faculties of body and behavior does an infant have when he first enters the world? Which responses are innate? How do his experiences change him?—and *which* experiences? Does the baby's later behavior grow out of an inherent potential? If so, to what degree?

These are some of the questions the present chapter on physical growth will explore, by following the development of the child's sensory capacities and experiences and his motor development, from crying and kicking to talking and running. Historically, the greatest emphasis in the study of motor growth, sensation, and perception has been on the controlling effects that maturation exerts. In more recent years, however, it has been discovered that although maturation certainly sets limits to what the child can do at any given time, sensory and motor stimulation do make a great difference in how quickly the child develops. The degree of stimulation that a child receives also affects the level of activity to which he will become accustomed and will enjoy; it is this level of activity that he will be able to utilize in his further development.

The State of the Newborn

The Infant's Senses

From his first breath, the child is remarkably well-equipped for life. He can see, hear, smell, touch, and feel pain. All his senses, except taste, are operating immediately, and even taste develops rapidly. From his first moment outside the womb, the human infant can feel most stimuli that adults experience. Unlike many mammals—the puppy, for instance, born deaf and blind—the senses of the newborn child are in good working order.

The Infant's Reflexes

The newborn comes into the world with a number of well-developed reflexes also. Some of these—the sucking reflex, for example—are needed for survival. Others, reflexes which are quite complex, are geared to the current state of his nervous system. Seemingly sophisticated reflexes appear very early. An infant 2 hours old will turn his head to follow a light reflexively, assuming it is not moved too quickly. The pupil of his eye will dilate in darkness and contract in light—the *pupillary reflex*. Further, his body will shudder at a loud noise—the *startle reflex*. And if you touch an infant's cheek, he will turn rather quickly to that side, demonstrating his *rooting reflex*, which brings his mouth into position so that his *sucking reflex* can draw nourishment from breast or bottle. If you press the infant's palm with your finger, his fingers will close around yours—the *grasp reflex*. Many an infant's grasp, in his first few weeks, is so strong—and his body so light—that he can hang by his hands for a minute or so, or inadvertently tear off your tablecloth as you get up from holding him at the table. He also can cough, cry, vomit, and wave his arms and legs. Lying on his stomach, he can raise his chin and turn his head. He can smack his lips noisily and munch his fingers—especially later when he anticipates a feeding. Also operating is his *withdrawal reflex*, which makes the infant recoil from pain, whether the source is an overheated nursing bottle or an open diaper pin. His jerking back from the pin or spitting out of the hot milk is soon followed by his shocked cry, which is an outlet for him and a clear distress signal to his parents.

One of the infant's clearly identifiable reflexes is the *Moro reflex*. In this reflex, the infant flings his arms to either side, extending his fingers at the same time. Then he quickly brings his arms back up, as if he were hugging a stuffed toy to his chest. Some infants display this common reflex whenever they are moved or surprised; most will display it when their head positions are suddenly changed. The curious thing about the Moro reflex is that it disappears within three to six months after birth. One theory explaining its disappearance is based on the belief that this reflex and all other basic reflexes are controlled by the brainstem, initially, and later by the cerebral cortex. The cortex, which houses memory, thought, and perception, probably does not operate completely until an infant is several months old. The cortex gradually assumes control over the more primitive brainstem by blocking or modifying the signals emanating from that area. Thus, when the brainstem becomes dominated by the cerebral cortex—some time between the third and sixth month—the Moro reflex ceases. A pediatrician therefore might suggest that the 1-year-old child who still displays the Moro reflex may be suffering from damage to his cerebral cortex or central nervous system.

The *Babinski reflex* is another prominent infant action. It consists of the spreading of the toes when the sole of the foot is touched. Like the Moro reflex, it disappears when the infant is 4 to 6 months old; its persistence beyond 6 months can again signal a malfunction in the nervous system.

The infant may display more than 20 reflexes. Relatively few, however, are significant. We can dismiss the eye blinks and coughs. These reflexes do not develop any further. Others, such as sucking, grasping, and eye-focusing, while unsophisticated in the newborn, improve rapidly, and are important in his development. As we shall see in the chapter on mental and cognitive development, it was Jean Piaget who described the central role these developing reflexes play in the infant's early growth.

The Infant's Needs

Like any living organism, the human infant's survival depends on the satisfaction of a handful of basic needs. First he needs oxygen and a constant air temperature somewhere above 70 degrees. His requirement for sleep is at first as much as 18 or 20 hours a day, but declines until 1 year of age, when the infant sleeps about as long as he stays awake. His earliest need for nutrition is for liquids. Then, in a few weeks, he eats semisolid foods. He eliminates urine frequently during the first few weeks after birth, with the number of urinations slowly declining and the volume of urine in each gradually increasing. By 7 months, he may not wet himself for as long as two or three hours, and by 1 year he may stay dry for an even longer time.

The infant's elimination of solid waste, like urination, is involuntary because the nerves and muscles he needs to control bowel and bladder functions have not yet fully developed. In the first three or four weeks, the infant's bowel movements are frequent, but after one month they usually decline to three or four a day; by two months, to two a day, one as he wakes in the morning and another during or near a mealtime. By four months, the infant's system has usually established a set pattern between eating and bowel movements. In earlier times, when mothers used to pride themselves on not having wet or soiled babies, they usually managed this achievement by paying close attention to these regularities. We would say today that it was the mothers who were trained rather than the babies.

Toilet training, which usually is accomplished in the infant's second or third year, requires the child to control his reflexive bowel and bladder movements. The child must learn—through whatever inducements parents devise—to replace reflex with control.

The infant's needs for food, drink, and elimination are the bases for his earliest relationships,

Figure 5.1 Some of the significant reflexes of the newborn infant.

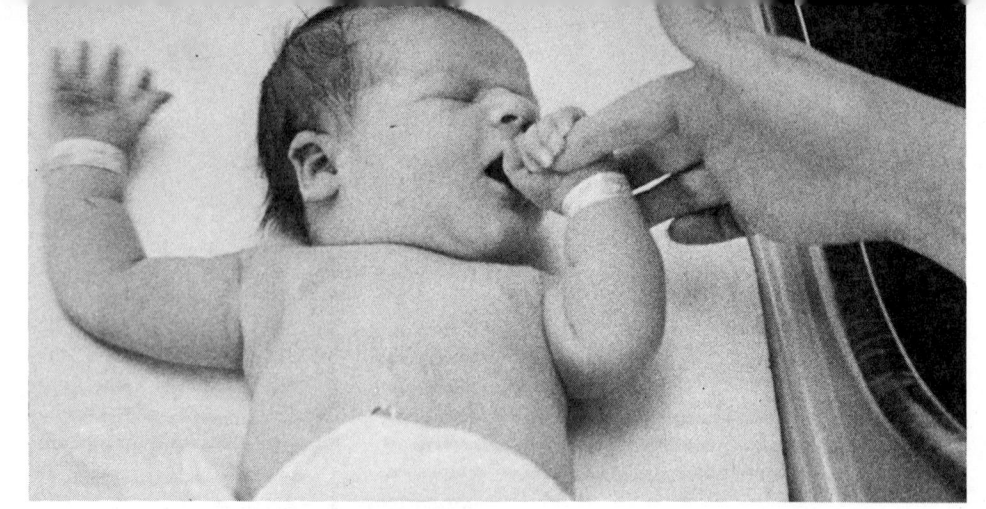

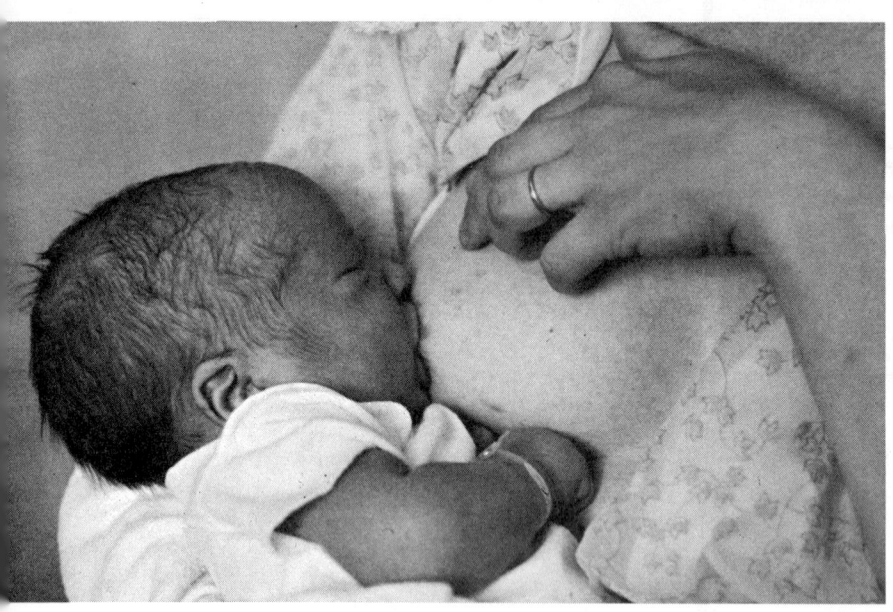

The rooting reflex. The infant turns his head to the side where his cheek has been touched. He grasps the finger and sucks it, thus combining the grasping and sucking reflexes. (Eve Arnold—Magnum)

The sucking reflex. Through the rooting reflex, the infant is put in a position to obtain nourishment by sucking breast or bottle. (Eve Arnold—Magnum)

The grasp reflex. When the infant's palm is pressed, his fingers will curl around the hand that touched him. (Pinney—Monkmeyer)

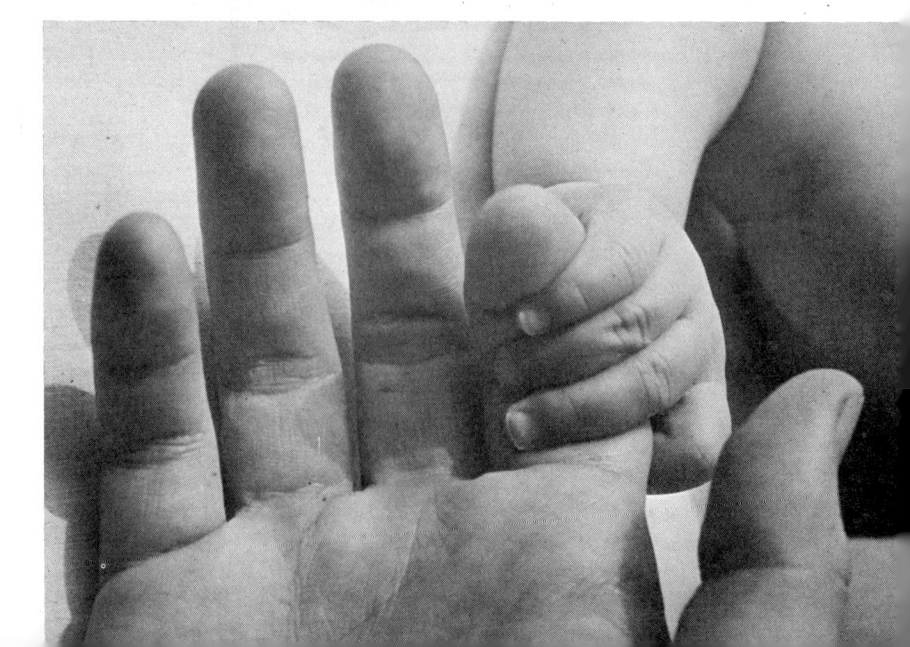

The Moro reflex. The infant flings his arms to either side and extends his fingers in response to being moved or surprised, or to having his head position changed. (Lew Merrim—Monkmeyer)

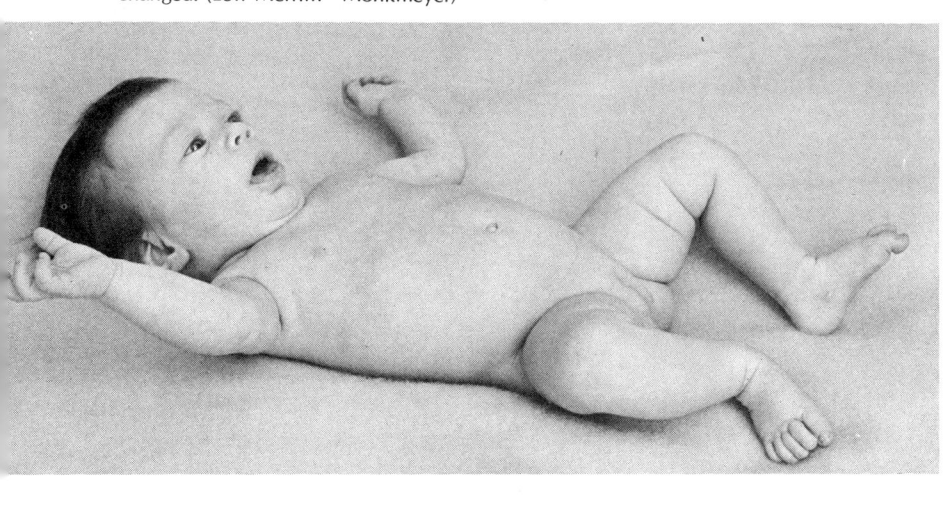

The withdrawal reflex. This infant's feet jerk back in response to a pinprick. (Nolan Patterson—Black Star)

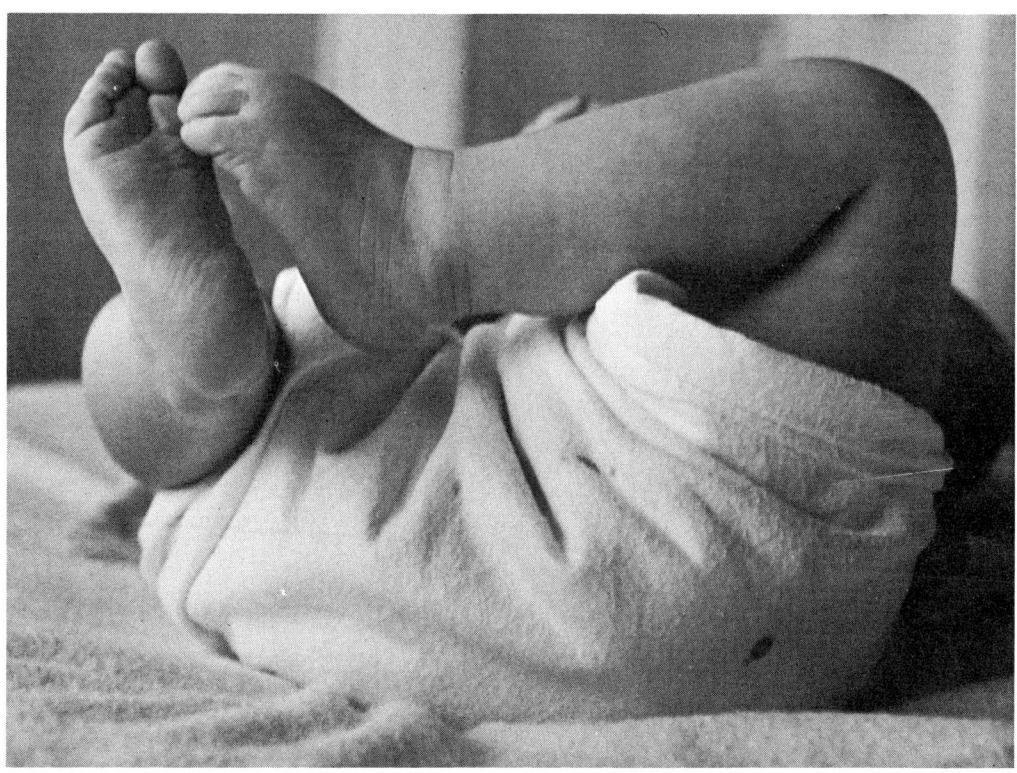

MOTOR DEVELOPMENT AND SENSORY EXPERIENCE

since to satisfy these three needs he must depend on others. In Chapter 7, we shall discuss these three needs as they affect the infant's social development.

Growth in Infancy

Norms and "Normal" Behavior

As the infant's physical growth and development are discussed, the phrases *average infant*, *normal behavior*, and *median age* will be used to indicate the child's age at his first step, or his other infant "firsts." These expressions are exactly what they say—averages, not absolutes. Many parents, misunderstanding the psychologist's use of the terms *norm* and *average*, become alarmed when they read or hear about a certain behavior and its established norm. A mother hears that the norm for standing with support is 12 months of age. Her son is 15 months old and has not yet pulled himself to his feet against a chair or an end table. Misconstruing what the norm means, the mother worries that her son is not developing properly. In the overwhelming majority of cases, her worry is unnecessary. The *norm* is not meant to be interpreted as an ideal. On the contrary, it is merely a statistical calculation referring to the middle two-thirds of all variations that are recorded.

Averages and norms are used because they are convenient summaries. An experimenter tests many infants to find how often the "average infant" turns his head toward a bright light. He finds two extremes—the infant who all but refuses to look at the light, and his opposite, the infant who whips his head about as if it were on a swivel. To summarize his findings, the experimenter uses an average head-turning frequency, derived by including all the infants. Thus he arrives at the "average infant" for that particular act of head-turning. No matter how often cited, that average infant remains a mythical child who exists only on the nether side of the experimenter's final "equal" sign. Real-life infants may considerably exceed or fall far behind the "average infant's" rating and still be completely normal, growing up into competent adults.

Physical Size

The infant's physical growth varies greatly. Babies' birth weights may vary by several pounds—both 5- and 10-pound babies are not uncommon. The same is true of their length. However, the average newborn male baby—who is a little bigger, overall, than the female—is about 20 inches long and weighs about 7½ pounds. Children will meet, exceed, or fall short of this statistical average, depending on their sex and on the genes their parents contribute. The quality of the mother's nutrition and her success at resisting infection during her pregnancy also will help determine the infant's length and weight at birth.

While the infant always seems to be changing rapidly, he grows most quickly in his first year. His length increases by about one-third. If he was born 21 inches long, for example, he would be about 28 inches long at 1 year. His weight nearly triples—the 7½-pound newborn becomes a 20-pound toddler. In addition to changes in length and weight, other great changes occur. The infant's body proportions and the structure of his skeleton, muscles, and nerves are radically altered during his first year of life.

Proportions

The infant's body proportions change quickly, especially from his sixth to twelfth month. The proportions change because his different parts are growing at different rates. At birth, for instance, the infant's legs are one-fifth the adult length and are short in comparison to the size of his head and the length of his arms. However, at about 8 weeks of age, leg growth begins to speed up, and by the end of the rapid development period culminating at about the infant's second birthday, his legs have assumed a body proportion very close to the adult's. On the other hand, his head and face grow less quickly during this period than the rest of his body, even though the size and shape of his skull do change a great deal. The head and face of the 3-month-old fetus, for example, is about one-third the length of its whole body. When the infant is born, the head and face unit has diminished to one-fourth of his full length. When he is 12, it is one-eighth; and when he is 25, his head and face are reduced to one-tenth of his total height.

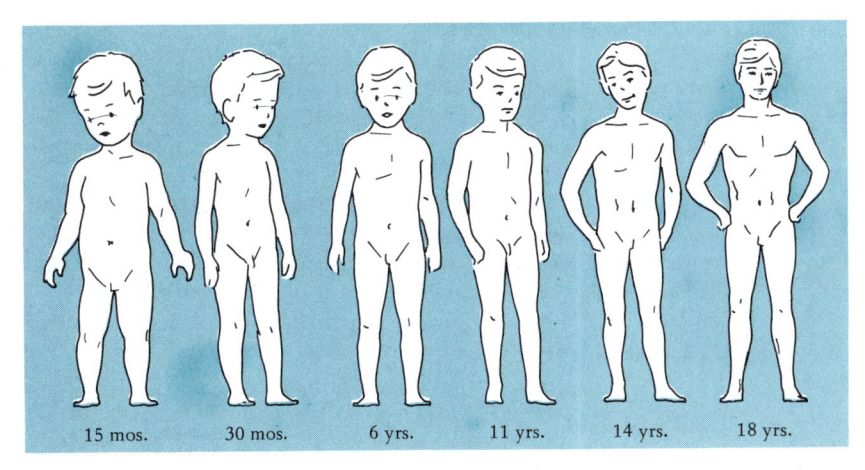

Figure 5.2 Changes in body proportions from 15 months to 18 years. (From N. Bayley. Individual patterns of development. *Child Develpm.*, 1956, *27*, 45–74.)

Skeletal System

The infant's changing body proportions are determined in large part by the growth of his bones. In the newborn, many parts of the skeleton are not actually bones but soft cartilage tissue. As minerals, drawn from the infant's food and drink, accumulate in this tissue, the tissue hardens, or ossifies, into bone. Ossification first starts when the infant is still in the womb, and some bones are still hardening when the "child" enters college. Because most of his bones are not extensively ossified, they bend rather than break—the salvation of many a fumble-fingered parent who turns away from the changing table only to hear his offspring crash, usually unhurt, to the floor. Because the infant's bones are lighter, softer, and somewhat rubbery, they also respond faster to muscular pull. These assets are balanced by the potential danger that unossified bones, if subjected to severe and extended stress, can become deformed as they harden. The once customary binding of baby girls' feet in Japan to produce exaggeratedly tiny feet in adulthood was successful precisely because the bones hardened in the approximate size and shape in which they were bound when soft.

The baby's bones ossify at different times and different speeds. However, the hardening of some bones is all but guaranteed by certain ages. By 1 year of age, for example, 3 of the 28 hand and wrist bones have already ossified. Other bones, such as those of the skull, take longer to harden. The six soft spots of the infant skull (called fontanelles) do not harden thoroughly until the child is about 2 years old. Still other bones take years more to ossify completely.

Ossification and skeletal growth, like weight and size, also vary markedly among individuals and groups. Sex is one important factor related to such variation. From birth, a girl's bones grow more quickly. Genes also strongly affect the timing and rate of skeletal development. For example, the bones of the broad-framed child ossify faster than those of the narrowly built child. While genes are prime determinants of bone hardening, sickness, malnutrition, and allergies also can affect ossification.

Muscles

The newborn infant has all the muscles he ever will have—a revelation that may distress those enthusiastic young fathers who show up in maternity wards waving baseball gloves for their newborn sons. They need not worry, however. While the number of muscle fibers will remain the same from birth, the fibers themselves will grow longer, wider, and thicker before they reach maturity, at which point they will weigh 40 times as much as they do in the newborn.

Some of the infant's muscles are voluntary, or striped, muscles, such as those in the arms, and some are involuntary, such as those in the stomach. During his first year, the infant does not have full control of his voluntary muscles. His arms, for example, flail in the Moro reflex, an act the infant does not will to happen. Also during this period, the voluntary muscles tire easily but recover from fatigue quickly as the infant first attempts to sit and walk. The total weight of the muscle tissue an infant possesses varies from one baby to the next. As a general rule, however, male infants have more muscle tissue than females, a sexually rooted difference that remains true at all stages of development (Garn 1957, 1958).

Teeth

While some babies do not show their first teeth until they are a year old, the average infant's teeth have begun to form months before he is even born. As early as 10 weeks after its conception, the fetus has the beginnings of baby teeth inside its gums. When the fetus is 5 months old, calcium has begun to accumulate. Nonetheless, the day of the first tooth varies widely among infants. Some, but only a very few, are born with a tooth, or with several. At the opposite extreme is the 1-year-old who is just cutting his first tooth. The average age for the first tooth—usually a lower front one—is 7 months. The coming of the first tooth has no relation to any other facets of the infant's physical development, such as height, weight, and the amount of muscle. A musclebound 1-year-old might be toothless as a hen, while a 15-pound weakling his age might flash an impressive, if gappy, grin. An infant's genetic makeup partially determines the sequence and arrival times of his teeth. Sex also helps establish when a tooth appears and how fast it grows. Generally, the female infant "teethes" before the male. Race, too, is a teething determinant. Oriental and black infants usually get their teeth earlier than Caucasians.

The Brain

Controlling the growth of the bones, muscles, and teeth is the brain, a mere three-quarter-pound mass in the newborn. Small as it may seem, the infant's brain is actually 10 percent of his weight—not at all small, relatively. The brain grows quickly, especially near birth. By the child's second birthday, his brain weighs almost two and one-half pounds. When he is 6, his brain will have reached nearly its adult size—four pounds for the adult male. It is slightly less for the female since the brain's mass is proportionate to the body's weight. Between birth and 6 years, the brain grows more rapidly than any other anatomical system. The infant brain develops so fast that by the time the child is 2, it is hard to distinguish—using brain tissue characteristics as the criterion—the 2-year-old's brain from an adult's.

Growth Variables

SEX. An infant's growth pattern is strongly determined by whether he is a male or female. Generally, girls grow faster than boys, and their skeletons mature sooner (Tanner, Whitehouse, and Healy 1962). In addition, a girl's skeletal development at age 2 is a more accurate indication of her later growth than is a boy's, because skeletal growth patterns in females are more stable than they are in boys (Acheson 1966). Furthermore, there is less variability of growth among girls than there is among boys (Garn and Rohmann 1960).

Besides growing faster and more predictably, female infants have less muscle tissue, as noted earlier, and more subcutaneous fat than males. This fat, which lies just under the skin, builds up in the fetus until birth, when it begins to disappear. Females have more of this "baby fat" at birth than males, and they lose it a little more slowly (Stolz and Stolz 1951).

FOOD AND GROWTH. Nutrition has a definite effect on growth rates. Undernourished infants, such as those born to poor families or born during a famine or war, are noticeably smaller and slower-growing (Dean 1951). Children of the upper social classes—who generally eat more nourishing food—are taller and heavier at age 3, or earlier, than their lower-class counterparts. The damage caused by early malnutrition can be permanent, as shown by a study of African children afflicted with *kwashiorkor*, a nutritional disease common among infants and older children whose diets are limited to protein-deficient grains or cereals. The study showed that while the afflicted infants gained weight and grew taller upon exposure to a sounder diet, they never did grow as tall or weigh as much as children well fed from birth (Dean 1960). In 1962, after further study, Dean put forward the additional suggestion that even when such undernourished children take adequate nourishment, their development may fall behind the average after 4 years of age (Dean 1962).

Visual Perception

Traditionally we think of ourselves as having five senses—vision, hearing, taste, smell, and touch—and perhaps a mysterious "sixth sense." We are underestimating ourselves. Science has shown that these are only a few of the many senses that every individual has. Even the infant has more than the customary five. Psychologists know that the newborn experiences sight, hearing, balance at rest, balance in motion, taste, smell, perception of heat, pain, and touch; and these senses may be only the beginning of a list that will grow as research techniques are further refined. While this discussion requires that the senses, each sense and its stimuli, be treated separately for the purposes of study, it is important at the same time to remember that, far from being separate units, the senses, and each sense and its stimuli, interact very closely. The stimulus has a great effect on the sense. An eye shut off from objects and light does not develop.

Vision is the sense most widely investigated by researchers. It has been found that the infant's eyes can quite sharply detect light, dark, and color. However, the nerves and muscles involved in vision are not working together smoothly in the newborn, though the basic nerves begin developing just three weeks after his conception.

The *pupillary reflex* is the most basic response of the eyes. Even premature babies display this reflex: a "closing" of the pupil when light is brightened, and dilation, or opening, when it is dimmed. This is the same principle a photographer uses as he adjusts his camera shutter to "shoot" in different lights. During the infant's first day or two, only a light or a dark room will make the infant's pupils contract or dilate, and even then the reflex may operate slowly. However, in a few weeks, changes from moderate light to darkness, and vice versa, will stimulate the pupillary reflex (Pratt 1934, 1954).

Infants of only 2 or 3 days will follow a flashlight's beam. This visual pursuit indicates that the muscles of the eyes are developed to the point where the infant can direct both his eyes at one moving light and track that stimulus—providing the light is strong enough. His eye movements will be jerky, however, shifting abruptly from one focal point to the next. While this behavior shows that *coordination*—the muscular direction of both eyes at one object—is present a few days after birth, it does not show whether the infant's vision has converged on the object.

Convergence is the focusing of both eyes to produce one image, as opposed to the simple muscular coordination of the eyeballs. Both coordination and convergence are indispensable to focusing the eyes and perceiving depth. Though the infant does not add the full power of convergence to coordination until he is about 2 months old, primitive kinds of coordination and convergence do begin operating within a few hours after birth (Ling 1942). The infant reaches the adult level of convergence, called binocular vision—that is, two-eyed vision—at the 2-month mark. He achieves binocular vision through a slow process of refining his erratic eye movements until his eyes converge smoothly and quickly.

While the newborn baby may "stare" intently at a red rubber elephant, he may be seeing something that looks more like a hippopotamus or an outsized tomcat. The infant's image is unclear. This blurring occurs because his ciliary muscles, which control the lenses of the eye, have not developed enough to produce the proper *accommodation*—the adjustment of his lenses' curvature to focus the light rays correctly on his retinas. By the time the infant is 3 to 4 months old, he will be able to see the elephant's every wrinkle. At 4 months he will also be shifting his focus well, seeing the clock on the wall as clearly as his mother's face when she feeds him (Haynes 1965).

Like a bright light, the color or black-white *contrast that a contour produces* catches and holds the infant's eye. Shown a black triangle, he will fasten his gaze on the "corners" of the triangle where the black cuts into the white background to create the strongest contrast (Salapatek and Kessen 1966). Since an infant usually gazes longer at objects with more contours, experimenters have used the length of his gaze to measure the sharpness of eyes. Robert Fantz did this with infants only a few weeks old. Nine inches from the infants' eyes, he held a gray patch and one made of one-eighth inch stripes, which, of course, gave the patch many contours. The infants spent considerably more time looking at the striped patch, indicating that their eyes were developed enough to detect—and continue examining—stripes that narrow at a viewing distance of nine inches. Later, when the infants were 12 weeks old, Fantz held up another gray patch and a striped patch, this time with mere pinstripes—one sixty-fourth of an inch wide. Still—and at a distance of 15 inches—the infants looked longer at the stripes, showing they could distinguish even such a finely striped patch (Fantz 1965).

These descriptions present a brief developmental picture of the infant's eyes in the first four months. During the first four weeks, the infant does not adjust the curvature of his lenses to view things at different distances from him. Instead, he locks his focus on objects roughly eight inches away. At 8 weeks he begins accommodating his eyes to sights far and near, and at 16 weeks he can accommodate as well as an adult. While the newborn does not accommodate at all, his eyes do react in other ways—they can track a moving light and respond to lights of varying brightness.

Attentional Preferences of the Infant

The infant's world is not the adult's well-ordered and familiar one. The difference between the two is rooted in the limited perceptions of the infant. Many stimuli surround the infant, but he sees only some of them. His daytime environment might be, for instance, a kitchen. As described by an adult, it might be a bright yellow room with a blue table and four orange chairs, a white sink, and a copper refrigerator and stove. That may not be what the child perceives. The infant's limited color perception, for example, may reduce the kitchen's visual content, watering the colors down to something more diffuse, without the distinctness each of these objects and colors has for adults. Equally important, the infant knows no relationships among things. He has none of the adult's knowledge of how the chairs relate to the table, the sink to the wall, the refrigerator to the stove. While he may detect objects, he is not as "at home" as his parents, or even his 4-year-old brother. It is important to realize that the child's world at this time is not our world. When we try to assess an infant's reaction to a smiling face, a whistled tune, or a red ball, we must ask: Is the infant perceiving the same thing I am presenting?

During his first 8 to 12 weeks, the infant is strongly attracted to objects with movement, contour lines, and sharp contrasts, such as the contrast of black and white. However, after his second or third month, these preferences no longer account for some of his eye actions.

COMPLEXITY THEORY. One proposed principle governing visual preferences is that infants like a fair amount of complexity in objects. It is true that they gaze longest at a moderately complicated object. Brennan, Ames, and Moore, taking up the complexity theory for testing, defined complexity by the *number of objects* and then by the *variety of objects*. They used three groups of infants—3 weeks, 8 weeks, and 14 weeks old—with 10 infants in each group. Taking number as the criterion of complexity, the experimenters presented the infants with patterns increasing in complexity in rough proportion to their age and supposed development. The 3-week-old infants received black-and-white checkerboards with 4 squares; the 8-week-olds, with 64 squares; and the 14-week-olds, with 576 squares. Next, taking variety as the criterion of complexity, the experimenters presented groups of infants with two circles, each containing nine objects, but the nine objects varied more in form in one circle than in the other. The more complex circle enclosed three stars, three squares, and three triangles, while the other enclosed nine triangles. In both experiments, the researchers, by recording the number and time of eye fixations, found that the simplest design appeals to the youngest child, the moderately complex to the older infants, and the most complex to the oldest (Brennan, Ames, and Moore 1966).

122 INFANCY

Clearly, these results point to a gradual change in the infant's interest in scanning patterns. Conclusive as it may seem at first glance, complexity itself has not been finally proven a determinant of infant interest. So far, no experiment has been able to eliminate the size and contour of the object itself—as opposed to the size and contour of its patterns—as possible influences on the maturing infant's tendency to choose more complex objects.

MEANING AND FAMILIARITY. In addition to contour, contrast, and movement, infants are attracted by the familiarity of objects. Year-old children sometimes will even prefer a familiar object over one with movement and contrast. A study by Haaf and Bell shows that even 4-month-old infants respond strongly to sights that have meaning for them or are familiar. The two experimenters in this case showed the children four face drawings. The first was similar to the human face, the second was missing an eye but had a rash of random, contour-contrast lines and dots covering the face, the third had no eyes or mouth, and the fourth had an oval enclosing a mass of squiggles with the same number of contour-contrast lines as the second face. The infants looked longest at the first face—which was most human—even though it did not have as many contour-contrasts or squiggles as the second and fourth faces. Of these two, the second face looked more human and the infants looked longer at it than at face four. The third face, lacking the mouth and both eyes, drew the least attention. These findings seem to indicate that the face's familiarity or meaning for the infant does do more to hold his eye than does the face's complexity (Haaf and Bell 1967).

Fantz and Nevis found that infants from 4 weeks to 6 months of age prefer an oval with correctly located "eye spots" to a plain oval or one with nonface patterns. However, until 5 months, the same infants were as likely to choose a photograph of a head as a painted model head. At the same time, they found that until infants were fully 6 months old, most did not consistently prefer an accurate drawing of a basic face over a face with its features strewn about (Fantz and Nevis 1967). These findings indicate that the child's emerging preference for faces is still at a quite diffuse level at this time.

Stimulus	Degree of Faceness	Amount of Detail	Percent Fixation Time
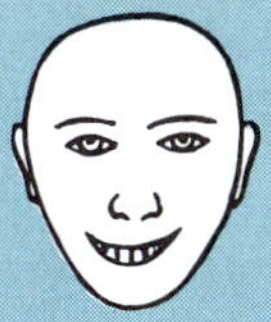	1	3	.33
	2	1	.28
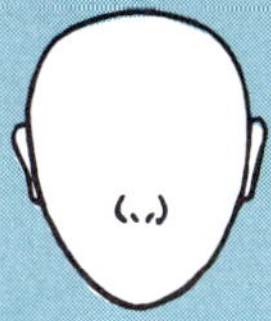	3	4	.19
	4	2	.20

Figure 5.3 Differences in fixation time for four different facial stimuli. (From R. A. Haaf and R. Q. Bell. A facial dimension in visual discrimination by human infants. *Child Develpm.*, © 1967 by The Society of Research in Child Development, Inc., *38*, 895. By permission.)

DISCREPANCY OF SCHEMA. After six months, and sometimes as early as four months, the infant recognizes things and people. Because psychologists are able to observe such recognition, they infer that the infant must be able to carry some internal representation in his mind of the people and things he recognizes. Otherwise, how could he remember them from one time to the next? This internal representation is referred to as a *schema* (the plural form is *schemata*). The term *schema* is usually preferred to *image* or *idea* because the other terms connote too many adultlike capacities. It is doubtful, for example, if the infant's remembrance is more than the sketchiest representation. Perhaps it is more like a caricature or a political cartoon than a photograph. The schema accents certain salient features of the object much as a cartoonist draws a banana nose, wildly bulging eyes, or elephant ears if the congressman or president he is depicting has even a hint of such features. The infant's schema of the human face may be an oval shape with two eyes at the same level.

Differences between an infant's schema and the object he is viewing can rivet his attention. The face missing an eye is a fascinating sight, possibly because it retains much of its "faceness" while it lacks one of the face's basic components. The object that differs only moderately from an infant's schema attracts him more strongly than one that is highly different from his schema. McCall and Kagan illustrated the attractive power of such a distorted or discrepant object. They showed one group of 4-month-old infants black-and-white shapes, and another group face drawings and two photographs. One drawing and one photograph had scrambled features. While the black-and-white shapes had much more contrast than either the face drawings or photographs, the infants looked longer at the distorted faces. It seems clear, then, that *objects moderately different from an infant's schemata will often draw and hold his gaze longest* (McCall and Kagan 1967). The game of "funny faces" that parents play with their children at about 10 months seems to be based on the child's capacities to recognize discrepancy but, at the same time, to recognize that what he is seeing is still the familiar face. The parent screws up his face into a contorted appearance—the child looks surprised, and then laughs gleefully. Here the discrepancy is both observed and, in a sense, discounted.

ASSOCIATIONS. The quality of associations an infant has learned for an object is another determinant of how long he will look at that object. Generally, the infant's associations do not become rich enough to affect his attention span until he is over a year old. At this age, a child presented with a discrepant face behaves differently from the younger infant. Besides having a cluster of face associations, he also knows some words. The sight of a discrepant face—a one-eyed man, for example—may provoke a host of partly formulated apprehensions or questions in his mind. Where did his eye go? Did it fall out? Is that why he does not smile? As he tries to explain the facial distortion in terms of the things he knows about faces, he is likely to keep his eyes fixed on the discrepant face.

THE HYPOTHESIS. Kagan and his associates at Harvard University have suggested that when the year-old child encounters such discrepancies, he tries to mentally transform the discrepant object or event into one that is more familiar to him (Kagan 1972). Kagan used the term *hypothesis* to refer to the mental structure the child uses in trying to make such a transformation.

The emergence of the ability to generate hypotheses explains why an infant is progressively less interested in a masklike representation of the human face from 2 to 9 months, and then suddenly becomes more interested in the same mask between 9 and 36 months. In the earlier months the infant's schema for the face is becoming more mature. This makes the realistic mask appear less and less discrepant, and so his attention drops. At about a year, however, when interest in the mask should continue to drop, the infant becomes more interested; Kagan suggested that his interest is held longer because he now is trying to form hypotheses about the mask in relation to his schema of the human face.

One of the ways in which this theory has been tested was to record the eye fixations and changes in heart rates of $11\frac{1}{2}$-month-old infants as they watched a toy car roll down a slope and knock over another toy, an event which for them was discrepant. After a few trials, some infants began to look ahead toward the toy that soon would be knocked over. In 73 percent of the infants whose eye fixations anticipated the car's motion, there was an increase in heart rate. Since an accelerated heart rate in infants probably means an increase in mental activity, just as it does in older children, Kagan concluded that the infants in these and similar tests may be forming hypotheses (Kagan 1972).

PART-WHOLE PERCEPTIONS. Researchers in perception also are interested in the question of whether the infant sees the whole object or only a part of it. Salapatek showed newborn babies shapes—black-and-white, outlined, and solid geometric shapes—of three sizes. He also showed them a flat, blank surface. The infants scanned the flat, blank surface a great deal, especially horizontally. When the experimenter introduced any of the shapes, the infants cut back quite a bit on the scope of their scanning. On smaller shapes, they scanned a smaller area than on larger shapes. Many infants confined their looking to a very small part of a shape, even when the shape itself was the smallest size shown them. This study and others indicate that newborn babies limit themselves to a small portion of anything they view (Salapatek and Kessen 1966).

All that we now know about the kinds of objects infants gaze at, when, and for how long—all this knowledge does not provide a complete picture of the infant's visual perception, but it does outline large areas in this rather strange landscape. We know more today than Piaget did when he published his first work almost 50 years ago. Yet we have much more to discover. We know that contour-contrast and movement are the first two qualities that attract an infant's eye. We know that at 2 or 3 months, the infant has developed visual schemata of things to the point where an object differing moderately from his schema will catch and hold his attention. Later in infancy he can digest information about the world and begin to hypothesize about oddities he sees. The length of time he spends looking at something is a fair guide to how actively he is trying to explain that thing to himself. The infant has begun to think about what he sees.

Depth Perception

Vital as the perception of depth is in our three-dimensional world, the infant is born without it and does not develop this aspect of vision until he is between 8 and 12 weeks old. At that age, the infant confronted with a flat, cardboard-mounted likeness of a human head, and then with a three-dimensional model of a head, will look more at the three-dimensional model (Fantz 1965). Infants younger than 10 weeks will look for the same length of time at a two-dimensional black circle as they will at a black ball. However, after 10 weeks, as the infant notices depth, he begins looking longer at the black sphere. Most infants under 10 weeks will react the same way when presented with a photograph of a person and the person's face, first looking equally at both picture and person, and then, after 10 to 12 weeks of age, smiling more and making more sounds to the real three-dimensional face than to the flat print.

THE VISUAL CLIFF. As an experimental device, the "visual cliff" dramatically displays the infant's depth perception in his first year. Experimenters placed an infant on a crawlway that was flanked by two other crawlways covered by heavy glass plates. One plate covered the crawlway's checkered pattern. The other plate covered a patterned extension of the crawlway that was several feet below the glass, creating a sensation of depth.

Infants 6 months old quickly recognized what they saw as a sheer drop and would not move off the crawlway on the "visual cliff" side, even though they could feel the heavy glass bridging the gap. They even refused to venture out when their mothers stood across the gap, calling and gesturing to them (Gibson and Walk 1960). Puzzled, perhaps, by this apparently unmotherly request, they nonetheless trusted their eyes and clung to the center crawlway.

When the experimenters replaced the checkered floor of the lowered crawlway with a gray pattern—which made it harder for the infants to detect depth—many of the infants lost their fear and crossed over to their mothers on the glass. They did the same thing when the experimenters made the cliff much less threatening by raising the checkered floor up to within inches of the glass (Walk 1966). These experiments have provided clear evidence that the infant does perceive depth as early as at 10 weeks of age, and will, at 6 months, trust his depth-perception judgments and act in accord with them against considerable inducements to go against them.

Since perception of depth does not appear for at least two months after birth, some psychologists maintain that depth perception is learned. According to this theory, the infant slowly becomes accustomed to depth by seeing objects at a distance. This hypothesis gained some support from the investigations of Walk, who found that babies who begin to crawl late in their infancy—

Figure 5.4 The "visual cliff" used to test depth perception in infants. (From E. J. Gibson and R. R. Walk. *Scientific Amer.*, April, 1961, *202*, 65. Photographer: William Vandivert. By permission.)

and thus presumably have little experience with objects around them—are more willing to crawl off the visual cliff than early walkers who are experienced with objects and know a bad spill when they see one (Walk 1966). While this seems to confirm that infants learn depth perception, other evidence indicates that an infant is equipped to perceive depth at birth. For instance, experimenters working with chickens and goats found that these animals did perceive depth at birth and would not step off the visual cliff. Since the infant locks his focus at eight inches and does not adjust his eyes to other distances until he is 12 to 16 weeks old, he may have the capacity for depth perception at birth, but, in practice, seldom sees any depth of field until the muscular coordination of his eyes becomes developed enough for him to see objects at distances other than eight inches. Just as he eventually develops his leg muscles enough to walk, he must develop his eyes to see depth of field.

When the individual components of the infant's sense of sight are reassembled after this separate examination of each one, it can be seen that together they provide him with quite a full picture of the world he has entered. He sees movement and images sharply, distinguishes colors, perceives depth at about 3 months, and is able to put together schemata for objects when he is barely over 80 days old. While he has not acquired anywhere near an adult's wealth of object associations, the infant at his first birthday may well be seeing the world in basically the same way as his parents.

Other Sensory and Perceptual Development

Auditory Perception

PITCH, DURATION, RHYTHM. We know much less about what the infant hears than about what he sees. And since the bulk of the existing research, which is not extensive, has focused on the newborn baby, we know little about the huge span from 2 weeks to 12 months of age. We do know that the newborn baby can hear and that he notices a sound's frequency and the direction it comes from. When an infant first hears a sound, he will stop what he is doing. Then he may kick his legs, breathe hard, or flex his abdomen. After many repetitions of the sound, he will become accustomed to it and stop reacting. A new tone, however, will again draw a response. A study by Leventhal and Lipsitt showed how 2- and 3-day-old babies demonstrate this cycle of behavior. The experimenters first adapted the infants to hearing a tone with a frequency of 200 cycles per second—about the pitch but not the loudness of a foghorn. When they increased the frequency to 1,000 cycles per second—the pitch of a clarinet—the infants responded immediately. They also responded when the "foghorn" was sounded in their right ears, not because it was a new sound, but because it came from a new direction (Leventhal and Lipsitt 1964).

Keen, Chase, and Graham tested infants under 13 days old to see if they could distinguish between brief and longer sounds. The experimenters sounded two tones of the same pitch, one lasting 2 seconds and the other 10 seconds. To measure the effect of each tone, they monitored the rate of the infant's heartbeat. The 10-second tone prompted a much greater increase in the heart rate than the 2-second tone—until repeated soundings made the infants indifferent to both. However, the initial increase in heart rate for the 10-second tone showed clearly that even infants 2 days old can tell the difference between long and short sounds (Keen, Chase, and Graham 1965).

Newborn infants also recognize and are affected by rhythm and pitch. Rhythmic sound, such as a heartbeat, will soothe an uneasy infant more effectively than an irregular sound, such as a radiator banging or a dog barking. The infant makes even finer distinctions between pitches. When the heartbeat, a low-frequency sound, is compared to a rhythmic click, which usually has a higher frequency, the heartbeat remains the better pacifier, indicating that the infant responds to pitch with considerable sensitivity. Some researchers have said that the heartbeat soothes an infant because it "reminds" him of his mother's heartbeat as he heard it in the womb. This is not as implausible as some critics have maintained. On the contrary, experiments have shown that newly hatched chicks that heard a beeping sound of 200 cycles per second for some time before hatching picked out that sound when presented with both it and a 2,000-cycle tone. In addition, chicks that were exposed to a 200-cycle tone before hatching trailed after a toy chick beeping at 200 cycles for a longer time than they followed a toy chick making a noise they had never been exposed to (Grier, Counter, and Shearer 1967).

While these studies give evidence that the human infant does learn its response to the heartbeat, other studies have not corroborated the finding that infants are quieted more readily by a heartbeat than by any other rhythmic, low-frequency sounds (Brackbill et al. 1966). Whether the response is learned or inherent, the earlier experiment and centuries of human experiences tell us that infants are effectively soothed by such slow, rhythmic chants as "Sleep now, sleep now, sleep now."

FAMILIARITY. While the newborn recognizes a sound's frequency, length, rhythm, and point of origin, the infant of 6 months or a full year also recognizes the familiar sound. Experimenters in one study read four sentences with different inflections and meanings to 8-month-old boys. Two sentences read with high and low inflections were deliberately nonsensical. The other two, which made sense and used familiar words such as daddy, baby, and smile, also were read with high and low inflections. Each infant heard each sentence three times in no particular order. Of all four, the one combining a high inflection with familiar words evoked the most babbling, even though it was read by a strange male voice (Kagan 1968).

As early as at 8 months, the infant's auditory schema of familiar sounds apparently affects his responses to other sounds resembling these. Interestingly, the infant's "understanding" of certain spoken words comes well before he himself can pronounce any words at all.

Perception of Changes in Position

As anyone who has ever held a baby knows, infants are very sensitive to how they lie, sit, or are carried. If held awkwardly or insecurely, they will struggle to adjust to a comfortable position. A baby laid on his stomach or rolled about—as in a fast diaper change—may move his head or roll his eyes from side to side. Even at birth, infants held up with their feet on a table will take steps.

These reflexes, the precursors of acts used in balancing and walking, show that even the youngest infant responds when his muscles and the "balance" mechanisms in his inner ear send out signals calling for certain changes in his position.

Perception of Taste

At birth, infants have no taste sense. They cannot distinguish between such different liquids as sugar water and fruit juice. However, the sense develops quickly. Within 2 weeks, the infant begins to pucker his lips and suck if a sweet food like sugar is put in his mouth; a bitter liquid like quinine or fruit juice, made sharp by its citric acid, evokes a shake of the head and a fierce grimace (Pratt, Nelson, and Sun 1930). In another indicative experiment, the researcher found that newborn babies will suck at the taste of milk, acidic milk, glucose, and sterile water, but they will slow down or stop sucking if they taste a salt solution. He also noted, as we would expect, that the baby who is fairly well fed distinguishes more carefully between foods than the ravenous infant (Jensen 1932).

Perception of Smell

While more research is still needed about the ability of the nose to detect odors—*olfactory perception*—some valuable information is available. It is known, first of all, that newborn infants do have a sense of smell. Though faint odors draw no response from the newborn, except perhaps to make him more active generally in his crib (Disher 1934), a sharp or offensive odor, such as ammonia or acetic acid (vinegar), will cause him to promptly turn his head away. He also distinguishes among smells. Engen and Lipsitt presented infants 10 times with a combination of two odors and found that at each scenting of the two mixed odors, the infants' breathing change—the guide to their responses—diminished somewhat as they grew used to the combined smell. Yet, when the infants were given only one of the two odors—a distinct change from the mixture—most of them drastically changed their breathing, showing they had smelled the difference between the mixed and single odors (Engen and Lipsitt 1965).

Perception of Heat and Pain

While infants differ quite widely in their sensitivity to heat and cold, they all respond to these stimuli. They feel temperature changes both externally, as when a warm or cold object touches their legs (Crudden 1937; Pratt, Nelson, and Sun 1930), or internally, as when a prepared formula is either too warm or too cold (Jensen 1932). Generally, the infant moves about more when he is cold than when he is warm.

The infant's perception of pain is a sensitivity that develops extensively in the first four or five days of life. A newborn infant might absorb as many as six pinpricks in the sole of his foot before pulling back his leg, but an infant only 8 days old will often jerk back his leg after the first touch of the pin (Sherman and Sherman 1925; Sherman, Sherman, and Flory 1936). The sex of an infant also seems to influence his sensitivity to pain, with females reacting more quickly and sharply to pain than males. Lipsitt and Levy tested newborn infants by applying a very mild electrical shock to a toe. They found that the female wriggled the shocked toe with a vigor that only a stronger shock could draw from an infant boy the same age (Lipsitt and Levy 1959). Further research may reveal whether such differences in pain perception are clearly distinguishable among individuals, regardless of sex, in the first days of life, and whether these inborn differences persist throughout a lifetime.

Motor Development

The young child's neuromuscular development is depicted quite clearly in the stages of his motor development in infancy. His progress, from sitting up to crawling on his hands and knees, to standing, to walking, is an outward reflection of the growth and coordination that are occurring in his nerves and muscles. The infant is usually able to perform these physical acts before his second birthday. By then, he has developed his behavior through his increased mobility. At the same time, his central nervous system has grown more complex and his muscles and bones have become larger and stronger. In this section we shall look closely at the development of these motor activities, as well as at the infant's growth in reaching for and grasping objects.

Sitting Up

While the newborn infant cannot perform the seemingly simple feat of sitting up, he develops the ability early—at 3 or 4 months—and sits up briefly with some help (Bayley 1935; Dennis 1941; Gesell and Amatruda 1941; Shirley 1933). By the time he is 7 or 8 months old, he can do it alone. Then he improves more rapidly, usually working up to "sits" of 10 minutes or more by 9 months of age (Gesell and Amatruda 1941).

Crawling

One experimenter, by watching films of 20 infants who had begun to creep on all fours, identified 14 stages that creeping and crawling infants pass through. Most infants, it seems, move through all these developmental levels, but at widely varying ages. In the first stage of crawling,

Table 5.1 Progress Indicators in the Development of Locomotion*

Indicator and Phase	Age Expected (Weeks)
I. Rollover from supine to prone	
A. While on back, raises head as if trying to roll over	8
B. First success in rolling over	21
C. Rollover not easy, *repeats* it over and over	24
D. Rollover easy, automatic, apparently without conscious direction in order to accomplish further purpose (to reach a toy, etc.)	25
II. Independent sit-up	
A. Pushes self up from stomach, apparently trying to sit up	11
B. First success in pushing self from stomach to sitting position	34
C. Practices feat over and over—not easily accomplished	35
D. Act of sitting up well organized and easily accomplished with attention apparently on some further purpose (as using hands to reach for object)	37
III. Independent walk	
A. Pulls self to stand, tries to take independent steps	36
B. First success with few independent steps	51
C. Persistently practices walking alone	54
D. Walks in grownup fashion, apparently without conscious direction, *with purpose* of going somewhere or doing something	60

*Adapted from research on locomotor development at the Merrill-Palmer School conducted by Leland H. Stott with the assistance of Marian K. Lampard, Research Assistant. (To be reported.)

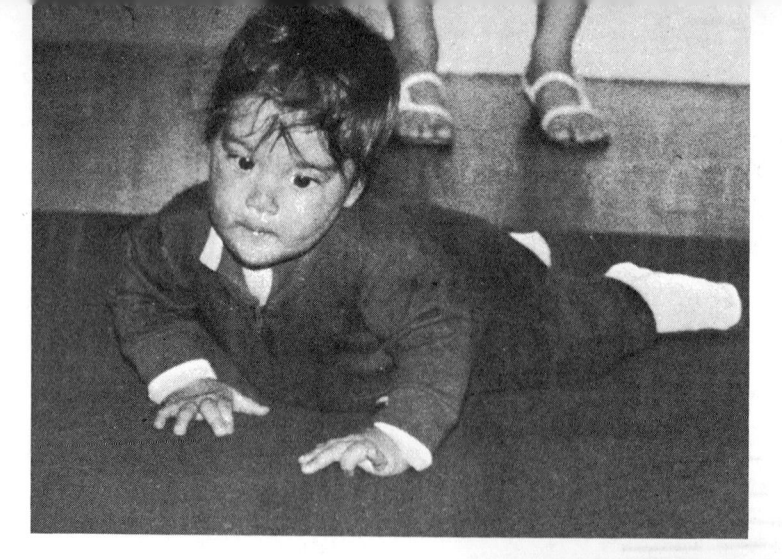

Figure 5.5 This infant gets into a crawling position, raising himself from his stomach to his hands and knees. (Betty Shapiro)

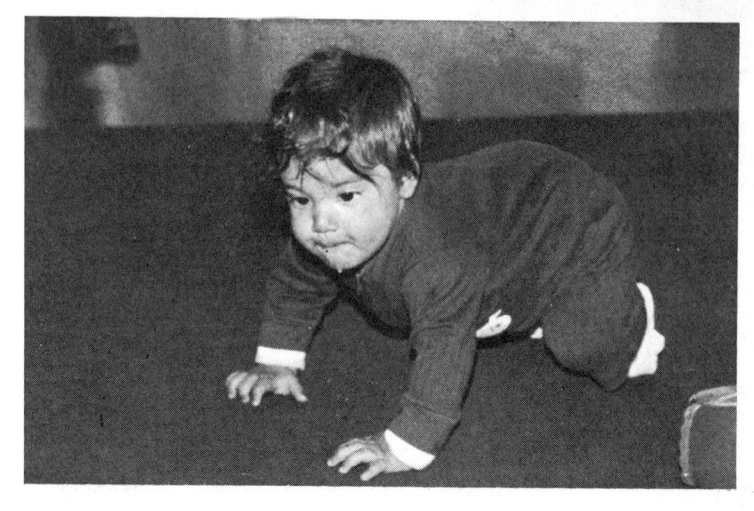

which occurs at about 28 weeks, the infant lies on his stomach and crooks one knee, froglike, and then the other knee. At 34 weeks, he begins a prone crawl. He moves in this slow, dragging crawl simply because his arm, leg, and trunk muscles are not strong or coordinated enough to hold his weight steady above the floor. At about 40 weeks, the infant's hands and knees become sufficiently strong for him to raise himself on them and creep along faster. The final stage in the crawling development occurs at an average age of 49 weeks when the infant arches his back slightly and begins to creep on his hands and feet (Ames 1937).

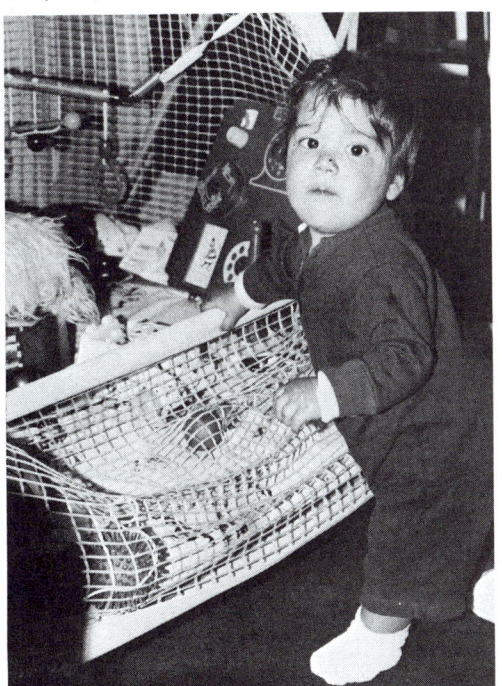

Walking

The norms for each "step" in the walking process also have been established. By 1 year, the average infant can haul himself to his feet and walk, holding on to sofas, coffee tables, and chairs. Two months later, he can stand by himself, and in his fifteenth month, he walks, carefully and none too gracefully, but alone and without props. The adult viewer watching children walk unsteadily at this age is sometimes reminded of Frankenstein movies in which the monster moves about with similar unsteadiness. Many children walk sooner—some as early as 10 months—than this nonexistent "average" child, the offspring of a mathematically computed norm. On the other hand, some children are almost 2 years old before they first sally forth alone. It is noteworthy that just as no evidence has emerged to link the walking age—or general motor development—to infant intelligence, so no proof has been produced to support the common assumption that large, heavy babies crawl, sit, stand, or walk more slowly than trimmer infants (Peatman and Higgons 1942). These locomotive skills also do not seem to be related to the two variables of sex and social background. A study of infant walking made a few years ago in Paris, London, Brussels, Stockholm, and Zurich showed that neither the infant's sex nor his family's social standing made any difference in these motor skills. The daughters of carpenters began walking at roughly the same time as the sons of socialites (Heinecke 1956).

While neither sex nor social standing made a

Figure 5.6 The final stage of crawling is often on hands and feet. (John Rees—Black Star)

Figure 5.7 This infant supports himself in a standing position by holding on to his playpen. (Betty Shapiro)

MOTOR DEVELOPMENT AND SENSORY EXPERIENCE   **131**

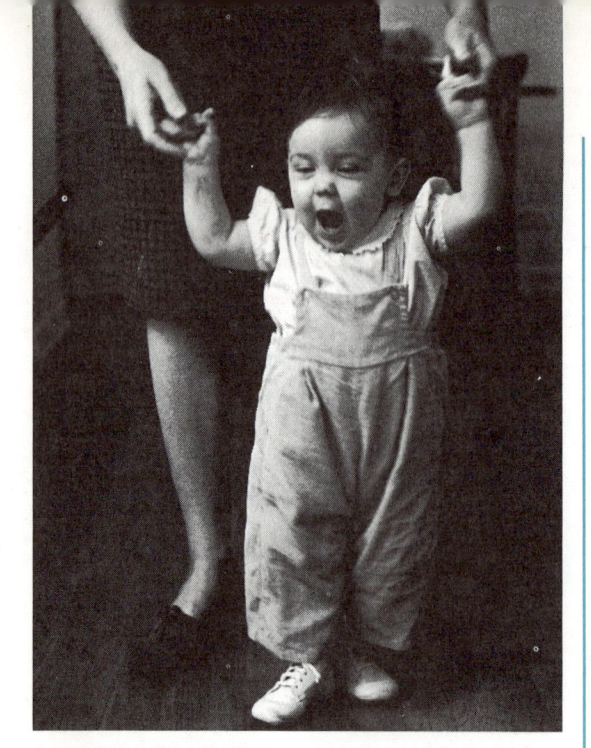

Figure 5.8 This infant takes some first steps, holding on for support. (Charles Harbutt—Magnum)

difference in how soon the child walked, geography did. In the above study, Swedish infants walked earlier than any; Parisians brought up the rear. Various theories have attributed these differences to such factors as racial and genetic determinants, nutrition, and child-rearing practices. While child-rearing practices do have some effect, the level of maturation is usually a much more significant factor in such physical achievements as walking. All the encouragement and practice in the world will not make a child's physically unready body perform an act. Trying to force performance too early is akin to tossing a 1-year-old into a swimming pool and expecting him to swim—and sometimes it is almost that dangerous. This is not to say that practice cannot improve performance. Practice can perfect performance, but only after the child has shown he can perform the basic action himself, however clumsily at first. The adult usually is not needed in the learning of motor movements. They develop without his coaching or help. Only in extreme cases, when the infant has been confined somehow physically—in a body cast or brace, perhaps, or reared in a severely deprived environment—is muscular and neural development so slowed down through lack of activity that walking comes late.

While most of the older studies in this field have emphasized the importance of maturation, it needs to be stressed that such an idea of maturation usually must take for granted an environment in which the child has some "normal" degree of stimulation and opportunity. We may contrast, for example, Wayne Dennis's early work, in which he emphasized maturation, with his more recent work, in which he has been able to demonstrate the great importance of a "normal" environment in allowing maturation to exercise its influence. In the older, not very well controlled study, Dennis left female twins on their backs from birth to 9 months, thus preventing them from practicing sitting and standing. This did not inhibit them from other actions, such as putting their hands to their mouths, laughing, or grasping their blankets. These acts, though given no encouragement, emerged nonetheless as they would in children in normal environments. The twins' sitting and standing, however, were a different story. Yet even here their performance suffered only slightly—in sitting more than standing. Encouraged at 37 weeks to try sitting alone, they could not do it; but several weeks later they could. Again, at 52 weeks, when given their first chance to stand with help, the twins could not perform, though most infants can at only 40 weeks. Still, in just three days, both twins stood for over two minutes with some assistance. One twin even performed normally in crawling, standing, walking hand-in-hand with an adult, and walking alone (Dennis 1941). As this study showed, some acts require no experience to emerge fully. Others are retarded slightly if the infant gets no practice. Thus, this study seemed to indicate that although motor activity requires some practice, maturation usually plays the major role in motor development.

CONFINED CHILDREN. In another study, Dennis worked with children 1 to 3 years old confined in institutions. At two of the three institutions, children were not given opportunities to sit up or even play lying on their stomachs. The infants in

132 INFANCY

the institution that allowed these infant amenities were measurably less retarded in their walking than the others. Dennis concluded that his findings opposed successfully the belief that motor development is reflected in a series of behaviors heavily dependent on maturation. Dennis contended that his data showed that besides affecting the age at which a certain motor behavior appears, practice and experience influence the form of the behavior itself (Dennis 1960).

Dennis subsequently performed two other studies in a home for children in the Middle East. The first study, conducted with Najarian, used subjects at an understaffed and poorly supported home for infants in Beirut. The infants were confined primarily to their beds, hurriedly fed, dressed, and changed, and usually not talked to. The infants were rarely sat up, sometimes not even when they began eating solid foods. Dennis and Najarian gave them a standardized infant performance test, including such manual skills as picking up a spoon or cubes. They then compared their scores with those of a group of home-reared Lebanese infants and an American group of comparable age. The institutionalized children were retarded in their motor development—such as the ability to sit up—from 2 to 12 months. They also were retarded in the test's manual skills. Dennis and Najarian concluded that retardation in these cases was caused by a lack of learning opportunities (Dennis and Najarian 1957).

After this work was published, some commentators suggested that emotional disturbances, and not a lack of experience in the institution, had caused the retardation. So, eight years after Dennis and Najarian had published their findings, Dennis and another researcher, Sayegh, returned to Beirut to reconfirm Dennis's experience-based hypothesis. Upon arriving at the institution they tested all the babies present. A month later, they tested them again. For 15 days between tests, one group of infants was taken out for an hour a day to a room where they were sat up and where they could play with and handle attractive objects. The second test showed that this group had improved greatly. The other infants also improved, but very slightly in statistical terms, and exclusively as a result of uncontrolled variable factors. In any case, their improvement was dramatically inferior to that of the infants in the experimental group (Dennis and Sayegh 1965).

The results of Dennis's experiments add up to a view of the child's development in which maturation and experience work together in producing behavioral outcomes. It is true that maturation initiates the sequences of major motor behaviors, but maturation cannot exercise this influence if the child does not have a normal degree of stimulation or experience so that he may practice his skills.

Manual Manipulation

REACHING AND GRASPING. An infant's ability to handle or manipulate objects with his hands, like his ability to crawl or walk, develops through set stages. Halverson, using films of infants—this time reaching out for and grasping objects—demonstrated that infants under 5 months did not

Figure 5.9 At an early stage of visual motor reaching, the infant sights his target but makes no attempt to reach for it. (Lew Merrim—Monkmeyer)

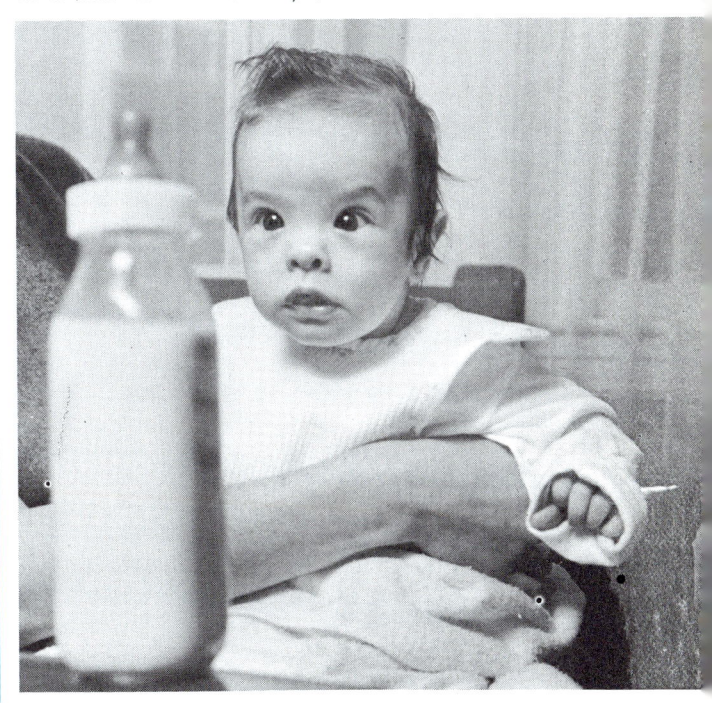

MOTOR DEVELOPMENT AND SENSORY EXPERIENCE   **133**

reach out for the blocks although they did watch them closely. Some 5-month-old infants reached out, but slowly and imprecisely, using their shoulders and elbows rather than their forearms and hands. As the infant matured, he used his arm, wrist, and hand more. By 15 months, his arm moved out and grasped accurately (Halverson 1931; Halverson 1936).

An important step in this reaching process is *visual-motor reaching*, which involves the coordination of eyes and hands. Piaget has demonstrated the role that this coordination plays in the development of intelligence. A 4-week-old infant with a studded rubber ball set before him stares at it, but never tries to take it in his hand. Six weeks later, he swings at it, missing it by a country mile. At 4 months, he lifts his hand near the ball and then glances back and forth between ball and hand. He slowly closes the gap between the two and may even touch the ball. Perhaps a month later, he will reach out and pluck up the object. At this point he has coordinated the measurements of his eye with the movements of his arm and hand. A more typical response between 4 and 6 months, however, is to bring together both hands onto the object in a lunging manner.

The growth of the grasping skill advances through several stages. The first is the loss, at about 16 weeks, of the early grasp reflex. At this stage, which lasts for three to four weeks, the infant does not grip anything firmly; he brushes objects ineptly and fumbles about, often without even opening his hand. Then, the infant begins to touch things again and awkwardly press them in his palm. At 7 months, he still closes his hand mainly by flexing his palm. But at 9 months, the forefinger begins to curl in and close down on the object. The thumb and forefinger begin to work together, and the other three fingers fall into place around the object. When all of these stages are fully developed, usually at about 15 months, the infant grasps a block as well as his mother or father would (Halverson 1931).

EXTRA STIMULATION. Although reaching and grasping develop in stages based on maturation, they also can be accelerated. The child who is exposed to attractive mobiles or has soft toy animals in his crib can often attain the 5- to 5½-month stage of reaching a full month early. This is a major acceleration when the time gained is considered as a percentage of the infant's lifetime to date (White and Held 1966). Of course, a child must be at the right maturational stage to benefit from any stimulatory help.

Interesting experiments on such sensory stimulation by Burton White seemed to show that stimulation must be graded to the child's capacity at the moment in order for it to be effective. In some of his work, however, infants who at first were irritated by overstimulating mobiles hanging above their cribs, designs on their sheets and crib bumpers, and toys attached to the sides of their crib later showed acceleration of development; they only required a short period to become accustomed to these new objects (White 1967).

This same study also unexpectedly revealed an acceleration in one area of development for the

Figure 5.10 Visual motor reaching. The infant looks at the object as he reaches for it and succeeds in grasping it. (Lew Merrim—Monkmeyer)

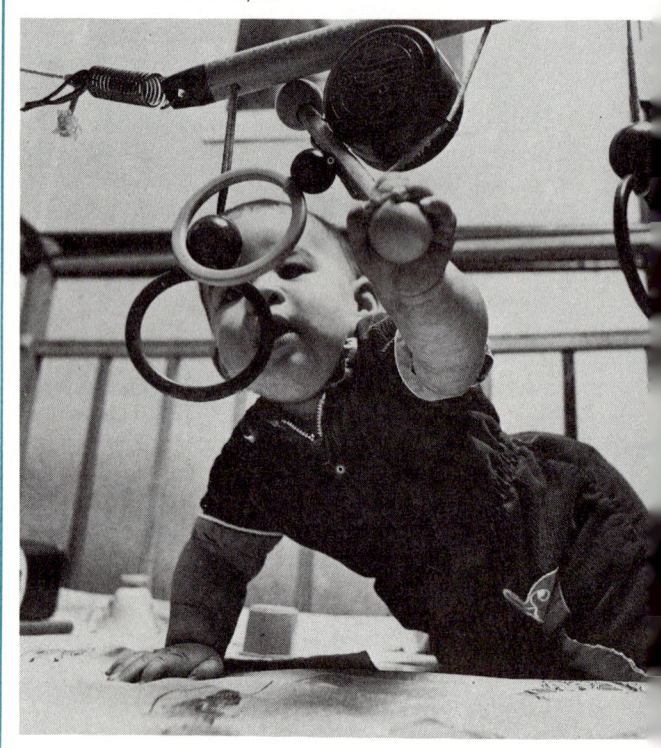

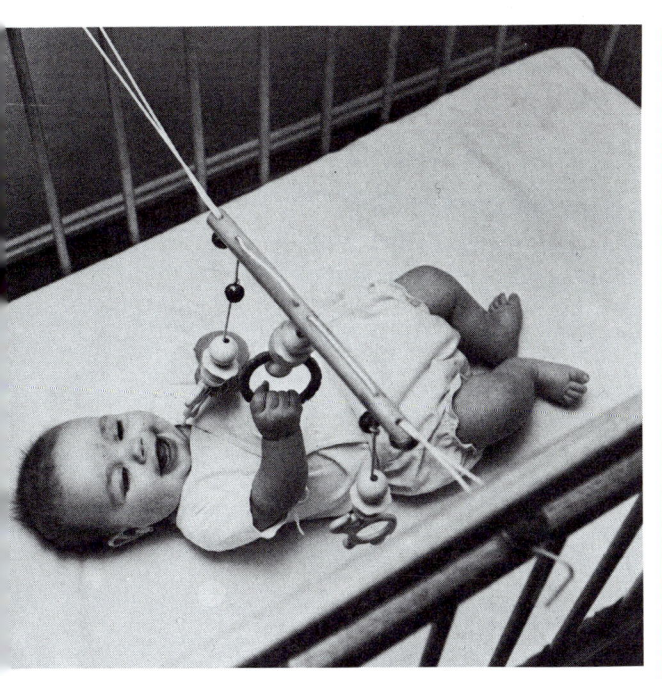

Figure 5.11 A child's development may be accelerated by stimulation: attractive mobiles may induce earlier reaching. (Lew Merrim—Monkmeyer)

control group—the infants who did not receive extra stimulation. The control infants, because they had virtually nothing else to look at, began to notice and play with their hands about a month sooner than average infants do, and about six weeks sooner than the infants in the experimental group did. Those whose visual and tactile surroundings were enriched began watching their hands only when they came into contact with the toys attached to their cribs. Later they noticed their hands independently of the toys. It appeared from these differences in the two groups that discovery of the hand in infants is partly related to the presence of other interesting visual stimuli (White 1967).

Increased stimulation above certain limits presumably makes no difference in an infant's development. Within these limits, however, there are upper levels of stimulation that may irritate and confuse the infant at first, but actually may have an accelerative effect after he has been exposed to this stimulation for a short time. White's work indicated that when a person wishes to stimulate an infant's development, he should probably look for the stimulus that is at the upper limit of the infant's present capacity, yet still is within his capacity.

Growth Trends

Psychologists use three general ways of describing body development. The first is the *cephalocaudal*, or head-to-tail, development trend. This means that the infant's body development starts with the early moving of his head, the fixing of his gaze, and his eye-hand coordination. All of these actions are performed by the upper portion of his body. Actions involving the lower portion of his body—crawling, standing, and walking—occur near the end of cephalocaudal development. Before they can occur, the infant's trunk, arms, hands, hips, and pelvis must develop. Even when he walks, the cephalocaudal trend is still visible: the infant's arms are coordinated to balance him before his legs are coordinated to carry him.

The second growth trend, called *proximodistal*, describes the infant's motor, or muscular, responses during his first year. The term *proximodistal* means radiating out from a center, as branches radiate from a tree's trunk. For our purposes, it means that the first limbs the child uses are those closest to his trunk: he moves his shoulders and elbows before he uses his wrists and hands. He uses his upper arm before his forearm, and his forearm before his hand and fingers. In the same order, he can coordinate his upper leg before his foreleg, and his foreleg before his foot or toes.

The third and last growth trend is the infant's development *from mass to specific acts*. In his early infancy, a child slaps at a ball or a dangling toy. He grasps in a clumsy, if firm, grip. As he approaches 1 year, his manual dexterity improves very noticeably. At this point, and even earlier, a child sitting on the floor may be seen fastidiously picking up such tiny objects as a stickpin or a bit of thread.

This trend from gross to more articulate hand use is clearly demonstrated in the 1-year-old's behavior. When he first begins feeding himself with a spoon, he makes many unnecessary, awkward gestures—perhaps tipping his plate or

MOTOR DEVELOPMENT AND SENSORY EXPERIENCE 135

scuttling a spoonful of peas. He usually gets more food on his face, sleeves, and shirt front than in his mouth. But in a month or two, he is using utensils much more adequately.

The Differences in Infants

Despite the many acts and behaviors attributed to the "average infant," he does not really exist, as we noted earlier, except as a useful statistic. The hypothetical infant who displays the "mean" or "normal" behavior or development is flanked on both sides by all the real babies who grow and respond in their own ways and at their own times. They often differ quite markedly, but these differences in their rates of development do not necessarily indicate either a deficiency or superiority in body or intellect. In the 1- or 2-year-old, the infant's inherited genes may explain the differences. For example, hereditarily acquired temperament may explain one infant's intense activity and his playmate's lassitude. Differences also may be explained by the infant's environment—either in the womb or in the world.

Of course, the infant's level of maturation significantly determines how he will behave at the various stages in his development. The child whose leg muscles, nerves, and bones mature at 9 months will be a walking prodigy—to his parents, at any rate. The child whose development in his upper body is slow may not be able to eat with utensils until he fork-feeds himself chocolate cake on his third birthday. Clearly, the rates and levels of maturation vary extensively.

Activity Level

As in every other respect, infants span the activity range from the "sleeper" to the hellion. The former will not only sleep like a stone, but will lie quietly for an hour at a time, content to watch his hands or examine a toy. The active infant kicks off his blankets in his sleep, twists and turns in his mother's arms, cries himself blue before feedings, and later nonchalantly heaves his drained bottle over his crib rail. The infant between these two extremes may show periodic distress, but it is provoked only by unusual circumstances, such as a diaper rash or a long lapse between feedings.

An infant's tendency to be active or inactive seems to persist, at least for a few years. One experimenter examined the behavior of 31 infants and then predicted how they would act at 3 and 6 years. After checking their behavior at those ages, he found some interesting correlations. Infants who moved slowly became children whose motor responses were slower than their other developmental responses (Escalona and Heider 1959). To a limited extent, then, the experimenter found that the level of infant motor activity persists into the preschool years.

Reaction to Stimuli

While all the newborn's senses—even taste to a limited extent—function at birth, each infant's senses require a different degree—however slight—of stimulation to react. One infant may wake at the creak of a floorboard, another may sleep through the noisiest party. As mentioned under "Perception of Heat and Pain," the pain stimulus draws different reactions from different infants, dividing them along sexual lines. According to Lipsitt and Levy, newborn girls are more sensitive to pain than newborn boys (Lipsitt and Levy 1959).

Another aspect of sensory responsiveness is reflected in the infant's tendency to get bored with a toy or any sensory stimulus. This, too, varies from child to child (Bridger 1961). How soon an infant adapts to a stimulus may help to predict how he will behave in later months, or even years. In one pertinent study, a researcher presented faces to several infants at 4 months of age. He assessed their reactions then, and again at ages 8 months, 13 months, and 25 months. He found that the 4-month-old boys who grew bored quickly shared three characteristics. They were shorter in height, weighed less, and were less inclined to smile than the boys who showed greater interest. At 8 months, these boys played restlessly with toys, moving rapidly from one to the next. The interested boys, on the other hand, thoroughly investigated one toy, turning it over and over, before moving on to others (Kagan 1968). Both these boys and the restless ones kept their play habits until at least 2 years of age. Apparently, then, early inclinations persist and may actually continue to play a role in patterns of behavior, possibly even in the adolescent and the adult.

Body Reactions

In the third group of seemingly inherited responses are those shown by the vital body systems under stress. Four such responsive body systems can be clearly identified: respiratory; cardiovascular (heart and blood vessels); gastrointestinal; and the skin itself. Predictably, the responses these body systems show under tension vary from infant to infant. Many young children, left lying in a cramped position, become so tense that their skin temperatures rise significantly and their heartbeats speed up—incidentally, they probably are also screaming at the top of their lungs. Other infants might struggle quietly, or perhaps upset their stomachs and spit up their milk and cereal. Some become red as beets because the tiny blood vessels just below the skin's surface inflate as tension builds up blood pressure. Some pant and snuffle. Still others will suddenly break out in a sweat, raise a crop of hives, or a "nervous rash." A few vomit.

While there are some indications, as we have noted, that an infant retains his activity level, his sensitivity to stimuli, and his vital system reactions, we do not have conclusive proof. In the cases which indicate that an activity level does remain static, the tests do not extend much beyond infancy. Therefore, it is hard to say that such behavior will typify him as he grows into a child, adolescent, or adult. Yet, if bodily reactions, such as profuse sweating or a fast heartbeat, do continue throughout the entire first year, there is a good chance these reactions could be retained as the infant develops further into childhood, and perhaps even beyond childhood. This argument is supported by the findings of longitudinal studies of individuals that have been carried out for over 20 or 30 years. They seem to show that such hereditarily determined variables as activity level, introversion, and extroversion are more consistent over time than those which are not considered to be inherited (Yarrow 1964).

With all his widely varying behavior and ability, the human infant remains a proficient and still mysterious organism. We know he prefers to look at very particular objects. He likes the familiar as well as the slightly odd sight. He also reacts to sounds, smells, tastes, and touches in his first few days of life. As he approaches his second birthday, he is walking confidently, chatting in two-word sentences about his observations and desires. With these traits and a growing hoard of images, he resembles nothing more than a miniature, sometimes inept adult, toddling out of his playpen to meet his rapidly expanding world. And psychologists now feel that the world he seeks and finds will play a much more important role in his development than was formerly supposed. Modern researchers still concede that maturation has a strong influence over the motor aspects of development, but increased understanding of sensory stimulation shows that experience can dramatically alter a child's development.

Summary

Contrary to the old-time notions of the infant as an insensitive, bumbling being, he is, rather, a rapidly developing being that within 18 months can remember, discriminate, walk, talk, and relate to other people. All senses except taste operate immediately upon the birth of infants, as do more than 20 well-developed reflexes, such as the pupillary, startle, rooting, sucking, grasp, and withdrawal reflexes. The Moro and Babinsky reflexes are unusual in that with time they disappear, ceasing to remain reflexes. Certain other reflexes, such as the infant's bowel and bladder functions, must be replaced, through learning, with control.

Averages and norms used to describe the infant's growth and **behavior** are merely statistical calculations used as **conven**ient summaries. They are not meant to be interpreted as ideals. Body proportions, the skeletal system, muscles, teeth, brain, as well as behavior, develop with great variability, and certain developmental differences appear to exist between males and females. All growth—physical and mental—can be severely retarded by poor nutrition in either the infant or his mother during pregnancy.

The pupillary reflex and some degree of muscular coordination are present at birth or almost immediately after birth in the infant; but convergence, indispensable to visual focusing and depth perception, and accommodation of the lens curvature to light rays, are achieved after the first few months of life. Studies have shown that first movement and contour-contrast, then complexity (the number and variety of objects) and the familiarity of any one object govern the infant's visual preferences. Discrepancy from the infant's schemata (his internal representations of objects and events he recognizes) and the quality of the associations he has for these stimuli will also affect how long he gazes at them. The perception of depth begins to function at about 2 months, but the infant is reluctant to trust his judgment and act accordingly until around 6 months, as the visual cliff test has shown.

Newborn babies can hear and respond to sound's frequency, direction, rhythm, pitch, and length; and by 6 months to 1 year, they will also be able to recognize familiar sounds. Balancing mechanisms, the sense of taste, and olfactory and pain perceptions develop extensively in the period immediately after birth.

Studies have proven that sitting up, crawling, and walking—skills involving the neuromuscular system of the infant—require some practice, but are generally influenced most by maturation. Dennis's experiments with confined children indicated, however, that maturation cannot exercise its usual influence if the child has not received a normal degree of stimulation. Similarly, reaching, then visual-motor reaching, and finally grasping, advance through maturational stages and can be accelerated with proper stimulation. Increased sensory stimulation of many types, in fact, can usually accelerate development if it is provided at the correct time and in amounts appropriate for the individual infant.

Babies differ markedly in their growth, their activity levels, their reaction to stimuli, and their perceptions of heat and pain, as well as in the responses of their vital body systems; in some cases differences are due to inheritance and in others, to environmental variables; or a combination of both may be responsible. While maturation is the accepted basic influence over all the motor aspects of development, sensory stimulation, along with gene and environmental differences, all give direction to the child's responses to the world around him.

Case Studies

The case studies following each chapter are intended to provide an added dimension of concreteness to selected developmental principles dealt with in the chapter. Each of the 22 cases has been carefully chosen to stress developmental variation as well as developmental regularity. These true-to-life verbal portraits highlight three crucial factors in the "formula" of human development:

—the incomparable variability of any individual child;
—the normally wide range of individual differences in every aspect of psychological development;
—the unique quality of each family's parent–child interactions.

To facilitate discussion—and further dramatize aspects of variability and regularity—a pair of cases is presented for each selected developmental area.

Bruce J.

Bruce J. is a first child, born to middle-aged parents after three miscarriages. Although of normal weight and size, Bruce was born with an abnormal congenital stomach condition which required simple surgery at 6 weeks of age. Such an early trauma made him an anxious baby for several months—easily tired, bothered by noises, and upset by overstimulation or sudden change in routine. Fortunately, Mrs. J. had the loving patience Bruce needed in order to make a 100 percent recovery.

Once over his early problems, Bruce developed his own style of motor activity. By his third month, he was trying to hold his bottle for himself. Thereafter, he liked to help guide his cereal spoon into his mouth—a time-consuming and messy activity, but one which his mother encouraged.

His mother, in fact, spared no effort to make Bruce comfortable, secure, and loved—although she was particularly anxious to avoid spoiling this child she had wanted so much. While she admittedly enjoyed caring for Bruce's needs, she did not believe, for instance, in "too much handling" for children, lest they become dependent on unnecessary attention. Mrs. J. read her child-care literature carefully in order that the love she gave her son might be as constructive as it was warm.

By the end of his first year, Bruce was in every way a smiling, responsive, babbling baby. Except for his lack of interest in crawling and his inability to stand from a seated or fallen position, which are occasional but quite normal variations in motor development, Mrs. J. noted that Bruce had progressed normally from turning himself over (4 months), to sitting upright, to standing with support, and then to walking (11 months). Although Mrs. J. was a bit concerned about Bruce's not being able to get himself up—she had never seen him even try to stand in his crib by holding on to the side bars—she saw no signs of frustration evidenced by the child.

In general, Bruce was coordinated and inquisitive, even if a bit cautious in his approach to his environment. For instance, although he would not roam from his sitting position to retrieve a dropped toy, his visual sensitivity urged him to explore with great interest things like the similarities between a visitor and the visitor's mirrored reflection.

As Bruce began his second year, he was articulating his first words—although he used them rather sparingly with strangers. His favorite play involved drumming his mother's pots and pans (Mrs. J. had "given" him one kitchen closet to explore at will), or carrying anything and everything to show to mother and grandmother. Only in the warm months was he allowed to play outside the house.

At his second birthday, Bruce was a normal, curious boy readily described as both good-natured and quiet-mannered. What we appear to see here is the counteracting of a potentially upsetting life event, and of potentially upsetting variations in a normal growth pattern, by excellent care on the mother's part (Soddy 1956).

Joan R.

Joan R. was the result of an unplanned pregnancy shortly before her father finished college on the G.I. Bill. Her mother showed little independence, often needing considerable support in daily life. Her father, outwardly a pleasant and affable man, was inwardly confused and anxious—occasionally to the point of physical incapacitation.

Joan's first several months of life proved an unsuccessful experience for her parents. Persistent crying during her first week home settled into a pattern of evening crying—just when Mrs. R. was most tired. Because her bellicose wailing was so totally consuming for her young body (as it continued to be throughout the first year), Joan's parents never let it go unattended. The mother sometimes became distressed enough to cry right along with her baby.

Mrs. R.'s reaction to this particularly threatening situation was to withdraw even further—hesitating to pick Joan up when she was quiet for fear of making her cry; holding Joan away from her body when nursing; and seldom caressing or cuddling her baby. She openly compared Joan unfavorably with the neighbor's more docile baby.

Although Joan quieted down as the mother-child relationship improved after their third month together, she continued responding to her parents' marital tensions, or to Mrs. R.'s impatience, with characteristic belligerence and tears.

Throughout her first four months, every physiological measure indicated that Joan was a highly active infant. At 5½ months, just as she had begun to crawl, Cattell and Gesell testing indicated that her intelligence and sensory-locomotor development were well above average. The next two months showed additional rapid development: by 6 months Joan was making strong efforts to pull herself upright to a standing position and to support herself while standing; and at 7 months she was taking steps with support.

In addition, Joan's clinic record noted that an unusual amount of exploratory activity was one of her most prominent characteristics. She was described as highly active and alert to even subtle changes in her social and physical environment. Never asleep during clinic visits, Joan was almost always engaged in either self-initiated or respondent activity. Her interest in interaction was indefatigable: she consistently maneuvered to maximize stimulation from her environment and to facilitate social interaction with her examiners. In fact, it seemed to the clinic staff that Joan's use of her rapidly developing postural and locomotor abilities followed not so much the random pattern normal for her age, but, rather, came from a need to exert some control over the persons and things in her environment. She was particularly responsive to interpersonal stimulation (her crying stopped almost immediately if the examiner talked to her kindly), showing more interest in exploiting social interactions than in physical objects.

Circumstances improved at home with the passing months. As feeding became less of a chore and Mrs. R.'s housekeeping schedule became more regular, her energy and composure increased. And, although she continued to be unsure of her abilities as a mother, Mrs. R. did begin to communicate a new sense of warmth and relaxation to her daughter—particularly when her own marital relationship was satisfying.

In this case an unpropitious family situation appears to be counteracted by the inborn and compensatory vigor of the baby reaching out and striving even harder for her own satisfactions (Soddy 1956).

References

Acheson, R. M. Maturation of the skeleton. In F. Falkner (Ed.), *Human development.* Philadelphia: Saunders, 1966.

Ames, L. B. The sequential patterning of prone progression in the human infant. *Genet. Psychol. Monogr.*, 1937, 19, 409–460.

Ashley, M. *Touching.* New York: Columbia Univer. Press, 1971.

Bayley, N. The development of motor abilities during the first three years. *Monogr. Soc. Res. Child. Develpm.*, 1935, No. 1.

Bayley, N. Individual patterns of development. *Child Develpm.*, 1956, 27, 45–74.

Bernard, H. *Human development in Western culture.* (3rd ed.) Boston: Allyn & Bacon, 1970.

Brackbill, Y., Adams, G., Crowell, D. H., and Gray,

M. L. Arousal level in newborns and preschool children under continuous auditory stimulation. *J. exp. child Psychol.*, 1966, *3*, 178–188.

Breckenridge, M. E., and Murphy, M. *Growth and development of the young child*. (8th ed.) Philadelphia: Saunders, 1969.

Brennan, W. M., Ames, E. W., and Moore, E. W. Age differences in infants' attention to patterns of different complexities. *Science*, 1966, *151*, 354–356.

Bridger, W. H. Sensory habituation and discrimination in the human neonate. *Amer. J. Psychiat.*, 1961, *117*, 991–996.

Chase, H. P., and Martin, H. P. Undernutrition and child development. *New England J. Med.*, April 1970, *282* (17), 933–939.

Crudden, C. H. Reactions of newborn infants to thermal stimuli under constant tactual conditions. *J. exp. Psychol.*, 1937, *20*, 350–370.

Dean, R. F. A. The size of the baby at birth and the yield of breast milk. Studies of undernutrition. Wuppertal, 1946–1950. *Spec. Rep. Ser. med. Res. Coun.*, London, 1951, No. 275.

Dean, R. F. A. Treatment of kwashiorkor with moderate amounts of protein. *J. Pediat.*, 1960, *56*, 675–689.

Dean, R. F. A. Nutrition and growth. *Mod. Probl. Paediat.*, 1962, *7*, 191–198.

Dennis, W. Infant development under conditions of restricted practice and minimum social stimulation. *Genet. Psychol. Monogr.*, 1941, *23*, 143–191.

Dennis, W. Causes of retardation among institutional children: Iran. *J. genet. Psychol.*, 1960, *96*, 47–59.

Dennis, W., and Najarian, P. Infant development under environmental handicap. *Psychol. Monogr.*, 1957, *71* (Whole No. 436).

Dennis, W., and Sayegh, Y. The effect of supplementary experiences upon the behavioral development of infants in institutions. *Child Develpm.*, 1965, *36*, 81–90.

Disher, D. R. The reactions of newborn infants to chemical stimuli administered nasally. *Ohio State Univer. Stud. Contr. Psychol.*, 1934, No. 12, 1–52.

Drillien, C. M. *Growth and development of the prematurely born infant*. Baltimore: Williams & Wilkins, 1964.

Engen, T., and Lipsitt, L. P. Decrement and recovery of responses to olfactory stimuli in the human neonate. *J. comp. physiol. Psychol.*, 1965, *59*, 312–316.

Escalona, S., and Heider, G. M. *Prediction and outcome*. New York: Basic Books, 1959.

Fantz, R. L. Visual experience in infants: Decreased attention to familiar patterns relative to novel ones. *Science*, 1964, *146*, 668–670.

Fantz, R. L. Visual perception from birth as shown by pattern selectivity. *Ann. N.Y. Acad. Sci.*, 1965, *118*, 793–814.

Fantz, R. L., and Nevis, S. The predictive value of changes in visual preferences in early infancy. In J. Hellmuth (Ed.), *The exceptional infant*. Vol. I. Seattle: Special Child Publs., 1967.

Flechsig, P. E. *Anatomie des menschlichen Gehirns und Rückenmarks auf myelogenestischer Grundlage*. Leipzig: G. Thieme, 1920.

Freud, S. *Drei Abhandlungen zur sexual Theorie*. Leipzig: F. Deuticke, 1905.

Garn, S. M. Roentgenogrammetric determinations of body composition. *Human Biol.*, 1957, *29*, 337–353.

Garn, S. M. Fat, body size, and growth in the newborn. *Human Biol.*, 1958, *30*, 265–280.

Garn, S. M., and Rohmann, C. G. Variability in the order of ossification of the bony centers of the hand and wrist. *Amer. J. Phys. Anthrop.*, 1960, *18*, 219–229.

Gesell, A. L., and Amatruda, C. S. *Developmental diagnosis*. New York: Hoeber, 1941.

Gibson, E. J., and Walk, R. R. The "visual cliff." *Scientific Amer.*, 1960, *202*, 2–9.

Grantham-McGregory, S. M., and Back, E. H. Gross motor development in Jamaican infants. *Develpm. Med. and Child Neurol.*, February 1971, *13*(17), 79–87.

Grier, J. B., Counter, S. A., and Shearer, W. M. Prenatal auditory imprinting in chickens. *Science*, 1967, *155*, 1692–1693.

Haaf, R. A., and Bell, R. Q. A facial dimension in visual discrimination by human infants. *Child Develpm.*, 1967, *38*, 893–899.

Hall, G. S. Notes on the study of infants. *Ped. Sem.*, 1891, *1*, 127–138.

Halverson, H. M. An experimental study of prehension in infants by means of systematic cinema records. *Genet. Psychol. Monogr.*, 1931, *10*, 107–286.

Halverson, H. M. Complications of the early grasping reactions. *Genet. Psychol. Monogr.*, 1936, *47*, 47–63.

Haynes, H., White, B. L., and Held, R. Visual accommodation in human infants. *Science*, 1965, *148*, 528–530.

Heinecke, C. M. Some effects of separating two-year-old children from their parents: A comparative study. *Human Relat.*, 1956, *9*, 106–176.

James, W. *The principles of psychology*. New York: Holt, 1890.

Jensen, K. Differential reactions to taste and temperature stimuli in newborn infants. *Genet. Psychol. Monogr.*, 1932, *11*, 363–479.

Kagan, J. Continuity in the first year. Unpublished manuscript, 1968.

Kagan, J. Do infants think? *Scientific Amer.*, 1972, *226*, 74–82.

Katz, V. The relationship between auditory stimulation and the developmental behavior of the premature infant. *Dissert. Abstr.*, January 1971, *31*(7-B), 4156–4157.

Keen, R. F., Chase, H. H., and Graham, F. K. Twenty-four-hour retention by neonates of an habituated heart response. *Psychon. Sci.*, 1965, *2*, 265–266.

Kilbride, J. E., Robbins, M. C., and Kilbride, P. L. The comparative motor development of Baganda, American white and American black infants. *Amer. Anthrop.*, December 1970, *72*(6), 1422–1428.

Korner, A. F. Individual differences at birth: Implications for early experience and later development. *Amer. J. Orthopsychiat.*, July 1971, *41*(4), 608–619.

Krogman, W. M. *Child growth.* Ann Arbor: Univer. of Michigan Press, 1971.

Leventhal, A. S., and Lipsitt, L. P. Adaptation, pitch discrimination, and sound localization in the neonate. *Child Develpm.*, 1964, *35*, 759–767.

Lewis, M., Wilson, C. D., and Baumel, M. Attention distribution in the 24-month-old child: Variations in complexity and incongruity of the human form. *Child Develpm.*, June 1971, *42*, 429–438.

Ling, B. C. I. A genetic study of sustained visual fixation and associated behavior in the human infant from birth to six months. *J. genet. Psychol.*, 1942, *61*, 227–277.

Lipsitt, L. P., and Levy, N. Pain threshold in the human neonate. *Child Develpm.*, 1959, *30*, 547–554.

Marietta, D. F., and Sandy, D. G. *Baby learns to listen.* Pittsburgh, Pa.: Stanwix House, 1971.

Matheny, A. P., and Brown, A. M. Activity, motor coordination and attention: Individual differences in twins. *Percept. and motor Skills*, February 1971, *32*(1), 151–158.

McCall, R. B., and Kagan, J. Attention in the infant: Effects of complexity, contour, perimeter and familiarity. *Child Develpm.*, 1967, *38*, 939–952.

McGraw, M. B. *Neuromuscular maturation of the human infant.* New York: Hafner, 1963.

Meredith, H. V. Body size of contemporary groups of 1-year-old infants studied in different parts of the world. *Child Develpm.*, 1970, *41*, 551–600.

Merminod, A. (Ed.) *The growth of the normal child during the first three years of life.* Basel: Karger, 1962.

Meyers, W. J., and Cantor, G. N. Infants' observing and heart period responses as related to novelty of visual stimuli. *Psychon. Sci.*, 1966, *5*, 239–240.

Mitchell, R. G. The Moro reflex. *Cerebral Palsy Bull.*, 1960, *2*, 135–141.

Munn, N. L., and Stiening, B. R. The relative efficacy of form and background in a child's discrimination of visual patterns. *J. genet. Psychol.*, 1931, *39*, 73–90.

Munsinger, H., and Kessen, W. Uncertainty, structure, and preference. *Psychol. Monogr.*, 1964, *78* (Whole No. 586).

Munsinger, H., and Weir, M. W. Infants' and young children's preference for complexity. *J. exp. child Psychol.*, 1967, *5*, 69–73.

Nelson, K. Organization of visual-tracking responses in human infants. *J. exp. child Psychol.*, 1968, *6*, 194–201.

Papoušek, H. Experimental studies of appetitional behavior in human newborns and infants. In H. W. Stevenson, E. H. Hess, and H. L. Rheingold (Eds.), *Early behavior.* New York: Wiley, 1967.

Papoušek, H. On the development of the so-called voluntary movements in the earliest stages of the child's development. *Česk. Pediat.*, 1962, *17*, 588–591.

Peatman, J. G., and Higgons, R. A. Relation of infants' weight and body build to locomotor development. *Amer. J. Orthopsychiat.*, 1942, *12*, 234–240.

Piaget, J. La première année de l'enfant. *Brit. J. Psychol.*, 1927, *18*, 97–120.

Pratt, K. C. The effects of repeated visual stimulation on the activity of newborn infants. *J. genet. Psychol.*, 1934, *44*, 117–126.

Pratt, K. C. The neonate. In L. Carmichael (Ed.), *Manual of child psychology.* (2nd ed.) N.Y.: Wiley, 1954.

Pratt, K. C., Nelson, A. K., and Sun, K. H. The behavior of the newborn infant. *Ohio State Univer. Stud. Contr. Psychol.*, 1930, No. 10.

Rubinfine, D. L. Maternal stimulation, psychic structure and early object relations. *Psychoanal. Study Child.*, 1962, *17*, 265–282.

Saint-Anne Dargassies, S. The first smile. *Develpm. Med. and Child Neurol.*, 1962, *4*, 531–533.

Salapatek, P., and Kessen, W. Visual scanning of triangles by the human newborn. *J. exp. child Psychol.*, 1966, *3*, 113–122.

Sameroff, A. J. An experimental study of the response components of sucking in the human newborn. *Dissert. Abstr.*, 1965, *26*, 2341.

Sameroff, A. J. Nonnutritive sucking in newborns under visual and auditory stimulation. *Child Develpm.*, 1967, *38*, 443–452.

Schaffer, H. R. Activity level as a constitutional determinant of infantile reaction to deprivation. *Child Develpm.*, 1966, *37*, 595–602.

Schaffer, H. R., and Parry, M. H. The effects of short-term familiarization of infants' perceptual-motor coordination in a simultaneous discrimination situation. *Brit. J. Psychol.*, 1970, *61*, 559–569.

Scott, W. C. M. The demonstration of object relations and effect in a set situation in infants of 6 to 12 months. *Proc. 3rd World Congress of Psychiatry.* Vol. I. Toronto: Univer. of Toronto Press, 1961.

Shapiro, H. The development of walking in a child. *J. genet. Psychol.*, 1962, *100*, 221–226.

Sherman, M., and Sherman, I. C. Sensorimotor responses in infants. *J. comp. Psychol.*, 1925, *5*, 53–68.

Sherman, M., Sherman, I. C., and Flory, C. D. Infant behavior. *Comp. Psychol. Monogr.*, 1936, *12*(4).

Shirley, M. M. *The first two years: A study of twenty-five babies.* Vol. I. *Postural and locomotor development.* Inst. Child Welf. Monogr., Ser. No. 6. Minneapolis: Univer. of Minnesota Press, 1933.

Shock, N. W. Physiological growth. In F. Falkner (Ed.), *Human development.* Philadelphia: Saunders, 1966.

Soddy, K. (Ed.) *Mental health and infant development.* Vol. 2. New York: Basic Books, 1956. Pp. 43–71, 97–122.

Stafford, P. *Psychedelic baby reaches puberty.* New York: Praeger, 1971.

Stechler, G., and Latz, E. Some observations on attention and arousal in the human infant. *J. Amer. Acad. child Psychiat.*, 1966, *5*, 517–525.

Stolz, H. R., and Stolz, L. M. *Somatic development of adolescent boys. A study of the growth of boys during the second decade of life.* New York: Macmillan, 1951.

Tanner, J. M., Whitehouse, R. H., and Healy, J. J. R. *A*

new system for estimating skeletal maturity from the hand and wrist, with standards derived from a study of 2,600 healthy British children. Parts I and II. Paris: Centre International de l'Enfance, 1962.

Walk, R. D. The development of depth perception in animal and human infants. *Monogr. Soc. Res. Child Develpm.*, 1966, *31*(5), 82–108.

White, B. L. *Experience and psychological development.* Englewood Cliffs, N.J.: Prentice-Hall, 1971.

White, B. L. An experimental approach to the effects of experience on early human behavior. In J. P. Hill (Ed.), *Minnesota symposia on child psychology.* Vol. I. Minneapolis: Univer. of Minnesota Press, 1967.

White, B. L., and Held, R. Plasticity of sensorimotor development. In J. F. Rosenblith and W. Allinsmith (Eds.), *Readings in child development and educational psychology.* (2nd ed.) Boston: Allyn & Bacon, 1966.

Williams, N. *Child development.* New York: Humanities Press, 1969.

Yarrow, L. J. Personality consistency and change: An overview of some conceptual and methodological issues. *Vita Humana*, 1964, *7*, 67–72.

6 Mental, Cognitive, and Language Development

For years, the infant's physical development has been the subject of detailed study. But it is only recently that the infant's cognitive and mental development has come under intensive scrutiny. Most of the research in this area dates from 1960. Like most subjects of burgeoning scientific inquiry, the study of cognitive development is not dominated by any one orthodox theory or system of thought. There are, appropriately, few absolute certainties; an ever-increasing amount of experimentation is providing findings that are expanding and shaping prevailing concepts of what the infant's mind can accomplish.

A number of these new findings have surprised some observers—though much less than they would have a generation ago. Just as the infant's physical sophistication was greatly underrated by early observers, his cognitive development was thought to be limited, at best. Today, the psychologist sees the infant as considerably more competent mentally. His studies have shown him that a baby's cognitive powers and processes are more organized than he had assumed. For example, it is now known that the infant devises behaviors of his own and even solves a few simple problems.

In this chapter, we shall trace first the evolution of language in the infant. Turning to mental development, we shall examine intelligence and then explore Jean Piaget's revolutionary—and still evolving—view of the infant's intellectual and cognitive development. Finally, we shall consider other voluntary infant behavior, such as play, that appears vital to the development of his cognitive faculties.

As in Chapter 5, it may seem at times that the development we are discussing is distinct from the other kinds of growth taking place simultaneously in the infant. Quite the opposite is true. Throughout the complex growth from infant to adult, the human's physical, mental, and emotional powers develop *interdependently*. Thus, despite the apparent isolation of each aspect of growth as we discuss it, these three facets of human development are very closely related. The diminution of any one strongly affects the other two.

Language Development

How a child learns to speak and understand his language is one of psychology's oldest and most persistent questions. It was already fascinating philosophers in the pre-Christian Golden Age of Greece. As prescientific thinkers, they explained language learning in terms of legends, curses, and the will of the gods. Many centuries later, other explanations, though drawn from empirical evidence rather than the cultural imagination, were hardly more illuminating.

In this century, the major step forward has been the development of systematic descriptions of the normative stages through which the child proceeds in language development. A dynamic new area of research known as *psycholinguistics* also is making important advances in the understanding of the process by which language is acquired and used. Most of the work in psycholinguistics, however, has focused primarily on the development of grammar and syntax. Because this chapter is concerned with the origin of speech in the infant—his first, pregrammatical sounds and single-word utterances—we shall discuss psycholinguistics more fully in the next chapter. This section traces the newborn's first cries and coos through the several stages of development that eventually result in that first celebrated word— usually *Da* or *Ma*.

Infant Vocalizing

EARLY SOUNDS. The infant begins making sounds at birth. In his first six months, he progresses from crying to cooing to babbling. At first, the cry is his only utterance. With it, he responds to stimuli—hunger, fatigue, and discomfort, such as wet diapers or gas pains. After six or eight weeks, the infant, while continuing to signal distress by crying, adds the cooing sound. Cooing differs from crying in two basic respects—it involves modulation of sound by the tongue, and it usually signifies pleasure or excitement, such as a warm bottle or musical toy might evoke. Although cooing does communicate, it is not language. It is an innate response occurring at a particular stage of maturation, and it lacks the flexible and varied structure of language. Its character is set by physical factors. For example, an infant lying on his back makes a consonantal cooing because, in that position, his tongue drops back in his mouth, blocking the vocal passage and producing that particular sound.

At first, the infant coos whenever he feels like it, for cooing is unchanged by the infant's sensory experience. This point has been proved by observations of the deaf infants of deaf-mute couples. Up to 2 months of age, these infants—who, like their parents, cannot hear their own voices—still coo as much as normal infants. In all infants, however, this reflexive vocalizing is short-lived. It begins to disappear about eight weeks after birth. As it does, there emerges a correlation between stimulation and vocalizing, a link that rapidly becomes firm and obvious. For example, an infant whose mother talks to him a great deal will make more sounds in greater variety than an infant whose mother ignores him. The correlation persists throughout the infant's first year. Orphans under 6 months—orphans are seldom talked to at any age—vocalize less, and with less variety, than infants who have parents. Moving further up the age scale, 6-to-12-month-old, middle-class babies "outtalk" lower-class infants—possibly because, as studies show, middle-class mothers talk more to their babies, prompting them to vocalize.

BABBLING BEGINS. After about 6 months, most mothers notice a form of vocalizing that resembles speech a bit more than cooing does. The baby has begun to babble. He strings together a great number and variety of sounds. An experimenter working with an infant of this age may feel that the baby, too, is experimenting—with his new sounds. Indeed, as he babbles and pauses, the infant-child sounds something like a composer of nonsense songs trying out short melodic phrases.

While almost all babies will babble somewhat

145

on their own, reinforcements or rewards can dramatically affect the degree of vocalizing. In one study, Rheingold, Gewirtz, and Ross (1959) confirmed the hypothesis that when an adult rewards an infant's babbling by smiling, clucking, and touching his stomach, the infant babbles a great deal more than otherwise. Though most infants will babble more for rewards, some children from 6 months to 1 year will babble unrewarded and alone for as long as an hour. It appears that the infant's hearing of his own voice stimulates him to go on babbling; the sound is its own reward.

Babbling, Vocabulary, and I.Q. Scores

Babbling in the first 4 months is not considered a reliable indicator of the size of an infant's later vocabulary or his volubility. However, between 4 and 12 months, babbling does seem to predict attentiveness and intelligence as measured by I.Q. tests — but only for girls.

A study by McCall and Kagan provided evidence of the relationship between babbling and attentiveness. They presented pictures of faces to 4-month-old boys and girls; the infants' responses differed widely. Some did not babble at all, and some babbled nonstop for several seconds at each face. At 8 months of age, the girls who had vocalized intensively to the pictured faces paid closer attention to a taped voice than the girls who had not babbled. At 13 months, the girls who earlier had babbled the most now continued to vocalize more in response to human likenesses; they also displayed greater attentiveness by settling down more readily than did the girls who were nonbabblers at 4 months of age. Again, at 27 months, the babblers among the girls played longer and remained interested by individual toys for longer spans than did the more silent girls. Throughout the experiment, babbling and nonbabbling boys also were compared in the same way. However, they did not demonstrate the relationship between babbling and attentiveness that the girls had displayed (McCall and Kagan 1967).

The connection between babbling and later vocabulary and I.Q. scores is supported by two other studies. Cameron, Livson, and Bayley found in 1967 that females who babbled often, when tested between 6 and 12 months, earned higher I.Q. scores as adults than girls who had not babbled. Again, boys' babbling predicted nothing — the frequency of their early babbling did not correlate with the distribution of higher I.Q. scores among them. An experiment that Moore conducted in London in 1967 provided similar results with a different criterion — vocabulary. Moore found that 6-month-old girls who babbled intensively displayed larger vocabularies when they were 2 and 3 years old than girls who had not babbled. Among the boys, however, many babblers and nonbabblers alike later developed vocabularies of the same size. Babbling, it appears, is related to syntax and verbal fluency, but only in girls does it forecast vocabulary size or scores on I.Q. tests, which primarily measure verbal ability.

SEX DIFFERENCES. Although it is known that girls respond more to auditory stimulation, that they babble more, and that increased babbling in girls predicts larger vocabularies and higher I.Q. scores, it is not clear why girls are so different from boys in these respects. Acheson maintained

Figure 6.1 A correlation has been found between stimulation — such as talking to the infant and touching his stomach — and frequency of vocalization. (Phoebe Dunn — D.P.I.)

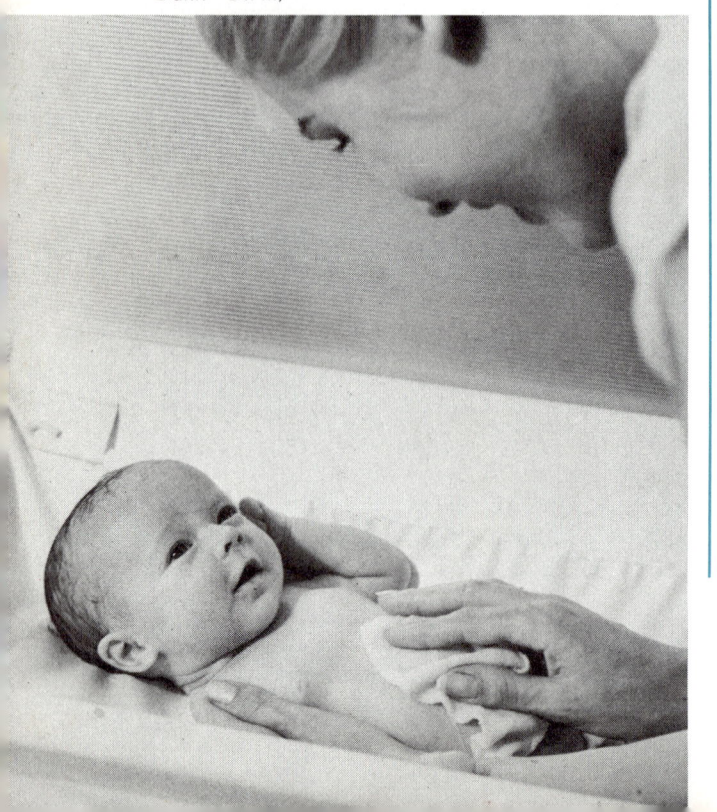

that female infants have a more regularly paced cognitive development than male infants. If it is assumed that frequent babbling indicates accelerated mental development for both the male and the female infant, the much steadier pace of the female's mental development would make her babbling a better indicator of her future I.Q. It may be that, like the female's more stable rates of physical growth, the greater predictability of I.Q. through her babbling simply demonstrates once again the female's generally more regular overall development (Acheson 1966).

A second theory of how sex affects the babbling-I.Q. relationship portrays males and females as having distinctly different modes of reaction, determined by different neuromuscular integration. The structure of the female's nervous system might be such that it leads infant girls to babble when excited. Thus, the female's babbling would be a reliable barometer of her awareness— possibly even of her adult intelligence to come. In contrast, the male infant's central nervous system may be organized so that visual, auditory, or tactile stimulation does *not* make him babble. In his case, the rate or extent of his babbling obviously would not be a reliable guide to his intellectual development. A study by Moss supports a third theory, which stresses the mother's treatment of her infant. Basic to this view is evidence that mothers treat their infant sons and daughters in different ways. Moss and his associates observed 26 mothers and their newborn sons and daughters in their own homes over a period of time, recording specific activities of the infants and the mothers' reactions to their sons and daughters. Moss found that the mothers of girls spent more time mimicking their infants' vocalizing (in effect, rewarding it) than did the mothers of boys, although at the time of the first observations—3 weeks of age—boys and girls were spending about the same amount of time vocalizing. By 3 months of age, however, girls were vocalizing much more than boys (Moss 1967).

A mother's frequent "conversations" with her daughter could explain the infant's more frequent babbling. In the same way, a mother's interest in her daughter's developing speech also could lead her to teach her daughter to pronounce words at an early age. Conceivably, the daughter's growth from vocal infant to verbally advanced young girl could be prompted by her mother's continued efforts. The predictive connection between a girl's babbling and her later verbal powers may depend on the mother's steady acceleration of her daughter. Moss attributed the lack of any predictive connection between a boy's early babbling and his speech development to the fact that mothers vocalize less with their boy infants than with their girls. He found that whereas the well-educated mothers he observed talked to their daughters much more than mothers with less schooling, all the mothers of sons talked to their boys approximately the same amount of time, which was less than the other mothers talked to their girls (Moss 1967).

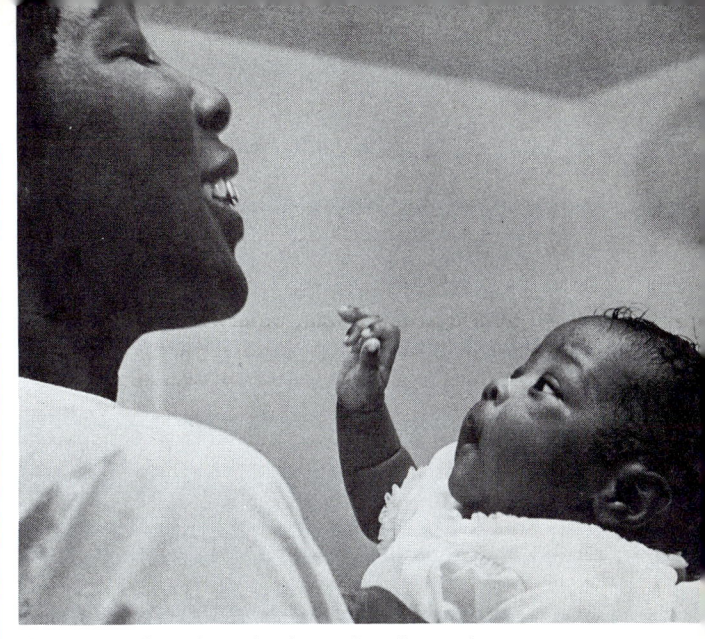

Figure 6.2 This infant, closely watching her mother's face, reaches out to the source of the sounds she hears. (Hanna W. Schreiber—Rapho Guillumette)

Babbling's Relationship to Language

While babbling is not language any more than cooing is, some psychologists believe that complex babbling may be the root of language. In support of this notion, some studies have shown that as an infant matures, his babbling begins to resemble his parents' speech. The question is: Does the infant's babbling become more articulate because his parents are rewarding only those sounds that resemble their own words? It would be tempting to answer yes, but it seems unlikely that this theory offers a complete explanation, since most parents, especially new ones, reward almost any sound with attention.

Other theories have explained babbling's relation to language in different ways. Mowrer, for instance, has observed that mothers usually speak or make sounds to their infants while they are comforting them, or feeding or changing them. Because the infant feels pleasure at the same time that he hears his mother's words, he mentally links the pleasure he feels to the words he hears. Later, when he makes a sound that resembles one of the pleasure-linked words, his hearing of that sound is itself a reward for making it, and this association increases the likelihood that he will repeat the sound (Mowrer 1952). Following this theory, the infant then begins modifying his sounds until they become more and more like his mother's words. While this explains partly how language is shaped over a period of time, recent evidence has shown that the baby also *invents* his own language, borrowing elements, of course, from those around him. This will be discussed further in the next chapter.

While babbling may contribute to the shaping of speech, it may do little to shape the infant's later understanding of language. Perhaps babbling is only the mechanical "warm-up" that shows the infant how the sound he makes relates to the movement of his tongue and mouth, and in this way contributes to his ability to produce speech rather than his ability to understand language. As Lenneberg showed in 1964, there are infants who have never babbled or uttered any bit of language and yet can understand new and complex sentences.

MATURATION AND SPEECH. Babbling can be considered as a precursor to language in the same way crawling is to walking. When walking replaces crawling, the baby's movement is radically changed; yet the two ways of moving are locked into a developmental sequence. In speech, as in walking and other body functions, the level of maturation limits the level of use. The maturation of the infant's nervous and muscular systems dictates when he will make particular sounds. For example, the sitting position—usually achieved at about 6 months—seems to change the shape of the inside of the mouth. This, in turn, affects the muscles the infant will use to form consonants a few months later (McCarthy 1954).

When the infant does begin to speak, at about 1 year of age, the sounds he makes are suddenly different from his babbling. When he had babbled, most of his sounds had been consonants shaped in the rear of the mouth. When the infant begins to talk, he shapes his most common consonants in the front of his mouth. The rhythms and inflections he played with when he babbled, however, can be heard as the "melody" of his new language.

Nature of Early Language Sounds

STARTING WITH PHONEMES. As early as the first 10 days of his life, the infant is able to sound four of the 35 basic phonemes that make up the American English language. Phonemes are the fundamental sounds of a language, and in English they include vowel and consonant sounds such as *o* and *t*. The newborn can be heard making the vowel sounds that are stressed in this sentence: "My p*e*t, a f*a*t m*u*tt, b*i*t me." Of these four sounds, the *a*, as in *fat*, is the most common during the first 10 days. The most frequently heard consonant, after 10 days, is the *h* as in *horse*, but *k* and *w* also are heard occasionally.

The first elementary sounds an infant utters seem to bear no relation to the sounds he hears about him. American, German, Italian, and Swahili babies all pronounce the same phonemes as they progress through the stages of babbling. For a while they all utter the German's vowels, the Frenchman's guttural *r*, and many other sounds they later will drop from their repertoires because their native languages do not use them. As adults they will be unable to reproduce some of these "foreign" sounds without training and practice.

Vowels outnumber consonants by about five to one in the infant's "speech" for the first four weeks. After that time, the use of vowels declines, and consonants begin to predominate. By the age of 6 months most babies are capable of making nearly all the vowel sounds (McCarthy 1954), but the production of consonants increases even more rapidly. Soon after his first birthday, the infant is uttering more consonants than vowels as he approaches the adult ratio of 1.4 consonants for each vowel (Irwin 1948). Of the infant's early consonants, 9 out of 10 are glottal noises or the *h* sound—all made in the throat. However, by 12 months, he has reduced these primitive sounds so that they are only about one-third of his store of consonants (Irwin 1947).

As he grows older, the infant also makes more and more sounds in any given period of time. At 8 weeks, he averages 63 sounds of all kinds in a 30-second breath-test time. At 24 weeks, his average rises to 74 sounds, and by 12 months he is up to 90 sounds (Irwin and Chen 1946; Irwin 1947, 1952).

From Phonemes to Morphemes. At about 12 months of age, the infant reveals that he can structure the sequence of his sounds, in an elementary fashion. Although his babbling had seemed to convey some meaning, the child had not made a consistent pattern of distinctions among his babbling sounds. Instead, he simply moved his mouth any way his whim took him, often running through his whole repertoire, purring slowly or peeling off a stream of chatter like an auctioneer. However, before he speaks his first word he learns to separate his utterances into distinct categories.

First, he distinguishes vowels from consonants, and then he combines them. His words assume a regular order of a consonant followed by a vowel. He says "ma" or "pa," not "ahm" or "ahp." Combinations of consonants and vowels like these are called *morphemes*, which are the shortest units of language that carry a definite meaning. A little later he learns to distinguish between consonant sounds—mother is consistently called "ma," and father, "da." Soon, his patterns become a little more complex as he adds a different vowel sound—for example, the long *e* as in *bee*. Having earlier developed the pattern of consonant followed by vowel, he applies this pattern again, making "me" rather than "em."

How the infant's speech structuring grows into the subtle verbal web that even a 4-year-old displays is not fully understood. One of the most intriguing theories, put forth by Leopold (1953-54), maintains that the infant learns differences between groups of sounds by learning the physical feelings associated with making each sound. The 1-year-old who pronounces the consonants *b* and *d* learns that he makes some sounds with his vocal cords vibrating and others without moving his vocal cords. By employing just this one physical difference, the infant could add four consonants—*b*, *p*, *d*, and *t*—to his speech. Plausible as Leopold's theory may seem, we do not, at present, know enough about the development of sound patterns to judge its accuracy or that of the other existing theories. More research into the emergence of sound patterns in the infant is needed before an authoritative evaluation of these potential explanations can be made.

The Talking Begins

FIRST WORD. While there are vast differences in the ages at which infants first begin to speak, the average infant usually says his first "mama" or "dada" at about 1 year of age. In uttering these two-syllable words, the infant is following his babbling pattern of pairing similar or identical sounds. His mouthing of *mama* may be more than simply naming the person he sees changing his diapers; some psychologists believe the infant's first word may be expressing a full thought (McCarthy 1954; Lenneberg 1967). Depending on his tone, volume, and the amount of kicking and arm-swinging he does, the thought may be equivalent to "I want my mother now!" or "Is that you, Mama?"

Although it is tempting to see these one-word utterances as complete sentences, expressing whatever the situation suggests might be in the infant's mind at the moment, there can be no proof, of course, that such a "sentence" actually exists in the infant's mind. Bloom (1970) has contended that earlier researchers have credited the infant with too much knowledge of grammar and syntax long before he displays this presumed knowledge in his speech. From her study of the speech development of three babies, Bloom argued that the use of one-word utterances is linked to the infant's cognitive structures rather than any ideas of grammar or syntax that the infant may have developed (Bloom, in press).

In relating the emergence and use of single

Table 6.1 Composite Table Showing Age in Months at Which Selected Language Items Are Reported in Eight Major Studies of Infant Development

	Strictly Longitudinal		Principally Cross-Sectional					
	Bayley (1933)	Shirley (1933)	C. Bühler (1930)	C. Bühler and Hetzer (1935)	Gesell, Thompson, and Amatruda (1938)	Gesell and Thompson (1934)	Gesell (1925)	Cattell (1940)
1. Vocal grunt		0.25						
2. Differential cries for discomfort, pain, and hunger						1		
3. Vocalizes small throaty noises					1.3			
4. Vocalizations	1.5							
5. Makes several different vocalizations						2		
6. Makes several vocalizations							4	
7. One syllable		2						
8. Vocalizes *ah, uh, eh* (See Items 26–33.)					1.3			
9. Attends readily to speaking voice						2		
10. Reacts positively to human voice				2				
11. Responds to voice	1.3							
12. Turns head on sound of voice					4			
13. Voice, attends (supine)								2
14. Voice, turns to (sitting)								4
15. Cooing			2	3				
16. Coos					3		4	
17. Babbles or coos								2
18. Returning glance with smiling or cooing				3				
19. Coos to music (See Item 22.)							6	
20. Two syllables		3						
21. Gives vocal expression to feelings of pleasure						3		
22. Actively vocalizes pleasure with crowing or cooing						6		
23. Vocalizes pleasure (See Items 15–19, 36–37, 43–44.)	5.9							

Table 6.1 (continued)

	Strictly Longitudinal || Principally Cross-Sectional						
	Bayley (1933)	Shirley (1933)	C. Bühler (1930)	C. Bühler and Hetzer (1935)	Gesell, Thompson, and Amatruda (1938)	Gesell and Thompson (1934)	Gesell (1925)	Cattell (1940)
24. Vocalizes to social stimulus	3.1							
25. Responds vocally when socially stimulated (See Items 38, 60.)						4		
26. Vocalizes in self-initiated sound play						4		
27. Articulates many syllables in spontaneous vocalizations							6	
28. Vocalizes several well-defined syllables						6		
29. Says several syllables	6.3							
30. Vocalizes *ma* or *mu*					6.5			
31. Vocalizes *da*					7			
32. Two syllables—2nd repetition of 1st—*mama* or *dada*	8				7			
33. Says *da-da* or equivalent	8.5					9		
34. Gives vocal expression of eagerness						5		
35. Vocalizes eagerness	5.6							
36. Vocalizes displeasure on withdrawal of coveted object						5		
37. Vocalizes displeasure	5.9							
38. "Talks" to a person (See Items 25, 60.)		6						
39. Distinguishes between friendly and angry talking				6				
40. Imitating sounds *re-re-re*—immediate or delayed response				6				
41. Imitates sounds								9
42. Incipient or rudimentary imitation of sounds (See Items 65, 66, 68.)						10		

Table 6.1 (continued)

	Strictly Longitudinal		Principally Cross-Sectional					
	Bayley (1933)	Shirley (1933)	C. Bühler (1930)	C. Bühler and Hetzer (1935)	Gesell, Thompson, and Amatruda (1938)	Gesell and Thompson (1934)	Gesell (1925)	Cattell (1940)
43. Vocalizes satisfaction	6.5							
44. Vocalizes satisfaction in attaining an object (See Items 21–23.)						7		
45. Singing tones		7.3						
46. Vocalizes recognition	7.4							
47. Gives vocal expression to recognition						8		
48. Single consonants (See Items 30, 31.)			8					
49. Adjusts to words (See Items 55, 62.)					8			9
50. Vocalizes in interjectional manner						8		
51. Vocal interjection	8.1							
52. Listens to familiar words (See Item 61.)	8.5							
53. Listens with selective interest to familiar words (See Item 62.)						9		
54. Understands gestures			9					
55. Responds to *bye-bye*					9			
56. Can wave *bye-bye* and often can say it							12	
57. Expressive sounds		9						
58. Expressive jargon	13.5							
59. Uses expressive jargon						15		
60. Uses jargon conversationally						18		
61. Differentiates words (See Item 52.)	9.8							
62. Makes conditioned adjustment to certain words (See Items 69–77.)						10		

Table 6.1 (continued)

	Strictly Longitudinal			Principally Cross-Sectional				
	Bayley (1933)	Shirley (1933)	C. Bühler (1930)	C. Bühler and Hetzer (1935)	Gesell, Thompson, and Amatruda (1938)	Gesell and Thompson (1934)	Gesell (1925)	Cattell (1940)
63. Vocalizes in cup-spoon situation					10			
64. Vocalizes in 2-cube situation					10			
65. Imitating syllables, *mama, papa, dada*			11					
66. Imitates words (See Items 40–42, 68.)	11.7							
67. One word		14						
68. First imitative word (*bow-wow*, etc.) (See Items 40–42, 65, 66.)		15						
69. Adjusts to commands					10			
70. Inhibits on command	11.5							
71. Adjusts to simple commands						12		
72. Places cube in or over cup on command						12		
73. Comprehends simple verbal commissions							12	
74. Understanding simple commands				13–15				
75. Understanding a demand ("Give me that" with gesture)				15–17				
76. Understanding a command ("Sit down" or "lie down" or "stand up" with gesture)				21–23				
77. Putting watch to ear on command (See Items 62, 95.)				21–23				
78. Responds to inhibitory words					12			
79. Understanding a prohibition				16–18				
80. Understanding a forbidding			18–20					

Table 6.1 (continued)

	Strictly Longitudinal		Principally Cross-Sectional					
	Bayley (1933)	Shirley (1933)	C. Bühler (1930)	C. Bühler and Hetzer (1935)	Gesell, Thompson, and Amatruda (1938)	Gesell and Thompson (1934)	Gesell (1925)	Cattell (1940)
81. Says 2 words	12.9					12		12
82. Says 2 words or more					12			
83. Says 2 words besides *mama* and *dada*							12	
84. Vocalizes when looking in mirror					12			
85. Says 3 words or more					13			13–14
86. Says 4 words or more					13	15		
87. Words, 5						18	18	15–16
88. Names 1 object (ball, pencil, cup, watch, scissors)	17.4							
89. Names picture in book (dog)		19						
90. Naming 1 object or more				19–24				
91. Names 1 picture	18.7					21		
92. Names picture in book (baby)		22.5						
93. Asks with words (See Items 101–103.)								17–18
94. Says "Hello," "Thank you," or equivalent							18	
95. Points to nose, eyes, or hair						18	18	
96. Comprehends simple questions (See Items 69–77.)							18	
97. Names Gesell watch on fifth picture (See Item 113.)	19.4							
98. Names 2 objects	19.6							
99. Repeats things said						21		
100. Repeats 4 syllables (2 words)				30				
101. Joins 2 words in speech						21		
102. Words, combines								21–22
103. Uses words in combination (See Item 93.)						24		

Table 6.1 (continued)

	Strictly Longitudinal		Principally Cross-Sectional					
	Bayley (1933)	Shirley (1933)	C. Bühler (1930)	C. Bühler and Hetzer (1935)	Gesell, Thompson, and Amatruda (1938)	Gesell and Thompson (1934)	Gesell (1925)	Cattell (1940)
104. Names 3 pictures	21.2							
105. Picture vocabulary 3								23–24
106. Names 3 objects	21.5							23–24
107. Names 3 objects in picture							36	
108. Identifies 4 objects by name								23–24
109. Names 3 of 5 objects (See Items 104–107.)						24		
110. Names familiar objects like key, penny, watch							24	
111. Points to 5 objects on card						24		
112. Names 5 pictures	24.4					30		
113. Names Gesell watch and picture (See Item 97.)	24.5							
114. Points to 7 of 10 simple pictures							24	
115. Points to 7 pictures	25.1					30		28–30
116. Picture vocabulary 7 (1937 Stanford-Binet)								25–27
117. Names 7 pictures	32.9							25–27
118. Pictures, points to 6								25–27
119. First pronoun		23						
120. Uses pronouns past and plural							36	
121. First phrase (See Items 124–126.)		23						
122. First sentence		23						
123. Uses simple sentences and phrases							24	
124. Distinguishes *in* and *under*							24	
125. Understands 2 prepositions	25							
126. Understands 3 prepositions	28							

Source: D. McCarthy, Language Development in Children. In L. Carmichael (Ed.), *Manual of Child Psychology*. (2nd ed.) New York: Wiley, 1954. Pp. 499–502.

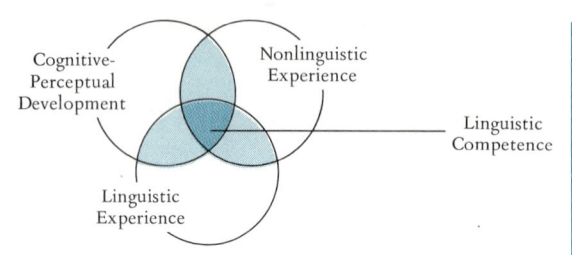

Figure 6.3 The roots of language development. (From L. Bloom. *Language development: Form and function in emerging grammars*. Research Monograph No. 59. Cambridge, Mass.: M.I.T. Press, 1970. P. 232.)

words to the infant's developing cognitive abilities, Bloom and other recent researchers have made use of important ideas presented ten years ago by Werner and Kaplan concerning the infant's ability to form symbols. Before an infant can speak a meaningful word, he first must be able to distinguish himself from the objects around him and then be able to understand that sounds can symbolize or stand for such objects. Sometimes between the fourth and tenth months the infant will begin to develop a concept of objects; until he does, he essentially sees the rest of the world as an extension of himself. (The object concept will be discussed in the section on Piaget in this chapter.)

The infant develops the use of symbols in the process of mentally separating himself from his mother, the primary object in his world. The objects that overlap his experience of himself and his mother and provide a link between them—such as food or a particular blanket—become his first primitive symbols.

From these "proto-symbols" or models of symbols, the infant progresses to the formation of other symbols and the use of "nonlinguistic representation," such as pointing and making call-sounds (Werner and Kaplan 1963). First the baby turns his body toward the object he is attempting to refer to, and then he develops the ability to point with his hand, and then with one finger. Call-sounds are refinements of babbling and are the vocal counterparts of pointing. Call-sounds are generally short, repetitive, barely modulated sounds that usually occur in a context that could be described as a goal-directed situation; it appears that the baby may be calling for a particular object or event. Werner and Kaplan believed that

these modes of nonlinguistic representation are the necessary precursors of linguistic representation or speaking. The infant's first words, and his use of single-word utterances, then, can be seen as a reflection of his developing ability to symbolize.

Although the 1-year-old generally can speak only a few words, his understanding of language far exceeds his ability to speak it. Maturation puts limits on the expression of his thoughts in words, but the 1-year-old can carry out many requests—such as, "Put the dog on the chair"—that show the extent of his language comprehension. Unexpressed comprehension can also be gauged by noticing how an infant solves simple puzzles or works out practical problems he encounters as he crawls or totters about. His actions indicate his understanding of how things relate to each other.

In his second year, he can begin articulating more of his thoughts; between his first and second birthdays, he learns words so rapidly that he seems to be adding a new word every other day. While his increasing physical maturation will allow him to enunciate these new words, his own urge to speak and the encouragement his parents give him will greatly influence how often and how well he actually uses those words.

For several months after delivering his first word, the infant continues to collect single words. Then, between his eighteenth and twenty-eighth month, he assembles his first simple sentence—such as, "Baby go" or "Baby eat." Though he forms these short sentences near the end of his second year, they actually signal the onset of a talking phase that blossoms fully in the child's third and fourth years—the next age level we shall discuss in this book. That section will consider the two-word sentence, as well as the questions relating to how the child gathers the elements of grammar and how he develops his sentence patterns.

Intelligence and the Infant

Scientific interest in the infant's intelligence has been active for over one hundred years. In the nineteenth century Charles Darwin, among others, kept baby biographies, one aim of which was to measure the baby's intellectual development as it was reflected in his physical behavior. Several concepts have emerged since those early efforts. Binet, early in this century, was the first of many to test infant intelligence; he focused on measuring the child's mental development by means of an extensive series of tasks the child performed in a set time. Guilford, a major contemporary figure in intelligence research, believes intelligence is a problem-solving ability made up of 120 factorial cells. His theory divides the mental process into five operations, including memory and evaluation; four products, such as memories; and four contents, which may be figural (actual images), symbolic (for example, a printed word), semantic (a grammar rule), or behavioral (actions, which also may be symbolic). Piaget, who began his research into intelligence in the 1920s and is still pursuing it, has taken another tack. Rather than assess the mental ability of individuals, Piaget has preferred to investigate the form of thought itself. We shall discuss his approach in considerable detail later in this chapter.

Testing Intelligence

In keeping with an often-cited American trait, the study of intelligence and the infant's cognitive workings in the United States has taken on a competitive note. In this country, an infant's intellectual rating is established by comparison with the group of children on whom the test was developed. This kind of comparative rating is accomplished by several infant intelligence tests. Some of the most prominent of these tests are the Cattell Intelligence Test for Infants and Young Children, the Minnesota Preschool Scale, the California Preschool Mental Scale, Merrill-Palmer, the Gesell Developmental Schedules, and Bayley's Scales of Infant Development.

These tests present the infant with a great number of tasks, selected to assess the power of his intellect. The standards of intelligence are established by first administering a newly constructed test to a group of infants large enough to be a cross section of the population. From such a tryout, the psychologists draw their norms—the average or median age at which most infants can perform each task. Using these norms, they rate the intellectual development of other infants as average, advanced, or below average. The Bayley Scale, for example, has 163 tasks for the infant. In one task—building a tower of two blocks—50 percent of the test children succeeded at the age of 13 months and 24 days. This age then became the norm for this task. In another task, 50 percent of 17-month-old infants used a stick to draw a toy to themselves. In still another, half the infants at 19½ months followed directions in pointing out the parts of a doll.

When the tester adds up the infant's performance on each task, he arrives at an overall assessment of his intelligence—the familiar I.Q. score. Most of the infant tasks require sensorimotor acts—muscular activity stimulated by sensory contact—and many are tests of manual dexterity. Some require a rudimentary grasp of language—identifying the doll's parts, for instance.

INFANT TEST SCORES: POOR PREDICTORS. Although infant intelligence tests are able to rank a baby in relation to his peers, they fall a good deal short of their target, which is to predict the intelligence of the infant several years from the test date. The reason for this failure is simple. While the infant tests primarily measure sensorimotor skills—the most efficient skills the infant then possesses—later tests move beyond these skills. Intelligence tests of 6- and 7-year-old children require the child to reason, remember, and use language and abstractions.

Bayley undertook a study spanning about six years to confirm the lack of predictive power for infant tests. First, she gave a group of infants tests made up of 185 tasks during their first few years. Then, at ages 6 and 7, she gave them the Stanford-Binet test, another well-known measurement of intelligence. Bayley found very few substantial correlations between the children's scores as infants and their scores as kindergarten and first-grade pupils. She concluded that test scores made by infants under 18 months are of no help whatsoever in predicting school-age abilities (Bayley 1943). Other experiments have shown that even scores earned at 21 months are not reliable in predicting the child's performance on the Stanford-Binet test four or five years later (Honzik 1938). In order to obtain a score correlation of any depth, in fact, intelligence tests should be given at age 2 or later.

MENTAL, COGNITIVE, AND LANGUAGE DEVELOPMENT **157**

Table 6.2 Items Drawn from Four Infant Tests for 6-Month-Old and 1-Year-Old Infants

Gesell & Amatruda (1941)	Bayley (1933)	Cattell (1940)	Griffiths (1954)
(Key age, 28 weeks) Lifts head. Sits erect momentarily. Radial palmar grasp of cube. Whole hand rakes pellet. Holds two cubes more than momentarily. Retains bell. Vocalizes *m-m-m* and polysyllabic vowel sounds. Takes solid food well. Brings feet to mouth. Pats mirror image.	5.8 mo. Exploitive paper play. Present a piece of paper to child so he may grasp edge of it. 5.8 mo. Accepts second cube. When child is holding one cube, place a second in easy reach. 5.9 mo. Vocalizes pleasure. 5.9 mo. Vocalizes displeasure. 6.0 mo. Reaches persistently. Place cube just far enough away from child so he cannot reach it. Credit if he reaches persistently. 6.1 mo. Turns head after spoon. Hold spoon so that it protrudes over edge of table by child's side and when he is interested, suddenly drop it to floor. 6.1 mo. Mirror image approach. Hold mirror before child, bringing it close enough so that he may reach it easily. 6.2 mo. Picks up cube deftly. 6.3 mo. Says several syllables.	(Key age, 6 months) Secures cube on sight. When child is sitting in upright position before table a one-inch cube is placed within easy reach. Lifts cup. Place straight-sided aluminum cup upside down within easy reach of child as he is sitting at table. Fingers reflection in mirror. While child is in sitting position, a framed mirror is held before him in such a manner that he can see his reflection but not that of his mother or other persons. Reaches unilaterally. Child sits with shoulders square to front and both hands an equal distance from examiner. A two-to-three-inch door key or peg is presented in perpendicular position. Reaches persistently. One-inch cube is placed on table just out of child's reach. Credit if child either reaches several times. Approaches second cube. Child is presented with one cube and as soon as he has taken it a second is held before him in such a position as to favor his grasping, but is not actually placed in his hand.	(Key age, 6 months) Plays with own toes. Sits with slight support. Anticipatory movements when about to be lifted. Manipulates bell. Makes 4+ different sounds. Secures dangling ring. Hands explore table surface. Holds two cubes.

It has been suggested, however, that an infant's attentiveness is related to his later intelligence. As Lewis (1971) has noted, "Attention is most necessary for any subsequent intellectual functioning, and individual differences in it will be predictive of differences in other learning phenomena." Measurements of attentiveness at 1 year, which tested specifically the infant's ability to distribute his attention and to switch his attention from familiar to new stimuli, were closely related to later I.Q. scores of the same infants at 4 years of age.

Whether or not infant tests of sensorimotor skills and attentiveness can predict an infant's future intelligence level, the tests may prove useful as detectors of the slow or retarded intelligence. Combined with a thorough observation of the infant's behavior and a comprehensive history of his development, the test scores can present quite an accurate picture of the infant's mental level at a specific stage in his growth. Experience has already shown that the tests can reveal mental abnormalities in infants very early—well before these defects would become apparent to an examining physician or a neurologist.

Intelligence as Action

When we speak of intelligence in infancy, we are referring to intelligence as a form of action—"sensorimotor action," in Piaget's terms. The infant retains this practical intelligence and uses it for the rest of his life. For instance, he exercises action-directed intelligence when, later in his life, he learns to ski, swim, play tennis, or drive a car. Because infant intelligence is a physically oriented faculty, we cannot, at this point, talk of symbolism; the ability to use symbols in thinking does not develop until near the beginning of the infant's second year. At this time, he begins to speak, play make-believe, and imitate. These activities are, in a sense, nonphysical in that they all refer to objects or actions that are not immediately present. Instead, the child "re-presents" these objects and remembered actions to himself and others through some act or sign—he *symbolizes* them.

Intelligence, like language, is as biological in infancy as are the motor behaviors that we discussed in Chapter 5. That is, just as sitting and crawling always occur in the normal human infant, so do intelligence and language. However, infant intelligence and language have important implications in later symbolic abstract thought.

Piaget: Intelligence in Infancy

Piaget has written that "intelligence is a particular instance of biological adaptation" (Piaget 1952). He also calls intelligence "the form of equilibrium toward which all the [cognitive] structures . . . tend" (Piaget 1950). These two statements present the briefest gloss of much of Piaget's basic attitude toward intelligence. The definitions suggest, first, that intelligence is the ability to adapt to an environment, and second, that the ability to adapt passes through a series of maturational stages as it develops. While all infants pass through the same stages, not all pass

Figure 6.4 Through his own physical actions, the infant discovers and constructs his knowledge of the world. (Charles Harbutt—Magnum)

through these stages at the same times. Some are slow in relation to the norms, others, fast. Piaget, however, is not interested in mapping the variations in rates of intellectual growth; instead, he is concerned with the sequences through which all must travel. Incidentally, while there is clearly a wide range in an infant's ability to adapt, studies have shown that early development predicts little in terms of linguistic or numerical ability.

A central belief underlying Piaget's theory of intelligence is that the infant's actions are essential to his development. It is solely through his own physical actions, Piaget contends, that the infant discovers and constructs his knowledge of reality.

Piaget's Basic Principles

Piaget bases his theory of intelligence on principles related to biological factors. We already have discussed two ways in which biological factors affect intelligence. First, hereditary physical structures establish broad limits on an infant's intellectual operations. Second, inherited behavioral reactions—reflexes—exert influence during the first days of life, although the infant's experience in his environment soon makes major changes in these reflexes. Piaget's theory adds another biological factor that affects intelligence. All species, he maintains, inherit two basic tendencies. Piaget calls them the tendencies to *adaptation* and *organization*.

ADAPTATION. All organisms, without exception, tend to adapt to their environments, though the methods of adaptation vary from species to species and among individuals within each species. Adaptation consists of two complementary processes: *assimilation* and *accommodation*. In the cognitive process of assimilation, the child modifies a new stimulus in his mind so that it will fit into the most appropriate schema he has at the time. An 18-month-old child is likely to refer to every woman as a "mommy," and to every child, regardless of age, as a "baby." The schemata of "mommy" and "baby" may be the only classifications he has for adult (or large) females and smaller humans of either sex. Piaget adapted the term *assimilation* from biology, and it can be thought of as the cognitive counterpart of digestion—food is taken in, is changed by digestive enzymes into usable substances, and then is absorbed or assimilated by the digestive tract. In the cognitive process, the new stimulus is assimilated into an existing schema, and the schema is thereby enlarged but not modified (Wadsworth 1971).

In the process of *accommodation*, on the other hand, the child will either modify an existing

Figure 6.5 Assimilation. The process in which the new stimulus is integrated into the existing schema. (After B. J. Wadsworth. *Piaget's theory of cognitive development: An introduction for students of psychology and education.* New York: David McKay Co., Inc., 1971. P. 14.)

Figure 6.6 Accommodation. The process in which the existing schema is changed to fit the new stimulus. (After B. J. Wadsworth. *Piaget's theory of cognitive development: An introduction for students of psychology and education.* New York: David McKay Co., Inc., 1971. P. 17.)

MENTAL, COGNITIVE, AND LANGUAGE DEVELOPMENT

schema in light of the characteristics of the stimulus he is trying to assimilate, or he will create a new schema that will allow him to assimilate the new stimulus. Thus, the child may refine his schema of "baby" so that it includes only infants and children who approximate his own size, and he may develop a new schema of "boy" or "girl" in order to assimilate people who are neither babies nor mommies and daddies. These processes of accommodation are different from assimilation because they produce changes in the child's cognitive structures, or schemata. The goal of accommodation, however, is the assimilation of a new stimulus. When the child achieves a balance between accommodation and assimilation—when he has satisfactorily dealt with a new stimulus—he has established what Piaget calls *equilibrium*. In Chapter 2, *equilibrium* was defined as the state in which the child has incorporated a new stimulus into his system of relationships with his environment.

ORGANIZATION. Organization is the second basic, inherited tendency, which, according to Piaget, affects intelligence in all species. Organization refers to the tendency of all species to order their processes into regular systems, either physical or psychological. A good example is the group of physical structures in the infant that permits him to breathe air—his mouth, nose, larynx, trachea, and lungs. All of these structures are closely related and coordinated into an efficient system that supplies oxygen to the blood. This kind of systematization is one result of the infant organism's tendency toward organization. This same tendency is present wherever organisms integrate themselves to form a composite system, such as a society, or family, which performs tasks of a higher order, tasks that none of the individual structures could perform alone.

The organizing tendency also exists at the psychological level. The infant's experience with reality prompts him to integrate his psychological structures into systems. The newborn infant, for instance, possesses separate behavioral structures for looking at a toy and for grasping it in his hand. At first, he simply looks. However, by 4 months of age, he is able to organize the looking and grasping structures into a single, higher-order structure. This structure permits him to hold a toy and look at it simultaneously. Organization, either physical or psychological, then, is the tendency of all life to integrate separate structures into higher-order systems.

Mapping a New World

Piaget has been widely criticized about the kinds of "data" that he uses to support his theory. His observations are sometimes based only on his own children and are highly subjective. They are not the sort of data with which most scientists would feel at all comfortable. In Piaget's case, however, what compels our attention is the way in which observations are linked together into an amazingly comprehensive account of how the child develops his own intelligence, how he comes to know objects, and how he begins to group events in the world around him.

In all cases, Piaget is attempting to describe logically the essential sequences through which a child must proceed in his development. It is the essence of developmental theory that it must show how each stage requires the preceding stage in order to function. The description of development is a listing of the prerequisites for each new competence.

Piaget's system is remarkable historically when contrasted to our prior understanding of the

Figure 6.7 Equilibrium. The state of balance between assimilation and accommodation, resulting in the integration of a new stimulus. (After B. J. Wadsworth. *Piaget's theory of cognitive development: An introduction for students of psychology and education.* New York: David McKay Co., Inc., 1971. P. 19.)

162 INFANCY

infant's intelligence. Until Piaget, there had been no such comprehensive realization of the steps taken in the development of thought. At the same time, Piaget's account should be seen for what it really is—a quite "primitive" map, in the scientific sense, opening up a new world for exploration, but not in itself a final, definitive, or validated account of that world.

Periods of Intelligence

Piaget divides intellectual development into two major periods. The first is the period of *sensorimotor intelligence*. It extends from birth to nearly 2 years of age and does not involve the use of language or symbols by the infant. In the period of sensorimotor intelligence, the infant is unable to use images, ideas, or words in his thinking; the dominant emphasis is clearly on overt physical action. The infant is busy encountering and mastering behaviors—such as sucking, sitting, and walking—that help him survive and adjust to his environment. Yet, physical as these acts are, Piaget is convinced that thought is derived from such actions, rather than from the infant's language. Furthermore, he emphasizes that such actions are the first forms of intelligence.

The second major period of intellectual development is *conceptual intelligence*. It is marked by the infant's systematic use of language and symbols. Conceptual intelligence begins to appear in the last half of the infant's second year. Its development follows the sensorimotor development phase of the first 18 months and occurs in three stages. The first is the preoperational stage, extending from about 18 months to 7 years. During this span, language emerges and becomes quite sophisticated. The child also becomes adept at the use of words and symbols to direct his action. This period is followed by the concrete operational stage, from 7 to 11 years, during which the child's orientation to objective reality increases to the point of understanding many systematic cause-and-effect relationships among objects and events. He knows how to use numbers, weight, volume, and measurement. At age 12, the child enters the last phase of intellectual development, called the stage of formal operations. From this time forward, he begins fully to employ and per-

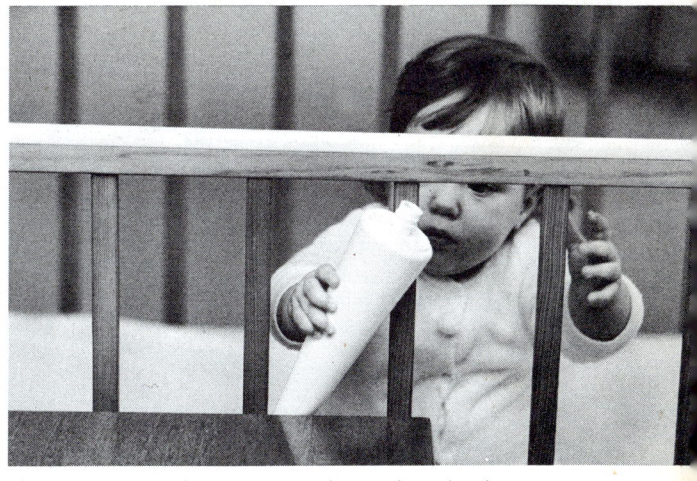

Figure 6.8 According to Piaget's theory, this infant has organized grasping and looking structures into a single, higher-order structure of grasping and looking at the grasped object simultaneously. (George Zimbel—Monkmeyer)

fect his developed abilities to understand and express reality, as he perceives it, in terms of ideas and abstractions. He can now work through ideas completely "in his head."

This section, which deals with the infant, will discuss only sensorimotor intelligence. Later chapters will describe the mental processes of older children and will investigate conceptual intelligence.

Sensorimotor Period: Six Stages

Piaget divides the 18-month-long sensorimotor period into six developmental stages. The first four stages occur during the first year, and the remaining fifth and sixth stages occur in the first half of the second year. Each stage is characterized by a new mode of behavior.

STAGE 1. This stage, encompassing the first month of life, is characterized by the newborn infant's fundamental mode of adapting to his environment—his innate reflexes, such as crying and sucking. Piaget maintains that the sucking reflex, as well as others, is not simply triggered by outside stimuli. It is the newborn infant himself, according to Piaget, who often initiates activity. Piaget also notes that, although the infant's reflexes do furnish a base for later development, they are emphatically only a starting point. As early as the first month of life, the infant's experience has

MENTAL, COGNITIVE, AND LANGUAGE DEVELOPMENT

begun to change and supplement the reflex mechanisms. For instance, infants often make sucking movements with their mouths just after they have been well fed. Piaget, observing his own son, noted this phenomenon:

During the second day also Laurent again begins to make sucking movements between meals. . . . His lips open and close as if to receive a real nippleful but without having an object. This behavior subsequently became more frequent. (Piaget 1952)

In the past, other instances of between-feeding sucking have been explained in terms of external stimulation, hunger, or the infant's association of pleasure with sucking which brings milk to allay his hunger pangs. However, in this particular instance, Laurent was not stimulated, nor was he hungry. Furthermore, the association between sucking and pleasure seems to have been established for too brief a time—less than two days—to prompt such extended and repeated nonnutritive sucking as Laurent displayed.

Piaget believes that Laurent's sucking is a demonstration of one particular form of assimilation—*functional assimilation*. The other two forms he has delineated are *generalizing assimilation* and *recognitory assimilation*. In its most general form, assimilation involves an organism's tendency to use its existing structures to deal with the environment. The principle of *functional assimilation* holds that when an organism possesses a structure, the organism has a basic tendency to use that structure, to make it perform. Thus, Laurent's nonnutritive sucking is simply a demonstration of the tendency of the infant's sucking reflex to activate itself. In some ways, functional assimilation parallels the concept of response generalization discussed in Chapter 2. In this instance, the sucking response becomes generalized when it occurs without a specific stimulus. The tendency of a response to activate itself is particularly strong in a structure or response which, like sucking in the month-old infant, is not yet well formed and needs to be perfected through practice.

Generalizing assimilation is a closely related tendency, and it parallels, to a certain degree, the process of stimulus generalization described in Chapter 2. Because structures need practice to develop, and the practice often involves objects, Piaget believes the infant tends to extend or generalize the range of objects that function as stimuli for a particular structure. For instance, the newborn at first will suck only a nipple or a finger inserted into his mouth, but later he will also suck on his blanket or furry toys.

The infant soon displays the ability to discriminate among stimuli, however. When he is hungry, for example, he can recognize, in a primitive way, the particular stimulus—the nipple—which will provide food. Piaget refers to this behavior as *recognitory assimilation*. He illustrates it by describing 20-day-old Laurent in the act of "recognizing" his mother's nipple as opposed to the skin around it. Laurent first bit the skin, sucked briefly, but quickly rejected it to search for the nipple with his mouth. When he found the nipple, he began sucking so rapidly that he appeared to have recognized immediately that this was what he had been searching for.

STAGE 2. During the second stage in the period of sensorimotor development, from 1 to 4 months, the infant forms habits, such as the extension of sucking beyond the breast or the bottle. While the infant's habits at this point are quite simple and related closely to his own body, they nonetheless are a step above his reflexive first-stage behavior. It is in this second stage that Piaget has defined the *primary circular reaction*, a phenomenon in which the infant's random behavior happens to cause something interesting or beneficial to happen. When this occurs, the infant immediately tries to rediscover or discriminate the act he has just performed, and after a series of attempts, he succeeds in duplicating the act. In the future, he may repeat the act, enjoying the result; these acts thus have become habits. Piaget's research documents the development of such a habit in his son Laurent:

At 0;1(1) [zero years; 1 month; 1 day] Laurent is held by his nurse in an almost vertical position. . . . He is very hungry. . . . Twice, when his hand was laid on his right cheek, Laurent turned his head and tried to grasp his fingers with his mouth. The first time he failed and succeeded the second. But the movements of his arms are not coordinated with those of his head; the hand escapes while the mouth tries to maintain contact. . . .

At 0;1(3) . . . after a meal . . . his arms, instead of gesticulating aimlessly, constantly move toward his mouth. . . . It has occurred to me several times that the chance contact of hand and mouth set in motion the directing of the latter toward the former and that then (but only then), the hand tries to return to the mouth. . . . [Later though,] it is no longer the mouth that seeks the hand, but the hand which reaches for the mouth. Thirteen times in succession I have been able to observe the hand go back into the mouth. There is no longer any doubt that coordination exists.

. . . . At 0;1(4) . . . his right hand may be seen approaching his mouth. . . . But as only the index finger was grasped, the hand fell out again. Shortly after it returned. This time the thumb was in the mouth. . . . I then remove the hand and place it near his waist. . . . After a few minutes the lips move and the hand approaches them again. This time there is a series of setbacks. . . . [But finally] the hand enters the mouth, the thumb alone is retained and sucking continues. I again remove the hand. Again lip movements cease, new attempts ensue, success results for the ninth and tenth time, after which the experiment is interrupted. (Piaget 1952)

Piaget's observations illustrate the steady development of thumb-sucking. At first, the infant cannot get his hand into his mouth. Next, he learns to do this, and then he learns to suck just the thumb instead of the entire hand. After the extended learning process, he can perform the thumb-to-mouth sequence smoothly and rapidly.

STAGE 3. The third stage stretches from 4 to 10 months of age. The infant's widening perceptions and motor capacities now permit him to crawl and manipulate objects around him. At this stage, the repetitive or circular reactions involve components of the infant's surroundings and are referred to as *secondary circular reactions;* the primary circular reactions of the previous stage centered on the infant's own body.

The infant still must rely on chance in his external environment to provide him with interesting objects or events, but now he has the capacity to enjoy the events and develop schemata to reproduce the events again and again. One of Piaget's observations of his son Laurent provides a good example of a secondary circular reaction. Laurent discovered by chance that he was able to move balls that were attached by strings to his hands. He appeared to be delighted when he saw the balls move, and quickly began repeating the motion that had first caused them to move.

Laurent was exhibiting not only a secondary circular reaction; he was also demonstrating once again the principle of functional assimilation: a functioning scheme needs to operate. The baby's ability to move his hand properly to cause the balls to move is an example of accommodation. However impressive this accommodation may seem in a 4-month-old, Piaget does not consider that the baby was acting intelligently. The infant's discovery that his hand could move the ball was at first accidental, not purposeful. However, the activity directed at duplicating the hand motions that resulted in pleasure was an example of intelligence.

Concept of Objects. During Stage 3, Piaget also detects four new behavior patterns that indicate the infant is fast forming a *concept of objects.* Until this point, the infant has seen the external world basically as an extension of himself. Gradually he has developed a rudimentary concept of self—he is conscious of where his body ends and his mother's body begins. Now he is capable of developing an idea of the nature of objects; he begins to understand that objects have an independent existence apart from himself, and he begins to make the connection between objects and his actions involving them.

From this point on, he will be able to perceive, accumulate, and process the endless information coming to him from his surroundings. The concept of objects is the foundation upon which our whole knowledge of the external world depends, and, as noted earlier, it is a necessary precursor to the formation of symbols and thus to the development of language (Werner and Kaplan 1963). A bit later in his development the infant will come to realize that objects also have permanence; that is, they continue to exist even when they are out of his sight.

The first of the four behavior patterns that show the infant is developing a concept of objects is his ability to anticipate where a dropped object will land, even if it falls very quickly. At first, he can only predict its landing place if he himself drops the object; later he can anticipate the land-

MENTAL, COGNITIVE, AND LANGUAGE DEVELOPMENT **165**

ing no matter who releases the object. The second behavior is a manual one that Piaget calls *interrupted prehension*. If an infant is reaching for an object, but loses it for some reason, he will continue the reaching motions in search for the object. However, if the infant was not reaching for an object that begins to disappear, he will not suddenly reach for it. He does not reach for the object because, as yet, it has no permanence for him. It exists only in relation to the action he is executing when the object slips from his fingers. The third behavior pattern is called the *deferred circular reaction*. Here, if an action involving an object is interrupted, the infant later resumes the action spontaneously. The infant's resumption of his action toward the object suggests that he expects the object to be where he saw it earlier. This development is an important forward step, for it shows that the infant now attributes a certain degree of permanence to the object, though his object concept is not yet mature. In the fourth behavior pattern, the infant recognizes a covered object when he can see certain parts of it still exposed. He now is able to reconstruct an invisible object from portions that may be visible. As might be expected, this behavior appears only after an infant has become skilled in handling objects and exploring them at close range and from various angles.

STAGE 4. The intelligence that is first revealed in this stage—which extends from approximately 10 to 12 months—occurs as the infant displays intent in his actions and adapts past sensorimotor accomplishments to master a new situation. In the following example, Laurent begins his activity with an objective in mind, rather than accidentally as he did in Stage 3. In approaching this activity he employs several of the principles of the previous stage. The earlier techniques (or schemata), however, are not successful in this instance, so Laurent modifies his old schemata to fit the requirements of the new stimulus, thereby displaying originality and intelligence.

. . . at 0;6(0) I present Laurent with a matchbox, extending my hand laterally to make an obstacle to his prehension. Laurent tries to pass over my hand, or to the side, but he does not attempt to displace it. As each time I prevent his passage, he ends by storming at the box while waving his hand. . . . Same reactions at 0;6(8), 0;6(10), 0;6(21), etc.

Finally, at 0;7(13) Laurent reacts quite differently almost from the beginning of the experiment. I present a box of matches above my hand, but behind it, so that he cannot reach it without setting the obstacle aside. But Laurent, after trying to take no notice of it, suddenly tries to hit my hand as though to remove or lower it; I let him do it to me and he grasps the box. I recommence to bar his passage, but using as a screen a sufficiently supple cushion to keep the impress of the child's gestures. Laurent tries to reach the box, and bothered by the obstacle, he at once strikes it, definitely lowering it until the way is clear. (Piaget 1952)

We see that Laurent's immediate reaction to the box was to attempt to assimilate it into his existing schemata—in action terms, to reach for and grasp the box. Here functional assimilation is evident. A working schema—grabbing the box—needs to function. But Piaget's hand blocks the way. At this point, Stage 4 behavior differs from Stage 3. Instead of reusing a behavior discovered accidentally, the infant displays originality—though limited—by trying to use as "obstacle removers" the schemata—striking, for example—that he has developed in other circumstances. This time, in an act of *generalizing assimilation*, the infant carries patterns of previously learned behavior to a new problem situation. In this generalizing process, he may modify old schemata and he may try out several for one purpose, but, finally, he will settle on one schema to remove the obstacle. His practical success at doing so determines the extent of the accommodation taking place in the action. When successful, as it was for Laurent, the result is a coordination of two secondary schemata—striking and grasping—that he learned earlier and has now slightly changed to suit the new situation. The infant's originality does not consist of inventing the two separate schemata, however; he already possessed them. When Laurent found the right schema and removed the obstacle, he then employed the familiar schema of grasping to get the matchbox. It is the novel combination of the two learned behavior patterns that carries the mark of intelligence at this stage.

STAGE 5. The infant's *tertiary circular reaction* emerges in this stage, which extends from 12 to 18 months. By this term Piaget denotes the infant's interest in novelty for its own sake. He is very curious about things themselves, how they feel and

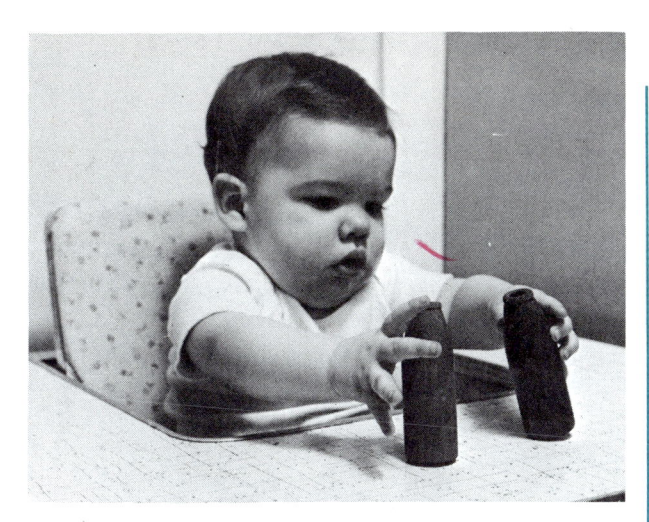

Figure 6.9 This infant displays curiosity about the nature of objects for their own properties—how they feel and behave. (Lew Merrim—Monkmeyer)

behave. He seems to want to absorb all he can about the nature of an object he examines. Piaget observed many different instances of such interest and curiosity.

. . . at 0;10(2) Laurent discovered in "exploring" a case of soap, the possibility of throwing this object and letting it fall. Now what interested him at first was not . . . the object's trajectory—but the very act of letting go. He therefore limited himself, at the beginning, merely to reproducing the result observed fortuitously.

At 0;10(10) . . . Laurent manipulates a small piece of bread. . . . Now in contradistinction to what has happened on the preceding days, he pays no attention to the act of letting go whereas he watches with great interest the body in motion [the falling bread]. . . .

At 0;10(11) Laurent is lying on his back. . . . He grasps in succession a celluloid swan, a box, etc., stretches out his arm and lets them fall. He distinctly varies the positions of the fall. Sometimes he stretches out his arm vertically, sometimes he holds it obliquely, in front or behind his eyes, etc. When the object falls in a new position (for example on his pillow), he lets it fall two or three more times on the same place, as though to study the spatial relation; then he modifies the situation. (Piaget 1952)

The action described above is much like the action in Stage 3. That is, by chance, the infant does something which produces an interesting result and thereafter he tries to repeat the action to achieve the same outcome. But at this point, the behavior in Stage 5 differs strikingly from that in Stage 3 because two notable aspects of the infant's novelty-seeking now come to the fore. First, rather than simply repeating the event he found interesting, Laurent in Stage 5 tries to vary the event. He drops the bread, the swan, and the box from new positions and heights. The second change from Stage 3 behavior is that the infant now is intrigued by the objects' new actions and actively searches out novelties. To all appearances, he regards the unexpected paths of the falling objects as things to be examined and understood.

STAGE 6. All of the infant's considerable progress to this stage is dwarfed by what begins to occur in this final period of sensorimotor development, which spans the ages from 18 months to 2 years. Before this stage, the infant could not think without actions; Stage 6 is the link between the purely sensorimotor phase of the infant's life and the coming, lifelong phase in which he will use mental symbols and language to identify objects and events that are not physically present to him. Through symbols, the infant will be able to move beyond the sensory world where physical things are the only reality. With symbols, the child can enter the vastly larger and more complex reality composed of thought and language. Stage 6, however, is only the transition to, not the fulfillment of, this level of operations. To illustrate the beginnings of thought, Piaget uses an anecdote in which he hides an attractive watch chain in a slightly opened matchbox and gives it to his daughter Lucienne, who was 16 months old at the time.

She looks at the slit [the narrow opening of the box] with great attention; then, several times in succession, she opens and shuts her mouth, at first slightly, then wider and wider!

Then . . . Lucienne unhesitatingly puts her finger in the slit, and instead of trying as before to reach the chain, she pulls so as to enlarge the opening. She succeeds and grasps the chain. (Piaget 1952)

Clearly, Lucienne has internalized actions she would earlier have performed physically. She now *thinks* about the ways to solve the problem instead. The mouth movement, to Piaget, means she

Table 6.3 Piaget's Theory of Cognitive Development: The Sensorimotor Period

Stage	General	Object Concept	Space	Causality
1. Reflex, 0–1 mo.	Reflex activity	No differentiation of self from other objects	Egocentric	Egocentric
2. First differentiations, 1–4 mos.	Hand-mouth coordination; differentiation via sucking, grasping	No special behavior re vanished objects; no differentiation of movement of self and external objects	Changes in perspective seen as changes in objects	No differentiation of movement of self and external objects
3. Reproduction, 4–8 mos.	Eye-hand coordination; reproduction of interesting events	Anticipates positions of moving objects	Space externalized; no spatial relationships of objects	Self seen as cause of all events
4. Coordination of schemata, 8–12 mos.	Coordination of schemata; application of known means to new problems; anticipation	Object permanence; searches for vanished objects; reverses bottle to get nipple	Perceptual constancy of size and shape of objects	Elementary externalization of causality
5. Experimentation, 12–18 mos.	Discovery of new means through experimentation	Considers sequential displacements while searching for vanished objects	Aware of relationships between objects in space, between objects and self	Self seen as object among objects and self as object of actions
6. Representation, 18–24 mos.	Representation; invention of new means via internal combinations	Images of absent objects, representation of displacements	Aware of movements not perceived; representation of spatial relationships	Representative causality; causes and effects inferred

Source: B. J. Wadsworth, *Piaget's Theory of Cognitive Development: An Introduction for Students of Psychology and Education.* New York: David McKay Co., Inc., 1971. Pp. 36–37.

is considering the options for action that she envisions. The infant's major accomplishment in this stage is being able to represent internally an event or an object not actually present. Through representation, he can try out solutions mentally, then perform the action he thinks will solve the problem.

Concept Development

OBJECT PERMANENCE. The infant's concept of object permanence grows out of his concept that objects have an existence independent from him. Once the infant discovers that he himself is a being separate from the other people and objects in his world, he then is capable of understanding that other people and objects also have permanence. First he learns that his mother returns to him after she leaves his sight, time after time, and he gathers evidence that she continues to exist when he cannot see her. The infant's concept of person permanence precedes the development of object permanence, and the quality of the infant's relationship with his mother contributes to his perception of external objects as independent constant entities (Bell 1970).

Piaget proposes that the concept of object permanence evolves through six stages, which correspond to the stages of intellectual development:

During the first two stages . . . the infantile universe is formed of pictures that can be recognized but that have no substantial permanence or spatial organization. During the third stage . . . a beginning of permanence is conferred on things by prolongation of the movements of accommodation (grasping, etc.) but no systematic search for objects which have been removed is yet observable. During the fourth stage . . . there is searching for objects that have disappeared but no regard for their displacements. During a fifth stage (about 12 to 18 months old) the object is constituted to the extent that it is permanent individual substance and inserted in the groups of displacements, but the child still cannot take account of changes in position brought about inside the field of direct perception. In a sixth stage (beginning at the age of 16 to 18 months) there is an image of absent objects and their displacements. (Piaget 1954)

Though Piaget's findings were based primarily on his observations of his own children, they often have been corroborated in principle by later studies. In 1966, for example, Charlesworth gathered data that supports Piaget's observation of object permanence in Stage 4 of sensorimotor development. Charlesworth's more systematic study focused on the infant's display of surprise when the experimenter's hand covered an object and made it "disappear." The resulting surprise reaction can be regarded as a relatively accurate barometer of the state of the infant's concept of object permanence. Since Piaget's personal observations were made, more precise measurements—such as changes in heart rate—have been used to measure such perceptions. These findings have portrayed the infant as much more perceptive than previously thought. Of course, this also indicates that Piaget, who devoted enormous care and precision to his painstaking observations, was aware of the infant's otherwise unsuspected receptivity.

IMITATION. Another significant aspect of infant behavior that Piaget sees as developing throughout the sensorimotor stages is imitation. He considers that it, like all other behaviors, is still another of the infant's attempts to comprehend and affect reality. As a result, imitation develops along with other aspects of cognitive growth, such as the concept of object permanence. Imitation first emerges in Stage 2 of sensorimotor development (extending from 1 to 4 months of age) when the infant imitates only actions he himself has already performed. These are confined to rudimentary sounds, eye movements, and grasping. From here, the infant progresses to Stage 3 (4 to 10 months) where he begins to imitate models with greater ease—though still performing only actions he already had mastered—and then to Stage 4 (10 to 12 months), where he begins to imitate the new actions of others around him. His imitation is clumsy at first, but by the end of Stage 5 (12 to 18 months), the infant is systematically imitating new actions he observes. By Stage 6, the infant has begun to internalize action. Thus, instead of physically trying to imitate an action, he can internalize the action and work it out mentally, evaluating many possible schemata very rapidly. This results in what seems to be immediate imitation of actions.

Another notable aspect of Stage 6 is the infant's ability to register a behavior without immediately imitating it. This *deferred imitation* means the infant can retain the absent behavior in some mental form, an image perhaps, and bring it into active use whenever he desires. This ability to form and retain an image or some type of mental construct is the beginning of representational and symbolic thinking.

CLASSIFYING OBJECTS. Piaget identified in Stage 3 the emergence of the infant's ability to classify objects into groups. These grouping activities, he believes, are the precursors for more complex classification—logic—later in life. Furthermore, as we noted in Chapter 2, the act of classification is the primary mode of cognitive thinking. Piaget observed an instance of classification in his daughter at about 6 months:

At 0;6(12) Lucienne perceives from a distance two celluloid parrots attached to a chandelier and which she had sometimes had in her bassinet. As soon as she sees them, she definitely but briefly shakes her legs without trying to act upon them from a distance. (Piaget 1952)

Thus, when Lucienne saw the familiar toy parrots, she did not carry through actions that would bring the parrots to her. Instead, she displayed a spontaneous, abbreviated behavior, apparently not expecting it to bring the parrots to her. Piaget sees the abbreviated behavior as a physical forerunner of the later classification activity. The infant has no mental concept of parrots and she cannot yet label the objects with a descriptive word. She is left to the more primitive device of her brief little kick, which says, in effect, "I know those things. They're parrots and they swing." At this point, the understanding of the concept *parrot* is not mental, but, nonetheless, the recognitory kick is the infant's first step toward thought because she has classified the parrots as objects she already has experienced.

RELATIONS BETWEEN OBJECTS. During Stage 3, Piaget also finds that the infant develops a primitive, nonmental understanding of how events and objects relate to and affect each other.

In the evening of 0;3(13) Laurent by chance strikes the chain while sucking his fingers . . . he grasps it and slowly displaces it while looking at the rattles. He then begins to swing it very gently which first produces a slight movement of the hanging rattles and an as yet faint sound inside them. Laurent then definitely increases by degrees his own movements: he shakes the chain more and more vigorously and laughs uproariously at the result obtained. On seeing the child's expression it is impossible not to deem this gradation intentional. (Piaget 1952)

Apparently, the infant can tell the difference between his own slight and more vigorous movements. He also can distinguish between a loud and muted rattle. He can even relate two movements or two sounds to each other. That is, the infant now recognizes that the muted and loud rattle and the slight and the vigorous movements are "lows" and "highs" on scales of sound and movement. He also seems to understand that the vigor of his movements is directly related to the volume of sound that his rattle makes. According to Piaget, these perceptions of differences in volume and intensity are the source of the infant's later quantitative thinking, and the recognition that variations in his activity produce variations in an object's response is a precursor of causal thinking.

In Stage 4, the infant establishes relationships of greater complexity than he had formed in Stage 3. When, at 7 months, Laurent removed an obstacle to get at his goal of the matchbox, he coordinated behavioral schemata to do it. Removing the obstacle to get at the goal shows Laurent "realized" a certain relationship between Piaget's blocking hand and the box.

Almost exactly two months after the matchbox incident, Piaget recorded another behavior pattern that reflects a grasp of more complex relationships among things:

. . . at 0;9(17), Laurent lifts a cushion in order to look for a cigar case. When the object is entirely hidden the child lifts the screen with hesitation, but when one end of the case appears Laurent removes the cushion with one hand and with the other tries to extricate the objective. The act of lifting the screen is therefore entirely separate from that of grasping the desired object and constitutes an autonomous "means," no doubt derived from earlier and analogous acts. (Piaget 1952)

In this instance the boy has learned not only how to get the cigar case; he also has discovered the relation between the obscuring cushion and the cigar case. Laurent's actions indicate he had grasped the physical relations—that the cushion was *on top of* the cigar case and the case was *under* the cushion. Unlike the adult, the infant does not possess this relationship as an abstraction; for him the relationship exists only as a specific incident within a particular behavior directed toward a goal.

Voluntary Behavior

Partly as a result of Piaget's work, the infant's voluntary behavior is a phenomenon that has been gaining increasing attention in the last decade. Jerome S. Bruner, an American child psychologist who is one of the leading researchers in this area, considers voluntary behavior to have five characteristics. Voluntary behavior implies, first, anticipation of a goal, or a result, and the selection of a means of reaching that goal; second, freedom from immediate sensory control; third, an ability to maintain a behavior beyond a single response; fourth, the sequential ordering of responses. Last, of course, voluntary behavior demands skill in making the desired response. The newborn infant usually can meet few, if any, of these requirements. His goal anticipation is not fully developed. He has automatic reflexes, rather than a choice of means to his goal. He is dominated by a flood of stimuli, and he is so engaged in activities that are immediately satisfying to him that it is hard to detect when his more goal-directed behaviors begin or end. Finally, the newborn lacks many instrumental skills, except his reflexive sucking and his early ability to follow a light with his eyes.

One technique Bruner has used to extend the research on voluntary behavior is to make films of infant activities. With such films, Bruner has revealed novel phenomena that no one had previously observed. For example, he found that in one film the infant's behavior clashed with a well-known observation by Piaget. Bruner's film shows that even a quite accomplished 7-month-old will commonly begin a reach after sighting his target, but then dispense with visual guidance as he completes the reach. The visual guidance the infant does use is a fixation on the target object, not a back-and-forth glancing from hand to object, as Piaget observed. Once the infant has begun his reach, he may no longer look at his target. If the reaching involves conflict between the infant's linear vision and the course his hand must follow, the infant may avert his gaze or close his eyes entirely as he executes the reach. Being able to cut off visual contact in this way is also one of the baby's first forms of control in relations with people. As early as 3 months, babies simply turn away when they have had enough contact or stimulation from someone.

While Bruner's observations add considerably to our knowledge of the structure of voluntary behavior, like Piaget's, they do not tell us precisely how such behavior is elicited. While we must suppose that the capacity for voluntary behavior is innate, it is clearly responsive to external influences. Here the work of Berlyne is of value.

Curiosity

Berlyne noted that it is difficult to link the exploration responses of organisms to the traditional motives of arousing or reducing thirst, hunger, or pain (Berlyne 1960). Where such conventional motives for responses seem to be lacking, Berlyne suggested that the actual motive may be a curiosity or exploratory drive. The cause of the drive may emerge from an arousal of conflicting responses. A large stuffed dog that barks when

Figure 6.10 The infant reaches for and grabs the object. After he has sighted his target and directed his hand toward it, he no longer needs to maintain visual contact with the object. (Wil Blanche—D.P.I.)

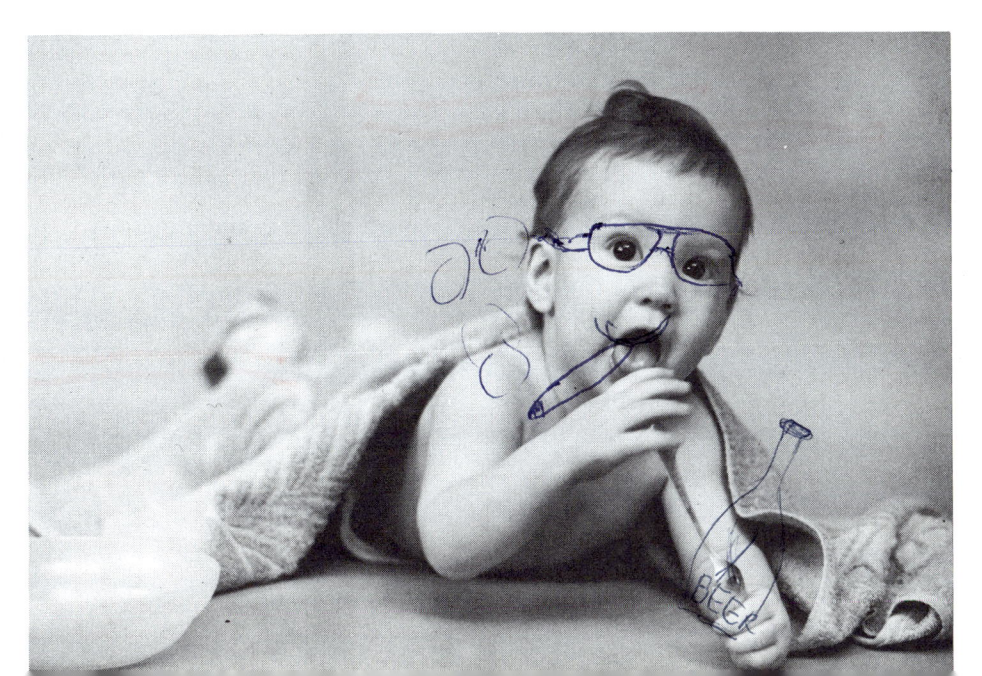

wound up may provoke a clash of incompatible responses in the infant—the desire to hold the furry toy and the impulse to scurry away from its barking sound. To reduce the conflict produced by the incompatible tendencies, the infant explores the novel object. In addition to novelty, Berlyne noted that an object's complexity, uncertainty, surprisingness, and incongruity also produce exploratory responses.

While novelty, complexity, and other qualities are quantitatively measurable, they are nonetheless primarily psychological rather than physical dimensions. It is difficult to define a variable such as complexity—is a triangle a simple shape and a hexagon a complex one?—yet it is clear that variations in an object's complexity or other qualities do prompt distinctly different responses in infants. A newborn, for instance, will look for a longer time at a checkerboard of only 4 squares than he will at a board with 16 or 144 squares. Several weeks later, the same infant will prefer the more complex checkerboard. Complexity can be defined also in terms of the number of different ways in which an object can transmit information. For example, a multicolored rubber ball that has indentations on its surface and a noisemaker inside that squeaks when the ball is squeezed or bounced is a much more complex toy than a smooth and silent red rubber ball.

In addition to its overall complexity, the squeaking rubber ball has another property that increases its interest-capturing value—an additional mode of responsiveness. When the baby squeezes, drops, or throws the ball, it not only will bounce—it will respond by making a funny sound as well. Responsiveness also is measured in terms of visual or tactile changes that a baby can produce in an object.

Novel or unfamiliar objects or events also have been found to hold the gaze of 6-year-old children much longer than a stimulus that had been presented fifty times before (Cantor and Cantor 1964). Furthermore, two days after this experiment, the "numbing" effects of the familiarization were still apparent; thus, the children continued to prefer the novel over the familiar stimuli.

Charlesworth (1964) used surprise as a measure of a child's curiosity. In the experimental situation, the child, expecting one thing, was deliberately presented with a discrepant object. The experiment showed that the discrepant object produced surprise in the infant, held his attention, and evoked persistence to a greater degree than did novel or familiar stimuli.

The level of curiosity and exploratory behavior an infant will display can be limited or increased by the variety and complexity of the objects he is exposed to at home. Rubenstein (1971) observed a group of 5-month-old infants in their own homes and found that those who regularly had the opportunity to see and handle the greatest variety of complex objects exhibited the most curiosity and exploration when she gave them new toys. The infants who were kept in unchanging, monotonous surroundings and had fewer and simpler objects to play with showed the least amount of interest in the new toys she presented. Rubenstein concluded that variety and complexity in an infant's environment, as early as the first 5 months of life, serve to keep him alert and receptive to new stimuli. Thus, an infant accustomed to high levels of variety and complexity in his environment has a greater capacity and inclination for seeking out new and varied stimulation.

A study that included institutionalized babies as well as those from homes in the lower and middle socioeconomic classes showed similar results (Collard 1962). The institutionalized babies, who had very little experience with varied and complex objects, explored the least and exhibited the fewest schemata when they were given new toys. Babies from the lower-class homes explored as much as those from middle-class homes, but the middle-class babies (who had been exposed to the greatest variety of complex objects) displayed the greatest number of schemata in playing with the new toys.

Play and Cognition

An infant slapping at a balloon or beating a spoon on a pan is demonstrating the essence of voluntary behavior—play. We call child's play "voluntary behavior" because it is a totally self-initiated program of varied behaviors. Until recently, the term *play* had been used indiscriminately to describe almost everything an infant or child does. Now, however, many behaviors that psychologists once labeled play are regarded as demonstrations of sensorimotor intelligence, as we noted in our discussion of Piaget's theories.[1]

Despite the greater selectivity now being shown in labeling behaviors as play, there remains the question of what precisely constitutes play. As yet, there is no generally accepted definition of what play is—or what it does. Because the word *play* can stand for so many activities—the infant shaking his rattle, the 7-year-old hosting a tea party, the college student playing basketball, the person solving a crossword puzzle—Berlyne (1968) has suggested dropping the term completely. Nevertheless, despite its inadequacies, developmental psychologists continue to use the term to record particular types of human voluntary activities.

THE FUNCTION OF PLAY. Just as there is no formalized definition of play, so there is no unified theory about precisely what function play serves in a person's life. Very little research has been devoted to answering this question until recently. Some think the investigation of play's function has been neglected so long because work—not play—has been more highly valued in our production-oriented industrial civilization (DeGrazia 1962). Despite the lack of research on its precise function, however, play is generally assumed to be important to the infant's cognitive development. The degree of importance, however, varies according to the general theoretical viewpoint being considered.

Compensation. Proponents of both the classical psychoanalytic theory and Piaget's theory feel that play serves primarily as compensation. Freudian psychoanalysts usually agree that play is related to intellectual growth, but only as it helps to reduce tensions that might impede intellectual activity. Piaget, however, attributes a more important role to play. He believes play permits the child to substitute an intellectual response through fantasy when he cannot make that response in reality. This substitution of a fantasy or make-believe response for a real one allows the child to experiment with ways of coping with the world without risking defeat or jeopardizing his feeling of independence. Piaget also believes that play helps a child to organize and retain information he has acquired in other situations.

Cognition. The view of play as compensation can be contrasted with others that attribute to the actual playing itself a more active cognitive function—even when the form of play may appear to serve mainly a social purpose. Sociologists, for instance, have long regarded play periods as model situations in which the child rehearses the roles he will assume later in life. The post-Freudian psychoanalyst Erik Erikson, however, sees a cognitive function being performed here as well. He believes the child's play serves an intellectual function parallel to the planning an adult does. Sociologists such as Mead also have pointed to the implications for cognitive development that social play may have. Mead has suggested that children develop social *understanding* by having to adjust their actions according to the role another person is playing. For example, a child cannot hide very well in the game of hide-and-seek unless he has understood and based his actions on what the others do when they are seeking (Mead 1934; Goffman 1961).

A NEW LOOK AT PLAY. In the past decade there has been a growing interest, along these lines, in the functional significance of play; play no longer tends to be subjugated to the minor role it so recently held. This change of attitude is a result of at least two shifts in psychological theory. First is the emergence of a new concept of the animal and human as stimulus-seeking organisms given to curiosity and exploration. And second is an increased awareness of, and interest in, the cognitive character and potential value of creativity and other expressive activities, and these, of course, include play.

Exploration and Cognition. In much of the true play research in the last few years, play has usually been linked to exploratory behavior. Both play and exploratory behavior are described as self-motivated activities whose reward to the "players" or "explorers" is the satisfaction they gain from participation in the play or exploration

---

1. The following discussion of play is based on the author's article, "The Role of Play in Cognitive Development," in *Young Children*, 1967, 22, 361–370.

itself (Berlyne 1960). For example, the discovery of new information about toys (the teddy bear growls when it is squeezed) or furniture (chairs can be tipped over) is a pleasure for an infant. This view parallels Piaget's belief that a child develops his cognitive powers by actively seeking new stimuli and is motivated by the pleasure of learning something new. And, as Maw and Maw pointed out in their 1965 study, exploratory and play behavior in children correlates highly with the children's information-seeking in general.

We know that more highly evolved animals spend a greater amount of time playing than do more primitive ones, and we also know that more play occurs in the more complex civilizations (Roberts and Sutton-Smith 1962). It appears, then, that play must have a role in increasing the infant's capacity for a larger range of responses and cognitive operations. Works that deal with the relations between exploration and cognition seem to support such a point of view (Piaget 1952; Welker 1961; Hutt 1966; Collard 1972). They describe a baby's, or young animal's, series of responses to novel objects or settings in the following manner:

If a baby is given a novel toy, say a bouncing ball, he first *examines* it. Then he makes potentially adaptive responses (touches, pokes, mouths, lifts, and drops it), and *repeats* those that are effective (poking, dropping). He continues those repetitions until he achieves mastery of the object, after which he habituates to the stimulus and decreases his rate of response (he becomes bored and stops playing with the ball). As an alternative approach, he might proceed as above, but after he has habituated to the stimulus he would change to *combinatory* activity: he applies the new responses (lifting and dropping) to old objects (teddy bear, bottle), applies old responses to the new object (hugging, fondling, babbling to the ball), combines new responses with old responses (dropping the ball while babbling to it), and the new object with old objects (hitting the teddy bear with the ball). Further, after the combinatory activity, he may make another shift to *transformational* activity (if he is older than about 3 years), which essentially is pretending. He transforms responses or objects into other responses or objects with a make-believe character—he might pretend the ball is a rocket ship as he throws it up in the air.

There are variations in children's approaches in carrying out the sequence of events. For example, children sometimes stop after the first two steps (examination and repetition) and do not proceed to the second two steps (combination and transformation). Sometimes a child's response is to reverse the last two steps or separate them with a considerable time interval, or separate them spatially. The explanations for these variations in approach have yet to be determined. It could be, for example, that if a child is relaxed when he approaches a stimulus that is novel but not anxiety-inducing, and when the situation is relaxed and familiar, it is possible for him to carry through the whole sequence. In circumstances where the child is somewhat apprehensive, however, he may feel that after he has accommodated to the first stimulus (steps one and two), he must transfer his interest to other novel stimuli in order to feel secure with them also.

When play is analyzed in this way—as the working through of novel responses and operations—it can be summarized as the *socialization of novelty*. This way of looking at play enables us to understand why in the work cultures of the world, such as early nineteenth-century Europe and some current tribal cultures of Asia and Africa, playing—of the sort described above—is regarded as trivial. In such cultures, requirements of adult behavior are quite rigid (factory work or herding, for instance), rather than novel; for survival reasons, children are socialized into these roles early. In the more diverse information culture of the Western world, however, children must be socialized so that they can manage a succession of novel contingencies and make their own novel transformations, and play seems to be related to this type of functioning.

Creativity. Other recent research has indicated that children who are taught to play imaginatively will score more highly on creativity tests than will children who have not had such play training (Feitelson and Rose, in press). This finding supports the interpretation above that play is related to the socialization of novelty. An earlier researcher who reached a similar conclusion is Nina Lieberman. She investigated the connection between playfulness (transformation activity) and creativity in 93 children from middle-class homes attending kindergarten classes in three New York schools. She rated the children's playfulness on scales that included these characteristics:

1. *How often does the child engage in spontaneous physical movement and activity during play?* This behavior would include skipping, hopping, jumping, and other rhythmic movements of the whole body or parts of the body like arms, legs, or head, which could be judged as a fairly clear indication of exuberance.
2. *How often does the child show joy in or during his play activities?* This may be judged by facial expressions such as smiling, by verbal expressions such as saying "I like this" or "This is fun," or by more indirect vocalizing, such as singing as an accompaniment of the activity, e.g., "choo, choo, train go along." Other behavior indicators would be repetition of activity or resumption of activity with clear evidence of enjoyment.
3. *How often does the child show a sense of humor during play?* By "sense of humor" is meant rhyming and gentle teasing ("glint-in-the-eye" behavior), as well as an ability to use a situation as funny as it pertains to himself or others.
4. *While playing, how often does the child show flexibility in his interaction with the surrounding group structure?* This may be judged by the child joining different groups at any one play period and becoming part of them and their play activity, and by being able to move in and out of these groups by his own choice or by suggestion from the group members without aggressive intent on their part. (Sutton-Smith 1967)

Lieberman concluded that the scales had sounded out a single factor of playfulness in children. More important here, however, is the significant relationship she discovered between playfulness and the ability to perform several creative tasks. She found that children rated as more playful also were more adept at (1) producing novel suggestions about how to modify a doll or toy dog to make it more fun to play with; (2) suggesting novel titles for two illustrated stories that were read and shown to the children; and (3) compiling novel lists of toys, food, and animals (Lieberman 1965).

More Play—More Responses. What, then, is the functional relationship between playfulness and creativity? We start from the assumption that when a child plays with particular objects, playfully varying his responses among them, he increases the range of his associations for those particular objects. He also discovers many more uses for those objects than he would without his play. Some of these uses may be completely private inventions. Many will be imaginative, fantastic, absurd, and perhaps serendipitous—that is, unexpected but very fortunate. Almost anything in the infant's repertoire of responses or cognitions can be combined in this way with anything else for a new result. Of course, recent and intense experiences can be expected to play more prominent roles. Most of the infant's associating and combining is probably of no use except as an expressive, rewarding exercise. It is also likely, however, that these two activities increase the child's repertoire of responses and cognitions, so that if he is faced with a situation or a "creativity" question involving a similar object, he is more likely to be able to make a unique, or creative, response. Thus, play increases the child's repertoire of responses, an increase that has potential value for later responses in different situations.

While most of the activities a player exercises in a game have an expressive value in and for themselves, such activities do occasionally show adaptive value—for example, when a healthy sportsman is required by emergency to run for help, or when the baseball pitcher is required to throw a stone at an attacking dog, or when a football player must fight hand-to-hand in war, or when the poker player has to consider the possibility that a business opponent may be merely bluffing. In such cases, it is not necessary to find a direct cause-and-effect connection between play and adaptive behavior. What can be found is the general evolutionary requirement that organisms or individuals with wider ranges of expressive characteristics, of which play is but one example, are equipped with larger response repertoires for use in times of adaptive need or crisis. It is in this sense as well, then, that we can define play as the socialization of novelty.

Summary

The newborn's first utterance, and generally his only one for about eight weeks, is the cry — his response to hunger, fatigue, and discomfort. Cooing, a response to pleasurable stimuli or excitement, begins in the second month; the infant now modulates sound with his tongue. By about 6 months these sounds become more like speech and are called babbling. Babbling involves stringing together a great variety of sounds and is dramatically increased by social rewards. There is evidence that the amount of babbling directly relates to later attentiveness and the size of vocabulary and I.Q. in females.

Phonemes, the fundamental vowel and consonant sounds from which all language is formed, are uttered almost from birth; vowel sounds predominate at first but consonants soon outnumber them. At about 12 months, the infant combines vowels and consonants to construct morphemes — the shortest meaning units of language. These become his first words.

Infant I.Q. scores based on sensorimotor performance before age 2 seldom correlate with later I.Q. scores. An infant's attentiveness may be a more reliable predictor of his later intelligence.

Piaget believes intelligence is a special type of adaptation, dependent at first on physical action. The infant seeks new stimuli, explores them, then mentally incorporates them into his world, by accommodation and assimilation, to achieve equilibrium. The separate cognitive structures thus formed become organized into higher-order systems.

From birth to about 2 years, according to Piaget, the infant develops sensorimotor intelligence; he primarily uses overt physical action, instead of language and symbolic thought, to adapt to his environment. This period is divided into six maturational stages. In the first, the infant uses only reflexive action to deal with stimuli. In the second and third stages, he develops primary and secondary circular reactions, and he acquires a concept of objects, as shown by interrupted prehension and deferred circular reactions. In Stage 4, the infant begins to combine two learned behavior patterns. In the fifth stage, tertiary circular reactions develop and the infant becomes interested in novelty for its own sake. In the sixth stage, symbolism emerges, enabling the infant to link action with thought. This stage provides the transition into the next major period, conceptual intelligence. Object permanence, imitation, deferred imitation, and object classification all develop throughout the sensorimotor period.

While various studies have investigated voluntary behavior — or play — in infants, we still do not know exactly how such behavior is elicited or what function it serves. Complexity, novelty, and discrepancy, however, are known to raise the infant's level of curiosity and exploratory behavior, which are expressed in "playful" activities. In turn, playfulness has been correlated with cognitive development and creativity. Playing provides the infant with opportunities to create new schemata and to increase his repertoire of responses to novel stimuli. Some of these responses may be simply expressive exercises, rewarding in themselves, and others may have potential value for later adaptations to other situations.

Case Studies

Debbie P.

Debbie was an unplanned, but eagerly awaited, firstborn. An alert, precocious child, Debbie was the center of attention for her middle-aged parents — particularly for Mrs. P., who had retired from active medical practice to become a mother. Debbie's father, an erudite psychiatrist, not only participated in her morning and evening activities, but had a good deal of free time to spend with his daughter each summer.

Within her first few weeks, Debbie showed unmistakable signs of unusual alertness. Her auditory sensitivity, for example, was demonstrated in her second week when she began to follow room sounds. And soon after her first month she was orienting discriminatively to the sound of her name or her nickname.

At 2½ months, Mrs. P. described Debbie's prolonged "conversations" with her parents, with Debbie's "total body straining prominent as she tries to vary her tonal range, or make various lingual and labial sounds." Debbie's range of vocal (and facial) expressions continued to widen throughout this third month to the point where Mrs. P. noted a definite—although undefinable—change "from infant to baby." During this same time period, Debbie had also begun to react appropriately to words and phrases in context—for instance, "Hold on" (with parents' hands outstretched), and "Take a bath."

At around 4 months Debbie seemed to be trying some "vocal magic" on her crib mobile—not yet having learned that things, unlike people, could not be influenced by her vocalizations. Mrs. P. also reported that Debbie apparently mistook a nearby curly-haired black jacket for the family poodle, and, straining toward it from her crib, uttered something "suspiciously like 'dg, dg, dg.' "

During the next several months Debbie's scope of vocalizations increased to include polysyllabic and vowel sounds strung together in monologues with a wide range of tones and volumes; nap-time humming; and an expressive "Ha!" to signify that she had done something she was pleased with. These were followed at about 9½ months by the introduction of considerable "expressive jargon"—Debbie's use of multisyllabic "pre-words" complete with appropriate cadences, melodic characteristics, and phonetic intonations. During this same time, Debbie recognized, and reacted to, phrases like "Go get it" and "Are you hungry?" She also knew the meaning of the admonition "No," often initiating her own warning as she approached any of the family's few forbidden objects.

Having already shown a "marked interest" in reading, Debbie's second year began with her learning to find things like noses, butterflies, and O's in magazine ads; to mimic the sounds of many pictured animals; and to watch her parents' mouths, attempting to copy sounds for words that intrigued her. Mrs. P. estimated that her daughter responded appropriately to about 80 words and 20 phrases.

Interestingly, however, from her fourteenth to eighteenth months, Debbie's progress seemed to reverse itself, and Mrs. P. noted a conspicuous *loss* of vocabulary. Debbie's style of speech was temporarily reduced to "dis" and "dat" with an accompanying pointing; words would appear for a day or two, then drop away as quickly as they came; and explanations to parents took the form of paragraph-long "patternless jargon," all enunciated extremely slowly and carefully. This idiosyncratic transitional period—possibly a preparation in expressive forms for syntax—soon gave way, however, to the introduction of new words and new combinations of words—at first in certain stock phrases ("How about that?" or "You're welcome."), and then in truly novel grammatical utterances which heralded a new stage of linguistic competence (Church 1968).

Benjamin C.

Like Debbie, Benjamin ("Benjy") was an unexpected, but welcome, late arrival for his middle-aged parents. His father, a warm and gentle man in his early fifties, worked as a college professor and traveling consultant. His conscientious mother had worked in a semi-executive capacity until Benjy's birth, and returned to that job on a part-time basis in her son's tenth month. Benjy had a brother and a sister—both teen-agers—and a playful dog named Sam.

From his earliest months, Benjy demonstrated an acute sensitivity to sounds around him, although noises outside of his immediate environment were often (and inexplicably) ignored. He also exhibited an early interest in attempting to imitate his mother's exaggerated mouth movements and sounds as she bent over his crib saying "Hi!" By his third month, Benjy's vocalizations included gurgles, coos, and some little shouts. His mother characterized him as "most" responsive to talking and singing, often "talking back" to adults verbalizing or singing to him. Mrs. C. reported her son's first consonant at 4 months—something between a *t* and a *d*, which he then repeated throughout one full day.

By his fifth month, Benjy was demonstrating his ability to differentiate his tones of crying, yelling, and cooing to coincide with specific sources of distress, anxiety, or pleasure. He also could consistently discriminate certain favored verbal sounds: his ready smile, for instance, at the mention of Dr. Doolittle's "Gubgub the Pig," or when his father asked him, "How are the Threeeeeee Bears?"

During the next couple of months Benjy expanded his vocabulary of consonants and wordlike sounds. Instead of long strings of vowels and randomly inflected babbling, Benjy now began to issue whole paragraphs of intonated syllables. Within a couple of weeks his mother had pretty well determined that her son reserved his "ma-ma-ma" sounds for times of distress, since he uttered no other *m* sounds except when he seemed to want her. She suspected no real naming sense of "ma-ma" as yet, however.

In Benjy's ninth month there were clear indications of solidifying "ma-ma" and "da-da" sounds, along with "goggie," which eventually developed into "dog." Later that month Benjy was obviously puzzled when Mrs. C. commented on the other "doggie" that had entered their yard to sit beside Benjy's Sam. Although Benjy repeated the word "doggie," he seemed unable to reconcile this same name with a very different-looking dog. Although the next two months brought a considerable increase in vocalizations and gamelike imitation of his parents' simple verbalizations, there was nothing in the way of intelligible speech. Benjy was beginning to respond to specific words and phrases, however, as he would willingly "Wave bye-bye" or react appropriately to "Open your mouth."

The first half of Benjy's second year, then, was a period of steady progress toward greater linguistic competence. More and more phrases drew appropriate responses; new words slowly became prominent and well articulated; the family noticed many more definite attempts to imitate adult utterances; and Benjy indulged in frequent all-day practice sessions for new sounds of the *g* or *th* or "chookachookachook" variety. By his sixteenth month, he could not only name familiar things but could comment when something was "all gone" and could request to get "down." Although Benjy occasionally continued to prattle in long stretches of expressive jargon, used almost no final consonants even with words he knew well, and was as yet uncertain that the name "Benjy" belonged exclusively to him, he was clearly on the threshold of true syntactic speech as he entered the second half of his second year.

Benjy's further language development will be described in Chapter 8 (Church 1968).

References

Acheson, R. M. Maturation of the skeleton. In F. Faulkner (Ed.), *Human development*. Philadelphia: Saunders, 1966.

Almy, M., et al. *Young children's thinking: Studies of some aspects of Piaget's theory*. New York: Teachers College Press, 1966.

Ames, E. W., and Silfen, C. K. Methodological issues in the study of age differences in infants' attention to stimuli varying in movement, complexity, and novelty. Paper read at Conference of Society for Research in Child Development, Minneapolis, April 1965.

Aronson, E., and Rosenbloom, S. Space perception

in early infancy: Perception within a common auditory-visual space. *Science*, 1971, *172* (3988), 1161–1163.

Banikiotes, F. G., Montgomery, A. A., and Banikiotes, P. G. Auditory reinforcement of infant vocalizations. *Proc. Ann. Conv. Amer. Psychol. Ass.*, 1971, *6* (Pt. 1), 135–136.

Bayley, N. *The California first-year mental scale.* Berkeley and Los Angeles: Univer. of California Press, 1933.

Bayley, N. Mental growth during the first three years. In R. G. Barker, J. S. Kounin, and H. F. Wright (Eds.), *Child behavior and development.* New York: McGraw-Hill, 1943.

Bayley, N. Comparisons of mental and motor test scores for ages 1–15 months by sex, birth order, race, geographical location, and education of parents. *Child Develpm.*, 1965, *36*, 379–411.

Beach, F. A. Concepts of play in animals. *Amer. Natur.*, 1945, *79*, 523–541.

Bell, S. M. The development of the concept of object as related to infant–mother attachment. *Child Develpm.*, June 1970, *41*, 291–311.

Bellugi, U., and Brown, R. (Eds.) The acquisition of language. *Monogr. Soc. Res. Child Develpm.*, 1964, *29*.

Berlyne, D. E. *Conflict, arousal and curiosity.* New York: McGraw-Hill, 1960.

Berlyne, D. E. Laughter, humor, and play. In G. Lindzey and E. Aronson (Eds.), *Handbook of social psychology.* (2nd ed.) Reading, Mass.: Addison-Wesley, 1968.

Bloom, L. *Language development: Form and function in emerging grammars.* Research Monograph No. 59. Cambridge, Mass.: M.I.T. Press, 1970.

Bloom, L. *One word at a time: The use of single word utterances before syntax.* The Hague: Mouton, in press.

Braine, M. D. S. The acquisition of language in infant and child. In C. Reed (Ed.), *The learning of language.* New York: Appleton-Century-Crofts, 1970.

Brockman, L. M., and Riccuiti, H. N. Severe protein-calorie malnutrition and cognitive development in infancy and early childhood. *Develpm. Psychol.*, May 1971, *4*(3), 312–319.

Bruner, J. *Processes of cognitive growth: Infancy.* Worcester, Mass.: Clark Univer. Press, 1968.

Bühler, C. *The first year of life.* Trans. by P. Greenberg and R. Ripin. New York: Day, 1930.

Bühler, C., and Hetzer, H. *Testing children's development from birth to school age.* New York: Farrar & Rinehart, 1935.

Cameron, J., Livson, N., and Bayley, N. Infant vocalizations and their relationship to mature intelligence. *Science*, July-August 1967, *157*, 331–333.

Cantor, J. H., and Cantor, G. N. Observing behavior in children as a function of stimulus novelty. *Child Develpm.*, 1964, *35*, 119–128.

Carroll, J. B. *Language and thought.* Englewood Cliffs, N.J.: Prentice-Hall, 1964.

Cattell, P. *The measurement of intelligence of infants and young children.* New York: Psychological Corporation, 1940.

Charlesworth, W. R. Instigation and maintenance of curiosity behavior as a function of surprise versus novel and familiar stimuli. *Child Develpm.*, 1964, *35*, 1169–1186.

Charlesworth, W. R. Development of the object concept: A methodology study. Paper presented at Conference of American Psychological Association, New York, September 1966.

Chomsky, N. *Language and mind.* New York: Harcourt Brace Jovanovich, 1968.

Church, J. (Ed.) *Three babies: Biographies of cognitive development.* New York: Random House, 1968. Pp. 3–106; 107–162.

Collard, R. R. A study of curiosity in infants. Unpublished doctoral dissertation, Univer. of Chicago, 1962.

Collard, R. R. Exploration and play in human infants. *Leisure Today*, 1972, *1*(2).

Corman, H. H., and Escalona, S. K. Stages of sensorimotor development: A replication study. *Merrill-Palmer Quart.*, 1969, *15*, 351–362.

Darbyshire, M., and Scott, P. M. Some cultural factors related to cognitive functioning: I and II. *Australian J. ment. Retard.*, June 1970, *1*(2), 40–45.

DeGrazia, S. *Of time, work, and leisure.* New York: Twentieth Century Fund, 1962.

DeLaguna, G. *Speech: Its function and development.* Bloomington: Indiana Univer. Press, 1963.

Eimas, P. D., Sigueland, E. R., Juscyzk, P., and Vigorito, J. Speech perception in infants. *Science*, January 1971, *171*(3968), 303–306.

Elkind, D., and Flanell, J. (Eds.) *Studies in cognitive development: Essays in honor of Jean Piaget.* New York: Oxford Univer. Press, 1969.

Erikson, E. H. *Childhood and society.* New York: Norton, 1963.

Feitelson, D., and Rose, G. S. *The neglected facts—play.* In press.

Fellows, B. J. *Discrimination process and development.* New York: Pergamon, 1968.

Fowler, W., and Lethwood, K. A. Cognition and movement: Theoretical pedagogical and measurement considerations. *Percept. and motor Skills*, April 1971, *32* (2), 523–532.

Furth, H. G. On language and knowing in Piaget's developmental theory. *Human Develpm.*, 1970, *13*(4), 241–257.

Gesell, A. *The mental growth of the preschool child: A psychological outline of normal development from birth to the sixth year, including a system of developmental diagnosis.* New York: Macmillan, 1925.

Gesell, A., and Amatruda, C. S. *Developmental diagnosis.* New York: Hoeber, 1941.

Gesell, A., and Thompson, H., assisted by C. S. Amatruda. *Infant behavior: Its genesis and growth.* New York: McGraw-Hill, 1934.

Gesell, A., Thompson, H., and Amatruda, C. S. *The psychology of early growth.* New York: Macmillan, 1938.

Ginsburg, H., and Opper, S. *Piaget's theory of intellectual development: An introduction.* Englewood Cliffs, N.J.: Prentice-Hall, 1969.

Goffman, E. *Encounters.* Indianapolis: Bobbs-Merrill, 1961.

Golden, M., Birns, B., Bridges, W., and Moss, A. Social-class differentiation in cognitive development among black preschool children. *Child Develpm.*, 1971, 42 (1), 37–45.

Gordon, I. J., et al. *Child learning through child play.* New York: St. Martin's Press, 1972.

Gouin Decarie, T. *Intelligence and affectivity in early childhood: An experimental study of Jean Piaget's object concept and object relations.* New York: International Universities Press, 1966.

Gratch, G., and Landers, W. F. Stage IV of Piaget's theory of infants' object concepts: A longitudinal study. *Child Develpm.*, June 1971, 42(2), 359–372.

Griffiths, R. *The abilities of babies: A study in mental measurement.* New York: McGraw-Hill, 1954.

Guillaume, P. *Imitation in children.* Chicago: Univer. of Chicago Press, 1971.

Herron, R. E., and Sutton-Smith, B. *Child's play.* New York: Wiley, 1971.

Honzik, M. P. The constancy of mental test performance during the preschool period. *J. genet. Psychol.*, 1938, 52, 285–302.

Hutt, C. Exploration and play in children. In P. A. Jewell and C. Loizos (Eds.), *Play, exploration and territory in mammals.* New York: Academic Press, 1966.

Ingram, D. Transitivity in child language. Unpublished paper, Stanford Univer., 1970.

Inhelder, B., and Piaget, J. *Early growth of logic in the child.* New York: Humanities Press, 1971.

Irwin, O. C. Development of speech during infancy: Curve of phonemic frequencies. *J. exp. Psychol.*, 1947, 37, 187–193.

Irwin, O. C. Infant speech: Development of vowel sounds. *J. Speech and Hearing Disorders*, 1948, 13, 31–34.

Irwin, O. C. Infant speech: The effect of family occupational status and of age on sound frequency. *J. Speech and Hearing Disorders*, 1948, 13, 320–323.

Irwin, O. C. Infant speech: Speech sound development of sibling and only infants. *J. exp. Psychol.*, 1948, 38, 600–602.

Irwin, O. C. Speech development in the young child: 2. Some factors related to the speech development of the infant and young child. *J. Speech and Hearing Disorders*, 1952, 17, 269–279.

Irwin, O. C., and Chen, H. P. Infant speech: Vowel and consonant frequency. *J. Speech and Hearing Disorders*, 1946, 11, 123–125.

Laurendeau, M., and Pinard, A. *Development of the concept of space in the child.* New York: International Universities Press, 1970.

Lenneberg, E. H. *Biological foundations of language.* New York: Wiley, 1967.

Lenneberg, E. H. (Ed.) *New directions in the study of language.* Cambridge, Mass.: M. I. T. Press, 1964.

Leopold, W. F. Patterning in children's language learning. *Lang. Learning*, 1953–54, 5, 1–14.

Lewis, M. Individual differences in the measurement of early cognitive growth. In J. Hellmuth (Ed.), *The exceptional infant.* Vol. II. *Studies in abnormalities.* New York: Brunner-Mazel, 1971.

Lewis, M., and Goldberg, S. Perceptual-cognitive development in infancy: A generalized expectancy model as a function of mother–infant interaction. *Merrill-Palmer Quart.*, 1969, 15, 81–100.

Lieberman, J. N. Playfulness and divergent thinking: An investigation of their relationship at the kindergarten level. *J. genet. Psychol.*, 1965, 107, 219–224.

Littenberg, R., Tulkin, S. R., and Kagan, J. Cognitive components of separation anxiety. *Develpm. Psychol.*, May 1971, 4(3), 381–388.

Maw, W. H., and Maw, E. W. *Personal and social variables differentiating children with high and low curiosity.* Cooperative Research Project No. 1511. Wilmington: Univer. of Delaware, 1965.

McCall, R. B., and Kagan, J. Attention in the infant: Effects of complexity, contour, perimeter and familiarity. *Child Develpm.*, 1967, 38, 939–952.

McCarthy, D. Language development in children. In L. Carmichael (Ed.), *Manual of child psychology.* (2nd ed.) New York: Wiley, 1954.

McKenzie, B., and Day, R. H. Operant learning of visual pattern discrimination in young infants. *J. exp. child Psychol.*, February 1971, 11(1), 45–53.

Mead, George H. *Mind, self and society.* Chicago: Univer. of Chicago Press, 1934.

Moore, T. Language and intelligence: A longitudinal study of the first eight years. *Human Develpm.*, 1967, 10, 88–106.

Morehead, D. M. Processing of phonological sequences by young children and adults. *Child Develpm.*, March 1971, 42(1), 279–289.

Moss, H. A. Sex, age and state as determinants of mother–infant interactions. *Merrill-Palmer Quart.*, 1967, 13, 19–36.

Mowrer, O. H. Speech development in the young child. 1. The autism theory of speech and some clinical applications. *J. Speech and Hearing Disorders*, 1952, 17, 263–268.

Murphy, L. B., et al. Children under three: Finding ways to stimulate development. *Children*, March 1969, 16 (2), 46–62.

O'Shea, M. V. *Linguistic development and education.* New York: Macmillan, 1907.

Piaget, J. *The psychology of intelligence.* Trans. by M. Percy and D. E. Berlyne. London: Routledge & Kegan Paul, 1950.

Piaget, J. *The origins of intelligence in children.* Trans. by M. Cook. New York: International Universities Press, 1952.

Piaget, J. *The construction of reality in the child.* Trans. by M. Cook. New York: Basic Books, 1954.

Ramey, C. T., and Ourth, L. L. Delayed reinforcement and vocalization rates of infants. *Child Develpm.*, March 1971, 42(1), 291–297.

Rheingold, H. L. *Maternal behavior in mammals.* New York: Wiley, 1963.

Rheingold, H. L., Gewirtz, J. L., and Ross, H. W. Social conditioning of vocalizations in the infant. *J. comp. physiol. Psychol.*, 1959 *51*, 68–73.

Roberts, J. M., and Sutton-Smith, B. Training and game involvement. *J. Ethnology*, 1962, *1*(2), 166–185.

Rubenstein, J. Dimensions of early stimulation and their differential effects on infant development: Dimensions of the inanimate environment. Paper presented at biennial meeting of the Society for Research in Child Development, Minneapolis, April 1971.

Schlesinger, I. M. Production of utterances and language acquisition. In D. I. Slobin (Ed.), *The ontogenesis of language: Some facts and several theories*. New York: Academic Press, 1971.

Shirley, M. M. *The first two years: A study of twenty-five babies*. Vol. II. *Intellectual development*. Minneapolis: Univer. of Minnesota Press, 1933.

Smitherman, C. The vocal behavior of infants as related to the nursing procedure of rocking. *Nursing Res.*, May 1969, *18*(37), 256–258.

Stott, L. H., and Ball, R. S. Infant and preschool mental tests: Review and evaluation. *Monogr. Soc. Res. Child Develpm.*, 1965, *30* (3, Serial No. 101).

Sutton-Smith, B. *The games of New Zealand children*. Berkeley and Los Angeles: Univer. of California Press, 1959.

Sutton-Smith, B. The role of play in cognitive development. *Young Children*, 1967, *22*, 361–370.

Sutton-Smith, B. Novel signifiers in play. Unpublished manuscript. Bowling Green State Univer., 1967.

Tizard, B., and Joseph, A. Cognitive development of young children in residential care: A study of children aged 24 months. *J. child Psychol. and Psychiat. and Allied Disciplines*, December 1970, *11*(3), 177–186.

Wachs, T. D., and Cucinotta, P. The effects of enriched neonatal experiences upon later cognitive functioning. *Develpm. Psychol.*, November 1971, *5*(3), 542.

Wadsworth, B. J. *Piaget's theory of cognitive development: An introduction for students of psychology and education*. New York: McKay, 1971.

Wallach, M. A., and Kogan, N. *Modes of thinking in young children*. N. Y.: Holt, Rinehart & Winston, 1965.

Welker, W. I. An analysis of exploratory and play behavior in animals. In D. W. Fiske and S. R. Maddi (Eds.), *Functions of varied experience*. Homewood, Ill.: Dorsey, 1961.

Werner, E. E., and Bayley, N. The reliability of Bayley's revised scale of mental and motor development during the first year of life. *Child Develpm.*, 1966, *37*, 39–50.

Werner, H., and Kaplan, B. *Symbol formation: An organismic-developmental approach to language and the expression of thought*. New York: Wiley, 1963.

White, B. L., Castle, P. W., and Held, R. M. Observations on the development of visually-directed reaching. *Child Develpm.*, 1964, *35*, 349–364.

White, B. L., and Held, R. M. Plasticity of sensorimotor development in the human infant. In J. F. Rosenblith and W. Allinsmith (Eds.), *The causes of behavior: Readings in child development and educational psychology*. (2nd ed.) Boston: Allyn & Bacon, 1966.

Wolff, P. H. *The causes, controls and organization of behavior in the newborn*. New York: International Universities Press, 1966.

7 Social Development

THE NEWBORN INFANT—though he has no experience outside the womb—already is capable of several responses to the world. He can cry, follow a moving light with his eyes, suck, and move his head, arms, and legs. The mother, who usually is the most constant observer of his behavior, also is the person who reacts most to it—feeding the infant when he cries in hunger, soothing him when he frets, smiling and laughing with him when he plays.

The mother's reaction (or the caretaker's in the absence of the mother) influences the infant's specific responses and, therefore, his social development. For example, the way a mother responds to her infant's crying, particularly by the second half of the first year, can influence his crying—how long, how intensely, and when he cries. However, most infants' crying in the first half year is triggered by internal discomfort of one sort or another and should be attended to.

In the first weeks and months of his life, the infant quickly develops more and more responses—such as smiling, lifting his head, reaching toward objects—as well as the self-initiated babbling and kicking which contented infants often indulge in, even when they are alone. These activities usually compel as quick a response from the mother as the infant's cries or his anxious fretting. The infant's babbling may be increased by his mother's reactions to his vocalizing. As we saw in the preceding chapter, babbling infants to whom someone reacted by smiling, clucking, or touching, babbled substantially more than infants without such reinforcements (Rheingold, Gewirtz, and Ross 1959).

It is the complex interplay of the infant's actions and reactions with those of his primary caretaker, usually the mother, that builds the foundation for the mutual attachment between parent and infant. This attachment increases and becomes more rewarding for the mother as the infant begins to respond to such social gestures as talking, smiling, nuzzling, and waving. For his part, the infant is "conservative" in that he likes to see behavior repeated; the repetition of his mother's reactions to his responses builds the attachment bond in him.

While the quality of the mother–child relationship becomes the basis for the child's future social capacities, this crucial first relationship is, in turn, affected by the set of norms or expectancies that the infant and mother bring to each situation. Their relationship has to be worked out in terms of these two sets of "rules." The infant has his innate temperament and the sequences of responses which maturation determines, and the mother has her expectations of the way infants should behave and should be treated, as well as her own temperamental capability for carrying out or not carrying out her own expectancies. The infant's norms and the mother's norms set the territorial limits for this process of mutual discovery and mutual adjustment. Together they have to settle what actually will occur as they go along from day to day.

Learning the social actions that produce attachments, first to his mother, and then to a wider spectrum of other persons, seems to be one of the major developmental achievements during the first two years. The influences of the child's peers and other persons outside his family will play an increasingly greater role after the age of 2; these relationships, therefore, will be discussed in the chapters that follow. The emphasis here will be on the infant's interactions with his parents. As we shall see, the idea that the infant influences the actions of his parents is a relatively new concept.

Figure 7.1 The interplay of the infant's responses with those of his parents or primary caretakers builds the foundation for mutual attachment. (Evelyne Heim — Rapho Guillumette; Mimi Forsyth — Monkmeyer; Bruce Roberts — Rapho Guillumette)

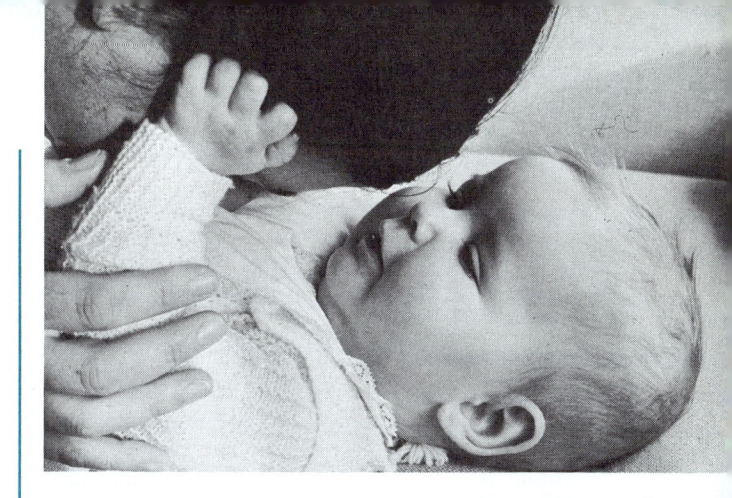

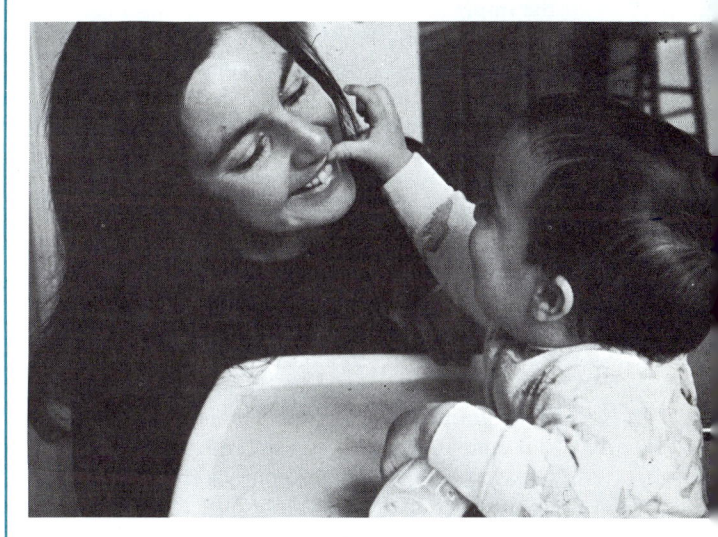

Child–Parent Interaction

Western society has always reflected a disagreement between those who felt that heredity best explained children's behavior and those who placed greater weight on their relationships with their parents. It is probably true, however, that the last few centuries have been somewhat unique in their emphasis on the parents' effect on children. Locke's seventeenth-century view of the infant as a blank tablet upon which parents make the impressions that form the child has been carried forward by similar attitudes of the learning theorists in our own times, such as Watson and Skinner. Within the last decade or so, however, the pendulum seems to have swung back somewhat from the simplicities of this *tabula rasa* position.

Various studies of child social development have indicated that children probably do inherit constitutional traits which differ from infant to infant and affect the individual's behavior. These findings suggest that the historical concept of the parents' role presents only half the story, leaving out the temperament of the infant as an important factor in his development. The infant's own special temperament plays a determining role in the two-way interaction between parent and infant—an interaction seldom entertained in historical views of human development.

In the study of offspring–parent interaction, investigators of animal behavior have been ahead of those who study children. In 1965, Noirot confirmed what other animal experimenters had found shortly before. In his work with mice, Noirot showed that a female's interest in her litter was closely linked to changes in the pups' behavior—that is, the varying stimuli they conveyed to her. Other animal studies have shown other effects of offspring on parents. Lactation, the secretion of milk by a female (Bruce 1961), plus licking and nest building (Noirot 1965), have been induced and sustained by presenting a female rat with a series of new litters. Certain behaviors of the mother and offspring evidently are synchronized and tend to regulate each other. The maternal responses of a female rat, it has been shown, can be lowered and then increased again by first removing her litter at birth, and a few days later returning the pups to her nest (Rosenblatt 1969). Then, as the pups mature and begin to produce new responses to the mother, such as playing, her maternal behavior declines; this leads, in turn, to more independent behavior on the part of pups.

These findings with animals have an important implication for human development. If mature animals, which are thought to respond to the rigid behavior patterns we call instincts, are affected by the varying behaviors of their young, it seems logical to expect human parents—whose behavior is noninstinctive and responsive to many more influences—to reflect to the same degree the variations in their children's behavior.

Influences on Parent–Infant Relationships

THE CHILD'S TEMPERAMENT. One of the most apparent aspects of the infant that will affect his relationship with his parents is his own temperament. A child's temperament is congenital—he inherits it from his parents—and it may include many qualities that can be seen as desirable or undesirable, depending on the situation. For example, assertiveness—active persistence in the face of obstacles—is a quality of temperament that affects the child–parent relationship in many ways each day. A parent faced with a mildly assertive child usually will try reasoning—"Stand still so you won't get stuck with the pin"—or an appeal—"Sit still and be a nice boy"—or threats to withdraw love—"Be still or you can't be Mama's little boy." The parents of a highly assertive child, on the other hand, may sometimes find themselves restraining physically, shouting at, or even striking their child if he persists in disruptive behavior when they are in no mood for nonsense. Parents of a passive, nonassertive child may enjoy more peace at home, but not much more peace of mind. They may react to the nonassertive child by prompting him to action, rewarding his occasional performance, and insisting that he avail himself of new toys, social activities, and a variety of playmates.

IRRITABILITY LEVEL. Other inborn personality traits besides temperament can influence the parent–child relationship. Just as activity or passivity can evoke different responses from the parent, so, too, will the infant's level of irritability, which he displays by crying and fretting. After observing 3- and 12-week-old infants in their homes, Moss concluded in 1967 that male infants slept less and were more irritable than female infants. Consequently, the sons received more attention than the daughters. Nonetheless, at 12 weeks of age the boys consistently showed fewer social responses in terms of smiles, coos, and eye-to-eye contact than the girls. This apparent contradiction —greater maternal attention resulting in less social response—may be explained by the observation that during most of the time the mothers spent with their sons, they were intent on soothing them. They tried to quiet them, alleviate pain or discomfort, and avoid stimulating them. For although stimulation might result in smiling or cooing, it also might prompt renewed crying or fretting, which the mothers naturally wanted to discourage. Thus, when the boys were awake but quiet, the mothers tended to give them wide berth. Here, then, apparently is an instance in which inherent, sex-linked behavior causes the mother to respond in a certain way—her response is caused by the child's irritability level, not by her own disposition. Of course, it is also possible the mother's response is in part determined by her feeling that males should be left to fend for themselves.

OTHER CONGENITALLY INFLUENCED TRAITS. There is some evidence that several other qualities of personality besides assertiveness and irritability level are inherited to a certain degree. Person-orientation is one such quality. The infant who is person-oriented seems to be a born "cuddler" who later displays a penchant for hugging soft stuffed animals and who likes to be held by others. He is attentive to his parents' behavior, and he readily adopts their social responses. For this kind of child, the parents' threat to withdraw their love would be a potent device for controlling his behavior (Bell 1968).

The infant who does not demonstrate person-orientation also dislikes being held, but likes objects and activity. He can be controlled by promising, or withholding, desired objects (a block; later a bicycle, a sports car), though the parents may resort fairly frequently to spankings. Needless to say, threats to withdraw love do not gain so much cooperation from this child (Bell 1968).

Goal-directedness and social responsiveness also may have a congenital basis. Goal-directedness—concentration on a task through its completion—has been found to be significantly inheritable in studies of twins conducted during the first year of life (Freedman 1965). Social responsiveness—a generalized version of person-orientation, or wider-ranging sociability—also has a high likelihood of being hereditary, according to studies that cut across social, sexual, age, and cultural lines (Scarr 1965).

MATERNAL ATTITUDE. Besides her child's congenital personality traits, a mother is open to other influences that affect her relationship with the baby. Her own maternal attitude is important—it could account for the amount and type of contact she initiates with her baby, as well as for the speed with which she responds to him. A mother who feels that a baby is a bother may leave an infant crying for hours in an upstairs room; she may justify her action by explaining, "I'm letting him cry it out—babies need to cry."

A study by Moss (1967) provided concrete evidence that a mother's acceptance of her maternal role and her image of babies corresponds closely to the way she answers her child's everyday needs. The mothers in this study first were rated on their "acceptance of the maternal role" and the extent of their positive attitude toward babies two years prior to giving birth. The ratings were based on interviews structured to render an attitudinal profile of their marriages. After these women gave birth they were observed at home with their infants. Moss found that the mother's attitude affected how often she held the infant close, how she fed the infant, how much affectionate contact she had with him, and how often she imitated the sounds he made.

Clearly, the mother's own attitude, as well as her infant's temperament, irritability level, and other inborn traits, influence the extent and kind of contact she will have with her child. Here again is an example of how the norms of each member of the pair can shape the interaction between them.

Responses that Affect Parent—Infant Interaction

SMILING. An infant's tendency to smile, even though it may not be recognized as an individual characteristic at first, can affect his relationship with his mother. If he smiles frequently, for whatever reason, he conveys contentment to his mother. This makes her feel successful in her maternal role. A gloomy, unsmiling child may have a contrary effect, possibly causing his mother to question her maternal competence. Her feeling of failure may possibly prompt the mother to be hostile to the infant's future demands because such demands only deepen her suspicion that she is incompetent at a task women are expected to perform successfully with natural ease.

While the infant smile has been recognized for some time as an important factor in the child–parent interaction, Bowlby (1958) went beyond the acknowledgment of its importance to assert that the infant's smile was an action to which the mother *had to respond* if she wanted to form a relationship with her baby. Whether or not Bowlby is correct in making the response of the mother so critically important, it is true that the mother's response actually does reinforce the infant's smiling. In 1958, Brackbill tested a group of infants 14 to 18 weeks of age to assess the effect of the mother's or caretaker's response. After establishing a base rate of smiling—that is, how frequently the unstimulated infant smiles—Brackbill placed each infant on its back in a crib. If an infant smiled a researcher smiled back, picked him up, and carried him for about 30 seconds. This reward was found to substantially increase an infant's smile frequency over the base-rate performance. Thus, it is clear that although smiling at first can be triggered by nonsocial stimuli—such as an intriguing mobile—it soon is controlled increasingly by social rewards, such as the experimenter's reciprocal smile.

While studies have made clear that the caretaker's response does affect how often the infant smiles, other research has shown that all infants smile with varying frequency, and that the *tendency* to smile is not learned through social conditioning. Among groups of infants raised in families—as opposed to institutions—a wide range of smiling frequency has been noted. Some infants, it was found, will smile often at a strange face or even at a mask; others, on seeing the same stranger or mask, will maintain a stony gaze. A critic might contend that these reactions are the result of early social conditioning. For a socially "uncontaminated" test group, we can examine newborn babies. However, we find that they, too, span a wide spectrum, from the enthusiastic smiler to the invincibly dour infant. Moving further from the possibility of social conditioning, we find that even premature babies display different smiling frequencies, some smiling readily, others not at all, even when coaxed and stimulated (Freedman 1966). Thus, the initial smiling tendency is obviously unlearned, for it is visible in many infants before they have any consistent contact with other humans. The fact that smiling is an unlearned response, however, does not mean that rein-

Figure 7.2 While the response of smiling is unlearned and the tendency to smile varies in different infants, smiling in the infant is affected by the mother's, or caretaker's, response. (Arthur Lavine—Monkmeyer)

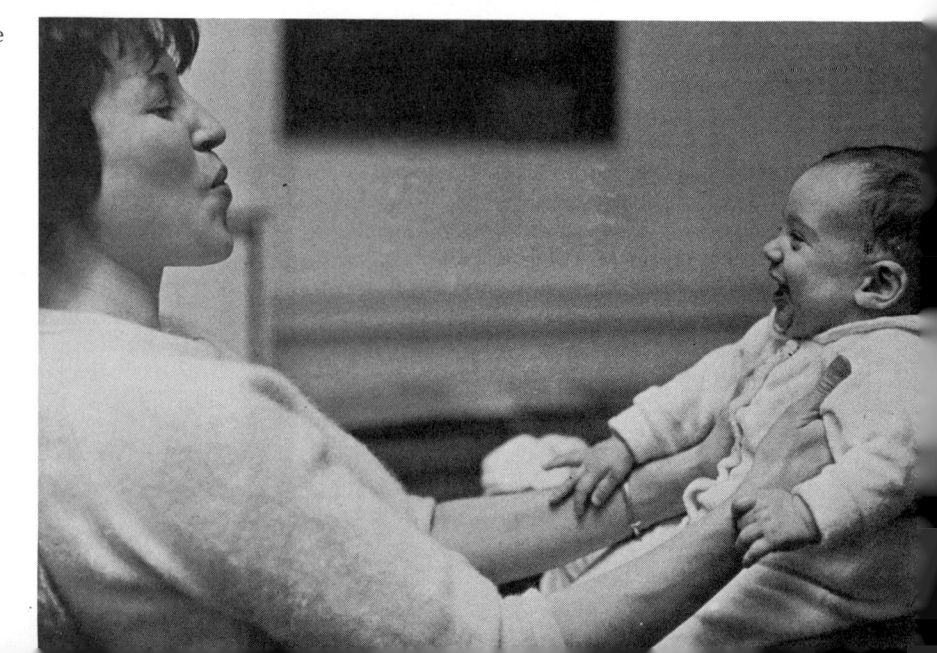

forcement has no effect on the infant's subsequent behavior. It remains true that the infant's smiling is conditioned by his caretaker's response, and this reciprocal pattern is a significant factor in the development of the child–parent interaction.

CRYING. Unpleasant as it sounds to a parent in the still of the night, crying is an important infant response. The infant's cry serves the same function as the animal's distress call—both draw the parent to the offspring. (Among animals, when the mother is near, the distress sound sharply diminishes.) When the distress call is granted this attracting function, a question arises: does the mother's rapid response to a distress call reinforce the offspring and encourage him to repeat that sound? To seek an answer to this question, Hoffman, Schiff, Adams, and Searle (1966) removed 18 ducklings from their mothers and imprinted them to follow a white plastic bottle mounted on a model-train engine. As we noted in Chapter 4, imprinting is the formation of a lasting social relationship, achieved when the offspring sees and follows a moving object (normally his mother) shortly after his birth—or his hatching, in the duckling's case. The object-stimulus in an experimental situation thus takes the place of the offspring's mother.

In the 1966 experiment, all the ducklings were exposed to the object-stimulus for four 45-minute periods during the first two days after their hatching. When the experimenters removed the object-stimulus to check for imprinting, the fowl showed that indeed they had formed strong social relationships with the plastic bottle. They made clear the loss they felt at its absence by immediately sending out distress calls. Similarly, they quieted when the moving bottle was returned. Next, the ducklings were paired, and each pair member was assigned to either an experimental or control group. Whenever a duckling in the experimental group made a distress call, he and his control partner were presented with the moving bottle. Calls from control pair members brought no responses. The investigators found that the experimental ducklings began to emit a greater number of distress calls than the control partners. They then reversed the conditions for the two groups. Calls from the experimental animals no longer caused the imprinted stimulus to appear. Instead, the stimulus was presented to pair members whenever the control partners made distress calls; calls from this group then increased significantly. It was concluded that the distress calls were reinforced by the contingent appearance of the imprinted stimulus. In other words, if a duckling's distress calls consistently caused the stimulus to appear, he would increase the number of such calls.

Similar behavior, centered about the infant cry, can be cited in the case of humans. A 1967 study with two infants demonstrated, for example, the efficacy of reward in the control of a baby's crying. Etzel and Gewirtz worked with two infants, one 6 weeks old and another 20 weeks old. They chose the infants from a children's hospital where their crying had been regularly reinforced—that is, rewarded with attention—in the nursery. The infants, like the ducklings, were attempting to attract their caretakers, or mother-figures, with their cries. Etzel and Gewirtz succeeded in replacing the crying with smiling by using the techniques of operant conditioning discussed in Chapter 4. That is, they discouraged crying by ignoring the infant when he cried and rewarding him when he smiled.

Every parent, of course, needs to interpret this finding rather carefully. It indicates a way in which only a certain type of crying can be decreased—crying that is primarily a call for social stimulation. Babies also cry because of internal pains, diaper pins, rashes, and other discomforts. Most parents would probably wish to respond to those cries and remove the babies' discomforts. After all, crying is an appeal for humane treatment, not merely a nuisance to busy adults. It is probably impossible to convert crying that has its source in pain into smiling with any conditioning technique.

In fact, the notion that parents will "spoil" their babies by answering most of their crying has been challenged by data collected recently by Ainsworth. Initial findings from her study of infant–mother interactions in 26 families indicate that "babies whose mothers respond promptly to crying from the outset tend to cry little by the end

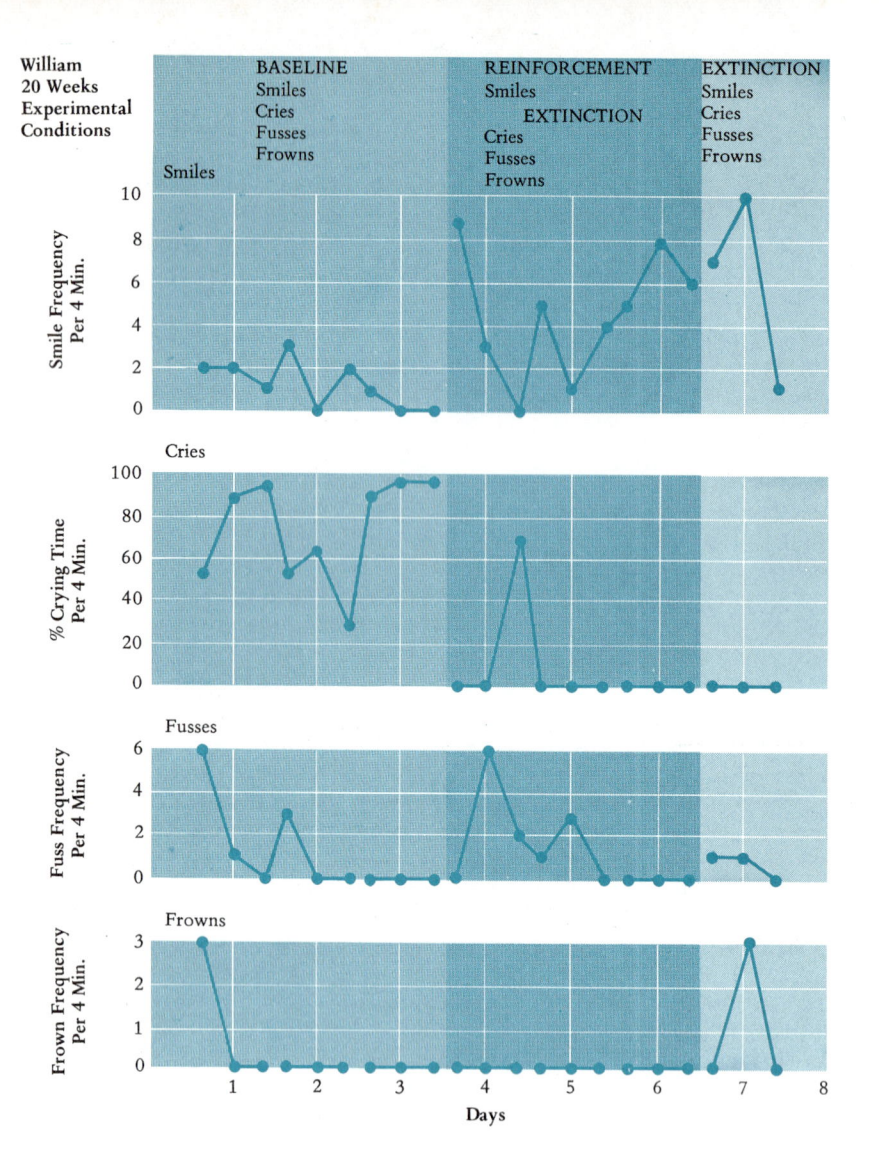

Figure 7.3 Three phases of an experiment that replaced the attracting mechanisms of crying, fussing, and frowning with smiling. (Crying had been reinforced previously with attention.) (From B. Etzel and J. Gewirtz. Experimental modification of caretaker-maintained high-rate operant crying in a 6- and a 20-week-old infant (*Infans tyrannotearus*): Extinction of crying with reinforcement of eye contact and smiling. *J. exp. child Psychol.*, 1967, 5, 303–317.)

of the first year and to have developed a rich variety of other modes of communication. Refusal to respond in the hope of not spoiling the child tends to have exactly the opposite effect" (Ainsworth 1972). Furthermore, in contrast to the findings of Hoffman and his associates, that ducklings' distress calls were reinforced by the appearance of the parent-figure, Ainsworth's data show that the human mother's responsiveness to distress calls resulting from separation tended to reduce such cries. "It's as though a baby who has learned to count on its mother as a secure base does not always seek to be close to her," she explained.

We have seen that in animals, the distress call is a cry for the parent, and that the appearance of the parent reinforces the distress cry in the future. As the Etzel and Gewirtz study has shown, not only are both of these observations also true of the human infant, but in addition, the human infant sometimes can be conditioned to supplant excessive crying with a social gesture—the smile.

188 INFANCY

HUNGER AND FEEDING. Another way the caretaker is involved with the infant is in satisfying the infant's hunger. The mother, in responding to this basic need, has a choice. She can breast-feed the baby or feed him with a bottle. Controversy has simmered over the two methods for years, but there is little evidence for the overriding superiority of either (Orlansky 1949). Advocates of breast-feeding maintain that it is the natural and, therefore, the preferred method of nourishing the infant. They cite the immunity to certain illnesses that mother's milk transmits from mother to infant. They stress the greater intimacy of the physical contact between mother and child. Some advocates of breast-feeding, on the offensive against the bottle theory, have even attempted to prove that psychic harm can come to an infant deprived of nursing at his mother's breast.

The advocates of bottle-feeding argue that breast-feeding is a primitive habit that reflects poorly on the sophistication of modern-day mothers. They also maintain that breast-feeding seriously disrupts the family schedule, thereby offsetting the nutritive and psychic benefits of breast-feeding—which they consider negligible anyway. Similarly, some critics contend that breast-feeding is undesirable because it imposes on the freedom of the mother, confining her to the immediate vicinity of the infant so that she will be readily available for feedings.

Another controversy related to infant feeding involves the advocates of the rigid, traditional feeding schedule, as opposed to the more contemporary supporters of the infant-demand schedule. By the former method, the infant is fed on a strict schedule, every three or four hours; he may be awakened for a feeding he does not want, and hunger cries between feedings may be disregarded. On a self-demand schedule, the infant is fed whenever he seems to want to eat. One practical benefit of this schedule is that the parents are subjected to less crying. As for behavioral results, no study to date has documented demand feeding as the source of later problems. On the other hand, a 1953 study by Williams and Scott suggests that infants raised on rigid feeding schedules are less active in their first and second years than infants fed when they expressed a desire to eat. However, doubt is cast on this finding because mothers following rigid feeding schedules are often restrictive in other areas of infant care. For this reason, the reduced activity level that appears later on may be caused by these restrictions rather than by the infant's inflexible schedule.

Each of these practices has attracted varying support over the years; successive generations have alternated between breast- and bottle-feeding, and between scheduled and demand feeding (Stendler 1950, Vincent 1951). In the late 1940s, for example, studies indicated that middle-class parents used more permissive feeding techniques. Recent studies, however, have indicated that this is no longer true of middle-class parents. Today their feeding schedules tend to be less flexible, though not so rigid as in former times—perhaps a compromise between these extremes.

Feeding methods vary among parents of different social classes as well as among generations of parents. In his 1966 study of California mothers, for instance, Heinstein reported that mothers from lower social and economic levels are more likely to breast-feed their infants than mothers from the higher social classes. On the other hand, the frequent need to return to work outside the home often forces the working-class mother to wean her infant—that is, to shift him from breast to bottle—earlier than the middle-class mother who may be able to stay at home all day and be available for nursing sessions.

Most expectant mothers quickly become aware of the choices to be made between bottle-feeding and nursing, and between demand and scheduled feeding. They often ask their obstetricians or the pediatricians they have selected which of the methods are best to use with their infants. These doctors will give their advice according to their own predilections and experience. Some will be distinctly partisan, others will say it is purely a matter of the mother's choice or convenience. Many psychologists today share the latter point of view. They believe that more important than the mode of feeding is the social interaction and stimulation between mother and infant, which seems to be a major determinant of the child's later social development. The quality of this interaction may hinge more on the mother's comfort with the mode of feeding than on the mode itself.

SUCKING. Another response that involves the caretaker is the infant's sucking reflex. Unlike smiling, which is a later response, sucking is fundamentally related to the infant's very survival. The sucking reflex of the breast-fed infant clearly brings him into intimate and regular physical contact with his mother. But the bottle-fed infant also is held in his mother's arms at first, and later in her lap or in an infant seat. In any event, the infant's sucking response brings him into consistent pleasurable contact—both physical and social—with one person, usually his mother. His satisfaction at these times reassures his mother in her maternal role and makes her eager for more such reassuring contacts. This maternal satisfaction is evidenced in patting, gentle handling of the infant, and quick responses to his nutritive sucking response. In this way, the feeding interaction between infant and mother is established and strengthened by repetition.

BABBLING. This form of vocalizing, which usually begins after 6 months of age, reflects the infant's relationship with his mother. As we discussed in Chapter 6, a mother stimulates more babbling by responding with attention, and by making sounds and gestures of her own when her baby babbles. Though such environmental objects as brightly colored mobiles may provoke babbling, it is the mother-infant interaction that reinforces and insures the retention of the babbling response.

SCANNING. The infant's visual scanning is another early response that links him to his mother by being mutually rewarding. As we saw in Chapter 5 on physical development, the infant is usually attracted to objects that move and contrast strongly—black on white, particularly. This is why an infant often seems to be searching his mother's gaze; he is visually fascinated by her eyes, which move rapidly and continuously and also have strong contrast value (between the iris and the surrounding white), no matter what their color. The infant's interest in his mother's eyes, and in her face in general, which is most obvious from about 6 or 8 weeks, evokes, in turn, the mother's greater interest in him as a person. Consequently, the mother spends more time near him, reinforcing his scanning response, as she does his babbling, smiling, and other responses.

Attachment to the Parent

Traditional Views: Feeding Most Important

The infant's perception of his mother as the source of food, care, and comfort traditionally has been regarded as the root of the close infant–mother relationship. Infants were thought to form an attachment to their mothers because they associated their mothers with good feelings—for example, being warm and well-fed. In this view, the mother is a pleasure stimulus. Because the infant sees his mother as a source of pleasure, he stays close to her and often protests her absence, however brief. At first, he cries out to his mother, and later goes to her, when he is hungry.

It is not long before he generalizes the hunger stimulus to include other discomforts, such as fatigue, sickness, cold, and injury. He turns to his mother to relieve these pains just as he turned to her to relieve his hunger pangs with food. However, it is essentially the feeding process, in the traditional view, that determines whether the infant regards his mother as a pleasing or displeasing stimulus. If feeding is an unpleasant experience—whether because the mother is brusque or anxious with the infant or because there is not enough food—the infant may begin to regard the mother as an unpleasant stimulus. If feeding remains a stressful experience for an extended time, the baby may reverse his normal response and avoid his mother. Such a negative response to feeding also may be generalized. That is, if the hungry child finds his mother can give him no relief from his hunger pains, he may extend his negative response to include other pains. Thus, instead of approaching his mother when he is tired or hurt, he may avoid her.

As the infant develops, he also generalizes his social experiences with his mother to include other people. He begins to accept and socialize with others. However, if the infant's relationship with his mother is again one of avoidance, he may avoid others as well, and never form close social relationships. Whatever the possibilities for behavior, the important point in the traditional view of the infant–parent relationship is its contention that the infant's social development begins with his central relationship with his mother—and specifically, with his early feeding experience.

Newer Ideas

In recent years this attractively simple concept of social development has been challenged by newer experimental evidence. Several important studies have introduced the importance of such variables as pleasurable physical contact and eye contact between mother and infant, as well as stimulation by the mother, to an understanding of the infant's attachment to his mother and his subsequent social development.

In one such set of experiments, Harlow (1959, 1966) worked with infant monkeys. He placed one group of infants with substitute "mothers" made of a roll of wire mesh, and another group with "mothers" made of the same material covered with terry cloth. Both kinds of artificial mothers "fed" the infant monkeys from bottles set into their "chests."

According to the traditional theory, the infants who fed from the wire-mesh mother should have preferred this mother to the terry-cloth mother because the wire mother relieved their hunger pains. Harlow's findings contradicted this expectation. He found, instead, that both the infants who fed from the wire-mesh mothers and those who fed from the terry-cloth mothers invariably went to the terry-cloth mothers and clung to them rather than the wire-mesh mothers. The monkeys originally grouped with the wire-mesh mother would feed from her, but would quickly abandon the wire-mesh mother and go to the terry-cloth mother to spend the time between feedings. Thus, the infant monkey seems to have a basic need that is second only to the hunger drive. Bowlby (1958) described this need in humans as the need to cling or to maintain physical contact. "There is in infants," Bowlby stated, "an in-built need to be in touch with and to cling to a human being." He maintained that clinging, along with crying, smiling, sucking, and mother-following (that is, keeping in visual or auditory contact with the mother) are the five instinctual responses with which an infant binds himself to his mother. Satisfying these responses seems to be vital to the infant in the first few months of his life.

Besides playing an important role in forming the initial mother–infant attachment, the clinging response also helps the infant deal with fears. Harlow tested infant monkey reactions to a fear-producing stimulus by placing a large model of a spider in the monkey cage, which also contained wire-mesh and terry-cloth mothers. At the appearance of the spider, the monkeys fled to the

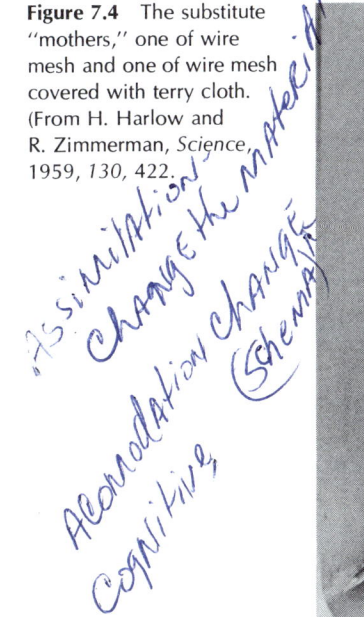

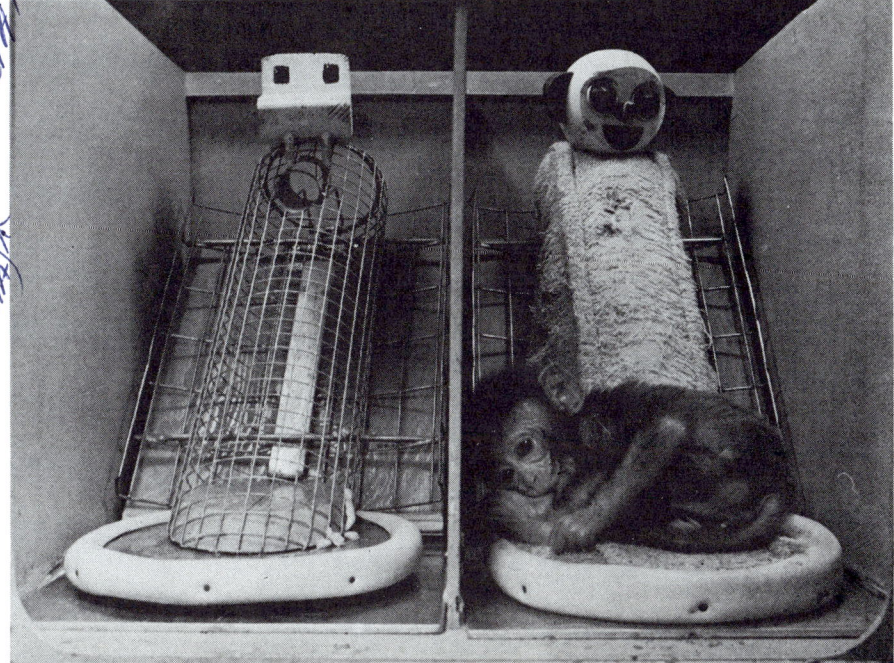

Figure 7.4 The substitute "mothers," one of wire mesh and one of wire mesh covered with terry cloth. (From H. Harlow and R. Zimmerman, *Science*, 1959, 130, 422.)

terry-cloth mother and clung to her. They ignored the wire-mesh mother. In further trials, Harlow found that clinging to the terry-cloth mother quieted fears more readily than clinging to the wire-mesh mother. He also found that the presence of the terry-cloth mother emboldened the monkeys to approach the feared spider model. When left with the wire-mesh mother, the monkeys hung back from the spider and were afraid to explore anywhere near it.

As Harlow's experiments made clear, the need to cling is a fundamental response in infant monkeys. The clinging response also has been found in other animals and in the human infant as well. We are all familiar with the 1-year-old infant who runs to his mother and clings to her when the postman appears.

Cuddling: A Congenital Trait?

As well as adding "contact comfort" or clinging to the category of primary needs, and thus challenging the earlier view of social development, recent evidence also has suggested that there may be innate differences in infants' needs for such comfort. Schaffer and Emerson (1964a) have drawn contrasting pictures of cuddlers and noncuddlers which have suggested such constitutional differences. They studied two groups of infants, between 1 and 2 years of age, who were described by their mothers as either "cuddlers" or "noncuddlers." The cuddlers found physical contact very satisfying and were eager for it; the noncuddlers resisted it vigorously.

Schaffer and Emerson tried to find social or maternal factors that accounted for these basic differences in the babies' responses, but were unsuccessful; instead, they arrived at a list of distinctive traits that appeared in babies of each group.

The noncuddlers were found to be restless and wakeful and did not like to be held close or hugged in a restraining embrace. They sat, stood, and walked earlier, disliked being physically confined, as in a car seat or infant sling, and ultimately scored higher in development on the Cattell Infant Scale than did the cuddlers. The cuddly infants, on the other hand, were not so active, liked soft playthings, displayed more autoerotic behavior, and slept more than the noncuddlers.

When Schaffer and Emerson found no determining social or maternal factors linked to cuddling—yet at the same time discovered distinctive traits such as either passive or restless behavior—they concluded that an infant's inclination toward physical contact is largely hereditary.

Visual Interaction

Investigators of social development also have examined the role of visual interaction between mother and infant. Looking at each other's face is clearly one of the most important forms of communication that the mother–infant pair can engage in when the infant is very young. Such mutual, face-to-face looks have long-range significance because they form the basic framework for the infant's later smiling, responsive babbling, and finally his talking.

When the mother–infant relationship is a healthy one, by 3 months there is a mutual synchronization of looking at each other and looking away. The mother and baby tend to look at each other at about the same time and look away from each other almost simultaneously. When there is not a good relationship, however, the baby may look away when his mother looks at him and then look at his mother when she turns away (Stern 1971).

A mother's prenatal maternal attitudes have been linked to the amount of time she and her infant later spend looking at each other's face (Moss and Robson 1968). In turn, this amount of time bears a relationship to the female infant's later visual activity. In the study that produced these conclusions, Moss and Robson interviewed 54 pregnant women, rating them on their positive perception of babies and on their interest in affectionate contact with infants. After the babies were born, the infants and their mothers were observed together in their homes to record how often the infant and mother looked at each other's face. The investigators found that the attitudes the mothers had expressed in the prenatal interviews correlated with the amount of mutual gazing between them and their babies at 1 month of age; mothers who had expressed the most favorable attitudes toward babies spent the most time in eye-to-eye communication with their infants. This was true for both males and females. At 3 months of age, the correlation was true only for the females.

At 3½ months of age, the infants' visual activity was measured in a laboratory, using a series of different checkerboards and three different pictures of faces. The visual-activity criterion was the total amount of time the infants looked at an object. The significant result was that female infants who had engaged in the most visual interaction with their mothers looked longest at the pictures of faces (social stimuli). Their scores for looking at the checkerboards (nonsocial stimuli) were not much higher than either the males or the other females.

Moss and Robson concluded, first, that the extent of mutual visual activity between the mother and infant reflects the attitude of the mother, and, second, that for girls, the early visual activity with the mother involves the learning of social behaviors.

Generalization of Social Responses

In the normal infant's social development, he gradually generalizes his response to his mother to include other adults. However, the infant's ability to accomplish this is not automatic. It is developed during his interaction with his mother, as the following experiment with institutionalized infants graphically illustrates (Rheingold 1956). For eight weeks, Rheingold played mother to eight out of sixteen 6-month-old infants. For eight hours a day, five days a week, she fed, changed, and bathed them, talked to them, smiled at them, and played freely with them. The remaining eight infants received routine, impersonal, institutional care from a changing variety of volunteers. The overall effect was that the eight experimental infants cared for by Rheingold had a single caretaker for an extended period and received more individual attention and care.

Each week during the test period and for four weeks after, all 16 infants were tested. Among other items, the test measured each infant's social responsiveness to people, specifically to Rheingold, to another adult who gave the other tests, and to a stranger who appeared at the end of the eight-week period of personal care. The results showed that the experimental infants were clearly more socially responsive to the three test figures than were the infants who received routine institutional care. They expressed their greater social responsiveness—especially to Rheingold—by smiling, "talking," or making some other recognitory facial gesture when any one of the three test figures smiled or talked to them. The actual physical care was not a determining factor according to Rheingold, who maintained that the experimental infants' greater social responsiveness was primarily prompted by the constant visual, verbal, and tactile exchanges between herself as the mother-figure and the infants.

These findings lend firm support to the hypothesis that the infant who learns social responses from an attentive and stimulating mother-figure will more readily generalize those social responses with other adults. Along with the evidence cited in this section, the Rheingold study considerably modified the earlier view that hunger reduction is the central condition for social development. Clearly, many variables are influential, such as physical and eye contact between mother and infant, and other forms of stimulation by the mother or caretaker.

Attachment and Stimulation

The degree of sensory stimulation the mother or caretaker provides the infant seems to be a major determinant of attachment. Schaffer and Emerson (1964b) discovered this when they studied how attachment behavior evolves, and what role is played by the mother's stimulation of the infant. As they did in their "cuddling experiment," the investigators interviewed mothers to assess their attitudes toward their infants and to gather other information about the care of the infants. In the trial portion of the experiment, Schaffer and Emerson measured the infant's attachment by noting his protests in seven different situations in which he was temporarily separated from his mother—for instance, when he was left alone in a room and when he was put down after being held. They compiled several interesting findings. Among them was the discovery that the depth of an infant's attachment to his mother is not affected by the number of persons who share the mothering tasks, nor by the amount of time the mother spends with the infant.

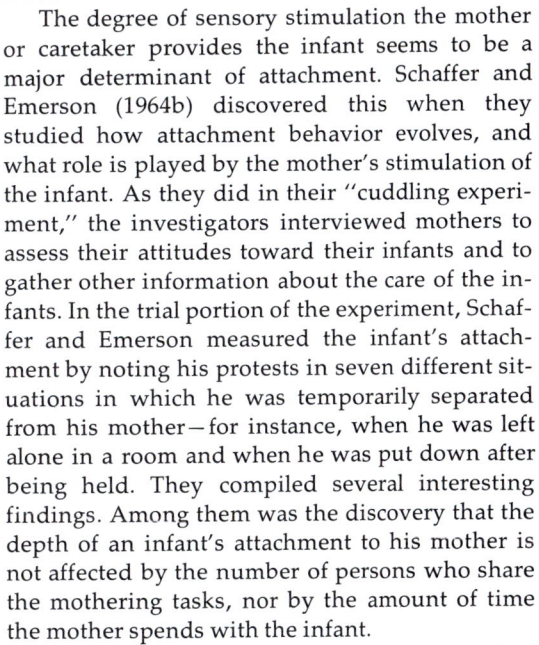

The investigators also found that very often the infants displayed more intense attachments to persons who did not actually satisfy their fundamental needs for food and comfort, but instead stimulated them by talking, smiling, teaching, and playing with them. This finding has a special interest because it amounts to another refutation of the earlier view of social learning, which we discussed in this section on attachment to the parent. This popular concept maintains that an infant establishes his strongest bond with the person who feeds, cleans, and comforts him, and puts particular stress on the feeding situation as a source of attachment. The findings of Schaffer and Emerson have discredited this common view and indicate, instead, that it is the *sensory stimulation* the caretaker provides that determines the intensity of the infant's attachment.

The investigators next attempted to discover if the kind of stimulation—cuddling, talking, or presenting toys, for example—affected the intensity of the attachment. Their results indicated that the kind of stimulation had no relation to the infant's attachment to his mother. More important was the sheer quantity of the stimulation she provided. Thus, it would seem that the developing infant does not need the presence of people so much as he requires a steady flow of changing sights, sounds, and tactile sensations. Yet it is hard to separate his need for stimulation from a need for persons. The infant is drawn to people since, among all possible stimuli, they can provide the greatest variety and intensity of stimulation. In turn, the infant's natural attraction to humans as providers of stimulation is a major factor in his social development.

Anxieties Related to Attachment

Stranger Anxiety

As the infant's attachment to his mother grows, he simultaneously assembles a visual schema for her. He is learning to associate his mother with comfort and pleasure, and he also seems to derive pleasure from matching the sight of his mother with his visual schema of her. Apparently this schema is quite sophisticated by the time the infant is 6 to 8 months old, especially in its depiction of the mother's face. We can assume its sophistication from the infant's fear reaction when a strange woman appears. This reaction is known as *stranger anxiety*. To tell a strange woman from his mother, the infant must remember and recognize a substantial amount of visual detail—such as face shape and contour, hair and eye color. Even moderate schema discrepancies, such as his mother's new haircut, may provoke uneasiness.

The schema discrepancies that account for stranger anxiety seem to involve primarily facial features, but may also involve size, the closeness of the strange person, or perhaps even a self-schema. These discrepancies alarm the infant, and since he cannot do anything directly to lessen his fear, he quickly begins to cry. Many a chagrined mother has seen her baby greet his grandmother for the first time by wailing and burying his head in her lap or arms. If the grandmother leaves the room, or perhaps if the mother holds and reassures the baby, he will stop crying. He can be expected to follow the same behavior pattern with all strangers, until the strangers become familiar to him or until he "outgrows" this response.

In American children, stranger anxiety usually begins at the end of the first 6 months, peaks toward the end of the first year, and decreases thereafter. After 1 year of age the situation is different, for the infant is now able to take some fear-reducing action on his own. For example, he may turn and run to his mother. By this time, too, it is possible that greater exposure to other faces will have generalized his face schema to the point where it includes almost all faces. Understandably, then, a strange face is much less discrepant, and therefore much less alarming, to the 1-year-old. Even at its extreme, however, the presence of the mother has a substantial calming effect on the infant.

THE DISSENTING OPINIONS. Several dissenting voices have been heard recently (and older ones recalled) that question the standard concept of stranger anxiety which we have just presented. Perhaps the most dramatic experiment backing the dissenters was conducted by Rheingold and Eckerman (1971), in which most of the 24 infants they tested "did not cry or fuss. They even allowed themselves to be held by the stranger." Rheingold and Eckerman pointed out that the same low incidence of stranger anxiety also could be seen in Shirley's 1933 report, which found a fearful response in only 6 of 20 subjects, and again in Gesell and Thompson's 1934 study, which found that the infants at any age who withdrew from a stranger made up less than 50 percent of the sample.

Rheingold and Eckerman in their report went on to criticize other studies showing stranger anxiety. They attacked, specifically, the variables in such trials, such as the quality of the setting, which in itself might induce anxiety. The last point in their critique of other stranger-anxiety studies "draws attention to the other side of the whole picture. The frequent reports of positive, friendly responses to strangers should not be ignored." Washburn (1929) is especially compelling on this point, as are Morgan and Ricciuti (1969).

"What emerges from this review and our data is that the proposition that the infant fears a stranger needs much qualifying. We are not the first to make the point; it has been made by others (for example, Stone and Church 1968; Nash 1970; Morgan and Ricciuti 1969). Ours is but a reminder."

A similar criticism has been made by Lewis and Brooks-Gunn (1972), who found that while the children in their study (7 to 19 months old) showed a fear response to adult strangers, they did not show that response to child strangers. Furthermore, the fear response depended on whether the infant was a boy or girl and the stranger a male or female, and whether they were close or far away. There were no fear responses as long as strangers remained at a distance. Most positive responses were made toward the mother and themselves alone as they were moved toward a mirror. Girls were more fearful of male strangers than were boys. All were delighted by another child. Lewis and Brooks-Gunn argued, therefore, that some schema for self must play a part in these reactions. Perhaps such a self-schema precedes the object concept we discussed in the preceding chapter. It might even be a logical prerequisite for such an object concept. It is this self-schema that dictates the infant's positive response to himself in a mirror and to a like-sized strange child. Perhaps the self-schema also is responsible for the different responses of the boys and girls to male and female adults. The apparent fear of strangers, therefore, may actually be more closely related to a discrepancy from self (particularly in terms of size) than a discrepancy from the mother's appearance. At least this formulation seems to account for more of these diverse phenomena than the mother-face discrepancy alone.

This approach to stranger anxiety makes use of certain principles of cognitive development, which were discussed in the previous chapter, such as incongruity, novelty, and familiarity and schema; and, as Lewis and Brooks-Gunn (1972) pointed out, it also

> . . . requires the introduction of such processes as object permanence, at least in terms of remembering the mother. This approach stresses that the child's response to a stranger is a part of the larger emerging cognitive functions. We would extend this position by considering the concept of self and using it as an additional referent in terms of social interactions and cognitions. . . . The positive response of the infants to the child stranger . . . suggests that infant-peer interactions may have a special quality. It is well known that infants often follow and learn faster from an older sibling (peer) than from their parents. In fact, peers may serve quite well as adult substitutes in the early attachment relationships (for example, Chamove 1966; Freud and Dann 1951). Infants not only show little or no fear toward peers, but, in fact, can engage in a meaningful attachment behavior. We would suggest that these facts have importance for a general theory of interpersonal relationships.

Separation Anxiety

The second type of fear that seems directly linked to the infant's attachment to his mother is *separation anxiety*, and examples are plentiful. The infant shopping with his mother is left sitting in the grocery cart while his mother goes into the next aisle. As she disappears around the corner, the infant begins to cry. Another mother feeds and changes her baby and then walks out the back door to hang the wash in the yard. Again, the infant protests by crying. Both infants felt separation anxiety.

The onset age for separation anxiety varies among different cultures. Generally, the closer the mother–infant bond, the sooner separation anxiety will appear. For example, Ugandan mothers have almost constant physical contact with their infants. They breast-feed them until they are 2 years old and carry them in close-fitting slings everywhere they go. Ugandan babies, who are completely unaccustomed to being parted from their mothers, exhibit separation anxiety as early as 6 months of age (Ainsworth 1967).

In Western cultures, the infant displays the same anxiety, but two to four months later than the Ugandan infant. The average American baby, for example, shows anxiety at separation from his mother at about 10 to 12 months of age. Anxiety becomes strongest at around 1 year and then declines. The lateness of the anxiety onset in the American infant compared to the Ugandan infant seems related to the relatively diminished physical contact between the American mother and the infant. For example, if American mothers nurse their children, they wean them much earlier, usually before 5 months. In addition, American infants have little physical contact with their mothers except when they are being cared for. At other times, the infants lie in their cribs or sit in infant seats, physically separated from their mothers.

Several explanations of why an infant undergoes separation anxiety have been offered. The concept of the discrepant schema is already somewhat familiar from our discussion of stranger anxiety; as applied to separation anxiety, the discrepant schema extends to more than just the mother's face or body. If a mother is always with her infant, as the Ugandan mother is, she soon becomes an integral part of each schema he develops. When she disappears from his view in the kitchen, his schema for that room is violated, anxiety is created, and the infant cries. However, the American infant, who spends substantially less time in contact with his mother than the Ugandan infant (though much more than infants in many other cultures), takes longer to integrate his mother as an essential part of his schemata. Therefore, he does not cry on separation until later in his infancy, when his schemata are developed to the point where his mother's departure will violate them. This interpretation, like one of the discussed interpretations of stranger anxiety, bases onset and intensity of separation anxiety on the state of the infant's schemata. The available data suggest that the mother-schema discrepancy may be more relevant to separation anxiety, and a self-schema discrepancy more relevant to stranger anxiety.

A recent series of studies by Rheingold (1969) has found that if an infant can do something to bring himself into closer contact with his mother, he seems to be less fearful in otherwise frightening circumstances. Rheingold placed 10-month-old infants in a strange, empty room. In the first trial, she left them with their mothers; in the second, with a stranger; in the third, with only toys; and in the fourth trial, they were completely alone. Infants left in the room with their mothers did not cry at all. Those left alone with a stranger or with toys usually began to cry within 60 seconds after entering the room. From these findings, we could conclude that the presence of the mother shields the infant from the anxiety he would otherwise feel in a strange room.

Further experiments in this study, however, added another dimension to this conclusion. Rheingold found that if an infant subjected to separation and strange surroundings can do something to bring himself into visual or bodily contact with his mother from time to time, he is less fearful. A 10-month-old infant was left with his mother in a room connected by an open door to the strange, empty room in which other infants had cried when left without their mothers. This infant frequently ventured into the empty room on his own, and without crying. Once inside, he would glance about and then crawl back to his mother. He did not cry because he was able to follow a path of action; when he became afraid, he simply crawled back through the open door to his mother. This alternative was not available to the infants in the earlier experiment. Consequently, when they became frightened by the empty room, they could make no response and therefore they cried. Of course, crying, too, is a response, but it is a last-ditch effort the infant resorts to when he cannot lessen his fear by seeing, hearing, touching, or moving toward his mother.

A second view of separation anxiety considers that before the infant resorts to tears, he may try to figure out why a separation situation is different from his familiar schemata. Kagan, in an article published early in 1972, noted that when an infant is confronted with a discrepant schema—whether a stranger or a separation situation—he hesitates for a few seconds before he expresses his fear in an outburst of crying. Almost always in the case of visually discrepant schemata—the sight of the gas meter man, for example—the few seconds of hesitation are filled by silence as the infant stares goggle-eyed at the object or person he finds discrepant. According to Kagan, this is not simply a petrified fixation, but evidence of a cognitive process that he calls hypothesizing, which he believes occurs as early as at 9 months of age in the human infant. The infant, according to Kagan, is examining closely the discrepant object and forming hypotheses about what has happened to the familiar object that otherwise fits his schema. When the infant cries it is because his hypothesizing—as he stared enrapt—has failed to interpret the reason for the discrepant person. Because the infant cannot interpret, assimilate, reject, or destroy the discrepant face of the meter man, his fear overcomes him and he resorts to crying, which as we have seen earlier, is an action he associates with comforting by his mother. Kagan has maintained that the same process seems to operate in separation anxiety. When the child fails to hypothesize the schema of his mother leaving him, or the schema of the room with her absent, he becomes frightened and cries. In both stranger and separation anxiety, the infant's negative reaction diminishes as he gets older because his experience broadens; therefore, he can succeed in producing hypotheses that explain discrepant schemata (Kagan 1972).

A third explanation draws on the habitual nature of the infant's—and indeed any human's—attachments. The explanation assumes that the infant quickly becomes a creature of habit through the responses he makes to particular stimuli. The 3-year-old prefers, to the point of tears, to be covered at night with a specific blanket, and he wants to sleep only with his soiled and shabby stuffed rabbit. An adult may habitually walk a particular route to his office, though alternate ways are just as short. For the infant, the strongest habitual responses are those associated with his mother. Changes in such simple habits can prompt anxiety, and infants often will cry if these habitual responses are frustrated. According to this explanation of separation anxiety, the infant's common responses to his mother—such as babbling, smiling, and looking—become habitual through repeated performance. When an infant's mother departs, he can no longer make these responses to her. His habitual pattern is broken, anxiety mounts, and the infant cries. Presumably, the infant who has more contact with his mother can form strong habitual responses to her at an earlier age—and therefore feel separation anxiety at an earlier age. This would explain the early separation anxiety—at 6 months—felt by the Ugandan infant. Since the American baby, on the other hand, has less contact with his mother than the Ugandan infant, he develops his habitual responses to her later in his infancy; therefore, he also exhibits separation anxiety at a later age.

A fourth explanation of separation anxiety holds that it is the mother's absence that conditions the infant to feel anxiety. Underlying this explanation is the assumption that the infant is much more likely to undergo discomfort or pain when his mother is gone. Granting this assumption, the infant would anticipate such pain and discomfort when his mother left him. Therefore, her leaving would create anxiety in him. However, the theory fails to explain the behavior of the infant who is seldom parted from his mother, such as the Ugandan infant in Ainsworth's 1967 study. According to this theory, the Ugandan infant who is almost never parted from his mother should not learn the anxiety of separation. Yet, he, too, exhibits it—even earlier than the Western infant who is more frequently separated from his mother and therefore has much more opportunity to learn the anxiety.

Although this fourth theory of conditioned anxiety may not prove to be correct, we still are left with three viable explanations of separation anxiety. The first is that the anxiety is determined by the intensity of the infant's attachment to his mother and, consequently, the development of his schemata that include or exclude her. The second and most recent explanation is that separation anxiety is the result of the infant's failure to produce a hypothesis that explains the discrepant schema of the absent or departing mother. And the third theory is that separation anxiety results from the interruption of habitual responses.

As in many areas of psychological explanation, these unidimensional accounts may actually complement each other by referring to different aspects of the same multidimensional process. It is noticeable that the first theory focuses on the infant's feelings or emotions, the second on his cognitive processes, and the third on his behavior. Each in its own terms predicates a discrepancy between the expected emotional, behavioral, and cognitive stimuli, and the stimuli that he discovers when his mother leaves or is absent. These theories ultimately are not inconsistent with each other; all probably can be thought of as aspects of a larger theory of the infant's expectations in general.

Effects of Long Separations

Separation from the mother can have profound effects on the infant, particularly when the mother's absences are extended. Bowlby, a leading investigator of these effects, recorded the reactions of infants 15 to 30 months of age who were separated from their mothers by hospital stays or by the mother's work schedule (Bowlby 1960). He found that the infants passed through three general phases as their situations wore on. At first, they fiercely protested the absence of their mothers by crying, rattling their cribs, and avoiding new persons or even other family members. At the same time, they were sharply alert for any evidence that their mothers had returned to them. The closer the attachment of the infant to his mother, the longer he kept up his protests.

In the next phase, the infants abandoned hope of reunion. As they despaired, they began to respond a little more to the new people around them—or so it seemed. They permitted others to feed and care for them, but at the same time, they seemed to have lost their vitality. They were quiet and uninterested, although they would play in a desultory way. When their mothers visited them, they were cool, almost indifferent. They hardly protested when their mothers left again. They did not seem to care for their mothers anymore; indeed, they appeared to be systematically distancing themselves from their mothers.

The third phase—permanent withdrawal from human relationships—can occur if the separation from the mother is extensive. It also can come about if the infant, during his mother's absence, passes through a series of brief relationships with caretakers, whether they are nurses, relatives, or babysitters. In both circumstances—a prolonged absence or a series of terminated attachments—the infant's ability to extend himself in new relationships is seriously impaired; he no longer is eager for his mother's comfort or contact with other humans. Though he maintains a veneer of sociability, he gravitates more and more toward narrowly defined, egocentric interests, often substituting objects for personal attachment. We should stress, however, that this series of events does not always occur during long separations. Bowlby's findings should be taken to mean, instead, that long separations increase the probability that this behavior will occur.

Other Infant Fears

Although stranger and separation anxieties receive the most attention in both the scientific and popular literature about children, they are not the infant's only fears, by far. They are simply his most common and most easily isolated ones. An infant's other fears usually are conditioned responses to disturbing experiences. The threat of repetition of those experiences, or the appearance of any stimuli associated with those experiences, arouses fear. For example, the toddler who has been knocked down by an unruly, if friendly dog, may be expected to fear other dogs and perhaps even such paraphernalia as their leashes, collars, and kennels.

Anxiety also is sparked by situations that make the infant expect the loss of his mother's presence. For example, the preliminaries of bedtime preparation tell the infant that his mother will leave him soon, an event that can prompt fear—and lead to tension-fraught bedtimes for the tired parents as well as the infant.

Infants of different ages fear some things more than others. A 1935 study by Jersild and Holmes recorded the fear reactions of 136 children from 3 months to 8 years of age. Children up to 12 months old showed fear of noises and the circumstances in which they were first heard. They also became anxious about falling or sudden movements, lights flashing, and people or things linked to painful experiences. Generally, they also feared animals, unfamiliar people, objects, and strange happenings. During their second year, the infants showed their strongest fear responses to noises, unusual happenings, and falling or the threat of falling. Their fear of flashing lights and surprise movements declined, while pain-linked persons, animals, objects, and situations elicited stronger fear reactions. A number of the infants showed fear of the dark and fear of solitude, apprehensions they had not demonstrated during their first year.

The Institutionalized Infant

Lack of a Caretaker

Children raised in institutions—whether they are called orphanages or foundling homes—have been a fruitful source of study, since those institutions provide a child-rearing situation in which the infant has no single caretaker. That is, while these infants are maintained physically and are exposed to a fair variety of adults, they very seldom form an attachment to a particular adult, and exhibit other differences, as well, from infants raised at home. The lack of a single caretaker is generally the prime variable investigated in assessing these differences.

While we must be cautious when drawing conclusions about cause and effect, studies have revealed definite behavior differences between institutionalized and home-reared infants. Uniformly, these differences have been cases in which the behavior of the institutionalized child is retarded. Specifically, experimenters have found that institution-reared infants are retarded in their social behavior and are relatively indifferent to their surroundings. Often, they are passive and withdrawn. They seldom utter sounds or demand attention. They generally are retarded in their motor development, lack an attachment to any adult, and consequently, perhaps, they exhibit little stranger or separation anxiety.

Developmental Impairment

While there are many studies of behavioral and developmental deficiencies among institutionalized infants, we shall confine our examination to a few representative pieces of research. Although these studies deal with children of different age levels in different kinds of institutions, they have one factor in common: all the children who were studied lacked a single, permanent caretaker.

PHYSICAL RETARDATION. Spitz, in 1945, was the first to conduct a large-scale examination of the development of infants under 12 months of age. He compared the infants of imprisoned mothers who cared for their own infants in a prison nursery with infants of women who could not support their babies and left them in a foundling home. The prison nursery infants were fed, nursed, cared for, and played with by their own mothers or by a full-time substitute mother-figure. The foundling-home infants, by contrast, encountered other people only at mealtimes, when busy nurses cared for them in a routine manner. They had few toys and were sealed off from visual stimulation by sheets hung over the front and sides of the cribs. They lay unmoved in these cribs for so long that their bodies made depressions in the mattresses; when their bodies were maturationally ready to allow them to turn over, at about 7 months of age, the mattress depressions prevented them from achieving that developmental step. As late as 1 year of age, some of these infants were still lying on their backs. This instance of retarded development typified the general condition of the foundling-home infants.

Spitz found that the difference between the developmental scores of nursery and foundling-home infants grew greater as the babies grew older. There was a sharp drop in progress for the foundlings between their 4-month test and the final test at 12 months; the nursery infants, on the other hand, continued to score at or above normal levels, along with two control groups of home-reared infants. Spitz also found that, despite the excellent hygiene at the home, the foundling infants were exceptionally prone to infection and disease. In fact, an epidemic of measles that swept the home while Spitz was there left many of the infants dead. It should be noted here that extremely high mortality rates among institutionalized infants have been common until fairly recently. However, with greater improvements in hygiene and advances in medical science, the death rate among institutionalized infants now compares with that among home-reared infants.

MINIMAL SOCIAL RESPONSE. The importance of personal attention for an infant's development of social responses such as vocalizing and playing was pointed up in a study of Provence and Lipton (1962). They observed 75 infants in an institution that adequately supplied the infant's physical needs, but provided almost no individual attention. Each attendant had responsibility for 8 to 10 infants during an 8-hour workday. During the remaining 16 hours, the infants saw no one, except at mealtimes when an attendant changed their diapers and propped their bottles. Although the infants had a few toys, the attendants did not have time for reciprocal play or vocalizing in response to the infant. Moreover, there was no close link between an infant's crying and the response of the attendants.

Provence and Lipton found that before 3 or 4 months of age, institutionalized babies were no different from home-reared infants. After this age, however, the infants showed many clear differences. The institutionalized infants seldom vocalized; they did not coo or babble, and they cried little. In addition, they did not accommodate themselves to the arms of an adult; when held, the infants moved their limbs in a satisfactory way, but their trunks were notably rigid and did not assume relaxed postures. By 8 months of age, these infants were very plainly not interested in grasping or approaching toys. They also lost interest in the rest of their surroundings. They showed very little stranger anxiety, fretted and whined rather than crying vigorously, and seldom tried to overcome physical obstacles. The most seriously affected of all behavior, however, was the infants' vocalization and speech development. At 1 year of age the infants did not use any words at all.

REDUCED VISUAL ACTIVITY. An experiment in which a group of institutionalized infants was given extra attention and handling showed that visual activity increased as the personal care increased (White and Castle 1964). The nursing staff at an institution was instructed to give 10 experimental babies (6 days old) two daily handling periods for 30 days. The attendants held the infants close against their chests and rocked them continuously for 10 minutes. The attendants were asked to handle the infants particularly when they cried; however, if the infants did not happen to cry within a certain period, the attendants were to pick them up and handle them anyway. Control infants, on the other hand, were to receive routine institutional care. After 30 days the special care was stopped and the investigators compared the visual attention of the experimental and control infants; assessments were made again at two-week intervals through the fourth month. Although the visual attention of the two groups dif-

Table 7.1 Comparison of Developmental Scores of Infants in Different Environments

Type of Environment	Cultural and Social Background	Developmental Quotients* Average of first four months	Average of last four months
Parental Home	Professional	133	131
	Village Population	107	108
Institution**	"Nursery"	101.5	105
	"Foundling home"	124	72

*Comparison of developmental and chronological age.
**Note that the scores for infants in the minimal-stimulation "foundling home" show a serious decline.
Source: R. Spitz. Hospitalism. *The psychoanalytic study of the child.* Vol. 1. New York: International Universities Press, 1945. Pp. 53–74.

Table 7.2 Degree of Retardation in Behavior Patterns of Institutionalized Infants

Motor Behavior

	Showing No Retardation	Showing Retardation	Showing Unusual or Deviant Behavior
0 mo. ↓ 12 mo.	Reflex responses Arm activation Hand engagement Rolling: prone to supine Emergence of hand-to-mouth maneuver Maturation of grasping patterns Lifting legs high in extension (supine) Head control in prone	Kicking activity Support of weight on lower extremities Head control: pull to sit Rolling: supine to prone Foot play (hand-foot; foot-mouth) Sitting erect Changing position: sitting to prone and back; pivoting Reaching out to people, toys Creeping (mild retardation) Pulling to stand Walking	Failure to adapt to holding Rocking (excessive) Disappearance of thumb-sucking Absence of self-touching Decreasing skill in coordination of movements Unusual motility patterns: hand waving, hand posturing, "athetoid" movements Inhibition of movement Poor modulation of movement (poor modulation of motor impulse discharge)

Language Behavior

	Showing No Retardation	Showing Retardation	Showing Unusual or Deviant Behavior
0 mo. ↓ 12 mo.	Early *ah*, *eh*, *uh* sounds Emergence of vowel sounds Emergence of consonants Changes in tonal range of voice (high pitch, low pitch, etc.)	Cooing Vocal social responses— chuckling and laughing Spontaneous vocalization to toys, to self, to adult Use of voice to initiate social contact Differentiation of vocal signs (pleasure, eagerness, recognition, displeasure, anxiety, etc.) Use of language for communication Specificity of mama, dada words Understanding verbalizations of others	Quietness Discrepancy between maturation and function

SOCIAL DEVELOPMENT 201

Table 7.2 (continued)

Responses to People

	Showing No Retardation	Showing Retardation	Showing Unusual or Deviant Behavior
0 mo. ↓ 12 mo.	Visual attentiveness Responsive smile Spontaneous smile	See also Motor Behavior and Language Behavior Recognition of nurse Discrimination of face versus mask Reflection of facial mimic Anxiety to the stranger Participation in social games (peekaboo, pat-a-cake, etc.) Initiation of social games Reaching out to adult to touch, caress, explore, or act aggressively	Intensity of visual regard of adult Failure to establish a personal attachment: tenuousness of emotional ties Failure to seek out the adult either for pleasure or when in distress

Responses to Toys (Inanimate Objects)

	Showing No Retardation	Showing Retardation	Showing Unusual or Deviant Behavior
0 mo. ↓ 12 mo.	Visual and acoustic attention Early grasping efforts	Memory for hidden toy Investigatory behavior Combining of toys Simultaneous attention to two or more toys Preference for one toy over another Recovering toy when obstacle is introduced	Decreasing interest in toys Rarity of spontaneous play with toys Rarity of mouthing of toys and other objects Absence of transitional object

Source: S. Provence and R. Lipton. *Infants in institutions.* New York: International Universities Press, 1962. Pp. 173–176.

fered less as more time elapsed between the extra handling and the testing, White and Castle found that in the early and middle comparisons, the infants who had been handled paid substantially more visual attention to their surroundings than did the control infants.

LASTING DAMAGE. Many reports have confirmed that the sustained absence of a mother-figure, particularly during the first three years, may cause permanent, serious developmental and emotional damage. Even placement in a foster home may not be able to reverse the effects of the child's early lack of mothering (Goldfarb 1945). In line with this conclusion is the statistical evidence that a disproportionately large number of adopted children, compared to children in the general population, are treated for emotional illness (Bostock 1961). It also should be noted that hyperactivity, hostility, and aggressive and delinquent behavior have been found to be significantly more common among adopted children than among children raised by their natural mothers (Menlove 1965).

Other Variables

The lack of the mother clearly is seen by many investigators as acutely destructive to the infant. There is, as we have noted, sound evidence to support this position. Yet, other investigators have placed less stress on the presence of the mother and point, instead, to the absence of other aids to development. They say—and correctly, as we have seen—that the institutionalized child suffers not only from the lack of a single caretaker or mother, but also from an environment that is generally barren of objects or sounds his senses can perceive. Others point out that the infant also gets little or no verbal or tactile stimulation from handlers or from other persons. They further cite the absence of stimuli that the infant can both clearly perceive in his environment and easily identify as separate.

When institutionalized infants are studied, these critics maintain that investigators may, in fact, be inadvertently measuring the effects of any of these variables rather than the lack of single-mothering. They might, for example, be measuring abnormal behavior resulting from a lack of toys that the infant can manipulate with his hands. Then, too, the investigators may be seeing the results of poor stimuli—specifically, those that are not distinct and varied. For example, an infant at home may be highly stimulated by the distinct sound of his mother humming a tune in the quiet of his bedroom. If the same tune were hummed by a busy attendant in a foundling home who was changing the listening child's diapers while 20 other children fretted in wet diapers and the radio played in the background—needless to say, the foundling-home child would not benefit from such indistinct humming to the same degree, if indeed, to any discernible degree. Similarly, if the humming sound continued, unvaried all day, it soon would cease to stimulate the infant.

Other factors sometimes thought to be significant in affecting the behavior of institutionalized infants are poor nutrition and disease. Even with the general improvement in diets and medical care, it is probably true that many infants are still undernourished in institutions. In conjunction with a lack of stimulation, poor nutrition and increased susceptibility to disease could account for some forms of abnormal behavior and development found among institutionalized infants.

Critiques

Many of the studies which conclude that the mother-figure's early absence is destructive to the infant's development have been seriously questioned. For example, Spitz's experiment has been taken to task because Spitz did not study whether the so-called retarded foundling-home children were afflicted with any congenital aberrations (Pinneau 1955). These defects, Pinneau argued, might have caused the infants' retarded development. He also criticized Spitz for not checking the personal histories of the mothers of the foundling-home and nursery infants. Differences such as the mother's social class, income level, and intellectual background could have influenced the infant's distinct behavior. Pinneau also doubted the dependability of the developmental tests Spitz had administered, specifically the fact that the test could not accurately predict an infant's later behavior as a child.

As to the high mortality rate among infants in

foundling homes, it may be that physical inactivity, rather than the absence of a mother-figure, leads to infant deaths from respiratory infections and other maladies. It also should be noted that institutionalized infants are not a random sample drawn from the general population; they are quite a special group of infants. Their mothers are most often from lower socioeconomic groups, which makes it likely that prenatal medical care and nutrition have been less than optimal. In addition, the mother who surrenders her baby often is not married. At least she probably does not want the child. In either event, she most likely was resentful and anxious during her pregnancy. Moreover, as a result of haphazard medical attention, she may have had a very painful labor and delivery which could have injured the infant at birth. Any or all of these factors may have handicapped the infant even before he was taken into a foundling home. It is known that the overall development of infants with damaged brains is more adversely affected by a lack of stimulation than that of normal infants (Bender 1950). Therefore, it is understandable that the infant whose brain had been damaged by inadequate nutrition before birth, or by difficult labor and delivery, would respond in a distinctly different way to isolation from people and other stimuli. This evidence is especially significant since brain-damaged infants may comprise a large percentage of an institution's population (Thompson and Grusec 1970).

On a more hopeful note, a team of investigators has concluded that the effects of mother-deprivation are not so bad as other studies indicate (Bowlby, Ainsworth, Boston, and Rosenbluth 1956). They drew their conclusion after conducting a follow-up investigation of 60 children who had spent from a few months to two years in a tuberculosis sanitarium before their fourth birthdays. The investigators tested them when they ranged from 6 to 14 years of age and found no indication that their intellectual functioning was lower than that of a social group of matched schoolmates. While more of the children in the follow-up study exhibited withdrawal, apathy, and temper than those in the control group, over half were capable of forming good social relationships with peers and few were delinquent. Therefore, the investigators maintained that deprivation of a mother-figure and institution life in general did not necessarily produce a cold and solitary individual, a conclusion that countered their own earlier views that psychopathic personalities almost inevitably resulted from these conditions of deprivation.

Several other experiments have supported the revised conclusion of Bowlby and his colleagues. Freud and Burlingham (1944) concluded that nursery-raised infants often demonstrated more advanced development than infants raised by their own mothers. A few years later, Freud and Dann (1951) studied six orphans who had grown up in a concentration camp. The investigators found that at 3 years of age, the children did not exhibit symptoms of retardation, psychosis, delinquency, or inability to form emotional relationships — at least the six children involved formed attachments among themselves. Similarly, in 1956, Rheingold tested a group of institutionalized infants with the Cattell Intelligence Test for Infants and Young Children. She discovered — in marked contradiction to other studies that indicated a serious reduction of intellectual development — that the average level of the institutionalized infants' intellectual development fell within the limits of the norm. Three years later, Rheingold and Bayley (1959) reexamined the children and found them intelligent and outgoing, with normal emotional and mental development. In a similar study of another group of institutionalized infants, Rheingold (1961) concluded that the subjects were as well developed and as engaged by their surroundings as infants raised in their own homes. She found that in many cases the institutionalized infants showed even stronger affirmative responses to the experimenters than the home-reared infants.

In connection with Rheingold's findings, it should be noted that no unassailable evidence to date has proven that rearing by one caretaker produces a child who is better developed emotionally or intellectually than the child raised by several caretakers at one time — as in a family where several generations live together. It is the total environmental situation and degree of appropriate stimulation that seem to be most im-

Table 7.3 Comparison between Home-raised and Institutionalized Infants Showing Similar Development on the Object Test

Response	Home Mean	Home Range	Institution Mean	Institution Range
Duration of attention	107.3"	70"–145"	104.2"	45"–175"
Smiles to object	0.1	0–1	1.1	0–11
Smiles to examiner	1.3	0–8	3.6	0–16
Vocalizations to object	3.5	0–10	2.6	0–7
Vocalizations to examiner	1.7	0–11	2.8	0–11
Negative responses to toy	2.3	0–17	1.5	0–9
Negative responses to examiner	1.0	0–7	0.5	0–4
Duration of quiet at first	43.0"	9"–74"	35.3"	14"–74"
Moves extremities	3.7	1–11	2.8	0–11
Bursts	4.3	0–13	13.3	0–54
Arm approaches	1.1	0–5	1.4	0–3
Hand contacts	0.5	0–4	0.9	0–3
Secures	0.4	0–2	0.5	0–1

Source: H. Rheingold. The effect of environmental stimulation upon social and exploratory behavior in the human infant. In B. M. Foss (Ed.), *Determinants of infant behaviour*. New York: John Wiley and Sons, Inc., 1961. Pp. 143–171.

portant to the infant's development. Several preliminary studies of collective caretaking (Gardner and Swiger 1958; Gardner, Pease, and Hawkes 1959, Rabin 1957, 1958) showed no adverse effects; in fact, one of the studies (Rabin 1958) indicated that there may be substantial emotional benefits to "multiple-mothering." For example, the children with many mother-figures escaped undue attachment to the parent of the opposite sex as well as feelings of hostility toward their natural mothers, and extreme competition with brothers and sisters (sibling rivalry). Following the conclusions of these studies of multiple-mothering—as well as those of Bowlby and his associates, and of Rheingold, Freud, Burlingham, and Bayley—we come to two conclusions of our own. The first is that since not all motherless infants suffer from poor development, there must be a reason other than maternal deprivation for the condition of those who do suffer such retardation. Second, we may conclude that it is not the deprivation of the mother alone that retards the infant. Rather, retardation may be caused by the lack of the stimulation which the infant's mother would have provided him, and which can be provided by caring and nurturant substitutes.

In examining the subject further, it is apparent that there are generally two kinds of stimulation—that which comes from the infant's environment itself, and that which is supplied by the caretaker. The effects of a low-stimulation environment were discussed in considerable detail in our reports of the numerous studies that found institutionalized infants far below home-reared infants in developmental scores. They were provided basic physical care, but not much more. They were fed from propped bottles and seldom were permitted to see beyond their barren cribs.

Information on the stimulation provided by the caretaker has been contributed by an evaluation of the effect of a mother's stimulation on her infant (Yarrow 1963). Yarrow found that I.Q. scores would have been proportionately lower without the stimulation the mother provided. Thus, stimulation, whether it is provided by the mother or the environment, is crucial to the infant's proper development.

The interactions of fathers with their infants—and the effects of such interactions—have not been investigated extensively. This reflects the mother-centered nature of child-rearing practices in our culture, especially during the period of infancy. One study, however, has examined the relationship between scholastic aptitude patterns of male college students and the absence of the subjects' fathers; the effects of this absence were found to be greatest if the father had left the family when his son was under 6 months of age (Carlsmith 1964).

Though the influence of fathers upon their infant sons may be great, as shown by the Carlsmith study, the amount of time fathers actually spend interacting vocally with their infants is quite small (Rebelsky and Hanks 1971). In a sample of 10 families of newborns, studied over a three-month period, the mean number of daily father–infant interactions was 2.7, and the average amount of time the fathers spent in these interactions per day was 37.7 seconds. As the infants grew older, 7 of the 10 fathers decreased their number of vocalizations, whereas mothers of these infants increased their vocal interactions during the same time period.

The fathers' interactions varied according to the sex as well as the age of their infants. Fathers of girls vocalized more than fathers of boys in the first 6 weeks, but the pattern was reversed in the second 6 weeks. Although vocalizations in both groups dropped at the 6-week mark, it dropped less among fathers of boys, so that by the age of 3 months the boys were ahead of the girls in attention from their fathers. In addition, fathers tended to vocalize with their girls more during caretaking activities than at other times, but most vocalizing with sons occurred at times other than at caretaking. It may be, as Rebelsky and Hanks have suggested, that the absence of the father in the first 6 months has a greater effect on a boy than on a girl because the father of a boy responds to his son in a manner that is more distinct from the mother's response.

It should be clear from this account of the many variables that enter into the baby's social development in the first year, that the early account of learning derived solely from hunger reduction now seems oversimplified. Each system of infant behavior, whether crying, smiling, sucking, or looking at his mother's face, has its own character and its own rewards for baby and mother. The baby has a particular temperament. The mother has a particular temperament. The mother has her sex role and other expectancies. In addition, when mother and infant relate to each other, their relationship is sustained by patterns of contact comfort, cuddling, and visual interaction, and by the contingencies of attachment, separation, and anxiety. Each behavior system comes with built-in rewards for its functioning, and each enters into relationships with the others (for example, cuddling sometimes helps or modifies visual activity), so that the outcome can certainly be interpreted in terms of social learning—but on a more complex series of schedules than was originally imagined. Again we must remember, however, the alternative argument of Piaget and others, that what may motivate development is not simply parental rewards and blandishments. Rather, the baby and the mother, and the baby and his environment, are continuously getting out of phase with each other; the infant makes efforts toward some new form of harmony or equilibrium, and it is these efforts that lead to learning. Either point of view, however, leads us to focus on the complex mutual regulations of caretakers and children as the major source of social development.

Socialization in Infancy

Up to this point we have dealt with the infant as the crib- or carpet-bound prewalker. But in the second year, with the onset of walking and talking, the infant's horizons broaden significantly. He toddles about, climbs stairs, turns over ashtrays, pokes into cabinets, pulls books from shelves, and turns on stereo sets. If he sees something frightening, he is able to run or crawl to his mother for reassurance. At the same time, he makes the general discovery that he now can satisfy more of his curiosities and desires by himself. (Table 7.4 lists some of the social behaviors that characterize different age levels in the first three years.)

It is probably because the infant becomes so mobile and inquisitive at this stage that our culture in the United States dictates that various social controls also should come into play at this time. Parents enforce these controls, which tell members of a culture—in this case, its youngest active members—which traits, behaviors, motives, and values the culture accepts and which it rejects. This process is known as *socialization*. The parent prevents the infant from acting out certain behaviors which the infant finds pleasurable, but which the culture, or a particular class within the culture, finds inappropriate. Thus, in his second year, the infant usually is no longer allowed to climb on the breakfast table, bang his cup on his dinner plate, play with his breakfast cereal, ransack drawers, or urinate and defecate at will. Basically, it is hard to control these actions because the infant enjoys performing them so much. In these supercharged activities we seem to see operating the Piagetian principle of functional assimilation that was discussed in the preceding chapter. That principle is: When an organism possesses a structure for performing an act, the organism has a basic tendency to use that structure, to make it

Table 7.4 Progress Indicators of Social Development, First 3 Years

Behavior Item	Age Expected
	(Weeks)
Responds to smiling and talking	6
Knows mother	12
Shows marked interest in father	14
Is sober with strangers	16
Withdraws from strangers	32
Responds to "bye-bye"	40
Responds to inhibitory words	52
Plays pat-a-cake	52
Waves "bye-bye"	52
	(Years, Months)
Is no longer shy toward strangers	1–3
Enjoys imitation of adult activities (smoking, etc.)	1–3
Is interested in and treats another child like an object rather than a person	1–6
Plays alone	1–6
Brings things (slippers, etc.) to adult (Father)	1–6
Shows beginning of concept of private ownership	1–9
Wishes to participate in household activities	1–9
Has much interest in and watches other children	2
Begins parallel play	2
Is dependent and passive in relation to adults	2
Is shy toward strangers	2
Is not sociable; lacks social interest	2–3
Is ritualistic in behavior	2–6
Is imperious, domineering	2–6
Begins to resist adult influence; wants to be independent	2–6
Is self-assertive; difficult to handle	2–6
Is in conflict with children of own age	2–6
Refuses to share toys; ignores requests	2–6
Begins to accept suggestions	3
Has "we" feeling with mother	3
Likes to relive babyhood	3
Is independent of mother at nursery school	3
Tends to establish social contacts with adults	3
Shows imitative, "me, too" tendency	3
Begins strong friendships with peer associates, with discrimination against others in group	3–6

Abridged from L. H. Stott. *The longitudinal study of individual development.* Detroit: Merrill-Palmer School, 1955.

perform. In the social-control period from 12 to 18 months of age, in a Piagetian sense it is the infant's structures that are restrained.

Parent—Child Relationships

When this socialization process begins to take place, a change in the parent—child relationship also begins to emerge. Up to this point, the mother has been a nurturant figure who comforted, consoled, and encouraged the infant. Now she tends to become more of a trainer who demands a certain level of performance. The curbs on his behavior which this performance requires may bring the infant into conflict with his mother for the first time. His norms and hers do not so easily mesh now. The potential for clashes between them is increased by the fact that several controls are imposed during the same transitional period in his social development. We need to remember, however, that parents may differ as greatly in the matter of establishing controls as they do in other responses to their children. Many parents derive considerable enjoyment from the vigor and spontaneity of their 2-year-olds. They see here the seeds of later enthusiasm and vitality, rather than potential destruction of the household.

The training techniques parents use to curb their infant's socially unacceptable acts are important because they seem to influence his later behavior. The effectiveness of any social training, however, hinges on the infant's physical, cognitive, and emotional state. In other words, his ability to learn new behaviors or to control established ones depends on whether he is physically ready. The American father who wants his son to "be a man" may urge the boy to stop playing with dolls or even stuffed toys—a behavior that many boys as well as girls enjoy—and take up so-called masculine toys, such as a ball and bat, which may be too advanced for him.

As we discussed in Chapter 2 in the section on learning and maturation, the child's response to any training will depend heavily on his maturational level, and in this instance on his ability to coordinate his limbs in physical action. If the boy is not prepared, all the father's urging toward the cultural goal of sporting behavior will do his son no good. Indeed, forcing premature behavior could do considerable harm. If the boy fails repeatedly, or even once, in a humiliating situation, his later performance may be inhibited by his frustration with his earlier effort, or his fear of failing again. The same overeagerness seen in some fathers may also jeopardize the "new" American mother's efforts to show her daughter that girls need not be limited to dolls and imitation housekeeping. If she is not sensitive to her daughter's capabilities and inclinations of the moment, she may force the pace unduly by overloading the child with trucks and airplanes. Maturational level is as important a determining factor in socialization as it is in walking or talking. Only when a child's body systems are ready to perform can any coaching be beneficial.

Difficult as it can be, the period of socialization might be even more trying were it not for several motives the young child has already developed. By the time he is about 2 years old, the child is eager to please his parents, and to earn the continuance of their love and comfort. Conversely, he has an equally strong motive to avoid the feelings of rejection and loss that would result either from his parents' disapproval or from physical punishment. Thus, the process of socialization is really an agreement; the child gives up his complete infantile freedom in exchange for continued love and protection from his parents. Of course, in order for socialization to be effective, the child must already be feeling love from his parents so that he knows he will be receiving something for his feats of restraint. A cold or unaffectionate mother can hardly expect to inspire control in her child with the threat of withdrawing love that has not been expressed. If there appears to be little or no affection for the child to earn by increasing his efforts, why should he bother?—unless his mother threatens to add to his misery by punishing him if he does not comply. Clearly, generous demonstrations of affection and pride in the child are central to the practical process of his socialization.

Autonomy and the Socializing Process

According to Erik Erikson, the widely regarded psychoanalyst, the socialization period is important to more than the practical "civilization" of the infant. This period in early life also is the time in which the young child develops his sense of autonomy—his ability to act by himself, independent of his mother—as well as his feelings of self-reliance and competence. The growth of all three qualities is basically dependent on the child's control of his elimination and on his expanded sensorimotor skills that allow for much more independence in manipulation, walking, and general movement and exploration. It is in this stage that the child begins the long process of emancipation from his mother. Erikson has stated that if a young child is expected to develop autonomy, he must "experience over and over again that he is a person who is permitted to make choices. He has to have the right to choose, for example, whether to sit or whether to stand, whether to approach a visitor or to lean against his mother's knee . . . to use the toilet or wet his pants" (Erikson 1953). We should note here that the child's desire for self-regulation and self-control becomes quite obvious in the way he organizes his toys and other possessions. During the second year he develops a strong penchant for arranging things precisely his own way in his own miniature universe. If the various conditions for the development of his autonomy are not favorable, Erikson believes, the child's subsequent behavior and feelings about himself may be marked by shame and doubt. This stage of autonomy versus shame and doubt is the second of Erikson's eight psychosocial crises that successively shape a person's life.

Overly protective parents may try to prevent their child from making and carrying through his own decisions, especially when the parents fear that the possibility of physical danger, no matter how slight, may be involved. However, removing the opportunity for the child to make and carry out decisions thwarts the growth of his sense of autonomy, according to Erikson. Overprotective parents constantly pull their children backward into the outgrown status of infancy. The child is not allowed to experience success in executing a new action, and he therefore may be prevented from maturing into a decisive and self-confident person. If a child is given a gradually increasing freedom to handle objects and investigate his world, he usually will set the appropriate pace for himself (although hazards beyond his experience need to be removed). Correctly guided, he will grow in confidence since he will have fewer mishaps and most likely will find his skills equal to his tasks. A child with such positive experience will welcome new circumstances and maintain a vigorous and enthusiastic attitude in the face of challenge. In the next section we shall illustrate the type of practical issue around which the child's striving toward autonomy and self-control often centers—as well as the alternative feelings of shame and doubt that may result when a measure of autonomy is denied the child.

Toilet Training: A Major Socializing Step

Perhaps the most important basic difference between the infant and the socialized child is the latter's control of his bladder and bowel functions. All cultures practice some kind of toilet training, but the cultures differ strikingly on many aspects of such training. In some societies the child is allowed essentially to train himself by imitating other children. It is interesting to note that in cultural history there is an association between severe toilet training and cultural complexity—including the possession of carpets. Even within cultures, there are strong differences in approach and emphasis. For example, working-class mothers in the United States usually start training their offspring earlier (Bronfenbrenner 1958) than middle-class mothers. The latter tend to begin toilet training at the same time that the infant becomes highly mobile and intensely curious—in his second year. More than half of the middle-class mothers interviewed by Sears, Maccoby, and Levin in 1957 said they began to toilet-train their infants when they were 9 to 14 months old and had successfully completed the process by 18 months of age. The law of maturation seems to be responsible for another finding in this study—training took a shorter time with infants whose instruction was begun later. The strong implication here is that the muscles and responses involved in controlling elimination were mature and ready in the older child, while they were immature in the younger.

Erikson, like Freud, recognizes the importance

of toilet training in the development of autonomy (Erikson 1968). Clearly, the elimination of wastes is a function to be controlled wholly by the child, once his muscles have sufficiently developed. Rushing his toilet training, or focusing undue attention on the control of bodily functions so important to a child's emerging autonomy, can serve only, according to Erikson, to cause a preoccupation with holding onto the desired material, and to overemphasize the value of its release. Relinquishing his control over his toilet habits and yielding to the wishes of his parents are seen as compromising the child's free will. For one to whom autonomy is of an increasing importance, this can cast a shadow of doubt over a period when he is otherwise enjoying his emergence as a person. Autonomy grows on trust, and strict toilet training implies a lack of trust. When a child at this age is deprived of his parents' trust, and his sense of autonomy is nipped in the bud, self-doubt is likely to characterize his future behavior. He may feel he is worthless and incompetent, doomed to dependency; and in varying degrees these attitudes may persist even into adulthood.

Erikson goes on to point out that a child's inability or unwillingness to use the toilet may sometimes cause the parent to shame him into compliance. Already quite aware of his subordinate position in his society, the child will resist this more pointed attack on his autonomy through such negative behavior as trying to get away with forbidden activity in secret or by losing all sense of shame entirely. Toilet training is a critical step in the development of personality. It is not, as many parents, regrettably, see it, simple indoctrination into a pattern of socially acceptable behavior, to be accomplished as quickly as possible.

Training that was begun too early or enforced too rigidly has been linked to subsequent frequent temper tantrums, bedwetting, bowel and bladder accidents, and resentment of the parent who punishes such accidents (Macfarlane, Allen, and Honzik 1954). Other studies also have shown that excessively harsh training may cause more diffuse and long-lasting side effects, such as an obsession with cleanliness (Huschka 1942) or undue timidity and conformity (Dollard and Miller 1950), a clear illustration of Erikson's concept of doubt. The infant who is punished often becomes hesitant to make any choices that might not coincide with his parents' desires. His solution to this dilemma is to act only when told to; hence, his only actions are conforming actions. His ventures into the world become few and timid.

Despite the many possible negative reactions to inappropriate training techniques, investigators have found no one training method in itself that invariably leads to specific symptoms of maladjusted behavior. The total context of the parent–child relationship, rather than the particular method used, is the most important influence here—just as it is in all other areas of interaction between parent and child.

Cultural Differences in Child Rearing

We have examined in substantial detail the social training of the Western, and especially the American, infant and young child. But this method of child rearing is only one of many. Around the world, in Africa, the Middle East, and the Orient, methods of mothering vary with, and are shaped by, the cultures in which the infants are reared. The differences pervade all areas of life. In America, infants and children usually sleep alone. By contrast, in about half of the Japanese families surveyed by Caudill and Plath (1966), children sleep with one or both of their parents until age 15. Another example of the cultural differences between the two countries is the way in which the mothers soothe their infants. The American mother talks to her baby, whereas the Japanese mother rocks her infant. "Thus," Caudill and Weinstein observed in another 1966 study, "the style of the American mother seems to be in the direction of stimulating her baby to respond by use of her voice, whereas the style of the Japanese mother seems to be more in the direction of soothing and quieting her baby by nonverbal means."

Whether the mother or other family members primarily care for the child is another culturally controlled child-rearing factor that varies widely. In a six-culture study by Minturn and Lambert in 1964, the proportion of time the mother spent caring for the baby clearly emerged as a disparate factor among the cultures. Only in the United States sample—the New England community of Orchard Town—did mothers spend most of their own time taking care of their infants. In the other five cultures (Okinawa, the Philippines, Mexico, India, and Kenya), other adults or older children took over the infant's care while the mother cooked, worked outside the home or in the fields, or performed other chores. The United States was the only culture in the study where child care was a full-time and exclusive occupation for the mother.

In our discussion of separation anxiety, it may be recalled, the point was made that because in Uganda mothers carry their infants with them everywhere in slings across their backs, these infants establish a strong attachment to their mothers earlier than do American infants. It is this culturally related difference that probably accounts for the earlier onset of separation anxiety in Ugandan infants. In a study of another African culture, Goldberg (1971) has reported on the higher degree of early stimulation received by infants in Zambia. This is in part a result of the fact that the infants accompany their mothers in slings all day. They are thus exposed early to a large variety of people and events. Zambian infants also are bounced a good deal in the sling and handled vigorously when they are removed from the sling. Their stimulation is varied even more by the fact that other family members play a large role in the infants' care. Goldberg noted that in the early months, Zambian infants thus received much more sensorimotor and social stimulation than American infants, who spend much of their time lying in a crib or supported in a semireclining infant seat, and are treated as if they were fragile. When Zambian infants are able to sit alone and spend less time in the sling, however, the amount of stimulation they receive drops markedly. Mothers seldom provide toys or objects for the infants to manipulate and explore, and the early training in obedience and conformity that these infants receive may inhibit stimulus-seeking activities. American infants, on the other hand, generally receive increased stimulation once they are able to sit alone, creep, and grasp at intriguing objects—which usually are provided in abundance by their parents.

There are literally hundreds of other cultural differences in the child-rearing practices of Zambians and Americans alone. The compounded differences among all the cultural groups of the world, if they were known, would certainly be vast. All of these differences contribute to shaping the physical or attitudinal tendencies that are easily detectable among distinct ethnic or cultural groups. Whether it is overt training—such as toilet training—or implicit practice shaped by centuries of habit, the acculturation process characteristic of a particular group begins at birth and has an enormous effect on all areas of development, from infancy through adulthood.

Prediction of Behavior

One of the most rapidly popularized and widely accepted beliefs of modern psychology is the theory that the behavior of an adult can be explained by his experience as a child. It is not uncommon to hear allusions to this theory. Thus, one person is aggressive because he never got along with his father and another is anxiety-ridden because her mother died when she was 2 and she was raised by indifferent relatives. And, indeed, the information we have examined in this chapter has shown that the interaction between mother and infant is vital to the infant's development. These studies, whether focusing on smiling, crying, feeding, babbling, sucking, scanning, attachment, cuddling, vision, stimulation, stranger and separation anxiety, autonomy, or toilet training, all convey the very consistent expression that the caretaker's responses to the infant are most formative in determining his subsequent behavior. The cumulative message of these studies is most substantial: What happens in early childhood is likely to influence the child's later life.

It is difficult to pinpoint the origins of this concept of personality predictability. The idea that the child shapes the man first was expressed in a definitive way in the sixteenth century when Saint Ignatius wrote that if he could have charge of a child's education until he was 6 years old, he would not be concerned about who taught him later (Stevenson 1956). The saint's statement set forth the concept that early training is the unshakable foundation of an entire lifetime. Since Saint Ignatius's day, many explanations of personality development—including Freudian theory and social learning theory—have stressed the role of infant and childhood experience in explaining adult behavior.

Despite the historical tenacity of the idea, the remarkable fact is that it nevertheless is difficult to find substantiating proof of predictability. Certain questions naturally arise. Since environment affects a human being from conception to death, why is the environment more influential at one period of a life than at another? Some proponents of predictability have pointed to the infant's helplessness as the reason for his alleged impressionability. Yet, as the behavior of the sick and aged shows, helplessness in itself does not make a person malleable or susceptible to the influences of his environment. Other proponents have maintained that the infant's lack of experience makes him more impressionable—with, it is implied, a particular leaning toward the retention of negative experience. But when evidence is sought, very little can be found that proves the infant derives any more negative significance from events than an adult does. The meanings an adult and an infant draw are simply different. Watching a priceless antique bowl shatter on the floor might be an exciting experience for an infant and a devastating shock for an adult.

Over the years, hundreds of studies have attempted to link adult behavior to early experience. Orlansky, having examined more than 100 such studies conducted before 1949, wrote: "This paper reviews some of the empirical data bearing on the theory that various features of infant care determine adult personality. Our conclusion has been largely negative." Similarly, McCandless concluded a 1961 review of child-rearing practices—feeding, toilet, sex, and aggression training—and their effects on child development with this statement: "Regrettably few solid conclusions can be drawn from these studies."

Several other studies make the same point in another way. They show that infants subjected to harrowingly abnormal early experiences have grown into well-adjusted children. For example, the study of World War II orphans mentioned in connection with separation anxiety found that a large number of these children were well adjusted in their postwar lives, despite their abnormal early years (Freud and Dann 1951). The investigators conceded that the children's well-being may have stemmed from their cohesion as a group and the nurturance they drew from one another. Nonetheless, considering the deviation from the norm of infant caretaking practice, these children should have been maladjusted. Yet they were not. Thus, in this test, too, early experience has failed to predict infants' developmental status as children. All this is not to say categorically that early experience does not affect later behavior; it is simply to point out that the cause-and-effect relationship has not been satisfactorily specified.

There is no question that infants and mothers affect each other in the ways shown in this chapter. But, as social learning theory itself stresses, these effects continue only so long as the particulars of the reward-producing situation are maintained. And, of course, as the infant grows older and new responses mature, or are demanded by society, and new socializers (peers, siblings, and other adults) enter his life and bring new rewards for new responses, hardly anything remains very consistent and unidimensional. Life becomes very complicated. The earlier friendships established by mother and infant are overlaid with innumerable new ones. It then becomes unreasonable to expect much of a clear-cut relationship between the mother's way of feeding the infant, for example, and all of the later developments in the child's life. If a child is not traumatized by his early relationships, he is always a *new* child responding to new incentives, always growing out of his past, rather than being predicted by it in any simple fashion.

It follows logically that if children are treated "normally" when young they will be open to new influences and will continue to grow; their subsequent behavior therefore will be more predictable on contemporary grounds than on historical grounds. They will be responsive to the present

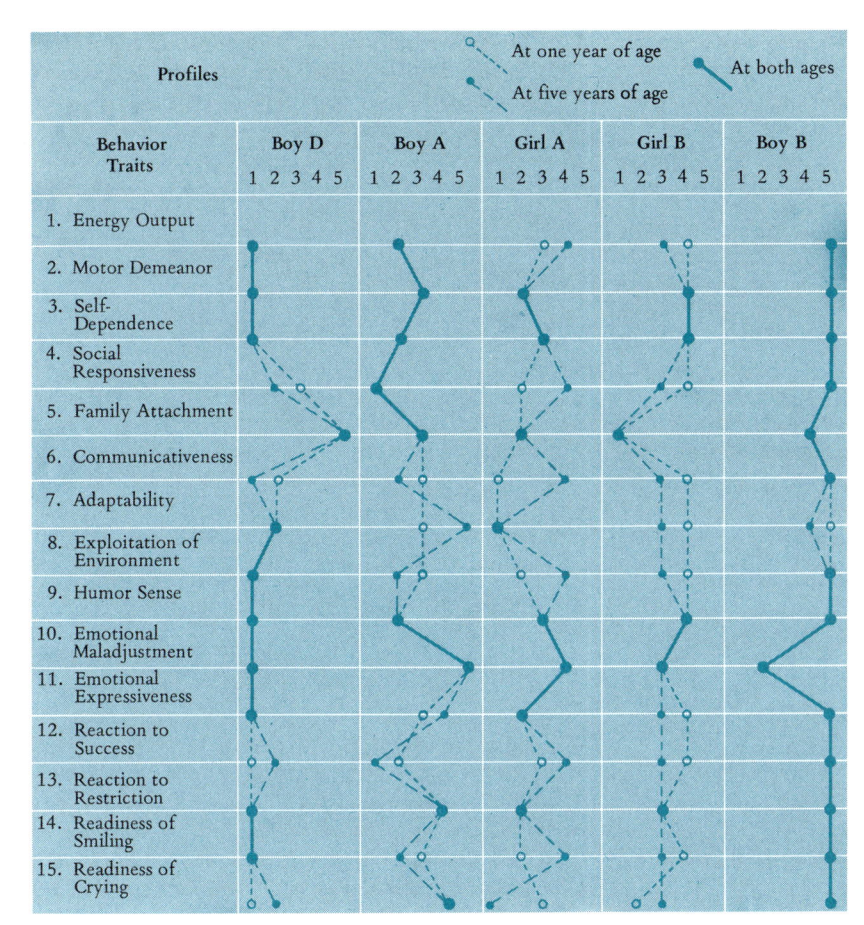

Figure 7.5 Predictiveness of individuality traits for five children as appraised in infancy and at 5 years (rated on a scale of 1–5). (From A. Gesell. Early evidences of individuality in the human infant. *Scientific Monthly*, 1937, *45*, 217–225.)

rather than determined by their past. There are, however, two exceptions—studies of animals that have had traumatic experiences, and studies of certain small societies in which, given the homogeneity of the society, the behavior of individuals correlates with their earlier treatment. We need to remember, as the philosopher Karl Popper said, it is only in a rigid society that behavior is predictable. Some psychoanalysts have contended that the behavior of traumatized humans, like the behavior of traumatized animals, can be predicted, and there is certainly more support for the infant-determination thesis when put in that negative fashion.

We can see, therefore, that all subsequent behavior need not be predictable in order to validate the theory of the mother's profound effects on her infant. These two ideas—maternal effects and predictability of the child's behavior—have been associated historically, but they are not necessary to each other. In fact, the better the mother, the less rigid influence she has.

This does not mean, on the other hand, that behavior is completely unpredictable. There is consistency in the environment over a period of time, and there is consistency in inherited characteristics.

Many human characteristics endure from infancy through adulthood. Infants, for example, may express marked humor, affection, curiosity, motor activity, or tolerance for frustration. These same traits have been identified clearly five years afterward in the same children in Gesell's 1937 study of early evidences of individuality in the human infant. Common parental observations support these findings. Parents frequently note

SOCIAL DEVELOPMENT **213**

that even as a baby, a son or daughter was always a happy, contented infant, or, conversely, that the child was always restless and curious. Such basic traits seem to endure with a high degree of consistency. "Thus," said Stevenson in his 1956 address to the American Psychiatric Association, "it seems reasonable to suppose . . . that many of the responses of infancy and childhood may not be the causes of character, but their expression. To say this is not to deny that character can be changed through experiences, but . . . it is changed by the way in which events are experienced rather than by the events themselves."

The consistency of characteristics from infancy through childhood, and even adulthood, has led some investigators to believe that the retained traits are based in the individual's genetic makeup, that they are as much a part of his personality as his hair color or his physical build. Yet these traits may also be subject to environmental influences, as Stevenson suggested. Yarrow, in his 1964 overview of personality consistency and change, noted that environment may be assumed to play on such genetically determined traits as good humor:

One assumption that is usually implicit in predictive statements about personality development is that the likelihood of personality consistency is greater, the greater the consistency in the environment. . . . the degree of personality continuity may be directly related to the extent to which the subsequent environment is reinforcing of given personality characteristics.

Essentially, then, we can say that consistency through infancy, childhood, and adulthood in any trait is likely to occur where it has a genetic basis or where the environment consistently evokes the same responses through the years.

Summary

A child's social development is rooted in his relationship with his mother in the first two years of life. This crucial relationship, in turn, is affected by the innate temperaments of mother and infant, and the mother's expectations of herself and her baby. The infant's inherited traits—such as assertiveness or passivity, irritability level, person-orientation, and tendency to smile—evoke certain responses from the mother, and these responses then influence other behaviors in the infant. A mother's acceptance of the maternal role also will affect her interaction with her infant. Furthermore, certain basic behaviors of the infant naturally involve the mother and thus shape the mother—infant relationship; these include smiling, crying, feeding, sucking, babbling, and scanning.

It first was thought that the infant's attachment to his mother grew primarily from his feeding experience, but evidence now suggests that a stronger attachment may be formed with the person who provides pleasurable physical contact and other sensory stimulation, rather than just food and basic care.

Two common fears experienced by all infants—stranger fear and separation anxiety—seem directly linked to the infant's attachment to his mother. Generally, the greater an infant's attachment to his mother, the more intense will be his fears of strangers and separation until he develops schemata to deal with these new stimuli. Stranger anxiety, however, may result more from a discrepancy from the infant's schema of himself than from a mother-schema discrepancy, since infants do not usually fear other infants.

Prolonged separation from the mother or a series of terminated attachments may impair the infant's ability to form close relationships in the future, as seen among institutionalized infants. The lack of a single caretaker usually is considered a cause of various other impairments as well, but this view is now challenged by some who question the validity of older studies and point to normal development among children raised by multiple mother-figures. The appropriate degree of individualized stimulation provided by the environment and the caretaker appears to be the relevant factor; although this usually accompanies single-mothering, it can be provided in other situations.

The infant's relationship with his parents changes when social controls are introduced in the second year. Because certain standards of behavior are now required, conflicts between parent and child may appear. In our culture, the first major step toward socialization is toilet training. The infant's willing accomplishment of this task is central to the development of his autonomy and self-confidence.

In some cultures the child is allowed essentially to toilet-train himself by imitating older children. There are countless other child-rearing practices that differ from culture to culture, reflecting the particular way of life in each society.

A child's early experience often is thought to determine his future, but a cause-and-effect relationship has not been satisfactorily proven. The determining factors, if they exist, may possibly be the innate personality traits that endure from infancy to childhood. Even given the consistency of these traits, however, if a child's early experience is within a normal range, he probably will remain responsive to whatever forces of change he encounters; and his future will not necessarily be determined by either his inborn personality or his early training.

Case Studies

Debbie P.

The precocious baby girl we studied in Chapter 6 also serves to illustrate one mode of coping with situations which typically bring about infants' separation and stranger anxieties. For whatever reasons, Debbie handled almost all such situations with the same alert confidence she showed in every other phase of her development.

Apparently able to discriminate strange faces from familiar ones by her third week, Debbie rarely exhibited any outward anxiety in the presence of strangers. By the fifth month, Mrs. P. characterized Debbie as "accepting" of strangers, but "not an automatic grinner at them." Although never frightened by new people, Debbie made no pretenses about "sizing them up" before making any advances. Familiar people, on the other hand, were welcome sources of social stimulation, even in groups. Mrs. P. reported, for instance, that her 7-month-old daughter mingled quite easily with neighbors and other children around the community pool, often interacting with them physically at her own instigation. By her first birthday, Debbie could even be comfortable with a roomful of new faces at her father's clinic Christmas party—where she readily gave her hand to a stranger so that she might be "introduced" to each of the partygoers.

Debbie's only signs of some subtle stranger anxiety were during scattered periods of major developmental transition, when her days seemed filled with considerable chaos and uncertainty. At 9½ months, for instance, when Debbie had just entered a period of "new assertiveness and self-expression," Mrs. P. noted an uncharacteristic frown when a strange visitor paid marked attention to the family poodle. Even as late as her twenty-third month, Debbie showed "real shyness" with strangers of all ages—complete with sidelong glances and back-turning—but this, too, was a transitional period of unusual confusion and inconsistency.

Likewise, Debbie exhibited very little of the normal separation anxieties—in part, at least, because she had developed early traits of autonomy. Full of independence and initiative from the moment she could crawl, Debbie was usually happy to amuse herself beyond the immediate supervision of her mother—although Mrs. P. was seldom more than a room or two away. Whenever Debbie wanted or needed her mother, however, Mrs. P. gave unstintingly of her time and energies.

Midway through Debbie's tenth month, some unforeseen circumstances obligated both Mr. and Mrs. P. to day-long absences for four consecutive days. Left at home with her grandmother (whom Debbie knew and liked, and who was familiar with Debbie's usual reactions as well as her schedule), Debbie passed most of each day quite as usual, except for some late afternoon restlessness and dissatisfaction. After more supervision than usual, she went to bed nearly an hour before schedule on all four days. She compensated, however, by waking during her 11 p.m. diaper change—which she normally slept through—and insisted on a half-hour's active play with both parents, just as she usually did at the end of her postsupper playtime. Mrs. P. noted more clinging and demands for attention than ever before during her first day back in the house, but Debbie's schedule was completely normal by the second day.

At 14 months, Debbie spent an unexpected weekend with her father and grandmother, since her mother had been caught in a blizzard. On Mrs. P.'s return, Debbie was decidedly cool and aloof, although there had been no fuss at all during the weekend itself. It took one entire day for Debbie to recover from her anger. Apparently, even the most autonomous of little girls resents being away from her mother for so long, snow or no snow (Church 1968).

Ruth S.

Like Debbie, Ruth was an unusually precocious child, particularly in her expressive and linguistic functions. Although raised in an atmosphere of strict parental expectations—both intellectual and behavioral—Ruth was also the object of much warm adoration. Her young, affluent parents were unusually active and social people, but also devoutly religious. Ruth's father worked long hours in his family's retail business. Mrs. S., always an intense and dynamic woman, managed to do some graduate study, volunteer work, and amateur painting even after Ruth's arrival.

An early case of colic and a history of respiratory infections made Ruth the object of considerable indulgence and overprotection throughout her first year and a half. Her mother reports that she was "excessively pampered" until she was 8 months old because her parents did not want her crying to disturb their apartment neighbors. (Only at that age, during a three-week vacation, was Ruth allowed to cry herself to sleep, "putting an end to her somewhat tyrannical ways at bedtime.") Throughout her first several years, Ruth was a tense, easily excitable girl who was quite sensitive to changes in emotional atmospheres—even to the point of vomiting and fever when major family events caused unusual parental tensions.

Although she was exposed almost exclusively to a wide variety of adults throughout infancy, Ruth's reactions to strangers were intermittently fearful and confident from her fourth month until nearly her second birthday. At 4 months, for instance, she cried disconsolately when her mother first handed her to the 300-pound woman who was to be her new nurse. It was several days before Ruth would let this stranger do anything for her without her mother being right in the room. During this same month, Ruth screamed her way through a visit to a neighbor's house, even though Mrs. S. held her the entire time.

At 7 months, Ruth was still crying when strangers—or even half-strangers—approached her, although just a month later she was playfully pulling their clothes to be sure they noticed her. By her first birthday, Ruth's stranger anxieties were restricted to times when she was picked up by a seeming stranger, in which case she would invariably cry for her "mama." By 19 months she seemed to have lost all of her fear of strangers (although Mrs. S. reports a brief fear of masks, face-doodles, and jack-o'-lanterns at 16 months). Toward the end of her second year, however, Ruth exhibited a sudden fear of a neighbor's cleaning woman by running to her mother and repeating insistently, "Good-bye, lady, go home."

Signs of separation anxieties in this willful little girl were somewhat more subtle, with one significant exception in Ruth's fifteenth month. At 9 months, for instance, Mrs. S. reported that whenever Ruth crawled from the room, she would repeatedly turn her head to keep her mother in view. At 11 months, Ruth would tearfully insist that she return to her mother if anyone else picked her up. And at 12 months, she would sob violently if Mrs. S. was not home when another adult brought Ruth back from a short visit.

Soon after her first birthday, however, Ruth was left with her maternal grandmother for seven weeks while her parents vacationed in Europe. Greeting them unhesitatingly on their return, she then did not let them leave the room, and kept repeating, "Mamma, Daddy, Mamma, Daddy. . . ." throughout her sleep that night. For many days afterwards, Ruth cried if her parents left the house; she demanded much more that she be picked up, and was generally more clinging and affectionate than ever before. Mrs. S. conjectured that the separation had "affected Ruth greatly."

In addition, both at 17 and 22 months Ruth reportedly grew very lonesome for her father while he was out of town. She asked for him repeatedly, resisted going to sleep without him, and waited at the door at his usual time of arrival. Perhaps Ruth was making it obvious that there were two people in her life she did not want to be without (Church 1968).

References

Ainsworth, M. D. S. Cited in: A scientific look at the origins of infant–mother attachment. *Johns Hopkins J.*, 1972, 6 (1), 1.

Ainsworth, M. D. S. *Infancy in Uganda*. Baltimore: Johns Hopkins Press, 1967.

Bakwin, H. Emotional deprivation in infants. *J. Pediat.*, 1949, 35, 512–521.

Bell, R. Q. A reinterpretation of the direction of effects in studies of socialization. *Psychol. Rev.*, 1968, 75, 81–95.

Bender, L. Anxiety in disturbed children. In P. H. Hoch and J. Zubin (Eds.), *Anxiety*. New York: Grune & Stratton, 1950.

Bender, L. Psychopathic behavior disorders in children. In R. M. Lindner and R. V. Seliger (Eds.), *Handbook of correctional psychology*. New York: Philosophical Library, 1947.

Bender, L., and Yarnell, H. An observation nursery: A study of 250 children in the psychiatric division of Bellevue Hospital. *Amer. J. Psychiat.*, 1941, 97, 1158–1174.

Bostock, J. Thieving in childhood. *Med. J. Aust.*, 1961, 1, 813–815.

Bowlby, J. The nature of the child's tie to his mother. *Int. J. Psychoanal.*, 1958, 39, 350–373.

Bowlby, J. Separation anxiety. *Int. J. Psychoanal.*, 1960, 41, 89–113.

Bowlby, J., Ainsworth, M., Boston, M., and Rosenbluth, D. The effects of mother–child separation: A follow-up study. *Brit. J. med. Psychol.*, 1956, 29, 211–247.

Brackbill, Y. Extinction of the smiling response in infants as a function of reinforcement schedule. *Child Develpm.*, 1958, 29, 115–124.

Bronfenbrenner, U. Socialization and social class through time and space. In E. E. Maccoby, T. M. Newcomb, and E. L. Hartley (Eds.), *Readings in social psychology*. (3rd ed.) New York: Holt, Rinehart & Winston, 1958.

Bruce, H. M. Observations on the sucking stimulus and lactation in the rat. *J. reprod. fert.*, 1961, 2, 17–34.

Carlsmith, L. Effect of early father absence on scholastic aptitude. *Harv. educ. Rev.*, 1964, 34, 3–21.

Casler, L. Maternal deprivation: A critical review of the literature. *Monogr. Soc. Res. Child Develpm.*, 1961, 26, No. 2.

Caudill, W., and Plath, D. W. Who sleeps by whom? Parent–child involvement in urban Japanese families. *Psychiatry*, 1966, 29, 344–366.

Caudill, W., and Weinstein, H. Maternal care and infant behavior in Japanese and American urban middle-class families. In R. Konig and R. Hill (Eds.), *Yearbook of the International Sociological Association*, 1966.

Chamove, A. S. The effects of varying infant peer experience on social behavior in the rhesus monkey. Unpublished master's thesis, Univer. of Wisconsin, 1966.

Church, J. (Ed.) *Three babies: Biographies of cognitive development.* New York: Random House, 1968. Pp. 3–106; 163–287.

Dennis, W., and Najarian, P. Infant development under environmental handicap. *Psychol. Monogr.,* 1957, 71, No. 7.

Dollard, J., and Miller, N. E. *Personality and psychotherapy.* New York: McGraw-Hill, 1950.

Durfee, H., and Wolf, E. Anstalspflege und Entwicklung im l. Lebensjahr. *Z. Kinderforsch.,* 1933, 42, 273–320.

Erikson, E. H. A healthy personality for every child: A fact-finding report: A digest. Midcentury White House Conference on Children and Youth. In J. Seidman (Ed.), *The adolescent: A book of readings.* New York: Dryden (Holt, Rinehart & Winston), 1953.

Erikson, E. H. *Identity: Youth and crisis.* New York: Norton, 1968.

Etzel, B. C., and Gewirtz, J. L. Experimental modification of caretaker-maintained high-rate operant crying in a 6- and a 20-week-old infant (Infans tyrannotearus): Extinction of crying with reinforcement of eye contact and smiling. *J. exp. child Psychol.,* 1967, 5, 303–317.

Freedman, D. G. The effects of kinesthetic stimulation on weight gain and on smiling in premature infants. Presented at annual meeting of the American Orthopsychiatric Association, San Francisco, 1966.

Freedman, D. G. Hereditary control of early social behavior. In B. M. Foss (Ed.), *Determinants of infant behavior.* Vol. III. New York: Wiley, 1965.

Freud, A., and Burlingham, D. T. *Infants without families.* New York: International Universities Press, 1944.

Freud, A., and Dann, S. An experiment in group upbringing. In R. Eisler et al. (Eds.), *The psychoanalytic study of the child.* Vol. 6. New York: International Universities Press, 1951.

Gardner, D. B., Pease, D., and Hawkes, G. R. Responses of two-year-old adopted children to controlled stress situations. Paper read at meeting of the Society for Research in Child Development, Washington, D.C., March 1959.

Gardner, D. B., and Swiger, M. K. Developmental status of two groups of infants released for adoption. *Child Develpm.,* 1958, 29, 521–530.

Gesell, A. Early evidence of individuality in the human infant. *Scient. Monthly,* 1937, 45, 217–225.

Gesell, A., and Thompson, H. *Infant behavior: Its genesis and growth.* New York: McGraw-Hill, 1934.

Goldberg, S. Infant care and growth in urban Zambia. Presented at meeting of the Society for Research in Child Development, Minneapolis, April 1971.

Goldfarb, W. Psychological privation in infancy and subsequent adjustment. *Am. J. Orthopsychiat.,* 1945, 15, 247–255.

Harlow, H., and Harlow, M. H. Learning to love. *Amer. Scientist,* 1966, 54(3), 244–272.

Harlow, H. F., and Zimmermann, R. R. Affectional responses in the infant monkey. *Science,* 1959, 130(3373), 421–432.

Heinstein, M. *Child rearing in California.* Berkeley, Calif.: Bureau of Maternal and Child Health, State of California Department of Public Health, 1966.

Hindley, C. B., Filliozat, A. M., Klackenberg, G., Nicolet-Meister, D., and Sand, E. A. Some differences in infant feeding and elimination training in four European longitudinal samples. *J. child psychol. Psychiat.,* 1965, 6, 179–201.

Hoffman, H. S., Schiff, D., Adams, J., and Searle, J. L. Behavioral control by an imprinted stimulus. *J. exp. Analysis Behav.,* 1966, 9, 177–189.

Huschka, M. The child's response to coercive bowel training. *Psychosom. Med.,* 1942, 4, 301–308.

Jersild, A. T., and Holmes, F. B. Children's fears. *Child Develpm. Monogr.,* 1935, No. 20, 358.

Kagan, J. Do infants think? *Scientific Amer.,* 1972, 226 (3), 74–82.

Kagan, J. Continuity in development in the first year. Unpublished manuscript.

Kessen, W. *The child.* New York: Wiley, 1967.

Korner, A. F., and Grobstein, R. Visual alertness as related to soothing in neonates: Implications for maternal stimulation and early deprivation. *Child Develpm.,* 1966, 37, 867–876.

Lewis, M., and Brooks-Gunn, J. Self, other, and fear: The reaction of infants to people. Presented at annual meeting of the Eastern Psychological Association, Boston, April 1972.

Lowrey, L. G. Personality distortion and early institutional care. *Amer. J. Orthopsychiat.,* 1940, 10, 576–586.

Macfarlane, J. W., Allen, L., and Honzik, M. P. *A developmental study of the behavior problems of normal children between twenty-two months and fourteen years.* Univer. of Calif. Publications in Child Development. Vol. II. Berkeley and Los Angeles: Univer. of Calif. Press, 1954.

McCandless, B. R. *Children and adolescence: Behavior and development.* New York: Holt, Rinehart & Winston, 1961.

Menlove, F. L. Aggressive symptoms in emotionally disturbed adopted children. *Child Develpm.,* 1965, 36, 519–532.

Minturn, L., and Lambert, W. W. *Mothers of six cultures: Antecedents of child rearing.* New York: Wiley, 1964.

Morgan, G. A., and Ricciuti, H. N. Infants' responses to strangers during the first year. In B. M. Foss (Ed.), *Determinants of infant behaviour.* Vol. IV. London: Methuen, 1969.

Moss, H. A. Early environmental effects: Mother–child relations. In T. D. Spencer and N. Kass (Eds.), *Perspectives in child psychology.* New York: McGraw-Hill, 1970.

Moss, H. A. Sex, age and state as determinants of the mother–infant interaction. *Merrill-Palmer Quart.,* 1967, 13, 19–36.

Moss, H. A., and Robson, K. S. Maternal influences in early social visual behavior. *Child Develpm.,* 1968, 39, 401–408.

Nash, J. *Developmental psychology: A psychobiological approach.* Englewood Cliffs, N.J.: Prentice-Hall, 1970.

Noirot, E. Changes in responsiveness to young in the adult mouse. III. The effect of immediately preceding performances. *Behavior*, 1965, *24*, 318–325.

O'Connor, N. The evidence for the permanently disturbing effects of mother–child separation. *Acta psychol.*, 1956, *12*, 174–191.

Orlansky, H. Infant care and personality. *Psychol. Rev.*, 1949, *46*, 1–48.

Palmer, R. R. *The age of the democratic revolution.* Vol. II. *The struggle.* Princeton: Princeton Univer. Press, 1964.

Pinneau, S. The infantile disorders of hospitalism and anaclitic depression. *Psychol. Bull.*, 1955, *52*, 429–452.

Provence, S., and Lipton, R. C. *Infants in institutions.* New York: International Universities Press, 1962.

Rabin, A. I. Personality maturation of kibbutz (Israeli collective settlement) and non-kibbutz children as reflected in Rorschach findings. *J. proj. Tech.*, 1957, *31*, 148–153.

Rabin, A. I. Some psychosexual differences between kibbutz and non-kibbutz Israeli boys. *J. proj. Tech.*, 1958, *32*, 328–332.

Rebelsky, F. G., and Hanks, C. Fathers' verbal interaction with infants in the first three months of life. *Child Develpm.*, 1971, *42*, 63–68.

Rheingold, H. L. The effect of a strange environment on the behavior of infants. In B. M. Foss (Ed.), *Determinants of infant behaviour.* Vol. IV. London: Methuen, 1969.

Rheingold, H. L. The effect of environmental stimulation upon social and exploratory behavior in the human infant. In B. M. Foss (Ed.), *Determinants of infant behavior.* Vol. I. New York: Wiley, 1961.

Rheingold, H. L. The modification of social responsiveness in institutional babies. *Monogr. Soc. Res. Child Develpm.*, 1956, *21*(2, Serial No. 63).

Rheingold, H. L., and Bayley, N. The later effects of an experimental modification of mothering. *Child Develpm.*, 1959, *30*, 363–372.

Rheingold, H. L., and Eckerman, C. O. Fear of the stranger: A critical examination. Presented at annual meeting of the Society for Research in Child Development, Minneapolis, April 1971.

Rheingold, H. L., Gewirtz, J. L., and Ross, H. W. Social conditioning of vocalizations in the infant. *J. comp. physiol. Psychol.*, 1959, *52*(1), 68–73.

Rosenblatt, J. S. The development of maternal responsiveness in the rat. *Amer. J. Orthopsychiat.*, 1969, *39*, 36–56.

Scarr, S. The inheritance of sociability. *Amer. Psychologist*, 1965, *20*, 524.

Schaffer, H. R. The onset of fear of strangers and the incongruity hypothesis. *J. child Psychol. Psychiat.*, 1966, *7*, 95–106.

Schaffer, H. R., and Emerson, P. E. Patterns of response to physical contact in early human development. *J. child Psychol. Psychiat.*, 1964, *5*, 1–13. (a)

Schaffer, H. R., and Emerson, P. E. The development of social attachments in infancy. *Monogr. Soc. Res. Child Develpm.*, 1964, *29*, No. 3. (b)

Sears, R. R., Maccoby, E. E., and Levin, H. *Patterns of child rearing.* Evanston, Ill.: Row, Peterson, 1957.

Shirley, M. M. *The first two years: A study of twenty-five babies.* Vol. II. *Intellectual development.* Inst. Child Welf. Monogr., No. 7. Minneapolis: Univer. of Minnesota Press, 1933.

Spitz, R. A. Hospitalism: An inquiry into the genesis of psychiatric conditions in early childhood. In A. Freud et al. (Eds.), *The psychoanalytic study of the child.* New York: International Universities Press, 1945.

Stendler, C. B. Sixty years of child-training practices. *J. Pediat.*, 1950, *36*, 122–134.

Stern, D. N. A micro-analysis of mother–infant interaction. *J. Amer. Acad. Child Psychiat.*, 1971, *10*(3), 501–517.

Stevenson, I. Is the human personality more plastic in infancy and childhood? Presented at annual meeting of the American Psychiatric Assoc., Chicago, April 1956.

Stone, L. J., and Church, J. *Childhood and adolescence: A psychology of the growing person.* (2nd ed.) New York: Random House, 1968.

Thompson, W. R., and Grusec, J. E. Studies of early experience. In P. H. Mussen (Ed.), *Carmichael's manual of child psychology.* Vol. I. (3rd ed.) New York: Wiley, 1970.

U.S. Dept. of Health, Education and Welfare. *Infant care.* Children's Bureau Pub. No. 8. Washington, D.C.: Government Printing Office, 1969.

Vincent, C. E. Trends in infant care ideas. *Child Develpm.*, 1951, *22*, 199–209.

Washburn, R. W. A study of the smiling and laughing of infants in the first year of life. *Genet. Psychol. Monogr.*, 1929, *6*, 397–537.

White, B. L., and Castle, P. W. Visual exploratory behavior following postnatal handling of human infants. *Percept. and mot. Skills*, 1964, *18*, 497–502.

Whiting, J. W. M., et al. The learning of values. In E. Z. Vogt and E. M. Albert (Eds.), *People of Rimrock: A study of values in five cultures.* Cambridge, Mass.: Harvard Univer. Press, 1966.

Williams, J. R., and Scott, R. B. Growth and development of Negro infants: IV. Motor development and its relationship to child-rearing practices in two groups of Negro infants. *Child Develpm.*, 1953, *24*, 103–121.

Yarrow, L. J. Personality consistency and change: An overview of some conceptual and methodological issues. *Vita Humana*, 1964, *7*(2), 67–72.

Yarrow, L. J. Research in dimensions of early maternal care. *Merrill-Palmer Quart.*, 1963, *9*, 101–114.

IV

Toddlerhood
Ages 2 and 3

Annan Photo Features

Motor, Cognitive, and Language Development 8

WHILE THE growing child is always somewhat in transition, he is especially so in the period between his second and fourth birthdays. At this age, he is no longer an immobile, helpless infant, yet he is not truly an independent, socially capable child. Psychologists have called this period of transition the *preschool or nursery years*. Another term commonly used, *toddlerhood*, highlights the increasing locomotive powers of the child in the third and fourth years.

It is the toddler's notorious ability to move about independently that so vividly marks the change from infancy to toddlerhood. Perhaps no other activity is so important to the child's sense of his own autonomy as his ability to move himself about, whether he does it by walking, running, or climbing. The toddler seldom lets those around him forget his new powers. He is always moving. Now he moves much like an adult. Having abandoned the cautious, hands-raised walking style of the infant, he runs full tilt, laughing and confident. He loves to transport lounge pillows and large stuffed animals and may even try to rearrange the furniture. He is eager to dress and undress himself, although his manual skills are not always adequate. He is assertive. He bullies pigeons off the pavement, and dashes boldly into strange alleys.

In keeping with his new expansiveness, the toddler's rapid cognitive development becomes more apparent. The child finds a good part of his amusement in investigating, talking, naming objects, colors, sounds, smells, and people. He also takes delight in his dawning awareness of the categories of things—toys, clothes, books, utensils—and how he can organize them by their likenesses.

The toddler is expansive in his social behavior

as well. He now turns outward to activity with other children, in a move away from the parent-oriented world of his infancy. However, the toddler is not yet able to engage in play very successfully with another child. He often seeks activity *among* his peers, in what is known as parallel play, rather than in cooperative play with them. For example, he does not, in this transitional stage, engage in such activities as hide-and-seek or tea parties, which are essentially cooperative games. Instead, each toddler amuses himself independently amid the cacophony of the sandbox crowd. True social activity develops in the years from 4 to 7, which we shall discuss in Chapters 10 and 11.

Despite the toddler's compelling drive to assert himself, even to the point of issuing a few orders now and then ("Go out!" "Cookie right now!"), he remains a baby in many ways. He retains a strong oral drive, tending to cram any feasible object into his mouth as if to taste-test it. Even as he defiantly bolts out of his stroller and into an intriguing doorway, the sudden absence of his mother may induce panic. A strange face may make him flee. He is an ambivalent, transitional person, both tiger and mouse.

It is in this active period, too, that the child's personality—inconsistent though it may be now—becomes more evident to his parents. Hints of permanent traits appear. His parents begin to know him as a quite complex, individualized person, and he develops an awareness of himself as a separate, increasingly independent being.

Although the proud toddler may be emerging as a distinct personality, with new powers of mind and body, he is far from "civilized." As his increasing abilities bring him into greater contact with the world around him, society—usually in the form of his mother—begins to impose its order on him. In our discussion of infancy, we were concerned with examining the care and feeding of the baby and the first steps toward socialization that were related to these areas of his life. In the second chapter of this section, we shall see evidence of how society further socializes the toddler; limits are set on his aggression and sexuality, and he is taught the social structures we broadly call etiquette. First, however, we shall trace the continuing development of the toddler's motor capabilities and his cognitive powers.

Physical and Motor Development

By age 3, the average toddler stands about 3 feet tall—boys at 38 inches and girls at 37.6 inches. The average weight is 33 pounds for boys and 32.5 pounds for girls. While height and weight differences between boys and girls are negligible, the tissue content of their bodies is distinctly different. Boys have more muscle tissue and girls have more fatty tissue.

A toddler's height gives a fair indication of what his stature will be as an adult. There is a .70 correlation between heights at these two stages, but even this relatively high correlation leaves room for the occasional pint-sized toddler to shoot ahead of his peers later in childhood to become an impressively tall adult.

While he is growing taller and adding weight, the upper half of the toddler's body is assuming the proportions of the adult's body. During this period, the growth speeds of different body parts change. The growth of the head slows down, the trunk grows faster, but the limbs accelerate more than any other part of the body. This stage transforms the 3-year-old with his protruding abdomen and short legs into the 6-year-old whose stomach has drawn in, whose legs have lengthened, and whose head size has come into proper proportion with the rest of his body. Now the child appears much like a scaled-down adult—he has roughly the same proportions, but a different body size.

Skeletal Growth

The child's skeletal system, too, is continuing to mature. Bones are forming out of the malleable cartilage at an increasing rate and in greater numbers. Existing bones also are becoming larger and, at the same time, harder. Teeth, too, are developing—between 2 and 3 years of age—toward the completion of the "baby teeth" that the child retains until the end of his sixth year. At 2½ or 3 years, the toddler is fully equipped dentally to eat the same food his parents eat.

Muscular Growth

The muscular system that supports and moves the bones grows in step with them. Up to about the fourth birthday, the growth of the muscles is proportional to the growth of the body in general. However, at the end of the fourth year, the muscles begin to grow at an accelerated rate—so rapidly that during the next year, three-quarters of the child's gain in weight is accounted for by additional muscle tissue (Thompson 1954). Not all muscles are growing at the same rate during this peak-growth year, however; the larger muscles develop more than the smaller ones. Thus, the child is better at gross actions—for example, a carefree, one-armed sweep of objects from his play table—than he is at turning the pages of a book or buttoning up a sweater.

The toddler also is physiologically better equipped to indulge in the persistent investigation and furious activity that characterize his age. His breathing has become slower and deeper, permitting sustained activity. His heart rate has steadied and slowed down, and, at the same time, his blood pressure has increased (Thompson 1954).

Nervous System

In conjunction with his bones and muscles, the toddler's nervous system is developing and becoming more refined. At the start of the toddler stage, his brain, the core of his nervous system, has reached 75 percent of its final weight (4 pounds for the adult male). During the next four years, the brain increases its size still more, until at age 6 the child's brain weighs about 3½ pounds, 90 percent of its adult weight. In the same period, between 2 and 6 years, the nerve fibers in the higher brain centers become myelinized—that is, they are sheathed in myelin, a fatty white substance that helps to speed up the transmission of nerve impulses. The myelinization of nerve fibers in the other regions of the child's body has been almost completed at this point.

Just as other characteristics of the toddler are becoming more like an adult and less like an infant, his physiological response to infections undergoes a marked change. Temperatures in illness are less dramatic than before, but the illness itself often afflicts the toddler for a longer time now. However, his more developed and generally stronger body is better equipped for these longer sieges of illness, and there is less risk than during infancy that any disease will affect his heart.

Psychomotor Development

The continuing development of muscles, bones, and nerves has expanded and refined the toddler's repertoire of physical skills. Now he runs in a smooth, regular rhythm, rather than jerkily as he did earlier. He can slow down, speed up, turn corners, and stop with greater finesse. He can climb upstairs as an adult does and leap off the sandbox seat with both feet at the same time, instead of putting one foot out ahead. He can jump a foot into the air and imitate the flamingo's one-legged stance—for a wobbly moment.

At 3, his manual skills, too, have become somewhat more sophisticated. Since these skills require small motor coordination, however, they

Figure 8.1 The increasing locomotive powers of the toddler give him new independence. (Black Star)

are not as advanced as his abilities that depend on the faster-developing large muscles. He is steady-handed enough to stack as many as 10 blocks, three or four more than he could manage when he was 2 years old. When he works with crayons or pencils, he makes strokes that are firmer and clearer, more organized and innovative. If shown how, he can fold a paper in half vertically or horizontally, but he cannot yet master the diagonal fold.

By his fourth birthday, the child is even more accomplished in locomotion because of the increasing ability of his legs to act independently of each other and the rest of his body. He can control his walking and running better, adjusting and changing his pace more quickly, and inserting such footwork as his newly acquired ability to skip. His up-and-down jumping has been outmoded by his new capacity to broad-jump from both running and standing starts.

The muscular independence evident in the leg movements of the 4-year-old also is present in other parts of his body. His arms operate in a much more articulate manner, working without heavy reliance on torso action, as they did at ages 2 or 3, when he threw a ball with his entire upper body.

Manual skills at age 4 show some refinement, although development of the small muscles is still not as advanced as that of the larger muscles. Pencil strokes are more precise, yet may be more wiggly than intended. The 4-year-old's drawings reflect his greater sense of relations among objects, both real and on paper. He can draw a cross and a circle and now can fold a sheet of paper diagonally. His manual as well as his body skills will continue to become more clearly defined and precise.

Intelligence and Its Measurement

The child's greatly expanded psychomotor development and sensorimotor intelligence give rise to a more complex mode of mental activity that depends less on physical action than it did during infancy. Tests that intend to measure the child's intellectual potential throughout childhood reflect the changes in his mental processes. In the first two years, as we saw in Chapter 6, the assessment of the infant's intelligence necessarily relied on the infant's performance of motor skills, since these skills were his primary mode of dealing with all stimuli.

Tests for Toddlers

Intelligence tests given at ages 2 and 3 take into account the toddler's new intellectual abilities by including cognitive and verbal as well as psychomotor items. Generally, these tests measure the extent of the child's vocabulary, his language understanding, instant recall, reasoning powers, perceptual organization, and his ability to solve problems.

The widely used Stanford-Binet intelligence test, for example, asks the 2-year-old to describe the uses of everyday objects, such as a spoon or a cup; to fit three blocks into matching recesses in a board; to put together a simple jigsaw puzzle; to indicate the arms, legs, head, and other parts of a doll's body; and to repeat two digits spoken by the test administrator. There are considerably fewer sensorimotor tasks than there were in the infant tests. Verbal tasks gain still greater predominance in the tests for 4-year-olds. They are asked to name common items from pictures and from memory. The children also must distinguish triangles, squares, circles, and other geometrical shapes; define common words like *hat* and *coat*; count four blocks or other such objects; and repeat a 10-word sentence read to them.

Because intelligence tests given to children up to 2 years old are composed primarily of sensorimotor tasks, they are not very useful as predictors of scores on school-age or adult intelligence tests (Bayley 1943), which rely heavily on verbal understanding and facility. However, starting with the tests given toddlers, where the measurement depends increasingly on verbal items, the tests begin to act as fairly reliable predictors of later performance. The tests given later in childhood are even more likely to be dependable advance profiles of adult performance. This correlation of later childhood tests with adult scores was confirmed in a study in which the subjects were given intelligence tests at intervals, starting when they were 21 months old. From this age until they began school, the children were tested with the California Preschool Schedule. In later childhood and adolescence, they took the Stanford-Binet test. When they were 18 years old, they concluded the study with the Wechsler Adult Intelligence Scale. Results showed that the later scores in the preschool period came closer to predicting future intellectual performance than did the earliest scores in that period. For example, at age 2 there was only a .37 correlation with the child's I.Q. at age 10, and a .31 correlation with his I.Q. at age 18. However, the tests taken just two years later, at age 4, showed a .66 correlation with the I.Q. at age 10, and a .42 correlation with the individual's I.Q. as an 18-year-old (Honzik, Macfarlane, and Allen 1948).

Although the predictive value of tests given to toddlers is greater than that of tests given during infancy, the toddlerhood tests never do achieve a fully desirable level of predictability. The dominant reason for this rather basic flaw is the nature of the tests themselves. Tests administered from infancy to adulthood necessarily measure different skills at each stage, because it is only in terms of his current abilities that the individual can respond to a particular test. Thus, an I.Q. measured largely in terms of motor skills at age 2 or 3 has limited value in predicting intelligence in a later age period when intelligence will be assessed in terms of language facility.

In addition to this primary handicap, the tests are subject to a number of outside variables that can influence their results and make them invalid as intelligence forecasters. For example, the child's physical, mental, or emotional condition on the day of the test may make a great difference. A child who has a headache, has to go to the bathroom, or is tired or emotionally upset will almost certainly score lower than he would on a day when he did not have these impediments. The warmth and encouragement of the examiner also may make a difference. The child's performance may further be affected by his parents' regard for intellectual accomplishment; his opportunities for cultural experiences; his language skills; and his motivation to perform well on tests, which may be linked to his attitude toward school in general. The general changeability of 2- and 3-year-olds makes them particularly susceptible to these and other influences. Despite these drawbacks, however, such tests nevertheless are capable of showing excessive degrees of retardation in sensorimotor skills, and thus can serve as an index of potential mental retardation.

Considerable activity is currently being devoted to designing intelligence tests based on Piaget's conceptions of intellectual development. These tests would possibly ask the toddler to perform such conceptual tasks as counting up to seven objects, grouping similar objects, telling which two of three objects are not the same, or determining which object of several is the largest or smallest, widest or thinnest, longest or shortest. There is hope among some psychologists that these new cognitive tests will be better predictors of future intellectual functioning.

Effect of Early Years on Intelligence

According to many investigators, the early years of the child's life are crucial to the successful development of his intellectual powers. Extreme conditions of deprivation in a child's environment—such as undernourishment or an emotionally disturbing home life—have been found to seriously affect the course of his intellectual development (Hebb 1949). As the child moves out of the preschool years, however, the effect of his environment diminishes (Bloom 1964). The early vulnerability of intellectual powers seems to be related to the course of intellectual development. The early life stages are the periods of most rapid intelligence development (in later childhood, the development of intelligence continues, but at a slower pace). Therefore, severe environmental deprivation in the early life stages could interrupt this development more drastically, stunting the child intellectually. Yet, the same degree of environmental deprivation, occurring at a later stage of development, might have little or no effect on the intellect.

Figure 8.2 The toddler's cognitive awareness expands as he investigates his world. (A. C. Forbes—D.P.I., Ivan Massar—Black Star)

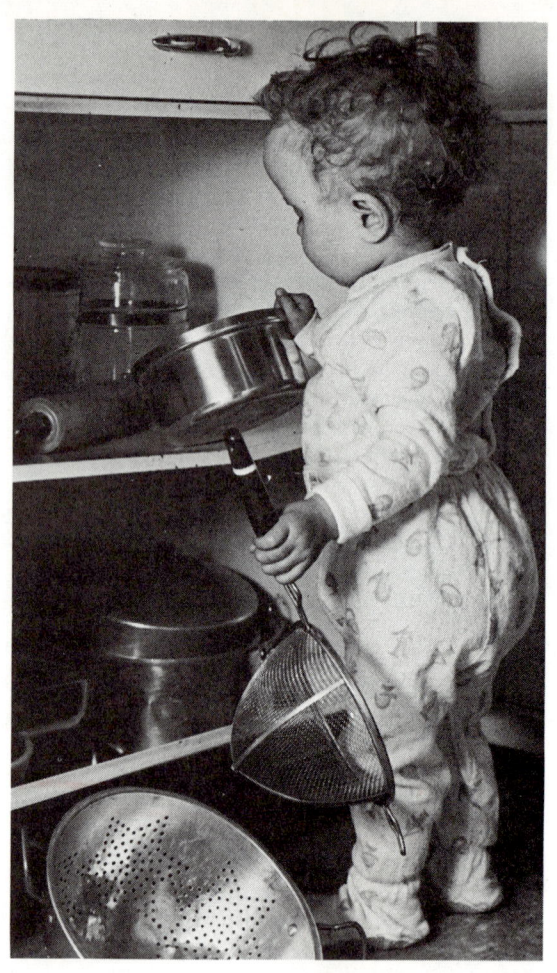

Elizabeth Hibbs—Monkmeyer

Cognitive Development

Thus far, we have traced the growth processes involved in the child's physical progress in the third and fourth years; and we have touched on the changes in his intellectual capacities and some of the methods of assessing these abilities. The child's intellectual growth is dependent upon, if not synonymous with, important cognitive processes that have been developing during this period. In the remainder of this chapter, we shall analyze these cognitive processes, which in toddlerhood center around the child's emerging ability to use representation, through language, cognition, and play.

Representation: Four Factors

The substitution of an act, word, or symbol for something else is known as *representation*. As we noted in Chapter 6, when we examined Stage 6 of Piaget's sensorimotor period, the first signs of representation usually appear between the twelfth and eighteenth months.

In focusing on the uses of representational or symbolic thinking in the child's language, cognition, and play, it is easy to forget what enormous achievements these acts of representation are for the child. The point is made most tellingly in the work of two developmental psychologists, Heinz Werner and Bernard Kaplan (1963). They demonstrated that the act of representation requires four prior achievements that are gradually developed during infancy, as we saw earlier in Chapter 6. First, the infant must discern that objects are separate from himself. Elementary as this may sound with the hindsight of age, the child's differentiation of self from objects and the differentiation of separate objects among the world's great variety is a slow process occurring throughout infancy. Integral to it is the development of a sense of *object permanence*—the sense that objects have an existence independent from the child's perception of them. The child knows that the toy screened by the walls of a toy chest still exists even though he cannot see it.

The second factor involved in acts of representation is the development of the ability to refer to objects, which is acquired by the child through reaching, pointing, touching, or looking. These acts are the basis for the linkage of symbol and its object.

From his sense of object permanence the child develops a third ability—the capacity to form mental images of real things. These images of acts or objects provide what showmen and dramatists call "routines" or "bits of business," which the child uses as symbolic vehicles to carry his intent. A child "washing" his face with a dry flannel cloth is one instance of the use of a symbolic vehicle; the child is pretending the cloth is wet, in accordance with his mental image of a washcloth. These nonverbal imitations are the precursors of later symbolization through words.

Finally, because symbolization is almost always part of the representational process, the child must gradually distinguish between himself, as the symbolizer, and the other person or persons as the audience to whom he is communicating. Thus, there are four factors involved in acts of representation—the child's sense of object permanence; his physical methods of referring to specific acts or objects; the symbolic vehicle; and the differentiation of the other person as the audience.

In the view of Werner and Kaplan, all four factors differentiate and develop from birth and then are reintegrated into the act of representation by a second, new process. The mechanics of this reintegration are still mysterious. Many assume the process is simply characteristic of the human species and occurs when the preceding experiences provide the optimal opportunity. This means, for example, that the child can imitate a face washing only if his image for that activity is well developed. Whatever the explanation for the reintegration process, it is most certainly a complex matter, as we shall see when we discuss current arguments over the origins of another kind of representation—speech.

REPRESENTATION BY METAPHOR. In their work, Werner and Kaplan emphasized that the child is much more enthralled by physical events than adults are. Because of his vivid engagement with action and movement patterns, his representation is, for him, imbued with the flavor and sensory quality of his original experience. Even after the child has verbalized a particular experience—"I fell down"—the event retains for the child an almost tangible aura, a "fallingness" which language cannot hope to reproduce. In what may be attempts to express this profoundly sensory apprehension, the growing child, and even the adult, often uses the more elementary system of representation by metaphor. The child looks at a burgeoning bee-sting and says, "See flower." The adult says, "I'm a bear when I get up in the morning"—a metaphor which probably would make a 3- or 4-year-old laugh or scowl in puzzlement because he does not understand the allusion to the bear's proverbial short temper.

Metaphor is the primary process of representation, preceding representation through the spoken word. Thus, when we express perceptions in poetry, motion, or other arts—all of which are basically metaphoric—we are about as close as the adult can come to the nature of the cross-modal representations that exist at the beginning of life.

Metaphoric thinking stands before logical thinking in its proximity to basic life experiences, because metaphoric thinking conveys feelings more fully by allowing one domain of experience to represent another domain. The child's bee-sting is, logically, not a flower. However, by using the flower image, which has many traits similar to the bee-sting (roundness, redness, outdoor association), the child produces an immediate transference of meaning, reflecting the visual similarity he detects between his sting and his flower image. His second domain of experience—the bee-sting—is expressed in terms of his first domain of experience, the sensory perception of the flower. To understand this synesthetic way of responding to an object or event—that is, responding to a single stimulus with more than one of the senses—we would have to examine the creative process of the artist. The art he produces is man's most sophisticated metaphoric thought, just as logic is the most sophisticated statement of verbal thought.

Piaget's Preconceptual Phase

In Piaget's view, the emergence of the symbolic function in the child at about 18 months marks the transition from sensorimotor intelligence to the beginnings of conceptual intelligence, which eventually will take precedence over the earlier form of intelligence. The major period of conceptual intelligence begins with the preoperational stage, which takes its name from the fact that during the time from about 18 months to 6 or 7 years the child is not yet capable of using logical "operations" in his thinking. In the development of this capacity, Piaget believes the child progresses through the preoperational stage in two phases, during which time his language develops and becomes quite complex and articulate. He also becomes adept in using his words and other symbols to direct his actions. The first phase of the preoperational stage is called the *preconceptual phase;* this gives way to the phase of *intuitive thought* at about age 4. We shall examine the preconceptual phase in this chapter, and intuitive thought in Chapter 10. The preconceptual phase, then, is the time when the child first begins to use representational thought and symbols, which, as Werner and Kaplan have also contended, is the first step in the development of mature thought.

New levels of reality become available to the child once he is able to substitute a mental symbol, a word, or an object for an object, person, or event that is not physically present. The child may develop a mental symbol to stand for his drum, or he may use the word *drum*, or symbolize a drum by demonstrating with a drum-beating flurry of his hands. Because he can symbolize the absent concrete object, he is less tied to the physical world—he now can pretend, imagine, and create fantasies.

One example of the way a toddler uses mental symbols is through deferred imitation. The child watches his father light his pipe. Several days later, the boy's mother may find him "puffing" on a stick and mimicking the motion of lighting a pipe. The aspect of this action which indicates progress in the child's cognitive development is the time lapse between his observation and his imitation of pipe-lighting. In an earlier stage the infant could imitate immediately some simple motions, but the imitation in this case was delayed—the father-model was not present—so the child must have formed a mental symbol or image of the pipe-lighting and based his imitation on the image. Thus, the ability to form an image permits the boy to store a "picture" of the pipe-lighting act and use it later. The mental "picture" is not necessarily a visual image. A child may represent objects or animals to himself by the sounds they make or by their movements.

The toddler's use of mental symbols also becomes apparent in his search for an object. In our discussion of Stage 6 sensorimotor development in Chapter 6, we briefly cited how Piaget's daughter sought out a watch chain in a matchbox. In a more complex example of a search for an object, Piaget hid a small pencil in his hand. He then put his hand under his beret, his handkerchief, and his jacket, where he left the pencil. Unlike the younger child, Piaget's daughter Jacqueline (about 18 months at the time) immediately looked under the jacket and found the pencil. This action demonstrated that the girl knew the pencil continued to exist, even though it was hidden in Piaget's hand and was moved consecutively under the beret, handkerchief, and jacket. Her action also meant that she had formed a mental image of the pencil and could mentally trace the image's path through the complex series of displacements.

DEVELOPMENT OF MENTAL SYMBOLS. How a child develops his mental symbols for real objects is not known. Piaget contends that symbolism is foreshadowed in the sensorimotor period, rather than suddenly appearing full-blown in the 2-year-old. In keeping with his general belief that intelligence has its roots in action, Piaget claims that the child draws his symbols from imitation. He cites this incident:

> . . . At 1;3(8) J. [Jacqueline] was playing with a clown with long feet and happened to catch the feet in the low neck of her dress. She had difficulty in getting them out, but as soon as she had done so, she tried to put them back in the same position. . . . As she did not succeed, she put her hand in front of her, bent her forefinger at a right angle to reproduce the shape of the clown's feet, described exactly the same trajectory as the clown and thus succeeded in putting her finger into the neck of her dress. She looked at the motionless finger for a moment, then pulled at her dress, without of course being able to see what she was doing. Then, satisfied, she removed her finger and went on to something else. (Piaget 1962)

In this observation, Jacqueline used her finger to imitate or symbolize the clown's movements. Such imitated movements are common in children, according to Piaget. For example, he observed that his daughter imitated the back-and-forth sway of her father's bicycle by performing a swaying walk at about the same speed as the bicycle. Such physical imitations, says Piaget, are the sensorimotor forerunners of mental symbols. In the older child, the mental image of a bicycle will serve the purpose the swaying serves in the younger child. As he nears the end of his sensorimotor development at about 18 months, the child's physical imitations become less pronounced. Gradually, the movements become very brief muscular acts, finally becoming almost undetectable as the child internalizes his imitations. At last, rather than mimicking actions in his behavior, the child imitates them "in his head." He now has mental symbols.

As Piaget uses the term *imitation*, it includes the use of *visual imagery* as internal symbols. When a child looks at a car, his eyes accommodate to the car. They follow the contour of the car body, register its color, and focus to fix the car in space. Such visual perception is an activity of the child, similar in purpose to the child's swaying in imitation of the bicycle. When the car is gone, the child may run through the visual acts he first used to perceive the car. This shortened version of the original perception *comprises* the visual imagery of the car in the mind of the child. But since a mental image is usually less vivid than the original object, the visual image of the car is actually more of a symbol of the car than it is a faithful representation.

Symbols are personal representations. Each child forms his own, and each symbol in some way resembles its correlative in the real world. One child, however, might easily fail to understand another child's mental symbol for a car. One may form his symbol in terms of the feel of the car's ride, another in terms of its sound, and a third in terms of the car's visual imagery. Therefore, one child's symbol may convey nothing about the object *car* to the other two children.

The word is a different kind of sign or symbol. Unlike the mental symbol, which resembles the thing it represents and is the personal creation of the child, the word is an arbitrary label for its correlative and a socially agreed-upon sign, not a personal creation. Thus, the word *car* can mean only one thing to all children. However, the sign *house* or *dog* could just as readily be used to signify car—if such a new sign were commonly agreed upon. In short, the word generally has no intrinsic connection with its correlative in reality.

All of the mental symbols the child develops, whether they are visual, auditory, or based on movement, represent or *signify* something about the real world to the individual who possesses them. His use of these symbols in play indicates that he knows the difference between real objects and their symbols.

SYMBOLIC PLAY. In the toddler stage, the use of symbolism in play constitutes a large portion of the child's total activity. Piaget defines symbolic play as the use of a concrete object in the place of another concrete object that the child encounters in his daily life. He offers an example:

At 1;3(12) Jacqueline . . . saw a cloth whose fringed edges vaguely recalled those of her pillow; she seized it, held a fold of it in her right hand, sucked the thumb of the same hand and lay down on her side, laughing hard. She kept her eyes open, but blinked from time to time as if she were alluding to closed eyes. (Piaget 1962)

It seems clear that Jacqueline was playing. The fringed cloth was the concrete object she had selected to stand in place of her everyday pillow. Knowing the two objects were not the same, she nonetheless applied her pillow behavior to the cloth. This constituted symbolic play. Piaget explains in terms of assimilation how this act came to have a meaning for Jacqueline and hence to be symbolic. In the past, the girl had lain down, kept still, sucked her thumb, and closed her eyes only when she had her pillow. In her play, she extended these schemata to the substitute object. Thus, she assimilated the cloth into schemata which she had used earlier exclusively with the pillow. This assimilation of the substitute object into the established schemata gives the symbol its meaning. Jacqueline was fully aware that she was performing a symbolic act; her laughter tells us this. Therefore, playful as it is, symbolic activity such as Jacqueline's indicates a growing understanding of the nature of symbols—a substantial intellectual achievement.

Although internal symbolization, as seen in the toddler's language and play, is a major step in his cognitive development, the resultant preconceptual thought is not sophisticated. In contrast with adult thought, it is rather primitive and action-oriented. The action, however, takes place in the child's mind rather than solely in his behavior as it did before.

SIX TRAITS OF TODDLER THOUGHT. As the toddler is strengthening his grasp of the symbolic function and working toward the ability to form concepts during this preconceptual stage, his mental processes are characterized by six general traits, according to Piaget's view. First, *children between the ages of 2 and 4 "think" about new situations in relation to their experiences in similar past situations.* For example, at about 29 months of age, Piaget's daughter Jacqueline saw her father drawing hot water. She concluded that he was going to shave because in the past she had watched him shave after he drew hot water. Her "thinking" about her observation was actually only a recollection of what had happened in similar past situations, not the deductive reasoning of the adult.

The second characteristic of preconceptual thought is its *lack of generality*. The toddler thinks in terms of particulars, not in terms of classes or categories. As Piaget noted, the preconceptual child views every snail as a separate class in itself, not as one of many individuals making up a common class. Since he cannot yet form concepts, the young child cannot organize his world on the basis of similarities among objects. He lacks the ability to generalize and thereby unite similar objects into classes and concepts. It is this inability of the child to form concepts that gives the preconceptual phase its name.

Egocentricity is the third characteristic of preconceptual thought. The child at this stage of cognitive development is not capable of seeing any point of view but his own. Parental appeals to "think how Jonathan feels when you knock down his tower" fall on deaf ears, for the child cannot extend himself in this way. His egocentricity also leads him to believe that cosmic events occur because of him. The sun shines because he is going on a picnic, the afternoon occurs because he is taking his nap, and the sun sets because he is going to bed. Because he has great difficulty seeing the needs of others, the child often fails to make himself clear; he does not supply vital information because he is not sufficiently aware of others to know that they need it. Finally, because he does not reflect on his own thoughts, or objectify them, he cannot examine his thinking for errors.

The fourth characteristic of preconceptual thought is the child's tendency to "center" on one aspect of an event to the exclusion of others. Piaget's famous example of the water jars remains the best illustration of this tendency to concentrate on a single, obvious aspect of a phenomenon. Piaget

TODDLERHOOD AGES 2 AND 3

presented a child with tall twin vases, both full of the same amount of water. When he poured the water from one of the tall vases into a squat, wide jar, the child refused to believe that the amount of water was equal in both containers. Instead, he said that the tall vase contained more water than the short jar. In this example, the child's attention had focused solely on the height of the tall containers, assuming that such vessels must always contain more water. When he grows out of the preconceptual phase—beyond 4 years of age—he will begin to decenter his attention and consider other aspects of the phenomenon—in this instance, the width of the vessels as well.

The distortion of reality by the child's desires is the fifth mark of the preconceptual phase. Again, Piaget has provided an apt example. At 34 months, his daughter Jacqueline wanted an orange. Her parents explained they were not ready to be eaten because they were still green. Jacqueline, accepting this, turned to her camomile tea and then suddenly burst out: "Camomile isn't green, it's yellow already. . . . Give me some oranges!" In her passion for oranges, the girl concluded that if the tea were yellow, then the oranges also must be yellow and thus edible. Her conclusion about the apparent parallel between yellow tea and yellow oranges was determined by her desire for the fruit.

Transductive reasoning is the sixth and final characteristic of preconceptual thought. Transductive reasoning is unlike either inductive or deductive reasoning, the two forms of reasoning commonly used by adults. Inductive reasoning moves from the specific to the general. An individual in a strange land encountering 100 men, all of whom wear gold earrings in their left lobes, might conclude that all men in that land practice that custom. Deductive reasoning works in the opposite way, from general to specific. For example, given the assumption that all men wear a gold earring in their left lobes, we would expect every individual to live up to the custom. Transductive reasoning is different from both of these forms of logical thought. According to Piaget, it falls between induction and deduction since it sets up a relationship between one particular and another where there is no connection. Lucienne, another of Piaget's daughters, provided an excellent example of transductive thought when she observed, "I haven't had my nap so it isn't afternoon." She jumped from one particular (nap) to a second particular (the afternoon), assuming that the afternoon occurred because she napped, whereas the actual relationship between them was coincidental.

CLASSIFICATION CONCEPT. Between the ages of 2 and 4 years, the child begins to develop his power to classify objects into logical collections. At this stage, his ability to sort is primitive. Rather than distinguishing on the basis of concepts—which he does not yet possess—he uses what Piaget has called the *preconcept.* Using this intermediate mental tool, the child often perceives two separate objects from the same class as being the same object. Similarly, he may exclude an object from a class for a superficial reason. In other words, the toddler does not understand how to form classes.

According to Piaget, classes have several basic qualities. Among them, these four are the most important:

First, *no object can belong to two classes at once.* A large blue square falls in the class of squares and not in the class of circles. Each class, no matter how many there may be, excludes dissimilar forms in this same way. Motor vehicles, for example, may be divided into several mutually exclusive classes: tow trucks, trailer trucks, buses, passenger cars, one-man racing cars, and motorcycles. Buses and motorcycles obviously belong in two separate classes, although both are motor vehicles.

Second, *all objects in a class have some common trait.* The large blue square and a small red square share "squareness." This property, then, is the definition of the class. Any square object meets that definition and therefore belongs in this class of squares. Piaget would call squareness the *intension* of that class. Circularity would be the intension of a class of circles.

Third, *a class also can be described by naming its members,* as opposed to its defining property. Thus, we can give the *extension* of the class *dog* by naming dachshund, Pekinese, poodle, Yorkshire terrier, Saint Bernard, and Samoyed.

MOTOR, COGNITIVE, AND LANGUAGE DEVELOPMENT 233

Fourth, *a class's defining property determines what objects can be placed in that class.* Intension (the definition) determines extension (the class contents). If we know that the intension of a class is "four-legged, hairy mammals that bark," we can assume the class will contain dogs. The intension "two-wheeled motor vehicles" would lead us to expect a class of motorcycles and motor scooters.

To determine if toddlers would form a class from many disparate objects, Piaget gave a group an assortment of flat squares, triangles, rings, and half-rings. The shapes, made of plastic or wood and in several colors, were mixed in a pile and Piaget instructed his experimental subjects to "put together things that are alike." The children grouped the objects in several ways. Some used *small partial alignment,* a selection method in which the child selected a number of the objects and assembled them with no particular attention to common characteristics of either shape or color. *Small partial alignment* satisfies none of the four basic qualities Piaget attributes to a class. It is clear that the child was not employing a consistent system of rules to guide the arrangements he selected for the geometric shapes.

Other children Piaget tested used the geometric shapes to create pictures. One depicted a tower and another a bridge, both *complex objects* in Piaget's lexicon. Like small partial alignments, complex objects are not classes. The elements of the complex object are selected not because they share common traits, but because they help fill out the picture the child envisions.

In a similar experiment, Piaget gave another group of toddlers model people, houses, and animals. As in the above experiment, the children again failed to form classes. Instead of sorting out people, animals, and houses, they mixed them together when asked to group them by likeness. In Piaget's terms, the children's intensions did not hold stable throughout the experiment. Instead, the children selected the models on the basis of one defining property, then another, and another. As a result, no class had a predictable extension. Piaget has suggested a simple reason for the toddler's inability to form a class of objects. He says that the child 2 to 4 years old often forgets quickly the defining property he was using to build a class of objects. This weakness of the memory, which may last through age 5, illustrates another of Piaget's persistent points—that age norms for classifying, as for every other act in the developing child, are only approximations. One child may form classes at age 4, another not until age 6. However, the order in which the stages of development occur does not vary. For example, before he can enter the preconceptual phase, a child must have passed through the six sensorimotor stages. Piaget also notes that a child may possess two different cognitive powers in two distinct stages of development. Accordingly, a child's ability to speak may be in a more advanced stage than his ability to classify objects.

Language Development

Toddler's Progress

Some of the most compelling evidence of the child's fast-developing cognitive abilities—specifically his capacity to form and use mental symbols—is the explosion of speech that occurs in the third and fourth years. As we saw in Chapter 6, the average baby begins speaking one- and two-word sentences at about 18 months ("Eat" or "Baby go," for example), and has begun to use pronouns and to name pictures of objects by about 23 months; by the time he is 2 years old he has acquired a fairly extensive vocabulary of about 270 words. But this progress, impressive as it may be, pales in comparison with the toddler's verbal achievements in the next two years. Each month he adds 40 to 50 new words, except for the six months before his third birthday, when his vocabulary jumps from about 450 words to almost 950. By his fourth birthday he will be using over 1,500 words.

After the toddler's vocabulary has expanded and he has successfully formed two-word sentences, his facility at combining words increases, but slowly at first. Then it surges ahead, in step with his accelerating vocabulary. Sentences become longer—up to five words or more at 4 years (McCarthy 1959). By the age of 4½, some children already are using all of the basic syntax of adults (Menyuk 1969). Certain nonessential words such as *the, and,* or *his* may be omitted, although more elaborate sentences ("Cat in house," "Doggy on bed") are now made possible by the ability

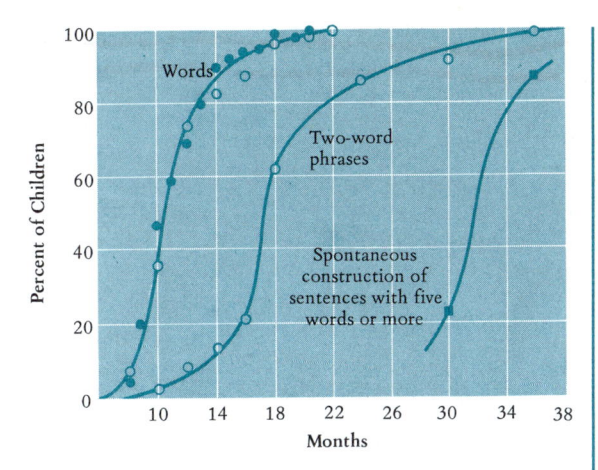

- 49 Austrian children (Bühler, 1931)
- 114 British children (Morley, 1957)
- 500 American children (Boston, Lenneberg's observation—no date)

Figure 8.3 Illustration of the regularity in attainment of the various developmental milestones in the acquisition of language. (From E. Lenneberg. *Biological foundations of language.* New York: John Wiley & Sons, Inc., 1967.)

of the average child over 28 months to understand and use a few prepositions. Vocabulary and sentence structure continue to develop as he matures.

Psycholinguistics

While we seem to know what the child does in assembling his vocabulary and making sentences, we do not as yet understand how he does it. Some of the possible answers to this ancient mystery of language development have been put forward by the proponents of a new field of study called psycholinguistics. Although psycholinguistics—the study of the acquisition and use of structured language—has been an area of concerted study for barely a decade, it has greatly illuminated the development of language in the young child. Research in psycholinguistics has been concentrated on the child's acquisition of grammar or syntax, the rules that control the building of sentences.

Traditionally, psycholinguists have viewed the grammar of a language as different from its meaning. They have considered language to be comprised of two major facets, structure and meaning. Grammar or syntax is an element of a language's structure—it is the set of rules for assembling words into sentences. Other structural elements are the language's system of sounds (its phonology) and its rules about the production of words from these sounds (morphology). Language meaning, on the other hand, resides in the definitions or associations of the arbitrary signs (words) attached to objects, people, or events. It is the structure of language, not the meaning, that the psycholinguist studies. More recently, psycholinguists have recognized that syntax and meaning are inseparable, and have shifted to the study of the grammatical meaning of the relationship between words in addition to the lexical meaning of individual words.

SOUNDS, WORDS, AND SENTENCES. A brief review of the primary structural elements of words that we discussed in Chapter 6 may be useful to a fuller understanding of psycholinguistics. The most fundamental sound in any language is the phoneme, a class that includes vowels and consonants, such as *o* and *t*. Phonemes are combined to form larger units called morphemes, which are the shortest units of a language that carry meaning. They may be words, such as *ma, pa, go,* or they may be used to form words. The grouping of words into sentences is governed by syntactic rules, or grammar.

Although, as noted above, the syntax of language is separate from its semantic meanings, one element of syntax—the *deep structure* of a sentence—is related to meaning. Even the simplest sentence has two types of structure—a *deep structure* and a *surface structure*. The surface structure is the order and relations among the words of a sentence; it operates at the phonetic level. The deep structure plunges below the literal level and indicates the sentence's underlying semantic meaning. The deep structure is much like a diagram of the semantic content of the sentence.

Acquiring Grammar

IMITATION THEORY. No one knows just how a child acquires the grammar of his language, but four major theories suggest a rich variety of possibilities. The first is the *imitation theory.* In essence, this theory proposes that the children build their vocabularies by imitating parents and others.

The imitation theory is correct to a point. Children do learn by copying adults, and they do hear adults speaking constantly. However, the theory fails to answer many other questions about grammar formation. For example, how can children speak and understand sentences—such as "All gone baby"—that they have never heard an adult say? What pattern of word arrangement are they following? They seem to be following some guide, innate or otherwise, but it does not seem to be imitation, since they do not always use adult word order. For example, children would not say "All gone baby" if they were patterning their speech on adult speech. In addition, if children learn syntax by imitation, they could be expected to refine their sentence structures by imitating appropriate elements of grammatical expressions. The child hearing "The baby is gone" could be expected to revise the order of his "All gone baby." Yet, it has been found that although children often attempt to mimic an adult sentence they have just heard, their imitations do not reveal any grammatical superiority over the children's natural, unprompted sentences (Ervin 1964). Moreover, there are simply too many possible word sequences for imitation to be the main principle involved. The child could not feasibly learn his grammar by memorizing the fact that "big" can precede "dog," that "good" can precede "boy," or that "here" can follow "come" in every case. The number of such possible sequences is infinite.

It is possible, however, that children learn grammar by imitating some element of language more abstract than the word arrangement. This seems to be the case in such sentences as, "All gone food," in which there clearly is a grammar functioning, although it is not the adult grammar. The concept of a more abstract or hidden grammar gains some support from the observation that children learn language elements not present in spoken sentences. For example, they learn to discover the unexpressed but logical bases of sentences. In "All gone food," the child is expressing a relationship of object and action which is intelligible despite the irregular order of the words, or the surface structure.

Another point argues for the abstractness of the language elements a child learns. The syntax that different children use is highly similar even though they often use quite different vocabularies. Thus, the common similarities of language, aside from vocabulary and sound, would seem to be abstract and not learned by the child through imitations of his parents' surface speech habits. There is also the possibility that the child's speech is not an imitation of the surface structure, but, instead, an inference of the deep structure of the speech he hears.

REINFORCEMENT THEORY. The second major theory—the reinforcement theory—holds that a child acquires correct speech patterns through a process of reinforcement or being rewarded for speaking as his parents do. This view has some of the same weaknesses as the imitation theory. As we noted above, children often say sentences they have never heard anyone say before, and these baby sentences usually are rewarded as much as standard sentences are. In fact, mothers frequently will correct a child's untrue, but grammatical, statements and disregard his ungrammatical ones if they are true (Slobin 1968). If, for instance, a 3-year-old were to say, "I drinked all my milk," his mother would probably reply, "Good." But if he said, "I'm asleep," she most likely would point out that this was incorrect.

Equally untenable is the notion that reinforcement of certain word sequences (red car, big dog, hot pan) results in the child's learning how words go together. As we observed in our critique of the imitation theory, the number of possible word sequences overwhelms the imagination. Learning

Table 8.1 Grammatical Novelty of Imitations*

	Percentage Imitated	Percentage Grammatically Consistent	
		Freely Generated	Imitated
Susan (1.10)	7	88	79
Christy (2.0)	5	91	92
Donnie (2.2)	6	93	100
Lisa (2.3)	15	83	65
Holly (2.4)	20	88	68
Donnie (2.5)	8	91	94
Donnie (2.10)	7	92	91

*Table shows little difference in grammatical consistency between freely generated and imitated sentences in 2-year-olds. Source: S. Ervin. Imitation in children's language. In E. Lenneberg (Ed.), New directions in the study of language. Cambridge, Mass.: M.I.T. Press, 1964. P. 170.

each sequence individually would be a superhuman feat. It becomes clear that an examination of the reinforcement theory brings us to the same conclusion as our probe of the imitation theory—that whatever language elements the child may learn through reinforcement, they are not spoken phrases or sentences but, rather, something quite abstract.

While the reinforcement theory, like the imitation theory, may be correct in some deeper way, current evidence suggests that it probably is not. For example, a congenitally mute child—who could not, therefore, have been rewarded for speaking—appears to have learned to understand English (Lenneberg 1964). Another phenomenon indicates that reinforcement alone is not enough to enable a child to acquire language. Congenitally deaf children babble during infancy just as normal children do. Even though they presumably are rewarded by being hugged, smiled at, or patted for their babbling and later vocalizations, they stop babbling prematurely and are slow to acquire all the elements of language (Lenneberg 1967).

Proponents of the reinforcement theory sometimes claim that a child learns his language by generalizing a linguistic response he has learned through reinforcement. Thus, the child might be rewarded for saying, "Baby go." In other brief sentences, he then would generalize the initial position of a noun when used with an active verb. Therefore he would say, "Daddy go," "Horsie run," "Baby see." This may actually be what the child does. Nonetheless, the generalization theory does not reveal the principles behind the generalizing act. This is a difficult problem for any theory of language acquisition—showing how the child learns an abstraction which he cannot experience directly.

Although the reinforcement and imitation theories clearly play a role in the child's vocabulary-building (later, for example, children pick up clichés and idiomatic expressions from their parents and peers), neither theory asks the basic questions about language acquisition. Therefore, neither can be construed as a complete account of how the child learns language structure.

INNATE THEORY. There are some psycholinguists, such as Chomsky and his associates, who have put forth the theory that *the human nervous system contains a mental structure that has an "innate" concept of human language* (Chomsky 1967). The theory has not been fully elaborated. For example, how this "mental structure" finds a common syntactic ground among the scores of human languages is not explained. Nonetheless, its espousal of an abstract method of learning—rather than one based on sensory perception—indicates that the theory may be the right kind of theory to answer the question of the origin of language structure.

Evidence for the existence of some kind of mental structure that is responsible for the acquisition of language comes from three generally acknowledged facts about language. First, considering the enormous number of errors it is possible to make in learning a language, the errors that children do make are relatively limited. Second, all children proceed through the same stages of language acquisition, despite great differences in their vocabularies or native language. And third, it is known that there are specific areas of the brain that control the ability to speak and understand language.

COGNITIVE THEORY. This fourth theory, based on cognitive principles, seems to come closest to fully accounting for the complexities of language acquisition. It is a continuation of the ideas of Piaget, and Werner and Kaplan, discussed above in the section on cognitive development, that the child first develops certain concepts, such as object permanence, through his sensorimotor experience. These concepts lead to the ability to form symbols. Once he can use symbols, the child is then able to attach words to the relations structured in his experience, first to name objects and later to express action or desires.

Bloom has applied these principles to the acquisition of language and has proposed that the child uses his existing and developing cognitive structures as a map for constructing his speech. The deep structure of a child's sentence then would be a reflection of his concepts of object permanence or person permanence, among others (Bloom 1970). Since, as we have seen, the cognitive structures develop in a precise sequence in all children, regardless of individual differences in nationality or culture, and this sequence is a fixed one, the theory of Bloom, and Werner and Kaplan, would account for the regularity and similarities in the acquisition of language by children from widely divergent backgrounds, and for the novel combinations of words that appear only in children's speech.

The Early Speech

Although at this point there may be no single theory of language acquisition which answers all questions and satisfies all investigators, there nevertheless is considerable information documenting the observable features of this process. From the theories that attempt to explain how language is acquired, we now turn to the language itself as it is spoken by the child.

TWO TYPES OF WORDS. As soon as the young toddler begins speaking two-word sentences, it is evident that he has a basic grammar guiding his verbal compositions. A number of experimenters have examined the structure of the toddler's early sentences. After recording many sentences spoken by a few children, Bellugi and Brown (1964) wrote a grammar for each of the children's recorded speech. Like any grammar, these contained the rules the children followed in constructing their sentences. The experiment is illuminating because the grammars revealed a distinct similarity in the kinds of sentence structures the various children used. Certain general principles seemed to be at work in the linguistic responses of all the children.

The grammars composed from the children's speech were quite simple. They contained two kinds of words: *pivot words* and *X-words*. Pivot words usually occupy a particular place—either first or second—in the toddler sentence and are used with many different words. In the sentences "Papa go," "Daddy go," and "Baby go," the pivot word is "go." Pivot words also can be adjectives, yielding expressions such as, "Pretty doggy," "Pretty car," "Pretty baby." Pronouns, too, may occur as pivot words—"Hit it," "See it," "Throw it." Most of a toddler's two-word sentences contain a pivot word that may be used similarly in scores of combinations. The X-words, or other words, which are numerically the bulk of the toddler vocabulary, are not all-purpose words

Table 8.2 A Grammar Derived from the 89 Utterances of One Child*

Initial Word	Second Word
A	+ C₁
Daddy	+ C₂
Mummy	+ C₃
's	+ C₄
Utterance → *See*	+ C₅
That	+ C₆
The	+ C₇
There	+ C₈
Two	+ C₉

C₁ → block, book, candle, cricket, dog, fall, kitty, meatball, nurse, pillow, reel
C₂ → bear, book, honey
C₃ → bear, dimple, do, go, puff
C₄ → bird, Daddy, picture
C₅ → boy, eye, Mummy, radio, rocker, that
C₆ → bird, boat, book, bowl, boy, broken, car, cookie, cow, Daddy, dirty, doggie, fuzzy, going, horsie, kitty, Mummy, Peter, pretty, puff, Rayma, rocker, sun, wire
C₇ → bird, book, girl, horsie, kitty, mike, peas, puppy, reel, rug, whistle
C₈ → bird, boat, book, boy, carriage, chair, Daddy, doll, dollie, Dru, go, goes, is, kitty, man, Mummy, pea, potty, radio, reel, 'tis
C₉ → Bobby, chair, Gale, men, reel

*A 2-year-old female.
Source: R. Brown and C. Fraser. The acquisition of syntax. In U. Bellugi and R. Brown (Eds.), *Monogr. Soc. Res. Child Develpm.*, 1964, 29(1), 43–79.

like the pivot words, nor are they fixed in a particular position in the toddler sentence as the pivot words are. The number of X-words is almost unlimited—*horse, bike, turtle, car, balloon,* and so on. Using his pivot words as a base, the toddler can readily add X-words to his vocabulary and form such sentences as, "See horse!" "See turtle!" or "See balloon!"

TELEGRAPHIC CONSTRUCTION. One obvious characteristic of these early two-word sentences is the omission of nonessential articles and conjunctives. The toddler never says, "The doggy gone"—simply, "Doggy gone." This telegraphic speech does not mean that the child is editing his thoughts, as a capable writer does, into the tightest possible communication. Instead, it probably reflects the developmental state of his grammar as an early toddler. As the child begins using prepositions, the telegraphic sentences expand, giving more information on relationships within sentences.

WORD POSITIONS. Another trait discovered in the toddler grammars is that most of the children constructed sentences in which the pivot word preceded the X-word (PW + XW). It seems that a child somehow learns the positions that particular words can take in a sentence. Thus, he might learn that a PW easily takes the first position. By putting the PW into the first position and then following it with a word he knows but does not know a position for, the child forms the PW + XW sentence structure (Braine 1963). Braine illustrated his theory by making up a simple language and then teaching the language to experimental toddlers. His results showed that children can learn the positions that words assume in sentences.

While children can learn word positions, it is not likely that this is how they learn to speak their language. The basis for such a criticism is that few languages have many consistent positions for words. English certainly does not. Any word can occur in almost any position in an English sentence. By listening to English sentences, a child would not learn that certain words always occur in certain positions. On the contrary, he would soon learn that a word can occur in any position in a sentence.

THEORY OF INNATE SYNTAX. Another theory has been advanced to show how the child selects his pivot and X-words. McNeill (1966a) contended that the child ready to learn language already knows innately the chief grammatical relations in a sentence. That is, he knows the three syntactic classes of subject, predicate, and modifier, which are universal in language. This view is an application of the theory of language acquisition discussed above which posits an inborn mental structure that is responsible for the learning of all language.

The theory of innate syntax, like the more comprehensive theory of an innate language-learning mental structure, has some definite strengths. In the first place, it is compatible with the information about language that is now available. In addition, it explains how children who speak seemingly different languages, notably Russian and Japanese, apparently begin their grammar formation with the same PW + XW arrangements that American children use. Yet, this theory fails, as do the others, in that it does not give basic answers. For example, to recognize the syntactic classes, as the theory maintains he does, the child would have to be able to make basic distinctions between words that represent actions and others that represent objects or people. Yet, this theory does not reveal how a child can distinguish a noun from a verb. Furthermore, the theory is based on the assumption that the child somehow acquires a substantial amount of information about his language, but it does not explain the path of experience which brings him to this information. Nevertheless, despite its shortcomings, the theory of innate syntactical classes is valuable because it envisions an abstract method of learning language structures.

ACTION-ORIENTED. Before discussing the toddler's longer sentences, it is worthwhile to note that early utterances reflect the child's awareness of actions taking place around him. The most common actions noted by the child involve acts of existence, disappearance, and recurrence (Bloom 1970).

In depicting existence, the child merely names objects or calls attention to them. He says, for example, "See doggy," or "See bottle." The "see" asserts the object's physical existence—an awareness that grows out of the child's developed sense of object permanence and his capacity to point to things or to refer to them. Often, a child will not have any other motive in naming an object. Since the objects are familiar to him and he knows their names, he spontaneously identifies them.

Besides naming objects that are present, the child's sense of object permanence, coupled with his vocabulary, enables him to name objects that have disappeared from view. The child expresses his perception that an object has disappeared, but still exists, by saying, "No bottle," or "No Daddy." Recurrence, of course, hinges on disappearance for the child. A bottle may have been placed

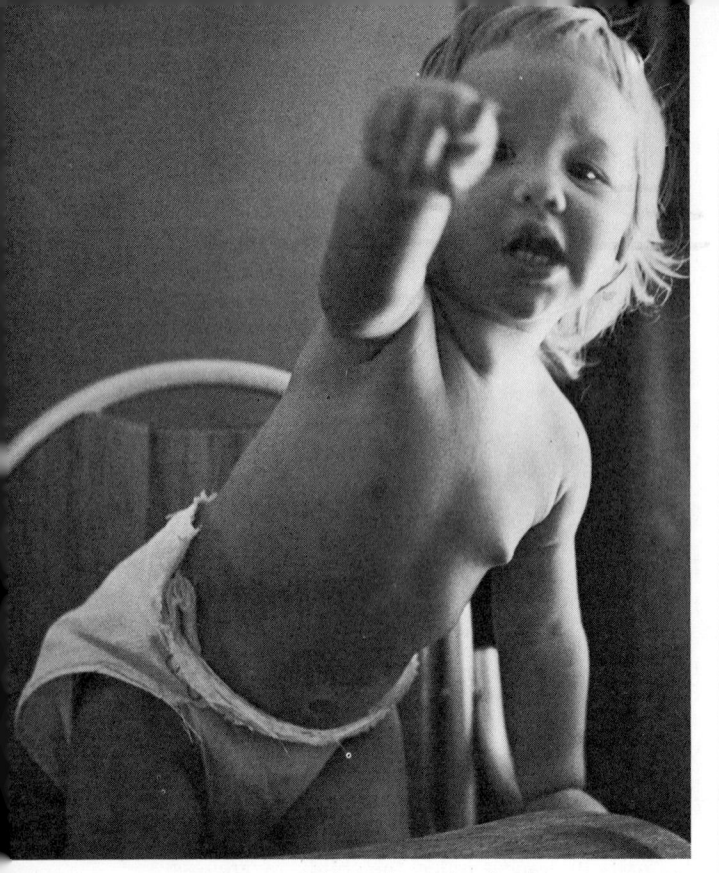

Figure 8.4 A child's early words reflect his awareness of the existence of objects. Earlier, his pointing served to identify objects, but now he names the objects as he points them out. (John Rees—Black Star)

in the refrigerator when the child stopped drinking. When the child, again hungry, says, "More bottle," he reflects his knowledge that the bottle can readily be brought back to him, that it can recur even though it has disappeared.

LONGER SENTENCES. With increasing maturity, the toddler expands his two-word sentences into longer utterances exhibiting more complex grammar. He assembles three-word sentences and begins to form negative sentences and to develop patterns of speech inflection. In developing his grammar, the toddler first divides his pivot and X-words into subclasses. For example, the child may form a subclass of pivot words including the articles *a* and *the*, the modifier *six*, and the possessive pronoun *my*. They are considered subclasses of pivot words because they are drawn from his group of pivot words, and the three are used in the same position in his utterances. In perhaps a month, the toddler has divided this subclass into three smaller classes—one for articles, another for demonstrative pronouns, and a third for miscellaneous words. The child no longer uses these three classes of words in the same way; his usage is becoming more specialized (Brown and Fraser 1964). Some investigators have hypothesized that the toddler continues subdividing his syntactical classes into more and more finely defined subclasses until his grammar reaches the sophistication of the adult grammar. However, the present data suggest that such progressive subdividing is probably an oversimplified explanation of the child's acquisition of grammar.

In the course of his early linguistic development, the toddler's sentences also begin to show a hierarchical structure. The simplicity of the first sentences begins to give way to sentences that can be divided into major elements, which are composed of smaller elements, and ultimately the single word (Brown and Fraser 1964); the words of the sentence are structured in a hierarchic fashion rather than forming simply a sequential string. In such speech, we find a sentence like, "That a brown horse, " "A doggy running," or "Where the cat go?" The first sentence contains the major elements "that" and "a brown horse." "A brown horse" is composed of two smaller elements, "a" and "brown horse." "A doggy running" is constructed from "a doggy" and "running," and the former element from "a" and "doggy." The child has developed the ability to build words into meaningful elements which, in turn, are used to construct major elements, and ultimately a rather complex sentence.

Other linguistic developments can be seen at this same stage. Sometimes a major element will be used as a sentence. "That horse" may be substituted for "That a brown horse." Pronouns may replace nouns or a complete noun phrase. "Throw ball" may become "Throw it," and "Catch the ball" may become "Catch it." Sometimes the child puts a pronoun in a sentence while retaining the noun to which the pronoun refers. The child says, "Daddy fix it truck," or "Mommy buy it soda." If there were any doubt of it, these permutations and refinements make it very clear that the toddler in his third year speaks sentences whose structure is fairly complex. They manifestly are not, as they are sometimes portrayed, simply daisy chains of words casually strung together.

NEGATIVE SENTENCES. It is not long after the use of pronouns that the child begins to form negative sentences. Unlike the adult, the toddler does not place his negatives deep within the sentence. Instead he begins with the negative "no" or "not" and adds the otherwise positive sentence: "No eat spinach," "No the car go," and "Not pretty doggy." The child does not say these sentences as an adult would say a sentence like, "No, we can't go now"—that is, the child does not drop his voice on the initial "no" as the adult does (Klima and Bellugi 1966). However, when children begin to use negative sentences, they are among the least complex sentences that they use. Most often, the first negative sentences consist of a noun or a verb preceded by a negative marker such as, "no," "no more," or "not." At the same time, affirmative sentences are more complex, with sentence subjects and predicate phrases. When a sentence subject first occurs in what appears to be a negative sentence (for example, "no doll sleep"), the "no" refers back to something else said or implied in the situation, and the rest of the sentence ("doll sleep") is actually an affirmative assertion. Subsequently, when the syntax of negation increases in complexity, sentence subjects are added, and they occur before the verb (for example, "Mommy no do it"). There is a developmental progression in the sequence in which different semantic categories are expressed in children's sentences. The first negative sentences usually express *nonexistence*, then *rejection denial* (Bloom, in press).

Although the child at first does not use, nor evidently understand, the negative that is seated within the sentence, he soon becomes more sophisticated. In a few months, he will have expanded his store of negative words—formerly confined to "no" and "not"—to include such negatives as "didn't," "don't," and "isn't." A word like "can't" now is used as a contraction of "can" and "not," rather than as a simple negative comparable to "no" or "not." The child uses these new negatives with abandon: "I can't find my shoe," "I don't want fish," and "Sissy isn't nice, she bad."

While the toddler is now beginning to add adult intonation, to introduce indeterminate nouns ("I ate something"), and to add passive verbs such as "do" and "have," he still has several steps to go before he is speaking truly adult English. Among the toddler's redundancies and verbal oddities are negative usages such as, "I can't eat something." In a matter of months, however, the average child increasingly acquires the adult use of negatives. Double, even triple, negatives are one exception. They tend to become widespread, producing statements like, "I can't share no toys with nobody." Earlier, double negatives appeared primarily in questions, such as, "Why not doggy not run?"

Gradually, as the toddler grasps the concepts behind adult usages, he brings his speech into line with adult speech (McNeill 1966b). This is not always a smooth and clearly progressive development. Sometimes the child's effort to use adult grammatical principles leads to sentences that sound more like his early speech than adult expression. In time, however, the child is able to integrate the adult principles into a complex syntactical guide to his entire language.

INFLECTIONS. At about 2½ years of age, the average toddler begins to add inflections, or endings, to his words. As we have noted, children seem to learn language by coding words onto underlying cognitive structures rather than by memorizing how individual words can be used with other individual words. The underlying structure is also behind the child's acquisition of inflections. Adults automatically add an *s* to pluralize many nouns (dogs, girls, cars, houses). Similarly, we add *s*, *ing*, and *ed* to verbs such as *talk*, and *er* and *est* to adjectives such as *fine*. In doing so, we follow specific grammatical rules. Toddlers, too, seem to follow such abstract guides. In a 1958 experiment, Berko tested children, ranging from 4-year-olds to first-graders, for their inflection usage. Using several nonsense words, which would be new to the children, the experimenter showed them several pictures. For example, presenting a birdlike creature, she said, "This is a wug." Showing a pair of wugs, she said, "Now here are two of them. There are two_____." The results showed that even younger children produced the appropriate inflection in a large portion of the test sentences. As might be expected, the first-graders performed more consistently than the preschoolers (Berko 1958).

As this experiment made clear, children know the guidelines for adding English inflections before they reach school age. Actually, the first inflections occur in their speech well before that age. An odd phenomenon in the child's acquisition of the inflectional system has been discovered, however. In examining the use of past-tense inflection, Ervin found that children selected strong verbs—those common in toddler usage—as the first words to receive inflections (in Lenneberg 1964). Thus, the children said, "goed," "sitted," and "comed" first, and only later did they put the same inflections on the correct words—*jumped*, *talked*, and *pulled*. It is possible that the strong verbs appeared to be inflected first because they were used more often and therefore were more likely to be detected by the experimenter. Despite the early and extended use of the incorrect inflections, the children in the experiment replaced them before long with the correct forms—*went*, *sat*, and *came*. Although, as we have noted, the child acquires his grammar by means of an abstract structure, he nonetheless is highly conscious of the individual words and phrases that adults about him use. He seems to assemble such forms as inflections by selecting the invariant forms in his language and applying them to as many words as he can.

How Are Language and Cognition Related?

While it is undeniable that the development of language and cognition in the young child are interrelated, there is considerable argument over which power develops first and which influences the other.

Figure 8.5 Illustration of method used in Berko's (1958) experiment to elicit inflections from nonsense syllables. (From U. Bellugi and R. Brown (Eds.). The acquisition of language. *Monogr. Soc. Res. Child Develpm.*, 1964, 29(1), 43–79.)

This is a wug.

Now there is another one.
There are two of them.
There are two_____.

Language Is Primary

Those who believe that language influences cognition have contended that the merger of speech and thought is crucial to further cognitive development. In their view, progressive improvements in language lead to more complex learning, thinking, concept forming, reasoning, and problem solving. Specifically, they maintain that verbal mediation greatly accelerates and upgrades these sophisticated cognitive processes. As the toddler's verbal facility rapidly improves, they point out, his cognition also improves—the toddler thinks and solves minor problems in much more sophisticated ways than does the 2-year-old.

In an extension of this view, the child's acquisition of basic language is seen as the beginning of the lifelong period of self-control through words. Whereas primitive speech formerly was only a way for the child to communicate with others, more articulate speech becomes a way of talking to himself. Through his words, the verbally competent child imposes order on his experience, instructs himself, regulates his actions, and uses words to mediate his actions (Luria 1957). Experiments with 3-year-olds have shown that, with only a short period of training, these young children can learn to verbally instruct themselves to respond appropriately to light signals and to stop or slow down a lever-pressing response (Bem 1967, Jarvis 1963). Thus, the controlling effect of language already can be seen halfway through the toddler stage.

INTERNALIZED SPEECH. The child seems to internalize speech in much the same way that he internalizes his imitations of actions or events. Just as a child first may sway his whole body as he walks, to imitate the movement of a bicycle, later on move just a few muscles, and eventually make the motions only in his mind, so does speech gradually become internalized. The first change in the internalization of the child's speech is the gradual shift from loud, full speech to a whisper which has a fractured syntactic structure. Soon the toddler whispers only single words to point out to himself particular objects or actions to be performed. After a while, his speech ceases altogether and he works or plays silently. Although the formerly overt speech becomes completely internalized, it still functions as did overt speech — organizing the necessary experience and guiding and controlling the desired actions. Internalized speech thus merges with the toddler's thinking process (Luria 1957).

Piaget: Cognition Comes First

Piaget opposes the view that language precedes cognition. He, and others such as Bloom, Werner, and Kaplan, have maintained that cognition occurs before language emerges. They see language development as dependent on cognitive operations that must precede speech in time. The basic cognitive structure that language depends on is the mental schema.

Schemata begin forming early in infancy as a result of an infant's sensory and motor activities. According to Piaget, such sensorimotor schemata are basic to the codes that we call language; the child applies words to the cognitive structures he is developing. During the second year of life, schemata are well developed, but language is lagging behind. Then, as the child enters the toddler stage, his language use suddenly speeds up dramatically and continues at a rapid pace through the fourth year. The work of Bloom (1970) has shown that sometimes the impetus of verbalization leads a child to produce sentences that he does not understand. Language jumps ahead of cognition, as when a child imitates a parent's words without knowing their meanings. For example, a child 2½ years old may say, "You came here *last* night. We go *next* Monday" — without knowing the meaning of either *last* or *next* in this context.

SUPPORT FOR PIAGETIAN VIEW. Studies of deaf children have lent support to the Piagetian view that language is not necessary to cognition, by offering evidence that such children can think and reason even though they have little language competence. Youniss and Furth (1965) taught both deaf and normal children by nonverbal means that a ball of color "A" would push a ball of color "B" down an incline, and similarly, that ball "B" pushes down a third ball of color "C." The key question was whether the children would learn by the logical principle of transivity (A is greater than B; B is greater than C; therefore, A is greater than C) that ball "A" would also push down ball "C." Deaf children at 8 and 9 years of age predicted that ball "A" would push down ball "C." On the other hand, normal children of 5 and 6 years could not make the logical connection. The experiment was interpreted as an indication of the spontaneous logical order which older, but not younger, children impose on a neutral event, with or without the use of language.

A review of a number of similar studies has pointed to the same conclusion (Furth 1971). These studies compared the performance of deaf — and therefore linguistically deficient — children with that of normal children in a number of tasks involving cognition, memory, and perception. Most of the studies reported that deaf children performed on a par with normal children. The reviewer of the studies concluded that language is not a necessary prerequisite to thought: "Deaf children construct their own symbols as they are needed for the development of thinking."

Furth admitted that deaf people are not entire-

Table 8.3 Comparative Performance of Deaf and Hearing Subjects on Cognitive Tasks

Task and Age	Study: Author and Number*	Topic	Performance of Deaf Versus Hearing Subjects Similar	Inferior/Different
Rule learning				
3–6	1. Blank and Bridger, 1966	Cross-modal transfer	X	
4–6	2. Weigl and Metze, 1968	Rule learning	X	
4–9	3. Pufall and Furth, 1966	Double alternation	X	X (5, 6)**
6–9	4. Youniss and Furth, 1966b	Discontiguity	X	
7–12	5. Andre, 1969	Reversal shift	X	
10–11	6. O'Connor and Hermelin, 1965	Visual rules	X	
9–13	7. Furth, 1964a	Combinatorial sequences	X	
6–10	8. Furth and Pufall, 1966	Combinatorial sequences	X (10)	X (6)
11–19	9. Goetzinger et al., 1967	Raven's matrices	X (18)	X (13)
17	10. Odom and Blanton, 1967	Sequential rules	X	
15–19	11. Michael and Kates, 1965	Social concepts	X	
Logical symbols				
9	12. Furth, 1966a	Logical symbol use	X	
16–20	13. Furth and Youniss, 1965	Symbol (a) use, (b) discovery	X (a)	X (b)
10–14	14. Youniss and Furth, 1967	Symbol use		X
Piaget-type				
5–8	15. Youniss and Furth, 1965	Transitivity	X	
5–8	16. Youniss and Furth, 1966a	Transitivity	X	
4–12	17. Piaget, 1966	Conservation tasks	X	X (2 tasks)
9–12	18. Furth, 1966a	Quantity of liquid		X
6–9	19. Youniss, 1967	Seriation		X
11–15	20. Ross, 1966	Probability	X (15)	X (11, 13)
8–12	21. Robertson and Youniss, 1969	Anticipatory images	X	
9–11	22. Youniss and Robertson, 1970	Anticipatory images	X	X (9)
13–19	23. Furth and Youniss, 1969	Formal operational tasks		X
Memory				
6, adults	24. Lantz and Lenneberg, 1966	Color recognition	X	X (6)
7–10	25. Youniss and Furth, 1966b	Recognition strategies		X
8–12	26. Withrow, 1968	Sequence (a) simultaneous, (b) successive	X (a)	X (b)
9–16	27. Rozanova, 1966	Pictures	X (15, 16)	X (9, 10)
7–15	28. Ross, 1969	Symbol span	X	
14–18	29. Goetzinger and Huber, 1964	Design reproduction	X	
13–20	30. Conrad and Rush, 1965	Type of encoding		X
12–17	31. Conrad, 1970	Type of encoding		X
Perception				
4–6	32. Oléron and Gumusyan, 1964	Embedded figures		X
6–11	33. Yashkova, 1966	Figure reversal	X (9–11)	X (6-8)
11–16	34. Gozova, 1966	(a) recognition, (b) drawings	X (a)	X (b)
7–12	35. Suchman, 1966	Preference (a) color, (b) form	X (a)	X (b)
8–18	36. Carrier, 1961	Color-weight association	X	
5½–10	37. Costa et al., 1964	RT (a) visual, (b) bimodal	X (a)	X (b)
Adult	38. Stoyva, 1965	EMG and REM in sleep	X	
Adult	39. Furth, 1961	Size-weight illusion	X	

*See original source (Furth) for complete references to studies.
**Numbers in parentheses in the last two columns indicate age in years.
Source: H. Furth. Linguistic deficiency and thinking: Research with deaf subjects, 1964–69. *Psychol. Bull.*, 1971, 76(1), 58–72.

ly without knowledge of the English language. However, he pointed out little-known data which show that

> the majority of people born deaf, even though they spend 10 to 15 years in schools concentrating almost exclusively on language learning, do not have competence in the natural language of their society. . . . However, the general conclusion seems abundantly clear that thinking processes of deaf children are similar to those of hearing children and therefore must be explained without recourse to verbal processes. This interesting fact implies that the current emphasis in psychology that attributes the growth of intelligence mainly to verbal factors is unquestionably inadequate and that undue emphasis on linguistic skill, particularly in early education, may not be a sound basis for nourishing intellectual development. Insofar as Piaget stated categorically that language is not a constitutive element of logical thinking, it is intriguing to consider that the evidence collected in this review provides as strong empirical support as can be reasonably expected for this theory. (Furth 1971)

Environmental Influences on Language and Cognition

Although language may be secondary to cognition in the earliest years of life, it seems probable that it greatly facilitates and extends cognition as development proceeds. A substantial body of literature supports the further contention that the development of language and cognitive powers is nurtured by certain environmental conditions and impaired by others.

The matter of environmental influence is of particular prominence in American society today when agencies of the federal government, educators, and many private individuals and organizations are earnestly seeking methods that can be employed to upgrade the standing of the disadvantaged. In our society, such upgrading depends in large part on higher levels of education, which, in turn, depend on sophisticated cognitive skills. According to some, it is precisely the basic cognitive skills that the economically disadvantaged are lacking. Others disagree, arguing that this judgment is a result of the tester's or researcher's middle-class performance standards, rather than any true absence of ability among such persons. Regardless of the judgments involved, however, it is useful to know how an individual's family and surroundings affect his language and cognitive development.

Social-Class Differences

Nearly all studies of language development in home-reared children, from infancy studies of vocalization onward, consistently find that children from lower-class homes score lower on tests of language development than do children from middle-class homes. You will recall that in Chapter 6 we found that infants from lower-class homes tend to vocalize significantly less than those from middle-class homes. This disadvantage continues to plague the lower-class child. Comparative studies covering articulation, sentence structure, vocabulary, and sound discernment have shown that lower-class children from 1 to 5 years of age perform less well in each respect than middle- and upper-class children (Templin 1957).

Deficit Theory

The study of poverty's effects on language and cognition has led to the development of a much debated and challenged *deficit theory*. This theory, in essence, maintains that members of disadvantaged groups display deficiencies in various aspects of language and cognition because their environments are deficient in certain important respects. For example, the father-model may be missing from the home. As applied to language, the deficit theory contends that the linguistic environment of poverty classes is also impoverished—that language is seldom used to discuss abstract social and material events, for example. Instead, language is used mainly in functional exchanges ("Give me the key," "Can you start the car?" "I'm going downtown"). Some studies have concluded that the single most important environmental factor influencing the rate of language development is the quality of the child's early linguistic environment (Carroll 1960). If the child's home environment is verbally stimulating—that is, if his parents speak often, with an interesting variety, and if they reward his speech—the child's language development will be greater than if he lives in a home where speech is monotonous or curt, or where the child's speech is ignored.

LOWER-CLASS SPEECH: TERSE, CLEAR, CAUTIONARY. Evidence of this lack of verbal stimulation was presented in a British class study (Bernstein 1967). The study illuminated a qualitative difference in the language of the two classes. It was found that the lower-class mother usually speaks to her child mainly when she wants to refer to objects and actions—"Don't step in the puddle!" "Don't run." "Be quiet." Characteristically, the sentences are terse, syntactically simple, and clear. Seldom is a lower-class child encouraged to express his feelings or his acute perceptions. Rather than pushing out barriers in life, lower-class speech seems to work at erecting more barriers; much of the speech is cautionary or otherwise more aggressively negative than positive. Some experimenters have concluded that because the concepts are rudimentary, the distinctions are few, and the chief attractions are specific, concrete, and immediate, the speech of the lower classes shows little indication of reasoning. Authority, they say, is substituted for winning arguments or cogent explanations.

Middle-class speech contrasts sharply. It is more elaborate, more shaped by the individual who is speaking it, more closely tailored to specific situations or people, and more precise than lower-class speech. Middle-class language is in itself more complex, and it carries a greater variety of complex communications, as well as emotional and intellectual information that is better articulated, according to this argument.

The study pointed out that the lower-class parent–child conversation often seems to be designed more to "keep the children in their place" than to communicate with them. A 3-year-old boy is crossing a busy street with his father:

Father: Take my hand.
Son: Why?
Father: Just take it or you'll get hit.
Son: By what?
Father: By me if you don't take my hand.

The same scene with a middle-class father and son might go more like this:

Father: Take my hand now, Billy.
Son: Why, Daddy?
Father: So you don't run in front of a car and get hit by it. Take my hand.
Son: I don't want to. I want to cross by myself.
Father: Billy, you're not old enough to cross by yourself. You've got to watch for cars.

The two exchanges are clearly different in tone. But the content, too, is very different. The middle-class father is not trying to force blind obedience as is the lower-class father. Instead of flat insistence, he offers responses and logical reasons for what he is asking, providing a good cognitive model for the son. In addition, the middle-class father encourages the child to ask future questions by answering his immediate ones. In a sense, too, he encourages the boy by speaking to him on what appears to the child to be an adult level; the child appreciates being talked to as a "big boy."

Critique of Deficit Theory: Different, Not Deficient

The portrayal of the speech of lower-class individuals as inferior, and the deficit theory underlying this attitude, have not gone unchallenged. Cole and Bruner (1971), for instance, have disputed the contention that the poverty environment, or the person living in such an environment, is deficient. Rather than deficient, the individual is merely different, they have contended. It is their opinion that it is the middle-class psychologist who demonstrates a deficiency in his approach to the study of class and linguistic ability.

To support this claim, the two commentators cited several criticisms of the linguistic deficit theory. Perhaps the most cogent and inclusive is a recent critique (Labov 1970) that made the following three points:

First, contrary to popular belief, all languages are functionally equal. In a study of nonstandard English spoken by blacks, it was shown that young blacks—who would be assessed as linguistically retarded by standard test methods—

enter conversations and present their arguments in a way that shows conclusively that they can speak adequately.

In an earlier study, Labov and Cohen (1967) analyzed the spontaneous and imitative speech of black lower-class subjects in New York City. Results showed that they were capable of perceiving, understanding, and reproducing the *meaning* of many standard English utterances, even though they could not spontaneously produce the language in its standard form. Since the blacks understood the meaning of the standard language and reproduced it in their own speech, neither their cognitive powers nor their language would appear to be inferior. On the contrary, it seems that their language may simply be different—a far cry from being deficient. Any American who has tried to speak with someone who is not very familiar with the English language probably will recognize in himself the almost unconscious assumption that this person is somewhat inferior, whereas, in fact, he might be highly intelligent and educated, but merely unfamiliar with our language. This is a common example of the unfortunate tendency to equate difference with inferiority or deficiency.

The second point in Labov's critique of the deficit theory was that psychologists are not familiar, as are linguists, with language in general, and nonstandard dialects in particular. What others may call a series of badly connected words can be an expression that follows very definite rules of the dialect that is being spoken.

Labov based this conclusion on research he carried out in south central Harlem from 1965 to 1968. Using two white and two black investigators, he sought to describe the differences between the standard English of the classroom and the black English vernacular. He discovered that rather than being an accumulation of errors caused by the failure to master standard English, black English, like all dialects, was a highly structured system with its own grammatical rules and its own vocabulary. Much of what some psychologists attribute to the complete absence of language in lower-class black preschoolers, Labov attributed to the psychologists' own ignorance of the rules of discourse and syntax.

Third, the critique argued against the entire testing procedure. It noted the widespread assumption that if the same questionnaire is administered to several groups of children of varying social backgrounds, all the children have been given equivalent tests—simply because they all received the same questionnaire. This assumption overlooks several differences. For example, the testing situation may mean different things to different groups of children. A black ghetto child who enters a plush, air-conditioned office and is given a verbal test may "freeze up." Contrary to what the test may indicate, the failure to score well may be due not to linguistic deficiency but to an unfamiliar, perhaps frightening, atmosphere and to the formality of the test. The same child taking the same test in his own home may perform very coherently and intelligently.

The critique concluded that before psychologists can accurately study the linguistic ability of minority groups, they must understand the minorities' languages and construct tests and testing situations that are free of culturally linked impediments to maximum performance. The sobering possibility must be admitted, however, that even when this is done, the disadvantaged may still be disadvantaged. Remembering Piaget's position, it follows that impoverished circumstances are probably associated with impoverished cognitive opportunities, with subsequent effects on language. But what must be kept clear is that this is an economic condition, not a racial one.

Are Environmental Effects Reversible?

When assertions are made about the effects of early environmental deprivations, a natural response is to ask if such effects can be reversed, if they do indeed exist as deficiencies. The question of reversibility is especially significant today when many social programs have set themselves the goal of helping the poor overcome cognitive and linguistic handicaps in their backgrounds.

To date, reversibility remains an open question. Results of one experiment show that the complexity of speech—as indicated by the number of words per communication—among both lower- and middle-class children increases as they grow older. However, the speech of middle-class children is consistently more complex than the speech of the lower-class children. This difference grows steadily with increasing age (Loban 1965).

Other studies, however, have given reason for guarded optimism. One such study (Blank and Solomon 1968) demonstrated that the cognitive activities of deprived preschool children could be substantially upgraded through brief, daily periods of individual tutoring. During the experiment's tutoring sessions, which were about 20 minutes long, the main effort was to sharpen the

Table 8.4. The Effect of Individual Tutoring on Cognitive Activities in a Group of Disadvantaged Preschool Children as Measured by Stanford-Binet I.Q. Scores

Sex	Age*	Total Hours Tutored	I.Q. Scores Pretest	Posttest	Change
Tutored group 1 (5 times/wk.):					
F1	3.8	11	70	98	+28
F2	3.11	11	100	109	+9
F3	3.4	13	104	115	+11
M1	3.3	12	111	127	+16
M2	3.11	14	90	109	+19
M3	3.7	14	111	115	+4
Mean			97.7	112.2	+14.5
Tutored group 2 (3 times/wk.):					
F4	3.9	8	89	105	+16
F5	4.7	6	86	98	+12
F6	4.5	7	103	103	0
F7	3.3	6	79**	96	+17
M4	3.11	9	94	93	−1
M5	4.0	5	107	105	−2
Mean			93.0	100.0	+7.0
Untutored group 1 (5 times/wk.):					
F8	4.1	13	107	111	+4
M6	4.4	10	101	99	−2
M7	4.2	11	80	84	+4
Mean			96.0	98.0	+2.0
Untutored group 2 (classroom):					
F9	4.6	. . .	97	99	+2
F10	3.5	. . .	105	107	+2
F11	3.11	. . .	105	103	−2
F12	4.2	. . .	117	114	−3
M8	4.2	. . .	115	124	+9
M9	4.2	. . .	88	88	0
M10	3.5	. . .	93	94	+1
Mean			102.8	104.1	+1.3

*Age at beginning of study.
**No basal score was achieved; a basal MA of 2 years was assumed for the calculations, thus overestimating the score.
Source: M. Blank and F. Solomon. A tutorial program to develop abstract thinking in socially disadvantaged preschool children. *Child Develpm.*, 1968, 39(2), 379–389.

child's skill at organizing his thoughts, thinking about situations, understanding events, and structuring his behavior so that he could choose his path of action. These intellectual skills were sharpened through training tasks in which the 22 children—who ranged in age from 3 years and 3 months to 4 years and 7 months—were asked to use and understand language, to respond to stimuli correctly on their own, and to talk about other possible solutions to the task at hand.

The 22 children were divided into four groups, all matched for age, sex, and I.Q. Group A was tutored five times a week, Group B three times, and Groups C and D served as control groups. Control Group C had daily meetings with the teacher but no structured tutoring, while Control Group D had only the usual nursery school program. All of the children were tested before and after the four-month trial period.

Among the children tutored five days a week, the average I.Q. increase was 15 points. Children tutored three days a week gained only 7 points. Control Group C averaged I.Q. gains of 2 points, while Control Group D averaged 1.3. The results seemed to show that the amount of tutoring directly affects the child's score on intelligence tests. In addition to improved intelligence test scores, a number of tutored children displayed sharply different behavior. Children who had spoken in disconnected words and phrases, as well as others who were extremely timid or emotionally affected, overcame these limitations as they became active in the training sessions. The tutored children also seemed to take great pleasure in learning and in their new sense of ability. The experimenter attributed great importance to these later responses—which the untutored children did not display—because the pleasure in learning and the sense of mastery apparently serve as rewards for the child, reinforcing his intellectual activity.

Despite such sanguine results in cases of individual tutoring, other problems, such as the sheer number of children to be tutored and the cost involved, somewhat dim the prospects for the reversibility of the effects of early deprivation. It is a general finding that even when such programs lead to improvement, the improvement is only maintained as long as the program continues. When the training program is over, there is a deterioration towards the original expected levels of response. As social learning theory would indicate, if the reinforcements for new behavior are not maintained, the new behavior will not be maintained. Those who would improve the education of the poor must not just engage in temporary remedial programs but in the long-term reform of education along such remedial lines. Ultimately, environmental effects are not reversible unless whole environments are reversed.

Summary

Between the ages of 2 and 4, the toddler's physical and mental skills improve dramatically, and through them he gains an increasing sense of his own autonomy. The most striking developments in this period are his new abilities to move himself about, by walking, running, and climbing, and to communicate in words. These developments are important to the emergence of his individual personality.

Intelligence tests given in toddlerhood are better predictors of future achievement than are infancy tests; but the later in childhood a test is given, the closer it comes to agreeing with test scores in later life. Despite their poor predictability, these tests nevertheless are useful in detecting possible mental retardation.

The capacity to symbolize and use representational and metaphoric thinking are the main characteristics of the period from 2 to 4 years, which Piaget classifies as the preconceptual phase. The symbolic function opens the way for the child's use of language. First he uses physical symbols, as in imitative activity and substitution of one concrete object for another; then he metaphorically expresses an event in one area of experience in terms of another; and finally he is able to form mental symbols and use speech.

Six traits characterize the child's thought in

this period: (1) the tendency to think about new situations in terms of past experience, (2) an inability to generalize, (3) egocentricity, (4) concentration on one aspect of a phenomenon to the exclusion of all others, (5) the distortion of reality to fit his wishes, and (6) transductive reasoning. The child in this phase also groups objects into classes by using faulty preconcepts, rather than the true concepts he will develop later.

One way the toddler's cognitive development is displayed is in his rapidly expanding powers of speech. In these two years, his vocabulary jumps from about 270 to over 1,500 words, and five-word sentences are common by age 4.

Just how the child acquires the syntax of his language is not yet fully understood. Current theories include imitation of adult speech, reinforcement by adults of his own correct speech, a mental structure that has the syntax "wired in," and the mapping of words onto cognitive structures he already has developed.

The child's early speech seems to be composed of two major classes of words—pivot and X-words—from which he constructs his sentences. Toward the end of toddlerhood these classes are refined and subdivided, and he is able to compose negative sentences and use inflections in a manner that approaches adult speech. Most of the toddler's speech centers around acts of existence, disappearance, and recurrence, providing the linguistic manifestation of his newly acquired concept of object permanence. Whether language or cognition appears first is an unsettled question, but there is no question that the two are intimately related.

Environmental conditions are known to influence the development of cognition and language, but whether this evidence has any relevance for bringing the cognitive and linguistic performances of lower-class children more into line with those of middle-class children is questionable. While some believe the home environments of lower-class children are deprived and therefore produce individuals with deficient cognitive and language skills, many others contend that their environments are not linguistically deprived and their skills are not deficient, but merely different. Programs to reverse the effects of assumed linguistic and cognitive deprivation are not likely to have enduring success without complete reform of the environment of the deprived person.

Case Studies

Benjamin C.

When we studied Benjy's language development in Chapter 6, we followed him to the threshold of an important new ability: the production of true syntactic utterances. At 18 months, Benjy's frequent use of phrases like "All gone" and "Whass dat?" seemed more like extended single-word utterances than grammatical combinations of words in appropriate circumstances. Rote qualities of Benjy's speech began to give way to more original utterances, however, in his twentieth month, as he started combining words into phrases like "All gone juice" (or toast, or whatever). He tried hard to increase his vocabulary, too, often repeating names of people and objects mentioned in adult conversation. He had not yet mastered final consonants, however, nor could he cope with double initial consonants (for instance, "gass" stood for both *glass* and *grass*).

Benjy's next couple of months saw a number of important new developments: more complex original phrases like "Benjy go upstairs sleep" and "All gone Frank bicycle"; improved abilities to imitate adult utterances; a few "Where . . . ?" questions including some use of possessives ("Where's Benjy's tractor?"); the advent of plurals; consistent distinctions between "up" and "down," but still some confusion between "big" and "little"; a fairly stable concept of what "two" means; and a couple of possible references to the future (for example, "See you tomorrow.")—although all of his few verbs remained in the present tense. Benjy's favorite book was now the trading stamp redemption catalog, and he could name practically every item pictured.

By the time Benjy had celebrated his second birthday, he was able to master all the consonants except *l* and *sh,* and never tired of demonstrating his vocal competence by parroting bits and pieces of conversation, commercials, and nursery rhymes. Having mastered the concept of "two-ness," he was working on three, although he could already do a creditable (if not completely accurate) job of counting because of his great fondness for numbers. Soon thereafter, Mrs. C. noted Benjy's grappling with the distinction between "my" and "yours"; the introduction of "the"; and Benjy's initial usage of "no" (but not "yes"). In addition, Benjy's primitive familiarity with negatives is illustrated in one of his typical self-admonishments: "What's-a trouble, Benjy? It's all right, Benjy. Don't cry anymore—don't cry, Benjy."

The three months which followed were primarily months of linguistic consolidation. New developments were restricted to infrequent uses of two past-tense verbs ("went" and "said"); discovery of "yes," but confusion with "no"; a few instances of "I" and "you," although he preferred using proper names; and a well-practiced usage of the comparative "like" on one afternoon as he described nearly 50 cars "like Ann's [the baby-sitter's] car." Mrs. C. also noted Benjy's improved ability to follow simple directions; his increased reference to the future (for example, "First have breakfast, then play vacuum cleaner."); his limited questioning format (restricted to "Where . . . ?"); and his persistent inability to master the consonant sounds of *l* and *sh.*

When Benjy entered nursery school (just prior to his third birthday), he was a fairly accomplished, well-practiced speaker. Past tenses were common; his usage of words like "yes," "yesterday/today/tomorrow," "I," "his/hers," and "himself/herself" was usually correct; he could relate an entire morning's events to his mother; and other forms of questions (such as, "Which ball you want?" or "Didja bump your toe on a fly?") had supplemented his old form. A somewhat indefatigable speaker, Benjy seemed verbally well equipped to deal with the experiences and challenges which lay ahead in the schoolroom world (Church 1968).

Sarah O.

Sarah was the third daughter of a well-to-do, socially prominent couple. Her participation in the "pleasant" family relationships was somewhat limited because her care was entrusted to the family nurse, who now devoted full time—and apparently her full emotional energies—to Sarah. In fact, Sarah was mothered almost 24 hours a day: although more than 2 years old, she had never, for instance, been encouraged to feed or dress herself. In addition, she had little opportunity to play with other small children or her school-age sisters.

At 27 months of age, Sarah was referred for professional help because of her inability to speak. Reportedly she had said only one word—"bye-bye"—and that only responsively. Except for a few scattered vocalizations during play and an occasional shrill "a-a-a-m!" to demand something, Sarah relied on vivid gestures to express herself quite clearly.

During her first visit to the clinic, it was determined that Sarah's comprehension of spoken words and her problem-solving abilities were normal, as were her motor and physiological development. It was noted, however, that her play was rather slow and deliberate, and that she showed signs of subtle, but constant, tension throughout every kind of activity. To begin the remedial process, the clinic set up home guidelines for Sarah's decreased dependency on adults; increased contact with other children; increased play to expand motor and limb activities; and constant encouragement to vocalize her wants and needs.

Because the nurse was unable to change her old ways, Mrs. O. found it necessary to replace her with someone who understood the problem more fully. By 33 months, however, there seemed little improvement, although Sarah had begun to say "all gone" and "yes" (in answer to questions), along with other scattered references to things ("keys," " 'up" [for cup]) and to people ("Daddy," "Mary"). She did try to repeat words occasionally.

At 35 months it became possible to schedule regular guidance nursery visits for Sarah so that she could be introduced to play groups, supervised free play, and carefully planned opportunities for free vocal expression. Both mother and nurse were encouraged to observe each nursery session.

Improvement in Sarah's speech patterns, although slow to begin, accelerated quickly. By her third birthday, Sarah had acquired a number of new words and short phrases: for example, "ki(ddy)-kar," "sank you," and "shee-shaw" (for see-saw). During the next couple of months, Sarah began combining words regularly, with more and more indication of syntactic competence: for example, "do this," "that's mine," "p'ease go," and "push Sa'ah." She also began to vocalize parts of favorite nursery rhymes, particularly finishing lines. By 39 months, it was not uncommon to record as many as 150 vocalizations per hour during Sarah's nursery visits.

A big jump in Sarah's linguistic performance came at 40 months. During one nursery session, it was noted that Sarah vocalized to herself almost constantly, although the words were seldom distinguishable. Just three weeks later, Sarah was talking in short sentences—complete with pronouns, adjectives, and prepositional phrases: "Dat turtle all green, I want it"; "De're more kitties in dere"; "No, you bring it." Despite occasional regressions, her language at home and at the nursery was judged well within the normal range for 40 months. What's more, during the next 20 months Sarah's articulation, vocabulary, and syntax all improved so markedly that her language was rated as "definitely superior" at 5 years of age.

It seems no coincidence that Sarah's linguistic gains were being made all the while she was being encouraged to mature in her personal and social adaptations to the world about her (Gesell, Amatruda, Castner, and Thompson 1939).

References

Bayley, N. Mental growth during the first three years. In R. G. Barker, J. S. Kounin, and H. F. Wright (Eds.), *Child behavior and development*. New York: McGraw-Hill, 1943.

Bellugi, U., and Brown, R. W. (Eds.) The acquisition of language. *Monogr. Soc. Res. Child Develpm.*, 1964, 29(1, Serial No. 92).

Bem, S. L. Verbal self-control: The establishment of effective self-instruction. *J. exp. Psychol.*, 1967, 74, 485–491.

Berko, J. The child's learning of English morphology. *Word*, 1958, 14, 150–177.

Bernstein, B. Social structure, language and learning. In J. P. De Cecco (Ed.), *The psychology of language, thought, and instruction*. New York: Holt, Rinehart & Winston, 1967.

Bever, T. G., Fodor, J. A., and Weksel, W. On the acquisition of syntax: A critique of "contextual generalization." *Psychol. Rev.*, 1965, 72, 467–482.

Blank, M., and Solomon, F. A tutorial language program to develop abstract thinking in socially disadvantaged children. *Child Develpm.*, 1968, 39(2), 379–389.

Bloom, B. *Stability and change in human characteristics*. New York: Wiley, 1964.

Bloom, L. M. *Language development: Form and function in emerging grammars*. Cambridge, Mass.: M.I.T. Press, 1970.

Bloom, L. M. *One word at a time: The use of single-word utterance before syntax*. The Hague: Mouton Press. In press.

Braine, M. D. S. On learning the grammatical order of words. *Psychol. Rev.*, 1963, 70, 323–348.

Braine, M. D. S. The ontogeny of English phrase structure: The first phase. *Language*, 1963, *39*, 1–13.

Brodbeck, A. J., and Irwin, O. C. The speech behavior of infants without families. *Child Develpm.*, 1946, *17*, 145–165.

Brown, R. W., et al. Language and learning: Special issue. *Harv. educ. Rev.*, 1964, *34*(2).

Brown, R. W., and Bellugi, U. Three processes in the child's acquisition of syntax. *Harv. educ. Rev.*, 1964, *34*(2), 133–151.

Brown, R. W., and Fraser, C. The acquisition of syntax. In U. Bellugi and R. W. Brown (Eds.), *Monogr. Soc. Res. Child Develpm.*, 1964, *29*(1), 43–79.

Bruner, J. S. The course of cognitive growth. *Amer. Psychologist*, 1964, *19*, 1–15.

Bruner, J. S., Olver, R. R., and Greenfield, P. M. *Studies in cognitive growth.* New York: Wiley, 1966.

Carroll, J. B. Language development. In C. W. Harris (Ed.), *Encyclopedia of educational research.* New York: Macmillan, 1960.

Chomsky, N. *Aspects of the theory of syntax.* Cambridge, Mass.: M.I.T. Press, 1965.

Chomsky, N. The formal nature of language. In E. H. Lenneberg (Ed.), *Biological foundations of language.* New York: Wiley, 1967.

Chomsky, N. *Language and mind.* New York: Harcourt Brace Jovanovich, 1968.

Church, J. (Ed.) *Three babies: Biographies of cognitive development.* N.Y.: Random House, 1968. Pp. 107–162.

Cole, M., and Bruner, J. S. Cultural differences and inferences about psychological processes. *Amer. Psychologist*, 1971, *26*(10), 867–876.

Conrad, R. The chronology of the development of covert speech in children. *Develpm. Psychol.*, Nov. 1971, *5*(3), 398–405.

Ervin, S. M. Imitation in children's language. In E. H. Lenneberg (Ed.), *New directions in the study of language.* Cambridge, Mass.: M.I.T. Press, 1964.

Ervin-Tripp, S. Language development. In L. W. Hoffman and M. L. Hoffman (Eds.), *Review of child development research.* New York: Russell Sage Foundation, 1966.

Flavell, J. H. *The developmental psychology of Jean Piaget.* Princeton, N.J.: Van Nostrand, 1963.

Fraser, C., Bellugi, U., and Brown, R. Control of grammar in imitation, comprehension, and production. *J. Verbal Learning and Verbal Behavior*, 1963, *2*, 121–135.

Freud, S. *A general introduction to psychoanalysis.* New York: Washington Square Press, 1964.

Furth, H. G. Linguistic deficiency and thinking: Research with deaf subjects, 1964–1969. *Psychol. Bull.*, 1971, *76*(1), 58–72.

Furth, H. G. Research with the deaf: Implications for language and cognition. *Psychol. Bull.*, 1964, *62*, 145–164.

Gesell, A., Amatruda, C. S., Castner, B. M., and Thompson, H. *Biographies of child development.* New York: Harper, Paul B. Hoeber, 1939. Pp. 139–146.

Ginsberg, H., and Opper, S. *Piaget's theory of intellectual development: An introduction.* Englewood Cliffs, N. J.: Prentice-Hall, 1969.

Goldfarb, W. Effects of psychological deprivation in infancy and subsequent stimulation. *Amer. J. Psychiat.*, 1945, *102*, 18–33.

Goldfarb, W. Infant rearing and problem behavior. *Amer. J. Orthopsychiat.*, 1943, *13*, 249–266.

Goldfarb, W. Psychological privation in infancy and subsequent adjustment. *Amer. J. Orthopsychiat.*, 1945, *15*, 247–255.

Gordon, J. *Child learning through child play.* New York: St. Martin's Press, 1972.

Gould, R. *Child studies through fantasy: Cognitive-affective patterns in development.* Cleveland: Quadrangle Books, 1972.

Hebb, D. O. *The organization of behavior: A neuropsychological theory.* New York: Wiley, 1949.

Higgens-Trenk, A., and Loft, W. R. Cognitive capacity of very young children: Yet another replication. *J. Psychol.*, Nov. 1971, *79*(2), 285–289.

Honzik, M. P., Macfarlane, J. W., and Allen, L. The stability of mental test performance between two and eighteen years. *J. exp. Educ.*, 1948, *17*, 309–324.

Inhelder, B., and Piaget, J. *The growth of logical thinking.* Trans. by A. Parsons and S. Milgram. New York: Basic Books, 1958.

Jarvis, P. E. The effect of self-administered verbal instructions on simple sensory-motor performance in children. Unpublished doctoral dissertation, Univer. of Rochester, 1963.

Kendler, T. S. Development of mediating responses in children. In J. C. Wright and J. Kagan (Eds.), Basic cognitive processes in children. *Monogr. Soc. Res. Child Develpm.*, 1963, *28*(2), 33–48.

Klima, E. S., and Bellugi, U. Syntactic regularities in the speech of children. In J. Lyons and R. J. Wales (Eds.), *Psycholinguistics papers.* Edinburgh: Edinburgh Univer. Press, 1966.

Klinger, E. *Structure and functions of fantasy.* New York: Wiley, 1971.

Krogman, W. M. *Child growth.* Ann Arbor, Mich.: Univer. of Mich. Press, 1971.

Kuenne, M. R. Experimental investigation of the relation of language to transportation behavior in young children. *J. exp. Psychol.*, 1946, *36*, 471–490.

Kuusinen, J., and Salin, E. Children's learning of unfamiliar phonological sequences. *Perceptual and motor Skills*, Oct. 1971, *33*(2), 559–562.

Labov, W. The logical non-standard English. In F. Williams (Ed.), *Language and poverty.* Chicago: Markham Press, 1970.

Labov, W., and Cohen, P. *Systematic relations of standard and non-standard rules in the grammars of Negro speakers.* Project Literacy Report No. 8. Ithaca, N.Y.: Cornell Univer. Press, 1967.

Lenneberg, E. H. The biological foundations of language. *Hospital Practice*, 1967, *2*, 59–67.

Lenneberg, E. H. (Ed.) *New directions in the study of language.* Cambridge, Mass.: M.I.T. Press, 1964.

Leopold, W. F. Patterning in children's language learning. *Lang. Learning*, 1953, *5*, 1–14.

Loban, W. Language proficiency and school learning. In J. D. Krumboltz (Ed.), *Learning and the education process*. Chicago: Rand McNally, 1965.

Luria, A. R. The role of language in the formation of temporary connections. In B. Simon (Ed.), *Psychology in the Soviet Union*. London: Routledge & Kegan Paul, 1957.

Markey, F. V. *Imaginative behavior of preschool children*. Child Develpm. Monogr., No. 18. New York: Teacher's College Bureau of Publications, Columbia Univer., 1935.

McCarthy, D. Language development in children. In L. Carmichael (Ed.), *Manual of child psychology*. New York: Wiley, 1954.

McCarthy, D. Research in language development: Retrospect and prospect. *Monogr. Soc. Res. Child Develpm.*, 1959, *24*(5), 3–24.

McNeill, D. The creation of language by children. In J. Lyons and R. J. Wales (Eds.), *Psycholinguistics papers*. Edinburgh: Edinburgh Univer. Press, 1966. (a)

McNeill, D. Developmental psycholinguistics. In F. Smith and G. A. Miller (Eds.), *The genesis of language: A psycholinguistic approach*. Cambridge, Mass.: M.I.T. Press, 1966. (b)

Menyuk, P. A preliminary evaluation of grammatical capacity in children. *J. Verbal Learning and Verbal Behavior*, 1963, *2*, 429–439.

Menyuk, P. *Sentences children use*. Cambridge, Mass.: M.I.T. Press, 1969.

Menyuk, P. Syntactic structures in the language of children. *Child Develpm.*, 1963, *34*, 407–422.

Oldfield, R. C., and Marshall, J. C. (Eds.) *Language*. Baltimore: Penguin, 1968.

Palthier, P. C. The developmental concepts of Piaget applied to nursing assessment and intervention with atypical children. *J. Psychiat. Nursing and Ment. Health Services*, Jan. 1970, *8*(1), 30–36.

Piaget, J. *Play, dreams and imitation in childhood*. New York: Norton, 1962.

Piaget, J. *The psychology of intelligence*. Totowa, N.J.: Littlefield, Adams, 1960.

Prentice, J. I. Is cognitive development a function of language? *Viewpoints*, July 1971, *47*(4), 195–205.

Rheingold, H. L., Gewirtz, J. L., and Ross, H. W. Social conditioning of vocalizations in the infant. *J. comp. physiol. Psychol.*, 1959, *52*(1), 68–73.

Rosenthal, T. L., Moore, W. B., Dorfman, H., and Nelson, B. Vicarious acquisition of a simple concept with experimenter as model. *Behavior Res. and Therapy*, 1971, *9*(3), 219–227.

Shine, D. N. Cognitive impulsivity and Piaget's theory of perceptual decentration. *Dissert. Abstr.*, Oct. 1971, *32*(4-B).

Sinclair-de-Zwart, H. Developmental psycholinguistics. In D. Elkind and J. H. Flavell (Eds.), *Studies in cognitive development*. New York: Oxford Univer. Press, 1969.

Skinner, B. F. *Verbal behavior*. New York: Appleton-Century-Crofts, 1957.

Slobin, D. Imitation and grammatical development in children. In N. Endler, L. Boulter, and H. Osser (Eds.), *Contemporary issues in developmental psychology*. New York: Holt, Rinehart & Winston, 1968.

Smith, M. E. An investigation of the development of the sentence and the extent of vocabulary in young children. *Univer. of Iowa Stud. Child Welf.*, 1926, *3*(5).

Stern, W. *Psychology of early childhood*. New York: Holt, 1924.

Sutton-Smith, B. Children at play. *Nat. hist.*, 1971, *80*, 54–59.

Templin, M. C. *Certain language skills in children*. Minneapolis: Univer. of Minnesota Press, 1957.

Thompson, H. Physical growth. In L. Carmichael (Ed.), *Manual of child psychology*. (2nd ed.) New York: Wiley, 1954.

Vygotsky, L. S. *Thought and language*. Trans. by E. Hanfmann and G. Vakar. Cambridge, Mass.: M.I.T. Press, 1962.

Weiner, I. D., and Elkind, D. *Child development: A core approach*. New York: Wiley, 1972.

Werner, H. *Comparative psychology of mental development*. (Rev. ed.) Chicago: Follet, 1948.

Werner, H., and Kaplan, B. *Symbol formation: An organismic-developmental approach to language and the expression of thought*. New York: Wiley, 1963.

Wickes, F. G. *The inner world of childhood*. New York: Appleton-Century-Crofts, 1966.

Winitz, H. *Articulatory acquisition and behavior*. New York: Appleton-Century-Crofts, 1969.

Youniss, J. Concept transfer as a function of shifts, age, and deafness. *Child Develpm.*, 1964, *34*, 695–700.

Youniss, J., and Furth, H. G. The influence of transitivity on learning in hearing and deaf children. *Child Develpm.*, 1965, *36*, 533–538.

Zimmerman, L. D., and Calovini, G. Toys as learning materials for preschool children. *Except. Children*, 1971, *37*(9), 642–654.

Personality and Social Development 9

During his third and fourth years, a toddler's individual personality becomes defined in greater detail than was possible earlier. His expanding abilities—in locomotion, language, and cognition—which we examined in the previous chapter, open new paths for him to develop and express the particular qualities that set each child apart from every other. He may be timid and soft-spoken or brash and loud, or he may seem timid one day and brash the next. He may pry into every cranny for a lost ball or react to its loss with considerable upset. He may be a toy-scattering, furniture-climbing dynamo, or he may prefer to work at puzzles and construct elaborate, careful castles with his blocks. Whatever his bent, individual personality traits are increasingly evident during this period, while at the same time they are quite susceptible to modification as a result of outside influences. The years between 2 and 4 are a critical time for the formation of personality characteristics and social behavior. These traits are shaped in part by the child's contact with other people, and in part by his genetic endowment.

Since the toddler spends almost all of his time in or near his home, his family greatly influences him. His parents, as well as his brothers and sisters, play a significant role in the development of his personality traits. Their attitudes, actions, and treatment of the child have a great deal to do with how he feels about himself—free or inhibited, competent or inadequate, wanted or ignored. The responses that parents make to their child's questions, for example, may lead him to be curious and questioning or indifferent and reticent.

We do not have to look far to find examples of marked family influence on offspring. We all have in our acquaintance at least one such family. To select a widely known family of this kind, though, we might cite the family of Rose and the late Joseph Kennedy. It appears likely that, in addition

255

to genetic heritage and financial position, the couple's three well-known sons also shared some other factors in their developmental periods. Those factors seem to have been a consistent and nurturant response from their parents and siblings as well as the family's advocacy of achievement and independence. This favorable combination could account for the positive, assertive personalities that permitted all three sons to become U.S. senators and one of them to become president.

While most parents do not produce senators and presidents, all clearly influence their children's personality development. A substantial amount of such personality shaping is interwoven with the socialization of the toddler. For example, a socially conscious mother's desire to mold her daughter into a quiet, well-mannered little lady could lead her to suppress the girl's spontaneous gaiety because somehow it appeared unbecoming in her eyes. The child's natural good cheer and humor, which have been an active, perhaps even a dominant trait in her personality, would seldom rise to the surface were she socialized harshly.

Although at times the toddler's personality emerges with the momentum of a fast freight, such seeming solidity and self-confidence may be misleading. In reality, the toddler often is characterized by instability in his physical, mental, and social prowess; at times he even seems uncertain of his standing in his parents' affection. All of his powers are far from being fully developed, and this unsatisfactory state adds to his tentativeness and occasional inadequacy. Thus, despite bursts of bravado, the toddler's personality may not be as firmly established as it appears to be. Instead, he may well be trying out different modes of living in his world. Stabilization comes as the child matures. In the next section, dealing with children 4 to 7 years of age, we shall see how the child's personality is manifested in his social behavior among his nursery school peers.

This chapter will explore the toddler's personality and social development from two perspectives. First we shall deal with some areas in which the parents' effects are dominant: the overall home environment created by the nature of the parents' interactions with the child; the child's identification with one of his parents; the degree of dependency the child feels toward his parents; and the level and type of aggression he exhibits. Then we shall turn to the areas in which the child's own growth and coping processes are dominant forces: the awareness that he or she is a boy or girl, and the adoption of behavior patterns considered appropriate for that sex; the sexual curiosity which accompanies this awareness; and the further development of the child's sense of self.

The Home Environment

From the hundreds of parent–child studies that have been conducted, several dimensions of the home environment and parental behavior emerge as especially influential in the development of the child's personality and social behavior. The Fels study of mother–child behavior, which will be discussed below, focused on the effects of four general dimensions of maternal behavior—restrictiveness, protection, hostility, and acceleration—upon several areas of the child's personality (Kagan and Moss 1962). Many other variables of parental behavior and home life also influence the child's development, however. Other studies have examined the effects of the parents' warmth or coldness; their willingness to express affection; the degree of democracy or authoritarianism in the home; and the consistency of the parents' behavior toward the child.

Before examining any of these aspects of parental behavior, and their effects on the child, we should note that the overall relationship between parent and child is affected in all of its dimensions by the existence of other children in the family. Elements of each child's relationship with his parents differ according to his position in the family. For example, parents are known to be more directive of firstborn than later-born children (Stout 1960). Parents also tend to expect more of their first children and to treat them inconsistently (Rothbart 1967; Hilton 1967). As a consequence of such distinct parental treatment, siblings behave differently from each other. First-

Figure 9.1 A child's position in relationship to siblings affects his development. This toddler is quite absorbed in his older brother's play activities. (Grete Mannheim—D.P.I.)

born children tend to associate strongly with their parents, act like little adults, and achieve to please their parents (McArthur 1956). Later siblings, on the other hand, act more like the conventionally imagined child. They learn to be noisier in their relationships with older brothers and sisters. They do not associate so closely with their parents, and they protest restrictions more (Sutton-Smith and Rosenberg 1970). Because sibling status prompts these and many other behavioral differences—in the parent and in the child—it is an important variable to be kept in mind while considering the young child's home environment.

Investigation: Methods and Problems

Researchers examining parent–child relationships have four basic tools for gathering information. They can interview parents and children, observe how the two interact, visit the home personally, or observe the child performing a particular task in a particular laboratory or naturalistic setting. While these are the most reliable means currently available, these four ways of gathering information seldom lead to unchallengeable results. Unfortunately, several problems are endemic to the gathering and evaluation of research data. Perhaps the first methodological problem is the chance that a study's evidence will be "contaminated" by a factor that the study is not intended to measure. For example, a parent may be asked to describe his own behavior. As we saw in our discussion of the retrospectional method in Chapter 1, personal accounts of one's own behavior are seldom completely accurate. Therefore, a study relying on this technique might be invalidated by the parent's wish to create a more favorable image than his actual behavior projects. This desire may lead him, unconsciously perhaps, to improve upon reality in the questionnaire or interview. Such alterations could distort the entire study.

A second common problem is the range of interpretations applied to a set of results. It is possible for three different investigators to give three different readings of the same evidence, depending on which factors in the evidence each investigator stresses.

A third shortcoming of many experiments is the character of the specific sample of subjects. For example, since most subjects in studies of parent–child relationships have been middle-class parents and children, rather than a comprehensive sampling from the upper, middle, and lower classes, it is difficult to generalize the results of most studies in their application to all children and their families.

Moreover, different research tools used in the same study may produce substantially different results. An example of such conflicts can be seen in an experiment that compared direct observation with other methods of assessing the parent–child relationship (Becker, Peterson, Luria, Shoemaker, and Hellmer 1962). The researchers compared the results gained in observations of parents and their 5-year-olds with the parents' ratings of themselves. The researchers also had available the results of interviews with the parents and the ratings that each parent made of the other. Data on the children came from ratings made by

PERSONALITY AND SOCIAL DEVELOPMENT   257

their teachers, parents, and trained observers. In comparing all of these results, little agreement could be found among the results of the various research tools. Although the interviewers' ratings of parents and the parents' self-ratings showed a high level of agreement, there was only a small correlation between the mothers' self-assessments and their husbands' assessments of them. And while parents' ratings of their children proved poor at predicting the children's school behavior, interviews with the parents yielded information that predicted this behavior fairly reliably. As this experiment shows, it is extremely risky to presume that different methods of measuring behavior will produce comparable information about that behavior and its effects on the child. In many instances, supplementary studies are necessary to eliminate ambiguities and produce an answer that is more conclusive.

THE LONGITUDINAL STUDY. The longitudinal study, unfortunately a rare event, focuses on the same individual over a substantial period of time, usually a number of years. It thus can be extremely useful in detecting trends and broad developmental patterns, as we saw in Chapter 1. For example, studies covering only a few weeks or months may suggest that a child exhibits certain traits because of a particular home environment. The longitudinal or long-range study, however, could determine whether the traits are temporary phenomena associated only with the child's developmental stage or whether they will persist throughout childhood and perhaps even have an identifiable effect on the adult personality. A long-range study of this sort was undertaken in 1929 by the Fels Research Institute at Yellow Springs, Ohio. In this study, 89 individuals were observed periodically from birth to maturity. Major results of the first 30 years of observation have been published, confirming the Fels study as one that is unique for its sample size, duration, and the range of behavior noted (Kagan and Moss 1962).

The Fels study serves to make two points for our discussion of research methodology. First, it illustrates the number of subjects and length of time required to complete a thorough long-range study; second, it exemplifies at the same time the difficulty of acquiring a representative sample.

The Fels sample. Let us look at the details of the sample group first. Of the 89 children enrolled for childhood observation during their first 10 years of life, 45 were girls and 44 boys, all drawn from a total of 63 Yellow Springs families of primarily Protestant stock. In terms of their occupations, the fathers were evenly distributed among several levels and kinds of employment categories. About 70 percent of the fathers were high school graduates and 38 percent were college graduates. During the Fels study, which, incidentally, is still continuing, 3 of the 63 sets of parents divorced. However, including the children of these divorced parents, only 8 of the children were separated from either the mother or the father before age 18. All measurement methods, ranging from observations to interviews, were used. The Fels staff had ample opportunity to observe the children since almost all of them were enrolled in the institute's experimental nursery school from ages 2½ to 5. From 6 to 10 years, they attended a summer day camp, also operated by the institute. After 10 years of age, the children were evaluated less frequently, although regularly. Thus, for 7½ years of childhood, researchers had plentiful opportunities to observe the children outside their homes, permitting much more systematic behavior analysis than is possible with home visits.

The Fels study was well planned, but it has its weaknesses. One is the unrepresentative character of its sample, which limits any generalization of the study's results to an entire population. The aim of the Fels study might have been to assemble a sample that would be a microcosm of the entire United States child population. Had it been possible to study such a scattered sample, the trends recorded by the Fels study could be generalized to apply to all American children. Unfortunately, the findings are necessarily restricted by time and place. The children assessed are representative not of all American children, nor of all midwestern children, nor even of all Ohio children. They represent children of Yellow Springs, Ohio, only. Their representativeness is further diminished by the fact that they were born in the particular decade between 1929 and 1939, subject to the events and stresses of that period. This shortcoming has been partly corrected by the fact that in subsequent years the Fels group has continued to introduce new babies into the study. Still, the first 89 children, who were the most intensively studied, cannot be seen as representative of individuals born outside their city or in times before or after their own. The Fels study, extended and comprehensive though it is, makes clear how difficult it is to gather evidence that is both uncontaminated and representative of an entire population. Nonetheless, the Fels study provides much useful information about what effects certain kinds of maternal behavior produced in the child, although it is unfortunate that the behavior of fathers was not examined as well. Since the young child usually spends more time with his mother than with his father, and since she has been more available for interviews and observation, investigators in this and other studies have dealt primarily with maternal behavior. There is a recent trend in research, however, to take into account the effects of the father's behavior as well, in evaluating the child.

Maternal Behavior

Because the Fels study covered the mother–child relationship from early childhood through 10 years of age, it permits us to see if maternal behavior tends to remain stable over that period of childhood. The data can be analyzed to detect, for example, whether a restrictive mother is likely to remain restrictive or shift to a more permissive manner. Observation extended in time also can show whether the relationship between parent and child over a period of years is affected at different stages by earlier interactions between them. It becomes possible, for example, to discover whether the mother who is hostile when her child is young creates an effect that is discernible in the child at age 10.

The Fels study measured several general aspects of the child's personality which his home environment seems to influence. Some of these personality patterns were dependency, aggression, sexuality, and achievement strivings. The institute's staff concurrently examined the effects of four types of maternal behavior on these areas of personality; they were maternal restrictiveness, protection, hostility, and acceleration, or active encouragement of achievement. Maternal restrictiveness—the degree of conformity to her wishes that the mother demands—has a multitude of consequences for the child's personality development and thus is a fruitful area to examine in some detail.

THE RESTRICTIVE MOTHER. The Fels study revealed that the restrictive mother, while demanding strict compliance, also tended to be hostile, and these two traits remained linked, with slight inconsistencies, throughout the first 10 years of childhood. Maternal protectiveness and acceleration also appeared together, with similar inconsistencies. When the first three years of childhood were omitted from the data, however, the mother's behavior in all four areas was stable with respect to boys and nearly stable for girls. It may be that after the first three years, which may serve as a training period for the mother and a stabilization period for the child, mother and child develop relatively consistent interactions together. As we noted in Chapter 7, prediction of behavior from infancy has been difficult.

Dependency and the restrictive mother. The Fels data indicate a link between maternal restrictiveness and dependency by the child. An interesting difference between dependency behavior in boys and girls emerged, however. Maternal restrictiveness correlated directly with the dependency in both boys and girls—up to age 10. At that point, boys began to change this dependent relationship. By age 14, there was some suggestion of the boys' rejection of their mothers' help—for example, a boy might turn down his mother's offer of a fast, cool car ride to the swimming pool in favor of a long, hot bicycle trip with his peers. Girls, on the other hand, maintained a functional dependence on their mothers beyond age 10.

In examining such data as the Fels study, it is always important to keep in mind other possible causes of behavior. For example, the breakdown of the boy's dependent relationship with his mother may be determined by a cultural factor— the West's accepted concept of male independence and dominance. It is entirely possible that the mother, responding to this cultural pressure, encourages her son to be more independent while retaining a more restrictive rein on her daughter, who in Western culture has been regarded as a person to be sheltered and protected. Such cultural dictates do change, though the process may be gradual. The growing emancipation of women in the United States illustrates how such ironclad cultural rules can be modified in the span of perhaps half a century. Women's Liberation seems to be a current manifestation of the same desire for equality that the suffragettes represented in their time. In societies that evolve less rapidly—the Australian aboriginal culture, to choose an extreme example—cultural changes occur over a much longer time span. Sometimes they may be so slow as to be imperceptible over several generations.

The pattern of restrictiveness in the parent and the child's consequent dependency can affect the child in several ways. His learning ability may be modified, for instance. The mother who is a walking rulebook—responding to less than instant and servile obedience with threats and punishments—more than likely will crush any spirit of independence in her child's behavior. Since her offspring seldom is permitted to act independently—and is in fact rewarded for acting dependently—the child probably will not develop much ability to take spontaneous action. Such inability tends to curb his curiosity, make him lethargic rather than vigorous, and timid rather than investigative. Of course, these effects are more likely to be produced in the child who by disposition is timid and passive, and less likely to be produced in the child of a more active and assertive nature.

From this one area of maternal influence, we now move to a necessary reciprocal process created in every normal child—that is, identification with an admired adult.

Identification

Identification is the process in which the child takes on the characteristics of someone else—usually a parent. Psychologists generally agree that identification is basic to the development of the child's personality and social behavior. Some, however, feel that the term *identification* is a superfluous one. They maintain it describes behavior that is simply imitation, which is controlled by the principles of learning that were discussed in Chapter 2. Others feel that the child does not just imitate particular behaviors of the parent for which he is rewarded, but that he demonstrates also a desire to be like the parent in a more total way; for this entire complex of behavior they prefer to use the term *identification*.

Conditions for Identification

In order for a child to identify with another person, that person must meet two requirements. First, the person must have some trait the child finds desirable. This trait—the power or skill of an adult, for example—according to most psychologists, is the initial motivation for the child to select that particular person as a model. Next, the child must detect some kind of emotional or physical similarity between himself and the other person. Since he is most often in the company of his parents, the toddler usually looks to them as models. The average child finds his mother and father admirable as the dispensers of warmth and love, and the possessors of skills and such mysterious commodities as money, which can bring the child the gumballs and ice cream cones he craves. Not only does the child recognize that his parents have these powers; he also understands that he himself does not. But he wants them. He especially desires the characteristics of a parent whom he personally finds positive and satisfying (Bandura and Huston 1961).

An important question here is how the child links his desire for a parent's specific traits—the parent's power or competence—to the act of imitating the parent's behavior. Presumably, the child believes that by imitating his parent, he acquires the parent's traits. For example, the boy who walks with his father's gait expects thereby to acquire his father's competence in driving a car and other adult skills. Thus, for the toddler, identification means not simply mimicking a person's behavior, but, in a sense, *becoming* that person. Because the child associates the nurturant parent with his own affirmative feelings, he is strongly rewarded and thereby prompted to sustain his identification with that parent. Therefore, for example, a boy who has a generous and demonstrative father is more likely to identify with his father than is the boy whose father is abrupt, cold, and aloof (Bandura and Huston 1961).

The ideal situation for identification exists when both parents are nurturant and affirmative toward the child. This toddler, rather than being

260 TODDLERHOOD AGES 2 AND 3

Table 9.1 Significance of Differences in Imitative Behavior Exhibited by Subjects in Nurturant and Nonnurturant Experimental Conditions

[a] p = probability of occurrence
[b] Aggressive behavior was quickly imitated in both nurturant and nonnurturant conditions.
[c] ns = not significant
Source: A. Bandura and A. C. Huston. Identification as a process of incidental learning. *J. abnormal soc. Psychol.*, 1963, 66, 315.

Response Category	Number of Subjects Imitating		p[a]
	Nurturant (N = 20)	Nonnurturant (N = 20)	
Nonaggressive behaviors	15	7	.04
Marching	13	5	.05
Verbal behavior	9	2	.05
Other imitative responses	6	1	.06
Aggressive behavior[b]	20	16	ns[c]
Partially imitative verbal responses	12	5	.04

puzzled as to which parent to identify with, will eventually select the one with whom he shares more characteristics. This selection of appropriate models can take varying lengths of time. Occasionally, in the case of male children, delayed identification with the father may cause the child, in our culture, to be teased and called a "Mommy's boy" by the father or an older male sibling. The great majority of children, however, spontaneously begin to identify more strongly with the parent of the same sex when they clearly see traits similar to their own (Kohlberg 1966). This is not to say that identification strictly follows sexual lines. A child does not suddenly begin identifying with one parent to the exclusion of the other. On the contrary, a boy, although he is thoroughly masculine and identifies strongly with his father, also may retain a substantial identification with his mother. For example, a burly fullback who mashes his opponents on the gridiron may raise African violets for enjoyment as his mother did. Similarly, a young woman who clearly feels a strong identification with her mother may take greater pleasure in working with a hammer and saw than in knitting or cooking.

In this rather abstract analysis of the process of identification, we need to be reminded of Heinz Werner's point that in the beginning the child does not clearly distinguish between himself and the other person. The relationship between himself and another is undifferentiated. It is out of this lack of separateness that identification is gradually delineated.

It follows, therefore, that identification depends on the child's increasing internal cognitive organization as well as on the adult's attractiveness and similarity. The child's perceptions must be sufficiently organized so that he will have begun separating himself from other people and objects in the world. Therefore, which adults the child identifies with depends on his own self-concept. He assimilates other models into his own behavior in terms of how he himself is constituted.

A Continuing Process

Identification is a continuing process. Toddlers notice and frequently comment on the things they have in common with their parent models. The girl notices that her dime-store ring is "just like Mommy's" or that her dress or raincoat resembles her mother's. The boy observes that he now has trouser cuffs or sneakers or a haircut similar to his father's. The sense of identity with his parent is further strengthened when others tell him that he resembles that parent. Elders, for example, may remark, "You're just like your daddy," or "You're the image of your mother." As the child grows and develops, these points of identity become deeply embedded in his personality; that is, the child retains the sense of identity with the parent while letting fall by the wayside the hairdo or sneakers that earlier provided the identification. Gradually, the child's imitative behaviors become so much a part of his personality that they are involuntary and reflexive. Over the years, the child continues to identify, picking up parental attitudes, fears, and mannerisms that range from ways of speaking and walking to ways of drinking from a cup.

Identification behavior may involve more than simple reproduction of a parent's acts. A child, even a young toddler, will exaggerate and caricature his parents' roles as he expresses such feelings as hostility, dependency, and aggression in his fantasies. Of course, the expression of mocking imitation is common in older children. In these stages, such flamboyant caricaturing is known by a more homely name—"plain sass."

Although for a considerable time—during the toddler period, particularly—the child chooses his parents as his primary models, he later may look to persons outside his family circle. His ability to assimilate more and more models into his behavior grows as his internal organization becomes more firm and articulate. At the same time, he makes wider social contacts in nursery school or on his block, with grandparents or favorite uncles. Of course, to become the child's model, these individuals, too, must be people whom he both admires and is similar to in some way. Thus, the older child may reflect a complex of many models, though one or two models tend to hold dominant positions in the child's pantheon of admirable adults.

The process of identification, according to the social learning theory we have been examining, is preceded by dependency. Unless the child finds dependency on the parent or another adult rewarding, he will find no motive for identification. We have seen that maternal restrictiveness, as measured in the Fels study, tends to foster overdependency. We shall now take a more detailed look at the subject of dependency.

Dependency

Need for the Adult

Every child has feelings of dependency. These arise out of his earlier reliance on adults for the basic assistance to sustain his life. Dependency feelings begin forming at the moment of birth. As an infant, the individual is completely dependent on others for his very survival. Without food, warmth, and his mother's general care, the infant would quickly die. The infant's needs and his mother's responses, especially during the first year of life, create a dependency bond between them. This emotional link continues to bind the child to the parent throughout childhood, though in progressively diminishing degrees.

As the child matures, his parents encourage him to take over many of the sustaining activities they have performed in the past. They teach him to feed himself, to drink from a cup, to use a toilet, to wash and dress himself. Performing all these behaviors increases the child's sense of his individuality and autonomy. At the same time, the toddler is trying out many of his own independent behaviors as a result of maturational readiness and his growing sense of capability. On the surface, the toddler often seems to be rapidly shedding his infant's dependency. Later in this chapter we shall see how the toddler struggles vigorously to assert his separateness from his parents and to establish his autonomy. At the same time, however, he remains deeply dependent, as shown in his frequent "babyish" demands for cuddling or reassurance. It is typical of this transitional toddler stage for an assertive, bold, or independent behavior often to be followed immediately by a complete reversion to the infantile desire to be held closely, consoled, and generally shielded from a world that is suddenly and mysteriously overwhelming. For example, the 4-year-old girl may serve her adult guests a snack, meticulously balancing a tray of cookies and juice mugs. Having executed this demanding and "grown-up" task, she may immediately climb into her mother's lap. Such fluctuations between independent and dependent behaviors are extremely common among toddlers, for the adoption of mature habits is not an overnight process. It is a gradual development of skill and confidence, in essence a fluctuating process that produces peaks and valleys of accomplishment.

Expression of Dependency in Toddlers

Children in their third and fourth years express their dependency in a variety of ways. Common dependent behaviors are negative at-

Figure 9.2 As the toddler asserts his independence from adults, at the same time he continues to need cuddling and reassurance from a warm parent. (Leonard Freed—Magnum)

tention-seeking, positive attention-seeking, approval-seeking, help-seeking, proximity-seeking, and physical contact-seeking. A child who is considered highly dependent, however, will not necessarily exhibit all of these behaviors. One study of dependency in preschool girls found that positive attention-seeking, approval-seeking, and help-seeking correlated significantly with one another in the same child. Similarly, proximity-seeking and physical contact-seeking correlated with each other; however, the first group of behaviors did not correlate with the second (Rosenthal 1965). Thus, a child may express his dependency in several ways, but these channels will probably fall into a distinct category, such as verbal contact as opposed to physical contact. He may, for example, desire an encouraging word or approval from his mother but have no need for a hug.

The frequency of various dependent and independent behaviors changes in the average child as he grows older. A comparison of specific behaviors of a group of 2-year-olds and a group of 4-year-olds has shown a decrease in some and an increase in others (Heathers 1955). Table 9.2 shows the difference in the frequency with which each dependent and independent behavior occurred in the two age groups. The older children simultaneously displayed less dependent teacher-oriented behavior and more social interaction with other children. While some of the interaction with peers was dependent in nature, such as seeking attention or approval from another child, much of it (structuring another child's play or resisting a peer's interference or aggression) demonstrated independence. Independence also is indicated by the decrease in the subject's interference in another's play. This development means that the older child no longer depends on interfering action, which is a negative way of seeking attention.

A child's display of a dependency behavior, however, may not mean that there is a general state of dependency in the child. That is, a child who is constantly clamoring for attention may appear to be dependent because he is exhibiting attention-seeking, a standard dependency behavior. However, this "symptom" could be complete-

PERSONALITY AND SOCIAL DEVELOPMENT 263

Table 9.2 Change with Age in Dependence and Independence Behavior, and in Type of Play Activities

Source: Abridged from G. Heathers. Emotional dependence and independence in nursery-school play. *J. genet. Psychol.*, 1955, 87, 37–58.

	Direction of Change from Age 2 to 4–5
Clings to or seeks affection from teacher	Decrease
Clings to or seeks affection from child	Decrease
Seeks attention or approval from teacher	Decrease
Seeks attention or approval from child	Increase
Ignores stimuli from teacher	Increase
Ignores stimuli from child	Increase
Plays alone intently	Increase
Structures child's play	Increase
Interferes with child's play	Decrease
Resists child's interference or aggression	Increase
Not playing	Decrease
Alone play	Decrease
Social play	Increase
Social interaction with children	Increase

ly misleading. It is possible that the child is at the same time quite independent in his other actions, but also is starved for attention or feedback. Whether or not a child displays general or quite specific dependency behavior hinges substantially on how his parents react to both his dependency advances toward them and his own displays of independence. Parents often differ markedly in their handling of each type of behavior. Furthermore, since dependence and independence are empirically separate behaviors, it is possible for a child to have high scores on both dependent and independent behavior, or low scores on both. The complexity of such an apparently simple variable, the difference between specific dependency and general dependency, is typical of the hazards in the study of human behavior.

Parental Influences on Dependency

RESTRICTIVENESS. Since every child is an individual with a different developmental history and a unique relationship with a unique set of parents, each feels and expresses a different degree of dependency. As we saw in our discussion of the Fels study, one determinant of the degree of a child's dependency can be the extent of his mother's restrictiveness. In that study, a high degree of parental control was generally linked to high dependency, and this relationship has been found in other studies as well (Watson 1957; Faigin 1958; Winder and Rau 1962). The Fels study also indicated that restrictiveness over a longer period has more lasting effects on the child. Some boys in the Fels sample who were restricted for the first three years of life became independent adults; however, most boys whose mothers continued to be restrictive through age 6 developed into dependent adults. Girls presented a different pattern. Maternal restrictiveness was associated with consistent dependency in girls, not only throughout childhood, but also into adulthood (Kagan and Moss 1962).

A study of dependency in boys found two distinct forms of this behavior in children whose mothers were overprotective and restrictive (Levy 1943). The boys were either passively dependent, letting their mothers direct them almost completely, or they were demandingly dependent on their mothers, constantly seeking attention and help, even with simple tasks.

PERMISSIVENESS. Since the polar opposite of restrictiveness is permissiveness, we might expect permissiveness to produce independence. Studies do show that permissive parents tend to raise children who are more independent. However, it is important to specify what is meant by permissive parental behavior. Simple indifference to a child is sometimes mistaken for permissiveness. It is true that such a neglected child often will not be dependent on adults—witness the extreme example of many children who lead a street life with a gang of their peers. Independent though he may appear, such a child often becomes dependent on his peers, conforming slavishly to their habits, talk, dress, and even to their hair styles.

While such peer-dependence is common in parentally neglected children, parents who combine permissiveness with guidance, trust, and understanding of their child's competence are likely to raise children who are independent of their peers as well as their parents. The important point is the quality of the permissiveness. Research has provided evidence of some of the parental behaviors that, along with permissiveness, correlate with independence in preschool children. One study reported that autonomy in male toddlers correlates with consistent discipline, high maturity demands, encouragement of independent contact, reasoning to gain obedience, and little restrictiveness or use of force. The same study showed that girls are more likely to develop autonomy when their parents make high socialization demands, use little force but are punitive, and when the parents, rather than the girl, initiate control of behavior (Baumrind and Black 1967). As these parental behaviors make clear, the permissiveness practiced by these parents was constructive and demanding, rather than indifferent or neglectful.

WARMTH. It is often heard that a mother's warmth and affection tend to increase the child's dependency on her. A number of studies, however, have found no relationship between warmth and dependency (Finney 1961; Cairns 1962; Baumrind and Black 1967; Sears et al. 1953, 1957, 1965; Siegelman 1966). Other studies indicate an inverse relationship between maternal warmth and dependency. In one of these experiments, 40 boys and girls of nursery school age were observed in two sessions with their parents (Hatfield, Ferguson, Rau, and Alpert 1967). Potential stress situations similar to possible home situations were contrived. In one session, for example, the mother was given a questionnaire, requiring her concentration, while her child was told to play with crayons nearby. Meanwhile, the dependency behavior of the child was observed through a one-way mirror. Information on the everyday relationship with the child was supplied by the mother's answers to the questionnaire. This information, assumed to reflect the warmth of the parent–child relationship, was correlated with the child's observed independence. Results showed that for both boys and girls, maternal warmth was related to independence, not dependence.

HOSTILITY. While warmth does not seem to induce dependency, its opposite trait, hostility, does. An experiment with over 100 children of nursery school age points to this link between parental hostility and child dependency (Marshall 1961). The parents of these children filled out a questionnaire designed to measure their hostility. For example, the answers to some questions indicated how the parents felt about avoidance of communication, suppression of sexuality, and the ascendance of the parent. Results showed that

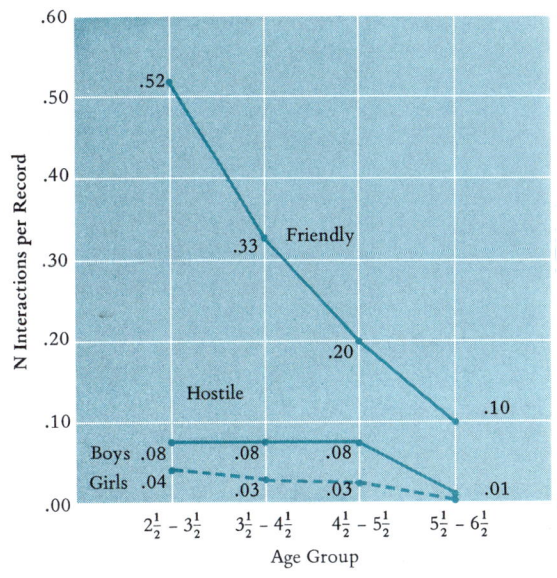

Figure 9.3 Mean number of all friendly interactions (association + friendly approach + conversation) and mean number of hostile interactions between children and teachers per 2-minute observation record for each age group. The youngest children had significantly more interactions with teachers than the oldest children. (From H. R. Marshall. Relations between home experiences and children's use of language in play interactions with peers. *Psychol. Monogr.*, 1961, 75, No. 5, 53.)

parents who scored high in hostility toward, or rejection of, their children had offspring who were very dependent on other adults, as indicated by observation. The children exhibited their dependence by frequently asking their teachers for help and seeking their approval. This relationship between hostility and dependency recalls the findings of the Fels study, mentioned earlier, that maternal hostility often correlates with restrictiveness, which also tends to produce dependency.

REINFORCEMENT. Based on what is known about reinforcement's role in the learning process, parental rewards or punishments also would seem to be determinants of dependency in the child. The mother who rewards her 4-year-old son for constantly asking to be fed by her, while scolding him for exploring the park's new "monkey bars," should produce a child who prefers dependence. His conditioning, it is supposed, will have taught him that dependence evokes a reward from his mother. Data supporting this theory have been drawn from studies of institutionalized children who were denied warmth and nurturance from birth. In addition, because of general institutional conditions, these children very seldom were rewarded for showing dependent behavior—for example, crying when they are hungry or need a diaper change. As a consequence, the children displayed such dependent behavior infrequently. From this data we can see that dependency seems rooted in early situations in which another person regularly satisfies the needs of the infant—in other words, rewards his dependent behavior.

In another study of dependency and reinforcement, mothers who initially punished a child for being dependent, but finally gratified him, produced the most dependent children (Sears, Maccoby, and Levin 1957). For example, a boy may approach his busy mother and ask her to tie his shoe. She reacts with irritation ("You're old enough to tie your own shoe," or "Don't bother me now!"), but she finally relents and ties the shoe. According to the study, this child is torn by conflict whenever he feels he has to call on his mother. Because of his experience with her, he expects his need will be satisfied. However, he also knows that his mother first will be angry with him, and this knowledge gives rise to anxiety. So his dependent gestures have the dual effect of making him anticipatory of gratification and at the same time anxious, thus increasing his general state of arousal.

SEX DIFFERENCES. The sex of the child, as we have seen in earlier chapters, tends to cause a mother to interact in certain ways with her child; for instance, a mother usually will vocalize more with a female infant. Other early differences in maternal treatment, based on the child's sex, may also have certain influences on the child's degree of dependence on her. Reflecting general cultural values, a mother may encourage, or at least tolerate, more independent behavior in a male child while discouraging similar activity in a female child. Or on the other hand, dependency behavior in boys is usually frowned upon but is actively rewarded in girls. As a result, greater dependency among girls has been widely observed. Nursery school teachers, for example, report that girls exhibit much more dependency behavior than boys do in the toddler and later preschool years (Emmerich 1966). Similarly, an experiment showed that in play situations, girls between 3 and 8 years approached adults for help more often than boys did (Crandall and Rabson 1960). Studies also have demonstrated that from age 3 to 14, dependency behavior is more stable in girls than in boys (Kagan and Moss 1960, 1962). Thus, a girl who is dependent as a 4-year-old toddler probably will remain dependent into puberty. Predicting a boy's dependency in childhood and at the same stage of adolescence is not so easy. The girl's more stable dependency seems to be prompted by our society's casting of the female in a generally dependent role. Similarly, the boy's less extended dependency period, or rather more inconsistent display of dependency, seems due to his opposite sex-determined role—the discouragement of his dependency by parents and peers as well as the encouragement that he be an independent male.

Dependence and Learning

Parents often exploit the dependency feelings of their toddlers when they want the children to learn a behavior of some kind. Understandably, the more dependent a child is, the more eager he will be to comply with their wishes. In a study of learning by means of dependency motivation, a female researcher provided constant comfort and assistance to one group of preschool children. A second group received similar attention for a while and then the researcher left them—an action expected to increase the child's desire for companionship and aid. At this point, all the children were presented with a simple task, the performance of which elicited praise from the researcher. The second group, which had been deprived of its nurturant companion, mastered the task before the first group, apparently because of their stronger motivation to earn the researcher's praise. In general, the investigators found that children who were very dependent worked more industriously at the trial task than children who had a fair degree of independence (Hartup 1958).

In this same experiment, as in learning through imitation (see Chapter 2), the sex of the researcher proved to be a significant factor in determining how fast a child performed the task. Boys performed best when they had a female nurturant figure who encouraged and rewarded them, and toddler girls responded best to a nurturant male. It may be argued that each sex finds the opposite sex a more arousing stimulus, or simply more rewarding.

In summing up our account of dependence, several separate elements must be kept in mind. First, the reinforcement of dependency is, in the early stages of life, a key to the child's identification with his parents and to the continuance of an element of dependency as a healthy component in subsequent personality. Second, some child-rearing methods (restriction and hostility) appear to maintain the more infantile types of dependency, while others (permissiveness, warmth, and guidance) are associated with the growth of healthy independence.

From this account of the child's basic dependency on his parents and the parental behaviors that lead to dependence or independence, we now move to the next step in the development of the child's personality and social behavior—the establishment of his conscience. Just as parental influences largely determine the degree of dependency in the child, so, too, does the parent play a significant role in developing his conscience, which essentially is the child's incorporation of his parents' morals and strictures as his own.

Conscience

As a toddler the child is forming internal structures that determine his external behavior. One of these internal structures is his *conscience*, which is a set of moral values and standards of behavior that the child attempts to adhere to independent of external enforcement. Another name for conscience is Freud's term, the *superego*. Both terms refer to an internal monitor that demands conformity to certain standards of behavior. Conscience does not concern itself solely with such clear-cut acts as lying or cheating. More subtle responses and attitudes also fall under the control of conscience—such as those linked to the well-being of others, acts of kindness or mercy, or consideration of the rights of others.

Development of Conscience

A widely held theory regarding the development of conscience is that conscience arises through the child's identification with his parental models. Thus, a child identifying with a parent will implicitly adopt the parent's behavior standards just as he may adopt the parent's manner of speaking. Incorporation of a parent's moral standards creates one more link that secures the child's identification with his parent. When he has internalized his parent's standards, the child begins to take over as his own moral guide. The newly created conscience becomes the parent *in absentia*. When the child does something that his parents would disapprove of or punish him for, the child now punishes himself—usually by means of the relentless reprimand of a guilty conscience (Whiting and Child 1953).

It seems likely, however, that the human conscience develops as a result of other processes besides identification alone, such as, for example, the child's ability to reason about causes and effects. His understanding of the reasons for behavior is critical in his ability to make moral judgments. We shall see this theory developed in greater detail in our discussion of morality in older children in Chapter 12.

Parental Effects on Conscience

The warmth of the parent–child relationship and the methods a parent uses to express disapproval and to punish unwanted behavior will affect the formation of the child's conscience. One survey of the literature of conscience development identifies the effects of certain common modes of discipline, such as power assertion, love withdrawal, induction, and affection (Hoffman 1954). The parent's assertion of power to discipline the child is considered the enforcement of rules by exploiting physical strength or control over material objects the child may desire. Withdrawal of love is an equally direct but nonphysical expression of the parent's disapproval or anger. Induction is the method of achieving discipline by giving a child reasons or explanations why a certain behavior is asked of him. Finally, affection—while not a mode of discipline—is a condition that affects adoption of parental standards. The child of affectionate parents will tend to emulate his parents and internalize their judgments and punishments of transgressions.

These types of discipline have been correlated with the level of conscience displayed by children whose parents were rated according to the method of discipline they most often used (Hoffman 1954). The child's personal orientation toward transgressions was the first measure of his conscience. One child may see an act as taboo because of its consequences—"You go to jail for doing that." This means his orientation is external. Another child may refrain from an act for internal reasons: "You did wrong—your father trusted you." The conscience with more internalized codes is regarded as more developed. Guilt intensity was the second measure of conscience. Guilt was measured by asking the child to make up the conclusion for a story in which a fictional child of the same age and sex had transgressed. It was assumed that a child with a well-developed conscience would identify with the fictional child and express a high degree of vicarious guilt. Resistance to temptation was the third method of assessing conscience. In this measurement, a child was assured that no one would know his response; he then was tempted to break a rule to win a prize. If he resisted breaking the rule, he was considered to have a highly developed conscience. The fourth and most widely used measure of conscience was the subject's confession and his acceptance of blame. These responses were assessed through such admittedly imperfect means as parents' reports of child behavior and the child's fantasy during experimental doll play.

Correlations of parental behaviors and the consequences for moral development showed most clearly that the frequent use of power assertion by the mother is associated with weak conscience development. In contrast, induction (reasoning and explanation) and affection were associated with advanced moral development. Love withdrawal was not consistently related to either weak or strong moral development. This lack of correlation, in contrast to induction's positive correlation with strong moral development, highlights the difference between the two parental behaviors. This finding seems to support Kohlberg's general contention that the greater part of morality is reasoning (see Chapter 12).

In the correlations, we saw that power assertion was not related to advanced moral development, whereas affection was. Since power-assertive parents have been shown to be "cold" or less affectionate (Hoffman and Saltzstein 1967), the next logical question is, would power assertion produce moral development if it were exercised in an affectionate atmosphere? In one study, 40 boys were given two 10-minute periods of play and rewarding contact with an experimenter on two successive days. Another 40 boys were placed in the same situation, but in their sessions the experimenter sat still and aloof. Then all the children were put into a room and subjected to various "punishments"—loud noises, for example—that kept them from playing with certain attractive toys. After a period of such exposure, they were left alone with the toys in the playroom for 15 minutes and their behavior was observed. Results showed that despite the "punishment," which would be expected to produce a weak conscience, the children who had had rewarding contact with the experimenter showed greater resistance to the temptation of playing with the toys than the children who had been denied such contacts (Parke and Walters 1967).

The results of this study would seem to support the contention that power assertion applied in an affectionate atmosphere will further moral development. While such positive notes are clearly sounded in this study, other interpretations of the study have questioned this contention. At this point in research, it is still the connection between parental reasoning and a child's advanced moral development that receives the strongest confirmation.

Just as conscience is generally taken as a measure of the child's identification with his parent, evidence now seems to show that aggression—which we shall examine next—also is strongly related to identification. As the child acquires qualities of the parental model, he adopts certain modes of expressing aggression as well. The parent's overall attitudes regarding aggression, as well as his own aggressive acts, are likely to become a part of the child's personality as he models himself after his parent.

Aggression

Aggression appears to have become an almost universal element in human behavior. This common tendency to injure or disturb another person, animal, or object begins to develop early in life. In the form of rage, it is noticeable in the infant's "temper tantrums." By 3 or 4 years of age, aggression has become more specific and clearly focused—as well as more common. It can take an infinite number of forms, some overt and some so subtle that even the aggressor often will not recognize his intent to cause injury or anxiety. For example, a toddler playing in his sandbox may become peeved with a playmate and strike him with a plastic shovel, clearly an overt act. On the other hand, a child whose mother is extremely neat and clean may aggress against his parent unwittingly by carelessly spilling food at every opportunity. Only on an unconscious level may the child sense that his carelessness disturbs his mother. Thus, the concept of aggression covers a wide range of behavior, from the most deliberate and overt to the more unwitting or unconscious.

Determinants of Aggression

There are several theories regarding the basic determinants of aggression. Each one emphasizes, to varying degrees, the importance of instinctual, constitutional, or social factors. The current popular view—that man's aggression is biologically based, or instinctual—is an outgrowth of conclusions drawn from subhuman animal studies. Such studies of the behavior of animals in their natural surroundings have concluded that in most species, aggression is an innate behavior (Ardrey 1966; Eibl-Eibesfeldt 1961; Lorenz 1966). Lorenz generalized this concept of natural aggression to apply to man as well (Lorenz 1966). He and other ethologists have maintained that particular events or stimuli invariably evoke various instinctive aggressions in the different species of animals. While this may be true of nonhuman animal behavior, it is risky to assume that the pattern applies to human behavior as well. It is known, for instance, that aggressive behavior varies markedly from species to species among animals. It is quite likely, therefore, that significant genetic differences also separate man's aggression from that of other species.

John P. Scott, an American psychologist, has attacked the popularized notion that man's aggression is rooted in his instinct as "a bloodthirsty carnivore":

Social fighting has most probably been evolved from defensive reactions to injury. Such reactions are almost universal and are adaptive against attacks by predators as well as against accidental injury by members of the same species. Starting at this point, the evolution of social fighting has proceeded independently in different species, with the result that fighting serves a variety of social functions. The most general of these functions is the regulation of social space, but agonistic [fighting] behavior may also regulate the availability of mates, as in deer and sage grouse; the division of food in dogs and wolves but not in mice; and the availability of breeding territories in many species of birds. (Scott 1970)

Therefore, Scott goes on to say,

> the hypothesis that man fights man because he is by nature a bloodthirsty carnivore is false. In carnivores the patterns of behavior involved in predation are distinctly different from those involved in social fighting, and agonistic behavior plays just as prominent a part in strictly herbivorous animals as it does in carnivorous ones. (Scott 1970)

Scott maintains that to discover the determinants and social functions of fighting in the human species, the only proper subject for study is not other animals, but man himself: "It is possible that man fights for any or all of the reasons that are found in other animal societies, and highly likely that other reasons are peculiar to human beings alone" (Scott 1970).

Scott's profile of human aggression refutes the concept of man as an aggressive brute among animals that are different only in their lower intelligence and adaptiveness. In effect, Scott says that man has used aggression because he has found it a useful social behavior. It brings in goods, slaves, and wealth (through raids and pillaging) and removes obstacles to goals quickly — whether the aggression used is a full-scale war or a verbally aggressive argument. From these effective actions, man has learned the benefits of aggressive behavior in certain circumstances. And this implies prophetically and optimistically enough that he can just as readily learn to avoid aggression if it is clearly not to his benefit. Man is not possessed by it. Yet he is not likely to give it up unless it is precluded by alternative strategies of reward.

Although it is questionable that man's aggressive drives are solely determined by his instinct, the biological constitution of the individual may play a significant role in his aggressive behavior. For example, evidence points out that the males of many animal species are more aggressive than the females. Furthermore, if females receive doses of male hormones they display aggressive behavior which resembles that of the male. In humans, most studies of young children conclude that aggression — and especially overt physical aggression — is more common among boys.

A child's constitution also includes his level of activity, which may vary from phlegmatic to hyperactive. Research has positively correlated activity level to frequency of aggression (Patterson, Littman, and Bricker 1967). Greater activity, it would seem, increases the child's contact with his environment and leads to more occasions when aggressive behavior will occur.

Social factors are important modifiers of aggression. One study, for example, showed that children rewarded for verbal aggression against an object will be not only verbally, but also physically, aggressive in a subsequent provocative situation (Bandura and Walters 1963). The effects of permissiveness are similar, leading to an increase in aggression (Hollenberg and Sperry 1950). On the other hand, parental disapproval seems to dampen aggressive behavior quickly. Parents' use of reasoning and affection also seems to induce internal control of aggression by the child, just as it tends to develop a strong conscience in the child, as we saw earlier.

The degree of frustration is another factor operative in the socialization of aggression. The level of frustration experienced in the same situation and leading to aggression can vary greatly among individuals. For example, a child who is heavily dependent on his mother will be more frustrated by her absence than a more independent child, and is likely to exhibit more aggressive behavior as a result of that separation. Similarly, some individuals can tolerate a substantial amount of frustration, while others explode in verbal or physical aggression at the slightest obstacles to their goals. The last major socializing factor to affect aggressive behavior is the behavior of the models with whom children identify. As we saw in Chapter 2 on learning and development, a child can learn to be aggressive or to inhibit his aggression by imitating an adult. Thus, the behavior of adults around a child is important in assessing the degree and form of aggression the child will display. The constitutional and social factors that affect the child's aggressiveness will be discussed in greater detail after we examine what may provoke his aggression and the forms this aggression may take.

Aggression in the Child

Aggressive behavior during the toddler years commonly arises as a result of the pressures inherent in the socialization processes he is subjected to at this time. For example, in the third year, severe toilet training or other obedience demands might result in temper tantrums or outbursts of verbal aggression toward parents. In the fourth year, rows with playmates begin to emerge as occasions for aggressive speech or behavior. As he begins to interact more with his peers, he is more likely to engage in conflict with them. This pattern of social aggression becomes a greater source of aggression as the child matures. Such aggressive behaviors as gossip, or the adroit "put-down," eventually surface in the speech of adolescents and often persist, in refined states, throughout adulthood. Like the causes of aggression, the ways in which the child expresses his aggression change as he matures. Temper tantrums are most common in children 2 years old and younger, although they remain a significant aggressive expression until the end of the third year. Between 2 and 4, verbal aggression increases, a reflection of developing speech abilities. While temper tantrums decline after age 3, efforts to gain verbal or physical revenge for immediate injuries increase with age. Thus, the infant's former diffuse rage at discomfort now focuses more closely as he seems to be developing a more clearly directed aggressive drive (Goodenough 1931).

STABILITY OF AGGRESSION LEVEL. An assessment of the stability of aggressiveness requires a study spanning a considerable number of years. Though such long-range studies are rare, two are available and both indicate a substantial stability in aggressive expression over a number of years. Tuddenham (1959) found a striking correlation between the ratings of aggressive motivation in a group of male adolescents and subsequent interview ratings of their aggression when they were approximately 33 years old.

Another study, extending and analyzing the data from the Fels Institute's longitudinal examination of human behavior, found that males maintained more stable aggressive behavior than females (Kagan and Moss 1962). Aggression in the Fels subjects was rated in four age groups: birth to 3 years, 3 to 6, 6 to 10, and 10 to 14. Then, ratings taken on 71 of the 89 subjects as young adults were compared with the earlier ratings. Correlations between the age periods indicated a fairly stable pattern of aggression manifestations. For example, for the first 14 years physical aggression toward peers was very stable. Interestingly, this sort of aggression was so negligible between the ages of 10 and 14 that the Fels study did not even rate the manifestation. However, a significant level of stability also was maintained by three more manifestations: dominance, competitiveness, and indirect aggression toward peers. In sum, the study using the early Fels data showed a

Table 9.3 Ratings for Aggressive Behavior in Males and Females for a Period of 14 Years*

Child Variable	Age	Males	Females	Total
Aggression to mother	0–3	.19	.11	.14
	3–6	.25	.00	.15
	6–10	.32	.09	.24
	10–14	.47	.13	.31
Physical aggression to peers	0–3	−.06	−.57	−.27
	3–6	.15	−.51	−.06
	6–10	.02	.23	.10
Indirect aggression to peers	0–3	.44	−.10	.11
	3–6	.30	.00	.16
	6–10	.27	.27	.26
	10–14	.31	.15	.28
Behavioral disorganization	0–3	.28	−.21	.03
	3–6	.12	.05	.13
	6–10	.37	.03	.22
	10–14	.51	.09	.34
Conformity	0–3	−.29	.01	−.15
	3–6	−.11	.05	−.04
	6–10	−.26	−.11	−.20
	10–14	−.24	.02	−.13
Dominance	3–6	.30	−.10	.06
	6–10	.44	.29	.37
	10–14	.48	.17	.37
Competitiveness	3–6	.17	−.37	−.11
	6–10	.33	−.12	.11
	10–14	.34	−.24	.10

*Note in the table that a fairly stable pattern between age periods is evident.
Source: J. Kagan and H. Moss. *Birth to maturity: A study in psychological development.* New York: Wiley, 1962. P. 96.

substantial stability in several aggressive behaviors over a broad time span. Early aggressive dispositions, particularly when manifested between 3 and 6 years of age, carry forward into the child's adolescence. A number of the childhood aggressions have their correlatives in adult aggression. Male children who were aggressive toward their mothers, in addition to displaying disorganized behavior between 6 and 14, yielded adult ratings showing revenge, anger arousal, and competitive behavior.

For girls, the comparison of Fels childhood data and adult aggression ratings produced less stable and more complicated correlations. Physical aggression toward peers by girls under 6 did not correlate with their adult competitiveness; after the age of 6, the girls' physical aggressive behavior showed a negative correlation with aggression anxiety. The changing pattern of aggression in girls seemed to reflect the fact that their early aggressive behavior (before age 6) is later thwarted, and that this inhibition produces anxiety and conflict. In males, on the other hand, early physical aggression is deemed the correct behavior for their sexual role. While we have thus attempted to explain the different degrees of aggression stability between boys and girls in terms of sex roles, other explanations have been offered. For example, the differences also have been attributed to constitutional factors. Boys are generally more muscular and less sensitive to pain than girls. This might account for the development of more physical aggression in boys than in girls.

Frustration and Aggression

It is commonly thought that frustration is the most common antecedent of aggression. The woman who missed an appointment as she waited for her husband, says to her friend: "I was so frustrated I could have killed him." While the woman probably was exaggerating the degree of aggression she felt toward her husband, this is basically the kind of frustration-aggression relationship that has been widely assumed by investigators; that is, frustration followed by aggression. Although there is no commonly accepted definition of frustration, most investigators view as frustrating those experiences or events that inhibit a person's movement toward a goal, undermine his self-regard, or create conflicts between incompatible responses. Apparently, the link between the removal of frustration and the aggressive act (and its frequent by-product, the infliction of pain on another) is learned through repeated trials. Although there is little empirical evidence to support this view, it is likely that the child quickly learns from experience and observation that aggressive acts can eliminate many sources of frustration (Feshbach 1964).

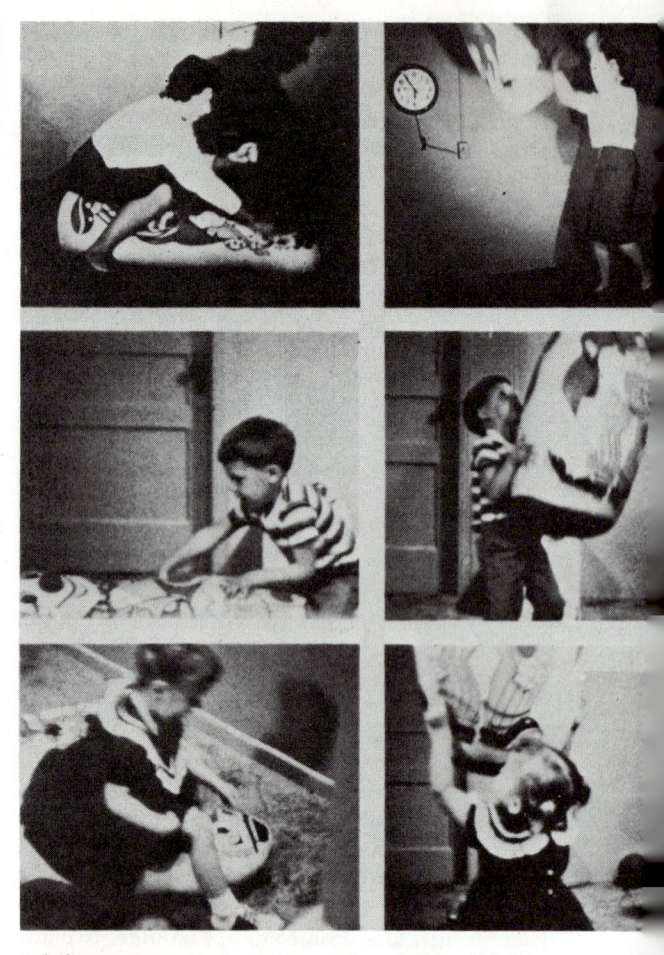

MODEL THEORY OF AGGRESSION. Other views of aggression hold that frustration is not a necessary antecedent to aggression. Some feel that a child's exposure to an aggressive model will, in itself, increase the child's aggressive responses.

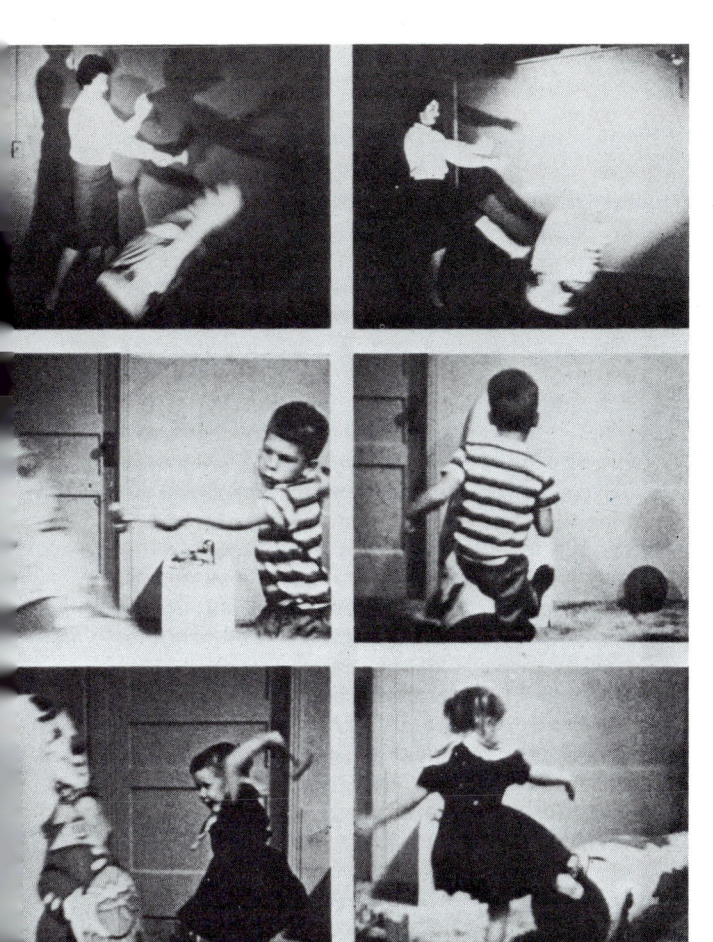

Figure 9.4 Photographs of the film shown to children of the imitation of aggressive behavior of an adult model. (From A. Bandura, D. Ross, and S. A. Ross. Imitation of film-mediated aggressive models. *J. abnorm. soc. Psychol.*, 1963, 66, 8.)

This argument recalls our discussion, in Chapter 2, of learning through imitation of an adult model. There, we reviewed a study in which three groups of preschool children saw three versions of adult aggression. The first saw a live adult abuse an inflated doll. The second saw a film of the same aggression, and the third saw a cartoon character, also on film, abuse the doll. After viewing these portrayals of the same aggression, the experimenters mildly frustrated these three groups, as well as a control group who had not witnessed any aggressive acts in the experiment. They then presented them all with an inflated doll. The children who had observed all three portrayals of aggression attacked the doll much more vigorously than the control group did (Bandura, Ross, and Ross 1963). In addition to the learned aggressive behaviors, children exposed to an aggressive model will perform new acts of aggression which were not previously demonstrated. Thus, the modeled aggression also can be generalized to other aggressive acts.

While a child's exposure to an aggressive model clearly increases his aggressive behavior regardless of earlier frustrations, we are still missing an important element in the aggression pattern—motivation. The children in this experiment beat up the inflated doll because they were "put up to the job." They were not frustrated by the doll, nor did they want to hurt it because of any feelings of revenge or retaliation, which are common motives at this age. The circumstances sim-

PERSONALITY AND SOCIAL DEVELOPMENT 273

ply were established in such a way as to take advantage of the child's natural drive to imitate an adult while expressing a mild frustration. Thus, though the model study tells us aggression will be increased when an adult provides a model for the behavior, it does not tell us about the child's internal motivation to commit acts of aggression in unconditioned situations in daily life. The frustration-aggression theory, on the other hand, gives us a sounder basis for understanding the motivation behind aggressive acts.

SOURCES OF FRUSTRATION. While generally all frustration may be said to arise from the blocking of a path to a goal, the intensity or level of all frustration is not necessarily the same. It usually is assumed that the intensity of the frustration is determined by the drive-instigated behavior that is being thwarted. The denial of ice cream to a child who was very hungry would produce more intense and more prolonged frustration than it would for a child who simply expressed a passing interest in ice cream after a succession of other treats.

The barriers that create frustration may be external or internal. A high wall, a steep stairway, or an unwieldy fork may be external blocks to the satisfaction of a child's drives. Internally, his own feelings of inadequacy or anxiety may thwart achievement of his goals. For example, a child may doubt his skills at dressing himself, or he may experience fear about climbing to the top of the playground slide. Either feeling may inhibit the achievement of a particular goal. Barriers to goals also may arise from internal conflicts between two responses that are incompatible. For example, a boy is caught out in the rain. His mother has just warned him not to stay out if it rains, yet she has also told him not to ring the doorbell and wake the baby. The two admonitions fight each other, preventing action and building frustration.

While there is support for the theory that the frustration level depends on the goal that is thwarted, evidence of intense frustration in children has not been produced experimentally. The lack of experimental situations that produce dramatic frustration in children is the result of ethical considerations: substantial pain or anxiety usually is required to elicit dramatic frustration. Even tests employing fairly mild frustrations have met resistance from humane adults (Frederickson 1942). Because of these restrictions—however admirable or valid they may be—we are left with low-frustration experiments that produce conflicting evidence about the aggression-provoking effects of frustration. Some positive evidence has emerged, however, from a study in which nursery school children were repeatedly frustrated at play (Otis and McCandless 1955). Eight times, a child and an experimenter pushed model cars toward each other and reached an impasse; the child's desire to continue down the length of the road was blocked each time. Over the last four trials, the child's dominant-aggressive responses increased, suggesting that the growth in aggression was prompted by continued frustration.

Other studies, however, seem to deny that increased frustration produces increased aggression. In one such study, nursery school children again were repeatedly frustrated (Jegard and Walters 1960). Then they were presented with an inflated toy punching bag on which to vent their frustrations. Although the investigator reported that several children showed anger at the repeated frustrations, he also reported that the frustrated children punched the inflated toy no more than they had in a previous trial run that had assessed the intensity of their unprovoked punching aggression. Thus, though it is difficult to state conclusively that increased frustration produces increased aggression, enough evidence does exist to make the correlation a strong probability.

REGRESSION IN RESPONSE TO FRUSTRATION. A common response to frustration is overt aggression, as we have seen, whether the aggression is physical, such as fighting, or verbal, such as quarreling. Another response that may arise from frustration is *regressive* behavior, in which the child reverts to earlier responses he has since surpassed. One important frustration-regression study recorded this type of response in nursery school children (Barker, Dembo, and Lewin 1943). The investigators recorded the children's behavior in two play situations. The first was a situation in which the children were free to play with a set of toys as they wanted. In the second situation, the children were frustrated by being presented with an additional, and even more attractive, toy set, and by then being deprived of the more attractive set after a period of exploration. The more attractive toys were locked behind a screen, out of reach, but plainly visible. The difference in behavior during the two play periods was striking. In the first period of uninhibited play, the children displayed interest and creativity. In the second, frustrating period, their play was substantially less creative and constructive, a sign of regression to earlier behavior. In addition, the children frequently tried to touch and retrieve the screened-off toys, begged to be let out of the room, and behaved aggressively toward both the wire screen and the investigators. It was also noted that the children most severely frustrated—that is, those who most often tried to escape from the room or who most often approached the wire screen—showed the greatest regression in their play. As this last finding indicates, there is a wide range of differences in the degree of frustration that will provoke regressive behavior in individual children.

FRUSTRATION TOLERANCE. The tendency to regress or engage in aggressive acts in the face of frustration is determined by the child's individual level of tolerance for frustration in general. The correlation between frustration tolerance and the tendency to regress has been supported by several studies. In one, a group of preschool children first were given two behavior tests to assess their frustration tolerance (Block and Martin 1955). Then each child was observed separately as he was permitted to play with an attractive toy set and later was thwarted by a wire screen. The results indicated that children shown by the two behavior tests as low in frustration tolerance were the subjects who, when frustrated, displayed the greatest degree of regression to infantile behavior. They did not play constructively with the remaining toys and frequently attacked the wire screen physically. On the other hand, children who tolerated frustration well on the two behavior tests also were able to maintain their constructive play with the toys that were left.

Correlations between frustration tolerance and particular personality traits also were obtained in the Otis and McCandless experiment described earlier. The test children first were classified, according to interviews with their teachers, as "dominant," "in need of power," "acquiescent," or "in need of love." In the course of the experiment with the model cars, the children with the dominant personality traits had lower frustration tolerances and consistently displayed more aggressive behavior. As these two studies demonstrate, then, frustration tolerance in the same situation may vary from individual to individual. Low tolerance for frustration is associated with the dominant personality in the child, and a low tolerance leads to higher levels of aggression and sometimes to regressive behavior.

Variables Affecting Aggressiveness

PUNISHMENT. A child's level of aggressiveness, as we have seen, is determined in part by his individual frustration tolerance; it is influenced, as well, by whether or not his aggressive acts are punished, and the method and degree of that punishment.

One important study found that reprimands temporarily lowered the aggression that nursery school children exhibited in their doll play (Hollenberg and Sperry 1950). In the first of four play periods, the base-line aggressive behavior was recorded. Next, 12 children were separated as the experimental group, and 11 remained as a control group. In the second session, the 12 experimental subjects were verbally punished, or reprimanded, for every aggressive behavior. The control children had complete freedom to aggress in any way. During the third play session, none of the 23 subjects was punished. Despite this reprieve, the 12 subjects who had been punished earlier displayed substantially less aggressive behavior than they had in the first free-play session. In contrast, the control group progressively increased its aggressive behavior from the first through the fourth play periods. In sum, punished aggressive behavior led to reduced aggression, while unhampered aggression led to more aggressive behavior. We should note, however, that though reprimands inhibited the 12 subjects' aggression in the third play session, by the fourth session they were showing as much aggressive behavior as the unpunished control group. Thus, while punishment has an inhibitory effect, the effect does not last long. The reason, incidentally, that verbal and not physical punishment was used in this study (in addition to obvious ethical considerations) is that other evidence has shown that, contrary to popular assumption, physical punishment is not consistently successful in inhibiting aggressive behavior.

The relative success of punishment in quelling aggressive behavior on a short-term basis would seem to indicate a rather direct relationship between punishment and aggression. However, other studies have indicated that the relationship is more complex and depends on the degree of punishment involved. In one, for example, investigators observed the level of aggression among three groups of nursery school children whose mothers had described their own punishments of their children (Sears, Whiting, Nowlis, and Sears 1953). The children in the first group had nonpunitive mothers. Those in the second had mothers who administered mild punishments. In the third group were children who were harshly punished. The results illustrate the complexity of the effects of punishment. The children whose mothers did not punish them displayed few aggressive behaviors; it was assumed this occurred because their permissive mothers rarely thwarted their desires at home, and therefore, the children did not develop pronounced aggressive drives. In contrast, the mildly punished children exhibited the most aggressive behavior. The harshly punished group displayed the fewest aggressions of any of the three groups. The investigators explained their results by noting the effects of various degrees of punishment. Mild punishment merely produces frustration to be expressed in later aggression. When a punishment is harsh, however, it taints the specific punished act and inhibits the child from repeating it. The frustration produced by the harsh punishment will be expressed only in aggressive behavior that is dramatically distinct from the earlier, punished activity (Sears 1961).

Displacement of aggression. When aggressive behaviors are expunged by harsh punishment, the frustration prompting those behaviors remains latent in the child. As suggested above, however, aggressive responses to such frustration may be *displaced* and emerge in other conditions entirely different from the situation in which the initial aggression was harshly punished. Thus, a boy's frustration, heartily punished when expressed as aggression toward a younger sister, may emerge the next day as a swift kick at his dog.

A study of 30 nursery school children showed how the degree of punishment and frustration experienced in the home relates to the amount of aggression expressed in their play with dolls (Sears, Maccoby, and Levin 1957). The subjects' mothers were thoroughly queried about their rules at home, their reactions to the child's needs or desires, and their insistence on their own demands. The mothers' responses furnished data on the amount of frustration the child experienced in his home. Their reported disciplining practices—spankings, threats of punishments and reprimands—provided ratings on home punishment of aggression. Results showed that children from homes in which either frustration or punishment was common exhibited displaced aggression more often and more strongly than children whose homes had low frustration or punishment ratings.

REWARD. While punishment tends to have a short-term inhibiting effect on specific acts of aggression, rewards for such behavior have been shown to have an overall reinforcing effect which increases the child's aggressiveness. Being rewarded for aggression prompts the child to generalize or extend his aggressive behavior into other situations. In one experiment, preschool children were rewarded when they reviled the dolls they were playing with as ''bad'' or made aggressive remarks such as, ''Doll should be spanked'' (Bandura and Walters 1963). A control group was rewarded for verbal responses that were not aggressive. The children rewarded for aggressive speech used such speech more frequently than the control children. After this was noted, all of the children played with other toys in another room. In this new situation the children who had been rewarded for aggressive speech were notably more aggressive than the control children, and at this point their verbal aggression had generalized to nonverbal aggression as well.

Permissive environment. It apparently is not necessary for a child to be rewarded directly for his own aggressive acts in order for him to conclude that aggression is acceptable or desirable. A general atmosphere in which aggression is tolerated has been noted as sufficient to raise a child's level of aggressiveness. In a study of aggression in the nursery school environment, three investigators recorded all the observed aggressive acts over a 26-week period (Patterson, Littman, and Bricker 1967). They also noted the aggression's consequences and the teacher's reaction to it. In the two schools they observed, the investigators found that, for the most part, aggressive behavior resulted in a positive reward for the aggressor. This finding suggests that the nursery school may foster aggressive behavior. When an analysis was made of the amount of aggressive behavior the children displayed between entering nursery school and the end of the 26-week experiment, the investigators' findings supported their assumption about the school's aggression-fostering qual-

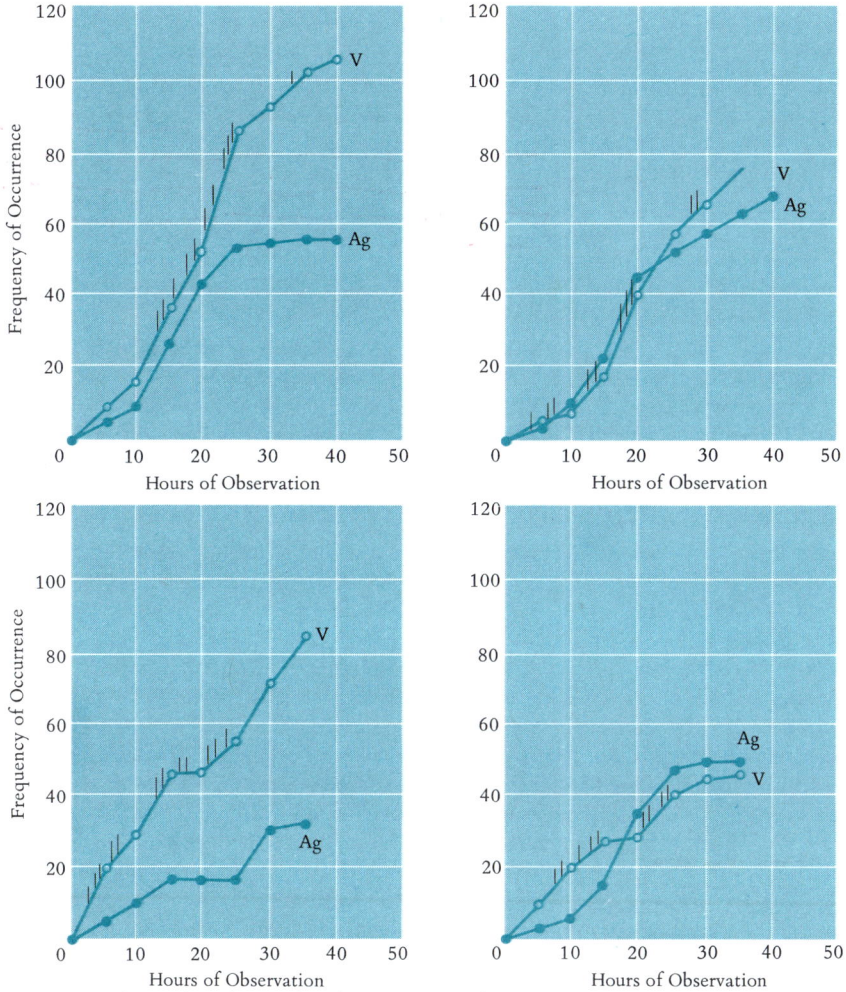

Figure 9.5 The increase in aggressiveness in four passive subjects conditioned in initiate assertive-aggressive behaviors. (From G. R. Patterson, R. A. Littman, and W. Bricker. Assertive behavior in children: A step toward a theory of aggression. *Monogr. Soc. Res. Child Develpm.*, 1967, *32*, No. 5, 24–25.)

V = The number of times the subject is victimized.

Ag = The number of aggressive acts.

|| (Vertical lines) = Occasions on which S successfully terminated the aggressor's attack by his own counterattack.

PERSONALITY AND SOCIAL DEVELOPMENT   **277**

ity. They discovered that children who entered nursery school with weak aggressive tendencies displayed a significant increase in aggressive behavior after the 26 weeks—provided they interacted socially with the other children. Thus, a rewarding environment as well as a specific reward for a specific aggression can cause an increase in aggressive behavior.

The reinforcing effect of a permissive environment has been further noted by another experiment that showed children's aggression levels increased when a permissive adult was present. The children were observed in a series of 10-minute play sessions with dolls. When a permissive adult was present, the children became progressively more aggressive in that session, and even more aggressive in the next play session (Bandura and Walters 1963).

Though the presence of a permissive adult can increase aggression, the absence of a known permissive adult also seems to reduce aggression. This seemingly contradictory effect was observed in a study of two groups of children in two play sessions (Siegel and Kohn 1959). In the first play period, both groups had a permissive adult present. In the second play period, the adult remained with the first group but was not present with the second group. Of the children playing in the presence of the permissive adult both times, two-thirds exhibited more aggression in the second play period than in the first. On the other hand, the children who had no adult present in the second session showed less aggressive behavior in that play period. It would seem that the permissive adult's presence was taken as an endorsement of aggressive activity. In the session without a permissive adult, the children apparently fell back on their own learned control of their aggression and checked much of their aggressive behavior. It appears, then, that the child gears his behavior to the standards of the adult who is in charge; if an adult is not present, the child relies on his own internalized standards, or his conscience.

Inconsistent treatment. Aggression also can be spurred by the parents' inconsistent treatment of a child's aggressive acts. An unpredictable pattern of punishment and permissiveness has been found to produce extremely aggressive children (Sears, Maccoby, and Levin 1957). The reason for this effect is not completely clear. It seems likely, however, that when a parent overlooks a previously punished behavior, the child's fear of future punishment for the same act diminishes. Then, too, inconsistent treatment produces additional frustration, which provides fuel for later aggression.

SEX DIFFERENCES. Aggression patterns vary significantly according to the sex of the child. One study reported that both boys and girls of 2 years display physically aggressive behavior, such as kicking and screaming. At 4 years of age, however, boys scream less and hit more than girls do (Hollenberg and Sperry 1950). Such sex differences in aggressive behavior become more marked and regular as the child grows older and learns the acts that are considered appropriate to his role. Another study confirmed the common knowledge that, at least during their preschool years, boys continue to be more aggressive than girls. Boys' play and fantasy contain more aggression, and they indulge in decidedly more fights, destruction, bickering, assaults—verbal and physical—and more negative responses (Maccoby 1966). Such differences appear to reflect the socialization processes that usually begin at about age 2. Aggression in boys in Western societies generally is condoned and even encouraged. In girls, aggression is regarded as an undesirable trait and is, therefore, more stringently inhibited, both by parents and peers.

We see, then, that many elements in the child's environment contribute to his feelings and expressions of aggression. Aggressive behavior cannot be accounted for solely by theories that stress one component alone, of the major components of aggression—whether it be instinct, or constitutional or social influence. Instead, a combination of these and other variables, such as modeling, frustration, displacement, punishment, reward, and sex differences, are all important determinants to be considered.

Sex-Typing

Unlike aggression, which seems largely dependent on external forces for its development, sex-typing appears to arise primarily from the

Table 9.4 Summary of Research Findings on Sex Differences in Aggression

Study*	Age	Differences	Comments
Observational Studies			
Dawe 1934	Nursery school	Boys	Boys participated in more quarrels.
Green 1933	Nursery school	Boys	Boys had more quarrels.
Sears et al. 1953	Nursery school	No diff.	Total aggressive responses—boys slightly higher, but not significantly so.
Sears et al. 1965	Nursery school	Boys / No diff.	In 7 out of 10 types of aggression. Verbal disapproval, tattling, and prosocial aggression.
Jersild and Markey 1935	2–5	Boys / No diff.	More physical quarrels. Verbal quarreling.
Muste and Sharpe 1947	2–5	No diff.	Boys slightly more physical and girls slightly more verbal aggression.
McKee and Leader 1955	3–4	No diff.	Pairs of children playing.
Siegel 1956	3–5	Boys	Like-sex pairs playing.
McCandless et al. 1961	3½–5	Boys	Initiated more conflicts and resisted attack more frequently.
Siegel et al. 1959	5	Boys	In type of interaction, aggression was rank order 3 for boys, and 7 for girls, out of 9 possible categories.
Walters et al. 1957	2–5	Boys	Aggressive contacts with peers.
Whiting and Whiting 1962	3–6	Boys	Physical aggression in six cultures.
Rating Studies			
Hattwick 1937	2–4½	Boys	Negativistic behavior.
Beller and Neubauer 1963	2–5	Boys	Mothers' reports of hyperaggression and hyperactivities in clinic children.
Beller and Turner 1962	Preschool	Boys	Several subscales of aggression.
Sears et al. 1957	5	No diff.	Mothers' reports.
Beller 1962	5½–6	Boys	General aggression.
Digman 1963	6–7	Boys	Teachers' ratings—more negativistic, aggressive, noisy.
Feshbach 1956	5–8	Boys	Teachers' ratings.
Toigo et al. 1962	8	Boys	Nominated by peers as more aggressive.
Tuddenham 1952	8 and 10	Boys	Considered more quarrelsome by peers.
Sanford et al. 1943	5–14	Boys	Teachers attributed aggression more to boys.
Experimental Studies			
Bandura et al. 1961	Nursery school	Boys / No diff.	Imitative physical aggression. Imitative verbal aggression.
Bandura et al. 1963	Nursery school	Boys	Total aggression and nonimitative aggression.
Bandura et al. 1963	Nursery school	Boys	Imitative and nonimitative aggression.
Bandura 1965	Nursery school	Boys	Aggressive acts.
Hartup and Himino 1959	Nursery school	Boys	More doll-play aggression with isolation as a precondition.

*See source of chart for complete references to studies.

Source: E. E. Maccoby (Ed.). *The development of sex differences*. Stanford, Calif.: Stanford University Press, 1966. Pp. 323–324.

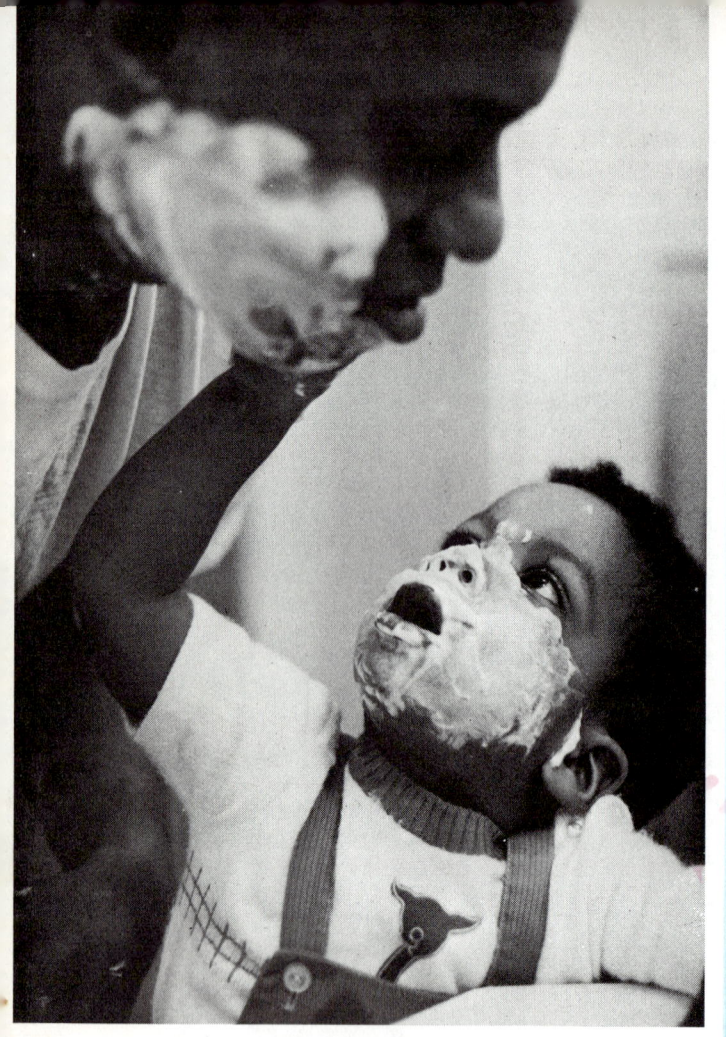

Figure 9.6 This toddler imitates the sex-role behavior of his father. (Burk Uzzle—Magnum)

child's internal organization of his world. Aggressive behavior is most often considered to be a response to what forces in the external world do to a person, whereas sex-typing is closely related to an individual's internal, cognitive structures. Of course, the distinction between external and internal forces is largely theoretical—in life these forces may not always be truly separable. But the distinction helps to explain why social learning theories seem more useful than others for understanding phenomena such as dependency and aggression, that are more dependent on external, social factors. By the same token, cognitive-developmental theories seem more appropriate for explaining processes that appear to be grounded in the child's internal organization, such as conscience and sex-typing. The traditional theory regarding sex-typing, however, explains the process in terms of social learning theory, as a result of identification. We shall first examine this theory and then explore the more recently formulated cognitive approach as an alternative view.

Identification Theory of Sex-Typing

In 1925, Freud introduced the term *identification* to explain an individual's ability to learn and adopt his parents' traits during the socialization process. Since that time, social learning theorists have developed the argument that a child learns his sex role through his identification with a male or female model. Thus, in social learning theory, identification leads to sex-typing. If a boy of 3 perceives his father as both attractive and similar to himself, he will begin to identify with that parent. As he begins noting and imitating his father's behaviors and mannerisms, he invariably will begin adopting many characteristics that are considered specific to the male personality.

Daily home activities, too, build the identity bond with the appropriate adult. Little girls may help their mothers bake cookies or make beds. Boys help their fathers rake the lawn or wash the car. By their fifth birthdays, most children have learned which behaviors and playthings relate to which sex (Brown 1956; Fauls and Smith 1956; Hartup and Zook 1960). A favorite form of childhood teasing—whose often-marked effect may indicate the importance of sexual identity to the child—involves mocking a child for behavior alien to his sex role. For example, the 5-year-old boy who plays with a doll often will be labeled a "sissy." The girl who roughs up aggressive peers or fights with boys will be singled out as a "tomboy."

In addition, the socialization process encourages behavior appropriate to a sex type. Boys are rewarded for being "tough," for "being a man," or for defending themselves against aggressors. They are discouraged from such "unmanly" acts as crying when they are hurt, physically or emotionally. Girls, on the other hand, are rewarded for avoiding fights and for being submissive. They are given the impression that crying is permissible, and, indeed, even expected of women (Sears, Maccoby, and Levin 1957).

CONDITIONS AFFECTING SEX-TYPING. Because the social learning theory of sex-typing hinges on identification, the conditions that affect identification also affect sex-typing. As we saw in our earlier discussion of identification, the behavior of the parent is important to this process and, therefore, to correct sex-typing. The parent must be nurturant, and this nurturance leads to dependency, which, in turn, leads the child to identify with the parent. One experiment found that young boys and girls who watched films in which the main characters were an adolescent boy and girl, remembered better the behavior of the figures of their own sex. The children also expressed preferences to be like the film heroes of their own sex (Maccoby and Wilson 1957). In everyday life, surface similarities are abundant. A child and parent may strongly resemble each other; this often prompts adult friends to point out such similarity to the child. In the same way, sex-appropriate characteristics also are mentioned by elders—"You're as strong (or as big) as your dad," or "You're just as pretty as your mother." Since behavior that is encouraged or rewarded tends to persist, sex-typed behavior becomes more firmly established through such encouragement. Boys are praised for being brave and strong, for running fast, climbing nimbly, and throwing well. Girls are rewarded for being kind, gentle, helpful, and quiet.

Children also form more positive sex-role identifications if the model parent is perceived as powerful. In a relevant experiment, a female model was introduced differently to two groups of preschool children. To the first group she was introduced as a visiting out-of-town teacher, who would therefore have no control over the children. In the second group, she was presented as their new schoolteacher, a person who would exercise great control over them in the future. The female model then played a game with all of the children. In the game she displayed some novel, aversive behavior—that is, behavior calculated to be distasteful to the child—and some novel but neutral behavior. When the children were observed later through a one-way mirror, the model's aversive behavior was copied only by the children in the second group, who thought of her as a person possessing power (Mischel and Grusec 1966). Thus, the power trait seems to be a strong motive for identification. The classic image of the henpecked, submissive husband therefore would not be an attractive model for a young boy. Such a person is seen as powerless, and the child—whose own position is virtually powerless—wants to gain power status, not move laterally from his own weak position to another of equal vulnerability. It becomes evident, then, that the social learning theory of sex-typing through identification places great stress on the role and behavior of the adult model.

Cognitive Theory of Sex-Typing

While the social learning theory of sex-typing enjoys wide acceptance today, another theory has been receiving increasing attention. This explanation, known as the *cognitive theory*, contends that the child does not acquire his sex type as an adjunct to his identification. Lawrence Kohlberg, the major proponent of the cognitive theory, maintains that, instead, the child first develops the idea of himself as a boy or girl and then perceives that certain attitudes and behaviors are categorized by sex type; he then begins to adopt those traits that are associated with his sex (Kohlberg 1966). Identification with the parent of the same sex, then, is a result of the child's developing interest in the activities and qualities of his own sex. This is a basic difference that distinguishes the identification theory from the cognitive theory of sex-typing. The identification theory assumes that a child's knowledge of his sex is the culmination of model identification, socialization, and cultural factors—in other words, that a child's sense of sex type is the last stage in the process. In contrast, the cognitive theory, which draws heavily on Piaget's concepts of mental development through experience, assumes this sequence: "I am a boy; therefore, I want to do boy things." The child then finds it rewarding to adopt the appropriate traits of his sex (Kohlberg 1966). In the cognitive theory, a child's sense of his sex comes first, not last, as in the identification theory.

The child develops his mental categories of boy and girl as a consequence of his being referred to as a boy or girl by his parents; his concept then gradually expands and becomes more sophisticated. Eventually, the child acquires the level of mental classification necessary to sort out people correctly on the basis of their sex traits. However, this sorting process does not result in sex-role certainty during the toddler years. On the other hand, the lack of certainty does not mean that a toddler will not label himself correctly. He does apply such labels, but they have little intrinsic meaning for him as yet. They simply are arbitrary labels, such as the name labels he applies to others (Kohlberg 1966). The toddler's use of "boy" or "girl" at first is determined by superficial traits—the individual's hair style or clothes—and young children generally do not realize that sex type persists while such surface characteristics change (Katcher 1955; Kohlberg 1966).

Uncertainty about sex stability persists until about school age. In one study, children 4 to 8 years old were presented with a picture of a girl. The researchers asked the children if the girl could be a boy if she wanted to; or if she played a boy's games; or if she wore a boy's clothes, or had short hair. The majority of the 4-year-old subjects said the girl in the picture could transform herself in these ways. However, the children 6 or 7 years old disagreed. They were convinced that the girl could not be a boy simply by behaving like one or making herself resemble one (Kohlberg 1966). These latter children were old enough to have formed firm mental categories based on intrinsic, rather than superficial, traits.

By extending the implications of the cognitive theory, Kohlberg refutes the psychoanalytic argument that a child's uncertainty about his own sex reflects emotional problems linked to sex. Kohlberg maintains that the uncertainty about sex-typing is simply an indication that the child has not yet worked out firm definitions of physical

FREUDIAN

1. Desire for mother
Fear of father's retaliation
2. Identification with father
3. Sex-typed identity

SOCIAL LEARNING

1. Attachment to father as major rewarder (and punisher-controller)
2. Identification modeling of father
3. Sex-typed identity

COGNITIVE DEVELOPMENTAL

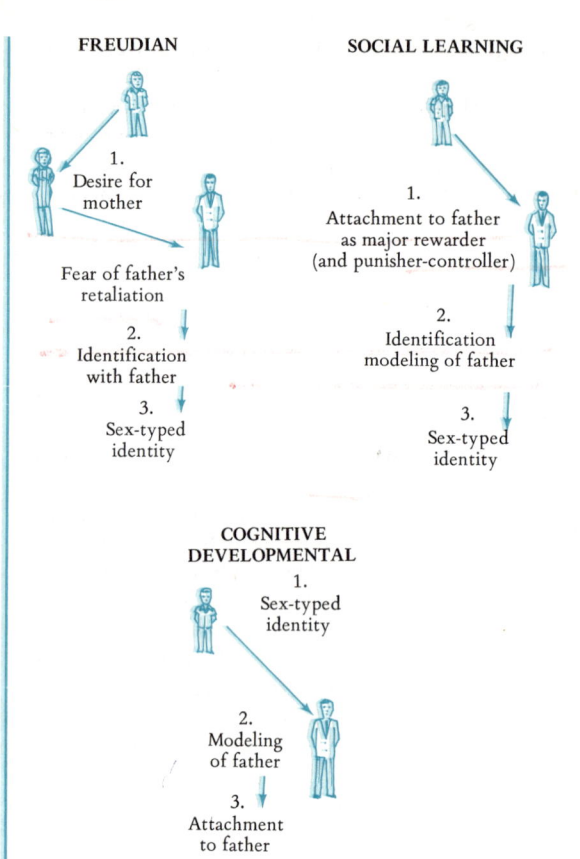

1. Sex-typed identity
2. Modeling of father
3. Attachment to father

Figure 9.7 Theoretical sequences in psychosexual identification. In identification theory (both Freudian and social learning), a child's sense of sex type is the last stage in the process. In the cognitive theory, his sense of sex type comes first. (From A. L. Kohlberg. A cognitive-developmental analysis of children's sex-role concepts and attitudes. *Genet. Psychol. Monogr.* V, 1966, 75, 128.)

concepts, including concepts of distinct sexes. In other words, a child's sexual uncertainty is merely a yardstick of his general cognitive development.

When a child's cognitive development reaches the stage—at about 6 or 7 years—at which he can classify persons accurately on the basis of sex (see Chapter 10), he begins to add more complicated and more abstract distinctions to his concepts of the male and female. For example, in Western culture, he develops concepts of the male as strong, aggressive, and controlling, and the female as predominantly passive and weaker.

The relative importance of internal cognitive factors as set forth by Kohlberg versus the external influence of parental reward and modeling on sex-typing cannot yet be established. Naturally, the proponents of each theory tend to assert that the variables on which they focus their research efforts are the primary ones. Until evidence clearly points to the unquestioned dominance of cognitive structures or social learning, we can accept the relevance of both. It is worth noting that in Chapter 12 we arrive at a similar impasse when dealing with problem solving.

In this account, we have taken for granted traditional sex differences. There is, however, much contemporary questioning of the continuing relevance of these differences. Many feel that at the very least girls should be encouraged to be as active and independent as boys have been. If girls are to fulfill new opportunities for legal and vocational equality, it is argued, they, too, must spend their childhood in appropriate independence training. On the other hand, there seems to be less concensus about advocating more "nurturance" and "affiliation" training (which are more typical female sex-role emphases) for boys, although any increasing humanization of mankind might indicate that this would be desirable. Again, few of those who advocate that girls be free to wear boys' clothes seem prepared to suggest that boys wear dresses. Perhaps the problem is being solved by a move to more neutral clothes for both sexes. All we need to note at this point is that the traditional sex-role distinctions seem to be in the process of considerable change.

Sexual Curiosity

Unlike sex-typing, sexual curiosity has not been a subject of great psychological research. This is not surprising, since sexual curiosity tends to be a taboo subject in Western civilization. However, as an important emerging activity among 3- and 4-year-olds, it requires our attention.

Early Interest and Activity

While the young child is beginning to understand his own sex role, he also is displaying an active interest in his own body. Interest in the genitals and often some genital handling occur even in the first two years, and male infants have erections. By the third and fourth years, genital play and exploration are not uncommon. In the immediate preschool years, genital stimulation becomes more frequent as children realize that this activity gives them intense pleasure. One study of middle-class children indicated that approximately 50 percent of preschoolers engage in some genital play (Sears, Maccoby, and Levin 1957). The actual incidence of sexual exploration and masturbation may be higher, however, since many parents may be unaware of their children's sex play or hesitant to contribute data concerning it. Once young children have found their genitals to be sources of pleasure, they pay more attention to them and develop an active curiosity. They want to know the function of the organs and the reasons for anatomical differences. They may wonder why they are different from their parents, as well as why they are different from the opposite sex. Another inevitable sex-related question—though not necessarily prompted by genital curiosity—is the classic query: "Where do babies come from, Mommy?"

Parent Responses

Parents react in different ways to such youthful sexual interest and activity. In some cultures, there is little or no restriction on youthful sexual play, individually or as a group. Western culture, however, ranks among the most restrictive in this regard. Social forces compel parents to restrain their children's sexual curiosity, excitement, and activity. Seldom, except among the very poor, will young children be seen playing naked in their yards. In no social class is there a laissez-faire attitude toward masturbation as there is in other cultures. Instead, mothers often reprimand their children for openly masturbating. Thus, the mother introduces a dilemma. Though the child knows from experience that genital play produces pleasant feelings, he also knows that he may be punished. Such incompatible feelings often begin to produce the conflicting attitudes toward sexuality that commonly are harbored by the adult population.

Another typical response to their children's sexual activity is for mothers to ignore the behavior while drawing the child's attention to another activity or toy. This technique probably reduces the incidence of sexual stimulation, but it may have other undesirable effects. If a child concludes that his sexual behavior and feelings—even his genitals—are taboo subjects, never to be mentioned, he will find it difficult to understand these matters. Lack of knowledge about his genitals, for instance, may create anxiety about them and the feelings associated with them. On the other hand, referring to them, but only in a negative fashion—such as associating them with urination or defecation—may lead the child to feel disgust for his sexual organs and activity. The familiar parental admonition that a child will harm himself by touching his genitals may substantiate for the child any connection he may have established between his sexuality and feelings of danger and fear of punishment. Needless to say, a child who forms any of these attitudes toward sexual feelings may have substantial difficulty in accepting the normality of sex as a young child and possibly as an adolescent and adult (Sears, Maccoby, and Levin 1957).

Some parents find effective ways to avoid making the sexual organs and sexual activity a source of conflict between pleasure and fear. A child whose questions are answered frankly and factually and without a parental show of embarrassment or secrecy generally will accept the answers with equanimity. After all, the child who has not been made wary of sex asks a question about his sex organs with the same ease that he asks why dogs bark or rain falls. Many parents who try an honest approach are relieved to observe this attitude and discover that the child does not want to know the whole story of the human reproductive system. Much more likely, he has a simple question which will be satisfied by a simple answer or analogy. When the answers are given on request, the child can gradually build up a proper understanding of his sex organs and sexual functions. In addition, the child will tend to trust his parent's assessment of sex and come to him or her when more serious sexual questions arise, as they inevitably will.

Sex raises larger social questions as well. For example, should pornography of any kind be available to adults and children alike? Should children observe their parents in sexual intercourse? Should unmarried adolescents be discouraged from premarital intercourse? What degree of sexual intimacy is advisable between dating adolescents? Is homosexuality simply another form of human sexual behavior, or is it abnormal? Many more such questions arise in our society, and the treatment of these issues affects public policy as well as private families. One study found that among the variables related to marital happiness, an important factor was the way in which a married individual's parents had responded to his childhood curiosity about sex. Study results indicated that parental secrecy, lack of information, or distortion ("dirtying") of sex caused marital problems later in an individual's life (Terman 1938). It is probable that the best answers to the important questions we have cited will come from people who themselves have been given a balanced view of the role of sex by their parents.

As in the case of traditional sex differences, this is another area in which our society is in the process of considerable change. It is already evident that sexual inhibitions are not so important to this generation as they were to previous ones. Sexual fulfillment seems to have become a more central focus for many younger adults, and this is likely to have implications for the future of child training in sexual attitudes.

OTHER CULTURES. As we have suggested, sexual attitudes and practices vary from culture to culture. "Our American middle-class . . . is rather extreme in the severity with which children are punished for masturbation, as they are given the same rating . . . as the most extreme of the primitive societies" (Whiting and Child 1953). Many societies are much more lenient in their treatment of genital stimulation. Cross-cultural studies show that among the Pukapukans of Western Polynesia open masturbation is accepted without qualms. Similarly, another tribal group, the Siberian Yakut, have practically no shame of nakedness and employ only slight modesty training (Whiting and Child 1953). The evolution of such sexual standards, whether they are restrictive or permissive, is almost always closely integrated with a people's view of the organization of their world, particularly how the role of sex is regarded in their religious concepts and practices.

Development of the Self

From an area of social learning we return once more to an aspect of development in which the child's internal cognitive structures are the primary determinants—the development of the self. The child's dawning self-awareness and sense of autonomy are at the heart of his feelings about his own existence. As the child begins to recognize himself, to make his own choices, and to live with them, so he determines the sort of human being he will become. Whether the development of the self is seen in this somewhat existentialist framework or, in contrast, as merely the sum of all other influences, it nevertheless involves a great deal of rather unstable experimentation in self-assertion and choice making, as we shall see.

Autonomy and Self-Awareness

The young child's developing individuality comes into sharper focus as he displays more identifiable personality traits and behaviors that are uniquely his own. These traits and behaviors appear in the child's personal bearing, in his social behavior, and in his ways of thinking, speaking, and playing. Just as others are becoming more aware of his individuality, the child's contact with other people and objects gradually gives him a sense of himself as a distinct being. This recognition of his separateness is the child's emerging sense of *autonomy*.

While the child begins to effectively manifest his autonomy in the toddler stage, it has been suggested that the concept of the self as the child's chief organizing force emerges much earlier. Lewis and Brooks-Gunn offer a profile of such early emergence of self:

Can one talk about the concept of the self at such early ages [4 months]? Consider two aspects of the self: the first and most common is the categorical self (I am female, or I am intelligent, or I am big or small, or I am capable); the second, and by far the more primitive, is the existential statement "I am." The basic notion of self—probably as differentiated from other (either as object or person, the mother being the most likely other person) . . . must develop first. There is no reason not to assume that it develops from birth and that even in the early months some notion of self exists. . . . this non-evaluative, existential self is developed from the consistency, regularity, and contingency of the infant's action and outcome in the world . . . . each time a certain set of muscles operates (eyes close), it becomes black (cannot see). . . . Action and outcome produce differentiation and self. . . . Touching the hot stove and the immediacy of the pain tell me it's my hand that is on the stove. . . . The infant's world is full of such relationships and they vary from its own action on objects to its relationship with a caregiver. . . . the highly directed energy of the caregiver (touch, smile, look, etc.) is contingent and specific to infant action (smile, coo, etc.). (Lewis and Brooks-Gunn 1972)

Though the child's self-concept may begin forming as early as 4 months, by the toddler years the child still is not yet fully certain who and what he is. He often appears to be oblivious to his own body as a physical presence. For example, the toddler often will stand in the middle of a doorway and not realize that he must step aside to permit others to pass through.

His very rudimentary self-awareness is aided in its development as he compares and contrasts himself with others. He may, for example, observe to a peer, "Your hair is the same color as mine," or complain to his father, "How come you can be bigger than me?" or make the bold statement, "When I get bigger, you'll get littler." As the child's self-awareness develops, he becomes more conscious of his common ground with nature, too. He may ask if the woodpecker's tapping hurts the tree or if the boxer pup's "docked" tail bled "when the man chopped it off."

PERSONALITY AND SOCIAL DEVELOPMENT   285

The toddler's emerging self-awareness and resulting sense of autonomy can be glimpsed in many behaviors and comments, when the observer is able to recognize the signs. These new dimensions of his personality are especially evident in certain characteristic activities of this period: recognizing himself in a mirror, using the pronoun *I*, naming himself, and making choices—usually in a negative manner, in opposition to his parents' choices.

SELF-RECOGNITION IN A MIRROR. The child who recognizes himself in a mirror quite literally "sees" himself as separate and autonomous—perhaps even as competent if he has hoisted himself up onto a chair or buffet to look in the mirror. After becoming aware that his own image is himself, a child may first speak of himself in the third person: "There's Alex." Occasionally, this second self will confuse and upset a child as well as give him the pleasure of self-recognition.

A child seldom understands what he is seeing in a mirror—a reflection or a real person, or both. A girl of 2½ is looking in the mirror: "Who is that?" her father questions. "Leslie," she says. "Will she be there when you go away?" "Yes." "Why?" "'Cause she can't get out. She would break the mirror." The same confusion between the real person and the child's image holds true for a drawing. For example, a 3-year-old was asked about a drawing of herself, "Can you get out of that?" She replied, "No, I can't get out of there because I'm in here."

Lewis and Brooks-Gunn suggest that even the infant may recognize himself in a mirror. They maintain that the child and the mirror have the same relationship as the child and the caregiver. That is, the mirror's "reaction" also is "contingent and specific to infant action":

Looking in the mirror is pleasurable because of the consistency, regularity, and contingency of the viewer's action and the viewed outcome. In no other situation is there such consistent action-outcome pairing. In other words, the mirror experience contains those elements that generally make up the fabric of the infant's growing concept of self. It is not possible for us to know if the infant is aware that the image is himself . . . . but it is clear that by the time one-word utterances emerge, such as "self" or "mine," the year-old infant has the concept of self. It is reasonable to assume that the concept existed prior to the utterance. In fact, if we consider the research on the development of object permanence (for example, Charlesworth 1968), we find that, for the most part, object permanence has been established by 8 months of life, in many cases even earlier. If the infant has the cognition available to preserve memory of objects no longer

Figure 9.8 This toddler gets a sense of her physical self and separateness as she studies her image in the mirror. (Inge Morath—Magnum)

present, how can we deny them the ability to have self-permanence? Indeed, is it reasonable to talk of object permanence capacity without self-permanence capacity? Given that this first self-other distinction is made very early, the various categorical dimensions of self [such as, I am big or small, I am intelligent, I am capable] may also proceed to unfold. (Lewis and Brooks-Gunn 1972)

Kohlberg, in his cognitive theory of sex-typing, also stresses early self-cognitive organization. It is conceivable that if the child begins to distinguish himself from others well before 1 year of age, as Lewis and Brooks-Gunn suggest, he may soon thereafter begin to accumulate knowledge of sex-appropriate traits. For our purposes, however, it is enough to note that both Kohlberg and Brooks-Gunn regard the self-concept as the central organizing force in the child's development.

USE OF THE PRONOUN *I*. Further evidence of such internal organization is the child's use of language to identify himself. At ages 2½ or 3 years, children make great strides in the use of words. In about their third year, they begin to use the word *I* for themselves. It would be difficult to overstress the importance this gives the child as a being. The pronoun use is a manifestation of the child's identification of himself within his social environment, and it signifies a great stride taken in his development.

Naming. The toddler's expanding self-concept is evident in the labels he applies to himself. At age 2 or 2½, the child will accept only some expressions and will stoutly reject others. As his self-concept becomes more sophisticated, he accepts more names for himself. For example, a father reports that his male toddler declared, "I'm a little boy." When the father saw he was wearing a cowboy hat, he added—thinking, perhaps, to humor the child—"You're a cowboy." Rather than be flattered and appreciative, the boy became annoyed. He shouted, "I am not a *cowboy*, I'm a *little* boy." Yet a few months later, when the boy was again wearing his western hat, the father again said, "You're a cowboy." "Where's my horse?" was the child's bright response this time. However, even at this later age, when the boy was asked to be a "big boy and pick up your clothes," the child insisted he was a *little* boy. At about the same time, the father said, "Go to bed, little fellow." The boy's immediate rejoinder was "I'm not a little *fellow*—I'm a little *boy*." Such gradual acceptance of different labels probably corresponds to the development of a more detailed and multidimensional self-concept. Moreover, as the child learns synonyms and generally expands his vocabulary and playfulness, he will broaden his repertoire of labels for himself.

MAKING CHOICES—NEGATIVELY. The toddler's sense of autonomy and self-awareness is also manifested in his desire to choose for himself in every area of his life. Most of the choices he feels compelled to make usually arise from the need to assert his will—in opposition to that of his parents. This behavior is often characterized as "negativism" and is heralded by the child's recurrent use of the word *no*. (An interesting note is that the child learns to say "No" before he says "Yes.") If you offer him his favorite food, he will push it aside. If you ask him to walk, he will want to be carried. At this stage of his development, he often must have his own way in everything. If his will is thwarted, or if he feels his fledgling independence threatened, he may protest or resist by going limp or rigid (whichever provides the most opposition at the time), or by biting, kicking, running away, or exploding in a total temper tantrum. As a rule, parental emotionalism triggers more of the same. The primary reason for such oppositional behavior or negativism is the child's drive to assert his sense of separateness from his parents. He is trying out his developing autonomy by pitting his will against his parents' at every turn. By insisting on making choices among activities or objects, absurd though they may often seem to a parent, he is carving out his independence and separateness. For example, in the course of a two-block walk with his mother, a 3-year-old may suddenly insist that they cross to the other side of the street. When the mother agrees and takes the child's hand to cross the street, the child may flop down on the sidewalk in "passive resistance" against his mother's firm request to hold hands. As he is forcibly carried across the street, the child may struggle and kick and scream until placed on his feet. Then he may streak ahead to the next corner, carefully stop short of the intersection, but place one foot in the gutter and both hands on his hips as a gesture of independence while he waits for his mother.

Such behavior is the child's means of defending and asserting his newly emerging self. It also gives the child an opportunity to experiment on his own. In these times, a wise mixture of support, ignoring, and, where necessary, firmness by the parent will usually contribute to an increase in more discriminating negation by the toddler.

Autonomy versus Shame and Doubt

Erikson describes the child's development during this stage as a series of attempts to achieve autonomy. If these attempts are blocked by parental overcontrol, he will be robbed of opportunities to develop a sense of autonomy and self-control. Instead, he will develop feelings of shame and doubt. Shame may arise from unremitting destructive criticism of the child's attempts at autonomous behavior, and doubt can result from the consequent lack of trust or confidence in himself.

This stage of autonomy is the second of Erikson's "eight stages of man," which were described in Chapter 1. (The first stage—or life crisis, in Erikson's terms—occurs in infancy, when the baby develops either a basic trust of the world or a lack of trust, which will shape the ways in which he interacts with his world in subsequent years.) Erikson's scheme of the alternatives open to a person at each stage in his life is based on the psychosexual stages of Freudian psychoanalytic theory. The contest between autonomy and its alternatives corresponds to Freud's anal stage. We saw in Chapter 7 how the issue of toilet training often is a crucial element in the child's achievement of self-control.

While Erikson stresses the development of the self to a greater extent than does the classical Freudian view, both have in common the clear realization that as the child struggles and overcomes the problems of his age level (toileting, walking, choosing, naming, negating), he is left with an emotional residue, which is the feeling tone of the person that he is becoming. Life crises, they both say, make or break people, and toddlers have life crises just as anyone else does. As Erikson describes the positive results of these early crises, the first stage "leaves a residue in the growing being which, . . . especially in the individual's sense of identity, will echo something of the conviction, 'I am what hope I have and give.' The analogous residue of the stage of autonomy appears to be 'I am what I can will freely'" (Erikson 1968).

The child's struggle to master his environment and strengthen his autonomy, then, is vital to the success of his further development. During this process, the child's personality structures change; he gains new ways of interacting with his environment in the future, even though the future may bring completely new tasks or fresh variations in the present. The child also acquires a sense of changing, of mastering his environment, which increases his ability to face new tasks with enthusiasm and to perform them successfully. Such mastery, endorsed by the child's social environment, encourages the development of his sense of self and autonomy. In addition to autonomy, this concept of the self includes the belief in one's physical integrity despite time, place, and distance. This belief is strengthened by the masteries the child achieves and the social approval they earn for him.

Effectance Motivation and the Self

For years, psychologists have generally assumed that children strive to master their environments because they are rewarded for such efforts or because such efforts help to satisfy their aggressive drives. In recent years, another theory has been advanced by Robert W. White. White has proposed that the child's motive for achievement is more intrinsic and closely tied to his developing sense of self. It reflects a basic need to interact effectively with the environment, independent of approval or disapproval, or the need to satisfy aggressive motives. White calls this intrinsic drive for achievement *effectance motivation*, because of the motive to *effect* an act (White 1959). Piaget, it should be noted, assumes a similar view of the child's intellectual motivation. Effectance motivation would seem to be at the root of the development of competence as a personality trait. That is, the child becomes competent at writing his name because of his inherent desire to master the task and advance his skills. The child has a need for competence. Thus, the infant's small, daily permutations and advances in such activities as reaching, grasping, and crawling—which Piaget observed in meticulous naturalistic detail—and the toddler's practice at climbing and sitting down are not casual or accidental acts. They are constant practice sessions in which the child's "lust for organization"—as White describes effectance motivation in the 2- and 3-year-old—demands that the inherent physical and intellectual powers be developed and used.

EFFECTANCE MOTIVATION AND ACHIEVEMENT. Effectance motivation is a major force in development because it leads to the learning of new acts, skills, behaviors, ideas, and concepts. Early encouragement and independence seem to strengthen this existing desire to achieve competence. They seem to be particularly effective at accelerating the motive to master intellectual activities, such as those encountered in school (Winterbottom 1958).

A study of the relationship between independence and achievement found that preschool children who spent a substantial amount of time engaged in activities classified as "achievement" activities—crayoning, painting, reading, and modeling clay—on the whole were less dependent upon their parents. These achieving children also asked for less help or emotional support than their nonachieving peers (Crandall 1963).

The children's high achievement motivation seems to be a direct result of parental treatment of their efforts. The high achievers in the experiment had mothers who had early begun a routine of urging and rewarding achievement and paying scant attention to requests for assistance. Ready praise and rewards for attempts at mastery produced children who often strove to achieve, outside as well as within the family circle.

Encouragement of mastery as early as infancy also increases later achievement motivation. Children who were encouraged in walking, talking, holding, and carrying objects achieved more in school than children whose mothers did not encourage these skills (Hollenberg and Sperry 1950). Furthermore, mastery striving is a persistent behavior, once developed. For example, an individual's strong preschool motivation to achieve in intellectual activities is most often retained throughout adolescence and into adulthood (Kagan and Moss 1960).

In the toddler years, as we have seen, the development of the child's personality, as well as his social behavior, becomes increasingly more complex, both for him and his parents, and for those who would study these developments. For the toddler and his family, this is a difficult time because he now is emerging as a more defined, though still fluctuating, personality; as such, he must test his growing selfness continuously, often against the grain of daily life in the family. For the psychologist, this period is difficult to assess because of the methodological problems endemic to assessing what is essentially the toddler's internal development.

In the course of our inquiry into this area, we have at times emphasized the determining effects of other persons upon the child, and at other times emphasized the child's own capacities. Obviously, they are both at work all the time. Obviously, also, social learning theory is more appropriate for explaining phenomena influenced largely by others, and cognitive theories are more appropriate for developments that are largely a result of the child's growing internal organization. In addition, however, the final section on the self and achievement suggests quite strongly that as children are permitted and encouraged in their independence by their parents (a social learning phenomenon), the children themselves accordingly become stronger, more independent, and better organized internally. The children then are best understood primarily in terms of the cognitive-developmental theory. Despite Kohlberg's often correct emphasis on the importance of the child's own cognitions, such cognitions would likely be poorly developed unless encouraged by the parents. In human independence and human

PERSONALITY AND SOCIAL DEVELOPMENT 289

development, man's growth as a rationally independent being does depend upon a groundwork of wise nurturance. When that is assured, however, explanations most relevant to this nurturance (the social learning theory) become less appropriate. The same type of struggle between alternative explanations will be taken up again in Chapter 12, where we discuss moral judgment both as a cognitive phenomenon and as a role-taking experience.

Summary

During the toddler's third and fourth years, his personality traits become more clearly defined. These traits and his social development are shaped in part by his contact with his family and in part by his genetic endowment.

Some of the variables of parental behavior that are known to influence the child's personality include restrictiveness, protection, hostility, acceleration, warmth, expression of affection, authoritarianism, and consistency. The Fels longitudinal study of maternal-child behavior, for example, found that warmth leads to less dependency; on the other hand, hostility, restrictiveness, and inconsistency induce dependency. Parental rewards and punishments for dependent and independent behavior also can influence the degree of the child's dependency.

Certain parental behaviors also affect the child through the process of identification. The child identifies with a nurturant parent because he associates that parent with his own strong, affirmative feelings. Identification also depends on the child's perceptions; most children soon begin to identify more strongly with the parent of the same sex, because they perceive that this parent has more traits similar to their own. Later on, wider social contacts provide more models for identification, and the older child reflects a complex of many models. Identification continues as the child grows, and the patterns of identification become deeply embedded in the personality.

Conscience develops through identification. Children of affectionate parents will tend to internalize parental values. Parents who explain the reasons for their demands, and do not rely on physical punishment, develop a strong conscience in their children; highly punitive parents are likely to develop a weak morality in theirs.

Aggression has biological and constitutional components, but it also has social components, which can be affected by parental behaviors. If the parents approve of aggression, or respond to it inconsistently, the child's aggressive behavior will increase; if they verbally disapprove, it will decrease. And parental reasoning and affection lead to the child's internal control of aggression.

There are two major theories as to how the child develops his sex role. Freud and the social learning theorists think that the child learns his sex-typing through identification with a masculine or feminine model, reinforced by rewards, daily home activities, and peer groups. The cognitive theorists, especially Kohlberg, believe that the child develops a knowledge of his sex type by being labeled a boy or girl by his parents; his concept then gradually expands and becomes more sophisticated. Whichever theory may be more valid, in our culture parents are apt to create anxiety about sex by punishing the child for sexual curiosity and activity, or by giving him false information, or no information at all. Simple, straightforward answers to questions about sex are appropriate and needed at this age.

As the child develops his identifiable personality traits and individual behaviors, he gradually becomes aware of himself as a distinct, autonomous being. He strengthens his autonomy by testing and exercising his power to make choices and to take independent action. The toddler seeks opportunities to learn and use new skills, yet his progress depends to a certain extent upon parental encouragement and reward.

Case Studies

Colin B.

Colin was the fourth of five children in a prosperous suburban family. His parents, economically and professionally secure amidst a status-conscious community, were socially active and influential. Considering herself a "natural mother," Mrs. B. made certain that Colin participated fully in their stimulating family life. She also attempted to handle his exuberance and volatility with a judicious amount of permissiveness—and an endless amount of understanding.

Colin's nursery school teachers pegged him almost immediately as one of the most imaginative of his group, for he proved equally expressive in his use of words, materials, and people. He was also a very active child, often darting about "as if he needed to do a great deal of running." Throughout most of his first year in nursery school his teachers considered him relatively carefree and quite charming.

As spring began, however, Colin, who was normally healthy, was sick for the better part of two months with a series of ailments, ending with a nasty ear infection which apparently disturbed his spatial orientation and caused him to scream in his sleep that he was "falling" or being "pushed backwards." For the first few school days following this frustrating bout with helplessness, he was noticeably changed—clinging to his mother in the morning, being afraid to drive to school with anyone but his mother, and needing more self-comforting body movements. As it happened, however, this behavior proved to be but a prelude to his forthcoming strivings for mastery and power.

The following September Colin was reassigned to a group in which he was one of the youngest, but also—more importantly—the smallest. From the year's outset Colin demonstrated new aspects of his personality: instigating frequent acts of aggression; insisting that he wanted and needed no help from adults; resisting or ignoring adult requests; appropriating and protecting the innumerable things he considered "mine"; and boasting of his emerging power with threats—"I'll push, I'm a big boy." Very much the self-contained child, Colin seemed aloof and withdrawn even when he played cooperatively. He almost never cried or asked for physical or emotional assistance of any kind. His volatility was such that he could be aggressive and pugnacious one moment, then dependent (on his teacher), consoling (of little girls or small animals), or cooperative and productive the next.

Throughout all this, Colin's fantasies showed recurrent notes of power, achievement, and consciousness of himself as a "near-man" who was beginning to identify strongly with the daddy-doctor so familiar to him from his own family. One particularly revealing theme was of big creatures (Halloween cats, owls, hawks, and eagles) stalking and killing smaller ones (mice and chipmunks). Another instance, which may have been prompted by memories of his previous long illness, occurred soon after Colin was absent with a spring cold: vivid dramatizations of a doll's eye having to be replaced and her nose removed.

While Colin's aggression at school became even more vigorous as the year progressed, his behavior at home became more volatile. Mrs. B. reported that he was sometimes violent over minor issues—matters that represented restrictions to him—but also suddenly dependent on his mother's help in his dressing and feeding. (He had also been exhibiting considerable reluctance to have her leave him at school each morning.) Mrs. B. reasoned that such contradictory behavior must have to do with Colin's timely desire for increased autonomy mixed with some jealousy over the amount of her time his 2-year-old sister was taking.

Surprisingly, there were signs of a new equanimity on Colin's fourth birthday. Obviously quite pleased with the new status of an added year, he proudly announced his new age to all of his classmates. His teachers noted an immediate "sense of release" as he became more cooperative and energetic (Murphy 1956).

Harriet H.

Unlike Colin's happy home situation, Harriet's family was no longer intact by the time she was 3½. Her father, a military man who spent substantial amounts of time traveling away from his family anyway, had made the separation permanent near the end of Harriet's first year in nursery school. Mrs. H., a rather matter-of-fact woman who was employed as a full-time secretary, was often obliged to leave Harriet in the care of a woman neighbor. A normally healthy, intelligent little girl, Harriet developed some rather marked ways of dealing with her frustrations and anxieties in her nursery school setting.

Most noticeable to her teachers (as she returned to a new nursery class the fall after her parents' divorce) was Harriet's preoccupation with order and neatness—particularly with the inanimate objects of her environment. She spent much of each day straightening her play area, or her locker, or even another girl's attempts at playroom cleanup. She would characteristically grumble throughout her efforts at orderliness, remarking, "It makes me dizzy when everything is jumbled," or "This house looks like there was a fire in it." (Mrs. H. also reported that Harriet began, soon after the divorce, to resist any efforts to repaint her room at home or to rearrange any of the furniture.) In addition, whenever Harriet was dissatisfied with the orderliness of one of her girl classmates, she did not hesitate to vocalize her unhappiness, and then try to impose her own system of neatness upon the situation. Similarly, when Harriet spied another girl's free-form painting of a flower garden, she did not hesitate to "show her how" such a subject should be painted: with rigid vertical flowers, each partitioned from the others by a green "name-tag pole."

Her behavior toward boy classmates was altogether different, however. As this nursery year began, Harriet was withdrawn and passive with boys, almost as if she was "stunned by their presence." Her reluctance gave way, however, to an unmistakable desire to be accepted by her male peers, even to the point of allowing a smaller, weaker boy to win a tug-of-war with her. Her compulsion for orderliness abated in the presence of the boys, too. For instance, she participated with considerable abandon in a frenzied, messy search for the tug-of-war rope, only to return to straighten the clutter as soon as the boys' interests had taken them elsewhere.

Harriet's teachers also noted the girl's differential attitudes towards them: she clearly sought warmth, affection, protection, and reassurance from her female teacher, sometimes wanting to be physically comforted or held. With her male teacher, however, she constantly sought acceptance and approval, even to the point of asking him many times a day if she had "done anything wrong" or if he was "maybe angry" with her. In addition, while Harriet was not normally given to crying, if she dropped something in sight of the male teacher, or missed an activity he led, she would break into a prolonged fit of inconsolable tears.

During this same time she also developed somewhat of a preoccupation with making contact with her father—writing him "letters" made of pictures and alphabet characters (but which she freely interpreted as, "Dear Daddy . . . I miss you. . . . Where are you now? . . . Do you live in a house?"), and listening intently whenever fathers of any sort, real or imaginary, were mentioned.

Only the passing of several months—during which Harriet found she could rely on the predictability of the school day and of her warm, reassuring relationships with her teachers—could make Harriet begin to relax her rigid attitudes toward the people and things in her environment. As she became more confident in the stability of her surroundings, she became more confident in her interactions with her peers. By the end of that nursery year Harriet could share her experiences, good and bad, with her playmates, and showed signs of incorporating others' attitudes into her own increasingly orderly world (Ostrovsky 1962).

References

Ahr, P. R. Moral development and social learning: Modeling effects on children's concepts of intentionality. *Dissert. Abstr.*, Oct. 1971, *32*(4-B), 2414.

Alexander, T., Stoyle, J., Roberge, J., and Leanerton, P. Developmental characteristics of emotional experience. *J. genet. Psychol.*, Sept. 1971, *119*(1), 109–117.

Alschuler, R. H., and Hattwick, L. W. *Painting and personality in young children.* (Rev. and abr.) Chicago: Univer. of Chicago Press, 1969.

Ardrey, R. *The territorial imperative.* New York: Atheneum, 1966.

Aronfreed, J. *Conduct and conscience: The socialization of internalized control over behavior.* New York: Academic Press, 1968.

Bandura, A., and Huston, A. C. Identification as a process of incidental learning. *J. abnorm. soc. Psychol.*, 1961, *63*, 311–318.

Bandura, A., Ross, D., and Ross, S. A. Imitation of film-mediated aggressive models. *J. abnorm. soc. Psychol.*, 1963, *66*, 3–11.

Bandura, A., and Walters, R. H. Aggression. In H. W. Stevenson (Ed.), *Child psychology. 62nd Yearbook Nat. Soc. Stud. Educ.* Chicago: Univer. of Chicago Press, 1963.

Barker, R. G., Dembo, T., and Lewin, K. Frustration and regression. In R. G. Barker, J. S. Kounin, and H. F. Wright (Eds.), *Child behavior and development.* New York: McGraw-Hill, 1943.

Baumrind, D., and Black, A. E. Socialization practices associated with dimensions of competence in preschool boys and girls. *Child Develpm.*, 1967, *38*, 291–328.

Becker, W. C., Peterson, D. R., Luria, Z., Shoemaker, D. J., and Hellmer, L. A. Relations of factors derived from parent-interview ratings to behavior problems of 5-year-olds. *Child Develpm.*, 1962, *33*, 509–535.

Block, J., and Martin, B. Predicting the behavior of children under frustration. *J. abnorm. soc. Psychol.*, 1955, *51*, 281–285.

Borke, H. Interpersonal perception of young children: Egocentrism or empathy? *Develpm. Psychol.*, 1971, *5*(2), 263–269.

Bronfenbrenner, U. Freudian theories of identification and their derivatives. *Child Develpm.*, 1960, *31*, 15–40.

Brown, D. G. Sex-role preference in young children. *Psychol. Monogr.*, 1956, *70* (421), 1–19.

Burton, R. V. Correspondence between behavioral and doll-play measures of conscience. *Develpm. Psychol.*, 1971, *5*(2), 320–332.

Cairns, R. B. Antecedents of social reinforcer effectiveness. Unpublished manuscript, Indiana Univer., 1962.

Charlesworth, W. R. Cognition in infancy: Where do we stand in the mid-sixties? *Merrill-Palmer Quart.*, 1968, *14*, 25–46.

Crandall, V. J. Achievement. In H. W. Stevenson (Ed.), *Child psychology. 62nd Yearbook Nat. Soc. Stud. Educ.* Chicago: Univer. of Chicago Press, 1963.

Crandall, V. J., and Rabson, A. Children's repetition choices in an intellectual achievement situation following success and failure. *J. genet. Psychol.*, 1960, *97*, 161–168.

Dorman, L., and Rebelsky, F. (Eds.) *Child development and behavior.* New York: Random House, 1970.

Edge, D. (Ed.) *Formative years: How children become members of their society.* New York: Schocken Books, 1970.

Eibl-Eibesfeldt, I. The fighting behavior of animals. *Scientific Amer.*, 1961, *205*, 112–122.

Elkins, F., and Handel, G. *Child and society: The process of socialization.* New York: Random House, 1972.

Emmerich, W. Continuity and stability in early social development: II. Teacher ratings. *Child Develpm.*, 1966, *37*, 17–28.

Erikson, E. H. Identity and the life cycle. *Psychol. Issues*, 1959, *1*, 18–164.

Erikson, E. H. *Identity: Youth and crisis.* New York: Norton, 1968.

Ermalinski, R., and Ruscelli, V. Incorporation of values by lower and middle socioeconomic class preschool boys. *Child Develpm.*, 1971, *42*(2), 629–632.

Faigin, H. Social behavior of young children in the kibbutz. *J. abnorm. soc. Psychol.*, 1958, *56*, 117–129.

Fauls, L., and Smith, W. D. Sex-role learning of five-year-olds. *J. genet. Psychol.*, 1956, *89*, 105–117.

Feshbach, S. Aggression. In P. H. Mussen (Ed.), *Carmichael's manual of child psychology.* Vol. II. (3rd ed.) New York: Wiley, 1970.

Feshbach, S. The function of aggression and the regulation of aggressive drive. *Psychol. Rev.*, 1964, *71*, 257–272.

Finney, J. C. Some maternal influences on children's personality and character. *Genet. Psychol. Monogr.*, 1961, *63*, 199–278.

Flapan, D. *Children's understanding of social interaction.* New York: Teachers College Press, 1968.

Fordham, M. *Children as individuals.* New York: Putnam's, 1971.

Frederickson, N. The effects of frustration on negativistic behavior of young children. *J. genet. Psychol.*, 1942, *61*, 203–226.

Freedman, A. M., and Kaplan, H. I. (Eds.) *The child: His psychological and cultural development.* Vol. 2. New York: Atheneum, 1972.

Gelfand, D. M. *Social learning in childhood.* Belmont, Calif.: Brooks-Cole, 1969.

Goodenough, F. L. *Anger in young children.* Minneapolis: Univer. of Minnesota Press, 1931.

Hamblin, R. L. *Humanization processes.* New York: Wiley, 1971.

Hartup, W. W. Nurturance and nurturance-withdrawal in relation to the dependency behavior of preschool children. *Child Develpm.*, 1958, *29*, 191–201.

Hartup, W. W., and Zook, E. A. Sex-role preferences in 3- and 4-year-old children. *J. consult. Psychol.*, 1960, *24*, 420–426.

Hatfield, J. S., Ferguson, P. E., Rau, L., and Alpert, R. Mother–child interaction and the socialization process. *Child Develpm.*, 1967, *38*, 365–414.

Hayes, N. A. The construction of an extraversion-introversion scale for the Personality Inventory for children. *Dissert. Abstr.*, Sept. 1971, *32*(3-B), 1844.

Heathers, G. Emotional dependence and independence in nursery school play. *J. genet. Psychol.*, 1955, *87*, 37–58.

Hilton, I. Differences in the behavior of mothers toward first and later-born children. *J. pers. soc. Psychol.*, 1967, *7*, 282–290.

Hoffman, M. L. Moral development. In L. Carmichael (Ed.), *Manual of child psychology.* (2nd ed.) New York: Wiley, 1954.

Hoffman, M. L., and Saltzstein, H. D. Parent discipline and the child's moral development. *J. pers. soc. Psychol.*, 1967, *5*, 45–57.

Hollenberg, E., and Sperry, M. Some antecedents of aggression and effects on doll play. *Personality*, 1950, *1*, 32–43.

Hoppe, R. A., Milton, G., and Simmel, E. C. (Eds.) *Early experiences and the processes of socialization.* New York: Academic Press, 1970.

Irwin, D. M., and Moore, S. G. The young child's understanding of social justice. *Develpm. Psychol.*, 1971, *5*(3), 406–410.

Isaacs, S. *Social development in young children.* New York: Schocken Books, 1972.

Jegard, S., and Walters, R. A. A study of some determinants of aggression in young children. *Child Develpm.*, 1960, *31*, 739–747.

Jensen, L., and Hughston, K. The effect of training children to make moral judgments that are independent of sanctions. *Develpm. Psychol.*, 1971, *5*(2).

Kagan, J. *Change and continuity in infancy.* New York: Wiley, 1971.

Kagan, J. The emergence of sex differences. *School Rev.*, 1972, *80*(2), 217–227.

Kagan, J., and Moss, H. A. *Birth to maturity: A study in psychological development.* New York: Wiley, 1962.

Kagan, J., and Moss, H. A. The stability of achievement and recognition-seeking behaviors. *J. abnorm. soc. Psychol.*, 1961, *62*, 504–513.

Kagan, J., and Moss, H. A. The stability of passive and dependent behavior from childhood through adulthood. *Child Develpm.*, 1960, *31*, 577–591.

Katcher, A. The discrimination of sex differences by young children. *J. genet. Psychol.*, 1955, *87*, 131–143.

Kellogg, W. N., and Kellogg, L. A. *The ape and the child: A study of environmental influence upon the behavior of the child.* New York: Hafner, 1933.

Kohlberg, L. A. A cognitive-developmental analysis of children's sex-role concepts and attitudes. *Gen. Psychol. Monogr.*, 1966, *75*, 128.

Levy, D. M. *Maternal overprotection.* New York: Columbia Univer. Press, 1943.

Lewis, M. Parents and children: Sex-role development. *School Rev.*, 1972, *80*(2), 229–240.

Lewis, M., and Brooks-Gunn, J. Self, other, and fear: The reaction of infants to people. Paper presented at Eastern Psychological Association annual meeting, Boston, April 1972.

Lorenz, K. *On aggression.* New York: Harcourt Brace Jovanovich, 1966.

Lovaas, O. Effect of exposure to symbolic aggression on aggressive behavior. *Child Develpm.*, 1961, *32*, 37–44.

Maccoby, E. E. (Ed.) *The development of sex differences.* Stanford, Calif.: Stanford Univer. Press, 1966.

Maccoby, E. E., and Wilson, W. C. Identification and observational learning from films. *J. abnorm. soc. Psychol.*, 1957, *55*, 76–87.

Marshall, H. R. Relations between home experiences and children's use of language in play interactions with peers. *Psychol. Monogr.*, 1961, *75*(5, Whole No. 509).

Masters, J., and Morris, R. J. Effects of contingent and noncontingent reinforcement upon generalized imitation. *Child Develpm.*, 1971, *42*(2), 385–397.

McArthur, C. Personalities of first and second children. *Psychiatry*, 1956, *19*, 47–54.

McGhee, P. E. Development of the humor response: A review of the literature. *Psychol. Bull.*, 1971, *76*(5), 328–348.

Mischel, W., and Grusec, J. Determinants of the rehearsal and transmission of neutral and aversive behaviors. *J. pers. soc. Psychol.*, 1966, *3*, 197–205.

Murphy, L. B. *Personality in young children.* Vol. 2. New York: Basic Books, 1956.

Ostrovsky, E. S. *Children without men.* New York: Collier Books, 1962. Pp. 79–93.

Otis, N. B., and McCandless, B. R. Responses to repeated frustrations of young children differentiated according to need area. *J. abnorm. soc. Psychol.*, 1955, *50*, 349–353.

Parke, R. D., and Walters, R. H. Some factors influencing the efficiency of punishment training for inducing response inhibition. *Monogr. Soc. Res. Child Develpm.*, 1967, *32*(1), 1–45.

Patterson, G. R., Littman, R. A., and Bricker, W. Assertive behavior in children: A step toward a theory of aggression. *Monogr. Soc. Res. Child Develpm.*, 1967, *32*(5), 1–43.

Rosenthal, M. K. The generalization of dependency behaviors from mother to stranger. Unpublished doctoral dissertation, Stanford Univer., 1965.

Rothbart, M. L. K. Birth order and mother–child interaction. Doctoral dissertation, Stanford Univer. Ann Arbor, Mich.: University Microfilms, 1967, No. 67–7961.

Scott, J. P. Biology and human aggression. *Amer. J. Orthopsychiat.*, 1970, *40*(4), 568–576.

Sears, R. R. Relation of early socialization experiences to aggression in middle childhood. *J. abnorm. soc. Psychol.*, 1961, *63*, 466–492.

Sears, R. R., Maccoby, E. E., and Levin, H. *Patterns of child rearing.* New York: Harper & Row, 1957.

Sears, R. R., Rau, L., and Alpert, R. *Identification and child rearing.* Stanford, Calif.: Stanford Univer. Press, 1965.

Sears, R. R., Whiting, J. W. M., Nowlis, V., and Sears, P. S. Some child-rearing antecedents of aggression and dependency in young children. *Genet. Psychol. Monogr.*, 1953, *47*, 135–234.

Siegel, A., and Kohn, L. Permissiveness, permission and aggression: The effect of adult presence or absence on children's play. *Child Develpm.*, 1959, *30*, 131–141.

Siegelman, M. Loving and punishing parental behavior and introversion tendencies in sons. *Child Develpm.*, 1966, *37*, 985–992.

Staub, E. The use of role playing and induction in children's learning of helping and sharing behavior. *Child Develpm.*, 1971, *42*(3), 805–816.

Stout, A. M. Parent behavior toward children of differing ordinal position and sibling status. Unpublished doctoral dissertation, Univer. of California, 1960.

Sutton-Smith, B., and Rosenberg, B. G. *The sibling.* New York: Holt, Rinehart & Winston, 1970.

Tasch, M. O. Modeling on prosocial behavior by preschool subjects of high and low self-esteem. *Dissert. Abstr.*, July 1971, *32*(1-B), 572.

Terman, L. M. *Psychological factors in marital happiness.* New York: McGraw-Hill, 1938.

Tuddenham, R. D. The constancy of personality ratings over two decades. *Genet. Psychol. Monogr.*, 1959, *60*, 3–29.

Watson, G. Some personality differences in children related to strict or permissive parental discipline. *J. Psychol.*, 1957, *44*, 227–249.

Weatherly, D. Maternal permissiveness toward aggression and subsequent TAT aggression. *J. abnorm. soc. Psychol.*, 1962, *65*(1), 1–5.

White, R. Motivation reconsidered: The concept of competence. *Psychol. Rev.*, 1959, *66*(5), 297–333.

Whiting, J. W. M., and Child, I. L. *Child training and personality.* New Haven, Conn.: Yale Univer. Press, 1953.

Winder, C. L., and Rau, L. Parental attitudes associated with social deviance in preadolescent boys. *J. abnorm. soc. Psychol.*, 1962, *64*, 418–424.

Winterbottom, M. R. The relation of need for achievement to learning experience in independence and mastery. In J. W. Atkinson (Ed.), *Motives in fantasy, action and society.* Princeton, N.J.: Van Nostrand, 1958.

Yamamoto, K. *The child and his image: Self-concept in the early years.* Boston: Houghton Mifflin, 1972.

V

Early Childhood

Ages 4 through 7

Hella Hammid – Rapho Guillumette

Intellectual and Cognitive Development 10

THE YEARS from 4 to 7 can be viewed as a period of transition between the diffuse, illogical thinking of the 2- to 4-year-old child and the systematic, practical thinking of the 7-year-old. Many of those who work with small children observe a significant change in their learning pace and ability between the ages of 5 and 7 (White 1965). The Russian psychologist Luria places the turning point somewhere between 4 and 5. According to Luria:

Something very important happens in the human being in this period. It is the period when speech is interiorized, when voluntary movements are developed and performed, and I think there may be some very intimate relation to maturation. (Luria 1960)

To Piaget, age 7 represents the watershed between two major phases in the child's development: the perceptual stage in which his thinking was largely intuitive, and a more sophisticated stage in which he will begin to understand the relationship between groups of objects and to commence concrete operations.

During the years from 4 to 7, the child seeks a more satisfactory balance between his interior and exterior worlds. His private play activities no longer appear as interesting to him as they once did; he replaces the symbolic play which formerly engrossed him with increasingly realistic imitations of what he sees happening in the world about him. If he attends kindergarten, he will come home and immediately begin playing school. According to Piaget, the play helps him to accommodate to his new situation. By converting that situation into a game, he assimilates it and relates it to his previous experiences. But at the same time that this realism is appearing in his observable behavior, he is developing the increasing capacity to continue his private play through internal fantasy.

By the time he is 6 or 7, the average child is

ready for elementary school and capable of learning reading and arithmetic. Even before this age, the nature of his thinking and his intense interest in the world around him enable him to profit from some type of schooling.

When psychologists want information about a child's thinking, they observe his speech and his actions. How well does he solve problems and answer questions? What scores does he receive on intelligence tests and on tests of academic achievement? How well does he write and speak? What are his drawings like? In what kinds of play does he engage? Because it is easy to observe activities, the tendency is to base estimates of the child's knowledge and ability exclusively upon them. Nevertheless, as we shall see when we study intelligence and I.Q. in greater detail, a child's I.Q. and his manner of answering questions are not always reliable clues to his mental ability. Generally, a child of 4 or 5 knows much more than he can produce. Because he draws a man with his arms attached to his head, for example, it does not necessarily mean that this is the way he thinks a man really looks. If he is shown two pictures, one with the man's arms where they belong and the other with the arms attached to the head, and asked to select the more accurate picture, he is able to pick it out. However, he may be incapable of drawing a man correctly himself. A considerable gap still separates his competence from his performance.

Numerous other intangibles affect his performance. One is his estimate of his own ability. The child who expects to succeed is more apt to do so than the child who expects to fail. Temperament, personality, motivation, and social class are among the other important performance variables which we shall consider in this chapter.

Figure 10.1 Play activities and drawings, as well as more standard measurements, yield information about the child's mental processes and content. The two children pictured here approach painting in very different ways. (Martin Helfer—D.P.I.; Lynn McLaren—Rapho Guillumette)

The Preoperational Stage: The Period of Intuitive Thought

Understanding the great shift in behavior and comprehension that occurs in the child between 4 and 7 years of age is a major challenge to psychologists. There are two schools of thought regarding this shift in behavior and comprehension. Each school claims the change comes about in a different way and for different reasons. According to Piaget, the founder and chief proponent of the first school, it is the shift in the capacity for thought that determines other changes in vocabulary, learning, memory, and imagery. Piaget regards these latter intellectual activities as determined by the larger shift in the cognitive structure.

The second school of thought maintains that the opposite may be true—that changes in memory or vocabulary could be the cause of changes in thought. We shall examine both contentions in this chapter. Whatever the relationships between the various functions may be, it is at least agreed that important shifts in all intellectual functions occur between 4 and 7 years and that a start to understanding them requires a description of them.

We shall begin with Piaget's position, which represents his effort to locate the child's capacity to reason at the root of the basic changes that take place. Throughout this discussion of Piaget's theories, we shall use as a base an excellent interpretive account of Piaget's theory of intellectual development written by Ginsburg and Opper, an American professor of developmental psychology and a psychologist who took her professional training with Jean Piaget.[1]

At about the age of 4, the child enters the second half of Piaget's preoperational stage—the period of intuitive thought. Behind him are the sensorimotor stage, which took him from birth until the age of 2, and the preconceptual phase of the preoperational period. At the beginning he had only the simple reflexes with which he was born. During the sensorimotor stage, the child made contact with the objects around him and developed a whole series of sensorimotor operations to help him deal with them. Gradually, his responses grew more sophisticated and he began to interiorize his actions; he began to think about how he would do something before he did it. During the initial half of the preoperational stage, he made his first tentative attempts to classify objects, but he did not yet understand the relationship between the individual representative of a class and the class itself. He tended to call all dogs by the name of his dog, to call all older women "Grandma."

Piaget describes the second half of the preoperational period—the intuitive stage—as follows:

. . . thought at this stage continues to be imaged and intuitive, and the equilibrium between assimilation and accommodation is not yet permanent. It is this intuitive thought, semi-reversible but without rigorous compositions, that constitutes the transition from preconcepts to concepts. . . . (Piaget 1962)

Characteristically, the child relies more upon immediate perception and direct experience than upon mental operations. Hence, his thinking tends to be egocentric and illogical. "However I perceive something, that is the way it is," he seems to be saying. One of the salient features of his thought at this time is *centration*. He thinks in terms of the parts of a given situation, but he cannot integrate these same parts into a satisfactory whole. Therefore, he can focus upon only one attribute of an object at a time. He cannot, for instance, think of beads as being simultaneously brown and wooden; either they are brown or they are wooden.

By the same token, he cannot reverse his thinking. Once he has divided something in two, he cannot then coordinate what he observed about the two halves with what he had observed about the object as a whole. His thinking also tends to be *static*. As a result, he seems unaware that when an object changes its shape a transformation process must occur. If, for example, a mass of dough is shaped into flat, round cookies, the child will focus upon the dough mass and then the cookies separately, without being able to form a mental picture of the change in form which occurred.

To Piaget, centration, irreversibility, and a

---

1. H. Ginsberg and S. Opper. *Piaget's theory of intellectual development: An introduction.* Englewood Cliffs, N. J.: Prentice-Hall, Inc., 1969.

static quality—the three hallmarks of intuitive thought—are interdependent. If the child concentrates upon objects at rest, he is insensitive to change. If he cannot picture change, he has no reason to reverse his thought. Hence, he will show only a comparatively limited ability to develop fully mature concepts concerning the world around him.

Classification of Objects and Events

Before discussing the 4- to 7-year-old's classificatory concepts, let us review Piaget's definition of a class. Borrowing his terms from the logician, Piaget tells us that a class has *intension*. By this he means that a class possesses a specific quality and excludes all objects lacking this quality. If, for instance, the defining quality or intension of a class is blueness, that class will include all objects that are in some way blue. A class also has *extension*; that is, it denotes a certain scope. Hence, a class may be described by the objects it includes. The class of triangles can include, among others, large red triangles, medium-sized yellow triangles, and small black ones. According to Piaget, intension defines extension, or, to put it another way, the defining property of a class determines the objects we will find in that class. Furthermore, no object can be a member of two classes simultaneously; it cannot be a circle and a square. Though this seems obvious to an adult, it is far from obvious to a small child.

Besides a knowledge of how to classify objects in accordance with the properties of intension and extension, mature classification also involves an understanding of *class inclusion*—the relationship between the different classes of a hierarchy. Thus, if a child begins with polygons and then goes on to separate them into squares and triangles, he should understand the connection between the original grouping and the new entities he has formed.

PIAGET'S EXPERIMENTS WITH CLASSIFICATION. Between the ages of 5 and 7, the child can produce rather elaborate hierarchical collections or true classes. Nevertheless, Piaget's findings indicate that a child of this age lacks the concept of class inclusion; he fails to grasp the relationship between one level of a hierarchy and another. In one experiment with 5- to 7-year-olds, Piaget gave each of the children being studied a number of pictures of flowers and other objects. He then told them to group the pictures in any way they wished. One child formed two collections, labeling the first "flowers" and the second "other things." Later the child divided his collection of flowers into primroses and "other flowers." Thus, he had produced a hierarchy with flowers at its apex and primroses and "other flowers" at its base. His ability to construct such a hierarchy seemed to imply a realization that flowers as a whole formed a larger group than primroses. Piaget's investigations, however, proved that this was not the case.

When asked if a little girl would have a bigger bouquet of flowers by using the yellow primroses or by using all the primroses, the child replied that the yellow primroses would yield the bigger bunch. Subsequently, the child counted the yellow primroses and then the other primroses and discovered there were four of each. "Oh! They're the same," he exclaimed (Piaget 1964). Apparently, he could not grasp the fact that "all the primroses" included the yellow primroses and the other primroses, that "yellow primroses" was a subdivision of a larger entity, namely primroses. Later, when asked which would be bigger, a bunch made up of all the primroses or a bunch made up of all the flowers, he again failed to see the relationship between the two. He replied that both bunches would be of equal size. To Piaget, the child's responses indicated that once a child of this age has divided an entity, he is unable to hold in his mind the original whole entity and the divisions into which he has separated it. The child who had divided his collection of flowers into primroses and "other flowers" found it impossible to move back and forth mentally between the original collection and the subdivisions he had created. Since he could no longer see the collection as the whole it had once been, while the subdivisions, on the other hand, were immediately present, he chose to refer to the subdivisions. Consequently, he gave incorrect answers to inclusion problems.

The Concept of Relations

Though a child can learn to add, subtract, and multiply by rote at an early age, Piaget believes that the same child cannot grasp the significance of what he is doing until he is around 7. In part this is because numbers are both cardinal (1, 2, 3) and ordinal (1st, 2nd, 3rd). In other words, a number represents not only a quantity such as, for example, five books, but also a position in a sequence—the fifth book. Piaget has conducted a series of studies on the ability of children 4 to 8 to comprehend and use ordinal relations. He detects three distinct stages in the child's mastery of this skill, the first beginning at age 4 and ending at 5, the second lasting from 5 to 6, and the third beginning at 7. For reasons which will become obvious when we study the stages in detail, he calls the first two preoperational, the third concrete. As in all his studies of concept development, he is careful to point out that the age at which a child enters a given stage may vary; the sequence of the stages, however, remains fixed.

STAGE 1. At this stage—beginning at 4 and ending at 5—a child can order five or six objects. Faced with a larger number, he will focus upon one aspect of the problem and appear oblivious to other equally important features. In one experiment, each child was given a collection of 10 sticks of varying lengths to which Piaget assigned the designations A to J. After scrambling the sticks, the Swiss psychologist asked the children to select the smallest and put that first, then find one a little bigger, and so on. Some children could not even pick out the smallest stick. Instead, they produced completely random arrangements. Others produced arrangements of the order of *ABCDHFE*. The more advanced selected a stick at random and then arranged the tops of all the other sticks in an orderly progression from shortest to tallest, meanwhile ignoring the bottoms of those same sticks (Piaget 1952).

The children's behavior illustrates what Piaget calls the "global" approach of Stage 1 children. In such an approach, we find neither an analysis of the details nor an understanding of what the problem calls for, only a haphazard attempt to manipulate objects.

STAGE 2. Children in Stage 2, from 5 to 6 years of age, generally succeeded in forming an orderly arrangement of sticks beginning with A and ending with J. This ordering did not, however, come easily. Usually the child appeared to lack an overall plan. Some children began by paying no attention to the bottoms of the sticks just as they had done in Stage 1. Others appeared more sophisticated in their approach. Whichever way they went at it, they had to continually shift sticks from one position to another before arriving at their final arrangements. In their handling of the problem, we see an example of what Piaget calls a perceptual reading of the situation, reliance upon trial and error and visual judgment to achieve the desired result.

Because the child bases his ordering upon intuition rather than upon a mental operation, he finds it difficult, if not impossible, to insert new elements. After correctly ordering sticks A to J, the children were then given another set of sticks, this time marked a to j, and told to put them into the previous arrangement. The correct ordering would then be *AaBbCcDd*, and so forth. One child produced the arrangement *CedD*, another produced *HgGIhjc*. Others succeeded in their task, but only after considerable trial and error.

Several factors contributed to their difficulties. Besides lacking any overall plan, they tended to view the original series as a unit; hence, they could not divide it into smaller units. They also had difficulty realizing that a given stick in their new series, let us say h, could be at one and the same time bigger than H and smaller than I. Since they could not coordinate this dual relationship, some children seeing h was bigger than B would place it next to B without considering whether it was also smaller than C.

STAGE 3. When he has reached the age of 6 or 7, the child has no difficulty either in ordering a series or in inserting new elements into an existing series. This is the beginning of a new major stage, the stage of concrete operations, which we shall examine in Chapter 12. At this stage, he no longer relies upon trial and error. Most often, he begins with the smallest stick and continues on with the next smallest until he has used up all his sticks. Furthermore, he can coordinate two inverse relationships such as taller and shorter, or bigger and smaller.

The Concept of Number

To understand the concept of *number*, Piaget believes the child must first grasp two basic concepts: one-to-one correspondence and conservation. By one-to-one correspondence, Piaget means the numerical equivalence of two sets of objects. For example, a subject might be given a first set—containing an orange, a flag, a bottle, and a doorknob—and a sack containing equally disparate objects. The subject would be asked to produce from the sack a second set of objects numerically equal to the first set. If he were an adult he simply would count the objects in the first set and take that same number of objects from the sack. If the subject was a child and could not count, he could achieve the same result by placing one object from the sack next to each object in the first set. Needless to say, he would not have to physically place each object from the sack next to one from the first set. Simply noting the one-to-one correspondence mentally would suffice. But in whatever way the subject solves the problem, he first must have a true conception of one-to-one correspondence, a conception which, as we shall see, the small child lacks.

To Piaget, the second basic concept essential for an understanding of number is the concept of *conservation*. Conservation is the ability to recognize that, despite changes in form, quantity is conserved. If, for instance, we place the objects in the first set close together to form a very short row or far apart to form a very long row, we still have the same number of objects. Similarly, if we roll a small, round ball of dough into a long snakelike shape, we still have the same quantity of dough.

Piaget's investigations have led him to conclude that the child's mastery of one-to-one correspondence and conservation occurs in stages. Before the child can fully understand these concepts, he needs to pass through three such successive stages (Piaget 1952).

STAGE 1. In Stage 1—beginning at age 4 and ending at 5—the child appears unable to use one-to-one correspondence. When comparing groups of objects, he tends to ignore density and to concentrate upon length. In one of Piaget's experiments, for example, the examiner placed a row of 6 or 7 pennies, candies, or other small objects before the child. The examiner then asked the child to select "the same number" or "as many" from a larger collection of similar objects. One child made a dense row of 10 candies which was shorter than the examiner's row of 6. When asked whether the two rows were the same, the child replied, "Not yet." After adding additional candies to his row, he declared that the two rows were equal because they were "like that," that is, equal in length.

In another experiment, Piaget attempted to make the child understand one-to-one correspondence before working out a conservation problem. Piaget showed the child 10 vases opposite which he placed 13 flowers. The vases were spaced out, but the flowers were bunched together. Although the child had counted the vases, he nevertheless thought that by spreading out his row of flowers to make it correspond in length to the row of vases, he had made the two rows equivalent in number. Later, Piaget made the child establish a one-to-one correspondence by having him put each flower in a vase. At this point, of course, the child realized that he had 3 extra flowers.

To see if this experience had helped the child to conserve the equivalency between flowers and vases, Piaget next removed the flowers from the vases and once again bunched them together. Once again the child concluded that there were more vases than flowers. He insisted on this even though he recognized that if he put the flowers back in the vases, there would be one flower in each vase. For him length was the crucial dimension in judging equivalency.

Piaget once more illustrated the child's focus

◉ ◉ ◉ ◉   ◉ ◉   Examiner's Row

◉◉◉◉◉◉◉◉◉◉   Stage 1 Child's Row

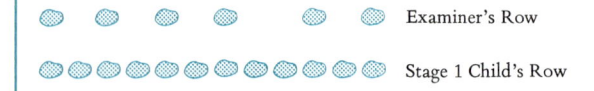

Figure 10.2 When asked to select the same number of objects as in the examiner's row, a Stage 1 child tends to concentrate on length of row and to ignore density.

on length when he investigated the role of counting at this stage. After counting two rows, one made up of six bottles and the other of six glasses, the child nevertheless pronounced the number of glasses bigger because the row was longer. Since the child plainly did not grasp the meaning of the numbers he had reeled off so blithely, Piaget concluded that at this stage counting was a meaningless act. No matter how often the child counts a series of objects, he continues to equate equality of length with equality of number.

STAGE 2. In Stage 2, the child 5 to 6 years old has no difficulty creating two numerically equal sets. When, however, the sets are rearranged, he does have difficulty conserving their equivalence. He appears unsure of which criteria to use in determining numerical equality. Sometimes he will assume that a longer row includes a greater number of objects merely because it is longer. At other times he will opt for a shorter row if it appears denser. He can concentrate on only one of these dimensions at a time. If he considers density, he must ignore length, and vice versa. In judging quantity, he therefore makes use of information relating to only one dimension. Such use of partial information persists until the child is ready to enter the third stage of his mastery of numerical concepts.

STAGE 3. This stage, extending from age 6 or 7 onward, represents the mastery of the child's concepts of one-to-one correspondence and conservation. Now he can coordinate the two dimensions of length and density. He can construct numerically equivalent sets and conserve their equivalency even after the examiner has rearranged them. At this point he is at the beginning of the concrete operational period.

Social Interaction and Cognitive Growth

The preoperational period has been called the period of egocentricity. The child's inability to see beyond himself leads the young child especially to assume that everyone thinks as he does, that the world was created for him. According to Piaget in *The Language and Thought of the Child* (1926), the child may be freed from his egocentricity through "inter-individual communication," that is, repeated communication conflicts with other children. In such conflicts, the young child is forced to pay attention to another's viewpoint, maintain another's perspective, and assume another's role.

ACQUIRING CONSERVATION THROUGH SOCIAL INTERACTION. In a recent article, Frank B. Murray has described the role of social interaction in cognitive growth (Murray 1972). In a study designed to help children acquire conservation concepts through social interaction, Murray studied 108 children about 6½ years old. In two experiments, he divided the children into groups of three (generally one nonconserver and two conservers). They replied to a series of standardized conservation problems. However, they were not permitted to reply individually. Instead, each group had to agree upon a collective answer, thus allowing for considerable interaction between group members. Each child was tested before being assigned to a group and then again at the end of his group experience. When tested upon parallel problems and new problems at this time, all of the children showed appreciable gains in both their conservation judgments and their explanations of the problems put to them. Nonconservers showed the greatest gains.

Murray's results indicate the importance of social conflict itself as an agent of cognitive growth—particularly since Murray and his associates made no effort to teach the children conservation. Instead, the investigators found that the children themselves often used reversibility explanations to convince the nonconservers among them. After the third problem, the nonconservers generally agreed with their peers. After their first conserving reply, most of the nonconservers replied in this fashion to succeeding questions.

It is not clear exactly what the nonconservers learned in the social situation that later sustained them in the individual situation. It is possible that as a result of the disorienting effect of the social conflict, the nonconserver then "models" after the conserver. Research which Murray currently has underway is attempting to probe this possibility. While the exact behavior is not clear, the necessity of the conflict to cognitive progress seems apparent. In a review of the many conditions thought to be related to attaining operational thought, Smeds-

Figure 10.3 Social interaction as an agent of cognitive growth: through interaction with other children, the child encounters other points of view and approaches. (Nicholas Sapieha—Rapho Guillumette)

lund concluded that the presence of communication conflicts is necessary for "intellectual decentration"—the transition from egocentric to operational thought (Smedslund 1966). Therefore, according to this view, the interaction crucial to the growth of intelligence is not between the individual and his physical environment. It is the interaction between the individual and those about him.

Problem-Solving Processes

Piaget favors a more unified, global view of the child's cognitive development than most investigators. Others have taken a more analytic approach, identifying more specific contributing variables such as vocabulary, attention, and memory. One such analytic approach is to study the processes involved in problem solving. At this point in the consideration of the question, it is difficult to sort out the relative value of the global and analytic approaches to cognitive development. It is possible that both approaches, focusing on different processes and outcomes, may in reality be less opposed than they seem. Undoubtedly, the more analytic variables, such as vocabulary, attention, and memory, also are part of the more global processes to which Piaget refers—even if such variables are not the simple causes of those global processes. Since the current issues are not always drawn clearly enough to make a resolution possible, the true nature of the interrelationship between the two orders of variables must remain a matter for investigation through further research.

Problem-oriented thought is highly directed. Its goal is a solution. A child's parents may present him with a problem—brushing his teeth, for example—or he may encounter problems on his own—for instance, how to get his trouser cuff out of his bicycle chain. In either case, the child is aware of the problem and he quickly seeks a solution.

In the studies of problem solving, several leading investigators have made use of five categories for mental processes, which we shall describe in some detail. The reader interested in further study of these processes should consult the review of this area of research by Kagan and Kogan[2] on which we have substantially based our approach.

The five mental processes which characterize effective problem solving are *encoding, memory, hypothesis-generation, evaluation,* and *deduction*—usually occurring in that sequence.

Encoding

Encoding refers to the comprehension and labeling of stimuli. Through the child's selective attention to a stimuli's specific aspects, these aspects are translated into perceptual images, words, and concepts. As the child develops during this period, words and concepts gradually become the dominant codes for labeling sensory information.

For example, a 1-year-old child presented with the shape

is likely to encode it only as an image. A 6-year-old, however, is likely to encode this shape as, perhaps, a boat, a bullet, or the bottom of a steam iron. As a result, when asked to select the same shape from a set of similar ones, the 6-year-old is apt to make errors which indicate that the shape had been labeled by one or more words. That is, once language is acquired, the child *assimilates* perceptions to his language labels. He relies on words as descriptions of objects rather than on the images as mental copies of those objects.

Nonliterate peoples, as well as the mentally retarded, do the opposite—they rely on images alone as codes for experience. The orientation toward the image seems to come about by necessity and to reflect a paucity of word skills. This assessment is based on studies of image-oriented persons who possess a remarkable facility, *eidetic*

2. J. Kagan and N. Kogan. Individual variation in cognitive processes. In P. H. Mussen (Ed.), *Carmichael's manual of child psychology.* Vol. I. (3rd ed.) New York: Wiley, 1970.

imagery, which is popularly called the "photographic memory." A person who has eidetic imagery can retain accurate mental pictures of sights he has seen only once and even then only for a short time. For example, he may be able to describe in detail the clothes worn by figures on a highway billboard or the print wallpaper in a relative's dining room. While eidetic imagery is fairly common in the normal population—perhaps 1 in 10 American school children exhibits it—it is especially prevalent among nonverbal, image-oriented persons. Approximately 1 out of 5 mentally retarded American children and several nonliterate peoples, such as the Ibo tribe of Eastern Nigeria (Wober 1967), possess eidetic imagery.

INFLEXIBILITY OF ENCODING. While encoding is a necessary step in problem solving, there is a tendency for children to adopt fixed or inflexible solutions to problems. Understandably, children, dominated by sense perception, try to solve problems by imposing a single order on their sense perceptions—even though that order may be quite arbitrary from the problem-solving point of view. A study by Gollin illustrates the child's tendency to fix on one set of units to encode all his experience (Gollin 1966). For this study, the experimental children were required to learn to associate pictures of animals and objects with sketchy drawings that depicted these animals only poorly. The pictures and partial drawings were presented in pairs. For example, a detailed drawing of an elephant was coupled with only a few lines vaguely suggesting an elephant. Then the child had to learn to guess the animal from the partial drawing. During the learning trials, a number of different animals and objects were shown, but always in the same order. Later, when the children were tested, the experimenter discovered that the number of correct responses depended on whether the pictures were presented in the same order in the test as in the learning period.

When the pictures were presented out of their original order, children who had been given fewer learning trials performed better than children who had more learning trials. Gollin concluded that this occurred because children who had been given fewer trials had not overlearned the original order of picture presentation. That is, they had not fixed inflexibly on the order, while the other children had learned both the association between pictures in each pair *and* the order of presentation of each pair. The results of similar encoding studies could affect certain educational practices that may encourage such inflexibility.

ATTENTION AND EXPECTANCY. The ability to focus the selective attention required for encoding is related to expectancy—as well as other variables, such as anxiety. If a child knows what is about to happen, he will be prepared to focus his attention on a particular event and to perceive and encode the event more accurately. Expectancy's role is illustrated by a study in which kindergarten children and second-, fourth-, and sixth-graders were asked to repeat words spoken by a man or woman (Maccoby 1967). In some instances, the illuminated face of a man or woman appeared before the words were spoken; in other instances, the face was illuminated after the words were spoken. The children proved better at repeating words spoken by voices they were prepared to hear, and this tendency grew more pronounced with increasing age.

ATTENTION AND OTHER VARIABLES. Data indicate that boys exhibit different biases from girls in their comprehension and labeling of experience. For example, boys were found more inclined than girls to analyze geometric designs into their component parts (Kagan, Rosman, Day, Albert, and Phillips 1964). Class as well as sex affects selectivity of attention. The data on social-class differences have shown, for example, that middle-class children were more likely than their lower-class peers to use descriptive and analytic language to sort out similar designs.

Another important variable is age. Research has repeatedly confirmed that children 6 and 7 years of age exhibit a dramatic increase in their ability to direct and sustain attention. This increase is so striking that some investigators have suggested that a change in the central nervous system during this period underlies the greatly extended attention span. Others explain this change in terms of the child's growing concern during this period about making mistakes and having his concepts agree with the accepted standard. Because of their heightened apprehension, children may apply themselves more diligently to performing tasks and gaining a better understanding of reality. Thus, for example, one study concluded that the best predictor of children's "achievement behavior" was their conviction that success or failure was due to self-imposed limitations or outside forces (Crandall, Katkovsky, and Preston 1962). Achievement behavior was defined as "behavior directed toward attainment of approval—or avoidance of disapproval—in meeting certain intellectual standards." Children who saw themselves as responsible for their own success or failure scored highest in achievement behavior; conversely, children who felt that their destinies were beyond their control scored lowest.

Memory

The next step in the problem-solving process is memory. A child's ability to register and retain encoded experience affects the store of information and knowledge he has to draw on in solving problems. Since remembering is often a great effort, the quality of a child's memory depends on his motivation, that is, his interest and determination. Therefore, anxiety and intervening thoughts generally reduce the child's ability to register or recall memories. This retardant effect on memory parallels the negative effect that anxiety exerts on verbal skill. On the other hand, experiments in which younger children's memory is facilitated by overlearning often have resulted in a marked increase in the problem-solving capacity of those children.

VOCABULARY AND MEMORY. Vocabulary, images, and concepts help a child associate events and fix them in his memory. Thus, a child with a good vocabulary recalls new information better than a child with poor language ability. Studies show, for example, that an older child can remember a longer series of numbers, but, more important, that the length of the series he can remember increases in proportion to the child's familiarity with words. Confirming these findings—children from language-poor environments have been found to perform poorly at remembering spoken or written words. While verbal ability coincides with facility at remembering, a better vocabulary does not guarantee a better memory. Instead, the child who wants to retain information must actively use words to reinforce and even rehearse his recent memories. This was demonstrated in a study of children in kindergarten and grades two and five in which they were shown a set of pictures in a given order, and then shown the same pictures in different orders. Finally the children were asked to point to the pictures in their original order. The older children repeated the names of the pictures to themselves as they were first presented or while trying to recall them. These children did better at recalling the original order than the younger children. The kindergarten children also knew the names of the pictures, but they did not use this information to reinforce their memories of the order. Children of 5 years, taught to use words to remember the pictures, did significantly better on recall—despite children's tendency not to use verbal mediators spontaneously until they are 7 or older (Flavell, Beach, and Chinsky 1966).

ANXIETY. Many experiments have demonstrated that anxiety, interfering with attention, diminishes a child's memory performance. Messer, in his study of this effect, divided third-grade boys into three groups. The first group was made anxious by causing its members to fail an anagram test; the second group was permitted to succeed in the test; and the third was not tested at all. Then a story was read to all the subjects, who later recounted it as accurately as possible. The "anxious" first group scored significantly lower than the other two, which scored the same (Messer 1968).

LONG- AND SHORT-TERM MEMORY. Short-term memory refers to newly encoded information that is available for no more than 30 seconds after it has been registered. These memories are generally lost unless they are transferred to long-term memory. One study showed that the short-term memory of children 5 or 6 years old is notably shorter than the short-term memory found in adults (Morrison, Eisenberg, Haith, and Mindes 1968). The experimenters presented children and adults with several geometric forms, displaying each for less than a second. Afterward, the subjects pointed out the forms they had seen on sheets showing 10 geometric forms. All the children could recall two forms with some ease, while many of the adult subjects could recall three or four. Adults had used the mnemonic aid of associating each form with a simple, familiar figure, and thus retained the forms in memory more easily. The immediate memory of number or word sequences also improves with age. Children 10 years old can recall a string of six or seven numbers read to them, whereas the 5-year-old remembers five at most.

Generation of Ideas and Hypotheses

Problem solving requires the ability to produce various possible alternative ideas and solutions. This implies that the child must possess a good knowledge of cognitive units—words, images, concepts, and the logical rules governing their use and relation to one another. Yet, the mere possession of this knowledge may only indicate that a child is *intelligent*. On the other hand, the child who combines these units in uniquely constructive ways is regarded as *creative*. Intelligence and creativity, therefore, do not necessarily appear together in a child. Indeed, insofar as these abilities have been measured, creativity is independent of intelligence. In all cases, the child's freedom and enthusiasm to generate ideas may be inhibited by the fear of making errors, so that measured performance in problem solving is sometimes misleading.

CRITICAL ATTRIBUTES. Much problem solving involves the recognition of similarities. The judgment that two objects are similar presumes the ability to perceive that they share certain salient features or *critical attributes*. These attributes provide a means for recognizing the conceptual similarity between things, as well as their literal and concrete likenesses. For example, a knowledge of critical attributes makes clear that the hummingbird as well as the giant condor, though vastly different in size and habits, are both members of the class of birds. The same knowledge would preclude the placement of the bat—which is a flying rodent—in the same class as the hummingbird, even though his wings make him superficially similar to a bird. Conceptual similarities permit objects and ideas to be sorted into classes that are more meaningful and more inclusive of different objects that may be unlike in specific details, and therefore more stimulating of new ideas and hypotheses. For example, although birds differ widely among the various individual species, they all possess the typical or critical attributes of the concept of bird.

Social experience also plays a role in the perception of certain critical attributes. Not uncommonly, for example, children who are led to believe that an adult's importance is based on his race may learn to prize lightness or darkness of skin. Other children will associate importance with creativity, character, education, social position, or wealth.

CREATIVITY IN PROBLEM SOLVING. As we have suggested, *creativity* can play an important, though little-understood, role in the generation of ideas and hypotheses. Creativity seems to be an ability that, in a sense, stands alone. Studies have found that, in addition to its independence from intelligence, creativity also is unrelated to academic aptitudes or achievement (Wallach and Kogan 1965). In these studies, four criteria of creativity were devised. Fifth-grade children were then tested against these criteria to assess their creativity. The children had to give examples of such concepts as "round things" (ladybugs, cookies, eyes) or "things that move on wheels" (cars, bicycles, carriages); propose practical uses for such items as a cork, a chair, and a newspaper (plug a leak, feed a fire, hit a dog); suggest possible similarities between such pairs as cats and mice (four feet, fur, sharp teeth) and milk and meat (come from animals, eaten as food, are kept in refrigerators); and lastly, view abstract designs and speculate on their meanings or interpretations. The researchers found that creativity performance in one of the tests could be used to predict performance in others. In addition, the subjects' overall creativity scores were found to be unrelated to standard measures of academic aptitude or achievement. It was equally likely that individuals with *low* scores in academic ability scored high or low in creativity; conversely, individuals scoring high in creativity may have scored either high or low in academic ability.

In this same study sex differences in creativity were correlated with social factors. Among boys, differences in creativity were not significantly related to social behavior. Girls, on the other hand, exhibited more complex interdependence between creativity and social relations. Girls who were highly creative as well as highly intelligent were popular with friends and self-confident in school. Girls with high creativity but low intelligence were socially less cautious and hesitant than the first group, but also less popular with their friends. Girls with low creativity and high intelligence, although sought out by their schoolmates, were more aloof and cautious than the two other groups of girls.

Another researcher also studied creativity in children 7 to 8 years of age, using similar creativity tests (Ward 1968). In this work, too, the experimenter found that although scores on each of the creativity tests correlated with one another, they were not related to the children's intelligence.

Most studies in this area reveal that some creative children may not display their creativity unless they can undertake problem-solving tasks in the spirit of a game. When challenged under serious test conditions, some of these otherwise creative children fail to score well. Thus, many investigators believe creativity is best expressed in an atmosphere where the child feels free to take chances and risk unusual ideas—and errors. In short, creativity blossoms where the child can be "playful"—a not unnatural connection considering our discussion in Chapter 6 on the relationships between play and creativity.

THE ROLE OF LEARNING SET. Another factor that plays a part in the generation of ideas and hypotheses is *learning set.* Learning set is the application of experience gained in solving one problem to solving other problems. A child's efficiency in using experience in this way improves steadily with age, continuing into the college years. For example, in one typical study of learning set, preschool children took six days to learn to solve a new problem in a progression of similar problems; but fifth-grade children required only three days (Levinson and Reese 1967).

Increasing efficiency in learning set follows on the child's expanding ability to generate hypotheses and mentally eliminate incorrect guesses. A child's growing confidence that problems have correct solutions also contributes to this improvement. Moreover, between the ages of 6 and 10, children learn that formal problems can be di-

Figure 10.4 A sample of abstract designs that children were asked to interpret in Ward's study of creativity. (From W. C. Ward. Creativity in young children. *Child Develpm.*, 1968, 39, 741.)

vorced from personal attitudes and solved logically.

Tests of learning set. In typical studies of learning set, children select one of two objects from a variety of different pairs of objects. The criterion for a "correct" selection is arbitrarily set by the experimenter, who chooses some attribute of the object, which is unknown to the subject. For each correct choice, the child is rewarded. Therefore, as the child progresses from one object pair to another, he can apply his previous criterion-learning experience to learning the criterion for the next selection between objects. For example, children may be shown a series of pairs of colored chips—perhaps red-green, red-yellow, and red-black. They then would be asked to select one chip from each pair. The criterion for the "correct" choice may be fixed as the "red one." After a number of trials the child is expected to recognize that color, not position, determines the proper selection. After learning this, the child may be shown a spoon and fork, both of the same size and color. The experimenter may decide that the spoon is the correct choice. The children now are expected to have learned from their previous experience to quickly discard certain hypotheses such as position. Therefore, they should choose more quickly on the basis of whether the utensil has tines or a scoop.

Dependence on age and I.Q. The type of experiment described above has been used to study the relation of learning set to chronological age (C.A.), mental age (M.A.), and I.Q. (Harter 1967). In one such experiment, two groups of children were studied, one with an M.A. of 5½ years and the other with an M.A. of 8½ years. The children were divided further into four subgroups, two subgroups with I.Q.'s of 100 and two subgroups with I.Q.'s of 130. At each I.Q. level, 5½-year-olds comprised one group and 8½-year-olds the other. A still further division was made: half of each subgroup was tested in a standard condition—with the experimenter hidden behind a screen. The other half was tested in a "social" condition—with the experimenter facing the children and praising them for making correct selections. The selection trials were arranged in this way: pairs of miscellaneous junk items to be discriminated were placed in a two-well tray. The pairs were placed to cover both wells. A marble, placed in one well of the tray, served as a token reward that could later be exchanged for a prize. The experimenter arbitrarily chose one of the junk items as the "correct" one to select. The selection trials were repeated until the child made the correct selection most of the time. It was found that younger subjects took longer than older ones to detect the criterion for making a selection. Those 5½-year-olds tested in the social condition, however, detected the criterion faster than those tested in the standard condition. Indeed, those 5½-year-olds in the socially tested group who had high I.Q.'s reached the criterion as quickly as the 8½-year-olds. The testing conditions did not affect the 8½-year-olds. On the average, children in the 130 I.Q. group improved their performance more rapidly than those in the 100 I.Q. group.

METHODS OF SORTING CONCEPTS. When generating hypotheses, children exhibit both formal developmental as well as individual differences in the ways that they classify information. Depending on their age and other personal factors, children indicate preferences among four approaches to the construction of concepts (Kagan, Moss, and Sigel 1963). Those four approaches are:

1. *Superordinate or categorical:* grouping objects as "wholes"; for example, categorizing car, train, and bus as "vehicles," or horses, mice, and birds as "animals."
2. *Functional-relational:* grouping objects according to some relation between their functions; for example, describing nine boys who play baseball together as "a team," or grouping gasoline with cars, since gasoline fuels cars.

3. *Functional-locational:* classifying objects because of common location; for example, classifying blackboard, desk, and notebook as "school things."
4. *Analytic:* grouping objects by some manifest, similar part; for example, all people with blonde hair, or all hoofed animals.

Age-related trends. Many studies have demonstrated certain age trends in the use of these approaches to concept construction (Sigel 1953; Kagan, Rosman, Day, Albert, and Phillips 1964). For example, children 4 to 6 years of age most often classify visually presented objects to functional-relational categories (the boys play ball together). Older children seem to prefer both superordinate and analytic groupings. Children in lower social classes tend toward functional-relational grouping more frequently than their middle-class peers. With increasing age the preference moves toward analytic groupings of visually presented objects.

In word-sorting tasks, the preference trends are opposite to those described above. When subjects 6 to 9 years old told of the likenesses they detected among word groups, the use of analytic groupings was found to have *decreased* with increasing age; on the other hand, the use of superordinate categories increased (Olver and Hornsby 1966). With exceptions, most investigations find that analytic concepts are used more frequently with pictures than with words.

Dependence on stimuli. While some studies suggest that age trends determine children's concept-sorting ability independent of what the stimulus is, other data seem to counter this contention. For example, one study found that while lower-class children could fairly easily categorize familiar three-dimensional objects, they had considerable difficulty sorting out pictures of those same objects (Sigel, Anderson, and Shapiro 1966; Sigel and McBane 1967; Sigel and Olmsted 1967). Thus, it would seem that the type of stimulus does influence a child's performance at concept sorting.

Another study contains an even clearer indication that the type of stimulus affects the child's classification processes (Wohlwill 1963). This study, using abstract representations of numbers as well as numerals themselves, compared two responses—the relational ("Select the larger number of dots") and the absolute ("Select the numeral 5"). When children were shown dot patterns or groups of triangles or crosses and asked to select the numerically smaller patterns or groups, they readily made selections based on such relative quantity—three dots being recognized as fewer than four, two triangles as fewer than three, and so on. However, using the same patterns and groups, the children had substantial difficulty selecting an absolute number as represented by the patterns and groups (five dots for the numeral 5, and so on). When shown the actual numerals, on the other hand, they made absolute responses much more readily, selecting, for example, the numeral 5 when it was requested.

It appears, then, that the stimuli definitely affected the child's ability to make desired responses. Therefore, unless the specific stimuli are taken into account, it is difficult to be certain that a child's observed responses are the only ones he can make in a concept area; given other stimuli, he might well make new responses.

Social influences. Children seem to be aware at an early time that adults regard certain ways of thinking as "good" and others as "bad." This understanding, investigators have found, results from the child's observation that frequently adults are more lavish in their praise when a child succeeds in difficult tasks or after a determined effort. As a result, children may associate success in difficult tasks with pleasurable feelings—and may therefore be motivated to develop more subtle skills in concept sorting. For example, if a situation makes functional groupings easier and analytic ones harder to determine, even a child of 6 or 7 may prefer the harder grouping if he thinks his parents or teachers regard it as more desirable. Such thought tendencies, established by expressed parental values, can result in habits of mind. Thus, an older child may have developed an analytical mind not because he had an inherent analytical cast to his character, but because his parents preferred such thinking and expressed their preference to him.

Evaluation

The next step in the problem-solving process is evaluation of the hypotheses generated. At 2 years of age, a child may already exhibit individual differences in the degree to which he evaluates the quality of his thinking. One child acts impulsively; he makes decisions on the basis of his first hypothesis. Another will pause and proceed cautiously, reflecting on the relative value of many different hypotheses. Whichever behavior the child displays—impulsive or reflective—this behavior tends to persist into later life and to emerge in most tasks that the child undertakes. Given training, however, children seem able to reverse either tendency.

A test in which the child matches familiar figures is the instrument most often used to evaluate impulsive and reflective behavior in problem solving. The child is shown a standard stimulus and six variants of the standard. He selects one variant that is identical to the standard, while the experimenter observes how long he takes to make his correct responses and how many responses he makes. Among American children the response time increases while errors decrease steadily between 5 and 12 years of age. The general rule is that the shorter the response time, the more errors a child makes. Reflective children respond slowly and make few errors. They also delay longer than impulsive children before describing pictures or answering an adult's questions; and they make fewer errors in tests of reading and deductive reasoning.

Studies of eye-tracking movements also reveal that reflective children make more systematic and thorough examinations of all the variants before they offer hypotheses. In contrast, impulsive children frequently answer even before they have scanned all the variants.

THE TEACHER'S INFLUENCE. A teacher's impulsive or reflective behavior may influence a child's behavior positively or negatively. A random group of 20 children from 20 classrooms was tested for impulsivity/reflectivity in the fall and then again in late spring (Yando and Kagan 1968). These children displayed behavior changes that paralleled their teachers' impulsive or reflective manners. The most pronounced effect was that of reflective teachers on impulsive boys; they showed the greatest increase in decision-making time.

Deduction

Deduction and hypothesis-generation complement each other. For example, the idea that trees and plants are similar because they both

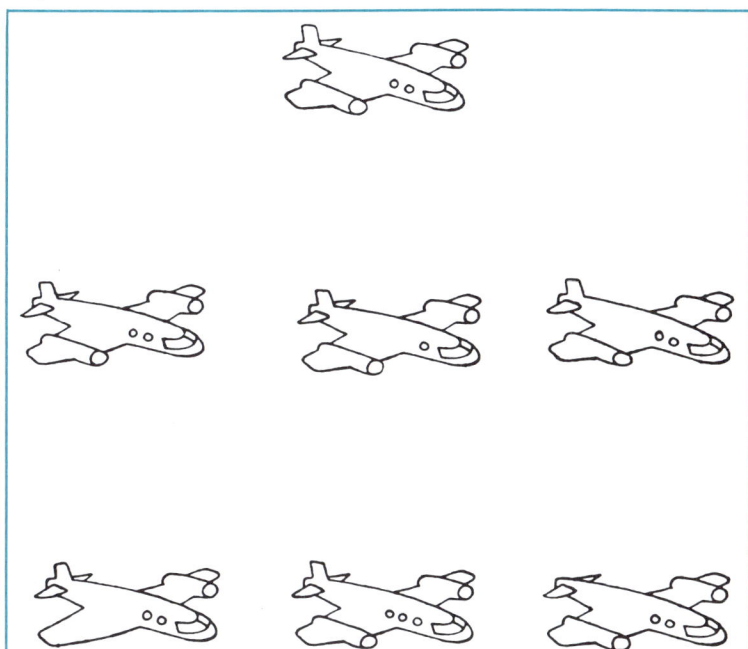

Figure 10.5 Illustrative item from the Matching Familiar Figures test for measuring reflective-impulsive tendency. (From J. Kagan, L. Pearson, and L. Welch. Modifiability of an impulsive tempo. *J. educ. Psych.*, 1966, 57(6), 361.)

have green leaves leads to the deduction that trees and plants both somehow use leaves in their life processes. Hence, the child's bank of rules (for example, knowing that green leaves relate to plant life) is the most important set of cognitive units determining deductive ability.

Still debated, however, is the question of whether a child's ability to use rules—not merely acquire them—changes significantly from 4 to 12 years of age. Some investigators feel that deductive ability continuously improves as new rules are absorbed, but that no fundamental change occurs in reasoning skill. Other psychologists, and Piaget is among them, contend that a child experiences a progressive development of reasoning skill. At first, therefore, the child possesses only a primitive ability to comprehend and apply elementary rules; thereafter, through experience, this ability is gradually elaborated to include very precise applications of extremely subtle rules.

Mediation

Up to this point, this section has dealt with various attempts to understand the important cognitive transition from age 4 to 7 by reducing the transition to an outcome of many subordinate processes; for example, memory, attention, vocabulary, learning set, concept-sorting preferences, and so forth. One other important subordinate process is *mediation*—an internal middle step in the thinking process. Mediation is more broad and inclusive than some of the other processes and may refer to any of several types of internal processing phenomena, whether they are words, concepts, images, or other mental realities.

A child's more advanced cognitive acts—problem solving as well as thinking, reasoning, and concept forming—are greatly aided by the process of *verbal mediation*. In verbal mediation, of course, the middle factor interposed between the outside stimulus and the final, overt response is the word.

A look at mediation's role in the common stimulus-response process may be a helpful prelude to understanding verbal mediation. To accommodate complicated developmental activities, such as concept formation, behavior-oriented psychologists have adapted the standard stimulus-response (S–R) theory—which had no third factor intervening between the stimulus and the response. The adapted theory is S–r–s–R, a longer chain of events (Kendler 1963). According to this theory, the outside stimulus (S) prompts an implicit response (r), which the learner makes internally as he detects the outside stimulus. His implicit internal response (r) modifies the outside stimulus by supplying an implicit stimulus (s). It is to this implicit stimulus that the learner makes his final, overt response (R). The mediating response (r) is important because it produces the implicit stimulus for the final, overt response.

Verbal mediation is common in the child's generalization of his responses. Through verbal mediation, he extends the same words or labels to include many objects which all evoke the same response. The child applies the word *game* to certain physical activities. Since he enjoys playing tag and blindman's bluff, he is well disposed toward other activities called games; thus, he can be expected to respond to them favorably. When his grandfather verbally offers to play "a game of checkers" with him—a game the boy has never played—the boy applies his acquired game response to the new stimulus of checkers and he decides to play checkers. Generalization, mediated by words, permits the child to respond—both negatively as well as positively, of course—to new stimuli the first time he encounters them. For this reason, verbal mediation is critical to the child's learning and to his problem solving.

A transposition experiment provides a good example. In such an exercise, the youngest subjects select an object because of its relationship to other objects. For example, the child is rewarded for selecting the largest of three black squares. Later in the experiment, the same children are shown three more squares, the smallest one exactly the size of the largest one selected earlier. They are told to select the largest square. Young children who do not have developed language ability cannot transpose the concept of relative size from the first trial to the second. Instead, they are attached to the specific square size, which they will select again for many trials even though they now receive no reward for doing so (Kuenne 1946). Kindergarten children in the same pair of trials are strikingly more advanced. Because they have verbal ability, they remind themselves to select the largest square in the second group. To do this, they use words as verbal mediators.

Once a child learns to use verbal mediators, he also can do well in an area of learning that involves *reversal-shift* problems. The child's basic task in such an exercise is to shift his responses and do the opposite of what he did earlier in the identical circumstance. Earlier he might have been rewarded for picking the larger of two blocks, one black and the other white. The size was the key characteristic, not the color. After the child learns to pick out the larger block regardless of color, the task is changed, introducing the reversal shift. The child must completely reverse his response and pick the *small* block this time. The *nonreversal shift* is another kind of change and demands a different response. This time the child would have to choose the block on the basis of color — previously an irrelevant characteristic — rather than on the basis of size. For example, the white block might be the correct choice.

The child who can make mediated verbal responses — in effect coaching himself by saying, "Look for the size of the block" — has no problem with the reversal shift. Accordingly, children over 7 are adept at reversal shifts. Preschoolers do better at nonreversal shifts because part of their earlier responses are still adequate: half the large blocks are the right color. Among kindergartners, fast learners — who tend to be proficient verbally and, therefore, good at verbal mediation — learn to perform reversal shifts more rapidly than their slower-learning peers. The difference between kindergarten and first-grade children suggests that in the period between ages 5 and 7 verbal mediation is developing into an effective cognitive tool for problem solving.

While verbal facility clearly seems to improve the child's cognitive ability, it has not been proven that language is essential for the child to think and solve problems. Such nonverbal mediators as pictures, symbols, and images serve deaf children — who have poor verbal skills — as well as words serve other children (Furth, 1964, 1971; Youniss 1964). (For a full discussion of the relationship between language and cognition, see Chapter 8.)

Though the mediating symbols used by deaf children are unknown, their performance in reversal shifts indicates that they have some sort of effective nonverbal symbolic system to guide them. Thus, rather than being the sole means of thinking and solving problems, verbal mediation seems to be one means among at least two that the child can use. The child who cannot use words as mediators may be falling back on a more basic method of representation.

Certainly, problem solving, with the subordinate processes we have examined, seems vastly more complex than we might have gathered from Piaget's account of it. While Piaget describes major operations, other writers try to explain facets of the competence needed to carry out such operations. Each focuses on problem solving at a different level. At the same time, the two points of view are perhaps complementary rather than alternative. However, we should not overlook the basic theoretical difference. Piaget assumes that cognitive operations come before the variables that affect them, whereas most other writers assume that the variables develop before the cognitive operations. Clearly, a fundamental question of causality divides the two points of view.

However, the transition that occurs between ages 4 and 7 holds still more changes to be explored. In addition to thinking, there are changes in many other functions, which may, in turn, have much to do with the changes in thought. Accordingly, we shall discuss next the area of mental imagery — again drawing heavily on the writings of Piaget — and then perception, where we shall deal with the work of other researchers.

Mental Imagery

As we saw in our study of children of 2 and 3, Piaget believes that until the middle of the second year, the child forms no mental images of his surroundings. As a result, he lives exclusively in the present. However, by the beginning of the 4-to-7-year period, imagery is well developed; the child can readily represent events and objects not actually present. According to Piaget, imagery results from imitation. At first the child imitates people and things overtly. Later, he internalizes and abbreviates his imitations, producing interior images of what he has seen or experienced.

The personal nature of children's images makes them difficult to study. No one but the child himself can "see" his images. Neither words nor pictures appear adequate to convey their substance to others. Asked to give a verbal report of an object, few children—or adults, for that matter—can satisfactorily describe what they actually see before their eyes, let alone something as ephemeral as a mental image. Nor does asking the child to draw an object he no longer sees in front of him prove a suitable alternative. Some children have poor memories. Since they are unable to fully remember what they have seen, they obviously cannot reproduce it on paper. Others may have no difficulty remembering but cannot adequately draw it.

To circumvent the problems inherent in the use of original drawings, Piaget has had the investigator show the child a number of drawings done by professionals. From these the child selects the one that most closely corresponds to the object he has seen. Even this method, however, has its limitations. The drawings are seldom exact copies of the child's images. Generally, they add details that were not present in the child's image and omit others that were there.

Because no one method is completely reliable, Piaget has used personal histories, original drawings, and collections of drawings singly or in combination in his studies of imagery. Usually he supplements these techniques with a clinical interview of his subject.

Kinetic Imagery

One of Piaget's experiments with children from the 4-to-7 age period was related to kinetic images—the mental representation of objects in motion. The children were given two identical blocks, the second of which was placed directly over the first. Generally, the children had no difficulty drawing the two blocks. When they had finished, the examiner moved the upper block so that it jutted out over the lower one, then he returned it to its former position. As long as children under the age of 7 saw the blocks in the new position, they had no difficulty drawing them. When, however, the blocks were returned to their original position and the children were asked to draw the second position from memory, they were unable to do so. Since they had been able to produce accurate drawings when the blocks were before their eyes, the inaccuracy of their subsequent rendition could not have been the result of a lack of drawing ability. Rather, it was the result of poor memory or of poor imagery.

The children's reactions to a group of professional drawings of the displaced blocks tended to reinforce this conclusion. Shown the drawings after the blocks had been returned to their original position, only children over 7 seemed capable of selecting a correct reproduction of the displaced blocks. As in the case of numerical relations, children under 7 appeared to form a "global" impression of what had occurred. They knew the blocks had moved, but how they had moved eluded them.

Transformational Imagery

Besides kinetic imagery, Piaget has studied transformational imagery, that is, changes in shape and form. In these studies the investigator showed the children semicircular pieces of wire. Then he bent the wires until they formed straight lines. The children were asked to draw the successive changes in shape between semicircle and straight line. They also were asked to give verbal descriptions of what had occurred and to select drawings depicting the transformation. All the children underestimated the length of the straight line. They frequently depicted the straight line as shorter than the curve and only rarely did they picture it as longer. Piaget interpreted their error in terms of boundaries; the children saw the ends of the curved wire as the boundary beyond which the straightened wire could not go. The children also were unable to picture the successive stages between curve and straight line. Here the tendency towards centration—the tendency to concentrate on only the first and last states of an object—as well as the generally static nature of the children's thought, was responsible for their failure to select the drawings depicting the wire's transformation.

In the last analysis, the only type of images with which children from 4 to 7 could deal successfully were static images. Shown pictures of objects or scenes that did not change either their shape or their position, they could produce reasonably faithful copies. Not until after the age of 7 can children produce kinetic and transformational images. At this time, their imagery becomes both reproductory and anticipatory; that is, children of this age can reproduce a person already seen and they also can anticipate changes in form or location. Since this growth in imagery coincides with the beginning of a new stage, the stage of concrete operations, the relationship between operative and imagistic thought becomes a matter of interest. It appears that the development of images assists operational thought, and the development of operational thought, in turn, enhances the ability to form better images. However, one must bear in mind Piaget's overriding emphasis in the area of mental imagery. He insists that while mental imagery flows from the child's cognitive operations, the imagery does not determine the state of these cognitive operations. Thus, when the child becomes capable of cognitive reversal of number or mass, he also becomes capable of transformational imagery.

Perceptual Growth

Perceptual growth, an area of study that has generated much controversy, has been defined by some psychologists as the increasing ability to recognize similarities and differences in visual stimuli. As this growth progresses, two changes have been noted. First, the child makes increasingly precise distinctions between objects on the basis of their appearance—that is, the child improves his ability to *differentiate* stimuli. Secondly, the child improves his ability to recognize both the details of a particular stimulus and the whole stimulus when he integrates these details. Thus, he develops the ability to see both "the forest and the trees."

Experimental data indicate that such visual perception develops gradually through learning. Hence, improvement comes with the child's experience, his increasing attentiveness, his skill at naming things, and perhaps even his growing

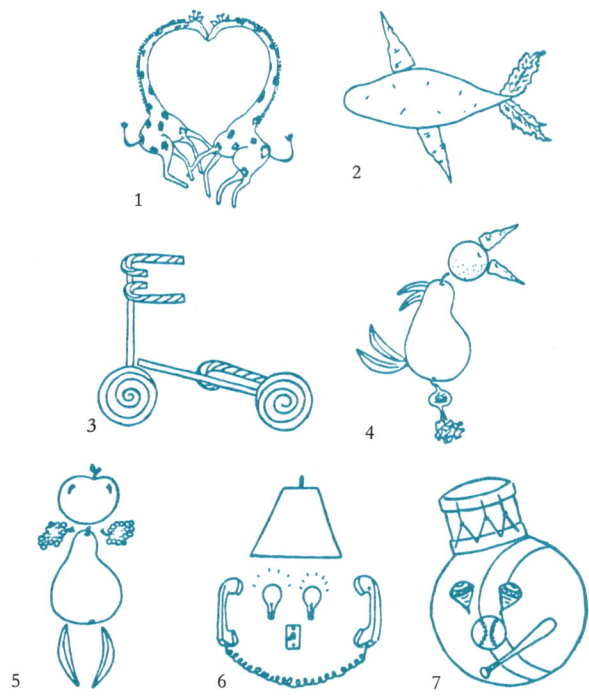

Figure 10.6 Drawings used in the study of part-whole perception. (From D. Elkind, R. R. Koegler, and E. Go. Studies in perceptual development: II. Part-whole perception. *Child Develpm.*, 1964, 35, 84.)

familiarity with letters of the alphabet—which aids his perception of graphic forms.

Characteristics of 4- to 7-year-olds

Several different theories attempt to explain how perceptual growth occurs and they all are still subject to debate. Broadly speaking, however, two tendencies can be seen in the child 4 to 7 years old. First, the younger children in this age group are apt to recognize the general features of an object only in a vague manner, or to recognize detailed parts and fail to perceive the whole object. Secondly, older children more often perceive both the details of an object and the whole object as well.

For example, when children were shown drawings of familiar objects made of still other familiar objects—for example, a drawing of a scooter made of candy canes—several results were noted. Most of the 4- to 5-year-old children saw only the candy and failed to recognize the scooter.

Table 10.1 Percentage of Part, Whole, and Part-Whole Responses for Five Age Levels and for Groups of Average (A) and Above Average (AA) Intelligence

I.Q. Group	N	D	W	W+D
Age 4–5				
AA	23	71.4	17.4	11.2
A	...	...	...	...
Age 6				
AA	24	49.4	27.4	23.2
A	20	50.0	8.6	41.4
Age 7				
AA	24	48.2	14.9	36.9
A	26	42.9	7.1	50.0
Age 8				
AA	24	32.3	7.5	60.2
A	26	35.2	2.2	62.6
Age 9				
AA	...	...	...	...
A	28	21.4	.0	78.6
Total				
AA	95	$\chi^2 = 109.6$**		
A	100	$\chi^2 = 264.9$**		

Note: N = number of subjects; D = part response (for example, only saw the candy canes); W = whole response (for example, only saw the scooter); W + D = whole-part response (for example, saw both the candy and the scooter).
**Significant beyond the .01 level.
Source: D. Elkind, R. R. Koegler, and E. Go. Studies in perceptual development: II. Part-whole perception. *Child Develpm.*, 1964, 35, 85.

By 8 years, more than half the children saw both the candy and the scooter. Finally, almost all 9-year-old children succeeded in integrating the parts into a whole. This study also found that individual differences in part-whole perception did not seem related to intelligence (Elkind, Koegler, and Go 1964).

Further evidence of the evolution of the perception of details and overall shape is provided by studies of children's eye movements during the perceptual process (Pick and Pick 1970). At ages when shape identification is poor, the child's eyes tend to concentrate on the interiors rather than the peripheries of objects, giving the movements little relation to an object's overall shape. In somewhat older children, eye movements usually conform to a shape's contours. It is traced by their eyes, as if the eyes have learned a way to identify objects. In still older children, eye movements jump quickly around the entire figure, including but not tracing contours, almost as if they had learned a shorthand for identification, or as if perhaps every facet of the figure was being viewed at once. Children's responses to visual stimuli also depend on whether these stimuli are either entirely new to them or otherwise without a known meaning.

SPATIAL ORIENTATION. Children also grow in their ability to recognize an object in many different spatial perspectives. For example, children 3 to 7 years of age were asked to identify pictures of objects presented both right side up and upside down (Ghent 1960). Forms shown right side up were identified more accurately than those shown upside down. However, the older the child, the more frequently he perceived both orientations as the same object.

LANGUAGE: ACQUIRED DISTINCTIONS. Many psychologists maintain that as children in the 4-to-7 age group acquire language, their new-found ability to label things promotes recognition of the distinctions between objects. The labeling of these distinctions—the attributes of objects—enables the child to focus his attention better on the distinctions and to compare objects according to their "acquired distinctions." For example, the different names applied to a couch and a chair—though they are similar in many respects and different primarily in size—help the child recognize these two objects as different. Similarly, the ability to label groups of trees as either "groves" or "forests" provides experience in integrating the parts of a stimulus into larger meanings or wholes.

Theories of Perception

There are two general types of theories of how children achieve the ability to distinguish between visual stimuli. One type contends that children first perceive select geometrical features of objects—corners, curves, and lines intersecting at various angles—and that through experience these distinctive features are compiled into a "dictionary" of translations in which every specific object translates into a unique combination of these features. The second type of theory contends that the child is able to perceive "gestalts," which are certain fundamental "whole" shapes such as squares, circles, or triangles. The gestalt theories tend to see the child's perceptual ability as progressing from the perception of wholes to the perception of parts. In contrast, the distinctive-feature type of theory tends to see the progression in the reverse order, moving from a part to the whole.

GIBSON'S THEORY OF DISTINCTIVE FEATURES. According to Gibson—who falls into the first group of perceptual growth theorists—perceptual growth depends on the acquisition of a dictionary of the kinds of distinctive features that we have mentioned. The idea has been tested by a study determining whether letterlike but meaningless graphic forms would be more easily identified by children who could read than by children who could not. Presumably, children experienced in recognizing the distinctive features of alphabetic symbols would transfer this experience in identifying the letterlike forms. Line drawings comparable to printed roman capital letters were constructed. Though these graphic forms contained joined lines and curves similar to those of roman capitals, the combinations of these lines and curves were meaningless. Children 4 to 8 years old were first shown a standard form of each line drawing. Then they were shown a set of pictures that included identical copies of both the standard and transformed versions of the standard. Finally the children were asked to pick out from the second set of pictures only exact copies of the standard form. Errors in selecting duplicates of the standard were found to decrease from age 4 through 8. More importantly, it was observed that the greatest decline in error rate occurred among children in the 5-to-6-year range. These children were just learning to read. This result was interpreted as supporting the concept that perception is built upon the recognition of distinctive features of shapes (Gibson 1969).

Interestingly, certain computers that are programmed to recognize objects also employ the distinctive-features concept. When an object is presented to the computer's photosensors, a "feature extractor" in the machine identifies the presence of elementary geometrical properties such as right angles, open curves, and so on. The computer then resorts to its "memory" where the list of features is translated into a specific object. Numerous efforts have been made to design computers that would identify whole shapes at once—that is, recognize certain gestalts—but no one has succeeded yet in accomplishing this.

WERNER'S THEORY. Werner—an example of the second type of perceptual-growth theorist—contends that at first the child's perceptions are vague and diffuse reactions to whole stimuli, with scant attention paid to specific parts (Werner 1957). With experience, however, the child learns to refine his perceptions, to differentiate a whole object according to its parts. These parts, Werner points out, are then coordinated with one another and reintegrated to form new perceptions. Such new perceptions are "wholes," in which parts are separate yet related. Thus, the theory states that the child begins with wholes, progresses to parts, and finally proceeds to more meaningful wholes.

According to this theory, differentiation and integration of stimuli proceed simultaneously, while in Gibson's theory, integration does not occur until the child has had significant experience in differentiating specific parts of stimuli. Werner's theory reflects the principle that wherever development occurs in biological systems, it proceeds from the global, undifferentiated state to one that is differentiated and integrated.

There are many experiments that demonstrate that the young child first reacts to whole stimuli rather than to their parts, thus giving support to the "gestalt" theories. One such study indicates that the child's focus on the whole interferes with his ability to notice changes in internal parts of objects. Children in the 4-to-8-year range were shown complete outlines of objects. Then they were shown the same outlines with inner parts added. The children were asked to indicate what part was added. The experimenters found that 4- to 7-year-olds did not do nearly so well as the 8-year-olds in identifying the added parts. With increasing age, however, the children demonstrated greater skill at seeing both the whole and its parts (Schober and Schober 1919). The difference between the theories of Gibson and Werner is one more illustration of one of the distinctions between the behavioral and structural approaches mentioned in Chapter 1 and earlier in this chapter—the preference for either an analytic or synthetic approach to cognition.

Figure 10.7 Children's drawings have personal meanings and, according to Kellogg and others, may not be aimed at copying real objects at all. (Syd Greenberg—D.P.I.)

KELLOGG'S THEORY. Kellogg's studies of over a million children's drawings, which show considerable universality across the world, have produced provocative and controversial results about perception. These drawings, according to Kellogg, indicate that children's first pictorial efforts are not aimed at copying real objects; instead, children spontaneously produce designs and forms that they only gradually realize resemble real objects. In Kellogg's words, as a result of inborn structures of the brain, children produce certain esthetically pleasing, universal forms—they produce their own "art" long before they are instructed to "draw from life" (Kellogg 1967).

These conclusions, if true, tend to support gestalt and gestalt-related theories that children possess an innate ability to perceive fundamental shapes, so that perception proceeds from the recognition of "wholes" toward progressive differentiation of parts.

Kellogg identifies four sequential stages of development of the child's self-taught art. First to appear are the early scribbles that demonstrate awareness of figure-background relationships; second, the child produces simple, overall gestalts or shapes (like circles or spheres); third, these shapes are combined to form designs; and finally, between the ages of 4 and 5, most children produce designs that begin to resemble recognizable real objects such as houses and people.

Kellogg's innatist point of view is controversial because it seems unlikely that children's drawings operate on principles differing from those in other areas of behavior. Detailed examination usually shows that behavioral outcomes in any area of performance are not "innate" but are rather a complex outcome of prior learnings and prior structural capacities. If children's paintings throughout the world are as similar as Kellogg maintains (which is yet to be precisely demonstrated), we might equally well argue that there is considerable similarity in the character of perceptual and motor learning throughout the world.

The competence-performance lag. This is the gap between the child's ability to recognize real objects (competence) and his lesser ability to draw these same objects (performance). A similar lag also appears in the area of language acquisition; the child understands spoken words before he can use them in his own speech.

The reason for the competence-performance lag is unknown. Many theories have been proposed, but none satisfactorily explains all the experimental data. Presently, however, several speculations seem to contain at least some part of the truth. One explanation is that drawing is a far more complicated process than perception. A child may be able to identify an object by noticing only its distinctive features, but to reproduce that object, many more detailed features must be placed in correct relationship. Another explanation of the inability to draw at the time of perception is simply that young children cannot draw; that is, they lack the motor control and the eye-hand coordination. There is some evidence to this effect. It has been found that children can reproduce forms when they are given pieces of the form to construct into a whole—pieces of a square that comprise a perfect square (Lovell 1960).

A third theory rejects the idea that children do not draw because of motor deficiency (Arnheim 1969). Instead, it maintains that children tend to reproduce their own characteristic visual thinking. They always tend to make circles because the circle is the first visual way of expressing an object—the first way to draw a "thing," that is, any object that stands out against its background. According to this theory, a child presented with triangles or squares should draw circles. Sometimes, experiments have shown, they do; more often they do not. Since children do not always reduce observed objects to simpler forms, this explanation can be only a partial answer to the question of what causes the competence-performance lag.

A fourth theory maintains that the child does not have difficulty discriminating an object. When a child draws a form, the child is really drawing an object which that form represents. Thus, when the child is shown a diagram of a square, he perceives the diagram as the square which the diagram only represents. He tries to draw that complete square, not just the diagrammatic representation of it, and he makes errors.

All these theories may be parts of the puzzle of the competence-performance lag. Reproducing does involve motor skill, paying attention to more features than in the discrimination process, possible confusion between the diagram and the object, and the preference for simpler forms. However, in addition to these four theories, we should note that drawing is not necessarily a realistic task to the child. Children observed at drawing seem to be mapping a fantasy or a story, only parts of which appear on the page. Fragments of the fantasy emerge in different parts of the representation. It is possible, therefore, that despite adult instructions on what to draw, the 4-year-old may be producing many things other than those we have in mind for him.

Interpersonal Perception

While the child of 4 to 7 years is developing his visual perception of objects, he also is developing social perceptions. His perception of others, both peers and adults, is a pivotal process in the progress of his social development. The popular belief is that the child under 7 years old is primarily egocentric—therefore unable to understand the feelings of others. Moreover, the child in this period is supposedly only rarely capable of conversing successfully with another child. Two recent studies, however, indicate that previous experiments have underestimated the child's ability both to converse and to empathize with his playmates. Both studies suggest that former experimenters failed to provide their child subjects with adequate means to express their true reactions.

EMPATHY IN CHILDREN. Borke (1971) provided children as young as 3 years old with means for articulating their emotional responses to the feelings of other children. First, she told 3- to 8-year-old children stories about other children who might be perceived as either happy, sad, afraid, or angry. The subject children then were to demonstrate their reactions by selecting a drawing of a facial expression that depicted the appropriate emotional reaction. The experimental stories were about such subjects as a child eating a favorite food, losing a toy, or being lost in the woods. The experimenter found that most of the children, as early as 3 years of age, responded appropriately to stories about happy children. However, these 3-year-olds could not respond to stories in which a child would feel fear, but by 4 to 5 years of age most of the children properly recognized these fearful situations. Responses to sadness and anger, on the other hand, failed to show a consistent trend with age—although the experimenter concluded that the stories that should have elicited those responses probably were ambiguous. Her chief conclusion, however, was that children, even as young as 3 years of age, are aware of other people's feelings and respond to a spectrum of such feelings.

When we realize that babies over 6 months old can respond contagiously to expressions of emotions in others (crying when someone else does), we need not be surprised by older children's perception of others' feelings. One can respond with appropriate feelings—that is, empathize—to the feelings of another long before responding with the appropriate understanding.

CHILDREN'S CONVERSATIONS. Mueller (1971) studied the conversations of 3½- to 5½-year-old children in free-play sessions. These sessions were recorded by hidden videotape cameras, so that experimenters were able to study at leisure the "success" or "failure" of the children's verbal interactions. Success in a conversation meant that the child listening appropriately replied to the utterance of the child speaking, or carried out directions specific to an utterance. Failure meant that the listener exhibited no behavior that might be an appropriate response to a speaker's utterance. Those experimenters who determined "success" and "failure" were not informed of the study's purpose. The experiment's results showed that a speaker who looked at a listener was guaranteed a successful response, whether or not his message related to the listener's activities. However, the speaker who did not gaze at his listener was unlikely to receive a reply. Overall, most utterances were answered or attracted the attention of the listeners, and almost all the speakers showed concern over their listeners' reactions. These findings contradict earlier experimenters' findings that children in this age group cannot communicate among themselves. One of the findings contradicted is that of Piaget—reported in *The Language and Thought of the Child*—suggesting that children are too egocentric to effectively communicate with their peers. As the Mueller experiment—which was considerably better controlled than Piaget's early work—shows, when the subjects of the discourse are tangible, such as observable actions or immediately present objects, communication among children is quite effective.

Changes in Thinking and Learning

Children in the 4-to-7-year range continue to think and learn by making simple associations between events, but now they also exhibit a gradual shift toward more complex and rule-controlled thinking (White 1965). During this transition period, the crude and impulsive association system is overlaid by a structure of more deliberate and sophisticated thought processes, and the child learns to curb his reflexive, less thoughtful reactions to stimuli. He begins to formulate more abstract rules than those of simple association.

Clearly, improving language skill also promotes the burgeoning development of more abstract thought, just as it promotes perceptual growth. Words, as internalized representations of external stimuli, may be pieced together to form expanded descriptions of events; these descriptions, in turn, permit more refined distinctions between events than those that can be drawn by simple association.

Overall, then, the associative and rule systems mesh together in a single, integrated structure; but within this structure the two different systems—one reflexive, the other cautious and rule-controlled—compete for expression. Stressful situations may cancel out the rules and call forth the first available reaction from the associative level. Regressions of this type may be caused either by emotional states, such as extreme fear, or the need to react quickly to rapidly changing or threatening stimuli—for example, a hard kick in the shins in response to the sudden threats of a schoolyard bully.

Behavioral Changes

The shift from spontaneous reactions to more controlled reactions is reflected in specific behavior changes (White 1965). In some of these behavior changes, we see language used to describe stimuli more fully. For example, an older child would be able to better define a toy that he wants so that it could be more readily identified by the adult purchasing it. In other behavior changes of this age period, there is a clear improvement in the child's ability to direct his attention to the basic characteristics of stimuli despite minor variations in the stimuli or other distracting factors. An older child looking for the word *football* would be less confused by having to select the word printed in five different typefaces. In a third type of behavior change, the child is more responsive to distant stimuli—visual and auditory—than to his more intimate perceptions, such as touch. Thus, older children prefer visual exploration to tactile, and their learning efforts are less reinforced by praise than by the satisfaction of being correct. These three types of behavior change indicate a general thrust towards greater inhibition of associative responses. That inhibition is, as we have mentioned, often exemplified in the child's acceptance and incorporation of rules into his

Figure 10.8 Between the ages of 4 and 7, children exhibit a marked cognitive transition from simple associations to more complex and rule-controlled thought, as well as an increase in attention for finer units of perception. (Mike Cantu—D.P.I.; Lynn McLaren—Rapho Guillumette)

own unmonitored daily life. Everywhere the child turns he finds rules he must apply to his behavior. When he speaks, he has to observe certain syntactical rules to make meaning clear. And he must speak audibly—another rule. When he gets dressed, he has to put his underwear on before his trousers, and his shirt before his jacket. When he plays darts he has to stand out of the line of fire; in three-cornered catch, he has to throw the ball to the right man. When he meets his grandmother, he has to say, "Hello," and when he wants to leave the table he says, "Excuse me, please." When he wants to judge a distance, he has to look with both eyes so that he can have the benefit of depth perception as well as vision. Thus, the child is surrounded by rules that he readily makes a part of his behaviors. This shift is evident both in the child's private intellectual life and in his social life with his peers and adults.

By age 7 the transition to rational, rule thinking is solidly established. At this point, children indicate that they are aware that events must be explained. They engage in logical argument and attempt to avoid self-contradiction, and finally, they can transcend the merely intuitive grasp of relations between objects by achieving a concrete understanding. A couch and a chair now are related by function as well as by color and size.

Intelligence and I.Q.

The Child's Intelligence

When we say that one child is more intelligent than another, exactly what do we mean? Like the words *love*, *hate*, and *tolerance*, the word *intelligence* connotes different qualities to different people. Psychologists such as Jean Piaget and J. P. Guilford basically construe intelligence as the child's capacity to build on his experience. From this ability arises the child's capacity to learn new concepts or sets of responses. The facility with which he learns these concepts and behaviors is a measure of his intelligence, according to the views of Piaget and Guilford. The concept of a point beyond which a child ceases to gain from a specific experience is another yardstick of intelligence shared by the two psychologists. Im-

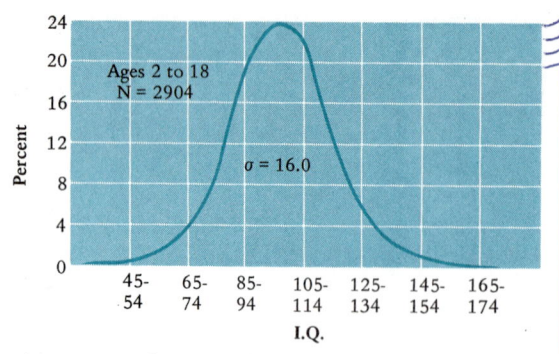

Figure 10.9 The range of I.Q.'s in the sample that was used to standardize the Stanford-Binet intelligence test. (From L. M. Terman and M. A. Merrill. *Measuring intelligence: A guide to the administration of the new revised Stanford-Binet tests of intelligence.* Boston: Houghton Mifflin, 1937.)

plicit in such a definition, of course, is the assumption that the point at which an experience stops yielding information is different for each child.

Though they may agree upon such a broad general description of intelligence, psychologists also advance other more individual interpretations. Piaget, for instance, calls intelligence the acquisition of operations that facilitate adaptation. To him, intelligence appears to be a gradually developing process which culminates in the stage of formal operations. In contrast, Guilford seems unconcerned with the idea of progression or development in intelligence. He believes that each child possesses a unique commingling of specific intellectual abilities. Hence, he has pictured intelligence as a cube containing 120 cells, each "containing" a specific ability.

The Stanford-Binet Tests

Piaget and Guilford have used their observations of children to theorize upon the nature of intelligence. Other scientists have sought to measure rather than define intelligence. The first man to suggest that mental ability ought to be measured was Sir Francis Galton, the nineteenth-century British scientist who laid the foundation for the new science of eugenics, which is concerned with the improvement of species, especially the human species, through the control of hereditary factors. Soon other scientists joined in the search for a satisfactory test of human intelligence. One of them was a French psychologist named Alfred Binet. Since intelligence obviously differed from person to person, Binet was interested in tests that would assess individual intelligence. As Piaget was to do later, Binet began by observing and testing his own children. In *The Experimental Study of Intelligence*, he described the essential psychological facts about his teen-age daughters in terms of the scores they earned on his tests of word-writing speed, mental imagery, sentence completion, and other related intellectual abilities. In 1904, the French Minister of Public Instruction asked Binet to devise a test which would identify subnormal children in the public schools of Paris. Since the Parisian schools were desperately overcrowded, a condition in which subnormal children could not benefit from regular instruction, the French government wished to set up special classes for them.

Binet and his collaborator, psychiatrist Theodore Simon, devised a series of graded tests which they standardized on normal children of different ages. If a child performed as well as his peers, he was presumed to be of average intelligence. If he did better, he was considered superior or bright; if worse, dull. Thus, the Binet tests were actually a measure of relative standing in a group.

The original Binet-Simon tests were based upon a generalized concept of intelligent behavior which Binet had derived from his intensive studies of children. The first test was actually a battery of 30 examinations of gradually increasing difficulty. These were intended to cover the range of mental capacity, from eye-head coordination in following a lighted match moved across the field of vision, to the ability to distinguish between abstract words such as *liking* and *respecting*.

The latest Stanford-Binet test, an American version, includes measures of information and past learning, verbal ability, perception, motor coordination, memory, and logical reasoning. In the 1960 revision of the test that is administered to 6-year-olds, the child is asked to count nine

324 EARLY CHILDHOOD AGES 4 THROUGH 7

blocks; to point out the path through a maze; to tell the ways in which a dog and a bird, or wood and glass, differ; to define six or more words including such words as *gown* or *orange*; and to recognize the missing parts in pictures of a rabbit and a shoe.

Calculating the I.Q.

Interestingly, Binet measured intelligence without ever saying precisely what it was. Soon after he devised his tests, a German psychologist, William Stern, developed the I.Q. or intelligence quotient, a numerical expression of the relationship between the child's chronological and mental age. The intelligence quotient is the ratio between mental and chronological age, multiplied by 100. Expressed mathematically, it looks like this:

$$I.Q. = \frac{M.A.}{C.A.} \times 100.$$

Thus, a child of 8 years 0 months whose mental age, as determined by the Stanford-Binet test, is 8.0 will receive a score of

$$\frac{8.0}{8.0} \times 100.$$

This gives him an I.Q. of 100, the average score for a child his age. An 8-year-old with a mental age of 10.0 will receive a score of

$$\frac{10.0}{8.0} \times 100.$$

This gives him an I.Q. of 125.

Figure 10.9 represents the range of I.Q.'s in the sample that was used to standardize the Stanford-Binet test. The graph's bell-shaped curve places the majority of the I.Q.'s at the midpoint—the 100–105 mark. Only a little over 12 percent of the group has an I.Q. over 120. Furthermore, the number of those who scored above 100 appears about equal to the number who scored below.

The WISC Intelligence Test

Though it is not as well known to laymen as the Stanford-Binet, the Wechsler Intelligence Scale for Children (WISC) is frequently used to test the intelligence of children between the ages of 5 and 15. Unlike the Stanford-Binet, the WISC uses the same items for children of all ages. More significantly, it has separate tests for verbal and performance skills. The WISC's five verbal tests measure reasoning, mathematical ability, ability in making comparisons, vocabulary, general knowledge, and common-sense judgments. The tests of performance include understanding of depicted scenes, basic copying, puzzles, detecting the missing parts of pictures, and building blocks into complex designs that stress spatial relationships.

The WISC differs from the Stanford-Binet in another way. It ignores the child's mental age in computing I.Q. Instead, it compares the child's test score with that of others in the same age group. To see how a child stands in relation to his peers, the examiner must consult the specially prepared WISC tables of I.Q. If, for example, a child of 6 receives an I.Q. of 81, he has scored above about 10 percent of his age peers, while the other 90 percent have scored above him.

While the two tests clearly differ in the methods of calculating the I.Q., as well as in content and organization, the score a child earns on the Stanford-Binet and the score he earns on the WISC often correlate very closely. Psychologists tend to use the Binet more frequently with children between 3 and 6 and then employ the WISC for children up to 12.

Group Tests

Although, as a general rule, the WISC is easier to administer and score than the Stanford-Binet, both tests are given to one individual at a time by

Figure 10.10 A facsimile of an item from the Object Assembly Test of the Wechsler Intelligence Scale for Children. (The Psychological Corporation, photo courtesy of CRM Books, Del Mar, California)

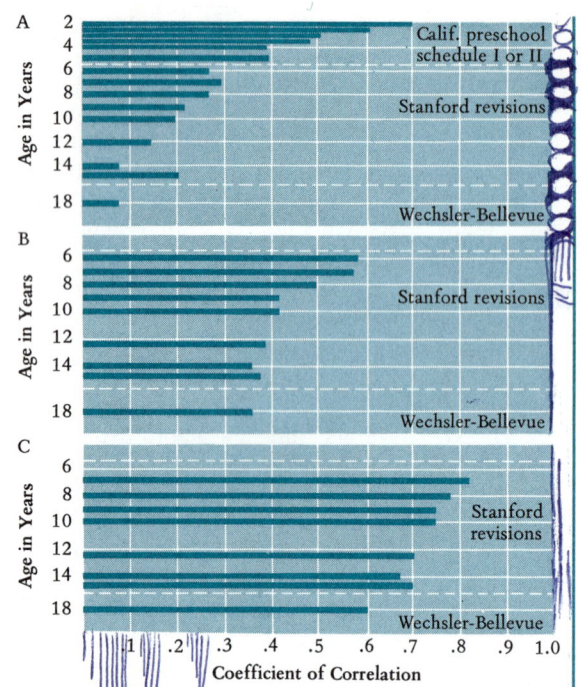

Figure 10.11 The correlation between children's mental test scores secured at (A) 21 months, (B) 3 years, and (C) 6 years, and the scores of the same children at other ages. In general, the closer the time interval, the greater the relationship between scores. (From M. P. Honzik, J. W. Macfarlane, and L. Allen. The stability of mental test performance between two and eighteen years. *J. exp. Educ.*, 1948, *17*, 309–324.)

a trained examiner. Group tests, however, can be administered by teachers or even clerks. Since 30 or 40 children can be tested at the same time by the same examiner, the tests also are more economical and take less time to administer to large numbers of students. But as indicators of future performance, they are not as reliable as individually administered tests. Reliance upon group test scores has frequently led to false assessments of mental ability and, consequently, misplacement in "track" classes or general misunderstanding of a child's ability. As a result, it is now felt that decisions concerning children who earn exceptionally low scores should await further testing by a trained psychologist. A child's general physical health, as well as other influences, clearly can affect his score and should be examined before other action is taken when a child scores abnormally low.

Strengths and Weaknesses of the I.Q.
Ever since the early 1900s when it was first put into use, the I.Q. test has been considered a good indicator of a child's knowledge, mental skills, and degree of general benefit from his environment. The test also can predict with a fair degree of accuracy how well a child will perform in school.

Critics of the I.Q. test generally attack it on the ground that it measures too few abilities to give a true picture of intellectual capacity. They point out that few questions on standardized intelligence tests require the child to learn anything new. Instead they measure skills and knowledge the child already possesses. As a consequence, the tests fail to evaluate one of the basic components of intelligence as defined by both Piaget and Guilford—the ease with which the child learns a new concept or a new set of motor responses.

Critics also argue that the tests primarily measure verbal and number skills and all but ignore other dimensions of intelligence—musical, artistic, and mechanical ability. Some consider the tests culturally loaded. Since every child grows up in a specific culture, his I.Q. would naturally reflect his sensitivity to that culture. Though social conditions have changed drastically during the last 60 years, the tests' cultural content has changed very little. They were originally standardized using white middle-class children living in western Europe and North America. As a result, lower-class children from distinctly different backgrounds are at a marked disadvantage when they take such tests.

The Predictive Value of the I.Q.
From the time Binet first developed the intelligence test, its major function has been to serve as an indicator of the child's future performance. Hence, the practical value of an I.Q. score depends upon its stability. The child who receives a high score on one test should receive a high score on all succeeding tests—otherwise his I.Q. tells us nothing.

As we noted in Chapter 8, I.Q. tests given to children under 2 years of age are useless as forecasters of performance because the test tasks change from sensorimotor to verbal as the child approaches school age. Although the more verbal tests of later childhood become increasingly more accurate predictors of performance and later childhood scores are substantially predictive of adult I.Q., they never achieve the status of absolute accuracy. When large groups of children between the ages of 6 and 18 were tested repeatedly, over half of one group showed a variation of 15 or more points at some time during the course of the testing; another group showed a variation of as much as 20 points (Honzik, Macfarlane, and Allen 1948).

I.Q. scores have been found to be better predictors of academic success in some areas than in others. In one study of I.Q. and academic performance, the correlation between the child's score on an intelligence test and reading comprehension was .73 (Bond 1940). In the case of I.Q. and history, the correlation dropped to .59. In biology, it dropped to .48. One reason for the poorer correlations is that I.Q. tests measure verbal skills and pay only minimal attention to other abilities. As a result, the correlation between I.Q. and success in fields such as art or a mechanical field is quite low.

Correlates of I.Q. and School Performance

Parental Attitudes and Background

Are I.Q. scores and achievement in school more affected by nature or nurture? Which is more important: the child's inheritance or his environment? To what degree do the child's surroundings and his parents' attitudes influence his intellectual growth?

In one study at Berkeley on parental attitudes and behavior and their effect upon achievement, a group of children was tested intermittently from 21 months of age to 30 years (Honzik 1967). At the start of the study the children's parents were observed and interviewed both at home and at work. On the basis of these interviews and observations, examiners evaluated them for a series of 64 variables. These included socioeconomic conditions, physical status, attitudes and concerns, social conflict, personality characteristics, and the amount of affection shown in the family situation. Only a small number of these variables correlated significantly with the I.Q.'s received by the children. Of these characteristics, one of the most significant in terms of grades obtained appeared to be parental concern with educational achievement. Such concern had a positive effect upon their children all the way up to the age of 30. Usually, the concern of the parent of the opposite sex provided the stronger motivation. For boys between the ages of 8 and 18, the mother–son relationship appeared crucial. Girls, on the other hand, seemed to require a good relationship with their fathers in order to perform well between the ages of 7 and 15. All aspects of socioeconomic status appeared to be intercorrelated and to affect the child's mental growth during the preschool years.

Certain other variables showed greater correlation with the children's test scores after the preschool years. Girls were affected by their mothers' educational level. A girl whose mother had gone to college appeared more interested in school than one whose mother had not. How the family felt about the father's occupation seemed to affect the sons. In one instance where the father felt trapped and hopeless in his job, his 15-year-old son, a boy of superior intelligence, was failing in school. "What's the use of trying? You don't get anywhere," he was quoted as saying.

Other studies corroborated the findings of the Berkeley group concerning the importance of parental concern with intellectual achievement. Some found a higher correlation for boys than for girls. In one study, children who consistently performed below the level their I.Q. scores had predicted were compared with children who consistently performed higher than their scores had predicted. A good parent–child relationship appeared to emerge as the crucial factor. Regardless of I.Q., there was a tendency for the achievers to come from loving parents and the underachievers to have been raised in homes where they were shown little affection or respect (Kurtz and Swenson 1951).

Personality Variables

In an analysis of changes in I.Q. scores, workers at the Fels Research Institute related such changes to the child's personality (Kagan and Moss 1962). Children whose I.Q.'s increased with each succeeding test were more independent, more competitive, and more verbally aggressive than others. They also worked harder in school and seemed eager to solve intellectual problems. In fact, this urge to master difficult problems rather than to shy away from them appeared to be a characteristic of the child whose I.Q. rose over the years.

Expectations of Success and Actual Performance

In general, the child who expects to succeed is more apt to do so than the child who expects to fail. Motives, expectations, and anxieties appear to be interrelated, and each in turn is related to performance. Thus, the child who is convinced he will fail worries about his anticipated failure and has less motivation to try; the child who is convinced he will succeed is free of anxiety in this area, and his motive for working increases. Often his view of his own potential for success or failure is influenced by how others behave toward him. In one widely known, but much disputed, experiment, all the children in a certain elementary school were given a group intelligence test. Their teachers then were given the names of those children who, on the basis of their scores, were expected to show "unusual" academic growth during the next year. In reality the I.Q.'s of these children were no higher than the I.Q.'s of their classmates. At the end of the year all the children were retested. Those children whose teachers had been told to expect "unusual" growth from them actually did score higher than their peers (Rosenthal 1966). Subsequent research, however, indicates the matter is somewhat more complex than this report suggested.

Social Class

In Chapter 8, we saw that many young children in the lower socioeconomic classes do not perform as well as their middle-class peers on standardized intelligence tests. In addition, when these children enter first grade, they seem less prepared for formal schooling. Teachers frequently find them less articulate, unable to organize complete sentences, unfamiliar with the names of common objects, and poor at dealing with the concepts of the middle-class curriculum. As time goes on, the gap between their academic achievement and that of middle-class children grows ever wider. By grade 6, many lower-class children score two years below their grade level on achievement tests; by grade 8, they are scoring three years below grade level (Hess and Shipman 1965).

There are several substantial reasons why lower-class children do so poorly on both I.Q. and achievement tests. One of the major reasons is the difference in use and exposure to language in lower-class and middle-class homes. (For a full discussion of this problem, see Chapter 8.) That I.Q. tests have been standardized on white middle-class children and reflect middle-class culture compounds the problem. Even the most intelligent child from a lower-class background may be unfamiliar with facts and word patterns a middle-class child of average intelligence has known all his life. Furthermore, middle-class children are constantly encouraged to learn those things that the I.Q. tests measure and the school believes important.

Compensatory Education Programs

Can the effects of the lower-class child's background be reversed, or must they shape his school experience and perhaps his entire life? During the last 10 or 15 years, numerous enriched training programs, such as Head Start, have been initiated all over the country, with the avowed purpose of compensating for the culturally impoverished milieu in which the typical lower-class child grows up. The United States Office of Education sponsored one of the best organized and most successful of these programs—the Early Training Program at Peabody College. The 87 black preschoolers who participated in the Peabody program all came from poor families; most of the parents were either unskilled or semiskilled workers who had never gone beyond grade school.

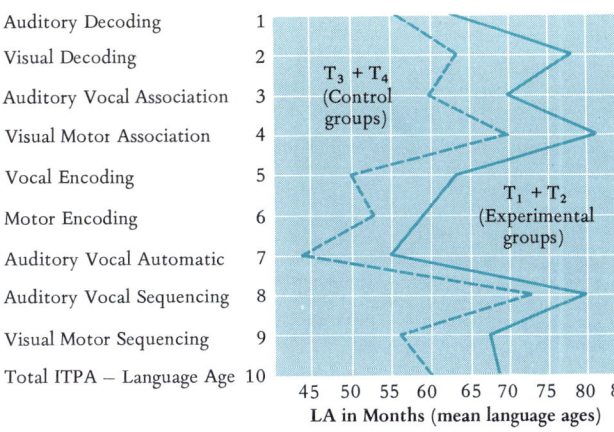

Figure 10.12 The influence of the Peabody early training program for culturally deprived children on cognitive abilities, as measured by the Illinois Test for Psycholinguistic Abilities. (From S. W. Gray and R. A. Klaus. An experimental preschool program for culturally deprived children. *Child Develpm.*, 1965, 36, (4), 896.)

Auditory Decoding	1
Visual Decoding	2
Auditory Vocal Association	3
Visual Motor Association	4
Vocal Encoding	5
Motor Encoding	6
Auditory Vocal Automatic	7
Auditory Vocal Sequencing	8
Visual Motor Sequencing	9
Total ITPA – Language Age	10

$T_3 + T_4$ (Control groups)
$T_1 + T_2$ (Experimental groups)

LA in Months (mean language ages)

To find out if the training program would benefit these children, investigators divided them into two experimental groups and two control groups. One experimental group was given special nursery school training for three summers; the other experimental group was given similar training for only two summers. Those in the control groups received no special attention. The special training consisted of efforts to motivate achievement and to encourage the children to think about, and form concepts of, the events and tasks that were part of their nursery school environment (Gray and Klaus 1965). Once a week a specially trained teacher talked with the mothers of the children in the two experimental groups to heighten the mothers' awareness of their children's motives and to encourage the mothers to reward their children's efforts. The preschoolers in both the experimental groups and the control groups were tested at the beginning of the program and biannually during the three years of the program. Plans also were made for two follow-up tests. In the original tests, the average Stanford-Binet I.Q. of the experimental group was 88, that of the controls 86. At the end of the third year, the average I.Q. of the experimental groups had risen to 95; that of the control groups had dropped to 81. Children in the experimental groups also scored higher on the Peabody Picture Vocabulary Test and the Illinois Test of Psycholinguistic Abilities (Dunn 1959; McCarthy and Kirk 1961–63).

Three years after the program had ended, the children were tested once again. On the Stanford-Binet, investigators still found a significant difference between the I.Q.'s of the children in the experimental groups and in the control groups. However, many I.Q.'s in the experimental groups had declined somewhat, now that the children were no longer receiving the special training. On the Metropolitan Achievement Test (MAT), which covered material more directly related to the elementary school program, the investigators found no significant difference between the scores of the children in the two groups. They felt that this was because most of the children were attending all-black schools where the quality of the instruction probably was not as high as that found in white, middle-class schools. In support of their conclusions, the investigators cited the case of eight children who had transferred to all-white schools. Every one of these children scored higher on the MAT than their classmates who had remained in the all-black schools.

From their data, the investigators concluded that while the preschool remedial program had had some effect, it was not able to counteract the adverse influence of the home and school environment. Consequently, once the enrichment program ceased, its good results gradually dissipated, unless the children were removed to other surroundings.

THE BEREITER-ENGLEMANN PROGRAM. Another attempt to help lower socioeconomic-class children, the Bereiter-Englemann program in Illinois, draws its inspiration from the restricted language code of Basil Bernstein, which we discussed in Chapter 8. Like Bernstein, Bereiter sees lower-class preschoolers as having almost no language of their own. He describes them as speaking in single words and grunts, or in a series of badly connected words or phrases, their speech really little more than a series of emotional cries. In the Bereiter-Englemann program, which is an extremely intensive and extended intellectual exercise for disadvantaged children, a trio of teachers spends two hours a day stressing and restressing the basics of arithmetic and language to about 15 preschoolers. In addition to vocabulary and idioms, the language workouts emphasize language as a way to think and learn—not simply as a way to express one's feelings. At the end of one year of such training, the children had raised their I.Q. scores an average of 17 points. Their scores on reading and arithmetic tests equaled those of the nation's average first-grade pupil.

CRITICISMS OF THE VERBAL DEFICIT THEORY. The assumption of linguistic deficiency and general lower-class inadequacy made by Bernstein, and Bereiter and Englemann, has been challenged by linguists and many anthropologists. (See Chapter 8 for a full discussion and critique of this theory.) As we saw in Chapter 8, critics of the deficit theory turn their attack on the psychologists examining the child of the poverty-stricken environment. Their argument contends that the poor environment is not deficient but simply different from the middle-class environment (Cole and Bruner 1970). Rather than finding the lower-class children deficient, this point of view finds the deficiency exists with the examining psychologists' approach to class and linguistic ability. It goes on to assert that all languages are functionally equal—the communication of the same information is possible in all of them—and that the present testing procedure constitutes a deck stacked against the lower-class child. Not only the tests' approach to content and the content itself must be changed, but the manner of their administration must be tailored to what the child is accustomed to in his environment—if they are truly to assess the intelligence of the disadvantaged child. Further, before teachers and psychologists can help black children, they need to understand that converting all first-graders into replicas of white middle-class suburban children is not the way to commence their education. Instead, those who work in the inner-city schools must begin to adapt the educational system to the language and learning styles of the children they are teaching.

Nursery School and Achievement in Middle-Class Children

Studies such as the Early Training Project cited earlier indicate that the I.Q.'s of lower-class children rise after they have attended nursery school. In addition, one study of Head Start children has shown the greatest gains in I.Q. were made by children whose teachers were rated as "warm" and "placing a high value on intellectual growth" (Connors and Eisenberg 1966).

On the other hand, nursery school's effect on the I.Q. and school performance of middle-class children is debatable. It is true that in a study of 5,000 British children, the 224 among them who had gone to nursery school scored higher than their peers on intelligence and educational achievement tests administered when they were 8 years old. However, by 11 years of age, the nursery school alumni had surrendered their higher standing. By age 15, their peers had a slight lead on them (Douglas and Ross 1964).

In a more recent study by the New York State Department of Education, children in eight school districts were tested for I.Q. and academic achievement. Some of the children had attended nursery school; others had not. Of those who had attended, some had gone to schools with traditional programs, others to schools with programs emphasizing social and psychological development, and still others to schools emphasizing cognitive development. All the children who attended the latter schools outscored their present classmates on every test. Lower-class white children who had gone to these schools appeared to make greater gains than their lower-class black classmates. However, neither group scored as high as middle-class children who had participated in the cognitive program. Nor did placing middle-class and lower-class children together appear to have affected the test results (DiLorenzo 1971).

Many investigators believe that comparing the performance of children who attend nursery school with that of children who do not is a futile exercise—unless the needs of the individual child are taken into consideration. For example, they point out that children with no siblings show a rise in I.Q. after they attend nursery school. Obviously, they need the social and intellectual stimulation they receive from other children in order to fulfill their potential (Truax 1966).

Still other investigators are impatient with the heavy stress placed on intellectual development as the end product of nursery school attendance. They are convinced that even if the child's I.Q. does not rise, attendance at a nursery school can have beneficial effects upon his social and psychological development—a question examined in our next chapter.

Summary

Significant changes occur in cognitive development in the years from 4 to 7. This period marks the transition between the diffuse, illogical thinking of the 2- to 4-year-old and the systematic thinking of the 7-year-old.

Two contending theories attempt to explain this change. Piaget maintains that it is the development of cognitive processes that determines changes in vocabulary, learning, memory, and imagery. Other psychologists take the stand that changes in memory or vocabulary cause the changes in cognitive and thought processes.

The 4-year-old child, according to Piaget, is entering the second half of the preoperational stage—the period of intuitive thought. Piaget describes the thinking of the preoperational child as egocentric and illogical because it relies more on perceptions and direct experiences than on mental operations. Some characteristics of the child's thought at this stage, according to Piaget, are: *centration*, focusing on one attribute of an object at a time; *irreversibility*; and a *static* quality. The child concentrates on states of objects at rest and does not consider transformational states. During this period of intuitive thought there is considerable growth in concepts of number, relations, and classification.

While Piaget's approach to cognitive development is more unified and global, other approaches tend to be analytic. Problem solving, an analytic approach to cognition, comprises five sequential mental processes: encoding, memory, hypothesis-generation, evaluation, and deduction. Other major processes, too, are shaping the child's thought.

By age 4, Piaget believes that mental imagery has developed sufficiently to allow the child to perceive and retain mental pictures of static parts of his surroundings; the perception of kinetic or transformational images, however, remains beyond the ability of the average 7-year-old. On the other hand, the visual perception of the older child in this age group permits him to perceive both the whole object and its parts. In the social realm, he becomes aware of, and shares, other people's feelings and is able to communicate with his peers.

Increased linguistic ability, apparent at this stage, also is a factor in the development of the child's intelligence. The child is gradually learning to label his experience in words rather than images. Words become internalized representatives of external stimuli and permit refined distinctions between events and objects. As vocabulary and attentiveness improve, memory also improves. Judgment and problem-solving ability develop from the child's growing mastery of words, images, concepts, and the logical rules that govern their use.

While Piaget has searched for the principles of intellectual development present in all children, other psychologists have been more interested in measuring individual differences in children's thinking. To measure intelligence—generally defined as an individual's ability to learn from experience, including the ease with which he grasps new concepts and ideas as well as new patterns of behavior—these psychologists have devised several standardized tests.

The first intelligence tests were developed early in this century by Binet and Simon. The Stanford-Binet is the American version of this test. Another commonly used intelligence test is the Wechsler Intelligence Scale for Children.

Intelligence tests give fairly reliable predictions of success in school; however, they have been criticized on the ground that they stress verbal and numerical abilities, excluding such abilities as the artistic and mechanical. The tests also have been faulted for being culturally loaded and for ignoring social changes in the compilation of their content.

Middle-class children do better on standardized tests than lower-class children. Middle-class children are exposed to and encouraged to learn the types of information that tests measure and schools teach. In addition, children who expect to succeed are most likely to do so. Motives, expectations, and anxieties are interrelated, and each, in turn, is related to performance. Early training programs can, to some extent, motivate and improve the performance of lower-class children, but they do not fully counteract the influence of the child's social environment.

Case Studies

Stanley T.

Stanley was a highly intelligent 4-year-old who showed many signs of creativity and originality. Described as possessing a "rich, open personality" and a "highly responsive temperament," Stanley seemed to present a balanced combination of drive, energy, and control. Although only slightly interested in motor activity, Stanley was perpetually sensitized to elements of form and visual design.

Midway into his fifth year, Stanley entered nursery school. His teacher's first impression was one of a "charming" boy, but also of a lad who was "silent, sitting, and serious." Quite satisfied to play alone most of the day, Stanley's interest heightened only when a familiar book was being read to the class. Somewhat later in the year the nursery staff noted that he continued to play alone, particularly indoors, and that he experimented little with any kind of gross motor activity. (He ran, in fact, "as if his body was tied together.") Staff professionals also noted that he tended to intellectualize his fears and exert his aggressive feelings through well-disguised, unobtrusive "magic" devices.

Stanley's true fascination was with words. He tended to verbalize his fantasies and soliloquize throughout any kind of play activity—often at the expense of the activity itself. For instance, Stanley had set up an elaborate network of fortresses and embattlements for his toy soldiers. With a bare minimum of cannon-type noises or troop activity, he talked his way through a "formidable" series of attacks and defenses. At another time, after he had led the way in the creation of a group poem about being "up high," Stanley asked if he could go on to create poems about "big things, and little things, and tiny things, and faraway things." His teacher noted that he seemed to enjoy the differences implicit in those concepts.

Stanley's way with words—particularly his charming formula-fashion commentaries (for example, "That's true, that's very perfectly true")—and his "delicious sense of humor" were his major modes of expression to the world about him, and usually gained him great favor with adults. In fact, the clinician who administered Stanley's series of Rorschach tests diagnosed an overdependence on verbal facility to compensate for a lack of confidence in the "propriety" of his creative abilities. In his opinion, Stanley's concept of the expectations placed on him necessitated suppression of his rich creativity in favor of a conformity he achieved most easily with verbal abilities.

There were other ways in which Stanley's creativity showed itself—most notably his art. His paintings were well unified, demonstrating good organization of form, many elements of movement, and a rich variety of color, form, size, and spacing. By the end of the year his paintings had taken on definite qualities of "vigorous, overall movements . . . wide smears, colors on top of each other. . . . " Typically, Stanley soliloquized as he painted, forever talking about the innumerable "storms, airplanes, zeppelins, lightning, fires, etc." that he found in even the smeariest of paintings. He also showed tremendous interest in the artistic process as well as in the product—for example, during his first fingerpainting session, he had endless questions about such things as why the paper was wet and what caused the white lines.

In the other expressive modalities, Stanley showed varying interests and aptitudes. He was an excellent and devoted carpenter, turning out a well-finished product with virtually no assistance. He seemed not to enjoy clay work, however, and insisted on making only simple functional items. And although he loved music and showed considerable creativity in his interpretive ideas, his tendency to "intellectualize" his musical sensitivity inhibited whatever emotional responses he attempted.

Another year or more of thoughtful supervision might well bring out the great depth of Stanley's creativity: he need only find in himself the necessary confidence to "be different" (Murphy 1956).

Adele J.

In contrast to Stanley, Adele was a very bright child who showed little of the creativity which often seems second nature to children. Throughout her first two classroom years, her teachers noted an obvious inability to make spontaneous responses to new situations or materials. Exhibiting "high degrees of organization and control" (perhaps at the expense of her personal needs and feelings), Adele approached her world rigidly. She was more concerned with social appearances, mores, manners, and smooth social-interaction patterns than with the everyday joys and frustrations of a typical 5-year-old. Particularly in her first few months of nursery school experience, Adele was characterized as prematurely concerned with the proper dress for different occasions; overly repetitious in conversation and play; almost totally devoid of vocal nuances; "rigidly neat" in her play with toys of any kind; and curiously limited in her propensity toward fantasy.

Although Adele was unquestionably cooperative in classroom play and participation—as well as unremittingly enthusiastic about coming to school each day—her involvement in any activity was severely limited by her own rigidity. With manipulative toys of any size, her primary concern was for their most "appropriate" usage. Her painting was entirely imitative except when her lack of imagination was ridiculed by other children—in which case she would halfheartedly attempt something different. She was not especially aware of color, although she seemed ever alert to clothes (only because they were new or different, not because of texture or design). Generally unmusical, Adele never sang spontaneously. Her involvement with spatial form and design was limited to imitative efforts at block building. Similarly, she apparently received no particular enjoyment from kinesthetic activity. She did, however, relish food and liquid of almost any sort—and she particularly enjoyed being taken out to restaurants.

Two experimental play incidents are especially revealing with respect to Adele's unimaginative behavior:

1. Each of the nursery children was individually introduced to several boxes of miniature lifelike toys and allowed to interact with them. In contrast to her peers (who dumped them out energetically, set them up in dramatic situations, or pawed through them excitedly), Adele labeled each from a stereotyped repertoire of seemingly embarrassed comments: "Oh pretty little things. . . . Cute little thing. . . . Cute. . . . Funny. . . . What's this? Isn't it cute? . . . Funny. . . . Bathtub. Isn't this a nice little bathtub? . . . Isn't it cute? . . . Cute. . . . [looking at a doll's torn dress] . . . Cute. . . . Nice. . . . Cute. . . ." and so on.

2. Each child was individually introduced to a variety of sensory-stimulating objects (for example, a music box, a strip of fur, colored excelsior, a kaleidoscope) which were to be enjoyed in whatever way the child saw fit. Although Adele seemed somewhat tense throughout her session, the experimenter felt she would have been no more receptive to stimulation under other circumstances. Once again, her comments—accompanied by her plastic, social smile—were stereotyped and unimaginative. Typically, she demanded only to know the function of several things (for example, skeins of colored wools and colored plastic sticks). Her only show of "strained" interest was when the experimenter played a game of "hiding the wools" with her—and her enjoyment here, however brief, was probably due most to the social nature of the activity.

Although Adele did represent a rather extreme degree of rigidity in her approach to her environment, two years of classroom experience had noticeable freeing effects on this bright little girl who was somehow eluding the most precious qualities of childhood (Murphy 1956).

References

Arnheim, R. *Visual thinking.* Berkeley and Los Angeles: Univer. of California Press, 1969.

Bereiter, C., and Englemann, S. *Teaching disadvantaged children in the preschool.* Englewood Cliffs, N.J.: Prentice-Hall, 1966.

Binet, A. *L'étude expérimentale de l'intelligence.* Paris: Schleicher Frères, 1903.

Bond, E. A. *Tenth-grade abilities and achievements.* New York: Columbia Univer. Press, 1940.

Borke, H. Interpersonal perception of young children: Egocentrism or empathy? *Develpm. Psychol.,* 1971, 5, 123–141.

Cole, M., and Bruner, J. S. Cultural differences and inferences about psychological processes. *Amer. Psychologist,* 1970, 25(10), 867–876.

Connors, K., and Eisenberg, L. *The effect of teacher behavior on verbal intelligence in Operation Head Start children.* Baltimore: Johns Hopkins Univer. School of Medicine, 1966.

Crandall, V. J. Katkovsky, W., and Preston, A. Motivational and ability determinants of young children's intellectual achievement behavior. *Child Develpm.,* 1962, 33, 643–661.

DiLorenzo, L. T. Which way for prekindergarten: Wishes or reality? *Amer. Educ.,* 1971, 7, 28–32.

Douglas, J. W. B., and Ross, J. M. The later educational progress and emotional adjustment of children who went to nursery schools or classes. *Educ. Res.,* 1964, 7, 73–80.

Dunn, L. M. *Peabody picture vocabulary test.* Minneapolis, Minn.: American Guidance Service, 1959.

Elkind, D., Koegler, R. R., and Go, E. Studies in perceptual development: II. Part-whole perception. *Child Develpm.,* 1964, 35, 81–90.

Flavell, J. Role-taking and communication skills in children. In W. Hartup and N. Smothergill (Eds.), *The young child.* Washington, D.C.: National Association for the Education of Young Children, 1967.

Flavell, J. H., Beach, D. R., and Chinsky, J. M. Spontaneous verbal rehearsal in a memory task as a function of age. *Child Develpm.,* 1966, 37, 284–299.

Furth, H. G. Research with the deaf: Implications for language and cognition. *Psychol. Bull.,* 1964, 62, 145–164.

Furth, H. G. Linguistic deficiency and thinking: Research with deaf subjects. 1964–1969. *Psychol. Bull.,* 1971, 76(1) 58–72.

Galton, F. *Hereditary genius.* London: Macmillan, 1869.

Ghent, L. Recognition by children of realistic figures presented in various orientations. *Canad. J. Psychol.,* 1960, 14, 249–256.

Gibson, E. J. *Principles of perceptual learning and development.* New York: Appleton-Century-Crofts, 1969.

Ginsburg, H., and Opper, S. *Piaget's theory of intellectual development: An introduction.* Englewood Cliffs, N.J.: Prentice-Hall, 1969.

Gollin, E. S. Serial learning and perceptual recognition in children: Training, delay and order effects. *Percept. and motor Skills*, 1966, *23*, 751–758.

Gray, S. W., and Klaus, R. A. An experimental preschool program for culturally deprived children. *Child Develpm.*, 1965, *36*(4), 887–898.

Greco, P. Quantité et quotité. In P. Greco and A. Morf (Eds.), *Structures numériques élémentaires. Etudes d'épistemologie génetique.* Vol. 3. Paris: Presses Universitaires de France, 1962.

Guilford, J. P. The structure of intellect. *Psychol. Bull.*, 1956, *53*, 267–293.

Guilford, J. P. Three faces of intellect. *Amer. Psychol.*, 1959, *14*, 469–479.

Guilford, J. P. *The nature of human intelligence.* New York: McGraw-Hill, 1967.

Guilford, J. P. Intelligence has three facets. *Science*, 1968, *160*, 615–620.

Harter, S. Mental age, I.Q., and motivational factors in the discrimination of learning set performance of normal and retarded children. *J. exp. child Psychol.*, 1967, *5*, 123–141.

Herrnstein, R. I.Q. *Atlantic Monthly*, Sept. 1971, *228* (3), 43–64.

Hess, R. D., and Shipman, V. C. Early experience and the socialization of cognitive modes in children. *Child Develpm.*, 1965, *36*, 869–886.

Honzik, M. P. Environmental correlates of mental growth: Prediction from the family setting at 21 months. *Child Develpm.*, 1967, *38*, 337–364.

Honzik, M. P., Macfarlane, J. W., and Allen, L. The stability of mental test performance between two and eighteen years. *J. exp. Educ.*, 1948, *4*, 309–324.

Kagan, J., and Kogan, N. Individual variation in cognitive processes. In P. H. Mussen (Ed.), *Carmichael's manual of child psychology.* Vol. I. (3rd ed.) New York: Wiley, 1970.

Kagan, J., and Moss, H. A. *Birth to maturity.* New York: Wiley, 1962.

Kagan, J., Moss, H. A., and Sigel, I. E. Psychological significance of styles of conceptualization. In J. C. Wright and J. Kagan (Eds.), Basic cognitive processes in children. *Monogr. Soc. Res. Child Develpm.*, 1963, *28*,(2, Serial No. 86), 73–112.

Kagan, J., Pearson, L., and Welch, L. Modifiability of an impulsive tempo. *J. educ. Psychol.*, 1966, *57*(6), 359–365.

Kagan, J., Rosman, B. L., Day, D., Albert, J., and Phillips, W. Information processing in the child. *Psychol. Monogr.*, 1964, *78* (1, Whole No. 578).

Kagan, J., Sontag, L. W., Baker, C. T., and Nelson, V. L. Personality and I.Q. change. *J. abnorm. Psychol.* 1958, *56*, 261–266.

Kellogg, R. Understanding children's art. In P. Cramer (Ed.), *Readings in developmental psychology today.* Del Mar, Calif.: CRM Books, 1967.

Kendler, T. S. Development of mediating responses in children. In J. C. Wright and J. Kagan (Eds.), Basic cognitive processes in children. *Monogr. Soc. Res. Child Develpm.*, 1963, *28*(2, Serial No. 86), 33–48.

Kuenne, M. R. Experimental investigation of the relation of language to transportation behavior in young children. *J. exp. Psychol.*, 1946, *36*, 471–490.

Kurtz, J. J., and Swenson, E. G. Factors related to overachievement and underachievement in school. *School Rev.*, 1951, *59*, 472–480.

Labov, W. Academic ignorance and black intelligence. *Atlantic Monthly*, June 1972, *229*(6), 59–67.

Levinson, B., and Reese, H. W. Patterns of discrimination learning set in preschool children, fifth graders, college freshmen, and the aged. *Monogr. Soc. Res. Child Develpm.*, 1967, *32*(7, Serial No. 115).

Lovell, K. A follow-up study of some aspects of the work of Piaget and Inhelder on the child's conception of space. *Brit. J. Educ.*, 1960, *29*, 104–117.

Luria, A. R. Verbal regulation of behavior. In M. A. B. Brazier (Ed.), *The central nervous system and behavior. Report of third Macy conference.* Madison, N.J.: Macy Foundation, 1960.

Maccoby, E. E. Selective auditory attention in children. In L. P. Lipsitt and C. C. Spiker (Eds.), *Advances in child development and behavior.* Vol. III. New York: Academic Press, 1967.

Maccoby, E. E., and Bee, H. L. Some speculations concerning the lag between perceiving and performing. *Child Develpm.*, 1965, *36*(2).

McCarthy, J. J., and Kirk, S. *Illinois test of psycholinguistic abilities. Experimental edition.* Urbana: Univer. of Illinois Press, 1961–63.

Messer, S. B. The effect of anxiety over intellectual performance on reflective and impulsive children. Unpublished doctoral dissertation, Harvard Univer., 1968.

Morrison, F., Eisenberg, K., Haith, M. M., and Mindes, P. Short-term memory for visual information in children and adults. Paper presented at meeting of Eastern Psychological Assoc., Washington, D.C., April 1968.

Mueller, E. Origins of success and failure in children's spontaneous communication. *Proc. 79th Ann. Con. Am. Psychol. Assoc.*, 1971, 153–154.

Murphy, L. B. *Personality in young children.* Vol. I. New York: Basic Books, 1956.

Murray, F. B. Acquisition of conservation through social interaction. *Develpm. Psychol.*, 1972, *6*, 1–6.

Neale, J. M. Egocentrism in institutionalized and noninstitutionalized children. *Child Develpm.*, 1966, *57*, 97–101.

Olver, R. R., and Hornsby, J. R. On equivalence. In J. S. Gruner, R. R. Olver, and P. M. Greenfield (Eds.), *Studies in cognitive growth.* New York: Wiley, 1966.

Piaget, J. *The language and thought of the child.* London: Routledge & Kegan Paul, 1926.

Piaget, J. *Judgment and reasoning in the child.* New York: Harcourt Brace Jovanovich, 1928.

Piaget, J. *The child's concept of the world.* New York: Harcourt Brace Jovanovich, 1929.

Piaget, J. *The child's conception of physical causality.* London: Routledge & Kegan Paul, 1930.

Piaget, J. *The moral judgment of the child.* London: Routledge & Kegan Paul, 1932.

Piaget, J. *Traité de logique.* Paris: Colin, 1949.

Piaget, J. *The origins of intelligence in children.* New York: International Universities Press, 1952.

Piaget, J. *The child's conception of number.* London: Routledge & Kegan Paul, 1952.

Piaget, J. *Logic and psychology.* New York: Basic Books, 1957.

Piaget, J. *Play, dreams, and imitation in childhood.* New York: Norton, 1962.

Piaget, J. *The early growth of logic in the child.* London: Routledge & Kegan Paul, 1964.

Pick, H. L., Jr. Perception in Soviet psychology. *Psychol. Bull.,* 1964, *62,* 21–35.

Pick, H. L., Jr., and Pick, A. D. Sensory and perceptual development. In P. H. Mussen (Ed.), *Carmichael's manual of child psychology.* Vol. I. (3rd ed.) New York: Wiley, 1970.

Pulaski, M. A. S. *Understanding Piaget: An introduction to children's cognitive development.* New York: Harper & Row, 1971.

Rosenthal, R. *Experimenter effects in behavioral research.* New York: Appleton-Century-Crofts, 1966.

Schober, G., and Schober, A. Über Bilderkennungs- und Unterscheidungsfähigkeit bei kleinen Kindern. *Beih. Z. angew. Psychol.,* 1919, *19,* 94–137.

Sigel, I. E. Developmental trends in the abstraction ability of children. *Child Developm.,* 1953, *24*(2), 131–144.

Sigel, I. E., Anderson, L. M., and Shapiro, H. Categorization of behavior of lower- and middle-class Negro preschool children: Differences in dealing with representations of familiar objects. *J. Negro Educ.,* 1966, *35,* 218–229.

Sigel, I. E., and McBane, B. Cognitive competence and level of symbolization among five-year-old children. In J. Hellmuth (Ed.), *The disadvantaged child.* Vol. I. Seattle, Wash.: Special Child Publications, 1967.

Sigel, I. E., and Olmsted, P. Styles of categorization among lower-class kindergarten children. Paper presented at meeting of American Educational Research Association, 1967.

Sigel, I. E., Roeper, A., and Hooper, F. H. A training procedure for acquisition of Piaget's conservation of quantity. *Brit. J. educ. Psychol.,* 1966, *36,* 301–311.

Smedslund, J. Les origines sociales de la centration. In F. Bresson and M. de Montmalin (Eds.), *Psychologie et épistemologie génetiques.* Paris: Dunod, 1966.

Templin, M. C. *Certain language skills in children: Their development and interrelationships.* Child Welfare Monograph Series, No. 26. Minneapolis: Univer. of Minnesota Press, 1957.

Terman, L. M., and Merrill, M. A. *Measuring intelligence: A guide to the administration of the new revised Stanford-Binet tests of intelligence.* Boston: Houghton Mifflin, 1937.

Truax, C. B. Factors affecting intelligence change associated with preschool attendance. Manuscript in preparation, 1966.

Wallach, M. A. Creativity. In P. H. Mussen (Ed.), *Carmichael's manual of child psychology.* Vol. I. (3rd ed.) New York: Wiley, 1970.

Wallach, M. A., and Kogan, N. *Modes of thinking in young children: A study of the creativity-intelligence distinction.* New York: Holt, Rinehart & Winston, 1965.

Ward, W. C. Creativity in young children. *Child Develpm.,* 1968, *39,* 737–754.

Wechsler, D. *Wechsler intelligence scale for children.* New York: Psychological Corporation, 1952.

Werner, H. *Comparative psychology of mental development.* New York: International Universities Press, 1957.

White, S. H. Evidence for a hierarchical arrangement of learning processes. In L. P. Lipsitt and C. C. Spiker (Eds.), *Advances in child development and behavior.* Vol. II. New York: Academic Press, 1965.

Wober, M. Adapting Witkin's field independence theory to accommodate new information from Africa. *Brit. J. Psychol.,* 1967, *58,* 29–38.

Wohlwill, J. F. The learning of absolute and relational number discriminations by children. *J. genet. Psychol.,* 1963, *101,* 217–228.

Yando, R. M., and Kagan, J. The effect of teacher tempo on the child. *Child Develpm.,* 1968, *39,* 27–34.

Youniss, J. Concept transfer as a function of shifts, age, and deafness. *Child Develpm.,* 1964, *35,* 695–700.

Zazzo, A. R. *Le devenir de l'intelligence.* Paris: P.U.F., 1946.

Personality and Social Development 11

BEFORE THE AGE OF 4, the child's personality and social development are determined largely by the home and the home environment, as well as by his own peculiarities of temperament. In the period from 4 to 7, the child begins to spend more time outside the private world of his home, with the result that many more new places, people, and experiences begin to play an important part in his life. During these years, sometimes called a transition to childhood, he moves into the public world—the neighborhood, the nursery school, the community—and he meets not only new adults, but also his peers. These outside people, situations, and places now have a profound effect on the shaping of his personality and social behavior.

One of the most noticeable differences that distinguishes children's social behavior during these years from that of toddlers is the more frequent and ready interaction with their peers, rather than with adults. Children under 4 are still predominantly home-centered and thus have little experience with other children, except perhaps siblings. Also, because of the state of their cognitive development, toddlers find it difficult to understand the wishes, feelings, or point of view of another person, an ability that is almost essential to satisfactory social interaction. After the age of 4, however, children begin to develop this capacity and find it rewarding to interact with peers, and these relationships take on a new and significant role. Children now begin to enjoy a group life of their own. New adjustments and behavior adaptations must be learned, though, before any genuine, long-term social give-and-take is possible. The years between 4 and 7 lead in this direction.

As their social life expands, children learn that the world has routines. There is a story of a 6-year-old who, after his first morning in school, proudly informed his mother, "I have a rule." When asked, "What is it?" he replied, "I have to be back by one o'clock." Now, when they begin to form groups of their own, children also construct their own rules and routines. Leadership emerges, which results in the formation of social hierarchies, with developing power relationships.

In this chapter, then, we shall concentrate on the shift children are making from primary ties with their parents to secondary ties with peers and adults outside the home. These new affiliations often occur in the nursery school setting, and the effects of this experience will be examined. We shall deal with the group life that, by ages 5 and 6, becomes measurable, while we look at the new social mastery and the changing patterns of social behavior that appear at this age. The pressures and conflicts of these years inevitably produce certain behavior problems, and these will be discussed along with the methods that are commonly used to treat them.

Patterns of Interaction with Peers

Although the infant responds to peers, his responses are primarily reactions, not true interactions. He is keenly interested in other babies or children and observes them avidly—often laughing or babbling or gesticulating at the antics of the other. As Lewis has shown, peers do not induce stranger anxiety in the infant, whereas adults do (see Chapter 7). Their similarity in size and actions apparently attracts him from the outset. The infant's social interaction, however, is almost totally limited to his mother. In his toddler years, also, he is oriented toward his mother at home, and at nursery school, toward his teacher. After the age of 3, however, there is an increase in group activities, and these sessions of group play last for longer and longer periods. The child's own continuing interest in other children, and his parents' and teachers' encouragement and expectations that he will learn to get along with other children, provide both intrinsic and extrinsic pressure toward the further development of peer activity. At 4 the child prefers to play in a small group, and at 5 he spends more than half his time with other children (Valentine 1956). Children at 5 and 6 seem to prefer groups of three, though they may play with as many as five or six (Green 1933), and will play even with people they do not particularly like rather than play alone. At this age they show signs of real cooperation, friendliness, and sympathy, but there is also a good deal of competition, fighting, and quarreling.

This change of orientation—from adults to peers, with social interaction patterns developing from simple to more complex—has been traced in a number of studies.[1] In her classic study of 42 nursery school children between the ages of 2 and 5, Parten (1932) found that social participation increased with the child's age. She classified and scored the children's play activity according to six categories: unoccupied behavior, solitary play, onlooker behavior (watches, but does not take part in the activity), parallel play (plays alongside rather than with other children, but uses the same toys), associated play (plays with others, sharing toys), and cooperative or organized play (takes part in games such as hide-and-seek). Parten's observations showed that as children grow older, they spend more time in associated and cooperative play and less in idleness, solitary play, and onlooker behavior.

Other related studies show that as the child grows older and engages in more associative and cooperative play, he also seeks attention and approval more often from peers than from adults (Hattwick and Sanders 1938; Heathers 1955). There is also an absolute, as well as relative, increase in the amount of attention and approval that 5- and 6-year-olds seek from their peers (Martin 1964).

The Role of Development

As the child moves into group situations, his physical development gives him a broader base for interacting socially. Another important basis for this interaction is his increasing cogni-

---

1. Because the period from about 1930 to 1950 was an especially fruitful one for research on preschool children in naturalistic settings, many of the studies cited in this section date from that time.

Figure 11.1 There is an increase in social interaction and cooperative play with peers in the 4- through 7-year-old period. (John Rees—Black Star; two photos by Hella Hammid—Rapho Guillumette)

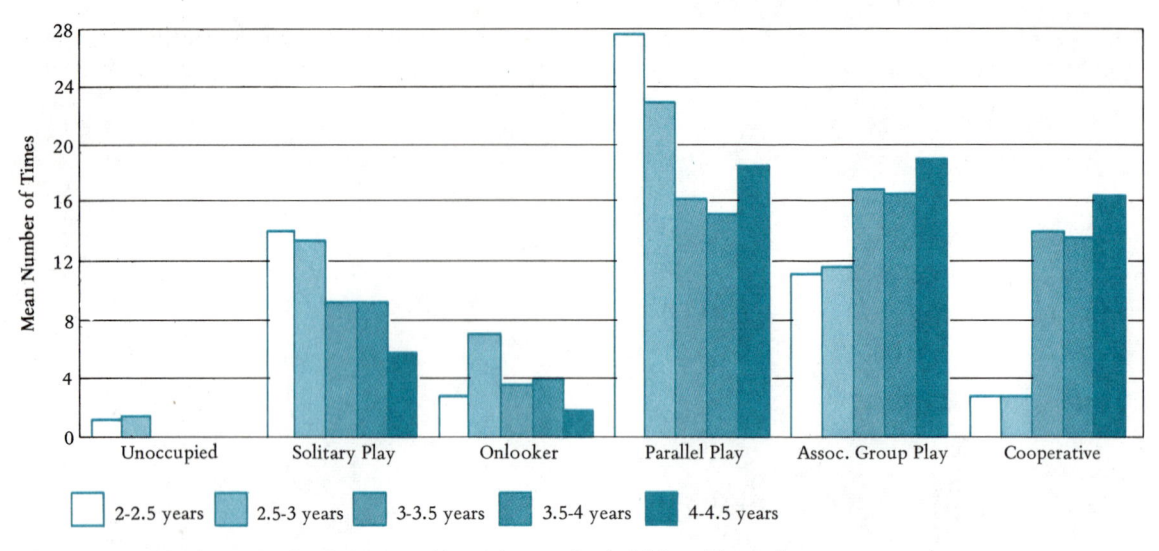

Figure 11.2 Social participation increases with age in preschool children. Figure shows mean number of times each activity was engaged in at different ages. (From M. B. Parten. Social participation among pre-school children. *J. abnorm. soc. Psychol.,* 1932, *27*, 243–269.)

tive maturity—the development of the processes of perceiving and knowing. Some psychologists feel, in fact, that the child develops socially in stages, as his cognition develops. Kohlberg, Selman, Flavell, and others have conducted research centered on children's social interaction as a form of social understanding. It should be pointed out, however, that while cognition is given a central role in these theories of social development, cognition itself is said to develop as a result of disequilibrium induced by role-taking.

ROLE-TAKING. Role-taking may be understood as the ability to put oneself in another's place, to see things from his point of view; it is an ability that seems a prerequisite for effective social behavior (Flavell 1966). For instance, in order to give a person directions, one must be able to identify with that person enough to perceive what he already knows and what he needs to know. Role-taking should be distinguished from empathy (which we discussed in Chapter 9), in which the child has only to have the same feelings as the other person. Empathy, which is observable even in infancy, is presumably one of the early bases for the development of role-taking.

Role-taking ability in children has been shown to be strongly dependent upon age. It is very difficult for children under 4. It is not uncommon, for instance, for a child of 3 to ask her mother to identify a picture in a book while she, the child, is pressing the book up against her own face. The 3-year-old clearly has trouble taking her mother's perceptual point of view—understanding what her mother can and cannot see (Flavell 1966). The ability to take the other person's point of view increases during middle childhood (Feffer and Gourevitch 1960), and therefore will be dealt with extensively in Chapter 12.

Social development, then, is seen by some investigators to depend partially on cognitive development, from which role-taking abilities emerge. Others in the field would assign cognition the major role. According to Kohlberg (1969), the primary meaning of the word *social* is the human activity of role-taking. Although this point of view has considerable merit and promise, it is quite recent and as yet there is little research work to support it. The small amount of research that has been conducted along these lines will be discussed in Chapter 12. Most of the investigation of social development in the past decades has made use of social learning theories, rather than cognitive theories, and this emphasis is reflected in this chapter.

Development of Social Order

We have seen that children between the ages of 4 and 7 begin to collect themselves into groups and to interact socially with each other. The strength shown by these groups, once formed, seems to be rather great. Although Merei, in a 1949 experiment, was more interested in studying interactions between "leaders" and the group, his findings caused him to diverge from this original aim. Merei found clear indications that a solidified group is stronger than a leader; under some circumstances, it even can make a follower out of one who formerly was a "leader."

In this study, the leaders among a class of nursery school children first were identified during a two-week observation period. Then the investigators created several groups of four to six children who were not leaders. These were children who got along reasonably well together and were of the same age and sex. Each group was observed as they played together for 30 to 40 minutes a day, in a room apart from the regular classroom where the identified leaders remained. After the experimental groups had seemed to form new group traditions and routines, a leader was brought in. The leader was someone who previously had been imitated, who was somewhat older, and who before had always given orders. Invariably these leaders first were ignored when they were brought into the new group. Then, one of a number of things happened: the ignored leader be-

Table 11.1 Progress Indicators of Social Development, Ages 4 through 10

Behavior Item	Age Expected (years)
Is assertive, boastful	4
Has definite preference for peer mates	4
Tries to gain attention; shows off	4
Tends to be obedient, cooperative; desires to please	5
Seeks approval; avoids disapproval of adults	5
Shows preference for children of his own age	5
Shows protective, mothering attitude toward younger sibling	5
Is sensitive to parents' and others' moods, facial expressions	6
Has strong desire to be with father and do things together (especially true of boys)	6
Insists on being "first" in everything with peers	6
Bosses, teases younger siblings	6
Has rich capacity to "pretend" in social play	6
Shows compliance in family relations	7
Desires to be "good"	7
Begins to discriminate between sexes	7
Forms close friendships with one of same sex; the age of "bosom pals"	8
Sex cleavage is definite; girls giggle, whisper; boys wrestle, "roughhouse"	9
The age of "clubs"	9
Sex differences are pronounced: girls show more poise, more folk wisdom, more interest in family, marriage, etc., and in their own personal appearance	10

Source: Abridged from L. H. Stott, *The longitudinal study of individual development.* Detroit: Merrill-Palmer School, 1955.

came a follower; the ignored leader maintained a front of leadership by ordering the children to do things they would have done anyway; or the ignored leader first adopted the group's traditions, then slowly began to introduce harmless orders and changes.

Most leaders in this experiment were absorbed by the groups they entered. Although each leader was more powerful than any single member of the groups he entered, the strength of the group traditions and mutually agreed-upon routines proved to be even greater.

Formation of Social Hierarchies

Beginning at about the age of 4, children form social hierarchies in whatever group they find themselves, whether it is the neighborhood, the block, or the nursery school. A hierarchy in a peer group develops quickly once a group forms and can be observed rather easily (Hartup 1970). Status in the group hierarchy is a many-sided thing, not just a matter of being popular or unpopular. Some children may be simply ignored, some disliked, some seen as powerful or as leaders.

Dominance–Submission Hierarchies. Dominance-submission hierarchies appear to be universal, in every type of human group, as well as in groups of subhuman primates. Japanese monkeys, for example, that have been observed for the past 20 years have been seen to establish hierarchies of strength. The strongest male leads the troop, and often a coalition of two or three well-established, mature males will share the lead position.

A similar dominance-submission pattern, based on strength, was found in over 30 classes of 3- to 9-year-old children (Freedman 1971). Although the difference between monkeys and humans is considerable, the basic structure had many parallels.

It was discovered that the children had established a hierarchy of strength by asking them to rate each other on the basis of various qualities. The question, "Which of you is toughest?" provoked the most enthusiastic and uniform answers. Among 4-year-old boys, the most frequent answer was, "Me!"; 6-year-olds, however, seemed to agree with each other on who, in fact, was the toughest. The major source of disagreements was the rank each boy gave himself, which generally was higher than the rank given him by the others. Throughout the study, girls were less interested in the question of toughness and in placing themselves in that hierarchy. The 6-year-old girls, though, also perceived toughness in boys with accuracy, while the teachers could not. A group hierarchy based on toughness or strength seemed to have been solidly formed by the age of 6.

In this same study, the children also were asked, "Who is the nicest?" and "Who is the smartest?" but at this age, these questions did not interest them to the extent that the toughness question did. In later years, "Who is the smartest?" presumably would provoke the most interest. In the preschool years, though, an important basis for the formation of hierarchies seems to be toughness, and boys are more involved in this process than girls are.

Facial Expressions Related to Status. Smiling and staring are two facial expressions that seem to be connected with position in the social hierarchy. To return to the monkey troops, it has been commonly observed that monkeys of a lower status exhibit a "fear-grin" before the stronger monkeys. The lower-status individuals also spend much more time watching the dominants than the dominants spend watching them. Scheinfeld (reported in Freedman 1971) observed the same behavior in street gangs on Chicago's West Side—dominant males never look at a lower-status male until he has proven himself worthy of the leader's gaze.

Children in grades one and three have been found to exhibit the same pattern. Lower-status boys and girls watched dominant boys and girls more than the dominants watched the lower-status children, and girls gazed more at boys than vice versa. Smiling, too, typified lower-status individuals. Lower-status girls smiled more than higher-status boys or girls, and lower-status boys more than higher-status girls. The lower-status boys, however, did not smile considerably more than the higher-status boys; in fact, in the first grade, they smiled less than the dominants (Freedman 1971).

To summarize, in human affairs as well as in

monkey affairs, dominance-submission patterns are present. Hierarchies are formed on the basis of toughness — though, with humans, the basis may be a different one in later years — and males seem to dominate. Smiling is more characteristic of those low in the hierarchy than it is of those higher up, and gazing is directed upward, toward the leaders.

POWER RELATIONSHIPS. Social hierarchies suggest the presence of some kind of politics, and politics suggests power and the seizing of power. Even before the formation of hierarchies, however, power-seizing is evident. Children under 4 simply claim power, assigning to others the inferior parts. The young child is an egoist and relates egocentrically to others. The psychoanalytic explanation of this phenomenon is that he is in competition with other children for the love and approval of parents. Not only does the young child grab leadership, but he grabs possessions as well, toys and other objects, apparently feeling that property gives power (Isaacs 1933).

Later, when groups are formed and rudimentary hierarchies established, we have seen that the quality of toughness is generally recognized and admired. The leaders that arise are generally aggressive and domineering, having initiative, strength, and courage. They are those, in short, who possess admired and desired qualities, and, for that reason, they are looked up to and imitated.

Sex differences in play and power. Freedman (1971) found that boys not only are more interested in power than girls, as we saw above, but also they display more power than girls do. Boys also show more aggression than girls. They form larger groups and their groups spread over greater areas. The boys' activities involve much more physical action than girls' activities. While girls are talking, boys are moving about. And boys are more likely to engage in activities that are a form of contest, producing a loser and winner.

A major argument of feminists is that most of the so-called differences between the sexes are really acquired differences in power and status: boys are trained for higher status, girls for lower status. If this is, in fact, true, then early sex differences in power tactics and power play become important, and we need to look at who is carrying out the power stratagems.

Pursuing the earlier work of Sutton-Smith and Roberts (1962), which studied games as models of power, Sutton-Smith and Savasta investigated sex differences in the use of power in games and play (1972). First, in a review of studies concerning the types of games played by children from ages 5 to 12, it was concluded that the games preferred by boys showed more emphasis on strength, body contact, and conflict in larger spaces, with clear outcomes of winning and losing. They were, in sum, the games of those who expect to be powerful, or at least expect to work toward power. The games of girls, on the other hand, were characterized by taking turns in ordered sequence, choral activity, and verbalism. Girls' games, it was theorized, were the games of those who expect to have restricted power and expect no need to fight for more. The study comments on the games of the girls as follows:

In their play sociability and inclusiveness seem to be more important considerations. There are, of course, some close parallels here with stereotypes about powerless groups, which means we are probably dealing with characteristics essential to powerlessness, rather than with femininity as such. (Sutton-Smith and Savasta 1972)

Observations were then conducted in an upper-status nursery school. The investigators this time focused on play rather than on games, and on children at the earlier age of 3. Contrary to the results of studies of older children, no sex differences in the type of play were found. Despite this lack of differences, however, there were differences in power. Boys spent considerably more time in social testing activities than girls did — activities in which the child seems to prove something about himself, as compared with others, as if to say: "See, I can do it." "You can't have it." "I'm biggest." One boy spent 43 percent of his time in this kind of testing, whereas the greatest percentage of time spent by any girl in such social testing was 20 percent (Sutton-Smith and Savasta 1972).

These differences are in accord with the very

general finding that boys are more aggressive in play and other behavior at all ages (Maccoby and Jacklin 1971). Perhaps, however, there is much more to the matter than mere physical aggression. The boys, it seems, are exploring dominance-submission arrangements, and it is skill in these contests that equips them for power in later years. Freedman's data showing that social hierarchies are established on the basis of toughness or power at the ages of 6 and 7 support this view.

Peers as Agents of Socialization

We have seen that social hierarchies appear quite quickly and obviously in groups of young children. Now we shall examine the effect of these groups and individual peer members on the socialization of behavior. Most studies in this area point to the conclusion that peers have a greater influence on a child than his nursery school teacher, and, in fact, may be almost as influential as his parents. Harlow's work with monkeys leads to a similar conclusion. Infant monkeys who were brought up without mothers but in the company of other infants showed social behavior that was considered fairly normal. Monkeys who were raised in total isolation from both mothers and peers, however, showed severe handicaps in their social behavior (Harlow and Harlow 1965). It seems clear that, among humans and monkeys as well, peers do have a significant potential for aiding each other's social development. A more intriguing question, however, is what determines the extent and kind of influence that children exert on one another.

Because children do, at this age, enter groups, they soon find they must adjust to other children and interact with them socially. At this point, a number of things may happen (although many individual differences may occur). Some of the behaviors the child has brought from home are reinforced. Others are not. The child may, in fact, be pressured to modify some behaviors. Also, he now finds new models for imitation and identification. And he undoubtedly will be subject to what has been called "educational friction"—upsets to his egocentricity, his personal assumptions and fantasies. That is, he will discover that other children may have purposes that conflict with his, that they have wills of their own, and this discovery will undoubtedly result in conflict. These confrontations and quarrels are, in the minds of some educators, as important as any other educational experience the child will have (Isaacs 1933).

A typical behavior that might be strengthened in a nursery school situation is the socially acceptable one of sharing. If sharing has been learned at home and is now brought into the school, it probably will be praised by adults and appreciated enough by peers so as to be reinforced and strengthened. A habit that may be weakened, on the other hand, is the self-centered one of always demanding the favored position in play. If a child insists that the ball always be thrown to him, he probably will soon find himself out of the game and will have to reconsider his behavior.

Peers as Reinforcers

As studies of age-related behavior in nursery school have demonstrated, children turn more frequently to peers than to adults for attention and approval as they mature and grow in social interaction. Because of this shift, peers become a significant source of positive social reinforcement. Some of the major studies in the area of peer interaction have been conducted by Hartup and his colleagues, whose work we shall examine here. Among other dimensions of peer interaction, their work has described the types of responses that tend to have a reinforcing effect on other children's behavior, the situations in which reinforcing responses occur most frequently, and in which children in a group are most effective in reinforcing another's behavior.

REWARDING ACTIONS AND SITUATIONS. From observations of 3- and 4-year-olds, Charlesworth and Hartup (1967) identified several types of behavior that served to reward or reinforce another child's actions. They included giving positive attention and approval, expressing affection and personal acceptance, submitting to another's demands, and giving tangible objects to other children. Behaviors that met with these reactions tended to be prolonged or repeated, and thereby strengthened. The investigators also found that the children who frequently gave such social rewards bestowed them among many peers, and these reinforcing children themselves received reciprocal social rewards. Similar findings have been reported by Kohn (1966) in his study of kindergarten children. These types of positive reinforcement by peers in nursery school seem to be related to certain situations. Charlesworth and Hartup (1967), for example, found that most social rewards occurred during free, dramatic play, rather than during activities that were structured by a teacher or required the children's attention to a project or to the teacher.

ARE BEST FRIENDS BEST REINFORCERS? To measure the relative effectiveness of reinforcement by liked and disliked peers, Hartup (1964) engaged 4- and 5-year-olds in a marble-dropping game. First, a child's performance in the game was noted when no peer was present. Then a reinforcing peer was introduced. In some cases the child dropping marbles was reinforced by a "liked" peer or "best friend"; in other cases, the child was reinforced by a "disliked" peer. Strangely enough, the subjects who were reinforced by a disliked peer increased their performance rate more than did the others. In fact, performance sometimes declined when reinforcement was given by a friend. Similar results were found by Titkin and Hartup (1965) for children slightly older, although some other studies are only partially consistent with these findings.

If, among preschool children, reinforcement from nonfriends is stronger than that coming from friends, it is natural to ask why. Hartup suggests, on the basis of this and similar studies, that "situations which are unexpected, unfamiliar, or in which the child is anxious produce the best performance under peer reinforcement" (Hartup 1970). (In the marble-dropping study, the presence of a disliked peer was taken as an anxiety-producing situation.) Other factors, of course, may be involved. For instance, Hartup noted in the same study that children tended to talk more to friends than to nonfriends during the game, in spite of instructions not to talk. This distraction when a friend was present might have caused their performance to decline. Possibly such talking

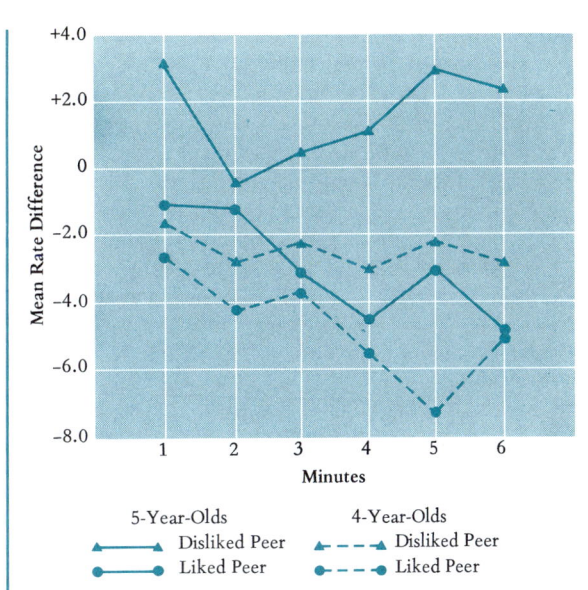

Figure 11.3 Differential effect of liked and disliked peers on marble-dropping performance by 4- and 5-year-olds. (From W. W. Hartup. Friendship status and the effectiveness of peers as reinforcing agents. *J. exp. child Psychol.*, 1964, *1*, 154–162.)

is an alternative form of reinforcement which competes with the original purpose of the experiment. So, in order to discover when best friends are best reinforcers, we would probably need to examine a variety of different task situations.

Peers as Models

Although peer reinforcement exerts a strong influence on the child's behavior during the preschool years, the direct imitation, or modeling, of peers seems to have an even greater influence. The effects of peer modeling are more pervasive simply because only the observation of another child is required to initiate a change in the child's behavior—no reinforcement or reward of the child's new behavior is necessary. It has been shown, however, that a behavior is more likely to be imitated if the child observes the model being rewarded for that action. (Later, when we discuss aggressiveness, we shall see that children who observe an aggressor rewarded for his acts will tend to imitate this behavior and become more aggressive themselves.) Once the child enters nursery school or other groups, he is surrounded by a variety of peers who serve as models, of both desirable and undesirable behavior.

In the realm of behavior regarded as socially positive, Hartup found that children become more altruistic when exposed to an altruistic model (1967). In this study, the subject watched a model solve some simple puzzles and receive six trinkets as a prize for each correct solution. The model then deposited the prizes in two boxes, one the model's, the other belonging to another boy in the class. The model always put five in the other boy's box. After finishing, the model left the room. The subject then played the game by himself, and his altruism—as measured by how many trinkets he put in the other boy's box—was indexed. It was found that the subjects who observed the model were significantly more altruistic than the control subjects who had not watched the model.

Hartup also noted, in this same study, that the amount of sharing a child (subject) imitated depended on two other factors: his past experience with reinforcement from the group, and his past experience with the model. If a child usually received reinforcement from his peers, he imitated a rewarding peer. On the other hand, if the child generally received little reinforcement from other children, he imitated nonrewarding peers.

A special type of altruism, involving the child's emotions as well as his material desires, was investigated by Aronfreed (1968). He observed the extent to which children would imitate a response that required sacrifice of personal gain to reduce the discomfort of a peer. It was found that at least two conditions must be met for the imitation of sympathy to occur. First, the child must have experienced that another person (the would-be model) was undergoing stress. And, second, the "distressed" model must have taken some action himself to relieve or reduce the subject's own stress. At the very least, this study concluded, a child must have observed another's distress while he himself experienced discomfort, in order for any imitative sympathy to occur.

The Growth of Competitiveness

Just as the young child learns cooperation and sharing from interacting with peers in his group, so, too, does he learn the fundamentals of competition. Very early, of course, in the home, the child shows some signs of competing—with one parent for the approval and love of the other, or with siblings for the love of parents. But a different sort of competitiveness begins to grow when the child enters the peer group. Now, though he may still be competing for the same rewards—the praise of adults, for example—he does so by striving for achievement and status in a group of peers outside his home. Everyone is familiar with the boasting cries of young children—"Mine's better than yours!" or "Mine's prettier!"—and with the verbal battles in which a child builds up his own abilities and prowess to the degree that his vocabulary will permit. These are, of course, evidences of competitiveness.

The culture in which the child is being reared naturally plays a part in the development, or lack of development, of competitive behavior. If, as it is in this country, competitiveness is extolled, encouraged, and rewarded, the child naturally will think of this quality as desirable. There are, however, some cultures where rivalry is discouraged, and clearly different attitudes are produced. The Zuñi and Hopi Indians of the American Southwest, for instance, display little, if any, competitive behavior, and value, instead, cooperative group activity (Honigmann 1954). The competitive drive found so widely in Western cultures appears to be a learned one. The time and rate of development of this drive in children has been associated with a number of variables: age, home background, and socioeconomic level.

VARIABLES AFFECTING COMPETITIVENESS. Competitiveness in young children tends to increase steadily with the child's age between the years of 2 and 7. In one classic experiment testing the age-dependency of this behavior, children from 2 to 7 were paired with agemates, and, one pair at a time, they were seated opposite each other at a table of construction blocks. They were allowed to play freely for a while, and then they were challenged to build something bigger or taller or better than their partner's. The 2-year-olds showed no competitive behavior and played with the blocks mostly in a random manner. Response to the challenge to compete began between the ages of 3 and 4, and the children from 4 to 7 were the loudest, most aggressive, and most hostile in their competitiveness. The percentages of the subjects in each age group who engaged in competition rose from about 40 percent at ages 3 to 4, to almost 100 percent at age 7 (Greenberg 1932).

The same study, however, also noted wide individual differences in competitiveness among the children. Some never competed at all, others competed quite violently, and others were moderate in their competitive actions. It would seem that other factors in addition to age have some influence on a child's competitiveness. Later studies show that home environment, sex of the child, and socioeconomic status exert some influence.

High competitiveness has been found more often in democratic homes rather than more restrictive, authoritarian ones. And the less competitive children tended to be those who got along well with their brothers and sisters (Baldwin 1948). Another study showed that sex and socioeconomic status can be correlated with a child's degree of competitiveness. As in the Greenberg study, pairs of nursery school children were led into a playroom where they found two piles of blocks and were encouraged to compete in building. This time all competitive and aggressive responses, including verbal responses, were recorded. The data showed the following: Not only did the older children compete more than the younger, but those from the lower middle class competed more than those from the upper middle class group, and boys competed more than girls. It might be concluded that sex stereotyping of competitiveness had already taken place; that is, both sexes had learned that highly competitive behavior is regarded as appropriate for males only. Also, there is the implication that children from the lower-middle status were encouraged in their homes toward more competition than were those from the higher-middle status.

Competitiveness in children, as these several studies have shown, seems to increase in intensity and to become more generally evident as the child approaches age 7. There are, however, great individual differences. Some of these differences are related to sex (boys seem more competitive than girls), some to social and economic status (those middle lower on the scale seem more competitive than those who are middle higher), and others are related to the kind of home the child comes from (democratic homes seem to foster more competitive behavior than authoritarian homes).

Aggressive Behavior

Competitiveness, though sometimes characterized by some aggression, nevertheless is not the same as aggression. Competition can, in fact, be closely related to cooperation; two children who compete with each other in one situation may well be quite friendly and sociable with each other in another. Aggressive behavior, on the other hand, is almost antithetical to cooperation, especially in the early years, when it is most often characterized by physical combat, pushing, hitting, and fighting. It should be remembered throughout this discussion that a certain degree of quarrelsomeness and threatening behavior is regarded as typical of 4-year-olds, and that 6-year-old children are, for a time, highly emotional in their reactions (Gesell and Ilg 1943). In short, some aggressive behavior is to be expected as normal.

REINFORCEMENT AND SPREAD OF AGGRESSION. If aggressive behavior already exists in a child when he enters nursery school, or any other group situation, it is not likely to be lessened by his experience in the group. In fact, it is more likely to be rewarded and, therefore, strengthened or even increased. And, if this behavior does not exist in the child when he enters the group, it may well be that he will learn it there.

As we have seen in the studies of reinforcement, if a trait receives peer reinforcement, that trait tends to remain and to become, possibly, even stronger than before. Aggressive behavior seems to be highly susceptible to peer reinforcement. When children give in to or retreat before an aggressor, they strengthen this behavior in him. One study of children in two nursery schools recorded a total of 2,583 aggressive acts and their consequences. The investigators found that very often the children gave in to an aggressor—gave him what he wanted, complied with his demands—which had the pronounced effect of reinforcing such aggression and making it virtually certain he would try the same tactics again (Patterson, Littman, and Bricker 1967).

Results of this study pointed also, quite un-

Table 11.2 Descriptive Data: Assertive Behaviors Output, Proportion of Positive Reinforcement, Number of High Asserters, Frequency of Assertive Bursts

Variables	I	II	III	IV	V
Nursery School C:					
Frequency, total assertions per hour	11.7	17.7	18.2	14.5	12.2
Proportion positive reinforcements	0.89	.86	.78	.71	.76
Number Ss with 3 or more assertive responses per hour	3	3	5	4	3
Number of bursts per hour	1.2	1.6	1.2	.7	1.1
Nursery School P:					
Frequency, total assertions per hour	13.0	20.4	28.2	40.0	13.2
Proportion positive reinforcements	0.76	0.83	0.82	0.85	0.73
Number Ss with 3 or more assertive responses per hour	2	5	4	5	3
Number of bursts per hour	0.2	0.6	1.4	6.0	0.4

(Blocks of Time)

Note: Number of subjects in each nursery school is 18. 1 burst = 5 or more attacks in rapid succession.
Source: G. R. Patterson, R. A. Littman, and W. Bricker. Assertive behavior in children: A step toward a theory of aggression. *Monogr. Soc. Res. Child Develpm.*, 1967, *32* (5), 1–43.

derstandably, toward a kind of contagion in aggressive behavior. If a child repeatedly finds himself to be a victim, sooner or later he may decide to strike back; in other words, a child who initially does not engage in aggressive acts may begin to do so—and may continue if he finds his new behavior successful. There were some children in this experiment, however, who did not acquire any aggressive habits at all; they were those who remained apart from the group and did not interact very often with the others. These findings would seem to support many parents' complaint that their children become more aggressive when they enter nursery school.

GENERAL FREQUENCY AND INDIVIDUAL DIFFERENCES. During this age period, aggressive acts seem to occur very frequently in groups of children, but there are also great differences in the number of conflicts engaged in by individual children. As to frequency, aggressive incidents were found to occur at the rate of once every five minutes in a study of American children (Jersild and Markey 1935), and once every six or seven minutes in a similar study of Australian children (Debus 1953). In the study of American children, 54 children, ranging in age from 2 to 4, were observed during 10 observations of 15 minutes each, over a period of time; the Australian study was much the same.

In both studies, wide individual differences were noted; some children never engaged in aggressive behavior, and others were almost always involved in aggression. As an example of the extremes, Jersild and Markey found that one child engaged in 141 aggressive incidents during the course of the observation (a total of 120 minutes), and another engaged in only 17. They also found one child who made 87 personal, physical attacks on other children—pushing, hitting, and throwing things—and one child who did nothing of that sort at all.

Influencing factors. The presence of these wide differences in the amount of aggressive behavior suggests that there must be variables which tend to influence the level of aggression in a child. As we have seen in our discussion of aggression in toddlers in Chapter 9, some of these variables—such as age, sex, type of home, and socioeconomic level—have been the subject of considerable research.

The most direct effect of age level seems to be a change in the form the aggression takes. Screaming, kicking, and crying are likely to be abandoned as the child grows older and substitutes language for sheer noise level and physical attack. Also, conflicts among older children tend to last longer than they do with younger children (Appel 1942).

Sex differences in aggressiveness are similar to those in competitiveness. Boys are more overtly aggressive than girls, in general, although this difference is much less marked at the age of 2 than it is at the older age levels (Jersild and Markey 1935). Older boys cry less than younger ones and more often use physical force instead. Another study, using a doll-play situation, found boys more aggressive physically and girls more aggressive psychologically (Sears 1951).

Homes where children are strictly trained in habits of politeness and neatness often produce children with a large amount of hostility (Isaacs 1933), and homes and families low on the socioeconomic scale tend to send out more aggressive children than those homes and families on a higher level. Those on the lower economic scale tend to fight more over possession of material objects than the children of higher socioeconomic status (Appel 1942).

In general, then, aggressive actions are, with wide individual differences, rather frequent in the child between the age of 4 and 7, as he begins to interact socially. The form, type, and length of aggressive acts often change with age, and the general aggressiveness or passivity of the individual child seems to be influenced by a number of other factors as well: his home, his sex, his socioeconomic level. Most important, perhaps, is the strong peer reinforcement that seems to be given this type of behavior, as well as the spread of aggressive behavior once the child is in the group and interacting with others.

Effects of Nursery School Attendance

Nursery school is generally regarded as a social situation in which the child's personality and social development, rather than intellectual or cognitive learning, is the primary focus. In most schools the child is guided in learning to adjust to others, to the extent that this is necessary for rewarding interaction, but he also is encouraged to maintain his own freedom as an individual in the group (Jersild and Fite 1939). Nursery school usually is the child's first regular experience with a group of children his own age, and, therefore, is his introduction to the influence of peers. Also, the nursery school teacher may be the child's first adult model other than his parents.

Both Positive and Negative Effects

Experience in a nursery school group has been found to have certain immediate beneficial effects, such as making a child more outgoing and more adaptable socially, more independent, self-reliant, and self-expressive, and more curious about the world around him. On the less positive side, however, some studies indicate that these benefits are short-lived and may not be attributable to nursery school attendance at all. And, as we have just seen, the imitation and reinforcement of the generally undesirable quality of aggressiveness frequently occurs in nursery schools. As we shall see, there are unresolved discrepancies, both in the research and in the attitudes of parents and teachers, concerning how much of a child's apparent advancement in nursery school is actually gained there, or how much would have occurred even if he had not been attending the school.

Finding true "control" subjects is one of the greatest obstacles in this area of research. Although studies of the effects of nursery school attendance can match the school and nonschool subjects for age, intelligence score, and socioeconomic status, other variables such as differences in temperament or home environment are difficult to control and may be responsible to some degree for differences in behavior between the two groups. The very fact that a child has been enrolled in nursery school, for example, may indicate significant differences, in both personality and parental interactions, between him and a child who is kept at home. Furthermore, the child who is sent to nursery school may be there because his parents hope the experience will help correct a certain behavior problem, such as an inability to play with others, either because of extreme shyness or excessive aggression.

Another research problem lies in the great variety of nursery schools and their programs. These differences are often subtle ones and are difficult to control. Also, since children's needs and level of social development vary so widely, different children may do better under some programs than others. The effectiveness of a school's program depends on its appropriateness to the particular child's level of social development.

In order to clarify and strengthen the research in this area, at least one investigator has suggested that specific aspects of the nursery school experience, rather than the total concept of nursery school, be studied (Thompson 1944).

IMMEDIATE POSITIVE EFFECTS. A number of studies seem to confirm the expectation that nursery school attendance will foster good social and personality adjustment. Babyish behavior may be eliminated and more independent behavior developed in the period of a year (Kawin and Hoefer 1931). Inhibitions and nervous tendencies such as tenseness and enuresis may be reduced, although the underlying anxiety will most likely remain (Hattwick 1936; Kawin and Hoefer 1931).

One early study found that children in a nursery school made greater gains in social and personality development than did a control group who were not in school. The subjects and controls were similar in age, intelligence, physical development, and socioeconomic background. Both groups were rated on the same behavior items when the nursery school children began their first term, and the ratings were repeated six months later. Results showed that after only these six months, the nursery school children outranked the control children in spontaneity, general socialization, initiative, self-assertion, self-reliance, curiosity, and interest in their environment (Walsh 1931). The investigator concluded that these developments were probably a result of the "social force of a large group of children who had to adjust to each other constantly" (Walsh 1931).

LONG-TERM EFFECTS. While some evidence exists that nursery school attendance facilitates social adjustment, there seems to be no evidence that these observed gains endure over a long period of time. In kindergarten and elementary school, for example, the nursery school graduate does not seem to have any particular advantages. In fact, the opposite has been shown to be true—though, once again, variables other than the actual preschool attendance may be playing a part.

One study of kindergarten children showed that those who had attended nursery school experienced more difficulties with social adjustment—which nursery school is supposed to foster—than did those who had not attended nursery school. The investigators point out, however, that their finding may not be so reliable as it appears. It is possible, they suggest, that the nursery school children were less well-adjusted originally than the others. Their nursery school attendance, then, would not be the only variable related to their observed social difficulties (Brown and Hunt 1961).

There is another point to consider in this brief look at the later success, or lack of success, of the child who attends nursery school—the probability that kindergartens and elementary schools may stress and try to develop rather different qualities and attitudes from those the nursery school encouraged in the child. For example, the freedom and spontaneity so valued in some nursery schools may not be so highly regarded by some kindergartens and elementary schools; indeed, the teacher in a highly structured and traditionally rigid elementary school may value conformity and compliance above all else.

Possibly this difference in aims and values accounts in part for the results of a study by Bonney and Nicholson (1958) which found that children with preschool experience (nursery school or kindergarten or both) showed no clear advantages over nonpreschoolers. Since the children were rated by their teachers and tested by sociometric techniques, it is possible that the preschoolers had received benefits not valued or measured by elementary school standards. All of this indicates that further and different kinds of studies must be made before the long-term effects of preschool education can be fully assessed.

Effects of Daily Separations

It might seem that daily separations from the mother would have harmful effects on the young child, and that these would outweigh whatever

Table 11.3 Comparison of Home Backgrounds of Nursery and Home Groups of Children

	Problem Children		All Children	
Home Backgrounds of Children Studied	Home (13)	Nursery (21)	Home (48)	Nursery (48)
Homes with low standard of child care	—	6	1	7
Anxious mothers	5	9	9	14
Aggressive mothers	—	5	—	5
Hostile attitude toward child	2	6	2	6
Lack of warmth toward child	3	2	5	3
Marital discord	1	5	2	5
Unsatisfactory discipline	5	13	7	14
Overprotection + unsatisfactory discipline	3	2	3	3
	19	48	29	57

Note: Some homes have more than one factor, some have no factors. Also, although the nursery group had more problems, they tended to come from more unfavorable home environments.
Source: From N. Glass. Eating, sleeping and elimination habits in children attending day nurseries and children cared for at home by mothers. *Amer. J. Orthopsychiat.*, 1949, *19*, 697–711.

benefits nursery school attendance would bestow on him. There is evidence, however, which seems to discount the assumption that such separations are harmful.

An English study comparing the eating, sleeping, and elimination habits of children who spent 6½ to 10 hours daily in nursery school with those of children cared for at home concluded that attendance at the nursery school had no unfavorable effects (Glass 1949). A slightly greater proportion of problems—such an enuresis, poor appetite, or nightmares—was found in the nursery school group, but home observations and interviews with mothers disclosed that these problems were closely associated with various unfavorable parental attitudes (maternal hostility, unsatisfactory discipline) and home environment. In some cases, preexisting problem behavior and related parental behaviors and attitudes were cited as the reasons for sending the child to the nursery.

Another study compared the effects of maternal separation on children from two different schools—one a residential school, the other a day school. Children in the residential school were found to have many behavior disorders (loss of sphincter control, hostility, excessive affection-seeking) that those in the day school did not have. It seems that short-term separation from the mother does not affect the child adversely, whereas long-term separation might (Heinecke 1956).

The Teacher's Role

To a large extent, the effects that the nursery school experience will have on a child are determined by the caliber of the teaching and the atmosphere of the school he attends. A sensitive, responsive teacher who is professionally trained to guide and facilitate the social and personality development of preschool children can create a happy, relaxed atmosphere, and, at the same time, provide a good model for imitative learning.

SOCIALIZATION. Because the teacher is, in effect, a substitute for the child's mother for the hours he is in school, she is in a powerful position to reward certain behaviors and discourage others, with the aim of fostering certain social and personality traits. The traits she reinforces are usually, but not necessarily, the ones that the child's parents are interested in seeing developed.

Some of the learning objectives in nursery schools are the development of self-reliance, spontaneity (both physical and mental), and assertiveness in the child, as well as the development of cooperative and sharing behaviors. The

Figure 11.4 The teacher can play an important role in helping children settle their conflicts and develop cooperative and sharing behaviors. (Lynn McLaren—Rapho Guillumette)

teacher may observe certain behaviors in the children and then encourage and discourage selectively by applying principles of reinforcement. Most nursery school teachers look to uncover, discover, and foster in the child such traits as joyfulness and humor, curiosity, and creativity. The professionally trained teacher notes such matters as the child's handling of routine, his reaction to frustration or failure, his ability to control his impulses, his initiative, and the nature of his interactions with peers and with adults. She may introduce the child to unfamiliar situations and people. She also tries to develop the child's level of competence in all the above kinds of behavior. Since these are the kinds of behavior that usually improve, often drastically, in the preschool years, it would seem that she is often successful (Sutton-Smith 1971).

At least one study has shown that the degree to which the teacher interacts with the children can have a decided effect on their progress. To investigate this effect, Thompson (1944) observed and rated two groups of 4-year-olds who were attending two nursery schools with different policies regarding the teacher's role in the classroom. The children were matched in intelligence, socioeconomic status, and general personality characteristics, as judged by their teachers.

The teachers for Group A were instructed to remain somewhat apart and to leave the children on their own as much as possible, while still expressing interest and understanding when approached by the children. In Group B, the teachers participated more actively and more warmly. They guided and helped the children, made more suggestions, and supplied materials in a constructive manner. At the end of the eight-month experiment, the two groups differed in many aspects of their behavior. Group B (in which the teacher participated more actively) excelled Group A (in which there was little teacher guidance) in constructiveness when faced with possible failure, in assertive behavior, in social participation, and in leadership. Fewer nervous habits were evident in Group B, although the difference here was not significant. Thompson concluded that the favorable changes in Group B may have been due to the more active guidance and participation of their teacher.

THE TEACHER'S THERAPEUTIC ROLE. In addition to the nursery school teacher's major role in the child's socialization, some experiments suggest that she also can play an important therapeutic role. It has been shown that the nursery school teacher can modify certain undesirable behaviors and strengthen positive ones through the judicious use of techniques such as reinforcement, or behavior therapy, and by giving a child special instruction in practical or social skills.

Some of the problems of social behavior that a teacher may be able to treat include low-frustration tolerance, too little self-direction, and excessively passive behavior, or, on the other hand, very dominating behavior with an accompanying lack of cooperation. For example, a highly individualized system of rewarding cooperative behavior or gradual approximations of it, and withholding rewards when the child is very dominating, could bring these two behaviors into a more constructive balance.

Special training and instruction in practical skills, and in social responses, also can help a child to modify his behavior. Keister (1938) succeeded in raising the level of frustration-tolerance, or persistence in the face of difficulty and possible failure, in a group of nursery school children by means of a series of special training sessions. In another experiment, children who were extremely submissive in play were given special training in certain skills they appeared to lack. After these play skills were mastered, the children showed an increase in self-confidence. Once their self-confidence was raised, their self-direction and dominance also increased (Jack 1934). Conversely, it has been shown that the behavior of children who are too dominant can be modified so that more cooperation can be elicited from them (Chittenden 1942).

The Chittenden study selected children who were very domineering, who were inclined to use force and threats in social situations. Each child took part in eleven 15-minute doll-play sessions with the experimenter. The dolls represented preschoolers in social situations similar to ones in which the child displayed very dominant behavior. By discussing, questioning, and playing out with the child various scenes of potential conflict, the experimenter helped the child to see that more cooperative responses were possible and encouraged him to resolve some of the frictional difficulties himself. It was found that these children did become more cooperative and considerably less dominant in a negative fashion.

A more complex problem of social behavior was shown to respond well to the regular use of reinforcement techniques. Ann, a 4-year-old in a university nursery school, seldom played with any of the other children in the first days of school, even though she interacted freely with adults. Although she was competent mentally and physically, and was similar in age, intelligence, and family background to the others in the class, she tended to isolate herself from her peers. Gradually, she began to exhibit more serious problems. She complained of imaginary cuts and

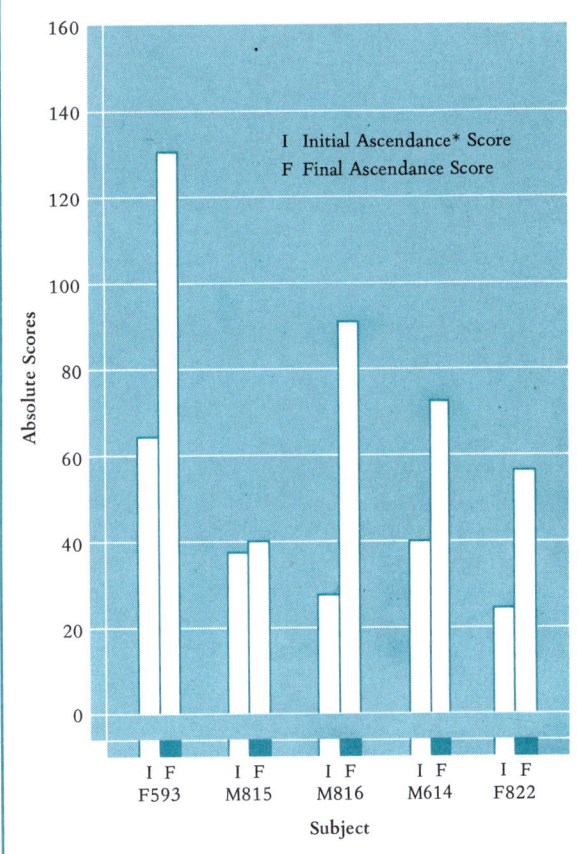

*Ascendance as measured by attempts and successes in securing materials and in directing others.

Figure 11.5 Comparison of ascendance scores in 5 preschool children before and after special training. (From L. M. Jack. An experimental study of ascendant behavior in preschool children. In L. M. Jack, E. M. Maxwell, I. G. Mengert et al., Behavior of the preschool child. Univer. of Iowa Stud. Child Welf., 1934, 9(3), 7–65.)

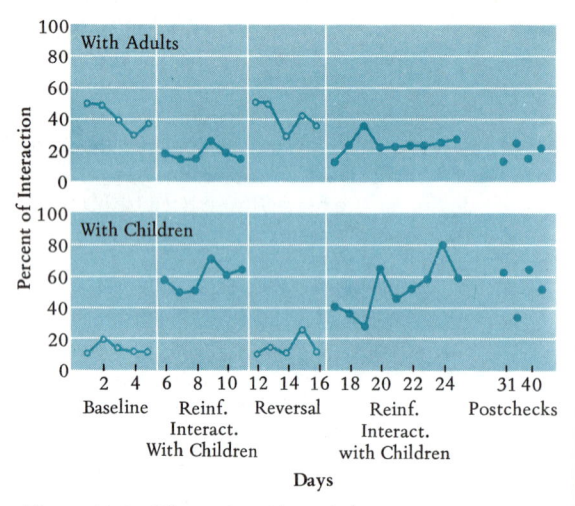

Figure 11.6 Effects of positive reinforcement on 4-year-old Ann's social interaction with children and with adults: percentages of time spent in social interaction during approximately two hours of each morning session. (From E. K. Allen et al. Effects of social reinforcement on isolate behavior of a nursery school child. *Child Develpm.*, 1964, *35*, 511–518.)

bruises, spoke in low, barely audible tones, and spent more and more of her time alone, standing apart and watching the other children. She also developed habits such as picking her lip and twisting a strand of hair.

Ann's isolation tendencies were changed through an intensive, carefully executed program of giving and withholding rewards. The teacher rewarded Ann with attention and approval whenever she played or talked with other children, but ignored her when she played alone. Whenever Ann began to leave the children she was playing with, the teacher turned her attention elsewhere and became occupied with another group. After six days of this training, Ann was spending a much greater percentage of her time playing with other children. To test the technique she was using, the teacher reversed her procedures for several days—she ignored Ann when she played with peers and gave her attention when she played alone or approached an adult. An immediate reversal in Ann's behavior occurred, which indicated that the techniques of reinforcement were responsible for the changes in her behavior.

The teacher then returned to her therapeutic training for nine more days; this produced a dramatic and lasting improvement in Ann's interaction with peers. Ann's baseline percentages of interaction had been 50 percent isolated play, 40 percent with adults, and 10 percent with other children. At the end of the program she was spending 60 percent of her time with other children, 25 percent alone, and only 15 percent with adults (Allen et al. 1964). This case indicates that techniques of reinforcement can effectively treat quite difficult behavior problems. Success is partly dependent, however, upon providing adequate time for the generally overworked nursery school teacher to focus closely on one of her 15 to 30 pupils over an extended period.

Emotional Development

The emotional life of the child has been the concern primarily of psychoanalysts rather than cognitive theorists or social learning theorists. Traditionally, psychoanalysts have found it desirable for purposes of discussion to separate the affective elements of a child's development from the cognitive and to consider them independently. Proponents of the cognitive theory, however, would not make this separation, any more than they would separate social development from cognition.

Psychoanalysts contend that not only is mental health dependent on emotional development, but it is primarily through the emotions, not the intellect, that the child begins to be aware of himself as a separate person, distinct from his surroundings and from other selves. At about age 5, this developing self-awareness is accompanied by feelings of rivalry with the parent of the same sex. Together, these developments contribute to the child's new concern for the intactness of his body and a fear of mutilation.

Sexuality

According to the theory of psychosexual development put forth by Freud, the child at 5 is in the phallic stage, the stage in which he seeks gratification from his sexual organs. (The term *phallic* is used here without sex differentiation.) This stage leads into and then culminates in the Oedipus conflict named for the hero of Greek legend, King Oedipus, whose fate it was to kill, unknowingly, his father and marry his mother. In the Oedipal period, the boy unconsciously is a rival with his father for his mother's love; while he loves his father, he also hates him and wishes to take his place. Feeling guilty about his hostile feelings, the child fears retaliation from his father. He begins at this time to fear mutilation or loss of his penis—a fear that Freud called *castration anxiety*. In girls, the same sort of conflict develops in connection with romantic feelings for the father; it is sometimes referred to as the Electra conflict, named for the heroine of the female counterpart to the Oedipus myth. Rather than fearing mutilation, however, the girl supposedly assumes, when she discovers that she has no penis, that she already has been castrated. She may even assume this is a punishment for her rivalry with her mother. Freud posited that girls inevitably envy the boy's penis, assuming it is superior both for urination and genital pleasure, but others have since disputed this view. Freud also believed that when a boy notices the girl's genital difference, his fear of castration is reinforced—the boy assumes the girl once had a penis but that it was cut off as punishment, and he fears the same fate will befall him.

In studying normal children directly, however, psychologists do not find great evidence for these suppositions about their emotional life, although disturbed children do indeed reveal such fantasies. Still, in a general way, it is highly probable that as a child asserts his independence, his close links to both parents and his fears lead him sometimes to interpret his vulnerability in these terms. For example, at this age both boys and girls express great concern for the wholeness of their bodies, their toys, and other objects. A dismembered doll, ignored at the bottom of the toy chest for many months, can cause extreme upset now, and personal injury often takes on magnified importance in the child's eyes. Surgery, such as a tonsillectomy, can cause greater fear and anxiety at this time than at any other, and for this reason it usually is postponed for a year or so if medical considerations permit.

By about age 6, the child begins to realize and come to terms with the fact that it is impossible to fulfill his desire for the parent of the opposite sex. He then turns his primary attention and attachment to the parent of the same sex and continues to strengthen his identification with that parent. In the psychoanalytic view, sex-role identity is developed in this manner.

In the early preschool years, the child knows he is a boy or a girl, but he hardly thinks of his sex as part of his identity. It does not embarrass a boy, for instance, to play the part of a girl, or vice versa, a girl to take a boy's role. Even at 4, when most children have noticed genital differences, they still do not appear to regard them as important. Sexual differences in clothing and haircut mean much more to them at this time. Stone and Church (1968) quote the story of a 4-year-old reporting to her mother on a neighbor's baby creeping around the lawn in the nude. When asked whether the baby was a boy or a girl, the child said she didn't know, that it was hard to tell at that age, especially since the baby's clothes were off.

At age 5, children seem to take sex differences more seriously. Some psychologists feel, however, that even at this age, sex-related personality differences and other social implications are much more important to them than are the anatomical differences (Stone and Church 1968).

Self-awareness

SHIFTING IMAGE. At age 4, the child has an idea of himself that is not steady but shifting. For instance, Stone and Church (1968) described one 4-year-old named Stuart who spent a number of months very persistently and cleverly being someone else—a 9-year-old boy whom he had heard of but never met.

At the same time, the identity of others is not yet fixed. A child may not recognize, or at least not acknowledge recognition of, a person out of his usual setting. Children have been known to ask questions such as, "What is your name when you have your hat on?" Of course, adults often have this same kind of difficulty. And the fact is that people do sometimes seem to be different people in different situations.

AWARENESS OF FEELINGS. Sometimes children between the ages of 3 and 6 have been shown to possess what might seem to be a surprising knowledge of their own feelings or mood at a particular time or in a particular situation. They seem to understand why they do what they do or how they should be handled in a particular situation. Jersild and Flapman collected anecdotes illustrative of this kind of reflective awareness of feeling. Among these anecdotes is one of a 4-year-old girl who laughed, then commented on her reasons for laughing, saying that people often laugh when they do not know what else to do. They also quoted a 6-year-old girl who told her teacher she was nervous and that the teacher would have to be patient with her and let her go at her own "fastness" if she was to learn. Other anecdotes in the study showed children criticizing themselves and predicting how they might feel in the future.

Jersild, a leading student of children's emotions, maintains that it is unfortunate that our own culture has so generally encouraged the suppression of emotion rather than its expression. "Don't cry" and "don't shout" are familiar admonitions. But it is through the recognition and expression of emotions that children grow into emotional health and well-being.

Emotion in Games

Besides the Freudian approach to the importance of sex-role relationships in emotional development, derived from psychoanalytic therapy and casework, another method of approach is through a study of children's emotions as they are expressed in games.

GAMES AS EXPRESSIVE FORMS. Between the ages of 4 and 7 the child imagines and plays in a way that allows us to see some of his dominant concerns and anxieties. His dreams, stories, folktales, nursery rhymes, and games—his imaginative and play life—seem to be expressive forms. They present and represent human experience and are consistent enough across individuals to allow formal analysis. The "flight" syndrome is one pattern that runs through these forms and is a central imaginative structure; the actions involve being chased, attacked, bitten, but without much counteraction or fighting back. Except for fully developed folktales where there is some form of redress, either through magical assistance or strategy, defeat seems to be "fatefully" accepted. In 5-year-old children, the feeling of being victim is a major dynamism; and in their dreams only the active agent, the monster or parent figure, and the passive counteragent, the child, seem to be differentiated.

This period, as we have seen, is one of emergence from the home, of growing more active in relation to the world and in response to feelings of being overwhelmed. It is a period, psychoanalysis has held, when the child represses his inclinations to family ties and begins to increase the number of secondary ties (to friends). It seems, therefore, that his flight and escape reactions and his concern for safe places may be brought forth by the fact that he is now required to be independent among strangers (Sutton-Smith 1959).

The motivation for game playing seems to be, according to Sutton-Smith and Roberts (1962), the presence in the player of anxieties and conflicts that may have been induced by previous child-training processes. The game is fun because it symbolizes these conflicts and also because the player gains, through playing it, some competence and confidence in the life situations he is anxious about. For example, they theorize that in games like tag and hide-and-seek there is a representation of the child's anxieties about being independent, since, in these games, the child can either run out into the dangerous open spaces and tackle strange persons, or he can stay in or near the safe areas (Sutton-Smith 1959).

In a cross-cultural test, these chasing types of games were found to be present in cultures with a significantly greater concern for independence training (Sutton-Smith and Roberts 1970). In addition, these same cultures had marriage customs requiring a girl to go out from her own kin group and marry among strangers.

Play expressions particular to sex. It appears that some of the games of young girls have more to do with feelings of love than with feelings of fear. Will I be chosen; will I be loved, married?

These are some of the concerns evident in games like the Farmer in the Dell and Sally Waters, in which players are either chosen or rejected. These are games in which a central person has the power to choose or reject those around her. In Farmer in the Dell, a number of persons get to choose and be chosen: the farmer takes a wife, the wife takes a child, the child takes the nurse, and on down a descending scale to the rat who takes the cheese—the cheese often being treated as a scapegoat. These games appear to mirror the girls' conflict over acceptance. This is in contrast with the pitting against each other of the central person and the counteractors in the chasing games, such as tag or hide-and-seek. At this time boys are also playing cops and robbers, Martians and Earthmen, and are showing an identification with culture heroes. Later they will be required to show real courage in games; now they are testing their conflict over competence in fantasy.

Imaginary companions. Many children, not by any means all solitary, timid children, have imaginary companions. As the term indicates, their prime function is to provide companionship for the child, and they usually appear somewhere between the ages of 3 and 10. From age 6 they begin to disappear, apparently having served their purpose. Besides companionship, that purpose also may be to perform rather extraordinary deeds that cause the public to applaud wildly, to dress in outstanding clothes, or simply to stand and let the real child talk as long as he wants without interference. Others may be used to act out impulses the child would like to act out but does not dare. Several studies have shown a large number of children of all temperaments to have imaginary companions.

GAMES AS LEARNING SITUATIONS. In addition to being expressive forms, the child's imaginative and play life seem to provide him with the chance to learn and to exercise the powers he will need in the new situations he is soon to meet. In the game he acts things out in a small, highly focused abstraction. Later he will confront the real situation.

In this sense, the game is similar to a school or college, in which experience is given in a packaged form since it is not possible to acquire it all directly. In the child's games we find a distillation of human relationships, particularly those having to do with power (Sutton-Smith and Roberts 1962). As models of power, games serve to prepare children for expected life experiences:

Games are, we suggest, models of ways of succeeding over others, by magical power (as in games of chance), by force (as in physical skill games), or by cleverness (as in games of strategy). We have speculated that in games children learn all those necessary arts of trickery, deception, harassment, divination, and foul play that their teachers won't teach them, but that are most important in successful human interrelationships in marriage, business, and war. (Sutton-Smith and Roberts 1970)

While psychotherapy and the study of children's games contribute a great deal to our understanding of emotions, a more characteristic approach has been the direct study of such feelings as fear and anxiety, with which the names of Jersild and Sarason, respectively, have come to be associated.

Fear

One of the emotions that children, especially boys, may be taught to hide or disguise is fear. Yet fear can serve an important purpose in life; in fact it often is necessary for survival—successful confrontation or avoidance of danger requires that the danger be recognized. The terms *fear* and *anxiety*, frequently used interchangeably, actually denote two emotions or feelings that are related, but have different qualities. Both are unpleasant. A specific fear—such as a fear of the dark—may be a prominent part of anxiety, but generally, anxiety is a more diffuse, free-floating, and subjective feeling that is expressed in a variety of ways. Fear is considered to be a localized response to an objective danger; a fear reaction is usually specific and directly associated with a particular stimulus or class of stimuli. Nevertheless, fear is a complex term, denoting feelings ranging from terror to quiet withdrawal.

Essential for survival in both primitive and modern life, fear provides the needed energy in a time of danger, moving a person out of the way of fierce animals or speeding automobiles. At the same time, fear can provide an impetus for learning—learning what the fierce animal is like and what can be done about him, or learning about traffic rules. However, if a fear continues too long or becomes too intense or generalized, remaining with the child long after the objective stimulus has disappeared, then it can become destructive. Fear can impair the child's ability to see and deal with his environment effectively.

AGE-RELATED FEARS. As a child grows older, both the intensity of his expressions of fear and the number of his overt expressions of fear decline. This does not necessarily mean a real decline in either the number or intensity of his fears. Instead, it may reflect the fact that a child expresses his emotions less openly as he grows older; furthermore, his fears become more imaginary and less provocative of overt reactions such as fleeing or crying. Between the ages of 2 and 7, a child shows a shift from fearing things that are a part of the objective world around him to fearing things that he imagines. All studies of fear in children are complicated by a number of factors: individual differences in susceptibility to fear; situational differences (a child may fear a loud noise when with a stranger but not when he is with his mother); the reluctance of some children to admit fear; and the fact that those who sometimes express it most may be less upset than the more reserved children. These limitations should be kept in mind.

One classic study reported, among other findings, the relative frequency of particular fears of children from 2 to 6. Information was gathered from reports and observations by parents and teachers. It included 146 records of observations of children for 21 days, combined with occasional records of 117 additional children. These records showed a clear decline with age in fears of noises, falling, specific objects, and strange objects and persons, but an increase in fears of imaginary creatures, plus the dark, robbers, death, and being alone, abandoned, or ridiculed (Jersild and Holmes 1935).

A study by Holmes (1936), using the same categories of fears as in the above study, found differences on two counts from the earlier study. This study showed fears of being left alone and being in a dark room to decrease with age. The discrepancies may be due to the differences in methods of obtaining the data—the first study relied on parents' and teachers' reports of children's reactions in natural settings, whereas the second study used semiexperimental situations, which may have been less frightening than real situations with similar components. Furthermore, the older experimental subjects may have inhibited their responses more than the earlier study's subjects did at home or in the familiar classroom.

Data obtained in private interviews with children from 5 to 12 years of age reveal that they mainly fear imaginary creatures and supernatural or remote dangers; this category represents about one-half of all fears expressed at this age level. All of these fears, however, were noted to decline with age and were highest at ages 5 and 6 (Jersild and Holmes 1935).

These fears, and others that arise with a child's growing self-awareness—such as fears of death and mutilation—may show up in the preschool years as painful timidity or in various physical complaints if they do not receive appropriate parental sympathy so that they may be outgrown naturally. Persistent fears may become transformed into a phobia, which is the attachment of existing nameless dreads or fears to some invented specific object. When a child is pressured to deny or hide his real fears, which may seem absurd to his parents, he may then attribute all his fears to one situation or object that will elicit concern from his parents, such as dogs, or thunder, or dark rooms. Older children frequently develop school phobias, which can be so severe as to render them physically incapable of attending school. Children who once experience this phobia have later interpreted their behavior at the time not as a fear of school but instead as an exaggerated concern for their mother's welfare and as an overwhelming desire to stay at home (Weiss and Burke 1970).

THE LEARNING OF FEARS. One conclusion to be drawn from the studies above is that a child may drop some fears and acquire new ones as he matures emotionally and cognitively. It is now generally held that most, if not all, fears are learned. This was not always so—fears at one time were regarded as instinctive. According to Hagman (1932), most fears are not only learned but also are learned in the home and from the mother, through identification or observation. Fear of dogs, insects, and storms, especially, have been shown to be acquired this way. Sometimes a fear also can be traced to a specific event; a child who is afraid of the water may have had an early frightening experience associated with water.

Wide individual differences among children in the number and kinds of fears they have are attributable to a number of variables. Girls seem more susceptible than boys—or, at least, they admit their fears more. And the physically disabled are more fearful than the healthy. The home environment, of course, plays an important role; one child may learn at home to be enormously frightened of a particular stimulus, but his friend may be completely unmoved by the same stimulus.

In the early years there is a relationship between the number of fears a child has and his I.Q. One study showed a positive correlation between number of fears and I.Q. between ages 2 and 3, but the correlation declined to zero by age 5 (Jersild and Holmes 1935). This finding would seem to reinforce others that relate fear to the child's maturing intellectual abilities. A young child who is more advanced intellectually may perceive fear of danger in a situation where a less advanced child does not see it, but later he may develop the understanding or skill to cope with the situation, or, at the later age, may be concealing his fear.

MODIFICATION AND GENERALIZATION. Once learned, a fear may later become generalized, or it may be modified. If a child once has a frightening experience with an automobile, he may become fearful of crossing the street even when there is no automobile in sight. Or his automobile accident may cause nightmares, which, even after they subside, could cause him to be afraid of the dark, although this had not frightened him earlier. In short, the process of learning a fear may be clear and direct and the cause clearly evident, or it may be quite complex and indirect.

ELIMINATING FEARS. In the cause of the fear may lie the cure. Interviews with parents seem to indicate that the best way to help a child overcome a fear is to help him understand the background of the fear and be actively sympathetic in his approach. Coercion, ridicule, and ignoring the fear have been shown to have negative results.

Anxiety

Unlike fear, anxiety is usually a more diffuse feeling and its causes are more subjective and hidden. It is, however, like fear in its inevitability and its potential for constructive as well as for destructive functioning. A moderate amount of anxiety, such as most people experience before an exam or a performance, can lead to action that is creative, inventive, and problem-solving. A large amount can nearly immobilize a person, making achievement difficult, if not impossible.

Inner conflict is a source of anxiety for young children, who often are filled with conflicting impulses. Some of the conflicts that children from 4 to 7 typically feel are the desire to be dependent on the parents and the desire to be independent of them; a feeling of anger against a parent who is loved; a desire to gain approval by complying and an impulse toward noncompliant self-assertion. All of these and many other incompatible feelings arise from the clash between the child's own impulses and the demands and restraints that are imposed from outside and are becoming a part of his own conscience. Conflicts are inevitable and normal, and the child usually develops some technique of coping with them. There is, of course, potential for trouble as well, as we shall see.

ANTECEDENTS OF ANXIETY. Early parent–child relationships provide soil for the growth of anxieties that often can be quite severe and regular in occurrence. Some antecedents of anxiety, according to clinical observation, are punishment and restrictions that are overly severe; the imposition of standards of behavior that are too high for the child; unfavorable and harsh judgments of the child's behavior and achievements; and quick and inconsistent changes of mood and reactions to the child by the parents (Kessler 1966; Ruebush 1963).

For example, it has been postulated that the child who is called "test-anxious" is one who has had his adequacy questioned in his home (Sarason et al. 1960). The same researchers present data suggesting that children's anxieties are "the result of a complex interaction between the parental threat of negative evaluation of the child's performance and the child's conflicting feelings of aggression toward his parents and his need to be dependent on them" (Sarason et al. 1960). The authors conclude that the anxious child experiences great difficulty in testlike situations, in which he is required to act independently and then be evaluated.

EFFECTS ON BEHAVIOR. Effects of anxiety on behavior in children between infancy and school age have not been studied extensively. However, the work that has been conducted on social behavior indicates that high-anxiety situations, such as being in a strange room, provoke an increase in proximity-seeking and other dependency behaviors (Rosenthal 1967). This correlation between high anxiety and dependency behavior has been found to be stronger in nursery school boys than in girls of the same age, and regression in play activities is a further characteristic of boys' behavior under high-anxiety conditions (Ruebush 1963).

In the area of cognitive behavior, the effects of anxiety are more complex. It has been found, for example, that anxiety can aid the learning process if the task is a simple one. If the task is difficult, however, anxiety seems to interfere with learning. One study comparing the effects of anxiety on verbal learning (a relatively complex type of learning) with its effects on classical conditioning (a simple type of learning) illustrates this relationship.

In this study the subjects were older students who were under stress because of certain conditions in their lives. Some of them were waiting to take oral exams, some were about to take part in a dramatic production in a university theater, and others were waiting to give oral reports in class. During this period of anxiety, each subject was asked to learn a list of nonsense syllables and to take part in a conditioned learning experiment. After all of the subjects' stressful situations were concluded, they then learned another list of nonsense syllables and participated in another conditioning experiment. Results showed that the verbal learning of the nonsense syllables was impaired by stress, but the conditioned learning was improved. The investigators concluded that stress is an impediment to difficult learning and an impetus to simple learning (Beam 1955).

Anxiety, therefore, is more apt to have a negative effect on the child's performance as he advances in school, because schoolwork becomes more verbal and complex in higher grades. This expectation was shown to be accurate by a longitudinal study in which high anxiety scores became increasingly correlated with low intellectual and school performance as the subjects advanced in school (Hill and Sarason 1966).

There are certain individual, personal variables, however, which contribute to the effects of high anxiety on the learning and performance of complex verbal tasks. For example, a person with high academic aptitude may perform better in a highly stressful situation, but a person of low aptitude for verbal learning may be hampered by stress (Katahn 1966). Furthermore, high anxiety can aid verbal learning in a person whose need for achievement is high, but low stress has been found to be more beneficial for persons with a low need for achievement (Schmeidler et al. 1965).

Defense Mechanisms

Since anxiety feelings are unpleasant and painful—often too much to bear—human beings learn ways either to handle or to defend against them, in order to reduce the pain and unpleasantness. The techniques used to accomplish this are called *defense mechanisms*. As the name indicates, this behavior is the opposite of an offensive strategy; in fact, it is more akin to retreat. When a child, for instance, blames another child for what is really his own fault, he is using a defense mechanism. He is retreating from or defending himself against a reality about himself that would be so painful to him that he does not wish to, or cannot, face it. Everyone has, and uses, such mechanisms.

Although preschool children use a variety of defense mechanisms, it is not until children reach the concrete operational stage (8 to 9 years old) that they seem able to recognize and understand the causality between their emotions and their actions, especially defensive responses. The emergence of this ability will be discussed in Chapter 12.

Whether defense mechanisms are constructive or destructive in their functioning depends on how they are used by the individual. First, the extent to which the individual uses them is important. Defense mechanisms usually involve distortion of some part of reality, but if not used too frequently, they may have an adaptive function; that is, they may assist the child in meeting some of life's vicissitudes and adapting to the world. The withdrawal response, for example, may be useful in removing the child from a situation that threatens him. He may withdraw and hide in his room when a congregation of strange relatives arrives to celebrate his birthday. If used pervasively throughout the child's behavior, however, defense mechanisms may remove the child from reality. He may be unable to cope with threatening situations. His defense mechanisms then would be maladaptive; they would operate against his adaptation to the demands of his life. Withdrawal, for instance, would be maladaptive if it became so frequent and automatic a response to anxiety that the child's activity became restricted to a smaller and smaller circle. Each withdrawal brings relief from anxiety, and thus is self-reinforcing. However, it also closes off avenues of growth for the child.

Besides the frequency with which a child uses defense mechanisms, the variety of such mechanisms used also contributes to whether his behavior is adaptive or maladaptive. If the child has a variety of defense responses and uses them with flexibility, in accordance with the demands of each situation, the chances are that his behavior will be adaptive. If, on the other hand, his repertory of responses is limited and he uses these few in a rigid manner—for example, always withdrawing, regardless of the nature of the anxiety or provocation—his defensive behavior is most likely to be inappropriate and maladaptive a large percentage of the time.

ANTECEDENTS. One study attempting to determine the antecedents of frequent and inflexible use of defense mechanisms in boys found a lack of communication between highly defensive boys and their parents. In the homes of boys whose defensive behavior was extreme, there were no open expressions of pleasure, displeasure, or other feelings between the child and his parents. Discussion of sex, death, and other emotionally tinged subjects was either absent or discouraged. The inadequacy of communication seemed to range widely across both emotional and cognitive areas. Even the motivation to communicate fully seemed to be missing in these homes. The investigators concluded that this early failure to communicate and thus alleviate normal anxieties seems to give rise to extremes of defensive behavior in subsequent years (Hill and Sarason 1966).

SOME COMMON DEFENSE MECHANISMS. Some of the classical "ego defenses" described by Freud are most easily seen in the behavior of young children because they are used in a less sophisticated form in these early years than they are later.

One of the defenses most often seen in the behavior of preschool children is *withdrawal*. If a situation is perceived as threatening, the child withdraws in some fashion. He may duck his head, or cover his eyes, or actually run off to his room. Although he may wish to face the situation, perhaps play with a group of unfamiliar children, he may refuse to go near them; thereby he avoids a situation he feels might be painful—finding his place in a new group. This response brings its own reward. The child, finding himself safely out of the feared situation as a result of his withdrawal, tends to use the same response again and again. Because he insulates himself in this manner, he may not learn to deal adequately with difficult or stressful situations.

The defense called *denial* is the refusal to acknowledge that an event has happened or that a certain situation exists. The child may maintain stoutly, for example, that his father or his brother or his pet did not die, although he really knows the death occurred and may even have witnessed it. It is almost as if by denying the validity of an event or situation the child hopes to reverse it.

Repression is similar to denial but has a deeper effect. A disturbing event is considered to be repressed when it is blotted out or erased completely from a person's awareness. In repression there is no denial that the event—maybe a family fight—took place because the child does not seem to be aware that it happened at all. He has repressed it, and the event is completely beyond his ability to consciously recall it.

Regression is the retreat to earlier babyish behavior. A child may return to bed-wetting, thumb-sucking, or extreme dependency in the hope that he may thus regain the more comfortable state he associates with such infantile behavior. Retreating to the remembered comforts of infancy may seem infinitely preferable to facing a situation that is threatening or painful. The preschool child often reacts in this manner when a new baby is anticipated or born. He may feel that the baby is displacing him or that his parents now are making too many demands on him to grow up and be more independent. If he behaves more like a baby, he may think, then he will receive the care and attention that his parents are giving the new baby.

Projection is easily and frequently seen in children's behavior. When a child attributes a thought or action to another person, when it actually is his own, he is projecting. This thought or action obviously is unacceptable to him. He cannot "own up to it" without anxiety and so he does not. In fact, the 5-year-old often really believes, "He did it—not me." This quick assignment of blame to someone else, even an imaginary companion, is typical of projection. Often the child displays "rapid-fire" imagination in his projections. For instance, if he overturns his glass of milk, he may tell his mother instantly, in convincing dramatic tones, that his baby sister let the pet rabbit out of its cage and the rabbit hopped onto the table and knocked over the glass. The child's projection is not in the least hampered by the fact that both his sister and the rabbit are sound asleep.

Displacement is the substitution, in the child's mind, of another object, person, or situation for the one actually responsible for his anxiety or fear. If a child fears his father, it may be painful for him to admit this fear to himself, since he also loves him and depends on him. Nevertheless, he does feel fearful of his father. Since he must place the cause of his fear somewhere, he chooses a substitute, which takes on symbolic significance, such as a dog, lion, snake, or monster. The child's response of fear may be appropriate, but he has displaced the emotion to an object that he finds more acceptable to fear than his father.

Reaction formation is an exaggerated display of behavior that is the opposite of an undesirable or taboo behavior the child has very strong impulses to engage in. A child may be reacting against a desire to be messy and dirty if he seems preoccupied with keeping himself spotlessly clean. He may even call attention verbally to his fastidiousness—"Look how clean I am." Or, in another instance, a child with strong feelings of hostility may display such extreme deference and solicitude that his actions seem to declare, "Look how nice I am!" In reaction formation, the true impulses are, for whatever reason, so unacceptable and frightening to the child that he is pushed to extremes of the opposite behavior in order to hide them.

Finally, *rationalization* is a widely used defense often made evident by the introduction, "You know why I did that?" What a child actually does when he engages in rationalization is to offer socially acceptable reasons for some unacceptable behavior. Or, the behavior may be acceptable, but it may have been provoked by reasons that are unacceptable to the child and would, if he admitted them, make him feel quite guilty and anxious. Sometimes rationalization is defined as giving good reasons instead of the real reasons. For example, one child might give another a hard push, then explain he was pushing him out of the way of some danger, doing it, in short, for his own good. And once the explanation has been given and seemingly accepted, the explainer is once again at peace.

The kinds of defense mechanisms a person will use are determined partly by his individual constitution and temperament, his family background, his prior experience, among other variables. There are also developmental and socioeconomic differences in preferences for defense mechanisms. Younger children, as well as the lower socioeconomic groups, show a preference for withdrawal, denial, and aggression, and older persons in the middle class show a preference for reaction formation and rationalizations. Projection and displacement appear to occupy a middle ground between both.

One interesting and yet unsolved question is whether or not the structures of defense mechanisms are parallel to the structures of the cognitive operations discussed by Piaget. According to Piaget, there must be such a parallel. But there are others who have argued that such "affective" structures operate on different principles from cognitive ones (Wolff 1963).

Behavior Problems and Disorders

Like fears and anxiety, which are usually associated with them, behavior problems are to be expected in the average child. Through the course of a child's development, problems arise but tend to work themselves out, given enough time and patience. In some cases, however, they may persist and require treatment. The words *normal* and *abnormal* have been used in the past to categorize behavior as if the two types of behavior were totally unrelated. However, there is a trend now to regard normal and abnormal behavior as coexisting on a kind of continuing scale, rather than being completely distinct from each other. In this view, a person moves from so-called normal behavior to so-called abnormal, and vice versa, by a matter of degrees, not by the radical abandonment of either mode of behavior.

There seems to be no standard, objective criterion for the judgment of normalcy and abnormality in behavior. In fact, the labeling of behavior as "disturbed" may result, according to Kanner (1960), more from the intolerant attitudes of the family and society than from any intrinsic qualities of the behavior itself. It has been pointed out that all children show signs of disturbed behavior at one time or another (Buckle and Lebovici 1960), and Kanner notes that many children who are "breath-holders, nail-biters, nose-pickers, and casual masturbators develop into reasonably happy and efficient adults because of tolerant and resourceful parental attitudes" (1960). When appropriate help from parents is missing and the child is referred to a clinic, the problem then may be magnified out of proportion to its importance in the everyday life of the child. Much of the basis for the labeling of behavior, then, may lie in the perceptions and reactions of those who are applying the labels.

A further sign that cultural or social factors often determine what is considered "abnormal" is the apparent changing styles in the diagnosis of such behavior. Nail-biting is an example. Once regarded as a "stigma of degeneration," later as "an exquisite psychopathic symptom," nail-biting was next found to be present in 66 percent of school children at one time or another. Commenting on this survey, Kanner (1960) observed that it hardly seemed possible to regard two-thirds of all children as degenerate, psychopathic, or victims of unresolved Oedipus complexes.

The concept of *behavior disorder*, as it was first used, referred to any departure from the behavioral norms of the growing child that seemed to come from "the way in which his relationship to himself and to his environment brought about difficulties in adjustment" (Anthony 1970). In 1956, Blau and Hulse revived Freud's view that primary behavior disorders are specific responses to conflict. They held that the anxiety resulting from the conflict was acted out in these disorders and could end in delinquency. In 1967, Anthony suggested that behavior disorders could be categorized into two classes: one, specifically localized in one particular stage of development when certain problems must be solved; and the other, a more diffuse kind, extending through every developmental stage.

Common Childhood Disorders

Childhood behavioral disorders often resemble those of adults, and, in fact, the consideration and treatment of these disorders as a separate category of maladaptive behavior is a relatively new development in psychology. This is attributable in large part to the fact that there is no distinct dividing line between behavioral patterns in children, adolescents, and adults. Although the development of behavior is a continuous process, the problems of childhood are different because the many unfamiliar and unique situations that a child encounters can lead to a variety of behavioral problems.

Because of their dependency upon others and their relative lack of experience in life, children have a tendency to become disturbed over problems that would appear insignificant to adults. Particular developmental requirements, such as the use of language and speech, toilet training, and adaptation to school and the learning situation in the classroom furnish the basis for many of the maladaptive behavior patterns of children. Children usually outgrow these problems, but maladaptive behavior emerging in later life is often more persistent. This point should be kept in mind during the following discussion of some specific examples of childhood disorders.

STUTTERING. Stuttering, an articulation difficulty marked by many stops and repetitions in the pattern of speech, is one of the major speech problems in children. About 1 percent of the people in the United States are estimated to be stutterers, and half of these are children (Barbara 1959). Ninety percent of stuttering begins before the child has reached the age of 6.

Lengthy words, words near the beginning of a sentence, and words starting with consonants are most commonly involved in stuttering (Taylor 1966). Stuttering usually occurs when the affected child feels frustrated, anxious, or self-conscious, as in the classroom or a new social situation with people he does not know very well. In nonthreatening situations, the stutterer often is able to speak in a normal fashion.

Although its origins are not completely understood, three basic theories of stuttering have been developed. The physical or constitutional explanation assumes that stuttering is the result of abnormal biochemical factors or a defect in the speech centers of the brain. Another view is that stuttering is learned, typically the result of the child's effort to conform to the wishes of parents who are hypercritical of his speech and other behavior. Also, stuttering has been explained as being a neurotic symptom, resulting from unconscious feelings of anxiety and conflict.

The treatment of stuttering involves various forms of speech therapy designed to improve vocal control and to produce greater clarity of speech, along with attempts to reduce the child's negative image of himself and his speech. Stuttering usually disappears in 80 percent of the cases as the child becomes older (Sheehan and Martyn 1970), and even the most difficult cases of stuttering generally can be cleared up or markedly improved with the proper treatment.

ENURESIS. Children over the age of 3 who have been successfully toilet-trained and then begin to show lack of nighttime bladder control are usually considered enuretic. About 10 percent of the cases of enuresis are caused by physical disorders (Pierce 1967). The other 90 percent of the cases seem to be the result of hereditary factors, improper learning, or response to situations of stress.

Conditioning procedures have proven successful in treating enuretics. An alarm or bell sometimes is attached to the child's mattress to awaken him at the onset of urination. Drugs, such as tranquilizers and others designed to increase bladder control, have also been helpful.

NAIL-BITING. As we noted above, nail-biting is very common in children. It appears to be related to attempts to reduce tension and to feelings of hostility or anxiety (Coleman and McCalley 1948; Coleman and Seret 1950). Nail-biting apparently serves to alleviate tension by giving the child something to occupy himself with in situations of stress.

In general, the treatment of nail-biting has been neglected. Methods such as the use of restraint and distasteful nail applications have been largely ineffective. Some improvements may be achieved with mild tranquilizers and behavior therapy, but more research on treatment methods is needed.

HYPERACTIVITY. A behavior problem that frequently is observed in school children is hyperactivity. The hyperactive child is characterized by a short attention span, distractibility, and seemingly uncontrollable restlessness (American Psychiatric Association 1968). This form of behavior is most common in younger children, usually appearing before the age of 8 (Jenkins 1969). It usually decreases or disappears during adolescence.

Hyperactive children typically have school-related problems, such as reading disabilities. However, a study by Burks discovered no dissimilarity between the I.Q.'s of a group of hyperactive children and a normal control group (Burks 1960). Hyperactive children frequently speak in a continuous and aimless fashion and are likely to demonstrate signs of immaturity and a lack of social control.

Learning programs using positive reinforcement techniques have been of value in modifying hyperactive behavior (Hewett 1968). Also, certain drugs, particularly amphetamines, have been used to treat hyperactive children. These drugs, paradoxically, decrease the child's activity level and enable him to concentrate on a subject for a longer period of time.

While this form of treatment has enabled children who previously had been unable to function in school or other social situations to do so, it has been criticized because of its possible side effects. Another criticism of drug therapy is that it supports two questionable assumptions: one, that the child and not the school needs to be modified; and two, that if an individual does not fit smoothly into his environment, he should be given medication so that he will. Further studies may show that behavior therapy is appropriate for certain cases, and drug therapy is necessary for others. It already is recognized that the origins of this problem are not the same for every affected child.

UNSOCIALIZED AGGRESSIVENESS. Children who are characterized by "overt or covert hostile disobedience, quarrelsomeness, physical and verbal aggressiveness, vengefulness and destructiveness . . . temper tantrums, solitary stealing, lying and hostile teasing of other children" are classified as unsocialized aggressive children (American Psychiatric Association 1968).

The unsocialized aggressive child frequently is the victim of a disturbed family situation in which the child receives little in the way of consistent affection or parental guidance. The parents of these children often have emotional problems and exhibit instability in their marital relationship. The child is made to feel that he is unwanted, and he often reacts to this parental rejection with an aggressive and antisocial pattern of behavior. Because of the unstable situation in the home, the unsocialized aggressive child is often difficult to treat. Successful treatment may necessitate placing him in an institution or a foster home, but this may be viewed by the child as a rejection by both his family and society as a whole. However, the successful treatment of the unsocialized aggressive child is very unlikely unless he is placed in a setting in which he can feel accepted and receive both affection and consistent discipline.

Unfortunately, past efforts to deal with the unsocialized aggressive child have tended to overemphasize punishment at the expense of treatment and rehabilitation. Placing these children in correctional institutions often causes their problems to be exacerbated and their level of antisocial activity to increase. This pattern of behavior is then likely to continue when the child reaches adolescence and adulthood.

Behavioral therapy and the use of parental control techniques have been effective in treating the unsocialized aggressive child. The child's parents can be instrumental in making him feel accepted by providing a suitable environment and by reinforcing the child's positive behavior.

WITHDRAWAL REACTION. An opposite type of behavior disorder is the *withdrawal reaction*. This behavior is considered maladaptive when it results in a lack of close personal relationships, detachment, seclusiveness, and extreme timidity, sensitivity, and shyness (American Psychiatric Association 1968). Children who exhibit this behavior seem to reject the world of reality and adopt a defensive posture that reduces their capacity to distinguish between fact and fiction. They are likely to be apathetic and to be preoccupied with idle thoughts and fantasies.

Withdrawn children are often found in homes in which the parents are overprotective. This situation can reduce the child's ability to deal effectively with objective reality. He may be plagued by feelings of inadequacy, particularly when he is faced with unfamiliar situations. The withdrawn child often discovers that attempts to establish relationships with others are extremely frustrating (Jenkins 1970). This failure can cause the child to turn even further within himself.

The withdrawn child typically outgrows this behavior as he gains confidence in his abilities and establishes friendships. Among other forms of treatment, techniques designed to aid the child in asserting himself and to improve his ability to perform certain tasks have been effective in helping the withdrawn child. The reasons for the child's withdrawal reaction, however, are the key to the selection of appropriate treatment. Here, as with other childhood behavioral disorders, the cooperation of the child's parents and teachers is an essential ingredient in helping him to overcome his problem.

Some children are divorced from the normal world in a manner that is far more profound than the child who is withdrawn. These children literally exist in a world of their own, and the unusual and sincere nature of their problem merits separate consideration.

Autism

Formerly called childhood schizophrenia, early infant autism is now considered to be distinct from schizophrenia (Kanner 1944). Though still uncommon, autism seems to be on the increase (an increase that may be due simply to improved diagnosis—some cases of autism once were classed erroneously as mental deficiency). This disorder may develop slowly from infancy, or it may appear quite suddenly between the ages of 2 and 3.

The feature that is most outstanding and most consistently present in cases of infant autism is a lack of any desire for human contact, almost a lack of humanity. Parents report that these children do not evoke the normal parental feelings in them, and the child himself seems to have no attachments to people, though he may, nevertheless, panic among strangers and in situations outside his home. The autistic child seems to be more closely attached to mechanical objects than to people, and he rarely displays the standard emotions of affection, anger, fear, or pleasure. He may show great manual skill and dexterity, as well as intelligence, in his precocious abilities to dismantle toys and household objects and put them back together again. He may spend long periods of time engaged in repetitive or rhythmic activity such as endlessly tearing paper into strips, or spinning a top again and again as if in a trance, or rocking back and forth for hours. One 9-year-old autistic child characterized himself as an electrical robot operated by remote controls (Bettelheim 1959).

The autistic child is not always hyperactive, but he often is. This high energy, combined with his mechanical ingenuity and an indifference to pain, often enables the autistic child to slip through standard safety devices and restraints, with the frequent result of severe injuries. Some psychiatrists consider indifference to pain one of the primary characteristics of autism.

The first indication of autism when it appears after the age of 2 may be the failure to talk. Often autistic children first are suspected of deafness. When autistic children do speak, their speech often is marked by *echolalia*, the automatic repetition of whatever words they hear. They characteristically repeat a question instead of answering it, and repeat isolated phrases, names, or verses of a song. This adoption of rigid, repetitive patterns of speech and behavior may take the place of absent emotional relationships for the child, giving him some security. These children may do well in mathematics, and sometimes they also perform amazing feats of memory. Their intelligence, it has been suggested, may be high but somehow flawed, perhaps by a subtle genetic defect (Rimland 1964). Others postulate as more plausible the theory that the usual responses and feedback from the environment that are necessary for emotional development may be missing. This theory draws support from the fact that all reports agree that the parents of autistic children tend to be cold and unresponsive. It is not clear at this point, however, whether parental rejection and neglect are the primary cause, or whether these reactions develop when the infant fails to respond affectionately from the very beginning.

Autistic boys outnumber girls 4 to 1, and the child is typically first-born. About a third grow into reasonably normal adulthood, though probably without enjoying real emotional relationships (Kessler 1966). The best indication that recovery will occur is the normal use of language by the age of 5, and the best help toward recovery seems to be acceptance by an understanding teacher. If a teacher can overcome the difficulties of relating to such a child, she can accomplish a great deal. Many cases are so severe, however, that treatment in specialized schools is required. Only the most simple conditions are responsive to behavior therapy, as the following discussion shows.

Treatment of Behavior Problems

Nearly all preschool children have minor behavior problems. Some are easily handled by parents or nursery school teachers, and some may spontaneously disappear in time. However, others may persist and grow worse, making it necessary for the parents or teachers to seek help for the child. There is today a variety of effective therapies, and making a choice among them is part of the diagnosis of the child's problem. Individual psychotherapy has been used for many years, but other forms of treatment are now being used more and more. Among these are play therapy, family therapy, group therapy, and, most recently, behavior therapy. The last is different from all the others in that its approach is not the psychoanalytic one; rather than trying to uncover and resolve the causes of the child's behavior problem, it simply treats and attempts to remove the symptoms—or maladaptive behaviors—themselves.

In all except behavior therapy, two approaches are possible, directive and nondirective. In directive therapy, the therapist identifies the problem, prescribes the activities, and directs the course of the treatment; the aim is to eliminate the problem the therapist has identified. In nondirective, or client-centered, therapy, the patient, or child, sets the direction and pace of each session. There is no manipulation by the therapist, and the session takes place in an open, permissive environment. Client-centered therapy was first developed in 1951 by Carl Rogers, who believed that given a free atmosphere, some encouragement and understanding, and the opportunity to examine himself, a person can identify and work out his problems.

PLAY THERAPY. Erikson has suggested that "the child's play is the infantile form of the human ability to deal with experiences by creating model situations" (Erikson 1964). Since young children cannot always express themselves effectively in words, the technique of allowing a child to speak through his play has proven useful. In play therapy, the child is brought into a yard or room filled with toys, dolls, and other playthings and is invited to choose what he wishes to play with. The child is the central figure in the situation. As the child plays, the therapist may talk with him about the feelings he is expressing by his actions, with the aim of clarifying and discovering the child's attitudes. At the same time, the understanding of the therapist tends to increase the child's confidence in himself and to encourage him to express more of his feelings and thoughts.

One case of highly successful client-centered play therapy is described by Axline (1966) in *Dibs: In Search of Self*. Before therapy, Dibs talked to no one, and in school was unresponsive to his teacher. He might, during class, hide under a table and was thought to be mentally retarded. His therapy sessions were completely nondirected; Dibs was allowed to play or not play, to talk or not talk. After therapy, he emerged as a highly talented child.

In the very first session, as described by Axline, Dibs spent a long time just looking around, touching and naming different objects; but before the end of the hour he had communicated to Axline that "he had had some unhappy experiences with closed and locked doors." This information was revealed in connection with a dollhouse in the playroom. As Dibs sat in front of it, he repeated over and over again, "No lock doors. No lock doors." Axline replied, "You don't like the doors to be locked?" Dibs added that he did not like walls around him, and then he took the mother and father dolls from the house and ordered them to "Go away to the store. Go away!" The play situation had provided Dibs with the tools and perhaps the impetus for opening one path to problems that were troubling him.

Therapists have found the play session an ideal place for children to release negative or hostile feelings not usually acknowledged or expressed. Some therapists encourage the expression of whatever emotions are pent up, a kind of catharsis technique. Others are more directive, often using doll play as a way of instructing children in better adjusted forms of behavior; for example, the therapist or the child will tell the dolls what to do and how to act in more adaptive ways.

FAMILY THERAPY. In this type of treatment, the therapist joins the family group and is, at the same time, an outsider, inviting, to an extent, company behavior. Attention is focused on communication among family members, both verbal and nonverbal, and on the contradictions between the two types of communication. At the same time, the therapist sets up a subgroup with each member to demonstrate the possibilities of communication and the potential richness to be found in human relations. Since participation by all members of the family is essential, this type of therapy is not usually used with families in which there are children under 9. Parental participation in solving the problems of younger children is, however, important and must be pursued somehow on a separate basis if not in family therapy.

GROUP THERAPY. There are various approaches to the use of group therapy with children. One technique places emphasis on the activity of the children in the group and the place of the individual within that group (Slavson 1964). Another emphasizes verbal communication with the children (Anthony 1957). The first concentrates more on play activities as expressions of emotions, whereas the second relies on the child's ability to talk about his feelings with the therapist and the other children in the group.

In the second type, the therapist must learn how to converse with children without talking down to them and without asking for factual data, which is the usual mode of adult–child conversation. Playthings are used in this therapy, too, to stimulate collective fantasies. Anthony has used a "small-table" technique in which the children are encouraged to use play materials together. He also uses a "small-room" technique to explore problems of closeness and restrictions. In order to encourage children to verbalize their feelings, he has used a barter method—giving them a period of playtime in exchange for a period of talking.

BEHAVIOR THERAPY. Behavior therapy has been rather recently introduced and differs fundamentally from other types of therapy in that it is based on learning theory. Proponents of this type of therapy believe that maladaptive behavior can be unlearned and adaptive behavior learned in its place. Whereas other therapies seek to find and eliminate the underlying causes and conflicts giving rise to behavior problems, behavior therapy focuses only on the symptoms. The symptoms are regarded as the problem itself, rather than an expression of, or result of, deeper problems. A combination of methods may be used to eliminate the behavior problem, including conditioning, gradual learning, and the promotion of sudden insights. Basically, the procedure is one of unlearning undesirable behavior and learning more adaptive habits. The technique of shaping behavior, as described in Chapter 2, is also utilized.

Behavior therapy is especially suited to the elimination of single symptoms, such as a nervous tic. The case of an 11-year-old boy who had displayed tics for six years illustrates how this can be accomplished. The tics, regarded as tension-reducing because they occurred when the boy was under some kind of pressure, were seen theoretically as being unconditioned originally. Since the boy evidently was experiencing some relief when he used the tic to reduce tension, however, the habit was reinforced and became stronger and more powerful.

On the basis of this theorizing, it was felt that the tic could be eliminated if the boy was conditioned to experience tension reduction—relief—when he stopped the tic. The treatment therefore consisted of sessions of mass practice of the tic; the patient was asked to practice it over and over

Figure 11.7 The effect of massed practice of a major tic on its frequency of occurrence. (From J. Walton. Experimental psychology and the treatment of a ticquier. *J. child psychol. Psychiat.,* 1961, 2, 148–155.)

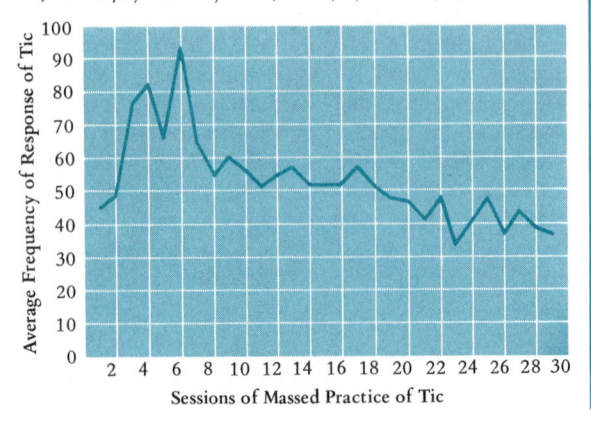

and then told to stop. When he stopped, the absence of the tic brought a reduction in tension, since tension had built up from the extended practice. As a result, the patient showed increasing inability to imitate the tic, and in his daily life showed a marked improvement. He was able to go three or four days with little evidence of the tic, which had been impossible before his treatment (Walton 1961).

The opponents of behavior therapy usually argue, however, that unless the underlying cause of a difficulty such as this is discovered and understood, other symptoms will soon take the place of the eliminated one. Though high percentages of success are claimed by behavior therapists, follow-up studies are scarce and lack comprehensiveness and reliability.

Some of the techniques of this therapy can be used by the teacher in the classroom, and they have been effective in treating some minor problems. Sometimes, in a specialized environment, behavior therapy has been successful in treating serious maladjustments including infant autism. Recently there have been attempts to draw analytic and behavior therapy together (Anthony 1970). The utilization of techniques from both may indicate a valuable direction for child therapy in the future.

In this chapter we have emphasized the social determinants of social and emotional behavior. We have stressed the importance of parents and peers and how they affect the personality of the developing child. Social learning arguments have been given precedence, in contrast to the previous chapter, where much greater weight was placed on the child's own cognitive formulations. While cognition certainly is not unimportant to the child's social and personality development, the current state of research does not allow for an equal presentation of the two types of information.

Summary

Between the ages of 4 and 7, the child's personality develops rapidly. Contributing to his personality development is the child's increasing social interaction with persons outside his family. The child can now see another person's point of view, and the communication which this role-taking ability fosters facilitates the formation of the children into groups.

The group plays an important part in the child's life. In it, some of the behaviors the child has learned at home are reinforced by group approval and acceptance, while other behaviors are not. The child may modify or drop the behaviors that are not rewarded. At the same time, the child learns new ways of behaving from the group. Here he has many models to imitate or identify with, and he may copy both desirable and undesirable behaviors.

The child also discovers that other children's purposes may conflict with his own. In the group, he learns both cooperation and competition. Competition arises from the striving for advancement and status in the group, which has its own social hierarchy. If the culture values competition, as our culture does, the competitive behavior will be further reinforced outside the group. Aggressive behavior also tends to be reinforced by groups. In our culture, boys are likely to be more overtly aggressive than girls.

At the same time that the child is learning to interact socially, he is strengthening his awareness of himself as a separate person. This self-awareness brings with it a concern for the intactness of his body and fears of mutilation and death. A child's fears and anxieties often are expressed in his games and play activities.

Although it is normal for all children to express their feelings in these symbolic ways, children should be encouraged to express them more openly as well. Sympathetic parents can help children overcome their fears. Parents who are unduly harsh, whose standards of behavior are too high, or who are inconsistent in their reactions to their children can heighten a child's anxiety.

Anxiety feelings are painful, and all children develop some defense mechanisms to deal with them. If the child uses a variety of defense mechanisms, and uses them with flexibility, the results are adaptive. But if he uses defense mechanisms too often and too rigidly, the effects are maladaptive. In extreme cases, such an individual becomes totally unable to cope with reality.

In all behavior, there is a continuum between "normal" and "abnormal." Behavior problems are to be expected in all children, and they usually work themselves out. If they persist they may require treatment. The types of therapy used with children are individual psychotherapy, play therapy, family therapy, group therapy, and behavior therapy. Each of these methods has its successes and its failures. The individual child and the nature of his behavior disorder are taken into consideration when a method of therapy is selected.

Case Studies

Paul S.

The only son of middle-aged working parents, Paul impressed his teachers as an independent, withdrawn little boy as he began kindergarten. For the first few days of school, his typical retort to any offers of assistance was, "I can do it myself."

Within a matter of a couple of weeks, however, Paul's personality took a turn toward vigorous—even aggressive—insistence on autonomy and authority. As other children began to form normal social groupings, Paul began to assert himself by dominating games and activities whenever he could. He also challenged the authority of the male teacher occasionally by insisting that he could be the better instructor—for instance, that he could better teach another boy how to use a saw (and, when his carpentry effort failed, that sawing was "no fun" compared to another activity he could teach the boy).

It soon became apparent that Paul was carving out his role as classroom "tough guy." He constantly tried to prove himself powerful and grown up. For example, he showed no emotional displays, even when he banged his head in a nasty fall. His teacher commented that he seemed "confused" if others showed their emotions—as when the injured classroom hamster hid under a pile of papers, and Paul's comment was that "man-hamsters, like real men, should not cry." Part of his "tough-guy" role also involved protecting the smaller children and animals of his classroom: he often admonished his peers not to take any unfair advantages lest he "beat them up."

Paul's teachers gained some further insights into this boy's needs and expectations when he commandeered a story session one day because he had "a better story." His tale was one of a valiant warrior who was friend to all animals, and who would kill anyone who got in his way. In an encounter with a belligerent giant, the warrior threw his adversary "so high that even the birds couldn't see him." Resting afterwards, the hero spied a little fox who had wept so hard for the warrior's safety that "even the fox's feet got all wet."

Likewise, Paul played out another "he-man" fantasy when he boasted, during an all-involving, make-believe shaving session, that his whiskers were tough enough to stick anyone who touched him. When one of the nearby girls chided him on his preoccupation with toughness, he retorted that girls were "silly" and not worth playing with.

A consultation with Paul's parents was revealing, in spite of their reluctance to talk. Ever since Paul's fourth birthday, his father had insisted that the boy learn to take care of himself—even to the point of leaving him home alone when he was sick. Mr. S. also mentioned that he tried in various ways to "toughen Paul's character."

As the year wore on, however, Paul (who had never been to nursery school) saw that there were other styles of manliness, other acceptable ways for adults—and children—to act. He began to exhibit less disdain for emotional displays, even to the point of helping to bandage a playmate's hurt finger or stroking a little girl's troubled brow. In one particularly dramatic episode, Paul's teacher found himself unexpectedly confronted with both tantrum and tears. Having had to remove Paul bodily from a dangerous—but attractive—situation, the teacher was the target of a fury of kicking and punching. In the middle of it all, when it was explained to Paul that he had been removed from his perilous perch because the teacher *liked* him, the boy suddenly burst into tears and sobbed in his teacher's arms for several minutes.

Perhaps the little fox was voicing Paul's fears that the warrior he hoped to be was not as invulnerable as the world sometimes demanded (Ostrovsky 1962).

Barbara A.

This highly intelligent little girl entered school three months before she was 5. Although a normally amiable child, Barbara seemed to have an unusual preoccupation with cleanliness. She would not, for instance, take part in any painting (although she loved to crayon), any work with clay, any collage activities, or any games that involved sand. Her general comment to any such undertakings was that she didn't like "those dirty games."

Barbara also avoided games that demanded any sort of physical dexterity or daring, although her preschool testing showed her to be in excellent physical condition, with good physical coordination and adequate muscle development. If, for instance, she was challenged to climb on the "monkey bars" she would refuse because her dress was "too short"; and if that excuse failed to satisfy her playmates, she would simply admit that her mother "did not like her to do such things."

Throughout the first two months of school, Barbara's teachers recorded several instances which typified her cautious approach to her world: her avoidance of a sandy mixture being prepared to "feed baby" during some housekeeping play, and her insistence that "baby" be scrubbed thoroughly beforehand; her careful efforts to hold her skirt down as she and others pirouetted around the dance floor and her immediate retirement when she thought there was a chance a boy might "see her panties"; and her reluctance to use the bathroom until others had vacated it because "when the boys were there it wasn't nice."

Not surprisingly, Barbara's mother echoed many of her daughter's concerns during a routine interview. Dwelling on topics of health, cleanliness, and safety, she expressed the attitude, "When you have a girl, you just can't be too careful." She mentioned, however, that her busy husband would have preferred Barbara to have as much freedom as he had had during his own childhood.

And by midyear it seemed that Barbara was showing a bit more of the father's influence in her behavior. She exhibited some unprecedented signs of risk-taking, for instance, when she experimented in isolation after refusing to "walk the [narrow] gangplank" to board an "African-bound steamer." She also ventured into some clay work, but only when she could use sticks—instead of fingers—to shape the clay. (One painstakingly decorated clay turtle—with no head and no feet because "he pulled them inside to sleep"—still proved unfit to take home because it was "too messy.") And, although she boycotted the class's efforts to turn a resident rabbit on its back to ascertain its sex, Barbara showed some surreptitious interest in examining the undersides of the fish abiding in a nearby tank.

One particularly revealing incident centered around the creation of take-home Easter cards. Having carefully prepared one rigidly designed, two-color card for her mother, she launched on a second for her father: a gay collage of colored papers, crayoned designs overpainted with watercolors, and a fuzzy cotton center. When a playmate asked why she did not make it "neat like the other one," Barbara replied that she knew her "daddy wouldn't mind. . . . He'd like it all right."

A year of careful guidance, selective reinforcement of her newfound adventurousness, and sensitive counseling for the mother brought encouraging results. As summer vacation neared, Barbara could be found painting, clay-modeling, playing almost any game, and—occasionally—venturing into the bathroom even in the company of her peers (Ostrovsky 1962).

References

Allen, K., Hart, B., Buell, J. S., Harris, F. R., and Wolf, M. M. Effects of social reinforcement on isolate behavior of a nursery school child. *Child Develpm.*, 1964, *35*(2), 511–518.

American Psychiatric Association. *Diagnostic and statistical manual: Mental disorders.* Washington, D.C.: American Psychiatric Association, 1968.

Ammons, R. B. Reactions in a projective doll-play interview of white males two to six years of age to differences in skin color and facial features. *J. genet. Psychol.*, 1960, *76*, 323–341.

Anthony, E. J. An experimental approach to the psychopathology of childhood: Encopresis. *Brit. J. med. Psychol.*, 1957, *30*(3), 146–175.

Anthony, E. J. Classification and categorization in child psychiatry. *Int. J. Psychiat.*, 1967, *3*(3), 173–178.

Anthony, E. J. The behavior disorders of childhood. In P. H. Mussen (Ed.), *Carmichael's manual of child psychology.* Vol. II. (3rd ed.) New York: Wiley, 1970.

Appel, M. H. Aggressive behavior of nursery school children and adult procedures in dealing with such behavior. *J. exp. Educ.*, 1942, *11*, 185–199.

Aronfreed, J. M. *Conduct and conscience: The socialization of internalized control over behavior.* New York: Academic Press, 1968.

Axline, V. M. *Dibs: In search of self.* Boston: Houghton Mifflin, 1966.

Baldwin, A. L. Socialization and the parent–child relationship. *Child Develpm.*, 1948, *19*, 127–136.

Baldwin, A. L. The effect of home environment on nursery school behavior. *Child Develpm.*, 1949, *20*, 49–62.

Barbara, D. A. Stuttering. In S. Arieti (Ed.), *American handbook of psychiatry.* Vol. I. New York: Basic Books, 1959.

Beam, J. C. Serial learning and conditioning under real-life stress. *J. abnorm. soc. Psychol.*, 1955, *51*, 543–551.

Beech, R. Stuttering and stammering. *Psychol. Today*, 1967, *1*, 48–51.

Bettelheim, B. Joey: A mechanical boy. *Scientific Amer.*, March 1959, *200*, 116–120.

Blau, A., and Hulse, W. C. Anxiety (actual) neuroses as a cause of behavior disorders in children. *Amer. J. Orthopsychiat.*, 1956, *26*, 108–118.

Bonney, M. E., and Nicholson, E. L. Comparative social adjustments of elementary school pupils with and without preschool training. *Child Develpm.*, 1958, *29*, 125–133.

Brown, A. W., and Hunt, R. G. Relations between nursery school attendance and teachers' ratings of some aspects of children's adjustment in kindergarten. *Child Develpm.*, 1961, *32*, 585–596.

Buckle, D., and Lebovici, S. *Child guidance centers.* Geneva: World Health Organization, 1960.

Burks, H. F. The hyperkinetic child. *Except. Children*, 1960, *27*, 18–26.

Charlesworth, R., and Hartup, W. W. Positive social reinforcement in the nursery school peer group. *Child Develpm.*, 1967, *38*, 993–1002.

Chittenden, G. E. An experimental study in measuring and modifying assertive behavior in young children. *Monogr. Soc. Res. Child Develpm.*, 1942, *7*(1).

Coleman, J. C., and McCalley, J. E. Nail-biting and mental health: A survey of the literature. *Ment. Hyg.*, 1948, *32*, 428–454.

Coleman, J. C., and Seret, C. The role of hostility in fingernail biting. *Psychol. Service Center J.*, 1950, *2*, 238–244.

Debus, R. L. Aggressive behavior in young children. *Forum of Educ.*, 1953, *11*, 95–105.

Dunnington, M. J. Behavioral differences of sociometric status groups in a nursery school. *Child Develpm.*, 1957, *28*, 103–111.

Elkan, B. Developmental differences in the manifest content of children's reported dreams. Doctoral dissertation, Columbia Univer., 1969.

Erikson, E. H. Toys and reasons. In M. R. Haworth (Ed.), *Child psychotherapy: Practice and theory.* New York: Basic Books, 1964.

Feffer, M. H., and Gourevitch, V. Cognitive aspects of role-taking in children. *J. Pers.*, 1960, *28*, 383–396.

Ferguson, N. Peers as social agents. Unpublished master's thesis, Univer. of Minnesota, 1964.

Flavell, J. H. Role-taking and communication skills in children. *Young Children,* January 1966, *21,* 164–177.

Freedman, D. C. The development of social hierarchies. Paper presented at meeting of World Health Organization on "Society, Stress, and Disease: Childhood and Adolescence," Stockholm, June 28–July 3, 1971.

Freud, A., and Dann, S. An experiment in group upbringing. In R. Eisler et al. (Eds.), *The psychoanalytic study of the child.* Vol. 6. New York: International Universities Press, 1951.

Gesell, A., and Ilg, F. L. *Infant and child in the culture of today.* New York: Harper, 1943.

Glass, N. Eating, sleeping, and elimination habits in children attending day nurseries and children cared for at home by mothers. *Amer. J. Orthopsychiat.*, 1949, *19,* 697–711.

Green, E. H. Friendships and quarrels among preschool children. *Child Develpm.*, 1933, *4,* 237–252.

Greenberg, P. J. Competition in children: An experimental study. *Amer. J. Psychol.*, 1932, *44,* 221–249.

Grosser, D., Polansky, N., and Lippett, R. A laboratory study of behavioral contagion. *Human Relat.,* 1951, *4,* 115–142.

Gump, P. V., and Sutton-Smith, B. The "it" role in children's games. *The Group,* 1955, *17,* 3–8.

Hagman, R. R. A study of fears of children of preschool age. *J. exp. Educ.*, 1932, *1,* 110–130.

Harlow, H., and Harlow, M. K. The affectional systems. In A. M. Schrier, H. F. Harlow, and F. Stollnitz (Eds.), *Behavior of nonhuman primates.* Vol. 2. New York: Academic Press, 1965.

Hartup, W. W. Friendship status and the effectiveness of peers as reinforcing agents. *J. exp. child Psychol.*, 1964, *1,* 154–162.

Hartup, W. W. Peers as agents of reinforcement. In W. W. Hartup and N. L. Smothergill (Eds.), *The young child: Reviews of research.* Washington, D.C.: National Association for the Education of Young Children, 1967.

Hartup, W. W. Peer interaction and social organization. In P. H. Mussen (Ed.), *Carmichael's manual of child psychology.* Vol. II. (3rd ed.) New York: Wiley, 1970.

Hattwick, B. W. The influence of nursery school attendance upon the behavior and personality of the preschool child. *J. exp. Educ.*, 1936, *5,* 180–190.

Hattwick, L. A., and Sanders, M. K. Age differences in behavior at the nursery school level. *Child Develpm.*, 1938, *9,* 27–47.

Heathers, G. Emotional dependence and independence in nursery school play. *J. genet. Psychol.*, 1955, *87,* 37–57.

Heinecke, C. M. Some effects of separating two-year-old children from their parents: A comparative study. *Human Relat.*, 1956, *9,* 105–176.

Hewett, F. M. *The emotionally disturbed child in the classroom.* Boston: Allyn & Bacon, 1968.

Hicks, D. J. Imitation and retention of film-mediated aggressive peer and adult models. *J. pers. soc. Psychol.*, 1965, *2,* 97–100.

Hill, K. T., and Sarason, S. B. The relation of test anxiety and defensiveness to test and school performance over the elementary school years: A further longitudinal study. *Monogr. Soc. Res. Child Develpm.*, 1966, *31*(2).

Holmes, F. B. An experimental investigation of a method of overcoming children's fears. *Child Develpm.*, 1936, *7,* 6–30.

Honigmann, J. J. *Culture and personality.* New York: Harper & Row, 1954.

Horowitz, F. D. Incentive value of social stimuli for preschool children. *Child Develpm.*, 1962, *33,* 111–116.

Isaacs, S. *Social development in young children.* London: Routledge & Kegan Paul, 1933.

Jack, L. M. An experimental study of ascendant behavior in preschool children. In L. M. Jack, E. M. Maxwell, I. G. Mengert el al., Behavior of the preschool child. *Univer. of Iowa Stud. Child Welf.*, 1934, *9*(3), 7–65.

Jenkins, R. L. Classification of behavior problems of children. *Amer. J. Psychiat.*, 1969, *125,* 1032–1039.

Jenkins, R. L. Diagnostic classification in child psychiatry. *Amer. J. Psychiat.*, 1970, *127,* 680–681.

Jersild, A. T., and Fite, M. D. *The influence of nursery school experience on children's social adjustments.* Child Develpm. Monogr., No. 25. New York: Teachers College, Columbia Univer., 1939.

Jersild, A. T., and Holmes, F. B. *Children's fears.* Child Develpm. Monogr., No. 20. New York: Teachers College, Columbia Univer., 1935.

Jersild, A. T., and Markey, F. V. *Conflicts between preschool children.* Child Develpm. Monogr., No. 21. New York: Teachers College, Columbia Univer., 1935.

Jones, M. C. A laboratory study of fear: The case of Peter. *Ped. Sem.*, 1924, *31,* 308–315.

Kanner, L. Early infantile autism. *J. Pediat.*, 1944, *25,* 211–217.

Kanner, L. Do behavior symptoms always indicate psychopathology? *J. child psychol. Psychiat.*, 1960, *1,* 17–25.

Katahn, M. Interaction of anxiety and ability in complex learning situations. *J. pers. soc. Psychol.*, 1966, *3,* 475–479.

Kawin, E. and Hoefer, C. *A comparative study of a nursery-school versus a non-nursery-school group.* Chicago: Univer. of Chicago Press, 1931.

Keister, M. E. The behavior of young children in failure: An experimental attempt to discover and to modify undesirable responses of preschool children to failure. *Univer. of Iowa Stud. Child Welf.*, 1938, *14*, 27–82.

Kessler, J. W. *Psychopathology of childhood.* Englewood Cliffs, N.J.: Prentice-Hall, 1966.

Kohlberg, L. Stage and sequence: The developmental approach to socialization. In D. Goslin (Ed.), *Handbook of socialization.* Chicago: Rand McNally, 1969.

Kohn, M. The child as a determinant of his peer's approach to him. *J. genet. Psychol.*, 1966, *109*(1), 91–100.

Leuba, C. An experimental study of rivalry in young children. *J. comp. physiol. Psychol.*, 1933, *16*, 367–378.

Maccoby, E. E., and Jacklin, C. N. Sex differences and their implications for sex roles. Paper presented at annual meeting of American Psychological Association, Washington, D.C., September 1971.

Martin, W. Singularity and stability of profiles of social behavior. In C. B. Stendler (Ed.), *Readings in child behavior and development.* New York: Harcourt Brace Jovanovich, 1964.

McCandless, B. R., and Hoyt, J. M. Sex, ethnicity, and play preferences of preschool children. *J. abnorm. soc. Psychol.*, 1961, *62*, 683–685.

McKee, J. P., and Leader, F. B. The relationship of socioeconomic status to the competitive behavior of school children. *Child Develpm.*, 1955, *25*, 135–142.

Merei, F. Group leadership and institutionalization. *Human Relat.*, 1949, *2*, 23–39.

Moore, S. G. Problem solving and the perception of persons. In R. Tagiuri and L. Petrullo (Eds.), *Person, perception and interpersonal behavior.* Stanford, Calif.: Stanford Univer. Press, 1958.

Moore, S. G., and Updegraff, R. Sociometric status of preschool children related to age, sex, nurturance giving, and dependency. *Child Develpm.*, 1964, *35*, 519–524.

Moore, S. G. Correlates of peer acceptance in nursery school children. In W. W. Hartup and N. L. Smothergill (Eds.), *The young child: Reviews of research.* Washington, D.C.: National Association for the Education of Young Children, 1967.

National Institute of Mental Health. Amphetamines approved for children. *Science News*, 1971, *99*, 240.

Ostrovsky, E. S. *Children without men.* New York: Collier Books, 1962. Pp. 50–56; 68–78.

Parten, M. B. Social participation among preschool children. *J. abnorm. soc. Psychol.*, 1932, *27*, 243–269.

Patterson, G. R., Littman, R. A., and Bricker, W. Assertive behavior in children: A step toward a theory of aggression. *Monogr. Soc. Res. Child Develpm.*, 1967, *32*(5), 1–43.

Piaget, J. *The language and thought of the child.* New York: Harcourt Brace Jovanovich, 1926.

Piaget, J., and Inhelder, B. *The child's conception of space.* London: Routledge and Kegan Paul, 1956.

Pierce, C. M. Enuresis. In A. M. Freedman and H. I. Kaplan (Eds.), *Comprehensive textbook of psychiatry.* Baltimore: Williams & Wilkins, 1967.

Rimland, B. *Infantile autism: The syndrome and its implications for a neural theory of behavior.* New York: Appleton-Century-Crofts, 1964.

Rosenthal, M. K. Effects of a novel situation and of anxiety on two groups of dependency behaviors. *Brit. J. Psychol.*, 1967, *58*(3–4), 357–364.

Ruebush, B. K. Anxiety. In H. W. Stevenson (Ed.), *Child psychology. 62nd Yearbook of the National Society for the Study of Education.* Part I. Chicago: Univer. of Chicago Press, 1963.

Sarason, S. B., Davidson, K. S., Lighthall, F. F., Waite, R. R., and Ruebush, B. K. *Anxiety in elementary school children.* New York: Wiley, 1960.

Schmeidler, G. R., Bruel, I., Ginsberg, S., and Lukomnik, M. Motivation, anxiety and stress in a difficult verbal task. *Psychol. Reports*, 1965, *17*(1), 247–255.

Sears, P. S. Doll play aggression in normal young children. *Psychol. Monogr.*, 1951, *65*(6), 42.

Selman, R. L. Conceptual role-taking development in early childhood. *Proc. 79th Ann. Conv. Amer. Psychol. Assoc.*, 1971.

Sheehan, J. G., and Martyn, M. Stuttering and its disappearance. *J. Speech and Hearing Disorders*, 1970, *13*, 279–289.

Slavson, S. R. *A textbook in analytic group psychotherapy.* New York: International Universities Press, 1964.

Smith, R. E., and Sharpe, T. M. Treatment of a school phobia with implosive therapy. *J. consult. Psychol.*, 1970, *35*, 239–243.

Stevenson, H. W. Social reinforcement of children's behavior. In L. P. Lipsitt and C. C. Spiker (Eds.), *Advances in child development and behavior.* Vol. 2. New York: Academic Press, 1965.

Stevenson, H. W., and Stevenson, N. G. Social interaction in an interracial nursery school. *Genet. Psychol. Mongr.*, 1960, *61*, 37–75.

Stone, L. J., and Church, J. *Childhood and adolescence.* New York: Random House, 1968.

Sutton-Smith, B. A formal analysis of game meaning. *Western Folklore*, 1959, *18*, 13–24.

Sutton-Smith, B. Preschool program and behavior objectives. Unpublished manuscript, 1971.

Sutton-Smith, B., and Roberts, J. M. Child training and game involvement. *Ethnology*, 1962, *1*, 166–185.

Sutton-Smith, B., and Roberts, J. M. The cross-cultural and psychological study of games. In G. Lüschen (Ed.), *The cross-cultural analysis of sport and games.* Champaign, Ill.: Stipes Publishing, 1970.

Sutton-Smith, B., and Savasta, M. Sex differences in play and power. Paper presented at annual meeting of Eastern Psychological Association, Boston, April 1972.

Taylor, I. K. What words are stuttered. *Psychol. Bull.*, 1966, *65*, 233–242.

Thompson, G. G. The social and emotional development of preschool children under two types of educational programs. *Psychol. Monogr.*, 1944, *56*(5).

Titkin, S., and Hartup, W. W. Sociometric status and the reinforcing effectiveness of children's peers. *J. exp. child Psychol.*, 1965, *2*, 306–315.

U.S. Department of Health, Education and Welfare, National Advisory Committee on the Dyslexia and Related Reading Disorders. *Reading disorders in the United States.* Washington, D.C.: Government Printing Office, 1969.

Valentine, C. W. *The normal child and his abnormalities.* (3rd ed.) Baltimore: Penguin Books, 1956.

Verville, E. *Behavior problems of children.* Philadelphia: Saunders, 1967.

Walsh, M. E. The relation of nursery school training to the development of certain personality traits. *Child Develpm.*, 1931, *2*, 72–73.

Walton, D. Experimental psychology and the treatment of a *ticquier. J. child psychol. Psychiat.*, 1961, *2*, 148–155.

Weiss, M., and Burke, A. A 5- to 10-year follow-up of hospitalized school-phobic children and adolescents. *Amer. J. Orthopsychiat.*, 1970, *40*, 672–676.

Wolff, P. H. *Developmental and motivational concepts in Piaget's sensorimotor theory of intelligence.* New York: Pergamon, 1963.

VI

The Middle Years Ages 8 through 12

James Carroll

Cognitive and Moral Development and Social Perception 12

A GREAT DEAL of attention has focused on the cognitive aspects of the child's social and moral development between the years of 8 and 12—years during which the child's awareness of others and of his surroundings greatly increases. While the cognitive and social aspects of personality development once were treated as distinct areas, the past three decades have witnessed an upsurge of scientific interest in the relationship between cognitive and social growth. This development has been prompted by two major forces: the influence of Jean Piaget's developmental theories, and an increasing concern shown for educational problems.

Since the early 1950s, public attention has been drawn to the performance of schools, particularly urban schools. In attempting to increase the effectiveness of the schools, especially in the ghetto, administrators and public officials have turned increasingly to professional psychologists and sociologists for scientific information on why children fail or do well in school. The demand for relevant information and theory has stimulated much research into the cognitive processes. Psychologists often have found that in order to solve educational problems, they must consider the "whole child." Naturally, this consideration has led to a probe for connections between cognitive and social development, and the processes and principles common to both.

In Jean Piaget's theory there are attempts to unite these two aspects of development. Piaget has developed several concepts which may be applied to the cognitive aspects of personality and to the social world of people and morals, as well as to the world of objects.

One of Piaget's pivotal ideas is the *centration-decentration* distinction. He maintains that in the course of cognitive development the child moves through cycles of egocentrism. As a young child, the individual is rigid and centered in the application of his own new concepts. Because he takes his own categories concretely, the child ties his objective view of the world too closely to his own perspective. Gradually, however, the child extends his range of perspectives until he possesses a more objective or realistic grasp of the world. To Piaget this reduction of egocentrism is cyclic, occurring repeatedly as different growth phases result in new cognitive functions.

As another major developmental shift, Piaget notes the increase in ability for *categorization*. As the child grows older, particularly between the ages of 8 and 12, he can subdivide his experience into many more categories. He becomes capable of isolating various phenomena and detecting similarities and differences between them. On the basis of these similarities and differences, he attaches more differentiated labels to things. This is the age of collections, of stamps, stones, and shells—collections which are primarily categorical exercises.

Another way of speaking about the cognitive changes of this age level is in terms of the increase in differentiation they represent. As it is employed by both Piaget and Heinz Werner, the term *differentiation* refers to two developments. It refers, first, to the child's learning to differentiate, or discriminate, between different types of experience and objects in his environment. Second, it refers to the growth in differentiation of the child's thought processes and personality. He develops different behaviors for different situations and becomes more flexible and structured in his response to external reality. While it might seem desirable to have one set of terms for these comparable processes (decentering, differentiation), each investigator uses them somewhat differently in his experiments, so at this stage in our understanding it seems wise to retain both.

In this chapter, we shall consider how the child develops from the egocentrism of early childhood toward a more differentiated and relative view of the world. This process, as we shall see, has wide implications for the child's social behavior as well as for his ability to perform cognitive tasks.

Cognitive Changes in Middle Childhood

Concrete Operationalism versus Preoperationalism

Piaget characterizes the cognitive development that takes place roughly between the ages of 7 and 12 as the concrete operational stage, named for the child's ability to perform *mental* acts or operations in response to environmental changes. Such acts are reversible—that is, the child can perform their opposites as well. He can mentally add up the members of his baseball team and then subtract the sick players. The preoperational child cannot perform such acts. However, there is also a limitation on the ability of the concrete operational child. He can perform mental actions only on objects that are immediately present. He cannot yet perform operations on objects that are not present or deal with operations in terms of hypothetical situations.

Piaget's experiment with physical objects, which we cited in Chapter 10, illustrates growth in the capacity for decentering characteristics of this age group. A 9-year-old child was asked which would make a bigger bouquet—all of the primroses he sees before him or all of the yellow primroses. Unlike the younger children, the 9-year-old said all of the primroses, adding that his bouquet would include the yellow primroses. When asked which was bigger—all of the primroses or all of the flowers—he answered all of the flowers, again adding that the second bouquet would include the primroses (Piaget 1964). As we saw in Chapter 10, the younger child is unable to hold in mind both the whole entity of the primroses and the subdivision that includes only the yellow primroses.

Because the 9-year-old child is able to focus simultaneously on the part and the whole, he can separate the flowers themselves into primrose and nonprimrose while thinking about the part and the whole. Thus, his thought has *decentered*. Instead of focusing on the part or the whole alone, he can focus on both at the same time. The child who is not exclusively egocentric is able to decen-

380 THE MIDDLE YEARS AGES 8 THROUGH 12

ter his attention from those aspects of the situation that relate solely to himself at the moment. He is able to think objectively—that is, to focus on several aspects of the situation at once.

Another example illustrates further how concrete operationalism functions. The 7- to 11-year-old, shown equal lines of pebbles and gumballs, will be able to count the number in each set and to place the pebbles and gumballs in one-to-one correspondence, assigning one pebble to each gumball, and vice versa, without repeating any pebble or gumball. Although the pebbles are squeezed densely into a tight lineup, he will be able to detect that the numbers of pebbles and gumballs are still equal.

As we saw in Chapter 10's similar example of bottles and glasses, the preoperational child cannot make this judgment. Instead, he will say there are more gumballs because the line of gumballs is longer than the tightly compressed line of pebbles.

Why does the concrete operational child succeed at this task where the preoperational child fails? The answer lies in the mental operations performed by the concrete operational child. He recognizes how the two dimensions of length and density relate, and that density compensates for length in the number of lined-up objects in the tightly squeezed-together group. Seeing that the pebbles gained in density what they lost in length, he can mentally balance them with the long line of gumballs. The density's counteraction of decrease in length brings about a reversal of the first condition in which there was an equal number of pebbles and gumballs, equally spaced. This ability to return to an earlier equality is *reversibility*. We should note here that the child's reversal is possible only because he can now decenter. He can focus on the two aspects of density and length, rather than merely on the length, or the density alone.

Negation is another mental operation that enables the concrete operational child to arrive at the correct answer. He knows that compressing the pebbles can be negated by its opposite—spreading them out again so that they will resume their earlier length. He is able to perform this action because he can see the sequence of changes in a transformation rather than merely perceiving the transformed line of pebbles. In other words, he sees that a physical operation was required to change the length of the row of pebbles, and understands that this physical operation can be reversed. The preoperational child, by contrast, is merely aware that the pebble row was first one length and then another. He pays no attention to the transition stages between one length and another.

Finally, the concrete operational child uses an *identity* operation. He sees that no pebbles have been added or taken away. Therefore, he reasons, their number must remain the same. These three concepts of *reversibility, negation,* and *identity* are essential to Piaget's discussion of the nature of conservation as a cognitive operation. They should be considered particular applications at this age level which underlie the more general process of decentration mentioned above.

TYPES OF IMAGERY. According to Piaget, concrete operational and preoperational children also differ in the way they form mental images. To understand his work in this area, it will be helpful to review Piaget's three major types of mental images—*kinetic,* involving an object's change of position; *transformational,* involving an object's change of shape; and *static,* involving an object that remains the same.

Piaget has found that most concrete operational children, in contrast to preoperational children, can accurately select and draw kinetic images such as those of the displaced blocks discussed in Chapter 10. Similarly, concrete operational children possess transformational imagery. Presented with semicircular wires, they are able to draw the sequence depicting the transformation from semicircle to straight line.

Piaget presents two reasons for this capacity of the concrete operational child. First, unlike the preoperational child, the older child can *conserve* a quantity such as length of wire. For the older child, change in shape does not entail a change in length. Second, the older child focuses on the process of transformation as well as on the first and final states of the objects. Seeing the process of change as continuous, he finds it easy to reconstruct the intermediate steps. He *decenters* from states to transformations.

SEQUENCES OF DEVELOPMENT. In distinguishing the concrete operational child from the preoperational child, we should note that these two stages are idealized abstractions. The actual sequence of development varies in different individuals and in different cultures.

In general, it has been found that children master conservation of quantity by the age of 7, but do not comprehend conservation of weight until age 9. Conservation of volume—perceiving, for example, that the same volume of substance can fit into containers of different shapes—takes even longer, typically occurring at around age 11. This lack of transfer of a given type of operation—*conservation*—to all kinds of situations shows the *concreteness* of the concrete operational stage. The child, not yet capable of generalizing an operation, is limited by specific situations.

Although the order of these stages of development is similar across many cultures, the age at which each stage appears varies with the differing experiences to which children are exposed in different cultures. Thus, in cultures where the conservation of water is critical for survival, children have been shown to conserve volume at an earlier age than would be expected (Goodnow and Bethon 1966; Lovell 1961).

Decentration and Social Growth

Having briefly reviewed Piaget's approach to cognition, we shift next to the social issues with which this chapter is largely concerned. Applying cognitive changes to social development, Piaget, Werner, and others maintain that the growth in decentration and differentiation leads to increased role-taking ability and new awareness in perceiving others. Werner maintains that with age the individual's thought becomes more differentiated, articulated, and hierarchically integrated. In other words, the individual can decenter from one limited aspect of a situation and make distinctions where at first his thought was both narrow and global. He also becomes capable of arriving at increasingly general principles or abstractions.

One study in this area applied Werner's concepts to the study of impressions that boys in first, third, and fifth grade formed of their peers (Scarlett, Press, and Crockett 1971). The boys were rated for the number of concepts they used to describe various peers, and for the degree of abstraction in the concepts they used. Their results confirmed both Werner's and Piaget's general notions. As age increased, both the number and abstraction of concepts used increased. There also was a shift from egocentric-concrete descriptions ("he lends me his pencil") to nonegocentric statements about the other's internal values and character ("he is generous").

Younger boys tended to describe girls very globally and superficially ("they're all silly," or "they're all alike"), whereas fifth-graders, to whom girls were more relevant, made more discriminations in their descriptions. In addition, the fifth-grade subjects described peers they disliked in greater detail than peers whom they liked.

Various researchers have investigated the development of role-taking in children at dif-

Table 12.1 Average Number of Constructs Used for Each of Four Categories by Each Age Group

Type of Construct	Grade 1	Grade 3	Grade 5	Mean
Egocentric-we	0.6	0.6	0.4	0.5
Egocentric-concrete	1.4	2.4	1.7	1.8
Nonegocentric-concrete	0.9	1.7	2.7	1.4
Abstract	0.3	1.2	3.6	1.7
Total	3.2	5.9	8.4	5.4

Note: N = 36 boys, each grade.
Source: From H. Scarlett, A. Press, and W. Crockett. Children's descriptions of peers: A Wernerian developmental analysis. *Child Develpm.*, 1971, *42*, 446.

ferent levels of concrete operational functioning. Role-taking requires the capacity to see things from another's perspective. Piaget, for example, has shown that young children could display awareness of another's perspective at one moment and fail to demonstrate this awareness in the next moment (1926). One of the most thorough series of studies of children's role-taking development has used communication skills as the measure. The reader is referred to the work of Flavell and his colleagues (1968).

Humor and Cognitive Development

One aspect of personality that shows a clear relation to cognitive development is the appreciation of humor. For example, very young children do not have the cognitive perceptions to appreciate riddles.

It has been shown that at the same age that riddles peak, children first manifest competence in verbal classification, reclassification, and multiple classification. When riddles were placed into various categories consistent with the Piagetian framework, Sutton-Smith (1971a) found that many riddles popular in third-grade circles (8 years) could be dealt with as types of classification problems. For example, the following riddle is an explicit reclassification:

> What has an ear but cannot hear?
> Corn.

However, the following is an implicit reclassification:

> Why did the dog go out into the sun?
> He wanted to be a hot dog.

The reigning principle for these apparently arbitrary answers is that homonyms are not synonyms. In the study, a number of other types were distinguished—all of them involving Piagetian categories. It was found that 80 percent of all responses to riddles among 4-year-olds were preriddles—that is, riddles which, although involving questions and arbitrary answers, are totally lacking in any systematic homonymic or synonymic connections between questions and answers. Only 7 percent of all responses among older children in grades 1 through 3 were preriddle answers. Furthermore, implicit reclassifications (such as the moron riddles) constituted the largest single group in grades 1 through 8 (60 percent). Goldstein and McGhee (1972) have shown that children laugh most at riddles or jokes whose basic operation, in this case *classification*, they have recently mastered. The incongruous nature of the joke's departure from the recently learned operation is a major source of laughter. Variations on operations that are thoroughly understood are not so funny.

Cognitive Aspects of Moral Development

Piaget's Theory

Piaget views morality as essentially developing out of peer relations. Unlike Freud, in whose theory morality is primarily a result of the parent–child relationship (an aspect discussed in Chapter 13), Piaget bases the growth of morality on the acquisition of autonomy as it grows out of the need to cooperate with peers in social situations. According to Piaget, true morality can result only from autonomy, not from heteronomy (rule by others rather than oneself), which is at the heart of the relationship between the parent and the very young child. For this reason, Piaget holds that morality begins to develop in earnest from around age 7, as the child's cognitive powers develop and his social interactions with peers increase.

In the view of Piaget, the individual, from early childhood through middle childhood (until about age 12), is developing his concept of justice. It changes from an inflexible view of good and bad acts—based on predetermined, and usually literally interpreted, parental codes—to a more rational, thoughtful view based on equity and the particular circumstances of a situation. Tracing this change, a 4-year-old boy, when asked, may regard the act of shouting as bad because of its loudness, whereas an 8- or 9-year-old is likely to realize that there are instances when the prohibition against shouting may be waived.

Piaget tested his theories about moral development by asking children such questions as,

"Why shouldn't you cheat in a game?" He also told them stories that involved an injustice of some kind, or another moral question. He then carefully studied the response patterns of different age groups and developed categories that characterized the types of morality at different ages.

One type of story that Piaget used involved a conflict between a sense of justice and obedience to parents. Predictably, the youngest children chose obedience to parents most frequently (95 percent at 6 years of age), while the older children—those between 7 and 12—chose obedience to parents less frequently. This result supported the Piagetian view that early conscience tends to be based on prohibitions (usually parental) against specific behaviors, whereas the morality that develops during the later years of childhood is based on internal sanctions and general principles.

Another study also produced significant results on the question of general principles versus specific prohibitions. Piaget asked a group of children between the ages of 6 and 12 what things they thought were unfair. Of children aged 6 to 8, 64 percent cited acts that their parents had prohibited, while only 7 percent in the 9- to 12-year age group did so. By contrast, 73 percent of the 9- to 12-year-olds mentioned inequities in their parents' treatment of them, while only 27 percent of the 6- to 8-year-olds did so. These results are in keeping with a view of morality in which the child's conscience develops out of premoral hedonism (doing whatever one wants to do and can get away with), through a period of reliance upon external rules and sanctions, and then to a period of greater reliance on internal moral principles.

As the earlier example about shouting suggests, the older the child grows, the less his judgments tend to be absolute and authoritarian. Instead, he begins to see that morality is based on the need for harmony between persons rather than conformity to an iron and arbitrary law. He begins to base his morality more on the needs and desires of the group as his interaction in the social world increases. Relativism replaces absolutism. The inviolable quality with which he once regarded rules gives way to a greater maturity in which a rule's value for him depends upon mutual agreement (Piaget 1932). Mutual agreement presupposes decentering and the growth of the ability to imagine another's viewpoint. Thus, very basic cognitive developments play a part in the growth of moral relativism.

In considering moral development, Piaget also studied the child's concern with intentions of others and consequences of an action. He found that concern with others' intentions increased with age. Older children, themselves acting upon internal principles, naturally will be more perceptive of the intentions of others. Again, we must note that the ability to consider others' motivations depends to a great degree on the child's ability to decenter, or, if you like, upon the quality of his imagination.

The difference between restitutive and expiative justice is another distinction that Piaget makes use of in his consideration of moral development (Piaget 1932). *Restitutive justice* is concerned with the redress of injuries and with maintaining a balance of justice between persons based on mutual agreement or social contract. *Expiative justice* is based on an inviolate and abstract rule and is focused more on punishment and the offender's relief from guilt. Again, older children—those in the 8- to 12-year age group—being more aware of the needs and desires of the group, will be inclined to employ notions of restitutive justice, since this is the more flexible, utilitarian view designed to maximize the good of all members of the group. Younger children, less concerned with group living, and more responsive to the demands of parents, may tend to act more on the basis of guilt and will thus tend toward expiative justice. For example, if one child has destroyed another's toy, expiative justice might demand that the destructive child's toy also be destroyed. Restitutive justice, on the other hand, might require the child who performed the misdeed to furnish the injured party with another toy.

The growth of morality in the Piagetian system also includes conformity to peers' expectations as opposed to obedience to adult authority. Here, as in conflicts between the child's sense of justice and his inclination toward blind obedience, social experience was a significant determining factor. The older a child is, the more he will rely on his peers for moral standards and judgments.

PIAGET-INSPIRED RESEARCH ON MORAL DEVELOPMENT. Many studies, in addition to Piaget's, have been conducted in the area of moral development. Some have been designed to test Piaget's hypotheses about the stages of moral development. One such study asked boys and girls, aged 2, 5, and 8, what was to be done when one child struck another child (Durkin 1959). Before replying, older children tended to ask for the offender's reason for striking the other child, as well as to inquire about the conditions surrounding the act. The younger children, on the other hand, seldom were concerned with these mitigating factors. Thus, the experiment supported Piaget's generalization that increased concern with intention correlates with age. Other studies of children have supported Piaget's theses about changes in moral judgment (Lerner 1937). Results were found to apply equally well to lower-class and middle-class children. It was found that in older children, fewer suggestions were made that conflicts be solved by acquiescence to adult demand or by obedience to authority.

Hoffman (1970) has tabulated some of the research that deals with Piaget's distinctions concerning moral attributes. He listed 21 studies conducted in Western countries, including one study done in 1894 (Schallenberger), that have dealt with restitutive and expiative justice. In addition to that theme, the studies were concerned with relativism and absolutism; an objective view of punishment and immanent justice; intentions and consequences; and conformity to peer expectations as opposed to obedience to adult authority. Piaget's views were upheld in all the studies except one (Medinnus 1959). That is, relativism, objective views of punishment, concern with intentions in moral judgment, concern with restitutive justice, and conformation to peer expectations, all were found to increase with age.

The studies gain significance from the fact that the subjects used were drawn from a wide variety of populations, differing in socioeconomic status, intelligence, and race. Thus, it would seem that Piaget's findings have considerable validity, cutting across a wide selection of variable individual and social factors.

CRITICISMS OF PIAGETIAN THEORY. Although Piaget's hypotheses about moral development have received a great deal of support, they also have been criticized on several grounds. One objection has been that each Piagetian stage of development involves a cognitive reorganization. It has been argued that if this were the case, moral development should occur in sharp breaks rather than gradually. Instead, evidence from cross-sectional studies has shown a rather gradual progression in age trends for moral judgment.

However, Hoffman argued, in support of Piaget, that cross-sectional studies have a built-in bias against revealing sharp breaks (1970). He claimed that sudden spurts in moral development occur at different times for different children, and that averaging by age norms tends to wash out these individual spurts. To adequately test the hypothesis of sudden moral growth, longitudinal studies of a number of individuals are needed.

Another objection to Piaget's theory contends that it is not clear that progression through the moral stages is invariant or irreversible. If this view is valid, it would seem that morality is not so closely tied to cognitive level as Piaget has indicated. Two studies appeared at first to support this second objection to Piaget's theory. In the first study, boys 5 to 11 years of age observed a model being reinforced for expressing moral judgments that were more advanced than the boys' judgments (Bandura and McDonald 1963). The boys were found to shift their own judgments toward the model's. When the model was reinforced for expressing judgments less advanced than the boys', the boys again shifted their judgments.

A similar result was obtained by two other experimenters who used adolescent models and subjects; they found the shift to last as long as three months (LeFurgy and Woloshin 1969). The moral dimension used in the second part of this study—conducted at the end of the three-month period—was the difference between viewing legal and social norms as inviolable, and seeing them as violable under extenuating circumstances.

The finding that children's behavior could be

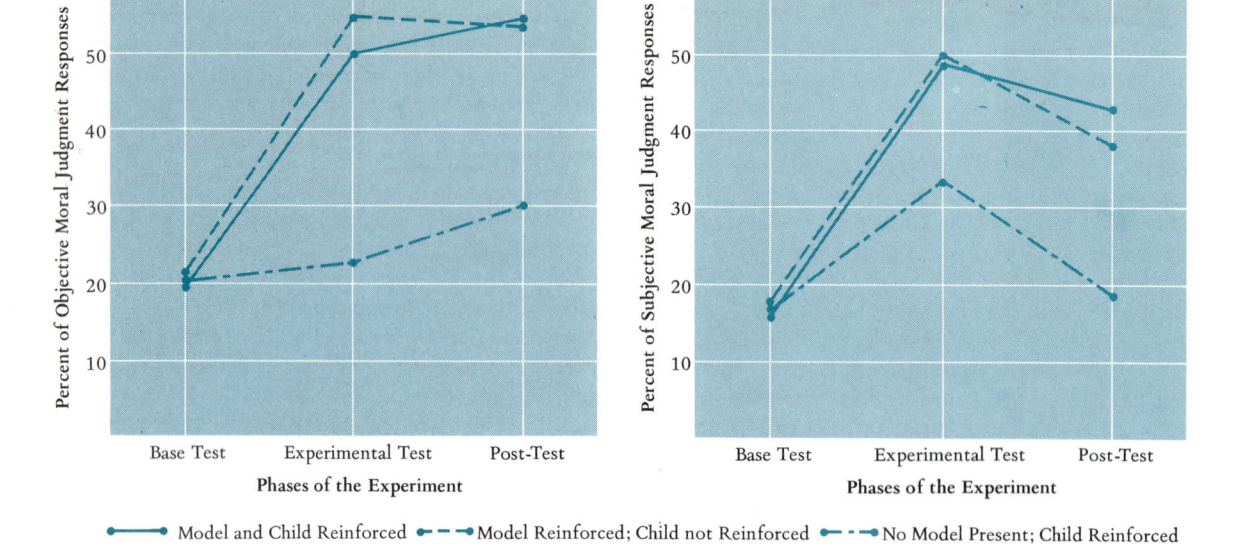

Figure 12.1 Moral judgment responses produced by "subjective" and "objective" children on each of three test periods for each of three experimental conditions. Regardless of level of moral development or amount of reinforcement, 5- to 11-year-old children were influenced to change their moral judgments toward those of a verbally reinforced adult model. Children who had been judging situations on the basis of intentions ("subjective" responses) reverted to judgments on the basis of damage done ("objective" responses), and vice versa. (From A. Bandura and F. J. McDonald. Influence of social reinforcement and the behavior of models in shaping children's moral judgment. *J. abnorm. soc. Psychol.*, 1963, 67(3), 274–281.)

changed so easily seems to contradict Piaget's assumption that the stages of moral growth are invariable, and that progression through a stage requires a series of cognitive syntheses. Reverses are, of course, easier to explain than progressions, because individuals do not necessarily forsake lower responses when acquiring higher ones.

However, there also is a problem related to the design of these studies that must be considered, as one researcher pointed out (Hoffman 1970). In all the studies of this kind, the items used in both the test before exposure to the model and the test after exposure were very similar. Thus, these studies may be showing merely that surface responses can be modified. The actual underlying cognitive structure may remain unchanged.

A study by Rothman (1971) has provided a partial answer to some of these dilemmas. Children of varying levels of moral judgment watched

models advocating courses of action that were at moral stages either higher or lower than their own. (Kohlberg's stages, which we shall discuss in the next section, were used.) Children at the more elementary stages—Kohlberg's Stages 1 to 3— were strongly influenced, both to progress and regress, by the models. Children at Kohlberg's higher stages—4 to 6—tended to follow their own moral judgment. These results seem to indicate that the relationship between moral action and moral judgment depends on the moral stage an individual already has attained. A child at a lower stage is affected much more by the actions and opinions of others—that is, by the principles of social learning. At more advanced stages of moral development, a child is more likely to follow his own cognitive understanding of the situation and be less easily influenced.

Thus, in the elementary stages, subjects' actions should vary in accord with what the models advocate because the subjects' morality still is determined by the immediate situation. However, in the more advanced stages, children should not display such wavering behavior. It is interesting to note here that each theory gains some support from children in the various age groups. Younger children behave as social learning principles suggest they should. Older children behave as cognitive theory suggests is appropriate.

Kohlberg's Theory of Moral Stages

While he has incorporated the Piagetian cognitive approach in the study of moral development, Kohlberg has amplified and extended Piaget's system of moral stages. Kohlberg's account of moral development employs six stages which are grouped in three major levels (Kohlberg 1958, 1963, 1969a). We shall discuss each level in detail, basing our discussion on the work of Martin L. Hoffman.[1]

PRECONVENTIONAL MORALITY. The first level is the preconventional level, which corresponds roughly to Piaget's premoral stage. Kohlberg divides the preconventional level into two stages. Stage 1 is the stage of punishment and obedience orientation. In this first stage of moral development, the child determines the goodness or badness of actions by their pleasure- or pain-producing consequences alone. He attempts to avoid punishment, and generally he defers to the superior power of his parents.

Kohlberg calls Stage 2 of the preconventional level the *instrumental relativist* orientation. Here the child judges the goodness or badness of actions by whether they satisfy his needs. Occasionally he also takes into account whether they satisfy the needs of others. In this stage are the elemental beginnings of a sense of fairness—reciprocity and sharing. However, the child always views these qualities in marketplace or exchange terms: "You can use my ball if I can use yours." General formulations of principles of justice or gratitude are still, for the most part, absent.

---

1. M. L. Hoffman. Moral development. In P. H. Mussen (Ed.), *Carmichael's manual of child psychology*. Vol. II. (3rd ed.) New York: Wiley, 1970.

At the preconventional level, the child's conduct is subject mainly to external control. He responds to pressures from peers, parents, and other adults. His main motives are to earn rewards, avoid punishment, and have favors repaid in kind. He fears punishment not because it implies that he has done wrong, or is disapproved of, but merely because of its physical unpleasantness.

CONVENTIONAL MORALITY. Kohlberg's next level of moral development is the conventional level, which coincides approximately with the stage of concrete operationalism in Piaget's cognitive system, the material being dealt with in this and the next chapter. At the conventional level, morality is defined as performing good acts and living up to the expectations of the existing social order as well as those of other important individuals, such as parents and teachers. At this level, the child considers good and bad as more than simple obedience or disobedience. Instead, he tries to live up to certain rules—propagated by these authorities—that have acquired value in themselves. Conduct control remains external insofar as the rules and expectations still are laid down by others. However, his motive for obeying the rules has shifted somewhat. The child has become concerned with others' opinions of him, with their praise or disapproval and not simply with their power to physically reward or punish him. He assumes the roles of others and respects their judgments.

These tendencies are reflected clearly in Stage 3, the first stage of the conventional level, which is the stage of "good-boy morality." The child desires approval and wants to help or please his parents and peers. When he judges another person's actions, he takes his intentions into account, usually in terms of their conformity to the rules and standards he himself accepts. To the Stage 3 child, a good person is a person of clear moral strength.

Stage 4 of the conventional level is the stage of clear-cut respect for authority and social convention. The child is concerned with fulfilling his tasks, respecting his elders, and blindly sustaining the existing social order. He has, by this time, largely internalized the moral code handed down to him by his parents and other persons, such as his teachers. He also is able to assume the place of others, and thus can show regard for their rights (according to the rules he accepts) and their expectations. Finally, he usually believes in the overall justice of the moral and social order, and believes, as well, in "poetic justice"—that goodness will be rewarded. As Kohlberg has pointed out, most people in our society remain at the conventional level throughout their adult lives.

POSTCONVENTIONAL MORALITY. The third level in the Kohlbergian system is the postconventional level of self-accepted moral principles. With the attainment of this level, the individual has exceeded mere acceptance of the standards of other individuals and of society. He is attempting, at this point, to find his own morality based on principles that he himself determines. He tries to conform to these standards, which he envisions as either actually or potentially shared by others. This level, usually reached some time in adolescence, is associated with Piaget's stage of formal operations.

Stage 5, the first plateau of such postconventional moral development, has a contractual, legalistic tendency. Although the individual recognizes that rules are arbitrary and conventional, he accepts them to maintain agreement and social harmony. He defines his duty in terms of contract, taking care not to violate the rights or will of others, or the will or well-being of the majority. Stage 5 thinking corresponds somewhat to the ideas of the nineteenth-century utilitarian John Stuart Mill. This stage may be approximately described in a paraphrase of Mill's philosophy: the greatest good for the greatest number.

Stage 6, the last stage in Kohlberg's scheme of moral development, is the stage of conscience or principle. The individual goes beyond the acceptance of social rules, and even the will of the majority, to embrace principles growing out of "inner necessity," such as universality, compassion, or logical consistency. At this stage, the dominant rule is, "Let your conscience be your guide." Therefore, moral codes are likely to vary greatly among individuals.

Kohlberg based his three major levels and six stages on his original studies (1958, 1963, 1969a) which consisted of interviews with boys aged 10 to 16. He presented his subjects with 10 situations in which conformity to the law, rules, or orders of authorities went counter to the requirements necessary for the well-being of other persons. The subjects chose between helping the other persons or conforming to the dictates of the authorities. After they had made their choices, they answered questions focusing on the reasons for making those particular choices. To every moral idea or utterance of the experimental subjects, Kohlberg assigned a trait and gave a rating. From this data, he derived 30 moral traits which he rated on a six-point scale that related to his six developmental stages. Since interjudge reliability varied from 68 percent to 84 percent, Kohlberg's system has a fair evidential base.

Comparison of Kohlberg and Piaget

Kohlberg, who, like Piaget, is a cognitive theorist, has attempted to explain many phenomena of behavior and personality—which are not exclusively cognitive in nature—by reference to their cognitive component. In addition, he believes, with Piaget, that the development of this cognitive component can be characterized in stages.

One study has explored the relationship between Kohlberg's measures of moral development and Piaget's measures of cognitive development (Lee 1971). Using Piaget's cognitive tasks, the experimenter administered a series of tests to 195 boys from kindergarten through twelfth grade in Worthington, a middle-class suburb of Columbus, Ohio. The Piagetian conceptual tasks included tests for conservation of mass and liquid, lateral discrimination, projected space, equilibrium or balance, and projected shadows. The boys also were given a series of tests using Kohlberg's stories involving moral choices. Then the results were examined to see if there were significant relationships between the measures of cognitive level and those of moral development. On the whole, the results supported Piaget's contention that cognitive and moral development can be correlated. The findings of the study showed that children functioning in the preoperational stage adhere cognitively to acceptance of authority in their moral conceptualizing, whereas children who were in the later concrete operational stage appropriately employed reciprocity—as seen in

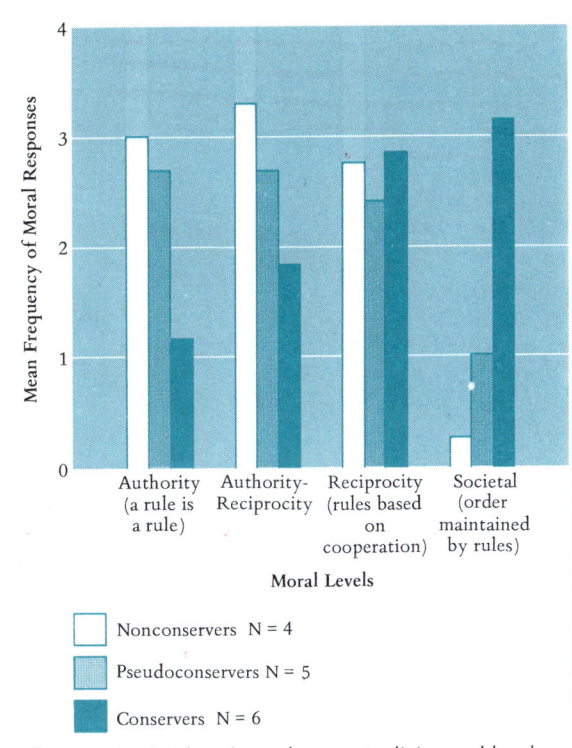

Figure 12.2 Modes of moral conceptualizing and levels of cognitive functioning are shown to be correlated in this group of 6-year-olds. (From L. C. Lee. The concomitant development of cognitive and moral modes of thought: A test of selected deductions from Piaget's theory. *Genet. Psychol. Monogr.*, 1971, 83, 13–146.)

the statement, "I am my brother's brother"—in dealing with moral questions. Subjects whose cognitive development had reached the level of formal operations tended to use higher social ideals as the basis for their moral reasoning. Thus, the study revealed a definite correlation between Kohlberg's moral levels and Piaget's cognitive stages.

Role-Taking and Moral Development

Kohlberg, in his investigation of moral development, has stressed, somewhat more than Piaget, the importance of role-taking which occurs in the 8-to-12 age span. Kohlberg's hypothesis is that role-taking is an essential skill for the development of morality. Since the ability to take the role of the other cannot develop outside the social situation, it would follow from Kohlberg's thesis that social experience and interaction, that is, social learning, also are crucial for moral development. This need not minimize the importance of purely cognitive aspects of role-taking and, therefore, of moral judgment, but it does put them in a larger social learning context. The cognitive component of role-taking, as Selman has pointed out, although less obvious than the social aspect, is still evident in the need to shift, balance, and evaluate perceptual and cognitive social information (Selman, in press).

The importance of role-taking to moral development can be seen in the 4-year-old child's inability to make an advanced moral judgment. This is clearly illustrated in one of Kohlberg's stories about a man who steals a drug for his dying wife. A 4-year-old lacks the ability to take the role of the story's desperate husband in both the general cognitive sense of being able to put himself in another's place, as well as in the specific social sense of having no conception of the experiences entailed by the role of the desperate husband.

The role-taking factor also is useful in helping to explain individual variation and cultural differences in the development of moral reasoning. According to Kohlberg, the more role-taking opportunities an individual has, the more his experience will facilitate his moral development. In the more complex societies and cultures, a greater number of role-taking opportunities will be open to the individual. This seems to account for the slower pace of moral development in rural and primitive cultures where social institutions are more simply structured. The occurrence of role-taking opportunities also would explain individual role-taking variation within a particular culture. For example, children with greater participation in peer groups and family structures are more likely to develop advanced moral reasoning at an earlier age.

A recent study examined the relationship between the role-taking ability and Kohlberg's moral judgment levels among 60 middle-class children—10 boys and 10 girls from each of three age groups: 8, 9, and 10 years (Selman, in press). The subjects were given two role-taking tasks,

Kohlberg's Moral Judgement Scale, and an intelligence test. The results of the two role-taking tasks were controlled for age and I.Q.; the results of the Moral Judgement Scale were not controlled for age, I.Q., or sex. The results of these tests were analyzed for correlation between role-taking ability and moral judgment.

In one of the role-taking tasks, a child, matched with a partner of the same sex, was shown two boxes. One box was marked 10 cents, the other 5 cents. Inside each was the corresponding coin, a dime and a nickel. The examiner told each child serving as an experimental subject that his partner would select one box and take the money in it. The subject was to trick his partner by taking the money out of the box he thought his partner would select. The examiner pointed out that the subject's partner knew that he (the subject of the experiment) was going to attempt to deceive him. The subject's task was to predict which box his partner, knowing the subject's intention, would select. When the subject had made his choice, the examiner asked him why he had thought his partner would choose that box.

Replies were classified into three categories of role-taking ability, the lowest score going to replies displaying no understanding that the task required a grasp of the other person's motives. These subjects could not or would not attribute any choice to their partners, or could give no explanation for the choice they felt their partners would make. The second category of role-taking ability included the child who was aware that his partner could have a motive, but still was not aware that this partner also might be aware of his motives. Thus, for example, the subject could state that his partner would select the 10-cent box, but was not able to see that his partner also might be aware that the subject would think this and would thus select the box marked 5 cents. The third category contained the highest level of role-taking scored for this task. This child was aware of both his partner's motives and the possibility that his partner was aware of his motives as well. At this stage of understanding, we find the reciprocal nature of role-taking. For example, one of the experimental subjects noted: "He will think I will take (predict) the dime box and so he will switch to the nickel box, so I better take the nickel box."

A positive correlation was obtained between results on the role-taking tasks and the Moral Judgement Scale, providing at least initial evidence for the thesis that role-taking and moral judgment are related. The study's next step took place one year later when 10 of the subjects who had scored low on both role-taking and moral judgment were located for a retest. Five of the 10 subjects rated at the higher level on role-taking this time, but only 2 of the 10 had attained the conventional level in moral judgment. (Both of these children also obtained the higher level in the role-taking tests.) Thus, no subject raised his moral judgment score without raising his role-taking score, although some raised role-taking without raising moral judgment. This result is consistent with the theory that role-taking is a precursor of moral development. This hypothesis is supported further by the finding that the correlation between role-taking and moral judgment is significant not only for the whole group but within each age group as well. Thus, it is shown that the relationship between the two scores occurs not simply because both role-taking and moral judgment increase with age.

In another study, the same experimenter compared the scores of 28 delinquent and 9 nondelinquent boys both on Kohlberg's Moral Judgement Scale and on an assessment of their understanding of the Golden Rule, a conventional moral principle that requires the ability to see things from another's point of view (Selman, in press). Again, it was found that subjects who did not show role-taking reciprocity on the Golden Rule were at the preconventional level on the Kohlberg scale.

We see, then, that role-taking is a significant determinant of moral level and can account for individual variations that a purely cognitive account does not explain. For example, a cognitive account would not explain why a mathematician who was extremely competent in the realm of quantitative abstraction—a formal operation, in Piaget's term—should insist on settling grievances by demanding expiative justice. Thus, factors other than the purely cognitive must be operative in the growth of morality. Selman, Kohlberg, and others have suggested that this missing factor is the role-taking ability which develops during the child's social activities. Likewise, Murray's study discussed in Chapter 10 points out the importance of such social interaction in cognitive judgment.

TRANSITION BETWEEN MORAL STAGES. The growth in role-taking ability, as defined by Kohlberg, also would help to explain the transition from the preconventional level of morality to the conventional level, which is reached at about the end of the 8- to 12-year age period (Kohlberg 1969b).

In Kohlberg's system, as we have noted, the beginnings of reciprocity lie in the second stage of the preconventional level of morality. At this stage, the child performs approved actions to gain reward and avoids disapproved actions to escape punishment. Thus, a child in Stage 2 will avoid scratching a coffee table because his mother will punish him when she discovers the damage. While the child's response does not represent true role-taking reciprocity—the child worries that his mother would discover the damage but does not put himself in his mother's place—his response does show the first awareness of the motives of others. This marks the beginning of role-taking.

Role-taking, then, can be considered the transitional means the child uses to move from one stage to the next in the 8- to 12-year age period, during which his role-taking increases dramatically. According to some studies, the child performs reciprocal role-taking by age 11 or 12 (Flavell 1971). With the motive-awareness he gains from role-taking, the child can use his own motives and judgments to understand the motives and judgments of others. He begins to consider others' opinions of him and realizes that others judge him as he judges them. In Kohlberg's terms, he seeks approval—the "good-boy" orientation—as he makes the transition to Stage 3, the conventional level of moral development.

This development brings the child to the start of his teen years. Beyond this point, which marks the end of middle childhood, the relationship between moral judgment and role-taking is not clearly understood. An individual's morality may continue to advance to the postconventional level, but it often does not. Similarly, the role-taking ability may continue to develop. Thus, while role-taking seems to be the transitional device by which the child moves from preconventional to conventional morality, it cannot, at present, be shown that role-taking continues to be the only device the child can employ to progress to more advanced moral levels. This remains an undertaking for future research.

ROLE-TAKING OPPORTUNITIES AND MORAL DEVELOPMENT. We have noted that role-taking develops out of social interaction, and that children in the 8- to 12-year age span show the most marked increase in role-taking. Given these findings, a hypothesis may be formed. If role-taking ability is crucial to the development of conventional morality, then intense social participation should predict high levels of moral development in 8- to 12-year-olds.

This hypothesis has been investigated by an experimenter who selected 75 boys and 69 girls from four sixth-grade classes and one fifth-grade class in a California public school (Keasey 1971). The subjects, predominantly white, were lower-middle-class children of average intelligence. They represented the ages at which the greatest diversity in moral level occurs. In terms of the Kohlberg Scale, the subjects ranged across Stages 1, 2, 3, and 4. All were given the Kohlberg Moral Judgement test and their scores computed, yielding their place in the developmental scale. About two months after the test was administered, each subject was rated for social participation, on the basis of the number of clubs and social organizations of which they had been members during the past two years as well as at the time of the rating. Each child also listed the leadership positions he presently held. Peers and teachers, too, rated each child for leadership and popularity. These results created a composite picture of each child's level of social participation.

The experimenter then compared each social rating to the test data on the level of moral development. All three ratings of social participation (self, teacher, and peer ratings) correlated positively with moral development. Thus, at least for the conventional stages of moral development, the experiment offered support for the hypothesis that social participation is a causal factor in moral development. On the entire matter of the evolution of the individual's morality, the general thrust of research findings indicates that the role-taking process is essential to cognition, and that,

COGNITIVE AND MORAL DEVELOPMENT AND SOCIAL PERCEPTION 391

in turn, cognition underlies the development of morality in the child. We should note, paradoxically, however, that role-taking is particularly susceptible to the type of influences (modeling and reinforcement) with which social learning theorists have been most concerned. Kohlberg's demonstration that cognition underlies morality, therefore, does not replace the need for social learning explanations. What it does show is that these explanations cannot step immediately from parental reinforcement to moral behavior, but must allow for the mediation of such learning both through role-taking and internalized cognition, each of which is also governed by its own principles.

Social Cognition

In our discussion of cognitive development, we have made several general observations about the rule orientations of children 8 to 12 years of age. We then illustrated these rule orientations in an area of development where rules are clearly vital—morality. On the whole, research has shown that the Piagetian thinkers have been able to support their belief that a child's cognitive level is a precursor of his moral level. In other words, a child's understanding determines his moral judgment.

In turn, there is evidence for the view that one's understanding, or cognitive level, is accelerated by role-taking experiences and demands. While the evidence for this thesis is less substantial, both Piaget and Kohlberg have supported such a view. Many of the studies related to social cognition were conducted within the Piagetian tradition of naturalistic observation—that is, they describe the child's progression in social cognition through his actions and discernible judgments. They do not, as a rule, provide information on why changes occur over the course of the various age spans. Specifically, although such studies contain important stage-by-stage descriptions of role-taking shifts, they do not tell us much about the role-taking pressures behind those significant shifts.

Nonetheless, these studies have much to offer.

Based on the work of Piaget and many other researchers in the field of nonsocial cognitive development, several investigators have undertaken the study of the development of social cognition. As they would in studying nonsocial cognition, they have proceeded from the hypothesis that social cognition develops in distinct stages whose sequence does not vary from child to child. They have tried to discover these stages and in some cases have attempted to formulate what events, processes, and mechanisms, both within the child and in his environment, prompt or inhibit the acquisition of the various sets of skills in each stage. For example, Flavell has done considerable research in the area of *inference*—what a child can conclude about another person from his contact with that person. While preschool and young grammar school children can infer information about others, their inferences are very elementary. However, this ability, according to Flavell, develops rapidly in middle childhood and adolescence. During this period, the richness and complexity, though not always the accuracy, of inferences about hidden psychological states—smoldering anger, repressed fear, feigned delight—is striking. Flavell cited two reasons for the increase in inferential ability. First, the greater social activity of middle childhood increases the need and stimulates the desire to make inferences about others. Flavell's second explanation for greater inferential ability in the 8- to 12-year age period is that general cognitive abilities—which are more fully developed in children of this age—come into play in the social sphere. The value of Flavell's analysis is that it attempts to focus on the cognitive development in the role-taking process. Just how such an element relates to role-taking processes, such as modeling and learning social actions through reinforcement, is not as yet clear.

Perspective-Taking and Inferences

The increase in ability to make inferences is most apparent in the area of visual perception. Here we are concerned with both the visual experiences that children of different ages and cognitive stages can attribute to others, and the child's own ability to take the visual perspective of others toward arrays of objects.

Various researchers, including Flavell and Piaget, have constructed a variety of visual tasks to test different aspects of the development of the perspective-taking ability. One such task is the well-known "three mountains" test (Piaget and Inhelder 1956). In this test, the child looks at a scale model of three mountains and is asked to imagine or represent the mountains' visual appearance from various perspectives other than his own. Piaget and Inhelder found that this task remained quite difficult even for 9- and 10-year-old children.

Another task, even more difficult than the "three mountains" test, was devised by Flavell and his colleagues (1968). They constructed an arrangement of three wooden cylinders of different heights, each painted red for half its circumference and white for the other half. The subject's task was to reconstruct a particular view of these cylinders with a duplicate set of cylinders. To solve the problem, he had to understand, for example, that when the display was viewed from the side opposite him, the middle-sized cylinder would present its white side full face and would be to the left and in front of the other two cylinders. Only eight out of twenty 16-year-olds achieved maximum scores in this perspective-taking task.

A third, two-part experiment—also rather demanding—required children in the 8- to 12-year age period to perform two tasks: to anticipate the appearance of an array of objects that had been rotated, and to anticipate how an array would look to an observer in a different position (Huttenlocher and Presson, in press). The experiments produced a comparison of the difficulty that children had in anticipating how positional changes of an object array and of an observer affected the array's appearance under various conditions. It was found that when the array was covered over and reversed, the children could say what it would look like, but when the children had to imagine themselves in a change of position, they made many errors. Even adults found the task hard to master. The explanation for this difficulty, the experimenters contended, is that adults as well as children anticipate an array's appearance on the basis of their own present position relative to the array. When a new position for themselves must be imagined (as well as the new perspective on the objects), the perspective-taking process becomes more complicated. The subjects must mentally merge themselves into an imagined observer in order to judge how the array would appear to the observer. Children in middle childhood found the "mental merger" impossible. However, in contradistinction to Piaget, the experimenters maintained that the children's failure was not the result of egocentricity peculiar to childhood, because the children could tell how the array would be when reversed. Instead, they contended, the children's failure to solve the perceptual tasks resulted from their specific inability to perform the mental merger of the imagined observer—who has a set position in relation to the

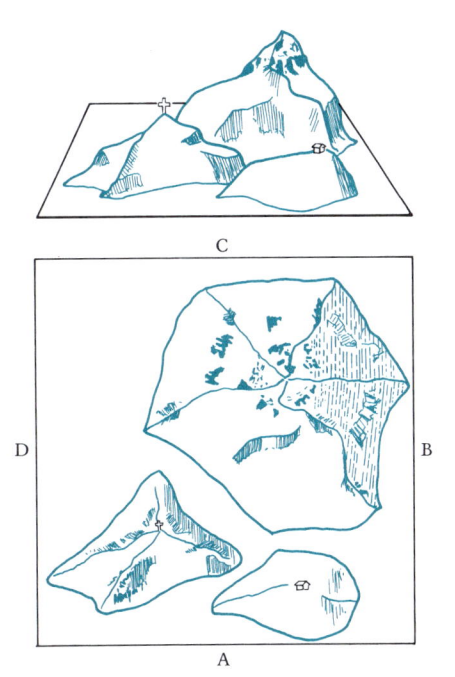

Figure 12.3 Three model mountains—all colored and marked differently—formed the basis of Piaget's and Inhelder's test of children's abilities to coordinate various spatial perspectives with their own. (From J. Piaget and B. Inhelder. *The child's conception of space.* London: Routledge & Kegan Paul, 1956.)

array—with their own positions in relation to the array.

DEVELOPMENTAL LEVELS OF PERSPECTIVE-TAKING. Flavell, using the work of Piaget, as well as extensive studies of his own, constructed a number of levels of perspective-taking ability.

Level 0, the lowest level, occurs in Piaget's sensorimotor (preoperational) stage. Knowledge from this level is composed largely of the child's sensorimotor expectancies as to his discoveries as he moves from place to place in his environment. The child is concerned primarily with *what* objects he will find, not with their appearance from different perspectives. He has no real ability to symbolically represent to himself what he will see in the future or what the experimenter is seeing in the present. His inference is based on his own action. The child can anticipate objects he has seen, but he cannot represent to himself anyone else's visual activities or experience.

At Level 1—generally the early school years—the child becomes capable of symbolically representing to himself the visual acts and experiences of others and himself. However, he still is concerned only with the appearance of the object itself, not with different perspectives of it. He can manage reversals in the object, but not in the viewer of the object. Thus, the child at this level can do the "three mountains" test if the mountains are reversed, but he cannot adequately comprehend the question—"How do these mountains appear to me from where I'm sitting?"—when asked by someone else. In the latter case, the child would expect the examiner to see the same thing he sees—the mountain, the thing itself, without permutation or variety.

With the attainment of Level 2, however, the child decenters from his exclusive concern with the objects he sees and is able to represent to himself the activity of seeing as executed by himself and others. He becomes aware of the inner experiences, the phenomenological fact of views or perspectives on an object. Thus, the child at Level 2 would be able to represent to himself, though not always accurately, the other's visual experience of the three cylinders in Flavell's perspective-taking task.

Level 3 is a further extension of the type of inference employed in Level 2. Whereas in Level 2 the sizes of objects viewed from different perspectives are vague and tied to the real size of the objects, in Level 3 the individual can represent a picture of the other's retinal image in complete size perspective. He can decenter from the objects' real size and imagine them the way an artist would.

A study by Laurendeau and Pinard (1970) charted the different age groups that can fall into a single level of perspective-taking ability. In the study's sample, 68 percent of the 5-year-olds, 52 percent of the 6-year-olds, and 17 percent of the 7-year-olds were found to be at Level 0 in their performance of the "three mountains" task. In other words, they could not comprehend the meanings of the questions asked.

Judging on the basis of behavior, it seemed that all of those at Stage 0 did understand that the other person looked at and saw the three mountains—a Level 1 inference—but they had no idea that he saw them in a particular way. Children over 7 years old seemed, on the whole, to be at least minimally aware of the existence of another's perspective, although they still displayed substantial egocentrism and made many mistakes in inference.

Interpersonal Perception

UNDERSTANDING EMOTIONS. Our discussion of social cognition up to this point has focused primarily on perspective-taking and role-taking. We have seen how the concrete operational child is able to recognize and make inferences concerning another's visual perspective, and also how the child in middle childhood is able to attribute intentions and awareness of intentions to others. An important aspect of attributing such motivations to others is an understanding of emotional causes of behavior. The ability to recognize another person's emotional state and to make inferences about it is a vital trait in social life. We would expect that this ability, too, would show marked development in the middle-childhood years.

Whiteman (1967) has investigated how and when children recognize the emotional causes of their own and others' behavior. The theoretical basis for this study came from two sources. The

Figure 12.4 The concrete operational child shows increased ability to understand emotional causes and motivations underlying his own and others' behavior. (Christa Armstrong—Rapho Guillumette)

first was psychoanalytic writings about the child's ability to identify mechanisms of personal adjustment. These adjustment mechanisms, which were discussed in Chapter 11, include: projection of emotions or traits onto other people; rationalizations of behavior; transfer of such emotions as anger to objects; wishful dreaming; denial of apparent emotions; repression of unpleasant thoughts or memories; and regression to earlier stages of emotional development.

The second theoretical source was Piaget's general insight that with the attainment of concrete operationalism, the child can decenter from the obvious, overt behavior of others to the less obvious, covert motivations underlying their behavior. According to Piaget, children 5 to 6 years old and children 8 to 9 years old show striking differences in their ability to comprehend physical causality. Therefore, the present experimenter reasoned, they also should reveal significant age differences in their understanding of psychological causality.

To test this thesis, Whiteman chose 21 East Harlem kindergarten children and 21 third-graders from the same school; all of the children were black or Puerto Rican. Each younger child was matched with a third-grader for sex and I.Q.; the average I.Q. in each group was 101. The experimenter tape-recorded each child's replies to questions about seven stories. Each story illustrated a different adjustment mechanism—emotion transfer or displacement, wishful dreaming, regression, and so forth. Each interview was prefaced with instructions to the child, such as: "I'm going to tell you some stories about a little girl (boy) named Jane (Johnny). In each one of these stories Jane (Johnny) does something different from what she (he) usually does. I want you to tell me why she (he) did it." The experimenter then told the first story—how Jane's mother promised ice cream for dessert but then forgot to buy it. After supper Jane did something she had never done before. She spanked her doll. Why did she do this? This story illustrates displacement or transfer of anger from the mother to an object—the doll.

In the second story, Jane's mother had bought her a pair of gloves. After Jane was warned not to lose this pair as she had lost the last pair, Jane lost the new gloves coming home from school. Although she knew she had to tell her mother, she forgot to do so. When she went out to play, she told her friends she had lost the gloves. But that night and again at breakfast the next day, she forgot to tell her mother. Why did she forget? This story illustrates repression.

Another story concerned a bowl of spinach Jane's mother gave her for lunch. Jane said she would not eat it because it would make her fat. Why did she say that when she liked to eat fattening things, such as candy? This story illustrates the mechanism of rationalization.

Similar stories illustrated denial, projection, wishful dreaming, and regression. After each story the child was asked why the story's main character acted the way he or she did. The responses, rated for degree of psychological understanding, disclosed that, in general, the third-graders showed more understanding of pyschological causes than the kindergartners. The third-graders generally were able to decenter from the overt behavior of the protagonist to uncover the masked emotions that moved the character to act as he did. Regarding the story in which the girl spanked her doll after the mother's failure to provide the promised ice cream, one third-grader responded in this fashion:

Interviewer: Why did she spank her doll?
Child: Because she didn't have any ice cream.
Interviewer: She didn't have any ice cream. Fine. Why did that make her spank the doll, though, if she didn't have any ice cream?
Child: Because she was mad.
Interviewer: She was mad. What was she mad at or whom was she mad at?
Child: Her mother.
Interviewer: Oh. She was mad at her mother. Very good. Now tell me why if she was mad at her mother did she spank the doll?
Child: 'Cause her mother didn't buy her any ice cream, and she was real mad; she took it out on the doll.

The child obviously understood that the story's character was displacing her anger onto the doll.

A kindergarten child responded to the same story in this way:

I: Why did she spank her doll?
C: Because she didn't have no ice cream.
I: Right. Now, why did she spank her doll though?
C: 'Cause she wanted ice cream.
I: Was she happy or mad, or how did she feel?
C: Sad.
I: She felt sad. Why . . . did she feel mad at anybody?
C: Uh-uh (negative).
I: Well, her mother forgot to bring the ice cream. Did she feel mad at her mother?
C: Yeah.
I: Why did she spank the doll if she felt mad at her mother?
C: Because she wanted ice cream.
I: Because she wanted ice cream. Now, when you spank a doll, does the doll spank back?
C: No.
I: When you spank your mother, does your mother spank back?
C: Yes.
I: So why did she spank the doll instead of her mother?
C: Because she wanted ice cream.
I: Because she wanted ice cream. Very good.

As the interview clearly demonstrated, the younger child had consistent difficulty decentering from the story's event itself to the internal state of the character. She volunteered no information about the character's emotional state unless she was closely questioned. Even then, the information elicited was vague. Finally, she was unable to link the character's feelings to the character's behavior.

An analysis of the total results showed that 76 percent of the third-graders could reach the highest level on at least one story. With prompting from the examiner, 90 percent could reach the highest level. In contrast, only 5 percent (one child) of the kindergartners was able to reach the highest level of psychological comprehension on at least one story. It seems, then, that the understanding of emotional causality probably grows with the progression of the concrete operational stage.

AWARENESS OF EXPRESSIONS OF EMOTION. The above data are consistent with the results of another study concerning children's ability to recognize external expression of emotions (Gates 1923, 1925). In this study, children ranging from 3 to 14 years of age were shown photographs of an actress expressing joy, anger, surprise, fear, scorn, and pain. Adults usually could identify all the emotions depicted in the photographs. However, of the children at the kindergarten level, only 70 percent could identify laughter, and less than 50 percent could recognize pain, anger, and fear. No kindergartners could identify surprise or scorn. Half of the children could recognize anger at age 7, fear at age 10, and surprise at age 11.

A more recent study found that children 5 to 12 years old identify the emotions of sadness and anger more aptly than expressions of happiness or lovingness (Dimitrovsky 1964). Using voice recordings and model figures, the experimenter tested the younger children's reactions to all four of these emotions. With few exceptions, the number of correct identifications of all four emotions increased with age. However, the identification of sadness and anger became more prevalent in the children at an earlier age—5 years—and remained more recognizable throughout the age groups.

A similar study examined the reactions of children to movies depicting various emotions (Flapan 1968). One film showed a girl practicing on her new roller skates while a neighbor boy asked to take a turn on them. The girl did not want to give them up, and there was a conflict between the two. The girl's parents appeared, and each parent attempted to shift responsibility for disciplining their daughter to the other. Then the father took away the skates and sent the girl to bed without supper. Later, the father regretted the punishment; finally the father made up for his injustice by taking his daughter to the circus.

Another film in the study showed a girl and a boy competing in stone-throwing. The girl threw a stone and accidentally killed a squirrel. Her father, seeing how upset she was, gave her a newborn calf to cheer her. Later her mother, unaware of these proceedings, all but took the calf away from the girl, seriously disappointing the child. Finally it was decided that the calf belonged to the whole family.

After these films were shown to three groups of middle-class girls of average intelligence, aged 6, 9, and 12 years, their accounts of the films were analyzed on a scale measuring the degree of psychological awareness. The scale ranged from literal statements about the action, dialogue, and the obvious emotions, such as crying, to statements attributing thoughts, feelings, or intentions—that is, psychological *explanations*—that could have been gained only by inference or interpretation. For example, an observer could only infer that the restlessness of the father in the first film meant he felt sorry about having punished his daughter so harshly. The three-point scale for this film ranged from 0 for the most literal responses, to 2 for complex inferences about thoughts, feelings, and motivations.

In their accounts of the movies, nearly every one of the 20 girls in each group was able to describe the film's situation and report the dialogue of the characters. Most could describe the obvious expressive reactions and feelings. Nineteen 6-year-olds and 9-year-olds, and all of the 12-year-olds, described the characters' obvious emotions. However, none of the 6-year-olds attributed feelings that were not obviously expressed, while thirteen 9-year-olds and eighteen 12-year-olds were able to do so. On the inference of thoughts and expectations, the scores were 2 for the 6-year-olds, 13 for the 9-year-olds, and 15 for the 12-year-olds. On the inference of intentions, the scores were 2, 6, and 10, respectively. In general, the scores for psychological explanations were 3, 12, and 14. Thus, there emerges a clear pattern in the age trends of responses. A large gap appears between the 6-year-olds and the 9-year-olds; another, though smaller gap, separates the girls 9 and 12 years old. These latter findings indicate a marked increase in interpersonal perceptive ability as the child moves into the stage of concrete operationalism, which occurs somewhere between the ages of 6 and 9.

NATURE OF SOCIAL PERCEPTION. From our account of children's reactions to social and emotional situations, we can draw some conclusions

Table 12.2 Consistency of Children in Using Various Types of Statements in Telling What Happened in the Movies

Categories of Statements	Number of 6-Year-Olds Who Used Category			Number of 9-Year-Olds Who Used Category			Number of 12-Year-Olds Who Used Category		
	For Both Movies	For One Movie	Never	For Both Movies	For One Movie	Never	For Both Movies	For One Movie	Never
Reporting and describing									
Situation-action	20	0	0	20	0	0	20	0	0
Verbal communication	20	0	0	20	0	0	20	0	0
Expressive behavior	10	6	4	8	9	3	11	6	3
Obvious feelings	15	4	1	15	4	1	19	1	0
Obvious intentions	5	8	7	18	2	0	19	1	0
Interpreting-inferring									
Feelings	0	0	20	6	7	7	10	8	2
Thoughts-expectations	1	1	18	7	6	7	9	6	5
Intentions-motives	1	1	18	3	3	14	5	5	10
Interpersonal perceptions	0	0	20	0	4	16	3	4	13
Explaining									
In situational terms	9	1	10	14	5	1	16	3	1
In psychological terms	1	2	17	5	7	8	10	4	6
In terms of interpersonal perceptions	0	0	20	0	6	14	2	4	14

Note: N at each age is 20.
Source: Adapted from D. Flapan. *Children's understanding of social interaction.* New York: Teachers College Press, Columbia Univ., 1968.

concerning the nature of social perception. One clear implication of these studies, especially the study employing films, is that the perceptions of another person's emotions are quite separate from inferences about a person's hidden intentions and feelings. In the film study, we saw that 6-year-olds are quite capable of describing another's emotions based on his obvious expressions, but are relatively incapable of making complicated inferences from a given social situation about another's psychological state. Thus, it would seem that perception of an actor's motives in a social situation requires more than merely being able to perceive emotion.

Role of reciprocity. The work of both Piaget and Asch suggests that social perception also involves the concepts of decentering and reciprocity. Piaget has contended that in the cognition of objects, the young child initially focuses on only one aspect of a situation. For example, the child who sees a certain volume of water poured from a squat to a tall container will conclude that there is more water in the tall container. When the child has matured to the stage of concrete operations, he can decenter from the height dimension and see the equality of the squat and tall containers. While Piaget deals primarily with reciprocity of relations between objects, Asch is concerned with the complementary nature of social roles.

Asch has suggested that a similar perception of part-whole relationships may take place in social perception (Asch 1952). Asch, using the example of two boys carrying a log, pointed out that their joint performance is completely different from what either would do separately. While log-carrying involves individual acts, it is more than the accumulation of these individual acts, but rather an "emergent" phenomenon on an entirely different level. According to Asch, the ability to perceive the reciprocity of such social relationships is vital to a mutually shared social situation. The individual incorporates within his own individual cognitive structure this "role complementarity"—the ability to see himself as both an actor and the object of another's actions. Thus he develops the idea of a coordinated group system. It would be reasonable to assume that social reciprocity, like object reciprocity—as Piaget views it—develops only with the attainment, in middle childhood, of concrete operations.

Rules and Peer-Group Interaction

Rule-Following Behavior. Another important aspect of group activity that involves cognitive functions is rule-following behavior. Rule-following passes through three distinct stages. First, the child is highly individualistic in his play. Although he may imitate the practices of his elders, he really does not understand rules or why they exist. In the second stage, the child begins to want to play in conformity with rules, which are still imposed from the outside. This orientation to rules comes about through imitation or verbal exchange and involves a number of such cognitive abilities as role-taking, reciprocity, and perspective-taking. In children from 5 to 8 years old, the consequences of rule-following can be seen in the types of societies they form. The group is paramount; individuality has little worth. As a result, the rules and activities of the group are the focus of attention. Because children 8 to 12 years old make little distinction between self and group, middle childhood can be a period of slavish conformity. Then, at about 10 years of age, the third stage of rule-following behavior emerges. The child begins to realize the arbitrary nature of rules. He realizes that he and others can change them by mutual agreement. This realization presupposes that the child differentiates between himself and others, and between himself and the group, distinctions which are characteristic of preadolescence and adolescence. This increased awareness of self is not a return to the child's earlier egocentrism. Instead, it is a new awareness that he is self-operating among many other selves who all share some of his attributes, but have differences as well. This self-awareness, in both play and other aspects of social life, appears only when the child attains the ability to decenter both from himself and from the group.

The parallel between cognitive development and social cognition is evident in Piaget's stages of social rule-following. Piaget distinguishes various rule-following stages in children's play—stages which were associated with the nonsocial cognitive levels—preoperational, concrete operational, and formal operational.

At the preoperational level, the child takes pleasure in purely egocentric motor exercise. His play has almost no structure, and he shows no awareness of the structures imposed by rules.

At a slightly later stage of egocentrism, but still within the preoperational level, games acquire rules and the barest structure. However, play often is improvised and rules ignored. There are only weak team and competitive relationships between players since rules are generally ignored, undercutting the possibility of officially winning the game. A successive egocentric stage occurs between ages 5 and 8 as the child advances to concrete operationalism. Games now have more complicated, adult-approved rules which are closely followed. Players keenly seek out rule infractions.

At the initial level of interpersonal cooperation, the game's structure becomes much more elaborate. The group establishes the rules before the game begins and individual exceptions are not permitted. A change in the rules requires a group decision. As the team relationship between players becomes more firmly fixed, the idea of winning emerges as the goal of the game. From this brief outline of game stages, it can be seen that the child's social rule-following in games parallels his cognitive development and demonstrably includes several such cognitive aspects as reciprocity and the understanding of conventions.

Role Differentiation. Along with the child's increasing differentiation between himself and others, and himself and the group, there develops a greater differentiation of roles that one can play in social activity. The group ceases to be monolithic, but becomes more articulated in its functioning. A good example can be drawn from the game behavior at various age levels. A recent study points out that in games played by young children, little differentiation in roles is likely to be detected (Sutton-Smith 1971b). Usually, there is a central player and an undifferentiated group, as in hide-and-seek, chain tag, stoop tag, and cross tag. A great deal of power is conferred on the central player, not because of skill but by virtue of his role. The other players are fairly powerless.

From this level, games evolve to the point at which—at about 10 years of age—the central player and the other players become more differentiated, as in "black magic" and ring-a-levio, where moments of group cooperation are possible. After this point, the child moves toward full-fledged team games and sports, which have varied roles and functions—for example, baseball, with its clearly defined positions of pitcher, catcher, basemen, and outfielders.

As the child grows older, the evolution of his games parallels the evolution of his groups from relatively primitive, undifferentiated mobs to articulated and functionally differentiated systems.

COMMUNICATION SKILLS. One of the cognitive factors influencing the transition, in the child's games, from undifferentiated mobs to articulated play systems is the quality of his communication with his peers. One study examined the extent to which school children of different ages listen to each other and respond to the other person's communication (Baker 1942). To do this, the experimenter evaluated class discussions carried on by elementary school children, for various types of responses: responses that were unrelated to the utterances of earlier speakers; responses that introduced new topics that seemed to be suggested by something previously mentioned; or responses that were logical continuations of previous topics. In grade 2, 87 percent of the responses were unrelated, 8 percent suggested by a previous speaker, and 4 percent a logical continuation of an earlier topic. The percentages for grade 4 were 33 percent, 24 percent, and 43 percent, respectively; and for grade 6, the percentages were 23 percent, 33 percent, and 44 percent, respectively. Thus, the expected relationship between advancing age, awareness, and the amount of attention paid to peers was borne out by the study. The older the children grew, the less they volunteered unrelated responses and the more they addressed themselves to the topic at hand.

Role-taking is one of the key abilities that underlies such communication skills as carrying on a discussion. As we have mentioned earlier, the ability to take the role of another person in any given situation involves the ability to distinguish between one's own perceptions and feelings and those of the other person. Thus, it requires decentering from exclusive concern with oneself. Role-taking also involves reciprocity—in communication, it is the realization that the other person must make sense of what the speaker says, and vice versa. This realization depends on the child's awareness of psychological properties; his ability to use these properties in a given situation; his ability to infer the listener's state from the situation's various cues; and, finally, his ability to modify his own behavior using these inferences as a guide.

The Development of the Peer Group

As the child's capability for social perception grows, so does his awareness of, and need for, the sense of belonging to a group. Thus, with the coming of middle childhood, an individual's circle of peers becomes an extremely important part of his social development.

Peer groups in middle childhood have a culture of their own that has endured for centuries. One reason for the staying power of this culture is the child's fascination with ritual. As Piaget has pointed out, when children reach the stage of concrete operations, they become preoccupied with the rules of the game, often considering them unchangeable. In addition, the tendency toward conformity during this period increases the likelihood that rules are followed to the letter. As a result of this childish zeal, the culture is transmitted from one generation of children to the next.

The child's love of ritual may arise from the feeling that ritual allows him to control reality. For the child, ritual is magical knowledge. Rituals make up for the various skills that he lacks in his dealings with the world. They also provide the child with a link to a group. By adopting the culture of his group, the child demonstrates to himself and to his peers that he belongs. Often the child who rebels against adult rules will accept rules imposed by his peers, probably out of his need to feel accepted by the group.

The peer group is an important context in

which the child learns social skills and behavior. Among other children, he discovers how to relate to people of his age, how to control or express his hostility, how to share his possessions and time, how to lead other children, and how to behave toward another child in a leadership position. In the group, he sometimes can see aspects of himself and realize that his internal emotional reactions—resulting in shyness or hurt feelings—are not peculiar to him. Knowing that his fears and interests are shared by others his age can be a comfort to the child, assuaging his uncertainty about the many aspects of physical development and emotional life that he does not fully understand.

In his peer group the child continues to build his self-concept. It is shaped, in part, from the emotional information he gains when he watches others react to him. For example, he may learn to change his behavior to succeed with his present friends or to win new ones. The peer group is both a refuge and a testing ground for the child beyond the limited sphere of his family. In our discussion of this vital aspect of development, we shall structure our approach on the intensive study of peer groups conducted by Willard W. Hartup.[2]

Types of Peer Groups

SEX-BASED GROUPS. From the preschool years to perhaps the sixth or seventh grade, children associate almost exclusively with peers of the same sex. This alignment continues until adolescence when boys and girls seek out members of the opposite sex.

Cultural patterns are one reason for sex-based peer groups. Either directly or indirectly, parents encourage their children to associate with other children of the same sex. Children who do not often are regarded as strange by peers and parents alike. Societies tend to impose stereotyped sex roles on children; urging children in middle childhood to associate exclusively with peers of the same sex is one way of facilitating such sex-typing. In American society, boys tend to play strenuous, "masculine" games together, and their rambunctious activities, while occasionally destructive, are regarded as natural and healthy. "Gangs" of girls, on the other hand, tend to be quieter, seldom engaging in physical or destructive activity.

SOCIAL-CLASS DIVISIONS. Social-class standing also is a parameter of the peer group. For the most part, investigation has indicated that lower-class children are less popular in a socially mixed peer group than upper- or middle-class children. However, the evidence on this point is not conclusive. Two experimenters reported a direct relationship between class status and popularity, but in their samples they neglected to control for I.Q. (Cannon 1957; Elkins 1958). However, an earlier study of sixth-graders controlled for I.Q. divided the subjects into three I.Q. levels and then tested for peer popularity (Grossman and Wrighter 1948). It was found that at each I.Q. level, the children of higher socioeconomic status were more popular than lower-class children with the same I.Q.

AGE GROUPINGS. Age is still another basis for peer-group divisions. Generally, children in middle childhood have been found to associate almost exclusively with children of the same age (Campbell 1964). However, among prepubertal girls there is a tendency to associate with boys who are slightly older.

The Development of Group Norms

Group norms—the behavior standards and activities the group accepts—play an important part in peer-group functioning during middle childhood. One study observed 12 groups of four children each in day-care centers (Merei 1949). In some of the groups were children as young as 4 years old, while other groups had children 11 years old. According to Merei, in all of the groups:

The children formed traditions such as permanent seating order (who should sit where); permanent division of objects (who plays with what); group ownership of certain objects; ceremonies connected with their use; expressions of belonging together; returning to certain activities; rituals; sequences of games; forming a group jargon out of expressions accidentally uttered, etc. (Merei 1949)

In short, some kinds of group norms appeared at all age levels.

---

2. W. W. Hartup. Peer interaction and social organization. In P. H. Mussen (Ed.), *Carmichael's manual of child psychology.* Vol. II. (3rd ed.) New York: Wiley, 1970.

Figure 12.5 Children in the middle years tend to associate almost exclusively with members of the same sex. (Irwin Rosen—Black Star; Burk Uzzle—Black Star)

GROUP NORMS AND CONFORMITY. Group norms are inculcated and enforced in early and middle childhood through two basic processes. The first is the preschool child's tendency to imitate; the second process is the development of social pressure which strengthens the 8- to 12-year-old's tendency toward conformity.

According to some social learning theorists, imitation of others' behavior is reinforced from early childhood onward (Miller and Dollard 1941). Although this may be true, such a statement does not predict the degree of conformity in each age or outline the various types of imitative behavior and the times at which they occur. Piaget's theories provide a somewhat more complete foundation for predicting and explaining social imitation at certain ages. According to Piaget, the child in the preschool years—the preoperative stage—has no clear concept of rules. Thus, although he will imitate his elders' behaviors, he really does not understand the reasons for these behaviors. With the development of concrete operationalism, and particularly with the appearance of reciprocity, the child begins to grasp the nature of rules. In his greater social experience, he begins to seek conformity with rules made by others. Thus, he grows increasingly susceptible to pressure to conform to group rules. The tendency to conform sometimes culminates in the rigid conformity of the 8- to 12-year-old child.

Several empirical studies have examined the various degrees of such conformity over age spans. In one study, Berenda (1950) used four separate experiments to assess conformity among children of different ages in terms of their agreement with false judgments on the lengths of lines on a card. In the first experiment, eight of the most intelligent children in each of two classes pressured the subject to conform. When the conformity behavior of the two groups—7- to 10-year-olds and 10- to 13-year-olds—was compared, children in both age groups were found to have agreed with significantly more incorrect answers when they were under peer pressure to conform than when they had been left to judge the questions by themselves. However, the children in the 7- to 10-year age group responded more readily to the pressure to conform than the older children.

The second and third experiments of the study examined the effects that a larger peer group had on the children who belonged to a smaller peer group. In the second experiment, the larger group was asked to overestimate the lengths of the lines—but not in unanimity; in the third experiment they all were asked to estimate the lengths of two lines, sometimes giving unanimously correct, and sometimes unanimously incorrect answers. The results showed that the younger child was more likely to be swayed by the larger group, particularly when those group members differed in their rehearsed false judgments. Thus, the pressure to conform seems to have a significant effect on the child, particularly in middle childhood. This result, it should be noted, coincides with Kohlberg's finding that the "good-boy" approval-seeking stage also occurs in middle childhood.

EFFECT ON MOTIVATION. In considering the peer group's influence on the child, we should point out that the differing norms of various kinds of peer groups will affect the child's behavior in various ways. For example, among middle-class children, achievement in school is prized and the middle-class child is motivated by his parents, teachers, and friends to perform well in school. The lower-class child, however, may be less highly rewarded by parents, teachers, and friends; he may actually be discouraged from academic achievement by the argument that only girls and sissies seek good grades.

Influences on the Peer Group

We have examined several characteristics of the peer group. Having thus noted such a group's salient traits, it would be valuable to see how the group acquires those characteristics. To gain an insight into this formative process, we shall turn our attention to some of the factors that affect the nature and existence of the peer group. Among these factors are the effects of physical proximity, competition, frustration, leadership style, and personality types.

HIERARCHY, HOSTILITY, AND OTHER FORMATIVE FACTORS. In a set of experiments, Sherif and his associates investigated some of the factors affecting peer-group formation. In their first study, they put forth three hypotheses: that a group of children who live together for any length of time and understand that they have a mutual aim will develop a hierarchy of leaders and followers in addition to relational patterns among group members and a pattern of labor assignments; that the group will evolve its own norms and attitudes; that two groups of this kind will become hostile to each other if they are subjected to a situation in which competition and frustration are strong (Sherif and Sherif 1953). This study's sample consisted of two groups of white, Protestant, middle-class, preadolescent boys who were moved, as groups, through three successive formative stages while living at a summer camp. In Stage 1, the two groups were separated for three days while casual social alignments formed and dissolved and individuals made friends. In Stage 2, the groups were split and two new groups formed. During Stage 2, which was five days long, the new groups were structured on the basis of personal data gathered in Stage 1. Members were selected for personality traits and capability; consequently, Stage 1 friendships were broken up. Once constituted, the new groups lived apart and engaged in different activities with little adult supervision or contact between the groups. The data on the new groups supported the hypotheses about peer-group formation. Both of the new groups had formed definite hierarchies—with the highest and lowest positions being filled first. The groups were very different in their cohesiveness. The "Red Devils," comprising more boys of low than high status, appeared to be only casually united; the "Bull Dogs," a more homogeneous group, seemed better integrated. The two groups also evolved their own norms and attitudes, resulting in the designation of outsiders as "they" and group members as "we," and the evolution of a code of laws and penalties. As practical extensions of their group identity, they each selected a group color and name. Stage 1 friendships were mostly abandoned and loyalties transferred to the new groups, resulting in a clear—though not hostile—competition between the groups.

Data support the contention that the frustrations and satisfactions of activity within the group lead to the formation of hierarchies and shared norms; these reactions act as binding forces that tie the individual members to the group. Of course, as Sherif and Sherif pointed out, a group's norms are not adhered to indefinitely by all the members. An individual may find his attitude toward a norm changed by an experience or new circumstance. When he defects from the group, it will change, either in its norms or in the alignment of its members (Sherif and Sherif 1964).

When the two groups of boys were placed in competition in Stage 3 of the experiment, they

Figure 12.6 Conformity to peer group behavior is characteristic of the years 8 through 12. (Magnum)

happened to be very unevenly matched; one group lost constantly and became frustrated. When the losing group encountered a contrived event, the experience seemed to trigger their excessive frustration. Bitter squabbles and grudges between the groups broke out. As a consequence, the morale and unity of the frustrated group were severely shaken; in contrast, the group that was more homogeneous in Stage 2 was more unified in its enmity.

Sherif and his colleagues explored the roles of peer-group competition and conflict more fully in another experiment similar to the earlier one (Sherif et al. 1961). Twenty-two fifth-grade boys were brought along in groups to the point at which group norms appeared. Then the groups were thrown into competition. Unlike the experiment above, the two groups were evenly matched—both groups had the same success-failure rate. Despite this equality, hostility between the two groups grew significantly while each group simultaneously became more unified and concerted.

Contrary to the experimenters' expectations that low-status boys would be more aggressive toward the other group, the data indicated that high-status boys demonstrated comparable aggression. The competition also changed the group's structure, promoting to leadership the boys who had performed well. Thus, success in achieving the peer group's aims emerged as a condition of leadership.

Another situation in this same study included a contrived water-supply blockage that required the competitive groups to cooperate in solving a problem important to both groups. The experimenters hypothesized that the cooperative project would break down the "they" characterizations of each group by the other, produce intergroup friendships, and generally lessen tension between the two groups. All three hypotheses were supported by the experimental data.

Likewise, Stendler, Damrin, and Haines (1951) found cooperation to be a factor influencing the peer group's cohesiveness. In this study, three groups of 7-year-old children were rewarded on a different basis from day to day. On the first day, the children were told they each would be rewarded if they worked together to paint a good mural. In successive meetings, a reward was promised to the individual child who painted the best picture. Results demonstrated that all cooperative painting periods produced many such constructive behaviors as sharing paints and brushes and friendly conversations. On the other hand, the competitive painting periods produced an excess of such negative or divisive behaviors as bragging or deprecating another's work. Thus, among young children, competition within a group fragments the group.

However, with age, the cohesiveness of such informal peer groups has been shown to increase. Smith (1960) found, for example, that grammar school children who were solving a mutual problem exhibit more behavior directed to others than do preschool children.

Thus, the Sherif experiments, as well as those of Stendler and Smith, point out several important influences on the formation of peer groups. First, a common aim, as well as physical proximity, is important. Second, cooperation can unify a group, while competition between two groups can bring out intergroup hostility and simultaneously unite each group more firmly. Third, the prevalent situation and the surrounding environment strongly affect a peer group's internal structure and norms, as well as its relations with other peer groups.

Group cohesiveness and performance. The cohesion of a peer group, whether or not it results from internal cooperation, affects individual performance. Lott and Lott (1966) found that group cohesiveness influenced children's verbal learning in accord with the ability of the children in the group. Among fourth- and fifth-graders with high I.Q.'s, those in cohesive groups performed better on a verbal learning task than those in noncohesive groups. However, the results for children with low I.Q.'s were exactly the opposite, though not so dramatically. The examiners hypothesized that the attraction to others, which appears in cohesive groups, is an incentive to perform. When the task is easy—as the verbal task would be for children with high I.Q.'s—the incentive would be likely to upgrade the child's performance. But when the task is difficult—as it would be for children with low I.Q.'s—the incentive would impede performance. Although the study does not reveal why this latter process takes place, it

COGNITIVE AND MORAL DEVELOPMENT AND SOCIAL PERCEPTION **405**

Figure. 12.7 In the middle years, the child becomes increasingly capable of carrying out projects that involve cooperation with others. Cooperation has been found to influence the cohesiveness of peer groups. (J. Cron—Monkmeyer; Mimi Forsyth—Monkmeyer)

does show that cohesion, in conjunction with other variables, affects performance.

LEADERSHIP STYLES. The group's leader is another important influence on group behavior. Several studies have examined the effect of different types of adult leadership on groups of 11-year-old boys (Lewin, Lippitt, and White 1939; Lippitt and White 1943, 1958). The experimenters analyzed adult leadership into three types: authoritarian, laissez-faire, and democratic. Through observation, they then attempted to determine the effects of each kind of leadership. They found that authoritarian leaders created two opposite social atmospheres, one apathetic and the other aggressive. Some boys with such leaders were excessively tense and nervous in their relations with others in the group; others were aggressive toward the leader or toward other groups. The boys with authoritarian leaders also made fewer suggestions related to the work at hand in the test sessions. Laissez-faire leaders, like authoritarians, produced more responses of annoyance and more aggression toward other group members than did the democratic leaders. On the other hand, laissez-faire leaders, as well as democratic leaders, created a condition in which more boys sought each other's help and approval than did boys with authoritarian leaders. While the brief absences of a democratic leader caused negligible changes in work concentration, the absence of the authoritarian leader immediately resulted in a marked decline in work activity. The boys with democratic leaders also showed more personal variation in their reactions than did the boys with laissez-faire or authoritarian leaders. Finally, while the kind of leadership seemed to have no effect on personal friendliness, the development of a sense of group identity ("*we* painted; *we* hammered") seemed to be retarded in the authoritarian atmosphere.

While these experimental results seem to clearly point out differences, positive and negative, among the three leadership styles, it is not certain that the same results are inevitable in various groups with these sorts of leaders. In the first place, as Hartup (1970) pointed out, the experiment's authoritarian leaders were cool and remote; one cannot help but wonder how the boys would have reacted to a warm and affectionate authoritarian. Similarly, the experimental author-

itarians were in reality adults with a strong democratic bent. If they had actually been rigid authoritarians, their behavior, as well as their effect on the boys, might well have been significantly altered. As a final note, most of the experimental boys came from homes that were primarily democratic; this basic orientation also could have affected the experiment's results.

Another study assessed the effectiveness of two kinds of leadership in imposing controls on the comic-book reading of fifth- and sixth-grade children (Kipnis 1958). The two forms of leadership were participatory leadership—in which the children had a voice in determining what was to be done—and nonparticipatory leadership—the children were told what to do by means of a lecture. At the start of the experiment, the children with both participatory and nonparticipatory leadership were told that certain comic books were good and certain ones bad. One-third of the children in both leadership categories were given movie passes for obeying the message about the comic books. Another third of the children from both categories were threatened with the loss of

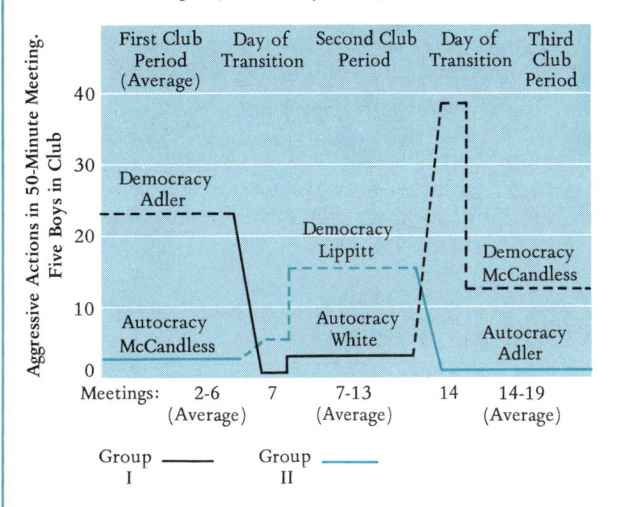

Figure 12.8 Group aggression undergoes marked changes as the group's leadership atmosphere varies from "apathetic autocracy" to democracy. (From K. Lewin, R. Lippitt, and R. White. Patterns of aggression in experimentally created social climates. *J. soc. Psychol.*, 1939, *10*, 271–299.)

their movie passes if they did not heed the message about the comic books. The last third, the control group, received neither reward nor punishment. All the children then rated their own preferences in comic books. The children in both groups who were punished and those who were rewarded obeyed the message about the comic books to about the same degree. However, both the punished and rewarded children had changed their minds about the comic books to a greater degree than the control children. A later assessment of preferences indicated that when participatory leadership was employed, both the rewarded and control groups changed their minds more significantly than when the lecture method was employed. In contrast, when children were punished for disobeying the messages, more attitudinal shifts resulted from the lecture than from participatory leadership. As this experiment reveals, a command's effectiveness in changing a child's behavior depends on whether the command ("if you read that comic book, you will lose your movie pass") is linked to the appropriate kind of leadership, limited in this experiment to participatory or nonparticipatory.

From these studies we can see that the impact of leadership is various and significant. As such, it is another major influence in the formation of peer groups, that vital testing ground on which the individual in middle childhood hones his cognitive and social powers.

From Peers to Cognitions

Although we must await further research to round out the particulars of the peer group's influence on the development of social conditions, it is evident that peer-group processes play a significant role. We can see that peer-group norms and leaders, as well as the child's desire for conformity and acceptance, bring tremendous pressure to bear upon him during these years. The child is forced to modify roles he has developed in the family. He is forced to acquire roles the peer group needs. The experience is bound to be disequilibrating and to force the child from earlier egocentricities. As he attempts to conceptualize his new social situation by more refined categorizations of others, by taking their perspectives more adequately, by understanding their feelings more validly, and by learning how to pursue their rules more effectively, so must his social cognition expand and become more insightful. What we have in this chapter are many mirrors of the changing dimensions of this process, as yet insufficiently detailed in research to make a meaningful whole. We also have a commentary on the ways in which the major theories interact with each other. Parents and teachers invite modeling for the use of cognitive processes through their rewards and power. Peers likewise invite modeling through their rewards and powers, their game rules and peer codes. Therefore, the child's own inherent cognitive processes are either facilitated or retarded by the role-taking requirements thus instigated. His cognitive attempts to put it all together, to equilibrate these influences, then become more directly predictive of his capacity for moral judgment and social cognition. The relevance of each theoretical approach depends on the point at which you enter this chain of causal influences.

Summary

The years from 8 to 12 are a time of great increase in the child's cognitive and social development. The relationship between these two aspects of personality has been illustrated in the developmental theories of Piaget.

Piaget characterizes the period from 7 to 12 as the concrete operational stage, in which the child can perform mental acts, or operations, in response to changes in his physical environment. Such cognitive development is brought about by maturation, experience, social transmission of knowledge, and equilibration, or harmony between the individual and his environment.

Two aspects of cognition which are particularly important for social development occur in this period. One is the shift from egocentrism to relativism, or from a subjective to an objective view of the world. The child is now more able to decenter, or detach his attention from one aspect of a situation and focus on several aspects simultaneously. The other aspect is the increase in categorization, the ability to subdivide experiences into many categories on the basis of their similarities and differences. Related to this is differentiation, in which the child learns to discriminate between types of experiences and to act differently according to the situation.

Social cognition is primarily the ability to make inferences about other people. This ability, based on an awareness of psychological states, increases markedly through middle childhood. This growth in social perception is attributed to increased social interaction, which develops the need to make inferences, and to the development of general cognitive skills, such as objective thinking. Children are able to decenter from the obvious, overt behaviors of other people to the less obvious, covert motivations that underlie them. The child becomes able to assume the role of other persons.

At this stage, too, the ability to perceive part-whole relationships leads to the ability to perceive the reciprocity of social relationships. Such reciprocity, plus the role-taking ability, underlie the child's growth in cognition which, in turn, underlies the development of morality. Piaget views morality as an outgrowth of the need for cooperation among peers. Cooperation depends on the decline of egocentrism and the ability to take on another's role.

As the child's capacity for social perception grows, so does his awareness of, and need for, belonging to a group. In middle childhood, the peer group becomes very important. It provides the child with the opportunity to learn how to relate to people of the same age, how to deal with hostility, how to lead and be led, and how to share.

Peer groups in our society tend to be homogeneous as to age, sex, race, and social class. Their norms are enforced through imitation and through social pressure playing on the children's tendency to conformity. Peer groups have different norms or structures and are shaped by such variables as competition, frustration, leadership, physical proximity, and personality. It is assumed that peer groups pressure the child toward role-taking, and that it is this pressure which helps to determine shifts in social cognition, including insight into others and moral judgment.

Case Studies

Barbara C.

A fifth-grader whose testing profile reveals a highly intelligent, highly creative little girl, Bobby shows a maturity that belies her age. As much at ease with adults as with her peers, this charming youngster exhibits unusual vitality in her many modes of expressing both personal freedom and self-control.

Socially, Bobby's confident manner and freedom of expression have brought her considerable recognition and popularity. Clearly a member of the social elite of her class, Bobby is often chosen for positions of leadership and responsibility. The genuine air of confidence that makes her stand out among her peers is even more impressive—and effective—in Bobby's comfortable relationships with adults. In fact, Bobby seems to treat everyone in her environment as if he or she were part of the warmth and security of Bobby's immediate family.

Bobby's emotional life evidences a freedom of expression unusual for child or adult. She is most perceptive of the feelings of others, and speaks unabashedly of her own. When describing an experience—either real or imaginary—Bobby energetically projects herself "inside it," apparently hoping to extract every possible ounce of understanding and empathy. In an experimental situation with stick figures, for example, Bobby easily identified with each of the "characters," seeming confident that her extra efforts would be rewarded by some new appreciation for her own experiences and those of others.

Almost any activity, in fact, is a good excuse for Bobby's "giving it all she has." With characteristic restlessness, she moves, talks, and thinks quickly and enthusiastically. She delights in expressing herself freely in all kinds of activity, and at every level of participation. Her enthusiasm for athletics, for instance, is equaled only by her considerable skill. At the conceptual level, on the other hand, she enjoys roaming through her own thoughts and associations, or exhausting the almost endless possibilities inherent in an experimental "creativity" situation.

One of the more obvious creative aspects of Bobby's personality is the sophisticated humor which she brings to interpersonal relations. While in some children this quality is more imitative than creative, Bobby's witty repartee seems the mature expression of a person sensitive to the wide range of motives and emotions in herself and in others. Consequently, Bobby's humor can also serve as a mature means of coping with her own effect, as well as with her awareness of effect in others. It is not surprising, then, that Bobby found several amusing ways to remind a team of psychological experimenters that she was most uneasy because of her suspicions about some unrevealed purpose to their "games."

In her daily activities—as well as in her psychological testing—Bobby shows her recognition of necessary limits on freedom of expression, however. She expends her considerable energies, for example, in ways that are socially appropriate: doing academic work during class time and enjoying social and physical activity during free time. In addition, her sense of discipline was displayed in her experimental descriptions of several stick figures engaged in "necessary" activities—like listening to camp counselors lecture about neatness. But at the same time, Bobby also showed an awareness that too much discipline, or too many boundaries, would indeed be harmful. She described, for instance, the hypothetical person who would make a perfectly straight path in the desert as "very sensible" and "very smart," but with a "blank personality" and "no imagination."

Unlike her desert traveler, Bobby will never have to choose between intelligence and imagination. Those native abilities, supported by the balance she seems to have struck between freedom and control, should make Bobby well prepared for the adolescent and adult years ahead (Wallach and Kogan 1966).

Jay M.

In contrast to Bobby, Jay, another fifth-grader, is a thin, frail-looking boy who avoids all sports and roughhousing. And, although Jay scores well on I.Q. tests, he is at the low end of the scale on creativity tests. Not surprisingly, his life seems to center around academic success—a focus quite acceptable to his aloof, but demanding, parents. Perhaps as a consequence of his family's emotional distance, Jay's academic strivings assume much more than their usual importance. For him, scholastic success means attention—and, therefore, some degree of adult acceptance—both at home and in school.

In the classroom, Jay is so eager for attention that he will speak up on any topic, whether or not his thoughts are relevant to the discussion. His teachers note that, although he grabs every chance to commandeer the floor with his rapid-fire speech, his thinking often reflects the "most superficial lines of associative connection."

Likewise, a team of psychological investigators noticed that Jay seemed overly anxious to please them. Never satisfied with the experimenters' disclaimers of any "testing" motive to their game-room atmosphere, Jay constantly inquired about whether he was "doing well," and he was anxiously alert for any cues to the experimenters' expectations, or to how he stood by their unrevealed criteria.

A look at Jay's academic record shows that his achievement problems evolved over a period of several years. His earliest teachers were unanimously enthusiastic about his intelligent interest in a wide variety of subjects, his articulateness, and his easygoing manner. The passing years, however, have witnessed Jay's increasing dependence on a "mechanical use of factual knowledge" instead of exercising his native intelligence; his reliance on a "superficial acquaintance" with many subjects instead of pursuing any in depth; and a degeneration of his linguistic facility into compulsive, often irrelevant, talking. Whatever vestiges remain of the "easygoing" first-grader now serve to cover for a frightened, lonely fifth-grader.

At home, Jay is painfully aware of an intense sibling rivalry for his parents' attention. Because his parents are so ambitious for their son, academic success has always been the surest way to gain their attention. Now, however, Jay's school productivity is falling, and he finds himself caught in a vicious circle of fear, failure, and rejection. If, perhaps, Jay began this period of academic laxity with the idea that unprecedented scholastic problems would trigger some positive protective reaction from his parents, his hopes were destined only for frustration: his "concerned" family simply hired a private tutor to help Jay through his exams.

No matter what the dynamics of Jay's behavior, however, it is undeniably clear that this little boy is caught in the unfortunate position of having his academic achievement and his emotional security mutually interdependent (Wallach and Kogan 1966).

References

Asch, S. *Social psychology.* Englewood Cliffs, N.J.: Prentice-Hall, 1952.

Baker, H. V. *Children's contributions in elementary school general discussions.* Child Develpm. Monogr. No. 29. New York: Teachers College, Columbia Univer., 1942.

Bandura, A., and McDonald, F. J. Influence of social reinforcement and the behavior of models in shaping children's moral judgment. *J. abnorm. soc. Psychol.,* 1963, 67(3), 274–281.

Berenda, R. W. *The influence of the group on the judgments of children.* New York: King's Crown Press, 1950.

Bonney, M. E. The constancy of sociometric scores and their relationships to teacher judgment of social success and to personality self-ratings. *Sociometry,* 1943, 6, 409–424.

Bonney, M. E. Relationships between social success, family size, socioeconomic home background and intelligence among school children in grades III to IV. *Sociometry,* 1944, 7, 26–39.

Campbell, J. D. Peer relations in childhood. In M. L. Hoffman and L. W. Hoffman (Eds.), *Review of child development research.* Vol. I. New York: Russell Sage Foundation, 1964.

Cannon, K. L. The relationship of social acceptance to socioeconomic status and residence among high school students. *Rur. Sociol.,* 1957, 22, 142–148.

Cooper, R. G., and Flavell, J. H. Cognitive correlates of children's role-taking behavior. *Merrill-Palmer Quart.,* in press.

Crane, A. R. Preadolescent gangs: A topological interpretation. *J. genet. Psychol.,* 1952, 81, 113–124.

Dimitrovsky, L. The ability to identify emotional meaning of vocal expressions at successive age levels. In J. R. Davitz (Ed.), *The communication of emotional meaning.* New York: McGraw-Hill, 1964.

Durkin, D. Children's concepts of justice: A comparison with the Piaget data. *Child Develpm.,* 1959, 30, 59–67.

Einhorn, J. A test of Piaget's theory of moral judgement. *Can. J. Behavioral Science,* 1971, 3, 102–113.

Elkins, D. Some factors related to the choice status of ninety eighth-grade children in a school society. *Genet. psychol. Monogr.,* 1958, 58, 207–272.

Feffer, M. A developmental analysis of interpersonal behavior. *Psychol. Rev.,* 1970, *77*(3), 197–214.

Flapan, D. *Children's understanding of social interaction.* New York: Teachers College Press, Columbia Univer., 1968.

Flavell, J. The development of inferences about others. Paper presented at Interdisciplinary Conference on Our Knowledge of Persons, State Univer. of New York, Binghamton, December 1971.

Flavell, J., Botkin, P., Fry, C., Wright, J., and Jarvis, P. E. *The development of role-taking and communication skills in children.* New York: Wiley, 1968.

Gates, G. S. An experimental study of the growth of social perception, *J. educ. Psychol.,* 1923, *14,* 449–462.

Gates, G. S. A preliminary study of a test for social perception. *J. educ. Psychol.,* 1925, *16,* 452–457.

Goldstein, J. H., and McGhee, P. E. *The psychology of humor.* New York: Academic Press, 1972.

Goodnow, J., and Bethon, G. Piaget's tasks: The effects of schooling and intelligence. *Child Develpm.,* 1966, *37,* 573–582.

Grossman, B., and Wrighter, J. The relationship between selection-rejection and intelligence, social status, and personality among sixth-grade children. *Sociometry,* 1948, *11,* 346–355.

Haines, A. C. Children's perception of membership roles in problem-solving groups: An exploratory study of interaction process in a third grade. Unpublished doctoral dissertation, Univer. of Illinois, 1952.

Hamsher, J. H. Children's understanding of emotions and interpersonal causality. *Proc. Ann. Conv. Am. Psychol. Assoc.,* 1971, *6*(Part 1), 159–160.

Hartup, W. W. Peer interaction and social organization. In P. H. Mussen (Ed.), *Carmichael's manual of child psychology.* Vol. II. (3rd ed.) New York: Wiley, 1970.

Hoffman, M. L. Moral development. In P. H. Mussen (Ed.), *Carmichael's manual of child psychology.* Vol. II. (3rd ed.) New York: Wiley, 1970.

Huttenlocher, J., and Presson, C. Mental rotation and the perspective problem. *Cognitive Psychol.,* 1973, *4*(2).

Kagan, J., and Kogan, N. Individual variation in cognitive processes. In P. H. Mussen (Ed.), *Carmichael's manual of child psychology.* Vol. I. (3rd ed.) New York: Wiley, 1970.

Keasey, C. B. Social participation as a factor in the moral development of preadolescents. *Develpm. Psychol.,* 1971, *5*(2), 216–220.

Kipnis, D. The effects of leadership style and leadership power upon the inducement of an attitude change. *J. abnorm. soc. Psychol.,* 1958, *57,* 173–180.

Kohlberg, L. The development of modes of moral thinking and choice in the years 10–16. Unpublished doctoral dissertation, Univer. of Chicago, 1958.

Kohlberg, L. The development of children's orientations toward a moral order: 1. Sequence in the development of moral thought. *Vita Humana,* 1963, *6,* 11–33.

Kohlberg, L. Stage and sequence: The cognitive-developmental approach to socialization. In D. Goslin (Ed.), *Handbook of socialization: Theory and research.* Chicago: Rand McNally, 1969. (a)

Kohlberg, L. *Stage in the development of moral thought and action.* N.Y.: Holt, Rinehart & Winston, 1969. (b)

Lambert, W. E., and Taguchi, Y. Ethnic cleavages among young children. *J. abnorm. soc. Psychol.,* 1956, *53,* 380–382.

Laurendeau, M., and Pinard, A. *Development of the concept of space in the child.* New York: International Universities Press, 1970.

Lee, L. C. The concomitant development of cognitive and moral modes of thought: A test of selected deductions from Piaget's theory. *Genet. Psychol. Monogr.,* 1971, *83,* 13–146.

LeFurgy, W. G., and Woloshin, G. W. Immediate and long-term effects of experimentally induced social influence in the modification of adolescents' moral judgments. *J. abnorm. soc. Psychol.,* 1969, *12,* 104–110.

Lerner, E. *Constraint areas and moral judgment of children.* Menasha, Wisc.: Banta, 1937.

Lewin, K., Lippitt, R., and White, R. Patterns of aggression in experimentally created social climates. *J. soc. Psychol.,* 1939, *10,* 271–299.

Lippitt, R., and White, R. K. The "social climate" of children's groups. In R. G. Barker, J. S. Kounin, and H. F. Wright (Eds.), *Child behavior and development.* New York: McGraw-Hill, 1943.

Lippitt, R., and White, R. K. An experimental study of leadership and group life. In E. E. Maccoby, T. M. Newcomb, and E. L. Hartley (Eds.), *Readings in social psychology.* New York: Holt, Rinehart & Winston, 1958.

Lott, A. J., and Lott, B. E. Group cohesiveness and individual learning. *J. educ. Psychol.,* 1966, *57,* 61–73.

Lovell, K. *The growth of basic mathematical and scientific concepts in children.* London: Univer. of London Press, 1961.

Masangkay, Z., McCloskey, K., Sims-Knight, J., and Flavell, J. The early development of inferences about the visual percepts of others. (In progress.)

Medinnus, G. R. Immanent justice in children: A review of the literature and additional data. *J. genet. Psychol.,* 1959, *94,* 253.

Merei, F. Group leadership and institutionalization. *Human Relat.,* 1949, *2,* 23–39.

Miller, N., and Dollard, J. *Social learning and imitation.* New Haven: Yale Univer. Press, 1941.

Opie, I., and Opie, P. *The lore and language of schoolchildren.* London: Oxford Univer. Press, 1959.

Piaget, J. *Judgment and reasoning in the child.* Trans. by M. Warden. New York: Harcourt Brace Jovanovich, 1926.

Piaget, J. *The language and thought of the child.* Trans. by M. Gabain. London: Routledge & Kegan Paul, 1926.

Piaget, J. *Child's conception of the world.* Trans. by J. Tomlinson and A. Tomlinson. New York: Harcourt Brace Jovanovich, 1929.

Piaget, J. *The moral judgment of the child.* Trans. by M. Gabain. New York: Harcourt Brace Jovanovich, 1932.

Piaget, J. *The psychology of intelligence.* Trans. by M. Percy and D. E. Berlyne. London: Routledge & Kegan Paul, 1950.

Piaget, J. *The child's conception of number.* Trans. by C. Gattegno and F. M. Hodgson. London: Routledge & Kegan Paul, 1952.

Piaget, J. *The early growth of logic in the child.* Trans. by E. Lunzer and D. Papert. London: Routledge & Kegan Paul, 1964.

Piaget, J. Response to Brian Sutton-Smith. *Psychol. Rev.*, 1966, 73(1), 111–112.

Piaget, J., and Inhelder, B. *The child's conception of space.* London: Routledge & Kegan Paul, 1956.

Radke, M. J., and Trager, H. G. Children's perception of the social roles of Negroes and whites. *J. Psychol.*, 1950, 29, 3–33.

Radke, M., Sutherland, J., and Rosenberg, P. Racial attitudes of children. *Sociometry*, 1950, 13, 154–171.

Roberts, J. M., and Sutton-Smith, B. Child training and game involvement. *Ethnology*, 1962, 1(2), 166–185.

Rothman, G. R. An experimental analysis of the relationship between level of moral judgment and behavioral choice. Doctoral dissertation, Columbia Univer., 1971.

Scarlett, H., Press, A., and Crockett, W. Children's descriptions of peers: A Wernerian developmental analysis. *Child Develpm.*, 1971, 42, 439–453.

Schallenberger, M. E. A study of children's rights, as seen by themselves. *Ped. Sem.*, 1894, 3, 87–96.

Selman, R. The importance of reciprocal role-taking for the development of conventional moral thought. In L. Kohlberg and E. Turiel (Eds.), *Recent research in moral development.* New York: Holt, Rinehart & Winston, in press.

Sherif, M., and Sherif, C. W. *Groups in harmony and tension.* New York: Harper, 1953.

Sherif, M., and Sherif, C. W. *Reference groups.* New York: Harper & Row, 1964.

Sherif, M., Harvey, O. J., White, B. J., Hood, W. R., and Sherif, C. W. *Intergroup conflict and cooperation: The Robbers Cave experiment.* Norman: Univer. of Oklahoma Press, 1961.

Smith, A. J. A developmental study of group processes. *J. genet. Psychol.*, 1960, 97, 29–30.

Stendler, C. B., Damrin, D., and Haines, A. C. Studies in cooperation and competition: I. The effects of working for group and individual rewards on the social climate of children's groups. *J. genet. Psychol.*, 1951, 79, 173–198.

Sutton-Smith, B. The psychology of games. *National Educ.*, 1955, 37(Part 1), 228–299.

Sutton-Smith, B. A cognitive approach to children's riddles. Paper presented at conference of the American Anthropological Association, New York, November 1971. (a)

Sutton-Smith, B. Plays, games and controls. In J. P. Scott and S. F. Scott (Eds.), *Social control and social change.* Chicago: Univer. of Chicago Press, 1971. (b)

Sutton-Smith, B., and Roberts, J. M. Rubrics of competitive behavior. *J. genet. Psychol.*, 1964, 105, 13–37.

Sutton-Smith, B., and Rosenberg, E. Sixty years of historical change in the game preferences of American children. *J. Amer. Folklore*, 1961, 74, 17–46.

Wallach, M. A., and Kogan, N. *Modes of thinking in young children.* New York: Holt, Rinehart & Winston, 1966. Pp. 261–262; 272–273.

Werner, H. The concept of development from a comparative and organismic point of view. In D. B. Harris (Ed.), *The concept of development.* Minneapolis: Univer. of Minnesota Press, 1957.

Werner, H. *Comparative psychology of mental development.* New York: Wiley, Science Editions, 1961.

Whiteman, M. Children's conceptions of psychological causality. *Child Develpm.*, 1967, 38(1), 143–155.

13 Personality and Social Development

SIGMUND FREUD, whose revolutionary ideas still form the basis of much of contemporary personality theory, called the period from 8 to 12 years the "latent period" (1949). He maintained that the powerful instinctual drives which were so critical during early childhood and adolescence lay dormant during middle childhood, and, therefore, that no important changes in personality could occur during this period.

It is not hard to understand why Freud arrived at such a conclusion. His theories of personality tended to emphasize the importance of the instincts—their expression or repression, and the consequences of these for the total psyche. A period of life during which the effects of the instincts are not clearly visible held relatively little interest or significance for Freud.

While the period of middle childhood is characterized by neither the imaginative play and fantasy behavior of preschool years nor the sexual preoccupation of adolescence, children of this age seem particularly concerned with the conscious mastery of the realities of the world around them. In contrast to Freud, other psychologists, more concerned with behavior, feel that this concern with mastering reality gives the period of middle childhood great importance in the development of the adult personality. It is during this period of development that the child seems to be constructing systems of rules about how one deals with the physical and social environment. How ought one to act in groups of people, particularly peers? What is moral and what is not moral? How much autonomy and independence ought one to have from one's elders? How does one deal with feelings of anxiety, frustration, and conflict? All these are tasks which the child masters during this period.

In this chapter, we shall examine the child's development in the mastery of his ever-expanding social world, as well as consider the influence of the family, the school, and the peer group on the child's development.

Personality Themes of the Middle Years

Industry versus Inferiority

Erik Erikson has called the middle childhood period *industry versus inferiority*. As we have seen in earlier chapters, Erikson regards each period of development as essentially the resolution of a conflict or "crisis" between two differing feelings or desires. It is the child's conflict between the pleasurable feelings of industry and the unpleasurable feelings of inferiority that Erikson sees as profoundly affecting the child's psychosocial development during this period.

At this stage, the child becomes more independent of his family and is able to engage in productive activities as well as the imaginative play of the younger child. During this period, the child learns mastery of social skills and rules (just as he learns to master words and technical skills). It is this characteristic of the child (mastery of skills) that Erikson labels *industry*. He sees inferiority as the competing danger, for while the child is mastering the realities of his physical and social environment, he may also be plagued by feelings of mediocrity or inadequacy. His friends may be better able to do certain things than he is, or they may be more adept at the social skills and more popular within the peer group than he is. Thus, the conflict between feelings of industry on the one hand, and inferiority on the other, affect the way he will behave.

Ciaccio (1971) submitted Erikson's theory to systematic analysis. In his study, children were selected from three age groups, 5-, 8-, and 11-year-olds. According to Erikson, children at each of these ages can be expected to mainly experience distinctive psychosocial stages. The 5-year-olds should be primarily concerned with issues of autonomy versus shame and doubt (Stage II); the 8-year-olds should be concerned with initiative versus guilt (Stage III); and the 11-year-olds should be concerned with industry versus inferiority (Stage IV). According to Erikson, children in one stage should not be expected to be overly concerned with issues from another stage. A finding that a significant number of older children were still concerned with issues which should have been, for the most part, resolved at an earlier age would be a contradiction of Erikson's developmental theory.

In Ciaccio's study, all the children were shown

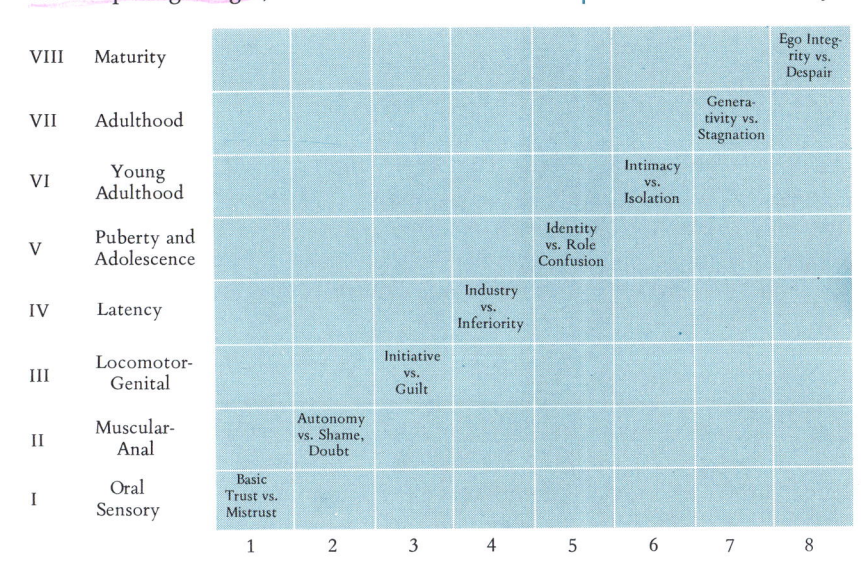

Figure 13.1 Erikson's psychosocial stages of development. (From E. Erikson. *Childhood and society*. New York: W. W. Norton & Co., Inc., 1963.)

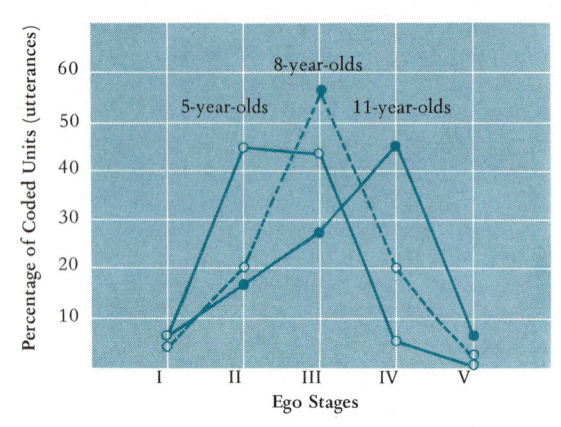

Figure 13.2 Frequency distribution of utterances from 5-, 8-, and 11-year-olds coded for pertinence to Erikson's various ego stages, showing age and stage-appropriate concern. (From N. V. Ciaccio. A test of Erikson's theory of ego epigenesis. *Develpm. Psychol.*, 1971, 4(3), 306–311.)

the same pictures and asked to make up a story about them. Their responses were coded to indicate whether the child was in Stage II, III, or IV. The results were interpreted to be a confirmation of Erikson's theory. The 5-year-olds seemed most concerned with issues of Stages II and III; the 8-year-olds seemed most concerned with Stage III questions; and the 11-year-olds seemed most concerned with Stage IV issues.

Other writers might describe the theme of industry versus inferiority in different ways, as, for example, the need for achievement in conflict with the fear of failure. But all would probably agree that some such forms of mastery are very important in this age group.

Stability of Personality Traits

While children undergo many changes between the ages of 8 and 12, there are some characteristics that are essentially stable. One example of a relatively stable characteristic is I.Q. By knowing a child's I.Q. at age 6 or 7, we have a fairly good idea what the same child's I.Q. will be when he is 21.

A number of personality characteristics have likewise been found to be stable and to undergo relatively little change during middle childhood and adulthood. For example, a study by Stott (1957) rated nursery school children on a scale which ranged from very bossy to highly submissive to other children. The children were followed for 12 years subsequent to the first rating, and the author concluded that consistency in behavior patterns occurred far more frequently than change. When changes did occur, they seemed for the most part to be temporary.

Another observational study rated children in seven categories (for example, social participation, efforts to affiliate with others in friendly and sharing ways). Over a two-year period, it was found that the frequency of each type of behavior increased in each child, but each child's *pattern* of responding with respect to the patterns of other children in the class remained stable (Martin 1964). It seems that although children in general acquire new social skills and new self-perceptions as they develop through middle childhood, many of the personality characteristics that determine what skills they develop remain essentially stable. Furthermore, the studies indicated that many of these personality characteristics already show a high degree of predictability by about kindergarten age.

Not only are different personality types clearly discernible by the time children have reached middle childhood, but also their concerns and interests seem to be fairly universal and convey a good deal of information about what children of this age are like. In one study, children expressed a great deal of interest in physical characteristics, clothing, home and family, recreation, and school. Interests in these matters subsequently declined with age. On the other hand, children in the early years expressed less interest in intellectual abilities, personality and character, and social relationships than interviewees who were older. These interests subsequently increased with age (Jersild). The choices of interests expressed in middle childhood can be viewed as reflecting both the concrete level of cognitive development described in Chapter 12 and the concern with industry typical of this period (Ciaccio 1971).

Awareness of Self and Others

One other key development in the period of middle childhood is the emergence of self-

Figure 13.3 During the years of 8 to 12, the child is involved more in productive activities, as well as in the imaginative play of the earlier years. His choice of activities reflects a concern with industry and an interest in mastering the realities of the world. (Charles Harbutt —Magnum; St. Louis Post Dispatch—Black Star)

awareness and the awareness of personality characteristics in others. The child begins to construct notions about "what he is like inside," and, by taking the role of others, he begins to formulate impressions of what they are like "inside" as well. He becomes conscious of his emotions—of being happy or sad, brave or frightened—and he becomes much more attuned to the emotions of others in social situations.

As a result of his increased awareness of personality traits, the child begins to form a stable picture of his own personality—for example, "I am a timid person," or "He is a kind person." And it is during the years 8 through 12 that the child becomes increasingly conscious of any problems that he may have—of his fears, anxieties, or other symptoms of emotional difficulty. Previous to this time, although the child may manifest his difficulties in his overt behavior, he is generally not aware of them on the conscious level. Some writers have spoken of children at this age having an "I am me" experience, a new self-consciousness of self.

Another important consequence of the increase in self-awareness and in awareness of others is the growth of conscious choice in the area of friendship. The child becomes aware of who is similar to him and who is different, of what characteristics he likes in friends, and what traits of his own will win him acceptance or disapproval.

As it will become evident in this chapter, these characteristics of middle childhood—the conflict between industry and inferiority, the achievement of relative stability of personality traits, and the increased awareness of self and others—all affect the child's growth in the various areas of personal and social development.

Personality Variables of the Middle Years

Self-esteem

Self-esteem, a person's judgment about his own capabilities, talents, and powers, influences much of an individual's behavior—what tasks he is willing to try, how he impresses other people, and what kinds of social relationships he will develop, for example. Coopersmith (1967) has examined this characteristic in children—how it is defined and what factors in the child's environment lead to high and low self-esteem.

Coopersmith describes children with high self-esteem as having a great deal of confidence in their own abilities and judgments. This confidence leads to a certainty in action and a high degree of initiative and assertive behavior in children. They participate actively in group discussions and projects, have little difficulty forming friendships, and express themselves freely even at the risk of attracting negative criticism. Because they are not overly self-conscious, they are able to take leadership and present new positions without worrying about approval. Not being preoccupied with themselves, they can devote more energies to external issues and other people.

The child with low self-esteem presents a different picture. Because he has little confidence in himself, he is wary of expressing his own ideas for fear of being criticized. In groups of children, he is usually very quiet and unlikely to participate for fear of attracting attention, and thus the possibility of negative opinions, toward himself. He is preoccupied with his own problems, and consequently has little time for those of other people. Thus, he does not interact very well with other children and has a hard time forming friendships.

Of course, most people fall between these two poles of self-esteem; but by studying children of these extreme types—very high self-esteem and very low self-esteem—Coopersmith was able to uncover some of the determinants of this trait.

DETERMINANTS OF SELF-ESTEEM. Perhaps the most important determinants of self-esteem are the attitudes and actions of the parents in rearing the child. Coopersmith found that parents of high self-esteem children manifested characteristics which indicated that they themselves were high in self-esteem. They interacted easily with their children and were consistent in their definitions of areas of authority. While they expected a great deal from their children, they were nevertheless encouraging and supportive. These parents expressed respect for their children and were willing to extend themselves into their children's lives and become participants along with them.

In contrast, mothers of children who scored low on measures of self-esteem avoided interaction with their children and participation in their activities. Rather than being supportive of their children, these mothers belittled them and what they did.

While parents of children with high self-esteem were not overly permissive, but always seemed to mete out punishment in a fair and rational manner, the children who were low in self-esteem were treated harshly and inconsistently by their parents. These parents vacillated between alternately expressing little concern over what their children did, or punishing them far in excess of the gravity of their offense, in a seemingly arbitrary fashion.

Sex-Role Development

One of the most fruitful approaches to the study of sex roles is the cognitive-developmental approach, most clearly articulated by Lawrence Kohlberg (1966). Kohlberg assumed that sex role can be conceptualized as a set of rules of behavior and can, therefore, be studied in the same way that the development of other sets of rules is studied in children. As the child matures, along with the other kinds of informal social rules he learns, he also learns a set of rules that apply to appropriate behavior for boys and girls. By middle childhood, children seem to be fairly set in their application of these rules.

According to Kohlberg, it is not until the child is about 6 years old, when, in Piagetian terms, he has moved into the stage of concrete operations, that he recognizes that a girl is a girl no matter what kind of clothes she wears. Just as the concrete operational child is able to judge that a quantity of water is the same no matter what shape container it is in, so he understands that a person remains the same sex no matter what he or she chooses to wear or do (Kohlberg 1966).

Prior to this, in the child of 2 to 4, sex identity is not conceived of as a constant, systematic thing. In other words, a boy knows that he is a boy only because his parents have told him so. At age 3, he may successfully label himself as a boy, but may at the same time be baffled as to whether his brother and his sister are boys as well. By the age of 4, few children have mastered the immutability of sex identity. In one study, a group of 4-year-olds claimed that a pictured girl could become a boy if she wanted to, simply by changing her clothes and her hairstyle. This suggests that they conceive of sex as something arbitrary which concerns only certain external attributes such as hair length (Kohlberg 1966). It is interesting, too, that even many 6-year-olds who have a fairly clear conception of sex identity remain at a superficial level in their concept of physical attributes. One study showed that even at 6 years, 31 percent of the children could not make correct identification of the gender of the genital region of a doll (Katcher 1955).

Along with a stable gender identity at 6 years, the child also shows a fairly well developed system of rules of behavior for the sexes. Studies have consistently shown boys to manifest more aggression than girls (Bandura 1962; Maccoby and Wilson 1957). Although a majority of the studies have found girls to be much more dependent, passive, and conforming than boys (Crutchfield 1955; Kagan and Moss 1962; Sears, Maccoby, and Levin 1957), Maccoby has recently challenged this material as resulting largely from sex stereotypes. Boys are more aggressive, she agrees, but not more active than girls (Maccoby 1971).

The data suggest that once a child has reached the stage of cognitive development where he can make stable categorical judgments, he is able to differentiate a system of rules, learned from his environment, with which he can decide which behaviors are appropriate and which are not. However, even before this age, observers have noted consistent sex differences among children, the origin of which is unclear. The child may have acquired these behaviors either through imitation of, or instruction from his parents; but, on the other hand, he may also have some constitutional tendency to behave in certain ways. In any case, while such consistencies do exist, it is not until middle childhood that the child becomes conscious of these social rules, as he does of other aspects of personality and social behavior.

Morality

Moral development encompasses cognitive and affective dimensions. In reality, these dimensions occur together and are inseparable; however, for purposes of analysis, they are generally separated. The previous chapter dealt with the

Table 13.1   Age Distribution of the Number of Subjects Making Genital Errors

Age	No Genital Errors N	No Genital Errors %	Man's Genital N	Man's Genital %	Woman's Genital N	Woman's Genital %	Boy's Genital N	Boy's Genital %	Girl's Genital N	Girl's Genital %	Total* N
3	10	12.0	36	43.4	40	48.2	31	35.3	21	25.4	83
4	32	31.4	39	38.2	37	36.3	36	35.3	27	26.5	102
5	23	51.1	13	28.9	13	28.9	12	26.7	7	15.6	45
6	26	71.2	8	22.2	7	19.4	2	5.6	1	2.8	36
Total:	91	34.2	96	36.1	97	36.5	81	34.4	56	21.1	266

*This column gives the number of subjects tested at each age.
Source: A. Katcher. The discrimination of sex differences by young children. *J. genet. Psychol.*, 1955, 87, 131–143.

cognitive aspect of moral development; here we shall discuss the affective aspect.

Moral development may be viewed from three different philosophic positions. In oversimplified terms, they are that of "innate purity," "original sin," and *tabula rasa*. The "innate purity" position contends that the child arrives in the world as a morally pure being, and it is society which corrupts him. In order to maximize moral behavior, therefore, it is necessary to minimize the corrupting influence of society. The "original sin" position assumes the opposite of the "innate purity" position. The child is born with evil instincts and impulses, and it is the job of society, whose rules represent the right moral values, to teach the child to keep these impulses under control and act morally. The *tabula rasa* ("blank slate" in Latin) view sees the child as being innately neither good nor bad, but as acquiring these moral values by society's teachings (Hoffman 1970).

These three philosophical views have given rise to distinct positions within the psychological investigations of moral development. They also represent real (although not always conscious) positions taken by parents in the rearing of their children. The "original sin" position leads to less love-oriented punishment on the part of the parent who believes that the child's natural impulses are evil and must be controlled. The "innate purity" position, which claims that the child is innately good, would probably lead to the most love-oriented behavior on the part of the parent. The parent who subscribed to a *tabula rasa* philosophy would probably fall somewhere in the middle, since he would find it necessary to extinguish bad behaviors learned from the environment, yet he would not attribute them to innate evil in the child.

The presence of warmth and love in the parent is perhaps the most important determinant of the development of conscience (Becker 1964). This love is translated into conscience in the child through two mechanisms. The first is the mechanism of identification with the parent, which has been discussed in Chapter 9. The loving parent, being more rewarding, is more likely to be imitated and identified with than the severe, punishing parent.

The second mechanism is the fear of losing the parent's love. The withdrawal of love is as severe a punishment as physical violence and normally more effective (Allinsmith 1960; Becker 1964). It has been reported that children who have well-internalized standards of morality were not subjected to physical punishment for misbehavior, but were punished in more love-oriented ways — for example, by being told, "what you did hurt me very much" (Hoffman and Saltzstein 1960). It seems necessary to assume that parent–child relationships of these sorts facilitate or retard the process of development through the moral levels which we described earlier. Probably a person's moral level is an outcome both of the way in which parent relationships facilitate subsequent learning from role-taking experience and the actual confrontation of that experience.

Competitiveness

As with other personality traits in this period, feelings of competitiveness take on a more stable expression, differing, of course, from one person to another. One child may attempt to monopolize whatever group activity he participates in, whereas another may consistently refrain from becoming involved in the struggle for ascendance.

The excitement of competing may motivate the child toward new discoveries and achievements, and may save him from giving up on a boring task which he is assigned in school. In addition, a sense of competition gives the child an opportunity to compare his own abilities with those of others and understand them better. The child's ability to continue competitively in the face of potential failure is one measure of the success of "industry" in the industry-versus-inferiority conflict. However, competition is not without its disadvantages as well. A child with wavering self-esteem may be severely hurt when put into a competitive situation. Such a child may become anxious and worried in highly competitive situations. Furthermore, competition may foster in the child a tendency to rejoice in the defeat of his peers.

Unfortunately, many school settings stress competition as a means of keeping the child involved in activities, rather than making the activities themselves more interesting in order to sustain the child's attention. Although this approach may motivate some children to greater achievement in areas in which they might otherwise have lost interest, it nevertheless teaches children that speed and quantity and winning are values in themselves. Moreover, it makes the weaker children even more insecure than they would be otherwise.

Leadership

Another personality trait that emerges more fully at this age is leadership among peers.

One study sampled children from all over the United States and classified them as either leaders or nonleaders according to teachers' reports of how often they were chosen to be leaders by their peers (Harrison, Rawls, and Rawls 1971). Additional information was then obtained about the particular characteristics of these children which it was thought might correlate with leadership.

The results showed that there were indeed several characteristics clearly associated with leadership. Leaders were significantly healthier than nonleaders, and their teachers reported that they displayed more physical activity and aggression. While these children required more disciplining in class than did nonleaders, they nevertheless were rated highly by their teachers on intellectual ability and academic achievement. In addition, the leaders scored significantly higher on various standard intelligence measures. Sex made no difference in leadership qualities. Finally, teachers rated leaders as being better adjusted emotionally than nonleaders.

Of course, not every child who was classified as a leader possessed all of the above-mentioned characteristics; however, leaders as a *group* displayed this pattern. Any child who was classified as a leader, therefore, could be counted upon to have at least one of these characteristics.

Peers: Acceptance and Friendship

The years 8 through 12 are a time of increasing social interaction among peers. The child becomes subject to the pleasures of friendship, the pain of exclusion, and the experience of innumerable social relationships. These new social relationships and their development may be presumed to constitute another important basis for social behavior throughout life.

Stability of Peer-Peer Relationships

Increased stability of friendship patterns among children is characteristic of peer-peer relationships in middle childhood. As children become more stable in their individual personal characteristics during this period, their choice of friends assumes a more distinctive and more stable character.

Figure 13.4 The peer group takes on increasing importance for the 8- to 12-year-old. The child learns the rules of group life and establishes his relationship to other group members. (Charles Harbutt — Magnum)

The stability of relationships between children in this period has been extensively investigated through the use of a sociometric technique. This technique involves asking every child in a group the same question—such as, whom he would like to have for a friend or a partner on a particular project. The results are expressed in what is known as a sociogram, a table indicating which children are chosen or rejected by each individual. Such tables yield a great deal of information about such questions as who is most and least popular; who is chosen but does not reciprocate; whether or not children tend to prefer other children from the same ethnic group or socioeconomic status; and whether children prefer or avoid children from the same or opposite sex.

A number of studies have shown a high degree of stability in childhood friendships and peer preferences. These studies have concluded: (1) that stability is related to the age of the peer group, older groups being more stable; (2) that stability is related to the degree of acquaintance, newly formed groups being less stable; and (3) that there is considerable stability of children's acceptance of others across groups (Witryol and Thompson 1953). However, in a study in which 400 sixth-grade children were tested twice, with an intervening interval of a few weeks, the results indicated that friendships were quite unstable. Sixty percent of the children rejected at least one of their earlier choices for best friend (Austin and Thompson 1948). Nevertheless, the bulk of the studies seem to suggest that friendships are relatively more stable with increasing age.

Correlates of Peer Acceptance and Rejection

Sociometric studies have yielded fairly consistent findings about which traits of children lead to peer acceptance and popularity, and which traits lead to peer rejection. While no single trait is a determining factor, in general, those traits which indicate a mastery of social reality as well as a mastery of physical and intellectual skills tend to be associated with acceptance by peers. By contrast, children who do not show signs of industry, but rather give evidence of inferiority and anxiety, tend to be rejected by peers.

FRIENDLINESS. Friendliness or sociability, a trait which indicates self-confidence and mastery of social reality, seems generally to promote acceptance by peers. The child who is outgoing and socially sensitive (Bonney 1944; Bonney and Powell 1953), who expresses kindness (Smith 1950), and who is willing to both give and receive friendly overtures from others (Campbell and Yarrow 1961) is usually well accepted in his peer group. It is important to note, however, that this result is not reversible; that is, a child who is not sociable will not necessarily be rejected by his peers (Hartup, Glazer, and Charlesworth 1967).

Table 13.2 Correlations between Types of Aggression and Popularity among White Lower-class Boys, Ages 10–13

	School A Grade 5 (N=19)	School B Grade 5 (N=10)	School B Grade 6 (N=16)	School C Grade 5 (N=16)	School C Grade 6 (N=13)	Over-all Mean for All Classes (N=74)
Provoked physical aggression vs. popularity	+.47*	+.42	+.57*	+.10	−.02	+.31
Outburst aggression vs. popularity	−.43*	+.07	+.12	−.60**	−.23	−.21
Unprovoked physical aggression vs. popularity	−.45*	−.22	+.05	−.62**	−.57*	−.36
Verbal aggression vs. popularity	−.48*	−.34	−.02	−.65**	−.75**	−.45
Indirect aggression vs. popularity	−.55**	−.56*	−.81**	−.68**	−.86**	−.69
Over-all mean for all aggression categories	−.29	−.13	−.02	−.49	−.49	−.28

*$P < .05$.
**$P < .01$.

Source: G. S. Lesser. The relationships between various forms of aggression and popularity among lower-class children. *J. educ. Psychol.*, 1959, 50, 20–25.

Table 13.3 Percentage of Children Ranking in Top Third on Specified Dimensions of Observed Behavior, by Effectiveness Rating*

Effectiveness Rating	Friendly, Sociable I**	Friendly, Sociable R	Aggressive, Disruptive I	Aggressive, Disruptive R	Assertive, Influencing I	Assertive, Influencing R	Submissive, Dependent I	Submissive, Dependent R	(n)
Very high	56	69	44	12	25	31	38	50	(16)
Moderately high	39	39	42	28	36	34	36	38	(36)
Average	36	24	32	41	40	36	34	30	(53)
Moderately low	24	24	24	40	16	24	16	28	(25)
Very low	24	36	36	40	32	32	28	36	(25)
Tau	+.14	+.15	+.11	−.03	+.04	+.07	+.03	+.13	..
p	.01	.01	.04	.56	.44	.22	.54	.01	..

*Recorded in each entry of the table is the percentage of children in each status group ranking among the top third on the given dimension of behavior.
**I and R refer to *initiated* and *received* behavior, respectively.
Source: J. D. Campbell and M. R. Yarrow. Perceptual and behavioral correlates of social effectiveness. *Sociometry*, 1961, 24, 11.

PROSOCIAL BEHAVIOR. Children who comply with the social norms also seem to be more popular. While one might postulate that the child who did all the "right" things might be classified as a "sissy," or a "goody-goody," this does not seem to be the case. One study showed that children who were widely accepted seemed to emphasize prosocial behaviors, such as neatness, sportsmanship, and a sense of humor (Klaus 1959). A later study, however, pointed out that the accepted child is the one who is able to choose a moderate level of conformity. A child who is overly compliant with the rules and norms loses out in popularity (Moore 1967).

SELF-ESTEEM. This choosing of a middle ground seems important also with respect to self-esteem. Children with very high or very low self-esteem are less popular than those who fall in the middle range (Reese 1961). It seems that a child must think well of himself in order for others to think well of him, but the child who acts too cocky or snobbish will put off other children. One study demonstrated that children with high self-esteem expected to be preferred by those children whom they preferred as friends, while children with low self-esteem did not expect that those they chose would reciprocate (Simon and Bernstein 1971).

ANXIETY. Anxiety is another factor that has been studied with respect to peer acceptance. However, the results are not conclusive. Some studies have suggested that a child who is more anxious or nervous is less likely to be popular among his peers (Iscoe and Garden 1961); yet other psychologists studying children in this age range found very little correlation at all between anxiety and peer acceptance (Hill 1963).

DEPENDENCE ON PEERS AND AGGRESSION. Most of the correlates discussed thus far have tended to be true of acceptance by adults as well as by peers. Dependency on peers, however, facilitates popularity among children, while at the same time it interferes with acceptance by adults. Moreover, children who manifest a great deal of immaturity and dependence on adults are less likely to be accepted by both peers and adults.

If a child who is dependent on peers stands a good chance of acceptance, one might expect that an aggressive child is likely to be rejected. In fact, most studies have shown that this tends to be true. Children who score high in tests of verbal aggressiveness and indirect aggressiveness receive low scores on tests of popularity among their peers (Lesser 1959). However, children who display friendly aggression or physical aggression when provoked tend to be the popular ones (Lesser 1959; Campbell and Yarrow 1961). Perhaps it is felt by the peer group that justified or playful aggression is admirable while impulsive or inappropriate aggression is not.

SOCIAL FACTORS. Race and social class are also important determinants of peer-group acceptance. In segregated schools, children from the racial majority group are more likely to express interest in having a friend of their own kind than are children who are members of the minority group (Morland 1966). Studies conducted in mixed-race peer groups have indicated that children from the minority group are significantly less popular (Morland 1966; Radke and Trager 1950). Lower-class children are less likely to be accepted in an integrated middle-class school situation than are their middle-class peers (Bonney 1942). It has been suggested, however, that this difference may be due not simply to labeling or stereotyping on the part of the dominant group, but to the fact that the lower-class child does not bring with him the kinds of characteristics which are so highly valued in the middle-class culture of the school (Feinberg, Smith, and Schmidt 1958).

OTHER FACTORS. In addition to the psychological and social factors described above, some other factors have also been correlated with peer acceptance. For example, children who have high I.Q.'s and do well in school seem to be more popular than those who do not (Sells and Roff 1967).

One study showed that the desirability of names is significantly correlated to their bearers' popularity. This result does not indicate, however, whether the undesirable name was responsible for the rejection by other children, or whether a child coming from a family that would give him such a name would also tend to have characteristics that would make him unpopular (McDavid and Harari 1966).

Choice of Friends

Observers of friendship groups among children have noted a number of similarities between members. Such similarities reveal which kinds of characteristics children see as important in their choice of companions.

A study of pairs of mutual friends among fourth-graders indicated that mutual friends tended to possess strong, aggressive personality traits and were recognized by observers as being good leaders. In addition, their classmates rated them above average in socially desirable traits such as neatness, daring, friendliness, good looks, enthusiasm, and activity in recitations. Children who were rated less well on these characteristics, who were slower and less dynamic, frequently sought out these more capable and industrious children for friends, but were rejected (Bonney 1944).

These results give rise to two possible interpretations. On the one hand, the industrious children may form mutual friendships because they share similar characteristics and are thus more understanding of each other's needs. On the other hand, those children who form mutual friendships may be the same children who find easy acceptance among peers, and thus, are more apt to form mutual friendships than other, less outgoing children.

Another study concluded that similarities in nonintellectual traits, such as social maturity, were more important than similarities in intelligence (Furfey 1927). However, a later study arrived at a conflicting conclusion, that intelligence was indeed a factor in which mutual friends resembled each other, although academic achievement was not (Bonney 1942).

SEX DIFFERENCES. Boys' responses about friendships have been reported to be very different from girls' responses. One boy said:

My best friend is John Corbett and the reason why I like him is that he is so nice to me and we both draw space ships and what's more he plays with me nearly every time in the playground. (Opie and Opie 1959)

Friendship here seems to be based on shared interests in activities. Girls' choices seem to be based largely on physical attributes:

I have two friends called Carol and Brenda. I like Brenda because she is very funny and very small. I also like Carol because when she has any sweets she always gives me some, and she has lovely curly hair, and she is very nice. (Opie and Opie 1959)

SITUATIONAL FACTORS. There are a number of situational factors influencing choice of friends. Mutual friends tend to resemble each other in socioeconomic background, lower-class children being friendly with others from the same status; this is true for middle-class children as well (Bonney 1942). In addition, children in the middle years usually choose friends of the same sex. This similarity highlights an important characteristic of the period, a segregation of the sexes not seen in older or younger children (Tuddenham 1952). Finally, physical proximity seems to be a determining factor. Children who are friends generally live in the same neighborhood or are in the same class at school. This similarity seems to decline with age and is another characteristic which sets this period off from earlier and later ones (Furfey 1927).

ADULT INFLUENCES. Adults—both parents and other significant figures—can have an important influence on the child's choice of friends. A study by Yarrow and Yarrow (1958), for example, showed that children in a summer camp were influenced to be more accepting of a racially integrated living situation by adult leaders who consciously attempted to alter the children's previous patterns of peer acceptance. Thus, while the data on peer acceptance patterns in middle childhood tell us how children tend to choose friends and form groups, we must bear in mind that adults can often intervene and alter the usual process.

Influences on Personality

As children from 8 to 12 form new relationships with peers and attempt to master the realities of their expanding social world, it is evident that some have an easy time, are well liked, and deal with general effectiveness in new social situations. Others are less successful, experiencing rejection by their peers, and being fearful and timid. Developmental psychologists have explored the factors in children's backgrounds that seem to have a bearing on the way children adjust to these new social demands.

Effects of Parents

It has been found that the child's relationship with his parents affects the way he gets along with his peers and his acceptance by them. Elkins (1958) reported that children who are accepted by peers express more satisfaction with their home lives than do children who are less accepted. The more popular children tend to have parents who express pleasure in the child's accomplishment. A study by Winder and Rau (1962) revealed that high-status boys experience little frustration and punishment from their parents while receiving a great deal of supportive reinforcement.

It has also been found that fathers of well-accepted boys tended to discourage rather than encourage aggressive or antisocial behavior in their sons, and were themselves less aggressive in punishing their sons (Winder and Rau 1962).

However, child-rearing patterns are far more predictive of boys' popularity than of girls'. It has been found that boys who come from mother-dominant homes show aggressiveness, unfriendliness, and a lack of influence among peers. By contrast, boys from father-dominant families tend to be good at initiating friendships and gaining influence in the peer group. These same differences between family types were not good indicators of girls' popularity (Hoffman 1961).

Effects of Birth Order

Along with his relationship to his parents in the family, the child's position with respect to his siblings is important in determining the course of

Figure 13.5 Percentage incidence of first-born, according to size of family. (From H. E. Jones. The environment and mental development. In L. Carmichael (Ed.), *Manual of child psychology*. (2nd ed.) New York: John Wiley & Sons, Inc., 1954. P. 669.)

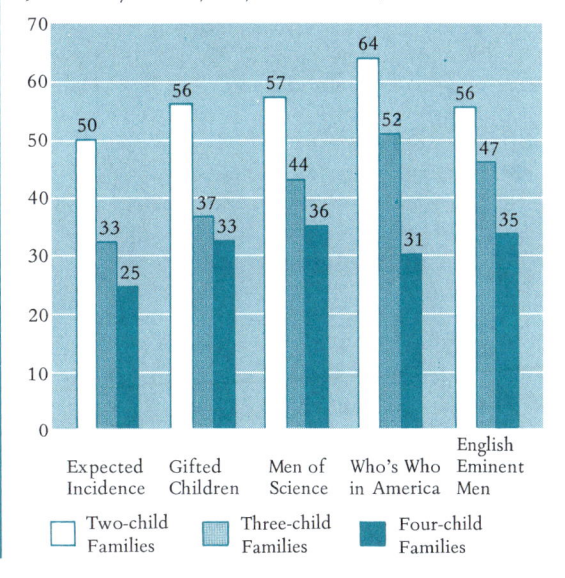

his development. Children who occupy similar role positions within families have been shown to exhibit similar personality traits not only during childhood but throughout life, although this is more true of females than males.

Being the first-born but especially the only child seems to carry with it certain advantages. First-borns tend to be more successful, as is evidenced by their disproportionate number in *Who's Who* (Jones 1954). Their thinking has been reported to reflect the notion that the world is an orderly and rational place (Harris 1964). Finally, these children attain significantly higher scores on achievement tests than do later-borns (Altus 1966).

Why should being the first-born or only child make such a difference? One reason is that first-borns probably have higher standards for their own achievements and competencies than later-borns do, since they have only adult performances to compare themselves with, not those of older siblings. A second, and related, hypothesis is that first-borns identify with, and model themselves after adults rather than other children, again because they have no older siblings with whom to compare themselves. Finally, the first-born is more likely to be exposed to an orderly world. His information comes from a fully developed adult mind which tends to be consistent in its interpretation of the world, while the later-born gains much of his experience from older siblings who are, although older, nevertheless children and interact with the world with the inconsistent thought and impulsive action of children (Sutton-Smith and Rosenberg 1970).

Being a first-born, as distinct from only child, is not, however, entirely advantageous. While he seems more likely than his younger brothers and sisters to have certain cognitive and intellectual advantages, the first-born also tends to have some personality traits which may not be so desirable. For example, first-borns express more fear of physical dangers and active sports (Helmreich and Collins 1967). They tend to be less aggressive than their peers, and have guilt feelings more than others (Cobb 1943; Sears 1951). One study reports that first-borns are more conforming (Becker, Lerner, and Carroll 1966). In addition, they are represented in disproportionately large numbers as patients in child guidance clinics (Rosenow and Whyte 1931), and display more nervous symptoms than children in any other position in the family (Garner and Wenar 1959). Contributing to the development of these characteristics of first-born children may be the fact that parents are often unsure and inconsistent in dealing with their first child. Usually parents have established patterns of behavior by the time their second child arrives and are more consistent in dealing with him.

Youngest children, in contrast to other children, have been characterized as popular and outgoing. They have some of the advantages of being the only children. Middle children show a rather inconsistent profile, appearing in some studies like neglected children but in others highly motivated to overcome this neglect.

How can we account for these kinds of differences in personality and emotional makeup? One factor is that the first-born is subjected to a great deal of anxiety early in life over the loss of parental attention upon the arrival of the sibling. A middle-born and later-born child has never known the status of only child; therefore the birth of another child in the family is not nearly so traumatic for him. Another factor that may account for such differences is that the first-born experiences more guilt over his hostility toward younger siblings than do later-borns over their hostility toward older siblings. The older brother or sister may show real aggression toward his younger rival, thus justifying the younger sibling's feelings of hostility toward him. However, an infant is a rather helpless individual, and the resentment that a jealous older sibling feels toward him cannot easily be justified, and so is more likely to give rise to feelings of guilt.

There are several factors that mitigate the effects of birth position. For example, one study showed that siblings who are close together in age and of the same sex show few differences, while siblings who are farther apart in age and of opposite sexes show a great many differences. This same study also showed that a two- to four-year age difference between siblings is threatening to the older child, who was himself a baby at the arrival of the sibling. However, if the older child was 7 or 8 years old when the infant was born, he was already much more independent of his parents and, therefore, less resentful of the sibling (Koch 1956). Unfortunately, many studies do not control adequately for such age-spacing effects nor for the fact that the sex of one's siblings, not just their position, also has an important impact. In general, we become more like our siblings, whether they are males or females. Furthermore, we tend to marry individuals with characteristics like both of our siblings.

School Influences

TEACHER BEHAVIORS. Children in the middle years spend a major part of their time in school. After the parents, teachers may sometimes be the most significant and influential adults in a child's life. For this reason, the effect of teacher behaviors on personality development has been the subject of a great deal of research. The effects of various kinds of teacher behaviors on the personality of the child are in many ways similar to the effects of parent behaviors. One particular advantage of studying teacher behavior as opposed to parent behavior is that a child normally changes teachers after each school year, whereas the parents remain a constant factor. It is, therefore, possible to follow the same child or group of children from year to year to see to what extent changes in teacher personality effect changes in the personality or behavior of the children.

Heil and Washburne (1961) classified teacher personality types into three categories, and then compared the progress of the children in various areas with different kinds of teachers. The teachers' personality types were: (1) Turbulent. This person is characterized as being independent, impulsive, unpredictable, and lacking in warmth. (2) Self-controlled. This person is generally methodical, pragmatic, calm, and sensitive, but lacking in dynamism. (3) Fearful. This person tends to fear impulses in himself and others. As a teacher, he is dependent, defensive, and conscientious to the point of rigidity.

Which kind of teacher is most effective? It was found that the self-controlled teacher is most effective both with respect to academic achievement and in encouraging friendliness in the children. A hostile or dominating teacher—as the turbulent individual is likely to be—generally has an adverse effect on the children. Pupils of such a teacher have difficulty adjusting to the school setting. They devote less energy to constructive activities and more energy to disruptive and aggressive behaviors. The fearful teachers were found to be least effective in the actual process of teaching. Their students scored the lowest of the three groups on academic achievement tests.

Another study of the effects of teacher personality on children traced the changes in the same children from teacher to teacher. For the purposes of this study, the teachers were classified into two categories: dominative, or authoritarian; and integrative, or approving and sensitive. The children were in second grade during the first year of the study. It was found that the children who had the integrative teacher engaged in more constructive activities, displayed initiative, and related well to others. By contrast, the children who had the dominative teacher paid less attention to their work and engaged in more disruptive activity in class. The following year the same children and teachers were studied. Teacher styles remained unchanged; however, children who had previously been placed with the dominative teacher showed more integrative behavior when placed with the integrative teacher, and vice versa (Anderson and Brewer 1946; Anderson, Brewer, and Reed 1946).

Children seem to perform well under the influence of both a warm parent and a warm teacher. Both aggressive or authoritarian parents and teachers seem to inspire counteraggression and antisocial behavior in children. Moreover, the parent or teacher who is more rational and consistent in his dealings with the child has the most peaceful and trusting relationship with him. Inconsistent discipline is frequently counterproductive or meaningless. These similarities between successful teacher and parent behaviors suggest that there are certain kinds of adult characteristics that are most effective in dealing with children.

SCHOOL EXPERIENCE AND ANXIETY. For many children, school may be an anxiety-producing experience, while for others, anxiety deriving

Figure 13.6 School life plays a major influence in a child's development. Children's involvement in school is affected by the teacher's behavior, the child's feelings of self-esteem, and other personality traits, as well as social and economic factors. (Roger Malloch—Magnum; Charles Harbutt—Magnum)

from other sources may have a serious effect on school performance. In most cases, the effects of anxiety on school performance seem to run in a vicious cycle. The source of anxiety is difficult to pin down. The child may bring some anxiety with him when he comes to school. This causes him to perform poorly in school, and his school failure engenders more anxiety, which, in turn, leads to further failure. Alternatively, the school situation may cause him to be anxious; and this anxiety then leads to failure. The failure leads to anxiety, and thus the cycle is repeated.

Research has shown that children who manifest a high degree of test anxiety obtain low scores on various measures of achievement and intelligence (Sarason, Hill, and Zimbardo 1964). As the child becomes more anxious, his performance declines; however, if the anxiety can be relieved, his performance improves (Hill and Sarason 1966).

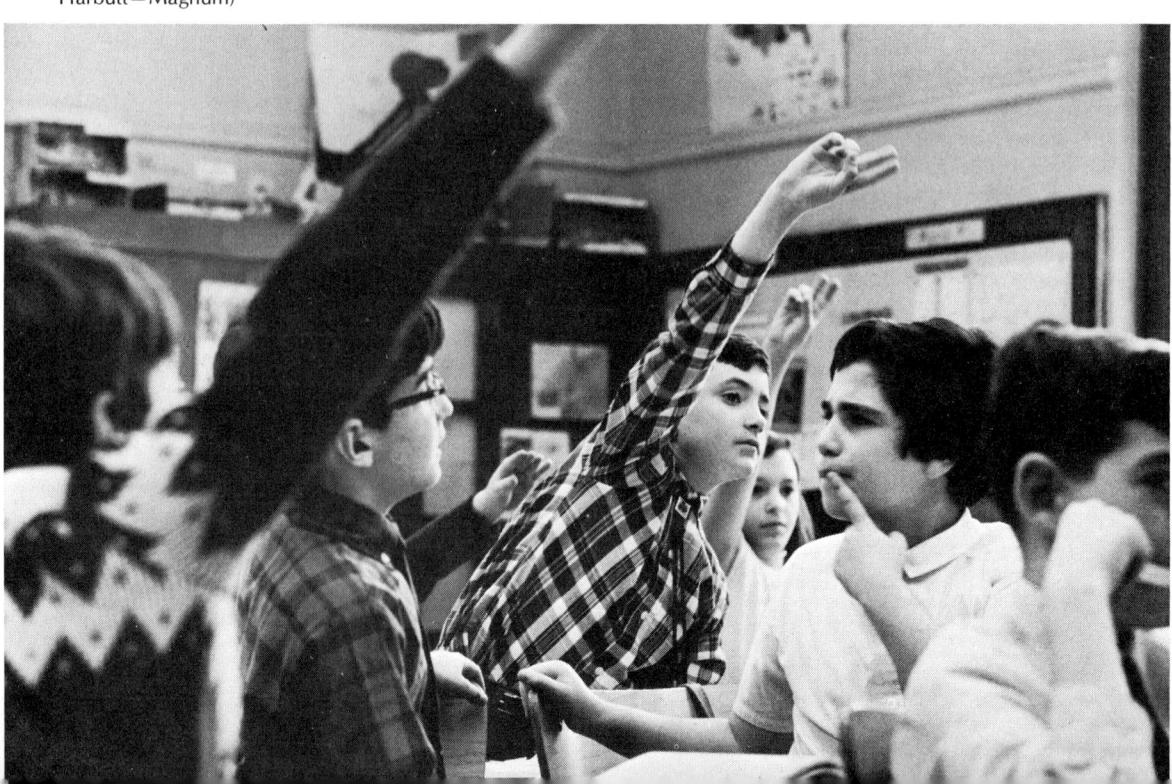

School experience also seems to bear a significant relationship to self-esteem. We have already discussed what happens to a child's self-esteem when he arrives at school with a set of values that are in conflict with those of the institution. Usually this is related to the sex or ethnic background of the child. However, frequently there are children whose personalities are not suited to the demands of the school environment. If a child does not have high intellectual aptitudes, for example, he is likely to be made to feel that he is of little worth and thus may suffer serious damage to his self-esteem. In one study, children were asked to evaluate themselves—what they liked and did not like about themselves. About one-fourth of the children mentioned school in their statements, and in most cases school was a source of self-disparagement rather than self-esteem (Jersild 1952).

By studying children's performances in games, we can see, in a more tightly controlled situation than the normal school setting, how the abilities of the child and the difficulty of the situation interact. Gump and Sutton-Smith (1955) examined the performances of children of varying abilities placed in the central role in the game situation. The central role was devised so that in one condition it was high-powered (that is, the nature of the role itself made it fairly easy for the role occupant to succeed), while in the other condition it was low-powered (that is, the role itself had little power, so the success of the role occupant depended on his own abilities). The results showed that highly skilled boys succeeded under either condition, whereas low-skilled boys succeeded only in the high-powered roles and suffered a good deal of humiliation by failing in the low-powered roles. These results suggest that the matching of abilities with roles in play situations, and even in school tasks, is very important in determining the development of self-esteem. If a child with low abilities in any sphere is given a task at which he is more likely to fail than his more highly skilled peer, he may suffer a debilitating blow to his self-esteem; in addition, his level of anxiety may increase in that and other situations.

Social-Class Influences

The very young child, while profoundly affected by the social conditions in his environment, is usually not aware of class difference. If his clothes are ragged or his family is the object of prejudice, he does not realize that life can be otherwise. However, by middle childhood, a time of increasing awareness of himself and things around him, the child recognizes more keenly that for some people life is different. He begins to understand what social dimensions make some people similar to him and others different. Since a real sense of societal awareness begins to emerge during middle childhood, this is a particularly interesting period for studying the effects of social conditions on the development of personality and social behavior.

However, in examining social-class influences on personality, we should not confuse class with race and ethnicity. Class is defined by one's economic status. In the United States, it happens that because of discrimination, groups such as blacks, Puerto Ricans, and Chicanos have disproportionate numbers in the lower class. We should not fall into the trap of identifying these groups as completely lower class.

PHYSICAL AND ECONOMIC FACTORS. Children raised in the lower classes are likely to live in crowded quarters, suffering many of the disadvantages associated with crowding, whereas middle-class children are more likely to have a room to themselves, affording them a more peaceful existence. The middle-class parent, less preoccupied with providing for the physical needs of the children, is able to devote more time to the psychological aspects of child care (Jersild, Woodyard, and del Solar 1949).

Lower-class children are also subject to more real fears than are middle-class children. Lower-class children may grow up in an environment in which realistic danger is common—rats, drunks, violence—while the middle-class child grows up in a relatively protected environment. One study asked older children to describe their earliest memories. In general, the middle-class children recalled fairly pleasant things about their early childhood; but the memories of the lower-class children, by contrast, were filled with images of anger, aggression, and overt sexual behavior (Epstein 1963).

ATTITUDES TOWARD AUTHORITY. Some early studies have described certain fairly consistent social-class differences between children in their perceptions of parents and other authorities. It was found that middle-class children are generally positive in their opinions of their parents and other people in authority positions, whereas lower-class children more often see their parents as severe and unreasonable. It follows, then, that lower-class children are themselves more likely to fear authority and to show greater concern for compliance with rules (Dolger and Ginandes 1946).

Meltzer (1936) also found differences in upper-, middle-, and lower-class children's attitudes toward their parents. His study revealed that middle-class children seemed to express the most positive attitudes toward their parents. Lower-class children were most ambivalent about their feelings toward their parents, and they expressed the greatest insecurity about themselves. These children viewed their parents as repressive and uninterested in their needs. The upper-class children were most variable and represented both extremes—some expressed adoration for their parents, while others were fearful of them. It is interesting to note that as a group, the upper-class children had the greatest number of instances of both overdependency and rejection (Meltzer 1936).

While the reasons for these class-based differences in children's attitudes toward parents and authority figures are undoubtedly complex, a number of contributing factors have been considered. One such factor is the larger family size of the lower classes. A recent study showed that as the number of children in a family increased, the mother became less accepting of the individual children. Large family size was also shown to lead to an increased amount of hostile psychological control on the part of the mother which was directed particularly toward daughters (Nuttall and Nuttall 1971).

The parent who is in the lower class is likely to be experiencing more economic strains and burdens than the middle-class parent, thereby leaving him less time and energy to devote to his children. Finally, the different value systems among classes may have a significant effect on philosophies of child rearing, and, ultimately, on the per-

Figure 13.7 The economic strain, burdens, and depressed conditions of the lower socioeconomic family greatly affect the child's primary relationships and his general social and personality growth. (Ken Heyman; Nicholas de Sciose—Rapho Guillumette)

430 THE MIDDLE YEARS AGES 8 THROUGH 12

sonality development of the child. For example, lower-class people tend to emphasize the value of obeying rules in socializing their children. It may be, in part, that they are anxious not to cause any trouble with the middle-class authorities — teachers, welfare workers, policemen, factory bosses — who can greatly affect their lives.

CHILD REARING. Several studies in which parents themselves, rather than an independent observer, have described their behavior are in general agreement with the studies which report children's perceptions of their parents' behavior. Working-class mothers are stricter in their child-rearing practices than are middle-class mothers. They put more pressure on the child to complete toilet training; they do not allow their children to wander about the neighborhood at will; and they are more restrictive of sexual and aggressive behaviors (Sears, Maccoby, and Levin 1957; Maccoby, Gibbs et al. 1954). However, one should be cautious in generalizing about these findings since there seems to be much variance within economic status groups (Havighurst and Davis 1955).

SCHOOLING AND ACHIEVEMENT. Social-class differences in academic achievement have stirred up a great deal of controversy among psychologists. As we have seen in earlier chapters, some contended that significantly lower I.Q. scores and achievement test scores among lower-class children are evidence that they are for genetic reasons less intelligent than middle-class children. However, most point to the disadvantages of growing up in an economically underprivileged environment and the inferiority of the schools in depressed areas as cause for these differences. It is generally assumed that until it can be shown that the environmental factors are not largely responsible for differences in intelligence, the genetic hypothesis is not a reasonable explanation. As long as gross environmental inequalities exist,

Charles Harbutt — Magnum

they should be considered first as the logical basis for differences. It would be a serious error to adopt a course that leads one to do nothing about social change.

What are some of the other environmental factors which might inhibit the academic progress of the lower-class child? One is transiency. Because of changing jobs, family disorganization, and economic insecurity, lower-class families are far more likely to move than middle-class families. Every time a family moves, the adjustments and ties which the child has made in school are disrupted. In some urban areas, the turnover rate may be as high as 100 percent during any given year, presenting problems for both the children and the teachers (Conant 1961; Levine, Wesolowski, and Corbett 1966).

Another factor is the poorer quality of schooling in impoverished areas. Not only is the physical plant dilapidated, but the schools are generally overcrowded, books and materials are lacking, and the staff is inadequate (Kerber and Bommarito 1965).

Furthermore, the class difference between the teachers and culture in the schools and the lower-class student is a significant factor. While the children in the city schools are largely from the lower class, bringing with them the set of values inherent in their communities, the teachers are generally from a middle-class background and tend to communicate its values. Frequently, conflicts between teachers and children may be attributable to differences in cultural values. Many middle-class teachers who may themselves feel a strong need for achievement are frustrated and puzzled by the fact that the children do not seem to share that need. They may then perceive the children as being deviant (Groff 1963).

The lower-class child's self-esteem can be seriously affected in school situations alien to him. A

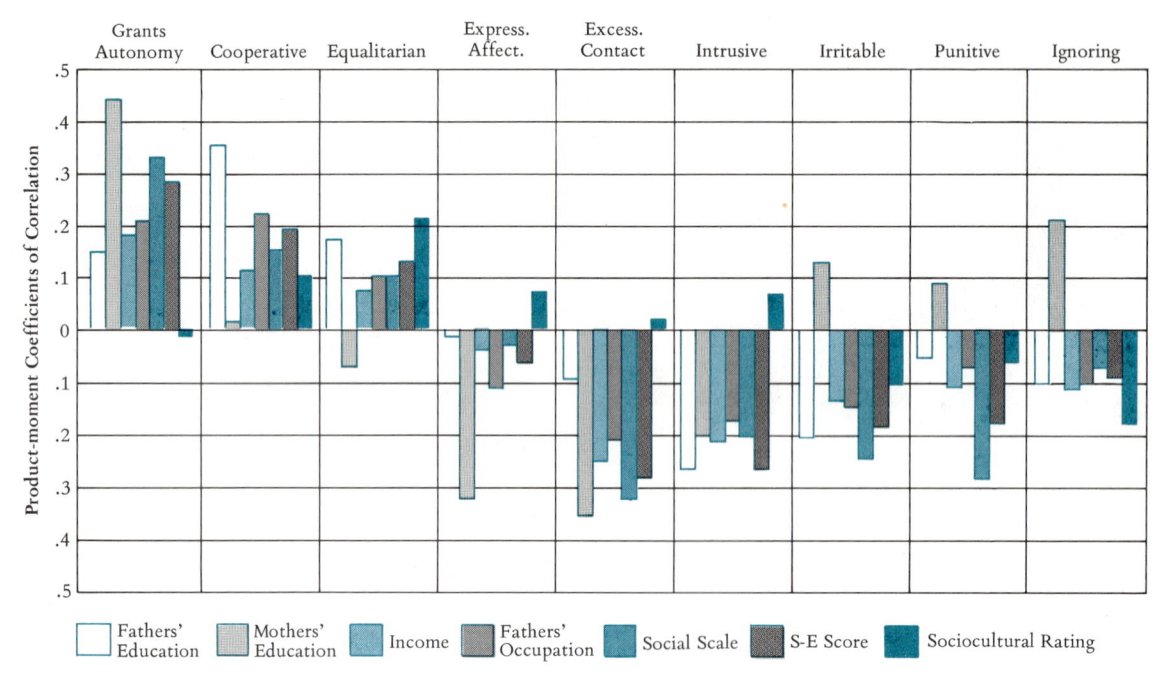

Figure 13.8 The relationship between the socioeconomic status of mothers and their behavior toward their infants (0–3 years). (From N. Bayley and E. Schaefer. Relationships between socioeconomic variables and the behavior of mothers toward young children. *J. genet. Psychol.*, 1960, 96, 61–77.)

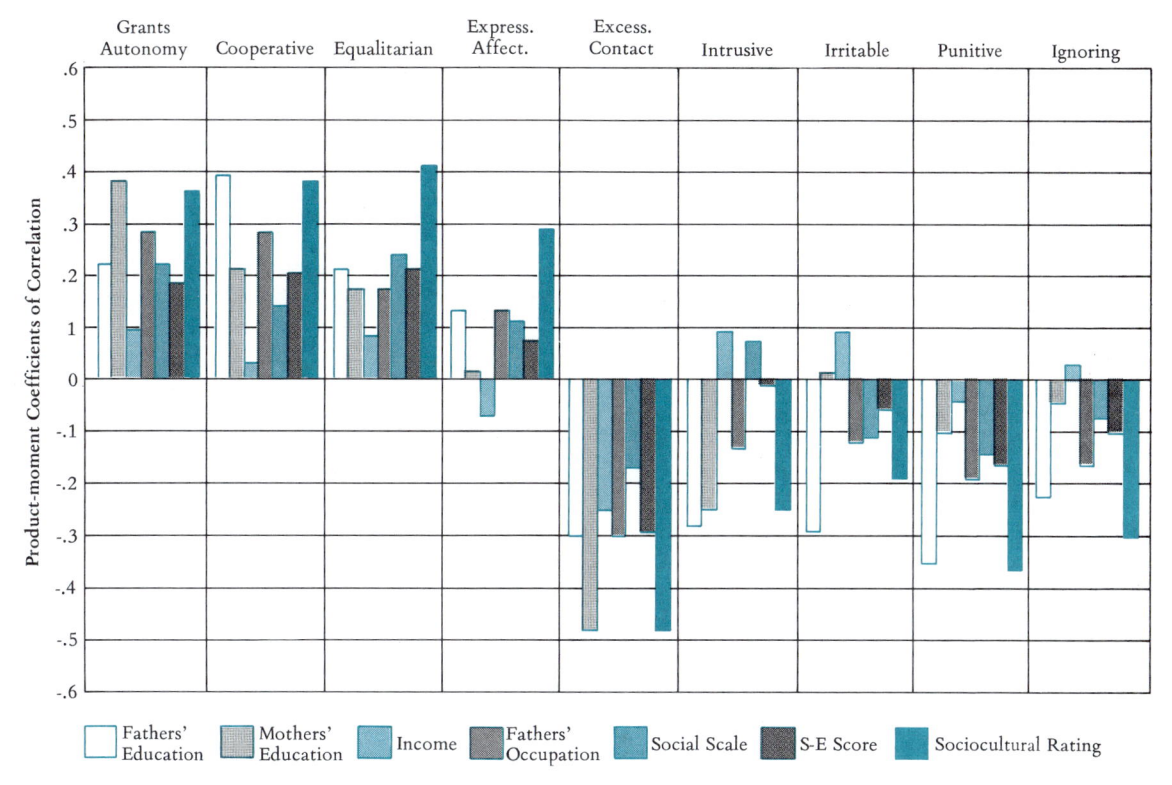

Figure 13.9 The relationship between the socioeconomic status of mothers and their behavior toward their children (9–14 years). (From N. Bayley and E. Schaefer. Relationships between socioeconomic variables and the behavior of mothers toward young children. *J. genet. Psychol,* 1960, 96, 61–77.)

child's self-esteem is closely related to his success in school. High self-esteem correlates with academic success, and low self-esteem is associated with difficulties and failures in school (Caplin 1966; Lourenso, Greenberg, and Davidson 1965). If a child's own values and characteristics are in conflict with those expressed by the school, he is likely to suffer low self-esteem and failure. The schools have been characterized as expressing the middle-class values of their (predominantly female) teachers, and so one might expect to find the greatest number of failures among lower-class boys whose own set of values would be most in conflict with the values of the institution. This is, in fact, the case. Boys from lower-class backgrounds have more disciplinary problems, lower grades, and a higher dropout rate than other children (Sgan 1967). Coopersmith, in his study, found that lower-class children tended to suffer low self-esteem for much the same reasons. In addition, the alien middle-class environment of the school culture may lead to a child's feeling inadequate or out of place (Greenberg, Gerver, Chall, and Davidson 1965; Lefevre 1966).

It is tempting to assign blame in such situations, but the problem is so complex that it lends itself to no simple interpretation. Some say that in order for lower-class children to succeed in a real and tangible way, it will be necessary for them to conform to middle-class values and master the skills necessary to get along in a middle-class world. They claim it is unfair to chain children to a "culture of poverty" by keeping them culturally isolated in ghettos and not exposing them to people from the middle class.

On the other hand, middle-class teachers, given little sociological training, tend to evaluate the children's behavior within a middle-class context, usually to the detriment of the children. However, it may be unjust to blame a teacher whose training never prepared him, in either educational methods or psychological sensitivity, to deal with the problems he confronts in the inner-city school.

A search for solutions. As with most complex problems, the solution to social-class differences in educational achievement is not simple. A number of solutions have been attempted. For example, it has been generally agreed that the textbooks used in schools are biased in favor of white middle-class children. They present a picture of suburban affluence and values foreign to most urban youngsters, particularly those of minority groups. In recent years there has been a growing awareness, within the educational system, and in our society as a whole, that this bias, with its consequent alienation of large groups of children in urban populations, has an adverse effect on learning ability. Publishers, reflecting this view, have begun to publish texts that more realistically relate to the lives of minority-group children. One researcher has pointed out, however, that in actual fact, most of these texts are basically unchanged—except that some of the people in the illustrations are depicted as having Negro features (Waite 1968).

Another possible solution—which has been highly controversial from its inception—is busing. A 1954 Supreme Court decision ordered equal educational opportunities for all children, and claimed that in reality, "separate is not equal." In order to integrate the schools, therefore, black children from urban areas are bused to more affluent white schools, while white children take their places in inner-city black schools. Proponents and opponents of busing have hotly disputed its merits, but no one has reached any firm conclusion as to its effectiveness on the basis of objective data. Some studies have shown that children bused out of inner-city schools have shown academic improvement, while other studies reveal that no improvement has occurred. However, children bused into the inner city have shown no academic decline. While the academic merits are as yet inconclusive, on the other hand, one significant argument maintains that allowing children to go to school in segregated environments would only perpetuate the prevalent racial hatred and misunderstanding in this country. In short, the value of busing may have more sociopolitical than academic importance.

Yet another solution is special preparation for school. The alternate successes and failures of various preschool "compensatory education programs," as they have been called, have left psychologists and educators more confused than they were at the outset. Initially, it was thought that ghetto children had been deprived in the very early years of the kinds of stimuli that would lead to the normal development of intellectual skills (Deutsch 1963). However, programs that have provided children experience with organized cognitive stimulation early in life—shapes, colors, language—have yet to demonstrate dramatic or lasting effects.

Although the results of such programs have been disappointing, they force us to consider the results of social-class differences. Lower-class children learn attitudes toward school from their parents different from those of middle-class children, frequently approaching school with fear and anxiety. If they have low self-esteem, they may take a defeatist attitude toward their own work and success; and when, for cultural reasons, their attitudes are misconceived by their teachers, school is likely to become a frustrating and unhappy experience. But at an even more basic level, lower-class children suffer many of the disadvantages of economic poverty. They are more likely than middle-class children to have health problems which go untreated (Bloom, Davis, and Hess 1965), and the schools they go to are dingy, inadequate, and often dangerous. In addition, their parents seldom have the time or money to spend on them that middle-class parents do.

In order for educational programs to be successful, many of the conditions of lower-class life will have to be rectified. We cannot really expect any changes to come about without more convincing steps toward social and economic justice in the United States. Most of the problems cited in this chapter ultimately revolve around poverty. Abolish poverty and we can rewrite this chapter on the child's social development.

Prejudice

One social behavior which psychologists and other students of social interaction have found both puzzling and insidious is prejudice. In very general terms, prejudice can be defined as the forming of judgments or opinions about some persons or issues before the facts are known. More specifically, it means that the assumption that a certain person is likely to have certain personality or character traits is made on the basis of his race or ethnicity, rather than through observation of actual behavior. Blacks, Puerto Ricans, and other minority-group members are greatly affected by the existing prejudiced attitudes toward them.

Most prejudice has serious consequences for the individual group members as well as for society as a whole. It is, therefore, important to understand the roots of such kinds of beliefs, for it may be the case that only if prejudice is reduced in the early years can it ever be minimized among adults. Consequently, prejudicial behavior among children has occupied the attention of many child psychologists. How early can it be observed among children? Is its development related to parental behavior? Is it correlated with other personality traits? And, finally, how can it be modified?

EARLY DEVELOPMENT OF PREJUDICE. Prejudiced attitudes toward members of other ethnic and racial groups have been observed among children as early as kindergarten age; and by the time they have completed the early years of school, these children's attitudes have come to resemble very closely those of their parents (Radke, Trager, and Davis 1949). These findings suggest two things. First, such attitudes must be

Table 13.4 Expressed Preference for Black and White Skin Color (in Pictures) by Black and White Boys and Girls, Ages 10 and 11

	Skin Color Preferred					
	Boys			Girls		
Subjects	Dark	Equal*	White	Dark	Equal*	White
Black	44	1	43	58	2	47
White	38	0	120	45	2	104

*Equal = those children who said they liked both equally.
Source: S. A. Richardson and A. Green. When is black beautiful? Coloured and white children's reactions to skin colour. Brit. J. educ. Psychol., 1971, 41, 62–69.

learned from either the verbal or the nonverbal behavior of the parents, who are the most important influence on the child's development in the early years. Second, interventions designed to change prejudiced behavior must take place even before the child enters kindergarten, for by that time he has already learned hostility toward other ethnic groups.

PREJUDICE AMONG CHILDREN. Studies have suggested that by the time children have reached middle childhood, they have successfully internalized the societal rules that determine which groups of people have high status and which groups have low status. For example, one study, conducted in London, asked black and white 10-year-olds to rank photographs of faces according to their own preferences. It was found that both black and white children ranked the pictures with respect to skin color, the lighter-skinned people being most preferred by both groups (Richardson and Green 1971). These children seemed to have learned that the people valued and rewarded most in their society have light skins.

A study by Mock and Tuddenham (1971) demonstrated quite dramatically the low regard in which both black and white children hold blacks in our society. Black and white children were placed into groups of five, in various degrees of integration ranging from all-black to all-white. However, boys and girls were not mixed. The

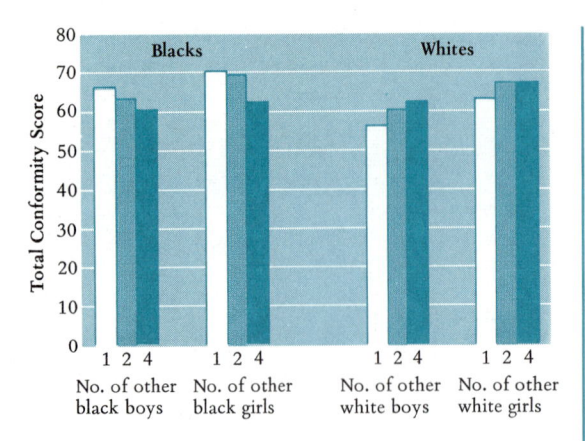

Figure 13.10 The influence of race on conformity to group norms in black and white boys and girls, aged 10 and 11. Both the black and white children conformed more to a predominantly white group. (From R. L. Mock and R. D. Tuddenham. Race and conformity among children. *Develpm. Psychol.*, 1971, 4 (3), 349–365.)

children were given a series of perceptual problems about which they had to make a judgment (for example, "Is line A the same length as line B?"). The experiment was devised so that each child thought he was the last one to respond and was given false information as to the responses of the other children. The extent to which children conformed to wrong answers in groups of various racial mixes was measured. The results showed that the more white subjects in the group, the more both black and white children conformed to what they thought was the group's opinion, regardless of their own judgments. However, when the group was composed of mostly black children, there was less conformity to the group norm by both blacks and whites.

These studies indicate that erroneous beliefs about the minority group are held not only by the majority, but by the minority as well. While it is unlikely that most blacks would express overtly beliefs that they are in various ways inferior to whites, prejudice is so pervasive in our society that blacks have been shown in subtle ways to express prejudiced views about themselves.

A final example of prejudice among children is drawn from a study cited in the section on leadership. When teachers were asked to name children who were most frequently and least frequently chosen as leaders among their friends, it was found that there were significantly fewer blacks than whites chosen in the leadership category (Harrison, Rawls, and Rawls 1971). These results suggest that blacks were held in lower regard than whites by most children. It is also possible that existing prejudice has led to black children having lower self-esteem and thus manifesting fewer of the characteristics which would tend to put them into leadership positions.

PERSONALITY CORRELATES OF PREJUDICE. Just as people manifest differences in other kinds of personality traits, they show large differences in susceptibility to prejudiced beliefs. Studies have revealed a number of characteristics associated with prejudice.

Frenkel-Brunswik (1948) tested 1500 children between the ages of 11 and 16, and concluded that prejudiced children tend to express a whole constellation of other beliefs which picture them as having rigid and authoritarian personalities. They also tend to believe in a firm delineation of sex roles, being highly intolerant of weak behavior in males or aggressive behavior in females.

Other studies of prejudice among children have dealt with self-concept. They have revealed that children who hold prejudiced beliefs are also plagued by doubts about their own abilities (Tabachnick 1962; Trent 1957). A related study showed that black children with poor self-concepts expressed fewer positive opinions about both blacks and whites than did those with more favorable self-concepts (Trent 1957).

PARENTAL BEHAVIORS AND PREJUDICE. One theory holds that childhood prejudice stems from parental authoritarianism and rigidity. In the study by Frenkel-Brunswik mentioned above, it was found that prejudiced children had relationships with their parents that were characterized by harsh, punitive treatment and lack of affection. This suggests that these children learned to deal with other people in the authoritarian and rigid manner in which their parents dealt with them;

and, therefore, they developed prejudiced opinions. Another study found that even if parents did not express overtly prejudiced attitudes toward other ethnic groups, children learned these attitudes from them anyway through the parents' own social relationships and restrictions on the child's relationships with other children (Radke-Yarrow, Trager, and Miller 1952).

However, the hypothesis that prejudice results from parental authoritarianism and rigidity has not been consistently confirmed by other studies. In one case, prejudice in children was shown to be related to moderate, as opposed to severe, disciplinary practices and high parental ethnocentrism, suggesting that a parent must be somewhat rewarding to be imitated (Epstein and Komorita 1966a). These same findings generally held true for black children as well, for whom the prejudice was directed against both blacks and whites. The investigators concluded that prejudice is a manifestation of a general misanthropy which is learned from the parents. In other words, the prejudiced person tends to dislike other people in any case, but attitudes learned from the parents give specific direction to these feelings (Epstein and Komorita 1966b).

PREJUDICE IN DIFFERENT CULTURES. The antecedents of prejudice are not the same in all cultures. What happens when prejudice is sanctioned openly by society, as it is in South Africa? A study conducted in that country, where racial discrimination is a policy of the government, found that children who identified strongly with the country expressed prejudice openly; however, these children did not score high on personality measures of authoritarianism and dogmatism as did children who expressed prejudice in studies conducted in the United States. The expression of prejudice is, therefore, not necessarily related to certain personality characteristics, but may be expressed by children without those characteristics if it is sanctioned by the society (Orpen 1971).

CHANGING PREJUDICED ATTITUDES. How can prejudice be stopped or changed? Several studies of this question have been conducted in summer camps in which interracial groups of children have lived together for periods of several weeks at a time. Mussen (1950) found that prejudice increased in some children while it decreased in others. The changes that took place appeared to be closely related to the children's personality structures. Those children whose prejudices increased were poorly adjusted socially and did not enjoy the camp experience in general. In contrast, the children whose prejudices decreased had good interpersonal relations with other people, enjoyed the camp experience, and seemed less hostile. These results suggest that the child whose personality characteristics tend to be related to prejudice is only encouraged in his belief by exposure to the actual objects of his hostility. It seems that something more than increased interaction with members of the other group is needed to dampen attitudes of prejudice.

Another experiment, conducted in a similar manner, was more successful in decreasing hostility between the groups. In this case, a counselor actively encouraged good interpersonal relations between the two groups. It seems that if a respected authority figure, who is also well liked, tries to teach the children to relate to each other as individuals rather than as group members, prejudice may be reduced (Radke-Yarrow 1958).

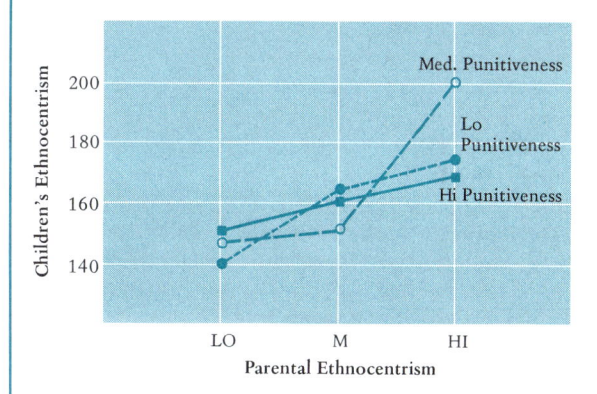

Figure 13.11 Relationship between children's prejudice (ethnocentrism) and parental prejudice and punitiveness. (From R. Epstein and S. S. Komorita. Childhood prejudice as a function of parental ethnocentrism, punitiveness, and outgroup characteristics. *J. pers. soc. Psychol.*, 1966, 3, 259–264.)

Of course, prejudice will not be eliminated by requiring all children to attend integrated summer camps. However, our increasing knowledge of the roots and antecedents of prejudice in children is of great value to those involved in structuring social and educational programs designed to minimize prejudiced behavior.

Interpreting Personality Studies

We have discussed a number of studies which have indicated the great variety of factors that may influence the development of personality. However, the very diversity of these factors can be confusing. Suppose we know that a child is a lower-class first-born with warm, loving parents. Can we predict what his personality will be like? Unfortunately, or perhaps fortunately, we cannot. All that these studies tell us is the *probability* that a child who is exposed to certain environmental factors will show certain personality traits; however, they do not make predictions about any individual child a certainty. Not only is the data probabilistic, but any given child is exposed to a unique combination of environmental factors likely to alter the probability of any one factor affecting the child. As we have seen in the previous chapter, these various influences ultimately reduce to the roles that the child can take and to his efforts to comprehend and assimilate them into his existing patterns of thought and behavior.

What is important about these studies is that they present information about how it is that personality develops—what kinds of influences shape it in one direction and what other kinds of influences shape it in another direction. For example, we have seen that warmth leads to high self-esteem, whereas dictatorial behavior does not. While we cannot predict that any given child with an authoritarian parent will necessarily have low self-esteem, we can nevertheless point to the relationship between a certain parental personality variable and a certain childhood characteristic. We can gain increased understanding of what influences the way different children master new social skills and realities and adjust to new relationships with peers.

Summary

Although some psychologists, like Freud, believe the years from 8 to 12 to be a "latent period" during which no important changes occur, there is considerable evidence that this period is significant for both childhood and adult personality and social behavior. Erik Erikson calls this stage *industry versus inferiority*. The industry lies in the child's mastery of social skills and rules, the inferiority in the accompanying feelings of inadequacy.

As he begins to master the world around him, the child develops new awareness of himself and other people. Peer relationships, which take on increasing importance during this stage, tell psychologists a great deal about both these factors. Sociometric studies show that the qualities children value in their friends are sociability, prosocial behavior, and social perceptiveness.

Sociability and social perceptiveness largely depend on a child's self-esteem. The way parents treat the child is very important in the development of these qualities. Parents of children with high self-esteem interact easily with their children and are consistent in their behavior towards them. Although they expect a lot, they are encouraging and supportive. Parents of children with low self-esteem avoid participation in the children's activities, tend to belittle their efforts, and treat them inconsistently.

Prosocial behavior relies greatly on the child's

development of conscience. Warm and loving attitudes in the parents are translated into conscience in the child through identification and also through the fear of the withdrawal of love.

Parental behavior is important in the development of other peer-related attitudes. Prejudice often predominates in children with poor self-concepts who have received harsh, punitive treatment and little affection from their parents.

Another factor influencing personality development is birth order, because the environment within the family changes with the birth of each child. First-born children tend to be more successful, but less aggressive and more guilt-ridden, than their younger siblings.

School also plays a part in the development of personality at this stage. School experience is related to self-esteem. If a child does not have high intellectual aptitudes, or if his values are different from those of the school, he is likely to suffer decreased self-esteem. A warm, self-controlled teacher can help the child feel accepted.

Social class has important consequences for personality development, too. Lower-class children are likely to live in crowded quarters and dangerous areas, have health problems, and attend inferior schools. Their parents tend to be more restrictive than middle-class parents. Their academic progress often falls below that of the middle-class child. This can be attributed to the inferiority of the schools in poor neighborhoods, to the conflicts of the lower-class child attending a school where middle-class values prevail, and to other environmental factors.

Case Studies

Tom L.

A bit on the small side for his 8 years, Tom is a determined little boy who is characterized by his parents as "very studious and serious" and "more stable" than his younger, but taller, brother. The two boys, who share many interests and activities, are unendingly delighted by their father's frequent participation in their evening and weekend play. A gentle man who works as a copywriter for an advertising agency, Mr. L. is considered a "magician" by all of Tom's friends because of his untiring ability to invent new games for everyone in the neighborhood.

Mrs. L. recalls that Tom has been an extremely active child for every bit of his 8 years—as he was, in fact, even during her pregnancy with him. Now rather high-strung and incessantly alert, Tom shows frequent signs of tension. (This has lessened in the last six months; at the same time his allergies have been improving.) He cries somewhat easily, especially if he feels he has been mistreated in school or by his playmates. (According to Tom, one of his biggest frustrations is having the bigger boys deny him a place on their baseball team.) Tom rarely resorts to fighting in order to settle disputes, although when driven to it he will usually kick because of his size. At home, his anger is vented by slamming things around or by bursts of loud complaining and talking back. Although his parents permit him to "get it out of his system," they later take the time to talk things over, reasoning with him in adultlike fashion. During many other times of stress, however, Tom will refuse all help from his parents, preferring to rely on his rather determined self-sufficiency (which, Mrs. L. notes, erupted when he entered first grade and "became suddenly aware of his small size").

Tom says he has no particular fears about, or anger toward, his parents. In more direct language than is usual for his age, he asserts that there is no real boss in his family, but that his father is the stricter of the two. Mrs. L., whose tendency toward rigidity is probably a holdover from her teaching days, observes that her boys undoubtedly favor their father to some extent, although this does not seem to bother her. She admits being reassured, however, that Tom customarily confides in her on a "man-to-man" basis, especially in view of his otherwise unaffectionate nature.

During his psychiatric interview, Tom was noted to be zestful, talkative, and respectful, although somewhat restless and given to nail-biting. He characterized his dreams as half good and half bad—particularly good when he had memorized parts of movies or television stories and could use his dreams to embellish upon these basic plots; particularly "scary" when he dreamed of falling off a drawbridge into a boat far below. When presented with a box of toys, Tom rustled through its contents (but took nothing outside its walls) and seemed most interested—even if somewhat restlessly—in the gun and in the mechanisms of the dolls' arms and legs. When asked what would be his favorite three wishes, he listed being captain of a baseball team, being a train engineer, and owning a ranch. And, if he could be 16 years old instead of 8, he said grinning, he could not only be an engineer but he could also skip a lot of school.

The one interview procedure he seemed to like best was drawing, for he participated freely, accompanying himself with a monologue of compliments on his work. And, as he completed his session with a particularly pleasing piece, he remarked matter-of-factly to his interviewer, "They don't allow cameras in submarines or else a spy could take pictures."

Although as unpredictable and individualistic as one expects of a boy his age, Tom clearly deserves the "well-adjusted" classification indicated on his school records (Harris 1959).

Caroline J.

Although tiny and somewhat frail for her 9 years, Caroline is a dainty girl who offers her parents an agreeable contrast to her younger brother's high-strung, roughhouse personality. Ever sensitive to the feelings of others, Caroline almost never plays practical jokes, nor willingly teases or fights with anyone except her brother. A "pleasure" to both her parents, this rather homely little girl bubbles with soft, warm personality and a quiet zestfulness.

The daughter of a retired dancer and a hard-driving Army career man, Caroline moved quite often during her first years. Although generally healthy, she suffers from hay fever and an allergy to weather changes. Mrs. J. reports that Caroline had a year of hysterical dreams some time ago, but these are only occasional now. Nevertheless, Mrs. J. avers that Caroline has always been a happy child. Usually very agreeable, Caroline does get emotional when she is angry, but she is soon over it. Eating is the only subject about which parents and daughter fight—and rarely, at that. Caroline will never talk back to Mr. J., whom she both fears and idolizes.

An extremely affectionate girl, Caroline usually gets along best with her demanding father, on whom she has a "terrific crush." Mrs. J. reports that Caroline not only calls her father "cute" and remarks on how well he dances, but also makes excuses for him when Mrs. J. is annoyed at something he has done.

Caroline has taken little notice of her sex up to this point, except to say recently that she "preferred being a girl" when she decided to stop bathing with her brother. Since Caroline takes dancing lessons with older girls, Mrs. J. is almost certain her daughter knows something of the coming physiological changes, but there have been no questions to introduce the subject of menstruation. When Mrs. J. recently found her daughter masturbating with a girl cousin who had given her the idea, she showed as little concern as possible, except to ask the girl's mother to keep them apart for a time, because she knows that Caroline tends to "sit and think about these things and get very concerned."

Perpetually concerned about how "nice" she looks, Caroline shows considerable preoccupation with wanting to be beautiful. At times she is even philosophical about the matter: although she hates her nighttime orthodontic headgear, she wears it willingly, saying that it could have been worse if she had been born with just one eye or leg, for instance. To the contrary, however, her two legs serve her quite well for skillful dancing, although Caroline never seems satisfied with her own performance.

During her psychiatric interview, Caroline made a point of getting along with everyone concerned. In addition to her delightful animation and obliging manner, she seemed quite open and nondefensive. Although she said she preferred arithmetic to playing, she readily professed to fondness for jumping rope, playing with dolls, and playing ball. She also likes going downtown with her mother. She rejected the toy-box dolls as "baby stuff," saying that she preferred to be grown up. She wants to be a dancer, although her most fervent wish is to "have a lot of fun." She would rather be 6 years old than 9, however, because "as a grown-up I have to give up those cute dresses and pinafores." Although she indicated some anger toward her mother and brother, similar questioning about her father evoked only her fear of disobeying him because "he'd feel bad or get angry and spank me more." And, after describing her dreams as "mostly nice," she proceeded to detail her nighttime adventures with quicksand, falling from a 1000-foot tower, and being attacked and buried alive by a mad, drunken strangler.

Caroline's dreams apparently create some problems during daylight, too, for Mrs. J. complains that her daughter's biggest fault is that she is a "dreamer"—to the point where she has no conception of time. Perhaps Caroline has found her own way to ignore that mysterious force that somehow prevents a little girl from being a coquettish 6, when she is, in fact, a "grown-up" 9 (Harris 1959).

References

Allinsmith, W. Moral standards: II. The learning of moral standards. In D. R. Miller and G. E. Swanson (Eds.), *Inner conflict and defense.* New York: Holt, Rinehart & Winston, 1960.

Altus, W. D. Birth order and its sequelae. *Science,* 1966, *151,* 44–49.

Anderson, H. H., and Brewer, J. E. Studies of teachers' classroom personalities. II. Effects of teachers' dominative and integrative contacts on children's behavior. *Appl. Psychol. Monogr.,* 1946, No. 8.

Anderson, H. H., Brewer, J. E., and Reed, M. F. Studies of teachers' classroom personalities. III. Follow-up studies of the effects of dominative and integrative contacts on children's behavior. *Appl. Psychol. Monogr.,* 1946, No. 11.

Austin, M. C., and Thompson, G. C. Children's friendship: A study of the bases on which children select and reject their best friends. *J. educ. Psychol.,* 1948, *39,* 101–116.

Ausubel, D. P. How reversible are the cognitive and motivational effects of cultural deprivation? Implications for teaching the culturally deprived child. *Urban Educ.,* 1964, *1,* 16–38.

Baldwin, A. P. The effect of home environment on nursery school behavior. *Child Develpm.,* 1949, *20,* 49–61.

Bandura, A. Social learning through imitation. In M. R. Jones (Ed.), *Nebraska symposium on motivation.* Vol. X. Lincoln: Univer. of Nebraska Press, 1962.

Bayley, N., and Schaefer, E. S. Relationships between socioeconomic variables and the behavior of mothers toward young children. *J. genet. Psychol.*, 1960, 96, 61–77.

Becker, H. The career of the Chicago public school teacher. *Amer. sociol. Rev.*, 1952, 17, 470–476.

Becker, S. W., Lerner, M. J., and Carroll, J. Conformity as a function of birth order and type of group pressure: A verification. *J. pers. soc. Psychol.*, 1966, 3, 242–244.

Becker, W. C. Consequences of different kinds of parental discipline. In M. L. Hoffman and L. W. Hoffman (Eds.), *Review of child development.* Vol. I. New York: Russell Sage Foundation, 1964.

Bloom, B. S., Davis, A., and Hess, R. *Compensatory education for cultural deprivation.* New York: Holt, Rinehart & Winston, 1965.

Bonney, M. E. A study of the relation of intelligence, family size, and sex differences with mutual friendships in the primary grades. *Child Develpm.*, 1942, 13, 79–100.

Bonney, M. E. Relationships between social success, family size, socioeconomic home background and intelligence among school children in grades III and IV. *Sociometry*, 1944, 7, 26–39.

Bonney, M. E., and Powell, J. Differences in social behavior between sociometrically high and sociometrically low children. *J. educ. Res.*, 1953, 46, 481–495.

Brim, O. G., Jr. Family structure and sex-role learning by children: A further analysis of Helen Koch's data. *Sociometry*, 1958, 21, 1–16.

Burger, G., and Armentrout, J. A factor analysis of fifth- and sixth-graders' reports of parental child-rearing behavior. *Develpm. Psychol.*, 1971, 4, 483.

Campbell, J. D., and Yarrow, M. R. Perceptual and behavioral correlates of social effectiveness. *Sociometry*, 1961, 24, 1–20.

Caplan, G. *Principles of preventive psychiatry.* New York: Basic Books, 1964.

Caplin, M. D. The relationship between self concept and academic achievement and between level of aspiration and academic achievement. *Dissert. Abstr.*, 1966, 27, 979–980.

Chazan, M. School phobia. *Brit. J. educ. Psychol.*, 1962, 32, 209–217.

Chess, S., Thomas, A., and Birch, H. G. Behavior problems revisited: Findings of an anterospective study. *J. Amer. Acad. Child Psychiat.*, 1967, 6, 321–331.

Cheyney, A. B. Teachers of the culturally disadvantaged. *Except. Children*, September 1966, 33, 83–88.

Ciaccio, N. V. A test of Erikson's theory of ego epigenesis. *Develpm. Psychol.*, 1971, 4, 306–311.

Cobb, E. A. Family press variables. *Monogr. Soc. Res. Child Develpm.*, 1943, 8, 327–361.

Cohen, S. An examination of frustration-aggression relations in boys during middle childhood. *J genet. Psychol.*, 1971, 118, 129–140.

Conant, J. B. Social dynamite in our large cities. In *Social dynamite: The report of the conference on unemployed, out-of-school youth in urban areas.* Washington, D.C.: National Committee for Children and Youth, 1961.

Coolidge, J. C., Tessman, E., Waldfogel, S., and Willer, M. L. Patterns of aggression in school phobia. *Psychoanal. Study Child.*, 1962, 17, 319–333.

Coopersmith, S. *The antecedents of self-esteem.* San Francisco: Freeman, 1967.

Crutchfield, R. S. Conformity and character. *Amer. Psychologist*, 1955, 10, 191.

Deutsch, M. The disadvantaged child and the learning process. In A. H. Passow (Ed.), *Education in depressed areas.* New York: Columbia Univer. Press, 1963.

Dolger, L., and Ginandes, J. Children's attitudes toward discipline as related to socio-economic status. *J. exp. Educ.*, 1946, 15, 161–165.

Dunlop, G. M. Certain aspects of children's fears. Unpublished doctoral dissertation, Columbia Univer., 1951.

Elkins, D. Some factors related to the choice status of ninety eighth-grade children in a school society. *Genet. psychol. Monogr.*, 1958, 58, 207–272.

Epstein, R. Social class membership and early childhood memories. *Child Develpm.*, 1963, 34, 503–508.

Epstein, R. C., and Komorita, S. S. Childhood prejudice as a function of parental ethnocentrism, punitiveness, and out-group characteristics. *J. pers. soc. Psychol.*, 1966, 3, 259–264. (a)

Epstein, R. C., and Komorita, S. S. Prejudice among Negro children as related to parental ethnocentrism and punitiveness. *J. pers. soc. Psychol.*, 1966, 4, 643–677. (b)

Erikson, E. H. *Childhood and society.* New York: Norton, 1950.

Feinberg, M. R., Smith, M., and Schmidt, R. An analysis of expressions used by adolescents of varying economic levels to describe accepted and rejected peers. *J. genet. Psychol.*, 1958, 93, 133–148.

Frenkel-Brunswik, E. A study of prejudice in children. *Human Relat.*, 1948, 1, 295–306.

Freud, A. *The ego and mechanisms of defense.* New York: International Universities Press, 1946.

Freud, S. *Outline of psychoanalysis.* New York: Norton, 1949.

Furfey, P. H. Some factors influencing the selection of boys' "chums." *J. appl. Psychol.*, 1927, 11, 47–51.

Garner, A. M., and Wenar, C. *The mother–child interaction in psychosomatic disorders.* Urbana: Univer. of Illinois Press, 1959.

Gordon, E. W., and Wilkerson, D. A. *Compensatory education for the disadvantaged. Programs and practices: Preschool through college.* New York: College Entrance Examination Board, 1966.

Gottlieb, D. Teaching and students: The views of Negro and white teachers. *Sociol. Educ.* 1964, 37, 345–353.

Greenberg, J. W., Gerver, J. M., Chall, J., and Davidson, H. H. Attitudes of children from a deprived environment toward achievement-related concepts. *J. educ. Res.*, 1965, *59*, 57–62.

Groff, P. J. Dissatisfactions in teaching the culturally deprived child. *Phi Delta Kappa*, 1963, *45*, 76.

Gump, P. V., and Sutton-Smith, B. The "it" role in children's games. *The Group*, 1955, *17*, 3–8.

Haller, A. O., and Thomas, S. Personality correlates of the socioeconomic status of adolescent males. *Sociometry*, 1962, *25*(4), 398–404.

Harris, I. D. *Normal children and mothers.* New York: Free Press, 1959. Pp. 183–195, 196–208.

Harris, I. D. *The promised seed.* London: Macmillan, 1964.

Harrison, C. W., Rawls, J., and Rawls, D. Differences between leaders and nonleaders in six- to eleven-year-old children. *J. soc. Psychol.*, 1971, *84*, 269–272.

Hartup, W. W., Glazer, J. A., and Charlesworth, R. Peer reinforcement and sociometric status. *Child Develpm.*, 1967, *38*, 1017–1024.

Havighurst, R. J., and Davis, A. A comparison of the Chicago and Harvard studies of social class differences in child rearing. *Amer. sociol. Rev.*, 1955, *20*, 438–442.

Heil, L. M., and Washburne, C. Characteristics of teachers related to children's progress. *J. teacher Educ.*, 1961, *12*, 401–406.

Helmreich, R. L., and Collins, B. E. Situational determinants of affiliative preference under stress. *J. pers. soc. Psychol.*, 1967, *6*, 79–85.

Hetherington, E. M. A developmental study of the effects of sex of the dominant parent on sex-role preference, identification, and imitation in children. *J. per. soc. Psychol.*, 1965, *2*, 188–194.

Hill, K. T. Relation of test anxiety, defensiveness, and intelligence to sociometric status. *Child Develpm.*, 1963, *34*, 767–776.

Hill, K. T., and Sarason, S. B. The relation of test anxiety and defensiveness to test and school performance over the elementary-school years: A further longitudinal study. *Monogr. Soc. Res. Child Develpm.*, 1966, *31*(2), 1–76.

Hoffman, L. W. The father's role in the family and the child's peer-group adjustment. *Merrill-Palmer Quart.*, 1961, *7*, 97–105.

Hoffman, M. L. Moral development. In P. H. Mussen (Ed.), *Carmichael's manual of child psychology.* Vol. II. New York: Wiley, 1970.

Hoffman, M. L., and Saltzstein, H. D. Parent practices and the child's moral orientation. Paper read at meeting of American Psychological Association, Chicago, 1960.

Hull, V., Krippene, B., and Porter, F. *Manitowoc story: A team approach to a school health study.* Fond du Lac, Wis.: Wis. State Board of Health, 1966.

Iscoe, I., and Garden, J. A. Field dependence, manifest anxiety, and sociometric status in children. *J. consult. Psychol.*, 1961, *25*, 184.

Jersild, A. T. *In search of self.* New York: Columbia Univer. Press, 1952.

Jersild, A. T. *Child psychology.* (6th ed.) Englewood Cliffs, N.J.: Prentice-Hall, 1968.

Jersild, A. T., and Tasch, R. J. *Children's interests.* New York: Teachers College, Columbia Univer., 1949.

Jersild, A. T., Woodyard, E. S., and del Solar, C. F. *Joys and problems of child rearing.* New York: Teachers College, Columbia Univer., 1949.

Johnson, A. M. School phobia. *Amer. J. Orthopsychiat.*, 1941, *11*, 702–711.

Jones, H. E. The environment and mental development. In L. Carmichael (Ed.), *Manual of child psychology.* (2nd ed.) New York: Wiley, 1954.

Kagan, J. Personality development. In I. L. Janis (Ed.), *Personality: Dynamics, development and assessment.* New York: Harcourt Brace Jovanovich, 1970.

Kagan, J., and Moss, H. A. *Birth to maturity: The Fels study of psychological development.* N.Y.: Wiley, 1962.

Katcher, A. The discrimination of sex differences by young children. *J. genet. Psychol.*, 1955, *87*, 131–143.

Kerber, A., and Bommarito, B. (Eds.) *The schools and the urban crisis.* New York: Holt, Rinehart & Winston, 1965.

Kessler, J. W. *Psychopathology of childhood.* Englewood Cliffs, N.J.: Prentice-Hall, 1966.

Klaus, R. A. Interrelationships of attributes that accepted and rejected children ascribe to their peers. Unpublished doctoral dissertation, George Peabody College for Teachers, 1959.

Koch, H. L. Some emotional attitudes of the young child in relation to characteristics of his siblings. *Child Develpm.*, 1956, *27*, 393–426.

Kohlberg, L. A cognitive-developmental analysis of children's sex-role concepts and attitudes. In E. E. Maccoby (Ed.), *The development of sex differences.* Stanford, Calif.: Stanford Univer. Press, 1966.

Lefevre, C. Inner-city school—as the children see it. *Elem. sch. J.*, 1966, *67*, 8–15.

Lesser, G. S. The relationships between various forms of aggression and popularity among lower-class children. *J. educ. Psychol.*, 1959, *50*, 20–25.

Levine, M., Wesolowski, J. C., and Corbett, F. J. Pupil turnover and academic performance in an inner-city elementary school. *Psychol. Sch.*, 1966, *3*, 153–158.

Lourenso, S. V., Greenberg, J. W., and Davidson, H. H. Personality characteristics revealed in drawing of deprived children who differ in school achievement. *J. educ. Res.*, 1965, *59*, 63–67.

Maccoby, E. E. Sex differences and their implications for sex roles. Address presented at convention of American Psychological Association, 1971.

Maccoby, E. E., Gibbs, P. K., et al. Methods of child-rearing in two social classes. In W. E. Martin and C. B. Stendler (Eds.), *Readings in child development.* New York: Harcourt Brace Jovanovich, 1954.

Maccoby, E. E., and Wilson, W. C. Identification and observational learning from film. *J. abnorm. soc. Psychol.*, 1957, *55*, 76.

Martin, W. Singularity and stability of profiles of

social behavior. In C. B. Stendler (Ed.), *Readings in child behavior and development.* New York: Harcourt Brace Jovanovich, 1964.

McDavid, J. W., and Harari, H. Stereotyping of names and popularity in grade-school children. *Child Develpm.*, 1966, 37, 453–459.

Meltzer, H. Economic security and children's attitudes to parents. *Amer. J. Orthopsychiat.*, 1936, 6, 590–608.

Meyers, C. E. The effect of conflicting authority on the child. *Univer. of Iowa Stud. Child Welf.*, 1944, 20(409), 31–98.

Mock, R. L., and Tuddenham, R. D. Race and conformity among children. *Develpm. Psychol.*, 1971, 3, 349–365.

Moore, S. G. Correlates of peer acceptance in nursery school children. In W. W. Hartup and N. L. Smothergill (Eds.), *The young child.* Washington, D.C.: National Association for the Education of Young Children, 1967.

Morland, J. K. A comparison of race awareness in northern and southern children. *Amer. J. Orthopsychiat.*, 1966, 36, 22–31.

Mussen, P. H. Some personality and social factors related to changes in children's attitudes toward Negroes. *J. abnorm. soc. Psychol.*, 1950, 45, 423–441.

Nuttall, E., and Nuttall, R. Effects of size of family on parent–child relationships. *Proc. Amer. Psychol. Assoc.*, 1971, 267.

Opie, I., and Opie, P. *The lore and language of schoolchildren.* London: Oxford Univer. Press, 1959.

Orpen, C. The effect of cultural factors on the relationship between prejudice and personality. *J. Psychol.*, 1971, 78, 73–79.

Radke, M. J., and Trager, H. G. Children's perception of the social roles of Negroes and whites. *J. Psychol.*, 1950, 29, 3–33.

Radke, M. J., Trager, H. G., and Davis, H. Social perceptions and attitudes of children. *Genet. Psychol. Monogr.*, 1949, 40, 327–447.

Radke-Yarrow, M. Interpersonal dynamics in a desegregation process. *J. soc. Issues*, 1958, 14, 3–63.

Radke-Yarrow, M., Trager, H. G., and Miller, J. The role of parents in the development of children's ethnic attitudes. *Child Develpm.*, 1952, 23, 13–53.

Reese, H. W. Relationship between self-acceptance and sociometric choice. *J. abnorm. soc. Psychol.*, 1961, 62, 472–474.

Reese, H. W., and Lipsitt, L. P. (Eds.) *Experimental child psychology.* New York: Academic Press, 1970.

Richardson, S. A., and Green, A. When is black beautiful? Coloured and white children's reactions to skin colour. *Brit. J. educ. Psychol.*, 1971, 41, 62–69.

Roberts, C. R. Ordinal position and its relation to some aspects of personality. *J. genet. Psychol.*, 1938, 53, 173–213.

Rogers, C. R. A study of the mental health problems in three representative elementary schools. In *A study of health and physical education in Columbus public schools.* Monogr. of the Bureau of Educ. Research, No. 25. Columbus: Ohio State Univer. Press, 1942.

Rosenberg, M. *Society and the adolescent self-image.* Princeton, N.J.: Princeton Univer. Press, 1965.

Rosenow, C., and Whyte, A. H. The ordinal position of problem children. *Amer. J. Orthopsychiat.*, 1931, 1, 430–434.

Sarason, S. B., Hill, K. T., and Zimbardo, P. G. A longitudinal study of the relation of test anxiety to performance on intelligence and achievement tests. *Monogr. Soc. Res. Child Develpm.*, 1964, 29, No. 7.

Sears, P. S. Doll play aggressions in normal young children: Influence of sex, age, sibling status, father's absence. *Psychol. Monogr.*, 1951, 65, No. 6.

Sears, R. R. The relation of early socialization experiences to aggression in middle childhood. *J. abnorm. soc. Psychol.*, 1961, 63, 466–492.

Sears, R. R., Maccoby, E. E., and Levin, H. *Patterns of child rearing.* New York: Harper & Row, 1957.

Sells, S. B., and Roff, M. Peer acceptance-rejection and birth order. *Psychol. Sch.*, 1964, 1, 156–162.

Sells, S. B., and Roff, M. *Peer acceptance-rejection and personality development.* (Final Report, Project No. OE 5-0417, U.S. Dept. of Health, Education and Welfare.) Washington, D.C.: Government Printing Office, 1967.

Sgan, M. L. Social reinforcement, socioeconomic status, and susceptibility to experimenter influence. *J. pers. soc. Psychol.*, 1967, 5, 202–210.

Simon, W. E., and Bernstein, E. The relationship between self-esteem and perceived reciprocal liking: A sociometric test of the theory of cognitive balance. *J. Psychol.*, 1971, 79, 197–201.

Smith, G. H. Sociometric study of best-liked and least-liked children. *Elem. sch. J.*, 1950, 51, 77–85.

Spock, B. *Baby and child care.* New York: Pocket Books, 1946.

Stott, L. H. Persisting effects of early family experiences upon personality development. *Merrill-Palmer Quart.*, Spring 1957, 3(Special issue, Seminar on Child Development).

Sutton-Smith, B., and Rosenberg, B. G. Age changes in the effects of ordinal position on sex-role identification. *J. genet. Psychol.*, 1965, 107, 61–73.

Sutton-Smith, B., and Rosenberg, B. G. *The sibling.* New York: Holt, Rinehart & Winston, 1970.

Tabachnick, R. Some correlates of prejudice toward Negroes in elementary age children. *J. genet. Psychol.*, 1962, 100, 193–203.

Trent, R. D. The relation between expressed self-acceptance and expressed attitudes toward Negroes and whites among Negro children. *J. genet. Psychol.*, 1957, 91, 25–31.

Tuddenham, R. D. Studies in reputation: I. Sex and grade differences in school children's evaluation of their peers. *Psychol. Monogr.*, 1952, 66, No. 333.

Vroegh, K. The relationship of birth order and sex of

siblings to gender role identity. *Develpm. Psychol.*, 1971, 4, 407–411.

Waite, R. R. Further attempts to integrate and urbanize first-grade reading textbooks: A research study. *J. Negro Educ.*, 1968, 37(1), 62–69.

White, W. F., and Richmond, B. O. Perception of self and peers by economically deprived black and advantaged white fifth-graders. *Perceptual and motor Skills*, 1970, 30, 533–534.

Winder, C. L., and Rau, L. Parental attitudes associated with social deviance in preadolescent boys. *J. abnorm. soc. Psychol.*, 1962, 64, 418–424.

Witryol, S. L., and Thompson, G. G. A critical review of the stability of social acceptability scores obtained with the partial-rank-order and the paired-comparison scales. *Genet. Monogr.*, 1953, 48, 221–260.

Yarrow, L. J., and Yarrow, M. R. Leadership and interpersonal change. *J. soc. Issues*, 1958, 14, 47–50.

VII

Adolescence

Sybil Shackman — Monkmeyer

Physical and Cognitive Development and Role Changes 14

WHEN CHILDREN reach the age of about 13 years, they begin to undergo marked physical, mental, and social changes. Generally, the period of these changes lasts until their early twenties. This is the time of life that has been termed *adolescence*. It is the period of transition from childhood to adulthood. During the adolescent years individuals show some of the characteristics of adults, such as the capacity for rational thought, and some of the characteristics of children, such as the failure to consistently use their rational faculties in appropriate situations. In general, adolescent behavior and appearance are marked by an uncertain status—neither completely child nor yet completely adult.

During this period of transition from childhood to adulthood, the adolescent is confronted with a number of developmental tasks. He must reject childhood behavior patterns and adopt new adult roles for interacting socially and organizing his life activities. Some of these adult roles and attitudes include: accepting his or her physique and its corresponding masculine or feminine role; establishing good relations with members of the opposite sex; achieving emotional independence from parents; choosing and preparing for a vocation; and developing a set of socially responsible attitudes and behaviors. Whether it is easy or difficult to assume these adult roles will vary with individual upbringing, the culture of the times, the economic situation, and the individual's own developing personality, among other factors.

Adolescence—A Time of Change

There seems to be some controversy among psychologists about how much change in roles and role expectations takes place in adolescence and the effect of these changes on the individual. The traditional view of the Freudian and ego psychologists stresses the difficulties and tensions of adolescence. Psychoanalytic thinkers often use the phrase *storm and stress*, borrowed from late eighteenth-century Romantic literature, to characterize this period. They see conflict and crisis arising from the clash of newly reawakened sexual wishes and fantasies with the defenses against these desires that were operative in the preadolescent period. Others attribute the crisis nature of this period to external pressures in the form of new social role expectations. In both views, the adolescent's identity is put in question as he experiences drastic change from within and without.

On the other hand, there are theories that do not characterize adolescence in "crisis" terms. While recognizing that many changes do indeed occur during this period, they contend that these changes do not necessarily create a crisis state in the individual.

Crisis Views

ERIKSON'S THEORY. One theorist who regards adolescence as a period of struggle is Erik Erikson. He has termed the adolescent period a time of *identity crisis*. The adolescent, encountering major physical and emotional changes, must continually struggle to reestablish a sense of himself—that is, the feeling that he is the same person that he has always felt himself to be. He must also try to adjust his sense of himself with the self that others perceive in him. The job of consolidating an identity can be hard or easy. To quote Erikson:

> In some young people, in some classes, at some periods in history, this crisis will be minimal; in other people, classes, and periods, the crisis will be clearly marked off as a critical period, a kind of "second birth." . . . Some young individuals will succumb to this crisis in all manner of neurotic, psychotic, or delinquent behavior; others will resolve it through participation in ideological movements passionately concerned with religion or politics, nature or art. Still others, although suffering and deviating dangerously through what appears to be a prolonged adolescence, eventually come to contribute an original bit to an emerging style of life. (Erikson 1958)

LEWIN'S THEORY. Another formulation of the changes and tasks of adolescence is that of Kurt Lewin (1935). Lewin's view of adolescence is based on his theory of the *life space*. The life space is the sum of physical and nonphysical environmental and personal factors that determine an individual's behavior. These factors are all interdependent. Therefore, a change in one of them will tend to bring about a change in the total life space. Within this life space there are negative and positive goals, objects to be sought and avoided, and forces that impel the individual toward or away from these goal objects.

According to Lewin, the adolescent life space is characterized by its great speed of change. The adolescent experiences a considerable speedup in body growth and drastic changes in physical characteristics. Thus, his self-image, which is closely tied to his body image, is disturbed. The life space of his own body, relatively stable throughout late childhood, becomes unreliable and unknown. This precipitates changes in other parts of the total life space.

Furthermore, according to Lewin, the adolescent is not merely confused about his body, but is also confused by his ambiguous social situation. In Western society, much of the adolescent's earlier, childish behavior is now deemed unacceptable. But, on the other hand, he has not been permitted many adult freedoms, such as sexual intercourse, driving a car, buying liquor, and so forth. His social life space, then, is not clearly defined and is not always easy for him to clarify and structure. As the scope of his life space expands, the adolescent must go through a process of increasing differentiation and structuring of the new territory.

In comparing the theories of Erikson and Lewin, it is evident that they are discussing the same phenomenon. For Erikson, the psychoanalyst, the key term is *identity*, while for Lewin, the Gestalt psychologist, the key term is *life space*, but both are dealing with the combined influences of internal physical and psychological change and of external societal pressures that compel the adolescent to develop mature adult behavior. And both theorists see these physical and psychological changes as being disruptive and disorienting, producing to some degree a crisis in identity and role formations.

Noncrisis Views

Although there is no doubt that rather drastic physical and psychological changes take place during adolescence, and although the adolescent must adapt to them, not all theorists depict this process as quite so difficult as do Erikson and Lewin. It is clear that while these changes are occurring, many adolescents are fortunate enough to be growing apace with their newfound skills and feelings, and have no sense of identity crises or of inarticulated life spaces through which they are being propelled. Several recent researchers support this view and contend that most adolescents in our society do not experience severe problems in growing up.

One such theorist is Gergen (1972). Gergen seriously questions the underlying assumptions of such crisis theories, particularly that of Erikson. According to Gergen, Erikson's faulty assumption is that the formation of a stable and coherent identity is the normal, healthy process, while any inability to do so is unhealthy or pathological. Gergen doubts "that a person normally develops a coherent sense of identity, and to the extent that he does, he may experience severe emotional distress" (Gergen 1972). Rather, he proposes that people can potentially develop many identities and roles, and that the healthy personality is multidimensional. Moreover, Gergen maintains that individuals are actually limited and constricted by external and internalized pressures if they adopt a single, consolidated self-concept.

Among others who challenge the "struggle" view of adolescence are Douvan, Gold, and Bandura. Douvan and Gold (1966), for example, reported that there is no sharp discontinuity between childhood and adolescence, and adolescence and adulthood. They maintain that research does not support the view that adolescents feel that too many demands are put on them or that they are overly constrained by their parents. This view is shared by many social learning theorists, such as Albert Bandura (1964), who stated:

The view that adolescents are engaged in a struggle to emancipate themselves from their family receives little support from our study....

No age group is free from stress or adjustment problems. Our findings suggest, however, that the behavioral characteristics exhibited by children during the so-called adolescent stages are lawfully related to, and consistent with, preadolescent social behavior. (Bandura 1964)

According to Douvan and Gold (1966), the "storm-and-stress" (crisis) view of adolescence stems from undue emphasis being placed on two subgroups of adolescents whose behavior, they maintain, is not typical of the population as a whole. These subgroups are the juvenile delinquents and those individuals psychologically disturbed to the degree of seeking, or being compelled to seek, professional help. These adolescents have problems in making the transition to adulthood, experiencing all kinds of conflicts with parents, authorities, and peers, as well as much internal confusion.

Since a great deal of our present-day thought regarding the subject of adolescence has been based on observations of such cases, it may partially explain, as Douvan and Gold have suggested, why experimental evidence from studies of normal populations is increasingly at odds with traditional theory.

Physical and Sexual Development

With the onset of puberty—that time in early adolescence when the sexual and reproductive system matures—there is a great spurt in the individual's rate of growth. These rapidly occurring changes in the adolescent's body have a great effect on the direction of the adolescent's emotional and social development.

A psychologist who has done extensive work in the area of physical and sexual development is J. M. Tanner. The following discussion on bodily

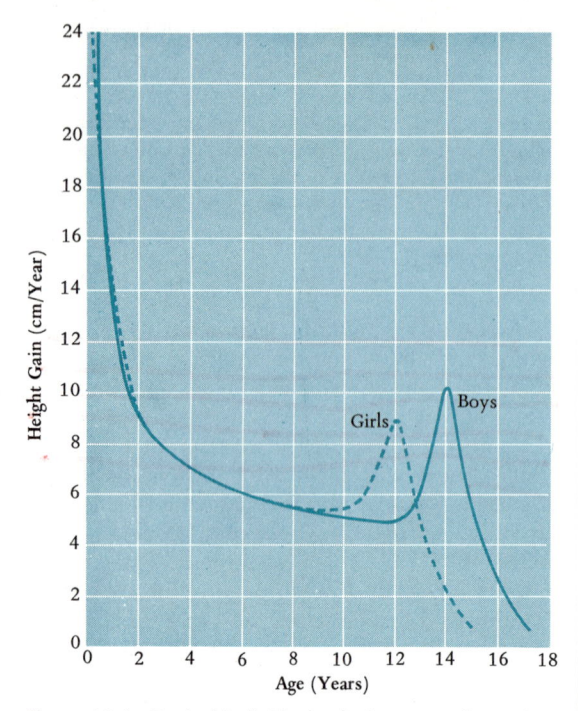

Figure 14.1 Typical individual velocity curves for supine length or height in boys and girls. These curves represent the velocity of the typical boy and girl at any given instant. (From J. M. Tanner, R. H. Whitehouse, and M. Takaishi. Standards from birth to maturity for height, weight, height velocity and weight velocity: British children 1965. *Arch. Dis. Child.*, 1966, *41*, 455–471.)

changes in the adolescent is based on Tanner's widely accepted treatment of this subject.[1]

Physical Changes in Adolescence

HEIGHT. One evidence of the adolescent's rapid growth rate is height increase. For at least a year, the rate of growth doubles, so that a boy will probably be growing at as fast a rate as he was during the years from birth to age 2. During the year of peak growth rate, the adolescent boy grows, on the average, between 2.7 inches and 4.7 inches, while the adolescent girl grows between 2.3 and 4.3 inches. Children who reach their peak growth rate early generally have higher peak rates than those who reach maximum growth rate at a later age. The age of peak growth in height varies, averaging in the United States about 13½ years for boys from middle-income groups and 11½ years for girls from the same socioeconomic groups (Tanner 1970).

The growth spurt in adolescence is under the control of body chemicals called hormones. These hormones are different from the hormones that controlled growth in earlier stages of development. Thus, the amount of height added during adolescence is relatively independent of the amount of height reached before adolescence. However, there is a .80 correlation between preadolescent and adult height.

For example, most children who were in, say, the fortieth percentile in height before adolescence eventually are in that same percentile as adults. On the other hand, a significant number of those children end up in lower or higher percentiles. Thus, some of the variability in adult height can be attributed to differences in the amount of adolescent growth spurt (Tanner 1970).

Although all muscular and skeletal dimensions share in the growth spurt, they do not all do so to the same degree. Most of the height spurt, for example, is caused by an increase in trunk length rather than an increase in growth of the legs. In addition, not all body parts reach their peak rate of growth at the same time. Usually leg length reaches its peak first, followed by trunk length and, lastly, by the width of the shoulders. This is why children continue to outgrow jackets long after they have stopped outgrowing pants.

The first body parts to reach their full adult size are the extremities—hands, feet, and head. Thus, many adolescent boys and girls seem strangely proportioned. As the other parts of their bodies reach adult size, the proportions between body parts assume their adult form.

MUSCLE AND BONE. Aside from a gain in height, other aspects of the body show dramatic changes in the adolescent years. One of the more evident changes is the increase in bone and muscle tissue relative to the amount of fat tissue. In a study by Tanner (1965), curves for muscle gain

---

1. J. M. Tanner. Physical growth. In P. H. Mussen (Ed.), *Carmichael's manual of child psychology*. Vol. I. (3rd ed.) New York: Wiley, 1970.

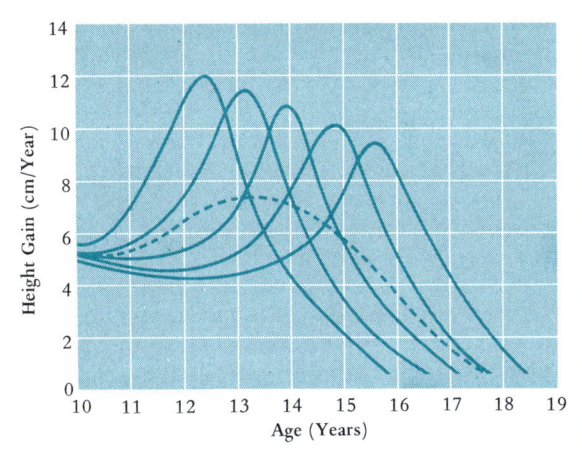

Figure 14.2 The relation between individual and mean velocities during the adolescent spurt. These curves (solid lines) represent the individual height velocity of five boys of the Harpenden growth study with the mean curve (dashed line) constructed by averaging their values at each age. (From J. M. Tanner, R. H. Whitehouse, and M. Takaishi. Standards from birth to maturity for height, weight, height velocity and weight velocity: British children 1965. *Arch. Dis. Child.,* 1966, *41,* 455–471.)

and fat loss over a number of years were established for 28 boys and 21 girls. The individual muscle growth patterns were aligned according to each child's point of peak height growth, rather than his chronological age. The growth pattern among adolescents is similar, while the chronological timing of the spurt may be different. Hence, to compare them in terms of chronological age would merely obscure the results.

The study demonstrated that the amount of muscle area in cross sections of the limbs shows the greatest gains in growth rate slightly after the point of peak height growth rate for both girls and boys. Boys, however, reach a considerably greater growth rate of muscle tissue than girls.

According to Tanner the average curve for bone width in the limbs shows a pattern similar to that for muscle tissue, but it peaks at the same time as does height. Similarly, fat loss is greatest at the time of maximum height gain. As Tanner pointed out, boys tend to lose fat absolutely during adolescence—that is, the velocity of fat loss is enough to reduce their gain of fat to below zero.

Girls, on the other hand, do not lose fat but rather gain fat in progressively decreasing amounts. In general, Tanner showed that maximum height growth is coincident, or nearly so, with changes in the muscle, fat, and bone proportions.

STRENGTH. As muscles increase in size, so, naturally, does strength increase. According to Tanner, boys and girls generally have the same strength relative to body size before puberty, but boys show a marked spurt in strength after the onset of puberty. Girls, on the other hand, show less growth in strength, generally reaching the maximum shortly after the beginning of menstruation.

Boys also tend to develop larger hearts and lungs than do girls, as well as higher systolic blood pressure, a lower heart resting rate, and a greater capacity for carrying oxygen in the blood. This greater capacity is a result of the fact that boys develop more red blood cells than girls. These cells contain the oxygen-bearing substance

Figure 14.3 Mean velocity of combined muscle cross-sectional area (calf, arm, and thigh). Longitudinal data, individual curves aligned on peak height velocity (PHV). (From J. M. Tanner. Radiographic studies of body composition. *Symp. Soc. Hum. Biol., 7,* 211–238. In J. Brozek (Ed.), *Body composition.* Oxford: Pergamon, 1965.)

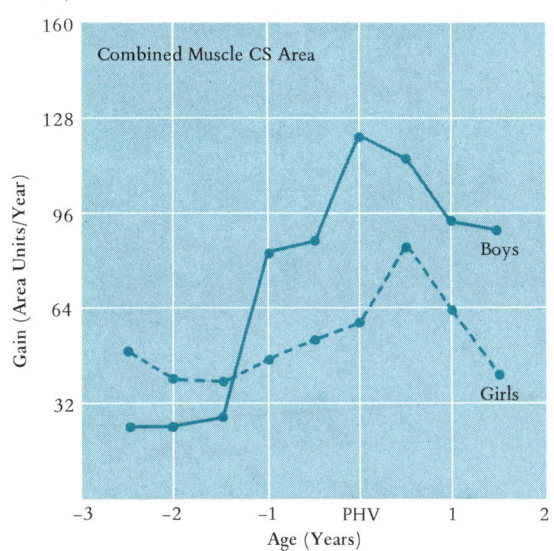

PHYSICAL AND COGNITIVE DEVELOPMENT AND ROLE CHANGES

called hemoglobin. Finally, the boys develop a greater ability for neutralizing chemical wastes produced by muscular exercise (Tanner 1970).

The result of these differences is that boys' muscles have more energy to burn and take longer to tire than do girls' muscles. Thus, boys, at the stage of adolescence, have greater strength and, hence, greater athletic capacity than do most girls. This fact has a number of consequences psychologically, socially, and culturally. One of the most obvious is that girls and boys do not, as a rule, participate in rough sports together. Also, girls who are exceptionally strong or athletic tend, unfairly, to be regarded as unfeminine.

Sexual Development

As we noted earlier, the body changes that we have been discussing are controlled by chemicals called hormones. In boys, increased production of the male hormone, testosterone, is directly responsible for the sharp rise in red blood cell production. Besides controlling growth and strength, hormones also determine the development of adult sex characteristics for both males and females.

At the same time as the spurt in muscular and skeletal growth takes place, there also occurs the development of adult sex organs and other adult sex characteristics. In girls, the reproductive organs—the ovaries, uterus, clitoris, and vagina—enlarge, as do the testes, penis, prostate, and seminal ducts in boys. Along with the development of the reproductive organs, there is also growth of pubic and axillary (armpit) hair, and, in girls, the enlargement of the breasts.

The ages at which these developments take place vary for different individuals. Penis growth, for example, begins to accelerate at about age 13 and end at about age 15. In some individuals, however, it begins as early as age 11 or as late as age 14 (Tanner 1970). Thus, within a given age group, it is possible to find individuals who are still preadolescent.

IN GIRLS. While the chronological ages of development can differ for both boys and girls, the order in which the specific developments occur varies considerably less. Generally, the first sign of puberty in girls is the appearance of the breast bud, usually at about age 11, although it can occur as early as 8 or as late as 13 years. Most girls begin to develop pubic hair shortly after the beginning of breast development. At the same time the breasts are developing, the uterus and vagina undergo their development, and the labia and clitoris enlarge.

Later in the developmental sequence, about two and one-half years after the appearance of the breast bud, the girl's first menstrual period, called menarche, occurs. Menarche usually takes place at about age 13, but can sometimes occur as early as 10 or as late as 16½. Sequentially, however, menarche usually comes slightly before breast development and pubic hair growth are complete, and, with few exceptions, comes after the peak in height growth spurt.

Menarche probably represents the mature stage in the development of the uterus. However, it is not necessarily a sign that full reproductive capability is attained. Early menstrual cycles may be irregular and are often unaccompanied by the

Figure 14.4 Mean velocity of combined subcutaneous fat cross-sectional area (calf, arm, and thigh). Longitudinal data, individual curves aligned on peak height velocity (PHV). (From J. M. Tanner. Radiographic studies of body composition. *Symp. Soc. Hum. Biol., 7*, 211–238. In J. Brozek (Ed.), *Body Composition.* Oxford: Pergamon, 1965.)

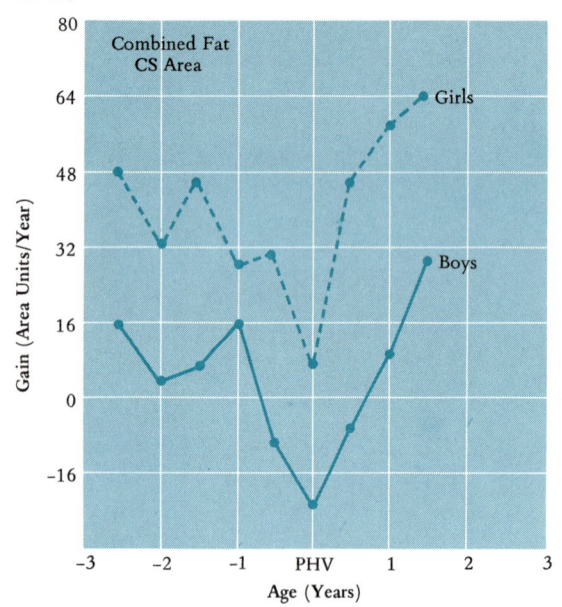

454 ADOLESCENCE

release of an egg. There is often a period of sterility for as long as 18 months after the first menstrual period.

IN BOYS. Just as adolescent girls go through a fairly standard sequence of development during puberty, boys also experience physical changes in a regular order. In boys, pubertal changes begin with accelerated growth of the testes and scrotum. Shortly thereafter, pubic hair begins to grow. Increased penis growth begins about one year after the start of accelerated growth of the testes. There is also a concurrent enlargement of the seminal ducts and the prostate gland. In addition, there is some growth of the Leydig cells, which secrete male hormones, but generally these reach their full development only when the testes have about reached adult size and active sperm are being produced. Finally, about a year after the acceleration in penis growth, the boy is usually capable of seminal ejaculation. Exactly when this first occurs is determined by psychological, cultural, and biological factors (Tanner 1970).

According to Tanner, the male breast also exhibits changes during adolescence. Before puberty the diameter of the areola (the area of darker pigmentation around and including the nipples) is equal for both sexes. However, during adolescence the size almost doubles for men — it about triples for women. Some boys also experience an enlargement of the whole breast midway through adolescence, but this enlargement usually recedes in a year or so.

With the onset of puberty, secondary sex characteristics also begin to develop. About two years after the first appearance of pubic hair, axillary hair begins to grow. In boys, the first evidence of facial hair appears at around this time, growing first at the corners of the upper lip, then over the whole upper lip, then on the upper cheeks and the middle of the chin, and finally on the lower cheeks and the rest of the chin. Body hair continues to grow for some time, often well beyond puberty; the amount is probably determined by heredity (Tanner 1970).

Voice change, another secondary sex characteristic, takes place somewhat late in the series of changes associated with puberty. Male hormones acting on the laryngeal cartilages cause an enlargement of the larynx and a lengthening of the

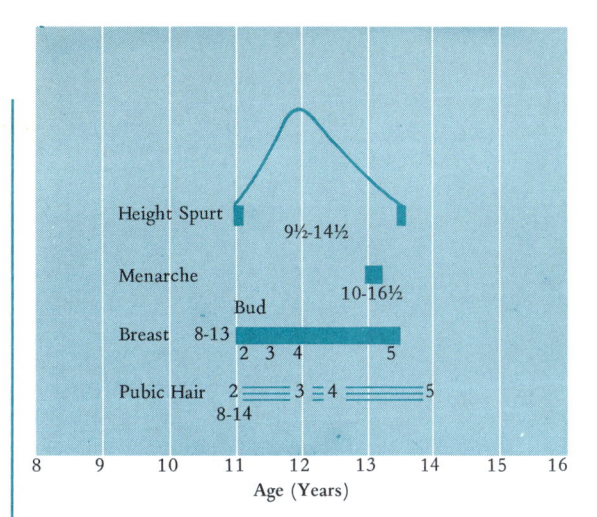

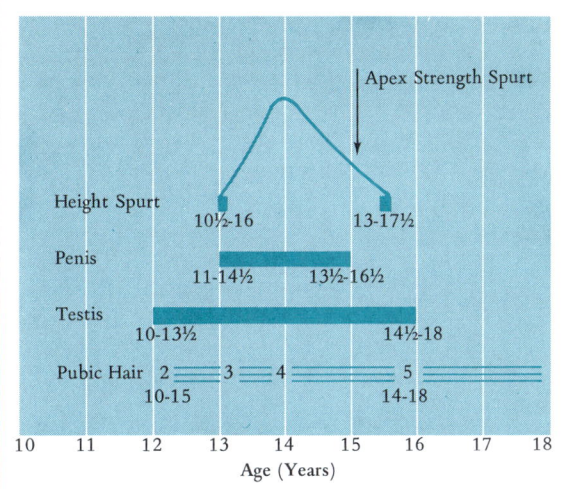

Figure 14.5 Diagram of sequence of events at adolescence in girls and boys. An average boy and girl are represented. The range of ages within which each event charted may begin and end is given by the figures placed directly below its start and finish. (From J. M. Tanner. *Growth at adolescence*. (2nd ed.) Blackwell Scientific Publications. Philadelphia: F. A. Davis Co., 1962.)

vocal cords, resulting in a lower pitch. The change is fairly gradual, producing at first a variable pitch, while the final adult pitch may not be attained until late adolescence (Tanner 1970).

RATE OF MATURATION. The time interval between the first signs of puberty and the stage of complete maturity varies from one and a half to six years for girls, and two to five years for boys. The speed of the maturation process is apparently

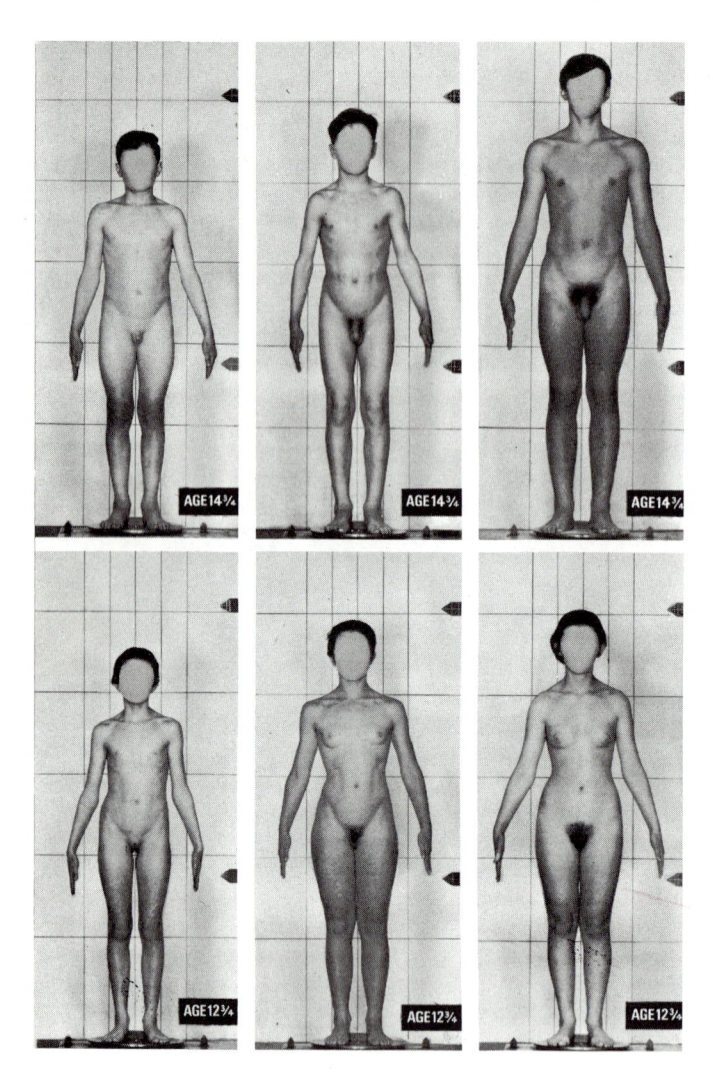

Figure 14.6 Differing degrees of pubertal development at the same chronological age. Upper row, three boys aged 14.75 years. Lower row, three girls aged 12.75 years. (From J. M. Tanner. Growth and endocrinology in the adolescent. In L. I. Gardner (Ed.), *Endocrine and genetic diseases of childhood.* Philadelphia: W. B. Saunders, 1969.)

independent of whether puberty begins early or late. For example, a girl may develop fully mature breasts and pubic hair rather rapidly and then be slow in experiencing menarche, while during the same period of time another girl may have completed the entire process. The same is true for boys—sometimes, though infrequently, the genitals may be well on their way to mature development before there is a sign of pubic hair, while during the same period of time another boy may have fully developed genitals and pubic hair.

Thus, the various events of puberty are closely related in some individuals, and more spread out in others. The reasons for this are not precisely known. It has been speculated that this phenomenon may have something to do with the degree of integration between various processes of the hypothalamus and pituitary glands (Tanner 1970). These glands, situated in the brain, control the secretion of hormones which determine height growth, pubic hair growth, breast development, and so on. Abnormalities in one or another of these areas may be due to glandular malfunction.

SEX DIMORPHISM. Since boys and girls develop different proportions of muscle, bone, and fat during puberty, body shape and composition tend to take on distinctly different, or dimorphous, forms. Boys develop longer bones and thicker skin, while girls have a smaller loss of fat. Boys develop greater size and width of shoulders, while girls develop wider hips.

Some sex dimorphisms, such as those mentioned above, become evident at puberty. Others are already present before puberty, while still others develop continuously throughout childhood and adolescence. For example, external genital differences develop during the fetal stage, as does part of the difference in pelvic shape. The greater length of the male forearm develops continuously throughout childhood and adolescence (Tanner 1970).

Early and Late Maturation

When we say that a girl is 13 years old or a boy is 14 years old, the statement tells us little about how physically mature that boy or girl is. Some boys at 14 are still preadolescent, having the muscles, genital development, and voice of a child. Similarly, some girls at 13 have hardly begun breast development and still have narrow hips. On the other hand, some boys and girls at these ages may have all the physical characteristics of mature adults.

Thus, chronological age is not necessarily a definite indicator of physiological or developmental age. According to Tanner, various criteria of physiological age have been used by researchers of growth. These include the number of erupted teeth and the percentage of water in muscle cells. One of the most generally employed indicators is that of skeletal maturity—that is, the shape of, and completeness of development of the bones. This is determined by means of X-rays, usually of the hand, since this body part has a large number of joints. Skeletal maturity has been found to correlate fairly well with other aspects of growth (Tanner 1970).

During the past century, there has been a trend toward increased size and earlier maturation in both Europe and America, probably due primarily to better nutrition in early life (Tanner 1970). According to Tanner (1971), one clear indication of earlier maturation is the trend of menarcheal age. In average populations in Western Europe and the United States, menarche has tended to occur three to four months earlier per decade since 1850. The relationship between nutrition and menarcheal age is demonstrated by differences between relatively prosperous Western populations and poorer countries. The median menarcheal age in industrial Western countries is 12.8, while the median age in the highland of New Guinea is 18, in central Africa, 17, and among the poorly nourished Bantu in southern Africa it is 15.5 (Tanner 1971).

EFFECTS OF EARLY AND LATE MATURATION. Having established the fact of variability in the timing and rate of maturation, we must now ask what are the psychological effects of different maturational ages among adolescents of our society. Do early maturers have a social advantage which lasts beyond adolescence? Do late maturers tend to be socially maladjusted in adolescence and later life? What personality factors are affected by late or early maturation?

Various studies have been conducted on this subject. Most support the thesis that early maturers tend to have an easier time with social adjustment in high school than do late maturers. Studies by Jones (1957, 1958, 1965) have revealed that early maturing boys exceeded late maturers on questionnaire measures of sociability, sense of wellbeing, dominance, achievement through conformity, and related areas. The same subjects continued to exhibit these traits into their midthirties. Moreover, it was found in this same longitudinal study that early maturers were more secure in their vocational status at the age of 30 than were late maturers. Thus, it would seem that early maturers possess a distinct advantage over late maturers in the adolescent years and that this advantage persists long after the actual physical differences have ceased.

It is not clear, however, that social and emotional differences between the two groups necessarily imply a difference in psychological health. The equation of social and psychological adjustment may not be entirely valid. For example, certain behaviors characteristic of late maturers, such as being more expansive, less inhibited, more animated and tense, more inclined to laugh, and so forth, have generally been attributed to childish hyperkinesis (that is, tension release), or to overcompensation for feelings of inferiority. However, there has been no clear evidence of differences between late and early maturers with respect to emotional disorganization, loss of control, or other signs of psychological problems (Peskin 1967). In the absence of significant group differences in maladjustment, the hypothesis concerning tension and feelings of inferiority lacks evidential support.

Further evidence that early maturers do not have everything in their favor comes from the same series of studies by Jones and others on early versus late maturation. These studies have shown that early maturers tend to be more rigid and more in control of impulses in later life. In contrast to late maturers, early maturers showed an inflexibility and lack of psychological insight.

One possible explanation for this last result is that early maturers experience social success early in life, and, thus, have less need to question themselves or modify their behavior. The early maturer tends to stick more rigidly to the behavior patterns that brought him to early success. The late maturer, on the other hand, has had to learn continually in order to compensate for his initially adverse social position. Thus, he has been forced to become more flexible and psychologically aware.

Intellectual and Cognitive Development

Intellectual Growth

Intelligence test scores of adolescents have generally shown improvement over scores made in preadolescence, but this growth is a part of a pattern that runs continuously from childhood into the early twenties (Douvan and Gold 1966).

The peak of intellectual development is usually reached in the postadolescent years. There is a certain amount of evidence that intellectual growth is related to maturation and not merely to an increase in training. Children who reach adolescence early do slightly better on intelligence tests than those who reach adolescence late (Freeman 1936). Girls who have reached menarche show slightly better scores than premenarcheal girls of the same age (Stone and Barker 1937).

The development of specific intellectual skills tends to follow the curve of overall intellectual growth. Peaks in some areas are reached earlier than in others. The top performances on common-sense questions, analogies, and numerical completion questions are reached in the late teens; peak performance on arithmetic problems and following oral directions are reached at about the age of 20; and vocabulary continues to improve into early adulthood (Douvan and Gold 1966). A skill such as vocabulary growth may take a longer period of training and experience, while the other skills require less training and are possibly more closely related to maturation.

No significant differences between the sexes have been found in overall intelligence. There are, however, certain differences related to specific skills. Adolescent girls tend to do better on tests of verbal skills, while boys tend to excel at numerical and scientific questions (Horrocks 1962). Preadolescent girls tend to excel in all mental abilities. Many regard these sexual differences as culturally induced; however, others feel they are largely biologically determined.

INTELLECTUAL ORIENTATION. A question distinct from that of intellectual ability is the subject of intellectual disposition. A study by Trent and Craise (1967) of late-adolescent college students found that liberal arts students were generally more disposed toward knowledge for its own sake and toward intellectual activities than were technical students or education majors. It was also found that a high degree of personal autonomy was present in students in the fields of the humanities and social sciences, with the highest scores in these areas obtained among student political activists. Finally, it was found in this study that college students were, on the whole, more re-

Table 14.1 Percentage of Students in the National Sample in Various Curricula at Each Level of Intellectual Disposition

Level of Intellectual Disposition	Liberal Arts (N=1096)	Major Education (N=572)	Technology and Business (N=899)
High	28	11	7
Middle	37	34	25
Low	35	55	68
Total	100	100	100

Note: $X^2 = 273.96$; $p < .001$
Source: From J. W. Trent and J. L. Craise. Commitment and conformity in the American college. *J. soc. Issues*, 1967, 23, 42.

flective and complex in their thinking, as well as more autonomous, than working people of the same age.

Abstract and Hypothetical Thinking

One of the primary features of cognitive development in adolescence is the newly developed capacity for abstract and hypothetical thinking. Prior to adolescence, the child's thought is for the most part characterized by its egocentrism. This means that the child sees things only as they relate to himself in the present. Younger children tend to be very literal-minded and incapable of fully understanding more abstract statements, about possibility, for example. Adolescents soon develop this ability, which has far-reaching implications for the development of thought and personality.

PIAGET'S FORMAL OPERATIONAL THOUGHT. One way of understanding this distinction between child and adolescent thought is in terms of Piaget's categories of *concrete operational* and *formal operational* thought. The former stage applies to the years from about 7 to 11; the latter becomes increasingly evident with the coming of adolescence.

As we have seen in earlier chapters, concrete operational thought is concerned with the here and now, with what is visible to the senses. The concrete operational child can solve problems by trial and error and can note physical changes in reality. However, he is not very good at forming hypotheses, at understanding contrary-to-fact propositions ("If this were true, then. . . ."), and at compensating mentally for *possible* changes in reality. While at the concrete operational stage he is capable of theorizing, it is only on a quite mundane level—"What would I look like if I had a mustache, and then if I took it off, what would people say?" Or, "If I shaved off my hair and was bald, what then would they say?" Any more sophisticated formulations would be considered formal operations.

In general, we can say that the concrete operational child is concerned with the reality or unreality of appearances, whereas the formal operational adolescent can go beyond appearance to deal with the truth or falsity of propositions. According to Piaget, formal operational thought begins to develop in late preadolescence and is nearly completely developed by the age of 16.

In addition to hypothetical and abstract thinking, the formal operational stage is also characterized by causal thought. The person capable of formal operations can isolate and distinguish various components of a concrete phenomenon and can determine cause and effect.

All of the attributes of formal operational thought are well illustrated by an experiment performed by Piaget and Inhelder (1958). In this experiment, subjects were presented with a pendulum formed by an object hanging from a string. Each subject was asked to find out which of four factors—length of string, weight of object, height

Figure 14.7 The adolescent, according to Piaget's system of classification, is in the period of formal operational thought. This stage is characterized by the capacity for abstract and hypothetical thinking. (Sybil Shackman—Monkmeyer)

from which pendulum was released, and force with which it was released—influenced the frequency of oscillation (how fast the pendulum would swing). The subjects' experiments and statements were recorded, and, occasionally, they were asked to prove their statements.

The experiment was administered to subjects of varying ages. Children below the age of 7, who had not yet reached the stage of concrete operations, were completely unable to perform the experiment. They made random tests such as first pushing a long pendulum with a light weight and then a short pendulum with a heavy weight. Needless to say, their tests yielded no information on the problem.

Children at the stage of concrete operations (7 to 11) did considerably better. One child varied the length of string and found, correctly, that the longer the string, the slower the oscillation. However, this same child then compared the oscillation of a 100-gram weight at lengths of 2 and 5 units to a 50-gram weight at a length of 1 unit, and found, incorrectly, that there was an inverse correspondence between weight and frequency of oscillation. This child did observe accurately, since the pendulum with the lighter weight in this case *did* swing faster. However, he did not set up a control for length, so that his results were not valid. His behavior illustrates the nature of concrete operational thinking. He could make judgments about appearances accurately. However, he could not abstract from appearances in order to form propositions which could then be tested for truth or falsity. In short, all he knew was what he saw, not what he could imagine.

Children at the formal operational stage were most successful. One subject (age 15 years) selected 100 grams with a long and short string; and finally 200 grams with a long and short string. She concluded that the length of string was the sole determinant of frequency of oscillation. (She set up controls for the other factors, height and force, in a similar manner.) Thus, through careful experimentation she was able to arrive at the correct answer.

This 15-year-old child's behavior illustrated a number of properties of formal operational thinking. First, she was able to consider the possible factors in the situation—height, force, weight, and length. Then, after constructing a set of hypotheses, she was able to isolate and test the various factors. This step required the ability to think abstractly—that is, to disengage thinking from the observed phenomena. In observation, weight and length are never separate—they are always observed together. The fact that the subject knew how to set up controls for these properties in her experiment showed that she could conceive of them separately. Finally, she was able to draw the logical conclusion from her experiment. This last operation involved the ability to judge the truth or falsity of propositions according to the laws of logic.

Her method of solving the problem—that is, imagining hypothetical situations, deducing their consequences, and then testing to see if the consequences hold true—is the essential method of modern science. It is called the *hypothetico-deductive method*, and it has a clear advantage over repeated trial and error.

Effects of the New Cognitive Processes

SELF-CONCEPT. One consequence of the ability to think abstractly and in terms of possibilities is that the adolescent becomes more aware of personal alternatives. He is capable of imagining an ideal self that is different from his present real self. Increasingly he projects himself into future social and occupational roles.

One study (Katz and Zigler 1967) has shown that the disparity between real self-image and ideal self-image is positively correlated with I.Q. and maturity measures. This finding can be explained by the developmental theory. As the child matures, he becomes more differentiated and articulate in his thinking. More possibilities open up to him. He is capable of making finer distinctions and thus can perceive his own inadequacies and possibilities for development.

CHANGES IN SOCIAL ATTITUDES. According to Piaget, another consequence of the adolescent's newfound capacity for abstraction is an inclination toward the construction of elaborate political and social doctrines. Since the capacity for abstraction is new to the adolescent, he may exercise these new mental powers without restraint and, at times, lose touch with reality. In short, the adolescent is captivated by the ideal. He becomes preoccupied with moral principles, with introspection, consciousness of self and others, self-criticism, and concern for future goals.

However, the development of rational propositional thinking also creates new social and psychological problems for the adolescent. He now is forced to examine many of his previous beliefs about himself and the world. He is less and less inclined to accept things on authority. Early sex taboos and religious beliefs, for example, may be put under severe strain by the adolescent's experience of sexual pleasure and his growing awareness that all is not right with the world. He begins to be aware of the irrationalities and inconsistencies in adult behavior, and may therefore come into more conflict with his parents and other authorities than he did as a young child. Elkind (1968) has suggested that many of the social and psychological phenomena of adolescence, such as ambivalence, self-consciousness, and conflict with parents, may be the result of the emerging capacity for theoretical thought.

CHANGING TIME PERSPECTIVES. Another result of the emerging capacity for abstract thought is a changed time perspective. As adolescents become more aware of possibilities and adult roles, they become more future-oriented. Mentally, they become capable of transcending present reality.

A study by Klineberg (1967) compared time perspectives of adolescents and preadolescents. Klineberg began with the hypothesis that future orientation in preadolescence is a brand of fantasy-escape or wish-fulfillment, while in adolescence it is realistic. The young child normally does not think in terms of possibilities and thus does not so readily distinguish between unattainable fantasies and realizable aims. The adolescent, by contrast, does make the fantasy-reality distinction. Now capable of formal operational thought, the adolescent can envision possibility, which is a form of thought about the future. Thus, he is more likely to be genuinely future-oriented, not as an escape from present reality, but as a realistic projection of his own possibilities.

Klineberg tested four groups of subjects for future-orientation. These groups were preadolescents who scored high on ratings of maladjustment, preadolescents who scored low in this respect, and midadolescents who scored high and low in this area. He found that future-orientation correlated positively with maladjustment in childhood, but negatively with maladjustment in adolescence. In other words, future-orientation was found to be a characteristic of the maladjusted child and the well-adjusted adolescent. From this it was inferred that adolescent future-orientation was realistic, a result of the development of the power of reason, whereas childhood future-orientation was grounded in fantasy and irrational thought processes.

INCONSISTENT USE OF FORMAL REASON. As we have seen, adolescence represents the stage of maturation of the reasoning process, or more specifically, the process of abstract thinking. Man's power of theoretical thought is an important factor in all aspects of his life. Adolescence, therefore, signifies the acquisition of one of the essential characteristics of adult humanity. However, there is some evidence that adolescents do not always apply formal operational thinking to all areas of life. At times they do not use the reasoning ability they have acquired and, instead, fall back on earlier modes of thinking.

A recent study (Higgins-Trenk and Gaite 1971) has shown that adolescents do not always use formal operational thought outside of their studies. In this study, 162 high school students aged 13 to 17 years were presented with two kinds of problems—situational problems involving themselves or friends in moral or social situations, and scientific problems relating to the conservation of volume. It was found that students who used formal operational thinking in one kind of problem did not necessarily do so in the other. Often students found it difficult to be objective or to hold certain factors constant in the situational problems, whereas they could do both of these things in the scientific problems. Forty-five percent of the total population studied used formal operations in the volume-conservation tasks, while only 32 percent used formal operations in the situational problems. Both figures increased with age. Thus, it was concluded that adolescents do not always make use of their reasoning ability. We could speculate here that such partial use of the power to theorize extends far beyond adolescence.

As the adolescent's cognitive abilities develop and he becomes more aware of his own *self* and personal alternatives, he also begins to feel a need for, and to seek, a sense of personal independence. The adolescent desires more and more to be free of any feeling of dependence on his parents. A feeling of personal autonomy becomes of growing importance to the adolescent.

Social and Cultural Changes

Personal Autonomy

Douvan and Gold (1966) distinguished between two types of personal autonomy—behavioral and emotional. They found that data in the area of behavioral autonomy—for example, dating, personal employment outside the home, access to independent finances, and choice of nonfamily companions—showed a marked increase in personal autonomy during adolescence. On the other hand, the evidence showed little increase in emotional autonomy—for example, valuing friendships over family relationships, choosing advisers and ideals outside the family, and disagreeing significantly with parental opinions.

It should be noted that adolescents tend to exhibit more emotional (or behavioral) autonomy in some areas than in others. For example, a teenager's attitude about the clothes he or she wears is more apt to agree with that of the individual's peers than with parents, while in another area the reverse might be true. A study by Kandel and Lesser (1969), for example, revealed that high school students were more influenced by their parents than by their friends on the question of educational plans. In responses to questions on this matter, the investigators found a higher agreement between mother and child than between child and friend (where the plans considered were the adolescents' own and not their plans for each other).

The failure of research to show a significant increase in emotional autonomy during adolescence seems to indicate either that parents generally refuse to give in to their children's demands for personal autonomy, or that theorists of adolescent psychology have overestimated the urgency of the adolescent's need for emotional independence. Douvan and Gold (1966) felt that the latter is the more realistic conclusion.

DEMOCRATIC VERSUS AUTHORITARIAN FAMILIES. According to Douvan and Gold, certain family conditions encourage the growth of autonomy, while other family conditions discourage it. They cited studies which indicate that families in which there is democratic decision making, parental warmth and concern, and consistency in rule enforcement foster autonomy. On the other hand, families where the parents lay down the law in autocratic fashion tend to produce dependent or rebellious children. They point out that adolescents from strongly autocratic families rarely ad-

Table 14.2 Indices of Emotional Autonomy for Girls, Ages 11 to 18, and for Boys and Girls, Ages 14 to 16

Item	Change in Girls from 11 to 18 (N=206) from %	Change in Girls from 11 to 18 (N=148) to %	Girls 14 to 16 (N=822) %	Boys 14 to 16 (N=1045) %
1. S thinks friendship can be as close as family relationship	53	71	61	42
2. S disagrees with parents about				
a. Ideas	12	46	34	
b. More than one issue out of six	54	59	56	
3. S would take advice of friends on more than one issue out of six				29
4. S chooses adult ideal				
a. Outside the family	22	48	38	36
b. Within the family	66	52	55	45
5. Projective: Response to request from lonely mother to give up good job and return to hometown				
a. Reject request	8	26	18	
b. Comply, conditionally comply	78	59	66	
6. Projective: Response to parental restriction				
a. Accept, reassure parents	51	38	36	
7. Projective: Response to conflict between parent-peer pressure				
a. Parent-oriented	78	61	63	
8. S chooses as confidante				
a. Friend	5	33	26	
b. One, both parents	67	36	45	
9. Part in rule making				
a. S has some part	45	64	58	
10. Attitude toward parental rules				
a. Right, good, fair	47	56	56	

Note: The data for boys are incomplete because some questions asked in the study of girls were not included in the boys' study.
Source: From E. Douvan and M. Gold. Modal patterns in American adolescence. In L. W. Hoffman and M. L. Hoffman (Eds.), *Review of child development research*. Vol. II. New York: Russell Sage Foundation, 1966.

mit to disagreeing with their parents, but they often show signs of deep hostility toward their parents.

As Douvan and Gold pointed out, part of the difference between the effects of democratic and autocratic families lies in the nature of the cognitive signals the child receives. Democratic families tend to help the child develop his reasoning ability. Since democratic parents verbalize rules and limits clearly, and give reasons for the rules, the child learns to reason about his own behavior. Children in autocratic families, on the other hand, are brought up to rely not on reason but on authority. They are forced either to accept the parents' standards or to rebel rather than to develop their own goals and behavioral standards independently (Douvan and Gold 1966).

Some other findings relating to parental authority versus parental permissiveness are particularly noteworthy. For instance, fathers tend to be more autocratic than mothers (Douvan and Adelson 1966). In both mothers and fathers there is a shift toward greater permissiveness with older adolescents, but the shift is greater among mothers. It has also been found that, in general, middle-class parents tend to be slightly more permissive and democratic than lower-class parents.

PARENTAL AMBIVALENCE. Many parents experience conflicts about how much independence they should allow their adolescent offspring. Some parents think that they want their children to be happy, but unconsciously they are jealous of their children and keep them tied to parental apron strings. Other parents are afraid their children will be hurt or disgraced if they are allowed to have complete freedom, particularly in sexual matters. Needless to say, parental ambivalence on such questions will tend to produce conflict and confusion in both the parent and the adolescent.

CROSS-CULTURAL DIFFERENCES. A look at other societies reveals great variations in the matter of personal autonomy from the family. In some cultures there is no discernible break from the family during the age of adolescence. Rather, the child gradually acquires skills and learns independence throughout his life.

A good example of this gradual growing-up process can be found among the Arapesh people of New Guinea. Here, adolescents assume much of the responsibility for support of the family, yet they do not leave home or experience changes in family relationships immediately. A boy's future wife is selected by his parents, and the choice is agreed to by the girl's parents while the children are still very young.

The Arapesh girl becomes acquainted with her future husband long before they marry, and she comes to know her in-laws almost as well as she knows her own parents. Her training in the tasks of motherhood and wifehood is very gradual. She experiences none of the confusion sometimes found in our society of moving into a strange home with a person she has known only for a short while and having to assume many burdens all at once.

On the other hand, adolescents of the Mudugumors (also of New Guinea) have a difficult time gaining independence from their families. Mudugumor society is characterized by hostility between members of the same sex — even between father and son, mother and daughter. Thus, the boy seeks independence chiefly to get away from a father he distrusts, while at the same time his mother tends to reinforce his distrust for girls his own age. The Mudugumor girl has to contend with a jealous and possessive father, as well as an often hostile mother. As a result, a smooth transition from adolescence to autonomous adulthood is very difficult (Mead 1939).

Western society falls somewhere in between these two extremes on the scale of emotional and behavioral autonomy.

Vocational Orientation

American culture presents a maze of occupational choices of bewildering variety to the adolescent. Unlike some cultures (such as the Arapesh), occupations in the American culture are not limited to family-centered tasks like tilling a plot of land for growing food. The American youth must seek a vocation outside the family and often has very little specific idea of what he can do or would like to do. It is no longer the rule for adolescents to follow in their parents' footsteps.

To an adolescent growing up in our increasingly complex and technological society, the choice of a lifetime vocation is seen as an extremely crucial decision. With the development of computer technologies and automation, there is less and less need for the unskilled and semiskilled factory worker of the assembly line. It is in the areas of service occupations, media, communications, and information processing that the vocational alternatives are to be found. Such vocations require more and more advanced education and longer periods of training. There is pressure, then, on the adolescent to decide early on his or her vocation in order to plan for the necessary education. At the same time, however, the individual is confronted with a culture accelerating to such a degree that a vocational choice of today may conceivably be made obsolete tomorrow by some new technological advancement. Thus, today an individual must continue to assess the trends in the vocation of his choice, consider vocational alternatives, and perhaps even change his mind several times before finally settling on any particular vocation.

Usually, as the adolescent matures he becomes more specific and realistic about his occupational plans. Ask a child what he wants to be when he grows up, and his answer will most likely be in terms of some vocational stereotype of excitement or adventure—say, an astronaut, a movie star, or the more traditional fireman or policeman, for example. An adolescent, on the other hand, is apt to be not only more realistic about his vocational choices, but also increasingly aware of and concerned with the education and training necessary to achieve them. As the adolescent matures, he becomes both more specific about his vocational goals and more thoughtful of the actual demands and rewards of the work involved (Douvan and Adelson 1966).

A number of other factors influence an adolescent's thinking about vocational alternatives and his eventual choice of occupation. Among these influences are the individual's sex and socioeconomic background.

CLASS DETERMINANTS OF OCCUPATION. Social class plays a significant role in determining the kinds of occupations with which an individual is familiar. His choices are determined to a great extent by his exposure. Children get first-hand ideas about work from hearing their parents talk about their jobs. Besides observing what their parents' working lives are like, adolescents are influenced by their parents' attitudes toward different occupations. These attitudes are often class-based. Rarely do we find upper-class or middle-class adolescents being encouraged to become firemen, policemen, or factory workers. Choices of lower-class occupations do not appeal to the aspirations of middle-class parents.

Lower- and working-class adolescents also show some tendency to aspire to the occupations of the dominant middle-class culture. These aspirations may be either encouraged or discouraged by their parents, depending on a number of factors—the parents' own desires for mobility or the nature of their relationship with their children, for example. One limiting factor on the aspirations of working-class adolescents is the inability of their families to afford the kind of education that is increasingly necessary to gain middle-class jobs. Nevertheless, it has been found that youths often aspire to job roles with a slightly higher socioeconomic status than those of their parents (Hollingshead 1949).

The same study by Hollingshead clearly showed the relationship of socioeconomic status to vocational choice. Adolescents in a midwestern city listed the occupations they were interested in. Seventy-seven percent of upper- and middle-class adolescents listed business or the professions, while only 7 percent of the adolescents in the lowest class listed such occupations. Only 1 percent of the youths in the highest classes listed services and trades, while 25 percent in the lower classes listed services and trades. Lower-class subjects exhibited much more indecision concerning vocational choice than did subjects from middle or higher socioeconomic classes.

Several hypotheses have been advanced to explain these results. One theory is that youths from different classes assign different relative values to the same occupations. This would mean that more lower-class youths actually prefer factory jobs than do upper-class youths. A different view maintains that youths from different classes value the occupations in the same manner, but lower-class youths do not choose the more prestigious occupations requiring more education because they perceive that the odds are against their achieving such goals.

It is important to note here that the Hollingshead study was conducted in 1949. While the results may still provide useful and valid information for consideration, obviously much has changed in our society since that time. Today more lower-class youths are seeking higher education, while higher education is being rejected by relatively large numbers of middle-class youths (the college dropouts). And the sometimes violently stated demands of students for educational reform undoubtedly indicate important shifts in attitudes and values since the Hollingshead study was conducted.

Sex-Based Determinants of Occupation. Sex-based differences also influence occupational choice. Douvan and Adelson (1966) found that girls' plans for the future centered less on work roles than did those of boys. In a national sample of youths from all classes, they found that girls were more concerned with marriage than with careers. Girls' status aspirations were closely tied to the status of the husband they hoped to marry.

Douvan and Adelson, in this same study, found that job preferences among girls tended to cluster around the traditionally female occupations such as schoolteaching, secretarial work, or nursing. They did find, however, a significant number of girls who had autonomous vocational goals, while not rejecting marriage. These girls tended to come from families that stressed personal autonomy and individuality.

Of course, since the time of this study, there have been changes in the family and sweeping changes in the attitude of women toward their position. With the growth of the Women's Liberation Movement it is likely that many more adolescent girls have definite occupational goals from a wider range of choices than was previously the case.

This hypothesis is partly borne out by a recent study by Hollender (1971). In a cross-sectional survey of 5200 subjects ranging in age levels from fifth to twelfth grades, he found that 69 percent of the girls expressed a definite occupational choice, as compared with 59 percent of the boys. For the boys, there were more definite choices in the sixth and the tenth through twelfth grades than in the seventh through ninth grades. (This difference held only for the lower-aptitude half of the population studied.) For both boys and girls it was found that the higher the scholastic aptitude, the greater the degree of vocational decisiveness.

Parental Influence on Occupational Choice. Parental influence is a fairly clear factor in determining vocational objectives. It has been found that children generally choose occupations in line with their parents' values and aspirations. Simpson (1962) reported, for example, that ambitious middle-class boys receive the most parental support for their goals; working-class boys who are upwardly mobile receive the second greatest amount of parental support; and unambitious middle-class and nonmobile working-class boys receive the least amount of support from their parents.

There is some evidence that with increasing autonomy and a widening generation gap in evidence between adolescents and parents, there may be some shifting away from middle-class success patterns. One recent study (Rose and Elton 1971) has shown that vocationally undecided freshmen who left college had higher scores on personality tests for nonconformity than those who remained in college. It was also found that they had lower standing academically and on American College Test scores. Thus, it is possible that vocational indecision is becoming increasingly associated with nonconformity and the search for personal autonomy.

Development of Political Awareness

We noted earlier that adolescents experience an increased ability for abstract moral thought. This, naturally, has some effect on how they perceive politics and their relationship to political questions.

In his discussion of adolescent political awareness, Adelson (1971) compared the responses of 12- and 13-year-olds to the question, "What is the purpose of laws?" with the responses of 15-year-olds to the same question. Typically, the younger adolescents gave responses such as, "So people don't steal or kill." Midadolescents, on the other hand, gave answers such as, "To insure safety and enforce the government," or "To limit what people can do."

Adelson pointed out that the responses of the younger adolescents are limited to concrete cases such as killing or stealing. Older adolescents are capable of dealing with general and abstract principles. Moreover, he concluded that younger adolescents tend to personalize societal processes and institutions. In other words, when asked about law, the young adolescent speaks of the judge, the policeman, and the criminal. When asked about education, he speaks about teachers, principals, and students. While his focus is not, strictly speaking, incorrect, it is clear that he has not yet grasped the notion of abstract social processes or institutions.

Insofar as the young adolescent limits himself to the personal and the concrete, it is difficult for him to take social viewpoints on political questions. Instead of being *sociocentric*, he is, at this stage, still largely *egocentric*. In this respect he differs from the late adolescent, who is better able to consider political questions from a broad social viewpoint, or, as Adelson put it, with "a sense of community" (1971).

The change in political awareness is closely related to cognitive growth. The more the adolescent is able to think in abstractions and consider possibilities, the more he will be able to deal with issues of how things should and *might* be run politically. A more cognitively mature adolescent will tend to respond to theoretical social or political questions in a fairly sophisticated manner. For example, in response to the question—"What would happen if there were no laws?"—Adelson reported one 14-year-old (obviously unusually mature for his age) as answering:

At first people would do as they pleased. But after a while someone or some party would come to power and impose laws, probably stricter ones than before. But a lot would depend upon the kind of society it was. Some societies have a strict social etiquette, like in ancient China, I think it was, where people were afraid to lose their place in society, because if they did something wrong everyone would look down on them. (Adelson 1971)

This response reveals an essentially adult ability to consider social questions. As Adelson commented, the adolescent here was able not only to "look past the immediate to remote second-order consequences," but also to challenge the assumption that laws are necessary for social control. He was also able to consider different types of society, as well as use a specific example to illustrate an abstract, general point.

PARTICIPATION IN POLITICS. Although late adolescents are capable of essentially adult cognitive processes, there is some question as to the degree to which this thinking will be directed toward the political arena. Recent research has suggested that adolescents are exhibiting greater interest in political knowledge and participation than they did in the 1950s and 1960s. Investigations conducted during the fifties and early sixties revealed, for example, that few adolescents in high school or college read anything about politics other than material assigned for schoolwork. Less than 14 percent of 14- to 16-year-old boys interviewed by Douvan and Adelson (1966) read newspapers; the findings for girls the same age were similar.

Douvan and Gold (1966) pointed out that while American schools inculcated citizenship and patriotism as primary virtues, adult behavior differed widely from the ideal of a good citizen. A 1960 survey of American voting habits revealed that under 66 percent of eligible adults participated in presidential elections and a mere 3 percent personally campaigned for a candidate (Campbell, Converse, Miller, and Stokes 1960). Thus, few teen-agers have had strong adult models of political participation.

Research in the fifties and sixties further indicated that adolescents at the time, while having little interest in, or knowledge of, politics and the operations of the government, often exhibited strongly patriotic opinions along with contradictory views on civil liberties. High school students in one survey expressed strongly negative attitudes about people who disrespect the American flag (Mainer 1963). And while denying police the right to imprison people without formal charges, teen-agers in another study affirmed the right of the FBI or the police to use extreme methods to make suspects talk (Remmers 1963).

RECENT POLITICAL ACTIVISM. However, it should be remembered that data for most of these studies were collected in times of relative social calm. Recent studies, such as the work of Lerner and his associates (1971), have shown more political knowledge and concern on the part of adolescents. The fact that adolescents had definite opinions on most of the issues investigated by the Lerner study indicates greater social and political awareness.

In a recent article, Kline (1972) maintained that data show that the recent radical student political activism of the late sixties and early seventies is a function of democratic family upbringing. He stated that families with affinities for open discussion produce active, questioning adolescents who become prime candidates for protests and political activism. In this he agrees with the theories of Kenneth Keniston, the noted psychologist and writer about student activism. Keniston has also maintained that democratic families foster political dissent. Adolescents raised in an atmosphere where appeals to authority are minimal are much less likely to accept established authority in the public sphere as well. Observed inequities grate against the sense of justice they have learned in practice at home, and thus they are stimulated to protest (Keniston 1968).

This explanation of the new youth life styles and political activist trends is not entirely in agreement with earlier psychoanalytic explanations of student radicalism as rebellion against male, parental, and social authority. Nevertheless, neither does it exclude such interpretations. Few families are purely democratic or purely authoritarian. Adolescents who have been brought up to have their own opinions and standards will often hold these opinions against the authority of their elders.

EFFECT OF THE LOWER VOTING AGE. There is some uncertainty over what the effects of the 18-year-old voting age will be in national, state, and local elections. An additional 950,000 18-year-old high school students, as well as 4 million 18- to 21-year-old college students, 4.1 million workers, and 1 million housewives will be eligible to vote. Kline (1972) predicts that the new voting age will produce little immediate change in electoral results. However, he believes that youthful skepticism about the existing political parties will be

Figure 14.8 There is evidence that today's youth are more concerned with political and social issues than the youth of the 1950s and 1960s. (Richard Stack—Black Star)

evidenced in the next five to seven years by many more ticket-splitters in voting and by many more independent candidates running for public office. One factor that may keep the immediate impact of the student vote down is the stringent residence requirement for registration. Young people, and particularly students, are among the most geographically mobile groups in the population.

Peer Relationships and the Peer Culture

Friendship

Friendship takes on a new and crucial significance in adolescence; at this time, the individual begins to detach his emotional life from the family. He seeks new authorities and sources of values to substitute for the old familial ones. He needs to establish an identity that is recognized and accepted by significant others. These others are his friends.

Whereas family relationships are often based on a mixture of love, guilt, and combativeness, friendships are generally freely chosen on the basis of mutual attraction. Guilt is normally not a factor among friends as it is in the family. Although there are expectations between friends concerning reliability and generosity, the obligations of friendship are usually freely assumed. Friendship requires a more mature form of sensitivity than does the relationship to parents. It is, ideally, an enlarging process that helps the adolescent find his adult self.

DIFFERENCES IN FRIENDSHIP. The nature of adolescent friendship is somewhat different from that of childhood friendship. Preadolescents select their friends on the basis of common activities, whereas with adolescents the mutuality of the relationship itself is emphasized. Girls between the ages of 14 and 16, in particular, are notable for their demands for loyalty and security in friendship. In one study by Douvan and Adelson (1966), it was found that indices of personal maturity were positively correlated with measures of maturity in friendship among girls, but less so with maturity in friendship among boys. Boys, it seems, persist longer in childhood patterns of activity-based friendships. This may be attributable in part to the fact that boys are not expected to verbalize about feelings to the extent that girls are.

The same study also found that girls' friendships tended to be more temporary than those of boys. This may be explained by the fact that adolescent girls' friendships are, as a rule, more intimate and demanding than those of boys. This kind of relationship is difficult to maintain for long stretches of time, particularly in a period when personalities are changing rapidly. Since boys' friendships are less closely connected with basic feelings, these less intimate, more casual relationships may be more easily maintained for longer time spans.

Finally, the Douvan and Adelson study (1966) revealed that adolescents choose friends from the same social class who are also similar in mental age, interests, moral values, and social maturity. Among girls, it was found that sexual attractiveness and popularity with members of the opposite sex is also a factor in friendship choice.

PEER-GROUP IMPORTANCE. Clique and peer-group evaluations become increasingly significant during adolescence. Common social and racial backgrounds, skills, and values are basic to clique formation (Douvan and Gold 1966).

Coleman (1961) found that students who were not members of an "in" crowd were usually aware of this fact and wished that they were members. These students tended to have lower self-esteem than members of the "in" crowd, while nonmembers who claimed that they did not want to be in the leading crowd had slightly less lower self-esteem (Coleman 1961).

Groups are particularly important for boys, supporting their need to assert their independence. Boys' groups tend to establish their own sets of values that often run counter to the official values of school authorities or parents. Girls, according to the Douvan and Adelson study (1966), tend to use groups in order to find close one-to-one friendships, and are less interested than boys in the group as such.

The differences in boys' and girls' behavior in groups are evident in their approaches to games.

According to Lever, boys tend to improvise new rules to meet new contingencies, in order to keep games going. Such behavior is an example of what Piaget called formal operational thought. On the other hand, girls tend not to use formal thinking in games. They either play games with simpler rules or break up over disputes (Lever, in progress).

As for the influence of peer groups on adolescent decisions, it has been found that adolescents generally depend on their parents' opinions for important occupational and educational choices, and on the influence of peers in questions relating to personal style and identity (Kandel and Lesser 1969).

Dating

With the coming of adolescence, the individual no longer spends all of his or her time in activities with peers of the same sex. Adolescence usually marks the beginning of heterosexual social life. Often there is a period of transition during which groups of boys and girls get together but maintain the separateness of their groups. Then, after a period of group heterosexual contact, pairing off begins.

In general, as Douvan and Gold (1966) pointed out, dating serves the purpose of reintroducing the adolescent to heterosexual social life after the preadolescent period of relatively sex-segregated activities. Adolescent dating is much more apt to be a means of social relationship between the sexes than strictly a process of mate selection prior to marriage.

It has also been suggested that the dating institution is in itself predominantly middle class and a transition between adolescence and adult courtship (Smith 1962). Smith pointed to the substantial evidence that adolescents from higher socioeconomic backgrounds date more often and with more partners than those of lower classes, whose dating behavior tends more toward courtship than conventional dating. However, many of the social patterns of dating and popularity are not as prevalent today as they used to be. There is growing evidence of changing attitudes and behavior patterns in dating and sexual behavior among adolescents since the 1960s. Particularly among urban, middle-class youth, the "dating game" seems to be receding in importance and is being replaced by more serious interpersonal relationships and earlier sexual relations. It should be kept in mind that research, even as recent as the last decade, may not fully reflect these changes; it is necessary, therefore, to view the findings of such research with some qualification.

Much research on dating habits and attitudes has centered around variations between adolescents of different socioeconomic classes. Such work has revealed, for instance, that middle-class dating generally begins earlier than lower-class dating, and is more socially oriented. Where a middle-class adolescent begins dating earlier and dates a number of peers of the opposite sex, the adolescent from the lower socioeconomic classes begins dating later and is more inclined towards serious steady dating of one individual (Lowrie 1961). This difference in dating patterns may be attributable to the greater middle-class concern with social status and prestige. Early dating may have little to do with emotional maturity or sexual interest and more to do with "being popular."

Research has explored other differences in dating patterns. According to Douvan and Adelson (1966), American girls begin to date at about the age of 14, while boys begin dating from one to two years later. The age of the first date has gradually lowered in the past quarter century, and it has been shown to be subject to many class and regional variations. For example, dating begins earlier in the South, where, as Broderick and Fowler (1961) have reported, there is extensive heterosexual social interaction among middle-class children as early as the fifth grade. Undoubtedly, as noted earlier, patterns of adolescent heterosexual relationships have continued to shift since the studies were conducted.

Sexual Behavior in Adolescence

Along with the rather rapid maturation of the sexual organs and the increased hormonal activity during adolescence, something of a sexual awakening occurs. The adolescent begins to be aware of his or her sex in new terms—an increased sexual urge gives rise to more sexual experimentation and fantasizing. The manner in which the child confronts and adjusts to these new sexual feelings

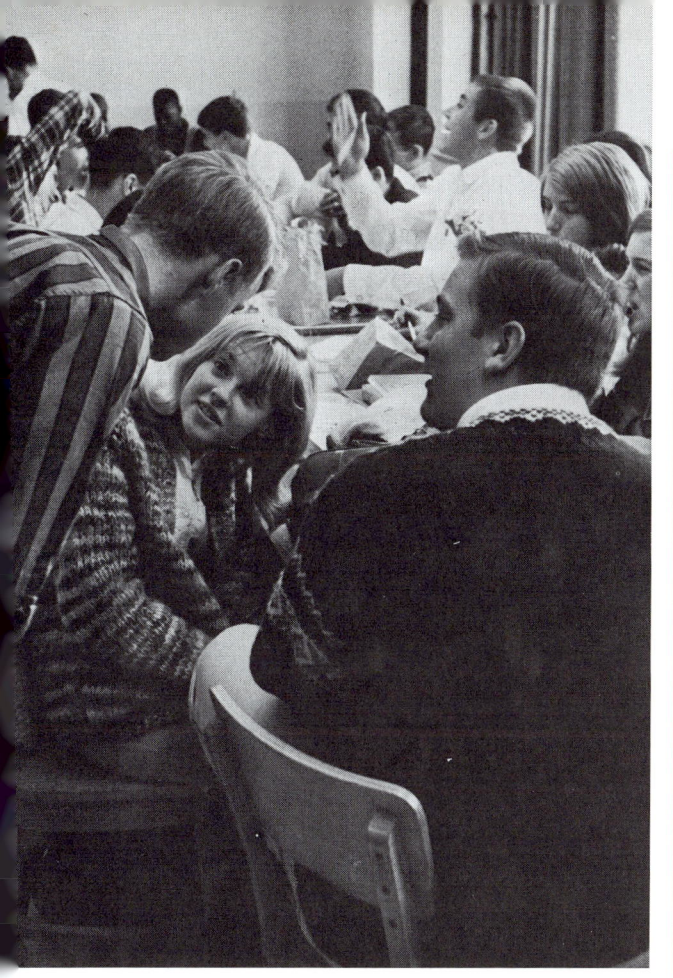

Figure 14.9 Clique and peer-group evaluation are important to the adolescent's development of self-concept and identity. (Burt Glinn—Magnum)

depends, of course, on a wide variety of psychological, cultural, and societal factors. We shall consider some of the ways in which the increased sexual drive affects adolescents of different sex, socioeconomic class, and cultures.

Once again, it is important to note that most of the conclusions about adolescent sexual behavior come from studies conducted during the fifties and sixties. Since that time, sexual values and attitudes have been undergoing fundamental changes which we shall examine later in the discussion.

SEX DIFFERENCES. Evidence concerning differences between the sexual behavior of males and females reveals that males exhibit more sexual drive than females at all ages, particularly during adolescence. Kinsey and his colleagues (1948, 1953) reported, for instance, that not only do adolescent boys express more sexual drive than do girls, but they also begin sexual activity earlier than girls. Kinsey's studies indicated that boys reach a peak in sexual activity three to four years after puberty and maintain this peak until about the age of 30. Females, on the other hand, often do not reach the peak of sexual activity until their late twenties or early thirties. Moreover, he reported that among his samples, fewer females than males achieved orgasm through any kind of sexual activity.

As Douvan and Gold (1966) pointed out, such results are surprising when compared to the fact that girls generally mature earlier than boys and are capable of increased sexual activity earlier. One explanation of such contradictory evidence is in terms of differences in societal controls on males and females. Girls presumably are more conditioned by societal pressures toward sexual restraint than are boys (Douvan and Gold 1966).

Various studies cited by Douvan and Gold (1966) suggest that boys may have more sexual fantasies than girls during adolescence. While less apt to freely fantasize about sexual matters than boys, girls seem to manifest more sexual anxiety during adolescence than boys. However, the studies from which such evidence comes are largely based on Rorschach and TAT protocols of relatively small samples, and, therefore, cannot be regarded as conclusive (Douvan and Gold 1966).

CLASS DIFFERENCES. There are several rather definite differences in sexual behavior between adolescents of different socioeconomic levels. Most notable among them are the differences between the sexual behavior of upper- and middle-class boys and that of boys from lower-class backgrounds. (Kinsey found no correlation between socioeconomic background and sexual behavior for adolescent girls.) Boys from upper- and middle-class families show a marked tendency toward masturbation and petting to climax as sexual outlets during adolescence. Though by no means approved by parents in the higher socioeconomic classes, masturbation and heavy petting are less objectionable than premarital intercourse.

On the other hand, adolescent boys from

lower-class backgrounds engage in heterosexual intercourse much more frequently than their middle- and upper-class peers. In the lower classes, sexual intercourse is considered the most normal sexual outlet, while there are strong taboos against masturbation or any other means of sexual release perceived as abnormal substitutes for direct intercourse (Kinsey 1948).

Where one type of sexual behavior is taboo, an alternative behavior may be positively reinforced. The boy from a lower-class background is likely to receive more positive reinforcement of sexual intercourse from his male adult models than the boy from middle- or upper-class families. A study by Bandura and Walters (1963), although not dealing specifically with class differences, does serve to illustrate the effect of reinforcement from an adult model. The study showed that boys whose fathers were permissive of heterosexual behavior during adolescence, sometimes even positively promoting sexual intercourse, engaged in heterosexual intercourse more frequently than boys with less permissive fathers, and tended to be less anxious about sexual matters in general.

CROSS-CULTURAL COMPARISONS. A look at how other cultures train their children with regard to sexual behavior will suffice to show that American middle-class attitudes and practices are by no means universal. The Samoan girl, in contrast to the American, receives continuous training in sexual freedom. Unlike the American girl, she has to unlearn no sexual taboos when she reaches the stage of adolescence. Aside from the incest prohibition, all forms of sexual experimentation, including masturbation, are permitted. Samoan girls postpone marriage in order to enjoy a carefree adolescence. Thus, sexual maladjustment in marriage and psychic impotence are virtually unknown in Samoa (Mead 1928).

Another contrast with American adolescent sexual practices is provided by Hogbin (1945). In this study of the Wogeo islanders of New Guinea, Hogbin found that homosexual relationships between male adolescents were both expected and encouraged. On the other hand, early heterosexual experiences were forbidden to boys, but not to girls. The boys were led to believe that sexual intercourse might cause serious illness or physical defects, while girls were actually rewarded for premarital affairs.

Such cultural comparisons also serve to support the thesis that human sexual practices are largely learned, and not, as in lower animals, chiefly the function of hormonal activity or inherited instinctual behavior (Bandura and Walters 1963).

CHANGING SEXUAL VALUES AND ATTITUDES. There is growing evidence of some rather fundamental changes in our society's attitudes toward sex and morality, particularly among adolescents. Where, not so very long ago, sex was not the subject for polite discussion in mixed company, it is now more openly and honestly discussed. It is the subject of countless debates, films, television programs, books, magazines, and protests as well. Where once adolescent sexual activity was hardly recognized as existent, now it is being nationally acknowledged and studied.

There is little doubt that the incidence of premarital sex among adolescents has increased in recent years. For instance, a study done for the Commission on Population Growth and the American Future (1972) revealed that 41 percent of unmarried American women have sexual intercourse before the age of 19. The same commission reported that although over 95 percent of the teenage girls in this age group had knowledge of birth control pills, only a few had ever used them. In view of this fact and the fact that about 25 percent of abortions performed under New York's liberalized abortion laws are accounted for by adolescents, the Commission recommended that birth control information and services be made available to teen-agers.

Because of such statistics on premarital sex among adolescents and the often excessive accent on sexual subjects in the entertainment media, it is sometimes argued that American morality is on the decline. However, there are fairly clear indications that while moral values may be changing, they are not necessarily lowering. For example, in a 1966 survey of 13- to 20-year-old youths asked about changing moral values, 75 percent agreed that they were developing a new sexual morality, and 82 percent believed that this new morality did not represent a lowering of standards (*Look* 1966).

A more recent survey of a cross section of American youth between the ages of 15 and 21 indicated that adolescents, while generally progressive and interested in change, were inclined to be thoughtful and cautious, rather than interested in radical change for its own sake. While 77 percent felt that sex education should be taught in school and 71 percent thought that there should be equal behavioral standards for both boys and girls, 63 percent stated that today's society put excessive stress on the importance of sex to happiness. Moreover, while 77 percent agreed with the concept of birth control, 78 percent of the high school students and 68 percent of the college students interviewed were negative about sexual relations between couples dating casually (*Life* 1971).

There is no doubt that the results of more serious and controlled scientific research are needed before any strong conclusions are drawn on the status of present adolescent sexual attitudes and behavior. Nevertheless, we can say that significant changes are obviously taking place, and have taken place within the last decade. In addition, there is at least some indication that these changing attitudes and values are in the direction of more honesty, openness, and freedom in adolescent (and adult) sexual behavior.

Summary

Adolescence begins at around the age of 13 and continues into the early twenties. During this transition from childhood to adulthood, the individual undergoes marked physical, psychological, and behavioral changes.

Various theories have been advanced concerning the psychological impact on the adolescent of these physical and cognitive developments. Erik Erikson, the psychoanalyst, sees adolescence as a time of identity crisis, a continual struggle to reestablish a sense of self in the midst of major physical and emotional changes. Kurt Lewin, the Gestalt psychologist, also sees adolescence as a period of crisis, with the rapid changes drastically altering the adolescent's self-image. On the other hand, more recent investigators challenge these crisis theories of adolescence, offering considerable evidence that the average adolescent experiences no severe problems in growing into adulthood. While definitely a time of change, adolescence, they feel, is not necessarily a time of crisis.

Most notable among the biological developments experienced by the adolescent is a rapid increase in the overall rate of physical growth, usually occurring simultaneously with puberty. Puberty is defined as the period, generally in early adolescence, during which the sexual and reproductive organs mature. While there is considerable variation among both boys and girls in the chronological ages at which specific biological developments occur, there is a fairly consistent order in which these developments take place.

Along with these physical and biological changes, and others related to them, the adolescent experiences changes in his cognitive and intellectual capacities. Chief among these changes is the development of the adolescent's capacity for abstract and theoretical thinking. Piaget has distinguished between the concrete operational thought of the preadolescent, and the adolescent's increasing capacity for formal operational thought.

As a consequence of his new cognitive abilities, the adolescent becomes more aware of personal alternatives, both present and future. With this new capacity for abstract thinking, the adolescent is inclined to be preoccupied with the ideal, in terms of moral, social, and political principles, as well as in his self-expectations. And he also begins to feel the need for, and to seek, a sense of personal autonomy and independence.

The psychological and behavioral changes the adolescent experiences are related to the individual's sex, socioeconomic background, and culture and society in which he lives. The degree of personal autonomy from the family particularly varies from culture to culture. Social class is an important factor in determining relationships with parents; it is also a major influence on the adolescent's vocational choices and sexual behavior.

Friendship assumes new and crucial significance in adolescence. The adolescent finds new authorities and sources of values among his peers to replace the old familial ones. And it is during this period that heterosexual social activity reappears and dating begins.

The adolescent experiences a kind of sexual awakening, with increased sexual behavior and experimentation. Adolescent sexual behavior and attitudes differ between boys and girls, and between individuals of different regional and socio-economic backgrounds.

While there is not yet enough scientific evidence to form strong conclusions, there are growing indications of profound changes in sexual attitudes and behavior in recent years. Statistics revealing increased premarital sex among adolescents are sometimes cited as evidence of a decline in American morality. However, although moral values may be changing, they are not necessarily lowering. These changes seem to be in the direction of greater honesty and freedom in both adolescent and adult sexual behavior.

Case Studies

Lois S.

The youngest of three girls, Lois is an intelligent teen-ager who has successfully competed with her intellectually gifted sisters since childhood. Her upper-middle-class home, well appointed in unobtrusively placed books and records, has been a source of unending stimulation and encouragement in all things creative and intellectual. Both older sisters have followed their father's lead by entering the academic profession after college. It is probably Mrs. S., however, who has had the strongest day-to-day influence on Lois.

A professional writer who plans to resume her career now that Lois is off to college, Mrs. S. claims a special affinity for her youngest daughter. It was she who had taken "much time to mold Lois's life," placing particular stress on the creativity she felt so beneficial to both social and personal well-being. Avowedly "determined" to nurture Lois's creativity to blossom, Mrs. S. has constantly encouraged her daughter to develop her promising literary talent. Now the mother regrets that Lois was encouraged to publish too early, for the resultant rejection notice was a "crushing blow" to her young talent, and Lois has since claimed "no interest" in the career "chosen" for her.

Mrs. S. has kept a steady surveillance—perhaps outright pressure—on Lois's academic and other achievements. Ever critical of all schools' social emphasis, Mrs. S. has always "shared in Lois's social life" by asking for a daily suppertime report of academic activities. Although she enjoys and encourages the success shown by Lois's straight-A record in high school, she also deplores her daughter's nervous tension before each and every exam. Mrs. S. relates that teachers have often advised Lois to relax in order that she might gain some new spontaneity and joy in learning, but her need for assured academic "success" has always precluded Lois's taking their advice to heart. Lois herself recognizes the anxiety in such striving, but feels that she has a "natural" drive for achievement and evidently counts these customary tensions as a fair price for her outstanding record.

So ingrained is Lois's sense of rivalry that even as a small child, Mrs. S. recalls, Lois had nightmares whenever she felt she was not competing successfully with her sisters. It is largely due to this unrelenting competition, Mrs. S. conjectures, that Lois has enjoyed her horses so very much: none of her family shared this interest. Though her daughter sometimes says that she will make a career of horses, Mrs. S. hopes that it is only a childish fantasy. She predicts, in fact, that at the age of 30 Lois will "have three or four children . . . a nice home . . . may give up riding . . . will take good care of her family."

As college selection came closer for Lois, she made it known that she did not want to follow the family tradition of attending a prestigious eastern college. Rather, she desired a low-prestige western college where she could pursue her riding; or she might prefer just to take a secretarial job, save money, and buy her own horse. Though she may never have been truly convinced of the merits of either idea, neither got even a second hearing at home.

Lois has now begun her career at a first-rate eastern college, and is reportedly cheerfully living up to her siblings' brilliant records. She continues with her horses, but is apparently content, at least for now, to live out her family's expectations (Getzels and Jackson 1962).

John B.

The oldest of three children, John divides his time between his love of music, his intellectual interests, and his enthusiasm for sports. Considered "outstanding" and "well-rounded" by teachers, peers, and parents alike, John has grown up with a deep regard for privacy and independence, a notably mature wit, and a strong sense of family affection. And, although his I.Q. of 127 is near the mean of 132 for his exceptional class, he is consistently in the top 20 percent on all achievement scores.

John's relationship with his parents has been characterized by a responsible freedom and a warm togetherness. He and his father, a well-known biologist, share a deep affection—as well as many interests and activities. His mother, formerly the editor of a small newspaper, is a woman of considerable vitality and few pretenses. She readily admits that her husband dominates family life, and that her only "absolute" family responsibility is the protection of her children's health. Otherwise, her attitude has been one of "live and let live," evolving primarily from a devout respect for her children's privacy. She is certain that her family appreciates her "permissive" attitude. All of her children are, she thinks, "secure" and "independent"; and family disagreements in no way jeopardize their shared feelings of respect and love.

A central question in John's life at this point is his plan for a career. Like his teen-age sister, he has a love for the arts, but he is not averse to a scientific profession either. Mr. B., not surprisingly, has been exerting some recent pressure for a decision toward the latter alternative, and he makes no pretense about his disdain for an entertainment career. Mrs. B. is inclined to let John make up his own mind. Meanwhile, in the face of his father's unaccustomed pressure, John's original ambivalence has now turned into a determined refusal to commit himself in either direction. In his resentment over Mr. B.'s intrusion on his privacy, John now evades any and all questions having to do with his future plans.

During his psychological testing, John revealed his humorous detachment toward his father's standards of ambition and success, but he does not simply reject all conventional criteria of achievement. Likewise, he shows some concern over his inability to decide on viable career plans. He feels he is doing "all right," however, and is determined to take any losses "philosophically." At this point, John's major goal in life is simply "knowing how to live."

Although John will have to make some major decisions about which role expectations he will fulfill and which he will ignore, it seems reasonable to assume that his family's contribution to his final goals will be genuinely supportive (Getzels and Jackson 1962).

References

Adelson, J. The political imagination of the young adolescent. *Daedalus: J. Amer. Acad. Arts and Sciences,* 1971, *100,* 1013–1050.

Bandura, A. The stormy decade: Fact or fiction? *Psychol. in the Schools,* 1964, *1,* 224–231.

Bandura, A., and Walters, R. H. *Social learning and personality development.* New York: Holt, Rinehart & Winston, 1963.

Broderick, C. B., and Fowler, S. E. New patterns of relationships between the sexes among preadolescents. *Marriage and Fam. Living,* 1961, *23,* 27–30.

Campbell, A., Converse, P. E., Miller, W. E., and Stokes, D. E. *The American voter.* New York: Wiley, 1960.

Coleman, J. S. *The adolescent society.* New York: Free Press, 1961.

Commission on Population Growth and the American Future. *Population and the American Future: The report of the Commission on Population Growth and the American Future.* New York: New American Library, Signet, 1972.

Douvan, E., and Adelson, J. *The adolescent experience.* New York: Wiley, 1966.

Douvan, E., and Gold, M. Modal patterns in American adolescence. In L. W. Hoffman and M. L. Hoffman (Eds.), *Review of child development research.* Vol. II. New York: Russell Sage Foundation, 1966.

Elkind, D. Cognitive development in adolescence. In J. F. Adams (Ed.), *Understanding adolescence.* Boston: Allyn & Bacon, 1968.

Erikson, E. H. *Young man Luther: A study in psychoanalysis and history.* New York: Norton, 1958.

Freeman, F. A. Intellectual growth of children as indicated by repeated tests. *Psychol. Monogr.,* 1936, *47,* 20–34.

Gergen, K. J. Multiple identity: The healthy, happy human being wears many masks. *Psychol. Today,* 1972, *5,* 31–35, 64–66.

Getzels, J. W., and Jackson, P. W. *Creativity and intelligence.* New York: Wiley, 1962. Pp. 176–183, 183–194.

Harrison, D. E., Bennett, W. H., and Globetti, G. Attitudes of rural youth toward premarital sexual permissiveness. *J. marriage and Fam.,* 1969, *31,* 783–787.

Higgins-Trenk, A., and Gaite, A. J. H. The elusiveness of formal operational thought in adolescents. *Proc. Ann. Conv. Amer. Psychol. Assoc.,* 1971, *6,* 201–202.

Hogbin, H. I. Marriage in Wogeo, New Guinea. *Oceania,* 1945, *15,* 324–352.

Hollender, J. W. Development of vocational decisions during adolescence. *J. counseling Psychol.,* 1971, *18,* 244–248.

Hollingshead, A. B. *Elmtown's Youth.* New York: Wiley, 1949.

Horrocks, J. E. *The psychology of adolescence.* (2nd ed.) Boston: Houghton Mifflin, 1962.

Jones, M. C. The later careers of boys who were early- or late-maturing. *Child Develpm.,* 1957, *28,* 113–128.

Jones, M. C. A study of socialization patterns at the high school level. *J. genet. Psychol.,* 1958, *93,* 87–111.

Jones, M. C. Psychological correlates of somatic development. *Child Develpm.,* 1965, *36,* 899–912.

Kandel, D. B., and Lesser, G. S. Parental and peer influences on educational plans of adolescents. *Amer. sociol. Rev.,* 1969, *34,* 213–223.

Katz, P., and Zigler, E. Self-image disparity: A developmental approach. *J. pers. soc. Psychol.,* 1967, *5,* 186–195.

Keniston, K. *Young radicals: Notes on comitted youth.* New York: Harcourt Brace Jovanovich, 1968.

Kinsey, A. C., Pomeroy, W. B., and Martin, C. E. *Sexual behavior in the human male.* Philadelphia: Saunders, 1948.

Kinsey, A. C., Pomeroy, W. B., Martin, C. E., and Gebhard, P. H. *Sexual behavior in the human female.* Philadelphia: Saunders, 1953.

Kline, F. G. New life styles versus political activism. *Current,* 1972, *137,* 23–28.

Klineberg, S. L. Changes in outlook on the future between childhood and adolescence. *J. pers. soc. Psychol.,* 1967, *7,* 185–193.

Lerner, R. M., Pendorf, J., and Emery, A. Attitudes of adolescents and adults toward contemporary issues. *Psychol. Reports,* 1971, *28,* 139–145.

Lever, J. Doctoral dissertation, in progress.

Lewin, K. *Dynamic theory of personality.* New York: McGraw-Hill, 1935.

Life. A new youth poll. 1971, *70*(1, Special issue, The new shape of America), 22–27.

Look. The open generation: Youth '66. Symposium. September 20, 1966, *30,* 29–44.

Lowrie, S. H. Early and late dating: Some conditions associated with them. *Marriage and Fam. Living,* 1961, *23,* 284–291.

Mainer, R. E. Attitude change in intergroup education programs. In H. H. Remmers (Ed.), *Anti-democratic attitudes in American schools.* Evanston, Ill.: Northwestern Univer. Press, 1963.

Masters, W. H., and Johnson, V. E. *Human sexual response.* Boston: Little, Brown, 1966.

Mead, M. *Coming of Age in Samoa.* New York: New American Library, 1950. (Originally published in 1928.)

Mead, M. *Sex and temperament in three primitive societies.* New York: Morrow, 1939.

Peskin, H. Pubertal onset and ego functioning. *J. abnorm. Psychol.,* 1967, *72,* 1–15.

Piaget, J., and Inhelder, B. *The growth of logical thinking from childhood to adolescence.* Trans. by A. Parsons and S. Seagrin. New York: Basic Books, 1958.

Remmers, H. H. (Ed.) *Anti-democratic attitudes in*

American schools. Evanston, Ill.: Northwestern Univer. Press, 1963.

Rose, H. A., and Elton, C. F. Attrition and the vocationally undecided student. *J. voc. Behavior,* 1971, *1,* 99–103.

Simpson, R. L. Parental influence, anticipatory socialization, and social mobility. *Amer. sociol. Rev.,* 1962, *27,* 517–522.

Smith, E. A. *American youth culture.* New York: Free Press, 1962.

Stone, C. P., and Barker, R. G. Aspects of personality and intelligence in postmenarcheal and premenarcheal girls of the same chronological ages. *J. comp. Psychol.,* 1937, *23,* 439–455.

Sutton-Smith, B. The kissing games of adolescents of Ohio. *Midwest Folklore,* 1959, *9,* 189–211.

Tanner, J. M. Radiographic studies of body composition. In J. Brozek (Ed.), *Body composition.* Oxford: Pergamon, 1965.

Tanner, J. M. Physical growth. In P. H. Mussen (Ed.), *Carmichael's manual of child psychology.* Vol. I. (3d ed.) New York: Wiley, 1970.

Tanner, J. M. Sequence, tempo, and individual variation in the growth and development of boys and girls aged twelve to sixteen. *Daedalus: J. Amer. Acad. Arts and Sciences,* 1971, *100,* 907–930.

Trent, J. W., and Craise, J. L. Commitment and conformity in the American college. *J. soc. Issues,* 1967, *23,* 34–51.

Whiting, J. W. M., Kluckhohn, R., and Anthony, A. The function of male initiation ceremonies at puberty. In E. E. Maccoby, T. Newcomb, and E. Hartley (Eds.), *Readings in social psychology.* (3rd ed.) New York: Holt, Rinehart & Winston, 1958.

15 Personality and Social Development

ADOLESCENCE is above all a time of change and transition. As we noted in the preceding chapter, the maturation of the sex and reproductive organs, the appearance of secondary sexual characteristics, and the spurt in physical growth gradually produce a marked alteration in the individual's body image. Along with these physical alterations, the adolescent is continuing to acquire new cognitive capabilities, as well as feeling the force of a new biological drive—the sex drive.

In addition to these physical and biological changes, the adolescent is confronted with new and different expectations about his behavior—expectations from his family, his school, and his peers. The adolescent's personality is forced to evolve by the pressures impinging upon him.

While in Chapter 14 we dealt with the changes and forces that confront the adolescent in our society, our focus in this chapter is on the ways in which adolescent personalities adapt to these new forces. We shall consider the degree to which the adolescent achieves emotional independence from his family and how this is accomplished, as well as the effects of these new forces on his self-concept, his sexual identity, and his attitudes and values. And we shall discover that many of the phenomena popularly associated with adolescents in general—alienation, juvenile delinquency, drug abuse, political radicalism—are characteristic of relatively small atypical minorities. Before we consider the specific areas of development, we begin with a brief review of some of the major theories about the processes of adolescent personality.

Theories of Adolescent Personality

Freudian Views

While Freud himself placed greater emphasis on early childhood development than on adolescence, his followers, particularly Anna Freud (his daughter), have devoted much attention to adolescent psychology. The orthodox Freudians stress the importance of a reawakening of Oedipal conflicts at the onset of puberty. The boy's infantile rivalry with the father for the attentions of the mother is now expressed in his first heterosexual relationships outside the family. His first choice of a girl friend is often a girl who reminds him to some extent of his mother. Similarly, a girl's first boyfriends often have characteristics in common with her father.

Anna Freud sees the adolescent personality in terms of the relationship between the id, governed by the pleasure principle; the ego, governed by the reality principle; and the superego, or conscience. The superego is made up of internalized moral values assimilated during childhood from parents and other adult authority figures. With the awakening of the child's sexuality at puberty, there is an increase in instinctual libidinal (sexual) energy, causing a conflict between the largely unconscious infantile and incestuous desires of the id, and the now-internalized moral values of the superego. The superego "punishes" the ego for any yielding to the impulses of the id by producing anxiety and feelings of guilt, as well as offering the "rewards" of a "clear conscience" when the ego resists these impulses (A. Freud 1948).

According to Freudian theory, the individual faces the problem of both repressing the incestuous Oedipal impulses and developing nonincestuous love relationships. The adolescent must successfully detach his sexual energy (libido) from the opposite-sex parent and transfer it to other love objects. Several potential dangers await the adolescent in this task, and these dangers can produce pathological results.

One such danger is that of overinhibition, which prevents the individual from establishing sexual relationships with any member of the opposite sex. Another danger is that the id may gain the ascendancy in the struggle of personality forces. The result may be a lapse into pregenital forms of gratification, perversion, criminality, and so on (A. Freud 1948).

On the whole, Freudian theory is primarily biologically based. That is, an individual passes through developmental stages that are genetically or biologically determined and thus, to a great extent, independent of environmental or cultural factors. Freud himself, for example, saw the Oedipus conflict as a universal condition. However, anthropological findings over the years have seriously questioned this assumption, and have provided considerable evidence that the structure and conditions of adolescent development—and development in general—differ from culture to culture.

Erikson's Theory of Adolescence

While the orthodox Freudian position emphasizes the sexual drive, particularly in terms of the internal, emotional conflict between instinct (id) and conscience (superego), many present-day psychoanalysts, among them Erik Erikson, stress the social side of adolescent personality development. Although Erikson considers sexuality very important, he regards the development of a solid ego-identity as the crucial task of the adolescent. And he believes that this process varies from culture to culture.

As we noted in Chapter 14, the adolescent struggles to establish a sense of continuity in light of the many physical and emotional changes that occur during this period. His vocational choices, sexuality, political and social values, tastes, and so on, will all be affected by this struggle. The peer group, for example, becomes an important means by which the individual gains a feeling of social belonging. The adolescent's sense of identification with a particular group or clique acts as a defense against the dangers of self-diffusion.

Moreover, Erikson considers the adolescent's romantic pursuits as being motivated more by his need to try out his developing ego-identity than by his sexual drive. Thus, in his "love affairs" the

479

Figure 15.1 In the view of Erikson, the adolescent uses romantic relationships to test his self-concept and identity. (Roger Malloch—Magnum)

adolescent uses the partner as a means of testing and reflecting on his own self-concept (Erikson 1950).

To Erikson, the mature individual is one who has successfully developed an independent and totally integrated sense of self-identity. The failure to do so will lead the individual to continual role confusion in his adult life. Thus, Erikson differs from the orthodox Freudians in that he places more emphasis on the struggle for an integrated ego-identity. In so doing, he also places more stress than do the Freudians on the social and cultural conditions within which the adolescent's identity struggle takes place.

Social Learning Theories

Social learning theorists view the psychological changes of adolescence as determined primarily by social and cultural factors. As we discussed earlier, the social learning theorists concentrate on behavior, which is considered the result of learning and not of biology. To the more extreme social learning theorists, such as B. F. Skinner, the source of all psychological and behavioral phenomena is the conditioning imposed on the individual by his environment. Development is regarded as the continuous and quantitative accumulation of behavioral patterns (Langer 1969). For example, in the view of social psychologist Allison Davis, the psychological and behavioral changes of adolescence are a continuation of the process of socialization. Through this process, beginning at birth, the child learns socially and culturally acceptable behavior by means of reinforcement and punishment. Davis speaks of "socialized anxiety" as the means by which the adolescent learns adult behaviors that his particular society considers normal (Davis 1944). Socialized anxiety is produced throughout childhood by social reinforcement—that is, by reward and punishment. The individual learns to anticipate punishment for certain kinds of behavior. He develops an internal mechanism, an "anticipation of discomfort" (Mowrer 1939), which guides his behavior. Like the superego in Freudian psychology, this anticipation of discomfort, or socialized anxiety, becomes internalized and less and less dependent on external reinforcement. And according to Davis, if enough socialized anxiety is internalized by the individual, it will lead him to mature and socially responsible behavior.

Thus, a key difference between social learning and Freudian and neo-Freudian views is that social learning theorists discount the existence of distinct, biologically determined stages of development. Instead, they view behavioral development as a relatively continuous learning experience. Adolescent behavior (and behavior in general) is the result of an accumulated history of reinforcement, and not something that suddenly appears at adolescence.

With these various theoretical positions in mind, let us now turn to some specific areas and issues in adolescent personality development.

Dependence versus Independence

The traits of dependence and independence are particularly important to an understanding of adolescent personality, since the achievement of personal independence or autonomy is one of the central tasks of adolescence. During the transition from childhood to adulthood, the individual evolves from one who is basically dependent on his family and adult authorities to one who is essentially autonomous. The individual's psychological capability for independent behavior is a basic part of his personality.

As we have noted in the social development chapters relating to earlier stages, psychoanalytic theory holds that the child is initially tied to the mother by its need for nurturance. This initial bond between mother and child often persists as a strong emotional attachment and dependency until much later in life. Although the mother does not remain the sole satisfier of such needs as food, warmth, or safety, the individual's emotional bond—according to psychoanalytic theory—remains to a greater or lesser degree.

When the child reaches puberty, his sexual needs mature. At this time, he must further break his dependence on the mother because of the incest taboo. Similarly, girls must begin to break the dependence on the father.

Factors Affecting Dependence

The capability for independent behavior is closely affected by a number of variables, including that of sex. While few sex differences in dependence are observed in early childhood, in middle and late adolescence, girls have been found to be generally more dependent than boys (Mischel 1970).

Another study found some evidence that passive and dependent behavior manifested by girls between ages 6 to 10 still persisted at ages 20 to 27. No such results were found for the male subjects (Kagan and Moss 1960). The authors used observational data from the subjects' childhoods and correlated this information with data obtained in adult interviews of the same subjects. They found that ratings of passivity for females from ages 6 to 10 correlated significantly with adult ratings for dependent vocational orientation, dependency on love object, dependency on parents, and withdrawal from situations likely to involve failure.

For men, they found only correlations between early instrumental dependency (that is, the constant need for guidance in tasks) and dependency on nonparental figures in adulthood. Thus, the stability of the dependency trait in men is much less marked than it is in women. As we noted before, such evidence of continuity of the dependency trait in women may change as the culture's attitude toward female roles changes and as social movements such as Women's Liberation affect women's traditional roles and attitudes. As women assume more of an equal economic role with men, it is likely that female dependency in adolescence—as well as in adulthood—will decrease.

Still another study, by Landsbaum and Willis (1971), indicated that dependency is a function of age and of the individual's perception of his own competence. These researchers studied 32 adolescents aged 13 to 14 and 18 to 21 years. The subjects were measured for conformity in an experimental judgment task. Each subject was given a "partner" who (he was told) had either high or low competency in the task. In general, more conformity to partner judgment was found for younger subjects, as well as for those who thought they had little competency and those who thought their partners had high competency.

One could point to several factors, universal throughout society, that can produce conflict in adolescent development of independence. For example, it is difficult to gain financial and vocational independence at an early age. The economy is constantly requiring more training and education for a limited total number of jobs. Thus, the adolescent is usually forced to remain financially dependent on his parents while he is in school. This situation often results in continued emotional dependence, as well as feelings of guilt and anxiety.

More subtle is the factor of parental inconsistency with regard to the child's emancipation. Since there are no specific rules for what behaviors are allowed at what ages (other than certain legal limits), parents are often confused about when to permit the child various adult behaviors. Moreover, many parents may be unconsciously jealous of their children and may strive to keep them dependent in order to gratify some of their own needs.

However, these kinds of conflict- and neurosis-producing situations, while found with some frequency (particularly among the urban middle and upper middle class), are not necessarily the rule. On the contrary, as we discussed in Chapter 14, there is a great deal of evidence that severe conflicts and crises arising out of adolescents' growth toward independence are relatively unusual and that the development of independence is gradual in our society. For instance, Douvan and Gold (1966) found that for the average, or modal, American adolescent, there are few strains or conflicts as a result of incomplete states of independence. They wrote:

But the modal pattern, the way of most American youngsters, is neither to act out nor to suffer the strains and conflicts, the guilts and anxieties of neurosis. It seems, rather, that the normal, the average, the modal youngster makes his bid for autonomy gradually and appropriately, and that his requests meet reasonable consideration and deference from parents who ally themselves (more or less) gracefully with the child's need to grow. (Douvan and Gold 1966)

Cross-cultural Data

RITES OF PASSAGE. In some cultures, the change from dependence on the parents to independence is acknowledged through a formal ritual, or *rite de passage*. Ethnographic studies have found a wide variety of pubertal initiation rites in different primitive societies. Frequently, such rites involve severe and painful hazing of pubertal boys by previously initiated men of the culture. Sometimes such rites include genital operations, tests of manhood, and isolation from the opposite sex for long periods of time (Whiting, Kluckhohn, and Anthony 1958). The Thonga of South Africa and the Kwoma people of New Guinea, for example, have such severe initiation rites. Other cultures have relatively minor pubertal rituals in which the boy is merely invested with some symbol of manhood such as a tatoo, as in the case of the Maori of New Zealand (Whiting et al. 1958). And still other cultures, like our own, have virtually no such rituals.

There has been much speculation on why pubertal initiation ceremonies exist in some cultures and not in others. Whiting and his colleagues provided an explanation based on psychoanalytic assumptions concerning the son's attachment to his mother and rivalry with his father (Oedipal conflict). These investigators found that pubertal initiation rites occur in cultures in which there is an exclusive relationship between mother and son during the first year or so of the child's infancy. Such relationships are characterized by the infant sleeping with the mother either alone or with the father present. In such cultures, the mother is usually subject to a relatively long post-birth sexual taboo. It is assumed that she therefore receives some sexual gratification from nursing her child.

As a result of these arrangements, a strong emotional dependence on the mother is engendered in the infant son. When the postbirth sexual taboo is lifted, the father abruptly terminates this exclusive relationship between the son and his mother and resumes his role as husband. Whiting and his associates assumed that considerable envy and hostility toward the father is thus generated in the son. This hostility becomes dangerous with the onset of puberty (biological manhood), and could conceivably lead to open rebellion. Therefore, the son's dependence on the mother must be finally broken, and he must be taught to identify with males of the society. Hence, the initiation rites (Whiting et al. 1958).

A number of alternative and/or complementary hypotheses have been offered to explain the phenomena of pubertal rites. Brown (1963), for example, dealt with the subject of female initiation rites. According to Brown, female rites tend to occur in societies where the mother and her daughter remain in the same household unit even after the girl's marriage. The rite serves to emphasize that the girl is grown up. Societies like our own, where the late-adolescent girl (and boy) generally leaves the parents' home, do not require puberty rites as proof of independence.

Moreover, according to Brown, female rites that subject the adolescent to painful genital operations are an attempt to deal with sex-identity conflict. Early mother–child sleeping arrangements reinforce maternal dependence. Then, rather abruptly, the child is introduced to a patriarchal social structure. The result is likely to be some degree of sex-role ambiguity. In order to force the child to make the proper sex-role identification, dramatic and painful ceremonies, including genital operations, are performed by adults of the same sex as the child (Brown 1963).

In addition, Brown noted that initiation rites are characteristic of those societies in which women play an important economic role. The rites educate and elevate the adolescent to adult status as a responsible and productive member of her society (Brown 1963).

Young (1962, 1965), on the other hand, offered an explanation differing from that of Whiting or Brown. He suggested that male initiation ceremonies occur in societies where strong solidarity among males as a group is a characteristic. Likewise, female initiation ceremonies are found in societies where there is institutionalized household solidarity—that is, where female work groups organize around household tasks. In both cases, according to Young, the initiation rites serve the function of dramatizing the status of the initiate as a member of a sex-group.

Development of Values in Adolescence

Another important component of personality is moral development—the growth of systematic beliefs about what is good and bad, right and wrong. There are a number of different theories about how morality develops in adolescence. These can be roughly divided into Freudian and neo-Freudian approaches and cognitive-stage approaches, as exemplified by the views of Piaget.

Freudian View of Adolescent Morality

In the classic Freudian view, morality results from the growth of the superego. The superego is seen as developing during the preadolescent period. As a way out of the Oedipus complex, the child identifies with the parent of the same sex and incorporates his or her standards into his own psychological makeup. Thus, the orthodox Freudian position is that morality is relatively well-formed by the time adolescence is reached (Freud 1933).

However, recent psychoanalytic thinkers have stressed that development of the superego and, hence, of morality continues in new ways into adolescence. This continuation takes the form of a

PERSONALITY AND SOCIAL DEVELOPMENT 483

"rebellion against the superego" in which the individual rejects his parents' standards and the part of himself that has unreflectively adopted his parents' morality (Blos 1962).

Another way in which morality develops in adolescence, according to the recent psychoanalytic view, is by integration of the ego and the superego. Erikson (1964, 1965), who has taken a modified psychoanalytic position, distinguishes an "ethical stage" of nonconventional, self-accepted moral principles which can develop out of the period of identity crisis. When the adolescent can no longer rely on his parents for his values and for his identity in general, he is forced to develop values of his own. Particularly in cases where the adolescent discovers hypocrisy in the conventional values of his parents or society, he may be compelled to find his own values.

Cognitive Stage Theories of Adolescent Morality

The work of Piaget (1948) has been prominent in cognitive-stage approaches to the study of moral development. Piaget has been mainly concerned with the cognitive aspects of moral reasoning. He has related adolescent moral reasoning to the growth of the ability for objective consideration of events, and the ability to consider the possibilities and isolate the various factors present in a given situation. Piaget has also shown that the adolescent appeals less to authority as he gets older.

Kohlberg has further developed the stage approach (1970). He has distinguished three stages of moral development,[1] which were described in Chapter 12. These are the preconventional stage of early childhood (doing what leads to personal gratification and what one can get away with); the conventional stage of later childhood (accepting the laws and standards of parents and community); and the postconventional stage (developing personal principles which are often abstract and conflict with society's conventional morality).

An article by Keniston (1970) cited data showing that the percentage of middle-class American males in these different categories varies with age. At age 16, 35 percent of the subjects were considered postconventional, 46 percent conventional, and 19 percent preconventional. At age 20, the breakdowns, in the same order, were 27 percent, 50 percent, and 23 percent. At age 24, again in the same order, the distribution was 36 percent, 52 percent, and 12 percent. Thus, it has been shown that most of the people studied did not reach the stage of postconventional morality.

An interesting sidelight to this data is a longitudinal study by Kramer (1968) which showed that some adolescents approaching postconventional morality actually go through a regressive period in which they return to earlier preconventional morality. This phenomenon is interpreted as the individual's attempt to free himself from irrational and crippling guilt attached to conventional morality. Kramer found that individuals who regress ultimately return to their previous stage of development and continue on from there.

According to Keniston (1970), three factors facilitate the development of postconventional morality. For one, a prolonged period of disengagement from adult institutions, such as that experienced by many college students, seems to facilitate higher moral development. Another facilitating factor is a confrontation with alternative points of view. Such confrontations often lead to skepticism about previously held conventional views. In this case, as with the first factor, the more mobile, urban middle-class adolescent is more likely to be exposed to alternative perspectives than, say, his lower-class rural counterpart. A third catalyst for higher moral development is the discovery of corruption or hypocrisy in society and, particularly, in trusted authorities (currently rather widespread). This last factor also can foster a regression in moral development by leading to cynicism about traditional values.

These factors, Keniston has claimed, are fostering the growth of postconventional morality in increasing numbers of young people, particularly among radical and hippie youth. His findings are consistent with those of Adelson (1971) who found, in a survey of English, German, and American adolescents, a marked decline in authoritari-

---

1. Actually, Kohlberg distinguishes six stages of moral development within the three general stages or levels we describe here.

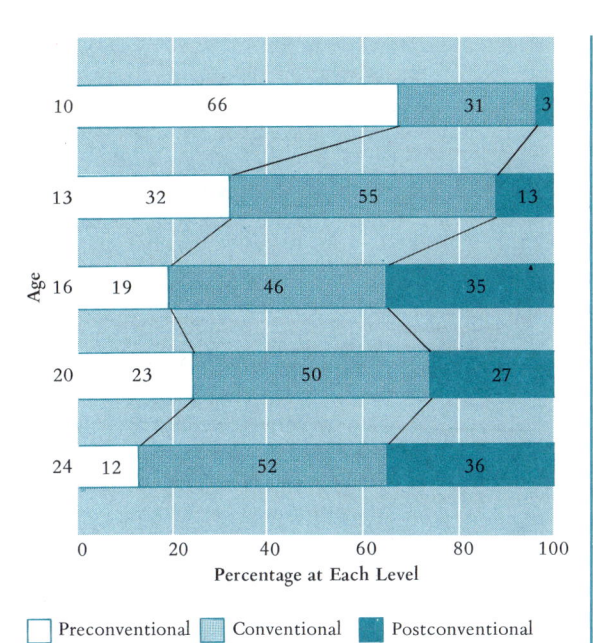

Figure 15.2 Level of moral reasoning at five age levels. Subjects were middle-class urban American males. All percentages are approximate; population sizes are not stated in original. (From K. Keniston. Student activism, moral development and morality. *Amer. J. Orthopsychiat.*, 1970, *40*, 580.)

an responses to political and social questions between early and late adolescence.

Keniston has suggested that while new technological, educational, and historical factors are fostering the increasing development of postconventional morality among today's youth, the meaning of this development may be paradoxical. For instance, if such development is not matched by the development of the capacity for love and compassion, it can lead to moral zealotry, dogmatism, and even fanaticism. Keniston pointed out that many crimes against humanity have been committed by those sincerely believing in high personal moral principles (1970).

Recent Trends in Adolescent Values

In 1957, Jacob presented evidence that 75 to 80 percent of American college students valued and were contented with their daily activity; aspired to material gratification for themselves; were tolerant of diversity but not crusaders for nondiscrimination; and valued traditional moral virtues such as honesty, sincerity, and loyalty, while being lax about departures from these virtues. Moreover, Jacob reported that the students saw a need for religion in their lives, but seldom applied religious ideas to their behavior. Similarly, they fulfilled the necessary obligations to the government (such as obeying its laws) without particular complaint or enthusiasm. And they exhibited little desire to have more voice in governmental decision making (Jacob 1957).

Since then, there have been innumerable student protests against a variety of social ills, ranging from racial discrimination to sexual discrimination. There have been highly publicized demonstrations by youth against the Vietnam war, as well as considerable media coverage of radical student political activism. Much has been made of the "new youth" and their often radical rejection of the values of the older generation. Such phenomena would seem to indicate a marked change in youthful values since Jacob's study in the fifties.

Several more recent studies do indicate some shift in adolescent values. For example, there is some evidence that today's youth are generally more interested in political and social issues, often holding strong opinions about political subjects (Lerner, Pendorf, and Emery 1971). In addition, as we have mentioned in the preceding chapter, they tend toward more openness and honesty in sexual matters. And, although there is evidence of an increase in premarital sexual experience among adolescents (Commission on Population Growth and the American Future 1972), there is also evidence that adolescents see more value in warm interpersonal relationships than those that are purely sexual (Reiss 1966).

However, there is little evidence that the majority of American adolescents are radically rejecting traditional values. In one cross-sectional survey, for example, over 60 percent of the adolescents interviewed said they place a "great deal" of faith in American social institutions, such as banks, the Supreme Court, higher education, and the medical and scientific communities. The same study revealed that only 25 percent had a "great deal" of faith in political parties, the press, organized labor, and television (*Newsweek* 1965).

A more recent national survey of adolescents between the ages of 15 and 21 was conducted by Louis Harris Associates for *Life* magazine (1971). This study revealed remarkably moderate views on a wide range of social questions. For example, 73 percent of the respondents agreed with their parents' values and ideals. While 80 percent felt that their parents lived up to their own ideals, 64 percent felt their parents approved of their (the adolescents') ideals.

This survey also revealed some differences between religious values of high school adolescents and those in college. For example, 77 percent of the high school students surveyed held religion to be important to them. For the college students the percentage dropped to 56 percent (*Life* 1971). That adolescent religious values tend to change during college is highlighted by another survey comparing religious values of college freshmen with those of college seniors. While 53 percent of the freshmen respondents said that college had not altered their religious beliefs, only 34 percent of the seniors made the same statement. Moreover, 45 percent of the seniors said college had raised doubts about their religious beliefs (*Newsweek* 1965). Such findings appear to support Keniston's feeling that the disengagement from adult institutions during the college years promotes changes in the previously held moral beliefs (Keniston 1970).

In general, then, recent trends seem to indicate that adolescents are less complacent about their values than they have been in the past. They seem somewhat more interested in social and political change and are perhaps better informed. On the whole, however, the majority tend to hold to rather conventional moral views.

Self-concept and Self-esteem

Theoretical Positions

Each major theoretical approach perceives changes in self-image development during adolescence, although each accounts for these changes in somewhat different ways. The orthodox Freudians view the development of self-concept as being closely tied to body-image and sex-role development. According to this view, high self-esteem results from good sexual adjustment—that is, an adequate resolution of the Oedipus complex and, beginning at puberty, a shifting of libidinal interest to object choices outside the family.

The Eriksonian view places more stress on the social aspects of self-esteem. If, at each stage of development, the child has received approval and has adequately mastered the tasks of that stage, the chances of his emerging from the adolescent identity crisis with a firm and positive sense of ego-identity are greater than if he has not experienced success and approval.

The cognitive approach to self-concept takes a different tack altogether from the Freudian and Eriksonian viewpoints. Thinkers such as Lewin, Werner, and Piaget may be construed as showing the consequences of cognitive development for the self-concept. For example, in the research that has focused on the disparity between real-self and ideal-self, the disparity might be explained as arising from the increased awareness of possibilities and deficiencies that comes with greater cognitive differentiation rather than from disturbances or conflicts in development.

For both Lewin and Werner, the adolescent's thinking is characterized by increased differentiation and articulation. Thus, the adolescent becomes capable of finer psychological distinctions which he can apply to himself and to others. In addition, he becomes more aware of social demands and expectations as a result of his increased cognitive powers. This, too, affects his self-concept.

Moreover, according to Piaget, the adolescent capable of formal operations is more aware of his own possibilities than the younger child who is limited to concrete operations. As a result, he does not merely accept what he is in the present, but can look forward to a future in which some of his present deficiencies will be filled. Piaget points out, however, that the adolescent is at first "egocentric" about his ideals, in the sense that he is unable to differentiate between his first ideals and possible future objective realities. There are thus recurring stages of egocentricity at each major level of thought—preoperational, concrete operational, and formal operational—as the child equates his own perspective, at each level, with the way things are for everyone.

Research in Theoretical Areas

DEVELOPMENTAL AND COGNITIVE RESEARCH. The cognitive and developmental theories have inspired a number of studies of self-image. One such study, that of Katz and Zigler (1967), took as its hypothesis that self-image disparity—discrepancy between real and ideal self-images—should increase with development. The hypothesis was based on two findings derived from previous research. The first was that as an individual matures, his capacity for incorporating social expectations, values, and mores increases, as does his capacity for making greater demands on himself. As the individual makes greater self-demands, his chances of being unable to fulfill all of them also increase. Consequently, he experiences more guilt feelings than an individual at a lower level of development (Katz and Zigler 1967; Phillips and Rabinovitch 1958; Phillips and Zigler 1961). The second finding was that of Piaget and Werner, that greater cognitive differentiation occurs as development proceeds to higher levels.

Katz and Zigler hypothesized that disparity in the self-image is related directly to level of development, or more specifically, that self-image disparity increases with increasing maturity. Fifth-, eighth-, and eleventh-graders were tested by questionnaires designed to determine their real-self, ideal-self, and social-self images.

It was found that the disparity between real-self and ideal-self increased with chronological age, as well as with I.Q. As Katz and Zigler pointed out, this finding is particularly surprising in view of the traditional theory that such disparity indicates maladjustment (the subjects in this experiment were considered normally adjusted). Their results also supported the thesis that self-image disparity is a function of both increased capacity for guilt and increased cognitive differentiation accompanying greater maturity.

The increase in the disparity between the real-self and ideal-self image with maturity was accounted for by both a lowering of self-evaluation and a more positive ideal-self image. According to Katz and Zigler, this finding contradicts the concept that only the real-self image varies with development, while the individual's ideal-self varies little, if any.

The findings of Katz and Zigler have received support from related studies by Mullener and Laird (1971) and Hess and Bradshaw (1970). Mullener and Laird found that there was a trend toward greater differentiation in the use of personal characteristics in self-evaluations with an increase in age (seventh- and twelfth-graders and young adults were tested). In addition, it was found that in all groups, individuals who gave less differentiated evaluations rated themselves more highly on given characteristics.

Hess and Bradshaw (1970) administered an adjective check list ("I am weak/strong; I should be weak/strong") to four groups: a high school group, a college group, a group aged 35 to 50, and a group aged 55 to 65. Each group was asked to go through the adjective list once to select adjectives describing self, and a second time to select adjectives describing ideal-self. The results showed a significant difference in each group between self and ideal, and that the older groups reflected greater disparity between real-self and ideal-self images than did the younger groups. Of all the four groups tested, the high school group (the youngest subjects) tended to have the least self-image disparity. There is support in these findings for the view of Gergen presented in Chapter 14, namely, that a healthy identity has multiple facets.

ERIKSON-INSPIRED RESEARCH. In a study by Marcia and Friedman (1970), a correlation was found between strength of ego-identity and both self-esteem and difficulty of college major, among a sample of 49 college women. The investigators defined ego-identity status in terms of the degree of crisis (or period of decision making which involves alternatives) in the areas of occupation and ideology, and the degree of commitment (the individual's personal involvement in the alternatives chosen).

Based on Erikson's emphasis on the identity

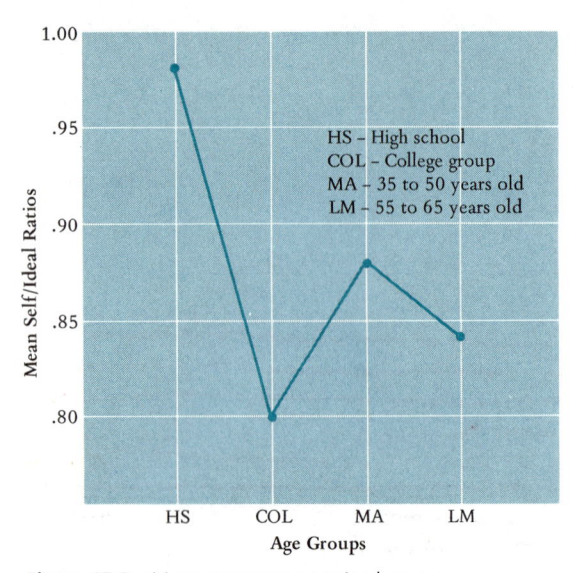

Figure 15.3 Mean congruency ratios between self-concept and ideal self-concept for four age groups. (From A. L. Hess and H. L. Bradshaw. Positiveness of self-concept and ideal self as a function of age. *J. genet. Psychol.*, 1970, *117*, 63.)

crisis and consequent ego-adaptation, Marcia and Friedman described four "identity statuses" for their study: *identity achievement*, the status held by those who have experienced a crisis period and subsequently committed themselves to an occupation and ideology; *moratorium*, the status of those individuals currently experiencing the crisis and not yet committed; *foreclosure*, the status of those who have experienced no crisis, but do have rather strong commitments (usually parentally determined); and *identity diffusion*, the status of those who have no apparent commitments and no sense of struggle to establish any. As the specific ideological issue, the experimenters chose the female subject's attitudes toward premarital intercourse.

The 49 subjects were interviewed concerning their attitudes about premarital intercourse and the degree to which they were committed to maintaining these attitudes. On the basis of these interviews, the subjects were placed in one of the identity-status categories and given various tests to measure their problem-solving ability, self-esteem, authoritarianism, and anxiety. The subject's major was rated by degree of difficulty (relative difficulty of various majors was determined prior to the main study by the ratings of 160 sophomore, junior, and senior women).

The findings showed that women in the identity-achievement category tended to have more difficult majors—for example, engineering, chemistry, biology, mathematics, pharmacy—than did those with identity-diffusion status. The foreclosure-status subjects had, on the average, the highest self-esteem and the highest degree of authoritarianism, and exhibited the lowest anxiety scores. Those with identity diffusions showed the highest anxiety scores.

Marcia and Friedman suggested that the high degree of ego-identity exhibited by the foreclosure-status subjects may indicate that such women are seeking social approval, thus adopting positions of high self-esteem and authoritarianism as a defense against self-exposure. On the other hand, as the investigators pointed out, traditional cultural expectations that girls become what their parents intend them to become may account for the higher self-esteem, higher authoritarianism, and lower anxiety scores of the foreclosure women. In that case, the lower self-esteem of the identity-achievement women might be due to possible feelings of alienation from their peers and family resulting from their actions against traditional expectations (Marcia and Friedman 1970).

OTHER RESEARCH ON SELF-ESTEEM. Other researchers have tried to determine what antecedent conditions foster self-acceptance among adolescents. A study by Medinnus (1965) measured late-adolescent boys and girls on the bipolar adjective scale ("I am . . . ." "I should be . . . .") for self-acceptance and perceived parental acceptance. The researcher also distributed questionnaires on parent–child relations to both the adolescent subjects and their parents.

Correlations were obtained between all the measures. While the correlations were not high enough to show that self-acceptance and perceived parental acceptance are determined by parent–child relations, they did confirm that these factors are related. In general, higher correlations for boys than for girls were found between self-regard and perceived parental acceptance, which "suggests that at late adolescence the boy's self-acceptance is more dependent upon perceived parental attitudes toward him than is the case for girls. For the boy, more than for the girl, the period of late adolescence involves an anxiety-provoking search for identity" (Medinnus 1965).

Another study of the child-rearing antecedents of self-conceptions, conducted by Rosenberg (1963), asked juniors and seniors in high school to report their remembrances of their parents' interest in them when they were 10 and 11 years old. Specifically, subjects were asked whether their parents had been interested in their friends, what had been their parents' reactions to good or bad report cards, and to what extent they (the subjects) had participated in dinner-table conversations. These responses were then compared with self-esteem scores.

The results revealed relatively few subjects at the low self-esteem end of the scale, and also relatively few who reported little or no parental interest. However, 45 percent of the low parental-interest group exhibited low self-esteem, compared to only 26 percent of the rest of the group. The difference was large enough to support the idea that parental interest (as perceived and remembered by the child) fosters high or moderate self-esteem. On the other hand, there were a substantial number of subjects who did not fit this pattern. It was also pointed out that a subject's current feelings of self-worth might possibly affect his memory of parental interest when he was a child (Rosenberg 1963).

Sex-role Identity and Self-concept

Closely related to the adolescent's self-identity is his sexual identification and sex-role development. The degree of security an individual feels in his sexual identity, and how consistent this identity is with the expectations of family and peers, cannot help but affect the adolescent's overall self-concept and feelings of self-esteem.

A study by Mussen (1961) revealed that adolescent boys exhibiting highly masculine interests on the Strong Vocational Interest Test tended to be more self-confident and have more positive self-concepts than boys of equal intelligence and from similar socioeconomic backgrounds who showed more feminine interests. However, Mussen found the reverse situation to be true with adult males. In a follow-up study, Mussen (1962) tested the same subjects, then in their thirties. Those who had shown highly masculine interests during adolescence, while still "masculine" in their interests, tended to lack the qualities of leadership, self-confidence, and self-acceptance as adults. On the other hand, boys who had feminine interests in adolescence showed more positive signs of leadership, self-confidence, and self-esteem as adults.

Mussen attributed this shift to the fact that many respected and well-rewarded adult vocational roles require a combination of what has been stereotyped as "masculine" and "feminine" characteristics. For example, a doctor or teacher must be both dominant and aggressive, as well as sensitive and receptive. Thus, while certain stereotypes of "masculine" characteristics may be of prestige value to adolescent boys, the same characteristics may inhibit the development of attributes important to successful vocational achievements in adulthood.

The results of a study by Heilbrun (1964) seem to support Mussen's earlier findings. Heilbrun found that male adolescents who had high masculinity ratings exhibited greater social-role consistency (an Eriksonian criterion of identity achievement) than did males with low masculinity ratings. It was felt that social reward for conformity to cultural stereotypes of masculinity seems to strengthen ego-identity, though perhaps at the expense of flexibility.

The same has been found to be true for adolescent girls. Douvan and Adelson (1966), for example, found that girls who indicated strong and unambiguous feminine sex-role identification seemed also to have the strongest sense of self-identity. In general, these girls identified with their mothers, choosing either the mother or another feminine relative as an adult ideal. Their relationships with their parents were amiable and ——————liancy with parental demands, usually identifying with their parents' point of view. The investigators pointed out that such girls were apt to gain self-esteem from parental praise more often than girls with more ambivalent feminine sex-role identifications.

On the other hand, the girls with the lowest scores for traditionally feminine interests were socially less at ease in their relationships with adults. These girls also exhibited generally weaker self-concepts and lower self-esteem than the unambivalent girls (Douvan and Adelson 1966). In general, these results suggest that greatest ego strength is not necessarily related to open-mindedness and flexibility. In fact, they may often be contrasting characteristics.

Atypical Groups

Although the majority of adolescents make their transition to adulthood with relative ease, experiencing no particular crisis or trauma, there are, of course, those who do not conform to this pattern. There are many individuals whose adolescent experience is marked by serious crises of one sort or another. The resulting deviant behavior is often the kind that creates wide public attention and alarm. The culture reacts because the adolescent deviants often do not seem amenable to existing systems and are seen as potentially capable of causing trouble and disturbance. We shall devote the remainder of this chapter to a discussion of some of these atypical groups, specifically the radical student activists, the dropouts, the juvenile delinquents, and the adolescent drug users.

Many of the problems experienced by the atypical adolescents are apt to be extensions or exaggerations of problems common to adolescents in general. However, unlike the majority of his peers, the atypical adolescent is either unable to successfully resolve the problem, resulting in a kind of arrested development, or he resolves it in a manner apparently incompatible with existing social systems.

For example, we have mentioned that as an individual develops into adolescence, he is at first inclined to be idealistic in his concept of himself, and in his hopes and goals for the future. Often this idealism clashes not only with the realities he perceives for himself personally and what he can realistically expect for his future, but also with the way he perceives society in general. This clash may become for some a major crisis, perhaps affecting the individual's overall concept of himself and his own worth, and/or his attitude about society and its worth.

Such a crisis unfavorably resolved may leave the individual with a profound sense of despair and alienation. It may result in the individual's rejection of some or all of the values of his society, leading him to rebel against those values to a greater or lesser degree. For some, the response might be a rebellion against what is perceived as society's demand for conformity in dress and social behavior. For others, it might take the form of intense protest against social injustice (such as racial discrimination), while still others may rebel against authority to the extent of exhibiting criminal behavior. In other words, various types of deviant behavior—even delinquency and violent behavior—may arise, at least in part, from disappointed idealism.

Radical Student Political Activism

The actual number of American students thoroughly committed to radical political activism is relatively small. For example, one study revealed that, at most, only 9 percent of any student body was involved in a protest movement (Peterson 1966). Moreover, such protests, by and large, occur only at select, high-quality institutions (Peterson 1966).

Peterson surveyed the deans of students or equivalent officers of 85 percent of the four-year colleges in this country. His data illuminate the nature and extent of student protests. He found that 38 percent of the deans reported activism over civil rights; 28 percent reported activism over campus living regulations; 21 percent over the war in Vietnam; 18 percent over student participation in campus decision making; 9 percent over rules governing controversial speakers on campus; 7 percent on curriculum matters; and 4 percent on academic freedom for the faculty.

Trent and Craise (1967) interviewed some 10,000 high school graduates in a national sample.

They found that most of those who went on to college had an uncritical acceptance of the status quo. While 23 percent considered themselves "nonconformists," 28 percent considered themselves as "common man," and only 1 percent labeled themselves as radicals.

The same study also found that the majority of students seemed to accept the general way their colleges were operated. For example, 68 percent of the students accepted campus rules and regulations as necessary; 70 percent reported that most of the faculty were intellectually stimulating; and 56 percent considered the faculty and administration successful in developing responsibility among students. It should be noted, however, that this survey was conducted in 1963, slightly before the full force of the student activism of the late sixties began to make itself felt.

SOME CHARACTERISTICS OF STUDENT ACTIVISTS. It has been found that frequently student activists are among the ablest students on the nation's campuses. Various studies of students involved in the Berkeley Free Speech Movement of 1964 have shown that such students ranked high in intellectual disposition, autonomy, flexibility, liberalism, level of ability, and qualities of individualism and social commitment (Heist 1965; Somers 1965; Watts and Whittaker 1966). They were distinctly higher than the general Berkeley student population in these categories. This finding is consistent with the findings of Haan, Smith, and Block (Haan, Smith, and Block 1968; Haan and Block 1969), who discovered that those involved in various protests at Berkeley and San Francisco State College rated higher than the general populations of these schools in moral development levels.

In the discussion of adolescent moral development, we mentioned Kohlberg's concept of three levels of morality—the preconventional, conventional, and postconventional. According to Kenneth Keniston (1970), most student protesters fall into the postconventional category. These students have gone beyond unquestioning acceptance of moral and social authority (parents, the college, the state) and are engaged in developing moral principles of their own. They are more likely to reject many more of the societal institutions than are those who are at the conventional level (the majority of students). However, as Keniston pointed out, a small but not entirely insignificant number of those involved in protests were at the preconventional level (what is right is what one can get away with). It is hypothesized that these students are experiencing what Kohlberg calls a "moral regression." Having previously approached postconventional moral development, these individuals may have regressed to the preconventional level as a reaction to guilt feelings arising out of their rejection of conventional morality.

An unpublished study by Kohlberg (cited by Keniston 1970) of the Harvard protests of 1969

Table 15.1 Comparison of the Mean Standard Personality Inventory Scores of Members of the Free Speech Movement and Other College Students

Scale	National College Persisters ('63) (N=1385)	Berkeley Seniors ('65) (N=92)	FSM Arrested (N=130)
Thinking Introversion	52	55	63
Complexity	51	54	66
Estheticism	51	52	61
Autonomy	53	61	67
Impulse Expression	51	54	64
Religious Liberalism	48	58	64
Lack of Anxiety	52	51	48

Note: FSM = Free Speech Movement. Study was conducted two months after the arrest of FSM members.
Source: From J. W. Trent and J. I. Craise. Commitment and conformity in the American college. *J. soc. Issues*, 1967, 23, 39. Source of Berkeley and FSM data: Heist, 1965.

predicted that postconventional students would not be overrepresented among those active—in contrast to the Berkeley findings. This prediction was based on an analysis of the Harvard issues which, according to Kohlberg, did not involve a clear appeal to abstract principles of justice. His prediction was validated. Thus, it seems that high moral levels do not automatically lead to involvement in all protests. Students at higher levels of moral development will tend to act only when principles are clearly involved.

FAMILY CORRELATES OF STUDENT ACTIVISM. We mentioned previously that student activists tend to come from families characterized by democratic decision making rather than authoritarian parental control. These students learn early to reason about goals and principles, and thus are more likely to question the authority and decisions of campus administrators, as well as national leaders.

Another family factor that may be important, according to Keniston (1970), is the discovery of moral hypocrisy on the part of parents. Such a discovery—also discussed by Erikson (1965)—may lead to a general questioning of the morality the adolescent learned from his parents.

School Dropouts

Most data on youth who fail to complete their high school education indicate a connection between economic deprivation and dropping out of school. The dropout rate is highest among ethnically and racially segregated youth in urban slums. Virtually half of the students in such areas drop out of school (Cervantes 1965). In general, the dropout rate is higher among the poor than among the more affluent (Bandura and Walters 1959). While only about 1 out of 50 upper-class youth drop out of school, the rate increases within each lower socioeconomic bracket. In the upper middle class it is about 1 out of 6; in the lower middle class, it is 1 out of 4; and among the lower class, it is 1 out of 2 (Cervantes 1965).

However, it is rarely economic conditions alone that are the major causes of dropping out. Cervantes (1965) found that less than 5 percent of lower-class dropouts withdrew specifically for financial reasons. Rather, it is the cultural, social, and family climate associated with the poor and the victims of racial discrimination that seems to be more directly responsible for the higher dropout rate. For example, large and uncohesive, often fatherless, families with few problem-free friends are characteristic of such backgrounds (Cervantes 1965).

OTHER FACTORS IN DROPPING OUT. Besides socioeconomic status, other factors such as achievement level, patterns of academic and social failure in school, and emotional problems play a role in causing school dropouts. (Some of these factors may be related to the social class conditions.)

Although a number of dropouts are below average intelligence (more so than for graduates), the majority fall within the average I.Q. range. According to Cervantes (1965), it is less a question of I.Q., and more a matter of the dropout's academic performance, that is an important factor in his withdrawing from school.

Typically, the dropout has had a history of failure, both academically and socially, during his years in school. He is generally two years behind the normal student in reading and arithmetic by the time he reaches the seventh grade. And he is likely to have failed at least one school year (Cervantes 1965). His performance in general is consistently below his potential.

In addition to academic failure, the school dropout has generally experienced some sort of social failure in school as well. Cervantes (1965) has found that dropouts are relatively unpopular with their peers in school and usually do not participate in extracurricular activities. The friends they have are usually not approved of by their parents, and are themselves not school-oriented.

Family problems, and particularly lack of communication within the family, are also important contributing factors in dropping out. Cervantes (1965) found that four out of five of the dropouts he studied felt their families understood and accepted each other "very little."

Delinquency

Another form of adolescent behavior that has received a great deal of attention in the popular media, and also serious social scientific study, is

Table 15.2 Comparison of Dropouts and Graduates of High School in Terms of Communication Within the Home, Happiness Within the Home, and Obstacles to Completion of High School

Communication Within the Home (in percentages)

	Very Infrequent	Infrequent	Moderate	Frequent	Very Frequent
Dropouts	43	38	11	6	2
Graduates	3	17	20	24	36

Happiness Within the Home (in percentages)

	Very Unhappy	Unhappy	Indifferent	Happy	Very Happy
Dropouts	35	27	25	10	3
Graduates	17	5	14	16	48

Obstacles to Completion of High School

	No Obstacles	Ordinary Obstacles	Serious Obstacles	Very Serious Obstacles	Impossible Obstacles
Dropouts	5	55	25	6	9
Graduates	12	56	22	10	0

Source: From L. Cervantes. *The dropout: Causes and cures.* Ann Arbor: Michigan Univer. Press, 1965. Pp. 29, 35, 95.

juvenile delinquency. Juvenile delinquents are unquestionably atypical of the majority of American adolescents; nevertheless, there is good reason for the attention this group receives. According to a report by the President's Commission on Law Enforcement and Administration of Justice (1967), a majority of all arrests in 1965 for major crimes against property were of individuals under 21 years of age.

THE STATISTICS. According to FBI figures for 1965, published in the report of the President's Commission, virtually half of all arrests in the United States for the crimes of burglary, larceny, and motor vehicle theft were of adolescents between the ages of 11 and 17. Arrests for these crimes were higher for this age group than for any other in the population.

As for crimes of violence, such as willful homicide, rape, robbery, and aggravated assault, the rates of juvenile arrests were considerably lower for the younger age groups, but increased with age. For example, of all arrests in 1965 for these crimes, 18.3 percent were accounted for by 11- to 17-year-olds, 31.7 percent by 18- to 24-year-olds, and 49.3 percent by persons over 25.

On the surface, such statistics seem to paint a rather awesome picture of American adolescents. However, some qualifications must be made. For instance, according to the President's Commission, juvenile arrest statistics tend to be exaggerated compared to those for adults because juveniles are probably more easily apprehended than adults. Also, juveniles are more likely to act in groups; thus, the number of arrests may outnumber the crimes committed. In addition, the statistics on larceny arrests include thefts of less than $50, which account for the majority of juvenile larceny cases. Moreover, most car thefts committed by adolescents are for temporary transportation, or "joy riding," and do not involve the permanent loss of the car.

Although adolescents do account for a significant number of serious crimes, the majority of juvenile crimes are of a less serious nature. According to the President's Commission, most juvenile offenses involve petty larceny, fighting, disorderly conduct, and misdemeanors such as violating curfew rules, truancy, and running away from home.

SOCIOECONOMIC ANTECEDENTS OF DELINQUENCY. As with the phenomenon of the dropout, delinquency seems to be closely associated with poverty (Short and Strodtbeck 1965). Racial and ethnic minority groups tend to have higher delinquency rates than the general population (Clark 1959). However, as Short (1966) pointed out, such high rates for ethnic minorities are related to the background of poverty and broken homes prevalent among these groups in urban ghettos, and tend to decrease as the general socioeconomic status of the minority group increases. For example, according to a study by Robison (1957), the rate of juvenile delinquency among Jewish youth in New York City accounted for 20 percent of the juvenile court cases in 1930, when the majority of the Jewish population in New York City were recent immigrants living in slum areas. However, as Jews attained social and economic advantages over the years, their delinquency rates dropped. Thus, in 1952, although Jews made up more than 25 percent of the white population under 15 in New York City, they accounted for only 3 percent of the juvenile court cases (Robison 1957).

The President's Commission (1967) found delinquency rates highest among lower-class adolescents living in large city slum neighborhoods. Based on arrest and court records, the rate of delinquency becomes lower as one travels away from inner-city slums to largely middle- and upper-middle-class suburbs, and is lowest in rural areas. However, as the Commission pointed out, slum offenders are more likely to be arrested than those in suburban areas and therefore, the rate of middle-class delinquency may indeed be higher than generally assumed. Short (1966), for instance, pointed out that disproportionately higher delinquency rates are not found among lower-class youth in small cities and towns, and thus more studies of delinquency among middle- and upper-middle-class adolescents are needed.

AGE AND SEX VARIABLES. In general, most juvenile offenders who come to the attention of the police and the courts are boys in their middle and late teens. For example, according to FBI figures, juvenile arrests are highest for adolescents between 15 and 18 years of age, and second for those between 18 and 21. Of the adolescents under age 18 arrested in 1965, there were five times as many boys as girls. As Short (1966) pointed out, there has been a considerable change in this ratio since the turn of the century—at that time the ratio of boys to girls involved in juvenile crimes was about 50 to 1.

It also has been found that while boys are apprehended most often for crimes against property, such as theft, property destruction, and so on, delinquent girls are most often involved in sexual offenses (Short 1966). One explanation for this finding is that sex is a culturally stereotyped way for females to gain attention and express themselves, and thereby also a means of ready exploitation by older males.

SOME CAUSES OF DELINQUENCY. Since delinquency rates, as we have seen, are highest in slum neighborhoods of large cities, a good deal of thinking and research on the causes of delinquency have concentrated on these areas. As the President's Commission pointed out, such studies have shown that delinquency rates have been consistently high in slum areas decade after decade, regardless of what particular ethnic population resided there. It is felt that the general conditions of slum life—the poverty, the unemployment, the overcrowding, the high percentage of fatherless and broken homes—are major contributors to juvenile delinquency.

On the other hand, delinquency is not entirely restricted to slums. Some researchers, therefore, have concentrated on specific family problems that also may contribute to adolescent delinquency. For example, Bandura and Walters (1959) compared highly aggressive delinquents, from intact families with no particular economic problems, with nondelinquents from similar backgrounds. They found that, compared to the nondelinquents, the delinquents exhibited far less identification with their fathers, who were inclined to be harsh disciplinarians. (The mother–son relationships were similar for both groups.) These investigators suggested that because of the lack, for the most part, of favorable father models, the delinquent boys failed to internalize a consistent set of moral values. The investigators also found that the delinquents had poorer relations with their peers than did the nondelinquents (Bandura and Walters 1959).

Generally, the research on causes of delinquent behavior has been divided between studies focusing on factors within the social background or milieu, and studies focusing on factors within the family relationships and the individual personality. Much more research is needed before it is possible to consistently predict all the factors that produce juvenile delinquency.

Drug Users

It is practically impossible to establish with any degree of certainty just how widespread drug use is among adolescents. Goldstein (1966) estimated that 10 to 15 percent of all American adolescents have taken some illegal drug of one kind or another. Although it is reasonable to assume that many of these adolescents have had only one-time experience with drugs, there are indications that heavy drug use is increasing among young people.

Some idea of the prevalence of drug use by adolescents is provided by a recent national survey of youth aged 15 to 21. This study seems to support the general consensus that marihuana is probably the most prevalently used illegal drug. For example, 62 percent of the high school students interviewed, and 83 percent of the college students, said they knew personally someone who had used marihuana. For other drugs the percentages were somewhat lower, but still significantly high. For instance, 41 percent of the high school students and 62 percent of those in college stated that they knew personally someone who used amphetamines. For LSD, the figures were 35 percent and 57 percent; and for heroin, 19 percent and 35 percent (*Life* 1971).

Such figures, while not providing any direct statistics on actual drug use, do provide an indication of the relative prevalence of various drugs in the milieu of American high schools and colleges. However, there are undoubtedly considerable variations between schools, as well as between regions and social classes, in the number of adolescents who experiment with or use drugs. For example, in one nonurban Michigan county high school, less than one in four high school students of 386 randomly selected had ever tried drugs (Frumkin, Cowan, and Davis 1969). But the apparent spread of drug abuse to significant numbers of middle- and upper-middle-class high school and college students has raised considerable public alarm in recent years.

EFFECTS OF VARIOUS DRUGS. One aspect of the drug problem is the number and variety of drugs involved. The drugs most often used differ both in the type of effect they produce and in the relative strength of that effect. The effects range from depressed to "high" states of varying degree. Thus different drugs may appeal to adolescents with different personality problems.

Some drugs, usually referred to as the "hard" drugs or narcotics, are physiologically addictive. That is, in order to avoid painful and often severe physical reactions of withdrawal, the addict must have continual doses of the drug. Heroin is the prime example of this type of drug, although barbiturates also can be addictive. Other drugs, such as marihuana and LSD, are not addictive, but are sometimes psychologically habituating.

Marihuana. Although marihuana is often associated with the "hard" narcotics in drug laws, it is technically not a narcotic and not physiologically addictive. According to current evidence, marihuana does not necessarily lead to the use of hard drugs such as heroin. Nor is marihuana linked to crimes of violence. However, its use is still illegal, and penalties in some states are severe.

Marihuana comes from the leaves and flowering tops of the female hemp plant, which grows wild or is cultivated in temperate or semitropical climates. Its strength varies according to the amount of a chemical, known as THC, present in the specific plant. Hashish is a more potent form of the drug, and the usual manner of taking either form is by smoking.

As a mild hallucinogen, marihuana, or "pot," apparently has some chemical effect on the brain and central nervous system, although specifically what effect is not known. Its subjective effects vary according to dosage, the individual metabolism and psychological mood, and the social setting in which it is taken. Generally, low or "social" doses produce a mild sense of euphoria or well-being, and a heightened sense of touch, sight, smell, taste, and sound. Larger doses can produce distortions of the body image, a sense of identity confusion or loss, and hallucinations. Most persons who continually use marihuana describe its effects in pleasurable terms (National Commission on Marihuana and Drug Abuse 1972).

LSD and the stronger hallucinogens. The exact physiological effects of LSD and other hallucinogens such as mescaline, peyote, and psilocybin are for the most part still unknown. Although there have been some reports of possible chromosomal damage resulting from the use of LSD, much more research is needed before any definite conclusions can be drawn.

Subjectively, LSD and related drugs produce various hallucinatory experiences, usually of a somewhat different and much more intense nature than those produced by strong doses of marihuana. These hallucinations are often described in aesthetic, religious, or mystical terms, in which the user describes a sense of "at-oneness" or unity with God or the cosmos. However, these drugs also can create states of acute anxiety, sometimes described as "bummers." They have also been known (especially in large doses) to produce acute psychosis, the effects of which may persist for some time. For instance, in a 10-month period in 1965, 65 persons were admitted to Bellevue Hospital in New York City with acute LSD-induced psychoses (Louria 1966).

"Ups" and "downs"—the amphetamines and barbiturates. Another variety of drugs used are the "pills"—notably amphetamines and barbiturates. In contrast to the other drugs we have mentioned, the "pills" are legal when prescribed by physicians for medical treatment. The amphetamines are medically useful for the control of overweight, for relief from fatigue, and in the treatment of mental depression. Barbiturates are often prescribed as sedatives, and to relieve excessive tension and anxiety.

The amphetamines are stimulants and are often referred to by users as "ups," "speed," or "pep" pills because of their antidepressant effects. These drugs, while not truly addictive, are often psychologically habituating and dangerous. They can cause aggressive behavior, intellectual impairment, hallucinations, and paranoia. They are likely to give the user a false sense of well-being and delusions of self-importance. Habitual use has been known to lead to self-neglect and, because of their reduction of the hunger drive, to malnutrition.

The barbiturates (sleeping pills), often called "downs," are habituating as well as physiologically addictive. Their use accounts for some 3000 deaths a year by accidental or intentional overdose. The habitual use of barbiturates produces noticeable self-neglect, slurred speech, defective judgment, chronic drowsiness, and ataxia—loss of muscle coordination (Goldstein 1966). Barbiturate withdrawal can often be more severe than heroin withdrawal, including such symptoms as extreme nausea, fever, hallucinations, convulsions, stupor, and coma. It is sometimes even fatal.

In addition to these pills, there are also a number of nonbarbiturate tranquilizers and sedatives which, while not generally addictive, are often psychologically habit-forming.

Heroin. A derivative of opium, heroin is the most widely used of the addictive or "hard" narcotics. It is described as a depressant, and produces a euphoria in the place of tension and anxiety. It also reduces the primary drives of sex and hunger. Among its other effects, heroin can produce chronic drowsiness, inability to concentrate, apathy, and a reduction in physical activity. It can also impair mental and physical performance. Heroin overdose, which is not uncommon, produces respiratory failure, coma, and is frequently fatal. As in the case of barbiturates and amphetamines, continued use of heroin (addiction) often produces self-neglect and malnutrition. Withdrawal from heroin addiction produces severe muscle aches, cramps, nausea, and sometimes convulsions (President's Commission on Law Enforcement and Administration of Justice 1967).

SOME CHARACTERISTICS OF DRUG USERS. The various research on adolescents who use drugs has often focused on clinical case studies. For example, a study by Kuehn (1970) reviewed 41 drug-related clinical cases. These students were predominantly passive and reactive in their interpersonal relationships. They tended to live excessively in the present, were often depressed for no immediate reason, and had serious difficulties in their studies that were not clearly attributable to reality problems or to difficulties in their environment. Moreover, the students exhibited unrewarding sexual behavior, repression and rationalization, overintellectualization, and isolation.

Kuehn suggested that the cause of the drug problems among these students was an arrested state of psychosocial development. This condition was related to strong feelings of general alienation. Kuehn also pointed to the fact that the drug users frequently spoke of family difficulties, such as a lack of communication and parental misunderstanding, as particular problem areas in their experience.

Other studies have emphasized the rising use of drugs by upper- and middle-class and increasingly younger adolescents (Shiller 1970; Smart and Fejer 1971).

A study by Smart and Fejer (1971) of Canadian teen-agers compared the drug use (frequency and prevalence) of 6447 seventh- to thirteenth-graders in 1968, to 8865 sixth- to thirteenth-graders in 1970. The investigators found that the use of barbiturates, tranquilizers, and stimulants remained fairly stable, while the use of alcohol, marihuana, opiates, LSD, and other hallucinogens increased by 1970. In general, more students used drugs in 1970, and more frequently. This study also showed that although more males than females used drugs, the ratio was apparently decreasing.

Of perhaps greater interest were these researchers' findings concerning individuals most likely to use drugs. For instance, such subjects most often had brothers or sisters who used drugs, were inclined to do poorly in school, did not participate in school activities, and tended to feel generally alienated (Smart and Fejer 1971). In addition, Smart and Fejer reported several correlations between specific personality problems and the use of particular drugs. For instance, the use of alcohol, tobacco, glue and other solvents, barbiturates, and tranquilizers was positively correlated with adolescents who had feelings of social isolation. Feelings of powerlessness were positively correlated with all drugs except the opiates, speed, and LSD (1971).

SOME CONTRIBUTING FACTORS IN THE SPREAD OF ADOLESCENT DRUG USE. We have already touched on some of the probable reasons for the increased use of drugs by adolescents—general alienation, psychosocial development problems, personality problems, family difficulties, association with peers using drugs, difficulties in school, and easy availability of drugs.

However, the fact that we live in what can only be termed a drug-oriented culture should not be underestimated. For instance, as one researcher pointed out, 60 percent of all prescriptions written in the United States are for medication whose primary intended effect is psychoactive (Cwalina 1968). Children grow up observing their parents and elders casually using a virtual plethora of drugs. Only recently has there begun to be some awareness on the part of many parents and adults that there is often very little difference between what is considered "medicine" and what is labeled "drugs."

Children and adolescents can hardly be expected to avoid the use of drugs when they are so often given inaccurate and false information in order to frighten them, by adults who smoke cigarettes, have cocktails, take diet pills, sleeping pills, and so on. The young people often may be encouraged to do the same.

It has been found that when programs of drug education have been truthful, up-to-date, and sophisticated, and have refrained from scare tactics, they have been effective in preventing the use of dangerous drugs. For example, a significant decline in the use of LSD in 1967–68 was achieved because of widespread, accurate information (Cwalina 1968).

Maturity

Having completed our account of the human developmental process through adolescence, we should be able to make some generalizations about the end result of this process—namely, the mature adult. However, it is precisely on this point, the determinants of mature adult behavior and character, that we must be especially wary of easy generalizations. For, if it teaches us anything, the study of human developmental processes should make us aware of the complexity of the forces that operate on the individual growing up in our culture. Bearing in mind the complexity of development, we may usefully consider how some of the various theories view the nature of emotional maturity.

The psychoanalytic view regards maturity as the successful resolution of conflicts engendered in the individual in early life. The mature adult, according to Freud, has mastered his infantile impulses for immediate (sexual) gratification and is thus capable of the discipline of work. At the same time, the emotionally mature adult is also capable of healthy and satisfying sexual relationships. Finally, through the sex act, the adult human being propagates his own species, creates a family, and participates in the dominant social order. Thus, the Freudian view defines maturity as the establishment of a balance between love and work, between id and ego.

Erikson's conception of maturity, while related to traditional psychoanalytic views, concentrates on the development of the adult ego and the nature of its relationships with others. According to Erikson, one of the major crises of young adulthood is the task of establishing intimacy and solidarity with others, as opposed to the adoption of a pattern of withdrawal and isolation. If the young adult is capable of establishing mutually rewarding relationships in sex, friendship, work, and so on, he will become capable of love relationships — losing and finding oneself in another.

For Erikson, the key attribute of adulthood is generativity. By this he means the ability to go outside oneself in order to create lasting relationships, meaningful work, children, and generally contributing to the social order. Generativity arises from the achievement of solidarity and intimacy with others. Only when an individual has the security and knowledge of connection with his fellow man does he become capable of losing himself in the sustained effort of work. The opposite course of withdrawal and isolation leads to self-absorption. Such a condition often creates stagnation within the person and in his relationships with others.

A successful attainment of generativity, according to Erikson, equips the person with the ego integrity or sense of completeness necessary to face the final crisis of life, that of disintegration in death. The sense of having created something with one's life, and of having achieved, leads to a feeling of at-oneness with oneself and with the rest of mankind. Such a person's life takes on significance. The person can, in the face of death, feel that he has truly "been," that his life has been worthwhile. The ability to face death with some sense of peace, as opposed to a feeling of despair associated with a lack of ego integrity, requires what Erikson terms wisdom. To Erikson, wisdom arises out of generativity. Thus, it includes the Freudian goals of productivity and sexual love, as well as the more general qualities of intimacy with one's fellow men and a feeling of unity with all of mankind.

In the light of these psychoanalytic interpretations of maturity, it is appropriate to consider the theories of Carl Jung concerning the different ways people characteristically seek ego integrity. According to Jung, full maturity does not come until the individual is in his forties, or sometimes even later. It is only around this time of life that the individual is in a position to place in perspective the various specialized aspects of personality that have been emphasized in early adulthood (such as practicality, lovingness, personal judgment, and so on). According to Jung, the young adult tends to opt for one or another dominant mode of character. He is either empiristic (practical), intellectualistic, emotive, or intuitive in his responses to others and to the tasks and problems of his life. As a result, the individual may find in middle age that certain important aspects of his makeup have been left out or only partially utilized. Some necessary, but previously neglected, element may need to be integrated into the personality. Thus, for example, one who has always been primarily intellectual and rational in his dealings with the world may find that he has trouble in experiencing and expressing his feelings. Given the widespread phenomenon of sensitivity groups, we may judge that this problem is quite common.

Similarly, Anna Freud notes that in adolescence and early adulthood there is often a tendency to emphasize one aspect of personality and life-functioning at the expense of others, in order to cope with anxiety. She, too, suggests that integrity, or a harmonious balance of diverse personality elements, is a goal of emotional development.

Outside of psychoanalytic theories, other views of maturity are less comprehensive. Piaget, for example, tells us little about maturity other than to indicate the kinds of skills the mature adult can be expected to have. However, an implication of both Piagetian and Kohlbergian views is that continuing disequilibrium or continuing novel role-taking requirements are probably necessary for the furthering of even higher levels of development and understanding. In these terms, a person who stops being challenged stops growing, and is thus never fully mature.

Kohlberg also has something of interest to say about moral maturity, as we have seen. He notes that the highest stage of moral development, one not usually reached by many people, is the attainment of personal principles. Such principles come from within and are based on consistency. We might note here that the attainment of such a level of morality would seem, at least partially, to depend on the achievement of some sense of self-worth. Thus, it would require some degree of the kind of ego integrity of which Erikson and other psychoanalytic thinkers speak.

But if we assume that ego integrity is a worthwhile goal of emotional development, we are still left with the practical question of how this integrity can be fostered in children. What can parents and teachers do to increase the chances of children becoming whole, emotionally mature adults? One way to look at the question is to recognize, with the neo-Freudians, that maturity is not the result of a conflict-free life, but is, rather, the end product of the successful resolution of conflict. Thus, shielding children from conflict and making their choices for them may have the effect of doing them more harm than good—the person creates himself by the choices he makes. If the choices are very easy or are made for the person by someone else, the individual has less of a chance to grow than if the choices involve real risks and some measure of struggle.

Although many parents believe, in principle, that it is important to allow children a measure of freedom to make their own choices and to experience both success and failure, it is remarkable how many parents let their anxiety interfere with their children's freedom. Many parents tend to err on the side of overprotection. As the child gets older and the choices become more serious, the parent may experience even more anxiety than when the child was young.

We all must recognize that there is no guarantee that the child will make the "right" choices. There is too much chance in life for there to be a final guarantee. Moreover, we must realize that what is right for us may not be right for our children. The most that one can do is to discuss the child's choices at each point of decision (and argue when we think he is wrong). In that way one can reasonably hope to develop in the child the habit of rational consideration of alternatives. Although many choices will have to be made for the young child, even at this very early stage, there are still a number of areas where the child can make real choices (for example, clothes, toys, and so on). If the habit of rational consideration is developed in the child about such matters, he may be able to apply them to other areas of life later on. By the time the child reaches late adolescence, the right to choose his style of life and his activities should be mainly his own. At this point, parents generally have to content themselves with an advisory role.

On the other hand, some parents commit the opposite mistake of overpermissiveness. These parents abdicate their responsibility and, indeed, their own standards, by allowing the child the spurious freedom of doing whatever he wants. This approach, too, is a mistake because the child then has little in the way of a model for his own behavior. He may come to feel that his parents have no standards of their own, and thus will lose respect both for them and for himself. The parent who is unclear about his own values in life cannot hope to give the child a good chance of developing clear values of his own.

In general, there must be some kind of rule for parents which says that first the parent must decide whether a given question is his responsibility or the child's. If it is the child's, then the parent should agree to live with the child's decision, while retaining the right to "appear in court" with his reasons for or against it. If this pattern is conducted in fairness throughout childhood, there is a reasonable hope that the parent will still be heard out in adolescence and early maturity.

However, this way of looking at the question may be somewhat overrational. At times, adult anxiety or adolescent impetuosity will disrupt this theoretically smooth and reasonable process. For these times, only patience and tolerance and a real concern for the child—a generativity and caring, as Erikson would put it—will see one through.

Summary

There are several major theories about the development of personality in adolescence. According to Freud, the adolescent is assailed once again by the infantile Oedipal desires of the id. But by now the superego, or conscience, has developed, and it represses these desires. The adolescent must transfer his sexual energy from the parent to other love objects. The dangers he faces are overinhibition, when he will not be able to form a relationship with a member of the opposite sex; or underrepression, which may lead to various forms of perversion and criminality.

Erik Erikson stresses the social side of personality growth. He emphasizes the necessity for establishing a solid ego-identity and squaring one's own perceptions of self with changed societal expectations as to one's roles and behavior.

Social learning theorists are concerned with socialized anxiety, which develops as a result of an accumulated history of reinforcement. Through socialized anxiety, the adolescent learns adult behaviors appropriate to his society.

Cognitive stage theorists, like Piaget, stress the growth of cognitive abilities and moral reasoning in childhood and adolescence.

But all theorists agree that the adolescent must adapt to new modes of behavior. For one thing, he must become more independent. The ways in which adolescents achieve independence vary from culture to culture. Some cultures have formalized initiation rituals to mark the child's transition to adulthood. In our society, the development towards independence is fairly gradual. Financial dependence on the parents may cause undue emotional dependence. In addition, parents are often confused about when to permit their children various adult behaviors, and parental inconsistency can cause problems.

Society expects adolescents to show increased moral awareness. Some theorists map stages of moral development. According to Kohlberg, the stages are: the preconventional, where the young child does whatever he can get away with; the conventional, where the older child accepts the standards of his parents and the community; and the postconventional, where the individual develops personal principles which sometimes conflict with conventional morality.

Adolescence is also a time of changes in self-image and self-esteem. The adolescent's self-identity is closely related to his sex-role development in which behavior and personality traits meet the appropriate standards of society.

Although the majority of individuals pass through adolescence experiencing no overwhelming difficulties, some atypical adolescents have serious problems, sometimes leading to alienation, dropping out, juvenile delinquency, and so on. It has been found that the highest dropout rate is among ethnically and racially segregated youth in urban slums, and that juvenile delinquency is also highest among these economically deprived groups. On the other hand, political activists tend to come from middle-class families who practiced democratic decision making. Drug users, too, tend to reflect middle-class alienation, as well as the general drug-oriented nature of our society.

There are various theoretical views on the nature of emotional maturity. The Freudians view maturity as the successful resolution of conflicts originating in early childhood. Erikson concentrates on the development of the adult ego and its relationships with others. His conception of maturity includes the Freudian goals of productivity and sexual love. It focuses on the adult's achievement of intimacy with his fellow man.

Both Jung and Anna Freud consider the attainment of a harmonious balance between diverse personality elements as an essential goal of emotional maturity.

Assuming that ego integrity is the goal of emotional development, it is important for the parent to consider how this integrity can be fostered in children. In general, parents should avoid both overprotectiveness (making all their child's decisions) and overpermissiveness (making none of them). It is important to permit the child a measure of freedom in making decisions. The parent, as a rule, should agree to live with those decisions which the child has been allowed to make. In this way the child can develop the habit of rational consideration of alternatives.

Case Studies

Keith Y.

Keith was referred to therapy late in his second year of high school by a teacher who suspected that an unhappy, insecure teen-ager lurked behind Keith's boisterous, exhibitionistic facade. The positive benefits from a year and a half of treatment surprised even Keith.

An only child born late in his parents' marriage, Keith withstood a disproportionate amount of tension at home. His mother—a self-educated, aggressive, highly emotional woman of many intellectual interests—made no effort to conceal her scorn for Keith's quiet, passive, and uneducated father. She often complained to Keith of Mr. Y.'s weak demeanor and unsuccessful career. In addition, the clinician inferred that Mrs. Y. had been overpossessive and highly stimulating during Keith's developmental years, and these traits probably resulted in more sexual feelings than such a young boy could handle. Since his father's weakness precluded any normal solution to this exaggerated Oedipal situation, Keith's solution was to remove himself as far as he could from his parents.

As a consequence, he became a member of a semidelinquent gang whose members openly abused all forms of conformity, education, and constructive work. Their free time was largely spent in their cars, cruising the city streets in search of new sexual conquests. Keith also took great pains to deny any association with his school's middle-class Jewish population by wearing disheveled clothes and a well-manicured ducktail haircut. Argumentative at home and decidedly unpopular even in his group, Keith's idea of being a man was "to be a sharp operator, to con, fake, and bluff your way through life." He shunned all schoolwork, but missed no opportunity to argue with his teachers about his poor grades or divert the class's attention with his wide variety of disruptive pranks.

The good results of Keith's counseling were undoubtedly aided by the fact that intervention began when these habits were still in their formative stages. Moreover, it was obvious—

even to Keith—that his defenses were not bringing the hoped-for results; there was, therefore, adequate motivation for change. He was also urged on by his rightful concern about the escalating unruliness of his gang and the increasing probabilities that he would have no other alternative but to escape from the school environment altogether.

Keith's exposure to a male counselor provided him with a new model of masculinity. The clinician was also careful to interpret much of Keith's problem so that the boy could understand it and deal with it more purposively—the reasons for the compensatory defense; what neurotic purposes that defense served; how he was presently acting out events from his past; and some of the Oedipal implications of his mother's deprecation of his father.

Keith participated freely in his own treatment, redirecting his manifold energies toward self-improvement. He began asking for help in acquiring acceptable social behavior for the groups he hoped to belong to. He became introspective. He began to taste the joy of discovering new intellectual interests, new social horizons, and a more comfortable relationship with girls. His efforts were reinforced from nearly every direction. And he seemed relieved to gain some mature understanding of true sexuality (as well as the compatibility of intellectual interests and manliness), for he had confided a deep concern about his own masculinity and his inability to deal with it honestly.

Although there were temporary setbacks along the way, Keith's progress was generally steady and quick-paced. His haircut, the last vestige of the old braggadocio, disappeared quite suddenly one day with the explanation that he thought it would hinder his search for summer employment.

While Keith's parents did not participate actively in his treatment, both were pleased to see his transformation. His mother found him more reasonable. And his father became the object of new respect for qualities Keith had previously overlooked. Amidst a more harmonious family atmosphere, Keith found himself active in a temple drama group, well-liked, intellectually motivated, and anxious to begin his college education (Lichter, Rapien, Seibert, and Sklansky 1962).

Betty R.

The oldest of six children, Betty comes from a physically comfortable, but emotionally draining, home environment. Amidst the impressive shelves of finely bound, but untouched, literary classics, the family endures the constant tension between parents who are out of touch with each other: Mr. R., the slum-born, self-made man who worked his way through law school and now enjoys wielding his political powers on the job and his tyrannical powers at home; and Mrs. R., the pretty—but uneducated and uncultured—"fashion plate" who boasts of leaving her family in the charge of the two full-time servants for long periods when she finds it necessary to "get away" from her husband's irritability. None of the children has any special responsibility around the house. Although Betty is the only "problem child" at this point, one senses that she is simply the first to have to deal with her feelings of pessimism and intense anger.

Before the start of this freshman year in public school, there had been considerable argument over whether or not to send Betty away to private school. Mr. R. rejected the proposal as "one of my wife's schemes," but Mrs. R. felt that Betty needed to get away from home because she had "grown up too fast." Now at the end of her first semester, Betty has failed all four of her subjects, and her teachers report her immature, lacking initiative, petulant, aloof, dilatory, sullen, and very unhappy. Mr. R.'s reaction is that his daughter is "determined to fail," and that her attitude is simply an extension of her having been always "too reserved," and having never wanted to be "shown off" to his friends. Earlier in the semester, when penalty cards had been sent home for Betty's first poor grades, Mr. R. admitted he had stormed around and "raised hell in general." Revoking all of Betty's privileges, he ranted that he had not striven to such heights to be disgraced by his daughter. The result of that episode was a note pinned to Betty's bedside lampshade: "I wish I was dead."

Betty's own explanation of her troubles is somewhat different, however. Although she was at first reluctant to confide in her counselor, she eventually admitted that she knows she can do much better in school, but that she hates everything about it. In particular, she dislikes the most popular teachers and girls—for no other reason than for their popularity. When asked to explain, she said simply, "They all dislike me. I'd like to be popular and smart, too." Although she attributes to herself qualities quite opposite to those attributed by her teachers, she recognizes her inclination toward pessimism and dissatisfaction. In fact, she sobbed as she finished her own personality sketch, saying, "Inside I'm all the good traits, outside I'm all the bad ones."

Her counselor found that Betty's troubles first became evident after the intense family bickering began. When Betty was 10 years old, her mother changed religions as a first major attempt to escape from her husband's domination. As tension waxed, Betty's confidence waned. She began to take the attitude that she could not do superior work, and, if she could, it would only lead to more "push, push, push." Her increasing commitment to the futility of her efforts forced her further into feelings of inadequacy. While her mother began to escape by leaving town, Betty could only withdraw into a shell of anger and disappointment. Going away to school held possibilities for a more satisfactory escape—at least in Betty's mind—and she apparently felt that academic expulsion was now her only means of attaining that hoped-for goal.

Although Mr. R. has admitted to Betty's counselors that his strong demands must share the blame for her negativism, it is clear that nothing short of an about-face in his attitudes will suffice to help Betty bring those good inner qualities to her troubled surface (Smithies 1933).

References

Adelson, J. The political imagination of the young adolescent. *Daedalus: J. Amer. Acad. Arts and Sciences*, 1971, *100*, 1013–1050.

Bandura, A., and Walters, R. *Adolescent aggression*. New York: Ronald Press, 1959.

Benedict, R. Continuities and discontinuities in culture conditioning. In W. Minter and C. Stanley (Eds.), *Readings in child development*. New York: Harcourt Brace Jovanovich, 1954.

Blos, P. *On adolescence*. New York: Free Press, 1962.

Brown, D. Sex-role development in a changing culture. *Psychol. Bull.*, 1958, *55*, 232–241.

Brown, J. Female initiation rites: A review of the current literature. In D. Rogers (Ed.), *Issues in adolescent psychology*. New York: Appleton-Century-Crofts, 1969.

Brown, J. K. Cross-cultural study of female initiation rites. *Amer. Anthrop.*, August 1963, *65*, 837–853.

Cervantes, L. *The dropout: Causes and cures*. Ann Arbor: Univer. of Michigan Press, 1965.

Clark, Kenneth B. Color, class, personality, and juvenile delinquency. *J. Negro Educ.*, Summer 1959, *28*(3), 240–251.

Commission on Population Growth and the American Future. *Population and the American future: The report of the Commission on Population Growth and the American Future*. New York: New American Library, Signet, 1972.

Cwalina, G. Drug use on high school and college campuses. *J. school Health*, 1968, *38*, 638–646.

Davis, A. Socialization and adolescent personality. In *Adolescence. Yearbook of the National Society for the Study of Education*, 1944, *43*, Part I.

Douvan, E., and Adelson, J. *The adolescent experience*. New York: Wiley, 1966.

Douvan, E., and Gold, M. Modal patterns in American adolescence. In M. L. Hoffman and L. W. Hoffman (Eds.) *Review of child development research.* Vol. II. New York: Russell Sage Foundation, 1966.

Erikson, E. H. *Childhood and society.* New York: Norton, 1950.

Erikson, E. H. The golden rule in the light of new insight. In E. H. Erikson (Ed.), *Insight and responsibility.* New York: Norton, 1964.

Erikson, E. H. Youth: Fidelity and diversity. In E. H. Erikson (Ed.), *The challenge of youth.* New York: Doubleday, Anchor, 1965.

Erikson, E. H. *Identity, youth and crisis.* New York: Norton, 1968.

Freud, A. *The ego and the mechanism of defense.* Trans. by C. Baines. New York: International Universities Press, 1948.

Freud, S. *New introductory lectures on psychoanalysis.* Trans. by W. J. H. Sprott. New York: Norton, 1933.

Freud, S. *An outline of psychoanalysis.* Trans. by J. Strachey. New York: Norton, 1949.

Frumkin, R. M., Cowan, R. A., and Davis, J. R. Drug use in a midwest sample of metropolitan hinterland high school students. *Corrective psychiat. and J. soc. Therapy,* 1969, *15,* 8–13.

Goldstein, R. *1 in 7: Drugs on campus.* New York: Walker, 1966.

Haan, N., and Block, J. *Further studies in the relationship between activism and morality. I: The protest of pure and mixed moral stages.* Berkeley, Calif.: Institute of Human Development, 1969.

Haan, N., and Block, J. *Further studies in the relationship between activism and morality. II: Analysis of cases deviant with respect to the morality-activism relationship.* Berkeley, Calif.: Institute of Human Development, 1969.

Haan, N., Smith, M., and Block, J. Moral reasoning of young adults: Political-social behavior, family background, and personality correlates. *J. pers. soc. Psychol.,* 1968, *10,* 183–201.

Harrison, D., Bennett, W., and Globetti, G. Attitudes of rural youth toward premarital sexual permissiveness. *J. marriage and Fam.,* 1969, *31,* 783–787.

Heilbrun, A. B., Jr. Conformity to masculinity-femininity stereotypes and ego identity in adolescents. *Psychol. Reports,* 1964, *14,* 351–357.

Heist, P. Intellect and commitment: The faces of discontent. In O. W. Knorr and W. J. Minter (Eds.), *Order and freedom on the campus: The rights and responsibilities of faculty and students.* Boulder, Colo.: Western Interstate Commission for Higher Education, 1965.

Hess, A. L., and Bradshaw, H. L. Positiveness of self-concept and ideal self as a function of age. *J. genet. Psychol.,* 1970, *117,* 57–67.

Hess, R. High school antecedents of young adult achievement. In R. Grinder (Ed.), *Studies in adolescence.* New York: Macmillan, 1963.

Jacob, P. E. *Changing values in college.* New York: Harper, 1957.

Jorgensen, E., and Howell, R. Changes in self, ideal-self correlations from ages 8 through 18. *J. soc. Psychol.,* 1969, *79,* 63–67.

Juvenile delinquency among Negroes in the United States. *J. Negro Educ.,* Summer 1959, *28*(3, Whole Issue).

Kagan, J., and Moss, H. A. The stability of passive and dependent behavior from childhood through adulthood. *Child Develpm.,* 1960, *31,* 577–591.

Katz, P., and Zigler, E. Self-image disparity: A developmental approach. *J. pers. soc. Psychol.,* 1967, *5,* 186–195.

Keniston, K. *The uncommitted: Alienated youth in American society.* New York: Harcourt Brace Jovanovich, 1965.

Keniston, K. *Young radicals: Notes on committed youth.* New York: Harcourt Brace Jovanovich, 1968.

Keniston, K. Student activism, moral development, and morality. *Amer. J. Orthopsychiat.,* 1970, *40,* 577–592.

Kohlberg, L. *Stages in the development of moral thought and action.* New York: Holt, Rinehart & Winston, 1970.

Kramer, R. Changes in moral judgment response pattern during late adolescence and young adulthood. Unpublished doctoral dissertation, Univer. of Chicago, 1968.

Kuehn, J. L. The student drug user and his family. *J. college stud. Personnel,* 1970, *11,* 409–413.

Landsbaum, J. B., and Willis, R. H. Conformity in early and late adolescence. *Develpm. Psychol.,* 1971, *4,* 334–337.

Langer, J. *Theories of development.* New York: Holt, Rinehart & Winston, 1969.

Lerner, R., Pendorf, J., and Emery, A. Attitudes of adolescents and adults toward contemporary issues. *Psychol. Reports,* 1971, *28,* 139–145.

Lewin, K. *A dynamic theory of personality.* New York: McGraw-Hill, 1935.

Lichter, S. O., Rapien, E. B., Seibert, F. M., and Sklansky, M. A. *The drop-outs: A treatment study of intellectually capable students who drop out of high school.* New York: Free Press, 1962. Pp. 232–236.

Life. A new youth poll. 1971(1, Special issue: The new shape of America), 22–27.

Louria, D. *Nightmare drugs.* New York: Pocket Books, 1966.

Marcia, J. E., and Friedman, M. L. Ego identity status in college women. *J. Pers.,* 1970, *38,* 249–263.

Mead, M. *Coming of age in Samoa.* New York: Morrow, 1928.

Medinnus, G. R. Adolescents' self-acceptance and perceptions of their parents. *J. consult. Psychol.,* 1965, *29,* 150–154.

Mischel, W. Sex-typing and socialization. In P. H. Mussen (Ed.), *Carmichael's manual of child psychology.* Vol. II. (3rd ed.) New York: Wiley, 1970.

Mowrer, O. H. A study of personality disorganization. *Amer. sociol. Rev.,* 1939, *4,* 475–487.

Mullener, N., and Laird, J. D. Some developmental changes in the organization of self-evaluations. *Develpm. Psychol.,* 1971, *5,* 233–236.

Mussen, P. H. Some antecedents and consequents of masculine sex-typing in adolescent boys. *Psychol. Monogr.,* 1961, *75*(2, Whole No. 506).

Mussen, P. H. Long-term consequents of masculinity of interests in adolescents. *J. consult. Psychol.*, 1962, 26 (5), 435–440.

National Commission on Marihuana and Drug Abuse. *Marihuana, a signal of misunderstanding: The official report of the National Commission on Marihuana and Drug Abuse.* New York: New American Library, Signet, 1972.

Newsweek, Campus '65, March 22, 1965, 43–54.

Peterson, R. E. *The scope of organized student protest in 1964–1965.* Princeton, N.J.: Educational Testing Service, 1966.

Phillips, L., and Rabinovitch, M. S. Social role and patterns of symptomatic behavior. *J. abnorm. soc. Psychol.*, 1958, 57, 181–186.

Phillips, L., and Zigler, E. Social competence: The action-thought parameter and vicariousness in normal and pathological behavior. *J. abnorm. soc. Psychol.*, 1961, 63, 137–146.

Piaget, J. *The moral judgment of the child.* New York: Free Press, 1948.

President's Commission on Law Enforcement and Administration of Justice. *The challenge of crime in a free society: A report by the President's Commission on Law Enforcement and Administration of Justice.* Washington, D.C.: Government Printing Office, 1967.

Reckless, W., Dinitz, S., and Kay, B. The self component in potential delinquency and potential non-delinquency. *Amer. sociol. Rev.*, 1957, 22, 566–569.

Reiss, I. L. The scaling of premarital sexual permissiveness. *J. marriage and Fam.*, May 1964, 188–189.

Reiss, I. L. (Ed.) The sexual renaissance in America. *J. soc. Issues*, 1966, 22(2).

Robison, S. A study of delinquency among Jewish children in New York City. In M. Sklare (Ed.), *The Jews: Social patterns of an American group.* New York: Free Press, 1957.

Rosenberg, B. G., and Sutton-Smith, B. Ordinal position and sex-role identification. *Genet. Psychol. Monogr.*, 1964, 70, 297–328.

Rosenberg, B. G., and Sutton-Smith, B. Sibling associations, family size, and cognitive abilities. *J. genet. Psychol.*, 1966, 107, 271–279.

Rosenberg, B. G., and Sutton-Smith, B. Family interaction effects on masculinity-femininity. *J. pers. soc. Psychol.*, 1968, 8, 117–120.

Rosenberg, M. Parental interest and children's self-conceptions. *Sociometry*, 1963, 26, 35–49.

Shiller, A. *Drug abuse and your child.* Public Affairs Pamphlet, No. 448. New York: Public Affairs Committee, 1970.

Short, J. F. Juvenile delinquency: The sociocultural context. In L. W. Hoffman and M. L. Hoffman (Eds.), *Review of child development research.* Vol. II. New York: Russell Sage Foundation, 1966.

Short, J. F., and Strodtbeck, F. L. *Group process and gang delinquency.* Chicago: Univer. of Chicago Press, 1965.

Smart, R. G., and Fejer, D. Recent trends in illicit drug use among adolescents. *Canada's Mental Health Supplement*, May 1971, No. 68.

Smithies, E. M. *Case studies of normal adolescent girls.* New York: Appleton, 1933. Pp. 200–215.

Somers, R. H. The mainsprings of the rebellion: A survey of Berkeley students in November 1964. In S. M. Lipset and S. S. Wolin (Eds.), *The Berkeley student revolt: Facts and interpretations.* Garden City, N.Y.: Doubleday, Anchor, 1965.

Sutton-Smith, B., and Rosenberg, B. G. Age changes in the effects of ordinal position on sex-role identification. *J. genet. Psychol.*, 1965, 107, 61–73.

Sutton-Smith, B., and Rosenberg, B. G. Sibling consensus on power tactics. *J. genet. Psychol.*, 1968, 112, 63–72.

Trent, J. W., and Craise, J. L. Commitment and conformity in the American college. *J. soc. Issues*, 1967, 23, 34–51.

Watts, W. A., and Whittaker, D. N. Some sociopsychological differences between highly committed members of the Free Speech Movement and the student population at Berkeley. *J. applied behav. Science*, 1966, 2, 41–62.

Whiting, J., Kluckhohn, R., and Anthony, A. The function of male initiation ceremonies at puberty. In E. E. Maccoby, T. Newcomb, and E. Hartley (Eds.), *Readings in social psychology.* (3rd ed.) New York: Holt, Rinehart & Winston, 1958.

Young, F. The function of male initiation ceremonies: A cross-cultural test of an alternative hypothesis. *Amer. J. sociol.*, 1962, 67, 379–396.

Young, F. *Initiation ceremonies: A cross-cultural study of status dramatization.* Indianapolis: Bobbs-Merrill, 1965.

Name Index

The page numbers in italics indicate the page on which the full reference appears.

Abrams, S., *106*
Achenbach, T., *50*
Acheson, R. M., 120, *140*, 147, *178*
Adams, G., 127, *140*
Adams, J., 187, *218*
Adelson, J., 464, 465, 466, 467, 469, 470, 476, 484, 489, 490, *503*
Ahr, P. R., *293*
Ainsworth, M. D. S., 196, 197, 204, 205, *217*
Albert, J., 308, 312, *335*
Alexander, T., *293*
Allen, K., 354, *372*
Allen, L., 210, *218*, 227, *253*, 326, 327, *335*
Allinsmith, W., 420, *441*
Almy, M., *178*
Alpert, R., 265, *294*
Alschuler, R. H., *293*
Altus, W. D., 426, *441*

Amatruda, C. S., 129, *141*, 158, *179*, 250, *253*
Ames, E. W., *178*
Ames, L. B., 122, 131, *140*, *141*
Ammons, R. B., *372*
Anandalakshany, S. G., *80*
Anastasi, A., 66, *80*
Anderman, S., *80*
Anderson, H. H., 427, *441*
Anderson, L. M., 312, *336*
Anthony, A., 477, 482, 483, *505*
Anthony, E. J., 102, *107*, 363, 368, 369, *372*
Appel, M. H., 349, *372*
Appley, M. H., *24*
Armentrout, J., *442*
Ardrey, R., *293*
Arena, J. M., *106*
Aries, P., 6, *24*
Arnheim, R., 320, *334*
Aronfreed, J. M., *293*, 346, *372*
Aronson, E., *178*
Asch, S., 398, *411*
Ashley, M., *80*, *140*

Assali, N. S., *106*
Auerbach, C., 68, *80*
Austin, M. C., 422, *441*
Ausubel, D. P., *24*, *441*
Axline, V. M., 367, *372*

Babson, S., *106*
Back, E. H., *141*
Bacon, H. M., *106*
Baer, D. M., *24*, 35, 40, *50*
Baird, D., 93, *106*
Baker, A. A., *106*
Baker, C. T., *335*
Baker, H. J., 78, *80*
Baker, H. V., 400, *411*
Bakwin, H., *217*
Baldwin, A. L., *24*, 347, *372*
Baldwin, A. P., *441*
Ball, R. S., *181*
Bandura, A., *24*, 40, 41, *50*, *51*, 260, 261, 270, 272, 273, 276, 277, 278, *293*, 385, 386, *411*, 419, 442, 451, 472, 476, 492, 494, 495, *503*

Banikiotes, F. G., *179*
Banikiotes, P. G., *179*
Barbara, D. A., 364, *372*
Barclay, A., *80*
Barnet, A. B., *106*
Barker, R. G., 17, *24*, 274, *293*, 458, 477
Barr, M. L., 76, *80*
Baumrind, D., 265, *293*
Bayley, N., *24*, 119, 129, *140*, 146, 157, 158, *179*, *181*, 204, 205, 219, 226, 252, *442*
Beach, D. R., 309, *334*
Beach, F. A., *179*
Beam, J. C., 360, *372*
Becker, H., *442*
Becker, S. W., 426, *442*
Becker, W. C., 257, *293*, 420, *442*
Bee, H. L., *335*
Beech, R., *372*
Bell, R. Q., 75, *80*, 141, 185, *217*
Bell, S. M., *179*
Bellugi, U., *179*, 238, 241, 242, 252, *253*
Bem, S. L., 243, *252*
Bench, J., *106*
Bender, L., 204, *217*
Benedict, R., *503*
Benjamin, J., *24*
Bennett, W. H., *476*, *504*
Benton, J. W., *106*
Bereiter, C., 329, 330, *334*
Berenda, R. W., 401, *411*
Berkman, P. L., *106*
Berko, J., 241, 242, *252*
Berlyne, D. E., 15, *24*, 171, 173, 175, *179*
Bernard, H., *140*
Bernard, R. M., 93, *106*
Bernstein, B., 246, *252*
Bernstein, E., 423, *444*
Berrien, F. K., *24*
Berry, H. K., *81*
Bethon, G., 382, *412*
Bettelheim, B., 366, *372*
Bever, T. G., *252*
Beyer, T. E., *106*
Biass-Ducroux, F., *80*
Bijou, S. W., *24*, 40, *51*
Biller, H. B., *80*
Binet, A., 324, 325, *334*
Birch, H. G., 93, 105, *106*, *442*
Birns, B., *180*
Bjarnason, S., *81*
Black, A. E., 265, *293*
Blackwell, L., 35, *51*
Blank, M., 244, 248, *252*
Blau, A., *372*

Blinick, G., *106*
Block, J., 275, *293*, 491, *504*
Bloom, A. D., *80*
Bloom, B. S., *80*, 227, 237, 239, 241, 243, *252*, 434, *442*
Bloom, L., 149, 156, *179*
Blos, P., 484, *503*
Blumberg, B. S., *80*
Bommarito, B., 432, *443*
Bond, E. A., 327, *334*
Bonney, M. E., 350, *372*, 411, 422, 424, *442*
Borgstedt, A. D., 100, *106*
Borke, H., *293*, 321, *334*
Bostock, J., 203, *217*
Boston, M., 204, 205, *217*
Botkin, P., 383, *412*
Bovet, M., *24*
Bowlby, J., 186, 191, 198, 204, 205, *217*
Brackbill, Y., 33, *51*, 127, *140*, 186, *217*
Bradley, R. A., *106*
Bradshaw, H. L., 487, *504*
Braine, M. D. S., 103, *106*, *179*, 239, 252, *253*
Braithwaite, R. B., *24*
Brazelton, T. B., 97, 99, *106*
Brearley, M., *51*
Breckenridge, M. E., *141*
Breland, K., *24*
Breland, M., *24*
Brennan, W. M., 122, *141*
Brewer, J. E., 427, *441*
Bricker, W., 270, 277, 295, 347, 348, *374*
Bridger, W. H., 136, *141*
Bridges, W., *180*
Brim, O. G., Jr., *442*
Brockman, L. M., *179*
Brodbeck, A., *253*
Broderick, C. B., 470, *476*
Broen, B. B., *107*
Bronfenbrenner, U., 209, *217*, *293*
Brooks-Gunn, J., 195, *218*, 285, 287, *294*
Broverman, D. M., 76, *80*
Brown, A. M., *142*
Brown, A. W., 350, *372*
Brown, D., *503*
Brown, D. G., 280, *293*
Brown, J., *503*
Brown, J. K., 483, *503*
Brown, R. W., *179*, 238, 240, 241, 242, 252, *253*
Brown, U. A., 99, *107*
Bruce, H. M., 184, *217*
Bruel, I., 360, *374*

Bruner, J. S., *24*, 171, *179*, 246, *253*, 330, *334*
Brunton, M., 77, *81*
Buckholdt, D., 35, *51*
Buckle, D., 363, *372*
Bühler, C., *179*
Buell, J. S., 354, *372*
Buick, H. G., *24*
Bulin, G. V., Jr., 99, *107*
Bunch, M. E., 100, *108*
Burger, G., *442*
Burke, A., 358, *375*
Burks, H. F., 364, *372*
Burlingham, D. T., 195, 204, 205, *218*
Burnham, S., 97, *107*
Burt, C., 73, *80*
Burton, R. V., 18, *25*, *293*
Butler, R. A., 48, *51*

Cairns, R. B., 265, *293*
Caldwell, B. M., 102, *107*
Caldwell, E. C., *51*
Calovini, G., *254*
Cameron, J., 146, *179*
Campbell, A., 467, *476*
Campbell, B. A., *51*
Campbell, H., 102, *108*
Campbell, J. D., 18, *25*, 401, *411*, 422, 423, *442*
Campbell, O., *107*
Cannings, C., *107*
Cannon, K. L., 401, *411*
Cantor, G. N., 39, *51*, 142, 172, *179*
Cantor, J. H., 39, *51*, 172, *179*
Caplan, G., *442*
Caplin, M. D., 433, *442*
Carey, M. J., *80*
Carlsmith, L., 206, *217*
Carmichael, L., 30, *51*
Carr, D. H., 76, *80*
Carr, S., *106*
Carroll, J. B., 245, *253*, 426, *442*
Casler, L., *217*
Cassirer, E., 11, *24*
Castle, P. W., *181*, 200, 203, *219*
Castner, B. M., 250, *253*
Cattell, P., 158, *179*
Cattell, R. B., *80*
Caudill, W., 210, *217*
Cavan, R. S., 18, *24*
Cervantes, L., 492, 493, *503*
Chall, J., 433, *442*
Chamove, A. S., 195, *217*
Charlesworth, W. R., 172, *179*, 286, *293*, 344, 345, *372*, 422, *443*
Chase, H. H., 127, *141*
Chase, H. P., *141*

Chazan, M., *442*
Chen, H. P., 149, *180*
Chess, S., 24, *442*
Cheyney, A. B., *442*
Child, I. L., 267, 284, 285, *295*
Chinsky, J. M., 309, *334*
Chittenden, G. E., 353, *372*
Chomsky, N., *179*, 237, *253*
Chow, B. F., 92, *107*
Christakos, A. C., 93, 104, *108*
Church, J., 177, 178, *179*, 195, 216, 217, *218*, 219, 250, *253*, 355, *374*
Church, R. M., *51*
Ciaccio, N. V., 414, 416, *442*
Clark, K. B., 494, *503*
Cobb, E. A., 426, *442*
Cochin, J., 98, *107*
Cofer, C. N., *24*
Cohen, D., 103, *109*
Cohen, P., 247, *253*
Cohen, S., *442*
Cole, M., 246, *253*, 330, *334*
Coleman, J. C., 364, *372*
Coleman, J. S., 469, *476*
Collard, R. R., 172, 175, *179*
Collins, B. E., 426, *443*
Collmann, R. D., *109*
Conant, J. B., 432, *442*
Connors, K., 330, *334*
Conrad, R., *253*
Converse, P. E., 467, *476*
Coolidge, J. C., *442*
Cooper, R. G., *411*
Coopersmith, S., 418, *442*
Corah, N. L., 102, *107*
Corbett, F. J., 432, *443*
Cord, E. L., *80*
Corman, H. H., *179*
Counter, S. A., 127, *141*
Covington, M., *25*
Cowan, R. A., 495, *504*
Craise, J. L., 458, *477*, 490, 491, *505*
Crandall, V. J., 266, 289, *293*, 308, *334*
Crane, A. R., *411*
Crockett, W., 382, *413*
Cronbach, L. J., *24*
Crowell, D. H., 127, *140*
Crudden, C. H., 128, *141*
Crutchfield, R. S., 419, *442*
Cucinotta, P., *181*
Curtis, M., *107*
Cwalina, G., 497, *503*

Dallapiciola, B., *80*
Damrin, D., 405, *413*

Dann, S., 204, 205, 212, *218*, 373
Darbyshire, M., *179*
Darlington, C. D., *80*
Davidson, H. H., 433, *442*, *443*
Davidson, K. S., 359, 360, *374*
Davis, A., 431, 434, *442*, *443*, 481, *503*
Davis, G. H., 98, *107*
Davis, H., 435, *444*
Davis, J. R., 495, *504*
Davison, A. N., *107*
Day, D., 308, 312, *335*
Day, R. H., *180*
Dean, R. F. A., 120, 121, *141*
Debus, R. L., 348, *372*
DeFries, J. C., *80*, *82*
DeGrazia, S., 173, *179*
DeLaguna, G., *179*
del Solar, C. F., 429, *443*
Dembo, T., 274, *293*
Demerec, M., *81*
Dennis, W., 24, 129, 133, *141*, *218*
Despres, M. A., 94, *107*
Deutsch, M., 434, *442*
Diamond, M. A., 78, *81*
DiLorenzo, L. T., 331, *334*
Dimitrovsky, L., 397, *411*
Dinitz, S., *505*
Discher, D. R., 128, *141*
Dobbing, J., *107*
Dobzhansky, T., 72, *81*
Dodge, P. R., *106*
Dolger, L., 430, *442*
Dollard, J., 8, 15, *24*, 210, *218*, 401, *412*
Dorfman, H., *254*
Doris, J., *81*
Dorman, L., *293*
Douglas, J. W. B., 330, *334*
Douvan, E., 451, 458, 462, 463, 464, 465, 466, 467, 469, 470, 471, *476*, 482, 489, 490, *503*
Dozier, J. E., 103, *108*
Drillien, C. M., 103, *107*, *141*
Dubignon, J., *107*
Dugdale, R. L., 59, *81*
Dunlop, G. M., *442*
Dunn, L. M., 329, *334*
Dunningham, M. J., *373*
Durfee, H., *218*
Durkin, D., 385, *411*
Dyk, R. B., *25*

Ebbs, J. H., 92, *107*
Eckerman, C. O., 194, *219*
Edge, D., *293*
Ehemann, B., 99, *107*

Ehrhardt, A. A., 96, 102, *107*, *108*
Eibl-Eibesfeldt, I., 269, *293*
Eimas, P. D., *179*
Einhorn, J., *411*
Eisenberg, K., 309, *335*
Eisenberg, L., 330, *334*
Elandt-Johnson, R. C., *81*
Elkan, B., *373*
Elkind, D., 24, *179*, 254, 317, 318, *334*, 461, *476*
Elkins, D., 401, *411*, 424, *442*
Elkins, F., *293*
Ellis, H. C., *51*
Ellis, R. W. B., 103, *107*
Elton, C. F., 466, *477*
Emerson, P. E., 192, 193, *219*
Emery, A., 476, 485, *504*
Emmerich, W., 266, *293*
Engen, T., 128, *141*
Englemann, S., 329, 330, *334*
Epstein, R. C., 39, *51*, 96, 102, *107*, 429, 437, *442*
Erikson, E. H., 13, 14, *24*, 173, *179*, 209, 210, *218*, 288, *293*, 367, *373*, 415, *442*, 450, *476*, 479, 480, 484, 492, *504*
Ermalinski, R., *293*
Ernhart, C. B., *107*
Ervin, S. M., 236, *253*
Ervin-Tripp, S., *253*
Escalona, S. K., 136, *141*, *179*
Estes, W. K., *51*
Etzel, B. C., 187, 188, *218*
Everett, J. W., *107*
Eysenck, H. J., 74, 75, *81*

Faigin, H., 264, *293*
Fantz, R. L., 122, 123, 125, *141*
Faterson, H. F., *25*
Fauls, L., 280, *294*
Feffer, M. A., *412*
Feffer, M. H., 340, *373*
Feinberg, M. R., 424, *442*
Feitelson, D., 174, *179*
Fejer, D., 497, *505*
Fellows, B. J., *179*
Ferber, P., 103, *109*
Ferguson, N., *373*
Ferguson, P. E., 265, *294*
Ferm, V. H., 100, *109*
Ferreira, A. J., 94, *107*
Ferritor, O., 35, *51*
Fesbach, S., 272, *294*
Fillozat, A. M., *218*
Finney, J. C., 265, *294*
Fischer, L. K., 103, *107*, *109*
Fite, M. D., 349, *373*

Flanell, J., *179*
Flapan, D., *294*, 397, 398, 412, *442*
Flavell, J. H., *51*, *253*, 309, *334*, 340, *373*, 383, 391, *411*, *412*
Flechsig, P. E., 113, *141*
Flory, C. D., 128, *142*
Fodor, J. A., *252*
Fordham, M., *294*
Forest, M., *81*
Foshee, J. G., 40, *52*
Fowler, S. E., 470, *476*
Fowler, W., *179*
Fraser, A., *81*
Fraser, C., 238, 240, *253*
Frazier, T. M., 98, *107*
Frederickson, N., 274, *294*
Freedman, A. M., 103, *106*, *294*
Freedman, D. C., 342, 343, *373*
Freedman, D. G., 74, *81*, 185, 186, *218*
Freeman, F. A., 458, *476*
Freeman, R. N., 72, *81*
Frenkel-Brunswik, E., 436, *442*
Freud, A., 24, 195, 204, 205, 212, *218*, *373*, *442*, 479, *504*
Freud, S., 4, 12, 13, 22, 23, *24*, *141*, *253*, 414, *442*, 483, *504*
Friedler, G., 98, *107*
Friedman, M. L., 487, 488, *504*
Friedmann, T., 68, 69, *81*
Friedrich, U., *81*
Froland, A., *81*
Frumkin, R. M., 495, *504*
Fry, C., 383, *412*
Furchtgott, E., *107*
Furfey, P. H., 424, 425, *442*
Furth, H. G., *51*, *179*, 243, 244, 245, *253*, *254*, 315, *334*

Gagné, R. M., *51*
Gaite, A. J. H., 462, *476*
Galton, F., *334*
Garden, J. A., 423, *443*
Gardner, D. B., 205, *218*
Garn, S. M., *107*, 120, *141*
Garner, A. M., 426, *442*
Gates, A. E., 92, *107*
Gates, G. S., 397, *412*
Gebhard, P. H., 471, *476*
Gelfand, D. M., *294*
Gentry, J. T., 99, *107*
Gergen, K. J., 451, *476*
Gerver, J. M., 433, *442*, *443*
Gesell, A. L., 21, 22, *24*, 129, *141*, 158, *179*, 195, 212, *218*, 250, *253*, 273, 347, *373*
Getzels, J. W., 475, *476*

Gewirtz, J. L., 33, 40, *51*, *52*, 146, *181*, 182, 187, 188, *218*, *254*
Ghent, J. H., 318, *334*
Gibbon, J., 92, *108*
Gibbs, P. K., *443*
Gibson, E. J., 125, 126, *141*, 319, *335*
Gilmour, G., *81*
Ginandes, J., 430, *442*
Ginsberg, H., *179*, *253*, 301, *335*
Ginsberg, S., 360, *374*
Glass, D. C., *24*
Glass, N., 351, *373*
Glazer, J. A., 422, *443*
Globetti, G., *476*, *504*
Go, E., 317, 318, *334*
Goffman, E., 173, *180*
Gold, M., 451, 458, 462, 463, 464, 467, 469, 470, 471, *476*, 482, *503*
Goldberg, I. D., 98, *107*
Goldberg, S., 102, *108*, *180*, 211, *218*
Golden, M., *180*
Goldfarb, W., 203, *218*, *253*
Goldstein, H., 98, *107*
Goldstein, H. J., *81*
Goldstein, J. H., 383, *412*
Goldstein, M. N., *81*
Goldstein, R., 496, *504*
Gollin, E. S., 307, *335*
Goodenough, D. R., *25*
Goodenough, F. L., 271, *294*
Goodnow, J., 382, *412*
Goodwin, B., *107*
Goodwin, D. A., 74, *82*
Gordon, E. W., *442*
Gordon, I. J., *51*, *180*
Gordon, J., *253*
Goss, A. E., *51*
Gouin Decarie, T., *180*
Gould, R., *253*
Goulet, L. R., *51*
Gourevitch, V., 340, *373*
Goy, R. W., 95, 96, *107*, *109*
Grady, K. L., 95, *107*
Graham, F. K., 102, *107*, 127, *141*
Grant, D. A., 32, *51*
Grantham-McGregory, S. M., *141*
Gratch, G., *180*
Gray, M. L., 127, *140*
Gray, S. W., 329, *335*
Greco, P., *335*
Green, A., 435, *444*
Green, E. H., 338, *373*
Greenberg, J. W., 433, *442*, *443*
Greenberg, N., 96, 102, *107*
Greenberg, P. J., 347, *373*
Greenfield, P. M., *253*
Grier, J. B., 127, *141*
Griffiths, R., 158, *180*

Grinder, R. E., *80*
Grobstein, R., *218*
Groff, P. J., 432, *443*
Grosser, D., *373*
Grossman, B., *412*
Gruenberg, E. M., 90, *107*
Grusec, J. E., 40, *50*, 95, 98, *109*, 204, 219, 281, *295*
Guilford, J. P., 324, *335*
Guillaume, P., *180*
Gump, P. V., *373*, *443*
Gynther, M. D., 93, 104, *108*

Haaf, R. A., *141*
Haan, N., 491, *504*
Haberman, S., *81*
Hagman, R. R., 358, *373*
Haines, A. C., 405, *412*, *413*
Haith, M. M., 309, *335*
Hall, G. S., *141*
Hall, J. F., *51*
Hall, V. C., *51*
Haller, A. O., *443*
Halverson, H. M., 134, *141*
Hamblin, R. L., 35, *51*, *294*
Hampson, J. G., 78, *81*
Hampson, J. L., 78, *81*
Hamsher, J. H., *412*
Handel, G., *293*
Hanks, C., 206, *219*
Hanson, H. M., 92, *107*
Hanson, V. H., *81*
Harari, H., 424, *444*
Harlow, H., 344, *373*
Harlow, H. F., 27, *51*, 191, *218*
Harlow, M. H., 191, *218*
Harlow, M. K., 344, *373*
Harper, P., 103, *108*
Harper, P. A., 103, *107*, *109*
Harrell, R. F., 92, *107*
Harris, F. R., 354, *372*
Harris, H., *81*
Harris, I. D., 440, 441, *443*
Harris, T. L., *51*
Harrison, C. W., 421, 436, *443*
Harrison, D. E., *476*, *504*
Hart, B., 354, *372*
Harter, S., 311, *335*
Hartmann, H., *24*
Hartup, W. W., 267, 280, *294*, 342, 344, 345, 346, *372*, *373*, 375, 401, *407*, *412*, 422, *443*
Harvey, O. J., 405, *413*
Hasson, J. E., *81*
Hatfield, J. S., 265, *294*
Hattwick, B. W., 350, *373*
Hattwick, L. A., 338, *373*

Hattwick, L. W., *293*
Hauscha, R. S., *81*
Havighurst, R. J., 431, *443*
Hawkes, G. R., 205, *218*
Hayes, N. A., *294*
Haynes, H., 121, *141*
Healey, J. J. R., 120, *142*
Heathers, G., 263, 264, *294*, 338, *373*
Hebb, D. O., 227, *253*
Hegmann, J. P., *80*
Heider, F., *24*
Heider, G. M., 136, *141*
Heil, L. M., 427, *443*
Heilbrun, A. B., Jr., 489, *504*
Heimer, C. B., 103, *106*
Heinecke, C. M., 131, *141*, 351, *373*
Heinstein, M., 189, *218*
Heist, P., 491, *504*
Held, R. M., 134, *141*, *143*, *181*
Hellmer, L. A., 257, *293*
Helmreich, R. L., 426, *443*
Hendricks, C. H., 104, *107*
Hernstein, R. I. Q., *335*
Herron, R. E., *180*
Hertzig, M., *24*
Hess, A. L., 487, *504*
Hess, E. H., 28, *51*
Hess, R., *504*
Hess, R. D., 328, *335*, 434, *442*
Hesser, J. L., *80*
Heston, L. L., *81*
Hetherington, E. M., *443*
Hetzer, H., *179*
Hewett, F. M., 365, *373*
Hicks, D. J., 42, *51*, *373*
Higgins-Trenk, A., *253*, 462, *476*
Higgons, R. A., 131, *142*
Hill, K. T., 360, 361, *373*, 423, 428, *443*, 444
Hilton, I., 256, *294*
Hindley, C. B., *218*
Hirschhorn, K., *81*
Hitchfield, E., *51*
Hockman, C. H., 94, *107*
Hoefer, C., 350, *373*
Hoffman, H. S., 187, *218*
Hoffman, M. L., 268, *294*, 385, 386, 387, *412*, 420, 425, *443*
Hogbin, H. I., 472, *476*
Hollenberg, E., 270, 275, 278, 289, *294*
Hollender, J. W., 466, *476*
Hollingshead, A. B., 465, 466, *476*
Holmes, F. B., 198, *218*, 358, 359, *373*
Holzinger, K. J., 72, *81*
Honigmann, J. J., 346, *373*
Honzik, C. H., 38, *52*

Honzik, M. P., 157, *180*, 210, *218*, 227, *253*, 326, 327, *335*
Hood, W. R., 405, *413*
Hooker, D., 89, *107*
Hooper, F., *52*
Hooper, F. H. A., *336*
Hoppe, R. A., *294*
Hornsby, J. R., *335*
Horowitz, F. D., *373*
Horrocks, J. E., 458, *476*
House, B. J., *53*
Houston, K. B., *107*
Howard, A. M., *24*
Howell, R., *504*
Hoyt, J. M., *374*
Hughes, J. G., 99, *107*
Hughston, K., *294*
Hull, V., *443*
Hulse, W. C., *372*
Hultgren, H. H., 100, *107*
Hume, D., 7, *24*
Humphrey, T., *108*
Hunt, R. G., 350, *372*
Huschka, M., 210, *218*
Huston, A. C., 260, 261, *293*
Hutchings, D. E., 92, *108*
Hutt, C., 175, *180*
Huttenlocher, J., 393, *412*

Ilg, F. L., 22, *24*, 273, 347, *373*
Illsley, R., *108*
Ingram, D., *180*
Inhelder, B., *24*, *180*, *253*, 374, 393, 412, 459, *476*
Irwin, D. M., *294*
Irwin, O. C., 149, *180*, *253*
Isaacs, S., *294*, 343, 344, *373*
Iscoe, I., 423, *443*
Ismajovich, B., 104, *109*
Ivanov-Smolensky, A. G., 33, *51*

Jack, L. M., 353, *373*
Jacklin, C. N., 344, *374*
Jackson, P. W., 475, *476*
Jacob, P. E., 485, *504*
Jacobs, P. A., 77, *81*
James, W., 113, *141*
James, W. H., *108*
Jarvik, L. F., 98, *108*
Jarvis, P. E., 243, *253*, 383, *412*
Jeffrey, W. E., 30, *51*
Jegard, S., 274, *294*
Jenkins, R. L., 364, 365, *373*
Jensen, A. R., 58, *81*
Jensen, K., 128, *141*
Jensen, L., *294*

Jersild, A. T., 198, *218*, 348, 349, 358, 359, *373*, 429, *443*
Joffe, J. M., 100, *108*
Johnson, A. M., *443*
Johnson, P. E., *51*
Johnson, V. E., *476*
Jones, H. E., *24*, *443*
Jones, M. C., *373*
Jorgensen, E., *504*
Jones, M. C. A., 457, *476*
Joseph, A., *181*
Juscyzk, P., *179*

Kaelther, C. T., *108*
Kagan, J., *24*, 124, 128, 136, *141*, *142*, 146, *180*, 196, 197, *218*, 256, 258, 264, 266, 271, 289, *294*, 307, 308, 311, 312, 313, 328, *335*, *336*, 412, 419, *443*, 481, *504*
Kahana, B., *80*
Kaij, L., *108*
Kallmann, F. J., 59, 68, 71, 77, *81*
Kandel, D. B., 462, 470, *476*
Kanner, L., 363, 366, *373*
Kant, I., 7, *24*
Kaplan, B., 10, *25*, 156, 165, *181*, 229, *254*
Kaplan, H. I., *294*
Karacon, J., *108*
Karp, S. A., *25*
Kasatkin, N. I., *51*
Katahn, M., 360, *373*
Katcher, A., *294*, 419, *443*
Katkovsky, W., 308, *334*
Kato, T., 98, *108*
Katz, P., 461, *476*, 487, *504*
Katz, V., *141*
Kawin, E., 350, *373*
Kay, B., *505*
Kay, H. E. M., *81*
Kaye, H., 31, *51*, *52*
Keasey, C. B., 391, *412*
Keeley, K., 94, *108*
Keen, R. F., 127, *141*
Keister, M. E., 353, *373*
Keller, F. S., *51*
Kellogg, L. A., *294*
Kellogg, R., 320, *335*
Kellogg, W. N., *294*
Kelsey, F. O., 97, *108*
Kendall, D. G., *108*
Kendler, H. H., *51*
Kendler, T. S., *51*, *253*, 314, *335*
Keniston, K., 468, *476*, 484, 485, 486, 491, 492, *504*
Kerber, A., 432, *443*

Kessen, W., 122, 125, *142*, *159*, *218*
Kessler, J. W., 359, 366, *374*, *443*
Khokhitva, A., *51*
Kilbride, J. E., *141*
Kilbride, P. L., *141*
Kimmel, H. D., 32, *51*
King, F. A., 100, *109*
Kinsey, A. C., 471, 472, *476*
Kintsch, W., *51*
Kipnis, D., 407, *412*
Kirk, S., 329, *335*
Klackenberg, G., *218*
Klaiber, E. L., 76, *80*
Klaus, R. A., 329, *335*, 423, *443*
Klausmeier, H. J., *51*
Klima, E. S., 241, *253*
Kline, F. G., 468, *476*
Klineberg, S. L., 461, *476*
Klinger, E., *253*
Kluckhohn, R., 477, 482, 483, *505*
Knobloch, H., 102, 103, 104, *108*
Kobayashi, T., 76, *80*
Koch, H. L., 427, *443*
Koch, J., *51*
Koegler, R. R., 317, 318, *334*
Kogan, N., *181*, 307, 310, *335*, *336*, 410, 411, *412*, *413*
Kohlberg, L. A., 261, 281, 282, *294*, 340, *374*, 387, 388, 391, *412*, 418, 419, *443*, 484, 491, *504*
Kohn, L., 278, *295*
Kohn, M., 345, *374*
Komorita, S. S., 437, *442*
Korner, A. F., *141*, *218*
Kozloff, M., 35, *51*
Kramer, R., 484, *504*
Kranz, P. L., *81*
Krippene, B., *443*
Krogman, W. M., *142*, *253*
Kruskal, W. H., *81*
Kuehn, J. L., 497, *504*
Kuenne, M. R., *253*, 314, *335*
Kurlord, A. A., *82*
Kurtz, J. J., *335*
Kusum, P. L., *80*
Kuusinen, J., *253*

Labov, W., 246, 247, *253*, *335*
LaDu, B. N., Jr., 69, *81*
Laird, J. D., 487, *504*
Lambert, W. E., *412*
Lambert, W. W., 211, *218*
Landers, W. F., *180*
Landreth, C., 35, *51*
Landsbaum, J. B., 482, *504*
Langer, J., *24*, *25*, 480, *504*
Langer, S. K., *25*

Lapidus, L. B., *108*
Latz, E., *142*
Laurendeau, M., *180*, 394, *412*
Lawson, P. R., *52*
Leader, F. B., *374*
Leanerton, P., *293*
Lebovici, S., 363, *372*
Lee, L. C., 388, 389, *412*
Lefevre, C., 433, *443*
Le Furgy, W. G., 385, *412*
Lenneberg, E. H., 148, 149, *180*, 235, 237, 242, 244, *253*
Leopold, W. F., 149, *180*, *254*
Lerner, E., 385, *412*
Lerner, M. J., 426, *442*
Lerner, R. M., 476, 485, *504*
Lesser, G. S., 462, 470, *476*
Lesser, M., 422, 423, *443*
Lethwood, K. A., *179*
Leuba, C., *374*
Leventhal, A. S., 127, *142*
Lever, J., *476*
Levin, H., 209, *219*, 265, 266, 276, 278, 281, 282, 283, *294*, *295*, 419, 431, *443*, 444
Levine, M., 432, *443*
Levinson, B., 310, *335*
Levy, D. M., 264, *294*
Levy, N., 128, 136, *142*
Lewin, K., *25*, 274, *293*, 407, *412*, 450, 476, *504*
Lewis, D. J., 40, *52*
Lewis, M., *52*, 102, *108*, *142*, 160, *180*, 195, *218*, 285, 287, *294*
Lichter, S. O., 502, *504*
Lieberman, J. N., 174, *180*
Lighthall, F. F., 359, 360, *374*
Lilienfeld, A. M., 102, 103, 104, *108*
Lindzey, G., *81*
Ling, B. C. I., 121, *142*
Lippett, R. A., *373*
Lippitt, R., *25*, 407, *412*
Lipsitt, L. P., 31, *52*, 127, 128, 136, *141*, *142*, 444
Lipton, R. C., 200, 202, *219*
Littenberg, R., *180*
Littman, R. A., 270, 277, *295*, 347, 348, *374*
Liverant, S., 39, *51*
Livson, N., 146, *179*
Loban, W., 248, *254*
Loevinger, J., *25*
Logan, F. A., *52*
Lonsdale, D., *81*
Lorenz, K. Z., 28, *52*, 269, *294*
Lott, A. J., 405, *412*
Lott, B. E., 405, *412*
Lourenso, S. V., 433, *443*

Louria, D., 496, *504*
Lovaas, O., *294*
Lovell, K. A., 320, *335*, 382, *412*
Lowrey, L. G., *218*
Lowrie, S. H., *476*
Lukomnik, M., 360, *374*
Luria, A. R., 243, *254*, 299, *335*
Luria, Z., 257, *293*

McArthur, C., 257, *294*
McAvoy, T., *29*
McBane, B., 312, *336*
McCall, R. B., 124, *142*, 146, *180*
McCalley, J. E., 364, *372*
McCandless, B. R., *218*, 274, 275, *295*, *374*
McCarthy, D., 148, 149, 155, *180*, 234, *254*
McCarthy, J. J., 329, *335*
McClearn, G., 66, *81*
McCloskey, K., *412*
Maccoby, E. E., 209, *219*, 265, 266, 276, 278, 279, 281, 282, 283, *294*, *295*, 308, *335*, 344, *374*, 419, 431, *443*, 444
McDavid, J. W., 424, *444*
McDonald, F. J., 385, 386, *411*
McDonald, R. L., 93, 104, *108*
Macfarlane, J. W., 210, *218*, 227, *253*, 326, 327, *335*
McGhee, P. E., *294*, 383, *412*
McGraw, M. B., *142*
McKee, J. P., *374*
McKenzie, B., *180*
McKusick, V. A., 68, *81*
McNeil, T. F., 103, *108*
McNeill, D., 239, 241, *254*
Mainer, R. E., 467, *476*
Malmquist, A., *108*
Malzmann, I., *25*
Manosevitz, M., *81*
Marcia, J. E., 487, 488, *504*
Margoles, C., *81*
Marietta, D. F., *142*
Markey, F. V., *254*, 348, 349, *373*
Marquis, D. P., 40, *52*
Marshall, H. R., 265, *294*
Marshall, J. C., *254*
Martels, B., 102, *108*
Martin, B., 275, *293*
Martin, C. E., 471, *476*
Martin, H. P., *141*
Martin, W., 338, *374*, 416, *443*
Martyn, M., 364, *374*
Marx, M. H., *52*
Masangkay, Z., *412*
Masica, D. N., 96, 102, *108*

Masters, J., *294*, *476*
Matarazzo, R. G., 102, *107*
Mateer, F., 32, *52*
Matheny, A. P., *142*
Mather, K., *80*
Maximilian, C., *80*
Mead, G. H., 173, *180*
Mead, M., 464, 472, 476, *504*
Medinnus, G. R., 385, *412*, 488, 489, *504*
Mednick, S., 71, *81*
Meier, G. W., 100, *108*
Meltzer, H., 430, *444*
Melville, M. M., 77, *81*
Menlove, F. L., 40, *50*, 203, *218*
Menyuk, P. A., 234, *254*
Meredith, H. V., *142*
Merei, F., 341, *374*, 401, *412*
Merminod, A., *142*
Merrill, M. A., 324, *336*
Merton, R. K., *25*
Meser, S. B., 309, *335*
Meyers, C. E., *444*
Meyers, W. J., *142*
Miller, J., *437*
Miller, N. E., 8, 15, 24, *52*, 210, *218*, 401, *412*
Miller, W. E., 467, *476*
Millett, K., 77, *81*
Milton, G., *294*
Mindes, P., 309, *335*
Minturn, L., 211, *218*
Mirzoiants, N. S., 31, *51*, *52*
Mischel, W., 281, *295*, 481, *504*
Mitchell, R. G., *142*
Mock, R. L., 435, *444*
Money, J., 77, 78, *81*, 96, 102, *107*, *108*
Montgomery, A. A., *179*
Moore, E. W., 122, *141*
Moore, J. M., *108*
Moore, S. G., *294*, *374*, 423, *444*
Moore, T., 146, *180*
Moore, W. B., *254*
Moralishvili, E., 98, *108*
Morehead, D. M., *180*
Morgan, G. A., 195, *218*
Morland, J. K., 424, *444*
Morris, R. J., *294*
Morrison, F., 309, *335*
Moser, H. W., *106*
Moss, A., *180*
Moss, H. A., 76, *81*, 94, 104, *108*, 147, *180*, 185, 192, *218*, 256, 258, 264, 266, 271, 289, *294*, 311, 328, *335*, 419, *443*, 481, *504*

Mowrer, O. H., *25*, 148, *180*, 481, *504*
Mueller, E., 321, *335*
Mullener, N., 487, *504*
Munn, N. L., *52*, *142*
Munroe, R. H., *108*
Munroe, R. L., *108*
Munsinger, H., *142*
Murphy, L. B., *180*, 292, *295*, 333, 334, *335*
Murphy, M., *141*
Murray, F. B., 305, *335*
Murray, H. A., *25*
Mussen, P. H., *25*, 437, *444*, 489, *504*, *505*
Myers, N. A., 40, *52*

Najarian, P., 133, *141*, *218*
Nash, J., 195, *218*
Neale, J. M., *335*
Neel, J. V., 99, *108*
Nelson, A. K., 128, *142*
Nelson, B., *254*
Nelson, K., *142*
Nelson, V., *335*
Nevis, S., 123, *141*
Newman, H. H., 72, 73, *81*
Nicholson, E. L., 350, *372*
Nicolet-Meister, D., *218*
Nielson, J., *81*
Nilsson, A., *108*
Nodine, C. F., *51*
Noirot, E., 184, *219*
Nolan, C. T., 100, *108*
Nowlis, V., 265, 276, *295*
Noyes, R. W., *108*
Nuttall, E., 430, *444*
Nuttall, R., 430, *444*

O'Connor, N., *219*, 244, *254*
Offord, D. R., *108*
O'Grady, D. J., *81*
Oldfield, R. C., *254*
Olmstead, P., 312, *336*
Olver, R. R., 253, *335*
Opie, I., *412*, 424, *444*
Opie, P., *412*, 424, *444*
Oppel, W. C., 103, *109*
Opper, S., *179*, 253, 301, *335*
Orlansky, H., 189, 212, *219*
Orpen, C., 437, *444*
O'Shea, M. V., *180*
Ostrovsky, E. S., 293, *295*, 371, 372, *374*
Otis, N. B., 274, 275, *295*
Ourth, L. L., *180*

Pahnhe, W. N., *82*
Painter, P., 102, *107*
Palmer, R. R., *219*
Palthier, P. C., *254*
Papoušek, H., *52*, *142*
Pardes, H., *81*
Parke, R. D., 269, *295*
Parker, A., *106*
Parkhurst, E., 99, *107*
Parry, M. H., *142*
Parten, M. B., 338, 340, *374*
Partington, M. W., *107*
Pasamanick, B., 90, 102, 103, 104, *108*
Patterson, G. R., 270, 277, *295*, 347, 348, *374*
Pavlov, I. P., 31, *52*
Pearson, L., *335*
Pease, D., 205, *218*
Peatman, J. G., 131, *142*
Peer, A., 93, *109*
Pendorf, J., 476, 485, *504*
Penk, W. E., *25*
Peterson, D. R., 257, *293*
Peterson, R. E., 490, *505*
Peskin, H., 458, *476*
Phillips, L., 487, *505*
Phillips, W., 308, 312, *335*
Phoenix, C. H., 95, 96, *107*, *109*
Piaget, J., 9, 10, 14, 15, 20, 22, 23, 24, 25, 46, *52*, 125, 134, *142*, 156, 157, 160, 164, 165, 166, 167, 169, 170, 175, *180*, 231, 232, 244, *253*, *254*, 301, 302, 303, 304, 305, 323, 324, *335*, *336*, *374*, 379, 380, 381, 382, 383, 384, 385, 393, *412*, *413*, 459, *476*, 484, *505*
Pick, A. D., 318, *336*
Pick, H. L., Jr., 318, *336*
Pierce, C. M., 364, *374*
Pinard, A., *180*, 394, *412*
Pinneau, S., 203, *219*
Plath, D. W., 210, *217*
Polansky, N., *373*
Pomeroy, W. B., 471, *476*
Porter, F., *443*
Powell, J., 422, *442*
Pratt, K. C., 121, 128, *142*
Prentice, J. I., *254*
Press, A., 382, *413*
Presson, C., 393, *412*
Preston, A., 308, *334*
Price, W. H., 77, *82*
Prokasy, W. F., 32, *52*
Provence, S., 200, 202, *219*
Pugh, T. F., *108*
Pulaski, M. A. S., *336*

NAME INDEX 513

Pumroy, D. K., 40, *52*
Pumroy, S. S., 40, *52*

Rabin, A. I., 205, *219*
Rabinovitch, M. S., 487, *505*
Rabson, A., 266, *293*
Radke, M. J., *413*, 424, 435, *444*
Radke-Yarrow, M., 437, *444*
Ramey, C. T., *180*
Rapaport, D., *25*
Rapien, E. B., 502, *504*
Rau, L., 265, 294, *295*, 425, *445*
Rawls, D., 421, 436, *443*
Rawls, J., 421, 436, *443*
Raynor, R., 39, *53*
Read, K. H., 35, *51*
Rebelsky, F. G., 206, *219*, *293*
Reckless, W., *505*
Reed, M. F., 427, *441*
Reese, H. W., 310, *335*, 423, *444*
Reinisch, J., *108*
Reiss, I. L., 485, *505*
Remmers, H. H., 468, *476*
Rheingold, H. L., 33, 52, 146, *180*, *181*, *182*, 193, 194, 196, 204, 205, *219*, *254*
Rhodes, A. J., 90, *108*
Riccuiti, H. N., 195, *179*, *218*
Richardson, S. A., *108*, 435, *444*
Richmond, B. O., *445*
Rider, R., 103, *108*
Rider, R. V., 103, *107*, *109*
Rimland, B., 366, *374*
Ripple, R. E., *51*
Robbins, E. S., *81*
Robbins, M. C., *141*
Roberge, J., *293*
Roberts, C. R., *444*
Roberts, J. M., 175, *181*, 343, 356, 357, *374*, *413*
Robison, S., 494, *505*
Roblin, R., 68, 69, *81*
Robson, K. S., 192, *218*
Roeder, L. M., 92, *107*
Roeper, A., *336*
Roff, M., 424, *444*
Rogers, C. R., 25, *444*
Rogers, H., *32*
Rogers, M. E., 102, 104, *108*
Rohmann, C. G., 120, *141*
Roizin, L., 98, *108*
Rose, G. S., 174, *179*
Rose, H. A., 466, *477*
Rosen, M. G., 100, *106*
Rosenberg, B. C., 426, *444*
Rosenberg, B. G., 77, *82*, 257, *295*, *505*

Rosenberg, E., *413*
Rosenberg, M., *444*, 489, *505*
Rosenblatt, J. S., 184, *219*
Rosenbloom, S., *178*
Rosenbluth, D., 204, 205, *217*
Rosenow, C., 426, *444*
Rosenthal, M. K., 263, *295*, 360, *374*
Rosenthal, R., 328, *336*
Rosenthal, T. L., *254*
Rosman, B. L., 308, 312, *335*
Ross, D., 24, 41, *51*, 272, 273, *293*
Ross, H. W., 33, *52*, 146, *181*, *182*, *218*, *254*
Ross, J. M., 330, *334*
Ross, S. A., 24, 41, *51*, 272, 273, *293*
Rothbart, M. L. K., 256, *295*
Rothman, G. R., 386, *413*
Rubenstein, J., 172, *181*
Rubinfine, D. L., *142*
Rudel, R. G., 102, *109*
Ruebush, B. K., 359, 360, *374*
Rugh, C. N., 99, *108*
Ruscelli, V., *293*
Russell, E. W., *82*
Rutt, C. N., *108*

Sainte-Anne Dargassies, S., *142*
Salapatek, P., 122, 125, *142*
Salin, E., *253*
Saltzstein, H. D., 268, 294, 420, *443*
Sameroff, A. J., *142*
Sand, E. A., *218*
Sander, G., 59, 68, *81*
Sandercock, J., *80*
Sanders, M. K., 338, *373*
Sandy, D. G., *142*
Sarason, S. B., 359, 360, 361, *373*, *374*, 428, *443*, *444*
Savasta, M., 343, *374*
Sayegh, Y., 133, *141*
Scarlett, H., 382, *413*
Scarr, S., 74, *82*, 185, *219*
Schachter, S., *25*
Schaefer, E. S., 74, *82*, *442*
Schaffer, H. R., *142*, 192, 193, *219*
Schallenberger, M. E., 385, *413*
Schegel, W. S., 77, *82*
Schiff, D., 187, *218*
Schlesinger, I. M., *181*
Schmeidler, G. R., 360, *374*
Schmidt, R., 424, *442*
Schober, A., 319, *336*
Schober, G., 319, *336*
Schuckit, M. A., 74, *82*
Schulsinger, F., 71, *81*
Schwahn, W., *51*

Scott, J. P., 269, 270, *295*
Scott, P. M., *179*
Scott, R. B., 189, *219*
Scott, W. A., 92, *107*
Scott, W. C. M., *142*
Searle, J. L., 187, *218*
Sears, P. S., 265, 276, *295*, 349, *374*, 426, *444*
Sears, R. R., 25, 209, *219*, 265, 266, 276, 278, 281, 282, 283, *295*, 419, 431, *444*
Segrames, R. T., *82*
Seibert, F. M., 502, *504*
Sells, S. B., 424, *444*
Selman, R. L., 340, *374*, 389, 390, *413*
Seret, C., 364, *372*
Serr, D. M., 104, *109*
Sgan, M. L., 433, *444*
Shapiro, H., *142*, 312, *336*
Sharpe, T. M., *374*
Shearer, W. M., 127, *141*
Sheehan, J. G., 364, *374*
Sheridan, M. D., 90, *109*
Sherif, C. W., 404, 405, *413*
Sherif, M., 404, 405, *413*
Sherman, I. C., 128, *142*
Sherman, M., 128, *142*
Shields, J., 73, *82*
Shiller, A., 497, *505*
Shine, D. N., *254*
Shipman, V. C., 328, *335*
Shirley, M. M., 129, *142*, *181*, 195, *219*
Shock, N. W., *142*
Shoemaker, D. J., 257, *293*
Short, J. F., 494, *505*
Siegel, A., 278, *295*
Siegel, P. S., 40, *52*
Siegelman, M., 265, *295*
Sigel, I., *52*
Sigel, I. E., 311, 312, *335*, *336*
Silfen, C. K., *178*
Simmel, E. C., *294*
Simmons, M. W., *52*
Simon, W. E., 423, *444*
Simonson, M., 92, *107*
Simpson, R. L., 466, *477*
Simpson, W. J., 98, *109*
Sims-Knight, J., *412*
Sinclair, H., *24*
Sinclair-de-Zwart, H., *254*
Singer, J. E., *25*
Siqueland, E. R., 33, *52*, *179*
Skinner, B. F., 8, *25*, 33, 34, 40, *52*, *254*
Sklansky, M. A., 502, *504*
Slavson, S. R., 368, *374*

Slobin, D., 236, *254*
Sluckin, W., *52*
Small, A. M., *81*
Smart, R. G., 497, *505*
Smedslund, J., 306, *336*
Smith, A. J., 405, *413*
Smith, E. A., 470, *477*
Smith, G. H., 422, *444*
Smith, M., 424, 442, 491, *504*
Smith, M. E., *254*
Smith, R. E., *374*
Smith, W. D., 280, *294*
Smitherman, C., *181*
Smithies, E. M., 502, *505*
Smock, C. D., *24*
Soddy, K., 139, 140, *142*
Solomon, F., 248, *252*
Somers, R. H., 491, *505*
Sontag, L. W., 93, *109*, *335*
Sørenson, A., *81*
Spence, J. T., *52*
Spence, K. W., *52*
Sperry, M., 270, 275, 278, 289, *294*
Spickard, W., 100, *107*
Spiker, C. C., *52*
Spitz, R. A., 199, 200, *219*
Spock, B. M., 4, 21, *25*, *444*
Staats, A. W., 34, *52*
Staats, C. K., 34, *52*
Stafford, P., *142*
Staub, E., *295*
Stean, L. P., 93, *109*
Stechler, G., 99, 102, 104, *109*, *142*
Steinberg, M. D., *81*
Stendler, C. B., 189, *219*, 405, *413*
Stern, D. N., 192, *219*
Stern, J. A., 102, *107*
Stern, W., *254*
Stevenson, H. W., 39, *52*, *374*
Stevenson, I., 212, 214, *219*
Stevenson, N. G., *374*
Stiening, B. R., *142*
Stokes, D. E., 467, *476*
Stoller, A., *109*
Stoller, R. J., 78, *80*
Stolz, H. R., 120, *142*
Stolz, L. M., 120, *142*
Stone, C. P., 458, *477*
Stone, L. J., 195, *219*, 355, *374*
Stony, R. R., *82*
Storm, L. H., *25*
Stott, L. H., *181*, 207, 341, 416, *444*
Stout, A. M., 256, *295*
Stoyle, J., *293*
Strodbeck, F. L., 494, *505*
Sullivan, E. V., *24*
Sun, K. H., 128, *142*
Suppes, P., 44, *52*

Sutherland, B. J., *81*
Sutherland, J., *413*
Sutton-Smith, B., 77, 82, 173, 174, 175, *180*, *181*, *254*, 257, *295*, 343, 352, 356, 357, 373, 374, 383, *399*, *413*, 426, 443, 444, *477*, *505*
Swenson, E. G., *335*
Swiger, M. K., 205, *218*

Tabachnick, R., 436, *444*
Tagucci, Y., *412*
Tanner, J. M., 120, *142*, 451, 452, 454, 455, 456, 457, *477*
Tasch, M. O., *295*
Tasch, R. J., *443*
Taussig, H. B., 97, *109*
Taylor, I. K., 364, *374*
Templin, M. C., 245, *254*, *336*
Tempone, V. J., *52*
Terman, L. M., 284, *295*, 324, *336*
Tessman, E., *442*
Teuber, H. L., 102, *109*
Thiessen, D. D., *81*, *82*
Thomas, A., *24*, *442*
Thomas, S., *443*
Thompson, G. C., 422, *441*
Thompson, G. G., 350, 352, *374*, 422, *445*
Thompson, H., *179*, 195, *218*, 250, 253, *254*
Thompson, W. R., 94, 95, 98, *109*, 204, *219*
Thurston, D., 102, *107*
Tijo, J. H., *82*
Tischler, B., *80*
Tisdall, F. F., 92, *107*
Titkin, S., 345, *375*
Tizard, B., *181*
Tolman, E. C., 38, *52*
Trager, H. G., *413*, 424, 435, 437, *444*
Trent, J. W., 458, *477*, 490, 491, *505*
Trent, R. D., 436, *444*
Truax, C. B., 331, *336*
Tuddenham, R. D., 271, *295*, 435, *444*
Tulkin, S. R., *180*

Valentine, C. W., 338, *375*
Vandenberg, S. G., 72, *82*
Verville, E., *375*
Vierck, C. J., Jr., 100, *109*
Vigorito, J., *179*
Vincent, C. E., 189, *219*

Vogel, W., 76, *80*
Vroegh, K., *444*
Vygotsky, L. S., 44, *52*, *254*

Wachs, T. D., *181*
Wadsworth, B. J., 161, 162, 168, *181*
Waite, R. R., 359, 360, *374*, 434, *445*
Waldsfogel, S., *442*
Walk, R. D., 125, *143*
Walk, R. R., 125, *141*
Wallach, M. A., *53*, *181*, 310, *336*, 410, 411, *413*
Walsh, M. E., 350, *375*
Walters, R. A., 274, *294*
Walters, R. H., *24*, 269, 270, 276, 277, 278, 293, *295*, 472, 476, 492, 494, 495, *503*
Walton, D., 368, 369, *375*
Ward, W. C., 310, 311, *336*
Washburn, R. W., 195, *219*
Washburne, C., 427, *443*
Watson, G., 264, *295*
Watson, J. B., 39, *53*
Watts, W. A., 491, *505*
Weatherly, D., *295*
Wechsler, D., *336*
Weiner, I. D., *254*
Weinstein, H., 210, *217*
Weir, M. W., 82, *142*
Weisberg, P., 33, *53*
Weiss, M., 358, *375*
Weksel, W., *252*
Welch, L., 313, *335*
Welker, W. I., 175, *181*
Wenar, C., 426, *442*
Werner, E. E., *109*, *181*
Werner, H., 9, 10, 11, 14, 20, 22, 23, 25, 156, 165, *181*, 229, *254*, 319, *336*, 382, *413*
Weslowski, J. C., 432, *443*
Weyl, N., *82*
Whatmore, P. B., 77, *82*
White, B. J., 405, *413*
White, B. L., 134, 135, *141*, *143*, *181*, 200, 203, *219*
White, R., 288, *295*, 407, *412*
White, R. K., *25*
White, S. H., *25*, 299, 322, *336*
White, W. F., *445*
Whitehouse, R. H., 120, *142*
Whiteman, M., 394, *413*
Whiting, B. B., 6, *25*
Whiting, J. W. M., *219*, 265, 267, 276, 284, 285, *295*, *477*, 482, 483, *505*
Whittaker, D. N., 491, *505*
Whittinghill, M., *82*

Whyte, A. H., 426, *444*
Wickes, F. G., *254*
Wiegerink, R., 103, *108*
Wiener, G., 103, *109*
Wilkerson, D. A., *442*
Willer, M. L., *442*
Williams, J. R., 189, *219*
Williams, N., *143*
Willis, R. H., 482, *504*
Wilson, C. D., *142*
Wilson, W. C., 281, *294*, 419, *443*
Winder, C. L., *295*, 425, *445*
Winitz, H., *254*
Winokur, G., 74, *82*
Winterbottom, M. R., 289, *295*
Witkin, E. M., 66, *82*
Witkin, H. A., *25*
Witryot, S. L., 422, *445*

Wober, M., *336*
Wohlwill, J. F., 312, *336*
Wolf, E., *218*
Wolf, M. M., 354, *372*
Wolfe, J. B., 37, *53*
Wolff, P. H., *181*, 363, *375*
Woodyard, E., 92, *107*, 429, *443*
Woolshin, G. W., 385, *412*
Wortis, H., 103, *106*
Wright, J., 383, *412*
Wrighter, J., *412*

Yamamoto, K., *295*
Yando, R. M., 313, *336*
Yarnell, H., *217*
Yarrow, L. J., 137, *143*, 205, 214, *219*, 425, *445*

Yarrow, M. R., 18, *25*, 422, 423, 425, *442*, *445*
Yates, A., *80*
Young, F., 483, *505*
Young, P. V., *25*
Young, W. C., 95, 96, *107*, *109*
Youniss, J., 243, 244, *254*, 315, *336*

Zazzo, A. R., *336*
Zeaman, D., *53*
Zigler, E., *50*, *53*, 461, 476, 487, *504*, *505*
Zimbardo, P. G., 428, *444*
Zimmerman, L. D., *254*
Zimmerman, R. R., 27, *51*, 191, *218*
Zitrin, A., 103, *109*
Zook, E. A., 280, *294*

Subject Index

abortion, 88
abstract and hypothetical thinking, adolescence, 459–461
acceptance and friendship of peers, middle childhood, 421–425
accommodation
   and intelligence, 161–162
   visual, in infancy, 121
achievement
   and effectance motivation, toddler, 289–290
   and schooling, social-class differences, 431–435
achievement behavior, 308
action concepts, 43
action orientation in early speech, 239–240
activity level, infants, 136
adaptation and intelligence, 161–162
adenine in DNA, 61, 62
adolescence
   atypical groups, 490–497
   case studies, 474–475, 501–503

changes, 449–451
crisis views, 450–451
dependence vs. independence, 481–483
Erikson's theory, 479–481
Freudian views, 479
identity crisis, 13–14, 450, 487–488
intellectual and cognitive development, 458–462
maturation rate, 455–457
noncrisis views, 451
peer relationships and culture, 469–473
personality theories, 479–481
physical and sexual development, 451–458
self-concept and self-esteem, 486–490
social and cultural changes, 462–469
value development in, 483–486
adrenogenital syndrome, 96

adults (see also parent(s); teacher)
   and middle childhood choice of friends, 425
   separation of child and, 5–6
   toddler need for, 262
affection and moral development, 268
age
   and competitiveness, 347
   and concept construction, 312
   and conditioning, 32
   and delinquency, 494
   and encoding, 308
   and fears, 358
   and I.Q. tests, 327
   and learning set, 311
   and peer groups, 401
aggression
   and dependence on peers, 423
   determinants, 269–270
   displacement of, 276
   early childhood, 347–349
   and frustration, 270, 272–275
   learned, 41–42

517

aggression *(continued)*
   man vs. animal, 269–270
   model theory of, 272–274
   and popularity, middle childhood, 422
   reinforcement and spread of, 347–348
   sex differences, 270, 271, 278, 279, 349, 419
   stability of level, 271–272
   toddler, 269–278
aggressiveness
   in peers, imitation of, 345
   unsocialized, early childhood, 365
   variables affecting, 275–278
alcoholism and heredity, 74
allele, heterozygous vs. homozygous, 63
altruism and peer models, 346
amaural idiocy, hereditary, 66
amniocentesis, 70
amnion, 85
amniotic sac, 85
amphetamines, 496, 497
androgen, effects on fetus, 95–97
androgen-insensitivity syndrome, 96
animals, operant conditioning, 32–33
anoxia, 100, 102
   fetal, 100
antigens, 91
anxiety
   and attachment to parents, 194–199
   early childhood, 359–360
   vs. fear, 47, 357
   and memory, 309
   and peer acceptance, middle childhood, 423
   and pregnancy, 93–94
   prenatal, and male births, 104
   socialized, 481
assimilation
   forms in sensorimotor development, 164, 165
   and intelligence, 161
associations and infant attentional preference, 124
attachment to parent, 190–194
   anxieties related to, 194–199
attention and expectancy in encoding, 308
attentiveness and babbling, 146
attitudes, conditioning of, 34
auditory perception, infant, 127–128

authority, attitudes toward, middle childhood, 429–431
autism, 71
   early childhood, 366
autonomy
   personal, adolescence, 462–464
   and self-awareness, toddler, 285–288
   vs. shame, 13, 288
   and socializing process, 208–209
awareness, *see* self-awareness

babbling
   early, 145–146
   and language, 147–148
   and parent–infant interaction, 190
   vocabulary, I.Q. scores, and, 146–147
Babinski reflex, infant, 115
barbiturates, 496, 497
behavior
   anxiety and, 360
   changes, early childhood, 322–323
   global, 11
   instinctive, 27–28
   learned, 26–30, 41–42
   measurement of change, 16
   mechanistic model, 8–9
   mother, and toddler personality, 259–260
   norms and "normal" in infant growth, 118
   of peers, as reward, 344–345
   prediction of, 211–214
   problems and disorders, early childhood, 363–369
   shaping, 33–34
   species-specific, 27
   teacher, and middle childhood personality, 427
   undifferentiated, 11
   voluntary, and sensorimotor development, 170–175
behaviorism, 9
behaviorist, 9
behavior therapy, 34–35, 368–369
binocular vision, 121
birth
   anoxia at, 102
   complications and other variables, 104–105
   effect of conditions of, 99–102
   and prenatal environment, 89–105

birth order and personality, middle childhood, 425–427
blacks, language difference, 246–247
blastocyst, 85
body cells, 60
body reactions, infants, 137
bond in conditioned learning, 31
brain
   fetal, 89
   growth in infancy, 120
   toddler, 225
brain damage
   and anoxia at birth, 102
   genetically caused, 70
   and learning, 102
breast-feeding vs. bottle-feeding, 189
busing and educational achievement, 434

California Preschool Schedule, 227
case studies
   adolescence, 474–475, 501–503
   early childhood, 332–334, 370–372
   infants, 138–140, 176–178, 215–217
   middle childhood, 409–411, 439–441
   toddler, 250–252, 291–293
castration anxiety, 355
categorization, middle childhood, 380
cathexis, 12–13
centration, 301
cephalocaudal direction, law of, 88
cephalocaudal growth trend, 135
cerebral palsy, 102, 103
childhood, early theories and views, 5–7
child psychology
   contemporary theories, 8–14
   historical overview, 5–8
   importance, 21–23
   mechanistic model, 8–9
   mechanistic theory, 9
   psychoanalytic theory, 9
   research methods, 15–21
   structural model, 9
   structural theory, 9–12
   tasks of, 4–5
child rearing
   cultural differences, 210–211
   and social class, 431
children
   and adult, separation of, 5–6

aggression in, 270–272
concept of, 5
confined, see institutionalized infant
defined, 3–4
empathy in, 321
interaction with parents, 184–190
latent learning, 38, 42–43
perceptions of, 4
prejudice among, 435–436
reasons for studying, 21–22
temperament, 184
what to study in, 22–23
chorion, 85
chromosomes
abnormality and criminality, 77
genes, DNA, and, 60–62
LSD damage to, 98
in mongolism, 70
replication, 60
in zygote, 59
circular reactions in sensorimotor development, 164–166
classical conditioning, 30–32
defined, 31
in infants, 31–32
classification
objects and events, preoperational stage, 302
toddler concept, 233–234
class inclusion, 302
cleft palate and prenatal emotional stress, 93
clinging response and attachment to parent, 191–192
cognition
components, 44–45
and language, toddler, 242–249
and play in sensorimotor development, 172–175
cognitive ability and sexual differences, 76
cognitive changes, middle childhood, 380–383
cognitive development
concrete operational stage, 46
formal operations stage, 46
and humor, middle childhood, 383
and intellectual development, adolescence, 458–462
Piaget's concept, 45–47
preconceptual stage, 230–234
preoperational stage, 301–306
sensorimotor stage, 46, 168
toddler, 228–234
cognitive growth
and political awareness, 467

and social interaction, 305–306
cognitive learning, 27, 43–47
cognitive operations and defense mechanisms, structure, 362
cognitive theory of grammar acquisition, 237–238
cohesiveness and performance, peer groups, 405–407
combinatory activity, 174
communication
and peer-group interaction, 400
and peers, early childhood, 322
companions, imaginary, 357
compensation, play as, 173
compensatory education programs, I.Q., and school performance, 328–330
competence-performance lag, 320–321
competition and conflict, peer groups, 405
competitiveness
early childhood, 346–347
middle childhood, 420–421
complexity and curiosity in sensorimotor development, 172
complexity theory of infant visual preference, 122–123
complex objects in classification, 234
concept(s)
analytic grouping, 312
development, 168–170
sorting, 311–312
conception, 59, 84
conceptual chaining, 44
conceptual intelligence, 163
concrete operational stage of cognitive development, 46
concrete operationalism vs. preoperationalism, 380–382
conditioning, see classical conditioning; operant conditioning
conflict
and behavior disorders, 363
and competition, peer groups, 405
conformity and group norms, 403
conscience, toddler, 267–269
conservation, 304
middle childhood, 381–382
and social interaction, 305–306
contiguity theorists, 38
control
by repression, 12
in research, 15
convergence, visual, in infancy, 121

conversation, children, 321–322
coordination, visual, in infancy, 121
correlation coefficient, 72
correspondence, one-to-one, 304
crawling in infant motor development, 129, 131
creativity
and play, 174–175
in problem solving, 310
criminality and chromosomal abnormality, 77
critical attributes in generating ideas and hypotheses, 309–310
crying and parent–infant interaction, 187–188
cuddling and attachment to parent, 192
cultural and social changes, adolescence, 462–469
culture
and autonomy, adolescent, 464
and child rearing, 210–211
and competitiveness, 346
and dependence vs. independence, adolescence, 482–483
and I.Q., 58
and maternal behavior, 259–260
and prejudice, 437
and sexual behavior, adolescent, 472
curiosity
and motivation for learning, 48
and sensorimotor development, 171–172
cytoplasm, 62
cytosine in DNA, 61, 62

dating, adolescence, 470
deaf children, mediating symbols, 315
deafness
hereditary, 66
and toddler language and cognition, 243–245
decentration
middle childhood, 380–381
and social growth, 382–383
decidua capsularis, 85
deduction and problem solving, 313–314
deductive reasoning, 233
defense mechanisms
and cognitive operations, structures, 362
early childhood, 360–362

SUBJECT INDEX 519

deficit theory of poverty's effect on language and cognition, 245–247
delinquency, 492–495
   causes, 494–495
denial as defense mechanism, 361
deoxyribonucleic acid, see DNA
dependence
   expression of, 262–264
   vs. independence, adolescence, 481–483
   and learning, 266–267
   parental influence on, 264–266
   on peers, aggression and, 423
   and restrictive mother, 259–260
   toddler, 262–267
deprivation response, 40
depth perception, infant, 125–127
despair vs. integrity, 14
development (see also cognitive development; intellectual development; language development; moral development; motor development; physical development; prenatal development; social development)
   adolescent values, 483–486
   anal stage, 13
   concepts, 168–170
   conscience, 267–268
   discontinuity, 10
   emotional, early childhood, 354–363
   heredity and, 68–79
   and interaction with peers, early childhood, 338–341
   laboratory experiments on, 16
   and mobility of operations, 11–12
   multilinearity, 11
   Oedipal, 13
   oral stage, 13
   orthogenetic, 10–11
   peer group, middle childhood, 400–408
   phallic, 13
   psychoanalytic theory of, 12–13
   psychosexual, 13
   theories vs. research methods, 20–21
developmental direction, law of, 89
developmental scores, infants in different environments, 200
diabetes and pregnancy, 91
differentiation, middle childhood, 380

dimorphism, sex, 457
disadvantaged children, individual tutoring and I.Q. scores, 248–249
discrimination, stimulus, 39
disease, hereditary tendencies, 68–69
displacement as defense mechanism, 362
distinctive features, theory of, 319
DNA, chromosomes, and genes, 60–62
dominance-submission hierarchies, early childhood, 342
double helix, see DNA
doubt and shame vs. autonomy, toddler, 288
Down's syndrome, see mongolism
drawing
   and imagery, 316, 317
   and perception, 320, 321
drives, 12
dropouts, school, 492, 493
drugs
   effects, 495–496
   heredity and reactions to, 69–70
   and pregnancy, 97–98
   users, 495–497

early childhood
   aggression, 347–349
   behavior problems and disorders, 363–369
   case studies, 332–334, 370–372
   characteristics, 317–318
   competitiveness, 346–347
   emotional development, 354–363
   intellectual development, 301–306
   intelligence and I.Q., 323–327
   interaction with peers, 338–344
   learning and thinking changes, 322–323
   mental imagery, 315–317
   nursery school attendance effects, 349–354
   peers as socialization agents in, 344–349
   perceptual growth, 317–322
echolalia, 366
economic factors and personality, middle childhood, 429
ectoderm, 87
educational friction, 344
effectance motivation and self, toddler, 288–290
ego, 12

egocentricity
   and communication with peers, 322
   and power relationships, 343
   preoperational stage, 305
   toddler, 232
Electra conflict, 355
elimination, infant needs, 115
embryo period of prenatal development, 85–88
emotion, understanding, middle childhood, 394–397
emotional development, early childhood, 354–363
emotional state and learning, 47–48
empathy
   in children, 321
   vs. role-taking, 340
empiricism, 7, 36
encoding in problem solving, 307–308
endoderm, 87
enuresis, 364
environment
   vs. heredity, controversy over, 57–58
   language, cognition, and, 245–249
   prenatal, and birth, 89–105
   reversibility of effects, 247–249
   toddler, 256–260
enzymes and hereditary disease tendencies, 68, 69
equilibrium, 162
   and cognitive learning, 45–46
erythroblastosis, 91
evaluation in problem solving, 312–313
expectancy and attention in encoding, 308
exploration and cognition in sensorimotor development, 173–174
exploratory behavior
   and curiosity, 171–172
   and play, 173–174
exploratory drive, see curiosity
extension, 302
   of class, 233
extinction response, 40
eye movement and perception, early childhood, 318

facial expression and status, 342–343
Fallopian tubes, 84, 85

familiarity
  and infant auditory perception, 127–128
  meaning, attentional preference, and, 123
familiarization, stimulus, 39–40
family, democratic vs. authoritarian, and adolescent autonomy, 463–464
family therapy in treating behavior problems, 367–368
fathers, influence on infant sons, 205–206
fear(s)
  vs. anxiety, 47, 357
  early childhood, 357–359
  infant, and attachment to parent, 198–199
  and learning, 47–48
  learning of, 358–359
feeding
  and attachment to parent, 190–191
  schedules, rigid vs. permissive, 189
Fels Research Institute longitudinal study, mother–child relationships, 258–259
fetus
  effects of androgen on, 95–97
  period of prenatal development, 88–89
  and prenatal influences, 83
fighting, social, 269–270
food and growth in infancy, 120–121
foreclosure status, 488
formal operational thought, 459–461
formal operations stage of cognitive development, 46
formal reason, adolescent use, 462
friends (see also peer groups)
  best, as reinforcers, 345
  choice, middle childhood, 424–425
friendship
  and acceptance, peers, middle childhood, 421–425
  adolescence, 469–470
frustration
  and aggression, 270, 272–275
  regression in response to, 274–275
  sources of, 274
  tolerance, 275
functional assimilation and sensorimotor development, 164, 165

functional-locational grouping of concepts, 312
functional-relational grouping of concepts, 311

games, 356–357
gamete, 59, 60
gametogenesis, 60
gene(s)
  alteration, 64
  and bone hardening in infants, 119
  chromosomes, DNA, and, 60–62
  and genetics, 58–59
generality, lack in toddler thought, 232
generalization, stimulus, 39
generalizing assimilation and sensorimotor intelligence, 164, 165
generativity and maturity, 498
genetic counseling, 70–71
genetic influence
  nature of, 65–67
  study methods, 67–68
genetics
  and genes, 58–59
  principles, 59–65
genital play, toddler, and parental responses, 283–285
genotype and phenotype, 63–64
German measles, hazard in embryo period, 88, 89, 90
gestalt theories of perception, 318–319, 320
goal(s)
  barriers, and frustration, 274
  satisfying, 48–49
goal-directedness and parent–infant relationships, 185
grammar
  vs. meaning, 235
  toddler speech, 238
grammar acquisition
  cognitive theory, 237–238
  imitation theory, 235–236
  innate theory, 237
  reinforcement theory, 236–237
  toddler, 235–238
grasp reflex, infant, 114
group(s)
  atypical, adolescence, 490–497
  norms, development of, 401–403
  therapy, in treating behavior problems, 368–369
growth
  beginnings of, 60

  in infancy, 118–121
guanine in DNA, 61, 62
guilt vs. initiative, 13

hallucinogens, 495, 496, 497
harelip and prenatal stress, 93
hashish, 495
Head Start, 328, 330
heat perception, infant, 128
height
  adolescent changes, 452
  toddler, 224
heredity
  and human development, 68–79
  vs. environment, 57–58
  and intelligence, 71–74
  Mendelian laws of, 62–63
hermaphroditism, progestin-induced, 96
heroin, 495, 496
  and pregnancy, 97
heterozygous alleles, 63
hierarchy
  dominance-submission, early childhood, 342
  and hostility, peer groups, 403–405
home environment, toddler, 256–260
homosexuality, 77
homozygous alleles, 63
hormones and pregnancy, 95–97
hostility
  and dependency, 265–266
  and hierarchy, peer groups, 403–405
humor and cognitive development, middle childhood, 383
hunger and feeding, parent–infant interaction, 189–190
Huntington's chorea, inherited susceptibility to, 66
hyperactivity, early childhood, 364–365
hyperkinesis, 21
hypotheses
  and ideas, generation of, 309–312
  and infant attentional preference, 124–125
hypothesizing and separation anxiety, 197

id, 12
ideas and hypotheses, generation of, 309–312

SUBJECT INDEX 521

identification
    conditions of, 260–261
    continuity of, 261–262
    and sex-typing, 280–281
    toddler, and personality and social behavior, 260–262
identity
    diffusion, 488
    middle childhood, 381
    sex-role, and self-concept, 489–490
identity achievement, 488
identity crisis, adolescence, 13–14, 450, 487–488
Illinois Test of Psycholinguistic Abilities, 329
imagery
    eidetic, 307
    kinetic, 316
    mental, early childhood, 315–317
    middle childhood, 381–382
    transformational, 316–317, 381
images in cognition, 45
imaginary companions, 357
imitation
    deferred, 169
    grammar acquisition theory, 235–236
    peers' aggressiveness, 345
    and sensorimotor development, 169
    toddler, 230–231
imprinting, 28–29, 78, 187
incentive and observational learner, 42
inconsistent treatment and aggression, 278
independence vs. dependence, adolescence, 481–483
induction and moral development, 268
inductive reasoning, 233
industry vs. inferiority, middle childhood, 415–416
infancy (see also infants(s); institutionalized infant)
    growth in, 118–121, 135–136
    intelligence in, 156–157, 160–170
    motor development in, 129–136
    socialization in, 206–210
    visual perception, 121–127
infant(s) (see also infancy; institutionalized infant)
    activity level, 136
    anticipatory responses, 41
    attachment to parent, 190–199
    attentional preferences, 122–125
    auditory perception, 127–128
    case studies, 138–140, 176–178, 215–217
    classical conditioning, 31–32
    depth perception, 125–127
    differences in, 136–137
    early language sounds, 148–149
    first words, 149, 156
    heat and pain perception, 128–129
    language development table, 150–155
    manual manipulation, 133–135
    Moro reflex, 115, 120
    needs, 115, 118
    operant conditioning, 33
    perception of position changes, 128
    premature, 102–104
    reflexes, 114–115
    senses, 114
    smell perception, 128
    state of newborn, 114–118
    taste perception, 128
    test scores as predictors, 157, 160
    vocalizing, 145–146
inferences and perspective-taking, 392–394
inferiority
    vs. industry, middle childhood, 415–416
    vs. mastery, 13
inflection in early speech, 241–242
inflexibility of encoding, 307–308
influenza and mumps during pregnancy, 90–91
inheritance, polygenic, 68
initiative vs. guilt, 13
innate theory of grammar acquisition, 237
innate syntax, theory of, 239
instinct, 27–28
institutionalized infant
    behavior pattern retardation, 201–202
    critique of studies, 203–206
    developmental impairment, 199–203
    motor development, 132–133
instrumental conditioning, see operant conditioning
integrity vs. despair, 14
intellectual development
    and cognitive development, adolescence, 458–462
    preoperational stage, 301–306
intelligence (see also intelligence tests; I.Q.)
    and accommodation, 161–162
    as action in infants, 160
    and androgen, 96
    conceptual vs. sensorimotor, 163
    effect of early years on, 227
    factors influencing, 58
    and heredity, 71–74
    and infancy, 156–157, 160–170
    and I.Q., early childhood, 323–327
    and measurement, toddler, 226–227
    periods of, 163
    and prenatal vitamin intake, 92
    and racial genetic factors, 58
    testing in infants, 157
    toddler, 226–227
intelligence tests
    Binet-Simon, 324
    group, 325–326
    infants, 158–159
    Stanford-Binet, 324–325
    toddlers, 226–227
    WISC, 325
intension, 302
    of class, 233
interaction
    child–parent, 184–190
    and cognitive development, 45
    with peers, early childhood, 338–344
intimacy vs. isolation, 14
intuitive thought, preoperational stage, 301–306
I.Q. (see also intelligence; intelligence tests; I.Q. scores)
    androgen and, 96
    calculating, 325
    and fears, early childhood, 359
    and intelligence, early childhood, 323–327
    and learning set, 311
    predictive value, 326–327
    racial and cultural differences, 58
    and school performance, correlates, 327–331
    strengths and weaknesses, 326
I.Q. scores
    babbling, vocabulary, and, 146–147
    and individual tutoring, disadvantaged children, 248–249
irradiation and pregnancy, 98–99

irritability level and parent–infant relationships, 184–185
isolation vs. intimacy, 14

justice, restitutive vs. expiative, 384

Klinefelter's syndrome, 76–77
Kohlberg's Moral Judgement Scale, 390, 391
kwashiorkor and growth in infancy, 120–121

labor, medication during, 99–102
language
   acquired distinctions, early childhood, 318
   and babbling, 147–148
   behavior, institutionalized infant, 201
   and cognition, toddler, 242–249
   development table, infants, 150–155
   differences, blacks, 246–247
   grammar vs. meaning, 235
   and thinking and learning changes, 322
language development
   infant, 145–156
   toddler, 234–242
leader and social group, early childhood, 341–342
leadership
   middle childhood, 421
   peer-group styles, 407, 408
learning
   and brain damage, 102
   cognitive, 27, 43–47
   concept, 43–44
   conditioned, see classical conditioning; operant conditioning
   conditions affecting, 47–49
   critical period, 28–29
   defined, 26
   and dependency, 266–267
   and fear, 47–48
   of fears, 358–359
   and games, 357
   latent, 38, 42–43
   and maturation, 29–30
   and motivation, 48–49
   observational, 41–43
   psychosocial, 13–14
   and reinforcement, 36–39
   theory, 9

   and thinking, early childhood, 322–323
   variable factors, 36–41
learning set in generating ideas and hypotheses, 310–311
libido, 12
life space, Lewin's theory of, 450
locomotion, progress indicators in development of, 129
LSD, 495, 496, 497
   and pregnancy, 97, 98
lysergic acid diethylamide, see LSD

male, vulnerability, 104
manual dexterity in infant motor development, 133–136
marihuana, 495–496
mass to specific acts, infant development growth trend, 135–136
mastery vs. inferiority, 13
masturbation, toddler, and parental response, 283–285
maturation, 29
   early and late, 457–458
   and infant motor development, 132
   and learning, 29–30
   and nutrition, 457
   rate, adolescence, 455–457
   and socialization in infancy, 208
   and speech, 148
maturity, 497–500
   psychoanalytic views, 498
meaning
   and familiarity, and infant attentional preference, 123
   vs. grammar, 235
mediation in problem solving, 314–315
medication during labor, 99–102
meiosis, 60
memory
   and anxiety, 309
   photographic, 307
   and problem solving, 308–309
   toddler, 234
menarche, 454, 456, 457, 458
Mendelian laws of heredity, 62–63
mental disease and retardation, genetically caused, 70–71
mental disorders and prematurity, 103
mental images, toddler, 229
mesoderm, 87
metaphor, toddler representation by, 229–230
methadone and pregnancy, 97–98

Metropolitan Achievement Test (MAT), 329
microcephaly and prenatal irradiation, 99
middle childhood
   acceptance and friendship, peers, 421–425
   attitudes toward authority, 429–431
   case studies, 409–411, 439–441
   cognitive aspects of moral development, 383–392
   cognitive changes, 380–383
   peer-group development, 400–408
   personality themes, 415–418
   personality variables, 418–421
   social cognition, 392–400
minority groups, testing, 247
mirror, toddler self-recognition in, 286–287
miscarriage hazard in embryo period, 88
mitosis, 60
mobility of operations, 11–12
model(s)
   in observational learning, 42
   peers as, 345–346
mongolism, 70
   and age of mother, 90
moral development
   and affection, 268
   cognitive aspects, middle childhood, 383–392
   criticisms of Piagetian theory, 385–387
   Kohlberg vs. Piaget, 388–389
   philosophical views, 420
   Piaget-inspired research, 385
   and role-taking, 389–392
morality
   adolescent, 483–485
   conventional, 387–388
   middle childhood, 419–420
   postconventional, 388
   preconventional, 387
   stages, 484
moral stages
   Kohlberg's theory of, 387–388
   transition between, 391
moratorium status, 488
Moro reflex, infant, 115, 120
morphemes, 235
   in infant language development, 149
mother (see also parent)
   age during pregnancy, 90

mother *(continued)*
   attitude and relations with infant, 185
   behavior, and toddler personality, 259–260
   emotional state, and pregnancy, 93–94
   physical size, and pregnancy, 92–93
   restrictive, and toddler dependency, 259–260
motivation
   effectance, and self, 288–290
   for game playing, 356
   and learning, 48–49
   and observational learner, 42
   and peer groups, 403
motor behavior, institutionalized infant, 201
motor development, in infancy, 129–136
mumps and influenza during pregnancy, 90–91
muscle and bone, adolescent changes, 452–453
muscular growth
   infancy, 119–120
   toddler, 225
mutations, 65
myelin, 225

nail-biting, early childhood, 363, 364
naming and self-recognition, toddler, 287
natural purposes, development principle, 7
nature-nurture controversy, 57–58
   and Women's Liberation Movement, 75
negation, middle childhood, 381
negativism, toddler, 287–288
nervous system, toddler, 225
nonreversal shift and verbal mediation, 315
number concept
   concrete operational stage, 305
   preoperational stage, 304–305
nursery school
   and achievement, 330–331
   attendance effects, 349–354
   influence, teachers vs. peers, 344
   sex differences in power and play, 343–344
   teacher's role, 351–354
nutrition
   infant needs, 115

   and maturation, 457
   and pregnancy, 91–92

object(s)
   concept of, 165–166
   grouping and classifying, 43, 169–170
   permanence, 168–169, 229
   relations between, 170
olfactory perception, infants, 128
ontogeny, 10
operant conditioning, 27
   in animals, 32–33
   applications, 34–36
   infants, 33
operations concept, 46–47
organization and intelligence, 162
ossification, infant bones, 119
ovum, 59
   fertilization, 60
   period of prenatal development, 84–85

pain perception, infant, 128–129
parent(s) *(see also* mother; parent–child relationships)
   and adolescent autonomy, 464
   attachment to, 190–194
   attitude toward, and social class, 430
   and conscience, 268–269
   and dependency, 264–266
   interaction with child, 184–190
   and I.Q. and school performance, 327–328
   and occupation choice, 466
   permissiveness, and peer-dependence, 265
   and personality, 425
   and prejudice, 436–437
   responses to sexual curiosity, 283–285
parent–child relationships *(see also* mother; parent)
   and anxiety, 359
   investigation methods and problems, 257–259
   and moral development, 420
   and socialization in infancy, 208
patterns, discovering, in concept learning, 44
Peabody Picture Vocabulary Test, 329
peer(s) *(see also* peer groups)
   acceptance and friendship, 421–425

   behavior as reward, 344–345
   dependence on, 265, 423
   interaction with, 338–344
   as models, 345–346
   as reinforcers, 344–345
   as socialization agents, 344–349
peer culture and relationships, adolescence, 469–473
peer groups
   development, 400–408
   importance, 469–470
   influences on, 403–408
   rules and interaction, 399–400
peer-peer relationships, stability, middle childhood, 421–422
peer relationships and peer culture, adolescence, 469–473
perception(s), 4
   auditory, 127–128
   early childhood, 321–322
   gestalt theories of, 318–319, 320
   of heat and pain, 128–129
   middle childhood, 394–399
   part-whole, and infant attentional preference, 124–125
   of position change, 128
   of smell, 128
   of taste, 128
   theories of, 318–321
perceptual growth, early childhood, 317–322
performance
   and cohesiveness, peer groups, 405–407
   school, 327–330
permissiveness
   and aggression, 276–278
   and dependency, 264–265
personality *(see also* personality traits)
   adolescence, theories of, 479–481
   and heredity, 74–75
   influences on, middle childhood, 425–438
   studies, interpreting, 438
   themes, middle childhood, 415–418
   toddler, 224, 256, 259–260
   variables, middle childhood, 418–421
personality traits
   congenitally influenced, 184–185
   and frustration tolerance, 275
   stability, middle childhood, 416
person-orientation and parent–infant relationships, 185
perspective-taking and inferences, 392–394

pharmacogenetics, 70
phenotype and genotype, 63–64
phenylalanine and phenylketonuria, 70
phenylketonuria (PKU)
    hereditary, 66
    and phenylalanine, 70
phobias and fears, 358
phonemes, 235
    in infant language development, 148–149
physical development
    and motor development, toddler, 224–226
    and sexual development, adolescence, 451–458
physical factors, personality, middle childhood, 429
physical retardation, institutionalized infant, 199–200
physical size, growth in infancy, 118
physical state and learning, 47
physical traits and heredity, 68
pitch and infant auditory perception, 127
placenta, 85, 86
play
    and cognition in sensorimotor development, 172–175
    and creativity, 174–175
    genital, toddler, 283–285
    and power, sex differences, 343–344
    symbolic, toddler, 232
play therapy in treating behavior problems, 367
political awareness, adolescence, 466–469
political activism, radical student, 490–492
politics, adolescent participation, 467–468
polypeptide, 62
popularity and aggression, middle childhood, 422
position changes, infant perception of, 128
poverty, effect on language and cognition, 245–246
power, parental assertion, and toddler moral development, 268–269
power relationships and social hierarchies, 343–344
preconcept in classification, 233
preconceptual stage, cognitive development, 230–234
pregnancy, conditions of, 90–99

prehension, interrupted, 166
prejudice and personality, middle childhood, 435–438
prematurity and disorders, 103–104
prenatal development, 84–89
prenatal environment and birth, effects of, 89–105
preoperationalism vs. concrete operationalism, 380–382
problem solving, early childhood, 306–315
productivity vs. self-absorption, 14
progestin-induced hermaphroditism, 96
programmed instruction, 35–36
projection, as defense mechanism, 362
proportions, changes in infancy, 118
prosocial behavior and peer acceptance, 423
proto-symbols in language development, 156
proximodistal growth trend, 135
psycholinguistics, 145, 235
psychologists, developmental, 11
    correlational research, 17–18
psychology (see also child psychology)
    associationistic, 7
psychomotor development, toddler, 225–226
puberty, 454–457
puberty rites, 482–483
punishment and aggressiveness, 275–276
pupillary reflex, infant, 114, 121

race, genetic factors and intelligence, 58
random assortment, law of, 63
rationalization, as defense mechanism, 362
reaction formation, as defense mechanism, 362
reaction to stimuli, infants, 136
reality distortion, toddler, 233
reasoning, transductive vs. inductive and deductive, 233
reciprocity and social perception, 398–399
recognitory assimilation and sensorimotor intelligence, 164
reflex(es)
    conditioned, 31
    in embryo, 88
    infant, 114–115

regression
    as defense mechanism, 361–362
    in response to frustration, 274–275
reinforcement
    and dependency, 266
    and learning, 36–39
    partial, 38
    and spread of aggression, 347–349
    timing, 38
reinforcement theory of grammar acquisition, 236–237
relations concept
    concrete operational stage, 303–304
    preoperational stage, 303
representation, toddlers, 229–230
representational stage, cognitive development, 46
repression, 12
    as defense mechanism, 361
reproductive cells, 60
research
    control in, 15
    developmental and cognitive, adolescent self-image, 487–489
    home environment, 257–259
    methods, 15–21
response, 30
    anticipatory, 41
    conditioned, 31
    extinction, 40
    hierarchy, 40–41
    and learning, 36
    natural vs. learned, 36
    satiation and deprivation, 40
    and stimulus, 36
restrictiveness and dependency, 264
retardation
    institutionalized infants, 199–202
    and mental disease, genetically caused, 70–71
retrospection in research, 17–18
reversal shift and verbal mediation, 315
reversibility, middle childhood, 381
reward(s)
    and aggression, 276–278
    and observational learner, 42
    primary and secondary, 37–38
Rh factor and pregnancy, 91
rhythm and infant auditory perception, 127
ribonucleic acid, see RNA
riddles and cognitive development, middle childhood, 383

ritual and middle childhood peer groups, 400
RNA in gene, 62
role differentiation and peer-group interaction, 399–400
role-taking
 and interaction with peers, 340–341
 middle childhood, 382–383
 and moral development, 387–392
rooting reflex, infant, 114
rubella, see German measles
rules
 in cognition, 45
 and peer-group interaction, middle childhood, 399–400
rule seeking and development, 46

satiation response, 40
scanning, visual, and parent–infant interaction, 190
schema, 43
schema discrepancy
 and infant attentional preferences, 123–124
 and separation anxiety, 196–197
 and stranger anxiety, 194
schizophrenia, genetically caused, 71
school
 dropouts, 492, 493
 performance and I.Q., correlates, 327–331
 and personality, middle childhood, 427–429
schooling and achievement, social-class differences, 431–435
segregation, law of, 63
self, toddler development of, 284–290
self-absorption vs. productivity, 14
self-awareness
 and autonomy, toddler, 285–288
 and awareness of others, middle childhood, 416–418
 early childhood, 355–356
self-concept
 adolescence, 461
 development in peer group, 401
 and self-esteem, adolescence, 486–490
 and sex-role identity, 489–490
self-esteem
 middle childhood, 418
 and peer acceptance, middle childhood, 423

and school experiences, middle childhood, 428–429
and self-concept, adolescence, 486–490
self-image, developmental and cognitive research on, 487–489
senses, infant, 114
sensorimotor action, intelligence as, 160
sensorimotor development, 46, 163–168 (see also cognitive development; motor development; physical development)
 cognition and play in, 172–175
 curiosity and, 171–172
sensorimotor operations, 43
sensory stimulation and attachment to parent, 194
sentences
 in early speech, 240–241
 words, sounds, and, 235
separation, effect on nursery school children, 350–351
separation anxiety and attachment to parents, 195–198
sex (see also sex differences; sex-typing; sexuality)
 and babbling, vocabulary, and I.Q. scores, 146–147
 determination of, 64–65
 dimorphism, 457
 drive, 12
 and occupation choice, 466
 play expressions particular to, 356–357
 role development, middle childhood, 418–419
 and social background in infant motor development, 131–132
sex chromatin and sexual anomalies, 76, 77
sex differences
 adolescent friendship, 469
 adolescent sexual behavior, 471
 aggression, 270, 271, 278, 279, 349, 419
 choice of friends, middle childhood, 424
 and cognitive ability, 76
 in creativity, 310
 dating, 470
 delinquency, 494
 and dependency, 266
 growth in infancy, 120
 learning and dependency, 267
 pain perception in infants, 128
 peer groups, 401

play and power, 343, 344
and sexuality, early childhood, 355
sex-typing, 278–283
 cognitive theory, 281–283
 identification theory, 280–281
 conditions affecting, 281
sexual anomalies, inherited, 76
sexual behavior, adolescence, 470–473
sexual curiosity, toddler, 283–285
sexual development, and physical development, adolescence, 451–458
sexuality
 early childhood, 354–355
 and heredity, 75–79
shame vs. autonomy, 13, 288
shaping in operant conditioning, 33–34
sickle-cell anemia, 69
sitting up in infant motor development, 129
skeletal growth
 infancy, 119
 toddler, 224–225
Skinner box in operant conditioning, 33
smell perception, infant, 128
smiling and parent–infant interaction, 186–187
smoking and premature birth, 89, 98
sociability and heredity, 74
social attitudes, changes, adolescence, 461
social changes, and cultural changes, adolescence, 462–469
social class
 and adolescent dating, 470
 and adolescent sexual behavior, 471–472
 and attitude toward parents, 430
 and child rearing, 431
 and competitiveness, 347
 and defense mechanisms, 362
 I.Q., school performance, and, 328
 language development differences, 245
 and occupation choice, 465, 466
 and peer groups, 401
 and personality, middle childhood, 429–435
social cognition, middle childhood, 392–400
social conflict and cognitive growth, 305

social development
   and decentration, middle childhood, 382–383
   indicators, 341
   progress indicators, first three years, 207
social factors, peer acceptance, middle childhood, 424
social hierarchies, early childhood, 342–344
social influences and concept sorting, 312
social interaction and cognitive growth, 305–306
socialization
   in infancy, 206–210
   nursery school teacher's role, 351–352
   peers as agents of, 344–349
social learning (see also learning; socialization; peer groups)
   adolescence, 480–481
   and moral development, 389
   theory, 9
social order, development in early childhood, 341–342
social perception, nature of, 397–399
social response(s)
   generalization of, and attachment to parents, 193
   institutionalized infant, 200
sounds, words, and sentences, 235
spatial orientation, early childhood, 318
speech
   beginnings of, 149, 156
   internalized, in toddler, 243
   lower vs. middle class, 246
   and maturation, 148
   as reinforcement, 345
   toddler, 238–242
spermatozoon, 59, 60
sperm cells, 84
S–R, 9
Stanford-Binet intelligence test, 226, 227
status and facial expressions, 342–343
stimulation
   and attachment, 193–194
   environment vs. caretaker, 205
   and infant motor development, 134–135
stimulus, 30
   conditioned, 31
   discrimination, 39
   familiarization, 39–40
   generalization, 39
   and learning, 36
   and response, 9, 36
   in sorting concepts, 312
stranger anxiety and attachment to parents, 194–195
strength, adolescent changes, 453–454
stress (see also anxiety)
   adolescence, 450, 451
   and pregnancy, animal studies, 94–95
student activism, family correlates, 492
student activists, characteristics, 491–492
stuttering, early childhood, 364
sucking
   and functional assimilation, 164
   and parent–infant interaction, 190
   reflex, infant, 114
superego, 12
superordinate grouping of concepts, 311
symbolic play, toddler, 232
symbols
   in cognition, 45
   mental, toddler development of, 231
sympathy, imitation of, 346
syntax, innate, theory of, 239
syphilis and pregnancy, 91

tabula rasa, 7, 184
talking, *see* speech
taste perception, infant, 128
teacher
   behavior, and middle childhood personality, 427
   influence in evaluation, 313
   nursery school role, 351–354
   vs. peers, influence, 344
teeth
   growth in infancy, 120
   toddler, 224–225
telegraphic construction, early speech, 238–239
temperament and relations with parent, 184
temper tantrums, 269, 271
teratogenes, 90
testing (see also intelligence tests; I.Q.)
   minority groups, 247
thalidomide and pregnancy, 86, 97

thinking
   abstract and hypothetical, adolescence, 459–461
   and learning, early childhood, 322–323
thought
   irreversibility, 301
   metaphoric, toddler, 230
   static, 301
   traits, toddler, 232–233
thumb-sucking and sensorimotor development, 165
thymine in DNA, 61, 62
time perspectives, changes in adolescence, 461–462
timing of reinforcement, 38
toddler(s)
   aggression, 269–278
   case studies, 250–252, 291–293
   cognitive development, 228–234
   conscience, 267–269
   dependency, 262–267
   development of the self, 285–290
   grammar acquisition, 235–238
   home environment, 256–260
   identification, and personality and social behavior, 260–262
   intelligence and its measurement, 226–227
   language and cognition, 242–249
   language development, 234–242
   personality, 256, 259–260
   physical and motor development, 224–226
   restrictive mother and dependency, 259–260
   sexual curiosity, 283–285
   shame and doubt vs. autonomy, 288
toilet training
   infant, 115
   and socialization, 209–210
toxemia and pregnancy, 91
trait(s) (see also personality traits)
   dominant vs. recessive, 63
   inheritance of, 66–67
   of instinctive acts, 27–28
   polygenic, 61
   transmission, RNA and DNA in, 62
transductive reasoning, toddler, 233
transfer RNA, 62
transformational activity, 174
transformational imagery, 316–317, 381
transiency, schooling, and achievement, 432

treatment, early childhood behavior problems, 367–369
Turner's syndrome, 77, 96
tutoring, individual, and I.Q. scores, disadvantaged children, 248–249
twins
   environmental influences, 67–68
   homosexuality studies, 77
   infant motor development studies, 132
   intelligence studies, 72–74
   personality studies, 74–75
   research using, 67–68
   schizophrenia concordance studies, 71
   similarities, identical vs. fraternal, 59

umbilical cord, 85, 86
undifferentiated behavior, 11
uniqueness, genetic, 64
unsocialized aggressiveness, early childhood, 365
uracil in RNA, 62

values, adolescent development of, 483–486
verbal deficit theory, criticisms of, 330
verbal mediation in problem solving, 314–315
vision, binocular, 121
visual activity, institutionalized infant, 200, 203
visual cliff and infant depth perception, 125
visual imagery and imitation, 231
visual interaction and attachment to parent, 192–193
visual-motor reaching in infant motor development, 134
visual perception in infancy, 121–127
vitamins and pregnancy, 92
vocabulary
   babbling, I.Q. scores, and, 146–147
   and memory, 308–309
vocalizing, infant, 145–146
vocational orientation, adolescence, 464–466

voluntary behavior
   characteristics, 171
   and sensorimotor development, 170–175
voting age and political awareness, 468–469

walking in infant motor development, 131–133
warmth and dependency, 265
Wechsler Intelligence Scale for Children (WISC), 325
withdrawal, as defense mechanism, 361
withdrawal reaction, early childhood, 365–366
withdrawal reflex, infant, 115
words
   position in early speech, 239
   sounds, sentences, and, 235
   types in early speech, 238

zygote, 84, 85
   chromosomes in, 59